Enhanced A+ Guide to Managing and Maintaining Your PC

Comprehensive Enhanced Third Edition

Jean Andrews, Ph.D.

A+™
CompTIA Certified

COURSE
TECHNOLOGY

THOMSON LEARNING

Australia • Canada • Mexico • Singapore • Spain • United Kingdom • United States

Enhanced A+ Guide to Managing and Maintaining Your PC, Enhanced Third Edition, Comprehensive is published by Course Technology.

Senior Product Manager	Lisa Egan
Managing Editor	Stephen Solomon
Senior Vice President, Publisher	Kristen Duerr
Senior Production Editor	Christine Spillett
Developmental Editor	Lisa Ruffolo, The Software Resource
Associate Product Manager	Laura Hildebrand, Elizabeth Wessen
Editorial Assistant	Elizabeth Wessen, Janet Aras
Manuscript Quality Assurance Manager	John Bosco
Manuscript Quality Assurance Engineer	Nicole Ashton
Associate Marketing Manager	Meagan Walsh
Marketing Manager	Toby Shelton
Text Designer	GEX, Inc.
Cover Designer	Abby Scholz

Disclaimer

Course Technology reserves the right to revise this publication and make changes from time to time in its content without notice.

The Web addresses in this book are subject to change from time to time as necessary without notice.

For more information, contact Course Technology, 25 Thomson Place, Boston, MA 02210;

or find us on the World Wide Web at *www.course.com*.

For permission to use material from this text or product, contact us by

- Web: www.thomsonrights.com
- Phone: 1-800-730-2214
- Fax: 1-800-730-2215

ISBN 0-619-03433-5

Printed in Canada

7 8 CODE 04 03 02

BRIEF CONTENTS

TABLE OF CONTENTS

CHAPTER TEN
Multimedia Technology   511

CHAPTER ELEVEN
Electricity and Power Supplies   555

CHAPTER TWELVE
Supporting Windows 9x   599

A+ Core Hardware Examination

A+ Core Hardware Examination

OBJECTIVES	CHAPTERS	PAGE NUMBERS
■ Network Interface Card (NIC)	17	912-915, 927-930
Portable system components:		
■ AC adapter	18	1010
■ Digital Camera	9, 10	467-471, 542-544
■ DC controllers	18	988
■ LCD panel	9, 18	491-493, 1008
■ PC Card	18	1016-1021
■ Pointing Devices	9	487-489
1.3 Identify available IRQs, DMAs, and I/O addresses and procedures for device installation and configuration. *Content may include the following:*		
■ Standard IRQ settings	2, 9, Appendix G	81-84, 89-90, 456, G1-G2
■ Modems	16	858
■ Floppy drive controllers	2, 5	89, 258-267
■ Hard drive controllers	2, 6	90, 278-281, 290
■ USB ports	3, 9	146-147, 467
■ Infrared ports	9, 18	459, 1016
■ Hexidecimal/Addresses	Appendix D	D1-D10
1.4 Identify common peripheral ports, associated cabling, and their connectors. *Content may include the following:*		
■ Cable types	9	464, 457-459
■ Cable orientation	5, 7, 9	265, 344, 458
■ Serial versus parallel	9	455
■ Pin connections	3, 5, 7, 9	170, 265, 344, 457-459, 463
Examples of types of connectors		
■ DB-9	9	455
■ DB-25	9	455
■ RJ-11	16	843
■ RJ-45	17	904-905
■ BNC	17	904-905
■ PS2/MINI-DIN	9	484-485

A+ Core Hardware Examination

A+ Core Hardware Examination

OBJECTIVES	CHAPTERS	PAGE NUMBERS
1.8 Identify hardware methods of upgrading system performance, procedures for replacing basic subsystem components, unique components and when to use them. *Content may include the following:*		
■ Memory	4	183, 219, 225-226
■ Hard Drives	7	350-351
■ CPU	3, 15	155, 794-797, 830-833
■ Upgrading BIOS	1, 3	22, 134-138
■ When to upgrade BIOS	3, 7	137, 350-351
Portable Systems:		
■ Battery	18	1013
■ Hard drive	18	1021
■ Types I, II, III cards	18	1016-1017
■ Memory	18	1014
2.1 Identify common symptoms and problems associated with each module and how to troubleshoot and isolate the problems. *Content may include the following:*		
■ Processor/Memory symptoms	8, Appendix E	415-418, E2-E6
■ Mouse	9, Appendix E	475-477, E10
■ Floppy drive	5, Appendix E	259-261, E8-E10
■ Parallel ports	9	462-465
■ Hard Drives	7, 8, Appendix E	355-357, 375, 378, 402, 418, E10-E12
■ CD-ROM	10	540-542
■ DVD	10	545-547
■ Sound Card/Audio	9, 10	475-477, 532-535
■ Monitor/Video	8, Appendix E	422-426, E13-E17
■ Motherboards	8	415-417
■ Modems	9, 16	475-477, 877-881
■ BIOS	8	415-417
■ USB	9	466-468
■ NIC	17	927-936, 974-975

A+ Core Hardware Examination

OBJECTIVES	CHAPTERS	PAGE NUMBERS
■ CMOS	8	415-417
■ Power supply	8, 11, Appendix E	414-415, 569-572, 574-576, E2-E8
■ Slot covers	11	566
■ POST audible/visual error codes	8, Appendix E	415-417, A1-A2
■ Troubleshooting tools, e.g., multimeter	11	566-567, 596
■ Large LBA, LBA	6	302, 306
■ Cables	9, 11	457-459, 464-465, 596
■ Keyboard	8, 9	421-422, 483-487
■ Peripheral	8, 9	421-431, 454-471
2.2 Identify basic troubleshooting procedures and good practices for eliciting problem symptoms from customers. *Content may include the following:*		
■ Troubleshooting/isolation/problem determination procedures	2, 8, 10, 19	82, 402, 408-421, 540-542, 1048-1049
■ Determine whether hardware or software problem	2, 8	87-91, 411-413
■ Gather information from user regarding, e.g.,		
■ Customer Environment	8, 20	410-411, 1073
■ Symptoms/Error Codes	8, 20	410-411, 1073
■ Situation when the problem occurred	8, 20	410-411, 1073
3.1 Identify the purpose of various types of preventive maintenance products and procedures and when to use them. *Content may include the following:*		
■ Liquid cleaning compounds	9, 19	488, 1028-1030
■ Types of materials to clean contacts and connections	8, 9	421-422, 488
■ Non-static vacuum (chasis, powersupplies, fans)	19	1028-1030
3.2 Identify issues, procedures and devices for protection within the computing environment, including people, hardware, and the surrounding workspace. *Content may include the following:*		
■ UPS (Uninterruptible Power Supply) and suppressors	11	581-584

A+ Core Hardware Examination

OBJECTIVES	CHAPTERS	PAGE NUMBERS
■ Determining the signs of power issues	8, 11	414-415, 574-576
■ Proper methods of storage of components for future use	3	165-167
Potential hazards and proper safety procedures relating to Lasers		
■ High-voltage equipment	11	574, 588
■ Power supply	11	574
■ CRT	19	1031
Special disposal procedures that comply with environmental guidelines		
■ Batteries	19	1031
■ CRTs	19	1031
■ Toner kits/cartridges	19	1032
■ Chemical solvents and cans	19	1032
■ MSDS (Material Safety Data Sheet)	19	1032
ESD (Electrostatic Discharge) precautions and procedures		
■ What ESD can do, how it may be apparent, or hidden	3, 11	165, 565-566
■ Common ESD protection devices	3	165-167
■ Situations that could present a danger or hazard	3	167
4.1 Distinguish between the popular CPU chips in terms of their basic characteristics. Content may include the following:		
■ Popular CPU chips (Intel, AMD, Cyrix)	3	115-116, 118-125
■ Characteristics	3	116-125
■ Physical size	3	127
■ Voltage	3	128
■ Speeds	3	120-121, 123-124
■ On board cache or not	3	119-121
■ Sockets	3	127-130
■ SEC (Single Edge Contact)	3	122-123, 127-130
4.2 Identify the categories of RAM (Random Access Memory) terminology, their locations, and physical characteristics. Content may include the following:		
■ Terminology:		
■ EDO RAM (Extended Data Output RAM)	3, 4	141, 185

A+ Core Hardware Examination

A+ Core Hardware Examination

OBJECTIVES	CHAPTERS	PAGE NUMBERS
4.4 Identify the purpose of CMOS (Complementary Metal-Oxide Semiconductor), what it contains, and how to change its basic parameters. *Example Basic CMOS Settings:*		
■ Printer parallel port		
■ Uni-, bi-directional	3, 9	158-159, 463-464
■ disable/enable	3, 9	158-159, 463-464
■ ECP, EPP	3, 9	158-159, 463-464
■ COM/serial port		
■ memory address	3, 9	158-159, 455-456
■ interrupt request	3, 9	158-159, 455-456
■ disable	3, 9	158-159, 459
■ Floppy drive		
■ enable/disable drive or boot	3	158-159
■ speed	3, 5	158-159, 240
■ density	3, 5	158-159, 238
■ Hard drive – size and drive type	6, 7	302, 347-350
■ Memory parity		
■ parity	3	159
■ non-parity	4	187
■ Boot sequence	3	159
■ Date/Time	2	97
■ Passwords	2	96-97
■ Plug & Play BIOS	3, 9	136, 470-472
5.1 Identify basic concepts, printer operations, and printer components. *Content may include the following:*		
■ Paper feed mechanisms	8, 18	429-430, 993-994
■ Types of Printers		
■ Laser	18	988-993
■ Inkjet	18	994-997
■ Dot Matrix	18	947
Types of printer connections and configurations		
■ Parallel	9, 18	463-464, 988
■ Network	18	1004
■ USB	9, 18	466-468, 988

A+ Core Hardware Examination

A+ OS Objectives

A+ OS Objectives

A+ OS Objectives

OBJECTIVES	CHAPTERS	PAGE NUMBERS
■ Partitioning/Formatting/File system (FAT, FAT16, FAT32, NTFS4, NTFS5, HPFS)	5, 6, 7, 13, 14	242-243, 281-282, 293, 298, 353-354, 672-673, 748-749
■ Windows-based utilities		
■ ScanDisk	6, 7	319-320, 386
■ Device Manager	12	633
■ System Manager	12	649-650
■ Computer Manager	14	766
■ MSCONFIG.EXE	12	652-653
■ REGEDIT.EXE (View information/Backup registry)	12, 13, 14	639, 718-719, 743, 762
■ REGEDIT32.EXE	13, 14	718-719, 743
■ ATTRIB.EXE	6	312
■ EXTRACT.EXE	5	257-258
■ DEFRAG.EXE	6, 7	317-318, 391
■ EDIT.COM	4	200
■ FDISK.EXE	7	352
■ SYSEDIT.EXE	12	608
■ SCANREG	12	636-638
■ WSCRIPT.EXE	19	1050
■ HWINFO.EXE	12	650
■ ASD.EXE (Automatic Skip Driver)	12	649-650
■ Cvt1.EXE (Drive Converter FAT16 to FAT 32)	12	620
2.1 Identify the procedures for installing Windows 9x, and Windows 2000 for bringing the software to a basic operational level. *Content may include the following:*		
■ Start Up	2, 12, 14, 15	71, 619-622, 748, 828-829
■ Partition	7, 13, 14, 15	352, 675, 750, 828-829
■ Format drive	7, 14, 15	354, 750, 828-829
■ Loading drivers	12, 14, 15, Appendix E	626, 629-632, 750, 828-829, E25-E29
■ Run appropriate set up utility	12, 14, Appendix E	620-622, 751, E5, E27
2.2 Identify steps to perform an operating system upgrade. *Content may include the following:*		
■ Upgrading Windows 95 to Windows 98	12	620-621

A+ OS Objectives

A+ OS Objectives

OBJECTIVES	CHAPTERS	PAGE NUMBERS
■ Missing or corrupt HIMEM.SYS	4, Appendix A	205-206, A3
■ SCSI	7	355-359, 390
■ Swap file	4	214-215
■ NT boot issues	13, 14, Appendix E	706-710, 755-763, E24, E29
■ Dr. Watson	12	644
■ Failure to start GUI	7	377
■ Windows Protection Error	12	603-604, 644
■ Event Viewer – Event log is full	13	725
■ A device referenced in SYSTEM.INI, WIN.INI, Registry is not found	12	614, 633-635
3.2 Recognize common problems and determine how to resolve them. *Content may include the following:*		
■ Eliciting problem symptoms from customers	8, 20	410-411, 1073
■ Have customer reproduce error as part of the diagnostic process	8, 20	410-411, 1073
■ Identifying recent changes to the computer environment from the user	8, 20	413-414, 1073
■ Troubleshooting Windows-specific printing problems		
■ Print spool is stalled	18	999-1004
■ Incorrect/incompatible driver for print	18	999-1004
■ Incorrect parameter	18	1003-1004
Other Common problems		
■ General Protection Faults	12	603-604, 644-645
■ Illegal operation	12	603-604
■ Invalid working directory	7, Appendix A	378, A2
■ System lock up	4, 7, 12, 14	217-218, 389-390, 605-606, 757
■ Option (Sound card, modem, input device) will not function	9, 12, Appendix A, E	471-473, 632-634, A3, E21
■ Application will not start or load	4, 12, Appendix A, E	203-204, 604-605, 647, A1, E5-E6, E28
■ Cannot log on to network (option – NIC not functioning)	17	973-975
■ TSR (Terminate Stay Resident) programs and virus	4, 19, Appendix E	203-205, 1037-1040, E5, E6
■ Applications don't install	12, Appendix E	643-647, E22-E23, E27-E28
■ Network connection	17	929-930, 933-937

A+ OS Objectives

Introduction

Enhanced A+ Guide to Managing and Maintaining Your PC, Comprehensive Enhanced Third Edition, was written to be the very best tool on the market today to prepare you to support personal computers. This book takes you from the just-a-user level to the I-can-fix-this level for the most common PC hardware and software concerns. This book achieves its goals with an unusually effective combination of tools that powerfully reinforce both concepts and hands-on real-world experience. It also provides thorough preparation for CompTIA's newly revised A+ Certification Exams.

This book includes:

- ◆ CoursePrep® A+ Test Preparation software contains 100 test prep questions like the ones found on the A+ certification exams.

- ◆ An A+ Table of Contents provides quick reference to all of the A+ exam content.

- ◆ Comprehensive review and practice end-of-chapter material, including an itemized summary, review questions, projects, and key-term definitions

- ◆ Step-by-step instruction guides on installation, maintenance, and optimizing system performance, which are presented throughout each chapter

- ◆ A wide array of photos and screen shots supporting the text, displaying in detail the exact hardware and software features you will need to understand to manage and maintain your PC

- ◆ A unique standalone troubleshooting guide (Appendix E), indexed for both hardware and software, which distills all troubleshooting information from the book and packages for one-stop troubleshooting guidance

- ◆ Several in-depth, hands-on projects at the end of each chapter designed to make certain that you not only understand the material, but can execute procedures and make decisions on your own

- ◆ www.findlearnmeasure.com/course: You can receive valuable certification resources and discounts on the A+ Exams by registering with this site.

In addition, the carefully structured, clearly written text is accompanied by graphics that provide the visual input essential to learning. Also, for instructors using the book in a classroom, a special CD-ROM is available that includes an Instructor's Manual, an Online Testing system, and a PowerPoint presentation.

Coverage is balanced—while focusing on new hardware, it also covers the real work of PC repair, where some older technology remains in widespread use and still needs support. For example, the book covers the various Pentium processors, but also addresses the capabilities and maintenance of 486 processors because many are still in use. Also included is thorough coverage of operating system and applications support. While Windows 9x is the primary OS of choice for many PCs, DOS is given comprehensive coverage because it is the foundation operating system for Windows 9x and is still used in troubleshooting situations when Windows 9x or other high-overhead operating systems are not appropriate. In addition, two chapters are dedicated to Windows NT and Windows 2000, which have many powerful capabilities that make them important options, especially in the business environment.

COMPTIA CERTIFICATION

This book provides thorough preparation for CompTIA's newly revised A+ Certification examinations. This book maps completely to all of the certification exam objectives. This certification credential's popularity among employers is growing exponentially, and obtaining certification increases your ability to gain employment and improve your salary options.

The logo of the CompTIA Authorized Quality Curriculum Program and the status of this or other training material as "Authorized" under the CompTIA Authorized Curriculum Program signifies that, in CompTIA's opinion, such training material covers the content of the CompTIA's related certification exam. CompTIA has not reviewed or approved the accuracy of the contents of this training material and specifically disclaims any warranties of merchantability or fitness for a particular purpose. CompTIA makes no guarantee concerning the success of persons using any such "Authorized" or other training material in order to prepare for any CompTIA certification exam.

The contents of this training material were created for the CompTIA A+ Hardware and A+ Operating System exams covering CompTIA certification exam objectives that were current as of February 2001.

How to Become CompTIA Certified: This training material can help you prepare for and pass a related CompTIA certification exam or exams. In order to achieve CompTIA certification, you must register for and pass a CompTIA certification exam or exams.

In order to become CompTIA certified, you must:

(1) Select a certification exam provider. For more information please visit http://www.comptia.org/certification/test_locations.htm.

(2) Register for and schedule a time to take the CompTIA certification exam(s) at a convenient location.

(3) Read and sign the Candidate Agreement, which will be presented at the time of the exam(s). The text of the Candidate Agreement can be found at www.comptia.org/certification

(4) Take and pass the CompTIA certification exam(s).

For more information about CompTIA's certifications, such as their industry acceptance, benefits, or program news, please visit www.comptia.org/certification

♦ **www.findlearnmeasure.com/course**: You can receive valuable certification resources and discounts on the A+ Exams by registering with this site.

CompTIA (the Computing Technology Industry Association) is a non-profit information technology (IT) trade association. CompTIA's certifications are designed by subject matter experts from across the IT industry. Each CompTIA certification is vendor-neutral, covers multiple technologies, and requires demonstration of skills and knowledge widely sought after by the IT industry.

To contact CompTIA with any questions or comments:
Please call + 1 630 268 1818
questions@comptia.org

FEATURES

To ensure a successful learning experience, this book includes the following pedagogical features:

- ◆ Learning Objectives: Every chapter opens with a list of learning objectives that sets the stage for you to absorb the lessons of the text.

- ◆ Comprehensive Step-by-Step Troubleshooting Guidance: Troubleshooting guidelines are included in almost every chapter. In addition, Appendix E is a unique compilation of troubleshooting information taken directly from the book, and indexed for both hardware and software. It provides a one-stop source for solving all PC problems.

- ◆ Step-by-Step Procedures: The book is chock-full of step-by-step procedures covering subjects from hardware installation and maintenance to optimizing system performance.

- ◆ Art Program: Numerous detailed photographs, three-dimensional art, and screenshots support the text, displaying hardware and software features exactly as you will see them in your work

 Tips: Tip icons highlight additional helpful information related to the subject being discussed.

A+os 4.1 **A+ Icons:** All of the content that relates to CompTIA's A+ Certification exams, whether it's a page or a sentence, is highlighted with an A+ icon. The icon notes the exam name and the objective number. This unique feature highlights the relevant content at a glace, so you can pay extra attention to the material.

- ◆ **A+ Table of Contents:** This table of contents indicates every page that relates to the each certification objective. This is a valuable tool for quick reference.

 Caution Icon: This icon highlights critical safety information. Follow these instructions carefully for your own safety.

- ◆ **End-of-Chapter Material**: Each chapter closes with the following features, which reinforce the material covered in the chapter and provide real-world, hands-on testing of the chapter's skill set:

  - ◆ **Summary**: This bulleted list of concise statements summarizes all major points of the chapter.

  - ◆ **Review Questions**: You can test your understanding of each chapter with a comprehensive set of review questions.

♦ **Key-Term List**: The content of each chapter is further reinforced by an end-of-chapter key-term list with definitions that are combined at the end of the book in a full-length glossary.

 Hands-On Projects: You get to test your real-world understanding with hands-on projects involving a full range of software and hardware problems. Chapters include exercises using Nuts & Bolts software as well. Each hands-on activity in this book is preceded by the Hands-On icon and a description of the exercise that follows.

♦ **Behind the Scenes with Debug**: For more detailed study of the subject at hand, Appendix F, using DOS DEBUG, makes for an exciting elective study.

♦ **CoursePrep® A+ Test Preparation software:** 100 test preparation questions mimic the testing enviroment so you can practice for exam day.

♦ **Web site:** For updates to this book and information about our complete line of A+ PC Repair topics, please visit our Web site at www.course.com/pcrepair

Supplements

For instructors using this book in a classroom environment, the following teaching materials are available on a single CD-ROM:

Electronic Instructor's Manual: The Instructor's Manual that accompanies this textbook includes a list of objectives for each chapter, a detailed chapter lecture notes, suggestions for classroom activities, discussion topics; additional projects and solutions.

Course Test Manager 1.2: Accompanying this book is a powerful assessment tool known as the Course Test Manager. Designed by Course Technology, this cutting-edge, Windows-based testing software helps instructors design and administer tests and pretests. In addition to being able to generate tests that can be printed and administered, this full-featured program also has an online testing component that allows students to take tests at the computer and have their exams automatically graded. The test bank that accompanies this book contains over 100 questions per chapter.

PowerPoint Presentations: This book comes with Microsoft PowerPoint slides for each chapter. These are included as a teaching aid for classroom presentation, to make available to students on the network for chapter review, or to be printed for classroom distribution.

ACKNOWLEDGMENTS

Thank you to the wonderful people at Course Technology who continue to provide support, warm encouragements, patience, and guidance. Lisa Egan, Stephen Solomon, Kristen Duerr, and Christine Spillett of CT: You've truly helped make this enhanced edition fun! Thank you, Lisa Ruffolo, the Developmental Editor, for your careful attention to detail. Thank you Tony Woodall of Omega Computer Systems for your above-and-beyond research efforts. Thank you, John Bosco and Nicole Ashton for your careful attention to the technical accuracy of the book.

Thank you to all the people who took the time to voluntarily send encouragements and suggestions for improvements to the previous editions. Your input and help is very much appreciated. The reviewers all provided invaluable insights and showed a genuine interest in the book's success. Thank you to:
Tom Bledsaw, ITT Technical Institute
Bill Bruyn, Devry Phoenix
Tracy Dearinger, Sheridan College
Pauline Duewekey, Baker College at Mount Clemens
Mary Fastner, Brown Institute
Bryant Grigsby, Brown Institute
Garrett Krueger, Brown Institute
Don Locke, Center for Disease Control
Scott Maikkula, Brown Institute
David Mansheffer, Brown Institute
Mary Ellen O'Shields, Central Carolina Community College
Timothy Peterson, Brown Institute
Greg Stefanelli, Carroll Community College
Sheri Schultz, Brown Institute
Mike Sthultz, CLCX
Arthur Tamer, Brown Institute
Doug Waterman, Fox Valley Technical College
Tony Woodall, Omega Computers

Thank you to Jennifer Dark and Ann Marie Francis who were here with me every step of the way making this book happen. I'm very grateful.

This book is dedicated to the covenant of God with man on earth.

Jean Andrews, Ph.D.

PHOTO CREDITS

1-12	© 2000 Quantum Corporation. All rights reserved.
3-5, 3-9	Courtesy of Intel Corporation
3-6	Courtesy of VIA Technologies, Inc.
3-7	© 2000 Advanced Micro Devices, Inc. Reprinted with permission.
8-11, 9-12	Photos courtesy of Larry Marchant.
9-32	Courtesy of Microsoft Corporation
9-33	© 1993 Steve Kahn. Used with permission.
9-36	© Logitech 2000. Used by permission.
9-36	Courtesy of Sharp Electronics Corporation
9-39	To come.
10-1	Courtesy of Adobe Systems Incorporated.
16-4	Courtesy of Diamond Multimedia Systems, Inc.
17-11	3Com Corporation.
18-1	Courtesy of Hewlett-Packard Company.
18-6	Courtesy of Hewlett-Packard Company.
18-27	Courtesy of IBM Corporation
19-7	Courtesy of Ecrix Corporation.
1-4, 1-5, 1-6, 1-7, 2-19, 3-1, 3-3, 3-8, 3-18, 3-30, 5-14, 9-6, 9-14, 9-29, 9-34, 11-7	Courtesy of Jennifer Dark

READ THIS BEFORE YOU BEGIN

The following hardware, software, and other equipment are needed to do the hands-on projects at the end of chapters:

♦ You need a working PC that can be taken apart and reassembled. Use a 486 or higher computer.

♦ Troubleshooting skills can better be practiced with an assortment of non-working expansion cards that can be used to simulate problems.

♦ DOS and Microsoft Windows 9x are needed to complete projects in Chapters 1 through 12. Microsoft Windows NT Workstation 4.0 is needed for Chapter 13, and Microsoft Windows Professional is needed for Chapter 14. Chapters 15 through 20 use a combination of all these operating systems and environments.

♦ Equipment required to work on hardware includes a grounding mat and grounding strap and flat-head and Phillips-head screwdrivers. A multimeter is needed for Chapter 11 projects.

♦ Before undertaking any of the lab exercises, starting with Chapter 3, please review the safety guidelines below.

 Caution Icon: This icon highlights critical safety information. Follow these instructions carefully for your own safety.

Protect Yourself, your Hardware, and your Software

When you work on a computer it is possible to harm both the computer and yourself. The most common accident that happens when attempting to fix a computer problem is the erasing of software or data. Experimenting without knowing what you are doing can cause damage. To prevent these sorts of accidents, as well as the physically dangerous ones, take a few safety precautions. The text below describes the potential sources of damage to computers and how to protect against them.

Power to the Computer

To protect both yourself and the equipment when working inside a computer, turn off the power, unplug the computer, and always use a grounding bracelet. Consider the monitor and the power supply to be "black boxes." Never remove the cover or put your hands inside this equipment unless you know about the hazards of charged capacitors. Both the power supply and the monitor can hold a dangerous level of electricity even after they are turned off and disconnected from a power source.

Static Electricity (ESD)

Electrostatic discharge (ESD), commonly known as static electricity, is an electrical charge at rest. A static charge can build up on the surface of a non-grounded conductor and on non-conductive surfaces such as clothing or plastic. When two objects with dissimilar electrical charges touch, static electricity passes between them until the dissimilar charges are made equal. To see how this works, turn off the lights in a room, scuff your feet on the carpet, and touch another person. Occasionally you'll be able to see and feel the charge in your fingers. If you can feel the charge, then you discharged at least 3,000 volts of static electricity. If you hear the discharge, then you released at least 6,000 volts. If you see the discharge, then you released at least 8,000 volts of ESD. A charge of less than 3,000 volts can damage most electronic components. You can touch a chip on an expansion card or system board and damage the chip with ESD and never feel, hear, or see the discharge.

There are two types of damage that ESD can cause in an electronic component: catastrophic failures and upset failures. A catastrophic failure destroys the component beyond use. An upset failure damages the component so that it does not perform well, even though it may still function to some degree. Upset failures are the most difficult to detect because they are not so easily observed.

Protect Against ESD

To protect the computer against ESD, always ground yourself before touching electronic components, including the hard drive, system board, expansion cards, processors, and memory modules. Ground yourself and the computer parts, using one or more of the following static control devices or methods:

♦ **Ground bracelet or static strap**: A ground bracelet is a strap you wear around your wrist. The other end is attached to a grounded conductor such as the computer case or a ground mat, or it can plug into a wall outlet (only the ground prong makes a connection!) The bracelet also contains a current-limiting device called a resistor that prevents electricity from harming you.

♦ **Ground mats**: Ground mats can come equipped with a cord to plug into a wall outlet to provide a grounded surface on which to work. Remember, if you lift the component off the mat, it is no longer grounded and is susceptible to ESD.

♦ **Static shielding bags**: New components come shipped in static shielding bags. Save the bags to store other devices that are not currently installed in a PC.

The best solution to protect against ESD is to use a ground bracelet together with a ground mat. Consider a ground bracelet to be essential equipment when working on a computer. However, if you find yourself in a situation where you must work without one, touch the computer case before you touch a component. When passing a chip to another person, ground yourself. Leave components inside their protective bags until ready to use. Work on hard floors, not carpet, or use antistatic spray on the carpets. Generally, don't work on a computer if you or the computer have just come inside from the cold.

Besides using a grounding mat, you can also create a ground for the computer case by leaving the power cord to the case plugged into the wall outlet. This is safe enough because the power is turned off when you work inside the case. However, if you happen to touch an exposed area of the power switch inside the case, it is possible to get a shock. Because of this risk, in this book, you are directed to unplug the power cord to the PC before you work inside the case.

There is an exception to the ground-yourself rule. Inside a monitor case, there is substantial danger posed by the electricity stored in capacitors. When working inside a monitor, you *don't* want to be grounded, as you would provide a conduit for the voltage to discharge through your body. In this situation, be careful *not* to ground yourself.

When handling system boards and expansion cards, don't touch the chips on the boards. Don't stack boards on top of each other, which could accidentally dislodge a chip. Hold cards by the edges, but don't touch the edge connections on the card.

Don't touch a chip with a magnetized screwdriver. When using a multimeter to measure electricity, be careful not to touch a chip with the probes. When changing DIP switches, don't use a graphite pencil, because graphite conducts electricity; a very small screwdriver works very well.

After you unpack a new device or software that has been wrapped in cellophane, remove the cellophane from the work area quickly. Don't allow anyone who is not properly grounded to touch components. Do not store expansion cards within one foot of a monitor, because the monitor can discharge as much as 29,000 volts of ESD onto the screen.

Hold an expansion card by the edges. Don't touch any of the soldered components on a card. If you need to put an electronic device down, place it on a grounded mat or on a static shielding bag. Keep components away from your hair and clothing.

Protect Hard Drives and Disks

Always turn off a computer before moving it, to protect the hard drive, which is always spinning when the computer is turned on (unless the drive has a sleep mode). Never jar a computer while the hard disk is running. Avoid placing a PC on the floor, where the user can accidentally kick it.

Follow the usual precautions to protect disks. Keep them away from magnetic fields, heat, and extreme cold. Don't open the floppy shuttle window or touch the surface of the disk inside the housing. Treat disks with care and they'll generally last for years.

CHAPTER

1

HOW COMPUTERS WORK

In this chapter, you will learn:

♦ About the functions performed by different hardware components of a microcomputer

♦ About the three kinds of software and how they relate to one another and to hardware

♦ How the CPU uses primary and secondary storage to manage software

Like millions of other computer users, you have probably used your microcomputer to play games, explore the Internet, write papers, build spreadsheets, or create a professional-looking proposal or flyer. You can perform all these applications without understanding exactly what goes on behind your computer case or monitor screen. But if you are curious to learn more about microcomputers, and if you want to graduate from simply being the end user of your computer to becoming the master of your machine, then this book is for you. This book is written for anyone who wants to understand what is happening "behind the scenes" in order to install and set up new software, install new hardware, diagnose both hardware and software problems, and make decisions about purchasing new hardware.

This chapter introduces you to the inside of your computer, a world of electronic and mechanical devices that has evolved over just a few years to become one of the most powerful technical tools of our society. The only assumption made here is that you are a computer user—that is, you can turn on your machine, load a software package, and use that software to accomplish a task. This book will help you see what goes on behind the scenes when you do those things.

In the world of computers, the term **hardware** refers to the physical components of the computer, such as the monitor, keyboard, memory chips, and hard drive. The term **software** refers to the set of instructions that directs the hardware to accomplish a task. In Figure 1-1, a passenger directs a chauffeur who directs a car, just as a computer user directs software which, in turn, controls hardware to perform a given task.

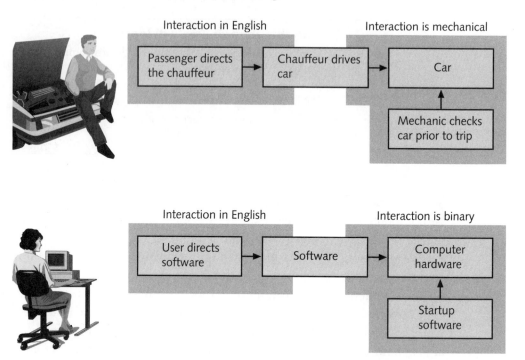

Figure 1-1   A user interacts with a computer much as a passenger interacts with a chauffeured car

In order to perform a computing task, hardware is used by software for four basic functions: input, processing, output, and storage (see Figure 1-2). Also, hardware components must communicate both data and instructions among themselves, and, since these components are electrical, an electrical system is required. In this chapter, we introduce the hardware and software components of a computer system. In Chapter 2 we address how they work together, with the primary focus on the sophisticated system of communication of data and instructions that includes both hardware and software.

Figure 1-2   The CPU is central to all computer activity, which consists of input, processing, storage, and output

Looking again at Figure 1-1, the interaction between the passenger and the chauffeur is in English, but the chauffeur must translate these directions such as, "Go to the airport," into mechanical directions that the car can "understand" such as pressing the gas pedal, braking when necessary, and turning the wheel to control the car until it reaches the airport. In the same fashion, a computer user interacts with a computer in a language that the user understands, but software must convert that instruction into a form that hardware can "understand" (see Figure 1-3). Hardware stores data and communicates with software by only one fundamental method—binary—and, in effect, speaks a language that only has two words, "on" and "off." Every communication that software has with hardware is reduced to a series of these two words.

Figure 1-3   All communication, storage, and processing of data inside a computer are in binary until presented as output to the user

It was not always so. For almost half a century, people attempted to invent an electronic computational device that could store all 10 digits in our decimal number system and even some of our alphabet. No one could invent a device that could effectively store all 10 digits. It was not until the 1940s that a breakthrough occurred when it was suggested that only two numbers be stored, reducing all counting and calculations to a number system that only needed two digits, 0 and 1. The technology to hold only two states, on and off, existed. Only two voltage levels were required for a functional switch, zero volts or some volts. Appendix D discusses this **binary number system**, which is the language of a computer. When you study how computers work, this one fact permeates everything, and keeping this binary concept in mind makes everything much clearer. A computer's world is a binary world, and communication of instructions and data by the devices that process them is always in binary.

> **TIP** Every communication, every process (including the storage of data and instructions) in a computer is a series of zeros and ones.

HARDWARE

Hardware without software is like a car with no driver; it's useless. So when we examine different hardware devices, we really don't see how to use them until we introduce software. In this section we cover the major hardware components of a microcomputer system used for input, output, processing, storage, electrical supply, and communication. Later in this chapter, we'll discuss how software is used to make the hardware work for us.

 A+ CORE 1.1 Most input and output devices are outside the computer case, and most processing and storage are done inside the case. The central, most important hardware device in a computer is the **central processing unit (CPU)**, the **microprocessor** or **processor**. As its name implies, this device is central to all processing done by the computer. Data received by input devices goes to the CPU, and output travels from the CPU to output devices. The CPU stores data and instructions in storage devices and performs calculations and other processing of data as well. Whether inside or outside the case, and regardless of the function the device performs, each device requires these things to operate:

- **A method for the CPU to communicate with the device.** The device must send data to and/or receive data from the CPU. The CPU might need to control the device by passing instructions to it, and/or the device might need to request service from the CPU.

- **Software to instruct and control the device.** A device is useless without software to control it. The software must know how to communicate with the device at the detailed level of that specific device, and the CPU must have access to this software in order to interact with the device.

- **Electricity to power the device.** Electronic devices require electricity to operate. Devices can either receive power from the power supply inside the computer case, or they can have their own power supply by way of a power cable to an electrical outlet.

In the next few pages, we take a sightseeing tour of computer hardware, first looking outside and then inside the case.

Hardware Used for Input and Output

A+CORE
1.2

Most input/output devices reside outside the computer case. These devices communicate with what is inside the computer case through cables attached to the case at a connection called a **port**, sending data and/or instructions to the computer and receiving them from the computer. Most computers have their ports located on the back of the case (Figure 1-4), but some models put the ports on the front of the case for easy access. The most popular input devices are a keyboard and a mouse, and the most popular output devices are a monitor and a printer.

On/Off switch
Power in
Mouse port
Keyboard port
USB ports
Parallel port
Serial ports
Video port (for monitor)
Network port
Microphone
Phone line connection for modem
Speaker

Figure 1-4   Input/output devices connect to the computer case by ports usually found on the back of the case

The **keyboard** is the primary input device of a computer (see Figure 1-5). The keyboards that are standard today are called enhanced keyboards and hold 102 keys. Some keyboards are curved to be more comfortable for the hands and wrists, and are called ergonomic keyboards. In addition, some keyboards come equipped with a mouse port—a plug into which a mouse (another input device) can be attached to the keyboard—although it is more common for the mouse port to be located directly on the computer case. Electricity to run the keyboard comes from inside the computer case and is provided by wires in the keyboard cable.

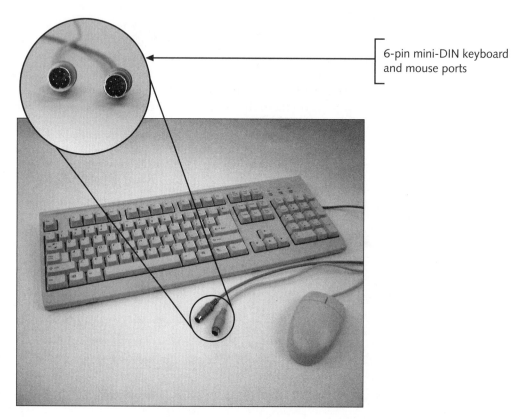

6-pin mini-DIN keyboard and mouse ports

Figure 1-5   The keyboard and the mouse are the two most popular input devices

A **mouse** is a pointing device used to move a pointer on the screen and to make selections. The bottom of a mouse houses a rotating ball that tracks movement and controls the location of the pointer. The one, two, or three buttons on the top of the mouse serve different purposes for different software. For example, Windows 98 uses the left mouse button to execute a command and the right mouse button to display information about the command.

Both the keyboard and the mouse receive input mechanically (you press a key or move the mouse), and this movement is converted into binary data that is input into the computer.

The monitor and the printer are the two most popular output devices (see Figure 1-6). The **monitor** is the visual device that displays the primary output of the computer. Once, all monitors were monochrome (one color), but today they display text and graphics in color.

Hardware manufacturers typically rate a monitor according to the size of its screen (in inches) and by the number of dots on the screen used for display. A **pixel** is a dot or unit of color that is the smallest unit of display on a monitor.

15-pin, 3 row video connector

25-pin parallel port connector for printer

Figure 1-6   The two most popular output devices are the monitor and the printer

A very important output device is the **printer**, which produces output on paper, often called **hard copy**. The most popular printers available today are ink-jet, laser, and dot matrix printers. The monitor and the printer each needs its own power supply. Their electrical power cords connect to electrical outlets. Sometimes the computer case provides an electrical outlet for the monitor's power cord to eliminate the need for one more power outlet.

Hardware Inside the Computer Case

Most storage and all processing of data and instructions are done inside the computer case, so before we look at components used for storage and processing, let's look at what you see when you first open the computer case. Most computers contain these devices inside the case (see Figure 1-7):

- A system board containing the CPU, memory, and other components
- A floppy drive, hard drive, and CD-ROM drive used for permanent storage

- A power supply with power cables supplying electricity to all devices inside the case

- Circuit boards used by the CPU to communicate with devices inside and outside the case

- Cables connecting devices to circuit boards and the system board

Power supply

Power cords

CD-ROM drive

Floppy drive

Hard drive

Data cables

System board

Expansion cards (circuit boards)

Figure 1-7   Inside the computer case

A+CORE
1.1

Among the things you first notice when you look inside a computer case are boards that contain electronic components. A **circuit board** is a board that holds microchips or integrated circuits (ICs) and the circuitry that connects these chips. All circuit boards contain microchips, which are manufactured in one of two ways: CMOS (complementary metal-oxide semiconductor) chips or TTL (transistor-transistor logic) chips. CMOS chips require less electricity, hold data longer after the electricity is turned off, are slower, and produce less heat than TTL chips do. Most CPUs are CMOS chips.

The other major components look like small boxes, including the power supply, hard drive, CD-ROM drive, and floppy drive. Devices that the CPU communicates with that are not located directly on the system board are called **peripheral devices** and are linked to the CPU through a connection to the system board. Some peripheral devices are linked to the system board by a circuit board designed for that purpose. These circuit boards, called **expansion cards**, are installed in long narrow slots on the system board called **expansion slots**.

There are two types of cables inside the case: data cables, which connect devices to one another, and power cables, which supply power from the power supply. Most often, you can distinguish between the two by the shape of the cable. Data cables are flat and wide, and power cables are round and small. There are some exceptions to this rule, so the best way to identify a cable is to trace its source and destination. All power cables originate from the power supply.

A+CORE
1.1

The System Board

The largest and most important circuit board in the computer is the **system board**, **mainboard**, or **motherboard** (see Figure 1-8), which contains the CPU, the component where most processing takes place. The system board is the most complicated piece of equipment inside the case and is covered in detail in Chapter 3. Because all devices must communicate with the CPU on the system board, all devices in a computer are either installed directly on the system board, linked to it by a cable connected to a port on the system board, or indirectly linked to it by expansion cards. Some ports on the system board stick outside the case to accommodate external devices such as a keyboard, and some ports provide a connection for a device inside the case, such as a floppy disk drive.

Chip set
RAM
AGP slot for video card
Battery
PCI slot for high-speed I/O devices
Slot for Pentium II CPU
ISA slot for slower devices
BIOS
Power supply connections

Figure 1-8   A Pentium system board. All hardware components are either located on the system board or directly or indirectly connected to it, because they must all communicate with the CPU.

Listed below are the major components found on all system boards, some of which are labeled in Figure 1-8 and are discussed in detail in the sections that follow.

Components used primarily for processing:

- Central processing unit (CPU), the computer's most important chip
- Chip set that supports the CPU by controlling many system board activities

Components used for temporary storage:

- Random access memory (RAM) used to hold data and instructions as they are processed
- Cache memory to speed up memory access (optional—depends on the type of CPU)

Components that allow the CPU to communicate with other devices:

- Bus used for communication on the system board
- Expansion slots to connect expansion cards to the system board

Firmware and setup information stored on the system board:

- Flash BIOS (basic input/output system) memory chip used to permanently store programs that control basic hardware functions (discussed in more detail later in the chapter)
- CMOS configuration chip

Electrical system:

- Power supply connections to provide electricity to the system board and expansion cards

Components Used Primarily for Processing

$A+$*CORE*
    1.1

The CPU or microprocessor is the chip inside the computer on which most computer processes must ultimately be executed (see Figure 1-9). Today most computers also contain microchips (called the **chip set**) that relieve the CPU of some low-level processing and provide careful timing of activities to increase the overall speed and performance of the computer. While this book will touch on different types of machines, it focuses on the most common personal computers (PCs), referred to as IBM-compatible, which are built around a family of microprocessors manufactured by Intel Corporation. The Macintosh family of computers, manufactured by Apple Computer, Inc., is built around a family of microprocessors manufactured by Motorola Corporation.

In addition to the CPU and the chip set, some older system boards also contain a chip that supports and enhances the function of some older CPUs. Many applications used this chip, called a **coprocessor**, to speed up the performance of certain CPU math functions. Most system boards manufactured before 1995 have a special socket for the coprocessor.

Figure 1-9   Processing of data and instructions is done by the CPU. This Pentium with fan on top is made by Intel.

Temporary (Primary) Storage Devices

$A^{+CORE}_{1.1}$ Figure 1-2 shows two kinds of storage: temporary and permanent. The CPU uses temporary storage, called **primary storage**, which is much faster to access than permanent storage, to temporarily hold both data and instructions while it is processing them. Primary storage is provided by devices on the system board and on other circuit boards, called memory or **random access memory** (**RAM**). RAM chips can be installed individually directly on the system board or in banks of several chips on a small board that plugs into the system board. The most common types of boards that hold memory chips are called **SIMMs** (**single inline memory modules**), **DIMMs** (**dual inline memory modules**), and **RIMMs** (see Figure 1-10). Whatever information is stored in primary storage is lost when the computer is turned off, because RAM chips need a continuous supply of electrical power to hold data or software stored in them. This kind of memory is called **volatile** because it is by nature temporary. By contrast, memory that holds its data permanently, such as that etched into ROM chips, is called **nonvolatile**.

Also part of primary storage is a special kind of very fast RAM called **cache memory**, which speeds up memory access by serving as a cache, or holding area, for data or instructions that are accessed frequently (see Figure 1-11). For newer CPUs, cache memory is stored inside the CPU housing on a memory chip that sits very close to the CPU microchip. For older CPUs, cache memory is stored on the system board either in individual chips or on memory modules called **COAST** (**cache on a stick**).

Figure 1-10   A SIMM or a DIMM holds RAM and is mounted directly on a system board

Figure 1-11   The speed of memory access is improved by using cache memory

Permanent (Secondary) Storage Devices

 As you remember, the RAM on the system board is called primary storage. Primary storage temporarily holds both data and instructions as the CPU processes them. These data and instructions are also permanently stored on devices such as hard drives and floppy disks, in locations that are remote from the CPU. Data and instructions cannot be processed by the CPU from this remote storage (called **secondary storage**), but must first be copied into primary storage (RAM) for processing. The most important difference between these types of storage is that secondary storage is permanent. When you turn off your computer, the information in secondary storage remains intact. Conversely, the information in primary storage, or RAM, is lost when you turn off the machine. The four most popular secondary storage devices are hard disks, floppy disks, Zip drives, and CD-ROMs.

> **TIP** Don't forget that primary storage is temporary; as soon as you turn off the computer, any information there is lost. That's why you should always save your work frequently into secondary storage, which is permanent. There, your work remains safe even after the computer is turned off.

A **hard drive** is a sealed case containing platters or disks that rotate at a high speed (see Figure 1-12). As the platters rotate, an arm with a sensitive read/write head reaches across the platters, both writing new data to them and reading existing data from them. Managing a hard drive and understanding how one works are the subjects of Chapters 6 and 7. A hard drive requires a controller to manage it. The **hard drive controller** is a set of microchips that contain software to manage the hard drive, and temporarily hold data that is passed to and from the hard drive. In the past, hard drives using older technology required a separate controller expansion card. Today, a controller on a circuit board attaches directly to the hard drive. In this case, the data cable from the hard drive connects to the system board or to a small hard drive adapter card in an expansion slot. The adapter card is the interface between the hard drive and the CPU; data passes from the hard drive to the adapter card to the system board to the CPU. Most system boards today have a connection for the hard drive data cable on the system board (see Figure 1-13).

The older hard drives that had a controller on a large interface card in an expansion slot used two cables to connect the controller card to the hard drive. One cable was used to transmit instructions that controlled the hard drive from the controller card, and the other passed data back and forth. The controller and the hard drive had to use the same type of technology for communication to be possible.

Figure 1-12 Hard drive with sealed cover removed

Data cable connecting
to system board from
hard drive

Figure 1-13 Most hard drives today connect to the system board by way of a data cable
connected directly to the board

1

Another secondary storage device almost always found inside the case is a floppy drive. Floppy drives come in two common sizes: 3½ inches and 5¼ inches (referring to the size of the disks the drives can hold). The newer 3½-inch disks use more advanced technology and actually hold more data than the older 5¼-inch disks did. Like hard drives, floppy drives are managed by controllers. These controllers can be on interface cards, or can be chips on the system board. You can tell which your computer has by following the data cable from your floppy drive to the board.

A+ CORE 1.1 Figure 1-14 shows a complete floppy drive subsystem in a microcomputer. A disk is inserted into the front of the floppy drive. Electricity to the drive is provided by a power cord from the power supply that connects to a power port at the back of the drive. A data cable also is connected to the back of the drive and runs either to a controller card inserted into an expansion slot on the system board or directly to the system board that contains controller chips, which completes the subsystem.

Figure 1-14   A floppy drive subsystem

Hard drives and floppy drives require power to operate. This power is received from the power supply through a power cord that connects at the rear of the drive.

System Board Components Used for Communication Among Devices

When you look carefully at the system board, you see many fine lines on both the top and the bottom of the board's surface (see Figure 1-15). These lines, sometimes called **traces**, are circuits, or paths, that enable data, instructions, and power to move from component to component on the board. This system of pathways used for communication and the protocol and methods used for transmission are collectively referred to as the **bus**. (A **protocol** is a set of rules and standards that any two entities use for communication.) The paths, or lines, of the bus that are used to carry data are the part of the bus that we are most familiar with. Binary digits (0s and 1s) travel down this data path side by side. Some buses have data paths that are 8, 16, 32, or 64 bits wide. For example, a bus that has 32 wires, or lines, that data can travel on is called a 32-bit bus. A system board can have more than one bus, each using a different protocol, speed, data path size, and so on.

Bus lines

Bottom of the CPU socket

Figure 1-15   On the bottom of the system board, you can see bus lines terminating at the CPU socket

One of the most interesting lines, or circuits, on a bus is called the **system clock** and is dedicated to timing the activities of the chips on the system board. A crystal on the system board (Figure 1-16), similar to that found in watches, generates continuous pulses to produce the system clock. These pulses are carried on wires over the system board to chips and expansion slots to ensure that all activities are performed in a synchronized fashion by providing a beat, much as a metronome keeps the beat for a musician. If you can imagine the system clock as the conductor maintaining the rhythm of a symphony, then you can imagine hundreds of symphonies occurring within the computer every second as all devices that make up your computer function in lock-step at the right time at an incredibly fast beat!

System board crystal, generates the system clock

Figure 1-16   The system clock is a pulsating electrical signal sent out by this component that works much like a crystal in a wristwatch. One line, or circuit, on the system board bus is dedicated to carrying this pulse.

The lines of a bus often terminate at expansion slots (Figure 1-17). The size and shape of an expansion slot are dependent on the kind of bus it is using. Therefore, one way to determine the kind of bus you have is to examine the expansion slots on the system board. In Figure 1-8, there are three types of expansion slots showing. With a little practice, you can identify these slots by their length, by the position of the breaks in the slots, and by how far from the edge of the system board a slot is positioned. Look for all three of these expansion slots in Figure 1-8:

- PCI (peripheral component interconnect) expansion slot used for high-speed input/output devices

- AGP (accelerated graphics port) expansion slot used for a video card

- ISA (Industry Standard Architecture) expansion slot used by older and/or slower devices

Pins on connector edge
of expansion card

PCI slot

Bus lines

Figure 1-17   The lines of a bus terminate at an expansion slot where they connect to pins that connect to lines on the expansion card inserted in the slot

Circuit board
mounted in slot

Expansion slots

System board

Figure 1-18   Circuit boards are mounted in expansion slots on the system board

Interface (Expansion) Cards

A+CORE
1.2

Circuit boards other than the system board inside the computer are sometimes called circuit cards, adapter boards, expansion cards, interface cards, or simply **cards** and are mounted in expansion slots on the system board (see Figure 1-18). Some common circuit boards you might find plugged into the expansion slots on your computer's system board are a card to control video, called a **video card** (see Figure 1-19), a sound card and a network card. These cards all enable the CPU to connect to an external device or, in the case of the network card, to a network. If your computer has an internal modem, that modem is installed as an expansion card. The modem technology is embedded on the card itself, and the card provides a port for a phone-line connection.

The easiest way to determine the function of a particular expansion card (short of seeing its name written on the card, which doesn't happen very often) is to look at the end of the card that fits against the back of the computer case. The card provides access to the outside of the case through a connector or port attached to the card (see Figure 1-19). A network card, for example, has a port designed to fit the network cable. An internal modem has one, or usually two, telephone jacks as its ports. A standard I/O controller card usually has at least one parallel port designed to fit a printer cable connection and a serial port designed to fit a modem cable connection or another serial device. (Parallel and serial refer to the way data and instructions are transmitted along a cable. With parallel transmission, streams of bits flow parallel to each other, while with serial transmission, single-file bits flow in one long stream. This is explained further in Chapter 5.)

15-pin, 3-row
video port

Figure 1-19   The easiest way to identify this video card is to look at the port on the end of the card

The Electrical System

A+CORE
1.1 The most important component of the computer's electrical system is the power supply, usu-ally located near the rear of the case (see Figure 1-20). This **power supply** does not actually generate electricity but converts it and reduces it to a voltage that the computer can handle. Older power supplies had power cables that provided either 5 or 12 volts of DC current. Newer power supplies provide 3.3, 5, and 12 volts of DC current. In addition to providing power for the computer, the power supply runs a conventional fan directly from the electri-cal output voltage to help cool the inside of the computer case. When a computer is running, this fan and the spinning of the hard drive are the two primary noise makers.

Figure 1-20   Power supply with connections

Every system board has one or a pair of connections to provide electrical power from the power supply to the system board and to other components that receive their power from ports and expansion slots coming off the system board (see Figure 1-21). Electricity travels over the system board on the buses. Each bus has wires, or lines, designated to carry voltage. Figure 1-22 shows the lines on the system board that are part of the bus ending at an expan-sion slot. Later, in Chapter 3, you will learn the specifics of which line carries what.

1

Power connectors from power supply to system board

Figure 1-21   The system board receives its power from the power supply by way of one or two connections located near the edge of the board

ISA expansion slots

ISA bus lines

Figure 1-22   Bus lines ending at expansion slots

Instructions and Data Stored on the System Board

Some very basic instructions and data are stored on the system board apart from secondary storage, just enough to provide rudimentary information about the setup of the computer and to start the computer and look for software (stored either on a floppy disk or hard drive).

These data and instructions are stored on special chips on the system board (called ROM, or read-only memory, chips). Some data is also retained on the system board by way of setting physical switches on the board. In the case of these special chips, the distinction between hardware and software becomes vague.

Most of the time, it's easy to distinguish between hardware and software. For example, a floppy disk is hardware, but a file on the disk containing a set of instructions is software. This software file, sometimes called a **program**, might be stored on the disk today, but you can erase that file tomorrow and write a new one to the disk. In this case, it is clear that a floppy disk is a permanent physical entity, whereas the program is not. Sometimes, however, hardware and software are not so easy to distinguish. For instance, a ROM (read-only memory) microchip on a circuit board inside your computer has software instructions permanently etched into it during fabrication. This software is actually a part of the hardware and can never be erased. In this case, hardware and software are married together, and it's difficult to separate the two, either physically or logically. Some even give a new name to such hybrid components, calling them **firmware**.

A+CORE 1.1, 1.8

These ROM chips hold programs or software that, among other things, tell the CPU how to perform many fundamental input/output tasks that manage the computer, and they are therefore sometimes called **BIOS (basic input/output system)** chips. See Figure 1-23 for an example of a **ROM BIOS** chip on a video expansion card. The system board contains a vital ROM BIOS chip (Figure 1-24) that contains the programming necessary to start the computer, and other fundamental BIOS programming for functions such as interacting with the floppy disk drive. If you want to upgrade these utility programs, usually you must buy new ROM chips. However, there are now ROM chips on the market that actually can be reprogrammed. Called **Flash ROM**, the software stored on these chips can be overwritten by new software that remains on the chip until it is overwritten.

Video BIOS chip
on a video card

Figure 1-23   A ROM BIOS chip on a video card holds programs that provide instructions
to operate the card

ROM BIOS chip

Figure 1-24   The ROM BIOS chip on the system board contains the programming to start up the PC as well as perform many other fundamental tasks

Another chip on the system board contains a very small amount of memory, or RAM, enough to hold configuration or setup information about the computer. This is called the **CMOS configuration chip**. This chip, shown in Figure 1-25, is responsible for remembering how memory is allocated, which hard drives and floppy drives are present, and so forth. When the computer is first turned on, it looks to this CMOS chip to find out what hardware it should expect to find. A similar function is performed on Macintosh computers by a chip called the parameter RAM (PRAM) chip. The CMOS chip is powered by a trickle of electricity from a small battery—located on the system board or computer case, usually close to the CMOS chip itself—so that, when the computer is turned off, the CMOS chip still retains its data.

Even though a computer has many CMOS chips, in the computer industry, the term "CMOS chip" has come to mean the one chip on the system board that holds the configuration or setup information. If you hear the following: "What does CMOS say?" or "Let's change CMOS," the person is talking about the configuration or setup information stored on this one CMOS chip. The program to change CMOS setup is stored in the ROM BIOS chip and can be accessed during the startup process.

A system board can also retain setup or installation information in different settings of jumpers or DIP (dual in-line package) switches on the board. **Jumpers** are considered open or closed based on whether a jumper cover is present on two small wires that stick up off the system board (see Figure 1-26). A **DIP switch** is similar to a light switch and is on or off based on the direction the small switch is set. Most system boards have at least one, often several, jumpers, and perhaps a single bank of DIP switches, although the trend is to include most setup information in CMOS rather than to have a jumper or switch on the board that has to be mechanically set.

Battery

CMOS setup chip

Figure 1-25   The CMOS setup chip, powered by a battery when the PC is turned off, contains data about the system configuration as well as the current time and date

Bank of jumpers

Jumper cover

Figure 1-26   Setup information about the system board can be stored by setting a jumper on (closed) or off (open). A jumper is closed if the cover is in place, connecting the two wires that make up the jumper; a jumper is open if the cover is not in place.

SOFTWARE

Let's return to the analogy used earlier (Figure 1-1) when we compared a car to computer hardware. If a car is like a hardware system, then the people who service and drive a car are like software that manages and instructs the hardware. The mechanic and driver make the automobile a functioning tool that can be used to accomplish a task. Without their intelligence, skill, and direction, the car is nothing more than an interconnected assemblage of electronic and mechanical devices. Software provides a similar function for hardware. Software is the intelligence of the computer; it determines what hardware is present, decides how it is configured and used, and then uses that hardware to perform tasks.

Three Types of Software and What They Do

Software consists of programs written by programmers that instruct computers to perform specific tasks. Almost all PC software falls into three categories: firmware (BIOS), operating system (OS), and applications software. The BIOS and OS perform tasks at startup that determine the overall health and functionality of the computer, just as a mechanic is responsible for the condition of a car before it is turned over to the driver. After startup, the OS, working with applications software and BIOS, provides instructions to the hardware to perform tasks, much as a driver operates the automobile.

As seen in Figure 1-27, first BIOS and then the OS is in control of preparing the computer for user interaction when it is first turned on. The user can then interact directly with the OS to perform simple tasks such as copying files from the hard drive to a disk or installing applications software. Or the user can use applications software to perform higher-level tasks such as word processing or database management. In this case, the OS is still working behind the scenes, serving as a middle layer between the applications software and the hardware.

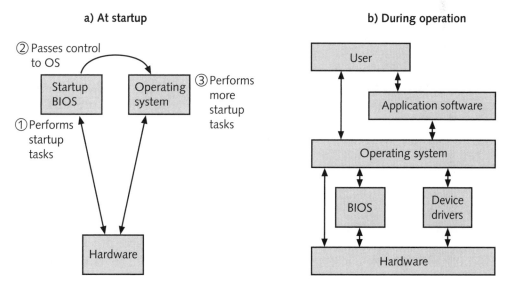

Figure 1-27 Not all software relates directly to hardware; some is dependent on other software to perform many basic functions

A+CORE
      1.1

Firmware or BIOS

BIOS on the system board and other circuit boards provides some fundamental instructions to hardware and often serves as the interface between higher-level software and hardware. The BIOS programs stored on the system board are together referred to as **system BIOS**, or **on-board BIOS**. Part of system BIOS is **startup BIOS**, which runs many computer startup functions and brings the computer to a state in which it can be managed by the OS. Once startup BIOS has completed its tasks, it turns control over to the OS, which stays in control as long as the PC is turned on. The process of powering up and bringing the PC to a ready state is called **booting** and is discussed in detail in Chapter 2.

Software Layers

Once the computer is running, a hierarchy determines how software interacts so that high-level software can depend on low-level software to manage the hardware for it. Looking again at Figure 1-27, you can see that applications software depends on the OS to interface with hardware. The OS might instruct the hardware directly, use BIOS to provide the instructions, or use special software designed to interface with specific hardware devices. These special software programs are called **device drivers** and serve the same functions as BIOS programs, but they are stored on secondary storage devices such as a hard drive rather than on ROM chips, as BIOS is. Some device drivers are provided by the OS, and some are provided by the manufacturer of the specific hardware device with which they are designed to interface.

> **TIP** You can find device drivers in a number of sources. Some come with the operating system. And the manufacturer provides some either with the device when it is purchased or over the Internet.

One advantage of using BIOS and device drivers to interface with hardware is that it frees the OS or applications software from knowing the specifics of how to communicate with the device. For example, different printers understand data and commands according to different sets of rules and standards called protocols. Applications software and the OS can pass print requests to the printer driver, which communicates with the printer, as in Figure 1-28. With the device drivers doing the interpreting, applications software developers do not have to include the specific protocol and standards for every printer that might be used by the applications they write.

Figure 1-28   Any specific protocols and commands sent to the printer are the responsibility of the printer device driver

The applications software does not even need to know which printer is being used, because Windows keeps track of the **default printer**, the currently selected printer. The application sends print jobs to Windows for printing. Windows uses the default printer unless the user selects a different one from the Windows printer list. Windows knows which device driver to call to execute the print job because the device driver was assigned to that printer when the printer was installed.

How Software Manages and Shares Information

Before the CPU can process data or follow software instructions, the data or instructions must first be stored in RAM. The CPU tracks where this information is stored in RAM by assigning an address to each unit of RAM that can hold one byte of information. These addresses are called **memory addresses** and are most often displayed on the screen as hexa-decimal (base 16) numbers in segment/offset form (for example, C800:5). See Appendix D for more information on the hexadecimal number system as it applies to memory addresses.

As you saw in Figure 1-27, BIOS, device drivers, the OS, and applications software are work-ing when a computer is running. During output operations, applications software must pass information to the OS, which in turn passes that information to a device driver or to BIOS. BIOS and device drivers managing input devices must pass information to the OS, which passes it to the applications software.

Using the CPU, software processes and shares data by referring to the memory address of the data, as seen in Figure 1-29. For example, if applications software wants to print data, rather than saying to the OS, "Please print data ABC," it says to the OS, "Please print the data at memory address 123." The OS then turns to the printer device driver and says, "Please send data at memory address 123 to the printer you control."

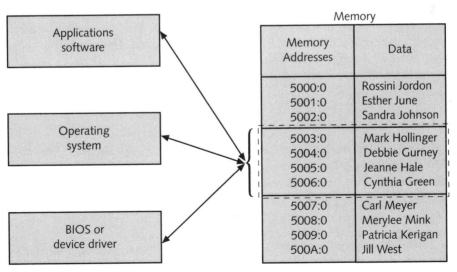

Figure 1-29   Software can exchange information by storing data in RAM that has been assigned memory addresses. Memory addresses can then be communicated to other software layers.

Operating Systems

Although there are several operating systems on the market, a microcomputer needs only one to operate. Different OSs support different types of hardware systems and user needs. The first OS among IBM computers and IBM-compatible computers was DOS, the disk OS. Because DOS was written for early PCs, it still has significant limitations. For years, DOS was used with Windows, a user-friendly intermediate program between DOS and the user. Versions of Windows include Windows 3.1 and Windows 3.11 (also called Windows for Workgroups), which together are referred to as Windows 3.x. With Windows 3.x, DOS is the OS. The more recent Windows 95 and Windows 98, which we call Windows 9x, provide a user-friendly interface and actually conduct OS functions. Other OSs include Macintosh for Apple computers, UNIX, OS/2, and Windows NT. UNIX and Windows NT are popular OSs used for high-end PCs on networks and to support applications used on the Internet. This section looks at different OSs, paying careful attention to their similarities and differences.

In general, OSs have evolved as hardware has improved. Software tends to run behind hardware in development, because software is generally designed to use current hardware, rather than vice versa. As we study the different OSs in this chapter, take note of that evolution process. Operating systems serve many functions. Among them are the following:

- Managing BIOS
- Managing files on secondary storage devices
- Managing primary memory (RAM)
- Diagnosing problems with software and hardware
- Interfacing between hardware and software (that is, interpreting applications software needs to the hardware and interpreting hardware needs to applications software)
- Performing housekeeping procedures requested by the user, often concerning secondary storage devices, such as formatting new disks, deleting files, copying files, and changing the system date

While DOS has served computing well, it has serious computing limitations, primarily because it has been modified extensively as hardware capabilities have increased. When computer users started using DOS in the early 1980s, computer systems were very small, and the power and usefulness of the software and hardware were limited. The computer industry made assumptions and decisions based on limitations in hardware complexity and amount of memory that still limit us today, even though the complexity and memory have increased astronomically. Such outdated limitations particularly affect the way hardware and software interact through the OS. Some drawbacks of DOS were partly solved by Windows 3.1 and Windows 3.11. Windows 95 and Windows 98, which contain parts of DOS and parts of a completely rewritten OS, offer even greater improvements.

Starting Up the Operating System

Operating systems are stored on hard drives, but applications software can be stored on hard drives, floppy disks, or CD-ROMs. Software is stored as files designated as **program files**.

A **file** is a collection of data or programmed instructions that is stored on a secondary storage device and assigned a single name, which the OS uses to identify it.

Although the OS is stored in files on the hard drive, these stored programs cannot be executed from their secondary storage locations. As explained above, these instructions first must be copied from secondary storage into RAM, or memory. The CPU can then read from one memory location in RAM to another to receive and follow instructions.

 TIP Remember that *all* programs must be copied into RAM before the CPU can read them. This includes even the operating system, which resides permanently on secondary storage (usually a hard drive) and must be copied or loaded into RAM each time the computer is started.

Figure 1-30 shows this two-step process. Recall that startup BIOS is in control when the computer is first turned on. When startup BIOS is ready to load the OS, it finds the OS program file stored on the hard drive and copies the file into RAM. The program file contains a list of instructions; each instruction is stored in a separate memory location with a memory address assigned to it. In the second step, control is given to these instructions in RAM. Beginning with the first memory address, the CPU executes the instruction stored at that address. Sometimes, an instruction causes control to be sent to a memory address other than the next one in sequential order. This action is called a **program jump**, as demonstrated in the move from Instruction 4 to Instruction 6 in Figure 1-30.

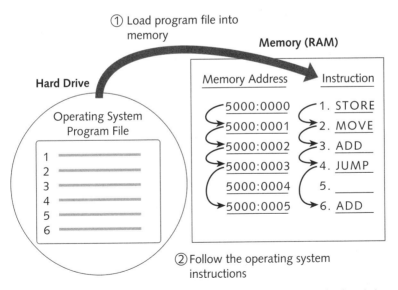

Figure 1-30 The operating system is stored in files on the hard drive but is executed from memory

Once the first OS program is in control, it will look for other OS program files on the hard drive and load them into memory. The OS consists of a group of programs, several of which are stored in RAM at any one time. Once the OS is loaded into memory and given control, as part of the booting process, it will perform its own limited startup routines.

Interfacing with the Operating System

After booting is complete, the OS either automatically executes an applications software program or turns to the user for its next instruction. If you are working with the OS, you will see an interface on the monitor screen. This interface can be one of three types:

A Command-driven Interface   With a command-driven interface, you key in command lines to tell the OS to perform operations (see Figure 1-31). For instance, the command-driven interface of DOS is the C prompt, which looks like this:

```
C> or C:\>
```

Computer users who are good typists and are very familiar with DOS commands often prefer this kind of OS interface.

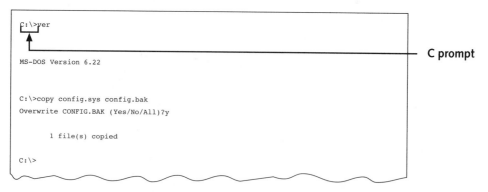

Figure 1-31   An operating system command-driven interface: the C prompt

A Menu-driven Interface   Some OSs allow you to choose from a list of options displayed on the screen. An example of such a menu-driven interface is Explorer in Windows 98. From the drop-down menus, you can format disks, rename files, copy and delete files, and perform many other operations to manage files and storage devices (see Figure 1-32).

An Icon-driven Interface   Today's OSs are more likely to use an icon-driven interface than a command-driven one. With an icon-driven interface, sometimes called a **graphical user interface** or **GUI**, you perform operations by selecting icons (or pictures) on the screen. When an OS is first executed, the initial screen that appears, together with its menus, commands, and icons, is called the **desktop**. Figure 1-33 shows the Windows 98 default desktop, which has an icon-driven interface. You double-click an icon with the left mouse button to execute an applications software program. Just about all OSs today offer icon-driven interfaces.

Figure 1-32   A menu-driven interface: Explorer in Windows 98

Figure 1-33   An icon-driven interface: Windows 98 desktop

Survey of Operating Systems

Operating systems continue to evolve as hardware and software technologies improve. As you look at several OSs, you will see the evolution process from DOS to DOS with Windows 3.x, to Windows 9x. To understand these gradual improvements in OSs, you need to understand the following terms:

- Multitasking. **Multitasking**, as it applies to hardware, refers to the ability of a CPU to do more than one thing at a time. The first CPU for microcomputers with this ability was the Pentium by Intel. The older i386 and i486 CPUs could do only one thing at a time (80386 and 80486 CPUs are often abbreviated as i386 and i486 in documentation; the i stands for the chip manufacturer, Intel). Earlier OSs did not need to support multitasking; newer OSs now need to support some form of multitasking.

- Cooperative multitasking. **Cooperative multitasking**, sometimes called **task switching**, is not true multitasking, in that the CPU is only doing one thing at a time. The CPU is switching back and forth between applications so that more than one application can be loaded at the same time. There is only one active application and one or more inactive applications sitting in the background waiting for the active application to relinquish control.

You observe cooperative multitasking when you have two applications open, each in its own window. You don't need to close one application before opening another. DOS does not handle cooperative multitasking, but Windows does (see Figure 1-34).

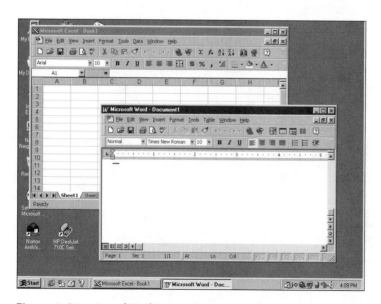

Figure 1-34   A multitasking environment allows two or more applications to run simultaneously

- Preemptive multitasking. **Preemptive multitasking** is another type of pseudo-multitasking whereby the OS allots CPU time to an application for a specified period, and then preempts the processing to give the CPU to another application. The end result is that the computer appears to be doing true multitasking.

- Environment. **Environment** refers to the type of support the OS provides to the applications software. For example, in order for applications software to offer you a window with mouse movement, buttons to click, and icons to view, it must be supported by a GUI environment, such as Windows. Such an application is said to need a "GUI environment" to work. Another example is the DOS environment that offers to its applications software only a "single-tasking environment." The software does not expect another applications software package to be running concurrently with it.

- Windows 3.x operating environment. There is a unique situation with Windows 3.x. It's not really an OS, but neither does it act like normal applications software. Windows 3.x provides an operating environment, which refers to the overall support that it provides to applications software, including cooperative multitasking and a GUI (which DOS does not offer). Windows 3.x is the "middleman" that manages this pseudomultitasking environment by passing tasks to DOS one at a time. DOS manages its single-tasking environment and relates to the hardware in single-task fashion. Windows provides the cooperative multitasking environment to the applications.

However, as Figure 1-35 shows, Windows 3.x both performs some of the functions of an OS and provides the environment within which applications software works. Figure 1-35 shows that the applications software relates only to Windows. There is usually no attempt to make applications software interact directly with DOS, system BIOS, or the hardware in a Windows environment. Windows 3.x sometimes interfaces directly with hardware, such as when printing with one of its own printer drivers. In this case, Windows 3.x is serving as the OS. Sometimes, however, Windows passes such functions to DOS. DOS can choose to relate directly to the hardware or it can choose to pass the hardware request to BIOS or a device driver to be processed.

Figure 1-35   Windows 3.x is unique in that it is an extra software layer between the OS and applications software. Compare this figure to Figure 1-27b.

With the above discussion of operating system characteristics in mind, we will compare several OSs based on these criteria:

- What kind of interface does the OS provide for the user?

- Can the OS support some form of multitasking?

- Can the OS easily manage large quantities of primary memory (RAM) and secondary storage?

- How many and what kinds of applications are written to work with the OS?

- How powerful must the hardware be to make efficient use of the OS?

- How does the OS perform in a network?

Tables 1-1 through 1-8 list the advantages and disadvantages of the most well-known OSs used in PCs and the OS used in Macintoshes. When choosing an OS, consider all the criteria discussed in these tables. Your choice will be determined by the size and type of your microcomputer system, your familiarity with the various OSs, and the applications software you plan to use.

DOS (Disk Operating System)   The first OS used by IBM microcomputers; for years DOS remained the unchallenged standard for OSs used by IBM and IBM-compatible machines. Most seasoned microcomputer users are comfortable and familiar with DOS. Table 1-1 summarizes its advantages and disadvantages.

Table 1-1   Advantages and disadvantages of DOS

Advantages	Disadvantages
• DOS runs on small, inexpensive micro-computers with a minimum amount of memory and hard drive space. • Some older applications are still in use today that were written for DOS and older hardware because of the low overhead of DOS compared to more modern OSs. • DOS is still a viable option for some specialized applications using a dedicated computer that does not involve heavy user interaction —for example, a microcomputer dedicated to controlling an in-house phone system. • DOS can be used to boot up and troubleshoot a computer when a more sophisticated OS is too cumbersome and has too much overhead.	• Memory management is awkward and sometimes slow. • DOS has no icon-driven interface. • DOS does only single-tasking; that is, it supports only one application running at a time. • DOS was not designed for use on networks. A separate applications software program is necessary for a DOS machine to access a network. • The last standalone version is DOS 6.22, which does not take advantage of the many new CPU features now available. (However, Windows 9x has a newer DOS core.) • Hardly any new software is being written for DOS.

DOS with Windows 3.1 and 3.11 Operating Environments   Written by the same software company that owns DOS (Microsoft Corporation), Windows 3.x was designed to allow applications to have a graphical interface, which is popular with users. DOS runs in the background as the true OS and uses Windows 3.x as a middle layer, or "go-between" program, between the application and DOS, providing the operating environment for applications software packages. When Windows is running, users can interact with applications directly with Windows or directly with DOS. A point of historical interest: Windows 3.11, called Windows for Workgroups, was the first Windows environment designed to interface with a network without depending on separate applications software to do the job. Table 1-2 summarizes the advantages and disadvantages of using DOS with Windows 3.x, which has been replaced with Windows 9x.

Table 1-2 Advantages and disadvantages of DOS with Windows 3.x

Advantages	Disadvantages
• DOS with Windows 3.x provides an icon-driven interface. • Windows supports cooperative multitasking as it manages more than one open application by passing segments to DOS, which then, in turn, interfaces with hardware. • DOS with Windows 3.x can run on relatively inexpensive microcomputer systems with present-day CPUs. • Many applications software programs are still in use that were written to run on Windows 3.x.	• Memory management is awkward and sometimes slow. • DOS with Windows 3.x is sometimes slow due to the complexity of the middle layer, or "go-between," concept. • The DOS/Windows 3.x combination does not take advantage of the full computing power of minimum amount of hard drive space. • There is no new software being written today specifically for Windows 3.x. • DOS and Windows applications tend to conflict with each other when sharing hardware devices.

Windows 95 and Windows 98 Windows 95 and Windows 98 (referred to as Windows 9x) take us two steps closer to a new OS but do not completely eliminate DOS. Windows 95 is the marriage of Windows for Workgroups (Windows 3.11) with an updated version of DOS sometimes known as DOS 7.0, together with some completely new additions and improvements to the OS. Windows 95 also introduced an improved and more automated method of installing new hardware devices, called **Plug and Play**. Windows 98 made several improvements on Windows 95 but is fundamentally the same OS. Windows 98 offers additional support for larger hard drives and more hardware devices, includes more software utilities, and is faster than Windows 95. The underlying DOS portion of Windows 98 is named DOS 7.1. Microsoft has announced that Windows 98 will be the last OS that it distributes that has a DOS foundation. Currently, there have been two editions of Windows 98 released. The third edition, code-named Windows Millennium Edition, is scheduled to be released before this book is in print. Table 1-3 summarizes the advantages and disadvantages of Windows 9x.

Table 1-3   Advantages and disadvantages of Windows 9x

Advantages	Disadvantages
• Windows 9x offers a very user-friendly and intuitive GUI interface. • Windows 9x offers almost complete backward compatibility for applications written for DOS and earlier versions of Windows. • Windows 9x is a mix of older and newer OS technology and allows both older and newer software and hardware to run. • Windows 9x offers the ability for one PC to talk with another over phone lines without additional software. It works well for low-end network use, such as when two users want to exchange files. • Disk access time under Windows 9x is improved over DOS and Windows 3.x. • Plug and Play features make installing some new hardware devices easier than with earlier OSs. • Windows 9x supports preemptive multi-tasking. While the hourglass is showing on the window of an application, you can make another application active by clicking on its window.	• Windows 9x requires at least a 386 CPU, 8 MB of RAM, and 30 MB of hard drive space, thus prohibiting its use on some older PCs. • Because of the attempt to bridge older and newer technology, there are some problems with failures and errors created in this hybrid environment.

UNIX Operating System   UNIX originally was written for mainframe computers in the early 1970s; only in the past few years has it become available for many different kinds of computers, including PCs, and it is now a popular OS for networking. UNIX computers are often used for Internet support. Problems with UNIX stem mostly from the lack of consistency from one vendor's version to another.

A variation of UNIX that has recently gained in popularity is Linux (pronounced "LIH-nucks"), an OS originally created by Linus Torvalds when he was a student at the University of Helsinki in Finland. This OS is free to everyone, and all the underlying programming instructions (called source code) are also freely distributed. For more information on Linux, see *www.linux.org*. Linux is popular as a low-end, scaled-down version of UNIX that can be used to support small networks or as a training tool to learn UNIX. Table 1-4 summarizes the advantages and disadvantages of the UNIX OS.

Table 1-4   Advantages and disadvantages of UNIX

Advantages	Disadvantages
• UNIX was written for powerful microcomputer systems and has strong multitasking capability, including preemptive multitasking. • UNIX manages large quantities of memory well. • UNIX performs very well in a networking environment.	• UNIX industry standards are not uniform, making it difficult for UNIX developers, administrators, and users to move from one UNIX vendor to another. • UNIX requires a powerful, large microcomputer system. • Few business applications software packages have been written for UNIX for PCs, although there are several very powerful database packages available under UNIX, such as Informix and Oracle.

Windows NT Windows NT (New Technology) breaks with previous versions of Windows. Although older applications written for DOS and DOS with Windows might work under Windows NT, Windows NT developers do not guarantee compatibility between the OSs. It takes an aggressive and altogether new approach toward managing hardware resources and interfacing with applications software. Windows NT completely eliminates the underlying relationship with DOS.

> Remember that Windows NT is the one Windows OS that does not guarantee compatibility with programs written for earlier Windows versions. That's because NT eliminates the connection to DOS. Whereas even Windows 98 contains some DOS in its programming code, NT does not. Older DOS and DOS with Windows applications *might* work with Windows NT, but you can't count on it.

Windows NT supports preemptive multitasking and also supports a system that contains two or more CPUs, called multiprocessing. Multiprocessing provides true multitasking because the OS can manage two or more processes happening at the same time, each using its own CPU.

Windows NT is designed to work within a powerful networked environment. Computers (called **servers**) are configured to store programs and data used remotely by other computers (called **clients**). With client-server arrangements, an organization's resources can be used more effectively, since computers are networked together to share these resources. Windows NT Workstation is an OS designed to run on the client, and Windows NT Server runs on the server. Table 1-5 summarizes the advantages and disadvantages of Windows NT.

Table 1-5   Advantages and disadvantages of Windows NT

Advantages	Disadvantages
• Windows NT is designed to run in powerful client-server environments and targets both the client and the server market. • Windows NT offers a completely new file management system, different from earlier Windows OSs. • Windows NT Workstation offers both networking over a LAN and dial-up connections over phone lines. • Windows NT Server offers powerful security both as a file server and for network administration. • Windows NT supports preemptive multitasking and multiprocessing.	• Windows NT requires at least a 486 CPU, 16 MB of RAM, and 120 MB of hard drive space, thus eliminating it as a plausible option for older, low-end PCs. • Windows NT is not compatible with some older hardware and software.

Windows 2000   Windows 2000 is actually a suite of operating systems, each designed for a different sized computer system. Windows 2000 is built on the Windows NT architecture and is designed to ultimately replace both Windows 9x for low-end systems and Windows NT for midrange and high-end systems. Windows 2000 includes four operating systems:

- **Windows 2000 Professional** This OS is designed to ultimately replace both Windows 9x and Windows NT Workstation as a personal computer desktop or notebook OS. It is an improved version of Windows NT Workstation, using the same new technology approach to hardware and software, and includes all the popular features of Windows 9x, including Plug and Play.

- **Windows 2000 Server** This OS is the improved version of Windows NT Server and is designed as a network operating system for low-end servers.

- **Windows 2000 Advanced Server** This network operating system has the same features as Windows 2000 Server, but is designed to run on more powerful servers. It supports up to eight processors on one machine, and up to 8 GB (gigabytes) of memory.

- **Windows 2000 Datacenter Server** This network operating system is another step up from Windows 2000 Advanced Server and is designed to support up to 32 processors and up to 64 GB of memory. It is intended to be used in large enterprise operations centers.

Table 1-6 lists the advantages and disadvantages of Windows 2000.

Table 1-6   Advantages and disadvantages of Windows 2000

Advantages	Disadvantages
• Windows 2000 provides powerful support to a network, including advanced security for the network and the ability to organize access to network resources in a centralized location on the network called an Active Directory. • Windows 2000 is backward compatible with all Windows NT and Windows 9x applications and most Windows 3.x and DOS applications. • Windows 2000 is really four operating systems, each targeting a different sized computer and different computing needs, therefore making the OS suite extremely versatile.	• Just as with Windows NT, Windows 2000 hardware requirements disqualify it as an option for an older, low-end PC operating system. Minimum requirements for Windows 2000 Professional are a 133 MHz Pentium-compatible CPU, 64 MB of RAM, and 650 MB of hard drive storage. • Windows 2000 is not scalable. Rather than having one OS that can easily handle a major computer system upgrade, the user must purchase one version of Windows 2000 for a small system and another to handle the upgraded system. • Windows 2000 is not as stable as other operating systems used to manage a large network.

OS/2   OS/2, written by IBM in cooperation with Microsoft Corporation, provides an altogether different OS in place of DOS. Errors in earlier versions and large computer hardware requirements have made OS/2 slow to gain popularity. Table 1-7 summarizes the advantages and disadvantages of OS/2.

Table 1-7   Advantages and disadvantages of OS/2

Advantages	Disadvantages
• OS/2 supports preemptive multitasking. • OS/2 can handle large quantities of memory directly and quickly. • OS/2 has an icon-driven interface. • OS/2 works well in a networking environment.	• Relatively few applications software packages are written for OS/2. Some consider it a dead or dying OS, although it is still used by some. • Many microcomputer users are not familiar with OS/2 and avoid it for that reason. • OS/2 requires a powerful computer system and large amounts of RAM and hard drive space to run efficiently.

Macintosh Operating System   Available only on Macintosh computers, several versions of the Macintosh OS have been written, the latest being Mac OS X (ten), which offers easy access to the Internet and allows any Macintosh computer to become a Web server for a small network. Table 1-8 summarizes the advantages and disadvantages of the Macintosh OS.

Table 1-8   Advantages and disadvantages of the Macintosh operating system

Advantages	Disadvantages
• The Mac OS has an excellent icon-driven interface, and it is easy to learn and use. • The Mac OS supports cooperative multitasking. • The Mac OS manages large quantities of memory. • Many applications exist for the Mac OS to create and edit graphics, build web sites, and manage multimedia.	• Historically, the Macintosh was not viewed as a professional computer but rather was relegated to education and game playing. Then the Mac gained a significant place in the professional desktop publishing and graphics markets. Most recently, the availability of more powerful IBM-compatible PCs and OSs to handle the high demands of graphics has reduced the demand for the Mac.

How an Operating System Manages an Application

An application depends on an OS to provide access to hardware resources, manage its data in memory and in secondary storage, and perform many other background tasks. Earlier OSs gave applications more latitude and power than later OSs do. For example, under DOS, a program could write data directly to RAM, but now, under Windows NT and Windows 2000, an application is not allowed direct access to RAM. Using today's OSs, the interaction among the hardware, the OS, and applications is more complicated than it was under DOS.

This book focuses on Microsoft operating systems: DOS, Windows 9x, Windows NT, and Windows 2000, by far the most popular OSs for microcomputers. It's true that DOS has become less popular as an OS in recent years. But because Windows has its beginnings rooted in DOS, it is important to understand DOS and the early assumptions and limitations of this OS that still affect Windows today. The two concepts in DOS discussed here are the rules DOS uses to name files (referred to as naming conventions) and how DOS manages memory addressing. Then, in leading up to discussing how applications software interacts with an OS today, we address how DOS interacts with a DOS application. The knowledge gained here will serve you well as you study how Windows 9x accomplishes these same tasks.

A+ OS
 1.2
Filenames Under DOS   Under DOS, a file's name has two parts. The first part, called the **filename**, contains up to eight characters. The second part, called the **file extension**, contains up to three characters. When you write the file extension in DOS commands, you separate the extension from the filename with a period. Acceptable file extensions for program files are .com, .bat, and .exe. For example, the WordPerfect program file is named WP.exe. Its filename is WP and its file extension is .exe.

With the introduction of Windows 95, long filenames traditionally used only by the Macintosh OS became available to IBM-compatible PCs. Under Windows 95 and later Windows generations, filenames can be as long as 255 characters and may contain spaces. You must be careful when using long filenames with Windows 9x because Windows 9x still contains a portion of DOS, which can only understand an 8-character filename, 3-character extension format. When the DOS part of the system is operating, it will truncate long filenames and assign new 8-character ones. More information about naming files appears in Chapter 5.

Memory Addressing Under DOS   In DOS, memory is divided into different areas, as shown in Table 1-9. This division of memory began with DOS and later was used by Windows 3.x and Windows 9x. The first versions of DOS could only access the first megabyte of memory (0 to 1024K) addresses. Later, DOS extenders were included with the OS so that memory above 1024K could be accessed.

Table 1-9   Division of memory under DOS

Range of Memory Addresses	Type of Memory
0 to 640K	Conventional or base memory
640K to 1024K	Upper memory
Above 1024K	Extended memory

Operating System Modes   Recall that an application, the OS, and BIOS can share data by communicating memory addresses, which point to the location of the data in RAM (see Figure 1-29). Also recall that memory addresses are communicated on the system board over a bus where a group of wires, or lines, in the bus are dedicated to this purpose. When DOS was first written, the system board bus only had 20 lines for this purpose. Since information is communicated over the bus in binary (0s and 1s), the largest memory address possible for these system boards was 1111 1111 1111 1111 1111 in binary, (2^{20}) which is 1,048,575 in decimal (see Appendix D for an explanation of this conversion). In effect, there were 1024K of possible memory addresses, and that was all that DOS was designed to use. Also, DOS assumed that only one application or program would be running at a time, so it gave that program direct access to these memory addresses and the data in RAM that they pointed to. Also, the CPU at that time (Model 8088 by Intel Corporation) could only process 16 bits of data at one time, so DOS was designed to pass segments of data to the CPU only 16 bits at a time. These standards of operation are collectively referred to as **real mode**, or MS-DOS mode, as seen in Figure 1-36.

Figure 1-36   Real mode is single-tasking program access to 1024K of memory addresses pointing directly to RAM using a 16-bit data path

    Real mode is limited to 16-bit data processing because originally only 16 lines on the system board bus were devoted to transmitting data to and from the CPU.

Later CPUs and system boards had buses that had as many as 32 wires devoted to memory addresses, allowing up to 4096 MB of addresses and data paths that were 32 bits wide. Both the CPU and the OS could support cooperative multitasking. These new operating methods are known as **protected mode** because the OS ensures that the memory assigned to one program is protected from interference by other programs. Figure 1-37 shows that, in protected mode, more than one program can run, and the programs have access to memory addresses up to 4096 MB (depending on the system board, CPU, and OS being used).

Figure 1-37   Protected mode is multitasking program access to more than 1024K of memory addresses using 32-bit data segments where the OS manages direct memory access

In protected mode, the OS does not allow a program direct access to RAM, but works as the mediator between memory and programs. This allows the OS some latitude in how it uses RAM. If the OS is low on RAM, it can store some data on the hard drive. This method of using the hard drive as though it were RAM is called **virtual memory**, and data stored in virtual memory is really stored in a file on the hard drive called a **swap file**. The OS manages the entire process, and the applications know nothing about this substitution of hardware resources. The programs running in protected mode just have "memory" designated by memory addresses and have no idea where it's located.

Even after protected mode was available, it was important for hardware and software to be **back-ward compatible** (able to support older technology), so real mode was still supported by the CPUs and OSs. In fact, most OSs start in real mode and switch to protected mode before allowing user interaction. DOS operates in real mode. All DOS programs use a 16-bit interface with the CPU, but can use memory addresses above 1024K by using a DOS extender, which will be discussed in detail in later chapters. Windows 9x starts out in real mode and then switches to protected mode. Some of Windows 9x uses 16-bit data access (called 16-bit programs) and some uses 32-bit data access (called 32-bit programs). Because the 32-bit programs access twice as much data at one time as 16-bit programs do, the 32-bit programs are faster. This fact largely explains why Windows 9x is faster than DOS or DOS with Windows 3.x. Windows NT is a true 32-bit OS; all its OS programs are written using 32-bit coding methods.

TIP   The main reason Windows 9x is faster than DOS or DOS with Windows is because it uses 32-bit data access, rather than the slower 16-bit access used by the older Windows software. However, Windows 9x still supports 16-bit software.

An OS will allow a 16-bit program to run in a 32-bit environment by providing it with an environment that appears to the program to be a 16-bit environment. This technique is called **virtual real mode** and will be discussed in Chapter 2.

Applications Software

Most applications software fits into eight categories: word processing, spreadsheet, database management, graphics, communications, games, mathematical modeling, and software development tools. Each software category contains many different products. For example, some popular database management packages include Access, Paradox, and Filemaker, and two popular word-processing packages include Word and WordPerfect. Some applications software manufacturers produce **suites** of software, which combine a word-processing program and spreadsheet program, and usually include a database management program, a presentation package, an e-mail package, and a World Wide Web browser package. Suites provide many advantages, including letting the programs use the same basic instruction sets; the programs are designed to make it easy to move data from one suite program to another; and files within a suite's programs can be linked, so that updates to data or text are automatically recorded in all linked files.

Applications software is designed to work on top of a particular OS. "On top of" here means that the application depends on the OS, such as MS-DOS or Windows 98, in order to run. For example, consider a situation in which Windows 98 loads an application and executes it. The application cannot run or even load itself without Windows 98, much as a document cannot be edited without a word-processing program. Windows 98 stays available to the application for the entire time the application is running. The application passes certain functions to Windows 98, such as reading from a CD-ROM or printing.

An application written to work with one OS, such as Windows 98, does not necessarily work with another, such as a Macintosh system. There are, however, some exceptions. For instance,

OS/2 is written so that any application designed to work with DOS also works with OS/2, an excellent early selling point for OS/2. However, to take full advantage of an OS's power and an application's power, buy applications software written specifically for your OS.

A+ OS
2.4

Applications software comes written on floppy disks or on CD-ROMs and usually must be installed on a hard drive in order to run. Installing a software package usually is very easy. For instance, under DOS, typically you insert the first disk of a set of floppies or a CD-ROM, and then type a command, such as A:INSTALL or D:SETUP at the DOS prompt. If you are working in Windows 9x, you click the Start button, click Run, and then follow the directions on the screen. We discuss software installation in Chapter 12.

How Applications Software Is Loaded and Initialized

Starting applications software seems like a simple task. For example, in Windows 98, you click the shortcut icon on the desktop, and the application window appears, ready for you to use it. But much happens behind the scenes between your click and the appearance of the application awaiting your next command. Recall that software or programs are stored in program files until needed. Before they can be executed, they must first be copied or loaded into RAM and assigned memory addresses. The CPU then works its way through RAM, following each instruction in turn. If the program uses data (and most do), the data is permanently stored in a data file in secondary storage, and must be copied or loaded into RAM and assigned memory addresses before the CPU can process it (see Figure 1-38). Understanding the process of loading and initializing software is important to those people responsible for supporting PCs. Listed below are the major steps that must take place. This section describes the process in detail for several OSs.

1. The OS receives the command to execute the application.

2. The OS locates the program file for the application.

3. The OS loads the program file into memory.

4. The OS gives control to the program.

5. The program requests memory addresses from the OS for its data.

6. The program initializes itself and possibly requests that data from secondary storage be loaded into memory.

7. The program turns to the user for its first instruction.

Figure 1-38   Both the operating system and applications software must be loaded into memory before execution, and existing data must also be copied from secondary storage into memory to be processed. After processing, data must be saved back to secondary storage.

We begin with DOS as our OS. Before we discuss the specific command to load software in DOS, let's first look at the command prompt the user sees and what information it provides. If DOS is your OS, the DOS prompt displays basic information and gives you the opportunity to enter some command for the OS to perform. Most of the time, DOS is loaded from the hard drive, which is designated with the letter C. It is common for computers to provide a DOS prompt that looks like this when the machine is first turned on:

```
C:\>
```

This prompt is called the C prompt. The DOS prompt (C:\>) displayed immediately after booting means that the OS was copied from drive C (where the OS is stored) when the machine was first turned on. As part of the startup process, drive C then becomes the **default drive** and **default directory**, sometimes called the current drive and directory, which DOS automatically uses to save and retrieve files. Sometimes the OS is copied from a floppy disk rather than the hard drive. In this case, the default drive and directory will be A:\ or B:\, and the command prompt will be A:\> or B:\>. A machine usually has at least two drives. The colon following the letter identifies the letter as the name of a drive, and the backslash identifies the directory on the drive as the main directory. The > symbol is the prompt symbol that DOS uses to say, "Enter your command here."

When a hard drive is first formatted for use by an OS, the format procedure creates a single directory on the drive. A directory is a table on a disk that contains a list of files that are stored on the disk. You can think of a directory as a list of files logically grouped together. When a hard drive is first formatted, the **root directory** (that is, the first or main directory on a drive) is the only directory that is created. This directory is written in DOS command lines as a single backslash (\) with no other directory name following. In the preceding DOS prompt, the backslash indicates that it is the root directory. After the drive is initially formatted, you can create other directories for file lists. These directories are given names and are listed in the root directory. These directories can, in turn, have other directories listed in them. These other directories are sometimes called **subdirectories** or **child directories** (see Figure 1-39). Any directory can have files and/or other directories listed in it. By creating different directories on a hard drive, you can organize your program files and data files by placing programs in one directory, and files created by those programs in a second directory. This organization is comparable to keeping paper records in separate folders.

Figure 1-39   A hard drive is organized into groups of files stored in directories. The first directory is called the root directory. All directories can have sub- or child directories. Under Windows, a directory is called a folder.

A drive with a list of directories pointing to a file is called a **path** when used in a DOS command. For instance, if the text file Myfile.txt is stored in the Data directory under the WP directory on the hard drive, the path to Myfile.txt is written as C:\WP\Data\Myfile.txt. The path is used to find the file. For instance, to see the contents of the text file Myfile.txt from any DOS prompt, we use the TYPE command, like this:

```
TYPE C:\WP\DATA\MYFILE.TXT
```

The TYPE command looks on drive C for a directory named WP. In that directory it looks for a subdirectory named DATA. DOS expects to find the file inside this subdirectory. It is appropriate to say that Myfile.txt is located in the path C:\WP\Data. If the file is located anywhere else on the hard drive, DOS will not find it, because we have given it only this one path to the file.

Launching the Program File   Now that you understand the DOS prompt and a path to a file, we turn our attention to giving DOS a command to execute a program. At the DOS prompt, when you type a single group of letters with no spaces, DOS assumes that you want to execute a program with the filename that you just typed, stored in a program file in the current directory. DOS first attempts to find the program file by that name, then copies the file into RAM, and then it executes the program. Let's use running WordPerfect in DOS as an example. In order to run WordPerfect in DOS, you type the letters WP when the OS displays the DOS prompt:

```
C:\>WP
```

A program file executed at the DOS prompt can have one of three file extensions: .com, .exe, or .bat. Therefore, in this example, DOS looks for a file with one of these names: WP.com, WP.exe, or WP.bat.

A+ OS 1.1 The first place DOS looks is in the default drive and directory—in this case, the root directory of the hard drive. If the A:\> prompt was displayed when you typed WP, then DOS would look in the root directory of drive A for the program file. DOS looks for the files in the following order: first WP.com, then WP.exe, and finally WP.bat. DOS executes the first one it finds. If DOS doesn't find any of these files, it stops looking and displays the error message:

```
Bad command or file not found
```

unless you have previously given DOS a list of paths in which to look for executable program files beyond the default directory. You give this list of drives and directories to DOS using the PATH command. You can cause the PATH command to be executed automatically during the booting process by storing the command in the Autoexec.bat file (to be discussed next). However, you can execute the PATH command at any time after booting. The last PATH command you execute overrides any previous one. To see the list of paths that are presently active, type PATH at the DOS prompt, and then press Enter. To enter a new list of paths, type the PATH command followed by each path name, separating one path from the next by a semicolon, as shown in Figure 1-40.

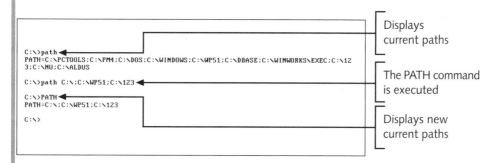

Figure 1-40   The PATH command

In Figure 1-40, the first PATH command displays the list of active paths. The second PATH command changes this list, giving DOS three directories in which to look to find executable files:

- Hard drive and root directory (C:\)
- Hard drive and directory named \WP51 (C:\WP51)
- Hard drive and directory named \123 (C:\123)

A+ OS
  1.1

The last PATH command in Figure 1-40 again displays the list of active paths.

When you tell DOS to execute a program, you can also include the path to that program file as part of the command line. For example, if the WP.exe file is stored in the directory \WP51, you can execute the program by typing the following:

```
C:\> \WP51\WP
```

Here you are telling DOS that the name of the program file is WP and that its location is in the directory \WP51. DOS assumes that the directory \WP51 is on the hard drive rather than on drive A or B, because C is the current default drive. With this method, the directory that contains WordPerfect need not be the default directory, nor do you need the \WP51 path in the PATH command line in the Autoexec.bat file. DOS used Rule 3 in the rules listed earlier for finding a program file.

Another way that you can tell DOS where the program is located is to make the directory containing the program file the current default directory, by using the CHANGE DIRECTORY, or CD, command. For example, you can use the following two commands to execute WordPerfect:

```
C:\> CD \WP51
C:\WP51> WP
```

The CD command directs DOS to make the directory \WP51 the default directory. This default directory appears as part of the DOS prompt. The next command executes the WordPerfect program stored in this directory. Because \WP51 is now the default directory, unless you direct WordPerfect otherwise, documents are saved to and retrieved from the \WP51 directory.

In summary, DOS searches for executable program files using the following rules:

1. If no path is given before the filename, DOS looks in the current directory.

2. If no path is given, and the file is not in the current directory, DOS looks in the paths given to it by the last PATH command executed.

3. If there is a path given in front of the filename in the command line, DOS looks in that path.

4. If there is a path given, but the file is not found in that path, DOS looks in the paths given to it by the last PATH command executed.

From this discussion, you can see that when you tell DOS to execute a program, DOS is unable to find that program unless you do one of the following:

- Include the path to the program file in the PATH command in Autoexec.bat

- Make the directory that contains the program file the default directory, using the CD command

- Include the path to the program file in the command line to execute the program

Copying the Program into Memory Recall that once DOS finds the program file, it copies the file into memory (RAM) in a location that DOS chooses (see Figure 1-41). After it copies the program into memory, DOS goes to the first address in memory occupied by the program, to receive its first instruction. If the program requests some memory for its data (and most will), DOS decides which memory addresses to give the program (usually the memory after the program).

Figure 1-41   Applications software is stored in files but executed from memory

If the program wants to write or read data to or from memory, DOS manages these tasks. If the program needs to print, display something on the screen, or read or write to or from the hard drive or a floppy disk, DOS does the work and returns to the applications software when finished. In other words, DOS is the "software behind the software," doing the background tasks for the application.

Loading Applications Software Using Windows 9x

Windows 9x has a different interface and methods to execute software than does DOS. Windows 9x offers four ways to execute software:

- Place a shortcut icon directly on the desktop for the applications you use often and want to get to quickly. These shortcuts contain the command line used to execute the application. To view this command line, right-click on an icon. A drop-down menu then displays. From the menu, select Properties. The icon's Properties box displays. See Figure 1-42. From this box, you can view the complete command line that the icon represents.

- Click the Start button, select Programs, and select the program from the list of installed software.

- Use the Run command: Click the Start button on the Windows 9x taskbar and then click Run to display the Run dialog box. See Figure 1-43. In this box, enter a command line or click Browse to search for a program file to execute.

- Execute a program or launch an applications file by double-clicking the filename in Windows 9x Explorer or My Computer.

A⁺ *OS*
 1.1

Shortcut icon

Shortcut Properties dialog box

Path to program file

Desktop

Task bar

Figure 1-42   Windows 9x has icons on the desktop that point to program files on the hard drive

Command line

Use Browse to search for a program file

Figure 1-43   The Windows 9x Run dialog box allows you to enter DOS-like commands

In summary:

- Applications software is executed by either the operating environment (Windows 3.x) or the OS software (DOS or Windows 9x).

- When an application is executing, you are interacting with the application.

- Applications software interacts with the OS software that is executing it.

- OS software interacts with hardware.

- OS software might interact with the hardware through BIOS or the device driver for this hardware.

1

CHAPTER SUMMARY

- The four basic functions of the microcomputer are input, output, processing, and storage of data.

- The four most popular input/output devices are the printer, monitor, mouse, and keyboard.

- The most important component inside the computer case is the system board, or motherboard, which contains the most important microchip inside the case, the central processing unit (CPU), a microprocessor, as well as access to other circuit boards and peripheral devices. All communications between the CPU and other devices must pass through the system board.

- Data and instructions are stored in a computer in binary, which uses only two states for data, on and off or 1 and 0.

- A ROM BIOS microchip is a hybrid of hardware and software containing programming embedded into the chip. These chips are called firmware.

- Each hardware device needs a method to communicate with the CPU, software to control it, and electricity to power it.

- Devices outside the computer case are connected to the system board by way of ports on the case.

- A circuit board inserted in an expansion slot on the system board can be used to provide an interface between the system board and a peripheral device, or can itself be a peripheral (an example is an internal modem).

- The chip set on a system board relieves the CPU of some of the system's processing demands and controls many components on the board.

- Primary storage, or RAM, is temporary storage used by the CPU to hold data and instructions while it is processing both.

- RAM is stored on single chips, SIMMs, DIMMs, and RIMMs.

- Cache memory is used on the system board or inside the CPU housing as fast RAM to improve processing speed.

- The buses on the system board are used to communicate data, instructions, and electrical power to components on the board.

- The system clock is used to synchronize activity on the system board, sending continuous pulses over the bus to different components.

- Setup or configuration information in a PC is stored in the CMOS chip on the system board and by means of jumpers and switches.

- Electricity is supplied to components both inside and outside the computer case by the power supply inside the case. Some components external to the case get their power from their own electrical cable.

❐ Secondary storage is slower than primary storage, but is permanent storage. The most common examples of secondary storage devices are floppy disk, hard drive, and CD-ROM drive.

❐ Three types of software are BIOS, operating systems (OSs), and applications software.

❐ BIOS is used at startup and after startup by the OS to provide software control of hardware devices.

❐ Applications software relates to the OS, which relates to BIOS and device drivers to control hardware.

❐ Operating systems utilize BIOS, manage secondary storage and primary storage, help diagnose problems with hardware and software, interface between hardware and software, and perform various housekeeping tasks.

❐ When a PC is first turned on, the startup BIOS is in control. It later loads the OS and then turns control over to it.

❐ Users interact with an OS by a command-driven, menu-driven, or icon-driven interface.

❐ The most well-known OSs for microcomputers are DOS, Windows, UNIX, Mac OS, and OS/2.

❐ True multitasking is not possible using CPUs built before the Pentium.

❐ DOS is being replaced by Windows as the most popular OS, but decisions made when DOS was designed still affect Windows 9x today.

❐ For DOS, the three types of logical primary memory are conventional (or base) memory, upper memory, and extended memory.

❐ Software manages memory by means of memory addresses that point to locations in RAM. The number of memory addresses is partly limited by the number of wires on the bus devoted to these addresses.

❐ The size of the data segment that software can access at one time is determined by the number of wires on the bus assigned for the data path.

❐ Real mode was used by DOS and is limited to single-tasking, a 16-bit data path, and 1024K of memory addresses.

❐ Protected mode allows more than one program to run at a time, can use a 32-bit data path, and has more than 1024K of memory addresses. In protected mode, the OS manages access to RAM and does not allow a program direct access to it.

❐ Virtual memory is "fake" memory whereby data is stored in a swap file on the hard drive. The OS makes applications think that they are using real memory.

❐ When an OS receives the command to execute a software program, it follows explicit rules as to where it looks to find the program file for the software.

❐ A program must first be loaded into memory before the OS can execute it.

KEY TERMS

Backward compatible — Refers to new hardware and software that is able to support older, existing technologies. This is a common choice of hardware and software manufacturers.

Binary number system — The number system used by computers; it has only two numbers, 0 and 1, called binary digits, or bits.

BIOS (basic input/output system) — Firmware that controls much of a computer's input/output functions, such as communication with the floppy drive, RAM chips, and the monitor. Also called RAM BIOS.

Booting — The process that a computer goes through when it is first turned on to get the computer ready to receive commands.

Bus — The paths, or lines, on the system board on which data, instructions, and electrical power travel.

Cache memory — A kind of fast RAM that is used to speed up memory access because it does not need to be continuously refreshed.

Cards — Adapter boards or interface cards placed into expansion slots to expand the functions of a computer, allowing it to communicate with external devices such as monitors or speakers.

Child directory — *See* Subdirectory.

Chip set — A group of chips on the system board that relieves the CPU of some of the system's processing tasks, increasing the overall speed and performance of the system.

Circuit boards — Computer components, such as the main system board or an adapter board, that have electronic circuits and chips.

Client — A computer that is connected to another computer and uses programs and/or data stored on the other computer.

CMOS (complementary metal-oxide semiconductor) — One of two types of technologies used to manufacture microchips (the other type is TTL, or transistor-transistor logic chips). CMOS chips require less electricity, hold data longer after the electricity is turned off, are slower, and produce less heat than do TTL chips. The configuration or setup chip is a CMOS chip.

COAST (cache on a stick) — Memory modules that hold memory used as a memory cache. *See* Cache memory.

Cooperative multitasking — A type of pseudomultitasking whereby the CPU switches back and forth between programs loaded at the same time. One program sits in the background waiting for the other to relinquish control. Also called task switching.

Coprocessor — A chip or portion of the CPU that helps the microprocessor perform calculations and speeds up computations and data manipulations dramatically.

CPU (central processing unit) — Also called a microprocessor or processor. The heart and brain of the computer, which receives data input, processes information, and executes instructions.

Default directory — The directory that DOS automatically uses to save and retrieve files.

Default drive — The drive that DOS automatically uses to save and retrieve files.

Default printer — The printer that Windows software will use unless the user specifies another printer.

Desktop — The initial screen that is displayed when an OS that has a GUI interface is loaded.

Device driver — A small program stored on the hard drive that tells the computer how to communicate with an input/output device such as a printer or modem.

DIMM (dual inline memory module) — A miniature circuit board used in newer computers to hold memory. DIMMs can hold 16, 32, 64, or 128 MB of RAM on a single module.

DIP (dual in-line package) switch — A switch on a circuit board or other device that can be set on or off to hold configuration or setup information.

Environment — As related to OSs, the overall support that an OS provides to applications software.

Expansion card — A circuit board inserted into a slot on the system board to enhance the capability of the computer.

Expansion slot — A narrow slot on the system board where an expansion card can be inserted. Expansion slots connect to a bus on the system board.

File — A collection of related records or lines that can be written to disk and assigned a name (for example, a simple letter or a payroll file containing data about employees).

File extension — A three-character portion of the name of a file that is used to identify the file type. The file extension follows the filename under DOS naming conventions.

Filename — The first part of the name assigned to a file. In DOS, the filename can be no more than eight characters long and is followed by the file extension.

Firmware — Software that is permanently stored in a chip.

Flash ROM — ROM that can be reprogrammed or changed without replacing chips.

GUI (graphical user interface) — A user interface, such as the Windows interface, that uses graphics or icons on the screen for running programs and entering information.

Hard copy — Output from a printer to paper.

Hard drive — The main secondary storage device of a PC, a sealed case that contains magnetic coated platters that rotate at high speed.

Hard drive controller — A set of microchips with programs that control a hard drive. Most hard drive controllers today are located inside the hard drive housing.

Hardware — The physical components that constitute the computer system, such as the monitor, the keyboard, the system board, and the printer.

Jumper — Two wires that stick up side by side on the system board that are used to hold configuration information. The jumper is considered closed if a cover is over the wires, and open if the cover is missing.

Keyboard — A common input device through which data and instructions may be typed into computer memory.

Main board — *See* System board.

Memory address — A number assigned to each byte in RAM. The CPU can use memory addresses to track where information is stored in RAM. Memory addresses are usually displayed as hexadecimal numbers in segment/offset form.

Monitor — The most commonly used output device for displaying text and graphics on a computer.

Motherboard — *See* System board.

Mouse — A pointing and input device that allows the user to move a cursor around a screen and select programs with the click of a button.

Multitasking — When a CPU or an OS supporting multiple CPUs can do more than one thing at a time. The Pentium is a multitasking CPU.

Nonvolatile — Refers to a kind of RAM that is stable and can hold data as long as electricity is powering the memory.

On-Board BIOS — *See* System BIOS.

Path — The drive and list of directories pointing to a file.

Peripheral devices — Devices that communicate with the CPU, but are not located directly on the system board, such as the monitor, floppy drive, printer, and mouse.

Pixel — The smallest dot that can be addressed by software on a monitor screen. An image is composed of many pixels.

Plug and Play — A feature of system BIOS, Windows 9x, and Windows 2000 that automatically installs new hardware devices and assigns resources to them.

Port — A physical connector, usually at the back of a computer, that allows a cable from a peripheral device, such as a printer, mouse, or modem, to be attached.

Power supply — A box inside the computer case that supplies power to the system board and other installed devices. Power supplies provide 3.3, 5, and 12 volts DC.

Preemptive multitasking — A type of pseudomultitasking whereby the CPU allows an application a specified period of time and then preempts the processing to give time to another application.

Primary storage — Temporary storage on the system board used by the CPU to process data and instructions.

Printer — A peripheral output device that produces printed output to paper. Different types include dot matrix, ink-jet, and laser printers.

Program — A set of step-by-step instructions to a computer. Some are burned directly into chips, while others are stored as program files. Programs are written in languages such as BASIC and C++.

Program file — A file that contains instructions designed to be executed by the CPU.

Program jump — An instruction that causes control to be sent to a memory address other than the next sequential address.

Protected mode — An operating mode that supports multitasking whereby the OS manages memory, programs have more than 1024K of memory addresses, and programs can use a 32-bit data path.

Protocol — A set of rules and standards that two entities use for communication.

RAM (random access memory) — Temporary memory stored on chips, such as SIMMs, inside the computer. Information in RAM disappears when the computer's power is turned off.

Real mode — A single-tasking operating mode whereby a program only has 1024K of memory addresses, has direct access to RAM, and uses a 16-bit data path.

RIMM — A type of memory module used on newer system boards

ROM (read-only memory) — Chips that contain programming code and cannot be erased.

ROM BIOS — *See* BIOS.

Root directory — The main directory created when a hard drive or disk is first formatted.

Secondary storage — Storage that is remote to the CPU and permanently holds data, even when the PC is turned off.

Server — A microcomputer or minicomputer that stores programs and data to be used remotely by other computers.

SIMM (single inline memory module) — A miniature circuit board used in a computer to hold RAM. SIMMs hold 8, 16, 32, or 64 MB on a single module.

Software — Computer programs, or instructions to perform a specific task. Software may be BIOS, OSs, or applications software such as a word-processing or spreadsheet program.

Startup BIOS — Part of system BIOS that is responsible for controlling the PC when it is first turned on. Startup BIOS gives control over to the OS once it is loaded.

Subdirectory — In DOS, a directory that is contained within another directory. Also called a child directory.

Suite — As applies to applications software, a collection of applications software sold as a bundle, whose components are designed to be compatible with one another. An example is Microsoft Office.

Swap file — A file on the hard drive that is used by the OS for virtual memory.

System BIOS — BIOS located on the system board.

System board — The main board in the computer, also called the motherboard. The CPU, ROM chips, SIMMs, DIMMs, and interface cards are plugged into the system board.

System clock — A line on a bus that is dedicated to timing the activities of components connected to it. The system clock provides a continuous pulse that other devices use to time themselves.

Task switching — *See* Cooperative multitasking.

Trace — A wire on a circuit board that connects two components or devices.

Video card — An interface card installed in the computer to control visual output on a monitor.

Virtual memory — A method whereby the OS uses the hard drive as though it were RAM.

Virtual real mode — An operating mode in which an OS provides an environment to a 16-bit program that acts like real mode.

Volatile — Refers to a kind of RAM that is temporary, cannot hold data very long, and must be frequently refreshed.

REVIEW QUESTIONS

1. Why is all data stored in a computer in binary form?
2. How does firmware differ from a software program stored on the hard drive?
3. What are the four primary functions of hardware?
4. What three things do electronic hardware devices need in order to function?
5. Name two input devices.
6. Obtain the manual for a system board and look for a diagram of the system board components similar to Figure 1-8. Identify as many components from the figure on your diagram as you can.
7. What is the purpose of an expansion slot on a system board?
8. Which components on the system board are used primarily for processing?
9. Which can hold the most memory, a SIMM or a DIMM?
10. What three things travel on a system board bus?
11. Give three examples of secondary storage devices.
12. Which OS (include version) does your home or lab computer use?
13. What does BIOS stand for, and what does it do?
14. List three well-known OSs.
15. Give three examples of OSs that use a GUI.
16. What might cause the error message "Bad command or file not found"?
17. What is the default directory of your home or lab computer immediately after bootup?
18. In the chapter, the concepts of primary storage and secondary storage are introduced. In Figure 1-38, a program was moved from secondary storage to primary storage before it could be executed. Based on this figure and concept, why do you think a hard drive is called secondary storage and memory is called primary storage?
19. Complete the following table. Refer to Appendix D as necessary.

Type of Memory	Beginning Memory Address in Hex	Ending Memory Address in Hex	Beginning Memory Address as a Decimal Number	Ending Memory Address as a Decimal Number	Ending Memory Address in Decimal Kilobytes
Conventional or base	0	9FFFF			
Upper	A0000	FFFFF			
Extended	100000	N/A		N/A	N/A

20. The number of memory addresses is limited by the _____ on the system board.
21. The amount of memory available to software is limited by the _____ on the system board.
22. In what three ways can configuration information be stored on a system board?

23. Name one way BIOS and device drivers are the same. Name one way they are different.

24. When one software layer passes data to another, it usually refers to the _____ of the data.

25. How does cooperative multitasking differ from preemptive multitasking?

26. Which OS was the first to introduce Plug and Play?

27. Using DOS, why is this not a valid file name?: EMPLOYEES.TXT

28. Memory above 1024K is called _____.

29. Real mode operates using a _____-bit data path, and protected mode uses a _____-bit data path.

30. Real mode allows programs direct access to _____, but protected mode does not.

PROJECTS

Observing the Boot Process and Hardware Components

1. Carefully watch your computer screen during the boot process (press Pause if necessary), and record which CPU is used by your home or lab computer.

2. Who is the BIOS vendor and what version of the BIOS are you using?

3. As the computer boots, memory is counted. Observe the memory count and record the amount of memory detected. What number system is used to count this memory?

4. Open the printer icon in the Windows Control Panel and find out which is the default Windows printer for your home or lab computer.

5. Look at the back (or the front if the ports are located there) of your home or lab computer and make a drawing. Label on the drawing the purpose of each port and connection you see. If you are not sure what the purpose of the port is, label the port "unknown port." In later chapters, the purposes of these unknown ports will become clear.

Using the Internet for Research

Linux is one of the fastest growing OSs today. What is the official mascot for Linux? Who chose it, and why? *Hint*: See *www.linux.org*.

Using Microsoft Diagnostics with Windows

1

DOS and Windows offer the Microsoft Diagnostics command. This utility examines your system, displaying useful information about ports, devices, memory, and the like. (For Windows 9x, search for the MSD.EXE utility on your Windows 9x installation CD and copy it to your hard drive.) Boot your PC to a DOS prompt. From the DOS prompt, execute this command:

```
C:\> MSD
```

You should see a screen similar to that in Figure 1-44. Browse carefully through all the menu options of this interesting utility and answer the following questions about your system:

a. List the following or print the appropriate MSD screen:

Manufacturer, version number, and date of your System BIOS, video BIOS, and mouse device driver.

b. What kind of video card is installed?

Use the information in Appendix D, "The Hexadecimal Number System and Memory Addressing," to answer these questions:

❐ How much memory is currently installed on this PC?

❐ Look under TSR programs (terminate-and-stay-resident programs, programs currently stored in memory but not running, will be covered in a later chapter) for the MSD.exe program that you are executing. What is the hex address of the beginning of this program? Convert the hex address to a decimal address.

❐ What version of DOS are you running?

❐ What CPU are you using?

Figure 1-44   MSD opening screen

When you are finished, exit the MSD utility and return to the C prompt.

Using Device Manager

Windows 9x provides a much more powerful tool than MSD, called Device Manager. From it you can view and print your hardware configuration. To access Device Manager, follow these steps.

1. Click the **Start** button on the taskbar, click **Settings**, and then click **Control Panel**.

2. When the Control Panel window appears, double-click the **System** icon.

3. In the System Properties dialog box, click the **Device Manager** tab.

The opening menu of Device Manager appears as shown in Figure 1-45. You can select an item from the list and then click Properties to view information about that item, or you can view the Properties by double-clicking the item. When you click the + sign to the left of an item, a list of the installed devices for that item appears beneath the item.

Figure 1-45   The Device Manager in Windows 98

Answer these questions about your computer:

1. Does your computer have a network card installed? If so, what is the name of the card?

2. What are three settings that can be changed under Device Manager?

3. What are all the hardware devices that Device Manager recognizes as present?

Use Shareware to Examine a Computer

Note: This exercise requires access to the Internet.

Good PC support people are always good investigators. The Internet offers a wealth of resources to those who take the time to search, download, and investigate the possible uses of software available there. This exercise is designed to help you learn to be such an investigator. Follow these directions to download a shareware utility to diagnose Windows 9x or Windows 3.x problems and print a report from the downloaded software about the hardware and software on your computer.

1. Access the Internet and go to this address:

   http://www.zdnet.com

2. Search for SANDRA. SANDRA stands for System Analyzer Diagnostic and Reporting Assistant and offers information about the hardware and software on your computer.

3. Follow the steps on the screen to download the file Sandra.zip to your PC. You can then disconnect from the Internet.

4. Uncompress Sandra.zip by double-clicking the filename and then extracting Setup.exe with its components.

5. Run the setup program, Setup.exe, which creates a new program in your Program Group.

6. Run the program SiSoft Sandra, and the screen shown in Figure 1-46 appears. You can execute each of the icons in turn by double-clicking them, or you can create a composite report of the results of each selection. Answer these questions:

   a. What is the model and speed of your CPU?

   b. Which version of Windows are you using?

   c. Which icons are not available to you because your copy of SANDRA is not registered?

Figure 1-46   Shareware utility for Windows 9x

You will use SANDRA again in later chapters, so don't erase her! By the way, try to find SANDRA through *www.shareware.com* and *www.sisoft.com*. Is the program available through these avenues as well?

Using Nuts & Bolts to Examine Your System

Follow the directions in the Preface to install Nuts & Bolts to your hard drive from the CD-ROM accompanying this book. Use Discover Pro to answer the following questions. (To access Discover Pro, click **Start**, **Programs**, **Nuts & Bolts**, **Discover Pro**.)

1. What CPU are you using?

2. What CPU speed does the manufacturer claim?

3. At what actual speed is the CPU running?

4. What is the BIOS manufacturer and production date?

5. How much RAM is in the system?

6. Which version of Windows are you using? Which version of DOS?

7. What software is currently running (Discover Pro calls these "tasks")? Are they 16-bit or 32-bit programs?

8. What is the size of your hard drive? How much of the drive is in use? How much is free?

9. What printers are installed on the computer? (An installed printer means that Windows has the printer device driver installed and available for use.)

10. Under Discover Pro Diagnostics, run the test of memory. Were any memory errors discovered?

2

HOW SOFTWARE AND HARDWARE WORK TOGETHER

In this chapter, you will learn:

♦ What happens when you first turn on a computer, so that both the hardware and the software are poised to follow your directions

♦ How hardware interacts with the system and how software manages hardware resources

♦ Practical and easy ways to protect hardware and software

In Chapter 1, you experienced "the grand tour" of all hardware and software components that make up a computer system. You saw hardware devices used for input, output, processing, and storage of data. You saw the hardware components that make up the electrical system of the computer and the components used for communicating both data and instructions from one device to another—buses on the system board being of paramount importance in that communication. The CPU was hailed as the central processing point for all data and instructions, and you learned that both must be stored in memory with assigned memory addresses before processing can begin.

On the software side, you learned that software works in layers, with the lowest layer (BIOS and device drivers) interfacing with hardware, and the highest layer (applications software) interfacing with the user. The OS is the middleman layer coordinating everything.

Chapter 1 surveyed individual components that make up a computer system. The focus of Chapter 2 is on learning how these individual components work together to perform tasks. If Chapter 1 is the grand tour, then this chapter invites you backstage to see firsthand how things work. First, the chapter continues with the boot process presented in Chapter 1. You will study booting in detail, and learn how you can customize the process, and troubleshoot and solve boot problems.

The boot process will serve as an introduction to thoroughly understanding how hardware and software components work together, which is the heart of this chapter. The major goal of this chapter is that, at its conclusion, you will say, "Aha, I finally understand the basics of how a computer really works!" Essential to this mastery is understanding how lines on a system-board bus are used, how hardware makes requests of the CPU to process its data, and how software, using the CPU, passes commands and requests for information to a hardware device. Before studying how this interaction takes place, we first look at the tools components use to do all that. These tools, including memory and other shared resources that peripheral hardware and software use for interaction, are both physical and logical; they're called system resources and are surveyed early in our discussion.

Our discussion of how computers work, presented in this chapter and Chapter 1, would be incomplete if we omitted a discussion of one of the most fundamental tasks of managing computer resources: protecting data, software, and hardware from the most common hazards. This chapter ends with a section describing how to make and use backups, how to protect a computer from hazardous electricity, and the practical precautions to take when troubleshooting a computer problem.

THE BOOT, OR STARTUP, PROCESS

Remember that computer hardware without software is about as useless as a car without a driver. Recall from Chapter 1 that the mechanic and chauffeur shown in Figure 2-1 were compared to startup software that prepared the hardware for action and other software that controlled the hardware once the startup process was completed. The user is like the passenger who directs the chauffeur. In this chapter, the analogy goes a step further. Software controls hardware by way of the CPU, much as a chauffeur controls a car with a steering wheel. Software (including firmware) is layered as shown in Figure 2-2. A user interacts with applications software, which interacts with the OS, which interacts with BIOS and device drivers, which interact with the hardware.

In this chapter, you will learn many of the details of the boot process, which is partly performed by startup BIOS, playing the role of a mechanic who prepares the car for a trip by thoroughly checking critical systems. When the car is in acceptable condition, the mechanic turns the car over to a chauffeur who does some additional minor checking of resources, such as determining the amount of gas in the car and whether the brakes work. This initial startup process performed by the chauffeur compares to startup routines performed by the OS after control is given to it by startup BIOS. Now all is ready to begin. The combination of software programs—applications software, the OS, the BIOS, and device drivers—play the role of a chauffeur, who in addition to keeping an eye on the status of the car, knows how to operate and direct the vehicle.

Figure 2-1   A user interacts with a computer much as a passenger interacts with a chauffeured car

Figure 2-2   The user interacts with applications software that interfaces with the OS; the OS uses either BIOS or device drivers to interface with the hardware

But, remember that the chauffeur will only go where his passenger—who is analogous to a computer user—tells him to go. Thus, the various players work together: the mechanic (BIOS startup program) checks the car (hardware) to make sure it is ready to be used; the passenger (user) provides specific instructions to the chauffeur (software) on what to do or where to go; and the chauffeur (software) interacts directly with the steering wheel (CPU) to control the various underlying mechanisms that make the car (computer) work as intended.

Just as a chauffeur has resources or tools to control a car (for example, controls on the console), and the car has resources to alert the chauffeur that it needs attention (for example, the oil warning light), software has resources to control hardware, and hardware has resources to alert software that it needs attention. Think of a system resource as a tool used by either hardware or software to communicate with the other.

System Resources Defined

There are four types of system resources: memory addresses, I/O addresses, interrupt request numbers (IRQs), and direct memory access (DMA) channels. Table 2-1 lists these system resources used by software and hardware and defines each.

Table 2-1   System resources used by software and hardware

System Resource	Purpose
IRQ	A line of a system-board bus that a hardware device can use to signal the CPU that the device needs attention. Some lines have a higher priority for attention than others. Each IRQ line is identified by a single number.
I/O addresses	Numbers assigned to hardware devices that software uses to get devices' attention and to interact with them. Each device "listens" for these numbers and responds to the ones assigned to it.
Memory addresses	Numbers that are assigned to physical memory located either in RAM or ROM chips. Software can then access this memory by using these addresses.
DMA channel	A number designating a channel whereby the device can pass data to memory without involving the CPU. Think of a DMA channel as a shortcut for data moving to/from the device and memory.

As you can see from Table 2-1, all four resources are used for communication between hardware and software. Hardware devices signal the CPU for attention using an IRQ. Software addresses a device by one of its I/O addresses. Software looks at memory as a hardware device and addresses it with memory addresses, and DMA channels are used to pass data back and forth between a hardware device and memory.

The Boot Process, Step by Step

The processes that occur when a computer is booted are vital to ensuring that it will operate as desired. The functions performed during the boot are:

- Startup BIOS tests essential hardware components. This test is called the **power-on self test** (**POST**).
- Setup information is used to configure both hardware and software.

2

- Hardware components are assigned system resources that they will later use for communication.

- The OS is loaded, configured, and executed.

- Hardware devices are matched up with the BIOS and device drivers that control them.

- Some applications software may be loaded and executed.

Booting comes from the phrase "lifting yourself up by your bootstraps," and refers to the computer bringing itself up to an operable state without user intervention. Booting refers to either a "soft boot" or "hard boot." A **hard boot**, or **cold boot**, involves initially turning on the power with the on/off switch. A **soft boot** or **warm boot** involves using the operating system to reboot. For DOS, pressing three keys at the same time—Ctrl, Alt, and Del—performs a soft boot. For Windows 95 or 98 (referred to here as Windows 9x), one way to soft boot is to click Start, click Shut Down, and then click OK.

A hard boot is more stressful on your machine than a soft boot because of the initial power surge through the equipment. Always use the soft boot method to restart unless the soft boot method doesn't work. If you must power down, avoid turning off the power switch and immediately turning it back on without a pause, because this can damage the machine. Most PCs have a reset button on the front of the case. Pressing the reset button starts the booting process at an earlier point than does the operating-system method and is, therefore, a little slower, but might work when the operating-system method fails. For newer system boards, pressing the reset button is the same thing as powering off and on except that there is no stress to the system caused by the initial power surge.

The most popular desktop operating system today is Windows 9x, but, because Windows 9x has its roots in DOS, we first cover the details of how DOS is booted and then explain the differences between booting it and Windows 9x.

A+ OS
2.3

The boot process can be divided into four parts: POST, loading the OS, the OS initializing itself, and finally loading and executing an application. Here is a brief overview of all four before we look at each one in detail.

Step 1: POST. The ROM BIOS startup program surveys hardware resources and needs, and assigns system resources to meet those needs (see Figure 2-3). The ROM BIOS startup program begins the startup process by reading configuration information stored in DIP switches, jumpers, and the CMOS chip, and then comparing that information to the hardware—the CPU, video card, disk drive, hard drive, and so on. Some hardware devices have BIOSs of their own that request resources from startup BIOS, which attempts to assign these system resources as needed.

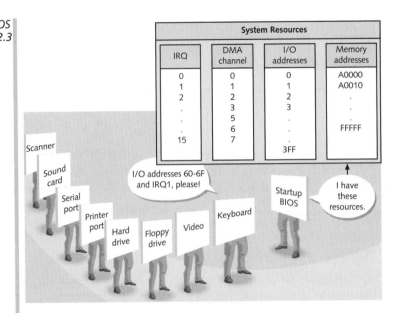

Figure 2-3   Boot Step 1: ROM BIOS startup program surveys hardware resources and needs and assigns system resources to satisfy those needs

Step 2: The ROM BIOS startup program searches for and loads an OS. Most often the OS is loaded from logical drive C on the hard drive (Figure 2-4). Configuration information on the CMOS chip tells startup BIOS where to look for the OS (Figure 2-5). The BIOS turns to that device, reads the beginning files of the OS, copies them into memory, and then turns control over to the OS.

Figure 2-4   A hard drive might contain more than one logical drive; the partition table at the beginning of the drive contains information about the location of each logical drive, indicates which drive is the boot drive, and holds the master boot record that begins the boot process for the operating system

Figure 2-5   Boot Step 2: BIOS searches for and begins to load an operating system (in this example, DOS is the OS)

Step 3: The OS configures the system and completes its own loading (see Figure 2-6). The OS checks some of the same things that startup BIOS checked, such as available memory and whether that memory is reliable. Additionally, the OS continues beyond that by loading the software to control a mouse, CD-ROM, scanner, and other

A+ OS
   2.3
peripheral devices. These devices generally have programs to manage them, called device drivers, stored on the hard drive. Figure 2-6 shows how DOS core components and applications are loaded. Details of this loading process are covered later in the chapter.

Figure 2-6   Boot Step 3: Operating system completes the boot process; DOS core components and applications are loaded

Step 4: The user executes applications software. When you tell the OS to execute an application, the OS first must find the applications software on the hard drive, CD-ROM, or other secondary storage device, copy the software into memory, and then turn control over to it. Finally, you can command the applications software, which makes requests to the OS, which, in turn, uses the system resources, system BIOS, and device drivers to interface with and control the hardware. Your trip has begun!

Step 1: Power-on Self Test (POST)

When you turn on the power to a PC, the CPU begins the process by initializing itself and then turning to the ROM BIOS for instructions. The ROM BIOS then performs POST. Listed below are the key steps in this process.

- When the power is first turned on, the system clock begins to generate clock pulses.

- The CPU begins working and initializes itself (resetting its internal values).

- The CPU turns to memory address FFFF0h, which is the memory address always assigned to the first instruction in the ROM BIOS startup program.

- This instruction directs the CPU to run the POST tests.

- POST first checks the BIOS program operating it and then tests CMOS RAM.

- A test determines that there has not been a battery failure.

- Hardware interrupts are disabled (this means that pressing a key on the keyboard or using another input device at this point will not affect anything).

- Tests are run on the CPU and it is further initialized.

- A check determines if this is a cold boot. If so, the first 16 KB of RAM is tested.

- Hardware devices installed on the computer are inventoried and compared to configuration information.

- Video, memory, keyboard, floppy disk drives, hard drives, ports, and other hardware devices are tested and configured, and IRQ, I/O addresses, and DMA assignments made. The OS will later complete this process.

- Some devices are set up to go into "sleep mode" to conserve electricity.

- The DMA controller is checked.

- Interrupt vectors are moved into the interrupt vector table (this table is covered later in this chapter).

- The interrupt controller is checked (its purpose is explained later in this chapter).

- CMOS setup (a BIOS program to change CMOS configuration data) is run if requested.

- BIOS begins its search for an OS.

A+CORE 2.1 During POST, before the CPU has checked the video system, errors encountered up to this point are communicated by beeps. Short and long beeps indicate an error. Appendix A lists some of these error codes and their meanings. After POST checks and verifies the video controller card (note that POST does not check to see if a monitor is present or working), POST can use the monitor to display its progress. After checking video, POST checks RAM by writing and reading data. A running count of RAM is displayed on the monitor during this phase.

Next, the keyboard is checked, and if you press and hold any keys at this point, an error occurs. Secondary storage, including floppy disk drives and hard drives, is checked. The hardware that POST finds is checked against the data stored in the CMOS chip, jumpers, and/or DIP switches to determine if they agree.

System resources are assigned to devices by more than one method. Jumpers and DIP switches might be set to request a resource (for example, a jumper might be set "on" if IRQ 5 is requested or "off" if IRQ 7 is requested), or the resources needed might simply be "hard coded" into the BIOS. "Hard coded" means that the values of resources are part of the ROM programming and cannot be changed.

For earlier computers, system resources were always assigned to the device during the boot-ing process (see Figure 2-3). Think of the process as a dialog: The startup BIOS recognizes that a hardware device is present. The BIOS asks the device, "What resources do you need?" The device says, "I need this IRQ, these I/O addresses, this DMA channel, and these addresses in upper memory for my BIOS." In almost all cases, a device is the sole owner of these resources. Problems occur when more than one device attempts to use the same resource.

Today, more cooperative Plug and Play devices (introduced in Chapter 1) simply say, "I need one IRQ, some I/O addresses, and this many memory addresses for my BIOS. Please tell me the resources I can use." Plug and Play is discussed in detail in Chapter 12.

Step 2: BIOS Finds and Loads the OS

Once POST is complete, the next step is to load an OS. Most often the OS is loaded from the hard drive (see Figure 2-4). The minimum information required on the hard drive to load an OS is:

A+ OS
1.1

- A small program at the very beginning of the hard drive called the master boot program that is needed to locate the beginning of the OS on the drive.

- A table that contains a map to the logical drives on the hard drive, including which drive is the boot drive. This table is called the partition table.

- At the beginning of the boot drive (usually drive C) the OS boot record that loads the first program file of the OS. For DOS, that program is IO.SYS.

- For DOS, MSDOS.SYS is needed next, followed by COMMAND.COM. These two files plus IO.SYS are the core components of DOS.

Often a hard drive is divided or partitioned into more than one logical drive—for example, drive C and drive D, as seen in Figure 2-4. Whether a hard drive has one or several logical drives, it always contains a single partition table located at the very beginning of the drive. At the beginning of the table is a small program used to start the boot process from the hard drive, which is called the master boot program, or master boot record (MBR). One logical drive on the drive is designated as the boot drive, and the OS is stored on it. At the begin-ning of this logical drive is the OS boot record that knows the names of the files that contain the core programs of the OS.

The process for BIOS to load the OS begins with BIOS looking to CMOS setup to find out which secondary storage device should have the OS (see Figure 2-5). Setup might instruct the BIOS to first look to drive C, and, if no OS is found there, then try drive A; or the order might be A then C. If BIOS looks first to drive A and does not find a disk in the drive, it turns to drive C. If it first looks to drive A and finds a disk in the drive, but the disk does not contain the OS (for DOS, that means the DOS boot record, IO.SYS, MSDOS.SYS, and COMMAND.COM), then this error message is displayed:

```
Non-system disk or disk error, replace and press any key
```

You must replace the disk with one that contains the OS or simply remove the disk to force the BIOS to continue on to drive C to find the OS. In the next section, we examine the details of booting using MS-DOS, Windows 95, and Windows 98. A discussion of booting using Windows NT is left to Chapter 13, and booting Windows 2000 is covered in Chapter 14.

Step 3: The OS Completes the Boot Process

This section describes what first happens during booting when DOS is loaded as the OS. In Step 2 of Figure 2-5, the BIOS locates the master boot record on the hard drive, which looks to the partition table to determine where the logical boot drive is physically located on the drive. It then turns to the DOS boot record of that logical drive.

The DOS boot record is a very short program; it loads just two hidden files which make up the core part of DOS (sometimes called the DOS kernel), into memory (see Figure 2-5, Step 3 and Figure 2-6). (A **hidden file** is a file not displayed in the directory list.) The DOS boot record program knows the filenames, which are IO.SYS and MSDOS.SYS for Microsoft DOS, and IBMBIO.COM and IBMDOS.COM for IBM DOS. You'll see IBM DOS on IBM and Compaq PCs and Microsoft DOS on other PCs. The IO.SYS file contains more BIOS software. MSDOS.SYS contains software to manage files, run applications software, and interface with hardware. Once these two files are loaded into memory, the boot record program is no longer needed, and control turns to a program stored in MSDOS.SYS. This program looks on the hard drive for a file named CONFIG.SYS. CONFIG.SYS is the first OS file that you, as a user, can change. This configuration file contains commands that tell DOS how many files it can open at any one time (FILES=) and how many file buffers to create (BUFFERS=). (A buffer is a temporary holding area for files.) CONFIG.SYS also includes the commands to load device drivers (DEVICE=) as well as other information. (Remember a driver is a program that instructs the computer how to communicate with and manage a peripheral device such as a modem or scanner.) An example of a typical command in CONFIG.SYS is the following:

```
DEVICE=C:\SCANGAL\SCANNER.SYS
```

This command line tells DOS to look in a directory named \SCANGAL on drive C for a file named SCANNER.SYS, copy it into memory, and save it there until an application requests to use a scanner. The SCANNER.SYS program tells DOS how to communicate with that scanner. Several drivers can be loaded into memory from commands in CONFIG.SYS. DOS puts these programs in memory wherever it chooses. However, a program can request that it be put in a certain memory location.

After CONFIG.SYS is executed, MSDOS.SYS looks for another DOS file named COMMAND.COM. This file has three parts: more code to manage I/O, programs for internal DOS commands such as COPY and DIR, and a short program that looks for another file named AUTOEXEC.BAT.

The filename **AUTOEXEC.BAT** stands for **automatically executed batch** program. The file lists DOS commands that are executed automatically each time DOS is loaded. The following two commands (or similar prompt and path commands) are typically in the AUTOEXEC.BAT file:

```
PROMPT $P$G
PATH C:\;C:\WINDOWS;C:\WP51;C:\DBASE;C:\123
```

The PROMPT command tells DOS to display the current directory name and the current drive name as part of the prompt. Without the prompt command, your prompt looks like this: C>. With the prompt command it might look like C:\WP51> where the WP51 tells you which directory is current.

Recall that you learned about the PATH command in Chapter 1. The PATH command shown above lists five paths separated by semicolons. This command directs DOS to look in five different directories for program files. Recall that without the benefit of the PATH command, you execute application programs in one of two ways: go to the directory containing the application by using the CD (change directory) command, or include the path with the name of the executable program file when you execute the software. Sometimes during the installation of a software package, the installation process automatically adds a new path to the existing PATH command in AUTOEXEC.BAT, telling DOS where the new application can be found.

Rather than appending an entry to the existing PATH command line, some software installation programs use the SET command to append a path to the PATH command without editing the existing PATH command line itself. It works like this:

```
SET PATH=%PATH%;C:\VERT
```

The path C:\VERT is appended to the existing PATH command.

The SET command is also used to create and assign a value to an environmental variable that can later be read by an application. A software installation program might add a SET command to your AUTOEXEC.BAT file. This command might look something like this:

```
SET MYPATH=C:\VERT
```

Later the software will use the environmental variable MYPATH in the program.

TIP Sometimes an installation program places the SET command too late in the AUTOEXEC.BAT file (after the WIN command to load Windows). If the application runs under Windows, Windows loads before the variable is set, which can cause an application error. The solution is to move the SET command before the WIN command in the AUTOEXEC.BAT file. Reboot the PC for the change to take effect.

Another typical use of AUTOEXEC.BAT is to load TSRs. A **TSR** is a "terminate-and-stay-resident" program that is loaded into memory but not immediately executed. The program later executes when some "hot" key is pressed or a special hardware action occurs, such as moving the mouse. An example of a TSR is a screen capture program. The program is loaded by entering the following command in AUTOEXEC.BAT:

```
C:\CAPTURE\SAVEIT.EXE
```

In this example, SAVEIT.EXE is the name of the program in the directory \CAPTURE. For this software, the hot key to activate the program is the Print Screen key. Later, when you are using any applications software and you press the Print Screen key, instead of the screen actually printing under DOS as it normally would, the SAVEIT.EXE program saves a copy of the screen to a graphics file or offers you other options. When you exit the screen capture program,

2

control returns to the application, where you continue working until you press Print Screen to evoke the TSR again.

Completion of the Boot Process

The boot process is completed after AUTOEXEC.BAT has finished executing. At this point, COMMAND.COM is the program in charge, providing you with a command prompt and waiting for your command. On the other hand, if a program was executed from AUTOEXEC.BAT, it might ask you for a command.

In a Windows 3.x environment, it is common to include in AUTOEXEC.BAT the following command to execute Windows each time the computer is booted. (The file extension is usually omitted, but can be included.)

```
C:\WINDOWS\WIN
```

The file that is executed above is WIN.COM found in the C:\WINDOWS directory. Windows software loads just like other software running under DOS. The program is first loaded into memory and then executed. WIN.COM then looks for several configuration files that contain user and environmental settings, such as the size of the screen display font, the desktop colors used by the monitor, and the speed of the mouse. These configuration files, sometimes called initialization files, or .ini files, are listed in Table 2-2 and are usually stored in the same directory as WIN.COM.

Table 2-2   Windows configuration files

Windows Configuration Files	General Purpose of the File
SYSTEM.INI	Contains hardware settings and multitasking options for Windows
PROGMAN.INI	Contains information about Program Manager groups
WIN.INI	Contains information about user settings, including printer, fonts, file associations, and settings made by applications
CONTROL.INI	Contains information about the user's desktop, including color selections, wallpaper, and screen saver options
MOUSE.INI	Contains settings for the mouse

Editing AUTOEXEC.BAT and CONFIG.SYS

When using DOS, you can change CONFIG.SYS and AUTOEXEC.BAT to configure your OS environment, install TSRs, or troubleshoot boot problems. You can change the contents of CONFIG.SYS and AUTOEXEC.BAT with any text editor. DOS provides EDIT, a full-screen text editor.

There is a risk in changing AUTOEXEC.BAT. If you make a mistake, your computer can stall during the boot process, making it impossible to use without rebooting. Because of this risk, never change AUTOEXEC.BAT without first making a bootable disk that you can use if your AUTOEXEC.BAT file on the hard drive fails or causes problems.

To make a bootable disk and a backup copy of AUTOEXEC.BAT:

1. From the DOS prompt, type:

   ```
   C:\> FORMAT A:/S
   ```

The command erases any files currently on the disk in drive A and the /S switch copies the two DOS hidden files and COMMAND.COM to the disk in drive A, making the disk bootable.

2. If your computer shows either drive A or B as the default drive, make drive C the default, as follows:

   ```
   A:\> C:
   ```

3. If the default directory is not the root directory, make it so, as follows:

   ```
   C:\WINDOWS> CD\
   C:\>
   ```

   No matter what the default directory was (in this example, it was \WINDOWS), the backslash (\) in the prompt indicates that the root is now the default.

4. Back up the current copy of AUTOEXEC.BAT to the hard disk, as follows:

   ```
   C:\> COPY AUTOEXEC.BAT AUTOEXEC.BK
   ```

   or to a disk in drive A, as follows:

   ```
   C:\> COPY AUTOEXEC.BAT A:
   ```

5. Edit the file on drive C, as follows:

   ```
   C:\> EDIT AUTOEXEC.BAT
   ```

Your screen should be similar to that shown in Figure 2-7. Follow the directions on the screen to use and exit the editor.

```
 File   Edit   Search   Options                                    Help
                              AUTOEXEC.BAT
LH C:\PCTOOLS\VDEFEND
C:\WINDOWS\SMARTDRV.EXE
@ECHO OFF
SET PCTOOLS=C:\PCTOOLS\DATA
path c:\;c:\dos;c:\windows;c:\wp51;c:\dbase:c:\winworks\exec;c:\123;c:\nu
rem   IMAGE
lh C:\DOS\MOUSE.COM /1
SET TEMP=C:\WINDOWS\TEMP
PROMPT $P$G



PATH = C:\PCTOOLS;C:\PM4;C:\DOS;C:\WINDOWS;C:\WP51;C:\DBASE;C:\WINWORKS\EXEC;C
rem c:\lantasti\startnet.bat




MS-DOS Editor  <F1=Help> Press ALT to activate menus          CN 00001:001
```

Figure 2-7   Edit AUTOEXEC.BAT

You must remove the disk from drive A and reboot your computer (using Ctrl+Alt+Del) to execute the new AUTOEXEC.BAT file on your hard drive. If the computer stalls during the boot, place the bootable disk in drive A and then reboot. Remember that if the disk does not have a copy of AUTOEXEC.BAT on it, you do not have an active PATH command.

Do not use word-processing software, such as Word or WordPerfect, to edit AUTOEXEC.BAT, unless you use the ASCII text mode, because word-processing applications place control characters in their document files that prevent DOS from interpreting the AUTOEXEC.BAT file correctly.

Today, most computers running DOS allow you to step through each line of the CONFIG.SYS and AUTOEXEC.BAT files if you press the F8 function key as soon as the "Starting MS-DOS" message appears during the boot process. This feature can be a very helpful debugging tool.

A^+ OS 1.1 Booting with Windows 95

Recall that if a computer takes full advantage of the Windows 95 OS, its BIOS is Plug and Play BIOS, meaning that BIOS configures the Plug and Play devices before it loads Windows 95. A Plug and Play device allows BIOS to select the device's computer resources, such as an IRQ, an I/O address, and DMA channels. BIOS then turns this information over to Windows 95 when it loads. The process is described below:

1. When you boot the machine, POST occurs just as it does for BIOS that is not Plug and Play.

2. The Plug and Play BIOS begins by examining the devices on the system and determining which ones are Plug and Play compliant. BIOS first enables the devices that are not Plug and Play, and then tries to make the Plug and Play devices use the leftover resources.

3. BIOS looks for a device containing the OS and loads Windows 95, making information about the current allocation of resources available to the OS.

4. Just as with DOS, the master boot record executes the boot record on the hard drive, which looks for the initial hidden file of Windows 95, called IO.SYS.

5. Again, just as with DOS, IO.SYS loads. In fact, IO.SYS is really a small core DOS module. IO.SYS looks for a CONFIG.SYS file, and, if found, the CONFIG.SYS file executes. Windows 95 does not require CONFIG.SYS because many of its functions are incorporated into Windows 95, but you can use CONFIG.SYS to load a device driver if you choose. However, CONFIG.SYS loads only 16-bit drivers which are slower than the 32-bit drivers that Windows 95 loads.

6. After CONFIG.SYS is complete, IO.SYS looks for MSDOS.SYS. The role of MSDOS.SYS in Windows 95 is much different from its role in DOS. In Windows 95, MSDOS.SYS is a hidden text file containing settings to customize the boot process. It follows a format similar to that of the .ini files of Windows 3.x.

A+ OS
1.1

Typical lines at the beginning of MSDOS.SYS look like those shown in Figure 2-8. The functions of the first few MSDOS.SYS entries are listed in Table 2-3.

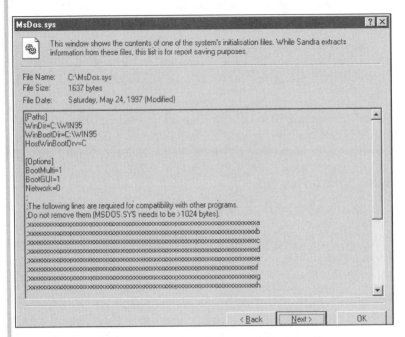

Figure 2-8 Sample MSDOS.SYS file from Windows 9x

Table 2-3 Entries in the MSDOS.SYS file for Windows 9x

Entry	Description
WinDir=	Location of the Windows 9x directory
WinBootDir=	Location of the Windows 9x startup files
HostWinBootDrv=	Drive that is the Windows boot drive
BootGUI=	When BootGUI=1, automatic graphical startup into Windows 9x is enabled When BootGUI=0, the system boots to a command prompt

7. Next, COMMAND.COM loads just as it does with DOS. COMMAND.COM provides a command interface for users and executes an AUTOEXEC.BAT file if it is present.

8. If AUTOEXEC.BAT is found, it now executes.

9. The heart of Windows 95 now loads, providing a desktop from which you can execute applications software. Further details regarding booting with Windows 95 are covered in Chapter 12.

$A+ \, OS \atop 1.1$ You can see from this description of loading Windows 95 that it still includes many DOS functions. In fact, by using the BootGUI entry in MSDOS.SYS, it is possible to backtrack from a Windows 95 installation to the underlying DOS 7.0, which comes with Windows 95.

Booting with Windows 98

Just as with Windows 95, Windows 98 goes through the boot sequence in the order listed above. First BIOS runs POST, then it loads a small DOS core, and then this DOS core loads Windows 98. Windows 98 has made some minor changes in what happens during startup to speed up the boot process. For instance, Windows 95 waits two seconds while "Starting Windows 95" is displayed so that you can press a key to alter the boot process. Windows 98 eliminated this two-second wait and, in its place, allows you to press and hold the Ctrl key as it loads. If you do that, you see the Startup Menu that is also available with Windows 95.

HOW SOFTWARE MANAGES HARDWARE RESOURCES

Recall from earlier in the chapter that the four system resources are IRQs, I/O addresses, memory addresses, and DMA channels. Their definitions are listed in Table 2-1. All four of these system resources are dependent on certain lines on a bus on the system board. Some lines on the bus are devoted to IRQs, some to addresses (both memory addresses and I/O addresses), and some to DMA channels. It's impossible to truly understand these resources without relating them to physical lines on the bus. Also, relating these logical resources to something physical (and visual) makes the concepts easier to understand. Therefore, we next turn our attention to a careful examination of one system-board bus before we look back at understanding system resources.

The 8-bit and 16-bit ISA Bus

Recall from Chapter 1 that all devices are directly or indirectly connected to the system board because they are all dependent on the CPU for processing their data. A device connects to the system board by a data cable, a slot, or a port coming directly off the system board. In any case, the device always connects to a single bus on the system board. Recall that there are several different buses on a system board, but our discussions here will be limited to only one bus, an older bus used on the early PCs of the 1980s, called the ISA (Industry Standard Architecture) bus, because this simpler bus is easier to understand. The first ISA bus had only eight lines for data and was called the 8-bit ISA bus. Figure 2-9 shows an expansion slot for this bus with some of the pinouts labeled.

$A+CORE \atop 4.3$

Some of the lines on the bus are used for data, addresses, and voltage, and others are a variety of control lines. Looking at Figure 2-9, you can see that 8 lines are used for data, and 20 lines are used for addresses. These 20 lines can carry either memory addresses or I/O addresses. The CPU determines which type of address is using these lines by setting control lines B11 through B14, as shown in Figure 2-9 (memory read/write and I/O read/write). Since this bus has only 20 address lines, the largest address value that can travel on the bus is 1111 1111 1111 1111 1111 or 1,048,576 (1024K).

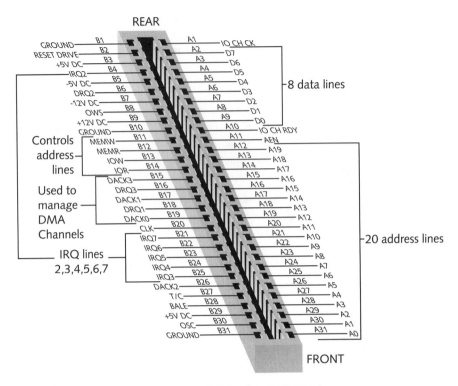

Figure 2-9   A 62-pin expansion slot for the 8-bit ISA bus

Two lines are required to manage a DMA channel: DRQ (Direct Request) and DACK (Direct Acknowledge). There are four DMA channels (0, 1, 2, and 3) on the 8-bit ISA bus.

As computer technology improved, the demand increased for more memory, more devices to be operating at the same time, and faster data transfer, making it necessary to provide more memory addresses, DMA channels, and IRQs. The 16-bit ISA bus was invented to meet these requests. Figure 2-10 shows the 16-bit ISA bus that added an extra extension to the 8-bit slot allowing for 8 additional data lines (total of 16), 5 additional IRQ lines, 4 more DMA channels, and 4 additional address lines (total of 24). Today, the 16-bit ISA bus is still used on system boards, although newer, faster buses are also used. An 8-bit expansion card (an expansion card that only processes 8 bits of data at one time) can use the 16-bit ISA expansion slot. It only uses the first part of the slot.

System boards also contain other newer buses that are faster and provide more options, but the basics haven't changed. You can still find lines on these buses for data, addresses, IRQs, and DMA channels, although it is common practice today for a line to perform several functions, making it not quite as easy (and not as much fun) to study the bus. Now that you've been introduced to what's on a bus, let's turn our attention back to the four system resources, what they are, and how they work.

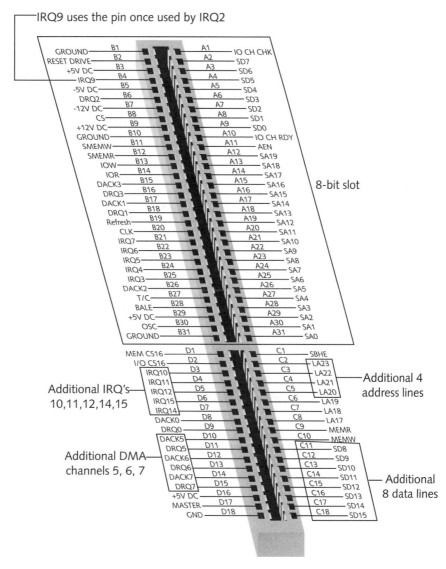

Figure 2-10   A 98-pin expansion slot for the 16-bit ISA bus

Interrupt Request Number (IRQ)

When a hardware device needs the CPU to do something, such as when the keyboard needs the CPU to process a keystroke after a key has been pressed, the device needs a way to get the CPU's attention and the CPU must know what to do once its attraction is turned to the device. These interruptions to the CPU are called **hardware interrupts** and the device handles them by placing voltage on a designated line on the bus it is connected to. These lines are numbered, and a line is referred to as an **interrupt request number**, or **IRQ**. This voltage on the line serves as a signal to the CPU that the device has a request that needs processing. Often, a hardware device that needs attention from the CPU is referred to as "needing servicing."

A+CORE
2.2 Look carefully at Figure 2-9 for the IRQ lines (IRQ 2, 3, 4, 5, 6, and 7). See Table 2-4 for a listing of the common uses for these IRQs. There are actually eight IRQs built into this bus, but IRQs 0 and 1 are not available for expansion cards (because they are used for system timer and keyboard), so they are not given a pin on the expansion slot. IRQ 2 was reserved in the early days of PCs because it was intended to be used as part of a link to mainframe computers. Thus, only five IRQs were available for devices, and each device had to have its own IRQ. This made it difficult for more than five devices to be connected to a PC at any one time. In Table 2-4, notice the COM and LPT assignments. COM1 and COM2 are preconfigured assignments that can be made to serial devices such as modems, and LPT1 and LPT2 are preconfigured assignments that can be made to parallel devices such as printers. You will learn more about these in Chapter 9.

On early system boards, the eight IRQs were managed by an Intel microchip called the interrupt controller chip and labeled the Intel 8259 chip. This chip had a direct connection to the CPU and signaled the CPU when an IRQ was activated. The CPU actually doesn't know which IRQ is "up" because the interrupt controller manages that for the CPU. If more than one IRQ is up at the same time, the interrupt controller selects the IRQ that has the lowest value to process first. For example, if a user presses a key on the keyboard at the exact same time that she moves the mouse installed on COM1, since the keyboard is using IRQ 1 and the mouse on COM1 is using IRQ 4, the keystroke is processed before the mouse action.

Table 2-4   Interrupt Request Numbers for devices using the early 8-bit ISA bus

IRQ	Device	IRQ	Device
0	System timer	4	COM1
1	Keyboard controller	5	LPT2
2	Reserved (not used)	6	Floppy drive controller
3	COM2	7	LPT1

When the 16-bit ISA bus appeared, more IRQs became available. A second interrupt controller chip was added to the system-board chip set, which hooked to the first controller. The second controller used one of the first controller's IRQ values (IRQ 2) to signal the first controller (see Figure 2-11). But there was a problem with that because there were some devices that used IRQ 2. Tying the new IRQ 9 to the old IRQ 2 pin on the 16-bit ISA bus solved the problem. The result was that a device could still use the pin on the expansion slot for IRQ 2, but it is really IRQ 9. (Look carefully at Figure 2-10 to confirm that.) Because of this, the priority level becomes: 0, 1, (8, 9, 10, 11, 12, 13, 14, 15), 3, 4, 5, 6, 7.

A+CORE
2.2 To see how the IRQs are assigned on your computer, use MSD for DOS and Windows 3.x, and Device Manager for Windows 9x. For Windows 9x, click **Start**, **Programs**, **Settings**, **and Control Panel**, and double-click **System**. Click the **Device Manager** tab. Select **Computer** and click **Properties**. Figure 2-12 shows the Computer Properties dialog box. Notice that IRQ 2 is assigned to the programmable interrupt controller, and IRQ 9 is used by the video card.

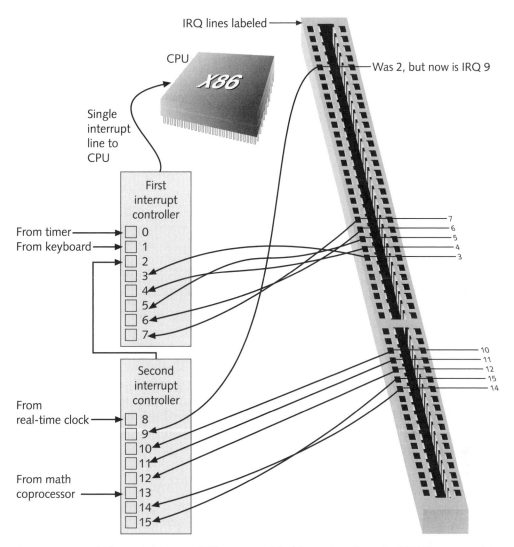

Figure 2-11 When eight more IRQs were added to system boards, IRQ 2 was used to receive all interrupts from these eight. IRQ 9 was wired to the pin on the ISA bus previously assigned to IRQ 2. You can say that IRQs 8–15 "cascade" to IRQ 2.

Newer buses are designed to allow more than one device to share an IRQ. In future chapters you will see how an entire bus only needs one IRQ for all devices and how the bus manages that feat.

Many processes that the CPU carries out are initiated by interrupts and are said to be "interrupt driven." Later in the chapter you will see how software can also issue an interrupt to the CPU so that the software can have access to a device.

IRQs 8 through 15 cascade to IRQ2

Figure 2-12   Use Device Manager to see how IRQs are used by your system

With interrupts, the hardware device or the software initiates communication by sending a signal to the CPU, but a device can be serviced in another way, called polling. With **polling**, software is constantly running that has the CPU periodically check the hardware device to see if service is needed. Not very many devices use polling as the method of communication. A joystick is one example of such a device. Software that is written to manage a joystick has the CPU check the joystick periodically to see if the device has data to communicate, which is why a joystick does not need an IRQ to work. Most hardware devices use interrupts.

Memory Addresses

Once the IRQ gets the attention of the CPU, its job is done, but memory addresses are used as the device is serviced. Recall that memory addresses are numbers assigned to both ROM and RAM memory so that the CPU can access that memory. Think of memory addresses as a single long list of hexadecimal numbers, as described in Appendix D. The CPU has a fixed number of memory addresses available to it as determined by the CPU and the bus it is using. These memory addresses can be assigned to any type of physical memory in the system that needs to be addressed by the CPU, including ROM and RAM chips on expansion cards and ROM and RAM chips on the system board, which can hold either data or instructions. Once addresses have been assigned, the CPU only sees this physical memory as a single list that can be accessed by using the memory addresses.

Also, remember from Chapter 1 that before the CPU can process data or instructions, both must be in physical memory, and the physical memory must be assigned memory addresses. In the case of ROM BIOS, these programs are already located on a memory chip, and so the only thing needed is for memory addresses to be assigned to them. Software stored on a hard drive or other secondary storage device must first be copied into RAM before processing, and memory addresses must be assigned to that RAM. Data coming from a keyboard or some other input device or stored in data files on a hard drive must also be copied into RAM before processing, and memory addresses must be assigned to that RAM. As one example of this process, Figure 2-13 shows that both RAM and memory addresses are needed so the CPU can load a program stored on the hard drive into memory before executing it.

Figure 2-13   RAM is a hardware resource, and memory addresses are a system resource; both are used when loading software into memory for execution

Table 2-5   Some ways memory addresses are used

Physical Location of Memory	Contents (Data and/or Instructions)
ROM BIOS chip on system board	• Startup BIOS program • System BIOS programs
RAM stored on SIMMs and DIMMs on system board	• Parts of the OS permanently stored on the hard drive • Applications software permanently stored on the hard drive • Device drivers permanently stored on the hard drive • Data used by the OS, device drivers, and applications software, either coming from input devices or copied from secondary storage devices
Video RAM stored on memory chips on a video card	• Video data
Video ROM BIOS chip on a video card	• Programs to control video (video BIOS)
RAM and ROM chips on other expansion cards	• BIOS and data used by the peripheral devices that the card supports (examples are network card, sound card)

How Are Memory Addresses Used?

Table 2-5 shows the ways that the CPU uses its list of memory addresses. Figure 2-14 shows a possible map that could result when all these items in Table 2-5 have claimed their memory addresses. Startup BIOS and **system BIOS**—also called **on-board BIOS**—stored in the ROM-BIOS chip on the system board must be assigned memory addresses so that the CPU can access these programs. RAM stored in SIMMs and DIMMs on the system board makes up the bulk of memory that is used by the CPU and uses the lion's share of available memory addresses. Many programs and data are copied into this RAM, including device drivers, portions of the OS, and applications software and data.

Notice in Figure 2-14 that some device drivers and BIOS are labeled 16-bit and some are labeled 32-bit. Using Windows 9x and DOS, all 16-bit programs including device drivers and BIOS must be assigned memory addresses in the first 1024K of addresses. Faster 32-bit programs can be assigned addresses in extended memory. DOS cannot support 32-bit programs without the help of Windows 3.x, so a pure DOS-based system can only use 16-bit programs. One goal of Windows 9x is to replace all older 16-bit device drivers with newer 32-bit versions. Also, newer devices contain BIOS that is written using 32-bit code rather than 16-bit code. Therefore, in a Windows 9x environment, most of the memory addresses below 1024K are not used.

Finally, note that Figure 2-14 applies to DOS and Windows 9x only. Windows NT and Windows 2000 use an altogether different memory-mapping design where there is no conventional, upper, or extended memory—it's all just memory. With this new approach to memory management, BIOS and device drivers have no say as to what memory addresses they are assigned.

Figure 2-14 shows that some memory addresses are used for video; every computer system has video. A **video controller card**, also called a **video card** or **display adapter**, might have RAM on it that the CPU must communicate with as the CPU passes data to the video card to be sent to the monitor. In addition to RAM, the video card also contains some programming to manage video stored in ROM chips on the card. This video BIOS requires some memory addresses so that the CPU can access this BIOS.

Lastly, expansion cards most often contain ROM chips with BIOS to control the peripheral devices they support. In addition, some cards might have RAM chips that also need memory addresses.

How Are Memory Addresses Assigned?

Memory addresses are, for the most part, assigned during the boot process. Recall from Chapter 1 that the boot process begins with startup BIOS on the ROM BIOS chip. This program in ROM is assigned addresses, as is the portion of ROM that contains the system BIOS. Video ROM and RAM get their address assignments early in the boot process so that the startup BIOS has the use of video while booting. Any other ROM or RAM chips on expansion cards can also request memory addresses during the boot process. Also during booting, addresses are assigned to RAM stored on DIMMs and SIMMs on the system board. Some of this RAM is used to hold the OS, device drivers, and data used by both. Most of this RAM is not used until applications and their data are loaded after booting.

2

Memory Addresses	Physical Location of Memory	Contents
8 MB	RAM	
		32-bit application's data
		32-bit application
		32-bit BIOS and device drivers
		portion of OS
1024K	ROM	system BIOS and startup BIOS
	RAM	16-bit sound card device driver
	ROM	16-bit network card BIOS
	ROM	16-bit video ROM
640K	RAM	16-bit video RAM
	RAM	
		16-bit application's data
		16-bit application
		16-bit mouse device driver
		operating system
0		data used by BIOS and OS

Left-side vertical labels: Extended memory; Upper memory; Conventional or base memory

Figure 2-14   Memory map showing how ROM and RAM, on and off the system board, might be mapped to memory addresses

A+CORE
2.2
OS
1.1

BIOS and Device Drivers That Request Specific Memory Addresses

Today's BIOS and software don't expect a specific group of addresses to be assigned to them. However, older BIOS and device drivers designed to run in a DOS real–mode environment sometimes required a specific group of memory addresses in order to load. You'll learn more about this in Chapter 4, but for now just know that BIOS or real-mode device drivers may

A+CORE
2.2
OS
1.1
only work if they are given a specific group of addresses. These addresses are usually in the upper memory address range between 640K and 1024K (see Table 1-8 in Chapter 1 for the memory divisions under DOS).

Shadowing ROM

Before leaving our discussion of memory, let's review one other interesting use of ROM and RAM, discussed in Chapter 1, that helps clarify how memory addresses are used. Remember that sometimes system BIOS programs are copied into RAM because reading from RAM chips is generally faster than reading from ROM chips. The process of copying programs from ROM to RAM for execution is called **shadowing ROM** or just **shadow RAM**. If the ROM programs are executed directly from the ROM chips, the memory addresses are assigned to this ROM. If the programs are first copied to RAM and then executed, the same memory addresses are assigned to this area of RAM. Either way, the instructions work the same way.

Input/Output Addresses

Another system resource that is made available to hardware devices is input/output addresses or I/O addresses. **I/O addresses**, or **port addresses**, sometimes simply called **ports**, are numbers that the CPU can use to access hardware devices, in much the same way it uses memory addresses to access physical memory. As you saw earlier in the chapter, the address bus on the system board sometimes carries memory addresses and sometimes carries I/O addresses. If the address bus has been set to carry I/O addresses, then each device is "listening" to this bus. See Figure 2-15. If the address belongs to it, then it responds; otherwise it ignores the request for information. In short, the CPU "knows" a hardware device as a group of I/O addresses. If it wants to know the status of a printer or a floppy drive, for example, it passes a particular I/O address down the address bus on the system board.

A+CORE
2.2
A few common assignments for I/O addresses are listed in Table 2-6. Because IBM made many address assignments when the first PC was manufactured in the late 1970s, common devices such as a hard drive, a floppy drive, or a keyboard have no problem with I/O addresses. Their BIOS can simply be programmed to use these standard addresses. Devices such as scanners or network cards that were not assigned I/O addresses in the original IBM list can be configured to use more than one group of addresses, depending on how they are set up during either the installation process or the boot process. More about this in Chapter 9.

1. CPU turns up signal on bus that says, "I/O addresses are on the address line"

2. All I/O device controllers listen for their addresses

3. CPU transmits an I/O address

4. The device that "owns" that address responds

Figure 2-15   I/O address lines on a bus work much like an old telephone party line; all devices "hear" the addresses, but only one responds

A+CORE 2.2   **Table 2-6**   Interrupt Request Numbers and I/O addresses for devices

IRQ	I/O Address	Device
0	040–05F	System timer
1	060–06F	Keyboard controller
2	0A0–0AF	Access to IRQs above 7
3	2F8–2FF	COM2 (covered in Chapter 9)
3	2E8–2EF	COM4 (covered in Chapter 9)
4	3F8–3FF	COM1 (covered in Chapter 9)
4	3E8–3EF	COM3 (covered in Chapter 9)
5	278–27F	Sound card or parallel port LPT2 (covered in Chapter 9)
6	3F0–3F7	Floppy drive controller
7	378–37F	Printer parallel port LPT1 (covered in Chapter 9)
8	070–07F	Real time clock

Table 2-6   Interrupt Request Numbers and I/O addresses for devices (continued)

IRQ	I/O Address	Device
9–10		Available
11		SCSI or available (covered in Chapter 6)
12	238–23F	System-board mouse
13	0F8–0FF	Math coprocessor
14	1F0–1F7	IDE hard drive (covered in Chapter 6)
15	170–170	Secondary IDE hard drive or available (covered in Chapter 6)

Direct Memory Access (DMA) Channels

Another system resource used by hardware and software is a **DMA (direct memory access)** channel, a shortcut method whereby an I/O device can send data directly to memory, bypassing the CPU. A chip on the system board contains the DMA logic and manages the process. In earlier computers there were four channels numbered 0, 1, 2, and 3. Later, channels 5, 6, and 7 were added when the 16-bit ISA bus was introduced. You can see the lines on the bus needed to manage these channels in Figures 2-9 and 2-10. Each channel requires two lines to manage it, one for the DMA controller to request clearance from the CPU and the other used by the CPU to acknowledge that the DMA controller is free to send data over the data lines without interference from the CPU.

DMA channel 4 is used as IRQ 2 was used, to connect to the higher IRQs. In Figure 2-16, note that DMA channel 4 cascades into the lower DMA channels. DMA channels 0–3 use the 8-bit ISA bus, and DMA channels 5, 6, and 7 use the 16-bit ISA bus. This means that the lower four channels provide slower data transfer than the higher channels, because they don't have as many data paths available. Also, an 8-bit expansion card that is only using the 8-bit ISA bus cannot access DMA channels 5, 6, or 7 because it can't get to these pins on the extended expansion slot.

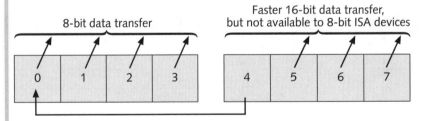

Figure 2-16   DMA channel 4 is not available for I/O use because it is used to cascade into the lower four DMA channels

Some devices, such as a hard drive, are designed to use DMA channels, and others, such as the mouse, are not. Those that use the channels might be able to use only a certain channel, say channel 3, and no other. Or the BIOS might have the option of changing a DMA channel number to avoid conflicts with other devices. Conflicts occur when more than one device uses

A+CORE 2.2 | the same channel. DMA channels are not as popular as they once were because their design makes them slower than newer methods. However, slower devices such as floppy drives, sound cards, and tape drives may still use DMA channels.

Tying It All Together

Let's take one more look at how system resources are allocated and used to manage hardware devices, and then we'll examine a comprehensive example to see how all the parts come together to perform a task. At startup, a hardware device is assigned (1) an IRQ by which it can signal the CPU that it needs attention, (2) some I/O addresses by which the CPU and the device can communicate, (3) some memory addresses that indicate where the program to manage the device can be stored, and (4) perhaps a DMA channel to speed up sending its data to memory. Later, when a hardware device needs attention from the CPU, the device raises its IRQ line to the CPU. When the CPU senses the IRQ, it stops what it is doing and handles the interrupt. The CPU looks at the location in memory where the device driver or BIOS program that services the device is stored. The CPU then executes this program, which will use the I/O addresses to communicate with the device.

Hardware Interrupts

And now for our comprehensive example of a hardware interrupt. For the keyboard shown in Figure 2-17 the process works like this:

Step 1. A key is pressed on the keyboard. The keyboard controller raises its assigned IRQ to the CPU, saying, "I need attention." The CPU sees the IRQ, acknowledges it, and turns its attention to servicing it. By sending the acknowledgment, it is requesting the device controller sends a number called an interrupt (abbreviated INT) that tells the CPU what service the device needs. There is more about interrupts coming up.

Step 2. The keyboard controller sends INT 9 to the CPU. The CPU uses this value to locate the program to handle the interrupt. This program, which may be either BIOS or a device driver, is called an **interrupt handler**.

Step 3. The CPU looks to a table in RAM called the **interrupt vector table**, or **vector table**, that contains a list of memory address locations of interrupt handlers. The INT value passed to the CPU by the controller points to the correct row in the table where the memory addresses in which the instructions to service the keyboard (a portion of system BIOS) are stored.

Step 4. The CPU looks to the location in memory of the request handler and begins to follow the instructions there.

Step 5. The CPU, following the interrupt handler instructions, processes the keystroke.

TIP

The BIOS and operating system initialize the interrupt vector table during booting, but later another program can modify the vector table to change the interrupt handler location to execute another program instead. This is a common method that a virus uses to propagate itself.

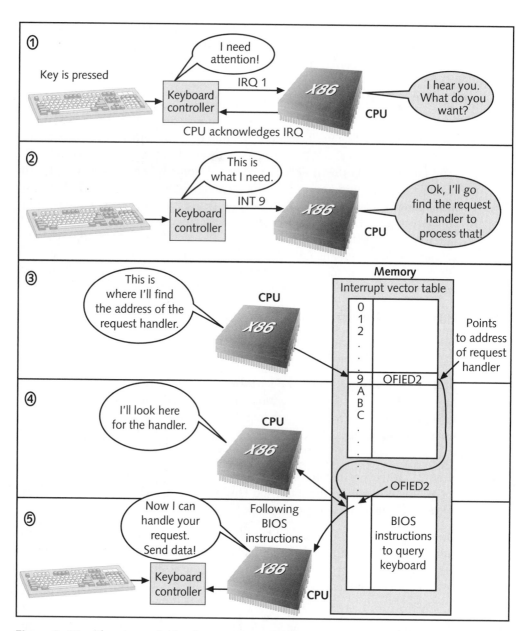

Figure 2-17   The story of a hardware interrupt, where the request handler is BIOS

Software Interrupts

In this last example, two of the four system resources were used (memory addresses and an IRQ). The keyboard controller used an IRQ to initiate communication, which means that this is an example of a hardware interrupt. When software initiates communication, such as when the user of word-processing software gives the command to save a file to the hard drive, this is known as a **software interrupt**, which is demonstrated in Figure 2-18.

Both hardware and software interrupts use the same numeric INT values to communicate their requests to the CPU. Appendix G contains a list of INT values.

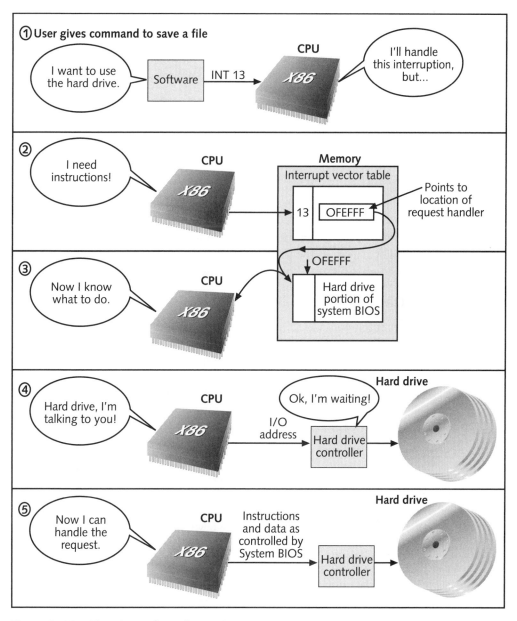

Figure 2-18   The story of a software interrupt

The interrupt value for a call to the hard drive for I/O interaction is INT 13. (1) The CPU receives the software interrupt, INT 13, and (2) turns to the interrupt vector table, using the INT value to locate the correct request handler. Next, (3) the CPU locates the handler in memory, (4) alerts the hard drive that instructions are forthcoming by sending its I/O address over the address bus, and (5) follows the instructions of the request handler, in this case, system BIOS, to manage the hard drive.

Incidentally, in Chapter 6 you will see how this process of software using INT 13 to interface with a hard drive has led to problems: more sophisticated methods of hard drive interface have been developed, but some legacy software still expects to use the INT method. Complex workarounds have become the solution to making hard drive interfaces backward-compatible.

Configuration Data and How It Is Stored

Recall from Chapter 1 that **configuration data**, or setup data, is stored in the computer in one of these devices: DIP switches, CMOS setup chip, or jumpers. This setup information can contain additional information such as system resources that a device requires or system date and time. This section takes a closer look at these storage methods.

Storing configuration information by physically setting DIP switches or jumpers on the system board or peripheral devices is inconvenient because it often requires opening the computer case to make a change. A more convenient method is to use the CMOS chip to hold the information in the small amount of RAM on the chip. A program in BIOS can then be used to easily make changes to setup.

Setup Data Stored by DIP Switches

Many older computers and a few newer ones store setup data using DIP switches on the system board, as shown in Figure 2-19. A DIP (dual in-line package) switch is a switch that has an ON position and an OFF position. ON represents binary 1, and OFF represents binary 0. If you add or remove equipment, you can communicate that to the computer by changing a DIP switch setting. When you change a DIP switch setting, use a pointed instrument, such as a ballpoint pen, to push the switch. Don't use a graphite pencil, because graphite conducts electricity. Pieces of graphite dropped into the switch can damage it.

Setup Data Stored on a CMOS Chip

Most configuration data in newer computers is stored in a CMOS microchip that is battery powered when the system power is off (see Figure 2-20). The advantage of a CMOS chip over other types of chips is that CMOSs require very little electricity to hold data. A small trickle of electricity from a nearby battery enables the CMOS chip to hold the data even while the main power to the computer is off.

On older computers (mostly IBM 286 PCs built in the 1980s), changes are made to the CMOS setup data using a setup program stored on a floppy disk. One major disadvantage of this method (besides the chance that you might lose or misplace the disk) is that the disk drive must be working before you can change the setup. An advantage of this method is that you can't change the setup unintentionally.

2

Figure 2-19   DIP switches are sometimes used to store setup data on system boards

On newer computers, you usually change the data stored in the CMOS chip by accessing the setup program stored in ROM BIOS. You access the program by pressing a combination of keys during the booting process. The exact way to enter setup varies from one system-board manufacturer to another. See the system-board documentation for the method to enter setup. A message such as the following usually appears on the screen:

```
Press DEL to change Setup
```

or

```
Press F8 for Setup.
```

Figure 2-20   The battery that powers the CMOS chip may be on the system board or attached nearby

When you do so, a setup screen appears with menus and Help features that is often very user- friendly. When you exit the program, you can exit without saving your changes or exit and save your changes to the CMOS chip.

Setup Data Stored by Jumpers

Most computers hold additional configuration information by using jumpers on the system board (see Figure 2-21). A jumper consists of two pins sticking up side by side, with a cover over the two pins making a connection. The two pins and the connection together serve as electrical connectors on the system board. If the pins are not connected with a cover, the setting is considered OFF. If the cover is present, the setting is ON. For older system boards, the presence of cache memory is a typical setting that was communicated to the computer by jumpers. Jumpers also are used to communicate the type and speed of the CPU to the system or to disable a feature on the system board, such as a keyboard wake up. (With this feature enabled, you can press a key to power up the system.) You change the jumper setting by removing the computer case, finding the correct jumper, and then either placing a metal cover over the jumper or removing the cover already there.

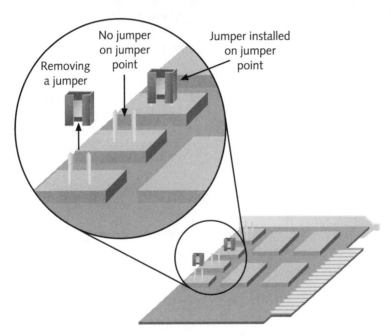

Figure 2-21   Jumpers on an add-on card

A+*CORE*
    4.4

Passwords Stored on CMOS

Access to a computer can be controlled using **startup passwords**, sometimes called **power-on passwords**. During booting, or startup, the computer asks for a password. If you do not enter the password correctly, the booting process is terminated. The password is stored on the CMOS chip and is changed by accessing the setup screen. Many computers also provide a jumper near the CMOS chip that, when set to "on," causes the computer to "forget" any changes that have been made to default settings stored in CMOS. By jumping these pins, you can disable a password.

PROTECTING DATA, SOFTWARE, AND HARDWARE

Although someone responsible for a computer must understand its operations to solve problems that can occur during use, another objective in maintaining a well-functioning system is to protect the data, software programs, and hardware from harm. Despite your best efforts, data is sometimes lost, software stops functioning correctly, and hardware fails. By taking a few practical measures, however, you can avoid some common causes of loss. Here are some practical guidelines that all computer users should follow. However, it is usually the computer support person who is called upon to save the day if something is lost. As a computer support person, you should take the time to train yourself and your users about preventive maintenance and practical precautions.

Saving and Restoring Setup Information in CMOS

A+CORE
4.4

Because the information stored in CMOS is so important to the successful operation of a computer, keep a backup of that information in case the CMOS data is lost. You can use several utility software programs to back up setup information to a disk you can use to recover lost setup information. In this chapter, we introduce two programs: Nuts & Bolts, which comes on the CD accompanying this book, and Norton Utilities, another popular PC utility program. Setup information on a PC can be lost if the battery dies or is replaced. Information also can be lost when errors occur on the system board, and a user can accidentally change setup without realizing how significant the consequences can be. Possible errors and events that might indicate that setup information is lost are:

- The battery is discharged. An early indication of a weak battery is that the PC loses the correct date and time when turned off.

- Message at startup says, "Hardware information is lost" or "CMOS checksum error." These errors can be caused by a dead battery or a poorly connected battery.

- The battery has been replaced. After the battery is replaced, restore the CMOS settings using a rescue disk.

Saving Setup Information Using Nuts & Bolts

Follow the steps below to create a rescue disk using Nuts & Bolts.

To save setup information to disk:

1. Select **Start**, **Programs**, **Nuts & Bolts**. The list of utilities included with the software appears, as shown in Figure 2-22. Select **Rescue Disk**.

2. The Welcome to Rescue Disk screen is displayed. Click **Next** to continue.

3. From the next screen (see Figure 2-23), you can choose to format the disk that will become your rescue disk or plan to use a previously formatted disk.

4. Click **Next**. Nuts & Bolts prompts you to insert the disk in drive A and creates the rescue disk.

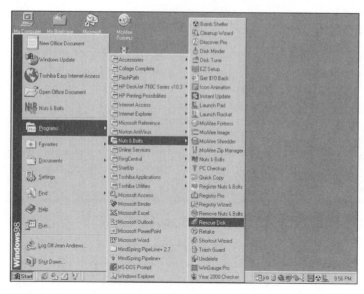

Figure 2-22   The Nuts & Bolts suite of utilities that is on the CD that accompanies this book

5. Click **Finish** when the process is complete.

The disk contains many files that can help rescue a system with problems. The file CMOS.DAT contains a backup of the data in CMOS setup.

Figure 2-23   The Nuts & Bolts Rescue Disk utility which, among other things, will save CMOS data to disk

To use a rescue disk to restore setup information when it is lost:

1. Insert the disk labeled Rescue Disk 1, which is a bootable disk, into the disk drive, turn the PC off and, after a pause, back on. This disk boots to drive A and provides an A prompt.

2. At the A prompt, type **RESCUE**, and then press **Enter**.

3. Select **CMOS Information** from the items to restore, and then press **Alt+R** to begin the process. Follow the instructions on screen.

4. Remove the rescue disk from the drive and reboot. CMOS information should now be restored. Return the rescue disks to a safe place.

Saving Setup Information Using Norton Utilities

Follow the steps below to create a rescue disk using Norton Utilities for Windows 9x. (Other uses of this software are found in later chapters.)

To save setup information to disk:

1. Select **Start**, **Programs**, **Norton Utilities**. The list of utilities included with the software appears, as shown in Figure 2-24. Select **Rescue Disk**.

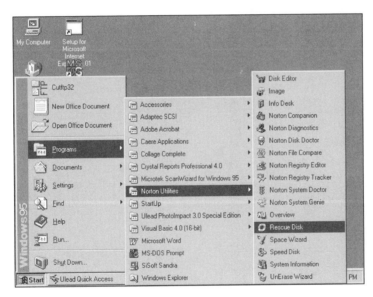

Figure 2-24   Norton Utilities lists a suite of utility programs

2. The Norton Utilities Rescue Disk window opens, as shown in Figure 2-25. To see the list of items that Norton Utilities saves to the set of rescue disks, click **Options**, which opens the dialog box shown in Figure 2-26. We have already introduced some of the items on the list, and will discuss others in future chapters. For now, notice the item CMOS Information, which will be saved to disk. Make sure that **Rescue** is checked to be included in the list, then click **OK** to return to the opening window.

3. Check that the appropriate disk drive is selected as the destination drive, and then click **Start** to begin the process.

4. Norton Utilities prompts you to insert the first disk.

5. When the information is saved to disk, the process ends and you are prompted to properly label and store the disk(s).

Figure 2-25   Creating a set of rescue disks using Norton Utilities

Figure 2-26   List of items to be stored on the rescue disks

To use a rescue disk to restore setup information when it is lost:

1. Insert the disk labeled Rescue Disk 1, which is a bootable disk, into the disk drive, turn the PC off and, after a pause, back on. This disk boots to drive A and provides an A prompt.

2. At the A prompt, type **RESCUE**, and then press **Enter**.

3. Select **CMOS Information** from the items to restore, and then press **Alt+R** to begin the process. Follow the instructions on screen.

4. Remove the rescue disk from the drive and reboot. CMOS information should now be restored. Return the rescue disks to a safe place.

Keeping OS Rescue Disks

A+ OS
2.3

An OS rescue disk, which allows you to boot a computer, is essential for every computer. You will learn later in the book about other software that should go on a bootable disk, but, at the least, a bootable disk should contain enough software to load the OS. A rescue disk can be created for DOS using the FORMAT A:/S command. Then copy the AUTOEXEC.BAT and CONFIG.SYS files from the root directory of your hard drive to the disk.

For Windows 9x, use Explorer to create a bootable disk. If you install Windows 95 from a CD rather than from floppy disks, be sure to include a DEVICE= line in a CONFIG.SYS file to load the driver for the CD-ROM and include the CD-ROM driver on the disk. A typical line might look like this (details of this command line are discussed in Chapter 10):

```
DEVICE=C:\CDSYS\SLCD /D:MSCD001
```

In either case, test the disk to make sure it works. To do this, insert the disk in the drive, hard boot, and verify that your OS does load. For Windows 95, verify that you can access your CD-ROM.

Windows 9x also offers a much better choice for creating a rescue disk. Follow these directions to create an emergency rescue disk for Windows 9x.

1. Click **Start** on the Taskbar, point to **Settings**, and then click **Control Panel**.

2. In the Control Panel window, double-click the **Add/Remove Programs** icon.

3. Click the **Startup Disk** tab, and then click the **Create Disk** button. The disk will then be created.

More details about rescue disks are included in later chapters.

Backing Up Your Hard Drive

How valuable is your data? How valuable is your software? In many cases, the most valuable component on the desktop is not the hardware or the software, but the data. Think about each computer you support. What would happen if the hard drive failed? Now create backups to prepare for just that situation. A **backup** is an extra copy of a file or files made to a different location or storage media.

Your backup policy depends on what you are backing up. If you use your PC to interface with a server, for example, and all data is stored on the server and not on the PC, then obviously, you should only back up software. (The person responsible for the server should back up the data.) If you keep original software disks and CDs in a safe place, and if you have multiple copies of them, you might decide not to back up the software. In this case, if a hard drive fails, your chore is to reload several software packages.

However, if you maintain a large database on the hard drive of your PC, you need to seriously consider a sophisticated backup method. Suppose this database is quite large and is edited daily, several times a day. If this database is lost, so are thousands of labor hours. Plan for the worst case! A good tape backup system is probably in order. Maintain 5 or 10 tapes, on which a complete backup of the database is made each night.

Even if the hard drive contains only a few important word-processing files, make backups. Never keep an important file on only one medium. Make a duplicate copy to a disk, to a file server, or to tape backup. Consider keeping some of your backups in an off-site location.

When protecting your data, the best plan is to back up. Assume that one day the primary medium you are using for this data will fail. Know the steps you will take when that happens and prepare for it.

Documentation

Make sure to keep the documentation that goes with your hardware and software. Suppose someone decides to tinker with a PC for which you are responsible and changes a jumper on the system board, but no longer remembers which jumper he or she changed. The computer no longer works, and the documentation for the board is now invaluable. If documentation is lost or misplaced, a simple job of reading the settings for each jumper and checking them on the board can become a long and tedious research task. Keep the documentation well-labeled in a safe place. If you have several computers to maintain, you might consider a filing system for each computer. Another method is to tape a cardboard folder to the inside top of the computer case and safely tuck the hardware documentation here. This works well if you are responsible for several computers spread over a wide area.

Damage from Electricity

Computers and data can be destroyed by two kinds of electricity—static electricity, known as **ESD** (**electrostatic discharge**), and power spikes, including lightning. You can do many practical things to protect from both.

ESD is most dangerous when the computer case is off. Never touch the inside of a computer without first taking precautions to protect the hardware from static electricity. Make sure both you and the computer are grounded before you touch anything inside. *Never* touch the inside of the computer when the computer is turned on. The Introduction to this book presents more extensive instructions on how to protect your computer when you work on it. Be sure to read this material before starting to work on your computer.

You can use several devices to protect the computer against electrical surges and lightning. These devices are discussed in Chapter 11.

CHAPTER SUMMARY

- ❑ Four system resources that aid in the communication between hardware and software are I/O addresses, IRQs, DMA channels, and memory addresses.
- ❑ An IRQ is a line on a bus that a device uses to alert the CPU that it needs servicing.
- ❑ A DMA channel provides a shortcut for a device to send data directly to memory, bypassing the CPU.
- ❑ Memory addresses are hex numbers, often written in segment/offset form, assigned to RAM and ROM so that the CPU can access both.
- ❑ The CPU sends a device's I/O address over the address bus when it wants to initiate communication with the device.

2

❏ Startup BIOS performs a power-on self test (POST) that surveys and tests hardware, examines setup information, and assigns system resources to the hardware. Startup BIOS then begins the process of loading the OS.

❏ When the OS loads from a hard drive, the first program BIOS executes is the master boot record (MBR), which executes the OS boot record, which, for DOS, attempts to find IO.SYS and MSDOS.SYS on the hard drive.

❏ IO.SYS and MSDOS.SYS together with COMMAND.COM form the kernel, or core, of DOS.

❏ AUTOEXEC.BAT and CONFIG.SYS are two files that contain commands used to customize the OS load process.

❏ After DOS is loaded, Windows 3.x can be executed from the WIN command stored in AUTOEXEC.BAT.

❏ Windows 9x uses Plug and Play to help install devices and assign resources to them during the boot process.

❏ In Windows 9x, the file MSDOS.SYS is a text file that contains parameters to customize the boot.

❏ One bus used on early PCs is the 8-bit ISA bus, which was later improved to become the 16-bit ISA bus that is still used on PCs today.

❏ Under Windows 9x, use Device Manager to find out how system resources have been allocated in your system.

❏ A hardware interrupt is initiated by a hardware device sending an IRQ to the CPU. A software interrupt is initiated by the software sending an interrupt number (INT) to the CPU.

❏ Setup data can be stored on the CMOS chip on the system board and by DIP switches or jumpers.

❏ There are several utility programs, such as Nuts & Bolts and Norton Utilities, that can save a copy of CMOS setup to disk. Use these to back up setup information.

❏ For safety's sake, back up important information on your hard drive, keep documentation in a safe place, and protect your computer against both static electricity and electrical power surges.

KEY TERMS

AUTOEXEC.BAT — One startup file on an MS-DOS computer. It tells the computer what commands or programs to execute automatically after bootup.

Back up, Backup — When used as a verb, to make a duplicate copy of important files or data. When used as a noun, refers to the file created when backing up. Backups can be made by saving a file with a different name or by copying files to a different disk or to a tape drive.

Cold Boot — *See* Hard boot.

Configuration data — Also called setup information. Information about the computer's hardware, such as what type of hard drive or floppy drive is present, along with other detailed settings.

Display adapter — *See* Video controller card.

DMA (direct memory access) controller chip — A chip that resides on the system board and provides channels that a device may use to send data directly to memory, bypassing the CPU.

ESD (electrostatic discharge) — Another name for static electricity, which can damage chips.

Hard boot — Restart the computer by turning off the power or by pressing the Reset button. Also called cold boot.

Hardware interrupt — An event caused by a hardware device signaling the CPU that it requires service.

Hidden file — A file that is not displayed in a directory list. To hide or display a file is one of the file's attributes kept by the OS.

Interrupt handler — A program (either BIOS or a device driver), that is used by the CPU to process a hardware interrupt.

Interrupt vector table — A table that stores the memory addresses assigned to interrupt handlers. Also called a vector table.

I/O addresses — Numbers that are used by devices and the CPU to manage communication between them.

IRQ (interrupt request number) — A line on a bus that is assigned to a device and is used to signal the CPU for servicing. These lines are assigned a reference number (for example, the normal IRQ for a printer is IRQ 7).

On-board BIOS – *See* System BIOS.

Polling — A process by which the CPU checks the status of connected devices to determine if they are ready to send or receive data.

POST (power-on self test) — A self-diagnostic program used to perform a simple test of the CPU, RAM, and various I/O devices. The POST is performed when the computer is first turned on and is stored in ROM-BIOS.

Power-on password — *See* Startup password.

Shadow RAM, Shadowing ROM — ROM programming code copied into RAM to speed up the system operation, because of the faster access speed of RAM.

Soft boot — To restart a PC by pressing three keys at the same time (Ctrl, Alt, and Del). Also called warm boot.

Software interrupt — An event caused by a program currently being executed by the CPU signaling the CPU that it requires the use of a hardware device.

Startup password — A password that a computer requires during the boot process used to gain access to the PC. Also called power-on password.

System BIOS — Basic input/output system chip(s) residing on the system board that control(s) normal I/O to such areas as system memory and floppy drives. Also called on-board BIOS.

TSR (terminate-and-stay-resident) — A program that is loaded into memory but is not immediately executed, such as a screen saver or a memory-resident antivirus program.

Vector table — *See* Interrupt vector table.

Video controller card — An interface card that controls the monitor. Also called video card or display adapter.

Warm boot — *See* Soft boot.

REVIEW QUESTIONS

1. List four system resources that software uses to manage hardware.
2. What Windows 9x utility allows you to see the IRQ assignments made to devices?
3. What must happen to a program that is stored on a hard drive before it can be executed?
4. Name some items that might be stored in physical RAM on a system board.
5. Name one system resource that a video card most likely will not need.
6. Where in memory are device drivers most often stored?
7. Is a mouse more likely to be controlled by a device driver or by system BIOS?
8. Name one device that is likely to be controlled by system BIOS.
9. Why is programming code that is stored in ROM BIOS sometimes copied to RAM? What is this process called?
10. How is a software interrupt initiated?
11. How is a hardware interrupt initiated?
12. Describe a request handler. Where in memory can you find a list of addresses where request handlers are located?
13. When the mouse initiates a hardware interrupt to the CPU, how does the CPU know where to find a program to service the mouse?
14. If memory addresses are used by the CPU to access memory, then what are I/O addresses used for?
15. What is the I/O address range for the keyboard?
16. Why are DMA channels not as popular as they once were with high-speed devices?
17. Name a device that uses polling in order to be serviced by the CPU.
18. List in detail the steps that happen when you press a key at the keyboard in order for the keystroke to be communicated to the current application.
19. When two expansion cards request the same system resources, what can be done to solve the problem?
20. Describe how Plug and Play BIOS can help resolve resource conflict problems.
21. How do you change a setting that is controlled by a DIP switch?
22. Describe how you access CMOS setup on your PC.
23. How can you add a startup password to your computer?
24. Why is Flash ROM easier to update than regular ROM BIOS?
25. What is a hidden file? Name a DOS file that is hidden.
26. List three commands that might be found in AUTOEXEC.BAT and the purpose of each.

27. How can you load a TSR that you want to remain in memory the entire time a PC is on?

28. Why is it dangerous to edit the CONFIG.SYS file with a word processor?

29. What is the purpose of IO.SYS in Windows 98?

30. Name a utility software that can be used to make a backup copy of CMOS setup information.

PROJECTS

Observing the Boot Process Using DOS

1. Use an operational computer with DOS installed. If your computer has a reset button, press it, and then watch what happens. If your computer does not have a reset button, turn it off, wait a few seconds, and then turn it back on. Write down every beep, light on/off, and message on the screen that you notice. Compare your notes to others' to verify that you are not overlooking something.

2. Unplug the keyboard and repeat the steps in Project 1. Write down what happens that is different.

3. Plug the keyboard back in, unplug the monitor, and repeat Project 1 again. After you reboot, plug the monitor in. Did the computer know the monitor was missing?

4. Put a disk that is not bootable in drive A and press the **Reset** button. If you do not have a Reset button, press **Ctrl+Alt+Del** to soft boot. Write down what you observe.

5. Print the AUTOEXEC.BAT and CONFIG.SYS files stored on the hard drive. Use one of the following methods, not Print Screen.

   ```
   C:\> TYPE filename.ext>PRN or C:\> PRINT filename.ext
   ```

6. Make a bootable disk using either of the two following DOS commands. If the disk is already formatted, but has no files stored on it, use this command:

   ```
   C:\>SYS A:
   ```

   To format the disk and also make it bootable, use this command:

   ```
   C:\>FORMAT A:/S
   ```

   Your disk should now contain a boot record, the two hidden files, and COMMAND.COM. Compare the bytes available on the disk to a disk that is not bootable. Calculate how many bytes must be in the two hidden files.

7. Test your bootable disk by inserting it in drive A and doing a soft boot. What prompt do you see on the screen?

8. At the DOS prompt, enter this prompt command as follows (where the space between P and $ can be used to customize the DOS command prompt):

   ```
   PROMPT $P    $G
   ```

   What prompt did you get? By examining the prompt, guess what $P in the command line accomplishes and what $G accomplishes. Test your theory by changing the PROMPT command, leaving first $P and then $G out of the command line.

9. Using EDIT, create an AUTOEXEC.BAT file on your bootable disk. Create a PROMPT command to include your first name. Test the command by booting from this disk.

10. Without the appropriate PATH command in your active AUTOEXEC.BAT file, you cannot execute software stored on drive C from the A prompt. Test this theory by trying to execute some applications software that you know is stored on your hard drive. For example, if you have WordPerfect on your hard drive, try to execute the software at the A prompt by using the following command:

```
A:\> WP
```

What error did you get? Why?

Using the Internet for Research

Microsoft offers a knowledge base of information on all its products. Learning to find information in the knowledge base is important to your success as a PC support person in a Windows environment. Go to the Microsoft support site at support.microsoft.com, follow these directions, and answer these questions:

1. Search for the specific article ID Q151667. Print the article and fill in the following chart for each file that Windows 9x might put in the root folder of the hard drive.

File name	Purpose of the file

2. What is the article ID of an article that describes the contents of the Windows 9x MSDOS.SYS file? Print the first page of this article.

3. List four articles that contain information about the Windows IO.SYS file.

4. Access the root folder of your hard drive and list the files in that folder that belong to Windows 9x. Mark the files that can safely be deleted without affecting Windows 9x functionality.

5. MS-DOS.SYS and IO.SYS must be in the root folder for Windows 9x to boot. Do you see them there? If they are not visible, what command would allow you to see them?

Observing the Boot Process Using Windows 9x

Hard boot your PC. If you are using Windows 95, when you see the message, "Starting Windows 95," press **F8**. If you are using Windows 98, press and hold the **Ctrl** key as the OS loads. Write down what happens when you execute each menu choice by booting several times.

Creating a Startup Disk Using Windows 9x

Use a startup disk in Windows 9x whenever you have trouble with the OS. Doing this allows you to boot from drive A. Follow these steps to create the disk:

1. Open **Control Panel**.

2. Double-click **Add/Remove Programs**.
3. Click the **Startup Disk** tab.
4. Click **Create Disk**.

After you have created the startup disk, test it by rebooting the computer with the disk still in the drive. Now, using a second disk, create a bootable disk using Explorer. Compare the contents of the two disks.

Using Shareware from the Internet

Refer to the Projects at the end of Chapter 1 for directions on how to download from the Internet the shareware utility SANDRA (System Analyzer Diagnostic and Report Assistant). Find the answers to the following questions using SANDRA and then print a report containing all the answers.

1. What is the name of the device driver file used to manage the serial ports under Windows?
2. What IRQ is your mouse using? What is the name of the mouse driver file?
3. How much conventional or base memory is free at this time?
4. What is the average access time to your hard drive?
5. If you are using Windows 9x, what is the current value of the BootMulti option found in the Msdos.sys file? What is the purpose of the BootMulti option?

Using Device Manager

Using Device Manager of Windows 9x, complete the following:

1. What is the filename and path of the device driver that is used to manage your printer port LPT1?
2. List the IRQs available on your computer, from 0 to 15.

Using MSD

Access MSD as you did in Chapter 1, with your home or lab computer, and then answer the following questions. You can print the appropriate screen in MSD showing the answers.

1. What is the IRQ assigned to the mouse?
2. What, if any, is the COM port used by the mouse?
3. What IRQ is assigned to the floppy disk drive?
4. What is the I/O or port address used by COM 1?
5. IRQ 2 points to, or "cascades" to, a higher IRQ. Which IRQ does it point to?

Using Norton Utilities to Save Setup Information

Using Norton Utilities, create a rescue disk containing setup information, following the directions given in the chapter. After the rescue disk is created, execute the RESCUE program on the boot disk and print the opening screen.

Using Nuts & Bolts to Save Setup Information

Using Nuts & Bolts, which comes on the CD accompanying this book, and following the directions in the chapter, create a rescue disk that contains a record of setup information.

3

THE SYSTEM BOARD

In this chapter, you will learn:

♦ Which physical components are on the system board

♦ How the system board transports data, follows programming logic, and coordinates the timing and execution of each processing task

♦ About the recent evolution of several system-board components

♦ How to set the CPU and system bus frequency for the system board

Chapters 1 and 2 surveyed the hardware and software that make up a personal computer and described how they work together to create a functioning computer system. In this chapter, we begin to examine in detail how the components of a computer work in harmony and with accuracy. Our starting point is the system board, the central site of computer logic circuitry and the location of the most important microchip in the computer, the CPU.

To understand the ideas in this chapter, you should (1) know the definitions of bit, byte, kilobyte, and hexadecimal (hex) number, and (2) be able to read memory addresses written in hex. Appendix D describes bits, bytes, and hex numbers used to address memory locations. If this is unfamiliar territory for you, turn to Appendix D before reading on.

Types of System Boards

A+CORE
1.1,
4.3

A system board's primary purpose is to house the CPU and allow all devices to communicate with it and each other. The two most popular system boards are the older AT and the newer ATX. The AT system board has a power connection for 5- and 12-volt lines coming from the power supply. To accommodate the newer CPUs that use less voltage, the ATX has lines for 5, 12, and 3.3 volts from the power supply. Figure 3-1 shows that the ATX system board uses a single P1 power connection, but the AT board uses two power connections, P8 and P9.

P1 on an ATX system board

(A)

P8 and P9 on an AT system board

(B)

Figure 3-1   ATX uses a single P1 power connection (A), but AT type system boards use P8 and P9 power connections

Each board is available in two sizes. The ATX boards include more power-management features and support faster systems. Table 3-1 summarizes these different boards and their form factors. ("Form factor" is computer jargon for the size and shape of a board or other device.)

A+CORE
    1.1,
    4.3

3

Table 3-1   Types of system boards

Types of System Boards	Description
AT	▪ Oldest type of system board still commonly used ▪ Uses P8 and P9 power connections (See Figure 3-1) ▪ Measures 30.5 cm × 33 cm
Baby AT	▪ Smaller version of AT. Small size is possible because system-board logic is stored on a smaller chip set. ▪ Uses P8 and P9 power connections ▪ Measures 33 cm × 22 cm
ATX	▪ Developed by Intel for Pentium systems ▪ Has a more conveniently accessible layout than AT boards ▪ Includes a power-on switch that can be software-enabled and extra power connections for extra fans ▪ Uses a single 20-pin power connection called a **P1 connector** (See Figure 3-1) ▪ Measures 30.5 cm × 24.4 cm
Mini ATX	▪ An ATX board with a more compact design ▪ Measures 28.4 cm × 20.8 cm

The main components on a system board are the following:

- CPU and its accompanying chip set
- System clock
- ROM BIOS
- CMOS configuration chip and its battery
- RAM
- RAM cache (only on older system boards)
- System bus with expansion slots
- Jumpers and DIP switches
- Ports that come directly off the board
- Power supply connections

A+CORE
    4.3

Of the components listed above, you can replace or upgrade the following five: CPU, ROM BIOS chip, CMOS battery, RAM, and RAM cache. Because you can exchange these items without returning the system board to the manufacturer, they are called **field replaceable units**.

Before examining the most important system board components, let's look at the system board itself as a component (see Figures 3-2 and 3-3).

$A^{+CORE}_{1.1}$

- Memory cache slot (COAST)
- CPU socket 7
- 16 bit ISA expansion slots (4)
- ROM BIOS
- PCI expansion slots (3)
- Keyboard port
- Connections to power supply
- RAM slots with two SIMMS

Figure 3-2   A typical AT system board with memory cache and socket 7 for the Intel Classic Pentium CPU. The CPU with a fan on top is installed as well as two SIMM memory modules

When you buy a system board, your selection determines the following components:

- Types and speeds of the CPU you can use
- Chip set on the board (already installed)
- Memory cache type and size
- Types and number of expansion slots: EISA, PCI, and AGP (explained below)
- Type of memory: ECC, EDO, SDRAM, SIMMs, or DIMMs (explained below)
- Maximum amount of memory you can install on the board and the incremental amounts by which you can upgrade memory
- Type of case you can use
- ROM BIOS (already installed)
- Type of keyboard connector
- Presence or absence of different types of proprietary video and/or proprietary local bus slots

- Presence or absence of IDE adapters and SCSI controller (explained below)
- Presence or absence of COM ports, LPT ports, and mouse port

3

A^{+CORE}
$_{1.1}$

P1 Power connector

Two IDE connectors

Floppy drive connector

DIP switches

16-bit ISA expansion slot

AGP slot

Five PCI expansion slots

Flash ROM
Parallel port

Two Serial ports

Two USB ports
Keyboard and mouse port

Slot 1 for Pentium III with
supporting braces

Four RAM slots with one
DIMM installed

Figure 3-3   An ATX system board with a Pentium III and one DIMM module installed

Selecting the system board is, therefore, a very important decision when you purchase a computer or assemble one from parts, because the system board determines so many of your computer's features.

Depending on which applications and peripheral devices you plan to use with the computer, you can take one of three different approaches to selecting a system board. The first option is to select the board that provides the most room for expansion so you can upgrade and exchange components and add-on devices easily. A second approach is to select the board that best suits the needs of the computer's current configuration, knowing that when you need to upgrade, you will likely switch to new technology and a new system board. The third approach is to select a system board that meets your present needs with moderate room for expansion.

Ask the following questions when selecting a system board:

- Is the system board designed so that long expansion cards don't get in the way of the CPU or other important devices you might want to access?

- How many different CPUs can the system board support—only those manufactured by Intel or also those made by Intel's competitors?
- What bus speeds, type of memory, and system BIOS does the board support?
- Does the board use many embedded devices (discussed below)?
- Does the board fit the case I plan to use?
- Does the board support my legacy cards?
- What is the warranty on the board?
- How extensive and user-friendly is the documentation?
- How much support does the manufacturer supply for the board?

Sometimes a system board contains a component that is more commonly offered as a separate device. A component on the board is called an embedded component. One example is support for video. The video port might be on the system board or might require a video card. The cost of a system board with an embedded component is usually less than the combined cost of a system board with an expansion card but no component. If you plan to expand, be cautious about choosing a proprietary board that has many embedded components. A proprietary design using many embedded devices often does not easily accept add-on devices from other manufacturers. For example, if you plan to add a more powerful video card, you might not want to choose a system board that contains an embedded video controller.

Even though you can often set a switch on the system board to disable the proprietary video controller, there is little advantage to paying the extra money for the on-board video controller.

If you have an embedded component, make sure you can disable the component so that you can use another external component if needed. You disable a component on the system board through jumpers on the board or through CMOS setup.

Table 3-2 lists some manufacturers of system boards with their web addresses.

Table 3-2   Major manufacturers of system boards

Manufacturer	Web Address
motherboard.com	www.motherboards.com
American Megatrends, Inc.	www.megatrends.com
ASUS	www.asus.com
Diamond Multimedia	www.diamondmm.com
First International Computer, Inc.	www.fica.com
Giga-Byte Technology Co., Ltd.	www.giga-byte.com
Intel Corporation	www.intel.com
Supermicro Computer, Inc.	www.supermicro.com
Tyan Computer Corporation	www.tyan.com

THE SYSTEM CLOCK

Remember from Chapter 1 that the system board contains a system clock that keeps the beat for many system-board activities. We use units called megahertz (MHz) to measure clock frequency. One megahertz (MHz) is equal to 1,000,000 beats, or cycles, of the clock per second. A single clock beat or cycle was once the smallest unit of processing the CPU or another device could execute, meaning that it could only do one thing for each beat of the clock. Some CPUs today can perform two activities per clock cycle. Even though how fast a CPU can operate is often referred to as the CPU speed, it is more accurate but less common to speak of the CPU frequency. For example, you might say that a CPU can operate at a frequency of 550 MHz.

A wait state occurs when the CPU must wait for another component, for example when slower dynamic RAM reads or writes data. To allow time for the slow operation, CMOS setup information specifies that the CPU maintain a wait state. If the CPU normally can do something in two clock beats, for example, it is told to wait an extra clock beat, meaning its cycle takes a total of three clock beats. It works for two beats and then waits one beat, which makes for a 50% slowdown. Wait states might be incorporated to slow the CPU so that the rest of the system-board activity can keep up. Wait states are initially set as part of the system board's default settings and are only changed in rare circumstances, such as when the board becomes unstable.

THE CPU AND THE CHIP SET

IBM and IBM-compatible computers manufactured today use a microprocessor chip made by Intel or one of its competitors. Early CPUs by Intel were identified by model numbers: 8088, 8086, 80286, 386, and 486. The next CPU introduced after the 486 was named the Pentium, and all Intel CPUs after that include Pentium in their name. The model numbers can be written with or without the 80 prefix and are sometimes preceded with an i as in 80486, 486, or i486. The name Pentium comes from the word *pente*, the Greek word for five, which Intel chose after a legal battle with two competitors, AMD and Cyrix. AMD and Cyrix won rights to continue using the X86 chip names, but are not allowed to use the word "Pentium" to name their CPUs.

You need to know how to identify a CPU installed in a system and what performance to expect from that CPU. The following attributes are used to rate CPUs:

A+*CORE*
1.1,
4.1

1. **CPU speed measured in megahertz.** The first CPU used in an IBM PC was the 8088, which worked at about 4.77 MHz, or 4,770,000 clock beats per second. An average speed for a new CPU today is about 550 MHz, or 550,000,000 beats per second. In less than a minute this processor beats more times than your heart beats in a lifetime!

2. **Efficiency of the programming code.** Permanently built into the CPU chip are programs that accomplish fundamental operations, such as how to compare or add two numbers. Less efficient CPUs require more steps to perform these simple operations than more efficient CPUs. These groups of instructions are collectively called the "instruction set."

A+CORE
1.1,
4.1

3. **Word size, sometimes called the internal data path size**. Word size is the largest number of bits the CPU can process in one operation. Word size ranges from 16 bits (2 bytes) to 64 bits (8 bytes).

4. **Data path**. The data path, sometimes called the external data path size, is the largest number of bits that can be transported into the CPU. The size of the data path is the same as the system bus size, or the number of bits that can be transported along the bus at one time. (The data path ranges from 8 bits to 64 bits.) The word size need not be as large as the data path size; some CPUs can receive more bits than they can process at one time.

5. **Maximum number of memory addresses**. A computer case has room for a lot of memory physically housed within the case, but a CPU has only a fixed range of addresses that it can assign to this physical memory. How many memory addresses the CPU can assign limits the amount of physical memory chips that the computer can effectively use. The minimum number of memory addresses a CPU can use is one megabyte (where each byte of memory is assigned a single address). Recall that one megabyte is equal to 1024 kilobytes, which is equal to 1024 $\times$ 1024 bytes, or 1,048,576 memory addresses. The maximum number of memory addresses for Pentium CPUs is 4096 megabytes, which is equal to 4 gigabytes.

6. **The amount of memory included with the CPU**. Some CPUs have storage for instructions and data built inside the chip housing. This is called internal cache, primary cache, level 1, or L1 cache.

7. **Multiprocessing ability**. Some microchips are really two processors in one and can do more than one thing at a time. Others are designed to work in cooperation with other CPUs installed on the same system board.

8. **Special functionality**. Special purpose CPUs, such as the Pentium MMX CPU, which is designed to manage multimedia devices efficiently.

Until Intel manufactured the Pentium series of chips, the three most popular ways of measuring CPU power were speed measured in megahertz and word size and data path size measured in bits. Our criteria for measuring the power of a CPU have changed since the introduction of the Pentium. The word size and path size are no longer distinguishing qualities, because these sizes have not changed significantly for the last few years. Currently, we are more interested in clock speed, bus speed, internal cache, and especially, the intended functionality of the chip, such as its ability to handle graphics well (MMX technology).

Relating CPU Attributes to Bus Architecture

A+CORE
4.1,
4.3

Two of the CPU attributes listed above work in relation to the bus architecture: number of memory addresses and data path size. The data path size is determined by the width of the bus data path, or the number of parallel wires in the bus data path, and the number of memory addresses is determined by the number of traces, or wires, on the bus that are used for memory addresses.

A+CORE
4.1,
4.3

Recall that if a data path is 16-bits wide, there are 16 wires on the bus, each used to transmit one bit, and 16 pins connecting to the CPU that can input and output single bits. If a bus has 20 wires dedicated to memory addresses transmitted over the bus, the CPU can transmit a maximum of 20 bits to define one memory address. The largest 20-bit base 2 number possible is then the maximum number of memory addresses the CPU can use. That number is 1111 1111 1111 1111 1111 in binary, or 1 MB of memory addresses (1,048,576 unique addresses).

3

The Earlier Intel CPUs

Table 3-3 lists specifications for some early CPUs made by Intel. Until the introduction of Pentium chips and their clones, most chips were rated by the criteria listed in this table.

Table 3-3   The power of the early Intel CPUs

Model (chronological order)	Approximate Speed (MHz)	Word Size (bits)	Path Size (bits)	Memory Addresses (MB)
80386DX	40	32	32	4096
80386SX	33	32	16	16
486DX	60	32	32	4096
486SX	25	32	32	4096
First Pentium	60	32 × 2	64	4096

Looking at the first two rows of Table 3-3, note that the 80386SX chip had a smaller path size than the 80386DX, although it was developed later. At the time Intel first manufactured the 80386DX with its 32-bit path size, system-board manufacturers could produce at a reasonable cost a system board with a path size of only 16 bits, or 2 bytes. Therefore the system-board manufacturers could not take advantage of the DX's 32-bit path size and chose not to use the first 80386DX chips. In response to this, Intel produced the cheaper 80386SX chip, which accommodated the smaller path size and kept the cost of the system more reasonable for personal computer users. The 80386SX chip used an internal 32-bit word size but an external 16-bit path size. (Internal refers to operations inside the CPU, and external refers to operations between the inside and outside of the CPU, such as those on the bus.) The smaller path size of the 80386SX is the reason that it is slower than the 80386DX chip (S stands for single and D for double).

Table 3-3 lists the earlier CPUs chronologically, based on their introduction in the marketplace. If you look at one of these CPUs, you see it is labeled as 80386SX-16, 80486DX2-50, or another number using a similar convention. The number at the end of the model number, 16 or 50 in the examples, refers to the speed of the CPU in megahertz. The 2 following the 486DX CPU indicates that the chip can work in overdrive mode, which doubles the external clock speed to increase the overall speed of the computer. (On some older computers, doubling the clock speed was called **turbo mode** and was accomplished by pressing a button on the computer case.) Sometimes, system boards and CPUs that work in this overdrive mode overheat, and heat sinks and/or fans must be mounted on top of the CPU.

For notebook computers, the CPU model number often has an L in it, as in 486SL-20. The L indicates that this microchip is a 486SX that requires a lower voltage than the regular SX. The 20 indicates that the speed is 20 megahertz.

Voltages Used by CPUs

Early CPUs all used 5 volts of electrical current to operate; these included the 486DX, 80486SX, 80487SX, and 80486DX2. Later versions of the 80486SX and the 80486DX4 CPUs ran on 3.3 volts. Because the power supply to the system board only supplied 5 and 12 volts, a voltage regulator was used to provide the 3.3 volts. The first Pentium running at 60/66 MHz used 5 volts. All other Pentiums, including the Pentium Pro and Pentium II, use 3.3 volts and 2.8 volts.

Coprocessor Used with Older CPUs

Some older CPU microchips were designed to work hand in hand with a secondary microchip processor called a coprocessor. The coprocessor performed calculations for the CPU at a faster speed than the CPU could. The coprocessor for the 80386 chip is the 80387. The 486DX has the coprocessor built into the CPU housing. The 486SX has the coprocessor portion of the chip disabled. Software must be written to make use of a coprocessor. Most software today assumes that you have a 486DX or Pentium chip and writes its code to take advantage of this coprocessor capability.

The Pentium and Its Competitors

A+CORE 4.1 The latest CPU microchips by Intel are the Pentium series of chips. A Pentium chip has two arithmetic logic units, meaning that it can perform two calculations at the same time; it is therefore a true multiprocessor. Pentiums have a 64-bit external path size and two 32-bit internal paths, one for each arithmetic logic unit.

Comparing Chips

To compare the Pentium family of chips and the Pentium competitors, you need to understand bus speed, processor speed, multiplier, and memory cache. Each of these is introduced here and then discussed in more detail later in the chapter.

A+CORE 4.1 Recall that **bus speed** is the frequency or speed at which data moves on a **bus**. Remember also that a system board has several buses; later in the chapter you will learn the details of each. Each bus runs at a certain speed, some faster than others. Only the fastest bus connects directly to the CPU. This bus goes by many names. It's called the system-board bus, or the system bus, because it's the main bus on the system board connecting directly to the CPU, or the Pentium bus because it connects directly to the Pentium. It's called the host bus because other buses connect to it to get to the CPU, and it's also called the **memory bus**

3

because it connects the CPU to RAM. This book uses the name memory bus because it is the most descriptive of the four, although system bus is probably the more popular term. However, the term system bus is used so loosely in the literature that its meaning can be confusing. The common speeds for the memory bus are 66 MHz, 75 MHz, 100 MHz, 133 MHz, and 200 MHz, although the bus can operate at several other speeds, depending on how jumpers are set on the system board.

> **TIP** When you read that Intel supports a system-board speed of 66 and 100 MHz, and that its competitors support bus speeds of 75 MHz, these speeds are all referencing the memory bus speed. In documentation you sometimes see the memory bus speed called the bus clock because the pulses generated on the clock line of the bus determine its speed. Other slower buses connect to the memory bus, which serves as the go-between for other buses and the CPU.

Processor speed is the speed at which the CPU is operating internally. If the CPU operates at 150 MHz internally, but 75 MHz externally, the processor speed is 150 MHz and the memory bus speed is 75 MHz. The CPU is operating at twice the speed of the bus. This factor is called the **multiplier**. If you multiply the memory bus speed by the multiplier, you get the processor speed or the speed of the CPU:

Memory bus speed × multiplier = processor speed

You can use jumpers on the system board to set the memory bus speed or bus clock. The jumpers set the multiplier, which then determines the CPU speed or processor speed. Common multipliers are 1.5, 2, 2.5, 3, 3.5, and 4.

A **memory cache** is a small amount of RAM (referred to as static RAM or SRAM) that is much faster than the rest of RAM, which is called dynamic RAM (DRAM) because it loses its data rapidly and must be refreshed often. Refreshing RAM takes time, making DRAM slower than SRAM, which does not need refreshing because it can hold its data as long as power is available. Therefore, both programming code and data can be stored temporarily in this faster static RAM cache to speed up the CPU processing of both. The size of the cache a CPU can support is a measure of its performance, especially during intense calculations.

A memory cache that is included on the CPU microchip itself is called **internal cache**, **primary cache**, **Level 1**, or L1 cache. A cache outside of the CPU microchip is called **external cache**, secondary cache, **Level 2**, or L2 cache. L2 caches are usually 128K, 256K, 512K, or 1 MB in size. In the past, all L2 cache was contained on the system board, but beginning with the Pentium Pro, some L2 cache has been included inside the Pentium physical housing—not on the CPU microchip like the L1 cache, but on a tiny circuit board with the CPU chip, within the same housing. The bus between the processor and the L2 cache is called the **backside bus** or cache bus and is not visible, because it is completely contained inside the CPU housing (see Figure 3-4). On the Pentium Pro and Pentium II, this cache bus runs at half the speed of the processor.

Backside bus or
cache bus

Processor
and
L1 cache

L2 cache

L2 cache

Processor
and L1 cache

Frontside bus or
system bus is 64
bits wide

Discrete L2 cache

Advanced Transfer Cache

Figure 3-4   Some Pentiums contain L2 cache on separate dies (discrete L2 cache), and
some contain L2 cache on the same die (Advanced Transfer cache)

A+CORE
4.1

In contrast, the bus that connects the CPU to memory outside the housing is called the **frontside bus** and can be seen on the system board. The frontside bus is the same bus as the memory bus. (Now the memory bus has one more name!)

More recently, some Pentium III CPUs contain L2 cache directly on the same die as the processor core and this is called **Advanced Transfer Cache (ATC)**, making it difficult to distinguish between L1 and L2 cache. ATC makes it possible for the Pentium III to fit on a smaller and less expensive form factor (the shape and size of a device). The ATC Cache bus is 256 bits wide and runs at the same speed as the processor. Pentium III L2 cache stored on a separate microchip within the CPU housing is called **discrete L2 cache** (see Figure 3-4). With discrete L2 cache, the Pentium III cache bus is 64 bits wide and runs at half the speed as the processor. All Pentium III processors have either 512K of discrete cache or 256K of ATC cache.

Table 3-4 lists the five types of Pentium CPUs, the Classic Pentium, Pentium MMX, Pentium Pro, Pentium II, and Pentium III. Variations of the Pentium II processor include the Celeron and Xeon. Each one is discussed below.

Table 3-4   The Intel Pentium family of CPUs

Processor	Current Processor Speeds (MHz)	Primary L1 Cache	Secondary L2 Cache	System Bus Speeds (MHz)
Classic Pentium	60, 66, 75, 90, 100, 120, 133, 150, 166, 200	16K	None	66
Pentium MMX	133, 150, 166, 200, 233, 266	32K	None	66
Pentium Pro	150, 166, 180, 200	16K	256K, 512K, or 1 MB	60, 66
Pentium II	233, 266, 300, 333, 350, 366, 400, 450	32K	256K, 512K	66, 100

Table 3-4   The Intel Pentium family of CPUs (continued)

Processor	Current Processor Speeds (MHz)	Primary L1 Cache	Secondary L2 Cache	System Bus Speeds (MHz)
Celeron	266, 300, 333, 366, 400, 433, 450 (mobile) 466, 500, 533, 566, 600	32K	Some have 128K	66, 100 (mobile only)
Pentium II Xeon	400, 450	32K	512K, 1 MB, or 2 MB	100
Pentium III	400, 450, 500, 533, 550, 600, 650, 667, 700, 733, 750, 800, 850, 866, 933, 1 GHz	32K	256, 512	100, 133
Pentium III Xeon	500, 550, 600, 667, 700, 733, 800, 866	32K	256K to 2 MB	100, 133

Classic Pentium

The first Pentium chip was introduced in March 1993, and has now become affectionately known as the "Classic Pentium." Early problems with this first Pentium (which Intel later resolved) could cause errors such as incorrect calculations on spreadsheets. The Classic Pentium is no longer manufactured.

Pentium MMX

The Pentium MMX (Multimedia Extension) targets the home market. It speeds up graphical applications and performs well with games and multimedia software.

Pentium Pro

Intel recommends the Pentium Pro for 32-bit applications that rely heavily on fast access to large amounts of cache memory. It was the first Pentium to offer Level 2 cache inside the CPU housing as well as other features not available on the Classic Pentium. The Pentium Pro is popular for computing-intensive workstations and servers but, because it does not perform well in real mode, it does not perform well with older 16-bit application software written for DOS or Windows 3.x.

Pentium II

The Pentium II is designed for graphics-intensive workstations and servers, and works well with 3-D graphic manipulation, CAD (computer-aided design), and multimedia presentations. The Pentium II is the first Pentium to use a slot (Slot 1) instead of a socket

A+CORE
4.1

to connect to the system board. (CPU sockets and slots are covered later in the chapter.) Intel chose to patent Slot 1, and, in doing so, forced its competitors to stay with the slower socket technology as they developed equivalent processors. The Pentium II can use the 100-MHz memory bus with processor speeds up to 450 MHz.

The Celeron processor is a low-end Pentium II processor that targets the low-end multimedia PC market segment. It uses Level 2 cache within the processor housing and works well with Windows 9x and the most common applications.

The Pentium II Xeon processor is a fast, high-end Pentium II processor designed exclusively for servers and powerful workstations. It can support up to eight processors in one computer and is recommended for use with Windows NT, Windows 2000, and UNIX operating systems.

Pentium III

The Pentium III (see Figure 3-5) uses either a slot or a socket and runs with the 100-MHz or 133-MHz memory bus with a processor speed up to 1 GHz. The Pentium III introduced Intel's new performance enhancement called SSE, for Streaming SIMD Extensions. (SIMD stands for single instruction, multiple data, and is a method used by MMX to speed up multimedia processing.) SSE is a new instruction set designed to improve multimedia processing even further. SSE will be an improvement over MMX as soon as operating systems and applications software are written to use it.

Figure 3-5   This Pentium III is contained in a SECC cartridge that stands on its end in Slot 1 on a system board

A+CORE
  4.1

The Pentium III Xeon is a high-end Pentium III processor that runs on the 133 MHz system bus and is designed for mid range servers and high-end workstations. It uses a 330-pin slot called the SC330 (slot connector 330), sometimes called Slot 2, and is contained within a cartridge called a Single Edge Contact Cartridge (SECC).

The Pentium Competitors

Intel's two primary competitors are AMD and Cyrix. Both companies have advertised goals to produce CPUs that are just as fast and powerful as Intel's, but at a lower cost. For the latest information about the Pentium and its competitors, see these web sites: *www.amd.com*, *www.cyrix.com*, and *www.intel.com*.

Table 3-5 lists the two early processors that competed with Intel's Classic Pentium. Neither of these processors is manufactured today, although plenty of them are still in use.

Table 3-5   Cyrix and AMD competitors of the Classic Pentium

Processor	Current Processor Speeds (MHz)	Bus Speeds (MHz)	Multiplier	Internal or Primary Cache
Cyrix 6x86 or M1	150	75	2	16K
AMD K5	75, 90, 100, 116, 133	50, 60, 66	1.5 or 1.75	24K

The AMD K5 offers an unusual assortment of clock speeds and bus speeds. One disadvantage of the Cyrix 6x86 is that it uses an external bus speed of 75 MHz, which is not supported by Intel for its chip set (that is, Intel does not guarantee this bus speed to be stable). Therefore, if a system uses this Cyrix chip, the system board must use another brand of chip set other than the popular Intel brand or, if the Intel chip set is used, the system board must be set to run at a bus speed that is not guaranteed by Intel to be stable.

Running a system board at a higher speed than that suggested by the manufacturer is called **overclocking** and is not recommended, because the speed is not guaranteed to be stable by Intel. VIA and SiS both have chip sets that support the memory bus speeds needed by the Cyrix CPUs.

Competitors of the Advanced Pentiums

Table 3-6 shows the performance ratings of five competitors of the Pentium advanced processors. Cyrix processors, such as the Cyrix III shown in Figure 3-6, use sockets that can also be used by Intel Pentium processors, but AMD has taken a different approach. AMD processors that can run on a 100-MHz system bus use a special type of socket called Super Socket 7 that supports an AGP video slot and 100 MHz system bus. AGP refers to a special port for video cards called the accelerated graphics port (AGP), which is discussed later in the chapter. The AMD Athlon, shown in Figure 3-7, uses a proprietary 242-pin slot called Slot A that looks like the Intel Slot 1, which also has 242 pins.

A+CORE 4.1

Table 3-6   Cyrix and AMD competitors of the advanced Pentiums

Processor	Current Clock Speeds (MHz)	Compares to	System Bus Speed (MHz)	Socket or Slot
Cyrix M II	300, 333, 350	Pentium II, Celeron	66, 75, 83, 95, 100	Socket 7
Cyrix III	433, 466, 500, 533	Celeron, Pentium III	66, 100, 133	Socket 370
AMD-K6-2	166, 200, 266, 300, 333, 350, 366, 380, 400, 450, 475	Pentium II, Celeron	66, 95, 100	Socket 7 or Super Socket 7
AMD-K6-III	350, 366, 380, 400, 433, 450	Pentium II	100	Super Socket 7
AMD Athlon	600, 650, 700, 750, 800, 850, 900, 950, 1 GHz	Pentium III	200	Slot A

Figure 3-6   The Cyrix III competes with the Intel Celeron and the Pentium III

Figure 3-7   The AMD Athlon competes with the Intel Pentium III

$A^{+CORE}_{4.1}$ **Intel's Itanium: The Next Generation Processor**

The next processor scheduled to be released by Intel before this book goes to print is the Itanium, Intel's first 64-bit processor for microcomputers. Recall from Chapter 1 that earlier computers always operated in real mode, which used a 16-bit data path. Later, protected mode was introduced, which uses a 32-bit data path. Almost all applications written today use 32-bit protected mode because all CPUs manufactured today for microcomputers use a 32-bit data path. The Itanium will change all that. To take full advantage of the Itanium's power, software developers must redo their applications to use 64-bit processing, and operating systems must be written to use 64-bit data transfers. Microsoft is expected to provide a 64-bit version of Windows 2000 when Itanium becomes available. Intel has promised that the Itanium will provide backward-compatibility with older 32-bit applications.

CPUs That Use RISC Technology

In addition to CPUs becoming faster and using a wider data path, another trend in chip design is the increased use of **RISC (reduced instruction set computer)** technology. RISC chips are challenging the monopoly in the chip market held by CISC (complex instruction set computer) chips. (CISC is the name given to traditional chip design.) The difference between the RISC and CISC technologies is the number of instructions (called the **instruction set**) contained directly on the CPU chip itself. With RISC technology, the CPU is limited to a very few instructions that can execute in a single clock cycle. One advantage that RISC chips have over CISC chips is that, because they have only a small number of operating instructions to perform, they can process much faster when few complex calculations are required. This feature makes RISC chips ideal for video or telecommunications applications. They are also easier and cheaper to manufacture.

Most Intel chips use the CISC technology to maintain compatibility with older systems and software, although the Pentium II uses a combination of both technologies. The K6 by AMD use the RISC technology. Cyrix, on the other hand, has chosen to stay with CISC technology, contending that it is better than RISC. Most CPU manufacturers for high-end servers have a version of a RISC chip. Sun Microsystems has the SPARC chip, Digital Equipment Corporation (DEC) has the MIPS and Alpha, and IBM Corporation has the RS 6000.

CPU Cooling Fans

Because a CPU generates so much heat, most computer systems use a cooling fan to keep the temperature below the Intel maximum allowed limit of 185° F (see Figure 3-8). Good CPU cooling fans can maintain the temperature at 90 to 110° F. Use cooling fans to prevent system errors and to prolong the life of the CPU. The ball-bearing cooling fans last longer than other kinds.

3

Cooling fan

Processor

Slot braces

Heat sink

Cooling fan power connection

Figure 3-8   A CPU cooling fan mounts on the top or side of the CPU housing and is powered by an electrical connection to the system board

The cooling fan usually fits on top of the CPU with a wire or plastic clip. Sometimes a cream-like thermal compound is placed between the fan and the CPU. This compound draws heat from the CPU and passes it to the fan. The thermal compound transmits heat better than air and makes the connection between the fan and the CPU airtight. The fan is equipped with a power connector that connects to one of the power cables coming from the power supply.

Some newer CPUs generate so much heat that they need extra cooling. The chips might have a heat sink attached to them and a large fan attached on top of the sink or to the side of the case, blowing over the heat sink. A **heat sink** is a clip-on device that mounts on top of the CPU. Fingers or fins at the base of the heat sink pull the heat away from the CPU.

Some system boards feature a power connection for the cooling fan that sounds an alarm if the fan stops working. Because the fan is a mechanical device, it is more likely to fail than the electronic devices inside the case. To protect the expensive CPU, you can purchase a heat sensor for a few dollars. The sensor plugs into a power connection coming from the power supply and is mounted on the side of the case. It sounds an alarm when the inside of the case gets too hot.

$A^{+CORE}_{4.1}$ ## CPU Form Factors

Intel currently has five form factors used to house its processors in desktop PCs:

- **SEP (Single Edge Processor)**. The processor is not completely covered by the black plastic housing, making the circuit board visible at the bottom of the housing. The first Celeron processors used the SEP form factor in Slot 1.

- **SECC (Single Edge Contact Cartridge)**. The processor is completely covered with a black plastic housing and a heat sink and fan are attached to the housing. You can't see the circuit board or edge connector in a SECC form factor. The Pentium II and Pentium III use a SECC form factor in Slot 1. You can see the SECC in Figure 3-5.

- **SECC2 (Single Edge Contact Cartridge, version 2)**. The processor SECC2 has a heat sink and fan similarly to the SECC, but the edge connector on the processor circuit board is visible at the bottom of the housing. Pentium II and Pentium III use the SECC2 form factor.

- **PPGA (Plastic Pin Grid Array)**. The processor is housed in a square box designed to fit flat into Socket 370 (see Figure 3-9). Pins are on the underside of the flat housing, and heat sinks or fans can be attached to the top of the housing by using a thermal plate or heat spreader. Current Celeron processors use this form factor.

- **FC-PGA (Flip Chip Pin Grid Array)** This form factor looks like the PPGA form factor and uses Socket 370. Heat sinks or fans can be attached directly to the top of the package. The Pentium III uses FC-PGA as one of its two form factors.

Figure 3-9   The Intel Celeron processor is housed in the PPGA form factor, which has pins on the underside that insert into Socket 370

CPU Slots and Sockets

A+CORE
1.1,
4.1,
4.3

Recall from Chapter 2 that a slot or socket is the physical connection used to connect a device (the CPU) to the system board. The type of socket or slot supplied by the system board for the processor must match that required by the processor. Table 3-7 lists several of the types of sockets and slots used by CPUs. Slots 1 and 2 are proprietary Intel slots, and Slot A is a proprietary AMD slot.

Table 3-7 CPU sockets and slots

Connector Name	Used by CPU	Number of Pins	Voltage
Socket 4	Classic Pentium 60/66	273 pins 21 × 21 PGA grid	5 V
Socket 5	Classic Pentium 75/90/100/120	320 pins 37 × 37 SPGA grid	3.3 V
Socket 6	Not used	235 pins 19 × 19 PGA grid	3.3 V
Socket 7	Pentium MMX, Fast Classic Pentium, AMD K5, AMD K6, Cyrix M	321 pins 37 × 37 SPGA grid	2.5 V to 3.3 V
Super Socket 7	AMD K6-2, AMD K6-III	321 pins 37 × 37 SPGA grid	2.5 V to 3.3 V
Socket 8	Pentium Pro	387 pins 24 × 26 SPGA grid	3.3 V
Socket 370 or PGA370 Socket	Pentium III FC-PGA, Celeron PPGA, Cyrix III	370 pins SPGA grid	1.5 V or 2 V
Slot 1 or SC242	Pentium II, Pentium III	242 pins in 2 rows Rectangular shape	2.8 V and 3.3 V
Slot A	AMD Athlon	242 pins in 2 rows Rectangular shape	1.3 V to 2.05 V
Slot 2 or SC330	Pentium II Xeon, Pentium III Xeon	330 pins in 2 rows Rectangular shape	1.5 V to 3.5 V

The 486 and earlier Pentiums used a **pin grid array (PGA)** socket where the pins were aligned in uniform rows around the socket. Later sockets use a **staggered pin grid array (SPGA)** where pins are staggered over the socket to squeeze more pins into a small space. Socket 7 is used on system boards that run at 66 MHz, and Super Socket 7 is used on the newer 100–MHz system boards. Super Socket 7 runs on 100–MHz system boards and supports AGP. It was designed to be used with AMD CPUs competing with the Intel Pentium II.

Socket 370 is used by two types of processors with two types of package form factors: PPGA (Plastic Pin Grid Array) and FC-PGA (Flip Chip Pin Grid Array). Both form

A+CORE
1.1,
4.1,
4.3

factors have pins on the underside of the processor that insert into the pin holes on the Socket 370 (see Figure 3-9). Socket 370 is also used by the Cyrix III and a version of the Pentium III designed for smaller computer cases called the Pentium III FC-PGA. For socket comparisons, see Figure 3-10.

Figure 3-10   CPU sockets use either a PGA or SPGA design; rows of pins are arranged on the socket either in even rows (PGA) or staggered (SPGA)

Earlier CPU sockets, called dual inline pin package (DIPP) sockets, were rectangular with two rows of pins down each side. PGA and SPGA sockets are all square or close to it. DIPP and some PGA sockets, called **low insertion force** (**LIF**) sockets, were somewhat troublesome to install because it was difficult to apply even force when inserting them. Current CPU sockets are called **zero insertion force** (**ZIF**) sockets and have a small lever on the side of the socket that lifts the CPU up and out of the socket. Push the lever down and the CPU moves into its pin connectors with equal force over the entire housing. The heat sink or fan clips to the top of the CPU. With this method, you can more easily remove the CPU and replace it with another if necessary.

Slot 1, Slot A, and Slot 2 are all designed to accommodate processors using the SEP or SECC housings that stand on their end much like an expansion card. The CPU is secured in the slot with clips on each side of the slot. You can attach a heat sink or cooling fan to the side of the CPU case. The Pentium II and Pentium III use Slot 1, and the Xeon versions of these processors use the longer Slot 2. AMD processors use Slot A.

The Celeron processor uses the PPGA form factor and Socket 370. Some system boards that have a Slot 1 can accommodate the Celeron processor by using a riser CPU card (see Figure 3-11). The riser card inserts into Slot 1, and the Celeron processor inserts into Socket 370 on the riser card. This feature allows you to upgrade an older Pentium II system to the faster Celeron.

The Pentium III processor uses two types of form factors: the SECC 2 and the FC-PGA. The SECC 2 is inserted into Slot 1, and the FC-PGA uses Socket 370. However, some older system boards that have a Socket 370 are not designed to support the Pentium III FC-PGA.

A+CORE
1.1,
4.1,
4.3

The Celeron processor uses 2.00 volts, and the Pentium III FC-PGA uses either 1.60 or 1.65 volts. A system board built only to support the Celeron may not recognize the need to step down the voltage for the Pentium III FC-PGA processor. This overvoltage can damage the Pentium III. Always consult the system board documentation to know what processors the board can support.

370-pin socket

CPU riser card

Clip to hold SECC processor or riser card in place

Slot 1

Figure 3-11   A riser card can be used to install a Celeron processor into a system board with slot 1

CPU Voltage Regulator

As you can see from Table 3-7, different CPUs require different amounts of voltage on the system board. Some CPUs require one voltage amount for external operations and another amount for internal operations. Those that require two different voltages are called **dual-voltage CPUs**. The others are called **single-voltage CPUs**. A CPU voltage regulator controls the amount of voltage on the system board. Some CPUs require that you set the jumpers on the system board to control the voltage, and other CPUs automatically control the voltage without your involvement.

Figure 3-12 shows sample documentation of what jumper settings to use for various CPU voltage selections on a particular system board that require jumpers to be set. Notice that two jumpers called JP16 located near Socket 7 on the board accomplish the voltage selection. For single voltage, for the Pentium, Cyrix 6x86, or AMD K5, both jumpers are open. Dual voltage used by the Pentium MMX, Cyrix M2, and AMD K6 is selected by opening or closing the two jumpers according to the diagram. Follow the recommendations for your CPU when selecting the voltages from the chart.

3

CPU TYPE	JP16	CPU Voltage	
		CORE	I/O
Single Voltage INTEL P54C/CQS/CT Cyrix 6x86 AMD K5	2 ○○ 4 1 ○○ 3 open	3.5V	3.5V
Dual Voltage INTEL P55C/MMX Cyrix 6x86L/M2 AMD K6	2 ○○ 4 1 ○○ 3 open	2.8V	3.4V
	2 ●○ 4 1 ●○ 3 1-2 closed, 3-4 open	2.9V	3.4V
	2 ○● 4 1 ○● 3 1-2 open, 3-4 closed	3.2V	3.4V

Figure 3-12   CPU voltage regulator can be configured using jumpers on the system board to apply the correct voltage to the CPU

THE CHIP SET

A chip set is a set of chips on the system board that collectively controls the memory cache, external buses, and some peripherals. Intel makes the most popular chip sets, which are listed in Table 3–8.

The Intel 440BX chip set is the first PC chip set to offer a memory bus that runs at 100 MHz, allowing a Pentium II running at 350 MHz or 400 MHz to reach its full potential for performance in desktop PCs. Before this, the memory bus slowed the CPU speed. The 440BX chip set is also the first chip set to use the mobile version of the Pentium II processor for notebooks. Often you see this chip set advertised with "AGP" in the name, as in the Intel 440BX AGP chip set. The 440GX chip set is an evolution of the 440BX.

Table 3-8   The Intel chip set family

Common Name	Model Number	Comments
Intel i800 Series	840	Designed for multiprocessor systems using Pentium II Xeon or Pentium III Xeon processors
	820	Designed for Pentium II and Pentium III systems
	810	First Intel chip set to eliminate the PCI bus as the main device interconnection
Orion	450GX, KX	Supports Pentium Pro (includes support for multiprocessors)
	450NX	Designed for servers with multiple Pentium II or Pentium II Xeon processors
Natoma	440FX	Supports Pentium Pro and Pentium II (Discontinued in January, 1999)
	440BX	Designed for servers and workstations (Pentium II and III)
	440GX	Designed for servers and workstations using the Pentium II Xeon and Pentium III Xeon
	440ZX	Designed for entry-level PCs using Pentium II
	440LX	Designed for Celeron processors
	440MX	Designed for notebook computers (M = mobile)
	440EX	Designed for smaller system boards such as the mini-ATX
Triton III	430VX	Value chip set, supports SDRAM
	430MX	Used for notebooks (M = mobile)
	430TX	Supports SDRAM, ultra DMA; replaced the VX and MX
Triton II	430HX	High performance, supports dual processors
Triton I	430FX	The oldest chip set, no longer produced

$A+$*CORE*
4.3

The 400 series of Intel chip sets uses the PCI bus as the interconnection between slower buses and the system bus. How the PCI bus does this is covered later in the chapter. The Intel i800 series of chip sets introduced a new way for I/O buses to relate to the faster system bus and ultimately to the CPU. With the i800 series, the interconnection between buses is done using a hub interface architecture, whereby all I/O buses connect to a hub, which connects to the system bus. This hub is called Hub Interface, and the architecture is called the Accelerated Hub Architecture (see Figure 3-13). The fast end of the hub, which contains the graphics and memory controller (GMCH), connects to the system bus and is called the hub's North Bridge. The slower end of the hub, called the South Bridge, contains the I/O Controller Hub (ICH). All I/O devices except display and memory connect to the hub by using the slower South Bridge.

Figure 3-13   Using Intel 800 series Accelerated Hub Architecture, a Hub Interface is used to connect slower I/O buses to the system bus

A+CORE
4.3

Chip sets are manufactured by the following companies:

- Intel Corporation
- Cyrix Corporation
- Silicon Integrated Systems Corp. (known as SiS)
- ALi, Inc.
- Standard Microsystems Corp.
- United Microelectronics Corp.
- VIA Technology, Inc. combined with AMD, Inc.
- VLSI Technology, Inc.

Chip Sets that Compete with Intel

SiS uses a similar faster North Bridge and slower South Bridge approach to managing slower I/O buses interconnecting with the faster system bus. The SiS620 chip set includes a digital video interface for digital flat panel display screens, and supports a 100 MHz system bus and an advanced hard drive interface called Ultra DMA (discussed in later chapters).

The Aladdin V chip set from ALi supports Socket 7 processors and the 100-MHz system bus speed. VIA in combination with AMD has the Apollo MVP3 chip set, which supports AGP, a 100-MHz bus speed, and Socket 7.

A+CORE
4.3

Currently, Intel dominates the chip set market for several reasons. The major advantage that Intel has over other chip set manufacturers is that they know more about their Intel CPUs than anyone else, and the chip sets are therefore more compatible with the Pentium family of CPUs. Intel's investment in research and development has let their engineers invent the PCI bus, the universal serial bus, the accelerated graphics port (AGP), and more recently the Accelerated Hub Architecture.

ROM BIOS

A+CORE
1.1,
1.8

Recall that there is one ROM chip on the system board that contains BIOS, which manages the startup process (startup BIOS) and many basic I/O functions of the system (system BIOS). Phoenix Software, Award Software, and American Megatrends, Inc. (AMI) write the most well-known and dependable ROM code for PCs. When selecting a PC clone, make sure to check who wrote the ROM BIOS code. If you select code written by one of these companies, your ROM BIOS will be compatible with most software.

An easy way to identify the name of the BIOS manufacturer without having to remove the case cover is to watch the boot process. The name of the BIOS manufacturer appears at the beginning of the boot process. You can also look for identifying information written on top of the chip. This ROM BIOS chip is easy to spot because it is larger than most chips and often has a shiny plastic label on it. On the label is the manufacturer's name, the date of manufacture, and the serial number of the chip. This information is important when you are trying to precisely identify the chip, such as when you're selecting the correct upgrade for the chip.

In the past, if the ROM BIOS needed upgrading—either because of new hardware or software added to the system or because the BIOS was causing errors, this meant exchanging the chip. The chip is usually socketed in, not soldered, for easy exchange. Recall from Chapter 1 that a newer kind of ROM, called Flash ROM, is now available that allows upgraded versions of the BIOS to be written to it without having to physically replace the chip.

You need to know the following about your BIOS:

- Does the BIOS support Plug and Play?
- Does the BIOS support large hard drives?
- Is the BIOS chip a Flash ROM chip?

This one ROM BIOS chip on the system board contains only a portion of the total BIOS code needed to interface with all the hardware components in the system. Understanding that BIOS programs can come from several sources helps in solving memory problems and other problems that arise from resource conflicts that will be considered in future chapters.

The Total BIOS in Your System

A+CORE
1.1,
1.8

Some expansion cards, such as a network interface card (NIC) or a video/graphics card, also have ROM chips on them containing BIOS code. The operating system uses the programs stored on these ROM chips to communicate with the peripheral devices. During the boot

A+CORE
1.1,
1.8

process, the expansion card tells the startup program how many memory addresses that it requires to access its ROM code. For protected mode firmware, any memory addresses will do, but, for older legacy cards using real mode, the BIOS must be assigned addresses in base memory or the upper memory area between 640K and 1024K. The ROM code from these boards becomes part of the total BIOS that the OS uses to communicate with peripherals. Problems referred to as hardware configuration conflicts can occur if two legacy boards request the same addresses in upper memory. We will address these hardware conflicts and offer possible solutions when we study managing memory in Chapter 4.

Figure 3-14 shows how the programming code from various ROM BIOS chips can be mapped onto the memory addresses managed by the CPU. The areas of upper memory are labeled the F range and the C range. In hex notation, upper memory addresses are numbered A0000 to FFFFF. Because of these hex numbers, the divisions of upper memory are often referred to as the A range, B range, C range, and so on, up to F range.

Recall from Chapter 2 that memory is viewed logically as a series of memory addresses that can be assigned to physical memory devices, such as a SIMM on the system board, a ROM BIOS chip on the system board, or a ROM chip on a network card or modem card. After booting is complete, most if not all of the BIOS on the system has declared that it exists and has requested memory addresses. In Figure 3-14, each memory device has been assigned a different address in base, upper, or extended memory.

Figure 3-14 The total ROM BIOS programs in a system can be assigned memory addresses in base, upper, and extended memory

A+*CORE*
  1.1,
  1.8

Remember from Chapter 2 that if the programming code from the ROM BIOS chips is also copied into RAM, this is called shadowing ROM or sometimes Shadow RAM. These terms indicate that RAM is shadowing ROM code. In the setup of your computer, you usually have the choice of whether to shadow System BIOS. For DOS and Windows 9x, accept the default setting for this option.

Plug and Play BIOS

Recall from Chapter 1 that **Plug and Play** (**PnP**) is a term that applies to both the Windows 9x OS and to some ROM BIOS. It means that rather than having you reset DIP switches and jumpers, the OS and/or the BIOS automatically configures hardware devices to reduce or eliminate conflicting requests for such system resources as I/O addresses, IRQs, DMA channels, or upper memory addresses. Windows 9x Plug and Play assigns these resources to a device only if the device allows it. For example, if a legacy sound card requires a certain group of upper memory addresses that are hard coded into its on-board BIOS, there's nothing that Windows 9x Plug and Play can do about that. (Hard coded is computer jargon for something being coded so that it cannot be changed.) Plug and Play simply tries to work around the problem as best it can. If two non–Plug and Play hardware devices require the same resource and their BIOS does not provide for accepting a substitute, these two devices cannot coexist on the same PC.

Newer devices that are Plug and Play compliant are more cooperative. At startup, they simply request to work and then wait for the OS to assign the resources they need. Windows 9x and Windows 2000 try to do that whether or not the system BIOS is Plug and Play BIOS. Plug and Play BIOS does some of the up-front work for Windows, the way that an efficient secretary organizes a boss's work for the day. At startup, it's the Startup BIOS that examines the hardware devices present, takes inventory, and then loads the OS. Part of the job of Plug and Play BIOS is to collect information about the devices and the resources they require and later to work with Windows 9x or Windows 2000 to assign the resources.

ESCD (extended system configuration data) Plug and Play BIOS goes even further, creating a list of all the things you have done manually to the configuration that Plug and Play does not do on its own. This ESCD list is written to the BIOS chip so that the next time you boot, the Startup BIOS can faithfully relate that information to Windows. The BIOS chip for ESCD BIOS is a special RAM chip called Permanent RAM, or PRAM, that can hold data written to it without the benefit of a battery, which the CMOS setup chip requires.

Most ROM BIOS chips made after the end of 1994 are Plug and Play. Windows 9x and Windows 2000 can use most—but not all—of their Plug and Play abilities without Plug and Play BIOS. If you are buying a new PC, accept nothing less than Plug and Play BIOS. As more and more devices become Plug and Play compliant, the time will come when installing a new device on a PC will be just as error-free and easy to do as it is on a Mac; Apple for years has known about and used the same concepts as are used in Plug and Play.

When BIOS is Incompatible with Hardware or Software

A+CORE
2.1,
4.4,
1.8

BIOS is a hybrid of two worlds. It's technically both hardware and software—it's really the intersection point of the two—and must communicate with both well, as shown in Figure 3-15. When hardware and software change, BIOS might need to change too. In the past, most users upgraded BIOS because new hardware was incompatible with it. Sometimes, however, you need to upgrade BIOS to accommodate new software, such as Plug and Play.

3

Figure 3-15   BIOS can serve as the hardware/software interface

Many years ago, when a new device became available, such as the 3½ inch floppy disk drive, your PC sometimes could not use the new device until you upgraded the BIOS. You did that by replacing the old BIOS chip with a new chip that supported the new device. Now, however, it's much easier. First, remember that most of today's new devices are not supported by the System BIOS at all, but by device drivers, which are software programs installed on the hard drive as an add-on part of the OS. But, if some new feature does require an upgrade to BIOS, you can do that with Flash ROM. Installing a larger hard drive is an example of a hardware upgrade that might require a BIOS upgrade because it is incompatible with the existing BIOS. Older BIOS supports only those hard drives with a 504-MB capacity. If you have this problem—large drive, old BIOS—you can solve it in one of two ways. Either upgrade BIOS or use special software designed to get around the problem. Often the device manufacturer supplies the software.

Flash ROM

Technically speaking, Flash ROM is called EEPROM (electronically erasable programmable read-only memory), which means you can change the programming on the chip through software on your PC. The updated programming will be retained—even when you turn off your PC for long periods of time—until you change it again. Flash ROM allows you to upgrade system BIOS without having to replace the ROM chip.

As more devices become Plug and Play compliant, Plug and Play BIOS will become more sophisticated. Additionally, makers of BIOS code are likely to change BIOS frequently because it is so easy for them to provide the upgrade on the Internet. You can get upgraded BIOS code from manufacturers' web sites or disks or from third-party BIOS resellers' Web sites or disks.

Figure 3-16 shows a sample Web site for Flash ROM BIOS upgrades. See the web site of the manufacturer of your BIOS or of the system board manufacturer for more information.

Figure 3-16 Flash ROM BIOS upgrades for most BIOS manufacturers can be downloaded from *www.unicore.com*

To upgrade Flash ROM, follow the directions that came with your system board and the upgrade software itself. Generally, you perform these tasks:

- Set a jumper on the system board telling the BIOS to expect an upgrade

- Copy the upgrade BIOS software to a bootable disk

- Boot from the disk and follow the menu options to upgrade the BIOS

- Set the jumper back to its original setting, reboot the system, and verify that all is working

Be *very careful* that you upgrade the BIOS with the correct upgrade and that you follow manufacturer instructions correctly. Upgrading with the wrong file could make your system BIOS totally useless. If you're not sure that you're using the correct upgrade, *don't guess.* Check with the technical support for your BIOS before moving forward. Before you call technical support, have the information that is written on the BIOS chip label available.

RAM (RANDOM ACCESS MEMORY)

A+CORE
4.2

Chapter 4 discusses how to manage RAM, but for now we present the essentials of where and what RAM is and how it is used. In older machines, RAM existed as individual chips socketed to the system board in banks or rows of nine chips each. Each bank held one byte by storing one bit in each chip, with the ninth chip holding a **parity** bit (see Figure 3-17). On older PCs the parity chip was separated a little from the other eight chips. (Parity, discussed below in more detail, refers to an error-checking procedure whereby either every byte has an even number of ones or every byte has an odd number of ones. The use of a parity bit means that every byte occupies nine rather than eight bits.)

3

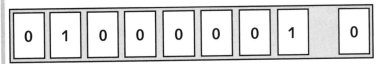

Figure 3-17   Eight chips and a parity chip represent the letter A in ASCII with even parity

Dynamic Memory

Recall that there are two types of RAM: **dynamic RAM** (**DRAM**) and **static RAM** (**SRAM**). Dynamic RAM chips hold data for a very short time; static RAM chips hold data until the power is turned off. Because DRAM is much less expensive than SRAM, most of the RAM on the system board is DRAM. DRAM comes in three types: parity, nonparity, or an altogether new method of error checking called ECC (error correcting code) that cannot only detect an error but also correct it. More about ECC in Chapter 4.

Parity is a method of testing the integrity of the bits stored in RAM or some secondary medium, or testing the integrity of bits sent over a communications device. When data is written to RAM, the computer calculates how many ON bits (binary 1) there are in the 8 bits of a byte. If the computer uses odd parity, it makes the ninth or parity bit either a 1 or a 0 to make the number of 1s in the 9 bits odd. Using even parity, the computer makes the parity bit a 1 or 0 to make the number of 1s in the 9 bits even.

Later, when the byte is read back, the computer checks the odd or even state. If the number of bits is not an odd number for odd parity or an even number for even parity, a **parity error** occurs. A parity error always causes the system to halt. On the screen you see the error message "Parity Error 1" or "Parity Error 2" or a similar error message about parity. Parity Error 1 is a parity error on the system board; Parity Error 2 is a parity error on a memory expansion board. Parity errors can be caused by RAM chips that have become

A+CORE
    4.2

undependable and that are unable to hold data reliably. Sometimes this happens when the chips overheat or power falters.

Recall that later, computers were made to hold RAM on a group of chips stored in a single physical unit called a **SIMM** (single inline memory module). A SIMM is a miniboard that stores an entire bank or banks of RAM. A SIMM can have several chips with 30 or 72 pins on the edge connector of the tiny board. RAM is then upgraded or changed by unplugging and plugging in SIMMs, which are much easier to work with than single chips. You will learn to upgrade memory using SIMMs in Chapter 4. RAM chips or SIMMs are located either on the system board or on memory expansion cards. SIMMs hold from 8 MB to 64 MB of RAM on one board.

All new system boards today use **DIMMs** (dual inline memory module), which have 168 pins on the edge connector of the board. A DIMM can hold from 8 MB to 256 MB of RAM on a single board. Figure 3-18 shows the two kinds of SIMMs and a DIMM module.

← 168-pin DIMM

← 72-pin SIMM

← 30-pin SIMM

Figure 3-18   Types of RAM modules

Most system boards today use 168-pin DIMMs. However, memory can be managed using several technologies that involve how memory is accessed, how timing the access is managed, and how the system board and the CPU relate to the memory modules. The more prevalent memory technologies (and some variations of each) used by the industry are listed in Table 3-9. Each of these technologies will be discussed in detail in Chapter 4. For now, know that the technology used by the memory modules must match the technology supported by the system board.

A+*CORE*
     4.2

Table 3-9   DRAM memory technologies

Technology	Description
Conventional	Used with earlier PCs but currently not available
Fast Page Memory (FPM)	Improved access time over conventional memory. FPM may still be seen today.
Extended Data Out (EDO)	Refined version of FPM that speeds up access time. Still seen on older system boards.
Burst EDO (BEDO)	Refined version of EDO that significantly improved access time over EDO. BEDO is seldom used today because Intel chose not to support it.
Synchronous DRAM (SDRAM)	SDRAM runs in sync with the system clock and is rated by clock speed, whereas other types of memory run independently of (and slower than) the system clock.
Rambus DRAM (RDRAM)	RDRAM uses a faster memory bus (up to 800 MHz), but only a 16-bit data path. The Intel Itanium processor will use RDRAM.
Double Data Rate (DDR) SDRAM	A faster version of SDRAM that can run at 200 MHz

3

Regardless of the type, dynamic RAM chips do not hold their data very long and must be refreshed about every 3.86 milliseconds. To **refresh** RAM means that the computer must rewrite the data to the chip. Refreshing RAM is done by the DMA (dynamic memory access) chip (discussed later in this chapter) or sometimes by circuitry on the system board other than the DMA chip.

Static Cache Memory

Recall that there are two kinds of static memory. L1 is contained on the CPU microchip, and L2 cache is external to the chip. L2 cache is housed either on the system board or, for newer CPUs, inside the CPU case. Look back at Figure 3-2 to see an example of an older CPU (the Pentium MMX) system board that has a memory cache slot. In Chapter 4 you will learn how to install extra L2 memory cache on one of these older boards.

BUSES AND EXPANSION SLOTS

As cities grow, so do their transportation systems. Small villages have only simple, two-lane roads, but large cities have two-lane and four-lane roads, and major freeways, each with its own set of traffic laws, including minimum and maximum speeds, access methods, and protocols. As microcomputer systems have evolved, so too have their "transportation" systems. The earliest PC had only a single and simple bus. Today's PCs have four or five buses, each with different speeds, access methods, and protocols. As you have seen, backward-compatibility dictates that older buses still be supported on a system board, even when faster, better buses exist. All this makes for a maze of many buses on a system board.

Bus Evolution

Just as a city's road system improves to increase the speed and number of lanes of traffic, buses have evolved around these similar issues, data path and speed. Cars on a freeway travel at a continuous or constant speed, but traffic on a computer's CPU or bus travels in a digital (on and off) manner rather than in an analog (continuous) manner. The system clock, run by a crystal on the system board, occupies one line of a bus and keeps the beat for components. Do something. Stop. Do something. Stop. Do something. Stop. With each beat, called a clock cycle, something can happen. Everything stops between beats, waiting for the next beat. The CPU is listening to this beat and working on these clock cycles. If another component on the system board also works by the beat or clock cycle, then it is said to be synchronized with the CPU. For example, earlier in the chapter, it was said that the backside bus of the Pentium II worked at half the speed of the CPU. This means that the CPU is doing something on each clock cycle, but the backside bus is doing something on every other clock cycle.

Some components don't attempt to keep in sync with the CPU, even to work at a half or a third of clock cycles. These components are said to be working asynchronously with the CPU. They might be working at a rate determined by the system clock or by another crystal on or off the system board. Either way, the frequency will be much slower than the CPU and not in sync with it. If the CPU requests something from one of these devices, and the device is not ready, it will issue wait states to the CPU until it can catch up.

$A+$CORE 4.3 Devices attached to the 8-bit or 16-bit ISA bus are an example of these slower devices. The 16-bit ISA bus works at a rate of 8.33 MHz, compared to memory bus speeds of 66 MHz to 200 MHz. Buses that work in sync with the CPU and the system clock are called **local buses** (sometimes called **system buses**). Buses that work asynchronously with the CPU at a much slower rate are called **expansion buses**. The memory bus is a local bus, and the ISA bus is an expansion bus.

Table 3-10   Buses listed by throughput in MB/sec (megabytes per second) or Mbps (megabits per second)

Bus	Bus Type	Data Path in Bits	Address Lines	Bus Speed in MHz	Throughput
FireWire	Local I/O or expansion	1	Addresses are sent serially	NA	Up to 1.2 GB/sec
Memory bus	Local	64	32	66, 75, 100 ...	Up to 1 GB/sec
AGP	Local video	32	NA	66, 75, 100 ...	Up to 528 MB/sec
PCI	Local I/O	32	32	33, 66	Up to 264 MB/sec

$A+CORE$
4.3

Table 3-10 Buses listed by throughput in MB/sec (megabytes per second) or Mbps (megabits per second) (continued)

Bus	Bus Type	Data Path in Bits	Address Lines	Bus Speed in MHz	Throughput
VESA or VL Bus	Local video or expansion	32	32	Up to 33	Up to 250 MB/sec
MCA	Expansion	32	32	12	Up to 40 MB/sec
EISA	Expansion	32	32	12	Up to 32 MB/sec
16-bit ISA	Expansion	16	24	8.33	8 MB/sec
8-bit ISA	Expansion	8	20	4.77	1MB/sec
USB	Expansion	1	Addresses are sent serially	3	1.5 or 12 Mbps

3

Why So Many Buses?

$A+CORE$
4.3

When the first PCs were introduced in the early 1980s, there was only one bus on the system board, called the system bus, which ran at the same speed as the CPU (4.77 MHz). Everything on the system board working with the CPU or the bus would simply keep the same beat, following the pulses of the one system clock. (This first bus is now called the 8-bit ISA bus.) Things today are not so simple. With the speeds of different hardware components evolving at different rates, a single speed for all components is no longer practical. The CPU works at one speed, the bus connecting the CPU to memory is working at a slower speed, and the bus communicating with I/O devices must work at an even slower speed. As manufacturers attempt to improve performance, new buses are invented to accommodate the characteristics of particular devices. In fact, there might be as many as five or six different buses working at different speeds on the same system board. Each bus will have a set speed that all components connected to it will work at. There are components that convert data moving from bus to bus to the speed of the new bus.

Table 3-10 lists the system-board buses, some outdated and some in use today, ordered from fastest to slowest. Historically, the 8-bit ISA (Industry Standard Architecture) bus came first, and was later revised to the 16-bit ISA bus to keep up with the demand for wider data path sizes. Then, in 1987, IBM introduced the first 32-bit bus, the MCA (Microchannel Architecture) bus, and competitors followed with the 32-bit EISA (Extended Industry Standard Architecture) bus. Because these buses are not synchronized with the CPU, they are all expansion buses. Of these buses, the only one still in use today is the 16-bit ISA. A relatively new expansion bus is the universal serial bus (USB), which targets slow I/O devices such as the mouse, digital camera, and scanner. Its advantage is that USB devices are easily installed and configured.

A+CORE
   4.3

A local bus is synchronized with the CPU. In the sense that a local bus is a bus that is close to or "local to" the CPU, there is only one "true" local bus, the memory bus or system bus, which connects directly to the CPU. All other buses must connect to it to get to the CPU. A local I/O bus is a bus designed to support fast I/O devices such as video and hard drives; it runs synchronized with the system clock, which means that it is also synchronized with the CPU. Local I/O buses did not always exist on a PC but were created as the need arose for a bus that was synchronized with the system clock, and was not as fast as the memory bus, but was faster than an expansion bus. The evolution of local I/O buses includes earlier proprietary designs, the VESA bus, the PCI bus, and the newer AGP bus. Of these, only the PCI and AGP bus are still sold. The FireWire bus is the latest local I/O bus and is not readily available as yet. It can work either synchronously or asynchronously and so is classified as either a local or expansion bus. The VESA bus could also be set to work either way.

What a Bus Does

Look on the bottom of the system board and you will see a maze of circuits that make up a bus. These embedded wires are carrying four kinds of cargo:

- **Electrical power**. Chips on the system board require power to function. These chips tap into a bus's power lines and draw what they need.

- **Control signals**. Some of the wires on a bus carry control signals that coordinate all the activity.

- **Memory addresses**. Memory addresses are passed from one component to another as these components tell each other where to access data or instructions. The number of wires that make up the memory address lines of the bus determines how many bits can be used for a memory address. The number of wires thus limits the amount of memory the bus can address.

- **Data**. Data is passed over a bus in a group of wires, just as the memory addresses are. The number of lines in the bus used to pass data determines how much data can be passed in parallel at one time. The number of lines depends on the type of CPU and determines the number of bits in the data path. (Remember that a data path is that part of the bus on which the data travels and can be 8, 16, 32, 64 or more bits wide.)

Most often when comparing buses users focus on the width of the data path and the overall bus speed. But you also should consider the type of expansion slot the bus allows. The number of fingers on the edge connector of the expansion card and the length of the edge connector are determined by the bus that controls that expansion slot. Various bus connections are shown in Figure 3-19.

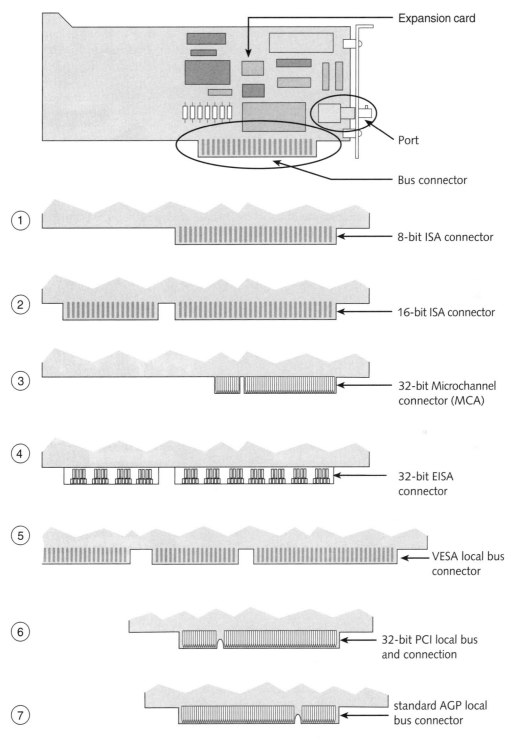

Figure 3-19   Seven bus connections on expansion cards

The ISA Bus

A+*CORE*
4.3

Used on the first IBM 8088 PCs in the early 1980s, the **ISA bus** had an 8-bit data path. Later, IBM revised the ISA bus to have a 16-bit path. The IBM AT personal computer used this bus and the 80286 chip, which is why the 16-bit bus is sometimes called the AT bus. IBM wanted this bus to be backward-compatible with the older 8-bit ISA bus so that the older 8-bit circuit boards would fit into the newer AT computers. To maintain compatibility, IBM kept the old 62-line slot connector and added another slot connector beside it to provide the extra 8 bits. Slots with both connectors are called 16-bit slots. A new system board today usually has at least one 16-bit slot, which can be used by either an 8-bit or 16-bit ISA card.

Microchannel Architecture (MCA) Bus

With the introduction of the line of PS/2 computers in 1987, IBM introduced the first 32-bit bus for personal computers, the **Microchannel Architecture (MCA) bus**. IBM did not intend the MCA bus to be compatible with ISA buses. Circuit boards used in older IBM computers could not be used in the PS/2 line. (The PS/2 Models 25 and 30 still included the older ISA bus in order to support legacy cards.)

IBM chose to patent the bus so that other companies could not economically manufacture and market it. IBM intended to control a subset of the bus market with MCA. In response, Compaq and eight other companies (called the "Gang of Nine") joined to design and build a competing 32-bit bus, the EISA bus.

The EISA Bus

Designed to compete with the MCA bus, the **EISA (Extended ISA) bus** (pronounced "ease-sa") has a 32-bit data path. The bus is compatible with older ISA buses so that expansion boards having 8-bit or 16-bit data paths work on the EISA bus. The speed of the EISA bus is about 20 MHz. To accommodate a 16-bit or 8-bit ISA circuit board, the 32-bit EISA has two slots that have the same width as 16-bit ISA slots. However, the EISA bus slots are deeper than 16-bit slots. All 32-bit circuit boards have longer fingers on the edge connectors that go deep into the EISA slot connecting to the 32-bit pins. A 16-bit circuit board reaches only partway down the slot connecting at a shallower level only to the 16-bit pins.

Universal Serial Bus

A+*CORE*
4.3,
1.3,
1.4

A relatively new I/O bus is the **universal serial bus** or **USB**, originally created by a seven-member consortium including Compaq, Digital Equipment, IBM, Intel, Microsoft, NEC, and Northern Telecom. It is designed to make the installation of slow peripheral devices as effortless as possible. USB is much faster than regular serial ports and much easier to manage, eliminating the need to manually resolve resource conflicts, since the host controller only uses one set of resources for all devices. It is expected that USB will ultimately replace both serial and parallel ports as the technology matures and more devices are built to use USB.

One or two USB ports are found on most new system boards today (see Figure 3-20), and older system boards that don't have USB ports can be upgraded by adding a PCI-to-USB controller card in a PCI slot to provide a USB port. USB allows for two speeds, 1.5 Mb per second and 12 Mb per second, and works well for slow I/O devices.

$A^{+CORE}_{\ 4.3,}$
1.3,
1.4

3

2 USB
ports

USB cable
connector

Figure 3-20   A system board with two USB ports and a USB cable; note the
rectangular shape of the connection as compared to the nearby
serial and parallel D-shaped ports

A **USB host controller**, which for the 400 series Intel chip set, is included in the PCI controller chip, manages the USB bus. As many as 127 USB devices can be daisy-chained together using USB cables up to five meters long. The host controller manages communication to the CPU for all devices, using only a single IRQ, I/O address range, and DMA channel. USB allows for **hot-swapping**, meaning that a device can be plugged into a USB port while the computer is running, and the host controller will sense the device and configure it without your having to reboot the computer. One USB device, such as a keyboard, can provide a port for another device, or a device can serve as a **hub**, allowing several devices to connect to it. There can also be a standalone hub into which several devices can be plugged. In USB technology, the host controller polls each device, asking if data is ready to be sent or requesting to send data to the device. The USB cable has four wires, two for power and two for communication. The two power wires (one carries voltage and the other is ground) allow the host controller to provide power to a device.

I/O devices that are now or are soon to be available with a USB connection are the mouse, joystick, keyboard, printer, scanner, monitor, modem, video camera, fax machine, and digital telephone.

USB must be supported by the operating system in order to work. Windows 95 with the USB update, Windows 98, and Windows 2000 support USB, but Windows NT does not. For more information about USB, see the forum web site at *www.usb.org*.

FireWire or i.Link or 1394

$A^{+CORE}_{\ 1.4,}$
1.7

FireWire and **i.Link** are the common names for another peripheral bus officially named **IEEE 1394** (or sometimes simply called 1394) after the group that designed the bus. The Institute of Electrical and Electronics Engineers was primarily led by Apple Computer and

A+CORE
1.4,
1.7

Texas Instruments in the initial design. FireWire is similar in design to USB, using serial transmission of data, but faster. FireWire supports data speeds as high as 1.2 Gbps (gigabits per second), much faster than USB. It is a viable option for connecting network cards, camcorders, DVD, and other high-speed, high-volume devices. Whereas USB is looking to replace slow serial and parallel ports, FireWire is likely to replace SCSI as a solution for high-volume multi-media external devices such as digital camcorders and hard drives. SCSI is a very fast, but difficult to configure, peripheral bus that will be discussed in Chapter 6.

Devices are daisy-chained together and managed by a host controller using a single set of system resources (an IRQ, an I/O address range, and a DMA channel). The one host controller can support up to 63 FireWire devices. Just as with USB, FireWire must be supported by the operating system. Windows 2000, Windows NT, and Windows 98 all support FireWire.

The 1394 Trade Association has developed a new standard, **IEEE 1394.3**, designed for peer-to-peer data transmission. Using this new standard, imaging devices, such as scanners and digital cameras, can send images and photos directly to printers without involving a computer.

Local I/O Buses

A+CORE
4.3

Recall that the primary intent of a local bus is to provide direct access to the CPU for a few fast devices, such as memory and video, that can run at nearly the same speed as the CPU. A local I/O bus must connect to the CPU by way of the memory bus. Figure 3-21 shows an example of a proprietary local bus that uses a 32-bit expansion slot created by adding an extra slot to a 16-bit ISA slot.

8-bit ISA slot

16-bit ISA slots

All three slots in this column together accommodate a proprietary local bus with 32-bit data path

Figure 3-21   Three kinds of legacy bus connections on the same system board

A+CORE
4.3

In an attempt to create a standard for local 32-bit buses, many manufacturers endorsed the **VESA (Video Electronics Standards Association)** VL bus. Many system boards offered the VESA local bus for video and memory circuit boards. The expansion slot for a VESA local bus includes the 16 bits for the ISA slot plus an added extension with another 116 pins (see Figure 3-22). The VESA bus has been replaced with the PCI bus.

Figure 3-22   VESA local bus expansion slot

PCI Bus

Another local I/O bus, the **PCI local bus (peripheral component interconnect bus)** is now the standard local I/O bus not only with Pentium CPUs but also with RISC CPUs. Standard PCI has a 32-bit data path and runs at 33 MHz when the system board runs at 66 MHz. However, the PCI specifications can also use a 64-bit data path and can run at a speed of 66 MHz when the system bus runs at 133 MHz. Also, an addendum to the PCI specifications, called PCI-X, released in September, 1999, enables PCI to run at 133 MHz.

A+CORE
4.3

One advantage of the PCI local bus is that devices connected to it can run at one speed while the CPU runs at a different speed. Devices connected to the VESA bus must run at the same clock speed as the CPU, which forces the CPU to endure frequent wait states. The PCI bus expansion slots are shorter than ISA slots (see Figure 3-23) and set a little farther away from the edge of the system board. Figure 3-24 shows the pinouts for the standard PCI slot.

PCI slots

16-bit ISA slots

Figure 3-23   PCI bus expansion slots are shorter than ISA slots and offset farther

3

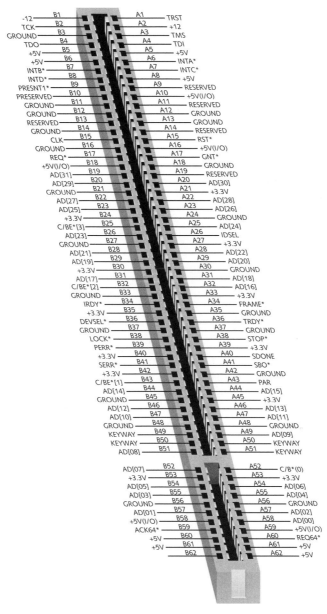

Figure 3-24 Standard PCI slot pinouts

As you learned earlier in the chapter, in addition to supporting I/O devices connected to it, the PCI bus also serves another function for the Intel 400 series chip set. The PCI bus interfaces with the expansion bus and the memory bus, serving as the go-between for the two, controlling the input and output to the expansion bus. As you can see in Figure 3-25, the memory bus is isolated from the ISA bus by the PCI bus. The connection between the two is the PCI bridge. The bridge allows the PCI bus to control the traffic not only from its own local devices but also from the ISA bus.

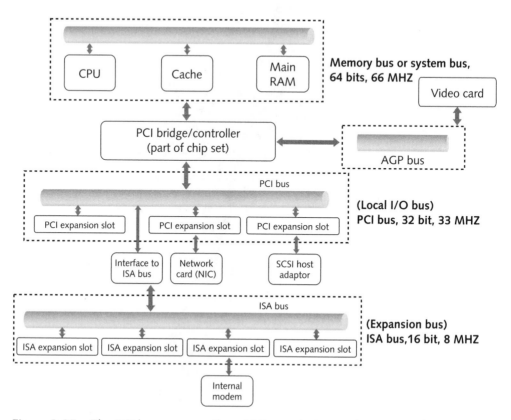

Figure 3-25   The PCI bus serves as the middleman between the memory bus and the expansion bus

In Figure 3-25, the SCSI (Small Computer System Interface) host adapter (discussed at length later in the book) and a network interface card (NIC) are connected to the PCI bus. (Physically, each card is inserted in a PCI expansion slot.) The PCI bridge/controller accesses the local bus where the CPU and memory are allowed to run at top speed without interference or wait states. If the CPU wants to send data to the network card, for example, it dumps it on the PCI bridge/controller at top speed. The controller puts the data in its own buffer or temporary memory storage and then writes it to the network card at a pace slower than the local bus. The bridge/controller eliminates interference with the local bus.

3

Figure 3-25 also shows the interface from the PCI bus to the ISA bus. This interface is a significant feature that distinguishes the PCI bus from other buses. The PCI bus was not designed to replace the traditional expansion bus, but to support it. The ISA bus in the diagram passes data through the interface to the PCI bus, which in turn passes the data on to the memory bus, to the CPU, and to memory.

The PCI bus also supports bus mastering. A bus master is an intelligent device (i.e., it has a microprocessor installed that manages the device) that, when attached to the PCI bus, can gain access to memory and other devices on the bus without interrupting the action of the CPU. The CPU and the bus mastering devices can run concurrently and independently of each other.

Because of the effective design of the PCI bus, the throughput performance, or the data transfer rate per second, is 132 MB when the bus is running at 33 MHz with a 32-bit data path. **Throughput performance**, or **data throughput**, is a measure of the actual data transmitted by the bus, not including error-checking bits or redundant data.

Accelerated Graphics Port

A+CORE 4.3 The **accelerated graphics port** (**AGP**) is designed to provide fast access to video. System boards have a single AGP slot to support an AGP video card (see Figure 3-26). AGP is more of a port than a bus, since it does not allow for expandability and can only support a single card. Notice in the diagram in Figure 3-25 that the faster AGP bus has a direct connection to the CPU without having to use the slower PCI bus.

AGP Slot

Figure 3-26   A system board will have only one AGP slot, which is used to support a video/graphics card

> **TIP** A slot or socket is the physical connector on a system board for a device and does not include logic to support the connected device. A port is a socket or slot but goes a step further and also includes the logic to support that connection (example: serial and parallel ports). A bus, among other things, provides the logic to support several devices connected to the system board, but does not include the physical connection itself. You need an expansion slot for that.

The AGP bus runs at the same speed as the memory bus, connects directly to it, and has a 32-bit-wide data path. AGP runs faster than PCI, running at half the memory bus speed, but also offers additional features that give it overall better performance for video than PCI. It offers an improved rendering of 3-D images when software is designed to use it.

AGP can share system memory with the CPU to do its calculations and, therefore, does not always have to first copy data from system memory to video memory on the graphics card. This feature, known as direct memory execute (DIME), is probably the most powerful feature of AGP. The first AGP specification defined AGP 2X, which allowed AGP to transfer two cycles of data during a single AGP clock beat. The AGP 2.0 specification defined AGP 4X whereby four cycles of data can be transferred during a single AGP clock beat yielding an overall data throughput of more than 1 GB/sec (gigabytes per second).

Figure 3-26 shows a 132-pin AGP slot on a system board. The latest AGP standard, called the AGP Pro, has provision for a longer slot. The new 188-pin slot has extensions on both ends that each contain an additional 28 pins that are used to provide extra voltage to the AGP video card in the slot. AGP Pro is used for high-end workstations that require powerful graphic accelerator cards for graphic-intensive applications.

In order for AGP to work at its full potential, the system board must be running at a minimum of 100 MHz, and the operating system must support AGP. Windows 98 and Windows 2000 both support AGP. See *www.agpforum.org* and *developer.intel.com/technology/agp/* for more information.

Audio Modem Riser

Newer system boards sometimes have an audio modem riser (AMR) slot that can accommodate a small modem card or sound card. These small cards are inexpensive since most of the logic to support audio or the modem is contained within the system board chip set. The AMR slot makes it possible to add the card at a low cost without using up a PCI or ISA slot.

Setting the CPU and Bus Speeds

A+CORE
1.8

You can, to some extent, control the speed of your system. Table 3-11 lists how the CPU and several bus speeds are controlled. There are two ways you can change the speed of a computer:

1. Change the speed of the memory bus. Whatever the memory bus speed is, the PCI bus speed is half or one third of that.

2. Change the multiplier that determines the speed of the CPU. The choices for the multiplier normally are 1.5, 2, 2.5, 3, 3.5 and so forth.

Table 3-11   System-board speeds and how they are determined

Bus or Device	How Speed Is Determined	How Controlled
CPU	Processor speed = memory bus speed x multiplier. Typical speeds are 350 MHz, 450 MHz, and 500 MHz	Multiplier is set by jumpers or DIP switches on the system board or in CMOS setup
Memory bus or system bus	System board manufacturer recommends the speed based on the processor and processors rated speed. Typical values are 66 MHz, 100 MHz, and 133 MHz	Set by jumpers, DIP switches, or in CMOS setup. Most commonly set by jumpers.
PCI bus	Memory bus speed / 2 (or for faster boards, it can be divided by 3)	The speed is set when you set the speed of the memory bus; either 33 MHz or 66 MHz
ISA bus	Runs at only one speed: 8.77 MHz	NA

Studies have shown that when the multiplier is large, the overall performance of the system is not as good as when the multiplier is small. This is a reasonable result because you are interested in the overall speed of the computer, which includes the CPU and the buses, not just the speed of the CPU. For example, a bus speed of 60 MHz and a multiplier of 5 yield a relatively fast CPU but a relatively slow bus. It's better to have a bus speed of 80 MHz and a multiplier of 3 so that the bus is running fast enough to keep up with the CPU.

See the system board documentation to learn how to set these speeds using jumpers, DIP switches, or CMOS setup. Figure 3-27 shows the documentation for one system board that uses one bank of jumpers to set the CPU-to-bus multiplier and another jumper bank to set the bus frequency. The steps to do that are:

1. Read the documentation of your CPU to determine its recommended frequency. In our example, we are using a Pentium II rated for 350MHz. Find the row labeled Pentium 350MHz in the table of Figure 3-27.

2. Read the multiplier from the selected row, which is 3.5x. Find the jumper settings for a multiplier of 3.5 in the possible jumper combinations for the CPU Core: BUS Frequency Multiple (fourth entry in first row).

3. The CPU type and speed also determine the bus frequency, which is 100MHz. To set the bus frequency to 100 MHz, find the jumper combination for the second jumper bank, which is the fourth entry in the list of selections for the CPU External Clock (Bus) Frequency Selection.

4. Set the jumpers in the two jumper banks. Figure 3-28 shows the jumper group for the multiplier set to 3.5.

❶ Begin with the speed of your CPU
❷ The CPU speed determines the ratio (multiplier)
❸ The CPU speed also determines the bus frequency

Set the jumpers by the Internal speed of your processor as follows:

Figure 3-27   Based on the advertised speed of your CPU, select the multiplier and the bus frequency from the table, which then determines the jumper settings to use

Figure 3-28   Jumper group that controls the CPU core-to-bus frequency. Compare this photo to the diagram in Figure 3-27. The jumpers are set for the multiplier = 3.5.

On-Board Ports

Many system boards contain **on–board ports** such as a keyboard port and a mouse port. In addition, a parallel printer port and one or two serial ports might be located directly on the system board. Few older system boards contain more ports than these. Some systems also have a video or network port, and newer system boards contain one or two USB ports.

You don't have to replace an entire system board if one port fails. Most system boards contain jumpers or DIP switches that can tell the CPU to disable one port and look to an expansion card for the port instead. Ports can also be disabled through CMOS setup.

When buying a new computer or system board, look for the ability to disable ports, floppy drive connectors, or hard drive connectors coming directly from the system board by changing the hardware configuration. You can easily tell if ports on the outside of the case are directly connected to the system board without opening the case; the ports are lined up along the bottom of the computer case, as shown in Figure 3-29.

Fan

Power cord connectors

Expansion slots

Printer port

Video

Serial ports
Keyboard

Figure 3-29   Ports along the bottom of the computer case usually come directly off the system board

Hardware Configuration

Recall that hardware configuration information communicates to the CPU what hardware components are present in the system and how they are set up to interface with the CPU. Hardware configuration includes information such as how much memory is available, what power management features are present, and whether disk drives, hard drives, modems, serial ports, and the like are connected. Remember that during POST, BIOS looks to the system configuration information to determine the equipment it should expect to find and how that equipment interfaces with the CPU. The CPU uses this information later to process data and instructions. Configuration information is provided on the system board in three different ways, as discussed in Chapter 2: DIP switches, jumpers, and CMOS. Earlier in the chapter you saw several examples of how jumpers are used to set configuration information on the system board. Here we look more closely at the CMOS setup screens.

Setup Stored on a CMOS Chip

A+CORE
1.1,
4.4

Computers today store most configuration information on one CMOS chip that retains the data even when the computer is turned off. (There are actually many CMOS chips on a system board, used for various purposes.) A battery near the CMOS chip provides enough electricity to enable the chip to maintain its data. If the battery is disconnected or fails, setup information is lost. Password information is also a part of the computer's setup that is stored in CMOS. The program to change the setup information is now stored in ROM but once was on a disk that came with the computer.

A+CORE
1.1,
4.4

System-board manuals should contain a list of all CMOS settings, an explanation of their meanings, and their recommended values. When you purchase a system board or a computer, be sure the manual is included for this purpose. If you don't have the manual, you can sometimes go to the system-board manufacturer's Web site and download the information you need to understand the specific CMOS settings of your computer.

Some CMOS settings are listed in Table 3-12.

3

Table 3-12   CMOS settings and their purpose

Category	Setting	Description
Standard CMOS Setup	Date and time	Use to set system date and time (called the real time clock).
	Primary display	Use to tell POST and DOS (but not Windows) the type of video being used.
	Keyboard	Use to tell system if keyboard is installed or not installed. Useful if the computer is used as a print or file server and you don't want someone changing settings.
	Hard disk type	Use to record size and mapping of the drive.
	Floppy disk type	Choices are usually 3½ inch and 5¼ inch.
Advanced CMOS Setup	Above 1 MB memory test	Use to disable POST check of this memory to speed up booting. The OS will check this memory anyway.
	Memory parity error check	If you have a parity system board, use to enable parity checking to ensure that memory is correct.
	Numeric processor test	Enabled unless you have an old 386 or 486SX computer
	System boot sequence	Use to establish the drive the system turns to first to look for an OS. Normally drive A, then C.
	External cache memory	Use to enable if you have L2 cache. A frequent error in setup is to have cache but not use it because it's disabled here.
	Internal cache memory	Normally enabled; disable only for old 386 computers.
	Password checking option	Use to establish a startup password. Use this only if you really have a problem with someone using your PC who can't be trusted.
	Video ROM shadow C000, 16K	For DOS and Windows 9x, shadowing video ROM is recommended because ROM runs slower than RAM.
	System ROM shadow F000, 64K	Enabling shadow system ROM is recommended.
	IDE Multi-block mode	Enables a hard drive to read or write several sectors at a time. Dependent on the kind of hard drive you have.
	Boot sector virus protection	Gives a warning when something is being written to the boot sector of the hard drive. Can be a nuisance if your software is designed to write to the boot sector regularly.

Table 3-12   CMOS settings and their purpose (continued)

Category	Setting	Description
Advanced Chip Set Setup	AT bus clock selection	Gives the number by which the CPU speed is divided to get the ISA or EISA bus speed
	ISA bus speed	Gives the number by which the PCI bus speed is divided to get the ISA bus speed
	Bus mode	Can be set to synchronous or asynchronous modes. In synchronous mode, the bus uses the CPU clock. In asynchronous mode its own AT bus clock is used.
	AT cycle wait state	The number of wait states the CPU must endure while it interfaces with a device on the ISA or EISA bus. Increase this if an old and slow ISA card is not working well.
	Memory read wait state	Number of wait states the CPU must endure while reading from RAM
	Memory write wait state	Number of wait states the CPU must endure while writing to RAM
	Cache read option	Sometimes called "cache read hit burst"
		The number of clock beats needed to load four 32-bit words into the CPU's internal cache. 4-1-1-1 is the usual choice.
	Fast cache read/write	Refers to external cache. Enable it if you have two banks of cache, 64K or 256K.
	Cache wait state	Refers to external cache. The number of wait states the CPU must use while accessing cache.
Power Menu	Power Management	Disable or enable all power management features. These features are designed to conserve electricity.
	HDD Power Down	Disable or enable the feature to shut down the hard drive after a period of inactivity
	Wake on LAN	Wake on LAN allows your PC to be booted from another computer on the same network. It requires an ATX power supply that supports the feature.
	Wake on keyboard	Allows you to power up your PC by pressing a certain key combination.

CHAPTER SUMMARY

◻ The system board is the most complicated of all the components inside the computer. It contains the CPU and accompanying chip set, the real-time clock, ROM BIOS, CMOS configuration chip, RAM, RAM cache, system bus, expansion slots, jumpers, ports, and power supply connections. The system board you select determines both the capabilities and limitations of your system.

◻ The most important component on the system board is the CPU, or central processing unit. The CPU is the microprocessor at the heart of a PC system, where almost all operations must ultimately be processed. The CPU is rated according to its speed, efficiency of programming code, word size, data path size, maximum memory addresses, size of internal cache, multiprocessing abilities, and special functions. Earlier Intel CPUs include the 80386DX, 80386SX, 80486DX, and 80486SX. The latest family of Intel CPUs is the Pentium family, including the Classic Pentium, Pentium MMX, Pentium Pro, Pentium II, Celeron, and Pentium III. AMD and Cyrix are Intel's chief competitors for the CPU market. CPUs can use either RISC or CISC technology or a combination of the two.

❏ Newer CPUs require extra cooling, which can be accomplished with a CPU heat sink and cooling fan located on top of or near the CPU.

❏ The common CPU sockets and slots today are Socket 7, Socket 370, Slot 1, Slot A, and Slot 2. A slot looks like an expansion slot.

❏ Because some CPUs require one voltage for internal core operations and another voltage for external I/O operations, system boards might have a voltage regulator on board.

❏ Some components can be built into the system board, in which case they are called on-board components, or they can be attached to the system in some other way such as on an expansion card.

❏ ROM chips contain the programming code to manage POST and system BIOS and to change the CMOS settings. The setup or CMOS chip holds configuration information.

❏ A chip set is a group of chips on the system board that supports the CPU. Intel is the most popular manufacturer of chip sets.

❏ The total BIOS of a system includes the ROM BIOS on the system board as well as BIOS on expansion cards. Plug and Play BIOS is designed to work in harmony with Windows 9x or Windows 2000 to resolve resource conflicts from expansion cards and other devices. Flash ROM allows the ROM BIOS to be upgraded without having to change the ROM chip.

❏ Dynamic RAM (DRAM) is slower than static RAM (SRAM) because dynamic RAM must be refreshed. RAM usually comes packaged as a SIMM or DIMM memory module.

❏ Two kinds of static RAM cache for the slower DRAM are internal and external cache, sometimes called Level 1 and Level 2 cache.

❏ Level 1 cache is contained on the CPU microchip, and level 2 cache is external to this microchip.

❏ A bus is a path on the system board that carries electrical power, control signals, memory addresses, and data to different components on the board.

❏ A bus can be 16, 32, 64 or more bits wide. The first ISA bus had an 8-bit data path. The second ISA bus had a 16-bit data path

❏ Some well-known buses are the 16-bit ISA bus, 32-bit MCA and EISA buses, and the two local buses, the VESA bus and the PCI bus. A local bus is designed to allow fast devices quicker and more direct access to the CPU than that allowed by other buses.

❏ The VESA local bus is a standard designed by the Video Electronics Standards Association. The PCI bus is presently the most popular local bus. To gain the maximum overall computer performance, the multiplier relating the bus speed to the CPU speed should be small.

❑ Expansion slots can be located on the system board, but they are sometimes stacked vertically in the computer case on a second board devoted to that purpose.

❑ Jumpers on the system board can be used to set the system-board speed and the CPU multiplier that determines the CPU speed.

❑ Sometimes the CPU must be slowed down to accommodate slower devices, enduring wait states that cause it to wait one clock beat. Wait states often mean a significant reduction in performance.

KEY TERMS

Accelerated graphics port (AGP) — A slot on a system board for a video card that provides transfer of video data from the CPU that is synchronized with the memory bus.

Advanced Transfer Cache (ATC) — A type of L2 cache contained within the Pentium processor housing that is embedded on the same core processor die as the CPU itself.

Backside bus — The bus between the CPU and the L2 cache inside the CPU housing.

Bus — Strips of parallel wires or printed circuits used to transmit electronic signals on the system board to other devices. Most Pentium systems use a 32-bit or 64-bit bus.

Bus speed — The speed or frequency at which the data on the system board is moving.

Chip set — A set of chips on the system board that collectively controls the memory cache, external buses, and some peripherals.

Clock speed — The speed or frequency that determines the speed at which devices on the system bus operate, usually expressed in MHz. Different components on a system board operate at different speeds, which are determined by multiplying or dividing a factor by the clock speed. The clock speed is itself determined by a crystal or oscillator located somewhere on the system board.

Data path — The number of bits of data transmitted simultaneously on a bus. The size of a bus, such as a 32-bit-wide data path in a PCI bus.

DIMM (dual in-line memory module) — A miniature circuit board that holds memory chips and has a 64-bit data path. Because Pentium system boards also use a 64-bit memory bus, it is possible to use only a single DIMM on these system boards.

Discrete L2 cache — A type of L2 cache contained within the Pentium processor housing, but on a different die, with a cache bus between the processor and the cache.

Dual voltage CPU — A CPU that requires two different voltages, one for internal processing and the other for I/O processing.

Dynamic RAM (DRAM) — The most commonly used type of system memory, it requires refreshing every few milliseconds.

EISA (Extended Industry Standard Architecture) bus — A 32-bit bus that can transfer 4 bytes at a time at a speed of about 20 MHz.

ESCD (extended system configuration data) — A list written to the BIOS chip of information about legacy devices that Plug and Play uses to configure these devices.

Expansion bus — A bus that does not run synchronized with the system clock.

External cache — Static cache memory, stored on the system board or inside CPU housing, that is not part of the CPU (also called level 2 or L2 cache).

3

Field replaceable unit — A component in a computer or device that can be replaced with a new component without sending the computer or device back to the manufacturer. Example: a DIMM memory module on a system board.

FireWire — An expansion bus that can also be configured to work as a local bus. It is expected to replace the SCSI bus, providing an easy method to install and configure fast I/O devices. Also called IEEE 1394 and i.Link.

Frontside bus — The bus between the CPU and the memory outside the CPU housing.

Heat sink — A piece of metal, with cooling fins, that can be attached to or mounted on an integrated chip (such as the CPU) to dissipate heat.

Hot-swapping — When a device can be plugged into a computer while it is turned on and the computer will sense the device and configure it without rebooting.

Instruction set — The set of instructions, on the CPU chip, that the computer can perform directly (such as ADD and MOVE).

Internal cache — Memory cache that is faster than external cache, and is contained inside 80486 and Pentium chips (also referred to as primary, Level 1, or L1 cache).

IEEE 1394 — *See* FireWire.

ISA bus — An 8-bit industry standard architecture bus used on the original 8088 PC. Sixteen-bit ISA buses were designed for the 286 AT, and are still used in Pentiums for devices such as modems.

Level 1 cache — *See* Internal cache.

Level 2 cache — *See* External cache.

Local bus — A bus that operates at a speed synchronized with the CPU speed.

Local I/O bus — A local bus that provides I/O devices with fast access to the CPU.

Low insertion force (LIF) — A socket feature that requires the installer to manually apply an even force over the microchip when inserting the chip into the socket.

MCA (Micro Channel Architecture) bus — A proprietary IBM PS/2 bus, seldom seen today, with a width of 16 or 32 bits and multiple master control, which allowed for multitasking.

Memory bus — The bus between the CPU and memory on the system board. Also called the system bus or the host bus.

Memory cache — A small amount of faster RAM that stores recently retrieved data, in anticipation of what the CPU will request next, thus speeding up access.

Multiplier — The factor by which the bus speed or frequency is multiplied to get the CPU clock speed.

North bridge — That portion of the chip set hub that connects faster I/O buses (for example, AGP bus) to the system bus. Compare to South bridge.

On-board ports — Ports that are directly on the system board, such as a built-in keyboard port or on-board serial port.

Overclocking — Running a system board at a speed that is not recommended or guaranteed by CPU or chip set manufacturers.

P1 connector — Power connection on an ATX system board.

Parity — An error-checking scheme in which a ninth, or "parity," bit is added. The value of the parity bit is set to either 0 or 1 to provide an even number of ones for even parity and an odd number of ones for odd parity.

Parity error — An error that occurs when the number of 1s in the byte is not in agreement with the expected number.

PCI (peripheral component interconnect) bus — A bus common on Pentium computers that runs at speeds of up to 33 MHz or 66 MHz, with a 32-bit-wide or 64-bit-wide data path. For most chip sets, it serves as the middle layer between the memory bus and expansion buses.

Pin grid array (PGA) — A feature of a CPU socket whereby the pins are aligned in uniform rows around the socket.

Plug and Play — A technology in which the operating system and BIOS are designed to automatically configure new hardware devices to eliminate system resource conflicts (such as IRQ and port conflicts).

Primary cache — *See* Internal cache.

Processor speed — The speed or frequency at which the CPU operates. Usually expressed in MHz.

Refresh — The process of periodically rewriting the data for instance, on dynamic RAM.

RISC (reduced instruction set computer) chips — Chips that incorporate only the most frequently used instructions, so that the computer operates faster (for example, the PowerPC uses RISC chips).

SECC (Single Edge Contact Cartridge) — A type of cartridge that houses the Pentium III processor.

SC330 (Slot Connector 330) — A 330-pin system board connector used to contain the Pentium III Xeon. Also called Slot 2.

SIMM (single in-line memory module) — A miniature circuit board that holds memory chips and has a 32-bit data path. Because Pentium system boards use a 64-bit memory bus, you must install two SIMMs at a time.

Single voltage CPU — A CPU that requires one voltage for both internal and I/O operations.

South bridge — That portion of the chip set hub that connects slower I/O buses (for example, ISA bus) to the system bus. Compare to North bridge.

Staggered pin grid array (SPGA) — A feature of a CPU socket whereby the pins are staggered over the socket in order to squeeze more pins into a small space.

Static RAM (SRAM) — RAM chips that retain information without the need for refreshing, as long as the computer's power is on. They are more expensive than traditional DRAM.

System bus — Today the system bus usually means the memory bus. However, sometimes it is used to refer to other buses on the system board. *See* memory bus.

Turbo mode — A means of doubling the external clock speed by pressing a button on the case of some older computers.

Universal serial bus (USB) — A bus that is expected to eventually replace serial and parallel ports, designed to make installation and configuration of I/O devices easy, providing room for as many as 127 devices daisy-chained together. The USB uses only a single set of resources for all devices on the bus.

VESA (Video Electronics Standards Association) VL bus — An outdated local bus used on 80486 computers for connecting 32-bit adapters directly to the local processor bus.

Wait state — A clock tick in which nothing happens, used to ensure that the microprocessor isn't getting ahead of slower components. A 0-wait state is preferable to a 1-wait state. Too many wait states can slow a system down.

Zero insertion force (ZIF) — A socket feature that uses a small lever to apply even force when installing the microchip into the socket.

3

REVIEW QUESTIONS

1. What are the two most popular types of system-board form factors?
2. How many power cords connect to a Baby AT system board have?
3. Name 10 components that are contained on a system board.
4. When is it appropriate to have a Slot 1 on a system board?
5. Why would you want both ISA and PCI expansion slots on a system board?
6. When people speak of bus size, what are they specifically referring to?
7. What characteristics of the system-board architecture determine the amount of memory that a CPU can address?
8. What was the first Intel CPU to contain internal cache?
9. If you know the system bus speed, how can you determine the CPU speed?
10. When is it appropriate to use a Celeron rather than a Pentium II in a computer system?
11. Which is more powerful, the Celeron or the Xeon processor?
12. What are the two major competitors of Intel in the CPU market?
13. Why did the competitors of the Intel Pentium II choose to stay with Socket 7 rather than use Slot 1 for their competing processors?
14. Contrast CISC and RISC technology.
15. In order to keep a CPU cool, which is better to use, and why: a heat sink or a cooling fan?
16. Describe the difference between a PGA socket and an SPGA socket.
17. Name a CPU that requires dual voltage. How are the two voltages used?
18. Why is AGP technology described as being more like a port than a bus?
19. What are the speeds of the most popular system boards currently available on the market?
20. Name three manufacturers of system-board chip sets.
21. Name the three most popular manufacturers of system BIOS programs.
22. When is Plug and Play not helpful in resolving a resource conflict?
23. Explain the difference between a local bus and an expansion bus.
24. How many bits are needed to store one byte when parity is used?
25. Why does memory need to be refreshed?

26. What is the name for the bus that connects L2 cache to the CPU inside the Pentium II processor housing?

27. Why don't all buses on a system board operate at the same speed?

28. Which is faster, the memory bus or the ISA bus?

29. What are the four categories of cargo that are carried over a bus?

30. Draw and label the ports that you find on the back of a typical computer.

31. Look in CMOS setup on your PC and list five things that you can change.

32. How can bus mastering improve overall computer performance?

33. What advantage does a USB have over serial ports?

PROJECTS

CAUTION

Unless you follow proper procedures, working inside your computer can cause serious damage—to both you and your computer. To ensure safety in your work setting, follow every precaution listed in the *Read This Before You Begin* section following this book's Introduction.

Important Safety Precautions

In some of the following activities, you remove the cover of a computer and examine the components. Before you perform the exercises in this chapter, carefully read the following precautions and procedures to protect yourself and the equipment. Remember that you can compound a problem, causing even more damage, by carelessly neglecting these safety precautions.

The most common threat to hardware is electrostatic discharge (ESD), commonly known as static electricity. Damage by ESD can cause a catastrophic failure, which can destroy components, or can cause an upset failure that produces unpredictable malfunctions of components, which are often difficult to detect or diagnose.

The three best protections against ESD as you work on a computer are a ground strap, a ground mat, and static shielding bags. A ground bracelet, sometimes called a ground strap or a static strap (see Figure 3-30), is worn on your wrist and is grounded to a ground mat, computer case, or a ground prong of a wall outlet. It contains a current-eliminating device, called a resister, that prevents electricity from flowing through the bracelet to you. A ground mat (see Figure 3-31) often comes equipped with a cord to plug into the ground prong of the wall outlet and a snap on the mat to which you can attach the end of your ground strap. New components come shipped in static shielding bags. Save the bags to store other devices not currently installed on your PC.

$A^{+CORE}_{3.2}$

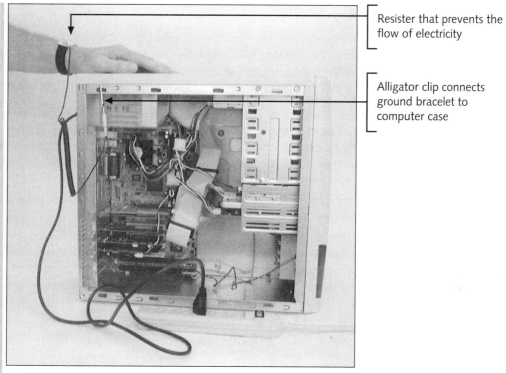

Resister that prevents the flow of electricity

Alligator clip connects ground bracelet to computer case

Figure 3-30   A ground bracelet, which protects against ESD, can clip to the side of the computer case and eliminates ESD between you and the case

Ground strap

Snaps to connect ground strap

Ground strap snaps to mat

To ground line in wall outlet

Ground mat

Figure 3-31   A ground bracelet can be connected to a ground mat, which is grounded by the wall outlet

Protect Against Electricity

A+CORE
3.2

You can actually destroy a computer chip with static electricity when you touch it, even though you might not feel a thing. You will learn more about this in Chapter 11, but for now, follow these rules to protect chips while you handle them:

1. Never touch the inside of a computer while it is turned on.

2. Never touch any component inside the computer without first grounding yourself to discharge any static electricity on your body. The best way to do this is to wear a ground bracelet or ground strap. If you don't have a ground bracelet, touch the metal case or power supply each time, before you touch any component, to discharge the electricity on your body.

3. Don't work on carpet. Work on a bare floor because a carpet collects static electricity, especially in cold weather.

4. Consider both the power supply and monitor to be a "black box." Don't open either unless you are trained to understand the dangers of and safety precautions for these devices. The power supply and the monitor have enough power inside them to kill you, even when they are unplugged.

Other Valuable Rules

1. When taking boards out of a PC, don't stack them. Stacking can loosen components.

2. Keep screws and spacers in an orderly place, such as a cup or tray.

3. Make notes as you work, so later you can backtrack.

4. In a classroom environment, after you have reassembled everything, before putting the cover back on, have your instructor check your work, *before* you power up.

5. Don't touch chips or edge connectors on boards unless absolutely necessary.

6. Don't touch chips with a magnetized screwdriver.

7. Don't use a graphite pencil to change DIP switch settings.

8. Don't put cards on top of or next to the monitor.

9. When setting down components, lay them on a grounded mat or static shielding bag.

10. Always turn off the PC before moving it (even a few inches) to protect the hard drive.

11. If you have been trained to work inside a monitor or power supply, while you are working inside either, be careful *not* to ground yourself.

12. When unpacking hardware or software, remove the packing tape from the work area as soon as possible.

13. Don't place a PC on the floor where it can be kicked.

14. Keep disks away from magnetic fields, heat, and extreme cold.

15. Don't open a disk's shuttle window or touch the surface of a disk.

16. Using a circuit tester, always verify that the ground plug in an outlet is physically grounded.

Examine the System Board

1. Look at the back of your computer. Without opening the case, list the ports that you believe to be coming directly from the system board.

2. Now look inside the case to verify your list.

    a. Follow these directions to remove the cover:

       ❒ Turn off the PC and unplug it.

       ❒ Unplug the monitor, mouse, and keyboard, and move them out of your way.

       ❒ For a desktop case or tower case, locate and remove the screws on the back of the case. Look for the screws in each corner and one in the top center, as in Figure 3-28. Be careful that you don't unscrew any other screws besides these. The other screws probably are holding the power supply in place (see Figure 3-32).

Figure 3-32 Locate the screws that hold the cover in place

       ❒ After you remove the cover screws, slide the cover forward and up to remove it from the case, as shown in Figure 3-33.

Figure 3-33   Power supply mounting screws

- ❑ For tower cases, the screws are also on the back. Look for screws in all four corners and down the sides (see Figure 3-34). Remove the screws and then slide the cover back slightly before lifting it up to remove it. Some tower cases have panels on either side of the case held in place with screws on the back of the case. Remove the screws and slide each panel toward the rear and then lift it off the case.

Figure 3-34   Removing the cover

3

b. Identify the following major components. Drawings in this and previous chapters should help.

❑ Power supply

❑ Floppy disk drive

❑ Hard drive

❑ System board

List the different circuit boards in the expansion slots. Was your guess correct about which ports come from the system board?

$A^{+CORE}_{1.4}$ 3. To expose the system board so you can identify its parts, remove all the expansion boards, following these procedures. (If you are working with a tower case, you can lay it on its side so the system board is on the bottom.)

a. To make reassembling easier, take notes or make a sketch of the current placement of boards and cables. You can mark a cable on a card with a marker if you like. Note the orientation of the cable on the card. Each cable for the floppy disk drive, hard drive, or CD-ROM drive has a color on one side of the cable called the edge color. This color marks pin 1 of the cable. On the board, pin 1 is marked either as the number 1 or 2 beside the pin or, on the back side of the board, with a square soldering pad (see Figure 3-35).

b. Remove the cables from the card. There is no need to remove the other end of the cable from its component (floppy disk drive, hard drive, or CD-ROM drive). Lay the cable over the top of the component or case.

c. Remove the screw holding the board to the case.

d. If you aren't wearing a ground bracelet, touch the case before you touch the board.

e. Grasp the board with both hands and remove the board by lifting straight up, and rocking the board from end to end (not side to side). Rocking the board from side to side might spread the slot opening and weaken the connection.

4. Examine the board connector for the cable. Can you identify pin 1? Lay the board aside on a flat surface.

5. You probably will be able to see most if not all the components on the system board now without removing anything else. Draw a diagram of the system board and label these parts:

❑ The CPU (include the prominent label on the CPU housing)

❑ RAM (probably SIMMs or DIMMs)

❑ Cache memory (probably one or more smaller SIMMs or DIMMs)

❑ Expansion slots (identify the slots as ISA, EISA, MCA, PCI, VLB, etc.)

❑ Each port coming directly from the system board

❑ Power supply connections

❑ ROM BIOS chip (Copy the writing on the top of the chip to paper. Identify the manufacturer, serial number, and date of manufacture of the chip.)

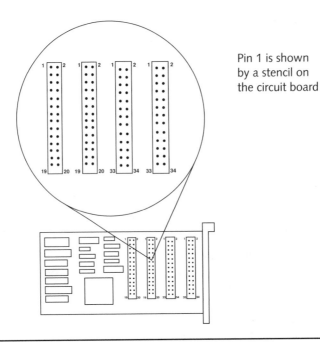

Pin 1 is shown
by a stencil on
the circuit board

Pin 1 is shown by square solder
pads on the reverse side of the circuit board.

Figure 3-35   How to find pin 1 on an expansion card

6. Draw a rectangle on the diagram to represent each bank of jumpers on the board.

7. You can complete the following activity only if you have the documentation for the system board: locate the jumper or jumpers on the board that erases CMOS and/or the startup password, and label it on your diagram. It is often found near the battery. Some boards might not have one.

8. You are now ready to reassemble. Reverse the disassembling activities above. Place each card in its slot (it doesn't have to be the same slot, just the same bus) and replace the screw. Don't place the video card near the power supply.

9. Replace the cables, being sure to align the colored edge with pin 1. (In some cases it might work better to connect the cable to the card before you put the card in the expansion slot.)

10. Plug in the keyboard, monitor, and mouse.

11. In a classroom environment, have the instructor check your work before you power up.

12. Turn on the power and check that the PC is working properly before you replace the cover. Don't touch the inside of the case while the power is on.

13. If all is well, turn off the PC and replace the cover and its screws. If the PC does not work, don't panic! Just turn off the power and go back and check each cable connection and each expansion card. You probably have not solidly seated a card in the slot. After you have double-checked, try again.

Saving and Restoring CMOS Settings

In Chapter 2, you used Nuts & Bolts to record CMOS settings to a rescue disk for later recovery. In this chapter, you use the Internet to download a shareware utility to record CMOS settings and later recover them.

1. Access the Internet and then go to this address: *www.shareware.com*. Search on "CMOS" to list the various shareware utilities available. Select and download CMOS.ZIP. You can then exit the Internet.

2. Explode the compressed file and print the CMOS.TXT documentation file. Three utility programs are included:

   ◻ CMOSSAVE.COM saves the CMOS settings to a file.

   ◻ CMOSCHK.COM compares the CMOS settings to the last saved version.

   ◻ CMOSREST.COM restores the CMOS settings from the file.

3. Access a DOS prompt and save the CMOS settings to a file on a floppy disk, using this command:

        CMOSSAVE.COM A:\MYFILE.SAV

4. Compare the settings stored in the file to the current CMOS settings, using this command:

        CMOSCHK.COM A:\MYFILE.SAV

The results of these commands are shown in Figure 3-36.

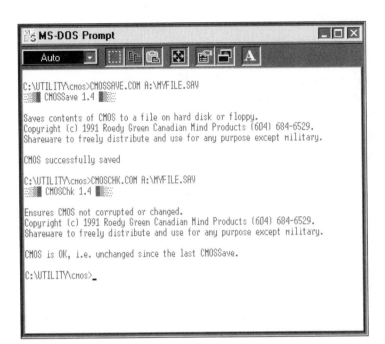

Figure 3-36   Using a shareware utility to save CMOS settings

Using a System Board Diagnostic Utility

A well-known diagnostic utility to help solve computer problems is AMIDiag from American Megatrends, Inc. The utility is DOS-based and works under both DOS and Windows 9x. You can download the utility from the Internet.

1. Access the Internet and then go to this address: *www.shareware.com.*

2. Locate the Quick Search text box and search on "amidiag" (don't enter the quotation marks). Download amidiag.zip to your PC. This file is a shareware version of AMIDiag for PC diagnostics.

3. Leave the Internet and expand the file by double-clicking it in either Windows 3.x or Windows 9x.

4. At a DOS prompt, change to the directory where the demo software files are stored.

5. Execute the first program by entering this command: AMIDIAG

6. The screen shown in Figure 3-37 should appear. Perform the test of processor speed. What is the detected speed?

Figure 3-37   AMIDiag opening menu

7. On the Memory menu, perform all the tests that this demonstration version of the software allows. Record any errors detected.

8. On the Misc menu, perform the serial port test. Write down any error messages that you get. If you get an unexpected error, perform the test more than once. Do you get the same results each time?

9. On the Options menu, select System Information. If you received errors in the test above, this program might lock up, and you might need to reboot. If you complete the information check successfully, write down the results.

10. On the system board menu, select DMA Controller Test. Why doesn't this test work?

11. Exit the program, returning to the DOS prompt.

Practice Activity

Using old or defective expansion cards and system boards, practice inserting and removing expansion cards and chips.

Print a Summary of Your System Hardware

1. In Windows 9x, right-click the **My Computer** icon.

2. On the shortcut menu, select **Properties**.

3. Click the **Device Manager** tab.

4. View devices by type.

5. Click the **Ports** (Com & LPT) icon.

6. Click the **Print** button.

7. Print **Selected class or device**.

Understand Hardware Documentation

Obtain the manual for the system board for your PC. (If you can't find the manual, try downloading it from the system-board manufacturer's web site.) List at least three functions of jumpers on the board as well as the corresponding jumper numbers.

Learn to Use the Windows 9x Help Feature

1. In Windows 9x, click the **Start** button on the Taskbar.
2. Click **Help**.
3. Click the **Contents** tab.
4. Double-click **Troubleshooting**.
5. Select and print **If you have a hardware conflict**.

Troubleshoot Setup Errors

Have someone change the DIP switches, jumpers, or CMOS configuration on a system board. (First make sure someone records the original settings, and don't attempt this project unless you have the system-board documentation.) Troubleshoot the system. Use this opportunity to learn to take notes as you work. List each error you encounter and what you did to work toward a solution.

Use the Internet for Research

1. Search the web site of Intel, AMD, or Cyrix and print information on the most recent offering of a CPU for microcomputers offered by the company.

2. Using your own or a lab computer, pretend that the system-board manual is not available, and you need to know the settings for the jumpers on the system board. Identify the manufacturer of the system board and research the web site for that manufacturer. Print the jumper settings for the system board available on the web site.

3. Does your current system BIOS support USB? To find out, go to the USB web site at *www.usb.org*. Have the BIOS manufacturer and version available.

4. Prepare a presentation about CPUs. Include the history of microprocessors, how a CPU is made, and how a CPU works. Use these web sites as resources:

   www.intel.com/education/mpuworks/index.htm

   www.intel.com/education/chips/index.htm

   www.intel.com/intel/museum/25anniv/index.htm

Research the Market

1. In a current computer magazine, find the speed and price of the fastest PC CPU on the market today.

2. In a current computer magazine, find the speed and price of the fastest PC RAM module on the market today.

Observe Hardware Conflict Errors

Have someone set up a troubleshooting practice problem by forcing two hardware devices on a PC to use the same IRQ. Troubleshoot the problem. Take notes as you go. Describe the errors that you see and what you do to solve the problem.

4

UNDERSTANDING AND MANAGING MEMORY

In this chapter, you will learn:

♦ About the types of physical memory housed on the system board and expansion boards

♦ How memory is used by DOS and Windows 9x

♦ How to manage memory using DOS and Windows 9x

♦ How to upgrade the memory in your computer

In the first three chapters, you saw memory chips and memory modules located on system boards and expansion cards and learned the basics of how software accesses this memory. In this chapter, you will learn how the operating system uses the memory on these boards, and how to manage this memory to meet the needs of applications software. You will also learn how to upgrade the RAM on your computer. Before turning to these topics, you will examine physical memory and its location, and what kinds of memory chips and modules are found in a computer.

PHYSICAL MEMORY

Recall that computer memory is divided into two categories: ROM and RAM. RAM is called primary memory, and temporarily holds data and instructions as the CPU processes them. All data stored in RAM is lost when the PC is turned off. (There is an exception; remember that one RAM chip, the CMOS setup chip, doesn't lose its data because it has its own battery, which powers it when the machine is turned off.) RAM is further divided into two categories: **static RAM (SRAM)** and **dynamic RAM (DRAM)**. ROM, on the other hand, stores system BIOS and startup BIOS programs in a microchip that does not lose data when the power is turned off. This section examines the different technologies of RAM and ROM, focusing on RAM technologies. Technology has steadily evolved to make RAM faster and increase its capacity (see Figure 4-1).

Besides the system board, recall that expansion boards can also have RAM chips to hold their data and ROM chips to provide the programming to drive their devices. For example, a network card contains ROM chips that provide the programming to communicate with the network. Similarly, video cards contain ROM chips with the programming that controls the monitor, and RAM chips to hold video data just before it is sent to the monitor.

DIMM

Two extra slots for additional DIMMs

Figure 4-1   DRAM on most system boards today is stored on DIMMs

ROM on the System Board

Recall that ROM, or read-only memory, consists of memory chips that contain programs that are acid-etched into the chips at the factory (see Figure 4-2). The programs on a ROM chip (sometimes called firmware) are permanent; they cannot be changed. **EEPROM (electrically erasable programmable ROM) chips** (also known as Flash ROM chips), do allow their programs to be changed. On EEPROM chips, a higher voltage is applied to a pin to erase its previous memory before a new instruction set or data is electronically written. **EPROM (erasable programmable ROM)** chips can also have their programs changed. They have a special window that allows the current memory contents to be erased with an ultraviolet light, so that the chip can be reprogrammed. However, for the discussions in this chapter, consider the EEPROM, EPROM, and ROM chips as providing BIOS that is not erasable during normal PC operations. In addition, when the text refers to ROM chips, they may be EEPROM, EPROM, or ROM chips.

4

ROM BIOS chip

Figure 4-2   The ROM BIOS on newer system boards can be upgraded using software provided by the BIOS manufacturer

When you purchased your computer, it contained several ROM chips on the system board and some on the expansion boards. These ROM chips contain the programming that the computer uses to start up (boot itself) and to do routine utility operations, such as reading from and writing to hardware devices and performing basic data manipulation. As discussed in earlier chapters, the ROM chips on the system board contain much of the BIOS for your computer. System BIOS is a set of programs that do the basic input/output chores. The operating system calls on the System BIOS programs to interact with input/output devices as they are needed. Startup BIOS manages the early stages of the boot process.

ROM chips are usually socketed onto the system board. Occasionally, you must replace a ROM chip either because it is faulty or the ROM must be upgraded. You can easily remove the chips, and insert a new one into the socket.

Flash Memory

Recall that upgrading the programming on an existing chip is much easier than physically exchanging a ROM chip. Flash memory makes this possible. **Flash memory** acts more like secondary storage than like other types of memory because it does not lose its data when the power is turned off. However, flash memory is different from a hard drive that holds its data as a magnetized area on a platter, because flash memory holds its data electronically. Also, flash memory is an electronic device and provides much faster data access than a mechanical device, such as a hard drive, though flash memory is more expensive.

Flash memory uses EEPROM chips, and is used on notebook computers and PC Cards (PCMCIA), which look like thick credit cards and attach peripherals to notebook computers. Flash ROM is one example of this kind of memory on a system board. Flash memory is also used to hold picture data in digital cameras.

RAM on the System Board

A+CORE 1.1   Recall that besides ROM, the other kind of computer memory is RAM, random access memory. In the 1980s, RAM chips were either socketed or soldered directly on system boards, but today all RAM used as main memory is housed on SIMMs or DIMMs. Memory chips on SIMMs or DIMMs can only hold their data for a few milliseconds. Also recall that this memory, because it constantly needs refreshing, is called dynamic RAM (DRAM), pronounced "DEE-RAM."

Besides serving as main memory, RAM also provides a memory cache. A system board can have a lot of main memory to hold data and instructions as they are processed, and a little memory cache to help speed up the access time to main memory. Cache memory is contained on the system board or inside the CPU housing. On the system board, it is either on individual chips or on a memory module called a **COAST** (**cache on a stick**; see Figure 4-3). Recall that these memory chips hold their data for as long as the power is on and are therefore called static RAM or SRAM, pronounced "S-RAM." The recent trend has been to put all cache memory inside the CPU housing, but you still see some system boards that have cache memory.

A typical COAST module

Figure 4-3   SRAM on the system board is stored on single chips or COAST modules

DRAM and SRAM use several technologies, summarized in Table 4-1.

Table 4-1   Types of memory

Main Memory	Cache Memory
DRAM, needs constant refreshing	SRAM, does not need refreshing
Slower than SRAM because of refreshing time	Faster, but more expensive
Physically housed on DIMMs and SIMMs	Physically housed on the system board on COAST modules or single chips or included inside the processor case
Technologies include: • FPM • EDO • BEDO • Synchronous DRAM (SDRAM) • Direct Rambus DRAM • Double Data Rate SDRAM (SDRAM II) • SyncLink SDRAM (SLDRAM)	Technologies include: • Synchronous SRAM • Burst SRAM • Pipelined burst • Asynchronous SRAM • Housed within the processor case (new trend)
Memory addresses are assigned	No memory addresses assigned here

SRAM and Memory Caching

SRAM provides faster access than DRAM because data does not need to be constantly rewritten to SRAM, saving the CPU time used to refresh data in DRAM every 4 milliseconds or so. SRAM chips are made up of transistors that can hold a charge, but DRAM chips are made up of capacitors that must be recharged. But because SRAM chips are more expensive than DRAM chips, all RAM does not use SRAM chips. As a compromise, most computers have a little SRAM and a lot of DRAM.

Memory caching (see Figure 4-4) is a method used to store data or programs in SRAM for quick retrieval. Memory caching requires some SRAM chips and a cache controller. When memory caching is used, the cache controller anticipates what data or programming code the CPU will request next, and copies that data or programming code to the SRAM chips. Then, if the cache guessed correctly, it can satisfy the CPU request from SRAM without having to access the slower DRAM. Under normal conditions, memory caching guesses right more than 90% of the time and is an effective way of speeding up memory access.

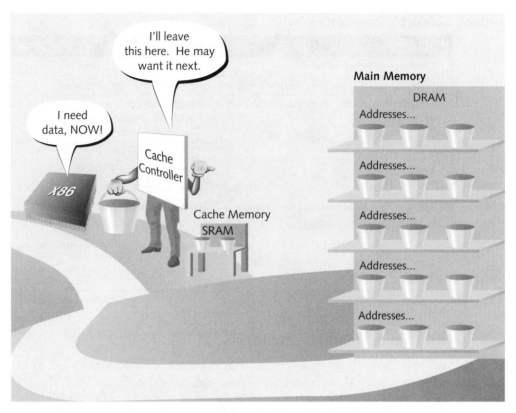

Figure 4-4   A memory cache (SRAM) temporarily holds data in expectation of what the CPU will request next

On older 386 computers, the cache controller was located on a single chip labeled the 385 chip, but 486 and later CPUs have the cache controller chip embedded in the CPU chip, housed together with some static RAM. This SRAM is called an internal cache, level 1 cache, or L1 cache, and is found in all 486 CPUs and higher. However, a system can have additional static RAM, called an external cache, level 2 cache, or L2 cache. This L2 cache may be on the system board of older computers or inside the CPU housing of newer systems.

If the cache memory is inside the CPU housing, you have no control over how much is present; it is dependent on the type of CPU you are using. However, older system boards were usually manufactured with some cache memory already installed, but with the option to add more in order to improve performance.

SRAM on the System Board

A+CORE
1.8

How much SRAM on a system board is enough without being prohibitively expensive? System boards often have 256K of SRAM installed with room for an additional 256K or more. The second 256K cache does not improve performance nearly as much as the first 256K does. For system boards running at 66 MHz, more than 512K of cache does not offer a significant improvement in access time. Figure 4-5 shows a system board that contains

256K of SRAM installed on the board in two single chips. A COAST slot is available to hold an additional 256K.

4

TAG SRAM chip manages cache

Jumpers for cache size selection

2 SRAM chips (128 KB each)

Memory cache slot (COAST)

Figure 4-5   SRAM on this system board is stored in individual chips, and the board also has a COAST slot

A+CORE 1.8   **Varieties of SRAM Memory on a System Board** SRAM is installed on a system board in increments of 64 KB, 128 KB, 256 KB, or 512 KB. See the documentation for the system board to determine which amounts of cache the board supports and what kind of memory to buy. Recall that all RAM sends data and control signals over the system bus. The methods used to coordinate how and when data and control signals are sent and read differ with various kinds of memory. SRAM uses a synchronous or asynchronous method (explained below). Synchronous SRAM is more expensive and about 30% faster than asynchronous SRAM.

A+CORE 4.2   **Synchronous SRAM** requires a clock signal to manage or synchronize its control signals. The cache memory can then run in step with the CPU. Synchronous SRAM can be either burst or pipelined burst SRAM. Burst SRAM is more expensive than pipelined burst SRAM and only slightly faster. With **burst SRAM**, data is sent in a two-step process: first the data address, and then the data itself is sent. Burst SRAM sends a burst of data without sending all the addresses of the data, only the first address, allowing a large amount of data to be sent without interruption. **Pipelined burst SRAM** uses more clock cycles per transfer than does the burst without pipelining, but it does not significantly slow down the process and is desirable because of the reduced cost.

A+CORE
4.2

Asynchronous SRAM does not work in step with the CPU clock speed. It must look up the address sent to it by the CPU and return the data within one clock cycle, which makes it unable to process as much data in one request and results in overall slower memory access.

To understand the difference between asynchronous and synchronous memory, think of this analogy. Children are jumping rope with a long rope, and one child on each end turns the rope. A child who cannot keep in step with the turning rope can only run through on a single pass, and must come back around to make another pass. A child who can keep in step with the rope can run into the center and jump a while, until he or she is tired and runs out. Which child can perform the most rope-jumping cycles in a given amount of time? The one who can keep in step with the rope. Similarly, synchronous memory can retrieve data faster than asynchronous memory can because it keeps time with the system clock.

A system board can support both asynchronous and synchronous SRAM, but not at the same time. Before you buy new SRAM, check the documentation for the system board to determine which kinds of SRAM the board can support, and then see what kind of SRAM the board already has. You might need to replace the existing SRAM on the board to upgrade to a larger or faster cache.

Main Memory: SIMMs and DIMMs

In earlier PCs, main memory was stored on the system board as single, socketed chips, but today RAM is always stored in either SIMMs (single inline memory modules) or DIMMs (dual inline memory modules), which plug directly into the system board. The major difference between a SIMM and DIMM module is the width of the data path that the module accommodates. A SIMM has a data path of 32 bits, and a DIMM has a data path of 64 bits.

The technology used by SIMM and DIMM microchips has evolved to improve speed and size. SIMMs first used FPM and then EDO technologies, first discussed in Chapter 3. Next came DIMMs using burst EDO, followed by SDRAM technology and Direct Rambus technology. The goal with each new technology is to increase overall throughput. FPM is used on system boards that range in speed from 16 to 66 MHz. EDO is used on system boards rated at about 33 to 75 MHz, and SDRAM and Direct Rambus are used on system boards rated 66 MHz and higher. The older the system board, the older the memory technology it can use, so, as a PC technician, you must be familiar with all these technologies even though the boards sold today only use the latest.

SIMM Technologies   Older SIMMs use FPM technology, have 30 pins on the edge connector, and come in sizes of 256K to 4 MB. Later FPM SIMMS had 72 pins on the edge connector and came in sizes up to 16 MB. Newer SIMMs use EDO technology, have 72 pins on the edge connector, are slightly longer, and come in sizes of 1 MB to 64 MB. A SIMM might have three or more chips, but this doesn't affect the amount of memory that the SIMM can hold. SIMMs are also rated by speed, measured in nanoseconds. A nanosecond (abbreviated ns) is one billionth of a second. Common SIMM speeds are 60, 70, or 80 ns. This speed is a measure of access time, the time it takes for the CPU to receive a value in response to a request. Access time includes the time it takes to refresh the chips. An access time of 60 ns is faster than an access time of 70 ns. Therefore, the smaller the speed rating, the faster the chip.

A+CORE
4.2

FPM (fast page mode) memory improved on the earlier memory types by sending the row address just once for many accesses to memory near that row. Earlier memory types required a complete row and column address for each memory access.

EDO (extended data output) memory is an improvement over earlier FPM memory. EDO memory is faster because it allows the memory controller to eliminate the 10-ns delay while it waited before it issued the next memory address. Without a memory cache, computer performance increases 10% to 20% when using EDO memory instead of FPM memory. However, if 256K of cache is used, the increased performance from FPM to EDO memory is only 1% to 2%. EDO memory does not cost significantly more than FPM memory, but your system board must be able to support it. Check your system board documentation or CMOS setup to determine if you should use EDO memory. If your system board does not support EDO memory, you can still use it, but it will not increase system performance. EDO memory is used on SIMMs and video memory, and is often used to provide on-board RAM on various expansion boards.

DIMM Technologies   DIMMs are also rated by speed and the amount of memory they hold. DIMMs have 168 pins on the edge connector of the board and hold from 8 MB to 256 MB of RAM. The first DIMMs used EDO or burst EDO (BEDO) and then used **synchronous DRAM** (**SDRAM**) technology. Recall from Chapter 3 that **BEDO** is a refined version of EDO with improved access time over EDO. BEDO is not widely used today because Intel chose to not support it.

Either 3.3 volts or 5.0 volts can power SDRAM modules. Purchase DIMMs that use the voltage supported by your system board. Your system board also determines if you can use buffered, unbuffered, or registered DIMMs. Buffers are used by EDO DIMMs and registers are used by SDRAM DIMMs. Registers and buffers amplify a signal just before the data is written to the module. To determine which feature a DIMM has, check the position of the two notches on the DIMM module. In Figure 4-6, the position of the notch on the left identifies the module as registered (RFU), buffered, or unbuffered memory. The notch on the right identifies the voltage used by the module. The position of the notches not only helps identify the type of module, but also prevents the wrong kind of module from being used on a system board.

A+CORE
4.2

168-Pin DIMM Notch Key Definitions (3.3V, unbuffered memory)

DRAM Key Position

Voltage Key Position

RFU ⌐ └ **Unbuffered**   5.0V ⌐ └ Reserved
Buffered   **3.3V**

20 Pins   60 Pins   88 Pins

Figure 4-6   The positions of two notches on a DIMM identify the type of DIMM and the voltage requirement, and also prevent the wrong type from being installed on the system board

Other RAM Technologies   Synchronous DRAM is currently the most popular memory type. SDRAM is rated by the system bus speed and operates in sync with the system clock, whereas older types of memory (FPM, EDO, and BEDO) all run at a constant speed. SDRAM currently comes in three variations: regular SDRAM, SDRAM II (DDR), and SyncLink (SLDRAM).

Regular SDRAM runs at the same speed as the system bus: 66 MHz, 100 MHz, 133 MHz, and so forth. The SDRAM data path is 64 bits wide, making SDRAM about 50% faster than its predecessor, EDO memory.

Double-data rate SDRAM (DDR SDRAM), sometimes called **SDRAM II**, runs twice as fast as regular SDRAM. Instead of processing data for each beat of the system clock as regular SDRAM does, it processes data when the beat rises and again when it falls, doubling the data rate of memory. If a system board is running at 100 MHz, then SDRAM II is running at 200 MHz with a data path of 64 bits. Future plans for DDR SDRAM include increasing this data path to 128 bits. DDR SDRAM is supported by a consortium of 20 major computer manufacturers. It is an open standard, meaning that no royalties need to be paid to use it. **SyncLink (SLDRAM)** was developed by a consortium of twelve DRAM manufactures. It improves on regular SDRAM by increasing the number of memory banks that can be accessed simultaneously from four to sixteen. Memory banks are discussed later in the chapter.

Direct Rambus DRAM (sometimes called **RDRAM** or **Direct RDRAM)** is named after Rambus, the company that developed it. The technology uses a narrow 16-bit data path rather than the wider 64-bit SDRAM data path. It works like a packeted network, not a traditional memory bus, and can run at speeds of 400 MHz to 800 MHz. The high speeds are possible because of the narrow bus width; wider buses cannot allow these high speeds. RDRAM uses a proprietary memory module called a RIMM and is not stored on a DIMM (see Figure 4-7). An earlier version of Rambus memory is Concurrent RDRAM, that is not as fast as Direct RDRAM. Manufacturers other than Rambus and Intel must pay licensing fees to use RDRAM, which might cause the industry to turn more toward SDRAM memory advancements over Rambus even though Intel is promoting RDRAM. The Intel 820

A+CORE
4.2,
4.4

and 840 chip sets both support RDRAM. Table 4-2 shows a comparison in data through-put of the current contenders for the memory market.

Figure 4-7   Direct Rambus DRAM is stored on a RIMM rather than a DIMM

Table 4-2   Comparing data throughput of current and future memory technologies

Memory Technology	Calculation of Throughput	Data Throughput
RDRAM	16 bits × 400 MHz	800 MB per second
RDRAM	16 bits × 800 MHz	1600 MB per second
SDRAM on 100 MHz board	64 bits × 100 MHz	400 MB per second
DDR-SDRAM on 133 MHz board	64 bits × 266 MHz	1064 MB per second
DDR-SDRAM on 166 MHz board	128 bits × 332 MHz	2656 MB per second

ECC, Parity, and Nonparity DRAM   Some SDRAM memory modules support a chip set feature called **ECC (error checking and correction)**. DIMMs that support ECC have a ninth chip on the module (the ECC chip), whereas it normally has only eight chips. The module is identified as a 71 or 72-bit DIMM instead of a 64-bit DIMM. ECC uses an extra 7 or 8 bits to verify the integrity of every 64 bits stored on the module and correct any error, when possible. ECC memory costs more than regular memory, but is more reliable. To see if your system board supports ECC memory, look for the ability to enable or disable the feature in CMOS setup or check the system-board documentation.

Some older system boards support **parity memory**, and some only use **nonparity memory**. If a SIMM has an odd number of chips, most likely it is parity memory; an even number of chips usually indicates nonparity memory. As discussed in Chapter 3, parity memory validates the integrity of the data stored in RAM by counting the number of bits set to 1, which determines whether the total is an even or odd number. Parity memory then sets a parity bit either to make the number of 1-bits even (called even parity) or to make the number of 1s odd (called odd parity). When data is read, the number of 1s is counted. If parity is even but the number of 1s is odd (or vice versa), a parity error occurs, and the CPU stops processing the data.

4

A+CORE
4.2

Most manufacturers use nonparity memory to save processing time, and therefore money. Some of the issues surrounding memory parity are discussed next.

When a computer first boots up, the system must detect what type of memory is installed. To do so, the system can use two methods: Parallel Presence Detect (PPD) that uses resistors to communicate the type of memory present, or Serial Presence Detect (SPD) that stores information about the memory type in EPROM. When purchasing memory for a system, you must match the method used by the module to what the system board expects. See the system board documentation to know which type to buy. If the board does not specify the method used, assume PPD.

Another feature of memory is called **Cas Latency (CL)** and reflects the number of clock cycles that passes while data is written to memory. Values are 2 or 3 clock cycles. CL2 (Cas Latency 2) is a little faster than CL3 (Cas Latency 3). Again, use the memory type recommended by the system board manufacturer.

What to Look for When Buying Memory Chips and Modules

Memory chips and memory modules are sold at different speeds and sizes and use different technologies and features. Chips can be high-grade, low-grade, remanufactured, or used. Poor-quality memory chips can cause frequent **General Protection Fault (GPF) errors** in Windows, application errors, and errors that cause the system to hang—so it pays to know the quality and type of memory you are buying. The following are some guidelines to follow to ensure that you are purchasing high-quality memory chips.

Memory Speed   Generally, use the fastest memory that your system board can support. The documentation for a system board states what speed of memory to use on the board, usually written as something like "Use 70 ns or faster." In this example, 60 ns will work on this board, but 80-ns memory will cause problems. It is possible, but not recommended, to mix the speed of memory modules on a system board, but don't mix the speeds within a single SIMM memory bank. You will learn more about this later in the chapter.

Tin or Gold Leads   Memory modules and the banks that hold them can be either tin or gold. On a system board the connectors inside the memory slots are made of either tin or gold, as are the edge connectors on the memory modules. You should match tin leads to tin connectors and gold leads to gold connectors to prevent a chemical reaction between the two different metals, which can cause corrosion. Corrosion can create intermittent memory errors and even make the PC unable to boot.

Choosing the Correct Size of Module   Not all sizes of memory modules fit on any one computer. Use the right number of SIMM or DIMM modules with the right amount of memory on each module to fit the memory banks on your system board. You can find more information about this later in the chapter.

Remanufactured and Used Modules   Stamped on each chip of a SIMM or DIMM module is a chip ID that identifies the date the chip was manufactured. Look for the date in the YYWW format, where YY is the year the chip was made and WW is the week of that year. For example, 9910 indicates a chip made in the 10th week of 1999. If you see date stamps on a SIMM or DIMM chip that are older than one year, these chips are probably used memory. If some chips are old, but some are new, the module is probably remanufactured. When buying memory modules, look for ones on which all chips have dates that are relatively close together and less than a year old.

Re-marked Chips New chips have a protective coating, which gives them a polished, reflective surface. If the surface of the chip is dull or matted, or you can scratch the markings off with a fingernail or knife, suspect that the chip has been re-marked. **Re-marked chips** have been used and returned to the factory, marked again, and then sold.

How DOS and Windows 9x View Memory

Now that you have reviewed the many ways memory can be physically installed on the system board and expansion boards, you can examine the logical organization of memory, a function of the OS. The following section explains how the OS categorizes, accesses, and uses memory.

Memory management under DOS and Windows 9x can seem complicated because of the way the process has evolved over the past 18 years or so. Like an old house that has been added to and remodeled several times, the present-day design is not as efficient as that of a brand new house. Decisions made by IBM and Microsoft in the early 1980s still significantly affect, and in some cases limit, the way memory is used today under Windows 98. Because Windows NT, followed by Windows 2000, has had the luxury of being designed from the ground up, they are free of those limitations.

Recall from Chapter 1 that earlier CPUs supported by DOS could only handle one program at a time, and that program had direct access to the first 1024K of memory addresses (see Figure 1-36 of Chapter 1). This processing mode is called real mode. Later, beginning with the i286 CPU, the CPU could manage more than one program at a time by switching among them (see Figure 1-37 of Chapter 1). Called protected mode, this mode allows for memory addresses above 1024K, 32-bit data transfers, and the OS managing access to memory for the programs. By managing memory, the OS could use the hard drive as virtual memory without a program's knowledge. However, needing to maintain backward compatibility with older real-mode applications software has slowed the transition from using real mode to protected mode. The process began with DOS, then continued to Windows 3.x and Windows 9x, and finally to Windows NT and Windows 2000, which provide a pure protected-mode OS whose program segments use 32-bit data flow.

Recall from Chapter 2 that earlier versions of DOS operated completely in real mode. Later, DOS added a memory manager extension (HIMEM.SYS) that allowed access to memory addresses above 1 MB. Early versions of Windows 3.x working with DOS could keep more than one program loaded at the same time by swapping them in and out of memory; this was called standard mode but was really real mode with some fancy maneuvering. Later versions of Windows 3.x let 16-bit programs share memory (more than one program could access the same memory and share its data) in a "virtual DOS machine" in 386 enhanced mode.

Windows 3.x could also perform virtual memory management by creating a swap file stored on the hard drive and using it as if it were memory.

Windows 95 was the first OS in this evolution of operating systems to support 32-bit protected mode applications software. Most of the OS code is written in 32-bit protected mode. It still allows 16-bit real-mode device drivers, and 16-bit software can run in a virtual DOS machine (VDM), just as with Windows 3.x, or can run in real mode. A VDM is an environment that a 32-bit protected-mode OS provides for a real-mode program to operate in.

Finally Windows NT made the break with the past. All its code is written in protected mode, and it does not allow other software to operate in real mode, but only in a virtual real mode that it tightly controls.

Table 4-3 summarizes the evolution of operating systems and software as it applies to memory. Notice that the first Microsoft OS to resolve the many issues involving real mode, particularly the 1024K limitation imposed by real mode, is Windows NT. With DOS and Windows 3.x, this limitation directly affects managing memory resources and, in some cases, can still be significant with Windows 9x. To explain how all this works, beginning with DOS and moving to Windows NT, you must understand basic memory concepts.

Table 4-3   Summary of how operating systems have evolved in managing memory

Operating System	Real Mode	Protected Mode
DOS	Operates totally in real mode, but later offered HIMEM.SYS, a device driver that allows programs access to extended memory	NA
DOS with Windows 2.x	Operated totally in real mode, but managed the process of switching programs in and out of memory	NA
DOS with Windows 3.x	Real mode is called standard mode. Allows only one 16-bit application at a time in memory	Protected mode is called 386 enhanced mode. Multiple applications can share memory. 16-bit applications share a virtual machine.

A+ OS 1.1

Table 4-3   Summary of how operating systems have evolved in managing memory (continued)

Operating System	Real Mode	Protected Mode
Windows 9x	Allows real-mode drivers to be loaded during startup. 16-bit DOS applications are allowed a real-mode session.	Switches back and forth between real mode and protected mode as necessary. Supports both 16-bit and 32-bit applications in a virtual machine.
Windows NT and Windows 2000	NA	All work is done in protected mode. Supports 32-bit applications. 16-bit applications can operate in a virtual machine only.

4

Physical Memory and Memory Addresses

The terms "memory" and "memory address" have significantly different definitions. **Memory** is physical microchips that can hold data and programming. It is located on the system board or on circuit boards as single chips or modules. Memory can be either ROM or RAM. A **memory address**, on the other hand, is a number the CPU assigns to ROM or RAM to track the memory it can use. Recall that a CPU has a limited number of memory addresses that it can assign to physical memory, determined by the number of memory address lines available on the memory bus.

Recall also that some older 16-bit programs work only when they can use certain memory addresses, such as a hexadecimal number like C80000. This address is part of the physical memory's ROM programming; no other address works for it. An example of this kind of memory is a ROM chip on an older video card. Some memory, usually ROM chips on expansion boards, must be assigned one of two—or sometimes three—sets of addresses. You make the choice by setting jumpers or DIP switches on the board or, in more recent cases, when you run an installation program for the board. New Plug and Play boards don't have this restriction. Their ROM code can be assigned any values chosen by the OS or system BIOS. Plug and Play cards are required to use whatever memory addresses are assigned to them. The system is free to assign any address it chooses to this physical memory.

Both RAM and ROM must be assigned memory addresses so the CPU can access this memory. System BIOS stored on system-board ROM chips must be assigned addresses by the CPU so that the CPU can access that programming. The assigning of addresses to both RAM and ROM occurs during booting, and is sometimes called **memory mapping**. In Figure 4-8, the memory addresses available to the CPU are listed on the left, and the physical RAM and ROM needing these addresses are on the right. These RAM and ROM chips and modules are located on the system board, a video card, and a network card in this example.

Programming stored on ROM chips is not usually copied into RAM, despite what many people believe. It is simply assigned memory addresses by the CPU. These ROM programs become part of the total memory available to the CPU, and do not use up part of total RAM. The resources they use are memory addresses. The RAM memory is still available to be assigned other addresses. **Shadowing ROM**, discussed in Chapter 3, is an exception because the programs stored on ROM are copied to RAM when the ROM is shadowed to improve performance.

Figure 4-8   CPU assigns memory addresses during booting

Finally, memory management in DOS and Windows 9x presents limitations not so much because of the operating systems themselves, but because their applications used the standards presented to the industry when DOS was first introduced. DOS (and the applications written for it in the 1980s that are still used today) incorporated assumptions that continue to affect memory management.

Compared to that of other operating systems, memory management in DOS and Windows 9x is handicapped because DOS has existed longer than most other operating systems. Therefore, DOS must maintain compatibility with software that has been around for a long time. Also, Microsoft made the commitment with Windows 9x that it, too, would be compatible with older software written for DOS and Windows 3.x using DOS. Probably the greatest limitation of DOS today is this commitment to maintain backward compatibility with older software and hardware.

Areas of the Memory Map

A+ OS
  1.1

The following section introduces several types of memory that the OS manages: conventional, upper, extended, and expanded memory. Except for expanded, these memory types are logical divisions or categories rather than physical ones, and the divisions are determined by their memory addresses rather than by their physical location. The following section covers this logical **memory management**. A segment of RAM can be assigned memory addresses in the upper memory range today but be assigned a range of addresses in extended memory tomorrow. It's still just RAM, no matter what address it's assigned. The difference is the way the CPU can use this memory because of the addresses assigned to it.

To get a clear picture of this memory-addressing schema, consider the memory map shown in Figure 4-9. The first 640K of memory addresses are called **conventional memory**, or **base memory**. The memory addresses from 640K up to 1024K are called **upper memory**. Memory above 1024K is called **extended memory**. The first 64K of extended memory is called the **high memory area (HMA)**. Memory that is accessed in 16K segments, or pages, using a window in upper memory is called **expanded memory**.

Figure 4-9   Memory address map showing the starting and ending addresses of conventional, upper, and extended memories, including the high memory area

$A^+ \begin{smallmatrix} OS \\ 1.1 \end{smallmatrix}$ | ## Conventional Memory

In the early 1980s, when IBM and Microsoft were designing the original PCs, they decided to make 640K of memory addresses available to the user, thinking that this was plenty for anything the user would ever want to do. This 640K of addresses were intended to hold the OS, the applications software, and the data being processed. At that time, 640K of memory addresses were many times more than enough to handle all the applications available. Today, 640K of memory addresses are inadequate, for the following reasons:

- Many applications are very large programs, requiring a considerable number of memory addresses to hold the programs as well as the data.

- Often more than one application is run at a time, each of which requires its own memory area for the program and data. Also, sometimes computers in a network serve more than one user at a time. In the early 1980s, a PC was expected to be used by a single user, operating one application at a time.

- Users expect software to provide a friendly graphical user interface, or GUI. Graphical user interfaces provide icons, graphics, and windows on a screen, all requiring large amounts of memory.

The problem caused by restricting the number of memory addresses available to the user to only 640K could have been easily solved by simply providing more addresses to the user in future versions of DOS. However, another original design decision ruled this out. The next group of memory addresses, the 384K above conventional memory, called upper memory, were assigned to utility operations for the system. The system requires memory addresses to communicate with peripherals. The programs (such as BIOS on the expansion boards) and data are assigned memory addresses in this upper memory area. For example, the video BIOS and its data are placed in the very first part of upper memory, the area from 640K to 768K. All video ROM written for DOS-based computers assumes that these programs and data are stored in this area. Also, many DOS and Windows applications interact directly with video ROM and RAM in this address range.

Programs almost always expect data to be written into memory directly above the addresses for the program itself, an important fact for understanding memory management. Thus, if a program begins storing its data above its location in conventional memory, eventually it will "hit the ceiling," the beginning of upper memory assigned to video ROM. The major reason that applications have 640K memory limit is that video ROM begins at 640K. If DOS and Windows 9x allowed applications into these upper memory addresses, all DOS-compatible video ROM would need to be rewritten, many existing video boards would be obsolete, and many DOS applications that access these video addresses would not work.

Windows NT and Windows 2000 are not backward compatible with older hardware and software because they do not manage memory the same way. You will learn more about how these operating systems manage memory later in this book.

Sixteen-bit applications under DOS and Windows 9x are boxed in the first 640K of addresses. Also, because the OS, BIOS, and TSRs use some conventional memory, not all the 640K of memory is available to applications. Several methods have been proposed and used to expand the 640K limit. These methods involve either freeing more conventional memory or providing memory outside of conventional memory. The ultimate objective is to provide more memory addresses to application programs and their data.

Upper Memory

A+ OS
1.1

The memory map in Figure 4-9 shows that the memory addresses from 640K up to (but not including) 1024K are called upper memory. In the hexadecimal number system (see Appendix D for an explanation of this system), upper memory begins at A0000 and goes through FFFFF. Video ROM and RAM are stored in the first part of upper memory, hex A0000 through CFFFF (the A, B, and C areas of memory). BIOS programs for other expansion boards are assigned memory addresses in the remaining portions of upper memory. BIOS on the system board (system BIOS) is assigned the top part of upper memory from F0000 through FFFFF (the F area of upper memory). Upper memory often has unassigned addresses, depending on which boards are present in the system. Managing memory effectively involves gaining access to these unused addresses in upper memory and using them to store device drivers and TSRs.

Figure 4-10 shows that video memory addresses fall between A0000 and CFFFF. For VGA and Super VGA video, the A and B areas hold data sent to the video card, and the C area contains the video BIOS.

Figure 4-10 Memory map of upper memory showing starting and finishing addresses and video ROM and RAM assignments

$A+$ *OS*
1.1

Extended Memory and the High Memory Area

Memory above 1 MB is called extended memory. The first 64K of extended memory is called the high memory area, and exists because a bug in the programming for the older 286 CPU (the first CPU to use extended memory) produced this small pocket of unused memory addresses. Beginning with DOS 5, the OS capitalized on this bug by storing portions of itself in the high memory area, thus freeing some conventional memory where DOS had been stored. This method of storing part of DOS in the high memory area is called "loading DOS high." You will see how to do this later in the chapter.

Extended memory is actually managed by the OS as a device (the device is memory) that is controlled by a device driver. To access extended memory, you need the device driver (called a memory manager) that controls it, and you must use applications that have been written to use the extended memory. DOS 5+ and Windows 3+ both offer memory management software that you will learn to use later in the chapter, and Windows 9x has automated the process. The amount of extended memory you can have on your computer is limited by the amount of RAM that can be installed on your system board and the number of memory addresses the CPU and the memory bus can support.

Expanded Memory

Few of today's applications software programs use expanded memory, but it is included in our discussion because occasionally you see an older program that needs it, and mainly because it is similar to the Windows NT memory model. Figure 4-11 shows that expanded memory falls outside of the linear addressing of memory. Linear addressing means that all memory is assigned addresses beginning with 1, and counting up. Expanded memory breaks out of this pattern. When first introduced in the 1980s, expanded memory was always physically located on the memory expansion boards that also contained the ROM BIOS that managed it. Expanded memory was made available through a small window called a page frame. A **page frame** is 64K of upper memory projected onto expanded memory in 16K segments called pages. It works as follows.

The system requests some expanded memory from the memory manager. The memory manager selects some expanded memory on the expanded memory card, say 32K of it, and assigns 32K of the 64K of upper memory addresses to this memory. The system now has actual physical memory (on the expanded memory card) assigned to the memory addresses in upper memory. The expanded memory manager keeps track of what memory on the card is being used, so that, on the next request for expanded memory, it will assign upper memory addresses to a different 32K of physical memory on the card. The same memory addresses in upper memory can be used over and over to access different memory addresses on the expansion board. These 64K of memory addresses can access several hundred kilobytes of physical memory during a single session. The relatively small 64K of upper memory addresses becomes the window that is moved around, over the larger amount of expanded memory, thus gaining access to it. (Think of this window as a picture frame moving over a large area, showing only a small space at any one time.) Applications software must be written in a way that makes use of this expanded memory.

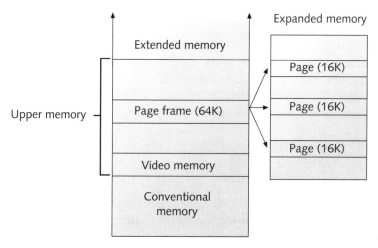

Figure 4-11   Expanded memory map showing page frame and pages; the page frame serves as a "window" into expanded memory

A+ OS
1.1   Expanded memory was developed by the Lotus Corporation in conjunction with Intel and Microsoft, because version 2.0 of Lotus 1-2-3 needed more memory. Other applications also make use of expanded memory. The term LIM (Lotus, Intel, Microsoft) memory is sometimes used for expanded memory. Incidentally, later versions of Lotus 1-2-3 don't use expanded memory, but instead use extended memory. Expanded memory is also sometimes called EMS memory (expanded memory specifications).

At one time, to have expanded memory for an application that required it, you installed an expanded memory card on your computer. There is, however, an alternative to an expanded memory card. The Windows and DOS extended memory manager for the i386 and later CPUs can emulate expanded memory by taking some extended memory and having the application treat this extended memory as expanded memory. You can then make either extended memory or emulated expanded memory available to your software, depending on which kind of memory the software requires.

Virtual Memory

A+ OS
1.1   **Virtual memory** is using hard drive space so that it acts like memory. Windows stores virtual memory in a file called a swap file, discussed later in the chapter. The purpose of virtual memory is to increase the amount of memory available. Of course, virtual memory works at a considerably slower speed than real memory, and uses hard drive space. For example, a hard drive may have a data access time of 10 ms (10/1,000,000 second), whereas RAM speed may be 60 ns (60/1,000,000,000 second).

For an OS to use virtual memory, it must be operating in protected mode. DOS and earlier versions of Windows work only in real mode. Windows 3.x uses 386 enhanced mode, which is protected mode and, therefore, provides virtual memory to applications.

RAM Drives

Creating a **RAM drive** makes part of memory act like a hard drive. A RAM drive is just the opposite of virtual memory. By loading the TSR that creates a RAM drive, you can make your computer appear to have a second hard drive, such as drive D. This drive D is really an area of memory set aside to act like a drive. A RAM drive was once useful to hold software that had to be loaded many times. Since software is so large today, RAM drives have become impractical. However, RAM drives still have value in a few instances, as you will see later. Since a RAM drive is not a real drive, but memory, nothing is really saved when data is stored to a RAM drive. Data written to a RAM drive is no safer than data still in RAM. Therefore, do not use a RAM drive to "store" data.

Another purpose for a RAM drive is to store programs. Programs are permanently stored on a real hard drive, such as drive C. On startup, the programs are copied to the RAM drive, such as drive D. The program is loaded from drive D (one part of memory) to another part of memory, where it is executed. (Remember that programs can't be executed from a hard drive, even if the hard drive is not a drive at all, but a RAM drive.) Loading the program from the RAM drive is faster than loading the program from the hard drive, because it is faster to copy from memory to memory than from the hard drive to memory.

The only gain in speed in this example is in the loading process. Once the software is loaded, the RAM drive is no longer used. You gain speed from using a RAM drive if you load the same software many times in one session.

With DOS and Windows 3.x, you create a RAM drive by using a DEVICE= command in the CONFIG.SYS file:

```
DEVICE=C:\DOS\RAMDRIVE.SYS 1024
```

The program that produces the RAM drive, RAMDRIVE.SYS, is stored on drive C in the \DOS directory. The 1024 in the command line tells DOS to create a RAM drive that contains 1024K of space. The RAMDRIVE program assigns the next available letter to the drive. Suppose you have a floppy disk drive and a hard drive, which are drives A and C respectively. The RAM drive then becomes drive D and is used just like any other drive in the system.

Summary of How Memory is Managed

This section introduced the different kinds of memory and the ways it can be used. Memory management makes the greatest amount of conventional memory available to an application. During the boot process, after ROM and RAM from expansion boards acquire upper memory addresses, any unused addresses in upper memory are used to hold TSRs and device drivers. Also, applications must be able to access extended and expanded memory. The next section details how DOS and Windows 9x manage memory effectively.

Managing Memory with DOS

A+ os
1.1

Beginning with DOS 5.0, memory management under DOS included access to upper and extended memory for device drivers and applications software. The TSRs that manage memory above 640K, HIMEM.SYS and EMM386.EXE, are loaded and used from the CONFIG.SYS and AUTOEXEC.BAT files at startup. The program file **HIMEM.SYS** is the device driver for all memory above 640K. The program file **EMM386.EXE** contains the software that loads user TSRs and device drivers into upper memory and makes extended memory emulate expanded memory for those applications that use expanded memory.

4

Using HIMEM.SYS

HIMEM.SYS is loaded into your system from the CONFIG.SYS file. Recall that the CONFIG.SYS file is executed during booting and loads device drivers into memory. Next, COMMAND.COM is executed and, in turn, runs AUTOEXEC.BAT. AUTOEXEC.BAT is the DOS batch file that automatically runs each time you boot the computer. It contains a list of DOS commands that are executed by COMMAND.COM. TSRs can be launched from AUTOEXEC.BAT. Remember that a TSR is a terminate-and-stay-resident program that is loaded into memory and lies dormant until activated by some later action, such as pressing a "hot" key.

HIMEM.SYS is considered a device driver because it manages a device, such as memory. It is executed by the DEVICE= command in CONFIG.SYS. Figure 4-12 shows an example of a very simple CONFIG.SYS file that loads HIMEM.SYS.

Figure 4-12   CONFIG.SYS set to use memory above 640K

A+ OS
3.2

In Figure 4-12, you can see the DOS EDIT command, which provides a full-screen text editor that can create or edit a file. To access CONFIG.SYS, at a DOS prompt or a Run dialog box in Windows 9x, enter this command:

```
EDIT C:\CONFIG.SYS
```

To exit from the editor, press the **ALT** key to activate the menus, and choose **EXIT** from the File menu. When asked if you want to save your changes, respond **YES** to exit the editor and save any changes. After editing the CONFIG.SYS file, boot the computer to activate the changes.

The last two lines in Figure 4-12 are usually found in a CONFIG.SYS file. The command FILES=99 tells DOS how many files it can have open at one time. The command BUFFERS=40 tells DOS how many buffers to maintain to transfer data to and from secondary storage devices. A **buffer** is an area of memory that serves as a holding area for incoming or outgoing data. When writing data to a device, DOS fills the holding area with data. When the area is full, DOS writes all the data at once to the device. When reading data, DOS reads enough data from the device to fill the holding area, or buffer, and uses all that data before going back for more. Buffers reduce the need for DOS to return again and again to the device for data; DOS only needs to access the device occasionally for data. Using buffers to speed up reading and writing data is largely outdated today. Disk caching, which is described in later chapters, is more common and effective. However, many software packages still use buffers, and so DOS must provide these buffers. The more files and buffers that are open, the less free memory is available, so limit the number of buffers to the smallest value that will still accommodate the DOS applications.

A+ OS
1.1

The first line in the CONFIG.SYS file is the one that loads the driver HIMEM.SYS into memory. HIMEM.SYS makes memory above 640K available to your applications as extended memory. Remember that you must be using applications software that can use extended memory.

The first line in the CONFIG.SYS file also contains the path that tells DOS where to find HIMEM.SYS. The path C:\DOS\ indicates that HIMEM.SYS should be stored on drive C in the directory named \DOS. If you are using the Windows version of HIMEM.SYS, your command line looks like this:

```
DEVICE=C:\WINDOWS\HIMEM.SYS
```

You should use the latest version of HIMEM.SYS that you have. Look in the \DOS or \WINDOWS directory, and use the latest file.

The second line in the CONFIG.SYS file, DEVICE=C:\MOUSE.SYS, tells DOS to load a device driver into memory. The driver that controls a mouse is stored in the file named MOUSE.SYS on drive C in the root directory. The mouse software is a TSR that is loaded into conventional memory; it does not execute until you use the mouse. The third line in the CONFIG.SYS file, DEVICE=C:\DOS\ANSI.SYS, tells DOS to load the device driver ANSI.SYS into memory. ANSI.SYS helps control the keyboard and monitor, providing color on the monitor and an additional set of characters to the ASCII character set. For more information about ASCII and ANSI, see Appendix C.

Using EMM386.EXE

A+ OS
1.1

In DOS and Windows, EMM386.EXE manages the memory addresses in upper memory and also emulates expanded memory. To provide the maximum amount of conventional memory to applications, store as many programs, TSRs, and device drivers as possible in upper memory, using upper memory blocks. To see which programs are loaded into conventional memory and which programs are loaded into upper memory, use a variation of the MEM command with the /C option. Also include the |MORE option to page the results to your screen. Figure 4-13 was produced using this command:

```
MEM /C |MORE
```

In Figure 4-13, the first column shows the programs currently loaded in memory. The second column shows the total amount of memory used by each program. The columns labeled Conventional and Upper Memory show the amount of memory being used by each program in each of these categories. This PC is not making use of upper memory for any of its programs. At the bottom of the screen is the total amount of free conventional memory (578,448 bytes) that is available to new programs to be loaded. Making this value as high as possible is the subject of this section.

```
                                MS-DOS Prompt

Modules using memory below 1 MB:

  Name         Total       =   Conventional   +   Upper Memory
  ----------   ---------       ------------       ------------
  MSDOS        15,565 (15K)    15,565 (15K)          0  (0K)
  SETVER          480  (0K)       480  (0K)          0  (0K)
  HIMEM         1,168  (1K)     1,168  (1K)          0  (0K)
  COMMAND       2,928  (3K)     2,928  (3K)          0  (0K)
  win386        6,704  (7K)     6,704  (7K)          0  (0K)
  SMARTDRV     27,488 (27K)    27,488 (27K)          0  (0K)
  WIN           1,520  (1K)     1,520  (1K)          0  (0K)
  SHARE        17,904 (17K)    17,904 (17K)          0  (0K)
  COMMAND       3,056  (3K)     3,056  (3K)          0  (0K)
  Free        578,448 (565K)  578,448 (565K)         0  (0K)

Memory Summary:

  Type of Memory      Total    =     Used    +    Free
  ---------------    -------        -------      -------
  Conventional       655,360         76,912      578,448
  Upper                    0              0            0
  Reserved           131,072        131,072            0
 -- More --
```

Figure 4-13   MEM report with /C option on a PC not using upper memory

Creating and Using Upper Memory Blocks

Figure 4-14 shows an example of a CONFIG.SYS file that is set to use upper memory addresses. The first line loads the HIMEM.SYS driver. The second line loads the EMM386.EXE file on drive C in the \DOS directory. EMM386.EXE assigns addresses in upper memory to memory made available by the HIMEM.SYS driver. The NOEMS switch at the end of the command line says to DOS, "Do not create any simulated expanded memory." The command to load EMM386.EXE must appear after the command to load HIMEM.SYS in the CONFIG.SYS file.

A+ OS 1.1

The command DOS=HIGH,UMB serves two purposes. The one command line can be broken into two commands like this:

```
DOS=HIGH
DOS=UMB
```

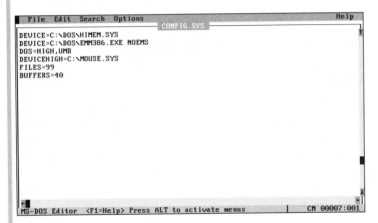

Figure 4-14 CONFIG.SYS set to use upper memory

The DOS=HIGH portion tells DOS to load part of DOS into the high memory area. Remember that the high memory area is the first 64K of extended memory. This memory is usually unused unless we choose to store part of DOS in it with this command line. Including this command in CONFIG.SYS frees some conventional memory that would have been used by DOS. Storing DOS in this high memory area is sometimes called "loading DOS high."

The second part of the command, DOS=UMB, creates upper memory blocks. An **upper memory block (UMB)** is a group of consecutive memory addresses in the upper memory area that has had physical memory assigned to it. DOS identifies blocks that are currently not being used by system ROM or expansion boards, and the memory manager makes these blocks available for use. This command, DOS=UMB, enables DOS to access these upper memory blocks. After the UMBs are created, they can be used in these ways:

- DEVICEHIGH= command in CONFIG.SYS
- LOADHIGH command in AUTOEXEC.BAT
- LOADHIGH command at the DOS prompt (explained below)

The next line in the CONFIG.SYS file in Figure 4-14 uses a UMB. The command DEVICEHIGH=C:\MOUSE.SYS tells DOS to load the mouse device driver into one of the upper memory blocks created and made available by the previous three lines. This process of loading a program into upper memory addresses is called **loading high**.

Loading Device Drivers High

A+ OS 3.2

Using the DEVICEHIGH= command in CONFIG.SYS, rather than the DEVICE= command, causes the driver to load high. With the DEVICEHIGH command, DOS stores these

A+ OS
3.2

drivers in UMBs using the largest UMB first, then the next largest, and so on until all are loaded. Therefore, to make sure there is enough room to hold them all in upper memory, order the DEVICEHIGH= command lines in CONFIG.SYS so that the largest drivers are loaded first. To determine the size of a driver, begin by simply looking at the size of the file. However, other factors also affect the size of a UMB needed for a driver.

A device driver needs some space immediately above it to hold its data. In addition, sometimes when the program first executes, it requires some extra room to initialize itself. This space may be released later, but it is still required in order to execute the driver. The largest amount of memory that a driver needs to initialize itself and to hold its data is called the maximum size, or the **load size**. It is almost always a little larger than the size of the program file. Since you don't always accurately predict what this maximum size will be, you can understand why a device driver might fail to load into upper memory even when the UMB is larger than the file size. If you include the DEVICEHIGH= command in CONFIG.SYS, but later discover that the device driver is still in conventional memory and did not load high, DOS did not find a UMB large enough for it.

You can determine the amount of memory a device driver allocates for itself and its data by using the DOS MEM command with the /M filename option:

```
MEM /M filename
```

The filename is the name of the device driver without the file extension. Later, this chapter will examine methods to determine just where in upper memory a driver is loaded, and what to do if things go wrong.

Loading TSRs High

Recall that a TSR is any program that remains loaded in memory, waiting to be executed at a later time. All device drivers are TSRs, but not all TSRs are device drivers. You can load TSRs that are not device drivers into upper memory either from AUTOEXEC.BAT or from the DOS prompt. In either case, the command is LOADHIGH followed by the path and name of the program file.

For example, suppose you want to print some screen captures like the screen capture that was used to produce Figure 4-13. While using DOS, you can press the Print Screen key to get a printout of the screen; while using Windows 3.x, use the Print Screen key to copy the contents of a screen into the clipboard, and print it using an applications software program such as Paint Brush. Sometimes the printout, however, looks very rough, is hard to read, and cannot easily be saved to a file. The screen capture in Figure 4-13 was created and printed with a software package called Pizazz Plus. Pizazz Plus is a TSR. It is loaded into memory by typing C:\PZP\PZP at the C prompt. This command tells DOS the name of the program file, PZP, and the path to it, drive C, \PZP directory. The program loads into conventional memory and immediately returns to the C prompt. It does not execute at the time it is loaded; it remains dormant until you press the Print Screen key.

You can then execute any software package and work until you are ready to use the screen capture software. When you have a screen ready to print, press the **Print Screen** key, the hot key for this TSR. Rather than printing the screen, the Print Screen key brings up the Pizazz menu, and you can save the screen to a file for printing later. When you exit from the Pizazz menu, DOS returns you to the software you are executing, and you pick up where you left off.

The Pizazz program, like all DOS applications, expects to use conventional memory, and a problem arises when you are running other software that requires a lot of conventional memory. The software might not run at all, might run unacceptably slowly, or might give errors. You can solve this problem by storing the Pizazz program in upper memory instead of in conventional memory. You do this by using the following command at the C prompt:

```
C:\> LOADHIGH C:\PZP\PZP
```

The command line can be shortened by replacing LOADHIGH with the shorter version, LH:

```
C:\>LH C:\PZP\PZP
```

The program is loaded into the largest UMB available and does not use up more precious conventional memory. Note that before the LOADHIGH command will work, these three lines must be added to CONFIG.SYS and executed by booting the computer:

```
DEVICE=C:\DOS\HIMEM.SYS
DEVICE=C:\DOS\EMM386.EXE NOEMS
DOS=UMB
```

If you intend to use the Pizazz software often, you can make it load into upper memory every time you boot the computer. To do this, the previous LH line is included in the AUTOEXEC.BAT file without any changes.

Figure 4-15 shows an AUTOEXEC.BAT file that loads the Pizazz software high every time the computer boots (LH C:\PZP\PZP). Note that the path to the PZP program must be included in the last command line, because \PZP is not included in the earlier PATH command.

Figure 4-15 AUTOEXEC.BAT loading a TSR high

> When TSRs are loaded high, two things can go wrong. Either the TSR might not work from upper memory, causing problems during execution, or there might not be enough room in upper memory for the program and its data. If the program causes the computer to hang when you attempt to run it, or if it simply refuses to work correctly, remove it from upper memory.

Simulating Expanded Memory

A+ OS 1.1

You can use HIMEM.SYS together with EMM386.EXE to simulate expanded memory. Some extended memory that is being managed by this memory management software can be allocated to "act" like expanded memory for software that requires it.

In Figure 4-16, the parameter 1024 RAM replaces the NOEMS parameter of Figure 4-14. By adding this parameter, you still have upper memory blocks available, but you also have told DOS to make 1024K of extended memory simulate expanded memory. Use this parameter when you are running software that can use expanded memory, instead of installing an expanded memory card. Consult the manual for the software that will use the expanded memory, in order to determine how much simulated expanded memory to allocate. Memory that simulates expanded memory is no longer available for extended memory applications.

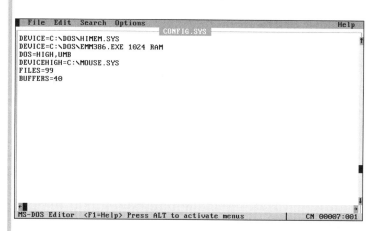

Figure 4-16   CONFIG.SYS set to simulate expanded memory

Memory Reports Using the MEM Command

A+ OS 3.1, 1.1

The DOS **MEM command** with the appropriate parameters shows exactly where in upper memory the UMBs are located, and what software has been assigned addresses in upper memory. In its simplest form, the MEM command looks like Figure 4-17. You will look at several examples of memory reports at different stages of memory management.

$A+$ OS
1.1,
3.1

```
┌──────────────────────────── MS-DOS Prompt ──────────────────── ▼ ▲ ─┐
│ C:\>mem                                                               │
│ Memory Type        Total   =   Used    +   Free                       │
│ ─────────────────  ──────     ──────      ──────                      │
│ Conventional         640K       75K        565K                       │
│ Upper                  0K        0K          0K                        │
│ Reserved             128K      128K          0K                        │
│ Extended (XMS)     3,328K    2,304K      1,024K                        │
│                    ──────    ──────      ──────                        │
│ Total memory       4,096K    2,507K      1,589K                        │
│                                                                       │
│ Total under 1 MB     640K       75K        565K                       │
│                                                                       │
│ Total Expanded (EMS)             1,024K (1,048,576 bytes)             │
│ Free Expanded (EMS)              1,024K (1,048,576 bytes)             │
│                                                                       │
│ Largest executable program size    565K (578,432 bytes)              │
│ Largest free upper memory block      0K       (0 bytes)              │
│ MS-DOS is resident in the high memory area.                          │
│                                                                       │
│ C:\>                                                                  │
│                                                                       │
│ ◄ █                                                                ► │
└───────────────────────────────────────────────────────────────────┘
```

Figure 4-17   MEM report without UMBs available

In Figure 4–17, upper memory blocks are not being used, and the total memory under 1 MB is reported to be only 640K. In Figure 4–13, you saw the same PC with no changes to memory management. The MEM command in Figure 4–13 includes the /C option:

    MEM /C |MORE

which shows a more complete report. You see several programs using conventional memory, and no use being made of the upper memory area.

To get a printed version of this report, use this command:

    C:\> MEM/C >PRN

You can read the report one screen at a time using this command:

    C:\> MEM/C x | MORE

In Figure 4–18, you can see how this upper memory area is helping to free some conventional memory after you have added the commands to CONFIG.SYS and AUTOEXEC.BAT to make use of upper memory. In Figure 4–19, the EMM386.EXE program was loaded from CONFIG.SYS, as in Figure 4–14, and two TSRs, SMARTDRV.EXE and SHARE.EXE, were loaded high from AUTOEXEC.BAT. Note that upper memory is now recognized by the system.

```
┌─────────────────────────────── MS-DOS Prompt ──────────────────────── ▼ ▲ ┐
│ C:\>mem                                                                     │
│ Memory Type       Total    =    Used   +    Free                            │
│ ─────────────────────────────────────────────────                         │
│ Conventional       640K          31K         609K                          │
│ Upper              155K         155K           0K                          │
│ Reserved           128K         128K           0K                          │
│ Extended (XMS)   3,173K       2,149K       1,024K                          │
│ ─────────────────────────────────────────────────                         │
│ Total memory     4,096K       2,463K       1,633K                          │
│                                                                             │
│ Total under 1 MB   795K         186K         609K                          │
│                                                                             │
│ Largest executable program size        609K (623,472 bytes)               │
│ Largest free upper memory block          0K       (0 bytes)               │
│ MS-DOS is resident in the high memory area.                                │
│                                                                             │
│ C:\>                                                                        │
└─────────────────────────────────────────────────────────────────────── ┘
```

Figure 4-18   MEM report on a PC using upper memory

```
┌─────────────────────────────── MS-DOS Prompt ──────────────────────── ▼ ▲ ┐
│ Modules using memory below 1 MB:                                            │
│                                                                             │
│ Name       Total      =    Conventional   +   Upper Memory                 │
│ ─────────────────────────────────────────────────────────                 │
│ MSDOS      15,581   (15K)     15,581  (15K)        0   (0K)                │
│ SETVER        480    (0K)        480   (0K)        0   (0K)                │
│ HIMEM       1,168    (1K)      1,168   (1K)        0   (0K)                │
│ EMM386      3,120    (3K)      3,120   (3K)        0   (0K)                │
│ COMMAND     2,928    (3K)      2,928   (3K)        0   (0K)                │
│ win386    117,088  (114K)      3,920   (4K)  113,168 (111K)               │
│ WIN         1,520    (1K)      1,520   (1K)        0   (0K)                │
│ COMMAND     3,056    (3K)      3,056   (3K)        0   (0K)                │
│ SMARTDRV   27,488   (27K)          0   (0K)   27,488  (27K)               │
│ SHARE      17,904   (17K)          0   (0K)   17,904  (17K)               │
│ Free      623,488  (609K)    623,488 (609K)        0   (0K)               │
│                                                                             │
│ Memory Summary:                                                             │
│                                                                             │
│ Type of Memory    Total    =    Used   +    Free                           │
│ ─────────────────────────────────────────────────                        │
│ Conventional     655,360       31,872      623,488                        │
│ Upper            158,560      158,560            0                        │
│ ── More ──                                                                  │
└─────────────────────────────────────────────────────────────────────── ┘
```

Figure 4-19   MEM/C report on a PC using upper memory

When you create upper memory blocks, you are reducing the total amount of extended memory available. This is because the amount of physical memory remains the same. What changes is the way DOS allocates memory addresses to this fixed amount of physical memory.

Compare Figure 4-13 with Figure 4-19. You see some interesting differences. EMM386 is requiring some memory in Figure 4-19, but was not used in Figure 4-13 since it had been omitted from CONFIG.SYS commands. Total conventional memory available for software increased from 578,448 in Figure 4-13 to 623,488 in Figure 4-19.

WIN386 is the Windows 3.x program responsible for managing virtual memory. Note the way WIN386 is using memory in both figures. In Figure 4-13, 6,704 bytes were being used when no upper memory blocks were available, but in Figure 4-19, WIN386 is using 117,088 bytes of memory. To see how this memory is being allocated, you use this command:

```
MEM /M WIN386
```

Figure 4-20 shows the results. Notice that all the upper memory area used by WIN386 is being used to store its data. WIN386 manages virtual memory for Windows and, in doing so, is able to decide to use upper memory area if it is available.

Using MemMaker with DOS 6+

DOS 6.0 and later versions offer an automatic way to manage upper and extended memory. MemMaker edits your CONFIG.SYS and AUTOEXEC.BAT files for you, placing the same commands in these files that were just discussed. It might edit an existing EMM386.EXE command line and change DEVICE= commands to DEVICEHIGH= commands. If it determines that a TSR loaded from AUTOEXEC.BAT can be loaded high, it adds the LH parameter to the beginning of the command line.

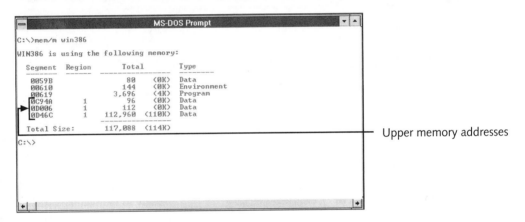

Upper memory addresses

Figure 4-20   How WIN386 is using memory

To execute MemMaker, type **MEMMAKER** at the C prompt. MemMaker will ask you some questions about your system and then tell you that it is ready to reboot. During the boot process MemMaker monitors the loading of device drivers and other TSRs. After the boot process is complete, it makes some calculations to decide the best way to configure memory, and then edits the CONFIG.SYS and AUTOEXEC.BAT files. Sometimes it will edit the Windows System.ini file. Again, it will ask you to reboot the machine. After this reboot, it will ask if you saw any error messages during the boot process, and if your machine appears to be working well. If you say "Yes" to the latter question, then MemMaker is finished.

MemMaker saves the original files before it edits them. AUTOEXEC.BAT is saved as AUTOEXEC.UMB, CONFIG.SYS is saved as CONFIG.UMB, and System.ini is saved as SYSTEM.UMB. To return to these original files, type this command:

        C:\> MEMMAKER /UNDO

The original copies of AUTOEXEC.BAT, CONFIG.SYS, and System.ini will be restored. Also, MemMaker offers a custom configuration. During this configuration, it will ask you what kind of video you are using. If you are not using a monochrome monitor, then it will use the B range of memory addresses normally designated for monochrome monitors for upper memory blocks.

If you have DOS 6+, you might want to compare your computer's performance before and after MemMaker has configured memory. Save the original CONFIG.SYS and AUTOEXEC.BAT files yourself, and compare the original and edited versions after MemMaker is finished. You might see some settings you might like to change in MemMaker's edited files; if so, you can make changes to the edited files yourself. It might take several iterations of MemMaker to completely optimize memory.

MANAGING MEMORY WITH WINDOWS 9X

Memory management has not changed fundamentally with Windows 9x; memory is still organized as conventional, upper, extended, and expanded. However, Windows 9x has made some improvements in the allocation of this memory and in the automation of the process that make it easier for us to manage memory. One of the major improvements takes us to a new level of 32-bit protected mode drivers. These 32-bit drivers are automatically loaded into extended memory (not conventional or upper memory) when Windows 9x loads, thus eliminating the need for DEVICE= entries in CONFIG.SYS.

Software written with 32-bit code is generally faster and takes up more memory than older software written in 16-bit code. Windows 9x offers many drivers written in 32-bit code that can replace older 16-bit drivers written for DOS in real mode. New 32-bit drivers are sometimes called **virtual device drivers** or **VxD drivers**; they have .vxd or .386 file extensions and operate in protected mode. For Windows 9x to use older 16-bit drivers, it must provide a real-mode environment for these drivers to operate in, by using entries in CONFIG.SYS and AUTOEXEC.BAT that normally are not needed with Windows 9x. When given the choice, always choose 32-bit drivers over 16-bit drivers to increase overall computer performance.

Another improvement in Windows 9x is that it frees up more of conventional and upper memory, because it no longer uses SMARTDRV.EXE or SHARE.EXE, two TSRs that required a lot of memory below 1 MB. SMARTDRV.EXE, a 16-bit driver to manage disk caching, was replaced by Vcache, 32-bit disk caching that is built into Windows 9x. The 16-bit SHARE.EXE was replaced by the 32-bit Vshare.386, a part of Vmm32.exe that is automatically loaded when Windows 9x starts.

If you are fortunate enough to be using all 32-bit drivers and applications in a Windows 9x environment, memory management requires no work on your part. Just let Windows 9x automate the process for you. However, if you are running older 16-bit applications under Windows 9x, you might need to provide some of the same memory management aids needed by DOS. Windows 9x does not need AUTOEXEC.BAT or CONFIG.SYS files to run. However, if these files are present when Windows 9x boots, Windows 9x processes them just as DOS did.

Windows 9x uses HIMEM.SYS to manage extended memory just as DOS does, but, instead of being loaded from CONFIG.SYS, it's automatically loaded by Io.sys without requiring an entry in CONFIG.SYS. When using this automatic method, Io.sys does not load HIMEM.SYS until after the commands in CONFIG.SYS have been executed. If you are using CONFIG.SYS to load EMM386.EXE, then you must include HIMEM.SYS in CONFIG.SYS along with EMM386.EXE because EMM386.EXE must find HIMEM.SYS already loaded before it can load.

If you need to load a 16-bit device driver into a UMB, then you must have a CONFIG.SYS file with these lines in it:

```
DEVICE=HIMEM.SYS
DEVICE=EMM386.EXE NOEMS
DOS=HIGH,UMB
```

However, if you are using all 32-bit drivers, you don't even need the CONFIG.SYS file. Windows 9x is much improved because it uses 32-bit drivers and software, but it is also backward compatible with 16-bit drivers and software that were written for DOS and Windows 3.x. When you are using these older programs, you have the same kinds of memory problems and require the same solutions as you did with DOS. All the commands for CONFIG.SYS and AUTOEXEC.BAT and the MEM command discussed earlier apply under Windows 9x using 16-bit drivers and older 16-bit software.

File extensions might help you to figure out whether you are using a 16-bit driver or a 32-bit driver to support a hardware device, but there is one way you can know for certain. Windows 3.x and DOS do not support 32-bit drivers, so if the driver works under DOS, you are using a 16-bit driver.

During the Windows 9x installation, Windows 9x setup tries to substitute 32-bit drivers for all 16-bit drivers it finds in use, and, if it can, to eliminate the CONFIG.SYS file altogether. However, if it can't substitute a 32-bit driver for the older 16-bit driver present, it puts (or keeps) the proper lines in the CONFIG.SYS file and sets itself up to use the older driver. More about this in Chapter 11.

When running DOS applications under Windows 9x, a DOS-like environment must be provided to the application. For example, to provide a DOS environment for the DOS program EDIT.COM on a PC running Windows 9x, go to Explorer and find the file EDIT.COM in the \Windows\Command directory. Right-click on the filename and select **Properties** from the drop-down menu that appears. Figure 4-21 is displayed, showing the Properties sheet for a DOS application. The entries on this sheet make up the **PIF** (**program information file**) for this application, which describes the environment the DOS program uses. Click on the **Memory** tab, and Figure 4-22 appears, listing the memory options available. From the Memory tab, you can specify how much conventional, expanded, and extended memory will be made available to the application, or leave the settings at Auto, which allows the application to use whatever is available. The last entry on the tab is MS-DOS protected-mode (DPMI) memory. This entry assigns the amount of protected-mode memory allowed the application. If you check Protected in the Conventional memory frame, the OS will protect memory used by the system from the application.

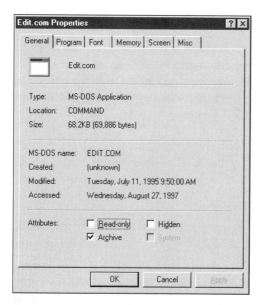

Figure 4-21   Properties sheet for a DOS application

Many DOS applications run with the default Auto settings with no problems. However, sometimes a DOS application has a problem with being given too much memory. Limit the amount of memory given the application using the Properties sheet shown in Figure 4-22.

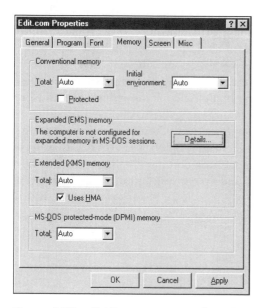

Figure 4-22   Setting up memory for a DOS application running under Windows 9x

Real Mode vs. Virtual Real Mode

When an OS that supports protected mode allows a 16-bit program that is written to work in real mode to run, this is called virtual real mode (sometimes referred to as virtual DOS mode). Figure 4-23 shows the difference between real mode and virtual real mode. In virtual real mode, the program "thinks" it is really working in a real-mode environment. It "thinks" that:

- It is the only program running

- It has all memory available to it, all 1024K of memory addresses that directly point to RAM

- It accesses data using a 16-bit data path

Underneath this environment, the OS is managing memory for the application. It receives the data in a 16-bit path, but is free to use a 32-bit data path to access memory and is also free to use virtual memory for the data.

Recall that there are two types of 16-bit applications: those written for DOS and those written for Windows 3.x. DOS 16-bit applications expect to run in real mode with no other applications running with them. A Windows 3.x 16-bit application expects to allow Windows to manage memory for it and expects that other applications might also be running in a cooperative multitasking environment.

When Windows 9x runs a 16-bit DOS application, ordinarily it is run in virtual DOS mode in a virtual DOS machine (VDM), sometimes called a DOS box, rather than in real mode. In a VDM, the application "thinks" it is running in real mode, but the OS is managing hardware resources using 32-bit drivers and providing virtual memory to the application. If you want a DOS application to have a "real" real mode rather than a virtual real mode, access the Properties box for the application. For example, once again using EDIT.COM as our example of a 16-bit application, right-click the program filename in Explorer (or you can right-click on the shortcut icon to the program) and select **Properties**. Click the **Program** tab and click **Advanced**. The Advanced Program Settings box is displayed as in Figure 4-24. Click **MS-DOS mode** to run the application in real mode. You can then choose to give the program its own private set of CONFIG.SYS and AUTOEXEC.BAT settings to be executed before the program runs. This information is stored in the PIF created for the shortcut. When you execute the shortcut or program, Windows 9x will shut down and reboot in real mode before executing the program.

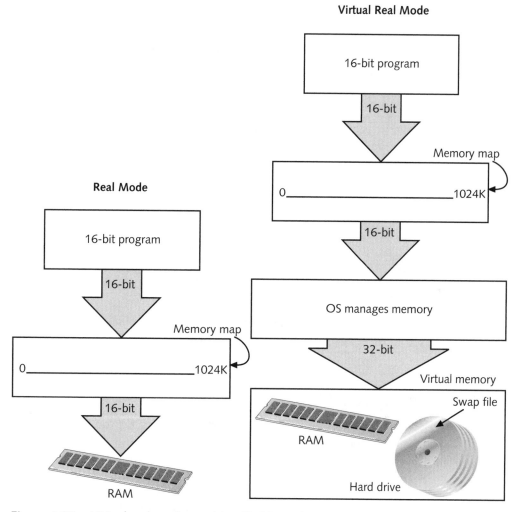

Figure 4-23   Virtual real mode provides "DOS in a box" to a 16-bit application that was written to run in real mode

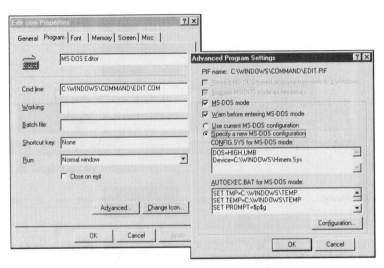

Figure 4-24   Use the Advanced Program Settings dialog box to run a 16-bit application in a real-mode environment in Windows 9x

> **TIP** To access real mode in Windows 9x, select **Start** and **Shutdown**. When the Shut Down Windows dialog box appears, select **Restart in MS-DOS mode**.

Windows 9x Swap File

Windows 9x automates the managing of virtual memory for you. Although you can override the automation, there is little reason to do so. To see what options Windows 9x offers, click **Start**, point to **Settings**, click **Control Panel**, then select **System** and select the **Performance** tab. A window similar to Figure 4-25 appears. Click **Virtual Memory**, and the dialog box in Figure 4-26 is displayed. Unless you have a very good reason to do otherwise, check **Let Windows manage my virtual memory settings**.

These settings are used to tell Windows how to manage the swap file. Notice in Figure 4-26 that you can specify the location of the swap file. You can choose to put the swap file on a compressed drive, but Windows does not compress the swap file itself in order to better ensure the safety of the file. Compressed drives, discussed in more detail in Chapter 6, are hard drives that have a portion of their data compressed in order to save space on the drive.

A^+_{OS} 3.1

Figure 4-25   System Properties Performance box in Windows 9x

Figure 4-26   Options for managing virtual memory in Windows 9x

THE ULTIMATE SOLUTION: WINDOWS NT AND WINDOWS 2000

A^+_{OS} 1.1

Memory management under Windows NT and Windows 2000, compared to memory management under DOS and Windows 9x, is like traveling on a freeway rather than an obstacle course. This new approach, which began with Windows NT, also applies to Windows 2000. The memory mapping for Windows NT is one continuous, linear, 32-bit address space that allows each program and driver using Windows NT access to any part of this memory. Obstacles, out of the way!

$A^+_{}$ OS
1.1

Although it is not the intent of this chapter to delve too deeply into managing Windows NT memory, because of the complexity of dealing with conventional, upper, extended, and expanded memory, you can appreciate the ultimate solution to memory management on PCs—Windows NT.

The Windows NT memory management model is shown in Figure 4-27. Earlier in the chapter it was explained that expanded memory is accessed, by page frames, from upper memory and mapped onto the expanded memory card. The application thinks it has addresses in upper memory stored in RAM on the system board, when it really has only a window from upper memory mapped onto memory on the expansion board. You can compare this process to the memory management model for Windows NT.

Figure 4-27   Windows NT and Windows 2000 memory management

Figure 4-27 shows the object-oriented approach to memory management. The application or device driver only says, "I want memory." It has no right to say to Windows NT which physical memory or which memory addresses it wants, or even the range of addresses that it wants to fall within. It can only say to Windows NT, "I want memory." Windows NT uses its Virtual Memory Manager to interface between the application or driver and the physical and virtual memory that it controls. Memory is allocated in 4K segments called **pages**. Applications and devices that are written for Windows NT only know how many pages they have. The virtual manager takes care of the rest. It is free to store these pages in RAM or on the hard drive in the swap file named Pagefile.sys. The only time an application would ever expect to run out of memory is when Pagefile.sys and RAM are full. Memory is only limited by the amount of physical memory available and the number of memory addresses that Windows NT can use, which is 4 GB.

With Windows NT and Windows 2000, struggles with "out of memory" errors should be a thing of the past.

Memory Management Troubleshooting Guidelines

A+ OS
3.2

This section describes what to do when things go wrong with memory management, and how to prevent potential errors.

When a TSR Will Not Load High   Sometimes after instructing DOS to load a TSR high, a MEM report will show you that the load high instruction did not work. You included the DEVICE=HIMEM.SYS, the DEVICE=EMM386.EXE, and the DOS=UMB command lines in the CONFIG.SYS file, and you attempted to load a TSR high, using either the DEVICEHIGH= command in CONFIG.SYS or the LOADHIGH command in AUTOEXEC.BAT. But, when you get a MEM/C report, you discover that the TSR is still in conventional memory. Probably, the problem is either that the TSR did not have enough space in the UMB assigned to it, or that there were no more UMBs available for it. Do these things:

1. Check that all command lines in CONFIG.SYS and AUTOEXEC.BAT are correct.

2. Make sure that the DEVICEHIGH= commands in CONFIG.SYS are ordered so that the larger TSRs are placed first, in the larger UMBs. Still, they might not all fit in upper memory. By putting the largest ones possible in upper memory, you have freed up the largest amount of conventional memory possible.

3. MEMMAKER does a very good job of choosing the best order of loading TSRs. Try it.

4. Some TSRs do not work from upper memory, so test them before assuming that all is well.

When Devices Do Not Work or the System Hangs   When DOS creates a UMB, DOS might "think" that no expansion board is using these memory addresses, when in fact they are being used by a card. If a TSR is loaded into this UMB, a memory conflict occurs. A memory conflict occurs when more than one program or their data have been assigned the same memory addresses. Memory conflicts can cause programs or devices to give errors, or can cause the computer to "lock up" and refuse to function.

There are two kinds of memory conflicts that cause a device to stop working or cause the system to hang:

1. Two expansion boards are using the same upper memory addresses.

2. DOS has created and is using a UMB in the same memory addresses used by an expansion board.

Two Expansion Boards Using the Same Upper Memory Addresses   You have a scanner card installed to drive your scanner, and it works well. But when you install a network card in this computer, the scanner refuses to work, and the network does not work properly.

A+ OS
3.2

It is likely that both the network card and the scanner card are using the same upper memory addresses. Consider the following approaches:

1. Some expansion boards have DIP switches or jumpers that allow you to substitute one set of memory addresses for another.

2. You might change the memory addresses by adding a parameter to the command line that loads the device driver for the expansion board.

3. When two devices use the same memory addresses, you can often change one to an alternate set of memory addresses. If neither device accepts an alternate address, then you cannot install the two devices on the same computer. To find out which memory addresses are assigned to the devices, whether an alternate set of memory addresses is available, and how to access it, consult the documentation for the device or the software that drives the device. It is very important to keep the hardware and software documentation in a place where you can find it. Without the documentation, your only recourse is to call technical support for the software or hardware.

TIP When reading the documentation, you will find that most addresses are given in hex rather than decimal form. (See Appendix D for an explanation of the hex number system.) Sometimes the memory addresses are written without the last hexadecimal numeral. For example, if the documentation says that the device uses C800 through CFFF, interpret this to mean that the upper memory address range is C8000 through CFFFF. Once you have discovered that the two devices use the same memory addresses, find out if one can use alternate addresses. If so, your problem is solved.

A+ OS
3.2

When UMBs and Expansion Boards Conflict   When DOS creates a UMB, it assigns memory addresses that it "thinks" are not being used by devices. However, some devices don't tell DOS what memory addresses they are using until the device is activated after booting. This delay causes DOS to think that the memory addresses assigned to a device are available, and DOS creates and loads a TSR into the UMB. If this conflict happens, the system might hang, the TSR might not work properly, and/or the device might not work properly. Try the following approach:

1. Read the documentation that came with the device to find out which memory addresses it is using. Some device drivers display the memory addresses they are using during the boot process as they are loaded. Carefully watch for this information on the screen while booting. Also, try using MSD to display how memory is being used. Once you know the memory addresses being used, you can change the EMM386.EXE command line so that this range of addresses is not used.

2. Use the Exclude option to the EMM386.EXE command line to exclude certain memory addresses. Do not use the last numeral in the hex address in the command line. For example, suppose you read from the documentation that came with the device that it uses addresses CC000–CFFFF. To exclude these addresses from the addresses used by UMBs, use this command line:

```
DEVICE=C:\DOS\EMM386.EXE NOEMS X = CC00 - CFFF
```

3. Reboot your computer to activate the change. The memory conflict problem should then be solved.

UPGRADING MEMORY

A+CORE 1.8, 4.2

Upgrading memory means to add more RAM to a computer. Many computers, when first purchased, have empty slots on the system board, allowing you to add SIMMs or DIMMs to increase the amount of RAM. If all the slots are full, sometimes you can take out small-capacity modules and replace them with larger-capacity modules. When you add more memory to your computer, ask yourself these questions:

- How much memory do I need?

- How much memory can my computer physically accommodate?

- What increments of memory does my system board support?

- How much additional memory is cost effective?

- What kind of memory can fit on my system board?

- What memory is compatible with the memory I already have installed?

With the demands today's software places on memory, the answer to the first question is probably, "All I can get." Both Windows 95 and Windows 98 need from 24 MB to 32 MB of memory. The minimum requirement is 8 MB, although performance will be slow with this little memory because the system is forced to write working files to the slower hard drive as virtual memory instead of using the much faster RAM.

How Much Memory Can Fit on the System Board?

To determine how much memory your computer can physically hold, read the documentation that comes with your computer. For example, one manual for a 486 computer explains that the system board can support up to 32 MB of memory, but there are only nine possible memory configurations. A table that describes these configurations might look like Table 4-4.

Table 4-4 shows that this system board has two banks. A **bank** is a location on the system board that contains slots for memory modules. On this system board, each bank can hold 256K, 1 MB, or 4 MB of memory. The first bank always has some memory in it, but the second bank might or might not contain memory. This computer, which is typical of many older 486 boards, uses SIMMs on the system board. Recall that a SIMM is a small miniboard that contains memory chips. The SIMMs are inserted into the slots in a bank. This computer can support these sizes: 256K, 1 MB, and 4 MB.

A+CORE
    4.2

Table 4-4   Memory configurations of a 486 system board

SIMM Size in Bank 1	SIMM Size in Bank 2	Total RAM on System Board
256K	0	1 MB
256K	256K	2 MB
1 MB	0	4 MB
1 MB	256K	5 MB
1 MB	1 MB	8 MB
4 MB	0	16 MB
4 MB	256K	17 MB
4 MB	1 MB	20 MB
4 MB	4 MB	32 MB

To determine how many slots are in one bank, you must know the computer's bus size. This 486 computer uses a 32-bit bus. When bits travel down a circuit on the system board to the bank to be stored in RAM, they are moving 32 bits abreast. The bank must receive 32 bits at a time to work with this bus. This system board uses 30-pin SIMMs. Each 30-pin SIMM receives one 8-bit byte at a time. Figure 4–28 shows that the 32-bit bus directs 8 bits to each of four SIMMs in the bank. The bank must contain four SIMMs to receive these 32 bits. Since each SIMM receives an equal part of the 4 bytes traveling down the circuit, all SIMMs within one bank must store the same amount of bytes.

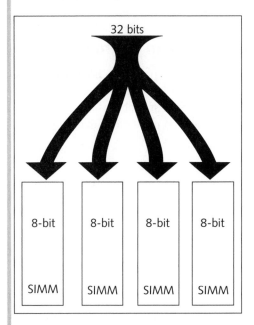

Figure 4-28   One bank on a 486 system board that uses a 32-bit bus and 8-bit, 30-pin SIMMs; each SIMM must hold the same amount of memory

A+CORE
4.2

In Table 4-4, you see in the first row of the table that bank 1 contains 256K SIMMs, and bank 2 is empty. Bank 1 contains four slots, each of which must contain a SIMM in order to accommodate the 32-bit bus. Hence, the amount of memory is 4 × 256K or 1 MB of memory. In the second row of the table, each bank contains four 256K SIMMs for a total of 2 MB of memory: (4 × 256K) + (4 × 256K) = 2 MB.

Notice that in the fourth row of the table, bank 1 contains 1-MB SIMMs, and bank 2 contains 256K SIMMs for a total of 5 MB of memory on the system board (calculations are left to the reader). The four SIMMs in a bank must be the same size, but the SIMMs can vary in size from one bank to another.

Our second example of a system board is one used by a Pentium, and it supports up to 128 MB of RAM. It has four SIMM sockets divided into two banks. Bank 0 holds SIMMs 1 and 2, and bank 1 holds SIMMs 3 and 4 (see Figure 4-29). Memory can be installed using 4-MB, 8-MB, and 16-MB SIMMs using either 72-pin EDO or FPM modules, which must have at least 70 ns speed.

Remember from Chapter 3 that the Pentium memory bus between RAM and the CPU is 64 bits wide (see Figure 3-23). Most 72-pin SIMM modules sold today accommodate a 32-bit data path so two SIMMs must be paired together to receive data from the 64-bit Pentium memory bus. One bank of memory on the Pentium system board must contain two 32-bit SIMMs. The other bank does not need to be filled, but, if it is used, both of the two SIMMs must be present in that second bank. As you study Figure 4-29, remember that this is the Pentium memory bus connecting the CPU and RAM, not the PCI bus, which is only 32 bits wide.

Figure 4-29   A Pentium memory bus is 64 bits wide and requires two 32-bit SIMMs to accommodate the bus width; each 64-bit bank can be used independently of the other

A+CORE
4.2

Table 4-5 shows half of the memory configurations supported by a Pentium system board using SIMMs. The other half is in a project at the end of this chapter with calculations left to the reader.

Pentium system boards that use DIMM modules use only one socket to a bank, since a DIMM module accommodates a data path of 64 bits. Single-sided modules (chips on only one side of the module) come in 8, 16, 32, 64, and 128 MB sizes, and double-sided modules (chips on both sides) come in 32, 64, 128, and 256 MB sizes. Figure 4-30 shows how one, two, or three sockets of DIMMs can be used by a Pentium system board.

Figure 4-30 Only a single DIMM is needed to fill one bank of memory for a Pentium memory bus; each DIMM can be a different size

Table 4-5 Memory configurations for a Pentium system board using SIMMs

SIMM Size in Bank 0	SIMM Size in Bank 1	Total Memory
4 MB	0	8 MB
4 MB	4 MB	16 MB
4 MB	8 MB	24 MB
4 MB	16 MB	40 MB
4 MB	32 MB	72 MB
8 MB	0	16 MB
8 MB	4 MB	24 MB
8 MB	8 MB	32 MB

Table 4-5   Memory configurations for a Pentium system board using SIMMs (continued)

SIMM Size in Bank 0	SIMM Size in Bank 1	Total Memory
8 MB	16 MB	48 MB
8 MB	32 MB	80 MB
16 MB	0	32 MB
16 MB	4 MB	40 MB
16 MB	8 MB	48 MB

Selecting Memory Types

When you are placing memory on the system board, match the type of memory to the system board requirements. For example, for the first Pentium system board just discussed, the documentation says that you must use 72-pin SIMMs, which can be either EDO or FPM modules. The speed must be at least 70 ns. Avoid mixing speeds on the same system board. If you use a SIMM having one speed in one bank and a SIMM having another speed in the other bank, your computer will only work as fast as the slower bank. Always put the slower SIMMs in the first bank. However, to ensure the most reliable results, use the same speed of SIMMs in all banks and also buy the same brand of SIMMs.

For the second Pentium system board just discussed, which uses 168-pin DIMM modules, the documentation says to use unbuffered, 3.3V, PC100 DIMM SDRAM modules. The PC100 refers to the speed of the modules, meaning that the modules should be rated to work with a system board that runs at 100 MHz. You have the choice of using ECC modules. If you choose to not use them, then CMOS setup should show the feature disabled. There are three DIMM sockets on the board, and each socket represents one bank. Figure 4-31 shows the possible combinations of DIMMS that can be installed in these sockets.

DIMM Location	168-pin DIMM		Total Memory
Socket 1 (Rows 0&1)	SDRAM 8, 16, 32, 64, 128, 256MB	x1	
Socket 2 (Rows 2&3)	SDRAM 8, 16, 32, 64, 128, 256MB	x1	
Socket 3 (Rows 4&5)	SDRAM 8, 16, 32, 64, 128, 256MB	x1	
	Total System Memory (Max 768MB)	=	

Figure 4-31   This table is part of the system board documentation and is used to show possible DIMM sizes and calculate total memory on the system board

Reading Ads About Memory Modules

Figure 4-32 shows a typical memory module ad listing 30-pin SIMMs, 72-pin EDO and FPM SIMMs, and BEDO and SDRAM DIMMs. When you are selecting memory, the number of pins, the speed, the size, and the type of module are all important. We will now examine the ad to see how all this information is given to us. The second column in the ad shows the total amount of memory on each module. For example, the first entry shows a 4-MB 30-pin SIMM.

Figure 4-32 Typical ad for memory modules

The third column gives the density of the module, which tells us the width of the data bus, if the module supports error checking, and the size of the module. Here's how it works. The density is written as two numbers separated by an $\times$, such as 8×32, and is read "8 by 32." Let's start with the second number. If the second number is 32 or 64, then it's the width of the data bus in bits grouped as 8 bits to a byte. If the number is 36 or 72, then it's the width of the data bus plus an extra bit for each byte that is used for either parity (for parity memory) or error checking and correction (for ECC memory). Look down the third column and note where you see 36 or 72, to verify that these are the values listed for parity or ECC memory. When calculating the size of the module, ignore the ninth bit and use only the values 32 or 64 to calculate size. Convert this number to bytes by dividing the number by 8, and then multiply that value (number of bytes) by the number on the left in the density listing to get the size of the module. For example, if the density is 8×32, then the size of the module is $8 \times (32/8) = 8 \times 4 = 32$ MB.

Here is another example: if the density is 16×36, then ignore the parity bit and use 16×32 to do your calculations, giving $16 \times 32 = 16 \times (32/8) = 16 \times 4 = 64$ MB. The size of the module is 64 MB; the data path is 32 bits, and the module does support parity.

Notice in the fifth column of the ad the big difference between the speed of SDRAM and that of other types of memory. Also notice the difference in price between SDRAM for a 100-MHz system board that has ECC and memory that does not have ECC functionality.

Installing Memory

A+CORE
1.2

When installing SIMMs or DIMMs, remember to protect the chips against static electricity. Always use a ground bracelet as you work. Turn the power off and remove the cover to the case. Handle memory modules with care. Ground yourself before unpacking or picking up a card. Don't stack cards, because you can loosen a chip. Usually modules pop easily into place and are secured by spring catches on both ends. Look for the notch on one side of the SIMM module that orients the module in the slot. The module slides into the slot at an angle, as shown in Figure 4-33. Place each module securely in its slot. Turn on the PC and watch the amount of memory being counted by POST during the boot process. If all the memory you expect does not count up correctly, remove and reseat each module carefully. To remove a module, release the latches on both sides of the module and gently rotate the module out of the socket at a 45-degree angle.

Figure 4-33   Installing a SIMM module

For DIMM modules, as shown in Figure 4-34, small latches on either side of the slot hold the module in place. Look for the notches on the DIMM module to orient it into the slot. Insert the module straight down into the slot, just as you would an expansion card.

For RIMM modules, the technology works so that the signal enters one end of the first RIMM socket and out the other end and then on to the next socket. For this reason, each socket must be filled so that continuity throughout all sockets is maintained. If the socket does not hold a RIMM, then it must hold a placeholder module called a C-RIMM (Continuity RIMM) to assure continuity throughout all slots. The C-RIMM does not contain any memory.

Figure 4-34   Installing a DIMM module

Most often, placing memory on the system board is all that is necessary for installation. When the computer powers up, it counts the memory present without any further instruction and senses what features the modules support, such as parity or ECC. For some computers, you must tell the setup how much memory is present. Read the instructions that come with your computer to determine what yours requires.

CHAPTER SUMMARY

- ❑ Memory can be viewed as both physical memory installed on the system board and circuit boards and as logical memory managed by the OS.

- ❑ The two kinds of physical memory are RAM and ROM.

- ❑ In order for ROM or RAM physical memory to be used by the computer, memory addresses must be assigned to it.

- ❑ System BIOS is stored on a ROM chip on the system board. In addition, expansion boards sometimes have ROM chips on them, holding BIOS programming to manage a device.

- ❑ The CPU uses memory in two ways, as main memory and as a memory cache.

4

- SRAM is fast, static RAM and is used as a memory cache, which speeds up the overall computer performance by temporarily holding data and programming that may possibly be used by the CPU in the near future. SRAM does not require constant refreshing.

- DRAM (dynamic RAM) is slower than SRAM because it needs constant refreshing.

- DRAM is stored on two kinds of miniboards: SIMMs and DIMMs.

- SIMM memory modules can use either EDO or FPM technology. EDO is faster and only slightly more expensive than FPM, but the system board must support this type of memory to make use of its increased speed.

- DIMM memory modules can use either BEDO or synchronous DRAM (SDRAM).

- Direct Rambus DRAM and Double Data Rate SDRAM (DDR SDRAM) are two technologies that are contending to be the next DRAM technology standard.

- Flash memory holds data permanently until it is overwritten, and is commonly used on Flash ROM chips and memory cards for notebook computers.

- Synchronous DRAM (which moves in sync with the memory bus) is a faster kind of memory than the less expensive asynchronous DRAM (which does not move in sync with the memory bus) found on SIMMs.

- When buying memory, use only gold edge connectors on memory modules that will be inserted in slots containing gold connections, and use only tin connectors in tin slots.

- When buying memory, beware of remanufactured and re-marked memory chips because they have been either refurbished or re-marked before resale.

- SRAM comes as either synchronous or asynchronous memory. Synchronous is faster and slightly more expensive than asynchronous memory.

- Synchronous SRAM can come as either burst or pipelined burst memory.

- COAST is a cache memory module holding pipelined burst SRAM chips.

- Logical memory is divided into conventional memory, upper memory, and extended memory, according to the memory addresses assigned to it.

- Upper memory is traditionally used to hold BIOS and device drivers. Drivers for legacy video cards normally fill the A, B, and C range of upper memory addresses (hex addresses beginning with A, B, and C).

- The beginning of extended memory is called the high memory area and can hold a portion of DOS.

- Expanded memory is located on an expansion board and is accessed by page frames given upper memory addresses.

- Windows can emulate expanded memory, taking some of RAM and presenting it to applications software as expanded memory.

❐ The practice of copying BIOS from slower ROM chips to faster RAM chips for processing is called shadowing ROM. The area of RAM holding the BIOS is called shadow RAM.

❐ Virtual memory is space on the hard drive that is used by the OS as pseudo-memory.

❐ A RAM drive is space in memory that is used as a pseudo-hard-drive.

❐ DOS and Windows 9x use the device driver HIMEM.SYS to manage extended memory.

❐ DOS uses EMM386.EXE to make more efficient use of upper memory addresses and to emulate expanded memory.

❐ An upper memory block (UMB) is a group of upper memory addresses made available to TSRs.

❐ Storing device drivers and TSRs in upper memory is called loading high.

❐ DOS can load device drivers into upper memory blocks by using the DEVICEHIGH command in CONFIG.SYS.

❐ DOS can load a TSR high by using the LOADHIGH command in AUTOEXEC.BAT.

❐ MemMaker is a DOS utility that can help in managing upper memory addresses.

❐ A swap file is the file on the hard drive that is used by the OS as virtual memory.

❐ Windows NT and Windows 2000 use an approach to memory management that is altogether different from that of DOS and Windows 9x. Conventional, upper, and extended memory concepts do not exist in Windows NT or Windows 2000.

❐ Memory modules must be installed on a system board in the slots of a memory bank according to the rules specified in the system-board documentation. There are a fixed number of memory configurations that a board supports.

KEY TERMS

Asynchronous SRAM — Static RAM that does not work in step with the CPU clock and is, therefore, slower than synchronous SRAM.

Bank — An area on the system board that contains slots for memory modules (typically labeled bank 0, 1, 2, and 3).

Base memory — See conventional memory.

Buffer — A temporary memory area where data is kept before being written to a drive or sent to a printer, thus reducing the number of writes needed when devices communicate at different speeds.

Burst EDO (BEDO) — A refined version of EDO memory that significantly improved access time over EDO. BEDO is not widely used today because Intel chose not to support it. BEDO memory is stored on 168-pin DIMM modules.

4

Burst SRAM — Memory that is more expensive and slightly faster than pipelined burst SRAM. Data is sent as a two-step process; the data address is sent, and then the data itself is sent without interruption.

COAST (cache on a stick) — Chips on a module available for pipelined burst synchronous SRAM.

Conventional memory — Memory addresses between 0 and 640K. Also called base memory.

Double-data rate SDRAM (DDR SDRAM or SDRAM II) — A type of memory technology used on DIMMs that runs at twice the speed of the system clock.

Direct Rambus DRAM — A memory technology by Rambus and Intel that uses a narrow, very fast network-type memory bus. Memory is stored on a RIMM module. Also called **RDRAM** or **Direct RDRAM**.

Dynamic RAM (DRAM) — Common system memory with access speeds ranging from 70 to 50 nanoseconds, requiring refreshing every few milliseconds.

ECC (error checking and correction) — A chip set feature on a system board that checks the integrity of data stored on DIMMs and can correct single-bit errors in a byte. More advanced ECC schemas can detect, but not correct, double-bit errors in a byte.

EDO (extended data output) memory — A type of RAM that may be 10-20% faster than conventional RAM because it eliminates the delay before it issues the next memory address.

EEPROM (electrically erasable programmable ROM) chip — A type of chip in which higher voltage may be applied to one of the pins to erase its previous memory before a new instruction set is electronically written.

EMM386.EXE — A DOS utility that provides both emulated expanded memory (EMS) and upper memory blocks (UMBs).

EPROM (erasable programmable ROM) chip — A type of chip with a special window that allows the current memory contents to be erased with special ultraviolet light so that the chip can be reprogrammed. Many BIOS chips are EPROMs.

Expanded memory (EMS) — Memory outside of the conventional 640K and the extended 1024K range that is accessed in 16K segments, or pages, by way of a window to upper memory.

Extended memory — Memory above the initial 1024 KB, or 1 MB, area.

Flash memory — A type of RAM that can electronically hold memory even when the power is off.

FPM (fast page mode) memory — An earlier memory mode used before the introduction of EDO memory.

General Protection Fault (GPF) error — A Windows error that occurs when a program attempts to access a memory address that is not available or is no longer assigned to it.

High memory area (HMA) — The first 64K of extended memory. The method of storing part of DOS in the high memory area is called loading DOS high.

HIMEM.SYS — A device driver that manages memory above 640K. It is often executed by the line DEVICE = C:\DOS\HIMEM.SYS in a CONFIG.SYS file.

Load size — The largest amount of memory that a driver needs to initialize itself and to hold its data. It is almost always a little larger than the size of the program file.

Loading high — The process of loading a driver or TSR into upper memory.

MEM command — A DOS utility used to display how programs and drivers are using conventional, upper, and extended memory (Example: MEM/C/P).

MemMaker — A DOS utility that can increase the amount of conventional memory available to DOS-based software applications, by loading drivers and TSRs into upper memory.

Memory — Physical microchips that can hold data and programming located on the system board or expansion cards.

Memory address — A number that the CPU assigns to physical memory to keep track of the memory that it has access to.

Memory caching — Using a small amount of faster RAM to store recently retrieved data, in anticipation of what the CPU will next request, thus speeding up access.

Memory management — The process of increasing available conventional memory, required by DOS-based programs, accomplished by loading device drivers and TSRs into upper memory.

Memory mapping — Assigning addresses to both RAM and ROM during the boot process.

Nonparity memory — Slightly less expensive, 8-bit memory without error checking. A SIMM part number with a 32 in it (4 $\times$ 8 bits) is nonparity.

Page — Memory allocated in 4K or 16K segments within a page frame.

Page frame — A 64K upper memory area divided into four equal-sized pages through which the memory manager swaps data.

Parity memory — Nine-bit memory in which the 9th bit is used for error checking. A SIMM part number with a 36 in it (4 $\times$ 9 bits) is parity. Older DOS PCs almost always use parity chips.

Pipelined burst SRAM — A less expensive SRAM that uses more clock cycles per transfer than nonpipelined burst, but does not significantly slow down the process.

Program Information File (PIF) — A file used by Windows to describe the environment for a DOS program to use.

RAM drive — A RAM area configured as a virtual hard drive, such as drive D, so that frequently used programs can be accessed faster. It is the opposite of virtual memory.

Re-marked chips — Chips that have been used and returned to the factory, marked again, and resold. The surface of the chips may be dull or scratched.

Shadow RAM or **shadowing ROM** — The process of copying ROM programming code into RAM to speed up the system operation, because of the faster access speed of RAM.

Static RAM (SRAM) — RAM chips that retain information without the need for refreshing as long as the power is on. They are more expensive but less volatile than traditional DRAM.

Swapping — A method of freeing some memory by moving a "page" of data temporarily to a swap file on the hard drive; it can later be copied from disk back into memory.

Synchronous DRAM (SDRAM) — A type of memory stored on DIMMs that run in sync with the system clock, running at the same speed as the system board. Currently, the fastest memory used on PCs.

Synchronous SRAM — SRAM that is faster and more expensive than asynchronous SRAM. It requires a clock signal to validate its control signals, enabling the cache to run in step with the CPU.

SyncLink (SLDRAM) — A synchronous memory technology that increases the number of memory banks from 4 to 16.

System variable — A variable that has been given a name and a value; it is available to the operating system and applications software programs.

Temp directory — A location to which inactive applications and data can be moved as a swap file, while Windows continues to process current active applications. (Avoid deleting Temp swap while Windows is running.)

Temporary file — A file that is created by Windows applications, to save temporary data, and may or may not be deleted when the application is unloaded.

Upper memory — The memory addresses from 640K up to 1024K, originally reserved for BIOS, device drivers, and TSRs.

Upper memory block (UMB) — A group of consecutive memory addresses in RAM from 640K to 1 MB that can be used by device drivers and TSRs.

Virtual device driver (VDD) or **VxD driver** — A 32-bit device driver running in protected mode.

Virtual memory — Hard disk space used when a system starts to run low on RAM. Because hard drives are much slower than RAM access, virtual memory is relatively slow.

REVIEW QUESTIONS

1. Where might flash memory be found on a system board?
2. Name two ways that a SIMM and a DIMM are alike. Name two ways they are different.
3. How many pins are on a DIMM? What are the two possible numbers of pins on a SIMM?
4. Which is faster, EDO memory or BEDO memory?
5. How does a memory cache speed up computer processing?
6. Explain the difference between a level 1 cache and a level 2 cache.
7. What types of memory can you use for a 100-MHz system board?
8. If your system board supports FPM memory, will EDO memory still work on the board?
9. Looking at a SDRAM DIMM, how can you know for certain the voltage needed by the module?
10. If your system board supports ECC SDRAM memory, can you substitute SDRAM memory that does not support ECC? If your system board supports buffered SDRAM memory, can you substitute unbuffered SDRAM modules?
11. What might be a symptom in Windows of unreliable memory on a system board?
12. If your system board calls for 60 ns memory, can you substitute 70 ns memory? Why, or why not?
13. When buying memory, what can you look for that might indicate that the memory is remanufactured?
14. What are the two major categories of static RAM memory?
15. When might there not be any SRAM on a system board?
16. Which operating system operates totally in real mode? Which OS operates totally in protected mode? Which OS can switch back and forth between the two?
17. Explain the difference between the terms memory and memory address.
18. What is memory mapping? When does it occur?
19. What area of memory does video BIOS use?
20. When might you configure Windows to provide emulated expanded memory?
21. Contrast virtual memory and a RAM drive.
22. How are the two commands DEVICEHIGH and LOADHIGH the same? How are they different?
23. Which is executed first in the boot process: CONFIG.SYS or AUTOEXEC.BAT?
24. When virtual memory is stored on a hard drive, what is it called?
25. Why do you want to use 32-bit drivers in Windows 9x rather than 16-bit drivers?

26. On a Pentium system board, why must you use SIMMs in pairs?

27. If the density of a 72-pin SIMM is 4 × 32, what is the size of the SIMM?

28. Using your home or lab computer, answer these questions:

    a. How much RAM is on the system board?

    b. How much virtual memory is used?

    c. Is the virtual memory permanent or temporary?

29. When installing a RIMM memory module, what must be installed in each empty RIMM slot? Why?

30. After installing new memory in a PC, how does the system know that the new memory is present?

PROJECTS

Unless you follow proper procedures, working inside your computer can cause serious damage to both you and your computer. To ensure safety in your work setting, follow every precaution listed in the *Read This Before You Begin* section following this book's Introduction.

Using Nuts & Bolts to Examine Memory

Use the Nuts & Bolts utility, Discover Pro, to answer the following questions about the memory on your PC. Using Windows 9x, click **Start**, point to **Programs**, **Nuts & Bolts**, and select **Discover Pro** from the list of Nuts & Bolts utilities. From Discover Pro, select **System** and then **Advanced**. Select the **BIOS/CMOS** icon in the Advanced section.

1. What memory addresses are currently being used by your computer to hold System BIOS?

2. Are any System BIOS programs being shadowed into RAM?

3. What is the memory address of the I/O address table where the keyboard buffer is located?

4. Convert this keyboard buffer address to decimal (see Appendix D).

5. Click **Summary** to return to opening screen.

From Discover Pro, select **Memory** and then **Advanced** to answer these questions.

6. What memory addresses are currently assigned to video?

7. What memory addresses in upper memory are available for UMBs?

Help Desk Support

1. A friend calls who is sitting at his computer and asks you to help him determine how much RAM he has on his system board. Step him through the process. List at least two different ways to find the answer. He is using DOS 6.22.

2. Answer Question 1 above, assuming that your friend is using Windows 98.

3. A customer calls who has Norton Utilities on her PC. She has an applications software program installed, and she wants to know whether it is a 16-bit or 32-bit application. Unfortunately, she does not have the documentation for the software available. Help her to find the answer to her question.

Planning and Pricing Memory

Read the documentation and look at the system board of your computer. What is the maximum amount of memory the banks on your system board can accommodate? How much memory do they now hold? Look in a computer catalog, such as *Computer Shopper*, and determine how much it costs to fill the banks to full capacity. Don't forget to match the speed of the modules already installed, and plan to use only the size modules your computer can accommodate.

Using Upper Memory

If you have access to a computer running DOS, does this computer make the best use of upper memory? Get a printout of the files CONFIG.SYS and AUTOEXEC.BAT and the results of the MEM/C command. Study the printouts to determine any improvements that could free more conventional memory for applications.

Installing a TSR

DOSKEY is a very handy TSR. When it is installed, you can retrieve previously issued DOS commands by pressing the Up Arrow key. See your DOS manual for other uses of DOSKEY. To install DOSKEY at the C prompt, use this command:

```
C:\>DOSKEY
```

To install DOSKEY so that it is available every time your computer boots up, you must include the command in your AUTOEXEC.BAT file. Installing DOSKEY in upper memory so that it does not use any conventional memory requires that you create upper memory blocks. List the commands in CONFIG.SYS and AUTOEXEC.BAT to install DOSKEY in upper memory.

4

Upgrading Memory

To practice installing additional memory in a computer in a classroom environment, remove the SIMMs or DIMMs from one computer and place them in another computer. Boot the second computer and check that it counts up the additional memory. When finished, return the borrowed modules to the original computer.

Using MSD to View Memory

Access MSD, and then access its view of memory on your computer. Get a printout of the MSD memory report.

How Memory is Allocated

Use the /M option on the MEM command to list the ways in which three TSRs currently installed in the memory of your computer are using this memory. For example, for a mouse driver named MOUSE.SYS currently installed, type this command:

```
MEM/M MOUSE
```

Using MemMaker

On a PC using DOS and Windows 3.x that does not provide access to upper memory, print a MEM report similar to Figure 4-17. Use MemMaker to create the commands necessary at bootup to manage memory effectively. Print a new MEM report to verify the improvement. Print copies of the AUTOEXEC.BAT and CONFIG.SYS files before and after using MemMaker.

Troubleshooting Memory

Loosen a memory module on a system board and boot the PC. What error do you get? Don't forget to follow rules to protect the PC against ESD as you work.

Plan Memory Installation

Fill out the following table, referring back to Table 4-5 in the text.

Memory Configurations for a Pentium System Board

Bank 0	Bank 1	Total Memory
16 MB	16 MB	64 MB
16 MB	32 MB	
32 MB		64 MB
	4 MB	72 MB
32 MB	8 MB	
32 MB	16 MB	
	32 MB	128 MB
0		8 MB
0	8 MB	
	16 MB	32 MB
0		64 MB

Assume that this system board is using EDO, 60-ns, 72-pin SIMMs and currently has 32 MB of memory in Bank 1. Find and make a copy of a memory module ad. Mark in the ad the memory module that is needed by this system board to upgrade to 64 MB. How many modules are needed, and what is the total cost?

Real Mode in Windows 9x

Create a shortcut on your desktop to provide a DOS prompt running in real mode. *Hint*: Create a shortcut for COMMAND.COM and then change the properties for this shortcut. List the series of events that happen when you execute the DOS prompt shortcut and then return to regular Windows 9x.

5

FLOPPY DRIVES

In this chapter, you will learn:

- ♦ How data is stored on floppy disks
- ♦ How to use DOS and Windows commands to manage disks
- ♦ How to replace or install a disk drive
- ♦ About removable drives

We now move from the system board and memory to our first encounter with secondary storage: floppy drives and removable drives. You will learn how data is stored on a floppy disk, how to manage that data, and how to install a floppy disk drive on a PC. Although many have predicted that floppy drives will become obsolete, their convenience and availability, the low cost of disks, and their proven usefulness and dependability have solidly rooted them in the marketplace and on almost every personal computer system.

Most of the concepts about secondary storage examined in this chapter apply to your study of hard drives in Chapters 6 and 7. In addition to discussing floppy drives and their support, this chapter serves as a foundation for the next two.

Recall that memory is organized in two ways: physical (pertaining to hardware) and logical (pertaining to software). Similarly, data is stored on a secondary storage device physically and logically. Physical storage involves how data is written to and organized on the storage media, while logical storage involves how the OS and BIOS organize and view the stored data. This chapter explains first how data is physically stored on a floppy disk and then how the OS logically views the data.

INTRODUCTION TO HOW DATA IS PHYSICALLY STORED ON A DISK

A+*CORE*
    4.4

Years ago, floppy drives came in two sizes: 5¼ inches and 3½ inches. Today, new computers are equipped with only 3½-inch drives. However, because some computers still have 5¼-inch floppy disk drives, this section refers to 5¼-inch disks as well. Although they are larger, 5¼-inch disks do not hold as much data as 3½-inch disks because they do not store data as densely. Table 5-1 summarizes the capacity of the four common types of floppy disks. The 5¼-inch double-density disks and the 3½-inch extra-high-density disks are hardly ever seen; most disks today are 3½-inch high-density and hold 1.44 MB of data.

Table 5-1   Floppy disk types

Type	Storage Capacity	Number of Tracks per Side	Number of Sectors per Side	Cluster Type
3½-inch extra-high-density	2.88 MB	80	36	2 sectors
3½-inch high-density	1.44 MB	80	18	1 sector
3½-inch double-density	720K	80	9	2 sectors
5¼-inch high-density	1.2 MB	80	15	1 sector
5¼-inch double-density	360K	40	9	2 sectors

Regardless of disk size and density, the physical hardware used to access a disk looks and works much the same way. Figure 5-1 shows a floppy disk drive and connections. The data cable leaving the floppy drive leads to a controller for the drive on the system board. In older computers, the controller board was plugged into the expansion bus in an expansion slot. The board communicated with the CPU, passing data to and from the floppy disk. These controller boards were called I/O cards, and often served multiple functions, having connections for a hard drive, floppy drive, and serial and parallel ports. You still see some today, so they are covered in this chapter. Today, the controller is built into the system board so that the data cable goes directly from the drive to the system board.

A floppy drive is connected to either the controller card or system board by a 34-pin data cable. The cable has the controller connection at one end and a drive connection at the other. A second drive connection is placed in the middle of the cable to accommodate a second floppy drive. Having two drives share the same cable is a common practice for floppy drives as well as hard drives and CD-ROM drives.

Floppy drives receive power from the power supply by way of a power cord. The power cord plugs into the back of the drive and has a smaller connection than the power cord for other drives in the system.

Power cord

Data cable
connects to
system board

34-pin
data cable

Floppy
drive

Figure 5-1   Floppy drive subsystem: floppy drive, data cable, and power connection

How Data is Physically Stored on a Disk

A+CORE
1.1

Floppy disks, no matter what density or size, store data in much the same way. When first manufactured, disks have nothing written on them; they are blank sheets of magnetically coated plastic. Before data can be written on the disk, it must first be mapped in concentric circles called **tracks**, and in pie-shaped wedges called **sectors** (see Figure 5-2). This process of preparing the disk to receive data is called **formatting** the disk. Figure 5-2 shows a formatted 3½-inch double-density floppy disk. According to Table 5-1, there are 80 tracks or circles on the top side of the disk and 80 more tracks on the bottom. The tracks are numbered 0 through 79. Each side of the disk has 9 sectors, numbered 1 through 9. Although the circles or tracks on the outside of the disk are larger than the circles closer to the center, all tracks store the same amount of data. Data is written to the tracks as bits, either a 0 or 1. Each bit is a magnetized, rectangular-shaped spot on the disk. Between the tracks and spots are spaces that are not magnetized. This spacing prevents one spot from affecting the magnetism of a nearby spot. The difference between a 0 spot and a 1 spot is the orientation of the magnetization of the spot on the disk surface.

A+CORE
1.1

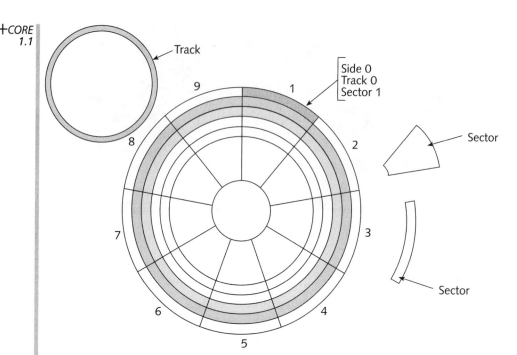

Figure 5-2   3½-inch double-density floppy disk showing tracks and sectors

Data is written to and read from the disk via a magnetic **read/write head** mechanism in the floppy drive (see Figure 5-3). Two heads are attached at the end of an actuator arm that freely moves over the surface of the disk. The arm has one read/write head above the disk and another below the disk. Moving in unison back and forth across the disk, the two heads lightly touch the surface of the disk, which is spinning at either 300 rpm (revolutions per minute) or 360 rpm, depending on the type of disk. (Note that the read/write heads of a hard drive never touch the surface.) Data is written first to the bottom and then to the top of the disk, beginning at the outermost circle and moving in. Eraser heads on either side of the read/write head, as shown in Figure 5-4, ensure that the widths of the data tracks do not vary. As the data is written, the eraser heads immediately behind and to the sides of the write head clean up both sides of the magnetized spot, making a clean track of data with no "bleeding" from the track. The magnetized area does not spread far from the track. All tracks are then the same width, and the distance between tracks is uniform.

Figure 5-3   Inside a floppy disk drive

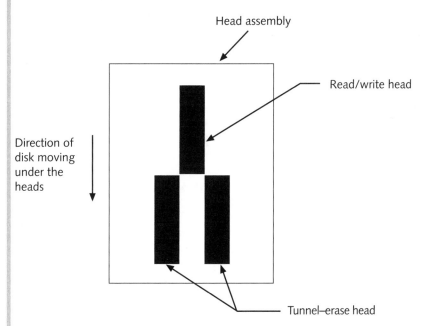

Figure 5-4   Uniform track widths are created by floppy drive read/write heads as the center head writes data while the two tunnel-erase heads clean up from behind

A+CORE
   1.1

The disk is actually a piece of Mylar similar to that used for overhead transparencies. Covering the surface of the Mylar is a layer of either cobalt oxide or iron oxide (rust) that can hold a magnetic charge. Some disks use another layer of Teflon to protect the oxide layer and to allow the read/write heads to move more smoothly over the surface. During formatting, the tracks are created by laying down a repeating character, the 3 (division) symbol in ASCII code, which is hex F6 or 1111 0110 in binary. The tracks are divided into sectors, and the sector that starts a new track is marked with a designated code. For 3½-inch floppy disks, the sector address mark written on the disk during formatting marks the beginning sector. After formatting, actual data is written on the disk by overwriting the F6h patterns on the tracks.

The different disk types use varying degrees of magnetic strength when data is written to a disk or when a disk is formatted. For example, a 3½-inch high-density disk can hold more data than a double-density disk because the data is written closer together. Data on the high-density disk is recorded at about twice the magnetic strength as data on the double-density disk. The high-density disk surface is not as sensitive to a magnetic field as the double-density is and therefore can handle data written to it with double the magnetic strength.

Many users have discovered that the less expensive double-density disks can be formatted as high-density, and that data can be written to the disk. Beware! Don't trust that disk with important data. The surface of a double-density disk is more sensitive to the magnetic field, and eventually the magnetic spots on the disk will affect each other, corrupting the data. The life span of an incorrectly formatted disk is very short. For this reason, always format a disk using the density for which it was manufactured.

When data is read from the disk surface, the read/write head changes roles. It passes over a track, waiting for the right position on the disk to appear. When the correct sector arrives, the controller board opens a gateway, and the magnetic charge on the disk passes voltage to the read/write head. The voltage is immediately amplified and passed to the controller board, which in turn passes the data to the expansion bus.

How Data is Logically Stored on a Disk

A+ OS
   1.3

In Figure 5-2, the part of a track that belongs to a single sector is marked; this segment of one track is also referred to as a sector. You can see that "sector" has two meanings: it describes the entire pie-shaped wedge on one side of a disk, as well as the single segment of one track or circle that falls within the wedge. In most of our discussions, sector means the segment of one track, unless we specify that we mean the entire wedge. A sector, or a segment of a track, as shown in Figure 5-2, always holds 512 bytes of data. This is true for all floppy disks, no matter what size or density. You will learn in Chapter 6 that this is also true for hard drives.

"Sector" refers to how data is physically stored on a disk, while "cluster" describes how data is logically organized. The BIOS manages the disk as physical sectors, but the OS considers the disk only as a long list of clusters that can each hold a fixed amount of data (see Figure 5-5).

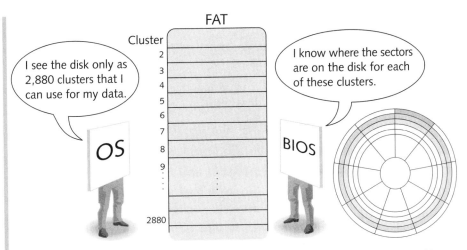

Figure 5-5   Clusters or file allocation units are managed by the OS in the file
allocation table (FAT), but BIOS manages these clusters as one or two
physical sectors on the disk

The OS reads data from and writes data to a disk in fixed-length chunks called clusters—a
cluster is therefore the smallest unit of data that can be read from or written to a disk at one
time. Because the OS manages a file on the disk as a group of clusters, a cluster is also called
a **file allocation unit**. The OS sees a disk as a long list of clusters, or file allocation units,
and keeps that list in a table called the **file allocation table** or **FAT**.

Look at a single track on the disk in Figure 5-2 to see how clusters relate to sectors. Recall
that there is a matching track on the bottom of the disk. The sector directly underneath the
top sector also holds 512 bytes of data. It is written to and read from at the same time as the
top sector. These two sectors together make up one cluster. On the 3½-inch double-density
floppy disk in Figure 5-2, each track has 9 sectors, and each side of the disk has 80 tracks. The
top side has 80 × 9, or 720 sectors, and so does the bottom. Because each cluster has two
sectors, the disk has 720 clusters. Each cluster holds 512 bytes × 2 = 1,024 bytes of data. One
disk has 1,024 × 720 = 737,280 bytes of storage space. Divide this number by 1,024 bytes
per kilobyte and you see that the storage capacity is 720 kilobytes.

Table 5-1 shows that a 3½-inch high-density floppy disk has 80 tracks and 18 sectors per track
on each side. Each side has 80 tracks × 18 sectors, or 1,440 sectors. This type of disk has only
one sector per cluster, making 1,440 × 2 sides, or 2,880 clusters. Because each cluster holds
512 bytes (one sector) of data, a 3½-inch high-density floppy disk has 2,880 × 512 = 1,474,560
bytes of data. Divide this number by 1,024 to convert bytes to kilobytes. The storage capacity
of this disk is 1,440 kilobytes. Divide by 1,000 to convert kilobytes to megabytes, and the storage is 1.44 MB.[1]

---

[1] There is a discrepancy in the computer industry regarding the definition of a megabyte. Sometimes
1 megabyte = 1,000 kilobytes; at other times, we use the relationship of 1 megabyte = 1,024 kilobytes.

The Formatting Process

The formatting of all disks is similar, no matter what size or density. During formatting, the Windows 9x or DOS FORMAT command without added options performs the following steps:

- Creates the tracks and sectors by writing tracks as a series of F6s in hex and, as necessary, writing the sector address mark to identify the beginning sector on a track

- Creates the master boot record (discussed below)

- Creates two copies of the file allocation table (FAT) (discussed in detail below)

- Creates the root directory

These basic steps are described in detail next. Later in this chapter you will learn how to add options to the formatting process.

Creating the Tracks and Sectors

The FORMAT command is a DOS and Windows 9x command that prepares a disk for use. The first step in the formatting process erases any data on the disk. In its simplest form, without adding any parameters, the FORMAT command always overwrites the data with the F6h character.

The Master Boot Record

During formatting, DOS or Windows 9x prepares the disk so that you can use it to read and write data. DOS and Windows 9x prepare a disk the same way. For the purposes of this discussion, you can think of Windows 95 as DOS 7 and Windows 98 as DOS 7.1.

At the beginning of each floppy disk, the first sector contains basic information about how the disk is organized, including the number of sectors, the number of sectors per cluster, the number of bits in each FAT entry, and other basic information that an OS or BIOS needs to read the data on the disk. This information is collectively called the **master boot record (MBR)**. At the end of the MBR is a small program that can be used to boot from the disk. Table 5-2 shows the layout of the MBR and its contents. The MBR, sometimes called the DOS boot record, indicates which version of DOS or Windows was used to format the disk, and is always located at the beginning of the disk at track 0, sector 1 (bottom of the disk, outermost track). This uniformity of layout and content allows any version of DOS or Windows to read any disk. A floppy disk has only one boot record, but a hard drive has at least two. On a floppy disk, the master boot record and the DOS boot record are the same record. On a hard drive, they are two different records, each with a different purpose. You will learn more about this in the next chapter.

Table 5-2   Contents of the master boot record

Bytes per sector
Sectors per cluster
Number of FATs
Size of the root directory
Number of sectors
Medium descriptor byte
Size of the FAT
Sectors per track
Number of heads (always 2)
Number of hidden sectors
Program to load the OS

5

A+ OS
3.1

The ninth item in Table 5-2 is the number of heads. A head refers to the read/write head that is a part of the physical components of the drive. Because the disk always has only one top and one bottom with a read/write head assigned to each, the number of heads is always two. The last item in Table 5-2 is the program that loads either DOS or Windows 9x. Some disks are bootable, meaning that they contain enough DOS code to load the OS—whatever it may be—into memory and to boot to the A or B prompt, depending on which drive contains the floppy disk. In Chapter 1, you learned that to make a disk bootable, it must include certain parts of the OS. For DOS, these parts are two hidden files and COMMAND.COM. These files can be loaded on the disk when it is formatted, or they can be loaded with the DOS SYS command. When Windows 9x creates a system disk (that is, a bootable disk), it copies COMMAND.COM and two hidden files, IO.SYS and MSDOS.SYS, to the disk to make the disk bootable.

All master boot records, however, are the same whether or not the disk is bootable. When the PC is looking for a bootable disk during POST, if a disk is in the drive, the program stored in the master boot record is executed. This program tries to load the startup files of the OS. On a bootable disk, the boot record contains the names of the two hidden files. For example, for IBM DOS 3.3, the filenames of the hidden files are IBMBIO.COM and IBMDOS.COM. The program looks for these two files on the disk. If it does not find them, the disk is not bootable and a message appears, such as the following:

```
Non-system disk or disk error...Replace and strike any key
when ready...Disk boot failure
```

POST terminates until the user intervenes. Only the program in the master boot record can determine if the disk is bootable.

The File Allocation Table (FAT)

Next, the FORMAT command writes two copies of the file allocation table (FAT) to the disk. The FAT lists the location of files on the disk in a one-column table. Because the width of each entry in the column is 12 bits, the FAT is called a 12-bit FAT or FAT 12. The FAT lists how each cluster or file allocation unit on the disk is currently used. (Remember that a cluster is the smallest unit of disk space allocated to a file.) A file is stored in one or more clusters that do not have to be contiguous on the disk. In the FAT, some clusters might be marked as bad (the 12 bits to mark a bad cluster are FF7h). These bits can be entered in the FAT when the disk is formatted or added later with the DOS RECOVER command. An extra copy of the FAT is kept immediately following the first. If the first is damaged, sometimes you can recover your data and files by using the second copy.

When the OS wants to write a file to a disk, the process works as follows. The name of the file, its size, and other attributes are written in a directory. Recall that a **directory**, in its simplest form, is a list of files on a disk. One piece of information kept in the directory concerning this file is the cluster number where the data begins (see Figure 5-6). Only the first cluster number is kept in the directory. The OS turns to the FAT to keep track of any additional clusters that are needed to hold the file.

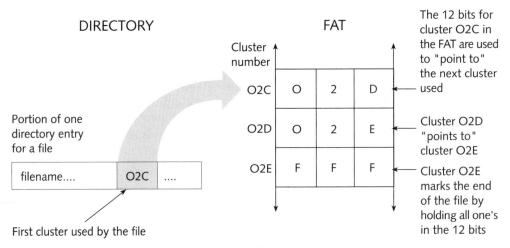

Figure 5-6   The OS keeps track of where a file is stored using a single entry in a directory and several entries in the FAT

In Figure 5-6, the beginning cluster number is 02Ch and is stored in the directory. The 12-bit FAT entry for cluster 02Ch contains 02Dh, or 0000 0010 1101 binary. This entry is interpreted as the next cluster, the second cluster, used by the file. Look in the FAT entry for cluster 02Dh to see what cluster is used next, if any. The entry in the FAT for cluster 02Dh is 02Eh, indicating that the file continues to a third cluster, 02Eh. The FAT entry for 02Eh is FFFh (binary 1111 1111 1111), the code for the last cluster used by the file. The file uses three clusters.

Figure 5-7 shows another FAT. In this example, the file contains 1,798 bytes. The file is stored beginning in cluster 4, then cluster 5, cluster 1C2, and cluster 1C3. Because this file is not stored in consecutive clusters, it is called a **fragmented file**. Recall that the beginning cluster number and the size of the file in bytes are stored in the disk's root directory. The disk is a 3½-inch high-density floppy disk, which has clusters equal to 1 sector, or 512 bytes.

Because the file is 1,798 bytes, this file requires 4 whole clusters or 2,048 bytes of disk space. The first FAT entry for the file tells you that the file starts in cluster 4. The cluster 4 table entry is 005, which points to the table entry for cluster 5. Remember that all disks have 12 bits for each FAT entry. The bits store 3 hex digits of 4 bits each. The location for cluster 5 has the hex numbers 1C2. In cluster 1C2, you see the hex numerals 1C3, which point to cluster 1C3. At cluster 1C3 you see FFF, which marks the end of the file. These four FAT entries are called a cluster chain. The **cluster chain** determines all cluster locations for a file on a disk.

5

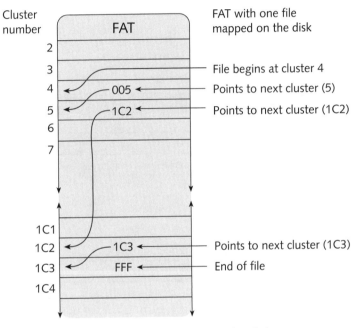

Figure 5-7   FAT with one file mapped on the disk

The Root Directory

After creating the file allocation tables, the formatting process sets up the root directory. Recall that the **root directory**, or **main directory**, is a table listing all the files assigned to this table. The root directory contains a fixed number of rows to accommodate a predetermined number of files and subdirectories; the number of available rows is dependent upon the disk type. The number of root directory entries for the four common disk types is listed in Table 5-3.

Table 5-3 Root directory entries (rows) for disk types

Disk Type	Number of Root Directory Entries
5¼-inch double-density	112
5¼-inch high-density	224
3½-inch double-density	112
3½-inch high-density	224

The root directory will later contain information about each file and subdirectory stored in it. Each directory entry is 32 bytes long, although only 22 bytes are used. Table 5-4 lists how the 22 bytes are used.

Table 5-4 Root directory information for each file

Root Directory Bytes	Usage
8	Name of file
3	File extension
1	Attribute byte (special meaning for each bit)
10	Not used
2	Time of creation or last update
2	Date of creation or last update
2	Starting cluster number in binary
4	Size of file in binary

A+ OS
1.2

Notice that the root directory contains only the starting cluster number. To find out what other clusters store the file, look in the file allocation table. By dividing the size of the file by the number of bytes per cluster and rounding up to the nearest whole number, you can determine how many clusters the file occupies.

Also note that there is no place for the period (often referred to as "dot") that we normally see between the filename and the file extension in DOS command lines. The period is not stored in directories but is only used in DOS command lines to indicate where the filename ends and the file extension begins. For the long filenames in Windows 9x, more room in the directory is required. This is provided by using more than one entry in the directory for a single file, enough to accommodate the length of the filename. Both the long filename and the DOS version short filename are stored in the directory.

Time and date of creation or last update are stored in a coded form that is converted to a recognizable form when displayed on the screen. The date and time come from the system date and time, which the OS gets from the real-time clock during the boot. For DOS, you can change these with the DOS DATE and TIME commands. For Windows 9x, change the date and time in the Control Panel. The earliest possible date allowed for both is 1/1/1980.

$A+ \begin{smallmatrix} OS \\ 1.2 \end{smallmatrix}$ The file attributes are used for various purposes. One file attribute byte is broken into bits; each bit has a specific meaning. The first two bits are not used. The meanings of the other 6 bits are listed in Table 5-5, beginning with the leftmost bit in the byte and moving to the right. You can use several Windows 9x and DOS commands to change the file attributes—you'll learn about many of them later in this chapter.

The root directory and all subdirectories contain the same information about each file. Only the root directory has a limitation on the number of entries. Subdirectories can have as many entries as disk space allows. Because long filenames require more room in a directory than short filenames, assigning long filenames reduces the number of files that can be stored in the root directory.

Table 5-5   Meaning of each bit in the directory attribute byte for each file (reading from left to right across the byte)

Bit	Description	Bit=0	Bit=1
1, 2	Not used		
3	Archive bit	Not to be archived	To be archived
4	Directory status	File	Subdirectory
5	Volume label	Not volume label	Is volume label
6	System file	Not system file	Is system file
7	Hidden file	Not hidden	Hidden
8	Read-only file	Read/write	Read-only

In summary, for DOS, the FORMAT command writes tracks and sectors on the disk, and creates a master boot record, an empty file allocation table, and an empty root directory. If you include the /S option in the FORMAT line, you add the two hidden files and COMMAND.COM that together make a disk bootable. The three files are referenced in the FAT and in the root directory. The two hidden files have their file attribute bit 7, the hidden bit, set to 1 (hidden). When you make a Windows 9x rescue disk, the two hidden files and COMMAND.COM are copied to the disk to make the disk bootable.

Using DOS to Manage a Floppy Disk

You can use several DOS commands to manage a floppy disk. DOS commands are categorized according to how the command is made available to DOS. **Internal DOS commands** are part of the COMMAND.COM program and so are automatically loaded into memory when COMMAND.COM is loaded. **External DOS commands** are stored as separate program files in the DOS directory. COMMAND.COM must search for and load these program files before the command can be executed. For more information about these and other DOS commands, type HELP followed by the command name at a DOS prompt, or type the command name followed by /? (slash and a question mark).

> **TIP** An external DOS command has a program file associated with it (such as FORMAT.COM), but an internal DOS command does not (for example, there is no program file named DIR.COM or DIR.EXE).

FORMAT drive: /U /V /S /Q /F:size Command

The DOS external FORMAT command discussed earlier in the chapter prepares a disk for use. If the drive is not specified, the command uses the default drive. The options for the FORMAT command are outlined in Table 5-6.

Table 5-6 DOS FORMAT command options

FORMAT Command Options	Description
/V	Allows you to enter a volume label only once when formatting several disks. The same volume label is used for all disks. A volume label is displayed at the top of the directory list to help you identify the disk.
/S	Stores the system files on the disk after formatting. Writes the two hidden files and COMMAND.COM to the disk, making the disk bootable. A bootable disk is called a **system disk**.
/Q	Recreates the root directory and FATs if you want to quickly format a previously formatted disk that is in good condition. /Q does not read or write to any other part of the disk.
/F:size	Specifies the size of a floppy disk. If the size is not specified, the default for that drive is used. The common values for size are: /F:360 is 360K, double-density 5¼-inch disk /F:1.2 is 1.2 MB, high-density 5¼-inch disk /F:720 is 720 K, double-density 3½-inch disk /F:1.44 is 1.44 MB, high-density 3½-inch disk
/U	Allows for an unconditional format of the disk, which does a more thorough job of formatting the disk by erasing all data. Use this option when you have been getting read/write errors on the disk.

LABEL Command

The LABEL command changes the volume label, or electronic name, on a disk. The volume label is stored at the beginning of the root directory and in the master boot record. Displayed at the top of the directory list when you use the DIR command, the label can be up to 11 characters long and can contain spaces.

DEL or ERASE Command

The **DEL** or **ERASE command** erases files or groups of files. Where the command does not include drive and directory information, like the following examples, DOS uses the default drive and directory when executing the command.

For example, to erase all the files in the A:\DOCS directory, use the following command:

```
C:\> ERASE A:\DOCS\*.*
```

To erase all the files in the current default directory, use the following command:

```
A:\DOCS> DEL *.*
```

To erase all files in the current directory that have no file extension, use the following command:

```
A:\DOCS> DEL *.
```

To erase the file named MYFILE.TXT, use the following command:

```
A:\> DEL MYFILE.TXT
```

UNDELETE Command

The **UNDELETE command** attempts to recover files that have been deleted. Following are some variations of the UNDELETE command.

To list the files that can be undeleted, without actually undeleting them, use the following command:

```
A:\>UNDELETE /list
```

To recover deleted files without prompting for confirmation on each file, use the following command:

```
A:\>UNDELETE /all
```

RECOVER Command

The **RECOVER command** attempts to recover a file from damaged sectors on a disk. Always specify the drive, path, and filename of the file you want to recover with the RECOVER command. If you want to recover several files, use the command on one file at a time.

To recover the file named MYFILE.TXT, use the following command:

```
RECOVER A:\DOCS\MYFILE.TXT
```

Whatever portion of the file that the RECOVER command can read is stored in the root directory and named A:FILE0000.REC (or the next available number). Copy this file to another disk before trying to recover the second file.

Because the RECOVER command might mark clusters as bad in the FAT, first use the DISKCOPY or copy command (described below) before using RECOVER. Data that might have been saved by other methods can sometimes be destroyed by the RECOVER command.

DISKCOPY Command

The **DISKCOPY command** makes an exact duplicate (sector by sector) of one floppy disk (called the source disk) to another disk of the same size and type (called the target disk).

To duplicate a floppy disk using only a single drive, use the following command:

```
C:\>DISKCOPY A: A:
```

DOS prompts you as many times as necessary to insert the source disk and then insert the target disk to make the exact copy. Data is copied from one disk to the other, byte by byte, including any hidden files, bad sectors, fragmented files, or other contents; everything is copied as is. For this reason, the copy can be faulty if the target disk has bad sectors. DISKCOPY ignores the fact that a sector is marked as bad in the FAT and copies to it anyway. The DISKCOPY command copies formatting information, so the target disk does not need to be formatted before executing the copy.

A+ OS 1.1 COPY Command

The **COPY command** copies a single file or group of files. The original files are not altered.

To copy a file from one drive to another, use the following command:

```
A:\>COPY drive:\path\filename.ext drive:\path\filename.ext
```

The drive, path, and filename of the original source file immediately follow the COPY command, and the drive, path, and filename of the destination file follow the source filename. If you do not specify the filename of the copy, DOS assigns the original name of the file. If you omit the drive or path of the source or the destination, then DOS uses the current default drive and path.

To copy the file MYFILE.TXT from the root directory of drive C to drive A, use the following command:

```
C:\>COPY MYFILE.TXT A:
```

Because a drive or path is not indicated before the filename MYFILE.TXT, DOS assumes the file is in the default drive and path.

To copy all files in the C:\DOCS directory to the floppy disk in drive A, use the following command:

```
C:\>COPY C:\DOCS\*.* A:
```

To make a backup file named SYSTEM.BAK of the SYSTEM.INI file in the \WINDOWS directory of the hard drive, use the following command:

```
C:\WINDOWS> COPY SYSTEM.INI SYSTEM.BAK
```

If you use the COPY command to duplicate multiple files, the files are assigned the names of the original files. When duplicating multiple files, no filename can be listed in the destination portion of the command line.

$A^+\substack{OS\\1.1}$ **XCOPY /M Command**

The **XCOPY command** is more powerful than the COPY command. It follows the same general command-source-destination format as the COPY command, but it offers several more options, as outlined next, with a couple of useful examples.

Use the /S option with the XCOPY command to copy all files in the directory \DOCS, as well as all subdirectories under \DOCS and their files, to the disk in drive A. Use the following command:

```
C:\>XCOPY C:\DOCS\*.* A: /S
```

To copy all files from the directory C:\DOCS created or modified March 14, 1999, use the following command:

```
C:\>XCOPY C:\DOCS\*.* A: /d:03/14/99
```

DELTREE

The **DELTREE command** deletes the directory tree beginning with the subdirectory you specify, including all subdirectories and all files in all subdirectories in that tree. Use it with caution!

```
C:\>DELTREE [drive:]path
```

Using Windows 9x to Manage a Floppy Drive

Windows 9x performs similar functions to those available with DOS and Windows 3.x. A few are covered here. Floppy disks as well as files and folders on the hard drive are managed using Windows Explorer.

Format a Disk and Make a System Disk Using Windows 9x

To format a floppy disk, follow these steps.

1. Click the **Start** button on the Taskbar, point to **Programs**, and then click **Windows Explorer**. Right-click either drive A or drive B. The menu in Figure 5-8 appears.

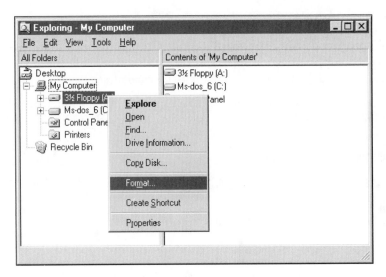

Figure 5-8   Menu to manage a floppy disk

2   Click **Format** on the menu. The dialog box shown in Figure 5-9 opens. Notice that you have three format options: Quick format (does not re-mark the tracks), Full format, or an option to copy just the system files to the disk (same as DOS SYS command).

3. Select the appropriate options to either format the disk or make the disk bootable.

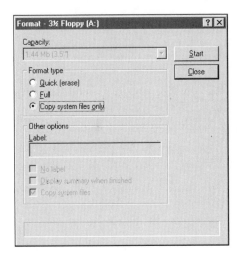

Figure 5-9   Format a disk in Microsoft Windows 9x

Copy Disk Command Using Windows 9x

If you select **Copy Disk** from the menu in Figure 5-8, a dialog box opens, as shown in Figure 5-10, where the disk listed under "Copy from" is the source disk, and the disk listed under "Copy to" is the target disk. Click **Start** to copy the disk.

Figure 5-10   Copying a disk using Windows 9x

Emergency Startup Disks

A+ OS 2.3

Although you normally boot from a hard drive, problems with the hard drive sometimes make it necessary to boot from a floppy disk. Always have a bootable disk called a **rescue disk** available for this purpose. For DOS, you must create your own disk, making sure it includes the necessary system files and any utilities (such as AUTOEXEC.BAT, EDIT.COM, and FDISK.EXE) that you might need in an emergency.

Beginning with Windows 95, the OS provided an automated method to create a system disk with useful utility programs on it. This rescue disk is called an **emergency startup disk (ESD)** and is created under the Control Panel, Add/Remove Programs group. Files that Windows 95 puts on an emergency startup disk are listed in Table 5-7, and files that Windows 98 stores on the disk are listed in Table 5-8. The use of some of these files will not be clear until Chapter 12.

The Windows 95 Emergency Startup Disk   When you create a Windows 95 emergency startup disk (rescue disk), the disk is formatted and system files are copied to the disk, just as when you make a bootable system disk. In addition to the files needed to boot in Windows 95, the files listed in Table 5-7 might be copied to the rescue disk, depending on the version of Windows 95 producing the disk. The table also describes the purpose of each file.

To create the disk, click **Start**, select **Settings**, and then click **Control Panel**. In the Control Panel, double-click **Add/Remove Programs**. When the Add/Remove Program Properties window appears, click the **Startup Disk** tab and then click **Create Disk**.

A+ OS
  2.3

Table 5-7   Emergency startup disk files created in Windows 95

File	Purpose
IO.SYS	Used to boot DOS
MSDOS.SYS	Startup configuration information
COMMAND.COM	Provides a DOS prompt
ATTRIB.EXE	Changes the attributes of a file
CHKDSK.EXE	Determines the status of a disk and repairs it
EDIT.COM	DOS Editor
EDIT.HLP	Help for EDIT.COM
FC.EXE	Compares files
FDISK.EXE	Used to partition a hard drive (covered in Chapter 6)
FORMAT.COM	Formats a floppy disk or hard drive
MEM.EXE	Displays information about memory
MORE.COM	Paginates the results of a command on screen
MSCDEX.EXE	CD-ROM driver
MSD.EXE	System diagnostics utility
SCANDISK.EXE	Checks and repairs hard drives
SCANDISK.INI	Initial parameters for SCANDISK.EXE
SETVER.EXE	Sets the DOS version for some programs
SYS.COM	Makes a floppy disk or hard drive bootable
XCOPY.EXE	Copy utility

Windows 98 Emergency Startup Disk   The Windows 98 emergency startup disk contains files similar to those in the Windows 95 version. It also contains additional support for CD-ROM drives, because Windows 98 assumes that you have installed the OS from a CD-ROM and will likely need the drive to recover from a problem.

A+ OS
2.3

Table 5-8   Emergency startup disk files created in Windows 98

File	Stored in Ebd.cab File	Purpose
Aspi2dos.sys		Adaptec CD-ROM drivers and supporting files
Aspi4dos.sys		
Aspi8dos.sys		
Aspicd.sys		
Attrib.exe	Yes	Manages file attributes
Autoexec.bat		Startup batch file
Btcdrom.sys		Mylex/BusLogic CD-ROM driver
Btdosm.sys		Mylex/BusLogic CD-ROM driver
Chkdsk.exe	Yes	Used to manage a disk
Command.com		DOS command interpreter
Config.sys		Startup file to load device drivers
Debug.exe	Yes	Used to examine a hard drive
Dryspace.bin		Used to manage a compressed hard drive
Ebd.cab		Cabinet file containing utility files
Ebd.sys		Identifies the startup disk to OS
Edit.com	Yes	DOS text editor
Extract.exe		Used to manage Ebd.cab
Extwrap.exe	Yes	New version of extract utility
Fdisk.exe		Partitions a hard drive (to be covered in Chapter 6)
Findramd.exe		Finds the RAM drive during startup
Flashpt.sys		Mylex/BusLogic CD-ROM driver
Format.com	Yes	Formats a disk
Himem.sys		Used to manage extended memory
Io.sys		Core OS file
Mscdex.exe	Yes	DOS utility to manage a CD-ROM drive
Msdos.sys		Information used to boot
Oakcdrom.sys		Atapi CD-ROM driver
Ramdrive.sys		Creates a RAM drive (to be covered in Chapter 6)
Readme.txt		Information to user
Scandisk.exe	Yes	Used to manage a hard drive
Setramd.bat		Used to create the RAM drive
Sys.com	Yes	Makes a disk bootable
Uninstal.exe	Yes	Uninstalls Windows 98

5

A+ OS
2.3,
3.2

Several files on the Windows 98 startup disk are compressed into a single cabinet file. A **cabinet file** has a CAB file extension and can store several files in a compressed form. Cabinet files are often used to distribute software. You can extract files from a cabinet file

A+ OS
2.3,
3.2

using the Extract.exe command that is included on the startup disk. To list the files that are compressed in a cabinet file, use this version of the Extract command:

```
Extract/d filename.cab
```

To extract a single file from a cabinet file, use the Extract command, specifying the name of the cabinet file and the name of the file you want to extract. For example, to extract myfile.txt from the cabinet file MYCABFIL.cab, use this command:

```
Extract MYCABFIL.cab myfile.txt
```

To extract all files in the cabinet file, use this command:

```
Extract MYCABFIL.cab *.*
```

The name of the cabinet file on the Windows 98 emergency startup disk is Ebd.cab. The files that are compressed into Ebd.cab are indicated in Table 5-8. In future chapters you will learn to use the startup disk to recover from a Windows 98 failure.

EXCHANGING AND SUPPORTING FLOPPY DRIVES

This section describes problems that can occur with a floppy drive and its support system, how to replace the drive, and how to add an additional floppy drive to a computer system. When a floppy drive cannot read a disk, the problem can have many causes. We cover several in detail.

Many computers today come with one 3½-inch floppy drive, a hard drive, and a CD-ROM drive. The machine might have one or two empty bays for a second floppy drive or for a Zip drive. If you don't have an extra bay and want to add another drive, you can attach an external drive that comes in its own case and has its own power supply.

Floppy drives are now so inexpensive that it is impractical to repair one. Once you've determined that the drive itself has a problem, open the case, remove the drive, and replace it with a new one. This procedure takes no more than 30 minutes, assuming that you don't damage or loosen something else in the process and create a new troubleshooting opportunity.

Using Floppy Drive Testing Software

Determining whether a drive is damaged takes only a short time if you have the proper software tools. You can use Nuts & Bolts diagnostic software, as well as MicroSystems Development Technologies, Inc.'s TestDrive at the end of the chapter. The explanation below of what the drive-testing software checks will help you solve drive problems and give you some insight into how floppy drives work. Working with floppy drive diagnostic software, you can test these criteria:

- **Azimuth skew:** Does the drive head align well with the tracks, or is it at a tangent (see Figure 5-11)?

- **Hub centering:** Does the disk wobble as it turns, or does it turn in a perfect circle?

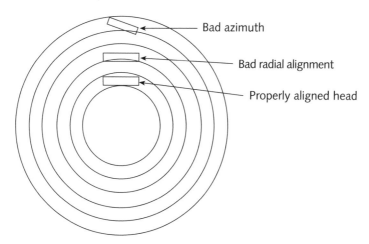

Figure 5-11   Alignment of floppy drive heads

- **Hysteresis:** Can the drive find a track regardless of the direction from which it approaches the track?

- **Radial alignment:** Is the drive head centered correctly on the track, or is it too far to the left or the right (see Figure 5-11)?

- **Rotational speed:** Does the drive turn the floppy disk at the proper speed?

- **Sensitivity:** How far from the data must the head be before it can read the data?

Over time, floppy drives can slowly shift out of alignment. A symptom of this problem is that a disk written by one drive cannot be read by another drive. To check thoroughly for these kinds of problems, the testing software must have a disk that it can use as its standard. The software determines how the drive reads the data from a disk that it knows to be written perfectly. These disks are known as **digital diagnostic disks** or **DDDs** and can be purchased at computer stores. The TestDrive software used in the end-of-chapter projects uses a DDD for several of its tests. You are asked to only complete those tests that don't require the DDD disk.

When a Floppy Disk Drive Doesn't Work

A+CORE
2.1

Sometimes a problem with the floppy drive arises during POST, and BIOS displays an error message. Error messages in the 600 range occur when the floppy drive did not pass the POST test. These problems can be caused by the power supply, the drive, the controller board, or the system board.

Even if POST finds no errors, you might still have a problem. If you put a disk in a faulty drive and issue a command to access the disk, an error message such as the following might appear on the screen:

```
General failure reading drive A, Abort, Retry, Fail?
```

A+CORE
  2.1

If nothing happens and the computer simply stops working, the problem might have several causes, including the following:

- The application you are running is pointing to a different drive.

- DOS or Windows 9x just encountered an unrelated error that has locked up the system.

- The System BIOS or CMOS setup is not correctly configured.

- The disk in the drive is not formatted.

- The floppy drive is bad.

- The shuttle window on the floppy disk cannot open fully.

- The floppy drive controller card is loose in the expansion slot or has a bad chip.

- The cable from the controller card to the drive is damaged or poorly connected.

- The edge color on the cable is not aligned with Pin 1.

- The power supply is bad.

- The power supply cable to the drive is loose or disconnected.

- The command just issued has a mistake or is the wrong command.

- The drive latch is not closed, or the disk is inserted incorrectly.

You might discover more items to add to this list. I once helped someone with a drive error. We took the 3½-inch floppy disk out of the drive and opened the shuttle window (the spring-loaded metal cover that opens to reveal the disk inside the plastic housing) to find a blade of grass on the disk surface. We removed the grass, and the disk worked perfectly. She then remembered that she had dropped the disk in the grass. When you have any computer trouble, check the simple things first. Here are a few suggestions for solving drive problems:

- Remove the disk. Does the shuttle window move freely? Do you see any dirt, hair, or blades of grass on the disk's Mylar surface? Does the disk spin freely inside the housing cover? Some new disks simply need a little loosening up. Put the disk back in the drive and try to access it again.

- Does the light on the correct drive go on? Maybe you are trying to access drive B, but the disk is in drive A.

- Does another disk work in the drive? If so, the problem is probably caused by the disk, not the drive. The exception is when the drive is out of alignment. When it is, the drive cannot read a disk that it did not format, although it might read a disk that it formatted with its own alignment. To test this possibility, try several disks, and note whether the drive reads only those disks that it has recently formatted. If so, then you might have identified the problem, and you can replace the drive.

- Does the drive light come on? If not, the problem might be with the software or the hardware. Try to access the disk with other software. Can DOS access the drive with a simple DIR A: command? Can File Manager or Windows Explorer access the disk? How about using the CHKDSK A: command? If the light doesn't come on even then, the problem might involve the power to the drive or the hardware connections inside the case. Does the other drive work? If both lights do not come on, consider the power supply or the floppy drive controller card as the source of your problem.

- Does the light come on and then stay on at boot? This is most likely caused by the cable not being attached correctly to Pin 1. Check the edge color to see that it is aligned with Pin 1.

- Has this drive been used recently? Perhaps the system setup has lost CMOS data. The system might think it has a 720K drive when it really has a 1.44 MB drive. Access setup and check the drive specifications.

- Reboot the machine and try again. Many problems with computers disappear with a simple reboot. If a soft boot doesn't do it, try a hard boot.

- Try cleaning the drive's read/write heads. Use a head-cleaning kit that includes a paper disk and a cleaning solution. Follow the directions that come with the kit. You can purchase a kit at any store that sells computer supplies.

- If the drive still does not work with any disk and any software, then you must dig deeper. Inside the case, the hardware that can cause this problem is the drive itself, the data cable from the controller card to the drive, the power supply, the power cable, or the system board. To find the culprit, replace each hardware component with a known good component, one component at a time, until the problem goes away. It is helpful to have access to another working computer from which you can borrow parts.

> **TIP** When you are trying to discover which device is causing a problem during a troubleshooting session, you can trade a suspected device for one you know is good (called a known-good device). You can also install the device you suspect is bad in a computer system you know is working. If the problem follows the device, then you know the device is bad.

- Turn off the computer and open the computer case. Check every connection from the system board to the drive. Check the power cable connection. Remove the controller card. If the second drive works, there is a chance (but not a guarantee) that the problem is not the card or its connection. Using a clean white eraser, clean the edge connector and reseat the board.

- Take the power cable from the second working floppy drive and put it on the nonworking one to eliminate the power cable as the problem.

- Replace the data cable and try the drive again. Make sure to align the cable correctly with Pin 1. Exchange the controller card. If that does not work, exchange the drive itself and try again.

- If the drive still does not work, suspect the system board or the ROM BIOS on the system board.

A+CORE 2.1 ## Some Common Error Messages and Their Meanings

Here are some common error messages that might be caused by problems with a floppy drive, together with what they mean.

```
Non-system disk or disk error. Replace and strike any key
when ready.
```

This message says that you are trying to boot from a disk that is not bootable. Remove the disk from the drive and press any key. The computer bypasses the floppy drive and loads the OS from the hard drive. If you intended to boot from the floppy drive, such as to boot DOS, the disk should have been formatted with the /S option, or you should have used the SYS command to place the two hidden DOS system files on the disk with COMMAND.COM. These three files are necessary to load DOS. To boot from a rescue disk in Windows 9x, first create the rescue disk as described earlier in the chapter.

If you had no disk in the floppy drive, you can assume that some of your critical OS files are missing from the hard drive. In this case, boot from a bootable floppy disk or rescue disk, and check whether the files have been erased accidentally from your hard drive.

```
Invalid or missing COMMAND.COM
```

This error appears when DOS is loading and the two hidden files are present, but COMMAND.COM is not present or is corrupt. Boot from a bootable disk that has COMMAND.COM and then copy the file to the disk that you want to be bootable.

```
Incorrect DOS version
```

This message appears when you try to use a DOS command such as FORMAT or BACKUP. Remember that these are external commands in DOS because they require a program to execute that is not part of COMMAND.COM. DOS contains a number of programs that reside on the hard drive in a directory named \DOS or, in the case of Windows 9x, in a directory named \Windows\Command. When you type the FORMAT or BACKUP command, you are executing these programs. DOS knows which version of DOS these programs belong to and the error message indicates that the FORMAT or BACKUP program you are using does not belong to the same version of DOS that you have loaded. To determine the version of DOS currently loaded, use the VER command.

```
Invalid Drive Specification
```

You are trying to access a drive that the OS does not know is available. For example, the error might appear in this situation: During booting, an error message indicates that BIOS cannot access the hard drive. You boot from a floppy disk in drive A and see an A prompt. You then try to access drive C from the A prompt, and you see the above message. DOS or Windows 9x is telling you that it can't find drive C because it failed the test during POST. As far as the OS is concerned, the hard drive does not exist.

```
Not ready reading drive A:, Abort, Retry, Fail?
```

This message means the floppy disk in drive A is not readable. Perhaps the disk is missing or is inserted incorrectly. The disk might have a bad boot record, errors in the FAT, or bad sectors. Try using Nuts & Bolts or Norton Utilities to examine the disk for corruption.

```
General failure reading drive A:, Abort, Retry, Fail?
```

A+CORE
2.1

This message means the floppy disk is badly corrupted or not yet formatted. Sometimes this error means that the floppy drive is bad. Try another disk. If you determine that the problem is the disk and not the drive, the disk is probably unusable. A bad master boot record sometimes gives this message.

```
Track 0 bad, disk not usable
```

This message typically occurs when you are trying to format a disk using the wrong disk type. Check your FORMAT command. Most manufacturers write the disk type on the disk. If you have a 3½-inch floppy disk, you can tell if you are using a high-density or double-density disk by the see-through holes at the corners of the disk. The high-density disk has holes on two corners; the double-density has a hole on only one corner. Don't try to format a disk using the wrong density.

```
Write-protect error writing drive A:
```

The disk is write-protected and the application is trying to write to it. To write to a 3½-inch floppy disk, the write-protect window must be closed, meaning that the switch must be toward the center of the disk so that you cannot see through the write-protect hole. To write to a 5¼-inch floppy disk, the write-protect notch must be uncovered.

If you have a damaged floppy disk, you can probably recover most, if not all, of the data on the disk, especially when you understand how the data is stored and have the right tools for the job. These data recovery techniques are covered in Chapter 7.

Replacing a Floppy Drive

A+CORE
1.2,
1.7

Following is a five-step summary of how to replace a floppy drive. Each step is described in more detail below:

1. Check that the computer and other peripherals are working. Can you boot to the hard drive or another floppy drive? You should know your starting point.

2. Turn off the computer and remove the cover.

3. Unplug the data cable and power cable from the old drive. Unscrew and dismount the drive.

4. Slide the new drive into the bay. Reconnect the data cable and power cable.

5. Turn the computer on and check the setup. Test the drive. Turn the computer off and replace the cover.

Now let's look at each step in detail.

Check that the computer and other peripherals are working. Can you boot to the hard drive or another floppy drive? You should know your starting point. Imagine yourself in the following situation. You are asked to install a floppy disk drive in a computer. You remove the cover, install the drive, and turn on the PC. Nothing happens. No power, no lights, nothing. Or perhaps the PC does not boot successfully, giving errors during POST that appear to have nothing to do with your newly installed floppy drive. Now you don't know if you created the problem or if it existed before you started. That is why you check

A+CORE 1.2, 1.7 the computer before you begin and make sure you know what's working and not working. The extra time is well worth it if you face a situation like this.

Here is a suggestion for a quick system check of a PC that you should do before you start to work:

- Turn on the computer and verify that it boots to the OS with no errors.
- For DOS systems with Windows 3.x, enter Windows 3.x to be sure it works well.
- Using Windows 3.x or Windows 9x, open a program and perform a task from the program.
- Get a directory listing of files on a floppy disk and a CD-ROM.
- For DOS with Windows 3.x, exit Windows and run the CHKDSK command.
- For Windows 9x, do a ScanDisk.

Turn off the computer and remove the cover. As you learned in Chapter 3, guard the computer against static electricity by using a ground bracelet, working on a hard floor (not on carpet), and grounding yourself before you touch any components inside the case. *Never* touch anything inside the case while the power is on. Remove the cover and set its screws aside in a safe place.

Next, prepare to remove the power cable. The power supply cable is a four-pronged cable that attaches to the back of the drive as in Figure 5-12. The cable can be difficult to detach because the connection is very secure. Be careful not to apply so much pressure that you break off the corner of the logic board. Steady the board with one hand while you dislodge the power cable with the other.

Floppy drive

Power cord

Figure 5-12 Power supply connection on the back of the drive (note how well this drive manufacturer has labeled Pin 1 on the data connection)

A+CORE
1.2,
1.7,
1.4

Unplug the data cable and power cable from the old drive and unscrew and dismount the drive. Before removing the cables and the drive, note carefully how they are assembled to help you reassemble later. The data cable might go to an adapter card or directly to the system board. Before removing the cable, note that the cable has a color or stripe down one side. This edge color marks this side of the cable as pin 1. Look on the board to which the cable is attached. Verify that pin 1 or pin 2 is clearly marked either by a number embossed on the board or by a square solder pad on the bottom of the circuit board and that the colored edge is aligned with pin 1 on both the board and the drive. Sometimes pin 1 on the floppy drive is marked, and sometimes the drive housing is constructed so that the cable built for the drive inserts in only one direction. Note the position of pin 1 on the drive.

Look at the cable connecting drive A to the floppy drive controller card or to the system board. There is a twist in the cable. This twist reverses these leads in the cable, causing the addresses for this cable to be different from the addresses for the cable that doesn't have the twist. The cable with the twist determines which drive will be drive A (see Figure 5-13). This drive is always the one that the startup BIOS looks to first for a bootable disk, unless a change has been made in CMOS setup, instructing startup BIOS to look to a different drive. By switching the cable with the twist with the cable without the twist, you exchange drives A and B. Some computers have two drives attached to the same cable. In this case, the drive attached behind the twist is drive A, and the one attached before the twist is drive B. After you are familiar with the cable orientation and connection, remove the cable from the floppy drive.

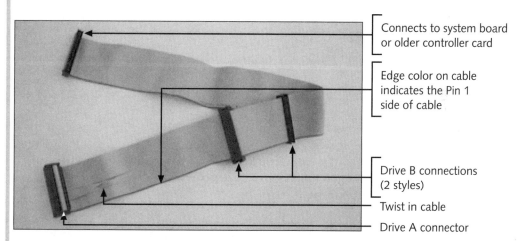

Connects to system board or older controller card

Edge color on cable indicates the Pin 1 side of cable

Drive B connections (2 styles)

Twist in cable

Drive A connector

Figure 5-13   Twist in cable determines which drive will be drive A

5

Floppy drive

Twist in cable

Colored edge connector

Pin 1 of edge connector

Power connector

Figure 5-14 Connect colored edge of cable to Pin 1

Now that the cables are detached, you can remove the floppy drive. Some drives have one or two screws on each side of the drive attaching the drive to the drive bay. After you remove the screws, the drive usually slides to the front and out of the case. Sometimes you must lift a catch underneath the drive as you slide the drive forward. Be careful not to remove any screws that hold a circuit card on top of the drive to the drive housing; all this should stay intact.

Slide the new drive into the bay. Reconnect the data cable and power cable. If the new drive is too narrow to fit snugly into the bay, you can buy an adapter kit with extensions for narrow drives that allow them to reach the sides of the bay. Screw the drive down with the same screws used on the old drive. You might have difficulty reaching the screw hole on the back of the drive if it is against the side of the case. Make sure the drive is anchored so that it cannot slide forward or backward or up or down even if a user turns the case on its side (as many users do).

Next you reconnect the data cable, making sure that the colored edge of the cable is connected to the Pin 1 side of the connection, as shown in Figure 5-14. Most connections on floppy drives are oriented the same way, so this one probably has the same orientation as the old drive. The power cable goes into the power connection only one way, so you can't go wrong here.

Turn the computer on, check the setup, and test the drive. Double-check all connections and turn on the computer. If you changed disk types, you must inform CMOS setup by accessing setup and changing the drive type. Test the drive by formatting a disk or doing a DISKCOPY. If you determine that all is well, replace the cover and you're done.

A+CORE
1.2

Note that you can run the computer while the cover is off. If the drive doesn't work, having the cover off makes it easier to turn off the computer, check connections, and try again. Just make certain that you don't touch anything while the computer is on. Leaving the computer on while you disconnect a cable and connect it again is very dangerous for the PC and will probably damage something.

Adding a New Drive

Adding a new drive is no problem if you have an empty bay, an extra power cable, and an extra connection on the floppy drive data cable. Slide the drive into the bay, screw it down, connect the cable and power cable, change setup, and you're done.

Let's consider the problems that might occur. If you don't have an extra power cable, you can use a "Y" splitter on the power cable for the existing floppy drive to provide the power connection. Most computers have only a single floppy drive cable with two connectors on it: one at the end of the cable and one in the middle.

In either case, look for the twist in the cable shown in Figure 5-14 and install the twist so that drive A is the top drive in the bay. In most cases, orient the drives so that drive A is on the left or on the top, and drive B is on the right or on the bottom. Though the computer really doesn't care where the drives are located; it's looking only for the twist in the cable, it's easier for you to have them placed this way. If you have A and B drives, you can exchange the drives to be B and A simply by exchanging the data cable connections.

REMOVABLE DRIVES

Using a removable drive provides several advantages: (1) It increases the overall storage capacity of a system, (2) makes it easy to move large files from one computer to another, (3) serves as a convenient medium for making backups of hard drive data, and (4) makes it easy to secure important files. (To keep important files secure, keep the removable drive in a safe when it is not being used.) A removable drive can be either an external or internal drive.

When purchasing a removable drive consider how susceptible the drive is when dropped. The **drop height** is the height from which the manufacturer says you can drop the drive without making the drive unusable. Also consider how long the data will last on the drive. The **half-life** (sometimes called life expectancy or shelf life) of the disk is the time it takes for the magnetic strength of the medium to weaken by half. Magnetic media, including traditional hard drives and floppy disks, have a half-life of five to seven years, but optical media such as CD-ROMs have a half-life of 30 years.

An internal removable drive should also be Plug and Play compliant, meaning that the drive can interface with Plug and Play BIOS and with Windows 9x and Windows 2000 installations without having to set switches and jumpers manually.

High-capacity Disk Drives

The Iomega 3½-inch Zip drive stores 100 MB or 250 MB of data on each of its disks and has a drop height of 8 feet (See Figure 5-15). An internal 100-MB Zip drive costs less than $100 and uses an IDE interface. An IDE interface is a way for a storage device to connect to a computer system and is covered in detail later. The external Zip drive plugs into the parallel port, a USB port, or a SCSI port. The drive and disk look like a traditional 3½-inch floppy disk drive and disk, but the disk is slightly larger. If you include a Zip drive on a new PC, consider it an add-on, not a replacement for the standard 3½-inch disk drive.

Another removable drive technology is SuperDisk LS-120 (laser servo 120 MB), developed by Imation. The disk holds 120 MB of data and is backward compatible with double-density (720K) and high-density (1.44 MB) floppy disks. The SuperDisk is really two disk drives in one. It can use the old technology to read from and write to regular floppy disks, and it can use laser technology to read/write 120 MB. SuperDisk is up to 27 times faster than regular floppy drives. One advantage SuperDisk has over Zip drives is its backward compatibility with regular floppy disks. SuperDisk drives can be purchased as external (parallel port and USB) or internal drives for about $150.

Figure 5-15   An internal Zip drive kit includes the IDE Zip drive, documentation, drivers on floppy disk, and one Zip disk

Hard Disk Removable Drives

The Iomega Jaz drive is one example of a magnetic media removable drive that stores 1 GB or 2 GB of data on each removable disk. Both the internal and external models use a SCSI connection. Iomega advertises that you can back up 1 GB of data from your fixed hard drive to the Jaz drive in as little as five minutes. The drop height is 3 feet.

Installing a Removable Drive

Installing an internal removable drive is similar to installing a hard drive and is discussed in later chapters. If the external or internal drive is a SCSI drive, the SCSI host adapter must already be installed and configured. How to install a SCSI host adapter is covered in Chapter 7. Do the following to install an external removable drive:

1. Identify the connectors. Many removable drives use either the parallel port, a USB port, or a SCSI port for connection. A parallel drive has a 25-pin connector for the cable to the 25-pin parallel port on the back of the PC and another 25-pin connector for the printer cable. A SCSI drive has a 25-pin, 50-pin, 68-pin connector on the drive for the cable to the PC and another connector for the next SCSI device on the external SCSI bus. For USB, there might be a second USB connection on the device for pass-through to another USB device.

2. For a parallel device, turn off your PC and connect the parallel cable from the drive to the parallel port on the PC. If you have a printer, connect the printer cable to the printer port on the drive. Go to Step 6.

3. For a USB device, connect the USB cable to the USB port. Go to Step 6.

4. For a SCSI device, with the SCSI host adapter installed, connect the SCSI cable to the drive and to the SCSI port on the host adapter.

5. For a SCSI drive, set the drive's SCSI ID. You might also need to set the host adapter to recognize an external device. See the documentation for the host adapter.

6. Check all your connections and plug the AC power cord for the drive into a wall socket.

7. Turn on your PC and install the software. See the installation procedures in the documentation that came with the removable drive. Most often, the software is on an accompanying disk.

8. If you have problems, turn everything off and check all connections. Power up and try again.

Chapter Summary

- ❏ Floppy disks are popular because they are cheap and convenient, and are considered a standard device.

- ❏ Data is stored on floppy disks in concentric circles called tracks or cylinders. Each track is divided into sectors. Each sector holds 512 bytes of data.

5

❑ Different types of floppy disks vary according to the organization of tracks and sectors, the density at which data can be stored, and the intensity of the magnetic spot on the magnetized plastic surface of the disk.

❑ The smallest unit of space allocated to a file is called a cluster. On 3½-inch high-density floppy disks, 1 cluster is the same as 1 sector, which is 512 bytes.

❑ When a disk is formatted for use, the formatting process creates tracks and sectors and places a master boot record, file allocation table (FAT), and root directory on the disk.

❑ For DOS, two hidden files and COMMAND.COM must be written on a disk for it to be a system, or bootable, disk.

❑ DOS and Windows 9x offer similar commands to manage files on a floppy disk.

❑ Installing a floppy disk drive in a PC involves firmly anchoring the drive in the bay, connecting the data cable and power cable, and informing CMOS setup of the new drive.

❑ The computer distinguishes drive A from drive B by a twist in the data cable. The drive with the twist is drive A.

❑ The three most popular removable drives are Zip, SuperDisk, and Jaz drives.

❑ External removable drives use either a USB port, parallel port, or a SCSI port to interface with the CPU.

KEY TERMS

Cabinet file — A file that contains one or more compressed files, and is often used to distribute software on disk. The Extract command is used to extract one or more files from the cabinet file.

Cluster — One or more sectors that constitute the smallest unit of space on a disk for storing data (also referred to as a file allocation unit). Files are written to a disk as groups of whole clusters.

Cluster chain — A series of clusters used to hold a single file.

COPY command — A command that copies files from one location to another (for example, COPY FILE.EXT A: is used to copy the file named FILE.EXT to the floppy disk in drive A).

DEL command — A command that deletes files (for example, DEL A:FILE.EXT deletes the file named FILE.EXT from drive A).

DELTREE command — A command used to delete a directory, all its subdirectories, and all files within it (for example, DELTREE DIRNAME deletes the directory named DIRNAME and everything in it).

Digital diagnostic disk — A floppy disk that has data written on it that is precisely aligned, which is used to test the alignment of a floppy disk drive.

Directory — A DOS table that contains file information such as name, size, time and date of last modification, and the cluster number of the file's beginning location.

DISKCOPY command — A command that copies the entire contents of one disk to another disk of the same type, while formatting the destination disk so that the two will be identical (for example, DISKCOPY A: A: uses drive A to duplicate a disk).

Drop height — The height from which a manufacturer states that its drive can be dropped without making the drive unusable.

Emergency startup disk (ESD) — A Windows 9x system disk that also contains some Windows 9x diagnostic and utility files. The ESD serves Windows 9x as a rescue disk. Also see rescue disk.

ERASE command — Another name for the DEL command.

File allocation table (FAT) — A table on a disk that tracks the clusters used to contain a file.

File allocation units — *See* Cluster.

Formatting (a floppy disk) — To prepare a new floppy disk for use by placing tracks or cylinders on its surface to store information (for example, FORMAT A:). Old disks can be reformatted, but all data on them will be lost.

Fragmented file — A file that has been written to different portions of the disk so that it is not in contiguous clusters.

Half-life — The time it takes for a medium storing data to weaken to half of its strength. Magnetic media, including traditional hard drives and floppy disks, have a half-life of five to seven years.

Internal DOS commands — DOS commands whose coding is contained within COMMAND.COM and therefore are automatically loaded into memory when COMMAND.COM is loaded.

Master boot record (MBR) (of a floppy disk) — The record written near the beginning of a floppy disk, containing information about the disk as well as the startup operating system programs.

Read/write head — A sealed, magnetic coil device that moves across the surface of a disk either reading or writing data to the disk.

RECOVER command — A command that recovers files that were lost because of a corrupted file allocation table.

Removable drives — High-capacity drives, such as Zip or Jaz drives, that have disks that can be removed like floppy disks.

Rescue disk — A floppy disk that can be used to start up a computer when the hard drive fails to boot. Also see Emergency startup disk.

Root directory — The main directory on a disk (often represented as C:\ on a hard drive), which typically contains other directories, such as Windows and MSOffice.

Sector — On a disk surface, one segment of a track, which almost always contains 512 bytes of data. Sometimes a single wedge of the disk surface is also called a sector.

System disk — A floppy disk containing enough of an operating system to boot.

Track — The disk surface is divided into many concentric circles, each called a track.

5

UNDELETE command — A command that resets a deleted file's directory entry to normal, provided the clusters occupied by the file have not been overwritten and the file entry is still in the directory list.

XCOPY command — A faster external DOS COPY program that can copy subdirectories (/S) (for example, XCOPY *.* A:/S).

REVIEW QUESTIONS

1. How many sectors per track are there on a 3½" high-density floppy disk?

2. What two cables are connected to a floppy drive inside a computer?

3. What symbol is written to a disk to indicate that the track is formatted and data can be written to it?

4. What is the difference between a sector and a cluster?

5. What is another name for a cluster?

6. What is the purpose of the master boot record on a disk?

7. If a file is fragmented, describe how the entries in the FAT will look.

8. What cluster information for a file is found in the directory entry for the file?

9. Which bit in the file attribute byte tells if the file is a hidden file?

10. What is the difference between an external DOS command and an internal DOS command?

11. How can you make an exact copy of a disk if you only have one floppy drive on your computer?

12. List the steps to create an emergency startup disk using Windows 95.

13. Why is it helpful to have EDIT.COM on the startup disk?

14. If a floppy drive is not working, why is it better to replace the drive than to repair it?

15. What might cause the error, "General failure reading drive A"?

16. How can you look at a 3½-inch floppy disk and tell if it is a high-density or double-density disk?

17. What do you check if you get the error, "Write protect error writing drive A:"?

18. List the steps that you would follow to install a new floppy drive as drive B.

19. How does the computer distinguish drive A from drive B?

20. Which holds more data, a Zip drive or a Jaz drive?

PROJECTS

Unless you follow proper procedures, working inside your computer can cause serious damage—to both you and your computer. To ensure safety in your work setting, follow every precaution listed in the *Read This Before You Begin* section following this book's Introduction.

Floppy Drive Troubleshooting and Installations

1. Use a PC with A and B drives. Reverse the drives so that drive A is B and drive B is the new A. Test by booting from the new drive A. When you are finished, return the drives to their original assignments to avoid confusing other users.

2. Use a PC with only a drive A. First, verify that you can boot from drive A with a bootable disk. Then turn off the computer and open the case and examine the data cable to drive A. Look for the twist in the cable. Verify that the cable is connected to the drive so that the twist is in line. Change the cable so that there is no twist between the drive and the controller. Turn on the PC and try to boot from drive A again. Describe what happens. After you are finished, turn off the computer and restore the cable to its original position.

3. Reverse the orientation of the floppy drive cable connection to the floppy drive controller so that the edge connector is not aligned with Pin 1. Boot the PC. Describe the problem as a user would describe it. Turn off the computer and restore the cable to the correct orientation.

4. In a lab setting, practice installing a floppy disk drive in a PC by working with a partner. Turn off the computer and remove a floppy drive from your PC and replace it with the floppy drive from your partner's PC.

5. Does the ROM BIOS for your computer support an extra-high-density 3½-inch floppy disk drive? List the drive types it does support. (*Hint*: See your setup screen.)

6. Change the floppy drive type in CMOS setup for one of the floppy drives on your PC to make it incorrect. (Make sure you don't change the hard drive type accidentally.) Reboot. What error did you see? Now correct the setting and reboot to make sure all components work again.

5

Using Nuts & Bolts to Examine a Floppy Disk

Using the Nuts & Bolts utility on the accompanying CD, follow these directions to examine a floppy disk.

1. In Windows 9x, click **Start**, point to **Programs, Nuts & Bolts,** and select **Discover Pro** from the list of utilities.
2. Click the **Drives** tab.
3. On the Drives tab, click **Advanced**.
4. On the left side of the Discover Pro Advanced window, click **drive A**. Print the Discover Pro report of the disk in drive A.

Using Diagnostic Software

MicroSystems Development provides a diagnostic program called TestDrive for examining and diagnosing problems with floppy drives and floppy disks. You can find a demo version on the Web that you can download from the company's site:

www.msd.com/diags/

When you download or copy the zipped file to your PC, explode it, and then do the following. (Most of the options on the TestDrive menu require that you have a DDD disk, but you can perform a few tests without one.)

Execute the TestDrive software by double-clicking the file **TESTDRIVE.COM** in Windows Explorer. The menu shown in Figure 5-16 appears. Select the option to perform the Write/Read test. The warning box shown in Figure 5-17 appears. Perform the test with a disk that has nonessential data on it that can be erased. While the test is running, answer these questions.

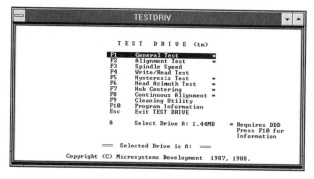

Figure 5-16   TestDrive main menu

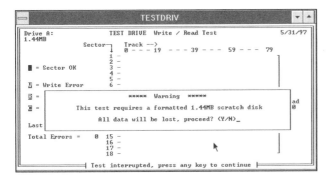

Figure 5-17   TestDrive's Write/Read Test

1. In what order are these components on the disk tested: heads, tracks, and sectors?

2. Did you get any errors? If so, where?

3. If you got a significant number of errors, try another disk. Do you see a pattern of errors when moving from one disk to another?

Troubleshooting Skills

1. Create a bootable system disk in Windows 9x. Boot from the disk. What version of the OS are you using? How can you enter Windows 9x from here?

2. Cause DOS to give you the error "Incorrect DOS version."

Working with a Cabinet File in Windows 98

1. Create a Windows 98 emergency startup disk.

2. Copy the cabinet file to a new directory on the disk.

3. Get a printed list of the files in the cabinet file.

4. Extract all files from the cabinet file into the new directory.

5. Get a printed list of the files in the new directory.

Comparing the Data Storage Cost of Devices

Research the market (using, for example, *Computer Shopper*) and fill in the following table to compare the storage costs of different secondary storage devices.

Type of Device	Zip Drive	Jaz Drive	SuperDisk
1. Manufacturer			
2. Capacity			
3. Price of drive and first disk			
4. Price of additional disks			
5. Cost per KB of drive and first disk			
6. Cost per KB of additional disks			

Using the Internet for Research

A friend of yours needs a successful way to carry very large files from one location to another location where he needs to access the files on either a Mac or a PC. You think that SuperDisk might be the technical solution, but you need to do some research. Can an external SuperDisk drive port from a PC to a Mac? If so, using what kind of connection? Use the Internet to find the answers to these questions and write a brief (less than one page) report to make your recommendation. *Hint:* See *www.superdisk.com*.

6

INTRODUCTION TO HARD DRIVES

In this chapter, you will learn:

♦ How data is stored on a hard drive

♦ How to use DOS and Windows commands to manage data on a hard drive

♦ How to identify the various types of hard drives and understand the advantages of each

♦ How to manage a hard drive to optimize its performance

In this chapter, the discussion of floppy disks from Chapter 5 is extended to hard drives. You can apply much of what you learned about the way floppy disks hold and manage data to hard drives. Just like a floppy disk, a hard drive has a file allocation table (FAT) and root directory, and stores data on tracks that are divided into sectors, each of which contains 512 bytes. In addition, many Windows and DOS commands that manage files on a floppy disk are used on hard drives as well. However, because of its size and versatility, a hard drive has more complicated methods of formatting and organizing data.

This chapter introduces hard drive basics and explains how to manage a healthy, previously installed hard drive. Chapter 7 continues our discussion of hard drives, examining installation, troubleshooting, and data recovery.

HARD DRIVE TECHNOLOGY

Hard drives used in today's microcomputers have their origin in the hard drives of early mainframe computers of the 1970s. These drives consisted of large platters or disks that were much larger and thicker than phonograph records. Several platters were stacked together with enough room to allow read/write heads to move back and forth between the platters. All heads moved in unison while the platters spun at a high speed. Applications programmers of the 1970s were responsible for how and where data was written to the platters. They wrote their programs so that data was spaced evenly over the disks, meaning the heads moved as little as possible while reading or writing a file. They could judge their success by standing over the clear cover of the hard drive and watching the heads. If they had programmed well, the heads moved smoothly over the platters; if not, they thrashed back and forth as data was processed. In today's systems, things are much more complicated. Several layers of software separate the data stored on a hard drive or floppy disk and the applications that read data from or write data to the disk. Learning about these layers, how they relate to one another, and how they manage the hard drive are the focus of this chapter.

A+CORE 1.1 Hard drive structure and function has not changed, however. Modern hard drives have two or more platters that are stacked together and spin in unison. Read/write heads are controlled by an actuator and move in unison across the disk surfaces as the disks rotate on a spindle (see Figure 6-1). PCs can use several types of hard drives, all using a magnetic medium; the data on all these drives is stored in tracks and sectors, and data files are addressed in clusters made up of one or more sectors.

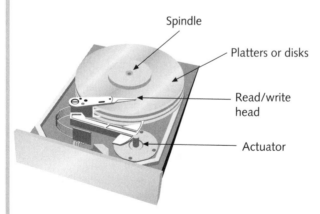

Spindle

Platters or disks

Read/write head

Actuator

Figure 6-1   Inside a hard drive case

Figure 6-2 shows a hard drive with four platters. All eight sides of these four platters are used to store data, although on some hard drives the top side of the first platter just holds information used to track the data and manage the disk. As with floppy drives, each side or surface of one hard drive platter is called a **head**. (Don't confuse this with the read/write mechanism that moves across a platter, which is called a read/write head.) The drive in Figure 6-2 has eight heads. Also as with floppy drives, each head is divided into tracks and sectors. The eight tracks shown in Figure 6-2, all of which are the same distance from the

A+CORE
1.1

center of the platters, together make up one cylinder. If a disk has 300 tracks per head, then it also has that same number of cylinders.

Figure 6-2   A hard drive with four platters

Just as with floppy disks, data is written to a hard drive beginning at the outermost track. The entire first cylinder is filled before the read/write heads move inward and begin filling the second cylinder. For older hard drives, even though tracks closer to the center of a platter are smaller, these tracks must store the same amount of data as the larger tracks toward the outside of a platter. As the heads move toward the center of the drive and the tracks become smaller, the read/write heads must adjust the way they write data so that sectors store a consistent number of bytes, even if they are different physical sizes. Two methods can be used to adjust for the smaller tracks: write precompensation and reduced write current.

Write precompensation speeds up the writing of data to the drive as the tracks become smaller near the center of the platters. If a hard drive uses write precompensation, it indicates at what track or cylinder the precompensation begins. Appendix B shows that some drives don't use this method. Some tables list the write precompensation as the total number of cylinders for the drive type. Interpret this to mean that precompensation is not used.

Reduced write current means just what it says. At a cylinder near the center of the platter, the read/write heads reduce the current used to place magnetized spots on the disk, because the spots are getting closer and closer together. Reduced write current is not as common as write precompensation.

IDE Technology

A+CORE
1.1

Almost all hard drives on the market today use **IDE (Integrated Device Electronics** formerly Integrated Drive Electronics) standards, but it was not always so. Older hard drive technologies, a few of which are still in use, include MFM, RLL, and ESDI. A variation of IDE technology is Enhanced IDE (EIDE). SCSI is one technology that manages the interface between the hard drive and the system bus.

The following sections discuss how IDE and SCSI work; MFM and RLL drives are covered for historical reasons only, to help you understand the basics behind today's drive technology.

As described earlier, a hard drive consists of two or more platters spinning inside a protective housing with read/write heads that move back and forth across the platters. The drive fits into a bay inside the computer case and is securely attached with supports or braces and screws. This helps prevent the drive from being jarred while the disk is spinning and the heads are very close to the disk surfaces.

A+CORE 1.2 A hard drive requires a controller board filled with ROM programming to instruct the read/write heads how, where, and when to move across the platters and write and read data. In IDE and SCSI drives, a controller is mounted on a circuit board on the drive housing and is an integral part of it. (Hence the term Integrated Device Electronics, or IDE.) Older RLL and MFM drives had the controller board as a separate, large expansion card connected to the drive with two cables. Today, the controller of an IDE drive usually connects to the system board by way of a data cable from the drive to an IDE connection directly on the system board. Older system boards did not have an IDE connection, so a small **adapter card** served as a simple pass-through from the drive to the system board. The data cable attached to the drive and the adapter card, which was inserted in an ISA slot on the system board. Sometimes an adapter card connects a hard drive to a system board to compensate for the system board BIOS not supporting a large-capacity drive. The adapter card contains the necessary BIOS to support the drive in the place of the system BIOS.

Figure 6-3 shows a hardware subsystem including an IDE hard drive and its connection to a system board. In addition to the connection for the 40-pin data cable, the hard drive has a connection for the power cord from the power supply.

IDE connection on system board

Power cord

IDE 40-pin data cable

Connection for a second drive

Hard drive

Figure 6-3 A PC's hard drive subsystem

Almost all drives on the market today are IDE technology. Although IDE technology is an innovative improvement over MFM and RLL type hard drives, it also introduces some new limitations. To understand how IDE technology differs from other drive technologies, examine the details of how drives are low-level formatted.

Tracks and Sectors on an IDE Drive

The MFM and RLL technologies use either 17 or 26 sectors per track over the entire drive platter (see Figure 6-4). The larger tracks near the outside of the platter contain the same number of bytes as the smaller tracks near the center of the platter. This arrangement makes the formatting of a drive and later accessing data simpler, but it wastes drive space. The number of bytes that a track can hold is determined by the centermost track, and all other tracks are forced to follow this restriction.

Sector

Track

Figure 6-4   Floppy drives and older hard drives use a constant number of sectors per track

One major improvement with IDE technology is that the formatting of IDE drives eliminates this restriction. The number of sectors per track on an IDE drive is not the same throughout the platter. In this new formatting system, called **zone bit recording** (Figure 6-5), tracks near the center have the smallest number of sectors per track, and the number of sectors increases as the tracks get larger. In other words, each track on an IDE drive is designed to have the optimum number of sectors appropriate to the size of the track. What makes this arrangement possible, however, is one fact that has not changed: every sector on the drive still has 512 bytes. If it weren't for this consistency, the OS would have a difficult time indeed communicating with this drive!

Because each track can have a different number of sectors, the OS cannot communicate with an IDE drive by contacting the hard drive controller BIOS and using sector and track coordinates, as it does with floppy disks and older hard drives. Newer, more sophisticated methods must be used that are discussed later in the chapter.

Formatting a Hard Drive

A+ OS
1.3

Recall from Chapter 5 that, when the OS formats a floppy disk, it writes sector and track markings on the disk. With IDE drives, since the track and sector markings no longer follow a simple pattern, they are written on the hard drive at the factory. This process is called

A+ OS
  1.3

low-level formatting. The OS still executes the remainder of the format process (creating a boot sector, FAT, and root directory), which is called the **high-level format** or **OS format**.

36 sectors per track

18 sectors per track

Figure 6-5   Zone bit recording can have more sectors per track as the tracks get larger

With older RLL and MFM technology, the system BIOS, OS, or utility software such as Norton Utilities and SpinRite could perform the low-level format; even now a low-level format routine is still part of standard system BIOS. For an IDE drive, however, using system BIOS or standard utility software to low-level format the drive would be a catastrophe. Formatting an IDE drive in this way could permanently destroy the drive unless the drive controller BIOS were smart enough to ignore the command.

Because of the unique way that an IDE drive is formatted and data is accessed, you must use a controller specific to the IDE drive. IDE drives thus have their controller built directly on top or on the bottom of the drive housing. The controller and the drive are permanently attached to one another.

Because IDE drives are low-level formatted by the manufacturer, they cannot be low-level formatted as part of preventive maintenance as older drives can be. The track and sector markings on the drive created at the factory are normally expected to last for the life of the drive. For this reason IDE drives are often referred to as disposable drives. When the track and sector markings fade, as they eventually do, you just throw the drive away and buy a new one!

A+ OS
  3.2

However, improvements for formatting the IDE drive are becoming more commonplace. Some better-known IDE drive manufacturers are offering a low-level format program specific to their drives. If an IDE drive continues to give "Bad Sector or Sector Not Found" errors or even becomes totally unusable, ask the manufacturer for a program to perform a low-level format of the drive. Sometimes these programs are only distributed by the manufacturer to dealers, resellers, or certified service centers.

 TIP   If an IDE drive creates problems, try using the manufacturer's low-level format software to re-create track and sector markings on the drive.

It's risky to low-level format an IDE drive using a format program other than one provided by the manufacturer, although some have tried and succeeded. Probably more drives have been permanently destroyed than saved by taking this risk, however. IDE drives last several

years without a refresher low-level format. By that time, you're probably ready to upgrade to a larger drive anyway.

System-Board Support for IDE Drives

A+CORE
4.3

When IDE drives first entered the marketplace, an adapter card in an expansion slot connected the drive to the system board. Nowadays, most system boards support IDE by providing one or two IDE connections directly on the system board. To alert a user when a hard disk is being accessed, a system board has a two-pin connection that connects to an LED on the front of the computer case. A lit LED means a hard drive is being accessed.

In summary, an IDE drive has its controller mounted directly on top of the drive. The OS does not communicate directly with the IDE drive, as is the case with drives that use older technology. Instead, the OS passes its requests to the drive controller, which is responsible for keeping up with where and how data is stored on the drive. As far as the OS is concerned, an IDE drive is simply a very long list of logical sectors, each 512 bytes long. The OS doesn't care where on the drive these sectors are located, since that information is maintained by the controller. Setup for IDE drives is very simple; the most important fact that setup and the OS need to know is how many sectors there are on the drive. It is important not to overestimate the number of sectors. You don't want the OS requesting use of a sector that does not exist. However, you can tell setup that you have fewer sectors than are present. If you do, some sectors will remain unused.

Enhanced IDE (EIDE) Drives

Early IDE drives followed the IDE/ATA (Integrated Device Electronics AT Attachment) standard[1] developed by ANSI. This standard is sometimes referred to as the IDE standard or the ATA standard. It involves how the drive interfaces with BIOS and software more than it does the actual drive technology. Using this ATA standard interface, drives were limited to 528 MB and could have no more than 1,024 cylinders. There could be no more than two hard drives on the same interface. This standard applied only to hard drives and did not include CD-ROM drives, tape drives, and so on. It has been improved several times as drive technology and methods of interface have improved.

Enhanced IDE (EIDE) drives support these newer, faster standards. The first standard supported by EIDE was ATA-2. This new standard allowed for up to four IDE devices on the same PC. These IDE devices could be hard drives, CD-ROM drives, or tape drives as well as other IDE devices. CD-ROM drives use the ATAPI standard. As standards were developed, different hard drive manufacturers adopted different names for them, which can be confusing. Standards today specify data transfer speed more than any other single factor. When selecting a hard drive standard, select the fastest standard you can, but keep in mind that the operating system, BIOS on the system board, and the hard drive must all support this standard. If one of three does not support the standard, the other two will probably revert to using a slower standard that all three can use.

[1]AT originally stood for advanced technology and refers to one of the early IBM PCs of the 1980s. The XT came before the AT PC. Sometimes you still hear the term XT/AT compatible or AT standard, which means the technology follows the standard established by this early AT PC.

A+CORE
4.3

Table 6-1 lists the different ANSI standards for hard drives.

Table 6-1   Summary of ANSI interface standards for hard drives

Standard (May Have More Than One Name)	Speed	Description
IDE/ATA ATA	Speeds range from 2.1 MB/sec to 8.3 MB/sec	The first ANSI hard drive standard for IDE hard drives. Limited to no more than 528 MB. Supports PIO and DMA transfer modes.
ATA-2 Fast ATA	Speeds up to 16.6 MB/sec	Breaks the 528-MB barrier. Allows up to 4 IDE devices. Supports PIO and DMA transfer modes discussed later in the chapter.
ATA-3	Little speed increase	Improved version of ATA-2
Ultra ATA Fast ATA-2 Ultra DMA DMA/33	Speeds up to 33.3 MB/sec	Defined a new DMA mode, but only supports slower PIO modes
Ultra ATA/66 Ultra DMA/66	Speeds up to 66.6 MB/sec	Uses a special 40-pin cable that provides additional ground lines on the cable to improve signal integrity

SCSI Technology

SCSI (pronounced "scuzzy") stands for **Small Computer Systems Interface** and is a standard for communication between a subsystem of peripheral devices and the system bus. The SCSI bus is a closed system that can contain, and be used by, up to seven or 15 devices, depending on the SCSI standard. The gateway from this bus to the system bus is an adapter card inserted into an expansion slot on the system board. The adapter card, called the **host adapter**, is responsible for managing all the devices on the SCSI bus. When one of these devices must communicate with the system bus, the data passes through the host adapter (see Figure 6-6).

The host adapter keeps up with the interchange between the devices on the SCSI bus and the system bus. SCSI technology has the added advantage of letting two devices on the SCSI bus pass data between them without going through the CPU. This method of data transmission provides a convenient way to back up a SCSI hard drive to a tape drive on the same host adapter without involving the CPU.

A+CORE
1.6

The maximum number of devices the SCSI bus can support depends on the type of SCSI being used. Some SCSI buses can link up to seven, others up to 15 devices. Each device on the bus is assigned a number from zero to seven called the **SCSI ID**, using DIP switches, dials on the device, or software settings. The host adapter is assigned a number larger than all other devices, either 7 or 15. Cables connect the devices physically in a straight chain. The devices can be either internal or external, and the host adapter can be at either end of the chain or somewhere in the middle. The SCSI ID identifies the physical device, which can

A⁺CORE 1.6 have several logical devices embedded in it. For example, a CD-ROM changer or jukebox device might have seven CD trays. Each tray is considered a logical device and is assigned a **Logical Unit Number (LUN)** to identify it such as 1 through 7 or 0 through 6. The ID and LUN are written as two numbers separated by a colon. For instance, if the SCSI ID is 5, the fourth tray in the jukebox is device 5:4.

Figure 6-6   SCSI hard drives communicate with the CPU through the SCSI host adapter, but IDE drives communicate directly on the system bus

A SCSI device such as a hard drive, tape drive, or CD-ROM drive, interfaces with the host adapter rather than directly with the CPU. The technology of a SCSI device can be the same as the technology of a similar device that is not SCSI, with the added ability to use the SCSI bus and communicate with the host adapter. A device is a SCSI device not because of its technology, but because of the bus it uses.

Just as with IDE drives, a SCSI drive has its controller mounted inside the drive housing and can have a variable number of sectors per track. Low-level formatting a SCSI drive is sometimes possible and even recommended by the manufacturer because the SCSI controller is likely to contain the firmware to do the job. See the drive's documentation. In theory, a SCSI drive can simply be an IDE drive with one more chip on the controller card in the drive housing and a different kind of data connection designed to fit the SCSI standard. In practice, however, SCSI drives are of higher quality, having higher rotational speeds and lower seek times than IDE drives. The SCSI chip within the drive housing that controls data transfer over the SCSI bus is called the **SCSI bus adapter chip (SBAC)**.

Figure 6-6 illustrates this concept of SCSI as a bus. On the left, the CPU communicates with the hard drive controller, which is contained in the hard drive case, through the system bus. On the right, the CPU communicates over the system bus to the SCSI host adapter, which communicates over the SCSI bus to the SCSI adapter in the hard drive case. The SCSI adapter communicates with the hard drive controller, which, in turn, communicates with the hard drive.

Sometimes a SCSI device is designed to be the only SCSI device on the SCSI bus and so has some of the host adapter logic built into the device. These devices are called **embedded SCSI** devices. The host adapter for the device is usually bundled with it and is much smaller and simpler than normal host adapters. Other SCSI devices on this computer must be separate from this SCSI bus system. Embedded SCSI devices often don't conform to standard SCSI specifications, because they do not accommodate any other SCSI device.

A^+CORE
1.6

To reduce the amount of electrical "noise," or interference, on a SCSI cable, each end of the SCSI chain has a **terminating resistor**. The terminating resistor can be a hardware device plugged into the last device on each end of the chain, or the chain can have software-controlled termination resistance, which makes installation simpler.

A^+CORE
1.6,
4.3

Differing SCSI Standards Just as with IDE/ATA standards, SCSI standards have improved over the years and use different names. The two general categories of all SCSI standards used on PCs have to do with the number of bits that travel on the SCSI bus, either 8 bits (narrow SCSI) or 16 bits (wide SCSI). In almost every case, if the SCSI standard is 16 bits, then the word "wide" is in the name for the standard. In most cases, the word "narrow" is not mentioned in names for 8-bit standards. Narrow SCSI uses a 50-pin cable, and wide SCSI uses a 68-pin cable.

A SCSI cable can be built in two different ways, depending on the method by which the electrical signal travels on the cable: single-ended and differential. A single-ended cable is less expensive than a differential cable, but the maximum cable length cannot be as long because data integrity is not as great. Cables for both narrow SCSI and wide SCSI can be either single-ended or differential. Single-ended cables and differential cables look the same, so you must make sure that you are using the correct cable. Single-ended cable is more popular than differential because it is less expensive.

Table 6-2 summarizes the different SCSI standards, including the three major standards: SCSI-1, SCSI-2 and SCSI-3 that are more commonly known as Regular SCSI, Fast SCSI, and Ultra SCSI, respectively. Other names used in the industry for these standards are also listed in the table. Both Fast SCSI and Ultra SCSI have narrow and wide versions.

Because there are several variations of SCSI, when you buy a new SCSI device, you must be sure that it is compatible with the SCSI bus you already have. All SCSI standards are not backward compatible with earlier SCSI standards. If the new SCSI device is not compatible, you cannot use the same SCSI bus, and you must buy a new host adapter to build a second SCSI bus system, increasing the overall cost of adding the new device.

The wide SCSI specification allows for a data path of 32 bits, although this has not been implemented in PCs. When you see a SCSI device referred to as wide, you can assume 16 bits.

Beginning with Ultra SCSI (SCSI-3), the SCSI standard supports **SCSI configuration automatically** (**SCAM**), which follows the Plug and Play standard. SCAM makes installing SCSI devices easier, if the device is SCAM-compatible.

$A+$*CORE*
1.6,
4.3

Table 6-2   Summary of SCSI standards

Names for the SCSI Interface Standard	Bus width Narrow = 8 bits Wide = 16 bits	Transfer ZRate (MB/sec)	Maximum Length of Single-ended Cable (meters)	Maximum Length of Differential Cable (meters)	Maximum Number of Devices
SCSI-1 (Regular SCSI)[1]	Narrow	5	6	25	8
SCSI-2 (Fast SCSI or Fast Narrow)	Narrow	10	3	25	8
Fast Wide SCSI (Wide SCSI)	Wide	20	3	25	16
SCSI-3 (Ultra SCSI or Ultra Narrow or Fast-20 SCSI	Narrow	20	1.5	25	8
Wide Ultra SCSI (Fast Wide 20)	Wide	40	1.5	25	16
Ultra2 SCSI	Narrow	40		12 LVD[2]	8
Wide Ultra2 SCSI	Wide	80			16
Ultra3 SCSI	Narrow	80		12 LVD[2]	8
Wide Ultra3 SCSI (Ultra 160 SCSI)	Wide	160		12 LVD[2]	16

[1]Bold indicates most common name
[2]LVD: Low voltage differential cable allows for lengths up to 12 meters

$A+$*CORE*
1.6

A sample configuration of a SCSI subsystem is shown in Figure 6-7. Because Ultra SCSI is backward compatible with SCSI-1 and SCSI-2, all three can coexist on the same SCSI bus. Note that the only connection this subsystem has to the overall computer system and the CPU is through the host adapter. You can see from the diagram why some people compare a SCSI system to a miniature LAN inside a computer.

Figure 6-7   Sample SCSI subsystem configuration

Other Variations of SCSI Hardware and Software

In addition to the differences in SCSI standards, other components of SCSI vary. Besides the cables already discussed above, there are also variations in termination, device drivers, and host adapters.

A +CORE 1.6 **Termination** **Termination** prevents an echo effect from electrical noise and reflected data at the end of the SCSI daisy chain, which can cause interference with the data transmission. There are several ways to terminate power:

- The host adapter can have a switch setting that activates or deactivates a terminating resistor on the card, depending on whether or not the adapter is at one end of the chain.

- A device can have either a single SCSI connection requiring that the device is placed at the end of the chain, or the device can have two connections. When a device has two connections, the second connection can be used to connect another device or to terminate the chain by placing an external terminator on the connection. This external terminator serves as the terminating resistor (see Figure 6-8).

Figure 6-8 SCSI subsystem showing terminators at each end of the SCSI chain

- The device at the end of the chain can also be terminated by a resistor that is physically mounted on the device in a specially designated socket.

- Some devices have built-in terminators that you can turn on or off with a jumper setting on the device.

- Termination can be controlled by software.

There are several types of terminators: passive terminators, active terminators, and forced perfect terminators. Forced perfect terminators are more expensive and more reliable than the other two are.

A+CORE
1.6 When buying terminating resistor hardware and cables for a SCSI bus (see Figure 6-9) get high-quality products even if they cost a little more. The added reliability and enhanced data integrity are worth the extra money.

SCSI Terminators

SCSI Peripheral Cable

SCSI System Cable

Figure 6-9   SCSI cables and terminators

SCSI Device Drivers   SCSI device drivers are needed to enable DOS or another OS to communicate with a host adapter. Although many drivers are available, it is best to use the drivers recommended by or provided by the host adapter vendor. Two popular drivers are the **Advanced SCSI Programming Interface** (**ASPI**) and **Common Access Method** (**CAM**). ASPI is probably the more popular of the two.

No SCSI device drivers are included with Window 3.1 or DOS. SCSI hardware manufacturers write their own drivers and include them with their devices. A SCSI driver is loaded in the CONFIG.SYS file just as other drivers are. Its DEVICE= command must appear in the CONFIG.SYS file before any device drivers for a SCSI device. For example, if you have a SCSI CD-ROM drive whose device driver must be installed in CONFIG.SYS, you must place the command for this driver after the one that installs the host adapter driver. The installation instructions for the CD-ROM drive offer similar instructions and give you the specific command. Windows 9x, Windows NT, and Windows 2000 all have built-in support for SCSI devices.

A+CORE
1.6 Many computers have some SCSI interface software in their system BIOS, enough, in fact, to allow a SCSI hard drive to be the boot device of the system. The system BIOS can access the SCSI drive, execute the load program in the drive's master boot record, and load the SCSI device drivers stored on the hard drive into memory. If a system has two hard drives, one being an IDE and one a SCSI, the IDE drive must be the boot device unless system BIOS can support booting from a SCSI drive even when an IDE drive is present. This is because the system-board BIOS takes precedence over the BIOS on the SCSI host adapter.

6

Host Adapter Issues An important issue when you install a SCSI bus system for the first time is the sophistication of the host adapter. More expensive host adapters are often easier to install because the installation software does more of the work for the installer and offers more help than does less expensive adapter software. When buying a host adapter, compare the installation procedures for different adapters, and also look for options, such as a built-in disk drive controller, software-controlled termination (eliminating the need for hardware terminating resistors), and configuration BIOS built into the adapter's ROM.

A SCSI host adapter controller has BIOS that loads into memory addresses on the PC and controls the operation of the SCSI bus. This SCSI controller uses a DMA channel, IRQ, and I/O addresses. You must install a SCSI device carefully to avoid resource conflicts with devices that are not on the SCSI subsystem.

In summary, to understand SCSI hard drive technology think of it as a SCSI bus system—a closed bus system that can include several devices as well as the host adapter that acts as the bridge to the system bus. SCSI drives are usually faster than IDE drives but also more expensive. When buying SCSI drives, determine if the host adapter is built into the drive (embedded SCSI), or if you must purchase it separately. When installing a new SCSI system, be aware of the many variations of SCSI and buy compatible components.

Although the installation of a SCSI system may sound complicated and requires many decisions about what components to buy, the installation instructions for SCSI devices and host adapters are usually very thorough and well written. If you carefully follow all instructions, SCSI installations can be smooth and problem-free.

Comparing SCSI Hard Drives and EIDE Hard Drives

Consider the following issues when choosing between using an EIDE hard drive and a SCSI hard drive:

- A SCSI hard drive with its supporting host adapter and cable costs more than an EIDE hard drive with its supporting adapter card.

- A SCSI subsystem provides faster data transfer than an EIDE drive, although the SCSI bus is the source of the performance rather than the hard drive technology.

- A SCSI bus supports multitasking, allowing the CPU to request data from more than one SCSI device at the same time, whereas when the CPU requests data from an EIDE drive on an ISA bus, it can only process data from one I/O device at a time. The CPU must wait until the ISA bus and EIDE drive have completed the request before it can tackle another task. With SCSI, the CPU can perform another I/O task while waiting for the SCSI bus to complete the first request.

- A good SCSI host adapter allows you to connect other SCSI devices to it, such as a printer, scanner, or tape drive.

- Without SCSI technology, if you have two IDE drives on the same adapter, only one of them can be busy at any one time. For instance, without SCSI, if one of your IDE devices is a CD-ROM, the hard drive must wait for the CD-ROM to complete a task before it can work again. With SCSI, two or more devices can operate simultaneously. If you plan to transfer a lot of data from CD-ROM to hard drive, this is a good reason to choose SCSI.

In summary, SCSI is more expensive than EIDE but gives you better performance. Chapter 7 covers installation of SCSI devices in detail.

Other Types of Hard Drive Interfaces

**A+CORE
1.1,
1.7**

In addition to the IDE and SCSI interface to the system bus, a hard drive can also interface with the system bus using IEEE 1394 and Fibre Channel. IEEE 1394, also known as FireWire and i.Link (named by Sony Corporation), was discussed in Chapter 3. It uses serial transmission of data and is popular with multimedia and home entertainment applications. For example, Quantum Corporation, a large hard drive manufacturer, makes a hard drive designed for home entertainment electronics that uses 1394 for the hard drive interface (Quantum in cooperation with Sony Corporation, calls it i.Link in the hard drive documentation). Another example of 1394 providing the interface for a hard drive is fireLINE External HotDrive by Evergreen Technologies. This external hard drive is intended for general-purpose storage and connects to a PC through a 1394 port provided either directly on the system board or by way of a 1394 expansion card. System board manufacturers have been slow to provide 1394 support on their system boards, mostly favoring support for USB instead. Generally, IDE is the slowest, SCSI is mid-range, and 1394 is the fastest, with some overlaps in these speeds. For a system to use 1394, the operating system must support it. Windows 98 and Windows 2000 support 1394, but Windows 95 and Windows NT do not.

Fibre Channel is another type of interface that can support hard drives. Fibre Channel is designed for use in high-end systems that have multiple hard drives. It competes with SCSI for these high-end solutions. As many as 126 devices can be connected to a single Fibre Channel bus as compared to 16 SCSI devices, including the host adapter. Fibre Channel is faster than SCSI when more than five hard drives are strung together to provide massive secondary storage, but is too expensive and has too much overhead to be a good solution for the desktop PC or workstation.

HOW A HARD DRIVE IS LOGICALLY ORGANIZED TO HOLD DATA

Recall that today's hard drives come from the factory already low-level formatted (that is, having track and sector markings already in place). During installation, after the hard drive is physically installed, the next step is to partition the drive into manageable areas. The high-level divisions are called **partitions**, and within the partitions, the drive is further divided into logical drives or volumes. This section discusses the different types of division and how they are organized and used by the OS.

**A+CORE
1.2**

Preparing a hard drive to hold data requires the following three steps:

1. **Low-level format.** This physically formats the hard drive and creates the tracks and sectors. For hard drives today, this has already been done by the time you buy the drive, and does not involve an OS.

2. **Partitioning the hard drive**. Even if only one partition is used, this step is still required. The FDISK program of Windows 9x or DOS sets up a partition table at the beginning of the hard drive. This table lists how many partitions are on the drive and their locations, and which partition is the boot partition. Within each partition, FDISK also creates logical drives, assigning letters to these drives.

3. **High-level format**. This can be done by DOS, Windows 9x, or some other OS for each logical drive on the hard drive. As each logical drive is formatted, the OS creates an OS boot record, a root directory, and the copies of FAT for the logical drive. (With floppy disks, the high-level format also creates the tracks and sectors, but with hard drives this has already been done by the low-level format.)

Hard Drive Partitions

Although you might have a 4-GB hard drive that is only a single physical drive, an OS can divide this single physical drive into more than one logical drive, which is called **partitioning the drive**. Two kinds of divisions take place. First the physical drive is divided into one or more partitions, and then each partition is further divided into logical drives or volumes. (A logical drive is sometimes called a logical partition; don't let the two uses of the term "partition" confuse you; partitions and logical partitions are divisions at different levels.) Figure 6-10 shows a typical example; the hard drive is divided into two partitions. The first partition contains one logical drive (drive C) and the second partition is divided into two logical drives (D and E). The **partition table** at the very beginning of the drive records all these divisions contained in the master boot sector (located in the very first sector at the beginning of the hard drive, on head 0, track 0, sector 1). Table 6-3 lists the contents of a partition table. Don't confuse the first physical sector of the hard drive with sector 1 as DOS or Windows 9x knows it. The OS's sector 1 comes after the physical sector 1.

The partition table is exactly 512 bytes long. During POST, the partition table program, sometimes called the **master boot record**, executes, checking the integrity of the partition table itself. If it finds any corruption, it refuses to continue execution, and the disk is unusable. If the table entries are valid, this program looks in the table to determine which partition is the active partition, and it executes the boot program in the boot record of that partition.

Figure 6-10   A hard drive is divided into one or more partitions that contain logical drives

Table 6-3   Hard drive partition table

Item	Bytes Used	Description
1	446 bytes	Program that calls the boot program on the OS boot record
2	16-byte total 1 byte 3 bytes 1 byte 3 bytes 4 bytes 4 bytes	Description of first partition Is this the bootable partition? (Yes = 90h, No = 00h) Beginning location of the partition System indicator; possible values are: 0 = Not a DOS partition 1 = DOS with a 12-bit FAT 4 = DOS with a 16-bit FAT 5 = Not the first partition 6 = Partition larger than 32 MB Ending location of partition First sector of the partition table relative to the beginning of the disk Number of sectors in the partition

Table 6-3   Hard drive partition table (continued)

Item	Bytes Used	Description
3	16 bytes	Describes second partition, using same format as first partition
4	16 bytes	Describes third partition, using same format as first partition
5	16 bytes	Describes fourth partition, using same format as first partition
6	2 bytes	Signature of the partition table, always AA55

Using DOS or Windows 9x, a hard drive can have only one primary partition and one extended partition, although the partition table can contain four partitions. Also, the primary partition can only have a single logical drive. In that case, the one logical drive in the primary partition is the only logical drive on the hard drive that can boot the operating system. The extended partition can have several logical drives.

The partition table must be created when the drive is first installed. This is done with the DOS or Windows 9x FDISK command or third-party software such as Partition Magic. Chapter 7 describes partitioning a hard drive in more detail.

A+ OS 1.3   When the drive is partitioned, FDISK assigns a drive letter to each logical drive. If only one logical drive is assigned, and this is the first hard drive installed in the system, this drive is called drive C. FDISK first creates a partition and then creates logical drives within the partition. You designate how many logical drives you want and how large they will be.

Logical Drives

Recall that both DOS and Windows 9x store data in files, each of which is allocated a group of whole clusters and cannot share a cluster with another file. The OS knows only the cluster numbers that it has assigned to a file; it does not track where these clusters are physically located. The OS keeps information about files and the clusters assigned to them in its file system. This arrangement is similar to a library where the readers are not allowed in the book stacks but must depend on a librarian to fetch the books for them (see Figure 6-11). When the OS requests BIOS to retrieve a file from the hard drive, BIOS, either on the system board or on the hard drive controller, determines where on the drive these sectors are located.

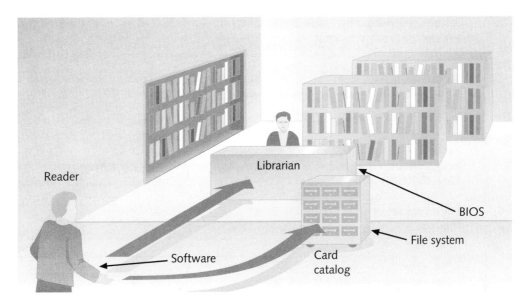

Figure 6-11 In some libraries, the reader (software) is not allowed in the stacks and depends on the librarian (BIOS) to know where to locate a book

A **logical drive** is a portion of a hard drive that an OS views and manages as an individual drive, much as it manages a floppy disk. The hard drive in Figure 6-10 is divided into three logical drives: drives C, D, and E. For a 3-GB drive, drive C might contain 2 GB, drive D 300 MB, and drive E 700 MB, to account for the entire physical drive capacity.

For the configuration in Figure 6-10, the three commands used to format these three logical drives are:

```
Format C:/S
Format D:
Format E:
```

The OS format for each logical drive creates these file system items at the beginning of each logical drive:

- Boot record

- FAT

- Root directory

These items are discussed below.

The Boot Record

A boot record is used during the boot process to inform the OS how a logical drive is organized. If the logical drive is the boot device, the boot program at the end of the boot record will load the hidden files (IO.SYS and MSDOS.SYS for DOS, and Msdos.sys for Windows 9x) during booting. Table 6-4 shows the complete record layout for the boot record. The medium descriptor byte tells the OS what type of disk this is. The values of this descriptor byte are given in Table 6-5.

 TIP The program in the boot record used to load the operating system is called the bootstrap loader; hence the phrase "booting the PC."

Table 6-4   Layout of the boot record

Description	Number of Bytes
Machine code	11
Bytes per sector	2
Sectors per cluster	1
Reserved	2
Number of FATs	1
Number of root directory entries	2
Number of logical sectors	2
Medium descriptor byte	1
Sectors per FAT	2
Sectors per track	2
Heads	2
Number of hidden sectors	2
Total sectors in logical volume	4
Physical drive number	1
Reserved	1
Extended boot signature record	1
32-bit binary volume ID	4
Volume label	11
Type of file system (FAT12, FAT16, or FAT32)	8
Program to load operating system (boot strap loader)	Remainder of the sector

Table 6-5   Disk type and descriptor byte

Disk Type	Descriptor Byte
3½-inch double-density floppy disk, 720K	F9
3½-inch high-density floppy disk, 1.44 MB	F0
Hard disk	F8

The FAT and the Root Directory

The OS uses two tables (the FAT and a directory, as seen in Figure 6-12) to keep track of which clusters are used for a file and other file information, including the filename and length, and whether the file is read-only or hidden. This high-level view of the file is all the OS needs to know. The physical location of the file is tracked by the BIOS or device driver managing the hard drive. The FAT and a directory are the vehicles of exchange between the

OS and the hard drive BIOS. The OS uses only one FAT for an entire logical drive but can have more than one directory on the drive. The main or root directory always present on a drive can have directories within it, called subdirectories in DOS or folders in Windows 9x.

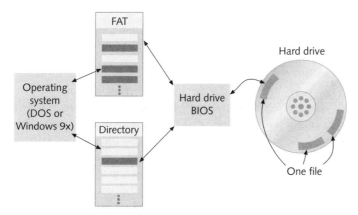

Figure 6-12   How the operating system views the hard drive when managing a file

To the OS, each logical drive looks like and is treated like a single floppy disk in this respect: as far as DOS or Windows 9x is concerned, a physical drive divided into three logical drives, C, D, and E, is equivalent to three separate physical drives (see Figure 6-13). The reason for this is that the OS manages a logical drive from the same high-level view whether it is a floppy drive, a part of a physical drive, or an entire physical drive. Each includes a FAT, one or more directories, and files that the OS tracks by using these tables.

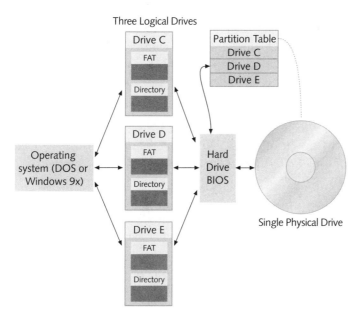

Figure 6-13   A single physical drive can be viewed by the operating system as one or more logical drives

A+ OS
1.3

For DOS and sometimes Windows 9x, each entry in a FAT for most hard drives is 16 bits, or a convenient 2 bytes, and the FAT is called FAT16. Besides FAT16, Windows 98 offers a FAT with 32-bit entries, and Windows NT offers an entirely different method of managing clusters called NTFS (new technology file system), which is discussed in Chapter 13. Windows 2000 supports FAT16, FAT32, and NTFS file systems. Windows 95 offers a version of FAT16 that can use long filenames, called virtual FAT or VFAT.

Remember that, as with floppy disks, each entry in a hard drive FAT tracks the use of one cluster. The number of sectors per cluster varies from one logical drive to another. Use the CHKDSK command to display the size of one cluster. There is another way to determine the size of a cluster with a simple test. First, use the DIR command and note how much space is available on your hard drive. Then, create a text file containing only a single character. Using the DIR command again, note how much disk space is available and compare the two values, before and after a single one-character file is written to the disk. The difference in the two values is the size of one cluster, which is the smallest amount that can be allocated to a file. In the FAT entries discussed below, we are using a hard drive that has one cluster equal to four sectors. A cluster is, therefore, 512 bytes/sector $\times$ 4 sectors/cluster, or 2,048 bytes.

Virtual File Allocation (VFAT)   Windows 95 and Windows for Workgroups feature some improved methods of hard drive access, called **VFAT**, or **virtual file allocation**. These enable Windows to use 32-bit protected-mode device drivers for hard drive access. In Windows for Workgroups, VFAT is called 32-bit file access. Windows 95 supports filenames up to 255 characters. As you learned in Chapter 5, the filename and extension are stored in the root directory or in a subdirectory list. Each entry in the directory is 32 bytes long, and each 32-byte entry is called a block. Long filenames require more than one block in the directory. The FAT is not affected, but still uses 16 bits per cluster entry.

Some DOS-based disk utility programs can damage the entries in a directory in these additional blocks because they are not programmed to manage the extra blocks used to hold long filenames. Even a simple DEL command under OS/2 can leave the extra blocks in the directory used to hold the long filename unavailable for later use. The Windows 9x ScanDisk utility can recover these unreleased blocks.

A+ OS
1.3

FAT32   Beginning with Windows 95, Service Release 2 (sometimes called Windows 95b or Windows 95 OSR2), Microsoft offered a FAT that contains 32 bits per FAT entry instead of the older 12-bit or 16-bit FAT entries. Actually, only 28 of the bits are used to hold a cluster number; the remaining 4 bits are reserved.

The 32-bit FAT allows better management of very large hard drives, because the number of clusters per logical volume can increase: The largest cluster number a 16-bit FAT entry can hold is 65,535. The value of a 16-bit number when all 16 bits are 1s, that is, 1111 1111 1111 1111, is 65,535, which is then the largest number of clusters that the OS can support on a single logical drive. The largest logical drive capacity is dependent on the size of a single cluster and the number of clusters that can be accessed through the FAT. For FAT16, logical drives can range in size from 16 MB to 2,048 MB. But in order to get the larger sizes, the cluster size must be very large, sometimes as large as 32K, which can result in a lot of wasted space

A+ OS
   1.3

for a hard drive that holds many small files. This wasted space is called **slack**. FAT32 makes it possible for cluster sizes to be smaller and still have very large logical drives, because there can be many more clusters to the drive. FAT32 is recommended for hard drives larger than 512 MB and is efficient for drives up to 16 GB. In this range, the cluster size is 8K. After that, the cluster size increases to about 16K for drives in the 16 GB to 32 GB range. You are then reaching a hard drive size that warrants a more powerful file management system than FAT32, such as NTFS supported by Windows NT and Windows 2000, discussed in Chapter 13.

If you are currently using FAT16 and are considering switching to FAT32, you can use Partition Magic, discussed in Chapter 7, to scan your hard drive and tell you how much of the drive is used for slack space. Knowing this can help you decide if the change will yield you more usable drive space. In Chapter 12 you will learn how to set up a new hard drive to use FAT32 or convert an older hard drive to it.

The Root Directory   The layout of the root directory is the same for hard drives as for floppy disks, discussed in Chapter 5. Recall that the total number of bytes for each file entry in a directory is 32. Refer back to Chapter 5 for a description of each entry in the root directory.

The maximum number of entries in the root directory for DOS and Windows 95 is fixed. The number of entries in a subdirectory, however, is not limited. The fixed reserved length of the root directory for current versions of DOS and Windows is 512 entries; early versions of DOS didn't allow as many entries in the root directory. Note, however, that the OS manuals recommend that you keep only about 150 entries in any one directory. Having any more entries slows access to the directory. The number of entries in the root directory is stored in the boot record of the hard drive. Using long filenames reduces the number of files that can be stored in this fixed number of entries in the root directory, because the long filenames require more than one entry in the directory. Windows 98 does not limit the size of the root directory.

Communicating with the Hard Drive BIOS

Recall that, beginning with IDE hard drives, the number of sectors per track varied from one track to another. Therefore, the OS and system BIOS could not count on using actual hard drive cylinder, head, and sector coordinates when making requests for data through the hard drive BIOS (which is how requests were made with early hard drives). Instead, sophisticated methods were developed so that system BIOS and the OS could communicate with the hard drive controller BIOS in familiar terms, but only the controller BIOS knew where the data was physically located on the drive.

In order to build a foundation for understanding these more complicated solutions, we begin our discussion of communicating with hard drive BIOS by looking at BIOS that uses older hard drive technology (using a consistent relationship among cylinder, head, and sectors on a hard drive). Looking at Figure 6-14, you can see the different stages in communication with these older hard drives. The OS and other software communicated the cylinder, head, and sector coordinates to system BIOS, which communicated them to the hard drive controller BIOS, which used these coordinates to locate data on the hard drive. All levels communicated the same cylinder, head, and sector information to locate data on the hard drive. No tricks, just straightforward communication. With this straightforward communication, drive capacity could easily be calculated and drive access was simple, when drives were small and all tracks on the drive had the same number of sectors. Subsequently, methods used to communicate among the different levels were altered to accommodate larger drives and new drive technology.

Figure 6-14   With older hard drives, cylinder, track, and sector information was communicated at each level

Calculating Drive Capacity

How much data can be stored on a hard drive? Back when hard drives used a constant number of sectors per track, measuring drive capacity was straightforward. Recall that the OS views the data as groups of sectors of 512 bytes each. The number of sectors present on the drive determined the drive capacity. Each surface or platter on a hard drive is divided into tracks and sectors. All sectors in a track hold 512 bytes regardless of the radius of the track. If you knew the number of tracks, heads and sectors per track, you could calculate the storage capacity of a drive, because all tracks had the same number of sectors. Software and operating systems were written to interface with BIOS, which managed a hard drive by this method of assuming that for each hard drive there was a fixed relationship among the number of sectors, tracks, heads, and cylinders.

The table in Appendix B, "Hard Drive Types," lists the drive types, first established by IBM and later added to by other companies, that were supported by system BIOS. Notice in Appendix B that most earlier and smaller drives have 17 sectors per track. Later in the list are a few drives that have 26 sectors per track (see types 33, 34, and 37).

Because some drives are not on the list, most system BIOS programs permit a user-defined hard drive type. When you choose a user-defined drive type, you must tell the setup the number of heads, tracks, and sectors that the drive has, as well as some other information, so that system BIOS knows how to address the drive. These drive types might seem like ancient history with respect to hard drive capacity today, but the concepts and calculations apply to today's modern drives in a similar fashion.

 When installing a hard drive, it was once necessary to tell CMOS setup the drive capacity. Today, most system BIOS offers **autodetection**, a method whereby the BIOS will detect the new drive and automatically select the correct drive capacity and configuration for you.

To learn how drive capacity is calculated with these older drive layouts, let's calculate the storage capacity of drive type 12 in Appendix B. The following table contains the information needed to calculate capacity:

Type	Number of Tracks	Number of Heads	Number of Sectors/Track
12	855	7	17

When you see an odd number of heads, you know that the first head is not used for data. The drive listed with seven heads really has eight surfaces, or four platters, with the top surface of the top platter used to record the layout information for the entire drive. You calculate the capacity of the drive as follows:

855 tracks $\times$ 17 sectors/track $\times$ 512 bytes/sector = 7,441,920 bytes

There are 7,441,920 bytes on one surface, or head, of the drive. Therefore, the drive capacity is as follows:

7,441,920 bytes/head $\times$ 7 heads = 52,093,440 bytes

To convert bytes to kilobytes, divide by 1,024, as follows:

52,093,440 bytes $\times$ 1 KB/1,024 bytes = 50,872.5 KB

To convert kilobytes to megabytes, divide by 1,024 as follows:[2]

50,872.5 KB $\times$ 1MB/1,024 KB = 49.68 MB capacity

Let's work through one more example, for drive type 37. From Appendix B, the specifications are as follows:

Type	Number of Tracks	Number of Heads	Number of Sectors/Track
37	1,024	5	26

The capacity of this drive is calculated as follows:

1,024 tracks $\times$ 26 sectors/track $\times$ 512 bytes/sector $\times$ 5 heads = 68,157,440 bytes

68,157,440 bytes/1,024/1,024 = 65 MB

Adjusting for More Complex Hard Drive Organization

As hard drive size and technology improved, the OS and other software required new methods to relate to hard drive BIOS because of two situations that arose:

- Beginning with IDE technology, the number of sectors per track varied depending on the location of the track, which made it impossible for the OS and software to address the data on the hard drive using actual cylinder, head, and sector parameters.

---

[2] For hard drive capacity, some tables use the relation 1 MB = 1,000K and others use 1 MB = 1,024K. There are no standards; in fact, sometimes both relationships may be used in the same table to calculate drive capacity. A close look at Appendix B demonstrates the lack of consistency.

- When hard drives were small, the maximum size of the parameters that the OS and software sent to hard drive BIOS was established. These maximum values placed self-imposed limitations on the size hard drive that software can address using actual cylinder, head and sector parameters.

A+CORE
2.1,
4.4

However, it was important for the industry to retain backward compatibility so that legacy operating systems and other software could work. As is common in the evolution of computers, clever methods were devised to "trick" older technology so that it could work in newer environments. The older, legacy technology (in this case, software) still sees its world unchanged because the newer technology (in this case, BIOS) shelters it from the new methodology. These "deceptions" can happen at several stages of communication, in the following ways:

- The hard drive can use a complex cylinder, head, and sector organization that only the controller BIOS knows. However, the controller BIOS communicates to system BIOS in terms of the older methodology. When this method is used, the actual organization of the hard drive is called the physical geometry of the drive, and the organization communicated to system BIOS is called the logical geometry of the drive. This method is called the **CHS mode** (cylinder, head, sector), or **normal mode**.

- The hard drive controller BIOS sends the logical geometry to system BIOS, but system BIOS communicates a different set of parameters to the OS and other software. This method is called **translation**, and system BIOS is said to be in **large mode**, or **ECHS mode (extended CHS)**.

- The hard drive controller BIOS and system BIOS communicate using a method entirely different from cylinder, head, and sector information. System BIOS sends cylinder, head, and sector information to the software, which is neither logical nor physical geometry. This method of translation is referred to as **LBA mode (logical block addressing)**.

- The OS and software can bypass the system BIOS altogether and communicate directly with the controller BIOS by using device drivers. This is the method used by Windows NT and Windows 2000. True to its compromising nature, Windows 9x has its own 32-bit protected mode device drivers to access hard drives, bypassing system BIOS. However, in order to support DOS and other older software, Windows 9x also supports using system BIOS to access drives.

Physical Geometry and Logical Geometry

Although today's hard drives no longer organize data on the drive in a straightforward manner (Figure 6-4), but rather use zone bit recording (Figure 6-5), drive capacity is calculated in the same way, as if the number of sectors per track were constant. Controller BIOS masks the actual organization of the drive, called its **physical geometry**, from system BIOS and software. It communicates to system BIOS and software a number of cylinders, heads, and sectors, which, when used in calculations, yields the actual capacity of the drive, although the physical geometry may be quite different. These bogus values for cylinders, heads, and sectors are called the **logical geometry** of the drive.

CHS or Normal Mode

Recall that CHS mode (cylinders, heads, sectors), or normal mode, is the method system BIOS uses to manage a hard drive—it communicates to the controller BIOS the logical geometry of the hard drive based on tracks (or cylinders), heads, and sectors. This was the only method available for several years. CHS mode can be used only on hard drives where the following is true:

- The number of cylinders does not exceed 1,024.

- The number of heads does not exceed 16.

- There are no more than 63 sectors/track, assuming a constant number of sectors/track.

- There must be 512 bytes per sector.

Based on these criteria, the maximum amount of storage on a hard drive using CHS mode is 528 MB or 504 MB, depending on how the calculations are done (1K = 1000 or 1K = 1024). This limitation exists because of a combination of two factors: the way software calls up system BIOS to access the drive and the IDE/ATA interface standard that many hard drives adhere to (see Figure 6-15).

Figure 6-15   In using CHS mode to access a hard drive, limitations exist at two stages of communication, resulting in a combined limitation of 504 MB

Recall from Chapter 2 and Appendix G that software calls BIOS by issuing a software interrupt. The interrupt number for input and output to hard drives is Int 13h. At the same time, software also sends to the interrupt request handler (BIOS) the CHS parameters giving the location of the data it wants to access. A decision was made early in the evolution of managing hard drives to allot these parameters a certain number of memory addresses, which limits the maximum values for these parameters (see Table 6-6). Notice in the last column of Table 6-6 that if all bits are ones (giving the largest possible values), then 7.88 GB is the largest possible drive supported by this process whereby software uses interrupt 13h to call system BIOS.

Table 6-6   CHS parameters used by a software interrupt for system BIOS to access a hard drive

Description	Cylinders	Heads	Sectors	Totals
Number of bits used to store the value	10 bits	8 bits	6 bits	24 bits
Value range	0 to 1023	0 to 255	1 to 63	NA
Maximum number of values	1024 cylinders	256 heads	63 sectors	7.88 GB

The second limitation is a result of the IDE/ATA interface standards for hard drives for communication between the hard drive controller BIOS and system BIOS. When IDE hard drives were first built, different manufacturers used different interface standards to communicate the logical geometry of their drives to system BIOS. This resulted in the possibility that two drives from two different manufacturers could not coexist using only one system BIOS. To eliminate this compatibility problem, the IDE/ATA standard was adopted by the **American National Standards Institute** (**ANSI**), a nonprofit organization dedicated to creating trade and communications standards. The IDE/ATA interface standard maximums are listed in Table 6-7. If all 28 bits are ones, the drive size is 128 GB, the largest size that the IDE/ATA standard supports.

Table 6-7   Limitation of the IDE/ATA standard for hard drives

Description	Cylinders	Heads	Sectors	Total
Number of bits used to store the value	16 bits	4 bits	8 bits	28 bits
Maximum number of values	65,536 cylinders	16 heads	256 sectors	128 GB

The software interrupt Int 13h supports 7.88 GB, and the IDE/ATA standard supports 128 GB. Unfortunately, each standard distributed bits differently, so communication across both standards is limited to the smaller value of the two parameters. Therefore, the maximum values allowed using both standards are 1,024 cylinders (smaller value comes from Int 13h), 16 heads (smaller value comes from IDE/ATA standard), and 63 sectors (smaller value comes from Int 13h), which give us the 504 MB limitation. It's amazing that this limitation is not at all a limitation of hard drive technology, but rather a limitation caused by poor collaboration of standards. Figure 6-16 shows the resulting overall limitation that is caused by a combination of the limitations of the two standards.

Figure 6-16   In using CHS mode, the three limitations on the number of bits to transfer cylinder, head, and sector information are caused by software interrupt parameters and IDE interface limitations

Translation Methods

With hard drives larger than 504 MB (called large-capacity drives), translation is used to bypass these limitations in our standards and maintain backward compatibility with older software. System BIOS that supports translation methods and, therefore, allows access to drives larger than 504 MB is called **enhanced BIOS**. Remember that system BIOS supports a hard drive in one of three ways:

- CHS, or normal, mode (for drives less than 504 MB)

- ECHS mode, or large mode (uses translation to access drives between 504 MB and 8.4 GB)

- LBA mode (uses translation to access drives larger than 504 MB)

Look at the CMOS settings of your computer to determine which modes your system BIOS supports. In Figure 6-17, you can see where the two major translation methods occur in the different stages of communication with the hard drive.

Figure 6-17   Translation methods must be supported by system BIOS and the hard drive controller BIOS within the hard drive housing

A+CORE 2.1

ECHS Mode or Large Mode   For large-capacity drives, using ECHS mode, or large mode, system BIOS translates the logical geometry of the drive given to it by the controller BIOS into parameters that the software interrupt Int 13h can handle. As you can see from Table 6-6, Int 13h allocates the number of bits that allows for a very large value for the number of heads. Using ECHS, system BIOS adjusts the parameters to use a larger value for heads and a smaller value for cylinders than the original logical geometry. It does this to (1) make the calculation of drive capacity correct, (2) still adhere to the Int 13h limitation, and (3) break the 504-MB barrier. ECHS is sometimes called Extended Int 13h. Using this method, the maximum logical geometry of a drive is 16,383 cylinders, 16 heads, and 63 sectors yielding a drive capacity of 16,383 cylinders × 16 heads × 63 sectors × 512 bytes per sector = 8,455,200,700 bytes or an 8.4 GB drive. This 8.4 GB drive capacity is the maximum size hard drive that can be supported using a DOS or Windows 9x FAT16 file system and system BIOS using the ECHS mode. The 8.4 GB barrier is broken using LBA mode for system BIOS and FAT32 for the OS file system.

ECHS mode is not as popular as LBA mode. If you are not sure which mode your large-capacity hard drive supports and you need to make a selection in setup, LBA mode is your best guess.

LBA Mode   In using LBA mode to support large-capacity drives, the hard drive controller BIOS does not present the logical geometry to system BIOS (based on cylinders, heads, and sectors), but rather communicates by using another method called logical block addressing (LBA). System BIOS simply views the hard drive as a long list of sequential numbers (0, 1, 2, 3,...) called LBAs or addressable sectors. If system BIOS is being used to interface with the software, it then uses a method of enhanced CHS to give to the software cylinder, head, and sector information consistent with the overall capacity of the drive. These parameters

A+CORE
2.1

will have no relationship to the actual physical location of the data on the drive. LBA mode is the most popular way of dealing with drives larger than 504 MB and is the only way of dealing with drives larger than 8.4 GB.

For hard drives greater than 8.4 GB, CMOS setup reports a drive capacity in cylinders, heads, and sectors that does not reflect the true size of the drive. Because of this, the normal way of calculating the size of the drive does not work. For example, a 20 GB hard drive contains the following information in CMOS:

> Cylinders: 1024
> Heads: 255
> Sectors: 63
> CHS Capacity: 8422 MB
> Maximum LBA capacity: 20525 MB

6

Though the cylinder, head, and sector information is incorrect, the LBA capacity reflects the true size of the drive.

 TIP To use the operating system to report the capacity of a hard drive, for DOS, enter the command CHKDSK at the DOS prompt. For Windows 9x, using Windows Explorer, right-click the drive letter and select Properties from the shortcut menu. Report the capacity of each logical drive on the hard drive and then add them together to get the entire hard drive capacity.

System BIOS Helps Manage Data Transfer

System BIOS is used in three different ways to support a hard drive:

- System BIOS provides the interrupt handler for software interrupts (discussed above).

- System BIOS can automatically detect and configure a hard drive (will be discussed in Chapter 7).

- System BIOS helps manage data transfer over the I/O bus between the hard drive and memory.

So far in our discussion, we have considered how data is accessed on the drive by using various methods of viewing the data on the drive. Now we turn our attention to how the data is transferred over the bus to memory, once the data is accessed. There are several data transfer methods and protocols used, many of which must be supported by system BIOS as well as the hard drive, in order to work. As hard drive technologies improve, so do the standards managing them. There is IDE/ATA, the first hard drive standard, followed by ATA-2, Fast ATA, Fast ATA-2, ATA-3, ATAPI, Ultra ATA, Ultra ATA/66, and Ultra ATA/100. In most cases, a PC technician does not need to know which standard a hard drive supports, because BIOS autodetection selects the best possible standard supported by both hard drive and BIOS.

Who's in Charge? Data transfer over the I/O bus can be managed in one of three ways, depending on which component controls the process.

- Using programmed I/O (PIO) mode, the CPU is in charge and manages data transfer. There are five different PIO modes (0 to 4) with transfer rates from 3.3 MB/sec to 16.6 MB/sec.

- Using DMA with the DMA controller in charge, data is transferred to memory without the involvement of the CPU.

- With bus mastering using DMA, the hard drive BIOS controls data transfer. The highest transfer rates are attained using this method. Transfer rates using DMA with bus mastering are 33, 44, 66, and 100 MB/sec. Speeds of 66 MB/sec and higher require the special 80-conductor IDE cable. Error checking is also done.

The latest advancement in data transfer is Ultra ATA (also called Ultra DMA) which involves bus mastering controlled by the hard drive BIOS. The hard drive controller, the system board chipset, and the operating system must support the transfer mode. For more information about this technology, see the web site of T13 Committee, the organization responsible for its standards, at www.t13.org.

How Much Can be Transferred at One Time? Using the IDE/ATA standard, data is transferred 16 bits at a time from the hard drive to the I/O bus over the hard drive cable. Once on the bus, data can be transferred at 16-bit access or 32-bit access.

How Much Overhead? Some BIOSs support a method of data transfer that allows multiple transfers of data on a single software interrupt. This method is called **block mode** and should be used if your hard drive and BIOS support it. However, if you are having problems with hard drive errors, one thing you can try is disabling block mode. Use CMOS setup to make the change.

OPERATING SYSTEM COMMANDS TO MANAGE A HARD DRIVE

DOS and Windows 9x have similar commands and methods of managing a hard drive. Below, DOS commands are discussed first, and then the same functions are covered in Windows 9x.

DOS Commands to Manage a Hard Drive

The DOS commands to manage a hard drive are described in this section, along with examples of how to use them. For more extensive discussions, see the *DOS User's Guide and Reference Manual*, or at the DOS prompt type HELP followed by the name of the command. In addition to the commands below, other DOS commands covered in Chapter 5 to manage files on a floppy drive can also be used on a hard drive. These are FORMAT, LABEL, DEL, UNDELETE, RECOVER, COPY, XCOPY, and DELTREE.

MKDIR [drive:]path or MD [drive:]path Command

The **MKDIR** (abbreviated MD, standing for make directory) **command** creates a subdirectory entry in a directory. This command can be used on both hard drives and floppy disks. Think of a subdirectory as a list within a list, much like the hierarchy of an outline or a company organizational chart. In an outline, there are major categories, and under some of these major categories more detailed subordinate items are listed. Parent directories are equivalent to the major categories. These parent directories can have subordinate directories, or subdirectories (sometimes called child directories) listed within them. When you move to these subdirectories, you see another list. This list too can have subdirectories.

You can use subdirectories to organize and categorize files. Long lists of unrelated items are tedious and difficult to manage. Putting related files under a single subdirectory heading simplifies your work. Software installation programs place an application it is installing in a separate directory to prevent mixing its program files with other files on the hard drive. Data that is created by a software package should not be put in the same directory as the software itself, for several reasons. If you are creating, copying, or deleting data files, you are less likely to erase or overwrite a software file if the data is in a different directory. Also, there is no question later about which files are data files and which are software files.

Another reason to keep data in one directory and the software in another is that it makes backing up easier. As soon as you have installed a software package and confirmed that it is working properly, you may want to back up your hard drive. This one backup of the software is all that's necessary unless you make a change to the software. The data, however, needs backing up as soon as you have several hours invested in it. If the data changes often, make regular backups. How often depends on how much data is changed and when it is changed. If the data is in its own directory, you can easily back up just that directory instead of having to back up the software with the data.

It's good practice to create a data directory in the software directory that manages that data. The software directory is called the parent directory, and the data directory is called a child directory. Just as with outlines, you commonly say that the child directory is "under," or subordinate to, the parent directory. When viewing the directory structure, it is easy, then, to see which data files belong to which software.

Another approach is to create one directory under the root directory named \Data. Put all data files under this directory, organized by type of data or by subject (see Figure 6-18). If you prefer to organize the data by file type, within the \Data directory, create one directory for each application program you are using and store the data for that application in that subdirectory. If you prefer to organize by subject, create a subdirectory for each subject (examples are personal, administration, Project 1, Project 2), and place all file types that pertain to that subject in that subdirectory. By putting all data files under a single subdirectory tree structure, it is easy to quickly back up all the data on your hard drive by selecting only this one directory, \Data. For example, to back up all the data on your hard drive to a Zip drive, select \Data and copy its contents to the Zip drive.

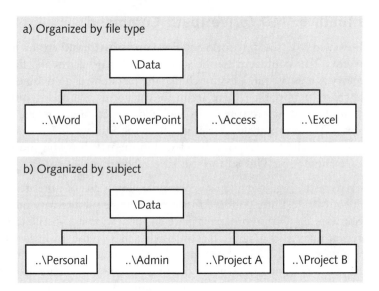

Figure 6-18   Two subdirectory trees to hold data on a hard drive

MKDIR Syntax and Some Examples   When using the MKDIR command, you need not specify the drive if the drive is the current default drive, and you need not specify the parent directory if it is the current default directory. To create a directory named \GAME on drive C, for example, use this command:

    MKDIR C:\GAME

The backslash indicates that the directory is under the root directory. To create a directory named CHESS under the \GAME directory, use this command:

    MKDIR C:\GAME\CHESS

DOS requires that the parent directory GAME must already exist before it can create the child directory CHESS.

Figure 6-19 shows the result of the DIR command on the directory \GAME. Note the two initial entries in the directory table, the . (dot) and the .. (dot, dot) entries. These two entries are created by the MKDIR command when DOS initially sets up the directory. You cannot edit these entries with normal DOS commands, and they must remain in the directory for the directory's lifetime. The . entry points to the subdirectory itself, and the .. entry points to the parent directory—in this case, the root directory.

A+ OS
1.1

```
C:\>DIR \GAME /P

 Volume in drive C has no label
 Volume Serial Number is 0F52-09FC
 Directory of C:\GAME

 .           <DIR>      02-18-93   4:50a
 ..          <DIR>      02-18-93   4:50a
 CHESS       <DIR>      02-18-93   4:50a
 NUKE        <DIR>      02-18-93   4:51a
 PENTE       <DIR>      02-18-93   4:52a
 NETRIS      <DIR>      02-18-93   4:54a
 BEYOND      <DIR>      02-18-93   4:54a
         7 file(s)              0 bytes
                        9273344 bytes free

C:\>
```

Figure 6-19   DIR of the \GAME directory

6

CHDIR [drive:]path or CD [drive:]path or CD..

The **CHDIR** (abbreviated CD, standing for change directory) **command** changes the current default directory. In its easiest-to-follow form, you simply state the drive and the entire path that you want to be current:

    CD C:\GAME\CHESS

If you have previously issued the PROMPT PG command, either from the DOS prompt or from the AUTOEXEC.BAT file, the DOS prompt will look like this:

    C:\GAME\CHESS>

To move from a child directory to its parent directory, use the .. variation of the command:

    C:\GAME\CHESS> CD..
    C:\GAME>

Remember that .. always means the parent directory. You can move from a parent directory to one of its child directories simply by stating the name of the child directory:

    C:\GAME> CD CHESS
    C:\GAME\CHESS>

Do not put a backslash in front of the child directory name; doing so tells DOS to go to a directory named CHESS that is directly under the root directory.

RMDIR [drive:]path or RD [drive:]path

The **RMDIR command** (abbreviated RD, standing for remove directory) removes a subdirectory. Before you can use the RMDIR command, three things must be true:

- The directory must contain no files.

- The directory must contain no subdirectories.

- The directory must not be the current directory.

The . and .. entries are present when a directory is ready for removal. For example, to remove the \GAME directory in the above example, the CHESS directory must first be removed:

```
C:\> RMDIR C:\GAME\CHESS
```

Or, if the \GAME directory is the current directory, use this command:

```
C:\GAME> RD CHESS
```

Once you remove the CHESS directory, you can remove the \GAME directory. You must first leave the \GAME directory like this:

```
C:\GAME>CD..
C:\> RD \GAME
```

TREE [drive:][path] [/F] [/A]

The **TREE command** displays the directory structure of a hard drive or disk. If you do not specify a drive or path, the TREE command displays the directory structure of the current drive and current directory. The command displays the structure in graphic form unless you include the /A option, which specifies text format. The /F option has the TREE command include the names of the files in a directory as well as the directory name.

For example, to display the subdirectory structure of the \Windows directory with files also listed, one screen at a time, use this command:

```
C:\> TREE \WINDOWS /F | MORE
```

The |MORE option at the end of the command line causes the output of the command to be displayed one screen at a time rather than continuously scrolled.

To send the output to a printer, use this command:

```
C:\> TREE \WINDOWS /F > PRN
```

A^+ *OS*
1.1,
3.2

ATTRIB

The **ATTRIB command** displays or changes the read-only, archive, system, and hidden attributes assigned to files. To display the attributes of the file MYFILE.TXT, use this command:

```
ATTRIB MYFILE.TXT
```

To hide the file, use this command:

```
ATTRIB +H MYFILE.TXT
```

To remove the hide status of the file, use this command:

```
ATTRIB -H MYFILE.TXT
```

To make the file a read-only file, use this command:

```
ATTRIB +R MYFILE.TXT
```

To remove the read-only status of the file, use this command:

```
ATTRIB -R MYFILE.TXT
```

A+ OS
1.1,
3.2

To turn the archive bit on, use this command:

```
ATTRIB +A MYFILE.TXT
```

To turn the archive bit off, use this command:

```
ATTRIB -A MYFILE.TXT
```

MIRROR

The **MIRROR command** saves partition table information to disk when used with the /PARTN parameter, like this:

```
MIRROR /PARTN
```

The MIRROR command is an older DOS 5 command that was not included with later versions of DOS. If you have access to DOS 5, even after you upgrade to a later version of DOS, keep the command file for MIRROR in your DOS directory as a quick and easy method of saving partition table information to floppy disk.

UNFORMAT

The **UNFORMAT command** not only reverses the effect of an accidental format, but also repairs a damaged partition table if the table has previously been saved with the MIRROR /PARTN command.

To unformat a disk, use this command:

```
UNFORMAT C:
```

To repair a damaged partition table if the table has previously been saved to a disk, use this command:

```
UNFORMAT /PARTN
```

PATH

As discussed in Chapter 2, the PATH command lists where DOS and Windows 3.x should look to find executable program files. This command is discussed here again to make the list of commands more complete. A sample PATH command is

```
PATH C:\;C:\DOS;C:\WINDOWS;C:\UTILITY
```

Each path is separated from the next with a semicolon. You should put the most-used paths at the beginning of the line, because the OS searches the paths listed in the PATH command line from left to right. The PATH command goes in the AUTOEXEC.BAT file and can be executed from the DOS prompt.

Using Batch Files

Suppose you have a list of DOS commands that you want to execute several times. Perhaps you have some data files to distribute to several PCs in your office, and, having no LAN, you must walk from one PC to another doing the same job repeatedly. A solution is to store the list of commands in a **batch file** on disk and then execute the batch file at each PC. DOS and Windows require that the batch file have a .BAT file extension. For example, store these five DOS commands on a disk in a file named MYLOAD.BAT:

```
C:
MD\UTILITY
MD\UTILITY\TOOLS
CD\UTILITY\TOOLS
COPY A:\TOOLS\*.*
```

From the C prompt, you execute the batch file, just as with other program files, by entering the name of the file with or without the file extension:

```
A:\>MYLOAD
```

All the commands listed in the file will execute, beginning at the top of the list. The batch file above will create a subdirectory under the C drive called utility\tools; change to that directory as the default directory, and copy all files from the disk in drive A into that new subdirectory. Look at any good book on DOS to find examples of the very useful ways you can elaborate on batch files, including adding user menus. AUTOEXEC.BAT is an example of a batch file.

Using Windows 9x to Manage a Hard Drive

Windows 9x Explorer is the primary tool for managing the files on your hard drive. Windows 9x calls a directory or subdirectory a **folder**. Windows 98 is used in the following examples, but Windows 95 works the same way. Open Explorer in Windows 98 (click **Start**, **Programs**, **Windows Explorer**, or right-click **My Computer** and select **Explore** from the menu) and follow the directions below to manage files and folders on your hard drive.

A+ OS 1.1 Create a New Folder

To create a folder (equivalent to the DOS MD command), do the following. Select the folder you want to be the parent folder by clicking the folder name. For example, to create a folder named Chess under the folder named Games, first click the Games folder. Then click the **File** menu. Select **New** from the menu. Then select **Folder** from the submenu that is displayed, as in Figure 6-20. The new folder will be created under Games, but its name will be New Folder. Click the folder name to open the text box and change the name of the folder. Change the name from New Folder to Chess, as in Figure 6-21.

Figure 6-20   Create a new folder

Figure 6-21   Edit the new folder's name

Delete a Folder

To delete a folder (equivalent to the DOS RD command) from Explorer, right-click the folder and select **Delete** from the shortcut menu. A confirmation dialog box like the one in Figure 6-22 asks you if you are sure you want to delete the folder. If you respond **Yes**, the folder and all of its contents, including subfolders, will be sent to the Recycle Bin. Empty the Recycle Bin to free your disk space.

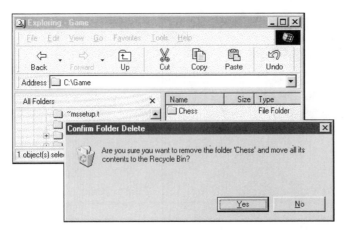

Figure 6-22 Delete a folder in Windows 98

A^+ OS 1.2 **File Properties**

To access file properties in Windows 98, from Explorer, right-click a file and select **Properties** from the shortcut menu. The Properties window appears, as shown in Figure 6-23. Windows 98 identifies the file type primarily by the file extension. From the Properties window, you can change the attributes of the file.

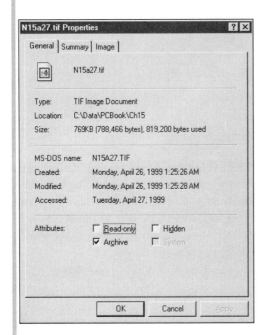

Figure 6-23 Properties of a file in Windows 98

The PATH Command and Batch Files

Although the PATH command and AUTOEXEC.BAT are not necessary in Windows 9x, you can use them the same way as in DOS and Windows 3.x. If you have an AUTOEXEC.BAT file in your root directory when Windows 9x starts, it reads the PATH command stored in that file. You can also store DOS commands in batch files and execute them from Windows 9x by double-clicking the filename of the batch file in Explorer.

Windows 9x uses a default path of C:\Windows; C:\Windows\Command if you don't have an AUTOEXEC.BAT file. Not all paths to program files must appear in the PATH command, as they do in DOS. To edit AUTOEXEC.BAT in Windows 9x, right-click the filename and select **Edit** from the shortcut menu. Notepad is executed. After making changes, restart your computer for the changes to take effect.

6

OPTIMIZING A HARD DRIVE

In the first part of this chapter, you saw how data is stored on a drive from the perspective of the OS, which sees the drive as a long list of clusters made up of 512-byte sectors. This section will delve more deeply into drive technology, looking at how a drive is formatted, the different ways data is stored, and some ways to optimize data access. Formatting a hard drive is introduced here in preparation for understanding some of the concepts of optimizing the drive discussed later in the chapter. A more detailed discussion of formatting a hard drive is left for Chapter 7, which covers installing a hard drive.

Fragmentation

A+ OS
1.3,
1.1,
3.2

Fragmentation is the undesirable placement of a single file in several cluster locations that are not right next to each other, so that data access time is increased. When a hard drive is new and freshly formatted, the OS writes files to the drive beginning with cluster 2, placing the data in consecutive clusters. Each new file begins with the next available cluster. Later, after a file has been deleted, the OS writes a new file to the drive, beginning with the first available cluster in the FAT. If the OS encounters used clusters as it is writing the file, it simply skips these clusters and uses the next available one. In this way, after many files have been deleted and added to the drive, files become fragmented. Fragmentation occurs when files are written to a drive in more than one group of contiguous clusters. The clusters that make up a file are together called a **chain**. For a well-used hard drive, it is possible to have a file stored in clusters at 20, 30, 40, or more locations. Fragmentation is undesirable because (1) when DOS has to access many different locations on the drive to read a file, access time slows down, and (2) if the file should become corrupted, recovering a fragmented file is more complicated than recovering a file in one continuous chain.

For these reasons, one routine maintenance task is to periodically **defragment** the hard drive. For DOS, the simplest way to do this is to use DOS 6+ DEFRAG or a utility software package, such as Nuts & Bolts or Norton Utilities, which reads the files on your drive and rearranges the clusters so that all files are written into contiguous chains. If you have utility software that does this, running it every six months or so is a good maintenance plan. To

A^+ *OS*
1.3,
1.1,
3.2

graphically see how badly a drive is fragmented, use Norton to view your FAT. Norton high-lights the clusters for each file in a different color so you can easily identify all the clusters that belong to a single file. By moving your cursor over the FAT, you can easily see whether your hard drive is badly fragmented.

For Windows 9x, the **Defragmenter** utility is also available. Choose **Start**, then **Programs**, then **Accessories**, and then **System Tools**. The menu in Figure 6-24 is displayed. (Two of the other menu items, ScanDisk and DriveSpace, will be discussed next.) Click **Disk Defragmenter** and select the drive from the dialog box that is displayed. Click OK. When the operation is complete, the message in Figure 6-25 appears; click **Yes** to exit.

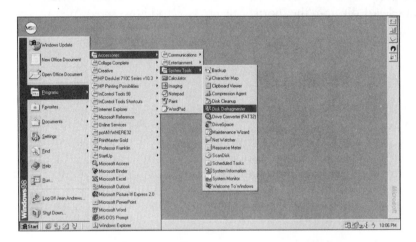

Figure 6-24   Windows 98 utilities

Figure 6-25   Disk Defragmenter results

TIP   Defragmenting a large hard drive may take a long time, so plan for this before you begin.

Cross-Linked and Lost Clusters

As you learned in Chapter 5, the directory on either a floppy disk or hard drive holds the number of the first cluster in the file. The FAT holds the map to all the clusters in a file. Occasionally, the mapping in the FAT becomes corrupted, resulting either in lost clusters or in cross-linked clusters, as shown in Figure 6-26. Here File 3 has lost direction and is pointing to a cluster chain that belongs to File 4. Clusters 29–31 are called **cross-linked clusters** because more than one file points to them, and clusters 15–17 and 28 are called **lost clusters** because no file in the FAT points to them.

Figure 6-26   Lost and cross-linked clusters

$A+$ *OS*
1.3,
1.1,
3.2

To repair cross-linked and lost clusters, use the ScanDisk utility in either DOS or Windows 9x. For DOS, enter the command **SCANDISK** from the DOS prompt. The screen in Figure 6-27 is displayed. When the program finishes scanning the disk, it returns you to a DOS prompt.

Figure 6-27   SCANDISK for DOS

A+ OS
1.3,
3.2

For Windows 98, click **Start**, then **Programs**, then **Accessories**, then **System Tools**, and then **ScanDisk**, as shown in Figure 6-24. The ScanDisk utility first asks which drive you want to scan and gives you the choice between a standard and thorough scan. The standard scan checks files and folders for errors. The thorough scan does all that the standard scan does plus checks the disk surface. Click **Start** to begin the scan. Errors are reported as in Figure 6-28, and results are displayed as in Figure 6-29.

Figure 6-28   ScanDisk reports errors

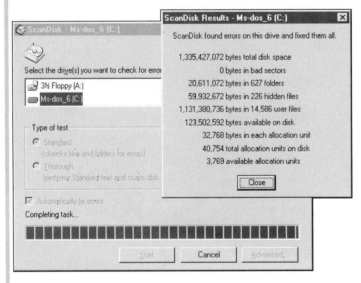

Figure 6-29   ScanDisk results

Disk Compression

Disk compression software can help meet the ever-increasing demands for more space on hard drives to hold improved software. Software packages requiring 100 to 150 MB of hard drive space were unheard of three or four years ago but are now common. The sizes of hard drives have increased proportionately. Even so, we often seek ways to cram more onto nearly full hard drives.

What Is Disk Compression?

Software to manage disk compression works by (1) storing data on your hard drive in one big file and managing the writing of data and programs to that file, and (2) rewriting data in files in a mathematically coded format that uses less space. Most disk compression programs, such as Stacker and DOS DriveSpace, combine these two methods.

Disk Compression in DOS and Windows 3.x

The first method listed above relies on the disk compression software provided by DOS and Windows 3.x, which uses a device driver loaded in the CONFIG.SYS file. The driver treats all the hard drive space as one big file called the host file. When DOS tries to write files to the hard drive, it passes these files to the driver, which does the actual writing. The driver keeps track of where the files are located on the drive. Normally with DOS the smallest allocation unit for a file is 1 cluster, which can be as large as 8 sectors or 4,096 bytes, so that even files physically smaller than one cluster still occupy a full 4,096 bytes. With a disk compression driver, the smallest allocation unit is one sector, or 512 bytes, and sometimes this is even reduced to one-half sector, or 256 bytes. The driver is free to place as many as eight small files into the 4,096-byte cluster space that DOS would use for one small file. This method of disk compression can be very effective if the drive contains many small files. If most files on the drive exceed 4,096 bytes, there may be little gain.

The second method of disk compression for hard drives listed above takes its idea from file compression software like PKZIP. File compression has been around for quite some time. It compresses one or more files into one small file for easy exporting to other systems. The file compression program looks for repeating characters in the data and eliminates the repetition by indicating how many times a character should be written instead of writing the character that many times. The program also writes characters that do not require an entire 8 bits by using only the bits that the character needs. For example, most ASCII characters only use 7 of the 8 bits (see Appendix C). File compression software uses the eighth bit for something else. By making use of every bit and by eliminating repeating characters, this software can compress data to as little as 65% of its original size.

All this sounds very good. You can make an older 500-MB hard drive magically hold 700 MB by adding just one more driver in your CONFIG.SYS file. Caution, however, is in order. Remember that the compression software is putting all your software and data into a single file. Occasionally, one or two files on a hard drive or floppy disk become corrupted. As long as this involves only a single file and rarely happens, you can deal with the loss by recovering the file from a backup, borrowing a fresh copy from a friend, or even reconstructing the file entirely. But with **data compression**, that one file is everything on your hard drive. All your eggs are truly in one basket!

You also have the added complexity of having one more layer of software manipulating your data. If this driver is incompatible with some application you happen to be using one day, the results could be disastrous. Also, because of this added complexity, disk access time is slowed down.

In summary, disk compression does save hard drive space, but you need to carefully consider the risks involved. If you do choose to use disk compression, keep good backups of both the data and the software. If the data and software on your drive are especially valuable, you may want to invest in a larger hard drive instead of using compression.

Disk Compression in Windows 9x

A+ OS 1.3

A **compressed drive** is not a drive at all; it's a file. Figure 6-30 shows the two parts of a compressed drive. The **host drive**, in this case drive H, is not compressed and is usually a very small partition on the drive, generally under 2 MB. The host drive contains a special file called a **CVF** (**compressed volume file**). The CVF holds everything on drive C, compressed into just one file.

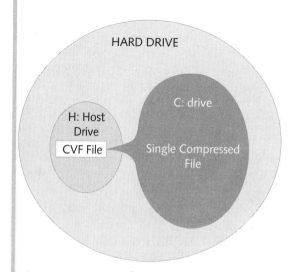

Figure 6-30   A compressed drive

Although there are several disk compression utilities on the market, Windows 9x offers its own, called **DriveSpace**. Others are STAC Electronics Stacker and DoubleSpace, both of which are supported by Windows 9x. DoubleSpace is also available under Windows 3.x. DriveSpace is used in the example here.

> **TIP**   DriveSpace does not work with FAT32 under Windows 98.

DriveSpace does the following things to compress a drive.

- Assigns a different drive letter to the hard drive, such as H
- Compresses the entire contents of the hard drive into a single file on drive H

- Sets up the drive so that Windows 9x and other applications view this compressed file as drive C

- Configures Windows 9x so that each time it boots, the DriveSpace driver will load and manage the compressed drive

Follow these steps to compress a drive in Windows 98 using DriveSpace: Click **Start**, then **Programs**, then **Accessories**, then **System Tools**, as shown in Figure 6-29. Click **DriveSpace** to display the dialog box in Figure 6-31. Drive A is used as the example here, but drive C gives similar results. Select drive A by clicking on it, and then choose **Compress** from the Drive menu. The dialog box in Figure 6-32 is displayed, showing how much space would be created by compressing the drive. Click **Options**, and the Compression Options box in Figure 6-33 appears. Note that you can allow extra space on drive H that will not be compressed. Click **OK** to return to the box in Figure 6-32. Click **Start** to begin compression. A dialog box displays suggesting that you make backups before compressing the drive.

Figure 6-31   Selecting drive using DriveSpace for Windows 98

Figure 6-32   Drive compression predictions

Figure 6-33   Drive compression options

> **TIP** If a Windows 9x utility such as DriveSpace is missing from a menu list, maybe the component was not installed when Windows was installed. To install a Windows component after Windows is installed, go to **Control Panel**, select **Add/Remove Programs**, and click the **Windows Setup** tab.

After a drive is compressed, you can use Explorer to monitor and manage the drive. Right-click the drive letter in Explorer and select **Properties**. Click the **Compression** tab to see information about the compressed drive. Click **Advanced** to see information about the host drive and to run DriveSpace (Figure 6-34).

You can also use Explorer to see how much space compressing a drive will create. Right-click the drive letter and select **Properties,** and then click the **Compression** tab (Figure 6-35). The amount of space made available when a drive is compressed depends on the amount of free space on the drive before compression. To get the most resources out of compression, begin with a relatively free hard drive.

Figure 6-34   The Advanced Properties box gives information about the host drive for a compressed drive

Figure 6-35   The Compression tab on the Properties box gives predictions about compressing a drive

Also notice in Figure 6-35 the option to create a new, empty compressed drive by using the free space on the existing uncompressed drive. Click **Create New Drive**, and Figure 6-36 is displayed. Select the amount of space you want to allot to the new compressed drive and click **Start**. This method is a relatively harmless way to experiment with hard drive compression.

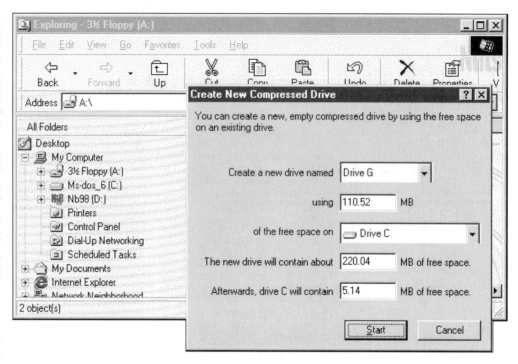

Figure 6-36   A new, empty compressed drive can be created by using free space on an existing drive

A drive can be uncompressed from the DriveSpace Drive menu if you first delete enough files so that the amount of data on the drive does not exceed the uncompressed capacity. If you compress a drive, the driver to manage the compressed drive is loaded only when Windows 9x senses that a compressed drive is present. After the hard drive is uncompressed, Windows 9x no longer automatically loads the mounting driver.

Disk Caching

A **disk cache** is a temporary storage area in RAM for data being read from or written to a hard drive to speed up access time to the drive. The idea behind a cache on a hard drive can be explained as follows:

The CPU asks for data from a hard drive. The hard drive controller sends instructions to the drive to read the data and then sends it to the CPU. The CPU requests more data, quite often data that immediately follows the previously read data on the hard drive. The controller reads the requested data from the drive and sends it to the CPU. Without a cache, each CPU request is handled with a read to the hard drive, as indicated in the top part of Figure 6-37.

Figure 6-37   A CPU asking a hard drive for data without cache (upper part) and with cache (lower part)

With a hard drive cache, the cache software handles the requests for data, as seen in the lower part of Figure 6-37. The cache program reads ahead of the CPU requests by guessing what data the CPU will request next. Since most data that the CPU requests is in consecutive areas on the drive, the cache program guesses correctly most of the time. The program stores the read-ahead data in memory (RAM). When the CPU requests the next group of data, if the cache program guessed right, the program can send that data to the CPU from memory without having to go back to the hard drive. Some cache software caches entire tracks at a time; others cache groups of sectors.

Hardware Cache or Software Cache

There are two kinds of hard drive caches: a hardware cache and a software cache. Some hard drive controllers have a **hardware cache** built right into the controller circuit board. The BIOS on the controller contains the cache program, and RAM chips on the controller hold the cache.

A **software cache** is a cache program that is stored on the hard drive like other software and is loaded into memory as a TSR, usually when a computer is booted. The software cache program uses system RAM to hold the cache.

There are advantages and disadvantages of each. A hardware cache does not use RAM on the system board, but a software cache uses RAM for both the cache program itself and the data being cached. Therefore, a disadvantage of a software cache is that RAM is used that might otherwise be used for applications software and its data.

On the other hand, a software cache is faster because of where the data is stored. Since data is stored in RAM, when the CPU is ready for the data, the data only needs to travel from RAM to the CPU on the memory bus, the fastest bus on the system board. Since the hardware cache is on the controller board, when the CPU is ready for data stored in this cache, the data must travel from the controller board over one or more buses to the CPU.

Another disadvantage of a hardware cache is that it is a permanent part of the hard drive controller, and today's hard drives have the controller built into the drive housing. If a faster software cache becomes available, upgrading software stored on your hard drive is a viable option, but exchanging hard drives to upgrade to a faster hardware cache is impractical.

When buying a new hard drive, check whether it includes hardware caches as an option. A controller with its own hardware cache is slightly more expensive than one without a cache.

Disk Cache in DOS and Windows 3.x

SMARTDrive is a 16-bit real mode software cache utility that comes with DOS and Windows 3.x. With DOS 6+, SMARTDrive is executed as a TSR from the AUTOEXEC.BAT file. With earlier versions of DOS, SMARTDrive worked as a device driver and was loaded from the CONFIG.SYS file with the DEVICE= command line. SMARTDrive caches data both being read from and written to the hard drive and caches data being read from floppy disks.

Other popular kinds of cache software for DOS and Windows 3.x are:

- Norton Cache, included in Norton Utilities
- Mace Cache, included in Mace Utilities
- Super PC-Kwik Cache from Multisoft

VCACHE in Windows 9x

Windows 9x has a built-in 32-bit, protected-mode software cache called **VCACHE**. **VCACHE** is automatically loaded by Windows 9x without entries in CONFIG.SYS or AUTOEXEC.BAT. VCACHE doesn't take up conventional memory or upper memory space the way SMARTDrive does, and it does a much better job of caching. Also, you don't need to tell VCACHE how much memory to allocate to disk caching, as you do with SMARTDrive; VCACHE allocates the amount of memory it uses on the basis of available memory and disk activity.

> **TIP** In speaking of disk caching, don't confuse a disk cache with a memory cache, discussed in earlier chapters. Memory caching is caching slow memory (DRAM) into fast memory (SRAM). Disk caching is caching slow secondary storage (hard drive) into faster primary storage (RAM).

DOS Buffers

Several years ago, before hard drive caching, buffers were used to speed up disk access. A **buffer** is an area in memory where data waiting to be read or written is temporarily stored. Disk caches do a better job of speeding up disk access than buffers, but many older software packages still in use require that DOS maintain buffers. To specify how many buffers DOS should maintain, use the BUFFERS= command in the CONFIG.SYS file. The only reason to use buffers today is to satisfy the requirements of older software that uses them. See the software documentation for the recommended number of buffers.

Using DOS under Windows 9x to Manage a Hard Drive

A word of caution: using some DOS commands on a hard drive that uses Windows 9x as the OS may cause damage to a hard drive's file structure. With a Windows 9x upgrade, some of these dangerous commands are erased from the \DOS directory on the hard drive. However, you will find DOS commands that come with Windows 9x stored in the \Windows\Command directory, and some of these should not be used. Here are the ones to avoid:

- Don't use disk utility software that does not know about VFAT, long filenames or FAT32, including older versions of Norton Utilities and Central Point PC Tools.

- Don't use FDISK, FORMAT C:, SYS C:, or CHKDSK while in a DOS session within Windows 9x. However, some of these functions are covered in the next chapter and will be useful to you when you learn what they do and how they do it.

- Don't optimize or defragment your hard drive using software that does not know about long filenames; look for the Windows 95 or Windows 98 compatibility message on the package.

- Don't run hard drive cache programs unless they are written especially for Windows 95 or Windows 98. Remember that Windows 9x has its own built-in caching software.

- Don't use the older DOS backup programs like BACKUP or MSBACKUP, because the long filename information might not be saved during the backup.

CHAPTER SUMMARY

- Most hard drives today use IDE technology, which has a complex method of organizing tracks and sectors on the disks.

- Older hard drives used either MFM or RLL technology, which used the same number of sectors on every track on the drive.

- The term SCSI hard drive refers more to the bus used by the drive than to the technology of the drive.

- There are several variations of SCSI buses and bus devices, including SCSI-1, SCSI-2, Wide SCSI, Ultra SCSI, and Ultra Wide SCSI.

- Every SCSI bus subsystem requires a host adapter with a SCSI controller and SCSI IDs assigned to each device, including the host adapter.

❏ Each end of the SCSI bus must have a terminating resistor, which can be either hardware or software.

❏ Hard drive capacity for drives less than 8.4 GB is determined by the number of heads, tracks, and sectors on the disk, each sector holding 512 bytes of data.

❏ The operating system views a hard drive through a FAT (file allocation table), which lists clusters, and a directory, which lists files.

❏ A hard drive is partitioned into logical drives, or volumes. A master boot record at the beginning of the hard drive contains a table of partition information. Each logical drive contains a boot record, FAT, and root directory.

❏ Physical geometry is the actual organization of heads, tracks, and sectors on the drive, whereas logical geometry is head, track, and sector information that the hard drive controller BIOS presents to system BIOS and the OS. The logical geometry may not be the same as the physical geometry, but, for drives less than 8.4 GB, should yield the same capacity when calculations are made.

❏ Drives larger than 8.4 GB use LBA mode in which (or "where") the drive is viewed by the BIOS and OS as addressable sectors. The capacity of the drive is calculated as the number of addressable sectors multiplied by 512 bytes per sector.

❏ System BIOS and software can use CHS, large mode, or LBA mode to manage a hard drive. The size of the drive and the drive manufacturer determine which mode is used.

❏ The FAT, or file allocation table, lists all clusters on the hard drive and describes how each is allocated. FAT16 uses 16-bit entries and FAT32 uses 32-bit entries to hold the cluster numbers.

❏ DOS and the first release of Windows 95 support the FAT16 file system for hard drives. Windows 95 Release 2, and Windows 98 support FAT16 and FAT32 file systems. Windows NT supports FAT16 and the NTFS file systems. Windows 2000 supports FAT16, FAT32, and the NTFS file systems.

❏ The FAT16 file system can be used for drives less than 8.4 GB, but for larger drives, the FAT32 or the NTFS file system must be used.

❏ Directories on a hard drive hold the information about each file stored on the drive. The main directory created when the drive is first formatted is called the root directory.

❏ Commands to manage a hard drive include those to create and remove directories, change the attributes on a file, and list paths where the OS can look to find software. DOS and Windows 9x offer commands or menu options to perform these tasks.

❏ Some ways to optimize drive space and access speed are to reduce fragmentation, to scan the disk for errors, to compress the drive, and to use disk caching.

KEY TERMS

Adapter card — Also called an interface card. A small circuit board inserted in an expansion slot and used to communicate between the system bus and a peripheral device.

Advanced SCSI programming interface (ASPI) — A popular device driver that enables operating systems to communicate with a SCSI host adapter. (The "A" originally stood for Adaptec.)

ANSI (American National Standards Institute) — A nonprofit organization dedicated to creating trade and communications standards.

ATTRIB command — A DOS command that can display file attributes and even lock files so that they are "read-only" and cannot be modified (for example, ATTRIB +R FILENAME).

Autodetection — A feature of system BIOS that automatically detects the presence of a new hard drive and identifies and configures the drive to CMOS setup.

Batch file — A text file containing a series of DOS instructions to the computer, telling it to perform a specific task (for example, AUTOEXEC.BAT, which contains a series of startup commands).

Block mode — A method of data transfer between hard drive and memory that allows multiple data transfers on a single software interrupt.

Buffer — A temporary memory area where data is kept before being written to a hard drive or sent to a printer, thus reducing the number of writes to the devices.

Burst transfer — A means of sending data across the bus, with one packet immediately following the next, without waiting for clock beats and/or addressing of the information being sent.

CD or CHDIR command — A DOS command to change directories (for example, CD\WINDOWS would change the directory to the Windows directory, and CD\ would return to the Root directory).

Chain — A group of clusters used to hold a single file.

CHS (cylinders, heads, sectors) mode — The traditional method by which BIOS reads from and writes to hard drives by addressing the correct cylinder, head, and sector. Also called normal mode.

Common access method (CAM) — A standard adapter driver used by SCSI.

Compressed drive — A drive whose format has been reorganized in order to store more data. A compressed drive is not a drive at all; it's actually a type of file, typically with a host drive called H.

Cross-linked clusters — Errors caused when files appear to share the same disk space, according to the file allocation table.

CVF (compressed volume file) — The file on the host drive of a compressed drive that holds all compressed data.

Data compression — Reducing the size of files by various techniques such as using a shortcut code to represent repeated data.

Defragment — To "optimize" or rewrite a file to a disk in one contiguous chain of clusters, thus speeding up data retrieval.

6

Disk cache — A method whereby recently retrieved data and adjacent data are read into memory in advance, anticipating the next CPU request.

Disk compression — Compressing data on a hard drive to allow more data to be written to the drive.

DriveSpace — A utility that compresses files so that they take up less space on a disk drive, creating a single large file on the disk to hold all the compressed files.

ECHS (extended CHS) mode —A mode of addressing information on hard drives that range from 504 MB to 8.4 GB, addressing information on a hard drive by translating cylinder, head, and sector information in order to break the 528 MB hard drive barrier. Another name for large mode.

Embedded SCSI device — A SCSI device designed to be a stand-alone SCSI device with some of the host adapter logic built in.

Enhanced BIOS — A newer BIOS that has been written to accommodate larger-capacity gigabyte drives.

Enhanced IDE technology — A newer drive standard that allows systems to recognize drives larger than 504 MB and to handle up to four devices on the same controller.

Folder — A Windows directory for a collection of related files (for instance, a person may find it convenient to create a Mydata directory, or folder, in which to store personal files).

Fragmentation — The distribution of data files, such that they are stored in noncontiguous clusters.

Hardware cache — A disk cache that is contained in RAM chips built right on the disk controller.

Head — The top or bottom surface of one platter on a hard drive. Each platter has two heads.

High-level format — Format performed by the OS that writes a file system to a logical drive. For DOS and Windows 9x, the command used is FORMAT, which writes a FAT and a directory to the drive. Also called OS format.

Host adapter — The circuit board that controls a SCSI bus that supports as many as eight or 16 separate devices, one of which is a host adapter that controls communication with the PC.

Host drive — Typically drive H on a compressed drive. *See* Compressed drive.

Integrated Device Electronics (IDE) — A hard drive whose disk controller is integrated into the drive, eliminating the need for a controller cable and thus increasing speed, as well as reducing price.

Large mode — *See* ECHS.

Logical block addressing (LBA) — A mode of addressing information on hard drives in which the BIOS and operating system view the drive as one long linear list of LBAs or addressable sectors, permitting drives to be larger than 8.4 GB (LBA 0 is cylinder 0, head 0, and sector 1).

Logical drive — A portion or all of a hard drive partition that is treated by the operating system as though it were a physical drive containing a boot record, FAT, and root directory.

Logical geometry — The number of heads, tracks, and sectors that the BIOS on the hard drive controller presents to the system BIOS and the OS. The logical geometry does not consist of the same values as the physical geometry, although calculations of drive capacity yield the same results.

Logical unit number (LUN) — A number from 0 to 15 (also called the SCSI ID) assigned to each SCSI device attached to a daisy chain.

Lost clusters — Lost file fragments that, according to the file allocation table, contain data that does not belong to any file. In DOS, the command CHKDSK/F can free these fragments.

Low-level format — A process (usually performed at the factory) that electronically creates the hard drive cylinders and tests for bad spots on the disk surface.

Master boot record (on a hard drive) — The first sector on a hard drive, which contains the partition table and other information needed by BIOS to access the drive.

MD or MKDIR command — A command used to create a directory on a drive (for example, MD C:\MYDATA).

MIRROR command — An old DOS command that saves information about deleted files as they are deleted. This information can be used later by the UNDELETE command to recover a deleted file. The command can be used to save the partition table to a floppy disk.

Normal mode — *See* CHS.

OS format — *See* high-level format.

Partition — A division of a hard drive that can be used to hold logical drives.

Partition table — A table at the beginning of the hard drive that contains information about each partition on the drive. The partition table is contained in the master boot record.

Physical geometry — The actual layout of heads, tracks, and sectors on a hard drive. *See* Logical geometry.

RD or RMDIR command — A DOS command to remove an unwanted directory (for example, RD C:\OLDDIR). You must delete all files in the directory to be removed, prior to using this command.

Reduced write current — A method whereby less current is used to write data to tracks near the center of the disk, where the bits are closer together.

SCAM (SCSI configuration automatically) — A method that follows the Plug and Play standard, to make installations of SCSI devices much easier, assuming that the device is SCAM-compatible.

SCSI (small computer system interface) — A faster system-level interface with a host adapter and a bus that can daisy chain as many as seven or 15 other devices.

SCSI bus adapter chip — The chip mounted on the logic board of a hard drive that allows the drive to be a part of a SCSI bus system.

SCSI ID — *See* Logical unit number.

Slack — Wasted space on a hard drive caused by not using all available space at the end of clusters.

SMARTDrive — A hard drive cache program that comes with Windows 3.x and DOS that can be executed as a TSR from the AUTOEXEC.BAT file (for example, DEVICE=SMARTDRV.SYS 2048).

Software cache — Cache controlled by software whereby the cache is stored in RAM.

Terminating resistor — The resistor added at the end of a SCSI chain to dampen the voltage at the end of the chain. *See* Termination.

Termination — A process necessary to prevent an echo effect of power at the end of a SCSI chain resulting in interference with the data transmission. *See* Terminating resistor.

Translation — A technique used by system BIOS and hard drive controller BIOS to break the 504 MB hard drive barrier, whereby a different set of drive parameters are communicated to the OS and other software than that used by the hard drive controller BIOS.

TREE command — A DOS command that shows the disk directories in a graphical layout similar to a family tree (for example, TREE/F shows every filename in all branches of the tree).

UNFORMAT command — A DOS command that performs recovery from an accidental FORMAT, and can repair a damaged partition table if the partition table was previously saved with MIRROR/PARTN.

VCACHE — A built-in Windows 9x 32-bit software cache that doesn't take up conventional memory space or upper memory space, as SmartDrive does.

Virtual file allocation table (VFAT) — A variation of the original DOS 16-bit FAT that allows for long filenames and 32-bit disk access.

Write precompensation — A method whereby data is written faster to the tracks that are near the center of a disk.

Zone bit recording — A method of storing data on a hard drive whereby the drive can have more sectors per track near the outside of the platter.

REVIEW QUESTIONS

1. If a hard drive has three platters, how many heads does it have?

2. What two types of tables do DOS and Windows 9x use to manage the data on a hard drive?

3. What is the purpose of the master boot record on a hard drive?

4. Given that there are 512 bytes per sector, calculate the hard drive storage for the following:

   heads: 32, tracks (cylinders): 1024, sectors/track: 63

5. Why does the logical geometry sometimes differ from the physical geometry of a hard drive?

6. How does an OS or other software communicate to the CPU that it wants to access data on a hard drive?

7. What organization is responsible for the IDE/ATA standard?

8. What two factors collectively are responsible for the 504 or 528-MB limit of the IDE/ATA standard?

9. In using large mode to access a hard drive, how is the 504 or 528-MB barrier broken?

10. How can you tell if your PC supports large mode?

11. Which is more popular, LBA mode or large mode? What is the difference between the two?

12. Name four ANSI standards for interfacing to hard drives.

13. How does block mode give faster access to a hard drive? How can you disable block mode?

14. What type of access mode must be used for a 20 GB hard drive?

15. List the steps to report the capacity of a hard drive using Windows 98.

16. What are the advantages of using VFAT?

17. When would it be appropriate to use FAT32 rather than FAT16 on a new hard drive?

18. Give a complete DOS command to create a directory called MYDATA on drive C.

19. Give a complete DOS command to make the file Resume.Doc read-only.

20. List the steps to create a new subfolder under the DATA directory in a Windows 9x system.

21. In Windows 98, how would you examine the file properties of the file Resume.Doc?

22. What causes a file to be fragmented?

23. In Windows 98, what steps would you use to defragment a hard drive?

24. What is the difference between a lost cluster and a cross-linked cluster?

25. Can Windows 98 use DriveSpace to compress a hard drive that is using FAT32?

26. What is one advantage and one disadvantage of a hardware cache over a software cache for a hard drive?

27. SMARTDrive is to Windows 3.1 as _____ is to Windows 98.

28. What ANSI hard drive interface standard does not use a traditional hard drive cable?

29. What is the difference between narrow SCSI and wide SCSI?

30. When is it not wise to use hard drive compression to increase the capacity of a hard drive?

6

PROJECTS

Using Nuts & Bolts to Manage a Hard Drive

1. Use the Nuts & Bolts Disk Tune utility to defragment your hard drive. Click **Start**, point to **Programs**, **Nuts & Bolts**, and click **Disk Tune**. Select the drive to defragment and click **Next**. When the visual presentation of your hard drive is displayed, answer these questions:

   a. What is the first cluster number that Nuts & Bolts is accessing to defragment?

   b. What is the last cluster number on your hard drive?

   c. Name at least one file on your hard drive that is fragmented.

   d. Name at least one file on your hard drive that is not fragmented.

Examine a Hard Drive's BIOS Settings

1. From the CMOS setup information on your computer, calculate the capacity of the drive. Show your method of calculation.

2. Does your hard drive use LBA mode? If so, compare the capacity of the drive as reported by LBA to the capacity of the drive as reported by ECHS. Are they the same? If they are different, explain why they are different.

3. Write down or print out all the CMOS settings that apply to your hard drive. Explain each setting that you can.

Examine the First Entries at the Beginning of a Hard Drive

(Refer to the optional "Behind the Scenes with DEBUG" sections in Appendix F before tackling this project.)

1. Print out the OS boot record of your hard drive. On the printout, label each item in the record and explain it.

2. Print out the beginning of the first FAT on your hard drive (see Figure F-7). (*Hint:* Use DEBUG and Print Screen.)

3. Calculate the memory location of the beginning of the second copy of the FAT. Show your method of calculation.

4. Calculate the memory location of the beginning of the root directory. Show your method of calculation.

5. Get a printout of the beginning of the root directory of your hard drive. Identify the first five entries in the root directory and the number of clusters in each entry that make up a file. For each of the five entries, explain the meaning of each ON bit in the attribute byte.

Using DOS to Manage a Hard Drive

1. Print the contents of SCANDISK.INI in the \DOS directory of your hard drive. SCANDISK.INI contains settings that SCANDISK for DOS reads and uses when it executes. The Windows 95 version of ScanDisk does not use these settings.

2. What is the setting that allows SCANDISK to delete the contents of a lost cluster without prompting you first?

3. From the INI file information, can SCANDISK repair a damaged boot sector of a compressed drive?

4. Run **SCANDISK** from a DOS prompt. What errors did it find?

5. From a DOS prompt, type **HELP DEFRAG**. What are the cautions listed concerning when not to use DEFRAG?

6. Following the directions from the Help utility, defragment a disk or hard drive using the DEFRAG utility.

7. From a DOS prompt, type **HELP SMARTDRV**, and then print the help information about the SMARTDrive utility.

8. Look in either the CONFIG.SYS or AUTOEXEC.BAT file of your computer for the SMARTDrive command. It should be in one or the other of the two files, but not both. Using your printout, explain each option used in the command line.

Using Windows 9x to Manage a Hard Drive

1. Using the chapter example of Windows 9x DriveSpace, practice disk compression by compressing two disks. Use one newly formatted disk and one disk about half full of data. Compare the results of the two compressions.

2. With your instructor's permission, use the Defragmenter utility to defragment the hard drive of your computer. Don't use this utility if your disk has been compressed by a utility program other than Windows 9x. If you haven't used Windows 9x to compress the drive, look at the documentation for your compression software to see if it offers a defragmenting utility, and use that to defragment the drive.

3. If you are not using add-on utility software to compress your hard drive, use Windows 9x ScanDisk to repair any cross-linked or lost clusters on the drive. If you are using utility software other than Windows 9x to compress your hard drive, use that software utility to scan for cross-linked or lost clusters.

4. Create a file on an empty disk with a long filename. Using DEBUG, display the root directory entries for this file. What are the two filenames in the root directory?

Recover a File

Using a word processor, create and save a short document under the name Test.del. Using Windows Explorer, delete the newly created document. Open the **Recycle Bin**, and select **File**, **Restore** to undelete the file Test.del.

6

Practicing DOS

Perform the following procedures and commands. For a dot matrix printer, adjust the paper in the printer to start exactly at the top of the page. If possible, attempt to complete all steps on one page only. Use the section on "Using DOS to Manage a Hard Drive" as a reference.

1. Cold boot the computer. Go to the DOS prompt.

2. List the directory of drive C in wide format.

3. FORMAT a new system disk in drive A. (Use your last name for the volume label.)

4. Switch to drive A. (Look for the A:\> prompt.) List the directory of the newly formatted disk.

5. Switch back to drive C. (Look for the C:\> prompt.)

6. Use the COPY command and the wildcard (*) to copy all files in the root directory to your disk in drive A.

7. Display the current DATE on the monitor.

8. Perform a SCANDISK of drive A.

9. Switch to Drive A. (Be sure the A:\> prompt appears.)

10. ERASE all .COM files from the disk in drive A.

11. List the directory of drive A.

12. Print the screen contents. Take the printer offline (press the Online button to make the Online light go off). Use the Line Feed or Form Feed button to eject the rest of the page from the printer.

7

HARD DRIVE INSTALLATION AND SUPPORT

In this chapter, you will learn:

♦ How to install a hard drive

♦ How to use diagnostic software

♦ How to recover lost data on hard drives

♦ How to apply hard drive troubleshooting skills

This chapter extends the discussion of hard drives in Chapter 6 to explain how to install a new hard drive and use software utility packages to help in managing a hard drive. The chapter addresses what to do when a hard drive fails or shows clear signs of impending disaster, or when data is lost. You will learn how important it is to keep good backups of software and data stored on your hard drive as well as backups of the partition table, boot record, root directory, and FAT. No amount of experience replacing a defective hard drive can substitute for good backups. The data itself is often the most valuable thing in your computer case.

As an additional resource for understanding how information is stored on a hard drive, see Appendix F, "Behind the Scenes with DEBUG," where you can use DEBUG to closely examine a hard drive. DEBUG is a DOS utility that lets you examine memory and hexidecimal data on a hard drive or floppy drive, including the boot record, FAT, and directories.

INSTALLING A HARD DRIVE

Hard drive installation is much easier now than it was a few years ago. Drives today come already low-level formatted with optimum interleave already established. (**Interleave** is a method of reorganizing sectors in a track to speed up data access.) When older technologies such as MFM and RLL drives were popular a few years ago, to install a hard drive, you had to purchase a controller that conformed to your type of drive. You then low-level formatted the drive, using either a format program stored in the controller BIOS or another utility such as SpinRite. During the low-level format, the software examined your drive, recommended the optimum interleave, and then changed the interleave to the optimum value. As explained in the last chapter, today's IDE drives are low-level formatted at the factory. Now you should low-level format a hard drive only as a last resort, using a specific low-level format program recommended by the manufacturer to refurbish a failing drive unless you have a SCSI drive and the manufacturer recommends you do a low-level format. This chapter will focus on today's IDE and SCSI hard drives.

Installation of IDE and SCSI hard drives includes:

- Installing the hardware and setting jumpers and DIP switches on the drive
- Informing CMOS setup of the new drive
- Creating one or more partitions on the drive
- High-level formatting the drive partitions
- Installing the OS and other software

Physical Installation of IDE or SCSI Hard Drives

A+CORE 1.2 To install an IDE drive, you need the drive, a 40-pin data cable, and perhaps a kit to make the drive fit into a much larger bay. If the system board does not provide an IDE connection, you also need an adapter card.

To install a SCSI drive, you need the drive, a cable compatible with the host adapter you are using, possibly an external terminator if the drive is on the end of the daisy chain, a host adapter if you don't already have one, and perhaps a kit to make the drive fit the bay.

Installing an IDE Hard Drive

Recall from the last chapter that IDE hard drives used today follow the EIDE standard that supports up to four IDE devices on the same system. These devices can be hard drives, CD-ROM drives, tape drives, Zip drives, or other drives that follow the EIDE standards of communication. There are four possible setups for each device:

- Primary IDE channel, master device
- Primary IDE channel, slave device
- Secondary IDE channel, master device
- Secondary IDE channel, slave device

A+CORE
1.2

When planning your system configuration, place the fastest devices on the primary channel and the slower devices on the secondary channel. If possible, allow the fastest hard drive to be your boot device and the only device on the primary channel.

The first step in any installation is to take some precautions. First, make sure that you have a good bootable disk or Windows 9x rescue disk; test it to make sure it works. As always, just in case you lose setup information in the process, make sure you have a record of your CMOS setup on a disk. The next step requires self-discipline. Before you take anything apart, carefully read all the documentation for the drive and adapter card, and the part of your PC documentation that covers hard drive installation. Look for problems you have not considered, such as IRQ or DMA conflicts if this is a second hard drive for your system, or an older, limited version of system BIOS. Also check the setup of your computer to be sure it accommodates the size and type of hard drive you want to install. If you plan to choose a user-defined drive type in the setup (where you must enter the drive specifications), make sure your PC accepts the values you want. Your PC documentation or system setup will provide this information. If your PC does not accommodate a large-capacity drive, you have three choices. You can upgrade your ROM BIOS before changing the drive, use only a part of the large-capacity drive by defining it as a smaller drive type in setup, or install a special adapter card to provide the BIOS you need.

Make sure that you can visualize the entire installation. If you have any questions, find answers to them before you begin. Either keep reading until you locate the answer, call technical support, or ask a knowledgeable friend. You may discover that what you are installing will not work on your computer, but that is better than coping with hours of frustration and a disabled computer. You can't always anticipate every problem, but at least you can know that you made your best effort to understand everything in advance. What you learn in thorough preparation pays off every time!

Having read the documentation for the hard drive, you should understand the meaning of each DIP switch or jumper on the drive. Then you can set the jumpers and DIP switches. For an IDE drive, note that the settings are usually correct for the drive to be the single drive on a system. Before you change any settings, write down the original ones. If things go wrong, you can revert to the original settings and begin again.

Although the settings on the drive can be configured by DIP switches, most settings use jumpers. Each drive type can have a different jumper configuration. Often a description of the jumper settings is printed on the top of the hard drive housing (see Figure 7-1). If they are not, see the documentation or visit the Web site of the drive manufacturer. (One end-of-chapter exercise allows you to practice this.) A typical jumper arrangement is shown in Figure 7-2. The three choices for jumper settings for this drive are listed in Table 7-1. Note that your hard drive might not have the first configuration as an option, but it should have a way of indicating if the drive will be the master device.

Some hard drives have a cable select configuration option. If you choose this configuration, you must use a cable-select data cable. When you use one of these cables, the drive nearest the system board is the master and the drive farthest from the system board is the slave. You can recognize a cable select cable by a small hole somewhere in the data cable.

7

A+CORE 1.2

> **TIP** CMOS setup determines which logical drive startup BIOS looks to first for the OS. Either the master IDE drive, the slave IDE drive, or a SCSI device can be a system's boot device. In fact, some systems allow a SCSI drive to be the boot device even when an IDE drive is present.

Table 7-1   Jumper settings on an IDE hard drive

Configuration	Description
Single-drive configuration	This is the only hard drive on this IDE channel. (This is the standard setting)
Master-drive configuration	This is the first of two drives; it most likely is the boot device
Slave-drive configuration	This is the second drive using this channel or data cable
Cable-select configuration	The cable select data cable determines which of the two drives is the master and which is the slave

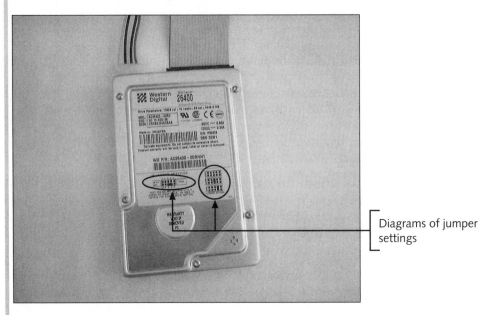

Diagrams of jumper settings

Figure 7-1   An IDE drive most likely will have diagrams of jumper settings for master and slave options printed on the drive housing

Figure 7-2   Jumper settings on a hard drive and their meanings

The next step is to prepare a large, well-lit place to work. Set out your tools, documentation, new hardware, and notebook. Remember the basic rules concerning static electricity. Ground yourself and the computer. Avoid working on carpet in the winter, when there's a lot of static electricity. Some added precautions for working with hard drives are:

- Handle the drive carefully.

- Do not touch any exposed circuitry or chips.

- Prevent other people from touching exposed microchips on the drive.

- When you first take the drive out of the static-protective package, touch the package containing the drive to a screw holding an expansion card or cover, or to a metal part of the computer case, for at least two seconds. This will drain the static electricity from the package and from your body.

- If you must set down the drive outside the static-protective package, place it component-side up on top of the static-protective package on a flat surface.

- Do not place the drive on the computer case cover or on a metal table.

Verify the state of the computer before you turn it off. Know where your starting point is. Does everything work that's supposed to work?

> **TIP** Verify which of your system's devices are working before installing a new one. Later, if a resource conflict occurs and causes a device to malfunction, the information will help you isolate the problem.

Turn off the computer and unplug it. Unplug the monitor and move it to one side. Remove the computer case cover. Check that you have an available power cord from the power supply.

A+CORE
1.2,
1.4

If you are using an adapter card, decide which expansion slot you will use for the adapter card. Don't use the one nearest to the power supply unless it's your only choice; heat can shorten the life of any card. Check that the cable you are using reaches from the drive to the adapter card. If it doesn't, you may need to use a different expansion slot. Next check that the wire that controls the drive light on the front of the computer case reaches from the adapter card to the front of the case or to where the connection for the wire is located on the system board. My experience has been that this wire often does not reach as far as it should. Either get a new wire or just don't use the drive light. Locate the pins on the system board for the wire. Use your system board manual to help you locate these pins.

For most installations, instead of using an adapter card, you use an IDE connection on the system board. If you are using an IDE connection on the system board (see Figure 7–3), use the primary IDE connection (sometimes labeled IDE1) before you use the secondary IDE connection (sometimes labeled IDE2). Find the connection and make certain the data cable reaches from the drive bay to the connection.

Pin1 aligns with edge
color on data cable

Figure 7-3   Two IDE connections on a system board, primary and secondary

Next look at the drive bay that you will use for the drive. You must be able to securely mount the drive in the bay; drive should not move when it is screwed down. Line up the drive and bay screw holes and make sure everything will fit. If the bay is too large for the drive, a universal bay kit can help you securely fit the drive into the bay. These kits are inexpensive and should create a tailor-made fit. In Figure 7-4 you can see how the universal bay kit adapter works. The adapter spans the distance between the sides of the drive and the bay.

A+CORE
1.2

Small drive   Bay adapter   Drive rails

External bay cover

Figure 7-4   Use a universal bay kit to make the drive fit the bay

7

Do not allow torque to stress the drive. For example, don't force a drive into a space that is too small for it. Also, placing two screws in diagonal positions across the drive can place pressure diagonally on the drive.

For tower cases, the drive can be positioned either horizontally or vertically. External bays can require a bay cover in the front of the tower, while internal bays do not (see Figure 7-5).

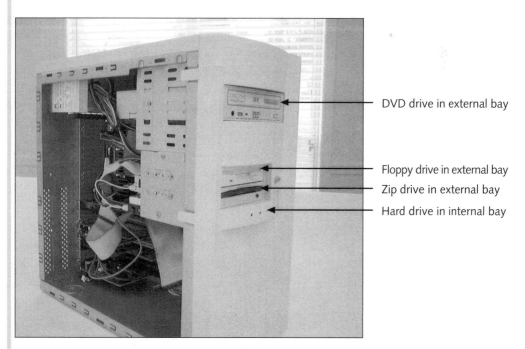

DVD drive in external bay

Floppy drive in external bay
Zip drive in external bay
Hard drive in internal bay

Figure 7-5   A tower case may have internal or external bays

A+$^{CORE}_{1.2}$

Be sure the screws are not too long. If they are, you can screw too far into the drive housing and damage the drive itself. After checking the position of the drive and determining how screws are placed, mount the drive in the bay. Decide whether to connect the data cable and power cord to the drive before or after you screw it down, depending on how accessible the connections are.

Once the drive is in place, if you are using an adapter card, insert the adapter card in the expansion slot, being careful not to touch the gold contact fingers on the edge connectors. Use one screw to secure the card to the case at the expansion slot. Don't eliminate this screw—without it cards can work themselves loose over time. Be certain to place the card securely in the slot. The most common error beginners make is not seating the card properly (see Figure 7-6).

Next, connect the data cable, making certain pin 1 and the edge color on the cable are aligned correctly at both ends of the cable. Connect the power cord to the drive. The cord only goes into the connection one way, so you can't go wrong here.

Figure 7-6   Place the adapter card in an expansion slot

When using an adapter card, connect the wire from the adapter card to the front of the case. This wire controls the hard drive activity light on the front of the case. When using a system-board connection, connect the wire from the computer case to the system board. If you reverse the polarity of the LED wire to the drive light at the front of the case, the light might not work. Unless the screw holes in the drive do not align with the screw holes in the bay, or there is some other unusual situation, physical installations go rather quickly.

TIP   If the drive light does not work after installing a new drive, try reversing the LED wire on the system board pins.

$A{+}\overset{CORE}{\underset{1.2}{}}$ Before you replace the computer case, plug in the monitor and turn on the computer. Verify that your system BIOS can find the drive before you replace the cover. If you have a problem, it will most likely involve a loose cable or adapter card. Here are some things to do and check in this case:

- Turn off the computer and monitor before you do anything inside the case.

- Remove and reattach all drive cables. Check for correct pin 1 orientation.

- Remove and reseat the adapter card.

- Place the adapter card in a different slot.

- Check the jumper or DIP switch settings.

- Inspect the drive for damage such as bent pins on the connection for the cable.

- To determine if the hard drive is spinning, listen to the hard drive or lightly touch the metal drive (with power on).

- Check the cable for frayed edges or other damage.

- Check the installation manual for things you might have overlooked. Look for a section about system setup and carefully follow all directions that apply.

Informing Setup of the New Hard Drive

$A{+}\overset{CORE}{\underset{4.4}{}}$ The newly installed drive is not available for booting until the installation is complete. If the new drive is the boot device, you must boot the computer from a floppy disk. You are now ready to use setup to tell CMOS the hard drive type you are installing. The text below first discusses setup for drives less than 528 MB, then setup for large-capacity drives, and finally setup when your BIOS does not support your large-capacity drive.

BIOS today offers a setup program that makes configuring hard drives easy. You can choose IDE **Auto Detection** and let the BIOS do the work for you. Recall that for this to work both the BIOS and the hard drive must be built to communicate this information. Figure 7-7 shows the four screens that are typical in setup programs that allow you to change hard drive parameters. In Figure 7-7a, you can see the choice for IDE HDD Auto Detection in the third item in the second column. Select this option then save and exit setup and continue with the installation. Later, after you have rebooted with the new drive detected, you can return to setup, view the selections that it made, and make changes where appropriate.

A+CORE
4.4

a) CMOS setup utility opening menu

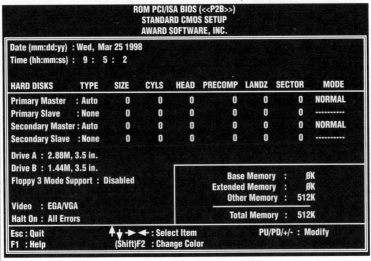

b) Standard CMOS setup

Figure 7-7   CMOS setup screens

A+CORE 4.4

c) CMOS setup for chipset features

```
                ROM PCI/ISA BIOS (<<P2B>>)
                     CHIPSET FEATURES
                    AWARD SOFTWARE, INC.

SDRAM Configuration      : By SPD    Onboard FDC Controller      : Enabled
SDRAM CAS Latency        : 2T        Onboard FDC Swap A & B      : No Swap
SDRAM RAS to CAS Delay   : 3T        Onboard Serial Port 1       : 3F8H/IRQ4
SDRAM RAS Precharge Time : 3T        Onboard Serial Port 2       : 2F8H/IRQ3
DRAM Idle Timer          : 16T       Onboard Parallel Port       : 378H/IRQ7
SDRAM MA Wait State      : Normal    Parallel Port Mode          : ECP+EPP
Snoop Ahead              : Enabled   ECP DMA Select              : 3
Host Bus Fast Data Ready : Enabled   VART2 Use Infrared          : Disabled
16-bit I/O Recovery Time : 1BUSCLK   Onboard PCI IDE Enable      : Both
8-bit I/O Recovery Time  : 1BUSCLK   IDE Ultra DMA Mode          : Auto
Graphics Aperture Size   : 64MB      IDE0 Master PIO/DMA Mode    : Auto
Video.Memory Cache Mode  : UC        IDE0 Slave  PIO/DMA Mode    : Auto
PCI 2.1 Support          : Enabled   IDE1 Master PIO/DMA Mode    : Auto
Memory Hole At 15M-16M   : Disabled  IDE1 Slave  PIO/DMA Mode    : Auto
DRAM are 64 (Not 72), bits wide
Data Integrity Mode      : Non-ECC   Esc  : Quit             ↑↓→← : Select Item
                                     F1   : Help      PU/PD/+/- : Modify
                                     F5   : Old Values  (Shift)F2 : Color
                                     F6   : Load BIOS  Defaults
                                     F7   : Load Setup Defaults
```

d) CMOS setup for BIOS features

```
                ROM PCI/ISA BIOS (<<P2B>>)
                     BIOS FEATURES SETUP
                    AWARD SOFTWARE, INC.

CPU Internal Core Speed  : 350Mhz    Video   ROM BIOS  Shadow  : Enabled
                                     C8000  - CBFFF   Shadow  : Disabled
Boot Virus Detection     : Enabled   CC000  - CFFFF   Shadow  : Disabled
CPU Level 1 Cache        : Enabled   D0000  - D3FFF   Shadow  : Disabled
CPU Level 2 Cache        : Enabled   D4000  - D7FFF   Shadow  : Disabled
CPU Level 2 Cache ECC Check : Disabled D8000 - DBFFF  Shadow  : Disabled
BIOS Update              : Enabled   DC000  - DFFFF   Shadow  : Disabled
Quick Power On Self Test : Enabled
HDD Sequence SCSI/IDE First : IDE    Boot Up NumLock Status      : On
Boot Sequence            : A,C       Typematic Rate Setting      : Disabled
Boot Up Floppy Seek      : Disabled  Typematic Rate (Chars/Sec)  : 6
Floppy Disk Access Control : R/W     Typematic Delay (Msec)      : 250
IDE HDD Block Mode Sectors : HDD MAX
Security Option          : System
PS/2 Mouse Function Control : Auto   Esc  : Quit             ↑↓→← : Select Item
PCI/VGA Palette Snoop    : Disabled  F1   : Help      PU/PD/+/- : Modify
OS/2 Onboard Memory > 64M : Disabled F5   : Old Values  (Shift)F2 : Color
                                     F6   : Load BIOS  Defaults
                                     F7   : Load Setup Defaults
```

Figure 7-7   CMOS setup screens (continued)

Setup for Hard Drives Less Than 528 MB

If you are using an older BIOS that only supports drives less than 528 MB, setup assumes you are using CHS mode, since that was the only available mode when these BIOSs were written. If you are using a newer BIOS, you must select CHS mode or normal mode, usually on the standard CMOS setup screen.

A+CORE
4.4

From this screen, you also enter the logical geometry of the drive. Your computer will probably list appropriate hard drive types and let you select a user-defined type as well. Follow the directions on your setup screen to scroll through the list of drives the BIOS supports. The list is similar to the one in Appendix B. The documentation that came with the hard drive tells you which type to choose, and it also tells you the number of heads and cylinders. The head and cylinder information is often written on the top of the drive housing. If your computer does not offer an exact match, you can enter your own values in the user-defined type.

If your computer does not offer an exact match or a user-defined type, you can improvise. You must choose the correct number of heads, but you can select a smaller number of cylinders than the drive actually has. Choosing fewer cylinders means some cylinders on your drive will remain unused. Choose the number of cylinders closest to the number you actually have without going over.

After you have identified the drive type, save the information to CMOS and reboot your computer from the floppy disk drive to the A prompt. You are now ready to partition the drive. If you see an error at POST when you reboot, turn off the computer and check the drive and card connections. Check the setup to make sure you have chosen the correct drive type.

Setup for Large-Capacity Hard Drives

A+CORE
1.8

Recall from Chapter 6 that the two ways BIOS relates to large capacity drives are LBA and large mode. Notice in Figure 7-7b the column labeled mode, referring to how BIOS relates to the drive. Choices are normal, LBA, large, and auto. Most likely, when auto is the choice, setup will automatically select LBA.

In Figure 7-7c (starting with the 10th item in the second column) you can see the hard drive features that the chip set on this system board supports. They are Ultra DMA, PIO, and DMA modes. Leave all these settings at Auto and let BIOS make the choice according to what it detects your hard drive supports.

In Figure 7-7d, you can see in the 12th item of the first column that BIOS on this system board supports block mode. From this screen you can also select the boot sequence (see ninth item in first column). Choices for this BIOS are A, C; A, CD ROM, C; CD ROM, C, A; D, A; F, A; C only; Zip, C; and C, A. Also notice on this screen (eight item of the first column) that this BIOS supports booting from a SCSI drive even when there is an IDE drive present. Booting from the IDE drive is the default setting.

When BIOS Does Not Support Large-Capacity Hard Drives

If you want to install a large-capacity drive on a PC whose BIOS does not support it, you have the following choices:

- Let the BIOS see the drive as a smaller drive.
- Upgrade the BIOS.
- Upgrade the entire system board.
- Use software that interfaces between the older BIOS and the large-capacity drive.
- Use an adapter card that provides the BIOS to substitute for system BIOS.

A+CORE
1.8

This first option may or may not work, depending on your BIOS. Some BIOSs that do not support large-capacity drives do not recognize a large drive, but simply see the larger hard drive as a smaller drive they can support. In this case, the BIOS assigns a drive capacity smaller than the actual capacity. You can use this method, although it wastes drive space.

Most large-capacity drives come with software that performs the translation between the older BIOS and a large-capacity drive. Examples of this translation or disk overlay software are Disk Manager by OnTrack, SpeedStor by Storage Dimensions, and EZ-Drive by StorageSoft. You can find the software on floppy disk with the drive or download it from the drive manufacturer's Web site. Boot from a floppy disk with the software installed and follow directions on the screen. A small partition or logical drive is created on the hard drive to manage the drive for the older BIOS. It's important to keep this disk in a safe place in case you need it to access the hard drive if the software on the drive becomes corrupted. A disadvantage of using this method is that if you boot from a regular bootable floppy disk, you might not be able to access the hard drive.

Some hard drives come with disk manager software already installed on the drive. For a drive manufactured by Maxtor, the disk manager software is found in a directory called \MAX in a 112-MB partition that BIOS recognizes as drive C. The rest of the drive is assigned to other partitions or logical drives such as drive D or drive E.

Adapter cards are available to provide the BIOS that substitutes for system BIOS. This is the recommended method if your system board does not have an upgrade for system BIOS. One manufacturer of these cards is Promise Technology, Inc.

The best solution is to upgrade BIOS. However, remember that the new BIOS must also relate correctly to the chip set on the system board. Follow the recommendations of the system-board manufacturer when selecting a BIOS upgrade.

A Note on Moving a Hard Drive or Changing BIOS

When you move a large-capacity hard drive from one computer to another, you can lose data. If you use large mode on the first computer and LBA mode on the other, you might not be able to access the drive's data. Also, the translation methods for LBA mode might not be the same from one BIOS to another. For this reason, back up the data on the drive before you move it. If the BIOS on the new computer does not let you access the data on the drive, you can partition and format the drive again and then move the backed-up data onto the newly formatted drive.

Don't change options in setup unless you are sure of what you are doing. You might also lose access to the data on the drive if you have formatted and stored data on a hard drive using one mode and then change to a different mode in setup. Returning to the correct mode might not solve the problem because changing modes can destroy data. To recover access to the hard drive (although data may be lost), repartition and reformat the drive using the correct mode.

7

Partitioning the Hard Drive

A+ OS
2.1,
3.2

After the hard drive is physically installed and setup knows about the drive, the next step is to partition the drive. Recall that the **partition table** is written at the very beginning of the drive and contains information about the size of each partition and identifies the partition that contains the OS from which the PC boots. Recall also that the partitions are created by the DOS and Windows 9x FDISK setup program.

Before you can use the Windows 9x CD for Windows 9x upgrades, you must first install DOS on the hard drive and boot from it. (You will also need the first Window 3.x setup disk because Window 9x setup asks for it during Window 9x installation.) Insert DOS disk 1 in drive A and boot the computer. FDISK is automatically executed by the install procedure on this disk. Or you can boot from any bootable disk and run FDISK from the disk. In either case, you see the FDISK opening menu shown in Figure 7-8. Select option 1 to create the DOS partition. The menu in Figure 7-9 appears. Use option 1 to create the primary DOS partition. If you plan to install Windows 9x later, be sure this partition is at least 150 MB, preferably more. Make this first partition the active partition. In DOS terms, the active partition is the partition that is used to boot DOS. The active partition will be drive C.

Figure 7-8   Fixed disk setup program (FDISK) menu

Next use option 2 to create an extended DOS partition using the remainder of the hard drive. Then use option 3 to create logical drives in the extended partition. They will be drive D, drive E, and so on.

The non-upgrade version of Windows 9x begins with DOS. The software comes with a DOS bootable disk. Boot from the disk, which prompts you to partition the drive, format it, and provide the necessary DOS files on the hard drive to install Windows 9x.

When FDISK is completed, the hard drive has a partition table, an active and extended partition, and logical drives within these partitions. As seen in Figure 7-8, you can choose option 4 of FDISK to display partition information (see Figure 7-10).

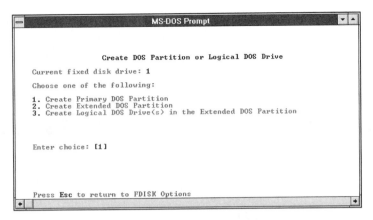

Figure 7-9   FDISK menu to create partitions and logical drives

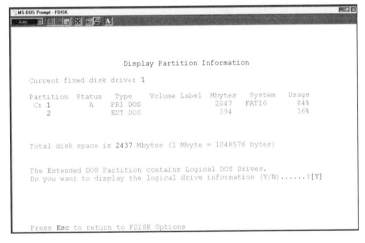

Figure 7-10   FDISK displays partition information

Using More Than One Logical Drive

A+ OS
1.3

DOS and Windows 9x can support only two partitions. The primary partition can hold only one logical drive, the boot device. If you want to have more than one logical drive or volume, create an extended partition and put the other logical drives in it.

Some people prefer to use more than one logical drive to organize their hard drives, especially if they plan to have more than one OS on the same drive. However, the main reason you need multiple logical drives is to optimize space and access time to the drive. Recall from Chapter 6 that, in general, the larger the logical drive, the larger the cluster size, and the more slack or wasted space. When deciding how to allocate space to logical drives, the goal is to use as few logical drives as possible and still keep cluster size to a minimum. You can also use FAT32 for very large drives, which results in an even smaller cluster size for the logical drive size. Table 7-2 gives the information you need to decide how to slice your drive. Recall from

A+ OS
1.3

Chapter 6 that the largest logical drive possible using FAT16 is 2 GB (this limitation is rooted in the largest cluster number that can be stored in a 16-bit FAT entry). However, you can see from the table that, to make a drive that big, the cluster size must be huge. Also, the largest hard drive that FAT16 can support is 8.4 GB; if the drive is larger than that, you must use FAT32.

Table 7-2 Size of some logical drives compared to cluster size for FAT16 and FAT32

File System	Size of Logical Drive	Size of Cluster
FAT16	Up to 128 MB	4 sectors per cluster
	128 to 256 MB	8 sectors per cluster
	256 to 512 MB	16 sectors per cluster
	512 MB to 1 GB	32 sectors per cluster
	1 GB to 2 GB	64 sectors per cluster
FAT32	512 MB to 8 GB	4 sectors per cluster
	8 GB to 16 GB	8 sectors per cluster
	16 GB to 32 GB	16 sectors per cluster
	More than 32 GB	32 sectors per cluster
NTFS	Up to 512 MB	1 sector per cluster
	512 MB to 1 GB	2 sectors per cluster
	More than 1 GB	4 sectors per cluster

Notice from Table 7-2 that the smallest logical drive that FAT32 supports is 512 MB. If you want to create a FAT32 volume using the Windows 9x FDISK program, answer yes when it asks you if you want to "enable large disk support."

After FDISK is done, reboot the system using a system disk or Windows setup CD, and you are now ready to format the drive.

OS or High-Level Format

After the hard drive has been partitioned, an OS must individually format each volume or logical drive within a partition. This is called the **high-level format** or the **operating system format**. The Windows 9x or DOS format writes the **boot record** in the first sector of each volume. Recall that this boot record is sometimes called the DOS boot record (DBR) or OS boot record. DOS or Windows 9x identifies this sector as sector 0 for each logical drive. Following the boot record, the OS creates two copies of the FAT as well as the root directory, just as it does on floppy disks. When the OS creates the FAT, the Format program scans the track and sector markings created by the low-level format of the drive performed by the manufacturer. If the low-level format encounters bad or unusable sectors, it marks these sectors so that the FORMAT program can recognize them as bad. FORMAT marks them in the FAT as bad sectors. The FFF7 entry in the FAT marks an entire cluster as bad so that the drive does not use that area.

For DOS, use this command: FORMAT C:/S. If you include the /S option in the FORMAT command, the program also writes the two hidden files and COMMAND.COM to the drive. The hard drive is now bootable. Use the FORMAT command for each logical drive. For example, for drive D, enter the command FORMAT D:.

For Windows 9x, the Windows 9x CD-ROM contains the real-mode drivers necessary to access the CD-ROM without having Windows installed. Place the Windows 9x Startup disk in the floppy drive and reboot. When you see the message, "Start computer with CD-ROM support," press Enter. The prompt indicates the CD-ROM letter. Insert the Windows 9x CD-ROM in the drive and type "setup" after the CD-ROM drive letter. If the setup process begins, follow the instructions on screen to install Windows 9x.

If you cannot access the Windows 9x CD, then the generic CD-ROM drivers on the Startup disk won't work with your CD-ROM drive. In that case, you must install the CD-ROM drivers before you can install Windows 9x from CD.

To install the drivers for your CD-ROM drive, see the instructions that came with your CD-ROM drive. The drive also comes with a floppy disk that has the drivers on it. Follow the instructions to install these drivers on the hard drive.

Installing Software

After your new hard drive is bootable and you have installed Windows 9x, you are ready to load the applications software, a subject that is addressed in later chapters. Once your drive has software completely loaded and working, there's no better time to make a complete backup of the entire drive—to tape or removable drive—using backup utility software. Also, for DOS, make a bootable disk that contains all the files in the root directory of the drive. This disk will be your emergency disk if you have trouble with the drive later. For Windows 9x, make an emergency startup disk, as discussed in Chapter 2.

Saving the Partition Table to Disk

If you have Nuts & Bolts, Norton Utilities, or other similar software, create a rescue disk to recover from a corrupted partition table. Saving the partition table using Nuts & Bolts and Norton Utilities is covered in the next section. To use DOS to make a copy of the partition table, follow these instructions:

Use the DOS 5 MIRROR command to save the partition table. The command line is:

```
C:\> MIRROR /PARTN
```

Recall that the DOS UNFORMAT command restores the partition table from the disk. Details were given in Chapter 6.

When Things Go Wrong

Sometimes trouble crops up during the installation process. Keeping a cool head, thinking things through carefully a second, third, and fourth time, and using all available resources will most likely get you out of any mess. Installing a hard drive is not difficult unless you have an unusually complex situation.

$A^{+CORE}_{2.1}$

For example, your first hard drive installation should not involve installing a second SCSI drive into a system that has two SCSI host adapters. Nor should you install a second drive into a system that uses an IDE connection for one drive on the system board and an adapter card in an expansion slot for the other. If a complicated installation is necessary and you have never installed a hard drive, consider asking for expert help. Know your limitations. Start with the simple and build your way up. Using what you have learned in this chapter and in Chapter 6, you should be able to install a single IDE drive in a PC, or install a second slave IDE master drive. After mastering that, tackle something more complicated.

Here are some errors that might occur during a hard drive installation, their causes, and what to do about them. This list has been compiled from experience. Everyone makes mistakes when learning something new, and you probably will, too. You can then add your own experiences to this list.

1. We physically installed an IDE adapter card and IDE hard drive. We turned on the machine and told setup what drive was present. When we rebooted from a disk, we received the following error message:

   ```
   Hard drive not found
   ```

   Although the hard drive was not yet bootable, POST should have found it. We turned off the machine, checked all cables, and discovered the data cable from the card to the drive was not tightly connected. We reseated the cable and rebooted. POST found the drive.

2. We got to the same point as in the previous situation except that we had replaced the cover on the computer case. When we rebooted from a disk, POST beeped three times and stopped.

   Recall that diagnostics during POST are often communicated by beeps if the tests take place before POST has checked video and made it available to display the messages. Three beeps on most computers signal a memory error. We turned the computer off and checked the memory SIMMs on the system board. A SIMM positioned at the edge of the system board next to the cover had been bumped as we replaced the cover. We reseated the SIMM and booted from a floppy disk again, this time with the cover still off. The error disappeared.

3. We physically installed a card and drive and turned on the computer. We received the following error:

   ```
   No boot device available
   ```

   We forgot to insert a bootable disk. We put the disk in the drive and rebooted the machine successfully.

4. We physically installed the card and drive, inserted a floppy disk in the disk drive, and rebooted. We received the following error message:

   ```
   Configuration/CMOS error. Run setup.
   ```

   This error message is normal. POST found a hard drive it was not expecting. The next step is to run setup.

5. We physically installed the card and drive and tried to reboot from a floppy disk. The error message 601 appeared on the screen. Any error message in the 600 range refers to the floppy disk. Because the case cover was still off, we looked at the

A+CORE
2.1

connections and discovered that the power cord to the floppy disk drive was not connected. (It had been disconnected earlier to expose the hard drive bay underneath.) We turned off the machine and plugged the cable in. The error disappeared.

6. The hard drive did not physically fit into the bay. The screw holes did not line up. We got a bay kit, but it just didn't seem to work.

We took a break, went to lunch, and came back to make a fresh start. We asked others to help view the brackets, holes, and screws from a fresh perspective. It didn't take long to discover the correct position for the brackets in the bay.

7. We physically installed a drive and card after changing jumper settings on the drive. We booted up, changed setup, and rebooted. We received the following error message:

`Hard drive not present`

We rechecked all physical connections and found everything was OK. After checking the jumper settings, we realized that we had set them as if this were the second drive of a two-drive system when it was the only drive. We restored the jumpers to their original state. In this case, as in most cases, the jumpers were set at the factory to be correct when the drive is the only drive.

One last warning. When things are not going well, you can tense up and make mistakes more easily. Be certain to avoid one costly error: turn off the machine before doing anything inside. A friend was in this situation once. After trying and retrying to boot for some time, he got frustrated and careless. He plugged the power cord into the drive without turning the PC off. Smoke went up and everything went dead. The next thing he learned was how to replace a power supply!

Calling Technical Support

To make calls to technical support more effective, have as much of the following information as you can available before you call:

- Drive model and description
- Manufacturer and model of your computer
- Exact wording of error message, if any
- Description of the problem
- Hardware and software configuration for your system

Installing a SCSI Hard Drive

Installing a SCSI hard drive is more complicated than installing an ordinary IDE hard drive, but having a SCSI bus on your system allows you to add other SCSI devices, such as a CD-ROM drive or a cassette tape for backups.

A+CORE
1.6

When you install a SCSI hard drive, make sure that your host adapter and the cables you are using are compatible with the SCSI drive. The vendor can help you here. Read the documentation for both the SCSI host adapter and the hard drive before beginning; most SCSI documentation is well written and thorough. In addition to the procedure already discussed for IDE hard drives, a SCSI installation requires that you configure the SCSI host adapter and the SCSI hard drive so that they can communicate with each other. This is done as follows:

1. **Set SCSI IDs.** Set the ID for each device on the SCSI bus. The host adapter documentation will probably explain that the host adapter must be set to ID 7. If the hard drive will be the boot device for the system, its ID is likely to be 0. The second hard drive ID is usually 1. These ID settings might be set by jumpers or DIP switches on the drive.

> **TIP**
>
> Jumpers on a SCSI device used to set the SCSI ID represent the binary value of the ID. For example, an ID of 6, which is 110 in binary, requires three jumpers set to on, on, and off.

2. **Disable or enable disk drive and hard drive controllers.** If the host adapter has a built-in disk drive controller that you are not using, it might be necessary to disable the controller with jumpers or DIP switches, or from the SCSI software setup program. The host adapter documentation will explain how to do this. Incidentally, if you are not using a hard drive or disk drive controller on your system board, you must disable these controllers by setting jumpers or DIP switches on the system board. See the documentation for your system board. Sometimes CMOS setup gives you the option of booting from the SCSI hard drive even if an IDE hard drive is installed.

3. **Terminating resistors.** Devices on both ends of the bus must have terminating resistors enabled so that the voltages to these devices do not spike from reflected signals at the end of the SCSI bus. The documentation will advise you to use terminating resistors that plug into a socket on the board or device, or to use terminating resistor connections where the cable plugs into the device. Some host adapters have jumper or DIP switches that enable or disable resistors on the card. Again, the documentation will be specific.

4. **CMOS setup for a SCSI system.** After you have physically installed the SCSI host and drive, tell setup that the SCSI system is present. Remember that for SCSI devices, the computer does not communicate with the hard drive directly but interfaces with the SCSI host adapter. To use a SCSI hard drive, some computers require that you tell setup that no hard drive is present. The SCSI host provides that information to the computer during start up. Sometimes, the computer setup lets you choose a SCSI hard drive type. That's all it needs to know, and the SCSI host adapter takes over from there. To recognize a SCSI drive, some computers require that the drive type be set to 1 in setup.

5. **SCSI device drivers.** A SCSI bus system on a computer using DOS is likely to require a SCSI device driver to be loaded in the CONFIG.SYS file of the bootable drive. Windows 9x offers its own SCSI driver, although if the host

adapter documentation recommends that you use the adapter's driver instead, then do so. As described in Chapter 6, the two well-known device drivers for SCSI systems are ASPI and CAM. After physically installing the drive and changing CMOS setup, the next step in any hard drive installation is to boot from a floppy disk. The hard drive package will include a bootable disk that loads the device driver to access the SCSI system. A SCSI installation disk includes the files necessary to boot to a DOS prompt, and a CONFIG.SYS file that contains the DEVICE= line to load the SCSI driver. The disk also includes the file containing the driver program. (It's a good idea to have more than one bootable disk available. If you have problems, you can boot from the one that doesn't have the SCSI driver on it.) After you have partitioned and formatted the drive, the installation disk will put this same device driver on your hard drive.

The procedure has more steps if the SCSI drive is installed on the same computer with an IDE drive. For this installation, the IDE drive must be the boot drive and the SCSI drive must be the secondary drive unless your system BIOS supports SCSI hard drives. Because the SCSI bus does not contain the boot device, you must communicate the location of the boot drive to the SCSI host adapter. Again, the documentation for the host adapter will explain how to do this. It may tell you to disable the SCSI host adapter BIOS and drive the SCSI bus (no pun intended) with a device driver loaded in the CONFIG.SYS file of the bootable non-SCSI hard drive.

If you have a CD-ROM drive or other device on the SCSI bus, install its device drivers in CONFIG.SYS so the device operates. Place the DEVICE= command for any SCSI device after the DEVICE= command that loads the SCSI host device driver.

Multiple Operating Systems

Sometimes a PC has more than one operating system on a hard drive, which is called dual booting. During the boot process, you decide which OS will load and complete the boot. The OS that controls the logical drive C (or whichever logical drive is specified in CMOS setup) always begins the boot process, because it is the one that BIOS turns to when searching for a boot device. During the boot, the OS on the boot partition offers the user the option of choosing another OS on the drive. Each OS manages a certain portion of the hard drive, which is accomplished by each OS formatting its own logical drive.

For example, you can install DOS with Windows 3.1 and Windows 9x on the same hard drive so that you can use software made for each operating environment within its native OS. To accomplish this dual boot, follow these general procedures:

1. Install DOS 6.x on your hard drive, using the DOS setup disk to partition and format the drive. DOS installs itself in a directory named \DOS.

2. Install Windows 3.x. By default, it installs itself in the \Windows directory.

3. Because Windows 9x deletes some DOS utility programs, back up your \DOS directory to a different directory, using this command:

```
XCOPY C:\DOS\*.* C:\DOSSAVE\*.*
```

4. Install Windows 9x. When asked for the directory name, choose a directory name different from the directory in which Windows 3.x is installed, such as \Win9x.

5. Restore your \DOS directory from the backup:

```
XCOPY C:\DOSSAVE\*.* C:\DOS\*.*
```

6. Edit the Windows 9x system file MSDOS.SYS in the root directory to allow for a dual boot. To do this, make MSDOS.SYS not hidden, not read-only, and not a system file, using this command:

```
ATTRIB -R -H -S C:\MSDOS.SYS
```

7. Now open MSDOS.SYS with any text editor, such as EDIT, and in the [OPTIONS] section, add this line:

```
BootMulti=1
```

This setting allows for a multiboot configuration. Save the file.

8. Reboot your PC. The PC normally boots to Windows 9x. If you want to boot to DOS and Windows 3.x, press **F8** when you see the message that Windows 9x is starting to load. You see a menu. Choose the "a previous version of MS-DOS" option. DOS then loads.

When a PC has both Windows 9x and DOS, a problem may occur because both OSs have files that have the same name but different purposes and contents. Windows 9x manages this potential conflict by renaming DOS files when it is installed.

When you halt the Windows 9x boot and reboot to the previous version of MS-DOS, Windows 9x restores the DOS files to the names that DOS expects. Table 7-3 lists the renamed files.

Table 7-3   DOS and Windows 9x files that are renamed by Windows 9x

Name When Windows 9x Is Active	Name When DOS Is Active	This File Belongs to
Autoexec.bat	Autoexec.w40	Windows 9x
AUTOEXEC.DOS	AUTOEXEC.BAT	DOS
Command.com	Command.w40	Windows 9x
COMMAND.DOS	COMMAND.COM	DOS
Config.sys	Config.w40	Windows 9x
CONFIG.DOS	CONFIG.SYS	DOS
IO.sys	Winboot.sys	Windows 9x
IO.DOS	IO.SYS	DOS
Msdos.sys	Msdos.w40	Windows 9x
MSDOS.DOS	MSDOS.SYS	DOS

TROUBLESHOOTING HARD DRIVES AND DATA RECOVERY

The rest of this chapter focuses on solving problems with hard drives and recovering corrupted data. We first take a quick look at four popular diagnostic and recovery software programs: Nuts & Bolts, Norton Utilities, Partition Magic, and SpinRite. Next we examine in detail what can go wrong with a hard drive and what to do about it. Special attention is given to recovering data lost through hard drive problems. Finally, a section on general troubleshooting guidelines summarizes much of the material in this section.

An Ounce of Prevention

A+ OS
1.3

Taking good care of your hard drive is not difficult, but it does require a little time. Before we begin a discussion of hard drive troubleshooting and data recovery, here are some precautions you can take to protect your data and software as well as the drive itself.

- **Make backups and keep them current.** It's worth saying again: keep backups. Never trust a computer; it'll let you down. Make a backup of your hard drive partition table, boot record, and CMOS setup. Whenever you install a new software package, back it up to disks or tape. Keep data files in directories separate from the software, to make backing up data easier. Back up the data as often as every four hours of data entry. Rotate the backup disks or tapes by keeping the last two or three most recent backups.

- **Defragment files and scan the hard drive occasionally.** A fragmented hard drive increases access time, and reading and writing files wears out the drive. If you are trying to salvage a damaged file, it is much more difficult to recover a fragmented file than one stored in contiguous clusters. Regularly scan your hard drive for **lost** or **cross-linked clusters**.

- **Don't smoke around your hard drive.** To a read/write head, a particle of smoke on a hard drive platter is like a boulder with a 10-foot circumference on the highway. Hard drives are not airtight. One study showed that smoking near a computer reduced the average life span of a hard drive by 25%.

- **Don't leave the PC turned off for weeks or months at a time.** Once my daughter left her PC turned off for an entire summer. At the beginning of the new school term, the PC would not boot. We discovered that the master boot record had become corrupted. PCs are like cars in this respect: long spans of inactivity can cause problems.

- **High humidity can be dangerous for hard drives.** High humidity is not good for hard drives. I once worked in a basement with PCs, and hard drives failed much too often. After we installed dehumidifiers, the hard drives became more reliable.

- **Be gentle with a hard drive.** Don't bump the PC or move it when the drive is spinning.

Utility Software

This section examines four popular **utility software** programs: Nuts & Bolts, Norton Utilities, SpinRite, and Partition Magic. The following descriptions tell you what to expect from the software with regard to recovery from a hard drive failure (note that this is *not* a complete listing of all the software's functions). You can find detailed instructions for performing the operations discussed here in the documentation for the software.

Nuts & Bolts

Nuts & Bolts by Network Associates, Inc., and McAfee are made up of four suites: Repair and Recover, Clean and Optimize, Prevent and Protect, and Secure and Manage. This limited discussion of recovering from a hard drive failure looks at only four of the 25 utilities in the suites:

- **Disk Minder** diagnoses and repairs hard drive problems, including those in the partition table, boot record, FAT, files, and directories.
- **Image** creates an image of critical disk information, which is written to a file on the hard drive to be used later if the disk is corrupted.
- **Rescue Disk** creates a disk from which you can boot and begin the recovery process if you can't start the system from the hard drive.
- **Disk Tune** defragments hard drives, consolidates free space, and reorganizes all files on the drive for optimal performance.

Figure 7-11 shows the main menu of Nuts & Bolts together with WinGauge, part of the Prevent and Protect feature, which continually monitors the system for conditions that may lead to problems (including applications software crashes).

The following is a look at the four utilities listed above.

Figure 7-11   Nuts & Bolts main menu showing Repair and Recover submenu options

Disk Minder From the main menu of Nuts & Bolts shown in Figure 7-11, first select **Repair and Recover** on the left and then click **Disk Minder** on the Repair and Recover submenu to access this feature of the software. Click **Properties** to display the Properties dialog box in Figure 7-12, listing some of the things that Disk Minder will check.

Figure 7-12   Nuts & Bolts Disk Minder scans drive for errors and can automatically repair them

Disk Minder includes the same functions as does Windows ScanDisk plus additional features, and is faster than ScanDisk. Disk Minder can check and correct problems with the partition table, boot sector, FAT, disk compression structure, directories, filenames, file dates and times, and clusters.

This version of Disk Minder is run under Windows 98, Windows 95, or Windows 3.x, but Disk Minder for DOS is also included in the software, in the event that you cannot boot from the hard drive. Look for directions below under the section "Rescue Disk." After you have recovered the hard drive so that you can boot from it again, use Disk Minder for Windows to complete the recovery process.

Image Select McAfee **Image** to create a snapshot of critical sectors of the hard drive and store this information on the hard drive in a .DAT file. You can set Image so that it takes this snapshot each time you boot. In case of a hard drive crash or destruction caused by a virus or other catastrophe, use Image to restore the directories and FAT to their state when the last snapshot was taken. Use Image frequently so that your snapshot will be current if it is needed. When you select Image from the Nuts & Bolts main menu, the Image dialog box appears. Click **Properties** to see the dialog box in Figure 7-13. From this Image Properties dialog box, you can choose to have Image take a snapshot of the hard drive every time the PC is booted.

Figure 7-13   The Image Properties dialog box shows how to have Nuts & Bolts take a snapshot of critical areas of the hard drive each time Windows is loaded

When you select **Restore drive from saved image** from the Image dialog box, you see the dialog box in Figure 7-14, listing files in the root directory that contain snapshots of the hard drive that Image has previously taken. By default, Image stores these files in the root directory. Select the image file that you want to use for the recovery.

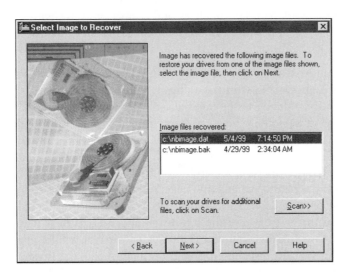

Figure 7-14   Nuts & Bolts Image creates the snapshot files in the root directory of the hard drive

Click **Next**, and the dialog box in Figure 7-15 appears, allowing you to select which areas of the hard drive to restore. Do no select the file allocation tables if many changes have been made to the file structure on the hard drive since the last snapshot was made. Use Disk Minder instead. However, the master boot sector and the partition table information should not have changed since the drive was last partitioned and formatted or drive compression was implemented. Click **Finish** to restore the selected areas of the drive. The Image restore process can also be implemented from the Nuts & Bolts rescue disk. Nuts & Bolts writes the Image snapshot file to the drive in such a way that it can read the file even from a drive that is severely damaged.

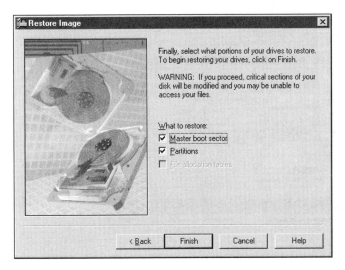

Figure 7-15   What Nuts & Bolts Image can restore on a damaged hard drive

Rescue Disk   Create a rescue disk you can use when you cannot boot from the hard drive. When you see the opening dialog box of the Rescue Disk utility, click **Next**, and then click **Advanced** to see the files that the utility will write to the disk, as shown in Figure 7-16. You can add other files to the list or remove files from the list. Click **OK** to return to the opening dialog box, and click **Next** to complete the process.

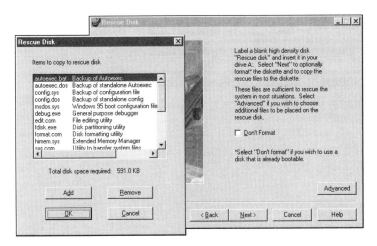

Figure 7-16   Items Nuts & Bolts stores on a rescue disk

When you cannot boot from the hard drive, boot from the rescue disk. After booting, the screen in Figure 7-17 appears, asking if the rescue disk was created on your system or on another PC. If the rescue disk was not created on your current PC, Nuts & Bolts can still be effective in recovering the drive. In either case, Nuts & Bolts examines the drive and then display the menu in Figure 7-18. From this you can use the DOS versions of Disk Minder, Image/Restore, and SysRecover to repair the drive.

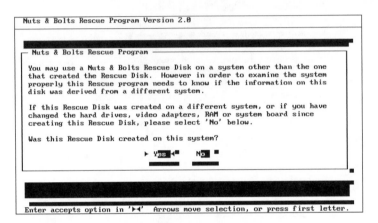

Figure 7-17   Using the Nuts & Bolts rescue disk

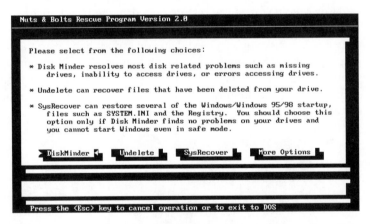

Figure 7-18   Utilities available on the Nuts & Bolts rescue disk

Disk Tune Disk Tune optimizes a hard drive by defragmenting it and moving files so that the most frequently used files are written near the beginning of the drive where access time is fastest. Free space is moved to the end of the drive. While Disk Tune is working, you can watch the progress as the color-coded grid changes color as clusters are read, written, moved, and optimized. Disk Tune can also set all unused FAT entries to zero, but this makes it impossible to use typical recovery procedures to recover deleted files. We will discuss this again later in the chapter.

To use Disk Tune, select **Clean and Optimize** from the Nuts & Bolts main menu, and then click **Disk Tune**. You see the dialog box in Figure 7-19 where you can select the drive to tune. Click **Next**, and the dialog box in Figure 7-20 appears, showing a map of the drive. Click any block to display the cluster numbers and contents of the block. Select the method for Disk Tune to use to optimize your drive, and then click **Start**. Don't use the drive or turn off the PC until the process is completed.

7

Figure 7-19   Nuts & Bolts Disk Tune lets you defragment and reorganize files on a hard drive

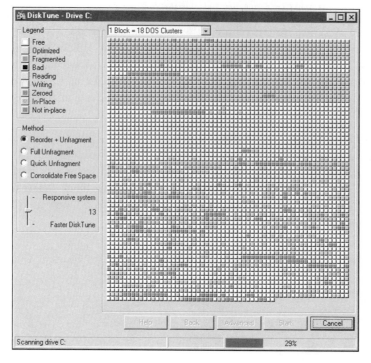

Figure 7-20   The color-coded grid of Disk Tune lets you visually inspect the drive to see how fragmented it is and watch as Disk Tune optimizes the drive

Norton Utilities

Norton Utilities offers several easy-to-use tools to recover data, resurrect a damaged hard drive, enhance hard drive speed and performance, and provide security. Figure 7-21 shows all the programs available under the Norton Utility software. Following is an overview of each Norton Utility program with reference to three main functions: prevention of damage, recovery from damage, and increased system performance. The discussion of the Windows 95 version of Norton Utilities below refers to Version 2.0, although other versions offer the same or similar functionality. The intent here is not to review all the features Norton Utilities offers, but simply to view and demonstrate some techniques to repair the disk and hard drive problems discussed later in the chapter.

If you are using Windows 98 and FAT32, be sure to purchase Norton for Windows 98 and FAT32. Don't try to use a version of Norton that does not support FAT32 on a system that uses FAT32. If you are using Windows NT, be sure to use the version that supports Windows NT.

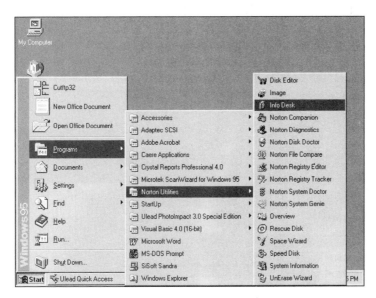

Figure 7-21   The programs of Norton Utilities

Prevention   Preparing for problems that might occur later is the key to making the best use of Norton Utilities. Four programs that help you do that are Norton System Doctor, Norton Protection, Rescue Disk, and Image.

- **Norton System Doctor**. Norton System Doctor detects potential disk and system problems and scans for viruses. By default it runs in the background at all times and informs you when it encounters a problem. You determine when Norton System Doctor should react to certain problems and what it should do about them. You can configure it to check the integrity of your hard drive routinely and to open Norton Disk Doctor if it encounters a problem. Figure 7-22 shows some sample alarms produced by Norton System Doctor while running in the background.

- **Norton Protection**. Norton Protection adds an extra layer of protection to the Windows 9x Recycle Bin.

- **Rescue Disk**. Norton Utilities allows you to create a rescue disk set that you can use to recover from hard drive disasters. Once these disks are created, you can use them to:
  - Format a hard drive
  - Make a bootable disk
  - Partition your hard drive using FDISK
  - Recover erased files
  - Recover accidentally formatted disks or heavily damaged disks, including a damaged partition table and boot record
  - Recover damaged files using Disk Editor

- Recover your CMOS setup
- Troubleshoot hardware conflicts using Norton Diagnostics

Figure 7-22   Examples of Norton System Doctor alarms

You can configure Norton System Doctor to alert you whenever the rescue disk information becomes out of date.

- **Image**. Image creates a snapshot of disk information, including the boot record, FAT, and root directory information. You can configure Image to record this data each time you boot.

Recovery   Norton Utilities offers five programs to help in recovering data and setup information and repairing damaged areas of the hard drive and disks. They are Norton Disk Doctor, UnErase Wizard, Norton Registry Tracker, Norton File Compare, and a DOS program called Disk Editor.

- **Norton Disk Doctor**. Norton Disk Doctor (NDD) automatically repairs many hard disk and floppy disk problems without your intervention. If you ask it to, it creates a backup of the disk before it makes any changes (called the Undo feature). Norton Disk Doctor examines and makes some repairs to the partition table, the DOS boot record, the FAT, directories, and files. It also scans the entire disk, looking for inconsistencies, and diagnoses disk problems, giving you a printed report of the results. If the disk is physically damaged, NDD can mark bad clusters in the FAT so they are not reused. However, Norton Disk Doctor is not a cure-all; some problems are beyond its capabilities.

- **UnErase Wizard**. UnErase Wizard offers added functionality to the Windows 9x Recycle Bin to help recover erased files.

- **Norton Registry Tracker**. Norton Registry Tracker monitors changes to the Windows 9x Registry and allows you to backtrack changes to the Registry.

> **TIP** The Windows 9x Registry is a database the OS uses to store configuration information about the OS environment, user preferences, application software configuration, and hardware configurations.

- **Norton File Compare**. Norton File Compare compares data files as well as Windows 9x Registry and INI files.

- **Disk Editor**. Disk Editor is a powerful tool for editing any part of a disk or hard drive, including the partition table, directory entries, DOS boot record, and FAT. Disk Editor can freely access any portion of the disk. You can reconstruct files manually, sector by sector, and Disk Editor can sometimes read a disk that DOS or Windows 9x refuses to read. Using Disk Editor requires an understanding of how data is stored on a disk, as explained in Chapters 5 and 6.

7

Performance   The four programs designed to improve overall system performance are Norton System Genie, Norton Registry Editor, Speed Disk, and Space Wizard.

- **Norton System Genie**. Norton System Genie allows you to change the way Windows 9x starts up, looks and feels, handles files, and runs applications software.

- **Norton Registry Editor**. Norton Registry Editor is an alternative to the Windows 9x Registry editor, offering improved user interface and functionality.

- **Speed Disk**. Speed Disk is an enhanced disk defragmenter that also allows you to affect the order in which files and folders are written to a disk.

- **Space Wizard**. Space Wizard scans the hard drive for duplicate files, infrequently used files, and temporary files and folders. It then suggests to you files that can be deleted or compressed.

The Help Features of Norton Utilities   Norton Utilities offers several ways to access its Help features. One method is direct access to Info Desk. Click **Start**, **Programs**, **Norton Utilities**, **Info Desk** to open the Info Desk window, shown in Figure 7-23. The Index tab works like the index of a book: type characters, and items appear that you can choose to display or print.

Another way to access the Norton Help features is from the utility programs themselves. For example, if you select **Rescue Disk** from the program list in Figure 7-21 to create a new rescue disk set, the Rescue Disk screen appears. From that window, if you click on the Options button, the Norton Rescue Options window appears, as in Figure 7-24. The third item in the list on the rescue disk is Rescue. To find out more about this item, right-click the item. You see the dialog box in Figure 7-25. Select **What's This** for information about the item, select **How To** for step-by-step procedures involving this item, and select **Info Desk** for a direct link to Info Desk and its information about this item. You can also click the **?** in the title bar of each window for general information about the window.

Figure 7-23 One Norton Help utility – Info Desk

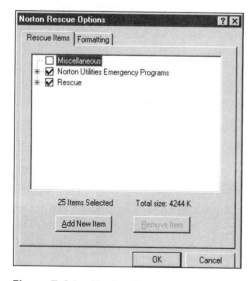

Figure 7-24 Norton Rescue Options

Figure 7-25   To find out more about a Norton Rescue Option, right-click on the item

Viewing the Contents of Norton Utilities Rescue Disk and Creating a Rescue Disk Set   To view the contents of Rescue Disk and create a set of rescue disks that contains, among other things, a backup of the hard drive partition table and boot records, follow these directions: Click **Start**, **Programs**, **Norton Utilities**, **Rescue Disk**. When the Rescue Disk opening screen appears, click **Options** (Figure 7-24). Click the + sign to the left of an item to see the list under that item. For example, to see a list of files that will be included on the rescue disks, click the + sign to the left of Rescue. Figure 7-26 shows part of the list. Note that Boot Record is in the list. Further down in the list the partition table is listed. From the Options window, you can include or exclude certain items from the list. When finished, return to the previous window by clicking **OK**. Click **Start** to create the rescue disk.

Partition Magic

Partition Magic by PowerQuest Corporation lets you manage partitions on a hard drive more quickly and easily than with FDISK. You can create new partitions, change the size of partitions, and move partitions without losing data or moving the data to another hard drive while you work. You can switch between FAT16 and FAT32 without disturbing your data, and you can hide and show partitions to secure your data.

Figure 7-26   Files and information for the Norton rescue disk

One advantage of Partition Magic is that you can quickly and easily rearrange partitions to get the least amount of slack. If you are responsible for many PCs and often find yourself building hard drives, this software as well as other programs from PowerQuest can save you a lot of time. Other PowerQuest products to manage hard drives include:

- **DriveCopy** lets you copy an entire old hard drive to a new hard drive. This software can be a time saver if you need to build several hard drives that contain identical software. The drives don't have to be the same size for DriveCopy to work.

- **DriveImage** helps you manage a compressed, backup copy of your hard drive.

- **DriveImage Professional** does the same thing as DriveImage, in addition to allowing you to download the compressed backup of the hard drive to many PCs over a network.

- **Lost & Found** recovers data from a corrupted hard drive caused by either software or hardware problems.

SpinRite by Gibson Research

SpinRite by Gibson Research is hard drive utility software that has been around for years. When older hard drives could be low-level formatted, SpinRite was the tool most technicians turned to for the job. Today, SpinRite is still a DOS application without a sophisticated GUI interface, but it has been updated to adjust to new hard drive technology. It supports FAT32, SCSI, Zip drives, and Jaz drives. You can boot your PC from a floppy disk and run SpinRite from a floppy, which means that it doesn't require much system overhead. Because it is written in a low-level language (assembly language), it is more likely to detect underlying hard drive problems than software that uses Windows, that can stand as a masking layer between the software and the hard drive. SpinRite analyzes the entire hard drive surface, performing data recovery of corrupted files and file system information. Sometimes, SpinRite can recover data from a failing hard drive when other software fails. For more information see Gibson Research at www.grc.com.

Problems with Hard Drives

A+CORE
2.1

Problems with hard drives can be caused by either hardware or software. Problems can also be categorized as those that prevent the hard drive from booting and those that prevent the data from being accessed. Hardware and software causes of hard drive problems can be summarized as follows:

1. Hardware Problems
   - Problems with the hard drive controller, power supply, data cable, BIOS, or setup—that is, with the supporting firmware and hardware needed to access the drive
   - Damage to the drive mechanism or physical damage to the disk surface where the partition table, boot record, directories, FAT, and/or the data itself are stored

2. Software Problems
   - Corrupted OS files
   - Corrupted partition table, boot record, or root directory, making all data on the hard drive inaccessible
   - Corruption of the area of the FAT that points to the data, the data's directory table, or the sector markings where the data is located
   - Corruption of the data itself
   - Data or access to it destroyed by a virus

Setting Priorities Before You Start

If a hard drive is not functioning and data is not accessible, setting priorities helps focus your work. For most users, the data is the first priority unless they have a recent backup. The software can also be a priority if it is not backed up. Reloading software from the original installation disks or CD-ROM can be time-consuming, especially if the configuration is complex or you have written software macros or scripts that are not backed up.

If you have good backups of both the data and software, the hardware might be your priority. It could be expensive to replace, and downtime can be costly. The point is, when trouble arises, determine your main priority and start by focusing on that.

Be aware of what resources are available to help you resolve a problem. Documentation lists error messages and their meanings. Technical support from the ROM BIOS, hardware, and software manufacturers can help you interpret an error message, or it can provide general support in diagnosing a problem. Most technical support is available during working hours by telephone. Check your documentation for telephone numbers.

An experienced computer troubleshooter once said, "The people who solve computer problems do it by trying something and making phone calls, trying something else and making more phone calls, and so on, until the problem is solved." There is a lot of truth in that statement.

The Internet can also help you diagnose hardware and software problems. Go to the Web site of the manufacturer of the product and search for an FAQ (frequently asked questions) list or bulletin board. It's likely that others have encountered the same problem and have posted the question and answer. If you search and can't find your answer, then you can post a new question.

Remember one last thing. After making a reasonable and diligent effort to resolve a problem, getting the problem fixed could become more important than resolving it yourself. There comes a time when you might need to turn the problem over to a more experienced technician.

Resolving Hard Drive Problems

Hardware problems usually show up at POST, unless there is physical damage to an area of the hard drive that is not accessed during POST. Hardware problems often make the hard drive totally inaccessible.

Sometimes older drives refuse to spin at POST. Drives that are having trouble spinning often whine at startup for several months before they finally refuse to spin altogether. If your drive whines loudly when you first turn on the computer, never turn the computer off. One of the worst things you can do for a drive that is having difficulty starting up is to leave the computer turned off for an extended period of time. Some drives, just like old cars, refuse to start if they are left unused for a long time.

Do not trust valuable data to a drive that is having this kind of trouble. Plan to replace the drive soon. In the meantime, make frequent backups and leave the power on.

Data on a hard drive sometimes "fades" off the hard drive over time. Also, the read/write heads at the ends of the read/write arms on a hard drive get extremely close to the platters but do not actually touch them. This minute clearance between the heads and platters makes hard drives susceptible to destruction. Should a computer be bumped or moved while the hard drive is in operation, a head can easily bump against the platter and scratch the surface. Such an accident causes a "hard drive crash," often making the hard drive unusable.

If the head mechanism is damaged, the drive and its data are probably a total loss. If the first tracks that contain the partition table, boot record, FAT, or root directory are damaged, the drive could be inaccessible although the data might be unharmed.

Here's a trick that might work for a hard drive whose head mechanism is intact but whose first few tracks are damaged. Find a working hard drive that has the same partition table information as the bad drive. With the computer case off, place the good drive on top of the bad drive housing, and connect a spare power cord and the data cable from the adapter to the good drive. Leave a power cord connected to the bad drive. Boot from a disk. No error message should show at POST. Access the good drive by entering C: at the A prompt. The C prompt should show on the monitor screen.

Without turning off the power, gently remove the data cable from the good drive and place it on the bad drive. Do not disturb the power cords on either drive or touch chips on the drive logic boards. Immediately copy the data you need from the bad drive to floppy disks, using the DOS COPY command. If the area of the drive where the data is stored, the FAT, and the directory are not damaged, this method should work. If the FAT is damaged, you might need to read sectors instead of files to retrieve the data, using either **DEBUG** (repeating the LOAD and WRITE commands for all sectors) or utility software.

Here's another trick for an older hard drive that is having trouble spinning when first turned on. Remove the drive from the case and, holding it firmly in both hands, give the drive a quick and sudden twist in such a way that the platters are forced to turn inside the drive housing. Reinstall the drive. It might take several tries to get the drive spinning. Once the drive is working, immediately make a backup and replace the drive soon.

For a hard drive to be accessible by DOS or Windows 9x, these items, listed in the order they are accessed, must be intact:

- The partition table
- The boot record
- The FAT
- The root directory

In addition to the preceding items, the following items must be intact for the hard drive to boot:

1. For DOS
   - The two DOS hidden files, IO.SYS and MSDOS.SYS (or IBMBIO.COM and IBMDOS.COM)
   - COMMAND.COM
   - CONFIG.SYS and AUTOEXEC.BAT (these are optional)

2. For Windows 9x
   - The two Windows 9x hidden files, IO.SYS and MSDOS.SYS
   - COMMAND.COM
   - CONFIG.SYS and AUTOEXEC.BAT (these are optional)
   - VMM32.VXD and several files that it uses to load the desktop

Windows 9x can be loaded to a command prompt, rather than a desktop. You can load just enough of the OS to attain a command prompt. If you press F8 as Windows loads, you can then choose the command prompt. Doing this gives you the C prompt provided by COMMAND.COM and prevents VMM32.VXD from loading.

The hard drive does not have to be bootable to access the data. You can always boot from a floppy disk and then access drive C. After Windows 9x or DOS accesses the drive, in order for the OS to access the data these items must be intact:

- The directory in which the files are located
- In the FAT, the sector information where the files are located

- The beginning of the file, sometimes called the header information, and the end of the file, called the end-of-file marker

- The data itself

Reviewing the preceding three lists, you can see that there are several opportunities for failure. To recover lost data due to a software problem, you must first determine which item is corrupted. Then you must either repair the item or bypass it to recover the data.

Preparing for Disaster   As discussed earlier, Nuts & Bolts and Norton Utilities both offer a version of Image, a utility program that makes a copy of important hard drive information, including the boot record, FAT, and root directory. You can configure your PC to execute Image each time you boot. The software can also track when you have made the last image and prompt you to make another when the information becomes outdated.

Figure 7-13 showed the Properties dialog box for McAfee Image, where you can choose to create an image each time you start Windows. Using the Image file to recover from a hard drive disaster was covered earlier in the chapter.

Damaged Partition Table

A+CORE
    2.1

A+ OS
    3.2

If the hard drive and its supporting hardware pass the POST tests done by startup BIOS, BIOS tries to load an OS from the hard drive if no floppy disk is in drive A. Even if the OS is loaded from a floppy disk, the partition table and the boot record must be intact for the OS to access the hard drive. The FAT and root directory must be readable for the OS to read data stored on the drive.

BIOS first reads the master boot program at the beginning of the partition table information on the hard drive. If the partition table is damaged, the error message is as follows:

```
Invalid drive or drive specification
```

In this case, you should still be able to boot from a floppy disk. When you get to the A prompt and try to access the hard drive by entering C:, you will get the same error.

If you suspect that the partition table is corrupted, use the FDISK command discussed earlier in the chapter to display the partition table information. The FDISK command will give an error when trying to display the information if the table is corrupted.

Restoring the partition table is impossible if the track is physically damaged. However, if you have previously saved the partition table and there is no physical damage, the process is simple. In Chapter 6, you learned that you can save the partition table to a disk using Norton Utilities, Nuts & Bolts, or the DOS 5 MIRROR command. If you have not saved this information, but you have another hard drive with a matching partition table, try saving the table from the good drive and writing it to the bad drive. Sometimes the UNFORMAT command will allow this.

If you have saved the information using the DOS MIRROR command, restore the partition table with this command:

```
UNFORMAT /PARTN
```

The command prompts you for the disk containing the file PARTNSAV.FIL, and it restores the partition table and boot records for all partitions on the drive.

Also, to recover the FAT, directories, and files, this variation of the UNFORMAT command sometimes gives results:

```
UNFORMAT /U
```

Nuts & Bolts Disk Minder, Norton Disk Doctor, and SpinRite also can repair a damaged partition table. You must have the utility software on floppy disks and execute the program from the disks. If you have made a set of rescue disks with Nuts & Bolts or Norton Utilities, use these disks to restore the partition table. If you have not made a set of rescue disks, try the Emergency Disks, which can sometimes correct the problem. If SpinRite instructs you to make a bootable disk on another PC, install SpinRite on the disk, and then use the disk to repair the hard drive.

A+ OS 3.2 Don't use FDISK to make a new partition table, because it will also overwrite the first few sectors on the hard drive that contain the FAT. Part of the partition information can be recovered using FDISK with the /MBR parameter. When the following error message is displayed, first boot from a floppy disk.

```
Invalid Drive or Drive Specification
```

Then to restore the boot program in the partition table (called the master boot record), which is at the very beginning of the partition table information, try this command:

```
A> FDISK /MBR
```

Oftentimes, this command solves the problem. Note that the /MBR option is not documented in the DOS or Windows 9x manuals. The FDISK program must be stored on the floppy disk in drive A; keep a copy of it on an emergency bootable disk for just this purpose.

You can, however, start over by repartitioning and reformatting the drive. Although the first few tracks are damaged, you might still be able to recover part of the storage space on the drive. The partition table is written on the very first sector of the hard drive, and this sector must be accessible. After that, you can skip as many sectors as you need to by making a non-DOS or non-Windows 9x partition at the beginning of the drive. This partition will never be used. Make the second partition, which will be the first DOS or Windows 9x partition, the bootable partition. All this is done using the FDISK command available in either DOS or Windows 9x, or you can use Partition Magic.

Don't perform a low-level format on an IDE or SCSI drive unless the drive is otherwise unusable. Use the low-level format program recommended by the manufacturer, and follow its instructions. Call the drive manufacturer's technical support to find out how to get this program, or check the manufacturer's Web site for details.

Damaged Boot Record

$A+\ OS$
3.1

If the boot record on a hard drive is damaged, you cannot boot from the hard drive. After you boot from a floppy disk and try to access the hard drive, you might get an error message such as "Invalid media type", "Non-DOS disk", or "Unable to read from Drive C."

If the boot record is damaged, the best solution is to recover it from the backup copy you made when you first became responsible for the PC. If you did not make the backup, try SpinRite, Norton Utilities Disk Doctor, or Nuts & Bolts Disk Minder. Figure 7-27 shows Help information from Norton Utilities about testing the boot record. Recall that a floppy disk has only one boot record, but a hard drive has one master boot record in the partition table area and a boot record at the beginning of each logical drive or volume on the drive.

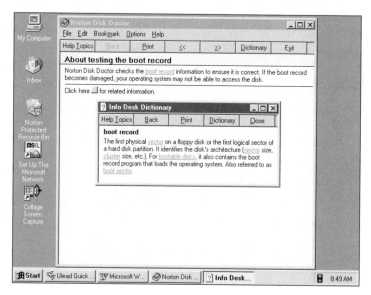

Figure 7-27   Help from Norton Utilities about testing the boot record

Norton Disk Doctor tests and repairs the damaged boot record if it can. The Norton Utilities Rescue Disk simply refreshes the boot record with the backup copy on the disk. To use Norton Disk Doctor, click **Start**, **Programs**, **Norton**, and **Norton Disk Doctor**. Select the hard drive from the list of drives displayed on the first screen of the program and click **Diagnose**. The dialog box in Figure 7-28 is displayed as Norton Disk Doctor tests the entire drive, including the boot record. If it discovers errors in the boot record or other areas of the disk, it asks permission to repair the damage or repairs it without asking permission, depending on how you have set the program options. Figure 7-29 displays the test results. When you click **Details** you can print a detailed report of the test and any corrections made.

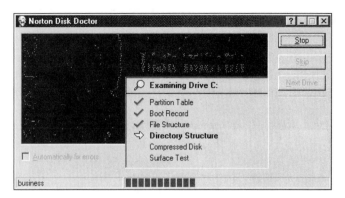

Figure 7-28   Norton Disk Doctor examining a hard drive

7

Figure 7-29   Norton Disk Doctor displays test results for drive C

Damaged FAT or Root Directory

A+ OS
3.1,
3.2

The partition table and boot record are easily backed up to disk; they will not change unless the drive is repartitioned or reformatted. Always back them up as soon as you can after you buy a new computer or become responsible for a working one.

Unlike the partition table and boot record, the FAT and the root directory change often and are more difficult to back up. SpinRite, Nuts & Bolts Disk Minder, and Norton Disk Doctor provide tools to repair a damaged FAT or root directory. Their degree of success is dependent on the degree of damage to the tables.

One message generated by a hard drive with a damaged file allocation table is:

```
Sector not found reading drive C, Abort, Retry, Ignore,
Fail?
```

Sometimes, however, you do not see an error message; files or directories are simply missing. Nuts & Bolts and Norton Utilities can be used to recover from a corrupted FAT.

If the physical areas of the FAT and root directory are damaged and you cannot repair them, you can still read data from the hard drive by reading sectors instead of files. With Norton Disk Editor, read one sector at a time and write each to a disk or use Lost and Found.

Norton Utilities   The two Norton Utilities programs that might be helpful in repairing a damaged FAT and other areas of the hard drive are Norton Disk Doctor and Disk Editor. Norton Disk Doctor does not require you to understand what the program is examining or doing to the drive. Disk Editor gives you more control, but this also means you must understand what you are doing as you make decisions and edit critical areas of the hard drive yourself.

Norton Disk Doctor   Norton Disk Doctor, discussed earlier in the chapter, offers an automated way to examine a disk or hard drive and to reconstruct it where the programs deem necessary. Norton Disk Doctor might be able to reconstruct a boot record, a copy of the FAT, a directory, and even files. In some situations it is an easy fix for a damaged disk.

Norton Disk Editor   Norton Disk Editor can automatically repair a damaged floppy disk or hard drive, including damage to the FAT, or you can make changes directly to a copy of the FAT and to the directory. As you move the cursor over the FAT entries, all the entries for one file change color so that they are easy to find and edit.

For example, Disk Editor allows you to take a damaged hard drive or floppy disk that has a fragmented file that you want to recover, and copy the file, sector by sector, to a floppy disk. Disk Editor creates a new file on the floppy disk and appends one sector from the damaged drive after another to that new file.

The time to learn how to use Disk Editor is not when you need it but before you need it. Learn how to use Disk Editor by practicing on floppy disks. Start with a floppy disk that has several files, and examine the root directory, the FAT, and the files themselves. Practice data recovery by copying a file one sector at a time to a new disk. The activities at the end of the chapter will help you gain experience by working with disks.

For a truly damaged floppy disk with important data on it, be sure to make a copy of the disk before you start working with it. Try Windows 9x Copy Disk or DOS DISKCOPY first. If they will not copy your disk, try Norton's UNDO feature before you begin editing the disk.

Nuts & Bolts   Use Disk Minder to recover a corrupted FAT on either a floppy disk or hard drive. The process is automatic but does give you the option to choose what to repair and what to leave as is. Under the Disk Minder Properties box, shown in Figure 7–30, remove the check from **Auto Fix Errors**. When Disk Minder finds errors on the hard drive, including errors in the FAT, it prompts you before making changes.

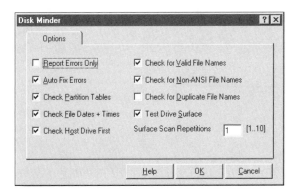

Figure 7-30   Nuts & Bolts Disk Minder will check these things on a disk

7

Using Norton Disk Editor to View a FAT   Viewing a FAT with Norton Disk Editor gives you a clear picture of how a data file is written to a disk. The FAT can also be used to recover a **corrupted file**, because you can locate each cluster of the file and copy the data, cluster by cluster, to a new disk.

One way to access Disk Editor is to click **Start**, **Programs**, **Norton**, **Disk Editor**. Windows 9x unloads, and Disk Editor loads from DOS. Another way to load Disk Editor is to type DISKEDIT at the command prompt. Norton Utilities puts a copy of DISKEDIT.EXE on the rescue disks, and it's also located on the Emergency Disks that come as a part of the software.

From the opening menu, select the **Object** menu (**Alt+O**) and select **A: 3½ Floppy** as the object. Click **OK**.

Select the **Object** menu again; this time select **1ST FAT** from the Object menu. The FAT is displayed as a table of entries, each entry representing one cluster on the disk, as shown in Figure 7-31. Look at the bottom of the screen for the current cluster in the FAT. The entry in that cluster location will either be <EOF> to mark the end of the file or the pointer to the next cluster in the file.

```
                              Disk Editor
     Object   Edit   Link   View   Info   Tools   Help
      708      709      710      711      712      713      714      715
      716      717      718      719      720      721      722      723
      724      725      726      727      728      729      730      731
      732      733      734      735      736      737      738      739
      740      741      742      743      744      745      746      747
      748      749      750      751      752      753      754      755
      756      757      758      759      760    <EOF>    <EOF>    <EOF>
    <EOF>    <EOF>    <EOF>    <EOF>      768      769      770    <EOF>
      772      773      774      775      776      777      778      779
      780      781      782      783      784      785      786      787
      788      789      790      791      792      793      794      795
      796      797      798      799      800      801      802      803
      804      805      806      807      808      809      810      811
    <EOF>      813      814      815      816      817      818      819
      820      821      822      823      824      825      826      827
      828      829      830      831      832      833      834      835
      836      837      838      839      840      841      842      843
      844      845      846      847      848      849      850      851
      852      853      854      855      856      857      858      859
      860      861      862      863      864      865      866      867
      868      869      870      871      872      873      874      875
  FAT (1st Copy)                                         Sector 3
  A:\MSDOS.B4                                 Cluster 767, hex 2FF
```

Figure 7-31   Norton Utilities Disk Editor in FAT view

Corrupted System Files

A+ OS
3.2,
3.1,
1.2

If the two OS hidden files are missing or corrupted, you should see the following error message for DOS:

```
Non-system disk or disk error...
```

or for Windows 9x:

```
Invalid system disk...
```

When this happens, first boot from a floppy disk, then access drive C, and begin looking for the problem. Use the ATTRIB command to unhide all files in the root directory, as follows:

```
C:\> ATTRIB -H *.*
```

You should see the two exposed hidden files if they are there. If they are missing or corrupted, you can use the COPY command to copy them from a disk to the hard drive root directory. (Unhide them on the disk first, so COPY can find them.) Once they are on the hard drive, hide them again with these commands:

```
C:\> ATTRIB +H IO.SYS
C:\> ATTRIB +H MSDOS.SYS
```

Substitute another filename as necessary. You can also use this command:

```
A:\> SYS C:
```

The SYS command copies the two hidden files and COMMAND.COM from the disk to the hard drive.

A+ OS
3.1

COMMAND.COM must be in the root directory. If COMMAND.COM is missing, you should get the following error message:

```
Command file not found
```

or something similar. You will probably find a spare copy in the \DOS directory or \Windows\command, or you can copy it from your bootable disk.

CONFIG.SYS and AUTOEXEC.BAT sometimes give errors when they are changed or accidentally erased. Keep a backup of these files so that you will not have to remember all the commands listed in them if you have to rebuild.

To prevent a user from accidentally erasing COMMAND.COM, CONFIG.SYS, and AUTOEXEC.BAT, you might want to hide these files, using the ATTRIB command in DOS or the Properties sheet in Windows 9x. You also can make them read-only files, using this version of ATTRIB for each file. For example, in COMMAND.COM you can use:

```
ATTRIB +R COMMAND.COM
```

Corrupted Sector and Track Markings

The first few bits of each sector are labels that the hard drive BIOS must read before it reads any data in that sector. The data might be perfectly fine, but, if the sector markings are faded, BIOS will not read the sector. DOS will give you the following error message:

```
Bad Sector or Sector Not Found
```

SpinRite, Nuts & Bolts, Norton Utilities, or Lost and Found might be able to read the sector. Try them first. If one can read the data, copy the data to a disk and have the utility mark the cluster as bad in the FAT so that it will not be used again. If the drive continues to report bad sectors, it needs to be low-level formatted. Only the low-level format will refresh these sector bits.

There are two kinds of **low-level formats**: a nondestructive and a destructive format. The nondestructive format does not destroy the data. It copies the data on one track to another area of the drive, rewrites the sector bits on that track, and then copies the data back to the track.

A destructive low-level format completely ignores old format information and starts all over again, writing track and sector markings to the drive and overwriting all data. The advantages of using a destructive format are that it's faster and does a better job of determining bad sectors and marking them than a nondestructive format. If you have a choice, choose the destructive format.

 TIP Remember that it is dangerous to low-level format an IDE drive because the track and sector locations can be specific to this drive. Only use a low-level format program recommended by the drive manufacturer.

Corrupted Data and Program Files

Data and program files can become corrupted for many reasons, ranging from power spikes to user error. If the corrupted file is a program file, the simplest solution might be to reinstall the software or recover the file from a previous backup.

To restore a data file that is not backed up, you have three options:

- Use operating system tools and commands to recover the file.
- Use Nuts & Bolts, Norton Utilities, Lost and Found, SpinRite, or other third-party software to recover the file.
- If neither of these approaches works, you can turn to a professional data recovery service. These services can be expensive, but, depending on how valuable the data is, the cost might be justified.

Using OS Tools and Commands to Recover Data

When a data file or program file is damaged, portions of the file may still be intact. The basic approach to recovering data in this situation is to create a new file on another disk or on the hard drive, containing all the sectors from the original file that can be read from the damaged disk or hard drive. Then edit the newly created file to replace the missing data.

How successfully an OS recovers data depends on how badly damaged the file is. A few examples of how data commonly becomes damaged and what can be done to recover it are discussed below. If a file has been accidentally erased, or the disk or hard drive is otherwise damaged, remember these two things: (1) don't write anything to the disk or hard drive, because you may overwrite data that you might otherwise recover, and (2) if you are recovering data from a disk, use DISKCOPY in DOS or, for Windows 9x, use Copy Disk in Explorer to make a copy of the disk before you do anything else. If Copy Disk or DISKCOPY doesn't work, try copying the disk with Norton Utilities or Nuts & Bolts.

Corrupted File Header   If an application cannot open or read one of its data files, the file header might be corrupted. Many applications place header information (called the file header) at the beginning of the file. This data follows a different format from the rest of the file. The application uses it to identify the file and its contents. If the file header is lost or corrupted and an application needs that header to read the file, you can sometimes recover the contents by treating the file as an ASCII text file. Most applications let you import a text file, and then convert it to the application's format. Read your application's documentation to learn how to import a text file.

Lost Allocation Units   A disk can develop **lost allocation units** or lost clusters if a program cannot properly close a file it has opened. For example, if you boot your computer while an application is running (not a good thing to do for this very reason), the application will not have the oppertunity to close a file and may lose clusters. Another way clusters can be lost is if you remove a floppy disk from a drive while the drive light is still on (also not a good thing to do).

A+ OS
3.2

Lost clusters make up a chain of clusters that are not incorporated into a file. The CHKDSK and SCANDISK commands take this chain of clusters, turn it into a file with the name FILE0000.CHK or a similar filename with a higher number, and store the file in the root directory. To use this utility in DOS to access lost clusters, use the command with the /F option, like this:

```
C:\> CHKDSK A:/F
```

Often the file created can be used by the application that it belongs to, although you might have to change the file extension so the application will recognize the file.

For Windows 9x, use the ScanDisk utility described in Chapter 6 to accomplish the same results.

Bad Sectors   Error messages that occur when a file is read might be caused by bad sectors on the floppy disk or hard drive. If a disk contains bad sectors, the COPY command can sometimes recover the remaining file data located in the good sectors. For example, if you have a disk in drive A that has bad sectors, and a file named DOCUMENT.DOC is unreadable by an application, for DOS try this command:

```
C:\TEMP> COPY A:DOCUMENT.DOC
```

Choose the **Ignore** option by pressing I when the following message appears:

```
Unable to read from Drive A: Abort, Retry, Ignore
```

DOS ignores that bad sector and moves on to the next sector. You should be able to copy at least part of the file on the disk.

For Windows, use the COPY command from File Manager in Windows 3.x or Explorer in Windows 9x.

Try the RECOVER command on only one file at a time. Don't use it at all unless you have made a backup copy of the disk or you have no other option. Sometimes the RECOVER command actually destroys data that might have been recovered by some other method. As with CHKDSK, you might have to rename the file created by RECOVER so that its application recognizes it.

Erased File   With DOS, if a file has been erased by the DOS DEL or ERASE command, it can sometimes be recovered. DOS offers the UNERASE or UNDELETE command that recovers some erased files. When DOS deletes a file from a disk or hard drive, it does so as follows:

- The first character of the filename in the root directory is overwritten with the character s, which has the hex value E5

- All entries in the FAT for this file are replaced with 00s

When you issue the DOS UNDELETE command, DOS looks for an entry in the root directory matching the filename and replaces the first character of the filename in the root directory. From the root directory, DOS can read the starting cluster of the file and the size of the file. If the file is not too fragmented and the disk is otherwise healthy, DOS can locate the sectors belonging to the file and reconstruct the FAT.

When you delete a file using Windows 9x, this OS handles floppy disk files differently from hard drive files. Windows 9x floppy disk files are treated the same way DOS treats any file that has been deleted; in other words, there's no Recycle Bin. (The Windows Recycle Bin is a special folder on the hard drive where Windows lists files that have been erased so that they can be unerased if necessary.) Windows 9x offers no tools to undelete a file from a floppy disk. However, for a hard drive, the file is moved to the Recycle Bin and stays there until you purge it. The file information is still retained in the FAT, and the file takes up space on the hard drive. You can recover the file simply by dragging it from the Recycle Bin to a new location. If the file has been deleted from the Recycle Bin, you might still be able to recover the file by using the DOS UNDELETE command. This command is not included with Windows 9x, so you must look for it in your older DOS 5.x or DOS 6.x directory. To undelete a file from Windows 9x using DOS UNDELETE, follow this procedure:

1. From the Windows 9x Start menu, choose **Shut Down**, and then choose **Restart the computer in MS-DOS mode**.

2. At the DOS prompt, type **LOCK**, which makes the FAT and directories available for DOS utilities without allowing other applications to access them.

3. Undelete the file using the DOS UNDELETE command. Don't forget to include the path in the command line as necessary.

4. Type **UNLOCK** to release the file system to applications.

5. Type **EXIT** to relaunch Windows 9x.

Using Utility Software to Recover Files

Norton Utilities and Lost and Found offer user-friendly ways to recover files. Norton Disk Doctor can often do the work (and the thinking) for you. You have more control, however, with Norton Disk Editor.

Norton Utilities   There are two approaches to using Norton Disk Editor to recover a file. One is to copy the file, sector by sector, to another disk or hard drive. You can locate the file by looking in the root directory for the starting cluster number and the size of the file. From the file size and the size of one cluster, calculate the number of clusters the file uses. Next, go to the FAT and look for the entries beginning with the first cluster in the file. The Disk Editor in FAT view is shown in Figure 7-31. If the FAT has been erased (for example, when the file was accidentally deleted), the FAT is virtually useless. However, clusters currently in use in the FAT can be eliminated as possible locations for the file, unless, of course, the file was overwritten after the deletion occurred. Write down or print all the information that you can get from the FAT.

Next go to the disk data area and read the disk as single sectors. Use the list from the FAT to locate the data. You need to know what you're looking for. Try to get the latest printout of the file if one exists. If there is no printout, you at least need to know what the data looks like so that you can recognize it. With Disk Editor, create a file on another disk and copy one sector after another to the new file, appending each sector to the file.

The second approach to using Disk Editor is to edit the root directory and FAT entries on the damaged disk to point to that area on the disk that is undamaged. Suppose, for example, you discover that only a few clusters of a 128-cluster file are damaged. The file begins at cluster 150. You can read the file, cluster by cluster, using Disk Editor, until you get to cluster 221. Good data picks up again at cluster 229. Here's what you do:

1. Edit the root directory of the original file, changing the size of the file to the number of bytes of the original file less the number of bytes in the damaged clusters. You need to know the number of bytes in one cluster for this disk.

2. Change the FAT entry at 220 to point to 229, not 221. Do the same for the second copy of the FAT.

3. Having altered the directory and FATs so that they do not read the damaged sectors, immediately copy the file to a new disk.

You can actually create files on a disk using the above method. By using a disk editor or DEBUG (a disk editor is much easier), you can add a new entry to the root directory and edit the two FATs to point to all the sectors on the disk you need for the file. The new file now exists! This method works well if you have a damaged data area of the disk but the root directory and FATs are still somewhat intact.

Lost & Found   Lost & Found by PowerQuest can recover data quickly and easily. This relatively new software does not attempt to fix disk problems; in fact, it does not write to the problem disk at all, but only reads and copies the data to another disk. PowerQuest offers a free demo that you can download from their Web site. Use the demo to determine if Lost & Found can recover your data before you have to purchase it. For more information, see *www.powerquest.com*.

SpinRite   SpinRite by Gibson Research can recover files on hard drives, floppy disks, and removable drives. You can run the program from within Windows, but, for best results, boot from a floppy and run the program from the floppy. For more information, see *www.grc.com*.

Virus Problems

If you suspect that a virus could be your problem, use a virus scan program to scan memory and your hard drive for an active or inactive virus.

HARD DRIVE TROUBLESHOOTING GUIDELINES

This section summarizes the steps to follow when troubleshooting a hard drive problem, listing several problems, their causes, and possible solutions. These and other troubleshooting guidelines are collectively listed in Appendix E as a quick reference while on the job to help give you ideas as to how to proceed when problem solving.

Begin troubleshooting by interviewing the user, being sure to include the following questions:

1. Was the computer recently moved?

2. Was any new hardware recently installed?

3. Was any new software recently installed?

4. Was any software recently reconfigured or upgraded?

5. Does the computer have a history of similar problems?

As you have learned in this chapter, hard drives can malfunction in many ways, including the ones discussed below.

Hard Drive Does Not Boot

A+ OS
3.1,
3.2

If the hard drive does not boot, proceed as follows:

- Confirm that both the monitor and computer switches are turned on.

- Sometimes startup BIOS displays numeric error codes during POST. Errors in the 1700s or 10400s generally mean fixed disk problems. Check the Web site of the BIOS manufacturer for explanations of these numeric codes.

A+ OS
3.1,
3.2

- For SCSI drives, numeric error codes 096xxxx, 112xxxx, 113xxxx, 206xxxx, 208xxxx, 210xxxx, or 1999xxxx generally mean problems with the host adapter.

- For SCSI drives, reseat the host adapter card and check terminators.

- Disconnect and clean the edge connectors on the adapter card, if present.

- Check CMOS setup for errors in the hard drive configuration.

- Try using a bootable disk, then log on to drive C. If you have a Windows 9x rescue disk, you can use SCANDISK, CHKDSK, or FDISK to examine the system.

- If the PC does not boot from the boot disk, verify that the boot disk is good. Try using it in a different computer. To protect against viruses, write protect the boot disk first.

- Check to be sure the power cable and disk controller cable connections are good.

- If the drive still does not boot, exchange the three field-replaceable units for a hard drive subsystem (the data cable, the adapter card, and the hard drive itself). Perform the following procedures in order.

- Reconnect or swap the drive data cable.

- Reseat or exchange the drive adapter card, if one is present.

- Exchange the hard drive for one you know is good (in computer jargon, this is called a known-good unit).

- If the hard drive refuses to work, but the hard drive light stays on even after the system has fully rebooted, the problem might be a faulty controller on the hard drive or system board. Try replacing the hard drive, then the system board.

A bad power supply or a bad system board also might cause a disk boot failure. If the problem is solved by exchanging one of the above field-replaceable units, you still must reinstall the old unit to verify that the problem was not caused by a bad connection.

Damaged, missing, or mismatched system files (COMMAND.COM, IO.SYS, MSDOS.SYS) can keep a hard disk from booting. You can see if they are of the same version by typing DIR/AH. This will show the hidden system files and their dates. If COMMAND.COM and the hidden files have different dates, then they are usually mixed and incompatible versions. You can replace the three system files using the following steps:

- Boot a rescue or system DOS disk from drive A (make sure you are using the same DOS version).

- Restore hidden system files on drive C (A:\>SYS C:).

- Older versions of DOS require you to copy COMMAND.COM separately. You can restore COMMAND.COM by typing:

```
A:\>COPY COMMAND.COM C:
```

- Run SCANDISK.

- Run a current version of an antivirus program.

Drive Retrieves and Saves Data Slowly

A+ OS
3.2

If the drive retrieves and saves data slowly, proceed as follows:

- Run DEFRAG to rewrite fragmented files to contiguous sectors. Slow data retrieval might be caused by fragmented files that have been updated, modified, and spread over different portions of the disk.

- Verify that the hard disk drivers are properly installed.

Computer Will Not Recognize a Newly Installed Hard Drive

If the computer will not recognize a newly installed hard drive, proceed as follows:

- Does the manual state that you must first do a "low-level" format or run a Disk Manager? IDE drives are already low-level formatted. Older drives require the user to perform this routine.

- Has the FDISK utility been successfully run? Choose "Display Partition Information" from the FDISK menu to verify the status.

- FORMAT C:/S is the last required "format" step. Has this been done?

- Has the CMOS setup been correctly configured?

- Are there any drivers to install?

- Are there any DIP switches or jumpers that must be set?

- Has the data cable been properly connected? Verify that the cable stripes are connected to pin 1 on the edge connectors of both the card and cable.

- Check the web site of the drive manufacturer for suggestions if the above steps are not productive.

7

CHAPTER SUMMARY

- Installing a hard drive includes setting jumpers or DIP switches on the drive; physically installing the adapter card, cable, and drive; changing CMOS setup; and partitioning, formatting, and installing software on the drive.

- An IDE hard drive can be installed as a master drive, slave drive, or single drive on a system.

- Protect the drive and the PC against static electricity during installation.

- The EIDE standards support two IDE connections, a primary and a secondary. Each connection can support up to two IDE devices for a total of four devices on a system.

- IDE devices under the EIDE standard can be hard drives, CD-ROM drives, tape drives, Zip drives, and others.

- Large-capacity hard drives must have either LBA mode or large mode set in CMOS in order for system BIOS to support the drive. Without this support, device driver software or a special EIDE adapter card specific to the drive must be used.

- Most BIOSs today can autodetect the presence of a hard drive if the drive is designed to give this information to BIOS.

- A drive must have one primary partition and can have one extended partition. The drive boots from the primary partition. The extended partition can be subdivided into several logical drive partitions.

- Use more than one partition to optimize the cluster size, to handle drives greater than 2 GB when using FAT16, or to improve the organization of the software on the drive.

- With FAT32, the hard drive can be partitioned using a single partition with a single logical drive.

- The OS, or high-level, format creates the FATs, root directory, and boot record on the drive and marks any bad clusters in the FAT that the low-level format had previously identified.

- A Windows 95 upgrade requires that DOS and Windows 3.x are previously installed on the drive or the Windows 3.x setup disk is available.

- You can make a backup of the partition table with the MIRROR command, Nuts & Bolts, Norton Utilities, or Partition Magic.

- Installing a SCSI drive involves installing the host adapter, terminating resistors, setting SCSI IDs, and configuring the SCSI system to consider whether the drive is the boot device or not.

- Windows 9x and DOS with Windows 3.x can be installed on the same hard drive, and you can boot to either OS.

- High humidity, smoking near the PC, and leaving the PC turned off for long periods can damage a hard drive.

- Utility software, such as Lost & Found and Norton Utilities, can sometimes be used to quickly recover lost hard drive information and data without extensive knowledge or an understanding of the problem.

- Sometimes the second copy of the FAT on a hard drive can be used when the first copy becomes corrupted.

- ScanDisk and CHKDSK can be used to recover lost allocation units caused by files not being properly closed by the application creating them.

- When data is lost on a hard drive, don't write anything to the drive if you intend to try to recover the data.

- Low-level formats should be used as a last resort to restore an unreliable IDE hard drive. Only use the low-level format program recommended by the drive manufacturer.

KEY TERMS

Auto detection — A feature on newer system BIOS and hard drives that automatically identifies and configures a new drive in the CMOS setup.

Boot record (of hard drives) — The first sector of each logical drive in a partition that contains information about the logical drive. If the boot record is in the active partition, then it is used to boot the OS. Also called DOS boot record or OS boot record.

Corrupted files — Data and program files that are damaged for any of a variety of reasons, ranging from power spikes to user error.

DEBUG utility — A DOS utility that shows exactly what is written to a file or memory, using the hexadecimal numbering system to display memory addresses and data.

Disk Editor by Norton — A powerful tool for editing any part of a disk, including the partition table, directory entries, DOS boot record, and FAT.

High-level format — Formatting performed by means of the DOS or Windows 9x Format program (for example, FORMAT C:/S creates the boot record, FAT, and root directory on drive C and makes the drive bootable). Also called OS format.

Interleave — To write data in nonconsecutive sectors around a track, so that time is not wasted waiting for the disk to make a full revolution before the next sector is read.

Lost allocation units — *See* Lost clusters.

Lost clusters — File fragments that, according to the file allocation table, contain data that does not belong to any file (in DOS, the command CHKDSK /F can free these fragments). Also called lost allocation units.

Low-level format — A process (usually performed at the factory) that electronically creates the hard drive tracks and sectors and tests for bad spots on the disk surface.

Operating system format — *See* High-level format.

Partition table — A table written at the very beginning of a hard drive, which describes the number and location of all partitions, and identifies the boot partition.

SCSI bus — A bus standard used for peripheral devices tied together in a daisy chain.

Utility software — Software packages, such as Nuts & Bolts or Norton Utilities, that provide the means for data recovery and repair, virus detection, and the creation of backups.

REVIEW QUESTIONS

1. When two hard drives are connected to the same data cable, how does BIOS know which is the master and which is the slave drive?

2. If a system board has two EIDE connections, how many IDE devices can the system support?

3. If a hard drive is too small to physically fit snugly into the drive bay, what can you do?

4. What is the purpose of the hard drive light on the front of a computer case?

5. How can you tell which side of a hard drive's data cable connects to pin 1 on the drive?

6. What are large-capacity drives? What are two methods that BIOS can use to support them?

7. What are the two limitations in standards that caused older BIOSs to not support drives larger than 528 MB?

8. If your BIOS does not support a large-capacity drive that you want to install, what four choices do you have?

9. How can you tell if your system board chip set supports Ultra DMA mode?

10. What OS utility is used to partition a hard drive?

11. How can you tell how many partitions a hard drive has been set up to have?

12. For a hard drive, describe the difference between a master boot record and a OS boot record.

13. Where on a hard drive is the information about the number and sizes of partitions stored?

14. What is the minimum number of partitions you can use for a 3-GB hard drive in a Windows 98 environment using FAT16? Why?

15. In Question 13 above, if you want to use only a single partition for the entire drive, what can you do?

16. When running FDISK under Windows 98, if you answer positively to the question, "Enable large disk support?" what does FDISK then do?

17. What is the cluster size for a 1.5-GB partition using FAT16? Using FAT32?

18. When would you be required to use FAT16 instead of FAT32 to partition a drive?

19. If a hard drive is using FAT16, what value is put in the FAT entry to indicate that the cluster is bad?

20. What is the difference between a bad cluster and a lost cluster?

21. What could cause a lost cluster?

22. What condition might prevent a deleted file from being undeleted?

23. Before you call the manufacturer's technical support for a hard drive during installation, what should you have in hand?

24. When you are installing a SCSI drive and an IDE drive on the same system, under what circumstances can the SCSI drive be the boot device?

25. In a dual boot situation between Windows 98 and DOS 6, when Windows 98 boots, what does it do with the DOS 6 system files?

26. Name two third-party utility software applications that can be used to manage and maintain hard drives.

27. What is one way that you can make a backup of partition information on a hard drive?

28. How can you tell if your hard drive is using normal, LBA, or large mode?

29. How can you unerase a file in Windows 98?

30. List three components to check or examine if a hard drive does not boot.

31. What is the one most important thing you can do to protect your data on a hard drive?

PROJECTS

Preparing for Hard Drive Hardware Problems

1. Boot your PC and make certain that it is working properly. Make sure you have a bootable disk available in case you need it. Turn off your computer, remove the computer case, and loosen the adapter card to your hard drive. Turn the computer back on. Write down the message that you get.

2. Turn the computer off and reseat the card. Disconnect the data cable and turn the computer back on. Write down the error that you get.

3. Turn off the computer and reconnect the data cable. Disconnect the power supply cord to the hard drive. Turn the computer on. Write down the error that you get.

4. Turn off the computer, reconnect the power cord, and turn on the computer. Rename COMMAND.COM in the root directory of your hard drive and reboot. Write down the error that you get. Reboot from the bootable floppy and rename the file on the hard drive back to COMMAND.COM. Reboot again to make certain that all is well.

5. Access Setup, write down the hard drive type and parameters you have, change the type, and reboot. Write down the errors you get. Access Setup, restore the drive type to the correct value, and reboot.

6. For DOS, add the following files to the rescue disk that you created in the Chapter 2 "Projects."

   ❐ FDISK.EXE (to display partition information and to refurbish the master boot record with the command FDISK/MBR)

   ❐ FORMAT.COM

   ❐ SYS.COM

   ❐ A copy of the partition table of your hard drive (use the DOS MIRROR command or some other utility software)

   ❐ DEBUG.EXE (to examine the hard drive)

   ❐ EDIT.COM (to create a new AUTOEXEC.BAT and other files)

   ❐ QBASIC.EXE (a program that EDIT.COM needs to work if you have an older version of DOS)

   ❐ Your current AUTOEXEC.BAT and CONFIG.SYS files if you have them on the hard drive

7. For Windows 9x, get a listing of all the files that Windows 9x puts on a rescue disk that it creates. Explain as far as you can the purpose of each file.

7

Data Recovery

The following exercises are designed to help you practice working with the tools used to recover data from floppy disks and hard drives.

1. The volume label is stored in two places on a floppy disk: the boot record and the root directory. Use a floppy disk that does not contain important information. To practice editing skills and test your knowledge of a floppy disk layout, change the volume label of a floppy disk, using either DEBUG or Norton Utilities disk editors.

2. Work with a partner on this problem. Separately alter an entry in the FAT of a file on a floppy disk, using Nuts & Bolts, DEBUG, or Norton Utilities. Don't tell your partner which file is damaged or what you did to the FAT. Exchange disks. Use DEBUG, Norton Utilities, SpinRite, Nuts & Bolts, or Lost & Found to repair the damaged FAT. Don't practice this exercise on a hard drive!

3. Use a healthy floppy disk that has at least one file stored on it. Edit the directory entry and the two FATs and divide the file into two files. Both files should be readable. Document or text files are better here than database or spreadsheet files that have header information.

4. Use a healthy floppy disk that is full of unimportant document or text files. Take a straight pin and make a small hole in the disk. Recover as much of the data on the disk as you can. When you're finished with this exercise, throw the disk away!

5. If a floppy disk has a damaged cover, it is still possible to recover the data on the disk. Cut the cover so you can remove the disk without damaging it. Sacrifice a good disk by cutting a slit carefully in the end of the cover, remove that disk, and insert the disk that had the damaged cover. Recover as much of the data on the disk as you can.

The Partition Table

Using Nuts & Bolts, Norton Utilities, or some other disk management software, get a printout of the partition table of your hard drive. On the printout, label each item in the table and explain it.

Research Using the Internet

Pretend you plan to install a Quantum Fireball CR 4.3-GB hard drive as a second drive on a PC. You want the drive to be the slave drive and know that you must change the current jumper settings. There are four jumpers on the drive, labeled DS, CS, PK, and Rsvd. From the description of the jumpers, you don't know how to set the jumpers so the drive is the slave. The documentation is not available. What do you do?

The best solution is to use the Internet to access the drive manufacturer's Web site for this information. In this case, the site is *www.quantum.com*. Use this example or some other example given by your instructor to determine the correct settings for the jumpers.

Recovering Data from a Floppy Disk

Use a floppy disk that contains data, but not important data that you cannot afford to lose. If you have Norton Utilities, use Disk Editor to alter the contents of the boot record on the disk so that the disk cannot be read by your OS. Recover the data on the disk.

Using Windows 9x Help

Using the Windows 9x **Start** button, **Help**, **Contents** tab, and **Troubleshooting** option, list specifically what to do if:

1. You run out of memory
2. You have trouble starting Windows

Troubleshooting a Hard Drive Problem over the Phone

A friend calls you to say that her hard drive does not work. She is using Windows 95 and has a rescue disk. Over the phone, walk her through the process of booting from the rescue disk and using the utilities on the rescue disk to examine the hard drive. List the utilities on the rescue disk that she should use in the order that she should use them, and write down for each utility what she should do with it.

In a lab environment, you can simulate this phone call by sitting with your back to a user sitting at a PC. Talk the user through the process without turning around and looking at the PC screen.

Hard Drive Troubleshooting

You have a virus scan program installed on your PC that executes each time you boot. The message it gives when it executes is "Unable to read boot record on drive C:". Is this the master boot record or the DOS boot record? What can you do to restore this information on the drive?

Using Nuts & Bolts

Using Nuts & Bolts utility software, make a snapshot image of the critical hard drive areas, using Image. Create a Nuts & Bolts rescue disk. Boot from the rescue disk. Use the DOS version of Disk Minder on the rescue disk to check the partition table for errors. Display the summary information from Disk Minder. Print the summary information screen.

From a DOS command prompt, delete a file on your hard drive that is expendable. Use Nuts & Bolts to recover the deleted file.

Using Nuts & Bolts Disk Tune, list the contents of clusters 20 through 29 on your hard drive.

7

Preparing for Disaster

Using Windows 9x Explorer, format a bootable system disk in drive A, and copy the following files from C:\Windows\Command to the new disk:

ATTRIB, CHKDSK, EDIT, FDISK, FORMAT, MEM, MSCDEX, SCANDISK

Create a directory and store a backup of critical Windows 9x startup files in it. Follow these directions.

1. On drive C, create a new folder called Win-bak.ini.
2. In the C:\Windows folder highlight all of the .ini files.
3. Copy them by pressing Ctrl+C.
4. Click the Win-bak.ini directory, then paste the copied .ini files into Win-bak.ini by pressing Ctrl+V.
5. Using Explorer, set the View, Options to "Show all files".
6. Copy C:\Windows\System.dat to C:\Win-bak.ini (do not drag!).
7. Copy C:\Windows\User.dat to C:\Win-bak.ini (do not drag!)

Research Third-Party Software on the Internet

Create a demo disk of Lost & Found. (Get the demo from *www.powerquest.com*, the PowerQuest Web site.) Execute the demo and print the list of all files that Lost & Found can recover in the root directory of your hard drive.

Data Recovery Services

Research the Internet for professional data recovery services. Report on three companies that offer this service. For each company include the following in your report:

❑ Name of company

❑ Contact information, including URL Web site address, mailing address, and phone number

❑ Short description of their service

8

TROUBLESHOOTING FUNDAMENTALS

In this chapter, you will learn:

♦ How to protect yourself, your hardware, and your software while solving computer problems

♦ What tools are needed to support personal computers

♦ How to isolate computer problems and devise a course of action

♦ The importance of good recordkeeping

♦ How to take a computer apart and put it back together

This chapter addresses some common-sense guidelines to solving computer problems. Before describing specific hardware or software problems, the chapter outlines some safety precautions to always follow as you work. In trying to solve a computer problem, you want to avoid making the situation worse by damaging hardware, software, valuable data, or yourself. The chapter goes on to discuss essential troubleshooting tools and others that are "nice to have." You will then learn strategies for solving computer problems, how to isolate each potential source of a problem, and general guidelines for dealing with problems. Next, the chapter methodically explains how to isolate the source of several problems and then resolve them.

The last part of the chapter covers defensive procedures that make computer problems easier to handle, such as backing up hardware and software, write-protecting application disks, and keeping records and documentation. These procedures minimize user losses if hardware or software fails, and reduce the time needed to get a system running again. In the end-of-chapter projects, you can hone your troubleshooting skills by disassembling and reassembling a PC.

Remember that every time you work on your PC, you risk hurting yourself, the hardware, and the software. Before attempting repairs, follow the important safety precautions at the end of Chapter 3 and in the "Read This Before You Begin" section following the introduction of this book. Remember that you can compound a problem, and cause more damage, by neglecting these precautions.

TROUBLESHOOTING PERSPECTIVES

As a PC troubleshooter, you might have to solve a problem on your own PC or for someone else. As a PC technician, you might fulfill four different job functions:

- A PC support technician working on-site who closely interacts with users and is responsible for ongoing PC maintenance

- A PC service technician who goes to a customer site in response to a service call and, if possible, repairs a PC on-site

- A bench technician working in a lab environment, who perhaps does not interact with users of the PCs being repaired, and is not permanently responsible for them

- A help-desk technician providing telephone support

A PC support technician is the only one listed above who is responsible for the PC before trouble occurs, and therefore can prepare for a problem by keeping good records and maintaining backups (or teaching the user how to do so).

PC service technicians are usually not responsible for ongoing PC maintenance, but usually can interact with the user.

Bench technicians probably don't work at the same site where the PC is kept. They may be able to interview the user to get information about the problem, or may simply receive a PC to repair without being able to talk to the user.

Help-desk technicians, who do not have physical access to the PC, are at the greatest disadvantage of the four. They can only interact with users over the phone and must obviously use different tools and approaches than the technician at the PC.

This chapter emphasizes the job of the on-site PC support technician. However, the special needs and perspectives of the service technician, bench technician, and help-desk technician are also addressed.

TROUBLESHOOTING TOOLS

Before we turn our attention to how to troubleshoot a PC problem, we will first look at the hardware and software tools needed to help you diagnose and repair computer problems. The tools you choose depend on the amount of money you can spend and the level of PC support you are providing.

Tools that are essential for PC troubleshooting are listed below. All but the bootable rescue disk can easily be purchased in one handy PC tool kit:

- Bootable rescue disk

- Ground bracelet and/or ground mat

- Flat-head screwdriver

- Phillips-head or cross-head screwdriver

- Torx screwdriver

- Tweezers for picking pieces of paper out of printers or dropped screws from tight places

- Chip extractor to remove chips (to pry up the chip; a simple screwdriver is usually more effective, however)

- Extractor, a spring-loaded device that looks like a hypodermic needle (when you push down on the top, three wire prongs come out that can be used to pick up a fallen screw, where hands and fingers can't reach)

The following tools might not be essential, but they are very convenient:

- Multimeter to check the power supply output (this is discussed in Chapter 11)

- Needle-nose pliers for holding objects in place while you screw (especially those pesky nuts on cable connectors)

- Flashlight to see inside the PC case

- AC outlet ground tester

- Small cups or bags to help keep screws organized as you work

- Antistatic bags to store unused parts

- Pen and paper for taking notes

- Diagnostic cards and diagnostic software

- Utility software

- Virus detection software on disks

Keep your tools in a tool box designated for PC troubleshooting. If you put disks and hardware tools in the same box, don't include a magnetized screwdriver, and be sure to keep the disks inside a plastic case. Make sure the diagnostic and utility software you use is recommended for the hardware and software you are troubleshooting.

Four tools from the list above are discussed here in more detail: bootable rescue disks, diagnostic cards and diagnostic software, utility software, and virus detection software.

Bootable Rescue Disk

An essential tool for PC troubleshooting is a **bootable rescue disk**. Not only can it boot the PC even when the hard drive fails, but you are assured the cleanest boot possible. By "clean boot," we mean that the boot does not load any extraneous software, drivers, or other memory-resident programs (TSRs), which might be loaded from startup routines on the hard drive.

A+CORE
2.2

Bootable Disk for DOS

For DOS, make a bootable disk using the same version of DOS that is on the PC's hard drive. Use this command:

```
C:\> FORMAT A:/S
```

The /S option tells DOS to copy to the disk the files needed to load DOS from it. This command also puts the two DOS hidden files and COMMAND.COM on the disk. The disk will include a small boot record that identifies the disk layout and the names of the two hidden files.

It's important that the boot disk have the same version of DOS that is on the hard drive. If you're consistent with versions, then once you're booted you can use some of the DOS loaded from the disk and some DOS program files on the hard drive, without DOS displaying error messages about using different versions. Use the VER command at the DOS prompt to display the current version of DOS.

You can also add some DOS utility commands to the disk so it can serve as a rescue disk if needed. In addition to the boot files, copy these files to the disk:

- ATTRIB.EXE
- CHKDSK.EXE
- EDIT.COM (which may also require QBASIC.EXE if you are using an older version of DOS)
- EMM386.EXE
- FDISK.EXE
- FORMAT.COM
- MSCDEX.EXE
- SCANDISK.EXE
- SYS.COM
- DEFRAG.EXE
- HIMEM.SYS
- UNDELETE.EXE

Rescue Disk for Windows 9x

For Windows 9x, make a rescue disk, as discussed in Chapter 2. To make a rescue disk for Windows 95, also include the files needed to access the CD-ROM without depending on the hard drive (see Chapter 9). Windows 98 places these real-mode driver files on the disk automatically.

Diagnostic Cards and Software

Although not essential, many hardware and software tools can help you diagnose a PC problem. Before purchasing these tools, read the documentation about what they can and cannot do, and, if possible, read some reviews about the product. The Internet is a good source of information. One hardware diagnostic tool is a diagnostic card, which is discussed next. Then we will look at several diagnostic software applications.

POST Diagnostic Cards

Diagnostic cards are designed to discover and report computer errors and conflicts at POST. If you have a problem that prevents the PC from booting, you can install the diagnostic card in an expansion slot on the system board and then attempt to boot. The card monitors the boot process and reports errors, usually as coded numbers on a small LED panel on the card. You then look up the number in the documentation that accompanies the card to get more information about the error and its source.

Examples of these cards are:

- POSTcard V3 by Unicore Software, Inc. (*www.unicore.com*)

- Post Code Master by MSD, Inc. (*www.msd.com*)

- POSTmortem Diagnostics Card by System Optimization, Inc. (*www.sysopt.com*)

Diagnostic Software

Diagnostic software is generally used to identify hardware problems. Although many diagnostic software programs are available, here we look at only a few. If the software rates itself as being at the professional level, it generally assumes greater technical expertise and also provides more features than end-user or novice-level software. The most effective diagnostic software does not run from the OS, because the OS may sometimes mask a hardware problem. Here are a few examples of diagnostic software.

PC-Technician by Windsor Technologies, Inc.

This professional-level PC diagnostic software loads and operates without using the PC's installed operating system, because it has its own proprietary OS built in. Results are thus unaltered by any errors in the PC's OS.

PC-Technician can relocate itself during testing and successfully test all of main memory. The ability to relocate is important, since software that tests memory cannot test the portion where it is currently loaded.

PC-Technician bypasses standard ROM BIOS when translation mode is used by the system, so that the diagnostic software communicates directly with the hard drive controller. Recall from Chapter 6 that translation mode is a method used by ROM BIOS to communicate with the controller BIOS of large hard drives. Any errors that might be masked by ROM BIOS translation methods are uncovered if the diagnostic software can communicate directly with the hard drive BIOS.

8

PC-Technician performs over 200 tests, including main memory, extended memory, expanded memory, hard drives, disk drives, video display, video cards, serial and parallel ports, and keyboards.

PC-Technician comes with test plugs (called loop-back plugs) that test parallel and serial ports by looping data out of and back to the port. These loop-back tests (also called wrap tests) determine that hardware ports are working.

There is a downloadable version of this software called TuffTEST-Pro. For more information, see the company Web site at *www.windsortech.com*.

PC-Diagnosys by Windsor Technologies, Inc.

This software is designed for less experienced PC technicians and end users. It contains a small subset of the features of PC-Technician discussed above, thus reducing the cost of the product. It's easy to use and includes its own proprietary OS so that the PC's OS will not mask results of the diagnostic tests.

Tests include main memory, extended memory, hard drives, disk drives, video display, video cards, and serial and parallel ports. See *www.windsortech.com*.

General Purpose Utility Software for Updates and Fixes

Utility software can be designed to diagnose problems, repair and maintain the software on a PC, recover corrupted or deleted data on the hard drive or floppy disks, provide security, monitor system performance, and download software updates from the Internet. The utility software might use the installed operating system or might provide its own. Examples of utility software include the following:

First Aid 2000 by McAfee

First Aid 2000 surveys and repairs problems with Windows 95 and Windows 98, including nonworking Windows 95 Shortcuts. It can connect to the Internet to update older versions of device drivers and Windows system files. It does not update applications software.

First Aid was originally written by Cybermedia, which is now a part of the McAfee Software Division of Network Associates. For more information on the product, see the McAfee Web site at *www.mcafee.com*.

McAfee Utilities Deluxe

McAfee Utilities Deluxe is a suite of utilities that includes protection from viruses using VirusScan, system performance monitoring, data backup, recovery from a corrupted file system or corrupted data, and software updates from the Internet. For more information, see *www.mcafee.com*.

Nuts & Bolts by Network Associates

Nuts & Bolts by McAfee Software of Network Associates is a comprehensive package including data recovery, security, system monitoring, and hard drive cleanup utilities. Nuts & Bolts was introduced in earlier chapters. The retail version of Nuts & Bolts is sold within the McAfee Office 2000 software suite. The company web site is *www.mcafee.com*.

Norton Utilities by Symantec

Norton Utilities by Symantec is general-purpose, user-friendly utility software that provides a variety of functions, including the ability to recover lost or damaged data from a hard drive. It is discussed in some detail in Chapter 7. The company web site is *www.symantec.com*.

CheckIt 98 Diagnostic Suite by Touchstone Software

CheckIt by Touchstone is a general-purpose software and hardware utility product that includes hard drive testing, performance testing, port testing (loop-back plugs are included), and setup, for resource conflicts. The product web site is *www.checkit.com*.

8

PartitionMagic by PowerQuest

PartitionMagic, first discussed in Chapter 7, lets you create, resize, and merge partitions on a hard drive without losing data. You can use the software to easily run multiple operating systems, convert file system types, and fix partition table errors. The product web site is *www.powerquest.com/partitionmagic*.

EasyRestore by PowerQuest

EasyRestore is a system recovery utility that allows any user to quickly and easily recover from a hard drive failure, if EasyRestore had been used earlier to back up the hard drive to CD when the drive was healthy. The product web site is *www.powerquest.com/easyrestore*.

Drive Image, Drive Image Pro, and DriveCopy by PowerQuest

Drive Image and Drive Image Pro both offer quick recovery from a failed hard drive if the drive has been backed up previously. These two applications, and the less powerful DriveCopy software, provide a way to easily copy software on one hard drive to another without having to install each software application on the new drive. This process, called cloning the hard drive, can be useful in a corporate or educational environment where many PCs contain exactly the same software loads. The manufacturer web site is *www.powerquest.com*.

Norton Ghost by Symantec

Norton Ghost by Symantec will also clone a hard drive, resize hard drive partitions without destroying data, create compressed hard drive backups, and restore a hard drive from a healthy image created earlier. The company web site is *www.symantec.com*.

Virus Detection Software

A+ OS
3.2

When you are troubleshooting PCs that show symptoms of either hardware or software problems, a virus is sometimes the cause, so virus detection software is an important tool to have. This section lists and describes some virus detection software and gives you background information about viruses in general.

A computer virus is a program that is transmitted to a computer, without the user's knowledge, with the intention of doing harm. Viruses can attach themselves to any executable program, but cannot become active until the host program is active. The programming code of the virus stays in memory or on disk as part of the host program until it executes. Then the virus either does its damage (called dropping its payload) or replicates itself into another program, either on the same medium or a different one. A virus can hide in an executable file such as COMMAND.COM or in any other program. A common place for a virus to hide is in a macro within a word-processing document or spreadsheet. They also can hide in the DOS boot record on a hard drive or floppy disk, or in the partition table load program on the hard drive. They can lie dormant for an extended time and, once active, can do mild or deadly damage. Viruses are usually transmitted by disks that contain program code, by program files downloaded from the Internet, or by documents with macros sent as e-mail attachments.

If you suspect that a virus may be involved in a computer problem, use a virus scan program to scan memory and the hard drive. Virus detection software, sometimes called antivirus software, searches hard drives and disks, informs you of the presence of a virus, and asks permission before deleting it. Some warning signs that a virus is present are:

- A program takes longer than normal to load.

- Disk access times seem excessive for simple tasks.

- Executable files that once worked no longer work and give unexpected error messages.

- Unusual error messages occur regularly.

- Less memory than usual is available.

- Files disappear mysteriously.

- There is a noticeable reduction in disk space.

- Executable files have changed size.

- The access lights on hard drives and floppy drives turn on when there should be no activity on those devices.

- You can't access a drive. This can be a hard drive, CD-ROM drive, Zip drive, or floppy drive.

- The system won't boot.

- Print services are not working properly.

An antivirus program is no better than the kinds of viruses it knows how to detect and erase. When choosing such software, check whether periodic updates are available from the company web site or another online service, so you can update the software for protection against new and different viruses as they arise. Some antivirus software programs on the market include the following:

- F-Protect (PROT) is rated as a high-quality antivirus product with excellent scanning and removal ability. The company web site is *www.complex.is*.

- McAfee VirusScan (SCAN) is probably the best-known antivirus software product. The company web site is *www.mcafee.com*.

- Norton AntiVirus (NAV) is popular because of its ease of use and graphical interface. The company web site is *www.symantec.com*.

Reducing the Threat of a Virus

Some things that you can do to reduce the threat of viruses are:

- Write-protect original software disks and backup copies.

- Boot from your hard disk or a write-protected disk only.

- Avoid downloading from the Internet or a bulletin board, or always use a virus scan program when you do.

- Use a scan utility such as Norton Anti-Virus or McAfee's SCAN on a regular or even daily basis.

> **TIP** Don't be a carrier yourself. When working on a PC, be careful not to transmit a virus from your own bootable disk. Make a practice of scanning your bootable rescue disk for viruses before using it to troubleshoot another PC.

HOW TO ISOLATE COMPUTER PROBLEMS AND DEVISE A COURSE OF ACTION

When a computer doesn't work and you're responsible for fixing it, you should generally approach the problem first as an investigator and discoverer, always being careful not to compound the problem through your own actions. If the problem seems difficult, see it as an opportunity to learn something new. Ask questions until you understand the source of the problem. Once you understand it, you're almost done, because most likely the solution will be evident. Take the attitude that you can understand the problem and solve it, no matter how deeply you have to dig, and you probably will. In this section we look at how to approach a troubleshooting problem, including how to interact with the user and how to handle an emergency.

Fundamental Rules

A+CORE
2.2

Here are a few fundamental rules for PC troubleshooting that I've found work for me.

- **Approach the problem systematically.** Start at the beginning and walk through the situation in a thorough, careful way. This one rule is worth its weight in gold. Remember it and apply it every time. If you don't find the explanation to the problem after one systematic walk-through, then repeat the entire process. Check and double-check to find the step you overlooked the first time. Most problems with computers are simple, such as a loose cable or circuit board. Computers are logical through and through. Whatever the problem, it's also very logical.

- **Divide and conquer.** This rule is the most powerful. Isolate the problem. In the overall system, remove one hardware or software component after another, until the problem is isolated to a small part of the whole system. You will learn many methods of applying this rule in this book. For starters, here are a few:

  - Remove any memory-resident programs (TSRs) to eliminate them as the problem.

  - Boot from a disk to eliminate the OS and startup files on the hard drive as the problem.

  - Remove any unnecessary hardware devices, such as a scanner card, internal modem, and even the hard drive.

  Once down to the essentials, start exchanging components you know are good for those you suspect are bad, until the problem goes away.

- **Don't overlook the obvious.** Ask simple questions. Is the computer plugged in? Is it turned on? Is the monitor plugged in? Most problems are so simple that we overlook them because we expect the problem to be difficult. Don't let the complexity of computers fool you. Most problems are simple and easy to fix. Really, they are!

- **Check the simple things first.** It is more effective to first check the components that are easiest to replace. For example, if the video does not work, the problem may be with the monitor or the video card. When faced with the decision of which one to exchange first, choose the easy route: exchange the monitor before the video card.

- **Make no assumptions.** This rule is the hardest one to follow, because there is a tendency to trust anything in writing and assume that people are telling you exactly what happened. But documentation is sometimes wrong, and people don't always describe events as they occurred—so do your own investigating. For example, if the user tells you that the system boots up with no error messages, but that the software still doesn't work, boot for yourself. You never know what the user might have overlooked.

- **Become a researcher.** Following this rule is the most fun. When a computer problem arises that you can't easily solve, be as tenacious as a bulldog. Read, make phone calls, ask questions, then read, make more calls, and ask more questions. Take advantage of every available resource, including online help, the Internet, documentation, technical support, and books such as this one. What you learn will be yours to take to the next problem. This is the real joy of computer troubleshooting. If you're good at it, you're always learning something new.

- **Write things down.** Keep good notes as you're working. They'll help you think more clearly. Draw diagrams. Make lists. Write down clearly and precisely what you're learning. Later, when the entire problem gets "cold," these notes will be invaluable.

- **Reboot and start over.** This is an important rule. Fresh starts are good for us and uncover events or steps that might have been overlooked. Take a break; get away from the problem. Begin again.

- **Establish your priorities.** This rule can help make for a satisfied customer. Decide what your first priority is. For example, it might be to recover lost data, or to get the PC back up and running as soon as possible. Consult the user or customer for advice when practical.

- **Keep your cool.** In an emergency, protect the data and software by carefully considering your options before acting, by not assuming data is lost even when hard drive and floppy drive errors occur, and by taking practical precautions to protect software and OS files. When a computer stops working, if unsaved data is still in memory or if data or software on the hard drive has not been backed up, look and think carefully before you leap! A wrong move can be costly. The best advice is: don't hurry. Carefully plan your moves. Read the documentation if you're not sure what to do, and don't hesitate to ask for help. Don't simply try something, hoping it will work—unless you've run out of more intelligent alternatives!

- **Don't assume the worst.** When it's an emergency and your only copy of data is on a hard drive that is not working, don't assume that the data is lost. Much can be done to recover data, as you learned in Chapter 7, but one important point is worth repeating. If you want to recover lost data on a hard drive, don't write anything to the drive; you might write on top of lost data, eliminating all chances of recovery.

- **Know your starting point.** Before trying to solve a computer problem, know for certain that the problem is what the user says it is. If the computer does not boot, carefully note where in the boot process it fails. If the computer does boot to an OS, before changing anything or taking anything apart, verify what does and what doesn't work, preferably in the presence of the user.

8

Devising a Course of Action

A+CORE 2.2 When solving a computer problem, the above rules prepare you to apply a successful course of action. This course of action is threefold:

1. Interact with the user. Gather as much information up front as you can before you start problem-solving. Have the user describe the problem in detail, and ask questions. Don't settle for secondhand information unless you have no choice. Later, as you work, consult the user before taking drastic action, such as formatting the hard drive.

2. Isolate the problem by (a) eliminating the unnecessary and (b) trading good for suspected bad.

3. Then follow established guidelines toward a solution. Many of these are listed later in the chapter, and you'll find many more in other chapters.

Interacting with the User

Ask the user to explain exactly what happened when the computer stopped working. What procedure was taking place at the time? What had just happened? What recent changes did the user make? When did the computer last work? What has happened in the meantime? What error messages did the user see? Re-create the circumstances that existed when the computer stopped, and in as much detail as you can. Make no assumptions. All users make simple mistakes and then overlook them. If you realize that the problem was caused by the user's mistake, take the time to explain the proper procedures, so that the user understands what went wrong and what to do next time.

Use diplomacy and good manners when you work with a user to solve a problem. For example, if you suspect that the user dropped the PC, don't ask "Did you drop the PC?" but rather put the question in a less accusatory manner: "Could the PC have been dropped?" If the user is sitting in front of the PC, don't assume you can take over the keyboard or mouse without permission. Also, if the user is present, ask permission before you make a software or hardware change, even if the user has just given you permission to interact with the PC.

When working at the user's desk, consider yourself a "guest" and follow these general guidelines:

- Don't "talk down" to or patronize the user.

- Don't take over the mouse or keyboard from the user without permission.

- Don't use the phone without permission.

- Don't pile your belongings and tools on top of the user's papers, books, etc.

- Accept personal inconvenience to accommodate the user's urgent business needs. For example, if the user gets an important call while you are working, delay your work until the call is over.

A+CORE
2.2

Whether or not you are at the user's desk, you should follow these guidelines when working with the user:

- Don't take drastic action such as formatting the hard drive before you ask the user about important data that may not be backed up.

- Provide users with alternatives where appropriate before making decisions for them.

- Protect the confidentiality of data on the PC such as business financial information.

- Don't disparage the user's choice of computer hardware or software.

- If you have made a mistake or must pass the problem on to someone with more expertise, be honest.

In some PC support situations, it is appropriate to consider yourself as a support to the user, as well as to the PC. Your goals may include educating the user as well as repairing the computer. If you want users to learn something from a problem they caused, don't fix the problem yourself unless they ask. Explain how to fix the problem and walk them through the process if necessary. It takes a little longer, but is more productive in the end because the user learns more and is less likely to repeat the mistake.

Here are some helpful questions to ask the user when you are trying to discover the problem:

- When did the problem start?

- Were there any error messages or unusual displays on the screen?

- What programs or software were you using?

- Did you move your computer system recently?

- Has there been a recent thunderstorm or electrical problem?

- Have you made any hardware changes?

- Did you recently install any new software?

- Did you recently change any software configuration setups?

- Has someone else been using your computer recently?

The goal is to gain as much information from the user as you can before investigating the hardware and the software.

Isolate the Problem

After gathering as much information as possible, try to isolate the computer problem. The two most effective approaches are eliminating the unnecessary and trading good for suspected bad.

8

Eliminate the Unnecessary   This rule can be applied in many ways—for example, when the PC will not boot successfully. In this case, it is often unclear if the problem is with the hardware or software. When using Windows 9x, you can boot into Safe Mode (press F5 at startup) and eliminate much of the OS customized configuration. But if you still have problems, you may be able to boot from your bootable rescue disk.

Boot from a disk that you know is good and that has a minimal OS configuration (i.e., no CONFIG.SYS or AUTOEXEC.BAT files). By doing so you eliminate all the applications software loaded at startup on the PC, all the TSRs loaded at startup, and much of the OS, especially in Windows 9x. If the problem goes away, you can deduce that the problem is with (1) the software on the PC or (2) the hard drive and/or its subsystem that is used as the boot device.

If you suspect the problem is caused by faulty hardware, eliminate any unnecessary hardware devices. If the PC still boots with errors, disconnect the network card, the CD-ROM drive, the mouse, and maybe even the hard drive. You don't need to remove the CD-ROM or hard drive from the bays inside the case. Simply disconnect the data cable and the power cable. Remove the network card from its expansion slot. Remember to place it on an antistatic bag or grounded mat—not on top of the power supply or case. If the problem goes away, you know that one or more of these devices is causing the problem. Replace one at a time until the problem returns. Remember that the problem might be a resource conflict. If the network card worked well until the CD-ROM drive was reconnected, and now neither works, try the CD-ROM drive without the network card. If the CD-ROM drive now works, you most likely have a resource conflict.

Trade Good for Suspected Bad   When diagnosing hardware problems, this method works well if you can draw from a group of parts that you know work correctly. Suppose the monitor does not work; it appears dead. The parts of the video subsystem are the video card, the power cord to the monitor, the cord from the monitor to the PC case, and the monitor itself. Also, don't forget that the video card is inserted into an expansion slot on the system board, and the monitor depends on electrical power. Suspect each of these five components to be bad; try them one at a time. Trade the monitor for one that you know works. Trade the power cord, trade the cord to the PC video port, move the video card to a new slot, and trade the video card. When you're trading a good component for a suspected bad one, work methodically by eliminating one component at a time. Don't trade the video card and the monitor and then turn on the PC to determine if they work. It's possible that both the card and the monitor are bad, but first assume that only one component is bad before you consider whether multiple components need trading.

In this situation, suppose you keep trading components in the video subsystem until you have no more variations. Next, take the entire subsystem—video card, cords, and monitor—to a PC that you know works, and plug each of them in. If they work, you have isolated

A+CORE
2.2
the problem to the PC, not the video. Now turn your attention back to the PC—the system board, the software settings within the OS, the **video driver**, etc. Knowing that the video subsystem works on the good PC gives you a valuable tool. Compare the video driver on the good PC to the one on the bad PC. Make certain the CMOS settings, software settings, etc., are the same.

An Alternate Approach to Trading Good for Suspected Bad   An alternate approach works well in certain situations. If you have a working PC that is configured similarly to the one you are troubleshooting (a common situation in many corporate or educational environments), rather than trading good for suspected bad, you can trade suspected bad for good. Take each component that you suspect is bad and install it in the working PC. If the component works on the good PC, then you have eliminated it as a suspect. If the working PC breaks down, then you have probably identified the bad component.

TROUBLESHOOTING GUIDELINES

8

Troubleshooting a PC problem begins with isolating it into one of two categories: problems that prevent the PC from booting and problems that occur after a successful boot. Begin by asking the user the questions listed earlier in this chapter, to learn as much as you can. Next, ask yourself, "Does the PC boot properly?" Figure 8-1 shows you the direction to take, depending on the answer. If the screen is blank and the entire system is "dead"—no lights, spinning drive, or fan, then proceed to troubleshooting the power system.

Recall from Chapter 1 that when POST completes successfully, it sounds a single beep indicating that all is well, regardless of whether the monitor is working or even present. If you hear the beep, then the problem is with the video, and the next step is to troubleshoot it. If you don't hear the beep or you hear more than one, then POST encountered an error. In that case, proceed to troubleshooting the system board.

If an error message appears on the screen, then the obvious next step is to respond to the message. An example of such an error is "Keyboard not present." If the error message occurs as the OS loads, and you don't understand the message or know what to do about it, begin by troubleshooting the OS.

If video is working but the boot message is confusing or unreadable, then begin to eliminate the unnecessary. Perform a clean boot. For Windows 9x, the simplest way is to boot to Safe Mode. If that doesn't work, use your bootable rescue disk.

If the PC boots up properly, turn your attention to the system that is not working and begin troubleshooting there. This chapter covers some of these systems, including the keyboard, video, and printer. Troubleshooting guidelines for other systems are spread throughout the book.

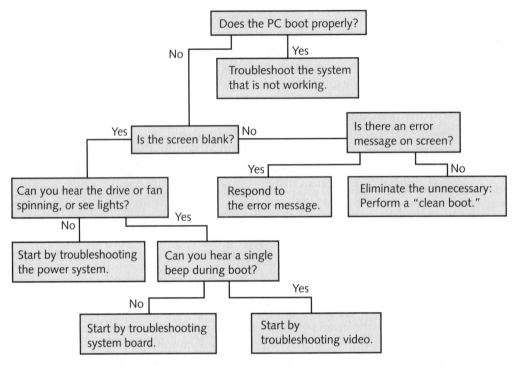

Figure 8-1   Begin PC problem solving by asking the question, "Does the PC boot up properly?"

Troubleshooting the Power System

A+CORE
2.1,
3.2

If the PC appears "dead," ask these questions:

- Are there any burnt parts or odors? (Definitely not a good sign!)
- Is everything connected and turned on? Any loose cable connections? Is the computer plugged in?
- Are all the switches turned on? Computer? Monitor? Surge protector? Uninterruptible power supply? Separate circuit breaker? Is the wall outlet (or surge protector) good?
- If the fan is not running, turn off the computer, open the case, and check the connections to the power supply. Are they secure? Are all cards securely seated?

Once you have answered these questions, if you still haven't isolated and fixed the problem, proceed this way:

For most of the newer ATX power supplies, a wire runs from the power switch on the front of the ATX case to the system board. This wire must be connected to the pins on the system board and the switch turned on before power comes up. Check that the wire is connected correctly to the system board. Figure 8-2 shows the wire, which is labeled

A+CORE
2.1,
3.2
"REMOTE SW," connected to pins on the system board labeled "PWR.SW." If you are not sure of the correct connection on the system board, see the system-board documentation. Next, check the voltage output from the power supply. (How to do this is covered in Chapter 11.)

Remote SW wire

8

Figure 8-2   For an ATX power supply, the remote switch wire must be connected to the system board before power will come on

Then, remove all nonessential expansion cards (modem, sound card, mouse) one at a time. This verifies that they are not drawing too much power and pulling the system down. It is possible that the expansion cards are all good, but that the power supply cannot provide enough current for all the add-on boards. Perhaps there are too many cards, and the computer is overheating. The temperature inside the case should not exceed 113° F.

Vacuum the entire unit, especially the power supply's fan vent, or use compressed air to blow out the dust. Excessive dust insulates components and causes them to overheat. Use an ESD-safe service vac that can be purchased from electronic tools suppliers.

Trade the power supply for another one that you know is good. For an AT system board, be certain to follow the black-to-black rule when attaching the power cords to the system board.

Is there strong magnetic or electrical interference? Sometimes an old monitor will emit too much static and EMF (electromagnetic force), and bring a whole system down.

Troubleshooting the System Board

A+CORE
2.1
When troubleshooting the system board, use whatever clues POST can give you. Recall that, before video is checked out, POST reports any error messages as beep codes. When a PC boots, one beep indicates that all is well after POST. If you hear more than one beep, look

A+CORE 2.1

up the beep code in Appendix A. Error messages on the screen indicate that video is working. Look up the error message in Appendix A if the message is not clear. If the beep code or error message is not in Appendix A, try the web site of the ROM BIOS manufacturer for information. Figure 8-3 shows the web site for AMI with explanations of beep codes produced by its startup BIOS.

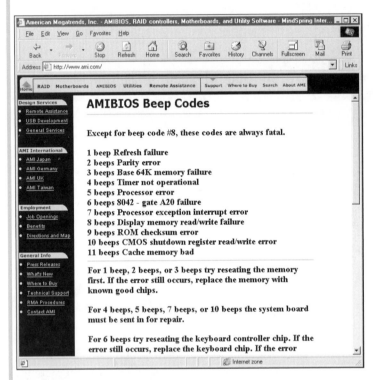

Figure 8-3   The ROM BIOS manufacturer's web site is a good source of information about beep codes

Remember that you can try substituting good hardware components for suspected bad ones. Be cautious here. A friend once had a computer that would not boot. He replaced the hard drive, with no change. He replaced the system board next. The computer booted up with no problem; he was delighted, until it failed again. Later he discovered that a faulty power supply had damaged his original system board. When he traded the bad one for a good one, the new system board also got zapped! Check the voltage coming from the power supply before putting in a new system board!

If the problem isn't improved, ask yourself, "Is the system in a Doze or Sleep Mode?" Many "green" systems can be programmed through CMOS to suspend the monitor or even the drive if the keyboard or CPU have been inactive for a few minutes. Pressing any key will usually resume operations exactly where the user left off.

A+CORE
   2.1

If this doesn't resolve the problem, try these things:

- If the fan is running, reseat or replace the CPU, BIOS, or RAM. Try installing RAM in a different slot. A POST code diagnostic card is a great help at this point.

- Sometimes a dead computer can be fixed by simply disassembling it and reseating cables, adapter cards, socketed chips, and SIMMs and DIMMs. Bad connections and corrosion are common problems.

- Check jumpers, DIP switches, and CMOS settings. Look for physical damage on the system board.

- If the battery is dead, or dying, it may cause problems. Sometimes, after a long holiday, a weak battery will cause the CMOS to forget its configuration.

- Reduce the system to essentials. Remove any unnecessary hardware, such as expansion cards, and then try to boot again.

- Exchange the system board, but before you do, measure the voltage output of the power supply in case it is producing too much power and has damaged the board.

8

The computer does not recognize all installed RAM or SIMMs

When the computer does not recognize all installed RAM or SIMMs, take the steps and answer the questions below:

- Are CMOS settings correct?

- Run diagnostic software such as PC-Technician to test memory.

- Are SIMM or DIMM modules properly seated? Remove and reinstall each one. For a DIMM module, try a different memory slot.

- Look for bent pins or chips installed the wrong way on cache memory.

- Place your fingers on the individual chips. Sometimes a bad chip may be noticeably hotter than the others.

- Make sure the SIMMs have correct or consistent part numbers. For example, if there are four installed SIMMs, they usually must be the same size (in megabytes) and same speed (in nanoseconds).

- Replace memory modules one at a time. For example, if the system only recognizes six out of eight megabytes of RAM, swap the last two SIMM modules. Did the amount of recognized RAM change? You might be able to solve the problem just by reseating the modules. Use SIMM modules with the same part number. Chapter 4 has more information about choosing the correct SIMMs or DIMMs for a system board.

- Sometimes a problem can result from a bad socket or a broken trace (a fine printed wire or circuit) on the system board. If so, you might have to replace the entire system board.

- A Windows error that occurs randomly and contains this or similar text, "exception fault 0E at >> 0137:BFF9a5d0", probably indicates a memory error. Test, reseat or replace RAM.

Troubleshooting the Operating System and Hard Drive

$A{+}CORE$
2.1 To troubleshoot the OS and hard drive, proceed as follows:

- Try a hard boot. A soft boot might not do the trick, because TSRs are not always "kicked out" of RAM with a soft boot.

- Learn to use the Windows 9x Startup Menu, which is described in other chapters and has the options displayed in Figure 8-4. Option 4 is displayed if the PC is configured for a network, and Option 8 is displayed if an earlier version of DOS is installed. Try Safe Mode first. If that doesn't work, use the step-by-step confirmation to identify the command causing the problem. Use the Logged option and examine the BOOTLOG.TXT file created. Try booting to just the command prompt. If nothing works, boot from the Windows 9x rescue disk or from a rescue disk created by utility software such as Nuts & Bolts or Norton Utilities.

1.	Normal	5.	Step-by-step confirmation
2.	Logged (\BOOTLOG.TXT)	6.	Command prompt only
3.	Safe Mode	7.	Safe Mode command prompt only
4.	Safe Mode with network support	8.	Previous version of MS-DOS
			Enter a Choice: 1

Figure 8-4   Windows 9x Startup Menu is displayed when you press F8 during startup

- When you boot from a floppy disk, you should boot to an A prompt. If you are successful, the problem is in the hard drive subsystem and/or the software on the drive.

- Can you access the hard drive from the A prompt? If you can get a C prompt, then the problem is in the software used on the hard drive to boot, including the partition table, master boot record, OS hidden files, and command interface files. See Chapter 7 for help diagnosing hard drive problems.

- Run diagnostic software to test for hard drive hardware problems.

- An error that contains the text "Kernel32.dll" probably indicates a corrupted kernel. Try restoring system files. If that doesn't work, reinstall Windows. More about this in Chapter 12.

Problems after the Computer Boots

Either hardware or software can cause problems after the computer boots.

- If you suspect the software, try diagnostic software such as Nuts & Bolts, ScanDisk, or Norton Utilities before reloading the software package. See Chapter 12 for more suggestions on diagnosing software problems.

- If you suspect the hardware, first isolate the problem by removing devices and substituting good components for suspected bad ones. Be aware that the problem might be a resource conflict.

- Check the voltage output from the power supply with a multimeter (to be covered in Chapter 11).

- Check jumpers, DIP switches, and CMOS settings for the devices.

- Suspect a corrupted device driver. Reinstall the driver.

- Suspect the applications software using the device. Try another application or reinstall the software.

$A^+ \, {}^{OS}_{2.4}$ ## Problems with the Software

Suppose the computer boots with no errors, and all but one software package on this computer work correctly. When you try to load the problem software package, however, you get an error message and the software terminates. If so, you can probably conclude that the software caused the error. Ask yourself: Has this software ever worked? If it has not, then try installing it again. Maybe wrong information was given during the installation. Be sure you check the requirements for the software. Maybe you don't have enough memory or space on your hard drive to create the necessary working files.

When was the last time the software worked? What happened differently then? Did you get an error message that seemed insignificant at the time? What has happened to your computer since the software last worked? Have you added more software or changed the hardware configuration?

Reinstalling software   Consider reinstalling the software even if it has worked in the past. Maybe a program file has become corrupted. Before you reinstall, however, ask yourself, "If I reinstall it will I erase data that this software has placed on my hard drive?" If you're not sure, back up the data. Maybe you can just copy the data to another directory while you reinstall the program. If the installation does erase the data in the original directory, you can copy one file and then another back to the original directory. If the problem reoccurs, then you've found the corrupted data file that caused the problem.

Software often uses configuration files and scripting files that are specific to a particular PC or user. If you reinstall the software, most likely you will lose the configuration information. Either save the configuration files before you begin or print the contents of the files. See the software documentation for the names and location of the configuration files (a file extension of .cfg is common). Consider that the problem with the software might be a corrupted configuration file.

If a particular software package doesn't work and everything else does, the problem might not be with the software. One user could not get a software package to work on his machine after many installation attempts. The video displayed only a blank screen. All other software worked properly on his computer, which he had purchased one year earlier. It was shipped as a complete system directly from the manufacturer and was equipped with a super VGA color monitor. During the software installation, the user correctly told the software to interface with a super VGA video card. After many phone calls to technical support at both the software and hardware companies, the problem was finally identified. The manufacturer had mistakenly sent him a computer with a super VGA monitor but a VGA (not super VGA)

8

A+ OS
2.4

video card. All the other software packages interfaced with the VGA card with no problems, but this one was more discriminating.

This is a case where Nuts & Bolts, Norton Utilities, or similar utility software could have helped. These utilities can display system hardware information and tell you what type of video card you have.

Problems Caused by Other Software

Software problems might be caused by other software. Windows 3.x and Windows 9x use files stored in the \Windows\System directory to support software files for many applications as well as Windows. These files can have extensions of .dll, .ocx, .oca, .vbx, etc. The most common are the DLL (dynamic-link library) files. Figure 8-5 shows the results of a search for these files on a hard drive: 938 DLL files were located. These files perform tasks for many software packages, such as displaying and managing a dialog box on screen. When you install an application, the installation program may write a DLL to the \Windows\System directory and overwrite an earlier version of the DLL used by another application. The original application may have problems because it cannot use the new DLL. If the software being investigated started to have problems after you installed another software program, the problem may well be the DLL it is unsuccessfully trying to use. Chapter 12 discusses solving DLL problems and similar difficulties created by "bad neighbor" software.

938 files found

Figure 8-5   DLL files can be shared by several applications, which can be a source of problems with software

A+ OS
  2.4

CORE
  2.2

Intermittent Problems

Intermittent problems can make troubleshooting challenging. The trick in diagnosing problems that come and go is to look for patterns or clues as to when the problems appear. If you or the user can't reproduce the problem at will, ask the user to keep a log of when the problems occur and exactly what messages appear. Show the user how to get a printed screen of the error messages when they appear. Here's the method:

- For simple DOS systems, the Print Screen key directs the displayed screen to the printer.

- In Windows, the Print Screen key copies the displayed screen to the Clipboard.

- Launch the Paint software accessory program and paste the contents of the Clipboard into the document. You might need to use the Zoom Out command on the document first. You can then print the document with the displayed screen, using Paint. You can also paste the contents of the Clipboard into a document created by a word-processing application such as Word.

Problems with the Keyboard and Monitor

A+CORE
    3.1

If peripheral devices such as a keyboard or monitor don't work, ask questions like these: Does the device work in situations other than the current one? Perhaps the problem is with the applications software interfacing with the device, rather than with the device itself. Has the device ever worked? Will another device work in this same situation? Exchange the keyboard or monitor for one you know works. If the good device now fails to work, you can eliminate the original device as the source of the problem. The problem must be the software, the cable, the computer, or the user. Check all connections and exchange cables.

Troubleshooting Keyboard Problems

Often dirt, food, or drink in the keyboard causes one or more keys to stick or not work properly. Because of their low cost, the solution for a keyboard that doesn't work is most often to replace it. However, you can try a few simple things to repair one that is not working.

A few keys don't work If a few keys don't work, remove the caps on the bad keys with a chip extractor. Spray contact cleaner into the key well. Repeatedly depress the contact in order to clear it out. Don't use rubbing alcohol to clean the key well, because it can leave a residue on the contact. If this method of cleaning solves the problem, then clean the adjacent keys as well.

Turning the keyboard upside down and lightly bumping multiple keys with your flat palm will help loosen and remove debris.

The keyboard does not work at all If the keyboard does not work at all, first determine that the cable is plugged in. PC keyboard cables may become loose or disconnected.

If the cable connection is good and the keyboard still does not work, swap it with another keyboard of the same type that you know is in good condition, to verify that the problem is in the keyboard and not in the computer.

A+CORE
    3.1

If the problem is in the keyboard, check the cable. If possible, swap the cable with a known good one, perhaps from an old discarded keyboard. Sometimes a wire in a PC keyboard cable becomes pinched or broken. Most cables can be easily detached from the keyboard by removing the few screws that hold the keyboard case together, then simply unplugging the cable. Be careful as you work; don't allow the key caps to fall out! In Chapter 11 you will learn how to use a multimeter to test a cable. This test is called a continuity test.

On the system board, the two chips that affect the keyboard functions are the keyboard chip and the ROM BIOS chip. You might choose to replace each of these chips on the system board. Otherwise the entire system board might have to be replaced.

Key continues to repeat after being released This problem can be caused by a dirty contact. Some debris may have conductive properties, short the gap between the contacts, and therefore cause the key to repeat. Try cleaning the key switch with contact cleaner.

Very high humidity and excess moisture will sometimes short key switch contacts and cause keys to repeat, because water is an electrical conductor. The problem will usually resolve itself once the humidity level returns to normal. You can hasten the drying process by using a fan (not a hot hair dryer) to blow air at the keyboard.

Keys produce the wrong characters This problem is usually caused by a bad chip. PC keyboards actually have a processor mounted on the logic board inside the keyboard. Try swapping the keyboard for one you know is good. It the problem goes away, replace the keyboard.

Major spills on the keyboard When coffee or other drinks with sugar in them spill on the keyboard, they create a sticky mess. The best solution is to thoroughly rinse the keyboard in running water, such as a bathroom shower. Make sure the keyboard dries thoroughly before you use it. Let it dry for two days on its own, or less if you set it out in the sun or in front of a fan.

A+CORE
    2.1

Troubleshooting Monitor Problems

For monitors, as well as other devices, do the easy things first. Make simple hardware and software adjustments. Also, remember the "trade good for suspected bad" method. Many monitor problems are caused by poor cable connections or bad contrast/brightness adjustments. Also check if the monitor is still under warranty. Remember that many warranties are voided if an unauthorized individual works inside the monitor. Typical monitor problems and how to troubleshoot them are described next:

Power light (LED) does not go on, no picture Is the monitor plugged in? Verify that the wall outlet works by plugging in a lamp, radio, etc.

If the monitor power cord is plugged into a power strip or surge protector, verify that the power strip is turned on and working and that the monitor is also turned on. Look for an on/off switch on the front and back of the monitor. Some monitors have both.

A+CORE
2.1

If the monitor power cord is plugged into the back of the computer, verify that the connection is tight and the computer is turned on.

A blown fuse could be the problem. Some monitors have a fuse that is visible from the back of the monitor. It looks like a black knob that you can remove (no need to go inside the monitor cover). Remove the fuse and look for the broken wire indicating a bad fuse.

The monitor may have a switch on the back for choosing between 110 volts and 220 volts. Check that the switch is in the right position.

If none of these solutions solves the problem, the next step is to take the monitor to a service center.

Power LED light is on, no picture on power-up   Check the contrast adjustment. If there's no change, then leave it at a middle setting.

8

- Check the brightness adjustment. If there's no change, then leave it at a middle setting.

- Is the cable connected securely to the computer?

- If the monitor-to-computer cable detaches from the monitor, exchange it for a cable you know is good or check the cable for continuity (Chapter 11).

- If this solves the problem, reattach the old cable to verify that the problem was not simply a bad connection.

- Confirm that the proper system configuration has been set up. Some older system boards have a jumper or DIP switch you can use to select the monitor type.

- Test a monitor you know is good on the computer you suspect to be bad. Do this and the previous step to identify the problem. If you think the monitor is bad, make sure that it also fails to work on a good computer.

- Check the CMOS settings or software configuration on the computer. When using Windows 9x, boot into Safe Mode (press F5 during the boot) to allow the OS to select a generic display driver and low resolution. If this works, change the driver and resolution. You will learn more about this in Chapter 12.

- Reseat the video card. Move the card to a different expansion slot. Clean the card's edge connectors using a contact cleaner or a white eraser. Do not let crumbs from the eraser fall into the expansion slot.

- If there are socketed chips on the video card, remove the card from the expansion slot and, using a screwdriver, press down firmly on each corner of each socketed chip on the card. Chips sometimes loosen because of thermal changes; this condition is called chip creep.

- Trade a good video card for the video card you suspect is bad. Test the video card you think is bad on a computer that works. Test a video card you know is good on the computer that you suspect may be bad. Whenever possible, do both.

- If the video card has socketed chips that appear dirty or corroded, consider removing them and trying to clean the pins. You can use a clean pencil eraser to

A+CORE
    2.1

do this. Normally, however, if the problem is a bad video card, the most cost-effective measure is to replace the card.

- Go into setup and disable the shadowing of video ROM.

- Test the RAM on the system board with diagnostic software.

- For an older system board that supports both VESA and PCI, if you are using a VESA video card, try using a PCI card.

- Trade the system board for one you know is good. Sometimes, though rarely, a peripheral chip on the system board of the computer can cause the problem.

Power on, but monitor displays the wrong characters   Wrong characters are usually not the result of a bad monitor but of a problem with the video card. Trade the video card for one you know is good.

Exchange the system board. Sometimes a bad ROM or RAM chip on the system board displays the wrong characters on the monitor.

Monitor flickers and/or has wavy lines   Monitor flicker can be caused by poor cable connections. Check that the cable connections are snug.

- Does the monitor have a degauss button to eliminate accumulated or stray magnetic fields? If so, press it.

- Check if something in the office is causing a high amount of electrical noise. For example, you might be able to stop a flicker by moving the office fan to a different outlet. Bad fluorescent lights or large speakers can also produce interference. Two monitors placed very close together can also cause problems.

- If the vertical scan frequency (the refresh rate at which the screen is drawn) is below 60 Hz, a screen flicker may appear.

- Use a different refresh rate. In Windows 9x, right-click the desktop and select **Properties** from the menu.

- For older monitors that do not support a high enough refresh rate, your only cure may be to purchase a new monitor.

- Before making a purchase, verify that the new monitor will solve the problem.

Check **Control Panel**, **Display**, **Settings** to see if a high resolution (greater than 800 × 600 with more than 256 colors) is selected. Consider these issues:

1. The video card might not support this resolution/color setting.

2. There might not be enough video RAM; 2 MB or more may be required.

3. The added (socketed) video RAM might be of a different speed than the soldered memory.

A+CORE
2.1

No graphics display or the screen goes blank when loading certain programs   This problem may be caused by the following:

- A special graphics or video accelerator card is not present, or is defective.

- Software is not configured to do graphics, or the software does not recognize the installed graphics card.

- The video card does not support the resolution and/or color setting.

- There might not be enough video RAM; 2 MB or more might be required.

- The added (socketed) video RAM might be of a different speed than the soldered memory.

- The wrong adapter/display type is selected. Start Windows 9x from Safe Mode to reset the display. (How to do this is explained later in this discussion.)

Screen goes blank 30 seconds or one minute after the keyboard is left untouched
A "green" system board (one that follows energy-saving standards) used with an Energy Saver monitor can be configured to go into a Standby or Doze Mode after a period of inactivity. This might be the case if the monitor resumes after you press a key or move the mouse. Doze times can be set for periods from as short as 20 seconds to as long as one hour. The power LED light normally changes from green to orange to indicate Doze Mode. Monitors and video cards using these energy-saving features are addressed in Chapter 9.

You might be able to change the doze features by entering the CMOS menu and looking for an option such as Power Management, or in Windows 9x by opening the **Control Panel** and selecting **Display**, **Screen Saver**.

Some monitors have a Power Save switch on the back of the monitor. Make sure this is set as you want.

Poor quality color display   For this problem, try the following:

- Read the documentation for the monitor to learn how to use the color-adjusting buttons to fine-tune the color.

- Exchange video cards.

- Add more video RAM; 2 MB or 4 MB might be required for higher resolutions.

- Check if a fan or large speaker (speakers have large magnets) or another monitor nearby could be causing interference.

Picture out of focus or out of adjustment   For this problem, try the following:

- Check the adjustment knobs on the control panel on the outside of the monitor.

- Change the refresh rate. Sometimes this can make the picture appear more in focus.

- You can also make adjustments inside the monitor that might solve the problem. If you have not been trained to work inside the monitor, take the monitor to a service center.

8

A+CORE 2.1

Crackling sound An accumulation of dirt or dust inside the unit might be the cause. Someone trained to work on the inside of the monitor can vacuum the inside.

To configure or change monitor settings and drivers in Windows 9x If the video card is supported by Windows 9x, you can change the driver and settings by double-clicking the **Display** icon in the **Control Panel**. For drivers not supported by Windows 9x, you can reinstall the drivers by using the CD or floppy disks that come with the video card. The settings for this type of driver can most likely be changed through the Control Panel's Display icon.

To change the video driver configuration Double-click the Display icon in the Control Panel. Select the Settings tab to change the color palette, resolution (for example, from 800 x 600 to 1024 x 768), or the driver for the video card or monitor type. Click Advanced on the Settings tab to show the Change Display Type window (see Figure 8-6). From this window, you can change the video card or the monitor type.

If you increase the resolution, the Windows icons and desktop text become smaller. Select **Large Fonts** on the Settings tab and increase the **Desktop Icon size** on the Appearance tab.

Returning to standard VGA settings When the display settings don't work, return to standard VGA settings as follows:

- For Windows 9x, reboot the system and press the F8 key after the first beep.

- When the Microsoft Windows 9x Startup Menu appears, select **Safe Mode** to boot up with minimal configurations and standard VGA display mode.

- Double-click the **Display** icon in the **Control Panel** and reset to the correct video configuration.

Figure 8-6 Changing the video card type in Windows 95 or Windows 98

Troubleshooting Printer Problems

A+CORE
5.2

When troubleshooting printer problems, first determine that the problem is truly with the printer. The problem might be the computer hardware communicating with the printer, the applications software using the printer, the printer driver, the printer cable, or the printer. Ask these questions and try these things:

- Is the printer turned on and online?

- Is the correct printer selected as the default printer?

- Can an applications software program other than the current program use the printer?

- Is the printer using the correct driver? Does the driver need updating? Is the driver correctly installed?

- Can you move the printer to another computer and print from it? Will another printer work on this computer?

Once you are convinced that the problem is not with the computer hardware or software, but is indeed a problem with the printer itself, you are ready for the following troubleshooting guide.

Laser Printer Problems

The printer documentation can be very helpful and most often contains a phone number to technical support for the printer manufacturer. A good test for a printer is to print the manufacturer's test page from the PC, not just directly from the printer. For example, using Windows 98, for an HP LaserJet 5L, access the **Control Panel** and double-click **Printers**. In the Printers window, right-click the printer you want to test. You see the shortcut menu shown in Figure 8-7. Select the **Properties** option. The Properties dialog box is displayed as in Figure 8-8. Click **Print Test Page** to send a test page to the printer.

Figure 8-7   Control menu for an installed printer

A+CORE
    5.2

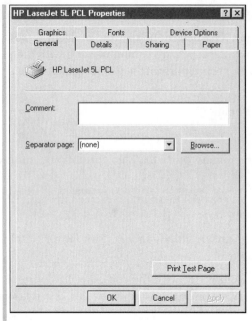

Figure 8-8   The properties box for an installed printer allows you to print a test page

Printer never leaves warm-up mode   The warming up message should go off as soon as the printer establishes communication with the PC. If this doesn't happen, try the following:

- Turn the printer off and disconnect the cable to the computer.

- Turn on the printer. If it now displays a Ready message, the problem is communication.

- Verify that the cable is connected to the correct printer port, not to a serial port.

- Verify that data to the installed printer is being sent to the parallel port. For example, open the Properties dialog box of the installed printer as described above. Verify that the print job is being sent to LPT1, as shown in Figure 8-9.

A+CORE
5.1,
5.2

Figure 8-9   Verify that print data is being sent to the correct parallel port

Check that the parallel port is enabled in CMOS setup and is set to the correct mode. More about parallel port modes in the next chapter.

Replace the cable.

A Paper Out message is displayed   Remove the paper tray. Be sure there is paper in the tray. Carefully replace the tray, being certain the tray is fully inserted in the slot.

Check the lever mechanism that falls into a slot on the tray when no paper is present. Is it jammed or bent?

A Toner Low message is displayed, or print is irregular or light   Remove the toner cartridge from the printer, tap the cartridge to redistribute the toner supply, and replace it in the printer. Don't shake the cartridge too hard, to avoid flying toner. This is really just a temporary fix for a cartridge low on toner. Eventually the user must put a new toner cartridge in the printer. Extreme humidity may cause the toner to clump in the cartridge and give the same error message.

A Paper Jam message is displayed   If paper is jammed inside the printer, follow the directions in the printer documentation to remove the paper. Don't jerk the paper from the printer mechanism, but pull evenly on the paper, with care.

If there is no jammed paper, then remove the tray and check the metal plate at the bottom of the tray. Can it move up and down freely? If not, replace the tray.

When you insert the tray in the printer, does the printer lift the plate as the tray is inserted? If not, the lift mechanism might need repairing.

8

$A+CORE$
5.1,
5.2

One or more white streaks appear in the print   Remove the toner cartridge, tap it to redistribute the toner supply, and replace the cartridge. Check the printer manual for specific directions as to what part might need replacing if this problem occurs.

Print appears speckled   Try replacing the toner cartridge. If the problem continues, the power supply assembly might be damaged.

Printed images are distorted   Check for debris that might be interfering with the printer operation.

Replace the toner cartridge.

Dot Matrix Printer Problems

Here is a troubleshooting guide for dot matrix printers:

Print quality is poor   Begin with the ribbon. Does it advance normally while the carriage moves back and forth? Replace the ribbon.

If the new ribbon still does not advance properly, check the printer's advance mechanism.

Adjust the print head spacing. Look for a lever adjustment you can use to change the distance between the print head and plate.

Check the print head for dirt. Make sure it's not hot before you touch it. If debris has built up, wipe each wire with a cotton swab dipped in alcohol or contact cleaner.

Printer self-test works, but printing from a computer application does not work   To perform a printer self-test, see the printer documentation. This test ensures that the printer itself is functioning correctly, and that the problem is communication from the PC.

Check cable connections. Is the printer online?

Print head moves back and forth, but nothing prints   Check the ribbon. Is it installed correctly between the plate and print head?

Does the ribbon advance properly?

Ink-Jet Printers

Here is a troubleshooting guide for ink-jet printers:

Print quality is poor   Is the correct paper for ink-jet printers being used?

Is the ink supply low, or is there a partially clogged nozzle?

Remove and reinstall the cartridge.

Follow the printer's documentation to clean each nozzle.

In the Printer Setup dialog box, click the **Media/Quality** tab, then change the **Print Quality** selection. Try different settings with sample prints.

Is the print head too close to or too far from the paper?

If you are printing on transparencies, try changing the fill pattern in your application.

Printing is intermittent or absent Is the ink supply low?

Are nozzles clogged?

Replace the ink cartridges or replenish the ink supply.

WHEN A PC IS YOUR PERMANENT RESPONSIBILITY

When you are the person responsible for a PC, either as the user or as the ongoing support person for the PC and the user, prepare for future troubleshooting situations. This section describes these tasks and procedures.

Accurate records of the configuration data on a PC, the hardware, the software, and the data are essential to effective troubleshooting. Make these records, or teach the user to make them, when all is well. Keep documentation on hardware and software in an easy-to-find location. Prepare a bootable disk that contains copies of the necessary startup files on the hard drive specific to this PC. Organize the hard drive to keep the number of files in the root directory to a minimum.

Organize the Hard Drive Root Directory

In the root directory, keep only startup files for your system and necessary initialization files for the software. Software applications or files containing data don't belong in the root directory, although these applications will sometimes put initialization files in the root directory to be used when they first load. Keep applications software and their data in separate directories.

Filenames and extensions can help identify files that applications software puts in the root directory to initialize itself. For example, PRODIGY.BAT is a DOS batch file that the Prodigy software uses to execute. Other software packages often use .BAT files for this same purpose. Other file extensions to look for as initialization files are .ini, .bin, and .dat. If you are not sure of the purpose of one of these files, leave it in the root directory. Some software packages might not work if their file isn't in the root directory. Also, it is common to find a mouse driver file, such as MOUSE.SYS, in the root directory. Don't move it unless you understand how to edit the CONFIG.SYS file to assign a path to this driver file.

In general, keep only a few utility-type files in the root directory on your hard drive. Remember to avoid storing data files or applications software in the root directory. Keep the number of files in the root directory to a minimum.

Create a Boot or Rescue Disk

After you have cleaned up the root directory, make a bootable system disk for DOS, and for Windows 9x make a rescue disk, as discussed in Chapter 2. Test your bootable disk to make sure that it works; label it with the computer model, date, and OS version, and keep it available at the PC. If you accidentally erase the files in the drive C root directory, you can boot up from drive A and restore the files to the hard drive from this disk.

Documentation

When you first set up a new computer, start a record book about this computer, using either a file on disk or a notebook dedicated to this machine. In this notebook or file, record any changes in setup data as well as any problems or maintenance that you do on this computer. Be diligent in keeping this notebook up to date, because it will be invaluable in diagnosing problems and upgrading the equipment. Keep a printed or handwritten record of all setup data for this machine, and store this with the hardware and software **documentation**.

If you are not the primary user of the computer, you might want to keep the hardware documentation separate from the computer itself. Label the documentation so that you can easily identify that it belongs to this computer. Some support people tape a large envelope inside the computer case, containing important documentation and records specific to that computer. Keep the software reference manuals in a location that is convenient for users.

Record of Setup Data

Keep a record of CMOS showing hard drive type, drive configuration, and so on. Use a CMOS save program similar to the one discussed in Chapter 3, or use Nuts & Bolts, Norton Utilities, or similar utility software to save the setup data to a floppy disk. This information should be stored on a floppy disk along with the software necessary to use it. Label the disk with the PC type, date, and any information needed to use the disk. Put the disk in a safe place.

If you don't have access to software to save setup, use the print screen key to print the setup screens. If the print screen key does not work while viewing setup on the PC, carefully copy down all settings on paper. On many machines there is an advanced CMOS setup screen. Copy that screen as well, even though you might never expect to change these advanced settings yourself. CMOS can lose these settings, and you will want to be able to reconstruct them when necessary. Also keep a record of DIP switch settings and jumper settings on the system board. You can record these settings the first time you remove the cover of the machine. At the very least, record the settings before you change them! Keep all this information in your notebook.

When installing expansion cards, write down in your notebook information about the card, and keep the documentation that came with it in your notebook. If you must change jumper settings or DIP switches on the card, be certain to write down the original settings before you change anything. When the card is configured correctly, write down the correct settings in your notebook or on the documentation for the card. It is unlikely that a user will accidentally change these settings and then ask you to fix them, but you never know!

Practical Precautions to Protect Software and Data

If software files become corrupted, the most thorough approach is to restore the software from backups or to reinstall the software. To simplify both of these time-consuming tasks, here are a few suggestions:

Before you install a new software package, back up the configuration files for DOS and Windows 3.x or make a backup of the Windows 9x Registry and the Windows 9x configuration files.

Because many software packages overwrite files in the \Windows\System directory during installation, if you have the hard drive space, back up this entire directory before you begin an installation.

Don't compress your hard drive, because compressed drives are more likely to become corrupted than those that are not compressed.

Don't store data files in the same directory as the software, so that there will be less chance of accidentally deleting or overwriting a software file.

At the very least, before beginning an installation, create a folder for the Windows 9x files that are likely to be altered during an application installation and back up these files to that folder. Figure 8-10 shows an example of such a folder, named Win-ini.bak. Store in this folder these files: Win.ini, System.ini, User.dat, and System.dat. The last two files make up the Windows 9x Registry, which is discussed in Chapter 12.

Figure 8-10   Back up Windows 9x files that are likely to be altered during an installation

Back Up Original Software

Many software packages today come stored on CD-ROM, which cannot be backed up easily. If you request a copy of the software on floppy disks, this can serve as your backup. If the software only comes on disk, most software copyright agreements allow the user to make a backup copy of the original disks. The copyright most likely does not allow you to distribute these backup copies to friends, but you can keep your copy in a safe place in the event that something happens to the originals. Many installation procedures that come with software on disk suggest that you make backup copies and then use the copy for the installation rather than using the original. To make an exact duplicate of a disk, use the Copy Disk command in Windows 9x or Windows 3.x or the DISKCOPY command in DOS.

Back Up Data on the Hard Drive

Don't expect the worst but prepare for it! If important data is kept on the hard drive, back up that data on a regular basis to tape (using utility software designed for that purpose), to removable hard drives, to floppy disks, or to a company file server. The procedures and methods for keeping good backups are beyond the scope of this chapter, but the principle needs stating: don't keep important data on only one medium.

CHAPTER SUMMARY

- ◘ While you are working on a computer, protect the computer and its components against ESD.

- ◘ Tools for solving computer problems include a repair kit, bootable disk, and diagnostic hardware and software.

- ◘ Two important rules when troubleshooting are to eliminate unnecessary hardware and software and to trade components you know are good for those you suspect may be bad.

- ◘ Learn to ask the user good questions (using good manners and diplomacy) that help you understand the history behind the problem.

- ◘ One good method of solving intermittent problems is to keep a log of when they occur.

- ◘ Troubleshooting keyboards, monitors, and printers should follow the general guidelines listed in the chapter.

- ◘ Problems with computers can be divided into two groups: the computer boots or it does not boot.

- ◘ Diagnostic cards give error codes based on POST errors.

- ◘ Diagnostic software performs many tests on a PC. Some of these software programs use their own proprietary operating systems.

- ◘ Utility software can update and repair device drivers and applications. Some utility software downloads these updates from the Internet.

- ◘ Keep a bootable disk containing the root directory files of your system.

- ◘ Keep backups of hard drive data and software.

- ◘ Protect documentation by keeping it in a safe place.

- ◘ Keep a written record of CMOS setup or save it on disk.

KEY TERMS

Bootable disk — For DOS, a floppy disk that can upload the OS files necessary for computer startup. It must have the two hidden system files IO.SYS and MSDOS.SYS, and also COMMAND.COM.

Diagnostic cards — Adapter cards designed to discover and report computer errors and conflicts at POST time (before the computer boots up), often by displaying a number on the card.

Diagnostic software — Utility programs that help troubleshoot computer systems. Some DOS diagnostic utilities are CHKDSK and SCANDISK. PC-Technician is an example of a third-party diagnostic program.

Documentation — Manuals, tutorials, and Help files that provide information that a user needs in order to use a computer system or software application.

Electrostatic discharge (ESD) — Another name for static electricity, which can damage chips and destroy system boards, even though it might not be felt or seen with the naked eye.

Ground bracelet — An antistatic wrist strap used to dissipate static electricity. Typically grounded by attaching an alligator clip to the computer chassis or to a nearby ground mat.

Ground mat — An antistatic mat designed for electronic workbenches to dissipate static electricity. It often uses a wire attached to the ground connection in an electrical outlet.

Static electricity — *See* Electrostatic discharge.

Video driver — A program that tells the computer how to effectively communicate with the video adapter card and monitor. It is often found on a floppy disk that is shipped with the card.

REVIEW QUESTIONS

1. Explain how to use a POST diagnostic card.

2. In Windows 9x, what key do you press to enter Safe Mode at startup?

3. Name two antivirus software packages. Why should you run a virus scan on the bootable disk that you use for troubleshooting?

4. List three good questions to ask a user when you are trying to discover a problem.

5. When a PC does not recognize all installed RAM, what are three things you can do?

6. List three things to do if you get the message "Unable to write to C:".

7. List three symptoms that might indicate that a virus is present.

8. Using the rule "trade good for suspected bad," describe how to easily troubleshoot a video problem.

9. Give five possible questions that should be asked of a user who is experiencing computer problems.

10. What are DLL files and why could they cause problems?

11. What is the best way to document intermittent problems?

12. List the steps to get a printed screen of an error message using Windows.

13. Starting with the easiest procedures, list five things to check if a monitor does not display a picture.

14. Identify three things that may cause monitor flicker.

15. What is the value of installing additional video RAM?

16. Starting with the easiest procedures, list five things to check if your printer does not print.

17. What can you do to temporarily solve streaking or light printing on a laser printer?

18. Starting with the easiest procedures, list five things to check if your PC does not boot.

19. Identify three things to check if your PC does not recognize all of the installed memory.

20. What is the rule to follow when connecting the power supply leads (P8 and P9) to the system board?

21. Using the Windows Control Panel or Windows 9x My Computer, System Properties, Device Manager, determine what specific controller (and/or driver) is used for your home or lab monitor.

22. Using the Windows Control Panel or the Windows 9x My Computer, System Properties, Device Manager, determine what specific controller (and/or driver) is used for your home or lab printer.

23. Describe what to do if you've just spilled soda pop on your keyboard.

24. Describe what to do to check that chips on a video card are properly seated in their sockets.

25. In Windows 9x, when troubleshooting problems with a monitor, why would you enter Safe Mode?

26. As a help-desk technician, list some good "detective" questions to ask if the user calls to say, "My PC won't boot."

27. A user calls your help desk complaining that a printer does not work. The printer power light is on, but the PC cannot send a print job to it. What questions do you ask?

28. With the printer problem in Question 27, you suspect that the cable is not correctly connected. List the directions to walk the user through checking the printer cable connections.

29. You are a support technician working at a user site. A user has just erased all the files in the root directory of a PC using DOS and Windows 3.1. Describe how you handle the situation.

30. What key do you press to bring up the Windows 9x Startup Menu during the boot process?

PROJECTS

Interacting with the User

Rob, a PC service technician, has been called on-site to repair a PC. He has not spoken directly with the user, but he knows the floor of the building where the user, Lisa, works and can look for her name on her cubicle. The following is a description of his actions. Create a table with two columns. List in one column the mistakes he made and in the next column the correct action he should have taken.

Rob's company promised that a service technician would come sometime during the next business day after the call was received. Rob was given the name and address of the user and the problem, which was stated as "PC will not boot." Rob arrived the following day at about 10 a.m. He found Lisa's cubicle, but she was not present. Since Lisa was not present, Rob decided not to disturb the papers all over her desk, so he laid his notebooks and tools on top of her work.

Rob tried to boot the PC and it gave errors indicating a corrupted FAT on the hard drive. He successfully booted from a disk and was able to access a C prompt. A DIR command returned a mostly unreadable list of files and subdirectories in the root directory. Next Rob used Norton Utilities to try to recover the files and directories but was unable to do so. He began to suspect that a virus had caused the problem, so he ran a virus scan program that did not find the suspected virus.

He made a call to his technical support to ask for suggestions. Technical support suggested that he try partitioning and formatting the hard drive to remove any possible viruses and recover the hard drive. Rob partitioned and formatted the hard drive and was on the phone with technical support and in the process of reloading Windows 98 from the company's file server when Lisa arrived.

Lisa took one look at her PC and gasped. She caught her breath and asked where her data was. Rob replied, "A virus destroyed your hard drive. I had to reformat."

Lisa tried to explain the importance of the destroyed data. Rob replied, "Guess you'll learn to make backups now." Lisa left to find her manager.

Using Some Nuts & Bolts Diagnostic Tests

Follow these directions to perform a series of diagnostic tests on your computer, using Nuts & Bolts.

1. In Windows 9x, click Start, Programs, Nuts & Bolts, and select Discover Pro.

2. From the Discover Pro main screen, select the Diagnostics tab.

3. Although you can perform the five diagnostic tests listed from this screen, to have more control over the tests, click the Advanced button on the bottom of the screen.

4. Select the hard drive test by clicking the HD Diag button on the left side of the screen. Select the hard drive from the list of drives on the right side. Click Start to perform the test. Print the results of the test by clicking Print.

5. Perform and print the results of each of the remaining four diagnostic tests.

8

Using the Windows Control Panel

1. Using the Windows Control Panel, set your monitor to Low power, Standby, or Doze Mode.

2. Using the Windows Control Panel, record the current video driver and video resolution settings. Then change the video driver to Standard VGA with a 640 3 480 resolution. Reboot the computer and change the video resolution back to the original settings.

3. Using the Windows Control Panel, add a new printer (choose any from the printer list). When done, remove the printer driver, then check to confirm that the correct printer is set as the default.

4. Log on to the Internet and download one of the diagnostic utilities mentioned earlier in the chapter. Use it to test your home or lab computer.

Take a Computer Apart and Put It Back Together

Follow these general guidelines to take a computer apart and put it back together:

1. Put the computer on a table with plenty of room. Have a plastic bag or cup available to keep screws from being lost. When reassembling the PC, insert the same screws in the same holes. (This is especially important with the hard drive. Screws that are too long can puncture the hard drive housing.) You'll need a Phillips-head screwdriver and a flat-head screwdriver, paper, and pencil.

2. Leave the computer plugged in so that it's grounded or follow the directions of the instructor to ground the computer as you work. If your computer uses CMOS for setup, print out all settings or save them to a floppy disk. Make a bootable disk if you don't already have one. Turn the computer off.

3. If necessary, remove the monitor from the top of the case. Unplug and remove the mouse and keyboard.

4. Remove the case cover. For some desktop computers, the case slides to the front; others lift off. For tower cases, from the back, lift the cover up and then slide it to the back before removing it (see Figure 8-11). After you set the top aside, ground yourself by touching the computer case to discharge any static electricity on your body.

Figure 8-11   To remove the cover of a tower case, lift up the backside and then slide the cover toward the rear

5. Draw a diagram of all cable connections, DIP switch settings, and jumper settings. You might need the cable connection diagram to help you reassemble. You will not change any DIP switch settings or jumper settings, but accidents do happen. Be prepared. If you like, use a felt-tip marker to make a mark across components to indicate a cable connection, board placement, system-board orientation, speaker connection, brackets, and so on, so that you can simply line up the marks when you reassemble.

6. Before removing the cables, note that each cable has a color or stripe down one side. This edge color marks this side of the cable as pin 1. Look on the board or drive that the cable is attached to. You should see that pin 1 or pin 2 is clearly marked. Verify that the edge color is aligned with pin 1. Look at the cable used to connect drive A to the floppy drive controller card. There is a twist in the cable. This twist reverses these leads in the cable, causing the addresses for this cable to be different from the addresses for the cable that doesn't have the twist. The connector with the twist is attached to drive A (see Figure 8-12). Remove the cables to the floppy drives and the hard drives. Remove the power supply cords from the drives.

8

Controller   Cable twist

Typical PC floppy cable

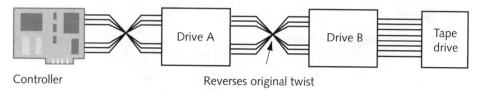

Controller   Reverses original twist

Figure 8-12   Twist in cable indentifies drive A

7. Remove the expansion cards. There is usually a single screw holding each card to the back of the case. Remove the screws first, and place them in your cup or bag. When removing a card, don't rock the card from side to side, because you can spread the card's slot, making connections more difficult. Don't rock the card from back to front. Don't put your fingers on the edge connectors or touch a chip. Don't stack the cards on top of one another. Lift the card straight up from the slot.

8. Remove the floppy drives next. Some drives have one or two screws on each side of the drive attaching the drive to the drive bay. After you remove the screws, the drive usually slides to the front and out of the case. Sometimes there is a catch underneath the drive that you must lift up as you slide the drive forward. Be careful not to remove screws that hold the circuit card on top of the drive to the drive housing. The whole unit should stay intact.

9. Remove the hard drive next. Look for the screws that hold the drive to the bay. Be careful to remove only these screws, not the screws that hold the drive together. Handle the drive with care.

10. You might need to remove the power supply before exposing the system board. Unplug the power supply lines to the system board. An ATX power supply only has a single power line, but for an AT power supply, carefully note which line is labeled P8 and which is labeled P9. You will want to be certain that you don't switch these two lines when reconnecting them, since this would cause the wrong voltage to flow in the circuits on the system board and can destroy the board. Fortunately, most connections today only allow you to place the lines in the correct order, which is always black leads on P8 next to black leads on P9. Remember, "black to black." Look for screws that attach the power supply to the computer case, as shown in Figure 8-13. Be careful not to remove any screws that hold the power supply housing together. You do not want to take the housing apart. After you have removed the screws, the power supply still might not be free. Sometimes it is attached to the case on the underside by

recessed slots. Turn the case over and look on the bottom for these slots. If they are present, determine in which direction you need to slide the power supply to free it from the case.

Figure 8-13   Removing the power supply mounting screws

11. The system board is now the last thing to be removed. It probably has spacers keeping it from resting directly on the bottom of the computer case. Carefully pop off these spacers and/or remove the three or four screws that hold the board to the case.

12. Now that the computer is fully disassembled, reassemble it in reverse order: first the system board, then the power supply, the hard drive, the floppy drives, the expansion cards, and the cables. Refer to your diagrams and marks on the cables as needed.

13. Before replacing the computer case, plug in the monitor and keyboard and have your instructor inspect your work. Do one last visual inspection before turning on the power. Then turn on the power and make sure everything works. If the computer doesn't work the first time, don't panic. You probably have not connected something snugly enough. Turn off the power and double-check all cards, cables, and power cords. Refer to your drawings and make sure that all cables are attached correctly. If the machine still doesn't work, it's possible you loosened a chip on a board as you were working. Use a screwdriver or your fingers and firmly but carefully push down all four corners of every socketed chip on the system board. As you work, be certain to turn off the power before touching the inside of the machine. Once the machine is working, replace the cover and you're done.

Practice Makes Perfect

Repeat the previous project using a different model of computer. You should feel comfortable disassembling and reassembling a computer before you leave this exercise.

Using the Help Feature in Windows 9x

Research the Help feature in Windows 9x. From the **Start** button, choose **Help**. The window shown in Figure 8-14 appears, showing the Index tab selected. Type the first few letters of the word you want to search for, and then click the index entry you want. Click **Display**.

Figure 8-14   The Windows 98 Help Index window

For Windows 95, Figure 8-15 displays the Find tab. Type the word to find, click on one of the topics listed, and select **Display**. Using the Windows 95 Help tool, list the steps for making a backup of the \Windows\System folder to disk. List the steps to restore the \Windows\System folder from disk.

Figure 8-15   The Windows 95 Help Find sheet

Using the Help Feature in Windows 98

Windows 98 offers a troubleshooter to help with problem solving, which is displayed in Figure 8-16. Research the feature in Windows 98. From the **Start** button, choose **Help**. Under the **Index** tab, enter the word **Monitor** or **Troubleshooting**. Print the list of problems that the Windows 98 Display Troubleshooter addresses.

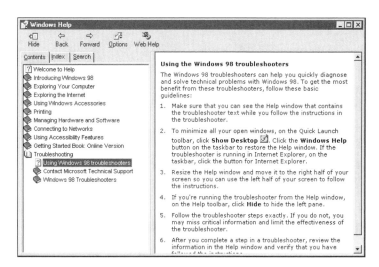

Figure 8-16   The Windows 98 Troubleshooter is an interactive tool to help solve computer problems

Troubleshooting a Modem Problem

Now let's apply what you've learned so far to a new situation. An external modem is connected to a PC. When you attempt to use the modem, you get the error message "Modem not found." There is a working PC and external modem nearby. List the steps to determine if the problem is with the PC, the modem, or the modem cable. Why can you assume that the problem is not with the phone line?

Troubleshooting a Boot Problem

Edit the CONFIG.SYS file on your PC. If you are using an installation of Windows 9x that does not use a CONFIG.SYS file, then create one. Enter a command line in the file that you know will cause an error. Boot the PC. Press F8 during the boot and walk through the boot process to demonstrate how this procedure can be used to diagnose a problem with startup files.

Correct the command line in CONFIG.SYS and boot again, walking through each command in the boot process.

Developing Help-Desk Skills

Work with a partner who will play the role of the user. Sit with your back to the user, who is in front of the PC. Troubleshoot the problem and talk the user through to a solution. Abide by these rules:

1. A third person has previously created an error on the PC so that the PC does not boot successfully. Neither you nor your partner knows what the third person did.

2. The user pretends not to have technical insight but to be good at following directions and willing to answer any nontechnical questions.

3. Don't turn around to look at the screen.

4. Practice professional mannerisms and speech.

5. As you work, keep a log of the "phone call to the help desk," recording in the log the major steps toward diagnosing and correcting the problem.

6. When the problem is resolved, have the third person create a different problem that causes the PC not to boot correctly, and exchange roles with your partner.

Adjusting a Monitor

Using the documentation that accompanies a monitor, learn to adjust the monitor using the buttons on the monitor. In a class situation, demonstrate your skills to the class and answer any questions others may have.

Save CMOS Setup Using Freeware

Research the Internet for freeware to save CMOS setup data to floppy disk. Print the web page of the product. Download the program and use it to save the setup data to disk. When you run the software, print the main menu of the software. Try these web sites when looking for software: *www.zdnet.com, www.geocities.com.*, and *www.download.com.*

9

SUPPORTING I/O DEVICES

In this chapter, you will learn:

♦ How to use standard resources on a computer system when installing add-on devices

♦ How to resolve resource conflicts

♦ How to install a new device on a computer

♦ About keyboards, pointing devices, and video subsystems

This chapter focuses on how to install and support I/O devices. You will first learn about procedures and guidelines that are common to most installations, including how to use serial, parallel, USB, IEEE 1394 ports, and expansion slots. You then turn your attention to the I/O devices common to every computer—a keyboard, pointing device, and monitor. This chapter builds the foundation for the next chapter, where multimedia devices are covered, including CD-ROM and DVD drives, sound cards, and digital cameras.

Basic Principles of Peripheral Installations

When you add new peripherals to a computer, the device needs a device driver or BIOS, system resources (which might include an IRQ, DMA channel, I/O addresses, and upper memory addresses), and applications software. Consider these fundamental principles:

- The peripheral is a hardware device that is controlled by software. You must install both the hardware and the software.

- The software might exist at different levels. For example, a device could require driver software that interfaces directly with the hardware device and an applications software package that interfaces with the driver. You must install all levels of software.

- Remember from Chapter 2 that more than one peripheral device might attempt to use the same computer resources. This conflict could disable one or both devices. Possible conflicts arise when more than one device attempts to use any of the following four system resources:
  - The same IRQ
  - The same DMA channel
  - The same I/O addresses
  - The same upper memory addresses (for 16-bit drivers)

A Review of System Resources

Before discussing principles of installation, let's review the concepts of the four system resources listed above that were first explained in Chapter 2. Recall that an IRQ is a line on a bus that serves as an interrupt request line and is assigned to a device. When the device needs attention, it signals the CPU through its assigned IRQ; it "raises" the IRQ line. The CPU then requests from the device an interrupt number (abbreviated INT). These numbers, used by hardware devices to request service from the CPU and by software to request that the CPU access a hardware device, are listed in Appendix G.

The CPU uses the INT to locate an entry in the interrupt vector table. This table, located in the lowest part of memory, stores the address of an interrupt handler, a program that handles the request. The program is either a device driver or BIOS and uses I/O addresses to communicate with the device. These I/O addresses are standard addresses always used by this program and device (for example, the keyboard always uses I/O addresses 60h–6Fh) or they are assigned to the program and device at startup.

Also remember that older device drivers and BIOS written in real mode require some upper memory addresses between 640K and 1024K. Some devices require a DMA channel to speed up transferring data across the bus. The DMA channel and upper memory addresses are also assigned at startup.

Sometimes devices connect to the system with a controller that manages the resources for it and other devices connected to the controller. One example of this type of setup is a PCI device installed in a PCI expansion slot on the system board. The PCI device is managed by the PCI controller which is also on the system board. The system resources needed by the device are assigned to the PCI controller, which then manages these resources. Other types of subsystems that have a controller to manage system resources for the devices connected to the controller include SCSI, USB, and IEEE 1394. In all these cases, the controller can be embedded on the system board as part of the chip set or can be on a host adapter in an expansion slot. Whether on the system board or host adapter, the controller is assigned system resources, which are used to manage the devices connected to it. With SCSI, USB, and IEEE 1394, only one IRQ and I/O address assignment is needed for the controller, and the devices managed by the controller don't need individual resources assigned to them; they all share the same resources assigned to the controller.

Installation Overview

A+CORE
1.2

You follow three basic steps to install an add-on device:

1. Install the device
2. Install the device driver
3. Install the applications software

9

The device can either be an internal (installed inside the computer case) or external device (installed outside the case). Devices installed inside the case are drives (hard drives, floppy drives, CD-ROM drives, DVD drives, Zip drives, etc.) or devices that are inserted in expansion slots on the system board (a modem card, video capture card, etc.). Drive installations are covered in other chapters. Using expansion slots to install a device is covered later in this chapter. You can install an external device using an existing port (serial, parallel, USB, or IEEE 1394 port), or a port provided by an interface card installed in an expansion slot.

An example of this last situation is a scanner, which is an external device. It uses an expansion card installed inside the case to interface with the system board. When you buy a scanner, the package might include an expansion card that provides a port for the scanner. You are buying (1) the scanner, (2) the expansion card that interfaces with the computer (for example, a SCSI host adapter to provide a SCSI port for the scanner), (3) the cable to connect the scanner to its expansion card, (4) the device driver on disk, (5) some applications software for using the scanner, and (6), very importantly, the documentation. Installing the hardware includes installing the expansion card in an expansion slot on the system board and then plugging in the scanner itself.

After physically installing the device, install the device driver. For DOS and Windows 3.x, installing the driver probably means executing a setup program from floppy disk or CD-ROM that copies the driver file to the hard drive and adds the DEVICE= command to CONFIG.SYS. For Windows 9x, start the setup program from the Start, Run command to install the device driver automatically. You also can open the Control Panel and choose the Add New Hardware option. A comprehensive example of these procedures is given at the end of this chapter.

A+CORE
1.2

The driver and the scanner expansion card are specific for each brand and model of scanner; however, the applications software does not have as narrow an application. Any application package that uses a scanner should work with most scanners. In fact, you might have several applications that use the same hardware device.

The rest of this section discusses hardware devices, device drivers, and applications software in detail before turning to using standard ports on a computer system for installing devices.

Hardware Devices

Consider a hardware device such as a modem. You know that a modem provides a way to connect one computer to another, forming a network. There are many kinds of modems and networks. Some modems use normal telephone lines for communication, whereas others use dedicated circuits. Internal modems are expansion cards installed inside the computer case; they provide one or (usually) two telephone-line ports that connect a telephone line directly into the back of the computer. External modems are contained in their own case with their own power supply. The external modem is connected to the computer by a cable that plugs into the back of the computer case, usually to a serial port. The telephone line then plugs into the back of the modem. In either case, the modem converts the computer's bits to a form that can be communicated over telephone lines and other circuits.

Most often internal devices are less expensive than external devices, which have the additional expense of the power supply and case. Internal devices also offer the added advantage of not taking up desk space, and their cables and cords are neatly tucked away. An advantage of external devices is that they can be moved easily from one computer to another.

If you've ever shopped for a peripheral device, such as a modem or a sound card, you know what a large variety of features and prices today's market offers. Research pays. First, know your own computer system. Know which CPU, system bus, and local bus you have, and how much memory and what size hard drive your system has. Know which OS you are using and what version it is (for example, DOS 6.22 or Windows 98 Second Edition). Determine how much space is available on your hard drive, and how many expansion slots and what kinds of slots are free in your computer.

In addition to a basic knowledge of your system, you might need some technical information. For example, most computers have a power supply that well exceeds the requirements of the standard system, making it possible to add internal devices without exceeding the total available wattage. However, if your computer is old (for computers, that's over five years), and you're adding more than one internal device, the power supply could limit your choices. If you install more internal devices than the power supply can handle, you might need to upgrade the power supply.

Unless you are using Plug and Play-compliant devices and a Plug and Play OS, know what IRQs, I/O addresses, DMA channels, and upper memory addresses your present devices use. Recall that a notebook dedicated to your PC, as discussed in Chapter 8, should have records of each device and the present settings of the device.

A+*CORE*
1.2,
1.3

> TIP To find out what IRQs, I/O addresses, DMA channels, and upper memory addresses your devices are using, use MSD for DOS and Device Manager for Windows 9x.

Generally, if you buy the device and other accompanying hardware (such as the interface board and cables) from the same source, they are more likely to be compatible.

Embedded BIOS on Devices

A peripheral device can require several levels of software to make it work. Recall from Chapter 1 that the most fundamental software needed is stored on ROM chips inside the device or on the interface board, and is called BIOS, or firmware. Some devices also contain some memory or RAM to temporarily store data moving through the device. Sometimes you must interface with the BIOS to set a parameter, such as the IRQ number. If the device and your system are Plug and Play, you do not need to change the resource parameters of the device. If you are not using Plug and Play, you can set a parameter of the BIOS by changing a DIP switch or jumper setting. However, for some sophisticated devices, you can interface with the BIOS using programs provided by the manufacturer, which present a chip setup screen similar to the system board CMOS setup screen. The documentation for the device should tell you what parameters you can change and how to communicate those changes to the BIOS. SCSI devices quite often use this method for setup.

The DIP switches and jumpers are normally set by the manufacturer in the most commonly used default settings. Don't change a DIP switch or jumper on a device without (1) writing down the original settings so you can backtrack, and (2) carefully reading the documentation.

Why change a BIOS parameter? The most common reason is to prevent a conflict in the assignment of computer resources. If you buy a second modem to install on your computer, and both modems are using the same IRQ by default, you might be able to instruct the new modem to use an alternate IRQ by changing DIP switches or jumpers on the modem. Making this change tells BIOS on the modem to use the alternate IRQ.

For example, Figure 9-1 shows a modem that has a bank of DIP switches on the back of the card and a bank of jumpers on the card itself (see Figure 9-2). By using combinations of these DIP switches and jumpers, you can configure this modem either to be Plug and Play compliant or to use a specific set of IRQ and I/O addresses.

9

Figure 9-1   Diagram of a modem card

In addition to BIOS on the device, system BIOS might also be involved. A good example of this is a hard drive. BIOS on the hard drive housing manages direct access to the drive, but system BIOS on the system board can manage communication between the hard drive BIOS and the OS.

Figure 9-2   Ports and DIP switches on the back of an internal modem

Device Drivers

The second level of software needed by a peripheral device is a device driver. As explained in Chapter 2, there are two kinds of device drivers: 16-bit real-mode drivers and 32-bit protected-mode drivers. Windows 9x contains 32-bit drivers for hundreds of hardware devices. Windows automatically loads these drivers into extended memory (memory above 1024K) at startup or when the device first needs them. However, not all devices are supported by Windows drivers, so you may need to use an older 16-bit real-mode device driver. These 16-bit drivers are loaded by entries in the CONFIG.SYS or AUTOEXEC.BAT file and use upper memory addresses.

Device Drivers under DOS

A common 16-bit DOS device driver is the mouse driver. For example, the device driver MOUSE.SYS is loaded in the CONFIG.SYS file with this command:

```
DEVICE=C:\UTIL\MOUSE.SYS
```

The DEVICE= command in CONFIG.SYS tells DOS that the program file named MOUSE.SYS stored in the \UTIL directory on drive C is a TSR needed to drive a device. Sometimes the device driver needs some parameters or switches listed at the end of the command line. For example, a device driver can direct a serial port mouse to use COM 2 instead of the default, COM 1, by adding a parameter to the end of the command line:

```
DEVICE=C:\UTIL\MOUSE.SYS /C2
```

See your documentation to find out what parameters you can use on the command line for a device driver.

Another type of mouse device driver is loaded from the AUTOEXEC.BAT file and the command line might look like this:

```
C:\UTIL\MOUSE.COM /C2
```

9

A+ *OS* *2.4,* *CORE* *1.7*

Device Drivers Under Windows 9x

Windows 9x provides 32-bit device drivers for a mouse, so you normally do not need to use a 16-bit driver in CONFIG.SYS as shown above for DOS. However, if you wanted to boot to DOS from a floppy disk and use a mouse, put the mouse device driver entry in the CONFIG.SYS file on your disk together with the driver file MOUSE.SYS.

For Windows 9x, the device driver is installed at the time the hardware device is installed, information about the driver installation is kept in the Windows 9x Registry, and then the driver is automatically executed each time Windows 9x starts or the device is used. Windows 32-bit drivers can be loaded into memory when the device is accessed and then unloaded to conserve memory when the device is disconnected or turned off.

Most often the device driver comes as part of the hardware package. For example, when you buy a video or sound card, a disk is enclosed that contains the driver. You want to use the latest 32-bit driver available. Windows 98 has added many drivers to the list of those supported by Windows 95. Select the latest driver available for that device, either provided by Windows or by the device manufacturer. Occasionally, a manufacturer releases a new, improved device driver for a device. You can most likely download these new drivers from the manufacturer's web site.

You can view and change current device drivers from the Control Panel. For example, in Windows 98, to view the current video driver, click **Start**, **Settings**, **Control Panel**, and double-click **Display**. Click the **Settings** tab to view the currently installed display driver, as seen in Figure 9-3.

A⁺ OS
2.4,
CORE
1.7

Figure 9-3   Use the Settings tab of Display Properties to view the currently installed display driver

To change the driver, click **Advanced**. Click the **Adapter** tab, and then click the **Change** button. You see the Windows 98 Update Device Driver Wizard. Click **Next** to see the dialog box in Figure 9-4, which includes options to let Windows 98 search for a new driver from its list of supported drivers or to let you perform the search manually. If you have a new driver that is not supported by Windows 98 (such as one that you just downloaded from the Internet), choose to perform the search manually. Select **Display a list of all the drivers in a specific location, so you can select the driver you want** and click **Next**. You see the dialog box in Figure 9-5, showing the currently selected driver. Click **Have Disk** to provide the new driver from a floppy disk, a CD-ROM, or a downloaded folder on your hard drive.

A+ OS
2.4,
CORE
1.7

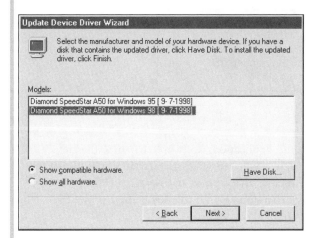

Figure 9-4   The Windows 98 Update Device Driver Wizard enables you to install a new device driver for a previously installed device

Figure 9-5   If you have a new driver for a device that Windows 98 does not offer, click Have Disk

TIP When you upgrade from DOS with Windows 3.x to either Windows 9x or Windows NT, use the latest 32-bit drivers. If Windows 9x or Windows NT does not support a hardware device installed on your system, the solution may be to use the Internet to locate a new 32-bit driver for your device. One of the projects at the end of this chapter shows you how.

Sixteen-bit drivers under Windows 9x can cause slow performance, so use 32-bit drivers when possible. To identify whether Windows 9x is using a 16-bit driver, click **Start**, **Settings**, **Control Panel**, double-click **System** and select **Device Manager**. Look for an

A+ OS
2.4,
CORE
1.7

exclamation point beside the device, which indicates that the driver has a problem. Table 9-1 summarizes basic information about device drivers under Windows 9x.

Table 9-1   Two types of device drivers and how to use them under Windows 9x

Characteristic	16-bit Device Drivers	32-bit Device Drivers
Operating mode	Real mode	Protected mode
Use of memory	May use upper memory addresses	Stored in extended memory
How loaded	Loaded by a command line in CONFIG.SYS or AUTOEXEC.BAT	Automatically loaded by Windows 9x at startup or when the device is used
How changed	Edit the CONFIG.SYS or AUTOEXEC.BAT file	From Device Manager, select the device and use Properties, Driver tab
How to identify the type	In Device Manager, look for an exclamation point beside the device name	Look for no exclamation point beside the device name in Device Manager. Also, typically "32" is included in the driver filename.
When to use this type	Use a 16-bit driver under Windows only when a 32-bit driver is not available. When operating under DOS, 16-bit drivers are required.	When you can, always use 32-bit drivers because they are faster

Applications Software

The next level of software is the applications software that uses the device. Most devices include applications software, such as voice messaging software to use with a modem or software to scan and manipulate images that comes with a scanner. You can use applications software other than the package that comes with the device, and, if you have other software, it isn't necessary to install the bundled software.

When you install older 16-bit applications software, you might need to provide some information about the hardware devices it uses. For example, for the 16-bit version of ProComm, a communications software package that can communicate with a modem, if an internal modem is configured to use COM2 by a DIP switch on the modem, ProComm must also be told to look for the modem on COM2. If the modem is communicating on COM2, and ProComm is communicating on COM1, ProComm will not find the modem. On the setup screen in ProComm, you can choose COM2 as the communications port.

USING PORTS AND EXPANSION SLOTS FOR ADD-ON DEVICES

Devices can be plugged directly into a serial, parallel, USB, or IEEE 1394 port, or they can use an expansion card plugged into an expansion slot. Some devices use a peripheral bus, called a SCSI bus, that interfaces with the local bus through a SCSI expansion card called the host adapter. The text below addresses the specific details of these kinds of installations.

All computers come with one or two serial ports, one parallel port, and, on newer comput-ers, a USB port and IEEE 1394 port. Newer system boards have serial, parallel, and USB ports and perhaps a IEEE 1394 port directly on the board (called on-board ports), but, on older system boards, an **I/O controller card** in an expansion slot supplied the serial and parallel ports.

Using Serial Ports

A+CORE
1.4,
4.3

Serial ports transmit data in single file, or serially. You can identify these ports on the back of a PC case by (1) counting the pins and (2) determining if the port is male or female. Figure 9-6 shows serial ports, a parallel port, and a game port, for comparison. On the top is one 25-pin female parallel port and one 9-pin male serial port. On the bottom is one 25-pin male serial port and a 15-pin game port. Serial ports are sometimes called DB-9 and DB-25 connectors. DB stands for data bus and refers to the number of pins on the connector. Serial ports are almost always male ports, and parallel ports are almost always female ports.

9

- 25-pin female parallel port
- 9-pin male serial port
- 15-pin female game port
- 25-pin male serial port

Figure 9-6   Serial, parallel, and game ports

To simplify the allocation of system resources, two configurations for these serial ports were designated as COM1 and COM2, and then later two more configurations were designated as COM3 and COM4. These COM assignments each represent a designated IRQ and I/O address, as seen in Table 9-2. Think of the serial ports as physical, and of COM1 and COM2 as logical assignments to these physical ports, much as a phone number is a logical assign-ment to a physical telephone (Figure 9-7). In reality, COM1 is just a convenient way of say-ing IRQ 4 and I/O address 03F8h. Also notice in Table 9-2 that the two parallel port configurations are named LPT1 and LPT2 and each is assigned an IRQ and I/O address. DOS, Windows, and most applications that use serial devices know about and comply with these assignments. For example, you can tell your communications software to use COM1

A+CORE
  1.4,
  4.3

to communicate with a modem, and it then knows that the modem is using IRQ 4 to sig-nal the CPU and "listening" for instructions by way of I/O address 03F8h.

Table 9-2   Default port assignments on many computers

Port	IRQ	I/O Address (in Hex)	Type
COM1	IRQ 4	03F8 – 3FF	Serial
COM2	IRQ 3	02F8 – 2FF	Serial
COM3	IRQ 4	03E8 – 3EF	Serial
COM4	IRQ 3	02E8 – 2EF	Serial
LPT1	IRQ 7	0378 – 37F	Parallel
LPT2	IRQ 5	0278 – 27F	Parallel

770-555-3233

COM2

Serial port   Telephone

Figure 9-7   A serial port is assigned COM2 much as a telephone is assigned a phone number

Serial ports were originally intended for input and output devices, and parallel ports were intended for printers. Serial ports can be configured for COM1, COM2, COM3, or COM4. Parallel ports can be configured as LPT1, LPT2, or LPT3.

To configure a serial port with a COM assignment, if it is on an I/O card, you would most likely set jumper switches on the card. If they are connected directly to the system board, most often the assignments are made in CMOS setup. Sometimes the setup screen shows the COM assignments, and sometimes you see the actual IRQ and I/O address assignments, as seen in Figure 9-8.

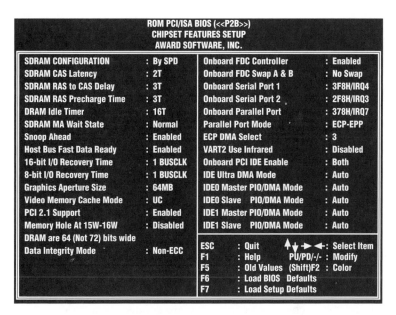

ROM PCI/ISA BIOS (<<P2B>>) CHIPSET FEATURES SETUP AWARD SOFTWARE, INC.			
SDRAM CONFIGURATION	: By SPD	Onboard FDC Controller	: Enabled
SDRAM CAS Latency	: 2T	Onboard FDC Swap A & B	: No Swap
SDRAM RAS to CAS Delay	: 3T	Onboard Serial Port 1	: 3F8H/IRQ4
SDRAM RAS Precharge Time	: 3T	Onboard Serial Port 2	: 2F8H/IRQ3
DRAM Idle Timer	: 16T	Onboard Parallel Port	: 378H/IRQ7
SDRAM MA Wait State	: Normal	Parallel Port Mode	: ECP-EPP
Snoop Ahead	: Enabled	ECP DMA Select	: 3
Host Bus Fast Data Ready	: Enabled	VART2 Use Infrared	: Disabled
16-bit I/O Recovery Time	: 1 BUSCLK	Onboard PCI IDE Enable	: Both
8-bit I/O Recovery Time	: 1 BUSCLK	IDE Ultra DMA Mode	: Auto
Graphics Aperture Size	: 64MB	IDE0 Master PIO/DMA Mode	: Auto
Video Memory Cache Mode	: UC	IDE0 Slave PIO/DMA Mode	: Auto
PCI 2.1 Support	: Enabled	IDE1 Master PIO/DMA Mode	: Auto
Memory Hole At 15W-16W	: Disabled	IDE1 Slave PIO/DMA Mode	: Auto
DRAM are 64 (Not 72) bits wide			
Data Integrity Mode	: Non-ECC	ESC : Quit ↑↓→←: Select Item	
		F1 : Help PU/PD/-/- : Modify	
		F5 : Old Values (Shift)F2 : Color	
		F6 : Load BIOS Defaults	
		F7 : Load Setup Defaults	

Figure 9-8   CMOS setup screen for chipset features

A⁺CORE 1.4 A serial port conforms to the standard interface called RS-232c (stands for Reference Standard 232 revision c) and is sometimes called the RS-232 port. This interface standard originally called for 25 pins, but since microcomputers only use 9 of those pins, a modified, 9-pin port was often installed by the manufacturer. Today some computers have a 9-pin serial port, and some have a 25-pin serial port, or both. Both ports work the same way. The 25-pin port uses only 9 pins; the other pins are unused. Serial 25-pin ports are often found on modems. You can buy adapters that convert 9-pin ports to 25-pin ports, and vice versa, to accommodate a cable you already have.

One of the 9 pins on a serial port transmits data in a sequence of bits, and a second pin receives data sequentially. The other 7 pins are used to establish the communications protocol. A protocol is a set of agreed-upon rules for communication that is established before data is actually passed from one device to another. Table 9-3 describes the functions of the pins of a serial port connection to a modem connected to another remote modem and computer. External modems sometimes use lights on the front panel to indicate the state of these pins. The labels on these modem lights are listed in the last column.

The table is included not so much to explain the use of each pin, as to show that more than just data is included in a serial communication session. Also, when the system is using serial ports, one of the devices is called the DTE (Data Terminal Equipment), and the other device is called the DCE (Data Communications Equipment). For example, a modem is called the DCE and the computer on which it is installed is called the DTE.

A+CORE
1.4

Table 9-3 9-pin and 25-pin serial port specifications

Pin Number for 9-Pin	Pin Number for 25-pin	Pin Use	Description	LED Light
1	8	Carrier detect	Connection with remote is made	CD or DCD
2	3	Receive data	Receiving data	RD or TXD
3	2	Transmit data	Sending data	SD or TXD
4	20	Data terminal ready	Modem hears its computer	TR or DTR
5	7	Signal ground	Not used with PCs	
6	6	Data set ready	Modem is able to talk	MR or DSR
7	4	Request to send	Computer wants to talk	RTS
8	5	Clear to send	Modem is ready to talk	CTS
9	22	Ring indicator	Someone is calling	RI

Null Modem Connection

When two DTE devices, such as two computers, are connected, software can transmit data between the two DTE devices over a special cable called a **null modem cable**, or a **modem eliminator**, without the need for modems. The cable is not a standard serial cable, but has several wires cross-connected in order to simulate modem communication. For example, based on the 9-pin specifications in Table 9-3, a 9-pin null modem cable would connect pin 2 on one end of the cable to pin 3 on the other end of the cable with a single wire, so that the sending data on one end is the receiving data on the other end. Similarly, pin 3 would be connected to pin 2 on the other end of the cable, so that the received data on one end is the sent data on the other end. Crossing pins 2 and 3 allows data to be sent from one computer and received by the other. Standard modem software can often be used to transmit data, but because there are no actual modems in the connection, very fast, accurate transfer is possible.

Table 9-4 describes the pins connected and crossed for a 25-pin null modem cable. Figure 9-9 shows the same information as a picture.

Table 9-4 Pin connections for a 25-pin null modem cable

Pin on one end is	Connected to the pin on the other end	So that:
2	3	Data sent by one computer is received by the other
3	2	Data received by one computer is sent by the other
6	20	One end says to the other end, "I'm able to talk"
20	6	One end hears the other end say, "I'm able to talk"
4	5	One end says to the other, "I'm ready to talk"
5	4	One end hears the other say, "I'm ready to talk"
7	7	Both ends are grounded

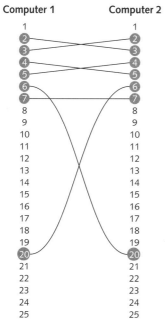

Figure 9-9   Wire connections on a 25-pin null modem cable used to transmit data

A+CORE
1.3,
4.4,
4.3

Infrared Transceivers

An infrared transceiver that supports infrared devices, such as wireless keyboards and printers, can connect directly to a serial port. If the transceiver is Plug and Play, connect the device and turn on the PC. Windows automatically detects and installs the infrared driver using the Add New Hardware Wizard. For legacy transceivers, install the transceiver using the Add New Hardware icon in Control Panel. The transceiver uses the resources of the serial port for communication and also creates a virtual infrared serial port and virtual infrared parallel port for infrared devices. During the installation, you are told what these virtual ports are and given the opportunity to change them. For example, if you physically connect the transceiver to COM2, the virtual ports will be COM4 for infrared serial devices and LPT3 for an infrared printer. The IRQ and I/O addresses for the infrared system are those assigned to COM2. To activate the transceiver, double click the **Infrared icon** in Control Panel. If the icon is not displayed, press F5 to refresh Control Panel.

In addition, some system boards provide a 5-pin connection for its own proprietary IRDA-compliant infrared transceiver. In this case, the transceiver mounts on the outside of the case and a wire goes through a small hole in the case to connect to the 5-pin connection. The system board manual instructs you to use CMOS setup to enable "UART2 Use Infrared." When you do that, COM2 serial port is disabled because the transceiver is using the resources or that port. The transceiver drivers are then installed and used the same way as described above.

The UART Chip

Serial ports are controlled by a chip called the **UART chip (universal asynchronous receiver/transmitter chip)**. This chip controls all 9 pins of a serial port, establishes the communications protocol, and converts parallel data bits coming from the system bus into serial bits for transmission. It also converts incoming serial data bits it receives into the parallel form needed by the system bus. The first UART chip was the 8250, and the next version was called the 16450 chip. The 16550 version of the UART chip contains a FIFO buffer (first in, first out buffer) that solves the problem of lost data that sometimes occurs with the 16450 UART. Also, look for improved versions of the chip labeled 16550A, 16550AF, and 16550AFN, each improving on the one before it. Some computers don't actually have the physical chip on the board, but the UART logic is contained in another chip. However, in all cases, utility software can tell you what is present.

Many inexpensive I/O cards and some system boards that have on-board serial ports still use the 16450 UART, which can cause lost data and slow transmission. The 16550 UART requires a driver that makes use of the FIFO buffer. Windows 9x uses this faster driver, but if you are using DOS or Windows 3.x, check the driver being used and upgrade if necessary.

The UART 16550 driver is built into Windows 9x. To verify that you are using the driver, click **Start**, point to **Settings**, and then click **Control Panel**. Double-click **System** and choose the **Device Manager** tab. Click the **+** sign beside **Ports** to reveal the list of ports. Click a communications port, such as **COM1**, and then click **Properties**. Click the **Port Settings** tab. You see the Properties dialog box in Figure 9-10. Note that the drop-down list shows the bits per second, or baud rate, of the port, which is currently set at 115,200 bps. Don't expect the port rate to exceed this value unless you are using the 16550A UART chip with buffering. Click **Advanced** to see the Advanced Port Settings illustrated in Figure 9-11. Note that **Use FIFO buffers** is checked. The standard FIFO buffer for the 16550 is 16 bytes long, which is indicated by the high range for the buffer size. Newer UART chips exceed this buffer size, so you should expect an improved version of the Windows 98 serial port driver to follow shortly. In the meantime, you can use third-party UART drivers such as TurboCom/95 Communications Drivers that support port speeds up to 921,600 bps. See *www.turbocom.com*.

Figure 9-10   Properties of the COM1 serial port in Windows 9x

Figure 9-11   Windows 9x Advanced Port Settings for the COM1 serial port, indicating FIFO option

One example of a newer UART chip by Texas Instruments, the TL 16C754, has a 64-byte buffer. Another example by Lava Computer Manufacturing, Inc., called the LavaPort 16650, increases speed by (1) using a faster clock speed, (2) increasing the buffer size (64 bytes), and (3) improving flow control. Lava puts the chip on a serial port accelerator card capable of a port speed baud rate of 460,800 bps. The web sites of these two manufacturers are *www.lavalink.com* and *www.ti.com*.

Also, some UART chips are Plug and Play compliant. These UART chips provide an interface with Plug and Play ROM so that they are automatically configured at startup. Texas Instruments now offers Plug and Play-compliant UART chips.

9

If you are losing data when using an external modem, first determine the kind of UART chip the serial port is using. You might need to upgrade to the 16550 or 16650 chip. Internal modems have their own UART chip on the card, or other chips that simulate the UART interface. If the UART logic is integrated into other chips, they most likely cannot be changed.

For older PCs using DOS and Windows 3.x, determine what kind of UART chip you have by using MSD.EXE. From the main menu of MSD, choose the **COM port** option. MSD displays information about each serial or COM port, including the UART chip used. However, if you execute MSD while Windows is running, the information can be deceiving. For example, Figure 9-12 shows the results of the MSD report taken while Windows was not running. Figure 9-13 is an MSD report from the same computer while Windows was running. Compare the results. With Windows running, the COM1 serial port shows the UART chip as the older 8250 chip. In fact, the UART chip on this general-purpose I/O card is the 16550AF chip, which, when Windows is running, is correctly reported for COM2 because COM2 is in use; it is incorrectly reported for COM1 because COM1 is not in use. On this computer, a serial port mouse is using COM2. Because COM2 is in use, Windows correctly recognizes the UART chip, and MSD can pick up the correct information. The information from MSD without Windows is correct.

```
Microsoft Diagnostics version 2.00  7/05/97  9:35am  Page  1


------------------- COM Ports -------------------
                        COM1:    COM2:  COM3:  COM4:

                        -----    -----  -----  -----
  Port  Address         03F8H    02F8H   N/A    N/A
  Baud  Rate            1200     2400
  Parity                None     None
  Data  Bits            7        8
  Stop  Bits            1        1
  Carrier Detect  (CD)  No       No
  Ring Indicator  (RI)  No       No
  Data Set Ready  (DSR) No       No
  Clear To Send   (CTS) No       No
  UART  Chip Used       16550AF  16550AF
```

Figure 9-12   MSD COM port report from DOS prompt without Windows

Figure 9-13   MSD COM port report from DOS prompt with Windows 3.x running

Another interesting fact about this particular computer is that the documentation that came with the I/O card stated that the UART chip is a 16450 UART. Here's a case where the manufacturer updated the product but not the documentation that came with the product.

Resources Used by Serial Ports

Table 9-2 listed the I/O addresses for standard serial and parallel ports. You can view I/O addresses using the DOS or Windows MSD command or from Device Manager of Windows 9x.

In summary, serial ports are used for various input/output data transfers, including data transferred over modems, to mice, to printers, and to other computers. Serial ports follow the RS-232c industry standard for communication. Each port is assigned a unique IRQ and a unique I/O address. The UART chip controlling the port is partially responsible for the speed of the port.

Using Parallel Ports

A+CORE
2.1,
4.3

Parallel ports, commonly used by printers, transmit data in parallel, 8 bits at a time. If the data is transmitted in parallel over a very long cable, the integrity of the data is sometimes lost because bits may separate from the byte they belong to. Most parallel cables are only 6 feet long, though no established standards sets maximum cable length. However, avoid using a parallel cable longer than 15 feet to ensure data integrity. Hewlett-Packard recommends the cables be no longer than 10 feet.

Parallel ports were originally intended to be used only for printers. However, some parallel ports are now used for input devices. These bi-directional parallel ports are often used for fast transmission of data over short distances. One common use is to download and upload data from a PC to a laptop. Some external CD-ROM drives use a bi-directional parallel port to transmit and receive data. If you use an existing parallel port to install a peripheral device, installation is very simple. Just plug the device into the port and load the software. To accommodate a second parallel port, configure the port as LPT2. An example of this is described in the next section.

A+CORE
1.4

The uses of the pin connections for a 25-pin parallel port are listed in Table 9-5.

Table 9-5   25-pin parallel port pin connections

Pin	Input or Output from PC	Description
1	Output	Strobe
2	Output	Data bit 0
3	Output	Data bit 1
4	Output	Data bit 2
5	Output	Data bit 3
6	Output	Data bit 4
7	Output	Data bit 5
8	Output	Data bit 6
9	Output	Data bit 7
10	Input	Acknowledge
11	Input	Busy
12	Input	Out of paper
13	Input	Select
14	Output	Auto feed
15	Input	Printer error
16	Output	Initialize paper
17	Output	Select input
18	Input	Ground for bit 0
19	Input	Ground for bit 1
20	Input	Ground for bit 2
21	Input	Ground for bit 3
22	Input	Ground for bit 4
23	Input	Ground for bit 5
24	Input	Ground for bit 6
25	Input	Ground for bit 7

A+CORE
4.4,
2.1

Types of Parallel Ports

Parallel ports fall into three categories: standard, **enhanced parallel port** (**EPP**), and **extended capabilities port** (**ECP**). The standard parallel port (SPP) is sometimes called a normal parallel port or a Centronics port, named after the 36-pin Centronics connection used by printers (see Figure 9-14). A standard port only allows data to flow in one direction and is the slowest of the three types of parallel ports. EPP and ECP are both bi-directional. ECP was designed to increase speed over EPP by using a DMA channel; therefore, when using ECP mode you are using a DMA channel. Over the years both hardware and software manufacturers have implemented several parallel port designs, all attempting to increase speed and performance. To help establish industry standards, a committee was formed in the early

A+*CORE*
4.4,
1.4,
2.1

90s supported by the Institute of Electrical and Electronics Engineers (IEEE), which created the **IEEE 1284** standards for parallel ports. These standards require backward compatibility with previous parallel port technology. Both EPP and ECP are covered under the IEEE 1284 specifications.

DB 25-pin connection (PC end)

36-pin Centronics connection (printer end)

Figure 9-14   A parallel cable has a DB-25 connection at the PC end of the cable and a 36-pin Centronics connection at the printer end of the cable

Configuring Parallel Ports

When configuring a parallel port, if the port is on an I/O card, then look to the documentation for the card to know how to assign system resources to the port. If the parallel port is coming directly off the system board, then look to CMOS setup to configure the port (see Figure 9-8). Setup can have up to three different settings for parallel ports. For the BIOS in this figure, choices for parallel port mode are Normal, EPP, ECP, and EPP 2 ECP. If you select ECP or EPP + ECP, you must also make an ECP DMA selection. Choices are DMA Channel 1 or 3. If you are having problems with resource conflicts, try disabling ECP mode for the parallel port. EPP mode gives good results and does not tie up a DMA channel.

Examining a General-Purpose I/O Card

Because you occasionally see the older technology when servicing a PC, this section briefly discusses a general-purpose I/O card, shown in Figure 9-15. The card is designed to be used with a system board that does not have serial or parallel ports, or floppy drive or hard drive connections, although it can be used to add extra ports to a system board that already has some of these. The card has one floppy drive connection and an IDE adapter supplying one IDE hard drive connector (labeled the IDE HDD connector), which can accommodate two hard drives by means of a two-connection cable. Directly on the back of the card is one 9-pin male serial port and one 25-pin female bi-directional parallel port. Short cables connect to an adjacent bracket that contains a 15-pin female game port and a 25-pin male serial port (see Figure 9-16). The card also has an internal game port connector.

Figure 9-15 General-purpose I/O card

Figure 9-16 Installing a general-purpose I/O card

This card is not Plug and Play compliant. The card has four banks of jumpers which allow you to configure the card's ports. To know which jumper controls a particular setting, read the documentation for the card.

The card allows no choices for hard drive or floppy drive I/O port addresses because the values are established standards that never change. For serial ports, when you select COM1, COM2, COM3, or COM4 for the port, you are also selecting the I/O port address. You can, however, select the IRQ separately from the COM assignment.

To configure the parallel port, you choose the I/O port addresses rather than LPT1, LPT2, or LPT3. The parallel port is assigned by the BIOS according to the I/O port address. The parallel port with the highest I/O address (3BCh) is LPT1. The next automatically becomes LPT2, and the port with the lowest I/O address is LPT3. The default I/O address for this card is 278h (sometimes the default is 378h), which is LPT1 if the system has no other parallel ports. If the system board has another I/O card or a parallel port, be certain that its address is not 278h. Depending on the setting of the I/O address of the other parallel port, the system may configure this parallel port set to 278h as LPT1 or LPT2. Figure 9-16 shows the card inserted in an expansion slot with the cables connected to all four external ports.

9

Using USB Ports

A^{+CORE}
5.1,
4.3,
1.7

Using USB ports is easier than using parallel or serial ports because the USB controller together with support from the OS manages the USB port resources for you. Newer system boards have one or two USB ports. For older system boards, you can purchase a PCI expansion card to provide a USB port.

Recall from Chapter 2 that all the USB ports and USB devices connected to them use a single IRQ, I/O address, and DMA channel, which is similar to the way a SCSI bus works. See Figure 9-17. The OS must support the USB host controller. Windows 95 OSR 2.1 was the first Microsoft OS to support USB, although Windows 98 offers much improved USB support. Windows NT and Windows 95a do not support USB. The current version of the USB standard is version 1.1 which supports speeds up to 12 Mbps. An improved standard, USB 2.0, is expected soon and will support speeds up to 480 Mbps. USB transfers data in packets and can partly improve the speeds of serial and parallel ports because it uses higher quality cabling. A USB cable has four wires; two are used for data, one is ground, and one provides up to five volts of power to the device.

You don't need to manually assign system resources to a USB device, because the OS and the USB host controller automatically do that at startup. To install a USB device, you need:

- A system board or expansion card that provides a USB port and USB firmware
- An OS that supports USB
- A USB device
- A USB device driver

Windows 98 provides many USB device drivers. If you are installing a USB device, don't use a device driver from the manufacturer that claims to work only for Windows 95. Windows 98

A+CORE
5.1,
1.7,
1.3

made several improvements in USB support that you should take advantage of. Sometimes setup on a system board lets you disable USB support.

Figure 9-17 Only one IRQ, I/O address, and DMA channel are needed for a USB host controller to manage multiple devices

Follow these steps to install a USB device:

1. Using Device Manager, verify that the USB host controller driver is installed under Windows 9x. See Figure 9-18. Note in the figure the symbol for USB. If the controller is not installed, install it from the Control Panel by double-clicking the **Add New Hardware** icon. If you have a problem installing the controller, verify that support for USB is enabled in setup.

2. Plug in the USB device and install its device driver. For example, for a scanner, insert the CD that came with the scanner in the CD-ROM drive and enter **D:\Setup.exe** in the Run dialog box, where D is the name of the CD drive. After the drivers are installed, you should see the device listed in Device Manager. Verify that Windows sees the device with no conflicts and without errors.

3. Install the applications software to use the device. Most scanners come with some scaled-down version of software to scan and edit images. After you have installed the software, use it to scan an image.

A+*CORE*
  5.1,
  1.7

Figure 9-18   Using Device Manager, verify that the USB host controller is installed

Using IEEE 1394 Ports

A+*CORE*
  1.4,
  1.7
IEEE 1394 ports are sometimes found on newer high-end system boards and are expected to become standard ports on all new system boards—as commonplace as USB ports are now. These ports have two types of connectors: a 4-pin port that does not provide voltage to a device and a 6-pin port that does. See Figure 9-19. The two extra pins in the 6-pin port are used for voltage and ground. The cable for a 6-pin port is fatter than the 4-pin cable.

(device requires AC adapter)

4-pin Cable

(2 pins are used for voltage and ground)

6-pin Cable

Figure 9-19   Two types of IEEE 1394 cable connectors; the 6-pin cable provides voltage to the device from the PC

9

A+*CORE*
   1.7

The four wires used for data in a 1394 cable are two pairs of shielded twisted pair cable wrapped in a common cord. Shielding refers to how wires are enclosed in a protective covering to reduce interference, and twisted pair refers to the fact that two wires are twisted to reduce interference. Some network cabling is also shielded and uses twisted pair wires. In fact, IEEE 1394 uses a design similar to Ethernet, the most popular network design. Just as with Ethernet, data is broken into small packets before it is sent over 1394 cable. Each device on the IEEE 1394 network can communicate with any other device on the network without involving the computer's CPU.

IEEE 1394 uses **isochronous data transfer** meaning that data is transferred continuously without breaks. This works well when transferring real-time data such as that received by television transmission. Because of the real-time data transfer and the fact that data can be transferred from one device to another without involving the CPU, IEEE 1394 is an ideal medium for data transfers between consumer electronics products such as camcorders, VCRs, TVs and digital cameras.

Figure 9-20 shows an example of how this might work. A person can record a home movie using a digital camcorder and download the data through a digital VCR to a 1394-compliant hard drive. The 1394-compliant digital VCR can connect to and send data to the hard drive without involving the PC. The PC can later read the data off the hard drive and use it as input to video editing applications software. A user can edit the data and design a professional video presentation complete with captioning and special effects. Furthermore, if the digital camcorder is also 1394 compliant, it can download the data directly to the PC by way of a 1394 port on the PC. The PC can then save the data to a regular internal hard drive.

Digital Camcorder

Personal Computer   IEEE 1394
                         Hard Disk   Digital VCR

Figure 9-20   IEEE 1394 can be used as the interface technology to connect consumer audio/visual equipment to a PC

The current standard for IEEE 1394 is IEEE 1394.A, which supports speeds of 100, 200, or 400 Mbps, allows for cable lengths up to 4.5 meters, and is hot-pluggable. **Hot-pluggable** means that you can plug in a 1394 device without rebooting your PC and remove the device without receiving an error message. A new standard under development, IEEE 1394.B will support speeds up to 3.2 gbps (gigabits per second) and extend the maximum cable length to 100 meters.

A+CORE
1.7

Windows 98 and Windows 2000 support IEEE 1394. Windows 98 Second Edition supports storage devices, but IEEE 1394 printers and scanners are not supported. Windows 2000 supports all these devices. For Windows 98 Second Edition, you can download an update from the Microsoft web site (*windowsupdate.microsoft.com*). The update solves previous problems when devices are removed while the PC is still running.

To use a 1394 port, follow these steps:

1. Verify that Windows 98 recognizes that an IEEE 1394 controller is present on the system board. Just as with the USB controller, using Device Manager, look for the 1394 Bus Controller listed as an installed device. Click the **+** sign beside the controller in Device Manager to see the specific brand of 1394 controller that the board contains. If the controller is not installed or is not working, then reinstall the driver. In the Control Panel, double-click the **Add New Hardware** icon. If you have problems installing the driver, verify that 1394 support is enabled in setup.

2. Plug the device into the 1394 port. Install the device drivers for the 1394-compliant device. For example, for a Sony camcorder, insert the CD that contains supporting software in the CD-ROM drive and execute **D:\Setup.exe** from the Run dialog box. When the device is plugged in and the drivers are installed, you should see the device listed in Device Manager under Sound, video and game controllers. If you don't see the device listed, turn the camcorder off and back on.

3. Install the applications software to use the device. A 1394-compliant camcorder is likely to come bundled with video editing software. Run the software to use the device.

For system boards that don't support IEEE 1394, you can install an IEEE 1394 host adapter to provide the support. For example, FireBoard by Unibrain, Inc. uses a PCI expansion slot and follows the IEEE 1394.A standard. See *www.unibrain.com*.

Using PCI Expansion Slots

A+CORE
4.3,
4.4

Recall from Chapter 3 that the PCI bus is a local bus that runs in sync with the CPU. The PCI slots are often white (see Figure 1-17 in Chapter 1), which easily distinguish them from the black ISA slots on the board. Because the PCI bus is faster than the ISA bus, PCI slots are often used for fast I/O devices such as a network card or SCSI host adapter. The PCI bus master, which is part of the system board chip set, manages the PCI bus and the expansion slots. The PCI bus master assigns IRQ and I/O addresses to PCI expansion cards, which is why you don't see jumpers or DIP switches on these cards. To be more accurate, the PCI bus assigns resources to a PCI slot; move the card to a different slot to assign new set of resources to it.

When installing a PCI card, most likely you do not need to configure the IRQ or I/O address for the card, because the startup BIOS and PCI bus controller do this for you.

A+*CORE*
4.3,
4.4

The PCI bus uses an interim interrupt between the PCI card and the IRQ line to the CPU. There are four of these interrupts, which PCI documentation calls A, B, C, and D. One interrupt is assigned to each PCI expansion slot. The PCI bus master then maps each of these internal PCI bus interrupts to IRQs, using IRQs that are available after legacy ISA bus devices have claimed their IRQs. The startup BIOS records which IRQs have been used by ISA devices and then assigns the unused ones to the PCI bus master during the boot process. In order for this to work, the system BIOS must be PCI-compliant. (Look for PCI on the BIOS chip; see Figure 1-24 of Chapter 1.)

Use Device Manager to see which IRQ has been assigned to a PCI device. For example, for Windows 95, Release 1, Figure 9-21 displays the resources assigned to a PCI video card. Notice that the IRQ assigned to the card is IRQ 9.

Figure 9-21   Use Device Manager to determine what IRQ has been assigned to a
PCI device

Sometimes BIOS gives the PCI bus master an IRQ that a legacy ISA device needs, which can prevent either device from working. In CMOS setup, you can specify which IRQ to assign to a PCI slot, or you can tell setup that a particular IRQ is reserved for a legacy device, and thereby prevent the PCI bus from using it. See Figure 9-22.

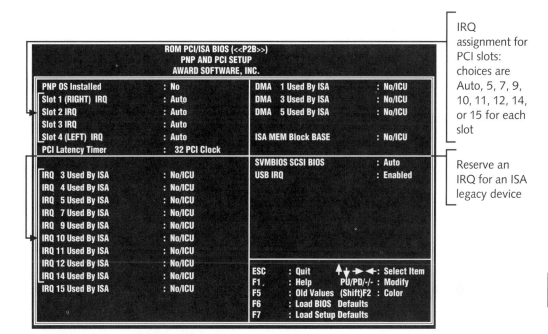

IRQ assignment for PCI slots: choices are Auto, 5, 7, 9, 10, 11, 12, 14, or 15 for each slot

Reserve an IRQ for an ISA legacy device

Figure 9-22   CMOS setup screen for Plug and Play and PCI options

PCI Bus IRQ Steering

A+ OS
3.2
CORE
4.4

PCI 2.1 specifications support **PCI bus IRQ steering**, a feature making it possible for PCI devices to share an IRQ, which can help solve the problem of not having enough IRQs to support all devices in a system. In order for the system to use the feature, both the system board BIOS and Windows must support it. During booting, startup BIOS records the IRQs used by ISA devices and the PCI bus in a table that Windows can read later when reassigning IRQs. Windows 95, release 2, (OSR2) and Windows 98 support PCI bus IRQ steering.

Sometimes an IRQ conflict can happen when startup BIOS is not aware that a legacy (not Plug and Play) ISA device is using a certain IRQ and assigns that IRQ to the PCI bus, which assigns it to a PCI device. With PCI bus IRQ steering, Windows can sometimes resolve the problem by reassigning another IRQ to the PCI bus, allowing the legacy device to be the sole owner of its IRQ.

In order to make this happen, Windows must detect an unused IRQ that it can use for the substitution. It then puts a holder on the IRQ, meaning that it reserves this IRQ for PCI only. The IRQ is no longer available for an ISA device as long as Windows has the holder on it. See Figure 9-23 for one example.

PCI bus IRQ steering can cause a particular problem. If Windows puts a holder on an IRQ, it might cause the PCI device using it to have problems. Also, if two PCI devices are having conflicts, sometimes PCI bus IRQ steering can mask the problem, making it difficult to diagnose. Finally, PCI bus IRQ steering can erroneously put a hold on an IRQ that is being used by an ISA device. Figure 9-24 shows an example of this, where IRQ 10 is needed by an Adaptec SCSI host adapter, but PCI steering has put a hold on the IRQ. In this case, you can

A+ OS 3.2 either claim IRQ 10 for the SCSI host adapter in CMOS setup (refer back to Figure 9-22) or you can disable PCI bus IRQ steering.

Figure 9-23   PCI bus IRQ steering has placed a holder on IRQ 10, making it unavailable to ISA devices

Figure 9-24   A conflict with IRQ 10 is caused by PCI steering putting a hold on the IRQ

> Sometimes problems with resource conflicts can be solved by enabling PCI bus IRQ steering, and sometimes they can be resolved by disabling the feature!

To either enable or disable PCI bus IRQ steering, use Device Manager. Do the following:

1. Click **Start**, **Settings**, **Control Panel**. Double-click the **System** icon. Select the **Device Manager** tab.

2. Select **View device by connection**. Select **PCI bus** and click **Properties**. The PCI bus Properties dialog box is displayed.

3. Select the **IRQ Steering** tab, as shown in Figure 9-25 for Windows 98.

4. To enable or disable PCI bus IRQ steering, use the check box beside **Use IRQ Steering**.

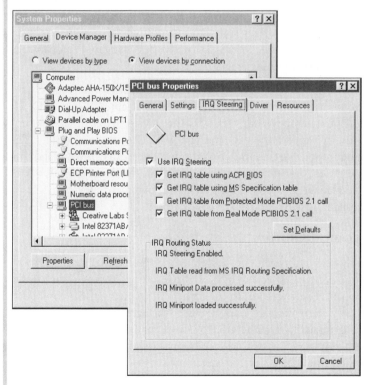

Figure 9-25   To enable or disable PCI bus IRQ steering, use the Properties box of the PCI bus

Using ISA Expansion Slots

Using legacy ISA bus devices is a little more difficult than using either USB or PCI, because the configuration is not as automated. The ISA bus itself does not manage the system resources, as do the USB and PCI bus masters. It is up to the ISA device to request system resources at startup. If the ISA device does not support Windows 9x Plug and Play, then you select the I/O address, DMA channel, and IRQ by setting jumpers or DIP switches on the card. If the ISA device is Plug and Play compliant, then at startup Windows 9x Plug and Play allocates the required resources to the device. To know if a device is Plug and Play compliant, look for "Ready for Windows 95" or "Ready for Windows 98" on the box, or read the documentation. You will learn more about this in Chapter 12.

When Device Installations Create Problems

A+CORE
2.1

Suppose you install a new sound card and it does not work. If you also discover that your network card has stopped communicating, it is likely the two devices have a resource conflict. Other problems also can prevent these devices from working, such as a poorly seated circuit card or a loose cable. Check all connections carefully before proceeding. You might also remove the sound card, and check that your network is working. You can then conclude that you most probably have a conflict.

The place to begin to diagnose a conflict is with the documentation. Read everything carefully, looking for what has been discussed earlier in this chapter. What IRQ, I/O address, DMA channel, or upper memory addresses does the device being installed use? What does your network card use? Compare the two, and you will discover your conflict. The fix might be easy, or it might be impossible if neither board offers alternatives. Fortunately, most devices today offer alternate choices for these settings. Again, read the documentation for directions. Plug and Play devices make this process much easier, but many devices today are still not Plug and Play compliant.

Resolving Resource Conflicts

When adding new devices to a system, probably the one most difficult problem you encounter is resolving a resource conflict, especially if the PC has several devices, some of which are not Plug and Play compliant. The two tools to use to help in resolving these conflicts are MSD in a DOS and Windows 3.x environment, and Device Manager in Windows 9x. However, neither of these tools is infallible because they both depend on what the OS knows about resources being used—and sometimes a device does not tell the OS what it's using. Follow this general approach when installing a new device:

1. Know the system resources already in use (see the documentation and/or use MSD or Device Manager).

2. Know what resources the new device will need (see the documentation).

3. Install the device using resources that are not already used by your system.

4. If you do have a conflict, use MSD, Device Manager, CMOS setup, and documentation for the system board and devices to first identify and then resolve the conflict.

A+CORE
2.1

To find out what resources are presently used by your system, for DOS and Windows 3.1, use the MSD diagnostics software. Figure 9-26 shows the results of displaying the IRQ settings. However, in the report in Figure 9-26, IRQs 10, 11, and 12 all have Reserved status. IRQ 11 and 12 are available, but on this computer, IRQ 10 is being used by a SCSI host adapter. MSD does not always tell all.

Figure 9-26 MSD report of IRQ settings

To know the full story, also depend on your knowledge of the system and the records you have kept in the notebook dedicated to this PC.

To find out what resources your system is using, for Windows 9x, follow the steps below.

1. Click **Start**, point to **Settings**, click **Control Panel**, **System**, and then **Device Manager**. Click **Computer** and then **Properties**. Select the **View Resources** tab. The window in Figure 9-23 is displayed, showing the IRQs currently in use.

2. Select **Input/output (I/O)** to display a list of I/O addresses currently in use (see Figure 9-27). Note that the keyboard is currently assigned the I/O address of 60h.

3. Select **Memory** to display the current upper memory addresses in use by devices. The A, B, and C range of upper memory addresses are normally reserved for video. The F range is reserved for system BIOS. Not all the memory addresses actually in use are listed on this screen, only those that are directly requested by a working hardware device.

Once you have found the conflicting resource, try these things to resolve the conflict:

- If the device is a legacy ISA device, physically set the device's jumpers or DIP switches to use a different resource.

- If a legacy device can only use one IRQ, then use CMOS setup to reserve that IRQ for the device.

- If your PC supports PCI bus IRQ steering, enable the feature. That alone might solve the problem.

- Using PCI bus IRQ steering, tell Windows 98 to use a different IRQ for a PCI device. To do that, use the Properties box for the device in Device Manager.

9

A+CORE
2.1

- Use CMOS setup to assign a specific IRQ to a PCI device.

- Move the PCI device to a different slot, which will cause the PCI bus to assign a different resource to the device.

- Disable PCI bus IRQ steering.

Figure 9-27 Use Device Manager to see I/O addresses currently in use

SCSI DEVICES

A+CORE
4.3,
1.6

The SCSI bus was first introduced in Chapters 6 and 7 as it pertained to hard drives. This section looks at SCSI as a bus that can support other devices. Installing a SCSI device is normally accomplished in one of two ways:

- Install the SCSI device using a simplified version of a SCSI host adapter designed to accommodate one or two devices. These adapters often come bundled in the SCSI device package.

- Install the SCSI device on an existing or new host adapter designed to handle several devices.

Matching the Host Adapter to the SCSI Devices It Supports

When selecting a SCSI host adapter or determining if an existing host adapter will work with a new SCSI device, consider the issues described below.

A+CORE
4.3,
1.6

SCSI standard   In Chapter 6, you saw that there are several SCSI standards, including SCSI-1, SCSI-2, SCSI-3, Fast SCSI, Wide Ultra SCSI, and Ultra 160 SCSI. SCSI-1, SCSI-2, and Fast SCSI use a 50-pin connection. All wide SCSIs use a 68-pin connection. Your device should match the host adapter according to the number of pins on the connections. Also, your device and host adapter should have compatible standards.

The host adapter must be made for the correct expansion slot   The host adapter must fit the expansion slot you plan to use. SCSI host adapters are made for 8-bit ISA, 16-bit ISA, 16-bit MCA, 32-bit MCA, 32-bit EISA, VL-Bus, and PCI buses. For a Pentium system board, you probably can choose either a 16-bit ISA host adapter or a PCI host adapter. Choose the 32-bit PCI bus for faster data transfer rate, instead of the 16-bit ISA bus.

Bus mastering   Choose a host adapter that uses bus mastering, discussed in Chapter 3, if your system bus supports it. For PCI buses that do support bus mastering, you have the added advantage that, when bus mastering is used, the SCSI host adapter does not require a DMA channel.

A host adapter that supports several SCSI standards   A host adapter that supports both 50-pin connections, 68-pin connections, and several standards allows you to choose a variety of devices without having to purchase a second host adapter.

Device driver standard   Select a host adapter that supports one of the two leading driver standards for SCSI, either the ASPI or the CAM standard. ASPI, a standard developed by Adaptec, a leading SCSI manufacturer, is probably the better known of the two. ASPI (Advanced SCSI Programming Interface) or CAM (Common Access Method) describes the standard for the way the host adapter communicates with the SCSI device driver. The ASPI or CAM standard has nothing to do with the SCSI-1, SCSI-2, or SCSI-3 types, but rather with the way the drivers are written. Be sure that the host adapter and all the device drivers meet the same standard. As shown in Figure 9-28, the ASPI or CAM standard also affects the way the host adapter relates to the OS. For Windows 9x, the SCSI driver is built-in, but many host adapters provide their own host adapter drivers to be used by Windows 9x, and by DOS with Windows 3.x. The manufacturer of the host adapter usually provides the SCSI driver on floppy disk or CD-ROM.

Single-ended and differential SCSI   Select a host adapter that matches the devices according to electronic signaling method. The two choices are single-ended SCSI devices and differential SCSI devices. Single-ended devices use single-ended cables and differential devices use differential cables. You cannot mix the two types of cables in the same system. Of the two, differential cables are more dependable. See Table 6-2 of Chapter 6 for details about cable length and maximum number of devices. Don't mix the two types of devices on the same SCSI system or use a host adapter that does not match. You can damage the devices if you do.

9

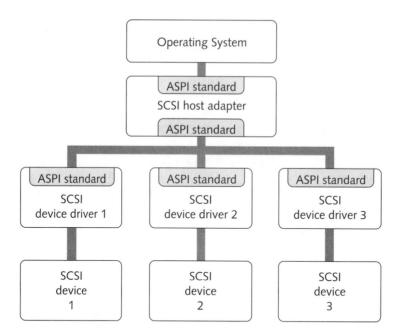

Figure 9-28   A SCSI device driver standard affects the interaction of the host adapter with the device drivers and the OS

SCAM-compliant SCAM (SCSI Configuration AutoMatically or SCSI Configuration AutoMagically, depending on the literature you're reading) is a method by which SCSI devices and the host adapter can be Plug and Play compliant. SCAM-compliant host adapters and devices can assign SCSI IDs dynamically at startup. Most SCSI devices currently in use are not SCAM compliant, and you will need to set the unique ID on the device, using jumpers, rotary dials, or other methods. Newer SCSI host adapters use software that comes with the card to configure the SCSI BIOS. With the software, you can set the SCSI IDs, SCSI parity checking, termination, and system resources used by the card.

There are two levels of SCAM. Level 1 requires that the devices, but not the host adapter, be assigned an ID at startup by software. Level 2 requires that the host adapter, as well as the devices, be assigned an ID at startup by software. SCSI-2 devices must be SCAM compliant to carry the logo "Designed for Windows 95" or "Designed for Windows 98."

A Sample Host Adapter for a Single Device

A+CORE 1.6   In the first example below, you look at installing a typical host adapter designed to be used by a single external device and one or more internal devices. In this case, you are installing the Adaptec 1505 ISA-to-SCSI host adapter that is Plug and Play compliant. It has one external 25-pin SCSI connection and one internal 50-pin connection and is shown in Figure 9-29. The card comes with software to control its BIOS that is run from a bootable floppy disk included with the card. A single jumper on the card can be used to control the I/O addresses assigned to the card if system BIOS is not Plug and Play compliant.

A+CORE
1.6

The card supports only one external device, hence the 25-pin connection; it uses only 25 of the 50 pins of the SCSI cable. The card comes with one 50-pin internal cable that has connections for the host adapter and two devices. The package also includes a 25-pin external cable for external devices.

Termination is achieved by three sets of sockets on the card that must be filled by three terminating resistors. One resistor is removed from a socket and is shown beneath the card. If you are installing both internal and external devices, remove all three resistors from the sockets and store them in a safe place. If you are only installing an external device or an internal device, but not both, then the host adapter is at the end of the SCSI chain and the three resistors should be in place.

J3 jumper used to control I/O addresses for a non Plug-and-Play system

50-pin internal connection for 1 or 2 internal devices

25-pin SCSI connection for single external device

3 sets of terminating resistors with one socket open

Terminating resistor

9

Figure 9-29   SCSI host adapter for a single external and multiple internal devices

A+CORE
1.6

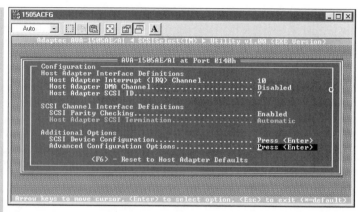

Figure 9-30   Setup software included with a SCSI host adapter is used to change SCSI BIOS settings on the card

For a Plug and Play system using Windows 98, follow these general steps to install this host adapter:

- Install the card in an ISA expansion slot.

- In most cases, the default settings for the host adapter are the correct ones, but you can change or verify these settings using the setup program on floppy disk. To use the setup program, boot the PC from the floppy disk included with the card. The disk boots the system (using DOS) and automatically executes the SCSI setup program. The two options on the opening menu are SCSI Disk Utilities (for installing a SCSI hard drive) and Configure the Host Adapter. Select **Configure the Host Adapter.** You see the host adapter configuration screen. See Figure 9-30.

- Verify the settings. Under the Advanced Configuration Options in Figure 9-30, you see two settings: enable or disable Plug and Play, and enable or disable SCAM support. Both are normally set to enable. Note in Figure 9-30 that the SCSI ID for the host adapter is 7 and that parity checking is enabled. After verifying settings, exit the setup program, remove the floppy disk, and reboot.

- When Windows 9x loads, it senses a new hardware device and automatically launches the Add New Hardware Wizard. Because Windows supports the host adapter, it loads the device drivers automatically and installs the host adapter.

To verify that the host adapter is correctly installed, click **Start**, **Settings**, **Control Panel**, and double-click **System**. Select **Device Manager**. Double-click **SCSI controllers**. The Adaptec host adapter should be displayed, as shown in Figure 9-31. Notice in the figure the broken diamond icon that stands for SCSI. Select the host adapter and click **Properties** to display the host adapter Properties dialog box also shown in Figure 9-31. Click the **Resources** tab to note the resources assigned the card by Plug and Play.

A+CORE
1.6

Figure 9-31   Device Manager displays the newly installed host adapter

9

After you have installed the host adapter, you are ready to install the external SCSI device. For example, if the device is a SCSI scanner, follow these directions:

1. Install the software to run the scanner, which will include the scanner driver.

2. Plug the SCSI cable into the host adapter port.

3. Plug the other end of the cable into the scanner.

4. Set the SCSI ID on the scanner.

5. Connect the scanner's power cord to a wall outlet, and turn the scanner on.

6. Restart your PC and test the scanner.

KEYBOARDS

In the rest of the chapter, we look at the essential I/O devices for a PC: the keyboard, a pointing device, and video display.

Keyboards have either a traditional straight design or a newer ergonomic design, as shown in Figure 9-32. The word "ergonomic" means designed for safe and comfortable interaction between human beings and machines. The ergonomically safer keyboard is designed to keep your wrists high and straight. Some users find it comfortable, and others do not. Figure 9-33 demonstrates the correct position of hands and arms at the keyboard. Keyboards also differ in the feel of the keys as you type. Some people prefer more resistance than others, and some like more sound as the keys make contact. A keyboard might have a raised bar or circle on the F and J keys to help your fingers find the home keys as you type. Another feature is the depth of the ledge at the top of the keyboard that holds pencils, etc. Some keyboards have a mouse port on the back of the keyboard, and specialized keyboards have trackballs or magnetic scanners for scanning credit cards in retail stores.

Figure 9-32   An ergonomic keyboard

Figure 9-33   Keep wrists level, straight, and supported while at the keyboard

Computer keyboards have been criticized by users who work with them for hours at a time because they can cause a type of repetitive stress injury (RSI) known as carpal tunnel syndrome (CTS). CTS is caused by keeping the wrists in an unnatural position and having to execute the same motions (such as pressing keys on a keyboard) over prolonged periods.

You can help prevent carpal tunnel syndrome by keeping your elbows at the same level as the keyboard and keeping your wrists straight and higher than your fingers. I've found that a keyboard drawer that slides out from under a desk surface is much more comfortable, because the keyboard is low enough for me to keep a correct position. If I'm working at a desk with no keyboard drawer, I sometimes type with the keyboard in my lap to relieve the pressure on my arms and shoulders.

Keyboard manufacturers use one of two common technologies in the way the keys make contact: foil contact or metal contact. With a foil-contact keyboard, when you press a key, two layers of foil make contact and close a circuit. A small spring just under the keycap raises the key again after it is released.

Metal-contact keyboards are more expensive and heavier, and generally provide a different touch to the fingers than foil keyboards. Made by IBM and AT&T, as well as other companies, the metal-contact keyboards add an extra feel of quality that is noticeable to most users, giving the keystroke a clear, definitive contact. When a key is pressed, two metal plates make contact, and a spring is again used to raise the key when it is released.

Keyboard Connectors

A+CORE
1.4

Keyboards connect to a PC by one of three methods: a PS/2 connector (sometimes called a mini-DIN), a DIN connector, or, more recently, a USB port. The DIN connector (DIN is an acronym of the German words meaning German industry standard) is round and has five pins. The smaller round PS/2 connector has six pins. See Figure 9-34. Table 9-6 shows the pinouts (position and meaning of each pin) for both connector types. If the keyboard you are using has a different connector than the keyboard port of your computer, use a keyboard connector adapter, like the one shown in Figure 9-35, to convert DIN to PS/2 or PS/2 to DIN. Also, some keyboards are cordless, using radio transmission to communicate with a sensor connected to the keyboard port. For example, a cordless keyboard made by Logitech uses a sensor that plugs into a normal keyboard port. (See *www.logitech.com*.)

Table 9-6   Pinouts for keyboard connectors

Description	6-Pin Connector (PS/2)	5-Pin Connector (DIN)
Keyboard data	1	2
Not used	2	3
Ground	3	4
Current (+5 volts)	4	5
Keyboard clock	5	1
Not used	6	–

9

$A^{+CORE}_{1.4}$

Figure 9-34 Two common keyboard connectors are a PS/2 connector and a DIN connector

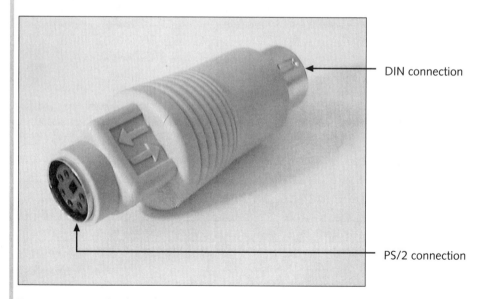

Figure 9-35 A keyboard adapter

Regardless of the type of connection or the construction of the keyboard, when a key is pressed, the same logical progression occurs. First, a code is produced called the **make code**. Releasing the key produces the **break code**. A chip in the keyboard processes these codes to produce a scan code that is sent to the CPU. The chip determines the location of the key pressed and sends that location together with the IRQ to the CPU. The scan code is temporarily stored in memory. The keyboard driver, which is most often stored in the system

BIOS, converts the scan code to the character assigned to that code, according to the keyboard driver selected. The different drivers available to interpret scan codes vary by language.

POINTING DEVICES

A device that allows you to move a pointer on the screen and perform tasks such as executing (clicking) a command button in applications software is called a pointing device. Common pointing devices are the mouse, the trackball, and touch pads (see Figure 9-36).

Figure 9-36   The most common pointing devices: a mouse, a trackball, and a touchpad

The two mouse technologies include a wheel mouse and an optical mouse. Inside a wheel mouse is a ball that moves freely as you drag the mouse on a surface. As shown in Figure 9-37, two or more rollers on the sides of the ball housing turn as the ball rolls against them. Each roller turns a wheel. The turning of the wheel is sensed by a small light beam as the wheel "chops" the light beam when it turns. The chops in the light beams are interpreted as mouse movement and are sent to the CPU. One of two rollers tracks the x-axis (horizontal) movement of the mouse, and a second roller tracks the y-axis (vertical) movement.

An optical mouse replaces the ball in a standard mouse with a microchip, miniature red light, and camera. The light illuminates the work surface, the camera takes 1500 snapshots every second, and the microchip reports the tiniest changes to the PC. An optical mouse works on most surfaces and doesn't require a mouse pad. The bottom of an optical mouse has a tiny hole for the camera rather than a ball and the light glows as you work. An example of an optical mouse is Intelli-Eye by Microsoft.

A mouse can have two or three buttons. Software must be programmed to use these buttons. Almost all applications use the left button. Windows 9x has made great use of the right button. The center button has recently been converted into a scroll wheel that you can use to move through large documents on screen.

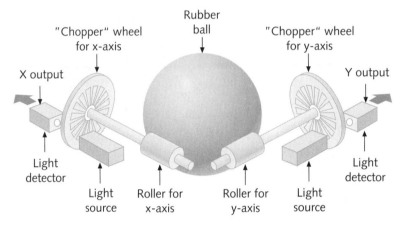

Figure 9-37 How a wheel mouse works

A+CORE
1.2

A mouse can connect to the computer by several methods:

- By using the serial port (the mouse is then called a **serial mouse**)

- By using a dedicated round mouse port coming directly from the system board (**system-board mouse** or **PS/2-compatible mouse**)

- By using a mouse bus card that provides the same round mouse port (**bus mouse**) as discussed above

- By using the USB port

- By using a Y-connection with the keyboard so that both the keyboard and the mouse can share the same port

- By using a cordless technology whereby the mouse sends signals to a sensor on the PC

Except for the cordless mouse, all of the above produce the same results (that is, the mouse port type is "transparent to the user"). Therefore, the advantages and disadvantages of each connection type are based mainly on the resources they require. The system-board mouse is the first choice for most users because the port on the system board does not take up any resources that other devices might need. If you are buying a new mouse that you plan to plug into the system-board port, don't buy a bus mouse unless the system-board documentation states that you can use a bus mouse. The system-board port and the bus port are identical, but a bus mouse might not work on the system-board port.

A+CORE
 1.2
If you have a system-board port, use it. If it becomes damaged, you can switch to a serial port or bus port. The system-board mouse port will most likely use IRQ 12. If you are not using a mouse on this port, the system board might release IRQ 12 so that other devices can use it. Check the documentation for your system board to determine how the unused IRQ is managed.

The serial mouse requires a serial port and an IRQ for that port. Most people prefer a bus mouse over a serial port mouse because they can assign the serial ports to other peripheral devices. A bus mouse can use a bus card if the system board does not have a mouse port.

Cleaning the Mouse

A+CORE
 2.1,
 3.1
The rollers inside the wheel mouse housing collect dirt and dust and occasionally need cleaning. Remove the cover to the mouse ball from the bottom of the mouse. The cover usually comes off with a simple press and shift or turn motion. Clean the rollers with a cotton swab dipped in a very small amount of liquid soap.

Other Pointing Devices

Another pointing device is a trackball, which is really an upside-down wheel mouse. You move the ball on top to turn rollers that turn a wheel sensed by a light beam. Touch pads allow you to duplicate the mouse function, moving the pointer by applying light pressure with one finger somewhere on a pad that senses the x, y movement. Some touch pads let you double-click by tapping their surface. Buttons on the touch pad serve the same function as mouse buttons. Use touch pads or trackballs where surface space is limited, because they remain stationary when you use them. Touch pads are popular on notebook computers.

9

COMPUTER VIDEO

The primary output device of a computer is the monitor. The two necessary components for video output are the video controller and the monitor itself.

Monitors

A+CORE
 1.1
The common types of monitors today are rated by screen size, resolution, refresh rate, and interlace features. Many older VGA (Video Graphics Adapter) monitors are still in use, but most sold today meet the standards for Super VGA. Monitors use either the older CRT (cathode-ray tube) technology used in television sets or the new LCD (liquid crystal display) technology used in notebook PCs and also available for desktop use. These LCD monitors for desktops are called **flat panel monitors**.

How a CRT Monitor Works

Most monitors use CRT technology, in which the filaments at the back of the cathode tube shoot a beam of electrons to the screen at the front of the tube, as illustrated in Figure 9-38. Plates on the top, bottom, and sides of the tube control the direction of the beam. The beam

A+CORE
1.1

is directed by these plates to start at the top of the screen, move from left to right to make one line, and then move down to the next line, again moving from left to right. As the beam moves vertically down the screen, it builds the displayed image. By turning the beam on and off and selecting the correct combination of colors, the grid in front of the filaments controls what goes on the screen when the beam hits that portion of the line or a single dot on the screen. Special phosphors placed on the back of the monitor screen light up when hit and produce colors. The grid controls which one of three electron guns is fired, each gun targeting a different color (red, green, or blue) positioned on the back of the screen.

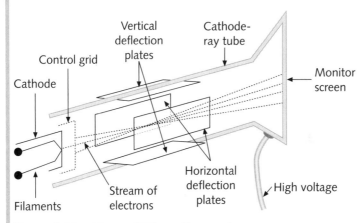

Figure 9-38   How a CRT monitor works

Choosing the Right Monitor

How a monitor works and what features are available on monitors are summarized in Table 9-7 and discussed next.

Table 9-7   Some features of a monitor

Monitor Characteristic	Description
Screen size	Diagonal length of the screen surface
Refresh rate	The number of times an electronic beam fills a video screen with lines from top to bottom in one second
Interlaced	The electronic beam draws every other line with each pass, which lessens the overall effect of a lower refresh rate.
Dot pitch	The distance between adjacent dots on the screen
Resolution	The number of spots, or pixels, on a screen that can be addressed by software
Multiscan	Monitors that offer a variety of refresh rates so they can support several video cards
Green monitor	A monitor that saves electricity and supports the EPA Energy Star program

A+CORE 1.1 Screen Size

The screen size of a monitor is the one feature that most affects price. Common sizes of monitor screens are 14-inch, 15-inch, 17-inch, and 21-inch. The 15-inch monitor is the most popular, and the small 14-inch monitor is losing popularity.

When matching a monitor to a video card, a good rule of thumb is to match a low-end video card to a small, 14-inch monitor, a midrange video card to a 15-inch monitor, and a high-end video card to a 17-inch or larger monitor to get the best performance from both devices. However, you can compare the different features of the video card to those of the monitor, such as the resolutions supported, the refresh rate, and the bandwidth. **Bandwidth** is the difference between the highest and lowest frequencies that an analog communications device such as a video cable can carry.

Macintosh computers can use special monitors designed for page layouts on legal-sized paper. The larger the screen size, the more expensive the monitor. The monitor I'm now using is advertised as having a 17-inch screen. The actual dimensions of the lighted screen are 9½ inches by 11½ inches. The diagonal measurement of the lighted area is 15 inches, and the diagonal measurement of the screen surface is 17 inches.

Refresh Rate

The refresh rate, or vertical scan rate, is the number of times in one second an electronic beam can fill the screen with lines from top to bottom. Refresh rates differ among monitors. The Video Electronics Standards Association (VESA) has set a minimum refresh rate standard of 70 Hz, or 70 complete vertical refreshes per second, as one requirement of Super VGA monitors. Slow refresh rates make the image appear to flicker while faster refresh rates make the image appear solid and stable.

Interlaced or Noninterlaced

Interlaced monitors draw a screen by making two passes. On the first pass, the electronic beam strikes only the even lines, and on the second pass the beam strikes only the odd lines. The result is that a monitor can have a slow refresh rate with a less noticeable overall effect than there would be if the beam hit all lines for each pass. Interlaced monitors generally have slightly more flicker than **noninterlaced** monitors, which always draw the entire screen on each pass. Buy a noninterlaced monitor if you plan to spend long hours staring at the monitor. Your eyes will benefit.

Dot Pitch

The **dot pitch** is the distance between the spots, or dots on the screen that the electronic beam hits. Remember that three beams build the screen, one for each of three colors (red, green, and blue). Each composite location on the screen is really made up of three dots and is called a triad. The distance between a color dot in one triad and the same color dot in the next triad is the dot pitch. The smaller the pitch, the sharper the image. A dot pitch of .28 mm or .25 mm gives the best results and costs more, although less expensive monitors can have a dot pitch of .35 mm or .38 mm. These less expensive monitors with dot pitches of .35 mm or .38 mm can still create a fuzzy image even with the best video cards.

Resolution

Resolution is a measure of how many spots on the screen are addressable by software. Each addressable location is called a **pixel** (for picture element) which is composed of several triads. Because resolution depends on software, the resolution must be supported by the video controller card, and the software you are using must make use of the resolution capabilities of the monitor. The standard for most software packages is 800 by 600 pixels, although many monitors offer a resolution of 1024 by 768 pixels or higher. The resolution is set in Windows from the Control Panel and requires a driver specific for that resolution. Higher resolution usually requires more video RAM.

Multiscan Monitor

Multiscan monitors offer a variety of vertical and horizontal refresh rates so they can support a variety of video cards. They cost more but are much more versatile than other monitors.

Green Monitor

A "green" monitor is a monitor that saves electricity, thus making its contribution to conserving natural resources. A green monitor meets the requirements of the EPA Energy Star program and uses 100 to 150 watts of electricity. When the screen saver is on, the monitor should use no more than 30 watts of electricity.

Monitors and ELF Emissions

There is some debate about the danger of monitors giving off ELF (extremely low frequency) emissions of magnetic fields. Standards to control ELF emissions are Sweden's MPR II standard and the TCO '95 standards. The TCO '95 standards also include guidelines for energy consumption, screen flicker, and luminance. Most monitors manufactured today comply with the MPR II standard, and very few comply with the more stringent TCO '95 standards.

Flat Panel Monitors

Increasing in popularity, though their cost is still three times that of comparable CRT monitors, are flat panel monitors, sometimes called flat panel display, that use LCD screens. See Figure 9-39. Flat panel monitors take up much less desk space than CRT monitors, are lighter, require less electricity to operate, and provide a clearer, more precise image. An LCD panel produces an image using a liquid crystal material made of large, easily polarized molecules. Figure 9-40 shows the layers of the LCD panel that together create the image. At the center of the layers is the liquid crystal material. Next to it is the layer responsible for providing the color to the image. These two layers are sandwiched between two grids of electrodes. One grid of electrodes is aligned in columns, and the other electrodes are aligned in rows. The two layers of electrodes make up the electrode matrix. Each intersection of a row electrode and a

A+CORE
1.1

column electrode forms one pixel on the LCD panel. Software can manipulate each pixel by activating the electrodes that form it. The image is formed by scanning the column and row electrodes, much as the electronic beam scans a CRT monitor screen.

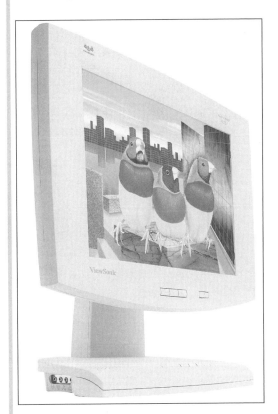

Figure 9-39 Flat panel display monitors use an LCD panel

The polarizer layers outside the glass layers in Figure 9-40 are responsible for preventing light from passing through the pixels when the electrodes are not activated. When the electrodes are activated, light on the back side of the LCD panel can pass through one pixel on the screen, picking up color from the color layer as it passes through.

There are two kinds of LCD panels on the market today: active-matrix and dual-scan passive matrix displays. A dual-scan display is less expensive than an active-matrix display and does not provide as high-quality an image. With dual-scan display, two columns of electrodes are activated at the same time. With active-matrix display, a transistor that amplifies the signal is placed at the intersection of each electrode in the grid, which further enhances the pixel quality.

A+CORE
1.1

Polarizer   Glass   Column electrodes

Color layer

Backlighting

Liquid crystal layer
(this layer blocks
or allows light to
pass for each pixel)

Row electrodes

Glass

Polarizer

Image is formed
on screen

A pixel is formed by the
intersection of the row and
column electrodes

Figure 9-40   Layers of an LCD panel

Flat panel monitors are built to receive either an analog signal or a digital signal from the video card and have two ports on the monitor to accommodate either signal. If the signal is analog, it must be converted to digital before the monitor can process it. Flat panel monitors are designed to receive an analog signal so that you can use a regular video card that works with a CRT monitor, thus reducing the price of upgrading from a CRT to an LCD monitor. As you will see in the upcoming discussion of video cards, video cards convert digital data from the CPU to analog before sending it to the monitor. Therefore, with analog flat panel monitors, the data is converted from digital to analog and back to digital before being used by the flat panel monitor. These conversions reduce the quality of the resulting image. To get the best output, use a digital flat panel monitor along with a digital video card designed to support the monitor.

Video Cards

A+CORE
1.7

Recall that the video controller card is the interface between the monitor and the computer. These cards are sometimes called graphic adapters, video boards, graphics cards, or display cards. Sometimes the video controller is integrated into the system board. If you are buying a system board with this integrated video controller, check that you can disable the controller on the system board if it needs replacement or gives you trouble. You can then install a video card and bypass the controller on the system board.

The quality of a video subsystem of a computer system is rated according to how it affects overall system performance, video quality (including resolution and color), power-saving features, and ease of use and installation. Because the video controller is separated from the core system functions, manufacturers can use a variety of techniques to improve performance without being overly concerned with compatibility with functions on the system board. An example of this flexibility is seen in the many ways memory is managed on a video controller. This section discusses the features available on video cards, especially video memory. The two main features to look for in a video card are the bus it uses and the amount of video RAM it has or can support.

How a Video Card Works

A video card performs four basic tasks, as seen in Figure 9-41. The RAM DAC (digital-to-analog converter) technology may be housed on a single RAM DAC chip on the video card or may be embedded in the video chip set. RAM DAC actually includes three digital-to-analog converters, one for each of the monitor's three color guns: red, green, and blue (RGB).

Four Basic Functions of a Video Card
① The digital data goes from the system bus to the video chip set on the video card.
② The video chip set writes the digital data to video memory on the card.
③ The data stored in video memory is passed to the digital analog converter (RAM DAC), where it is converted from digital data to analog data.
④ RAM DAC passes the analog data to the monitor.

Figure 9-41   Four basic functions of a video card

The Bus Used by the Video Card

The speed and performance of a video card are partly a function of the bus that the card is using. Since 1995, video cards have been designed to use only the PCI bus and more recently to use the AGP slot. Older video cards were made to run on VESA local buses (VL-bus), a proprietary local bus, ISA buses, and EISA buses.

Recall from Chapter 3 that the fastest bus for video on a system board today is AGP with a 32-bit-wide data bus, running at up to 1 GB/sec, depending on the AGP standard used. The regular AGP slot has 132 pins and AGP Pro has 188 pins. The added pins used by the AGP Pro standard provide voltage for high-end graphic accelerator cards discussed in the next section. After AGP, the PCI bus is next in throughput, providing either 132 or 264 MB/sec. If you play computer games or use extensive graphics software, such as that for CAD or desktop publishing, invest in a fast video card that uses a fast bus and has plenty of memory.

On the video card itself, performance is affected by the chip set, memory, and the RAM DAC, as well as by the bus speed and size. One method to improve performance is to allow both the video chip set and the RAM DAC (both the input and the output processes) to access video memory at the same time. This method, called **dual-porting**, requires a special kind of video RAM discussed later in this section. Another method of increasing performance is to place a processor on the video card, making the card a **graphics accelerator**.

The bus external to the video card is the PCI bus or the AGP bus, but the card itself also has an internal video bus. The volume of data that can travel on the bus is called bandwidth. Current video buses use a data path that may be 32 bits, 64 bits, 128 bits, or even 256 bits wide. The effective bandwidth of the bus is partly determined by the width of the data path and the amount of memory on the card.

Graphics Accelerators

One of the more important advances made in video cards in recent years has been the introduction of graphics accelerators. A graphics accelerator is a type of video card that has its own processor to boost performance. With the demands that graphics applications make in the multimedia environment, graphics accelerators have become not just an enhancement, but a common necessity.

The processor on a graphics accelerator card is similar to a CPU, but specifically designed to manage video and graphics. Some features included on a graphics accelerator are MPEG decoding, 3-D graphics, dual porting, color space conversion, interpolated scaling, EPA green PC support, digital output to flat panel display monitors, and applications support for popular high-intensity graphics software such as AutoCAD, Quark, Windows 9x, Windows NT, and Windows 2000. All these features are designed, in some way, to reduce the burden on the system board CPU and perform the function much faster than the system board CPU.

For more information about graphics accelerator cards, see these manufacturers at their web sites: ATI Technologies at *www.ati.com*, Matrox Graphics, Inc, at *www. matrox.com*, and 3-Dfx Interactive, Inc. at *www.3-Dfx.com* (makers of the popular Voodoo graphics card).

Video Memory

Older video cards do not have memory, but today they must so they can handle the large volume of data generated by increased resolution and color. Video memory is stored on video cards as memory chips. The first video cards to have memory all used DRAM chips, but now video memory chips can use several technologies. This section discusses how much video memory is needed and what kinds of video memory chips can be used on a card for the best possible performance.

How Much Video Memory Is Needed?

The amount of data received by a video card from the CPU for each frame (or screen) of data is determined by the screen resolution (measured in pixels), the number of colors, which is called the **color depth** (measured in bits), and enhancements to color information called alpha blending. The more data required to generate a single screen of data, the more memory is required to hold that data. Recall that this memory is called the frame buffer. The video card has other needs for memory besides the frame buffer, including the memory used by some cards to store font or other graphical information. Aside from these other uses of memory, Table 9-8 shows the amount of memory needed to hold the frame buffer, which is determined by the screen resolution and number of colors.

Table 9-8   Video RAM required for different video resolutions and color depths

Video Resolution	4-bit Color Depth (16 colors)	8-bit Color Depth (256 Colors)	16-bit Color Depth (65,000 Colors)	24-bit True Color (16.7 Million Colors)	32-bit (24-bit True Color with 8-bit Alpha Channel)
640 × 480	256K	512K	1 MB	1 MB	2 MB
800 × 600	512K	512K	1 MB	2 MB	2 MB
1,024 × 768	1 MB	1 MB	2 MB	4 MB	4 MB
1,152 × 1,024	1 MB	2 MB	2 MB	4 MB	4 MB
1,280 × 1,024	1 MB	2 MB	4 MB	4 MB	6 MB
1,600 × 1,200	2 MB	2 MB	4 MB	6 MB	8 MB

Color depth is directly related to the number of bits used to compose one pixel and can be 4, 8, 16, or 24 bits per pixel. The larger the number of bits allocated to storing each piece of data, the more accurate the value can be; in like manner, the greater the number of bits allocated to store the value of pixel color, the greater the number of color shades you can use and color depth you can have.

To determine the number of colors that can be represented by these numbers of bits, use the number of bits as the power (exponent) of the number 2. For example, to calculate the number of colors represented by 4 bits per pixel, raise 2 to the 4th power, which equals 16 colors. (Note that the largest 4-bit number is 1111, which equals 15 in decimal. If you include 0, then the number of values that can be stored in a 4-bit number is 16.) A color depth of 24 bits per pixel equals 2 to the 24th power, or 16.7 million colors.

To determine the amount of RAM needed for one frame buffer, multiply the number of bits per pixel times the number of pixels on the screen, giving the total number of bits per screen. Divide the number of bits by 8 to determine the number of bytes of RAM needed for the buffer.

For example, for a screen resolution of 1,024 × 768 and 256 colors, Table 9-8 shows that the amount of RAM required is 1 MB. The way that number is derived is illustrated below:

- The number of pixels for one frame buffer: 1,024 × 768 = 786,432 pixels

- For 256 colors, you need an 8-bit color depth, or 8 bits per pixel. (Remember that 1111 1111 in binary equals 255 in decimal, which, along with the value zero, provides 256 options.)

- Number of bits for one frame buffer: 786,432 pixels × 8 bits/pixel = 6,291,456 bits

- Number of bytes of memory needed: 6,291,456 bits/8 bits per byte = 786,432 bytes

- Since most video RAM comes in either 512K, 1 MB, 2 MB, or 4 MB increments, you must have 1 MB of video RAM to accommodate the frame buffer of 786,432 bytes.

In building a pixel on screen, each pixel uses three channels for color: red, green, and blue. However, when building 3-D graphics, a fourth channel is sometimes added called the alpha channel. The alpha channel controls the way the three colors are displayed and can add transparency or opacity to the image. The term for adding these effects is alpha blending, which can create the effect of shading or making one color partly visible behind another color, such as when you are looking through colored glass at a different color behind the glass. The alpha channel adds another 8 bits to the information kept for each pixel. When using 24-bit true color with an 8-bit alpha channel, 32 bits per pixel is needed, resulting in 32-bit graphics used by high-end video cards. The memory required for these cards is listed in the last column of Table 9-8.

Another factor that determines how much video memory is required is the bus width on the card. Just as with system boards, the RAM configuration on the card must conform to the bus width so that data can move from the bus to the card. A normal 1-MB memory chip on a video card has a bus width of 32 bits. In Figure 9-42, because each 1-MB video RAM chip is 32 bits wide, you can see why 2 MB of memory are needed if the video bus is 64 bits wide. In fact, this bit width of the video chip is the reason that a video card that has a 64-bit bus width and only 1 MB of installed memory is so slow. If your video card uses a 64-bit bus, be sure to install at least 2 MB of RAM.

Figure 9-42   Video bus with 64-bit width addressing two 1-MB memory chips with 32-bit widths

In Figure 9-43, 4 MB of RAM are required to make the most efficient use of the 128-bit video bus width. Some manufacturers of video chip sets have developed a method to use a 128-bit bus with less than 4 MB of memory. For example, the Tseng Labs ET6000 chip set uses a special kind of video RAM called **Multibank DRAM (MDRAM)** that is able to use the full 128-bit bus path without requiring the full 4 MB of RAM.

9

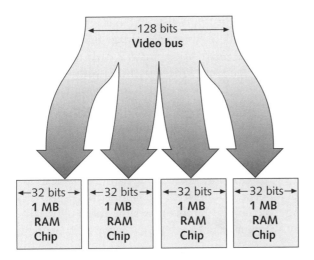

Figure 9-43   128-bit video bus addressing 4 MB of video memory

All these factors affect how much memory is required to build a single frame buffer. In Table 9-8, you can see that the most memory needed to build a single frame buffer is 8 MB. However, in addition to needing memory to hold each frame buffer, a graphics accelerator card might also need memory for other purposes. Software that builds 3-D graphics on screen often uses textures, and sometimes a graphics card holds these textures in memory to build future screens. Large amounts of video RAM keep the card from having to retrieve these textures from the hard drive or system RAM multiple times. In addition, the graphics card might use double or triple buffering to improve performance in which the card holds not just the frame being built, but the next one or two frames. Because of texturing and triple buffering, a card might need as much as 32 MB of RAM. See the graphics card documentation for information about memory recommendations for maximum performance.

A+CORE 4.2 Types of Video Memory

You have already been introduced to several different versions of video memory. Dual-ported memory, one type of which is sometimes called **video RAM** or **VRAM**, is designed so that video memory can be accessed by both the input and output processes at the same time. MDRAM memory chips are designed so that the full width of the video bus can be used with fewer memory chips than needed to provide the full bus width access to RAM. Three other types of memory chips designed to improve performance of video cards are: WRAM, SGRAM, and 3-D RAM.

SGRAM (synchronous graphics RAM) is similar to SDRAM, discussed in Chapter 4, but designed specifically for video card processing. SGRAM, like SDRAM, can synchronize itself with the CPU bus clock, which makes the memory faster. SGRAM also uses other methods to increase overall performance for graphics-intensive processing, but is not dual-ported memory. It is used on moderate to high-end cards where the very highest resolutions are not required.

WRAM (Window RAM) is a type of dual-ported RAM, but is faster and less expensive than VRAM. WRAM was named more for its ability to manage full-motion video than for its ability to speed up Microsoft Windows video processing. WRAM's increase in speed is primarily due to its own internal bus on the chip, which has a data path that is 256 bits wide. WRAM is used on high-end graphics cards with very high resolutions and true color.

Some video processing involves simulating 3-D graphics; **3-D RAM** was designed specifically to improve this performance. Much of the logic of 3-D processing is embedded on the chip itself. A graphics card chip set normally calculates which pixel of a 3-D graphic is to be displayed, depending on whether or not the pixel is behind other pixels and, therefore, out of sight in a 3-D graphic. After the pixel is drawn and a calculation is made as to whether or not the pixel is seen, if the pixel is not to be displayed, the chip set writes it back to memory to be used later. With 3-D RAM, the chip set simply passes the data to the 3-D RAM chip that draws the pixel and decides whether or not to display it without involving the chip set.

CHAPTER SUMMARY

❑ Adding new devices to a computer requires installing hardware and software and resolving possible resource conflicts.

❑ Most hardware devices require similar resources from a computer, including an IRQ, DMA channel, I/O addresses, and some upper memory addresses to contain their device drivers.

❑ Use MSD under DOS and Device Manager under Windows 9x to determine what resources currently installed devices are using.

❑ 16-bit real mode device drivers are loaded from command lines in CONFIG.SYS and AUTOEXEC.BAT, and 32-bit protected mode drivers are automatically loaded by Windows 9x because of entries in the Registry.

❑ Most computers provide two serial ports and one parallel port to be used for a variety of devices. Newer system boards also provide one or two USB ports and an IEEE 1394 port.

❑ A null modem connection is used to connect two computers using their serial ports and a cable, but no modems.

❑ The UART chip controls serial ports.

❑ Because data bits in parallel might sometimes lose their relationship with the byte they represent, parallel cables should not exceed 15 feet in length.

❑ Three types of parallel ports are standard, EPP, and ECP. The ECP type uses a DMA channel.

❑ Older general-purpose I/O cards provided serial and parallel ports as well as IDE adapters because these were not included on a system board.

❑ The USB bus only uses one set of system resources for all USB devices connected to it.

❑ The IEEE 1394 bus provides either a 4-pin or 6-pin connector, uses only one set of system resources, and is hot-pluggable.

❑ A system board can have up to four PCI slots. IRQs are assigned to PCI slots during startup.

❑ If the system board and the OS both support PCI bus IRQ steering, IRQs can be reassigned by the OS after booting, in order to resolve a conflict.

❑ When selecting a SCSI host adapter, consider the bus slot the adapter will use, the device driver standard used by the host adapter, single-ended versus differential SCSI, SCAM compliance, and whether or not the host offers bus mastering.

❑ Some inexpensive SCSI host adapters are sold bundled with hardware devices that only support one or two SCSI devices.

❑ A keyboard can use a DIN, PS/2, or USB connector.

❑ Two types of monitors are CRT and LCD. CRT costs less, but LCD yields better quality and takes up less desktop space.

❑ A video card is rated by the bus that it uses and the amount of video RAM on the card. Both features affect the overall speed and performance of the card.

KEY TERMS

3-D RAM — Special video RAM designed to improve 3-D graphics simulation.

Bandwidth — the range of frequencies that a communication cable or channel can carry. In general use, the term refers to the volume of data that can travel on a bus or over a cable.

Break code — A code produced when a key on a computer keyboard is released. *See* Make code.

Bus mouse — A mouse that plugs into a bus adapter card and has a round, 9-pin mini-DIN connector.

Color depth — The number of possible colors used by a monitor. Determines the number of bits used to compose one pixel. One of two characteristics (the other is resolution) that determines the amount of data sent to the video card to build one screen.

Dot pitch — The distance between the dots that the electronic beam hits on a monitor screen.

Dual ported — When the video chip set (input) and the RAM DAC (output) can access video memory at the same time. A special kind of video RAM is required.

ECP (extended capabilities port) — A bi-directional parallel port mode that uses a DMA channel to speed up data flow.

EPP (enhanced parallel port) — A parallel port that allows data to flow in both directions (bi-directional port) and is faster than original parallel ports on PCs that only allowed communication in one direction.

Flat panel monitor — A desktop monitor that uses an LCD panel.

Graphics accelerator — A type of video card that has an on-board processor that can substantially increase speed and boost graphical and video performance.

Hot-pluggable — A characteristic of 1394 devices that let you plug in the device without rebooting your PC and remove the device without receiving an error message.

Interlace — A display in which the electronic beam of a monitor draws every other line with each pass, which lessens the overall effect of a lower refresh rate.

IEEE 1284 — A standard for parallel ports developed by the Institute for Electrical and Electronics Engineers and supported by many hardware manufacturers.

I/O card — A card that often contains serial, parallel, and game ports on the same adapter board, providing input/output interface with the CPU.

Isochronous data transfer — A method used by IEEE 1394 to transfer data continuously without breaks.

Make code — A code produced by pressing a key on a computer keyboard. *See* Break code.

Modem eliminator — A technique that allows two data terminal equipment (DTE) devices to communicate by means of a null modem cable in which the transmit and receive wires are cross-connected, and no modems are necessary.

Multibank DRAM (MDRAM) — A special kind of RAM used on video cards that is able to use a full 128-bit bus path without requiring the full 4MB of RAM.

Multiscan monitor — A monitor that can work within a range of frequencies, and thus can work with different standards and video cards. If offers a variety of refresh rates.

Non-interlace — A type of display in which the electronic beam of a monitor draws every line on the screen with each pass. See interlace.

Null modem cable — *See* Modem eliminator.

Parallel port — A female port on the computer that can transmit data in parallel, 8 bits at a time, and is usually used with a printer. The names for parallel ports are LPT1 and LPT2.

PCI bus IRQ steering — A feature that makes it possible for PCI devices to share an IRQ. System BIOS and the OS must both support this feature.

Pixel — Small spots on a fine horizontal scan line that are illuminated to create an image on the monitor.

PS/2 compatible mouse — A mouse that uses a round mouse port (called a mini-DIN or PS/2 connector) coming directly off the system board.

Resolution — The number of spots called pixels on a monitor screen that are addressable by software (example: 1024 2 768 pixels).

Serial mouse — A mouse that uses a serial port and has a female 9-pin DB-9 connector.

Serial ports — Male ports on the computer used for transmitting data serially, one bit at a time. They are commonly used for modems and mice, and in DOS are called COM1 or COM2.

SGRAM (synchronous graphics RAM) — Memory designed especially for video card processing that can synchronize itself with the CPU bus clock.

System-board mouse — A mouse that plugs into a round mouse port on the system board. Sometimes called a PS/2 mouse.

UART (universal asynchronous receiver/transmitter) chip — A chip that controls serial ports. It sets protocol and converts parallel data bits received from the system bus into serial bits.

Video RAM or VRAM — RAM on video cards that holds the data that is being passed from the computer to the monitor and can be accessed by two devices simultaneously. Higher resolutions often require more video memory.

Window RAM (WRAM) — Dual-ported video RAM that is faster and less expensive than VRAM. It has its own internal bus on the chip, with a data path that is 256 bits wide.

9

REVIEW QUESTIONS

1. Name four system resources that a device might need and that offer the potential for a conflict with another device.

2. Why would an external modem cost more than an internal modem?

3. In DOS, what command loads a device driver? Where is the command located?

4. Name three possible ways a scanner might interface with a system board.

5. By definition, what system resources does COM1 use? COM2? COM3? COM4?

6. To what does RS-232 refer?

7. How many pins are on a typical serial mouse port?

8. What is a null modem cable, and what is it often used for?

9. What chip controls the speed of serial ports? What DOS utility program can you use to determine what version of this chip you have installed?

10. Why might you choose to use ECP mode for your parallel port rather than EPP mode?

11. When might you need to disable ECP mode for a parallel port?

12. How are system resources assigned to ports on a typical, general-purpose I/O card?

13. In order for your system to support a USB device, what three resources must you have?

14. What OS supports USB?

15. What is the maximum number of PCI slots that a system board might have?

16. What utility tool can help resolve system resource conflicts in DOS? In Windows 9x?

17. When installing a device, why would you prefer to use a PCI expansion slot rather than an ISA expansion slot?

18. Explain what PCI bus IRQ steering does. When might you disable it?

19. If PCI is attempting to use an IRQ that is used by a legacy ISA device, how can you force PCI to not use the IRQ?

20. If the port on a SCSI host adapter has only 25 pins, what does this tell you about the adapter?

21. How much video RAM is required to produce a resolution of 800×600 with 65,000 colors?

22. Give three examples of monitor screen sizes. How are monitor screen sizes measured?

23. Which provides better quality, an interlaced monitor or a noninterlaced monitor? Why?

24. What type of monitor can offer a variety of refresh rates?

25. What size frame buffer is needed on a video card to hold the data for $1,280 \times 1,024$ screen resolution and 65,000 colors?

26. What makes a device an ergonomic device?

27. Describe the size and pins on a DIN connector and a PS/2 connector for a keyboard.

28. What three colors are used to build all colors on a color monitor screen?

29. Which gives better image quality, a .25-mm dot pitch monitor or a .28-mm dot pitch monitor? Why?

30. If a mouse begins to be difficult to operate, what simple thing can you do to help?

PROJECTS

Unless you follow proper procedures, working inside your computer can cause serious damage—
to both you and your computer. To ensure safety in your work setting, follow every precaution
listed in the *Read This Before You Begin* section following this book's Introduction.

Supporting a Mouse in DOS

Prepare a bootable DOS floppy disk that provides access to a mouse. Test that you can use
the mouse by booting from the disk and using the mouse when executing MSD. What driver file must be on the disk in order for it to support a mouse?

Protected-Mode and Real-Mode Drivers

Windows 9x provides 32-bit protected-mode drivers for a mouse. Using either Windows 98
or Windows 95, print the screen showing the drivers currently used for your mouse. Now
substitute a 16-bit real-mode driver for your mouse. How does the icon for the mouse
change in Device Manager? Print the screen showing the current driver in use. *Hint*: Real-
mode drivers are loaded from CONFIG.SYS.

9

Research Hardware and Software on Your Computer

Know the computers for which you are responsible. Gather the documentation for your
computer and/or use the Nuts & Bolts software on the accompanying CD-ROM and fill in
the following chart. Copy the chart and put it in the notebook that is kept for this computer.
To use Nuts & Bolts to gather information about your computer, click **Start**, **Programs**,
Nuts & Bolts, and **Discover Pro**.

Computer Fact Sheet

Location of computer: _____

Owner: _____

Date purchased: _____

Warranty expires: _____

Size and speed of CPU: _____

RAM present: _____

Type of monitor: _____

Type of video card: _____

Hard drive type: _____

Hard drive size: _____

Disk drive A size: _____

Disk drive B size: _____

Software Installed:

Name	Version	Installed by	Date
1.			
2.			
3.			
4.			
5.			

Other Devices:

Name of Device	IRQ	I/O Address	DMA Channel	Device Driver Filename
1. Serial port 1				
2. Serial port 2				
3. Parallel port				
4. Mouse				
5. Modem				
6. CD-ROM drive				
7.				
8.				

Install a Device

Install a device on a computer. If you are working in a classroom environment, you can simulate an installation by moving a device from one computer to another.

Research a Computer Ad

Pick a current magazine ad for a complete, working computer system including computer, monitor, keyboard, and software, together with extra devices such as a mouse or printer. Write a four- to eight-page report describing and explaining the details in this ad. This exercise will give you a good opportunity to learn about the latest offerings on the market as well as current pricing.

Compare Two Computer Ads

Find two computer ads for computer systems containing the same processor. Compare the two ads. Include in your comparison the different features offered and the weaknesses and strengths of each system.

Using Nuts & Bolts to Examine Multimedia Devices

1. Using Nuts & Bolts Discover Pro, print a full description of your PC's sound, video, and printer functions. Include in the printout the amount of RAM that is stored on the video card.

2. What are the current resolution and number of colors of your monitor? Calculate the size of the frame buffer required for these settings. Compare your results to the calculation made by Nuts & Bolts under System in Discover Pro.

Search the Internet for an Older Video Driver

You have a 486DX computer with a VESA local bus video card by Avance Logic, Inc. You upgrade your DOS 6.22 and Windows 3.1 operating systems to Windows 95. When you install the video, you discover that Windows 95 does not support Avance Logic video drivers. You temporarily substitute a standard super VGA driver so you can complete the installation, but you notice that the video and color are not as clear as you think they should be. How do you resolve the problem? Follow these steps to a solution.

1. On the Internet, find the web site for Avance Logic, Inc. Here's where some educated guessing can be effective. Try *www.avance.com*.

2. Look for drivers for Windows 95. Your video card is labeled Avance Logic 2228. After a little searching, you arrive at the screen shown in Figure 9-44.

3. Download and explode the file labeled ALG2228.

4. Print the Readme.txt file that lists the instructions to use to install the new device driver in Windows 95. If you follow the instructions, don't apply the driver unless you really do have this particular video card.

Plan the Design of a 9-Pin Null Modem Cable

Draw a chart similar to Table 9-4 showing the pinouts (functions of each pin) for a 9-pin null modem cable.

Parallel Port Modes

Examine CMOS setup on your PC and answer the following questions about your parallel port:

1. Is there a parallel port coming directly off the system board?

2. What modes are available for the parallel port?

3. What is the currently selected mode?

4. If the parallel port supports ECP, what DMA channels can be selected for this mode?

5. Disable the parallel port using CMOS setup. Reboot the PC and attempt to use the port by executing a print command. What is the error message that you get?

Figure 9-44   Video drivers for Windows 9x

Troubleshooting Skills

Produce a troubleshooting situation by assigning the same IRQ to two devices. In some computer systems that use mostly PCI and Plug and Play devices, creating a conflict can be a real challenge. Older systems that use several legacy devices will prove to be much less of a challenge. Attempt to use the two devices at the same time and note what happens when you do that. Possible devices to use are a serial mouse, a modem, or a parallel port connected to a printer. Answer these questions:

1. What two devices did you use to create a conflict?

2. How did you create the conflict?

3. When you attempted to use both devices, what happened?

Working with a Monitor

1. Using Windows 9x, list the steps to change the monitor resolution. If you make a mistake when changing the monitor resolution, Windows 9x is much better about not allowing you to lock up your video than is Windows 3.x.

   □ Double-click the **Display** icon in the Windows **Control Panel** and practice changing the background, screen saver, and appearance. If you are not using your own computer, make sure to restore each setting after making changes.

   □ Pretend you have made a mistake and selected a combination of foreground and background colors that makes it impossible to read the screen. Solve the problem by booting Windows 9x into Safe Mode. Correct the problem and then reboot.

2. Windows 9x offers many new 32-bit video drivers for most video cards. When Windows 9x is first installed, it selects the driver for you based on the video card it detects. To see a list of available video drivers, follow these procedures:

   ❐ Right-click the **desktop**, and click **Properties** on the shortcut menu to open the Display Properties dialog box.

   ❐ Click the **Settings** tab. The choices available depend on the resources you have on your computer.

   ❐ Change the resolution by using the sliding bar under **Display area**. The changes are immediate; you don't have to exit and reenter Windows, as you did in Windows 3.x. Make a change and then make the change permanent. You can go back and adjust it later if you like.

3. Work with a partner who is using a different computer. Unplug the monitor in the computer lab or classroom, loosen or disconnect the computer monitor cable, and/or turn the contrast and brightness all the way down, while your partner does something similar to his/her PC. Trade PCs and troubleshoot the problems.

4. Turn the PC off, remove the case, and loosen the video card. Turn the PC back on and write down the problem as a user would describe it. Turn off the PC, reseat the card, and verify that all is working.

5. Insert a defective monitor adapter card provided by your instructor into a system. Describe the problem in writing, as a user would describe it.

9

CHAPTER

10

MULTIMEDIA TECHNOLOGY

In this chapter, you will learn:

♦ About the fundamental workings of multimedia technology

♦ About many multimedia standards and how they have helped shape the industry

♦ How to support many multimedia devices, including CD-ROM drives, sound cards, and DVD drives

The ability of PCs to create output in a vast array of media—audio, video, and animation, as well as text and graphics—has turned PCs into multimedia machines. The multimedia computer offers much to take advantage of, from video conferencing for executives to teaching the alphabet to four year olds. This chapter examines multimedia devices, what they can do, how they work, and how to support them.

The goal of **multimedia** technology is to create or reproduce lifelike representations for audio, video, and animation. Remember that computers store data digitally, and ultimately as a stream of only two numbers: 0 and 1. In contrast, sights and sounds have an infinite number of variations. The challenge of multimedia technology is to bridge these two worlds. The key to doing this is twofold: reduce the infinite number of variations to a finite few, and record as many as needed to reproduce an approximation of the original sight or sound, without overloading the capacity of the computer to hold data. These tasks require (1) a lot of storage capacity and (2) the ability to process large quantities of data at high speed and at the lowest cost possible. This chapter focuses on how the industry is attempting to meet the challenge.

When studying multimedia technology, look for these two features: the need for large amounts of storage capacity and the ability of a computer to handle this large volume at high speeds, including sophisticated methods of sampling sight and sound. Also, as you study, look for the attempts of the industry to standardize methods of sampling and storage so that different types of software and hardware are as interchangeable as possible, considering the fast-changing technology that manufacturers must contend with.

THE RIGHT TOOLS FOR THE JOB

Desktop computer systems are designed for three major purposes: low-end systems designed as e-machines and thin clients, mid-range systems designed for desktop publishing, home computing, and general business needs, and high-end systems designed for computer-intensive engineering applications. E-machines simply access the Internet and use its applications, and thin clients use the data and applications served to them by network application servers. Generally these machines are not intended for upgrade and might include a system board that has many proprietary components with no room for expansion. High-end systems meant for engineering applications focus on powerful and sometimes multiple CPUs, large amounts of memory and hard drive space, and use powerful operating systems such as Windows 2000 or UNIX.

This chapter focuses on the mid-range computer system designed for desktop publishing, graphics design, home entertainment, multimedia presentations, and entertainment from the Internet. These systems benefit from a CPU designed with multimedia in mind and from powerful graphics accelerator cards and sound cards. In addition, most of these systems can interface with multimedia devices such as camcorders, digital cameras, and scanners. Applications for these systems include web-authoring software, desktop publishing, multimedia presentations, and games. This section looks at the hardware and software requirements for each.

Technicians who help make purchasing decisions about multimedia hardware and software need to stay abreast of the latest innovations in the marketplace as the technology changes rapidly and choices and price ranges abound. Before you purchase or make a recommendation about the purchase of a new computer system or a peripheral, research the purchase. Some of your best resources are:

- Other satisfied users, retailers, books, the Internet, and computer service centers

- Trade magazines, such as *PC Computing, PC World, Home PC, Computer Shopper, PCNovice, PC Magazine*, and *PC Today*. Look for reviews describing hardware and software, how they work and popular features.

- Special-interest web sites such as *www.imaging-resource.com*, which focuses on digital imaging, or Tom's Hardware Guide at *www.tomshardware.com*, which focuses on hardware

- Magazine web sites, including:

www.zdnet.com	*Several technical magazines*
www.cshopper.com	*Computer Shopper*
www.pcmag.com	*PC Magazine*
www.pcworld.com	*PC World*
www.pccomputing.com	*PC Computing*
www.pcguide.com	*PC Guide*

Typically, the minimum software and hardware requirements for an adequate desktop-publishing, Web-authoring, entertainment, or multimedia presentations system include:

- A Pentium II-compatible computer or higher with a hard drive and a minimum of 64 MB of RAM, a mouse, and a high-resolution color monitor and video card

- A word-processing software package

- A scanner and related software

- A laser printer or ink-jet photo-quality printer

- A graphics software package to create and/or edit graphics

- Optional equipment for web authoring and multimedia presentations such as a video-capturing card and a digital camera

- For desktop publishing, a page composition software package, such as Adobe PageMaker (see Figure 10-1), to bring together all the individual elements of text, graphics, and scanned images into an easy-to-read and visually appealing finished document

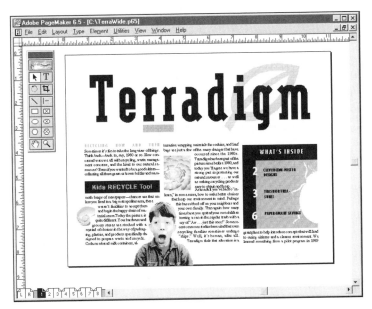

10

Figure 10-1   A page composition software package

- For web authoring, an authoring tool such as Microsoft FrontPage or Netscape Publisher, which brings together individual elements of text, graphics, video, scanned images, and sound into one or more web pages

- For multimedia presentations, a presentation package such as Microsoft PowerPoint, which ties individual elements of text, graphics, video, and sound into a sight and sound presentation

- For entertainment, access to the Internet with a fast enough connection to play streaming audio and video data and, for game playing, a fast graphics accelerator card

If your budget is limited, spend money on the computer itself rather than the peripherals. A computer system is no faster than the CPU, no matter how sophisticated the peripherals. A laser printer is an expensive item; you can use an ink-jet or dot matrix printer for rough drafts and then take your work on disk to another system with a photo-quality laser printer. By postponing the purchase of the laser printer, you may be able to afford a faster Pentium processor or more memory on the system board. The speed and reliability of the computer are invaluable.

Bits Are Still Bits

Just as with every other component of a microcomputer, multimedia devices represent data as a series of 0s and 1s. For example, a black-and-white scanner sends a light beam across an image and reads that image as a series of black and white dots. Each dot is represented as a 1 or 0, and is stored in a file called a **bit map file**. A sound card captures sound, converts each segment of the sound into a series of 0s and 1s, and stores these in a MIDI file that can later be interpreted once again as sound. A video-capturing card captures a segment of video and converts it to—you guessed it—a series of 1s and 0s, when it is stored in a file.

Another uniform quality of multimedia devices is that each device transfers its data over the same bus to the CPU; the CPU processes the data in the same way and sends it as output to a multimedia device, just as it does with other devices. So each device may require an IRQ, a DMA channel, an I/O address, and room in memory for its BIOS or drivers. When working with these devices, don't be intimidated by their complexity. All their basic computing needs are the same.

MULTIMEDIA ON A PC

Multimedia has traditionally targeted the home market, with games and more games at the top of the list of multimedia software. Until recently, the trend in the business market has been to acquire more powerful PCs for computing, networking, and remote management.

Now, however, business use of multimedia PCs is the norm. Video conferencing, computer-based training (CBT), and multimedia presentations are now common on the corporate scene. This trend affects the development of hardware and software, as both attempt to satisfy market demands.

Another important fact that helps to understand development trends is that, in the evolution of computers, hardware must improve in advance of the software designed to use it. A good example of this is the MMX (multimedia extensions) technology used with the Intel MMX Pentium CPU. When the hardware technology arrived, more software became available to use the technology. In the future, you can expect continuing improvements in multimedia hardware, which will continue to lead to the development of new software.

Evidence of the inroads multimedia technology is making into the business market is the introduction of the Pentium III CPU, which is marketed as a high-end CPU for servers, yet includes SSE, which is technology designed to improve on MMX multimedia processing.

Multimedia Fundamentals

Before you study multimedia technology, examine the special challenge confronting multimedia technology: reproducing something that is continuously changing (referred to as analog, as discussed below) such as sights and sounds, on a PC, which is incapable of making continuous changes because it is digital. It has only two states and can only change from one state to another, with no gradations in between.

We have been comparing the word "analog" to "digital," but what exactly do we mean by that? Analog comes from the same word as "analogous," and means "the same," implying smooth, continuous transition that lacks distinctly defined gradations. "Digital" comes from the Latin word *digitus*, which means a finger or toe. The term "digital" originates from our 10 counting digits and implies distinct and separate gradations. As you recall, all computer communication must be expressed in binary digits (or bits). And because a computer is binary, it is also digital. Thus, to be produced on a computer, sound and images must be converted into bits; it must cross the bridge from analog to digital.

Understanding the distinction between analog and digital signals is essential to grasping the challenges facing multimedia technology. Figure 10-2 illustrates the difference between using digital communication to describe the shape of a loading ramp and a staircase. A loading ramp is essentially analog because the changes in height of the ramp are gradual, continuous, with smooth transition, making the number of different heights of the loading ramp infinite. A staircase is essentially digital because changes in height move abruptly from one state to another, with no transition in between, in a way similar to counting. Figure 10-2 shows that it is easy to recreate the shape of the staircase because it is easy to measure the exact height of every part of the staircase, and there are a finite number of these heights. It is not so easy to recreate the shape of the loading ramp, because its height continuously gradually changes over the entire ramp. You can measure the height at any particular point of the ramp, but it is impossible to measure the height at every point of the ramp. Therefore, you are forced to measure the height at only some representative points. Measuring the heights at a series of representative points on the ramp in order to approximately reproduce the shape of the ramp is called **sampling**.

10

Figure 10-2   Expressing analog phenomena in digital terms is a challenge of multimedia

 TIP   When analog data is converted to digital data for a PC, the data is sampled, meaning that samples are taken at discrete intervals and stored individually as digital data. This process is called digitizing the data, and the resulting data is an approximation of the original data.

Look at the sound wave in Figure 10-3a. To record and store this sound wave in a PC, to reproduce it as closely to its original analog nature as possible, you must first record the sound wave as numbers—that is, digitize the analog wave—because your PC can only store data that way (see Figure 10-4). To digitize the wave, first select how many samples you want to take (how frequently you will take a sample), how accurate your measurements will be, and how you will store these numbers. Later, you must follow the reverse process to retrieve these numbers and use them to reproduce a sound wave as close to the original as possible.

When digitizing the sound wave to produce the best possible reproduction, the more samples taken over a period of time and the more accurate each measurement, the more accurate the representation of the sound. However, there is a trade-off between the quality of a reproduction and the cost of the resources needed to create that reproduced sound. In other words, you need more resources both to store more samples and to store more accurate measurements of these samples, both of which lead to creating better sound. This trade-off is important in the multimedia world and drives many purchasing decisions.

a) Many samples

b) Few samples

c) More accurate sample
   (nearest quarter of a unit)

d) Less accurate sample
   (nearest whole unit)

Figure 10-3   Sampling a sound wave

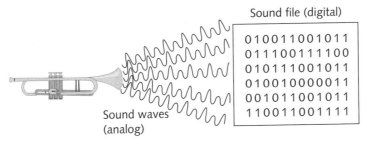

Figure 10-4   Sound has analog properties, but sound files store sound digitally

To understand why more accurate measurements require more storage, look back at Figure 10-2. If you measure the ramp height to the nearest foot, you need to store only a two-digit number in the table of heights, because the highest point of the ramp is only 10 feet. The range of sampling values in feet is 0, 1, 2, 3, 4, 5, 6, 7, 8, 9, and 10. If you choose to be more accurate, say to the nearest inch, then the range of sampling values increases to 0, 1, 2, 3, 4...120 inches, and the table must now hold three digits to store one number, which translates into a 50% increase in storage space to obtain greater accuracy. The number of samples and the accuracy of each sample determine the amount of storage needed to hold the values. The amount of storage needed to hold each measurement is called the **sample size**. However, you can use techniques to compress the data.

You need a compression method that does not lose too much information, and another method to decompress the values when you are ready to use them.

The impact of increasing measurement accuracy can be even greater in the binary world of the computer. Increasing the accuracy of the ramp measurement from feet to inches increased the storage space needed by 50% (from 2 digits for feet to 3 digits for inches). But remember that computers use bits instead of digits. So, 10 (feet) in binary is stored as 1010 (in 4 bits), but 120 inches is stored as 1111000 (7 bits) in binary. Since bits are stored in most multimedia files in even numbers of bits and not odd, measurements in feet would require 4-bit values, but measurements in inches would require 8-bit values, which creates a 100% increase in the storage requirement to gain added accuracy. In this chapter, look for the size in bits of the numeric values being stored as an indication of the accuracy of the data and the storage requirements.

In the two examples discussed above, the process is not very complicated, and the calculations are extremely easy. You just do the same thing many times, which is called "repetitive looping." However, you can see that the volume of data can get quite large when many samples are taken over a period of time.

> There are basically two types of data processing: repetitive looping with high input/output volume used by multimedia technology, and computer-intensive data processing, which involves many and/or complex calculations and a relatively low volume of data. A CPU is designed to best support one type of data processing or the other.

As you study the remainder of the chapter, this model of measuring the height at selected points along a curve, storing these values in a list, and using them to approximately duplicate the original curve in digital terms is applied often. Multimedia applications vary in the methods they use to determine the type and number of samples, to digitize the samples, to compress the measurements, to decompress them later, and finally to reproduce the original analog entity, be it image or sound.

Early on, the multimedia industry tried to standardize hardware and software. In the early 90s, the Multimedia Marketing Council established the **MPC (Multimedia Personal Computer) guidelines**. Sponsored by the Software and Information Industry Association (SIIA), three levels of standards were developed, the last one being MPC3 released in 1996. Today, no standards organization has attained enough prominence in the marketplace to have an impact, resulting in many methods for capturing, compressing, storing and processing multimedia data. Also, the technology is improving at such a fast pace that a standard today is likely to be outdated tomorrow. For these reasons, look for new and different technologies emerging in the industry.

What CPU Technologies Do for Multimedia

Two enhancements by Intel to CPU technology designed with multimedia applications in mind are MMX, which is used by the Pentium MMX, Pentium Pro, and Pentium II, and SSE, which is used by the Pentium III. Multimedia software tends to use input/output operations more than it performs complex computations. Both MMX and SSE were designed to speed up the repetitive looping of multimedia software manage the high-volume input/output of graphics, motion video, animation, and sound. MMX technology added three new architectural enhancements to the Pentium, all designed to speed up the repetitive looping of multimedia.

- **New instructions**. Intel added 57 new instructions to the CPU logic, all designed to handle the parallel, repetitive processing found in multimedia operations.

- **SIMD process**. A process called **single-instruction, multiple-data (SIMD)** was added that allows the CPU to execute a single instruction on multiple pieces of data rather than having to repetitively loop back to the previous instruction many times.

- **Increased cache**. Intel increased the size of the internal cache to 32K on the processor, reducing the number of times the CPU must access slower, off-chip memory for information.

The Pentium III introduced **SSE (streaming SIMD extension)**, which is designed to improve the performance of high-end multimedia software. SSE can improve 3-D graphics, speech recognition, MPEG, and some scientific and engineering applications.

To compete with SSE, AMD introduced 3DNow!, a CPU instruction set that helps AMD processors perform better in 3D graphics and other multimedia data processing. 3Dfx, the manufacturer of the Voodoo graphics accelerator card, was the first hardware manufacturer to use the 3DNow! instruction set, although it is now being used by many hardware and software manufacturers.

To know that software or hardware is taking advantage of a CPU enhancement, look on the product package for the Intel MMX, Intel SSE, or 3DNow! symbols.

DEVICES SUPPORTING MULTIMEDIA

Now that you have an understanding of the fundamentals of multimedia technology and insight into some of the early decisions made concerning hardware and software, you are ready to learn about several multimedia devices. This section looks at five popular multimedia devices: CD-ROM drives, sound cards, digital cameras, video capture cards, and Digital Video Disc (DVD) drives.

CD-ROM Drives

A+CORE 1.1 Of the multimedia components discussed in this chapter, the most popular is the CD-ROM drive. The technology of a CD-ROM drive is different from that of a hard drive, even though both are designed to hold data. CD-ROMs are popular media used to distribute software and sound files. CD-ROM drives are read-only devices. Read/writeable CD drives are discussed later in the chapter.

A+CORE
1.1

During the manufacturing process, data can be written to a CD-ROM disc only once, because the surface of the disc is actually embedded with the data. Figure 10-5 shows a CD-ROM surface that is laid out as one continuous spiral of sectors of equal length that hold equal amounts of data. The surface of a CD-ROM stores data as pits and lands. **Lands** are raised areas, and **pits** are recessed areas on the surface, each representing either a 1 or a 0, respectively. The bits are read by the drive with a laser beam that distinguishes between a pit and a land by the amount of deflection or scattering that occurs when the light beam hits the surface.

Figure 10-5   The spiral layout of sectors on a CD-ROM surface

A small motor with an actuator arm moves the laser beam to the sector on the track it needs to read. If the disc were spinning at a constant speed, the speed near the center of the disc would be greater than the speed at the outer edge. To create the effect of **constant linear velocity (CLV)**, the CD-ROM drive uses a mechanism that speeds up the disc when the laser beam is near the center of the disc, and slows it down when the laser beam is near the outer edge so that the beam is over a sector for the same amount of time no matter where the sector is. (Since the outer edge has more sectors than the inner edge, the light beam needs more time to read near the outer edge than it does near the inner edge.) The transfer rate of the first CD-ROM drives was about 150K per second of data, with the rpm (revolutions per minute) set to 200 when the laser was near the center of the disc. This transfer rate was about right for audio CDs. To show video and motion without a choppy effect, the speed of the drives was increased to double speed (150K per sec 3 2), quad speed (150K per sec 3 4), and so on. It is not uncommon now to see CD-ROM drives with speeds at 40 times the audio speed. Audio CDs must still drop the speed to the original speed of 200 rpm and a transfer rate of 150K per second.

Because of the problems of changing speeds using CLV, newer, faster CD-ROM drives are using a combination of CLV and **constant angular velocity (CAV)**, the same technology used by hard drives, whereby the disc rotates at a constant speed.

When you choose a CD-ROM drive, look for the multisession feature that the drive to read a disc that has been created in multisessions. To say a disc was created in **multisessions** means that data was written to the disc at different times rather than in a single long, continuous session.

Some CD-ROM drives have power-saving features controlled by the device driver. For example, when the drive waits for a command for more than 5 minutes, it enters Power Save

Mode, causing the spindle motor to stop. The restart is automatic when the drive receives a command.

Caring for CD-ROM Drives and Discs

Most problems with CD-ROMs are caused by dust, fingerprints, scratches, defects on the surface of the CD, or random electrical noise. Don't use a CD-ROM drive if it is standing vertically, such as when someone turns a desktop PC case on its side to save desktop space. Use these precautions when handling CDs:

- Hold the CD by the edge; do not touch the bright side of the disc where data is stored.

- To remove dust or fingerprints, use a clean, soft, dry cloth.

- Do not write on, or paste paper to, the surface of the CD. Don't paste any labels to the top of the CD, because this can imbalance the CD and cause the drive to vibrate.

- Do not subject the CD to heat or leave it in direct sunlight.

- Do not use cleaners, alcohol, and the like on the CD.

- Do not make the center hole larger.

- Do not bend the CD.

- Do not drop the CD or subject it to shock.

- If a CD gets stuck in the drive, use the emergency eject hole to remove it. Turn off the power to the PC first. Then insert an instrument such as a straightened paper clip into the hole to manually eject the tray.

How a CD-ROM Drive Can Interface with the System Board

CD-ROM drives can interface with the system board in one of several ways. The drive can:

- Use an IDE interface; it can share an IDE connection and/or cable with a hard drive

- Use a SCSI interface with a SCSI host adapter

- Use a proprietary expansion card that works only with CD-ROMs from a particular manufacturer

- Use a proprietary connection on a sound card

- Be a portable drive and plug into an external port on your PC

Most CD-ROM drives are Plug and Play compliant. These drives allow a system to avoid resource conflicts. Boxes marked "Ready for Windows 95" or "Ready for Windows 98" indicate Plug and Play CD-ROM drives.

10

$A^{+CORE}_{1.2}$ **Installing a CD-ROM Drive**

Installing a CD-ROM drive is easy, especially when the adapter is already present. If you are using a SCSI CD-ROM drive, install the host adapter or sound card first, and then install the drive. If you are using a proprietary adapter, install both at the same time. If you are using an existing IDE adapter card or connection on the system board, simply install the CD-ROM drive using an existing connection on the board or an extra connection on the hard drive data cable.

Figure 10-6 shows the front of a typical CD-ROM drive, and Figure 10-7 shows the rear view, where the power cord, data cable, sound cord, and ground connector attach. Also note that there is an "audio out" connection that supports a direct connection to a sound card. The jumper pins on a SCSI CD-ROM drive can:

- Control the SCSI ID for the drive

- Enable or disable SCSI parity checking

- Enable or disable the built-in SCSI terminator on the drive

The example shown is a SCSI CD-ROM drive. However, for IDE CD-ROM drives, expect to find jumpers that can set the drive as either the single drive, a slave drive, or the master drive in the IDE subsystem.

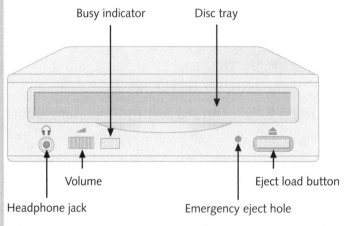

Figure 10-6   Front view of a typical CD-ROM drive

A+CORE
1.2,
4.3

SCSI bus connector

Jumper pin

Audio Out
connector

DC (In)
connector

DC power
connector

Frame ground terminal

Frame grounding
connector

Interface cable

Figure 10-7   Rear view of a typical SCSI CD-ROM drive showing drive connections

The CD-ROM drive documentation is your best installation guide, but here are a few general guidelines. The CD-ROM drive becomes another drive on your system, such as drive D or E. After it is installed, you access it just like any other drive by typing D: or E: at the DOS prompt, or by accessing the drive through Explorer in Windows 9x. The major differences are (1) the CD-ROM drive is read-only—you cannot write to it, (2) a CD-ROM is a little slower to access than a hard drive.

Configuring an IDE CD-ROM Drive

An IDE CD-ROM drive uses the **ATAPI** (Advanced Technology Attachment Packet Interface) standard, an extension of the IDE/ATA standard that allows tape drives and CD-ROM drives to be treated just like another hard drive on the system. With hard drives, IDE refers to the integrated drive electronics, but IDE as applied to a CD-ROM drive refers to the interface protocol between the drive and the CPU that requires software at the OS level to complete the interface. Windows 9x supports this protocol internally.

Figure 10-8 shows the rear of an IDE CD-ROM drive. Note the jumper bank that can be set to cable select, slave, or master. Recall from Chapter 7 that, for enhanced IDE, there are four choices for drive installations: primary master, primary slave, secondary master, and secondary slave. If the drive will be the second drive installed on the cable, then set the drive to slave. If the drive is the only drive on the cable, since single is not a choice, choose master.

When given the choice of putting the CD-ROM drive on the same cable with a hard drive or on its own cable, choose to use its own cable. If the CD-ROM drive shares a cable with a hard drive, it can slow down the hard drive's performance. Most systems today have two IDE connections on the system board, so most likely you will be able to use IDE2 for the CD-ROM drive.

10

Figure 10-8 Rear view of an IDE CD-ROM drive

Inserting the CD-ROM Drive

Some systems use rails on the drive to slide it into the bay. If you have them (the rails should come with your computer), screw the rails in place and slide the drive into the bay. If you have no rails, then put two screws on each side of the drive, tightening the screws so the drive can't shift, but avoiding overtightening them. Use the screws that come with the drive; screws too long can damage the drive. If necessary, buy a mounting kit to extend the sides of the drive so that it will fit into the bay and be securely attached.

Connect the Cables and Cords

Find an unused four-prong power cord from the power supply and plug it into the drive. For IDE drives, connect the 40-pin cable to the IDE adapter and the drive, being careful to follow the Pin 1 rule: match the edge color on the cable to Pin 1 on both the adapter card and the drive.

Some CD-ROM drives come with an audio cord that attaches the interface card to a sound card, which then receives sound input directly from the CD-ROM. Attach the audio cord if you have a sound card. Don't make the mistake of attaching a miniature power cord designed for a 3½-inch disk drive coming from the power supply to the audio input connector on the sound card. The connections appear to fit, but you'll probably destroy the drive by doing so.

Some drives have a ground connection, with one end of the ground cable attaching to the computer case. Follow the directions included with the drive.

Verify Power to the Drive

Check all connections, and turn on the power. Press the eject button on the front of the drive. If it works, then you know power is getting to the drive.

A+CORE 1.2

Install the Device Driver for DOS

To operate in a DOS environment, a CD-ROM drive needs a device driver that is loaded from the CONFIG.SYS file. The driver interfaces with the drive and with a real-mode program called the Microsoft CD-ROM extension for DOS (MSCDEX.EXE), which must be loaded from AUTOEXEC.BAT. Both of these programs come on floppy disk with the CD-ROM drive. Run the installation program that is also on the disk. It copies the files to the hard drive and edits both the CONFIG.SYS and the AUTOEXEC.BAT files. Restart the computer so that the changes take effect. If you have problems accessing the drive after you have restarted, check the items listed under "Troubleshooting Guidelines," later in the chapter.

Install the Device Driver for Windows 9x

Windows 9x supports CD-ROM drives without add-on drivers. Click **Start**, **Settings**, **Control Panel**, and double-click **Add New Hardware**. Click **Next** when you are prompted to begin installing the software for the new device. Complete the installation by following the directions on the Add New Hardware sheet.

When Windows 9x starts up, it assigns the next available drive letter to the drive. To dictate what the drive letter should be, use Device Manager. Click **Start, Settings, Control Panel**, and select **System**. Click the **Device Manager** tab. Select the CD-ROM drive and click **Properties**, then the **Settings** tab (see Figure 10-9), where the drive is designated E:. Select a range of letters to be used by the drive and click **OK**.

> When you update or install additional features on applications software, some software expects the same drive letter for the CD-ROM drive that was used when it was first installed. Permanently setting the CD-ROM drive letter satisfies the requirements of this software.

Test the Drive

The drive is now ready to use. Press the eject button to open the drive shelf, and place a CD in the drive. Since data on CDs is written only on the bottom, be careful to protect it. Now access the CD using Explorer (use the assigned drive letter).

If you have a problem reading the CD, verify that the CD is placed in the tray label-side-up, and that the format is compatible with your drive. If one CD doesn't work, try another—the first CD may be defective or scratched.

A CD-ROM drive can be set so that when you insert a CD, software on the CD automatically executes, a feature called Autorun. To turn the feature on, from Device Manager, right click on the CD-ROM drive and select Properties. From the Properties window, select the Settings tab and select Auto insert notification. To prevent a CD from automatically playing when the feature is enabled, hold down the Shift key when inserting the CD.

10

Figure 10-9   You can specify the drive letter assigned to the CD-ROM drive from the Properties box for the drive

A+ OS 1.1   Update Your Windows 95 Rescue Disk to Include Access to the CD-ROM Drive

The Windows 9x emergency startup disks you created in earlier chapters to start a system in the event of a hard drive failure need to include access to the CD-ROM drive, because Windows 9x is normally loaded from a CD-ROM. Windows 98 automatically adds the real-mode CD-ROM device drivers to this rescue disk, but Windows 95 does not. This section explains how to add this functionality to the rescue disk.

Windows 9x has its own built-in 32-bit protected-mode drivers for CD-ROM drives, but when booting from a rescue disk, you are using older 16-bit real-mode drivers. Two files are required, the 16-bit device driver provided by the manufacturer of the CD-ROM drive (or a generic real-mode driver that works with the drive) and the 16-bit real-mode OS interface to the driver, MSCDEX.EXE. The device driver is loaded from CONFIG.SYS, and MSCDEX.EXE is loaded from AUTOEXEC.BAT.

If you have run the DOS installation program that came with the CD-ROM drive, then your AUTOEXEC.BAT and CONFIG.SYS files should already have the correct entries in them. You can add these lines to these same files on your rescue disk, correcting paths to the two files as needed. Copy the two files to your rescue disk so you can access the CD-ROM drive when you boot from this disk, even when the hard drive is not accessible.

A+ OS
  1.1

For example, on a rescue or boot disk designed to access the CD-ROM drive without depending on any files or commands on the hard drive, the CONFIG.SYS file might contain this command (the parameters in the command lines are explained below):

```
DEVICE = SLCD.SYS /D:MSCD001
```

The AUTOEXEC.BAT file might contain this command line:

```
MSCDEX.EXE /D:MSCD001 /L:E /M:8
```

The explanations of these command lines are as follows:

- Two files needed to manage the drive are MSCDEX.EXE and SLCD.SYS, which must be copied to this disk.

- When the program MSCDEX.EXE executes, it uses the MSCD001 entry as a tag back to the CONFIG.SYS file to learn which device driver is being used to interface with the drive—in this case, SLCD.SYS.

- To MSCDEX.EXE, the drive is named MSCD001 and is being managed by the driver SLCD.

- MSCDEX.EXE will use SLCD as its "go-between" to access the drive.

- MSCDEX.EXE also assigns a drive letter to the drive. If you want to specify a certain drive letter, use the /L: option in the command line. In our example, the CD-ROM drive will be drive E. If you don't use the /L: option, then the next available drive letter is used.

- The /M: option controls the number of memory buffers.

- If the files referenced in these two commands are stored on the floppy disk in a different directory from the root directory, then include the path to the file in front of the filename.

If your hard drive fails and you start up from your rescue disk, once the CD-ROM drivers are loaded and the CD-ROM drive is recognized, you can install or reinstall Windows 9x from CD. To do this, insert the Windows 9x CD into the CD-ROM drive, and from the CD-ROM drive prompt (either D:, E: or some other letter), type **Setup** and then press **Enter**. Once Windows 9x is installed, it will often ignore existing CONFIG.SYS lines (turning them into comment lines by adding REM to the beginning of the line) and handle the CD-ROM drivers through its own protected-mode drivers.

Optimizing CD-ROM Cache

Recall that for Windows 9x, VCACHE replaced SmartDrive in Windows 3.x as the disk-caching software. For removable drives, VCACHE caches when reading data but not when writing. VCACHE decides how much memory to use when caching data, based on the speed of the CD-ROM drive and how much memory is installed in the system. You can affect this decision using the Performance tab in System Properties. Click **Start**, **Settings**, **Control Panel**, and select **System**. In the Properties dialog box, click the **Performance** tab and then click **File System**. Click **CD-ROM** on the File System Properties box, as seen

10

in Figure 10-10. By changing the CD-ROM speed in this box, you are changing the amount of memory allotted to the cache. The amount is displayed in the last sentence on this box.

Figure 10-10   By changing the CD-ROM speed in the File System Properties box, you can change the amount of memory VCACHE uses

CD-R and CD-RW Drives

A CD-ROM is a read-only medium meaning that CD-ROM drives can only read, not write. In the past, writing to a CD required expensive equipment and was not practical for personal computer use. Now, **CD-Recordable** (**CD-R**) drives cost around $300, and the CD-R disc costs less than $5, making "burning" your own CD a viable option. These CD-R discs can be read by regular CD-ROM drives and are excellent ways to distribute software or large amounts of data. Besides allowing for a lot of data storage space on a relatively inexpensive medium, another advantage of distributing software and/or data on a CD-R disc is that you can be assured that no one will edit or overwrite what's written on the disc.

A regular CD-ROM is created by physically etching pits into the surface of the disc, but a CD-R disc is created differently. Heat is applied to special chemicals on the disc and causes these chemicals to reflect less light than the areas that are not burned, thus creating the same effect as a pit does on a regular CD. Referring to writing data to a CD-R as burning the CD-R is actually fairly accurate. When you purchase and install a CD-R drive, good software to manage the writing process is an important part of the purchase, because some less robust software can make burning a disc a difficult process. Also, some CD-R drives are multisession drives and some are not.

Also available at a higher cost is a **rewriteable CD** (**CD-RW**), which allows you to over-write old data with new data. The process of creating a CD-RW disc is similar to that used by CD-R discs. The chemicals on the surface of the CD-RW disc are different, allowing the process of writing a less-reflective spot to the surface of the disc to be reversed so that data can be erased. One drawback to these CD-RW discs is that the medium cannot always be read successfully by older CD-ROM drives.

CD-RW discs are useful in the process of developing CDs for distribution. A developer can create a disc, test for errors, and rewrite to the disc without having to waste many discs during the development process. Once the disc is fully tested, then CD-R discs can be burned for distribution. The advantages of distributing on CD-R discs rather than CD-RW discs are that CD-R discs are less expensive and can be read by all CD-ROM drives.

Sound Cards

A sound card is an expansion card that records sound, saves it to a file on your hard drive, and plays it back. Some cards give you the ability to mix and edit sound, and even to edit the sound using standard music score notation. Sound cards have ports for external stereo speakers and microphone input. Also, sound cards may be Sound Blaster compatible, which means that they can understand the commands sent to them that have been written for a Sound Blaster card, which is generally considered the standard for PC sound cards. Some play CD audio by way of a cable connecting the CD to the sound card. For good quality sound you definitely need external speakers and perhaps an amplifier.

Sound passes through three stages when it is computerized: (1) digitize or input the sound, that is, convert it from analog to digital, (2) store the digital data in a compressed data file, and later (3) reproduce or synthesize the sound (digital to analog). Each of these stages is discussed next, followed by a discussion of sound card installation.

Sampling and Digitizing the Sound

Remember that converting sound from analog to digital storage is done by first sampling the sound and then digitizing it. Sampling and digitizing the sound are done by a method called **pulse code modulation** (**PCM**) and involves a component called an **analog-to-digital converter** (**A/D** or **ADC**). It follows that the opposite technology, which converts digital to analog, is also needed, and that conversion is done by a **digital-to-analog converter** or **DAC**. The DAC technology on a sound card converts digital sound files back into analog sound just before output to the speakers.

When recording sound, the analog sound is converted to analog voltage by a microphone and is passed to the sound card, where it is digitized. As explained earlier in the chapter, the critical factor in the performance of a sound card is the accuracy of the samples (determined by the number of bits used to hold each sample value, which can be either 8 or 16 bits). This number of bits is called the **sample size**. The **sampling rate** of a sound card (the number of samples taken of the analog signal over a period of time) is usually expressed as samples (cycles) per second, or **hertz**. One thousand hertz (one kilohertz) is written as kHz. Remember that a low sampling rate provides a less accurate representation of the sound than does a high sampling rate. Our ears detect up to about 22,000 samples per second or hertz. The sampling rate of music CDs is 44,100 Hz, or 44.1 kHz. When recording sound on a PC, the sampling rate is controlled by the software.

As explained above, sample size is the amount of space used to store a single sample measurement. The larger the sample size, the more accurate the sampling. The number of values used to measure sound is determined by the number of bits allocated to hold each number. If 8 bits are used to hold one number, then the sample range can be from –128 to +128. This is because 1111 1111 in binary equals 255 in decimal, which, together with zero, equals 256 values. Samples of sound are considered to be both positive and negative numbers, so the range is −128 to +127 rather than 0 to 255. However, if 16 bits are used to hold the range of numbers, then the sample range increases dramatically because 1111 1111 1111 1111 in binary is 65,535 in decimal, meaning that the sample size can be −32,768 to +32,767, or a total of 65,536 values.

An 8-bit sound card uses 8 bits to store a sample value, or uses a 256 sample size. A 16-bit sound card has a sample size of 65,536. Sound cards typically use 8- or 16-bit sample sizes, with a sampling rate from 4,000 to 44,000 samples per second. For high-quality sound, use a 16-bit sound card. Samples may also be recorded on a single channel (mono) or on two channels (stereo).

Don't confuse the sample size of 8 bits or 16 bits with the ISA bus size that the sound card uses to attach to the system board. A sound card may use an 8-bit sample size but a 16-bit ISA bus. When you hear people talk about an 8-bit sound card, they are speaking of the sample size, not the bus size.

Storing Sound in Files

Sound cards store sound in files in two ways: MIDI and WAV files. **MIDI (musical instrument digital interface**, pronounced "middy") technology, a standard for digitizing sound, dictates a specific number of sound samples and the quality of those samples. MIDI files have a .mid file extension. Nearly all sound cards support MIDI. The MIDI standard is supported by most synthesizers, so sounds created on one synthesizer can be played by another. Computers with a MIDI interface can receive sound created by a MIDI synthesizer and then manipulate the data in MIDI files to produce new sounds. The MIDI standards include storing sound data, such as a note's pitch, length, and volume, and can include attack and delay times. Data compression is used because sound files can be quite large.

Sampled files, which Microsoft calls **WAV** files (pronounced, and stands for, "wave"), have a .wav file extension. When Windows records sound using a sound card, the sound is stored in a .wav file. Most game music is stored in MIDI files, but most multimedia sound is stored in WAV files.

Sound files are often large. For example, CD-quality sound is recorded using a 16-bit sample size and 44.1 kHz sampling rate with stereo. The calculations of data size are:

16 bits $\times$ 44,100 samples/sec $\times$ 2 = 1,411,200 bits/sec or 176,400 bytes/sec

This yields more than 30 MB of disk space for a 3-minute song. Because of these large file sizes, methods of compressing data have evolved. Several are discussed next.

Compressing Data

You can compress data using several standards. Some apply to just audio and others to audio and video. To see the standards currently installed under Windows, double-click the **Multimedia** icon in Control Panel, and then click the **Devices** tab. See Figure 10-11. Click the plus sign next to **Audio Compression Codecs**. Compressing and later decompressing data is called **CODEC (Compressor/DECompressor)**. A CODEC method that does not drop any data is called **lossless compression**, and a method that works by dropping unnecessary data is called **lossy compression**. The term CODEC can also refer to hardware that converts audio or video signals from analog to digital or from digital to analog. When the term is used this way, it stands for coder/decoder.

Figure 10-11   Use the Multimedia icon in Control Panel to see the codecs supported by Windows

One of the better-known data compression standards is MPEG, an international standard for data compression for motion pictures. Developed by the **Moving Pictures Experts Group** (**MPEG**), it tracks movement from one frame to the next, and only stores what changes, rather than compressing individual frames. MPEG is a type of lossy compression. MPEG compression can yield a compression ratio of 100:1 for full-motion video (30 frames per second, or 30 fps).

There are currently several MPEG standards, MPEG-1, MPEG-2, MPEG-3, and MPEG-4. MPEG-1 is used in business and home applications to compress images. MPEG-2 is used to compress video films on DVD-ROM. MPEG-3 is best known for audio compression. MPEG-4 is used for video transmissions over the Internet.

MPEG level 3 audio compression, better known as **MP3**, is a way to compress sound files to a compression ratio of 1:12 and even as low as 1:24 for stereo sound without losing sound quality. This compression is possible because the data is compressed in such a way that sound that is not normally heard or noticed by the human ear is cut out or drastically reduced. Sound files downloaded from the Internet are most often MP3 files. MP3 files have a .mp3 file extension. For more information about MPEG and MP3, see *www.mpeg.org*.

Digital-to-Analog Conversion

Sound cards use two methods to convert digitally stored sound into real analog sound: **FM (frequency modulation)** synthesis and **wavetable** synthesis. The difference between the two is that FM synthesis creates a sound by artificially creating a wave similar to the sound wave produced by the instrument. With FM synthesis, sound is reproduced by making a mathematical approximation of the musical sound wave. For example, the sound of a trumpet would be produced by imitating the sound wave produced by the trumpet, through a series of mathematical calculations. Wavetable synthesis produces the sound by using a sample recording of the real instrument. This table of stored sample sounds is called the wave table, and a group of samples for each instrument is called a **voice**. Wavetable synthesis produces better sound than does FM synthesis, but is also more expensive.

Sound Playback   Once the sound has been converted back into an analog signal, you need speakers to play back the sound using a sound card. Unlike speakers used for other sound equipment, speakers made for computers have built-in amplifiers and extra shielding to protect the monitor from the magnetic fields around regular speakers.

> If you plan to put speakers close to a monitor, be certain they are shielded. Speakers that are not shielded cause the monitor to display strange colors, and can eventually do permanent damage to the monitor. Also, setting floppy disks on top of unshielded speakers can damage the data on the disks.

A+CORE 2.1 | Installing a Sound Card and Software

Most sound cards come with a device driver as well as all the software needed for normal use, such as applications software to play music CDs. The installation of a sample sound card is described below. The sample card used is the Creative Lab's Sound Blaster PCI128 shown in Figure 10-12. It is Plug and Play compliant, uses a PCI slot, and supports a 128-voice wavetable. It will work under DOS 6+, Windows 9x, Windows NT, or Windows 2000. The card comes with drivers and software on a CD-ROM and a user's guide.

$A^{+}_{2.1}\!\!\!\!^{CORE}$

Input from TAD (telephone answering device)

CD audio connector

TV/IDE connector-input from video card or IDE CD-ROM

Jumper to enable/disable speaker amplifier

Front speakers

Rear speakers

Microphone

Joystick/MIDI connector

Stereo, CD player, tape deck, etc.

10

Figure 10-12   A Sound Blaster sound card

The three main steps in this example of a sound card installation are to install the card itself in an empty PCI slot on the system board, install the driver under Windows 98, and then install the applications stored on the sound card's CD.

Installing a Sound Card   Follow these steps to install a sound card:

1. Turn the PC off, remove the cover, and locate an empty expansion slot for the card. Since this installation uses the connecting wire from the sound card to the CD-ROM drive (the wire comes with the sound card), place the sound card near enough to the CD-ROM drive so that the wire can reach between them.

2. Attach the wire to the sound card (see Figure 10-13) and to the CD-ROM drive.

3. Remove the cover from the slot opening at the rear of the PC case and place the card into the slot, making sure that the card is seated firmly. Use the screw taken from the slot cover to secure the card to the back of the PC case.

4. Check again that both ends of the wire are still securely connected, and replace the case cover.

5. Plug in the speakers to the ports at the back of the sound card and turn on the PC. The speakers may or may not require their own power source.

$A^{+CORE}_{2.1}$

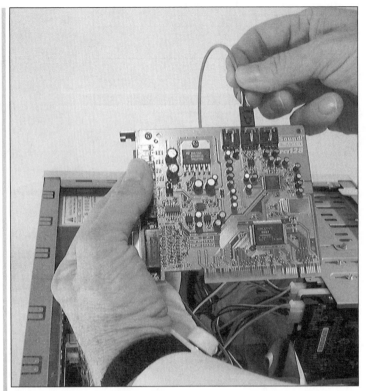

Figure 10-13   Connect the wire to the sound card that will make the direct audio connection from the CD

Installing the Sound Card Driver   Once the card is installed, the device drivers must be installed. When Windows 98 starts, it detects that new hardware is present. The New Hardware Found dialog box opens, indicating that it has discovered the Sound Blaster PIC128. Follow these steps to install the sound card driver:

1. The New Hardware Wizard gives you this option: **Search for the Best Driver for Your Device (Recommended)**. Select this option and click the **Next** button.

2. Clear all check boxes and check only the **Specify a Location** check box.

3. Click the **Browse** button and point to the driver path: **D:\Audio\English\Win95drv**.

   In this example, the CD-ROM drive is drive D, and the sound card's user guide listed the location of the driver on the CD. Substitute your CD-ROM drive letter and, for other sound card installations, see the documentation for the location of the driver on the CD-ROM.

A^+_{CORE}
2.1

4. Click **Next** to continue the driver installation.

5. Click **Finish** when the installation is complete and reboot your PC.

With most sound cards, on the CD containing the sound card driver, you can find some special applications software to use the special features offered by the card. Sometimes, as is the case with this Sound Blaster card, this software is installed at the same time as the drivers so you can use the software at this point in the installation. With other sound cards, after the driver installation is complete and the sound card is working under Windows 9x, you can then install the additional software. See the documentation that comes with the sound card to learn if applications software is present and how and when to install it.

After you have installed the driver, rebooted, and entered Windows, verify that the device and the driver are correctly installed in Windows 98 by using Device Manager.

1. Click **Start**, point to **Settings**, click **Control Panel**, and then double-click **System**.

2. Select the **Device Manager** tab. Figure 10-14 shows the sound card installed.

3. To see the resources used by the card, select the card and click **Properties**. The Properties box displays. Click the **Resources** tab.

10

Figure 10-14   Device Manager shows the sound card installed and the resources it is using

Using Sound with Windows 9x   Windows 9x offers some support for sound, such as playing a music CD or a WAV file or providing sound when performing certain Windows functions (such as starting an application or exiting Windows). This section will look at these features.

To configure the Windows 9x sound system to use the new sound card, first determine that sound control is installed under the Windows 9x Multimedia section, and then test the sound using Windows 9x:

1. Click **Start**, point to **Settings**, click **Control Panel**, and then double-click **Add/Remove Programs**.

2. Click the **Windows Setup** tab. From this tab, shown in Figure 10-15, you can install components of Windows 9x that were not installed at the original installation.

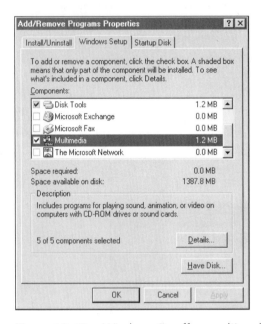

Figure 10-15   Windows 9x offers multimedia support

3. Click **Multimedia**, and then click **Details** to see the components of Windows 9x multimedia support (see Figure 10-16). Installed components are checked.

4. If CD Player, Volume Control, and Sound Recorder are not installed, then install them now. Select the files by clicking the check boxes.

5. Click **Apply** to install these components. You might be asked to insert the Windows 9x CD or floppy disks.

To test the sound, access the Multimedia group of Windows 95 or the Entertainment group of Windows 98. Note that the controls and windows displayed might be slightly different depending on the Windows 9x components, sound card drivers and other audio software installed:

1. For Windows 95, click **Start**, point to **Programs**, **Accessories**, and click **Multimedia**. For Windows 98, click **Start**, point to **Programs**, **Accessories**, and click **Entertainment**. Figure 10-17 shows the components for sound under Entertainment for Windows 98, which are the same for Windows 95 Multimedia.

Figure 10-16   The components of Windows 9x multimedia support

Figure 10-17   Controlling sound using Windows 98

2. To play a music CD, click **CD Player**. The CD Player window is displayed. See Figure 10-18.

3. Insert a music CD in the CD-ROM drive and click the play button which is a forward arrow.

4. To adjust the volume of the sound card, click **Start**, point to **Programs**, **Accessories**, **Entertainment**, and click **Volume Control**. The Volume Control window in Figure 10-19 appears. Adjust the volume and close the dialog box when finished.

Figure 10-18 Windows CD Player

Figure 10-19 Windows 9x volume control

A handy way to adjust the volume is to have Windows keep the volume control on the taskbar. To do this, use the Multimedia control in Control Panel: Click **Start**, **Settings**, **Control Panel** and then double-click **Multimedia**, and then click the **Audio** tab of the Multimedia window (see Figure 10-20). Check **Show volume control on the taskbar**.

Figure 10-20   Windows 98 multimedia audio selection includes the option to put volume control on the taskbar

Recording Sound   In addition to being able to play sound, a multimedia system must be able to record it, for which you need a microphone. You can attach a microphone to the MIC port on the back of the sound card. Windows 9x saves sound files in the WAV file format. To record sound using Windows 9x, follow these steps:

1. Click **Start**, point to **Programs**, **Accessories**, **Multimedia (or Entertainment)**, and click **Sound Recorder** (see Figure 10-21).

Figure 10-21   Recording sound using Windows 9x

2. Click the **Record** button (the red dot on the right side of the dialog box) to record. Sound enters the microphone and moves as an analog signal to the sound card, which samples and digitizes it before passing it on to the CPU by way of the system bus.

3. Click the **Stop** button when finished recording.

4. Click **File** and **Save As** to save the sound file for later use.

Controlling Windows 9x Sounds   When certain events occur, Windows 9x plays sounds that are controlled by the Sounds control of the Windows 9x Control Panel. To customize these sounds and the times at which they occur, access Control Panel (click **Start**, **Settings**, **Control Panel**), and then double-click the **Sounds** icon. Items listed that have a horn icon beside them cause a sound. The sound for this item is defined in the Name list. For example, in Figure 10-22, for the event Exit Windows, the sound will be The Microsoft Sound.wav. To preview the sound, click the **Play** button to the right of the filename. You can develop your own customized choices of sounds for chosen events using this box. Save the scheme as a file using the **Save As** option at the bottom of the box, and use it to create a multimedia sound experience when working with Windows 9x!

Figure 10-22   Controlling sound events under Windows 9x

Troubleshooting Guidelines

A+CORE 2.2   This section covers some troubleshooting guidelines for CD-ROM drives and sound cards.

Problems with a CD-ROM Installation

The following are general guidelines to use when a CD-ROM drive installation under DOS presents the problems described:

The Error Message "Invalid Drive Specification" Appears While the System Is Starting Up   Check that in the command lines in the CONFIG.SYS or AUTOEXEC.BAT files have no errors according to the documentation that came with the

A+CORE
2.2

CD-ROM. Did you get an error message during startup, such as "Bad Command" or "File Not Found"?

Turn off the computer, reseat the adapter card, and check cable connections.

The MSCDEX.EXE program might not be loaded because it is placed too late in the AUTOEXEC.BAT file. Sometimes when an installation program edits the CONFIG.SYS or AUTOEXEC.BAT files, the command is added too late in the file. If AUTOEXEC.BAT has the command to load the CD-ROM program after the command to execute Windows, the CD-ROM command will not execute. If this is the case, move the command up near the beginning of the AUTOEXEC.BAT file.

You might be using a version of the MSCDEX.EXE program that is different from the version that comes with DOS. If you have DOS 6+, use the version of MSCDEX.EXE that is in the \DOS directory. Change the path to the command in AUTOEXEC.BAT so it accesses the DOS MSCDEX.EXE. For example, if the command line looks like this:

```
C:\CDROM\MSCDEX /D:MSCD001 /M:10
```

change it to read:

```
C:\DOS\MSCDEX /D:MSCD001 /M:10
```

The Install Process Is Terminated with the Message "MSCDEX.EXE Not Found"
MSCDEX.EXE must be copied onto the hard drive. Put it in the \DOS directory, then restart the install process. Sometimes MSCDEX is placed in the Windows directory, and sometimes a copy is put in the newly created CD-ROM directory.

The Error Message "Not Enough Drive Letters" Appears During the Startup Process
By default, DOS only allows five logical drive letters (A through E). If you have used these up, then you must tell DOS to accept more drive letters, with the LASTDRIVE line in CONFIG.SYS. The line can look like this:

```
LASTDRIVE=Z
```

Conflict Errors Exist These appear during startup as error messages, or they can cause some other device to fail to operate. The IRQ and I/O address of your CD-ROM should be in the documentation. If not, call the manufacturer's technical support for this information or check the manufacturer's web site.

Computer does not recognize the CD-ROM drive (no D: prompt in DOS, or no drive D listed in Windows 9x Explorer)

- Check the data cable and power cord connections to the CD-ROM drive. Is the stripe on the data cable correctly aligned to pin 1? (Look for an arrow or small 1 printed on the drive. For a best guess, pin 1 is usually next to the power connector.)

- For an IDE drive, is the correct master/slave jumper set? For example, if both the hard drive and the CD-ROM drive are hooked up to the same ribbon cable, one must be set to master and the other to slave. If the CD-ROM drive is the only drive connected to the cable, then it must be set to single or master.

10

- For an IDE drive, is the IDE connection on the system board disabled in CMOS setup?

- If you are using a SCSI drive, are the proper IDs set, and is the device terminated if it is the last item in the SCSI chain?

- If you are using DOS, check drivers including entries in CONFIG.SYS and AUTOEXEC.BAT, and verify that MSCDEX.EXE is in the correct directory.

- Is another device using the same port settings or IRQ number? For Windows 9x, see Control Panel, System, Device Manager.

- Suspect a boot virus. Run a virus scan program.

There is no sound Is the sound cable attached between the CD-ROM and the analog audio connector on the sound card?

- Are the speakers turned on?

- Is the speaker volume turned down?

- Are the speakers plugged into the line "Out" or the "Spkr" port of the sound card?

- Is the transformer for the speaker plugged into an electrical outlet on one end and into the speakers on the other end?

- Is the volume control for Windows turned down? (To check, click **Start**, **Programs**, **Accessories**, **Multimedia**, **Volume Control**.)

- Does the sound card have a "diagnose" file on the install disk?

- Reinstall the sound card drivers.

- Is another device using the same I/O addresses or IRQ number?

- To check for a bad connection, turn off the computer and remove and reinstall the sound card.

- Replace the sound card with one you know is good.

Digital Cameras

A recent introduction to multimedia, with markets in both business and home computing, is the digital camera, which is becoming more popular as quality improves and prices decrease. Digital camera technology works much like scanner technology, except that it is much faster. It essentially scans the field of image set by the picture taker, and translates the light signals into digital values, which can be stored as a file and viewed with software that interprets the stored values appropriately.

TWAIN (technology without an interesting name) format is a standard format used by both digital cameras and PCs for transferring the image. Transfer the image to your computer's hard drive using a serial cable supplied with the camera, a parallel cable, or some external disk medium such as a flash RAM card, which is faster and more convenient than the other methods. Figure 10-23 shows a SmartMedia card from a digital camera inserted into a FlashPath card that can then be inserted into a floppy disk drive to upload images to the PC.

FlashPath

SmartMedia

Figure 10-23 The small SmartMedia card holds the digital images from a digital camera. FlashPath allows a PC to read SmartMedia by way of a floppy disk drive

10

Once the images are on the PC, use the camera's image-editing software or another program such as Adobe PhotoShop to view, touch up, and print the picture. The picture file, which is usually in **JPEG (Joint Photographic Experts Group)** format, can then be imported into documents. JPEG is a common lossy compression standard for storing photos.

Most digital cameras also have a video-out port so that you can attach the camera to any TV using a serial cable. You can then display pictures on TV or copy them to videotape.

The image sensing can be done by two kinds of technology: infrared sensor or charge-coupled device (CCD). The image sensor captures light reflected off the subject and converts that light to a serial stream of small DC voltages. The image sensor is made up of three sensors, each filtering a different color (red, green, or blue). Figure 10-24 shows the process a digital camera uses to create a picture. The figure shows only one channel of the three channels used (one channel for each color). The image sensor captures the light and converts it into voltage signals that will become pixels. These signals move through the DC restore or DC clamping stage and then on to the gain stage, where the signals are amplified and buffered. Next, the signals enter the ADC (analog-to-digital converter), where they are digitized. The digital pixels are then processed by the image processor and sent on to storage through the I/O process. The controller in the diagram controls all processing of the digital signals.

Figure 10-24   The signal chain used by a digital camera

MP3 Player

A popular audio compression codec is MP3, an advanced method of MPEG-3, that can reduce the size of a sound file as much as 1:17 without a noticeable loss in quality. An MP3 player is a device or software that plays these MP3 files. Portable MP3 players store the MP3 files on a compact storage device such as a SmartMedia card by Toshiba. When using a digital camera, data is transferred or uploaded from the camera to the PC, but when using a portable MP3 player, data is downloaded from the PC to the player.

You can purchase MP3 music files on the storage media suitable for your MP3 player, from regular CDs, or from web sites on the Internet such as eMusic at *www.emusic.com*. From the Internet, download them to your PC and then either play them on your PC using MP3 player software such as Windows Media Player or MusicMatch Jukebox (see *www.musicmatch.com*). You can also play the MP3 files directly from the Internet without first downloading them, which is called **streaming audio**.

Traditional music CDs store music files in CD format. You can use software that copies the music file from the CD and converts it to a WAV file, which is not compressed. This software is called a ripper because you're "ripping off" the CD. Once the file is in WAV format on your hard drive, use encoder software to compress the file into MP3 format. Next copy the MP3 file to a SmartMedia card or other type of flash storage device. For example, I-Jam portable MP3 players use a flash card smaller than SmartMedia called SanDisk. Data is downloaded to the card by way of a serial port interface. For more information about I-Jam MP3 players, see *www.ijamworld.com* and for information about the SanDisk flash card, see *www.sandisk.com*. CD rippers, MP3 encoders, and MP3 player software can be downloaded from the Internet. For example, see the MusicMatch site at *www.musicmatch.com*.

Video-Capturing Card

An NTSC (National Television Standards Committee) video-capturing card is another multimedia option. With this card, you can capture input from a camcorder or directly from TV. Video can be saved as motion clips or stills, edited, and, with the right card, copied back to video tape for viewing by a VCR and television. Look for these features on a video capture card: an IEEE 1394 port to interface with a digital camcorder, data transfer rates which affect the price of the card, capture resolution and color-depth capabilities of the card, ability to transfer data back to the digital camcorder or VCR, stereo audio jacks, and the video editing software bundled with the card. Other options include a TV tuner which makes it possible to turn your PC into a television complete with instant replay and program scheduling. Ports on a video capturing card might include an antenna or cable TV port for input and a TV or VCR port for output. Other ports are a PC monitor video port and possibly an IEEE 1394 port for a camcorder. Expect the card to fit into an AGP slot and take the place of your regular video card. For an excellent example of a video capturing card, see the All-in-Wonder card from ATI Technologies at *www.ati.com*.

Digital Video Disc (DVD)

With multimedia, the ability to store massive amounts of data is paramount to the technology's success. The goal of storing a full-length movie on a single unit of computerized, inexpensive storage medium has been met by more than one technology, but the technology that has clearly taken the lead in popularity is **digital video disc**, or digital versatile disc (**DVD**) technology (see Figure 10-25). It takes up to seven CDs to store a full-length movie, and only one DVD disc. A DVD disc can hold 8.5 GB of data, and, if both the top and bottom surfaces are used, can hold 17 GB of data, which is enough for more than 8 hours of video storage.

Figure 10-25   A DVD device

Both DVD and CD-ROM technologies use patterns of tiny pits on the surface of a disc to represent bits, which are then readable by a laser beam. When looking at the surface of either disc, it is difficult to distinguish between the two. They both have the same 5-inch diameter and 1.2-mm thickness, and the same shiny surface. But, because DVD uses a shorter wavelength laser, it can read smaller, more densely packed pits, which increases the disc's capacity. In addition, there is a second layer added to DVD discs, an opaque layer that also holds data, which almost doubles the capacity of the disc. Also, a DVD disc can use both the top and bottom surface for data.

DVD uses MPEG-2 video compression and requires an MPEG-2 controller card to decode the compressed data. Audio is stored on DVD in Dolby AC-3 compression. This audio compression method is also the standard to be used by HDTV (high-definition TV), soon to be introduced into the marketplace. Dolby AC-3 compression is also known as Dolby Digital Surround or Dolby Surround Sound and supports six separate sound channels of sound information for six different speakers, each producing a different sound! These speakers are known as Front Left and Right, Front Center, Rear Left and Right, and Subwoofer. Because each channel is digital, there is no background noise on the channel, and a sound engineer can place sound on any one of these speakers. The sound effects can be awesome!

10

The DVD controller card decodes both MPEG-2 video and Dolby AC-3 audio data and outputs them to a video port and speaker port, respectively. This PCI controller card can be configured to work in more than one way. Figure 10-26 shows one configuration demonstrating how the flow of data can come from a DVD disc through the PC to speakers and monitor. The DVD drive is attached to the system board by way of a SCSI controller that enables the data to bypass the CPU and to be routed directly to the MPEG-2 decoder card. The MPEG-2 decoder separates the video data from the sound data, decodes both, and sends the video data to the video controller card and on to the monitor. The DVD controller is also acting as a sound card. The sound data is sent to a DAC on the card that directs the analog sound signal to the speakers.

Figure 10-26   How a PC can use DVD data

Other DVD Devices

Besides DVD ROM, new DVD devices are coming on the market that are read-writeable. Table 10-1 describes these devices.

Table 10-1 DVD devices

DVD Device	Description
DVD-ROM	Read-only device. A DVD-ROM drive can also read CD-ROMs.
DVD-R	DVD recordable. Uses a similar technology to that used by CD-R drives. Holds about 4.7 GB of data. Can read DVD-ROM discs.
DVD-RAM	Recordable and erasable. Multifunctional DVD device that uses phase-dual (PD) technology. Can read DVD-RAM, DVD-R, DVD-ROM, and CD-R discs.
DVD-RW or DVD-ER	Rewritable DVD device, also known as erasable, recordable device. Uses phase-dual technology. Media can be read by most DVD-ROM drives.
DVD+RW	A technology similar to and currently competing with DVD-RW. Can read DVD-ROM and CD-ROM discs, but will not be compatible with DVD-RAM discs.

The last three items in Table 10-1 are competing with one another. All have similar, yet different, features, and compatibility and standards are issues. It's yet to be seen which of these three media will prevail in the marketplace. When purchasing one, pay close attention to compatibility with other media, such as CD-ROM, and availability and price of discs.

10

CHAPTER SUMMARY

❑ Multimedia PCs and devices are designed to create and reproduce lifelike presentations of sight and sound.

❑ Magazines, books, the Internet, retailers, and satisfied users are excellent resources for information when you are looking into purchasing multimedia devices.

❑ MPEG is a lossy compression method for files storing full-motion video and sound; lossy compression refers to compressing data by eliminating some of the data.

❑ MP3 is a version of MPEG compression used for audio files. Portable MP3 players stored MP3 files on flash storage devices.

❑ When analog data is converted to digital data for a PC, the data is sampled, meaning that samples are taken at discrete intervals and stored individually as digital data. This process is called digitizing the data, and the results are an approximation of the original data.

❑ When converting from analog to digital, the greater the number of samples and the more accurate each sample, the better the approximation of the original analog data.

❑ Interpolative scaling and color space conversions are two methods used by video controllers to improve video output.

❑ MIDI is a standard for the transmitting and storage of synthesized sound and is used by many sound cards.

❑ A sound card uses pulse code modulation or PCM, which is a sampling method, to convert analog sound to digital.

- Two methods of synthesizing sound are FM and wavetable. The wavetable method is more expensive and more accurate than FM.

- MMX and SSE by Intel and 3DNow! by AMD improve the speed of processing graphics, video, and sound, using improved methods of handling high-volume repetition during I/O operations.

- In order to take full advantage of MMX, SSE, or 3DNow! technology, software must be written to use its specific capabilities.

- CD-ROMs are read-only devices with data physically embedded into the surface of the disc.

- The speed of some CD-ROM drives slows down as the laser beam moves from the inside to the outside of the disc.

- CD-ROM drives can have an IDE or SCSI interface, or they can connect to the system bus through a proprietary expansion card or through a connection on a sound card.

- The most common interface for CD-ROM drives is IDE, which uses the ATAPI standard, an extension of the IDE/ATA standard developed for tape drives and CD-ROM, so that they can be treated just like another drive on the system.

- Data is only written to the bottom of a CD-ROM, which should be protected from damage.

- If you have installed Windows 95 from CD, be sure that your Windows 95 emergency startup disk has the necessary real-mode drivers on it to support a CD-ROM drive when this disk is used as the boot device. Windows 98 normally puts these drivers on the rescue disk for you.

- Installing a sound card includes physically installing the card, then installing the sound card driver and sound applications software. Windows 9x supports multimedia sound without using other applications software, but applications that usually come with sound cards enhance the ability to control various sound features.

- Digital cameras use light sensors to detect light and convert it to a digital signal stored in an image file using JPEG format.

- A DVD can store a full-length movie and uses an accompanying decoder card to decode the MPEG-compressed video data and Dolby AC-3 compressed audio.

- Video capture cards can be used to capture video images from VCRs, camcorders, and TVs for storage and manipulation on your PC.

Key Terms

Analog-to-digital converter (A/D or ADC) — A component on a sound card that samples and converts analog sound into digital values that can be stored on hard drives.

ATAPI (Advanced Technology Attachment Packet Interface) — An interface standard that is part of the IDE/ATA standards, which allows tape drives and CD-ROM drives to be treated like an IDE hard drive by the OS.

Bit map file — A type of graphics file in which the image is written as a series of 0s and 1s. These files have the extension .bmp and can be loaded into paint programs to be edited and printed.

CD-R (recordable CD) — A CD drive that can record or write data to a CD. The drive may or may not be multisession, but the data cannot be erased once it is written.

CD-RW (rewriteable CD) — A CD drive that can record or write data to a CD. The data can be erased and overwritten. The drive may or may not be multisession.

CODEC (compressor/decompressor) — Compressing and later decompressing sound, animation, and video files. MPEG is a common example. Also stands for coder/decoder when referring to digital-to-analog conversions.

Constant angular velocity (CAV) — A technology used by hard drives and newer CD-ROM drives whereby the disc rotates at a constant speed.

Constant linear velocity (CLV) — A CD-ROM format in which the spacing of data is consistent on the CD, but the speed of the disc varies depending on whether the data is reading near the center or the edge of the disc.

DAC (digital-to-analog converter) — A component that converts digital data back into analog signals just before output from the computer. For example, DAC technology is used to convert digital sound to analog sound just before playback to the speakers.

Digital video disc (DVD) — A faster, larger CD-ROM format that can read older CDs, store over 8 gigabytes of data, and hold full-length motion picture videos.

10

FM (frequency modulation) method — A method of synthesizing sound by making a mathematical approximation of the musical sound wave. MIDI may use FM synthesis or wavetable synthesis.

Hertz (Hz) — Unit of measurement for frequency, calculated in terms of vibrations, or cycles, per second. For example, a Pentium CPU may have a speed of 233 MHz (megahertz). For 16-bit stereo sound, 44,100 Hz is used.

JPEG (Joint Photographic Experts Group) — A "lossy" graphical compression scheme that allows the user to control the amount of data that is averaged and sacrificed as file size is reduced. It is a common Internet file format. *See* Lossy compression.

Land — Microscopic flat areas on the surface of a CD or DVD that separate pits. Lands and pits are used to represent data on the disc.

Lossless compression — A method that substitutes special characters for repeating patterns without image degradation. A substitution table is used to restore the compressed image to its original form. *See* Lossy compression.

Lossy compression — A method that drops unnecessary data, but with some image and sound loss. JPEG allows the user to control the amount of loss, which is inversely related to the image size. *See* Lossless compression.

MIDI (Musical Instrument Digital Interface) — Pronounced "middy," a standard for transmitting sound from musical devices, such as electronic keyboards, to computers where it can be digitally stored.

MMX (Multimedia Extensions) technology — A variation of the Pentium processor designed to manage and speed up high-volume input/output needed for graphics, motion video, animation, and sound.

MP3 — A method to compress audio files that uses MPEG level 3. It can reduce sound files as low as a 1:24 ratio without loosing sound quality.

MPEG (Moving Pictures Experts Group) — A processing-intensive standard for data compression for motion pictures that tracks movement from one frame to the next, and only stores the new data that has changed.

Multimedia — A type of computer presentation that combines text, graphics, animation, photos, sound, and/or full-motion video.

Multisession — A feature that allows data to be read (or written) on a CD during more than one session. This is important if the disc was only partially filled during the first write.

Pit — Recessed areas on the surface of a CD or DVD, separating lands, or flat areas. Lands and pits are used to represent data on the disc.

Pulse code modulation (PCM) — A method of sampling sound in a reduced, digitized format, by recording differences between successive digital samples instead of their full values.

Sample size — Refers to samples taken when converting a signal from analog to digital. Sample size is a measure of the amount of storage allocated to a single measurement of a single sample. The larger the sample size, the more accurate the value and the larger the file sizes needed to store the data.

Sampling — Part of the process of converting sound or video from analog to digital format, whereby a sound wave or image is measured at uniform time intervals and saved as a series of smaller representative blocks. *See* Sampling rate.

Sampling rate — The rate of samples taken of an analog signal over a period of time, usually expressed as samples per second, or Hertz. For example, 44,100 Hz is the sampling rate used for 16-bit stereo.

Single-instruction, multiple-data (SIMD) — An MMX process that allows the CPU to execute a single instruction simultaneously on multiple pieces of data rather than by repetitive looping.

SSE (streaming SIMD extension) — A technology used by the Intel Pentium III designed to improve performance of multimedia software.

Streaming audio — Downloading audio data from the Internet in a continuous stream of data without first downloading an entire audio file.

Voice — A group of samples for a musical instrument stored in a wavetable.

Wavetable — A table of stored sample sounds used to synthesize sound by reconstructing the sound from digital data using actual samples of sounds from real instruments.

REVIEW QUESTIONS

1. Describe the methodology used to convert analog data into digital data.

2. What two factors determine how accurately digital data represents analog data?

3. MPEG is used to compress what type of data? Describe the compression technique.

4. Typically, how many frames per second are displayed with MPEG?

5. What term refers to the standard interface for computers to electronic sound devices, such as musical keyboards?

6. Compare a DAC to an ADC. Where would you expect to find either of these components?

7. Compare the two methods to synthesize sound, wavetable and FM.

8. What must be true before MMX, SSE, and 3DNow! technology can improve multimedia performance on a PC?

9. Compare the speed of a hard drive platter turning on the spindle to the speed of a CD-ROM.

10. Name three ways a CD-ROM drive can interface with a system board.

11. Which side of a CD contains data?

12. If a CD-ROM drive and a hard drive are sharing the same data cable in a computer system, what type of connection is the CD-ROM drive using? Which of the two drives should be set to master? Which to slave?

13. When you are installing a CD-ROM drive, what is the solution when the DOS error message at startup reads, "Not enough drive letters"?

14. How do you access the volume control under Windows 9x for sound?

15. What is the difference between a CD-R drive and a CD-RW drive?

16. What hardware device that is a field replaceable unit converts sound from analog to digital?

17. When sound is digitized, what is the number of bits to hold each sample called?

18. The purpose of a microphone is to convert _____ sound to _____ voltage, which is then passed to a sound card.

19. What unit of measure is used to express the sampling rate of a sound card?

20. Sound samples recorded on a single channel are called _____, on two channels are called _____, and on six channels are called _____.

21. What is the sampling rate (in Hz) of music CDs?

22. What are the two most common file extensions for uncompressed sound files?

23. What effect could unshielded or very large speakers have on a monitor if they were placed too close to the monitor?

24. What would be a quick, short test to see if a sound card was successfully installed?

25. List several common file extensions used with graphics files.

26. For each of the following pairs, state which item is analog and which is digital:

    a. Text stored on a floppy disk, handwritten note

    b. MIDI file, sound

    c. Monitor display, video memory

    d. A loading ramp, a flight of stairs

    e. A serial cable, a telephone line

10

27. In Windows 95, sound controls are under the _____ option of Accessories, but in Windows 98, the controls are under the _____ option of Accessories.

28. Describe the purposes of FlashPath and SmartMedia technology.

29. What two things does a DVD controller decode? What compression methods are used for both?

30. What is the size of an uncompressed audio file that contains 3 minutes of music captured using CD-quality sound?

PROJECTS

Preparing for a Windows 95 Crash

Suppose you have Windows 95 stored on a CD-ROM and you don't have it stored on floppy disks. Your hard drive fails, or for some other reason Windows 95 on your hard drive will not load. How do you recover Windows 95 from the CD-ROM if the only way to access the CD is through Windows 95 on the hard drive? Prepare a recovery disk with which you can do these things:

a. Boot from the disk to a command prompt

b. Access the CD-ROM drive without using the hard drive

Include on the disk AUTOEXEC.BAT and CONFIG.SYS files that make no reference to drive C. As resources, use the current AUTOEXEC.BAT and CONFIG.SYS files on the hard drive and the documentation to the CD-ROM drive.

Sound When Starting Windows 9x

1. Load the Windows Sound Recorder: click **Start, Programs, Accessories, Multimedia/Entertainment, Sound Recorder**.

2. Connect a microphone to the MIC jack on the sound card at the back of the computer.

3. Press the **Record** button and record a greeting message such as "Welcome to my computer." Keep the greeting short, as the file can get quite large.

4. Click **File, Save as**, and then save the file as "Greeting" in the directory of \Windows\Start Menu\Programs\Startup.

5. Reboot the computer, and your greeting should automatically play.

Comparing Sound Quality

1. Load the Windows Sound Recorder: click **Start, Programs, Accessories, Multimedia/Entertainment, Sound Recorder**.

2. Insert a music CD in the CD-ROM drive.

3. Press record in the sound recorder window and record a 15-second sound clip.

4. Click **File**, **Save As** and save it as "SoundEx."

5. Open Windows Explorer, find "Sound Ex," and note its file extension and also its file size.

6. From the Sound Recorder window, click on **Edit**, **Audio Properties**, and **Performance**. Change the **Sample Rate Conversion Quality** and save the file with a different name. Compare both the sound quality and file sizes of the two saved files.

Windows 9x Sound Properties

Using a PC with a sound card and speakers, create your own customized Windows 9x sound scheme using at least six events and four different sounds. Save the sound scheme file to a floppy disk. Take the file to another PC and install the sound scheme there.

Using MMX Technology

Research the market and list five software packages that claim to use MMX technology. *Hint*: See the Intel Web site for a list of software that uses MMX. The Web site is *www.intel.com*.

Troubleshooting Skills

1. A friend calls to say that he has just purchased a new sound card and speakers to install in his PC and wants some help from you over the phone. The PC already has a CD-ROM drive installed. Your friend has already installed the sound card in an expansion slot and connected the audio wire to the sound card and the CD-ROM drive. List the steps you would guide him through to complete the installation.

2. Suppose, in the previous situation, the audio wire connection does not fit the connection on the CD-ROM drive. You think that if the problem is that the audio wire will not work because of a wrong fit, perhaps you can improvise to connect audio from the CD-ROM drive directly to the sound card. You notice that the CD-ROM drive has a port for a headphones connection, and the sound card has a port for audio in. How might you improvise to provide this direct connection? Check your theory using the appropriate audio wire.

3. Work with a partner. Each of you set up a problem with a PC and have the other troubleshoot the problem. Some suggestions as to what problem to set up are:

   ❑ Speaker cables disconnected

   ❑ Speaker turned off

   ❑ Speaker cable plugged into the wrong jack

   ❑ Volume turned all the way down

   ❑ MSCDEX.EXE not called in the AUTOEXEC.BAT file for DOS

   ❑ MSCDEX.EXE file missing

   As you troubleshoot the problem, write down the initial symptoms of the problem and the steps you take towards the solution.

10

Using the Internet for Research

Make a presentation or write a paper about digital cameras: what features to look for when buying one, and how to compare quality from one camera to another. Use these web sites and also include in the results of your research three more web sites that were useful.

www.imaging-resource.com

www.pcphotoreview.com

www.steves-digicams.com

Entertainment from the Internet

Use the *www.on2.com* web site by on2.com, Inc. to view a video clip from the web site. This web site uses Shockwave, a software product of Macromedia, Inc. (*www.shockwave.com*). Shockwave downloads a web browser plug-in (software that a browser can use to display data from a web site) to your PC and uses the Shockwave software on the PC and on the web site to attain streaming video.

Additional Activities

1. On your home or lab computer, find out what IRQ is used for the CD-ROM.
2. Play a music CD with the Windows CD Player.
3. Change Windows sounds through the Control Panel Sounds icon.
4. Record a voice message using the Sound Recorder.
5. Set up one of the following troubleshooting practice problems and have a fellow student discover the problem and the solution.
   a. Speaker cables disconnected
   b. Speaker turned off
   c. Speaker cable plugged into the wrong jack
   d. Volume turned all the way down
   e. MSCDEX.EXE not called in AUTOEXEC.BAT file
   f. MSCDEX.EXE not on drive
6. Use the Hardware Wizard to remove the CD-ROM drivers, and then reinstall the CDROM.

11

ELECTRICITY AND POWER SUPPLIES

In this chapter, you will learn:

♦ How electricity is measured

♦ How to measure the voltage output of the power supply

♦ How to change a power supply

♦ How a computer system can be protected from damaging changes in electrical power

---

Earlier chapters discussed most hardware components of the computer except the power supply, which provides the power to all other components inside the computer case. To troubleshoot problems with the power system of a PC, you need a basic understanding of electricity. This chapter begins by discussing how to measure electricity, and the form in which it comes to you as house current. The chapter then addresses the power supply, how to measure its output, and how to change a defective power supply. Lastly, the chapter considers backup power sources so that you understand what to look for when buying one to protect your computer system from electrical variations and outages.

INTRODUCTION TO BASIC ELECTRICITY

To most people, volts, ohms, watts, and amps are vague, ambiguous words that simply mean electricity. If these terms are mysterious to you, they will become clear in this section as electricity is discussed in nontechnical language, using simple analogies.

Electricity is energy; water is matter. However, the two have enough in common to make some analogies. Consider Figure 11-1. The water system shown in Part (a) is closed, that is, the amount of water in the system remains the same because no water enters and no water leaves the system. The electrical system in Part (b) is similar in several respects. Think of electricity as a stream of tiny charged particles (electrons) that flow like water along the path of least resistance.

Figure 11-1   Two closed systems: a) water system with pump, wheel, and pool; b) electrical system with battery and light bulb

Water flows down because of the law of gravity, and electricity flows from negative to positive because of the law of like charges repelling one another. The water pump produces water pressure in the system by lifting the water, and a battery produces electrical pressure in the system by creating a buildup of negative charges in one location (in the form of electrons) that are driven to move. This difference in charge, which is similar to water pressure in a water system, is called potential difference. Water seeks a place of rest, moving from a high to a low elevation, and electrons seek a place of rest by moving from a negatively charged location (called "hot") to a positively charged location (called "ground"). In the figure, as the water flows through the closed system, some of its force is harnessed by the water wheel and is converted to a form of energy, motion. Also in the figure, as the electrons flow in the closed electrical system, some of the force of the moving electrons is harnessed by the light bulb and converted to another form of energy, light. Once the water returns to the pool, water pressure decreases and the water is at rest, and, once the electrons arrive at the positive side of the battery, electrical potential difference decreases and the system is at rest.

 TIP When speaking of electron flow, the flow is from the hot point or negative terminal to the ground or positive terminal. Because early theories of electricity assumed that electricity flowed from positive to negative, most electronics books show the current flow from positive to negative. This method is called conventional current flow and, if it were used in Figure 11-1, the positive and negative symbols would be reversed in the figure.

Electricity is energy that has properties that can be measured in various ways. The description above (of an electrical system that includes a battery and a light bulb) illustrates some simple principles of how electricity works that apply to the most complex electrical systems. We next use this simple electrical system to define four properties of electricity, all of which can be measured (see Table 11-1).

A+CORE
2.1

Table 11-1   The measures of electricity

Unit	Definition	An Example as Applied to a Computer
Volts (measures potential difference)	Abbreviated as V (for example, 110 V). Volts are measured by finding the potential difference between the electrical charges on either side of an electrical device in an electrical system.	An AT power supply supplies four separate voltages: +12 V, -12 V, +5 V, -5 V. An ATX power supply supplies these and also 3.3 V.
Amps or Amperes (measures electrical current)	Abbreviated as A (for example, 1.5 A). Amps are measured by placing an ammeter in the flow of current and measuring that current.	A 17-inch monitor requires less than 2 A to operate. A small laser printer uses about 2 A. A CD-ROM drive uses about 1 A.
Ohms (measures resistance)	Abbreviated with the symbol Ω (for example, 20 Ω). Devices are rated according to how much resistance they offer to electrical current. The ohm rating of a resistor or other electrical device is often written somewhere on the device. The resistance of a device is measured when the device is not connected to an electrical system.	Current can flow in typical computer cables and wires with a resistance of less than 20 ohms. This condition of low resistance that allows current to flow is called **continuity**.
Watts (measures power)	Abbreviated W (for example, 20 W).Watts are calculated by multiplying volts by amps.	A computer power supply is rated at 200 to 600 watts.

11

Voltage

The first measure of electricity listed in Table 11-1 is potential difference. First consider how to measure the water pressure. If you measure the pressure of the water directly above the water wheel, and then measure the pressure just as the water lands in the pool, you find that the water pressure above the wheel is greater than the water pressure below it.

Now consider the electrical system. If you measure the electrical charge on one side of the light bulb and compare it to the electrical charge on the other side of the bulb, you see a difference in charge. The potential difference in charge creates an electrical force that drives the electrons through the system between two points, and is called **voltage**, which is measured in units called **volts**.

In Figure 11-2, the leads of a **voltmeter**, a device for measuring electrical voltage, are placed on either side of a light bulb that is consuming some electrical power. The potential difference between the two points on either side of the device is the voltage in the closed system. Voltage is measured when the power is on.

12 volt

Figure 11-2 A voltmeter measuring the voltage across a bulb and a battery

Amps

The volume of electrons (or electricity) flowing through an electrical system is called current. Look back at Figure 11-1. The volume or amount of water flowing through the water system does not change although the water pressure changes at different points in the system. To measure that volume, you pick one point in the system and measure the volume of water that passes through that point over a period of time. The electrical system is similar. If you measure the number of electrons, or electrical current, at any point in this system, you find the same value as at any other point because the current is constant throughout the system. (This assumes that there is only a single pipe or a single wire in the entire closed water or electrical system.) Electrical current is measured in **amperes**, abbreviated **amps**. Figure 11-3 shows the measuring device called an **ammeter**, which measures electrical current in amps. You place the ammeter in the path of the electrical flow so that the electrons must flow through the ammeter. The measurement is taken with the power on and might not be completely accurate because the ammeter can influence the circuit.

12 volt

Figure 11-3   Battery and bulb circuit with ammeter in line

 TIP Because the current flows through an ammeter, check the rating of the ammeter before measuring amps to make sure it can handle the flow of electricity. More flow than the ammeter is designed to handle can blow the meter's fuse.

11

The Relationship Between Voltage and Current

Refer again to the water system in Figure 11-1. To increase the volume of water flowing through the system, you increase the difference in water pressures between the low and high points (which is referred to as the pressure differential). As the pressure differential increases, the water flow or current increases, and as the water pressure differential decreases, the water flow or current decreases. Another way of saying this is: there is a direct relationship between pressure differential and current. An electrical system has the same relationship. As the electrical potential difference (or voltage) increases, the electrical current increases; as the voltage decreases, the current decreases. There is a direct relationship between voltage and current.

Ohms

Suppose you are working your water pump to full capacity. If you still want to increase the overall power of your water system so the wheel turns faster to produce more mechanical energy, you can decrease the resistance to water flow, which allows more water to flow to push the wheel faster. You might use a larger pipe, a lighter water wheel, or, if the system has a partially open water valve, you can open the valve more, all of which would lower resistance to water flow. As resistance decreases, current increases. As resistance increases (smaller pipes, heavier wheel, partially closed valve), current decreases.

Similarly, **resistance** in an electrical system is a property that opposes the flow of electricity. As the electrical resistance increases, the electricity decreases. As the resistance decreases, the electricity increases. When there is more resistance to the flow of electricity, the flow of electrons decreases. Also, when too much electricity flows through a wire, heat energy is created in the wire (similar to friction). This heat energy can cause the wire to melt or burn, which can result in an electrical fire, just as too much water current in a pipe can cause it to burst. Reducing the size of a wire reduces the amount of electricity that can safely flow through. Electrical resistance is measured in **ohms**.

Resistors are devices used in electrical circuits to resist the flow of electricity. (Sorry, I couldn't resist saying that!) Resistors control the flow of electricity in a circuit, much as partially closed valves control the flow of water.

Relationships Among Voltage, Current, and Resistance

Voltage and current have a *direct* relationship. This means that when voltage increases, current increases. Resistance has an *inverse* relationship between voltage and current. This means that as resistance increases, either current or voltage decreases. As resistance decreases, either current or voltage increases. This last statement is known as Ohm's Law. A similar statement defines the relationship among the units of measure—volts, amps, and ohms. One volt drives a current of one amp through a resistance of one ohm.

Wattage

Our discussion of electricity would not be complete without covering one last measure of electricity. **Wattage** is the total amount of power needed to operate an electrical device. When thinking of the water system, you recognize that the amount of water power used to turn the water wheel is not just a measure of the water pressure that forces current through the system. The amount of power is also related to the amount of water available to flow. For a given water pressure, you have more power with more water flow and less power with less water flow. A lot of power results when you have a lot of pressure and a lot of current.

As with the water system, electrical power increases as both voltage and current increase. Wattage, measured in **watts**, is calculated by multiplying volts by amps in a system.

AC and DC Current

Electricity can be either AC, alternating current, or DC, direct current. **Alternating current (AC)** is current that cycles or oscillates back and forth rather than traveling in only one direction. House current in the U.S. oscillates 60 times in one second (60 hertz), changing polarity from +110V to −110V, and causing current to flow in different directions depending on whether it's positive or negative in the cycle. AC current is the most economical way to transmit electricity to our homes and workplaces. Alternating current can be forced to travel great distances by decreasing current and increasing voltage (high pressure and low volume). When it reaches its destination, the voltage can be decreased and the current increased (low pressure and high volume) to make it more suitable for driving our electrical devices.

Direct current (**DC**) travels in only one direction and is the type of current required by most electronic devices, including a computer. A **rectifier** is a device that converts alternating current to direct current. A **transformer** is a device that changes the ratio of current to voltage. Large transformers are used to reduce the high voltage on power lines coming to your neighborhood to a lower voltage before entering your home. Because the transformer does not change the amount of power in this closed system, if it decreases voltage, then it increases current. The overall power stays constant, but the ratio of voltage to current changes.

A computer power supply changes and conditions the house electrical current in several ways, functioning as both a transformer and a rectifier (see Figure 11-4). It steps down the voltage from the 110-volt house current to 3.3, 5, and 12 volts or to 5 and 12 volts, and changes incoming alternating current to direct current, which the computer and its peripherals require. The monitor, however, receives the full 110 volts of AC current, converting that current to DC.

Recall that direct current flows in only one direction, from hot to ground. For a PC, a line may be either +5 or −5 volts in one circuit, or +12 or −12 volts in another circuit, depending on whether the circuit is on the far or near end of the power output (the hot point). Several circuits coming from the power supply accommodate different devices with different power requirements.

Figure 11-4   ATX power supply with connections

Hot, Neutral, and Ground

When AC current comes from the power station to your house, it travels from the power source at the power station to your house on a hot line and completes the circuit from your house back to the power source on a neutral line, as seen in Figure 11-5. When the two lines get to your house and enter an electrical device, such as a lamp or radio, the electricity flows through the device to complete the circuit between the hot line and the neutral line. The device contains resistors and other electrical components that control the flow of electricity between the hot and neutral lines. The hot source is seeking ground and finds that by returning to the power station on the neutral line.

Figure 11-5   Normally hot contacts neutral to make a closed circuit in the controlled environment of an electrical device such as a lamp. An out-of-control contact is called a short, and the flow of electricity is then diverted to the ground.

A short circuit, or a short, occurs when the electricity is allowed to flow uncontrolled from the hot line to the neutral line or from the hot line to ground. Electricity naturally finds the easiest route to ground. Normally that path is through some device that is controlling the current flow and then back through the neutral line. If an easier path (one with less resistance) is available, the electricity follows that path. This can cause a short, a sudden increase in flow that can create a sudden increase in temperature, which can start a fire and injure both people and equipment. Never put yourself in a position where you are the path of least resistance between the hot line and ground!

A fuse is a component included in a circuit and designed to prevent too much current from flowing through the circuit. A fuse is commonly a wire inside a protective case, which is rated in amps. If too much current begins to flow, the wire gets hot and eventually melts, breaking the circuit and stopping the current flow. Many devices have fuses, which can be easily replaced when damaged. You will learn to test a fuse later in the chapter.

To prevent the uncontrolled flow of electricity from continuing indefinitely, which can happen because of a short, the neutral line is grounded. Grounding a line means that the line is connected directly to the earth so that, in the event of a short, the electricity flows into the earth and not back to the power station. The grounding serves as an escape route for out-of-control electricity. The earth is considered to be at no particular state of charge and always capable of accepting a flow of current.

The neutral line to your house is grounded many times along the way (in fact at each electrical pole) and is also grounded at the breaker box where the electricity enters your house. You can look at a three-prong plug and see the three lines, hot, neutral, and ground (see Figure 11-6). Generally, electricians use green or bare wire for the ground wire, white for neutral, and black for hot in home wiring for 110 volt circuits. In a 220-volt circuit, black and red are hot, white is neutral, and green or bare is ground. To verify that a wall outlet is wired correctly, use a simple receptacle tester as shown in Figure 11-7.

Figure 11-6   A three-prong plug showing hot, neutral, and ground

 TIP   Beware of the different uses of black wire. In PCs, black is used for ground, but in home wiring, black is used for hot!

Figure 11-7   Use a receptacle tester to verify hot, neutral, and ground are wired correctly

It's very important that PC components be properly grounded. Never connect a PC to an outlet or use an extension cord that doesn't have the third ground plug. The third line can prevent a short from causing extreme damage. In addition, the bond between the neutral and ground also helps eliminate electrical noise (stray electrical signals) within the PC sometimes caused by other electrical equipment sitting very close to the computer. This electomagnetic interference is covered later in the chapter.

> **TIP**   Even though you might have a three-prong outlet in your home, the ground plug might not be properly grounded. To know for sure, test the outlet with an inexpensive outlet tester.

Some Common Electronic Components

A PC contains many electronic components. It's interesting to understand what basic electronic components make up a PC and how they work. Basic electrical components in a PC include transistors, capacitors, diodes, and resistors. Figure 11-8 shows the symbols for these four components. Materials used to make these and other electrical components can be:

- **Conductors**. Material that easily conducts electricity such as gold or copper

- **Insulators**. Material that resists the flow of electricity such as glass or ceramic

- **Semiconductors**. Material such as silicon with an ability to conduct electricity that falls between that of conductors and insulators

Figure 11-8   Symbols for some electronic components and ground

A **transistor** is an electronic device that can serve as a gate or switch for an electrical signal and can amplify the flow of electricity. Invented in 1947, the transistor is made of three layers of semiconductor material. A charge (either positive or negative, depending on how the transistor was designed) placed on the center layer can cause the two outer layers of the transistor to complete a circuit to create an "on" state. An opposite charge placed on the center layer can cause the reverse to happen, causing the transistor to create an "off" state. By manipulating these charges to the transistor, it can be used to hold a logic state, either on or off (translated to 0 or 1 in binary). When the transistor is maintaining this state, it requires almost no electrical power. Because the initial charge sent to the transistor is not as great as the resulting current created by the transistor, sometimes a transistor is used as a small amplifier. The transistor is the basic building block of an integrated circuit (IC) that is used to build a microchip.

A **capacitor** is an electronic device that can hold an electrical charge for a period of time and is used to smooth out the uneven flow of electricity through a circuit. Capacitors inside a PC power supply create the even flow of current needed by the PC. Capacitors maintain their charge long after current is no longer present, which is why the inside of a power supply can be dangerous even when it is unplugged.

A **diode** is a semiconductor device that allows electricity to flow in only one direction. (A transistor contains two diodes.) One to four diodes used in various configurations can be used to convert the AC to DC. Singularly or collectively, depending on the configuration, these diodes are called a rectifier.

As explained above, a resistor is an electronic device that limits the amount of current that can flow through it.

ESD and EMI

Recall that ESD (electrostatic discharge) is a brief flow of electricity caused by two objects that have a difference in voltage potential coming in contact with one another. Now that you better understand the concept of grounding, you can see why it is important that you be grounded before you work with computer components. If both you and the component

11

A+CORE
3.2,
2.1

you are going to work with are grounded, then there will be no potential voltage difference between you and the component, and no electrical discharge will occur when you touch it.

There are exceptions to the rule of always being grounded when you work with PCs. You *don't* want to be grounded when working inside a monitor or with a power supply. These devices maintain high charges of electricity, even when the power is turned off. *Don't* wear a ground bracelet when working inside these devices, because you don't want to be the ground for these charges!

Another problem with computers that can be caused by electricity is **electromagnetic interference** (**EMI**). EMI is caused by the magnetic field that is produced as a side effect when electricity flows. EMI in the radio frequency range is called radio frequency interference (RFI), which can cause problems with the radio and TV reception. Data in data cables that cross this magnetic field can become corrupted, which is called crosstalk. Crosstalk is partly controlled by using shielded data cables covered with a protective material. Power supplies are also shielded to prevent them from emitting EMI. PCs can also emit EMI to other nearby PCs, which is one reason a computer needs to be inside a case, and the case should not have holes—so always install face plates in empty drive bays or over empty expansion slots.

If a PC persists in giving mysterious, intermittent errors, one thing to suspect is EMI. Try moving the PC to a new location. If the problem persists, try moving it to a location that uses an entirely different electric circuit. One simple way to detect the presence of EMI is to use a small inexpensive AM radio. Turn the tuning dial away from a station into a low-frequency range. With the radio on, you can hear the static produced by EMI. Try putting the radio next to several electronic devices to detect the EMI they emit.

If EMI in the electrical circuits coming to the PC is a significant problem, you can use a line conditioner that filters out the electrical noise causing the EMI. Line conditioners are discussed later in the chapter.

MEASURING THE VOLTAGE OF A POWER SUPPLY

If you suspect a problem with a power supply, one thing you can do is measure the voltage output. When a power supply is working properly, voltages all fall within an acceptable range (plus or minus 10%). However, be aware that even if measured voltage is within the appropriate range, a power supply can still cause problems. This is because problems with power supplies often come and go. Therefore, if the voltages are correct, you should still suspect the power supply to be the problem when certain symptoms are present. To learn for certain whether the power supply is the problem, replace it with a unit you know is good.

Using a Multimeter

A+CORE
2.1

A voltmeter measures the difference in electrical potential between two points in volts, and an ammeter measures electrical current in amps. Figure 11-9 shows a **multimeter**, which can be used as either a voltmeter or an ammeter, or can measure resistance or continuity (the presence of a complete circuit), depending on a dial or function switch setting. Less expensive multimeters commonly measure voltage, resistance, and continuity, but not amps.

A+CORE
 2.1

Measure voltage and amps while the electricity is on. Measure resistance and continuity while the electricity is off. For the specific details of how to use your multimeter, consult the manual, which explains what you can measure with the multimeter and how to use it.

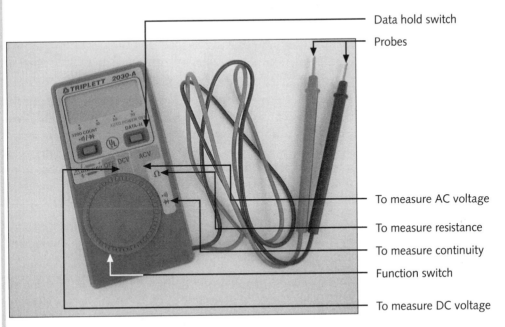

Figure 11-9   A digital multimeter

A multimeter can provide either a digital or an analog display. A digital display shows the readings as digits displayed on an LCD (liquid crystal display) panel. A digital multimeter is sometimes called a DMM (digital multimeter) or a DVM (digital voltage meter). An analog display shows the readings as a needle moving across a scale of values. Multimeters are sometimes small portable battery-powered units. Larger ones are designed to sit on a countertop and are powered by a wall outlet.

When you use a multimeter, you must tell it three things before you begin: (1) what you want it to measure (voltage, current, or resistance), (2) whether the current is AC or DC, and (3) what range of values it should expect. If you are measuring the voltage output from a wall outlet (110–120 V), the range should be much higher than when measuring the voltage output of a computer power supply (3–12 V). Setting the range high assures you that the meter can handle a large input without pegging the needle (exceeding the highest value that the meter is designed to measure) or damaging the meter. However, if you set the range too high, you might not see the voltage register at all. Set the range low enough to assure you that the measure is as accurate as you need, but not so low as to be less than the expected voltage. When you set the range too low on some digital multimeters, the meter reads OL on the display.

11

A+CORE
2.1

For example, to measure the voltage of house current, if you expect the voltage to be 115 volts, set the voltage range from 0 to somewhere between 120 and 130 volts. You want the high end of the range to be slightly higher than the expected voltage. Most meters do not allow a very large voltage or current into the meter when the range is set low to protect the meter. Some multimeters are **autorange meters**, which sense the quantity of input and set the range accordingly.

A meter comes with two test probes. One is usually red and the other black. Install the red probe at the positive (+) jack on the meter and the black probe at the negative (−) jack.

To measure voltage, place the other end of the black probe at the ground point and the other end of the red probe at the hot point, without disconnecting anything in the circuit and with the power on. For example, to measure voltage using the multimeter in Figure 11-9, turn the function switch dial to DCV for DC voltage measurement. This meter is autoranging, so this is all that needs to be set. With the power on, place the two probes in position and read the voltage from the LCD panel. The DATA-H switch (data hold) allows you to freeze the displayed reading.

To measure current in amps, as in Figure 11-3, the multimeter itself must be part of the circuit. Disconnect the circuit at some point so that you can connect the multimeter in line to find a measure in amps. Not all multimeters can measure amps.

You can also use a multimeter to measure continuity, which indicates if there is little or no resistance (less than 20 ohms gives continuity in a PC) in a wire or a closed connection between two points, meaning that the path for electricity between the two points is unhindered or "continuous." This measurement is taken with no electricity present in the circuit.

For example, if you want to know that pin 2 on one end of a serial cable is connected to pin 3 on the other end of the cable, set the multimeter to measure continuity, and work without the cable being connected to anything. Put one probe on pin 2 at one end of the cable and the other probe on pin 3 at the other end. If the two pins connect, the multimeter indicates this with a reading on the LCD panel, or a buzzer sounds (see the multimeter documentation). In this situation, you might find that the probe is too large to extend into the pinhole of the female connection of the cable. A straightened small paper clip works well here to extend the probe. However, be very careful not to use a paper clip that is too thick and might widen the size of the pinhole, which can later prevent the pinhole from making a good connection.

To determine if a fuse is good, you actually measure continuity. With a multimeter set to measure continuity, place its probes on each end of the fuse. If the fuse has continuity, then it is good. If the multimeter does not have a continuity setting, set it to measure resistance. If the reading in ohms is approximately zero, there is no resistance and the fuse is good. If the reading is infinity, there is infinite resistance and the fuse is blown and should not be used.

How to Measure the Voltage of a Power Supply

To determine that a power supply is working properly, measure the voltage of each circuit supported by the power supply. First open the computer case and identify all power cords coming from the power supply. Look for the cords from the power supply to the system board and other power cords to the drives. Follow the directions described in the next section to measure the voltage of the power supply output to the system board (see Figure 11-10).

- Probes
- Multimeter
- Power supply
- Hard drive connection
- Unused miniature power connector for floppy drive
- System board
- P8 and P9

11

Figure 11-10 Multimeter measuring voltage on an AT system board

A+CORE
2.1

Testing the Power Output of the Power Supply

The computer must be turned on to test the power supply output. Be very careful not to touch any chips or disturb any circuit boards as you work. The voltage output from the power supply is no more than 14 volts, which is not enough to seriously hurt you if you accidentally touch a hot probe. However, you can damage the computer if you are not careful.

You can hurt yourself if you accidentally create a short circuit from the power supply to ground through the probe. If you touch the probe to the hot circuit and also to ground, the current is diverted from the computer circuit and through the probe to ground. This short might be enough to cause a spark or to melt the probe, which can happen if you allow the two probes to touch each other while one of them is attached to the hot circuit and the other is attached to ground. Make *sure* the probes only touch one metal object, preferably only a single power pin on a connector, or you could cause a short.

Because of the danger of touching a hot probe to a ground probe, you might prefer not to put the black probe into a ground lead that is too close to the hot probe. Instead, when the directions say to place the black probe on a lead that is very close to the hot probe, you can use a black wire lead on an unused power supply connection meant for a hard drive. The idea is that the black probe should always be placed on a ground or black lead.

A+CORE 2.1 All ground leads are considered at ground, no matter what number is assigned that lead. Therefore, you can consider all black leads to be equal. For an AT system board, the ground leads for P8 and P9 are the four black center leads 5, 6, 7, and 8. For an ATX system board, the ground leads are seven black leads in center positions on the ATX P1 power connector. The ground leads for a hard drive power connection are the two black center leads, 2 and 3.

We first discuss how to measure the power output for AT and ATX system boards and then for a secondary storage device.

Measuring Voltage Output to an AT System Board

1. Remove the cover of the computer. The voltage range for each connection is often written on the top of the power supply. The two power connections to the system board are often labeled P8 and P9. Figure 11-11 shows a closeup of the two connections, P8 and P9, coming from the power supply to the system board. Each connection has six leads, for a total of 12 leads. Of these 12, four are ground connections, and lead 1 is a "power good" pin, used to indicate that the system board is receiving power. A common arrangement for these 12 leads is listed in Table 11-2.

Table 11-2 Twelve leads to the AT system board from the AT power supply

Connection	Lead	Description	Acceptable Range
P8	1	"Power Good"	
	2	Not used or +5 volts	+4.4 to +5.2 volts
	3	+12 volts	+10.8 to +13.2 volts
	4	−12 volts	−10.8 to −13.2 volts
	5	Black ground	
	6	Black ground	
P9	7	Black ground	
	8	Black ground	
	9	−5 volts	−4.5 to −5.5 volts
	10	+5 volts	+4.5 to +5.5 volts
	11	+5 volts	+4.5 to +5.5 volts
	12	+5 volts	+4.5 to +5.5 volts

A+CORE
2.1

Figure 11-11 AT power supply connections

2. Set the multimeter to measure voltage in a range of 20 volts and set the AC/DC switch to DC. Insert the black probe into the – jack and the red probe into the + jack of the meter.

3. Turn on the multimeter, and turn on the computer.

4. To measure the +12-volt circuit and all four ground leads:

   ■ Place the red probe on lead 3. The probe is shaped like a needle (alligator clips don't work too well here); insert the needle down into the lead housing as far as you can. Place the black probe on lead 5. The acceptable range is +10.8 to +13.2 volts.

   ■ Place the red probe on lead 3, and place the black probe on lead 6. The acceptable range is +10.8 to +13.2 volts.

   ■ Place the red probe on lead 3, and place the black probe on lead 7. The acceptable range is +10.8 to +13.2 volts.

   ■ Place the red probe on lead 3, and place the black probe on lead 8. The acceptable range is +10.8 to +13.2 volts.

5. To measure the −12-volt circuit, place the red probe on lead 4, and place the black probe on any ground lead or on the computer case, which is also grounded. The acceptable range is −10.8 to 13.2 volts.

11

A+CORE
2.1

6. To measure the −5-volt circuit, place the red probe on lead 9, and place the black probe on any ground. The acceptable range is −4.5 to −5.5 volts.

7. To measure the three +5-volt circuits:

   ▪ Place the red probe on lead 10, and place the black probe on any ground. The acceptable range is +4.5 to +5.5 volts.

   ▪ Place the red probe on lead 11, and place the black probe on any ground. The acceptable range is +4.5 to +5.5 volts.

   ▪ Place the red probe on lead 12, and place the black probe on any ground. The acceptable range is +4.5 to +5.5 volts.

8. Replace the cover.

Measuring Voltage Output to an ATX System Board

To measure the output to the ATX system board, follow the same procedure as with the AT system board. Recall that the ATX board uses 3.3, 5, and 12 volts coming from the power supply. Figure 11-12 shows the power output of each pin on the connector. Looking at Figure 11-12, you can see the distinguishing shape of each side of the connector. Notice the different hole sizes on each side of the connector, ensuring that the plug from the power supply is oriented correctly in the connector. Table 11-3 lists the leads to the system board and their acceptable voltage ranges.

Table 11-3   Twenty leads to the ATX system board from the ATX power supply

Unnotched Side			Notched Side		
Lead	Description	Acceptable Range	Lead	Description	Acceptable Range (volts)
1	+12 volts	+10.8 to +13.2	1	+5 volts	+4.5 to +5.5
2	+5 volts standby	+4.5 to +5.5	2	+5 volts	+4.5 to +5.5
3	"Power good"		3	−5 volts	−4.5 to −5.5
4	Black ground		4	Black ground	
5	+5 volts	+4.5 to +5.5	5	Black ground	
6	Black ground		6	Black ground	
7	+5 volts	+4.5 to +5.5	7	Pwr supply on	
8	Black ground		8	Black ground	
9	+3.3 volts	+3.1 to +3.5	9	−12 volts	−10.8 to −13.2
10	+3.3 volts	+3.1 to +3.5	10	+3.3 volts	+3.1 to +3.5

+12.0 Volts — 1 | 11 — +5.0 Volts
+5V Standby — 2 | 12 — +5.0 Volts
Power Good — 3 | 13 — -5.0 Volts
Ground — 4 | 14 — Ground
+5.0 Volts — 5 | 15 — Ground
Ground — 6 | 16 — Ground
+5.0 Volts — 7 | 17 — PWR Supply On
Ground — 8 | 18 — Ground
+3.3 Volts — 9 | 19 — -12.0 Volts
+3.3 Volts — 10 | 20 — +3.3 Volts

Notches

Unnotched side   Notched side

Figure 11-12   Power connection on an ATX system board

Testing the Power Output to a Floppy or Hard Drive

The power cords to the floppy disk drive, hard drive, and CD-ROM drive all supply the same voltage: one +5-volt circuit and one +12-volt circuit. The power connection to any drive uses four leads; the two outside connections are hot, and the two inside connections are ground (see Figure 11-11). The power connection to a 3.5-inch floppy disk drive is usually a miniature connection, as shown in Figure 11-10. Follow these steps to measure the voltage to any drive:

1. With the drive plugged in, turn the computer on.

2. Set the multimeter to measure voltage as described above.

3. Place the red probe on lead 1 shown in Figure 11-11, and place the black probe on lead 2 or 3 (ground). The acceptable range is +10.8 to +13.2 volts.

4. Place the red probe on lead 4, and place the black probe on lead 2 or 3 (ground). The acceptable range is +4.5 to +5.5 volts.

You may choose to alter the method you use to ground the black probe. In Step 4 above, the red probe and black probe are very close to each other. You may choose to keep them farther apart by placing the black probe in a ground lead of an unused hard drive connection.

PROBLEMS WITH THE POWER SUPPLY

If you assemble a PC from parts, most often you purchase a computer case with the power supply already installed in it. However, you might need to exchange the present power supply because it is damaged, or because you need to upgrade to one with more power. In this section, you will learn how to detect a faulty power supply and how to exchange one.

11

Power Supplies Can Be Dangerous

A+CORE
3.2

The power supply has capacitors inside it, which hold their electrical charge even after the power is disconnected. Never open the case of the power supply unless you have been trained how to protect yourself from high-voltage equipment.

>
> **TIP** If you do open the case to work inside the power supply itself, don't wear your anti-static bracelet. Recall that the bracelet grounds you, and you don't want to be a ground for the high voltage (110 to 120 volts) of the power supply!

Power Supply Troubleshooting Guidelines

A+CORE
2.1

Problems with the PC's power supply or the house current can express themselves in the following ways:

- The PC sometimes halts during booting. After several tries, it boots successfully.
- Error codes or beep codes occur during booting, but the errors come and go.
- The computer stops or hangs for no reason. Sometimes it might even reboot itself.
- Memory errors appear intermittently.
- Data is written incorrectly to the hard drive.
- The keyboard stops working at odd times.
- The system board fails or is damaged.
- The power supply overheats and becomes hot to the touch.

An overheated system can cause intermittent problems. Use compressed air to blow the dust out of the power supply and the vents over the entire computer. Dust acts like an insulator and retains heat inside the computer case. Check that the power supply fan and the fan over the CPU are both working.

The symptoms of electrical power problems might be caused by a brownout (reduced current) of the house current or by a faulty power supply. If you suspect that the house current could be low, check the other devices that are using the same circuit. A copy machine, laser printer, or other heavy equipment might be drawing too much power. Remove the other devices from the same house circuit.

A system with a standard power supply of about 250 watts that has multiple hard drives, multiple CD-ROM drives, and several expansion cards is most likely operating above the rated capacity of the power supply, which can cause the system to perform unexpected reboots or give intermittent, otherwise unexplained errors. Calculate the total wattage requirements of all devices drawing power from the power supply and compare it to the rated capacity of the power supply.

Wattage is calculated as volts $\times$ amps. The power supply is rated in watts, and it should run at about 60% its rated capacity or less. When operating at this capacity, the power supply lasts

A+CORE
    2.1

longer, runs cooler, and provides more consistent (or cleaner) power. In most cases, the computer's power supply is more than adequate if you add only one or two new devices. A project at the end of this chapter gives you practice calculating total wattage needs of a computer system. Upgrade the power supply as needed to accommodate an overloaded power system.

If these suggestions don't correct the problem, check the power supply by measuring the voltage output or by exchanging it for one you know is good. Remember that the power supply might give correct voltages when you measure it, but still be the source of problems.

An electrical conditioner might solve the problem of intermittent errors caused by noise in the power line to the PC. Try installing an electrical conditioner to monitor and condition the voltage to the PC. Conditioners are discussed later in the chapter.

The fan on the power supply stops working   Usually just before a fan stops working, it hums or whines, especially when the PC is first turned on. If this has just happened, replace the fan if you are trained to service the power supply. If not, then replace the entire power supply, which is considered an FRU (field replaceable unit) for a PC support technician. If you replace the power supply or fan and the fan still does not work, the problem might not be the fan. The problem might be caused by a short somewhere else in the system drawing too much power. Don't operate the PC with the fan not working. Computers without cooling fans can quickly overheat and damage chips.

Turn the power off and remove all power cord connections to all components, including the connections to the system board, and all power cords to drives. Turn the power back on. If the fan comes on, the problem is with one of the systems you disconnected, not with the power supply or its fan.

Turn the power off and reconnect the power cords to the drives. If the fan comes on, you can eliminate the drives as the problem. If the fan does not come on, try one drive after another until you identify the drive with the short.

If the drives are not the problem, suspect the system board subsystem. With the power off, reconnect all power cords to the drives.

Turn the power off and remove the power to the system board by disconnecting P8 and P9 or P1. Turn the power back on.

If the fan comes back on, the problem is probably not the power supply, but a short in one of the components powered by the power cords to the system board. The power to the system board also powers interface cards.

Remove all interface cards and reconnect plugs to the system board.

If the fan still works, the problem is with one of the interface cards. If the fan does not work, the problem is with the system board or something still connected to it.

The system board, just as all other components inside the computer case, should be grounded to the chassis. Look for a metal screw that grounds the board to the computer case. However, a short might be the problem with the electrical system if some component on the board is

11

A+CORE
2.1

making improper contact with the chassis. This short can cause serious damage to the system board. Check for missing standoffs (small plastic or metal spacers that hold the system board a short distance away from the chassis), the problem that most often causes these improper connections.

Shorts in the circuits on the system board might also cause the problem. Look for damage on the bottom side of the system board. These circuits are coated with plastic, and quite often damage is difficult to spot.

Frayed wires on cable connections can also cause shorts. Disconnect hard drive cables connected directly to the system board. Power up with P8 and P9 or P1 connected, but all cables disconnected from the system board. If the fan comes on, the problem is with one of the systems you disconnected.

> **TIP** Never replace a damaged system board with a good one without first testing the power supply. You don't want to subject another good board to possible damage.

Upgrading the Power Supply

If you are installing a hard drive or CD-ROM drive and are concerned that the power supply is not adequate, test it after you finish the installation. Make both the new drive and the floppy drive work at the same time by copying files from one to the other. If the new drive and the floppy drive each work independently, but data errors occur when both are working at the same time, suspect a shortage of electrical power.

If you prefer a more technical approach, you can estimate how much total wattage your system needs by calculating the watts for each circuit and adding them together as discussed earlier. In most cases, the computer's power supply is more than adequate if you add only one or two new devices.

Power supplies can be purchased separately. Power supplies for microcomputers range from 200 watts for a small desktop computer system to 600 watts for a tower floor model that uses a large amount of multimedia or other power-hungry devices.

Installing a New Power Supply

A+CORE
1.2

The easiest way to fix a power supply you suspect is faulty is to replace it. You can determine if the power supply really is the problem by turning off the PC, opening the computer case, and setting the new power supply on top of the old one. Disconnect the old power supply's cords and plug the PC devices into the new power supply. Turn on the PC and verify that the new power supply solves your problem before installing it.

If a new power supply is needed, follow these procedures:

1. Turn off the power.

2. Remove all external power cables from the power supply connections.

A+CORE
1.2

3. Remove the cover.

4. Disconnect all power cords from the power supply to other devices.

5. Determine which components must be removed before the power supply can be safely removed from the case. You might need to remove the hard drive, several cards, or the CD-ROM drive. In some cases, you may even need to remove the system board.

6. Remove all the components necessary to get to the power supply. Remember to protect the components from static electricity, as described in Chapter 8.

7. Unscrew the screws on the back of the computer case that hold the power supply to the case.

8. Look on the bottom of the case for slots that are holding the power supply in position. Often the power supply must be shifted in one direction to free it from the slots.

9. Remove the power supply.

10. Place the new power supply into position, sliding it into the slots used by the old power supply.

11. Replace the power supply screws.

12. Replace all other components.

13. Before replacing the case cover, connect the power cords, turn on the PC, and verify that all is working.

14. Test the voltage output of the new power supply and verify that it falls within acceptable ranges.

15. Turn off the PC and replace the cover.

11

ENERGY STAR COMPUTERS (THE GREEN STAR)

Energy Star computers and peripherals have the U.S. Green Star, which indicates that they satisfy certain energy-conserving standards of the U.S. Environmental Protection Agency (EPA). Devices that can carry the Green Star are computers, monitors, printers, copiers, and fax machines. Such devices are designed to decrease the overall consumption of electricity in the U.S. to protect and preserve our natural resources. These standards, sometimes called the **Green Standards**, generally mean that the computer or the device has a standby program switches the device to sleep mode when it is not being used. During **sleep mode**, the device must use no more than 30 watts of power.

Office equipment is among the fastest growing source of power consumption in industrialized nations. Much of this electricity is wasted, because computers and other equipment are often left on overnight. Because Energy Star devices go into sleep mode when they are unused, they create an overall energy savings of about 50%.

Energy Star PCs

Computer systems use three power management methods to conserve energy:

- Advanced Power Management (APM), championed by Intel and Microsoft
- AT Attachment (ATA) for IDE drives
- Display Power Management Signaling (DPMS) standards for monitors and video cards

These energy-saving features are designed to work in incremental steps, depending on how long the PC is idle. The features can sometimes be enabled and adjusted using CMOS setup or using the OS. In CMOS setup, a feature might not be available, setup might include additional features, or a feature might be labeled differently from those described below.

Green Timer on the System Board

This sets the number of minutes of inactivity that must pass before the CPU goes into sleep mode. You can enable or disable the setting and select the elapse time in number of minutes.

Doze Time

Doze time is the time that elapses before the system reduces 80% of its power consumption. This is accomplished in different ways by different systems. For example, when one system enters Doze mode, the system BIOS slows down the bus clock speed.

Standby Time

The time before the system reduces 92% of its power consumption is **Standby time**. For example, a system might accomplish this by changing the system speed from turbo to slow and suspending the video signal.

Suspend Time

The time before the system reduces 99% of its power consumption is **Suspend time**. The way this reduction is accomplished varies. The CPU clock might be stopped and the video signal suspended. After entering suspend mode, the system needs a warmup time so that the CPU, monitor, and other components can reach full activity.

Hard Drive Standby Time

Hard drive standby time is the amount of time before a hard drive shuts down.

Sample Power Management Setup Screen

Figure 11-13 shows the Power Management Setup screen of the CMOS setup for Award BIOS for an ATX Pentium II system board. Using the Video options on the left of the screen, you can enable or disable power management of the monitor. When power management is enabled, you can control Energy Star features. The PM Timers feature controls doze, standby, and suspend modes for the hard drive. The Power Up Control determines the way the system can be controlled when it is started or when power to the computer is interrupted. The features on the right side of the screen monitor the power supply fan, CPU fan, optional chassis fan, temperatures of the CPU and the motherboard (MB), and voltage output to the CPU and system board.

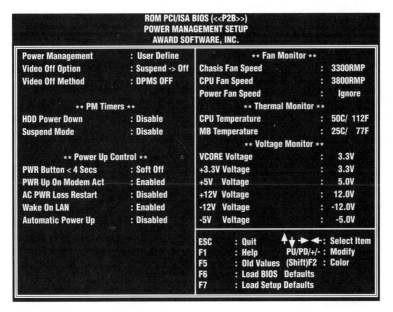

ROM PCI/ISA BIOS (<<P2B>>) POWER MANAGEMENT SETUP AWARD SOFTWARE, INC.			
Power Management	: User Define	** Fan Monitor **	
Video Off Option	: Suspend -> Off	Chasis Fan Speed	: 3300RMP
Video Off Method	: DPMS OFF	CPU Fan Speed	: 3800RMP
		Power Fan Speed	: Ignore
** PM Timers **		** Thermal Monitor **	
HDD Power Down	: Disable	CPU Temperature	: 50C/ 112F
Suspend Mode	: Disable	MB Temperature	: 25C/ 77F
		** Voltage Monitor **	
** Power Up Control **		VCORE Voltage	: 3.3V
PWR Button < 4 Secs	: Soft Off	+3.3V Voltage	: 3.3V
PWR Up On Modem Act	: Enabled	+5V Voltage	: 5.0V
AC PWR Loss Restart	: Disabled	+12V Voltage	: 12.0V
Wake On LAN	: Enabled	-12V Voltage	: -12.0V
Automatic Power Up	: Disabled	-5V Voltage	: -5.0V
		ESC : Quit ↑↓→◄: Select Item	
		F1 : Help PU/PD/+/- : Modify	
		F5 : Old Values (Shift)F2 : Color	
		F6 : Load BIOS Defaults	
		F7 : Load Setup Defaults	

Figure 11-13   A Power Management Setup screen showing power management features

Energy Star Monitors

Most computers and monitors sold today are Energy-Star-compliant, displaying the green Energy Star logo onscreen when the PC is booting.

In order for a monitor's power-saving feature to function, the video card or computer must also support this function. Most monitors that follow the Energy Star standards adhere to the **Display Power Management Signaling** (**DPMS**) specifications developed by VESA, which allow for the video card and monitor to go into sleep mode simultaneously.

Windows 9x sometimes recognizes that a monitor is an Energy Star monitor by its brand and model. To see if Windows 95 has identified a monitor as Energy-Star-compliant, open the **Display Properties** dialog box. One way to do this is to right-click anywhere on the desktop and select **Properties** from the shortcut menu. In the Display Properties dialog box, click the **Settings** tab, and then select **Change Display Type** (or, for OSR 2, select **Advanced Properties**). The Change Display Type dialog box opens, as shown in Figure 11-14. If you know that your monitor is Energy-Star-compliant, check the appropriate box. For Windows 98, right-click the desktop, select **Properties** from the shortcut menu, click the **Settings** tab and click **Advanced**. The monitor Properties dialog box opens. Click the Monitor tab and the dialog box in Figure 11-15 is displayed showing the Energy Star check box.

11

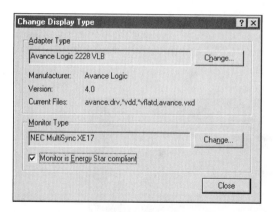

Figure 11-14 Windows 95 setting for an Energy Star monitor

Figure 11-15 In Windows 98, the Energy Star check box is grayed for this monitor and cannot be unchecked

To use the Energy Star features of your monitor, click the **Screen Saver** tab in the **Properties** dialog box to open the dialog box shown in Figure 11-16. Click the **Settings** button of the Energy savings feature. You can set system standby to activate after a specified number of minutes. Select the minutes under **Turn off monitor**. This feature causes your Energy Star monitor to go into sleep mode. Some monitors have an additional feature that allows the PC to shut off the monitor after a selected number of minutes of inactivity. Read the documentation that comes with the monitor to learn what features a monitor has and how to use them.

Problems might occur if CMOS is turning off the monitor because of power management settings and Windows 9x is also turning off the monitor. If the system hangs when you try to get the monitor going again, try disabling one or the other.

Figure 11-16   Using the monitor's Energy Star features

SURGE PROTECTION AND BATTERY BACKUP

A+CORE
3.2

A wide range of devices on the market filter the AC input to computers and their peripherals (that is, condition the AC input to eliminate highs and lows) and that provide backup
power when the AC current fails. These devices, installed between the house current and the
computer, fall into three general categories: surge suppressors, power conditioners, and uninterruptible power supplies (UPSs). All these devices should have the UL (Underwriters
Laboratory) logo, which ensures that the device has been tested by this agency, a provider of
product safety certification.

11

Surge Suppressors

A **surge suppressor**, also called a **surge protector**, provides a row of power outlets and an
on/off switch that protects equipment from overvoltages on AC power lines and telephone
lines. Surge suppressors can come as power strips, as seen in Figure 11-17 (but not all power
strips have surge protection), wall-mounted units that plug into AC outlets, or consoles
designed to sit on a desk top (Figure 11-18) with the monitor placed on top. Some provide
an RJ-11 telephone jack to protect modems and fax machines from spikes.

TIP   Whenever there is a power outage, unless you have a reliable power conditioner or UPS
installed, unplug all power cords to the PC, printers, monitors, and the like. Sometimes
when the power returns there are sudden spikes accompanied by another brief outage.
You don't want to subject your equipment to these surges.

A+CORE
3.2

Figure 11-17   A surge suppressor can protect a device against overvoltage or spikes

Figure 11-18   A surge suppressor might be designed to sit underneath the monitor on the
desk top

Surge suppressors are not always reliable, and once the fuse inside the suppressor is blown, a surge suppressor no longer protects from a power surge. It continues to provide power without warning you that the protection is lost. The performance of a surge suppressor as protection against spikes is measured in two ways: let-through voltage and joules.

The maximum voltage that is allowed through the suppressor to the device being protected is called the **let-through**. Less is better. The better units are expected to let through under 330 volts. Less expensive suppressors let through 400 volts or more.

The degree of protection of a surge suppressor can be measured in **joules**, a measure of energy that takes into account both voltage and current over a one-second interval. More is better. Look for devices that offer at least 240 joules of protection.

A surge suppressor might be a shunt type that absorbs the surge or might be a series type that blocks the surge from flowing, or it might be a combination of the two. The shunt-type suppressor is measured by **clamping voltage**, a term that describes the let-through voltage.

When buying a surge suppressor, look for those that guarantee against damage from lightning and that reimburse for equipment destroyed while the surge suppressor is in use.

Data Line Protectors

A **data line protector** serves the same function for your telephone line to your modem that a surge suppressor does for the electrical lines. Telephone lines carry a small current of

A+CORE
3.2
electricity and need to be protected against spikes, just as electrical lines do. The let-through rating for a data line protector for a phone line should be no more than 260 volts.

Measuring Power Ranges of Devices

The next two types of protective devices are power conditioners and uninterruptible power supplies. They both condition (alter so as to provide continuous voltages) the power passing through them. Both provide a degree of protection against spikes (temporary surges of voltage) and raise the voltage when it drops during brownouts (temporary reductions of voltage). These devices are measured by the load they support in watts, volt-amperes (VA), or kilo-volt-amperes (kVA).

To determine how much VA is required to support your system, multiply the amperage of each component by 120 volts and then add up the VA for all components. For example, a 17-inch monitor has 1.9 A written on the back of the monitor, which means 1.9 amps. Multiply that value times 120 volts and you see that 228 VA is required. A Pentium PC with a 17-inch monitor and tape backup system requires about 500 VA of support.

Power Conditioners

In addition to providing protection against spikes, **power conditioners** also regulate, or condition, the power, providing continuous voltage during brownouts. These voltage regulators, sometimes called **line conditioners**, can come as small desktop units (see Figure 11-19).

Low-cost line conditioners use a stepped transformer to adjust the output voltage. Higher priced models use a **ferroresonant regulator**, which contains a magnetic coil that can retain a charge of power to be used to raise the voltage during a brownout.

These electricity filters are a good investment if the AC current in your community suffers from excessive spikes and brownouts. However, if the device is rated under 1 kVA, it will probably only provide corrections for brownouts, and not spikes. Line conditioners, like surge suppressors, provide no protection against a total blackout.

11

Figure 11-19   A power conditioner can protect a device against overvoltage (spikes) and provide continuous voltage during brownouts

Uninterruptible Power Supply

A+CORE
3.2
Unlike a power conditioner, the **UPS (uninterruptible power supply)** provides a backup power supply in the event the AC current fails completely. The UPS also offers some filtering of the AC current. A UPS device suitably priced for personal computer systems is designed as either a standby device, an inline device, or a line-interactive device (which combines features of the first two). Among these three UPS devices, there are several variations on the market, whose prices vary widely.

A common UPS device is a rather heavy box that plugs into an AC outlet and provides one or more outlets for the computer and its peripherals (see Figure 11-20). It has an on/off switch, requires no maintenance, and is very simple to install.

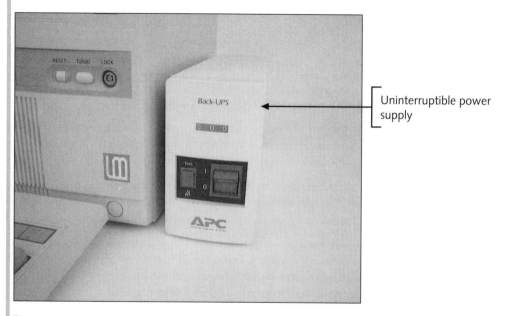

Uninterruptible power supply

Figure 11-20   Uninterruptible power supply (UPS)

Standby and inline UPSs differ in the circuit the devices use as the primary circuit, and in the way they function when the AC power fails. A **standby UPS** switches circuits from the AC circuit to the battery-powered circuit. In contrast, the **inline UPS** continually provides power through the battery-powered circuit and therefore requires no switching, which ensures continuous power.

UPS prices increase dramatically depending on the features offered. A UPS device is rated according to the amount of power it can provide, in VA during a complete blackout, and the length of time it can sustain that power. Most UPSs for microcomputer systems claim to provide backup power for only about 15 minutes, only enough time to save any work in progress and to do an orderly shutdown. The high cost of a UPS prohibits greater power.

The Standby UPS

Figure 11-21 shows how UPSs work. The solid line represents the primary circuit by which electricity normally flows. The dashed line represents the secondary circuit that is used when the AC current fails. For the standby UPS, the primary circuit is the house AC current circuit with an inline surge suppressor and filter. A relatively small amount of the current flows to the secondary circuit to keep the battery charged in case it is ever needed. When the AC current fails, the UPS switches from the primary to the secondary circuit and the battery provides the power, which is converted from DC to AC before it leaves the UPS.

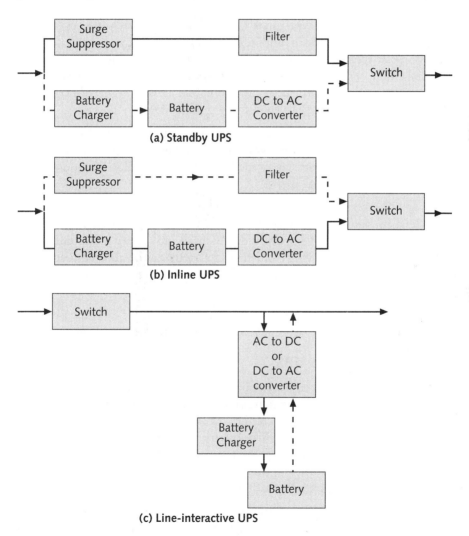

Figure 11-21   Standby, In-line, or Line-interactive UPS

The switching time (the time it takes for the UPS to switch from the AC circuit to the battery-charged circuit) caused problems for earlier computers, even causing the PC to reboot.

Today, however, computer power supplies are better designed and able to keep the computer running during the fraction of a second it takes to switch the power in the UPS. One variation on a standby UPS uses a ferroresonant regulator that delivers power to the circuit during the switching time, to virtually eliminate any interruption of power.

Other variations of this type of UPS reduce costs by eliminating the filter. The purpose of the filter is to condition the AC current, reducing the effect of brownouts and spikes. These electricity filters, or line conditioners, must be purchased separately.

The Inline UPS

In Figure 11-21, notice that the inline UPS uses the battery-powered circuit as the primary circuit, instead of the AC circuit. With most devices, the AC circuit is only used if the battery-powered circuit registers any error conditions caused by the failure of some component in the circuit. These conditions are not related to spikes, brownouts, or blackouts of the AC current, but rather to the performance of the components. With some inline UPS devices, both circuits are continuously used to collectively provide power.

With inline UPSs, when the AC current fails, no switching is needed because the primary circuit continues to be the battery-powered circuit. The only thing that is lost is the battery's recharging. These UPS devices are sometimes called true UPSs, because they truly do provide uninterruptible power.

The inline UPS also provides more line conditioning than does the standby UPS, and, because of the clean, constant 120-volt current it produces, it can extend the life of computer equipment. Because the inline UPS converts the AC power to battery power in DC and then back to AC power, the inline design is sometimes referred to as **double conversion**. Because the battery is in constant use, the inline UPS battery tends to wear out sooner than does the standby UPS battery.

The inline UPS is more expensive than the standby UPS; one less expensive variation eliminates the secondary circuit altogether, leaving the battery-charged circuit with no backup.

The Line-Interactive UPS

The **line-interactive UPS** is a variation of the standby UPS that shortens the switching time by always keeping the inverter working, so that there is no charging-up time for the inverter. An inverter is a device that converts DC to AC. However, during regular operation, the inverter filters electricity and charges the battery by converting AC to DC. See Figure 11-21c. If the power fails, the switch breaks the normal circuit and the inverter switches roles and begins to convert the battery's DC to AC. The delay for the inverter to switch roles is shorter than the delay for a standby UPS that must start up the inverter.

The line-interactive UPS also offers good line conditioning because there is an automatic voltage regulator, called the **buck–boost** feature. During spikes in electrical power, the regulator decreases (in other words bucks) the voltage, and it boosts it during brownouts. The boost feature means that the line-interactive UPS does not need to draw on battery power to respond to a brownout, as does the true standby UPS.

The Intelligent UPS

Some UPSs can be controlled by software from a computer, to allow for additional functionality. For example, from the front panel of some UPSs you can check for a weak battery. If the UPS is an **intelligent UPS**, you can perform the same function from the utility software installed on your computer. In order for a UPS to accommodate this feature, it must have a serial port connection to the PC and a microprocessor on board. Some of the things this utility software and an intelligent UPS can do are:

- Diagnose the UPS
- Check for a weak battery
- Monitor the quality of electricity received
- Monitor the percentage of load the UPS is carrying during a blackout
- Automatically schedule the weak-battery test or UPS diagnostic test
- Send an alarm to workstations on a network to prepare for a shutdown
- Close down all servers protected by the UPS during a blackout
- Provide pager notification to a facilities manager if the power goes out during weekends
- After a shutdown, allow for startup from a remote location over phone lines

Windows NT and Windows 2000 offer support for intelligent UPSs. You can monitor and control the devices from the UPS dialog box accessible through Control Panel. The Windows 2000 controls were developed by Microsoft and Amercian Power Conversion (APC), a leading manufacturer of UPSs.

When Buying a UPS

The power supplies in most computers can operate over a wide range of electrical voltage input, but operating the computer under these conditions for extended periods of time can shorten the life not only of the power supply, but also of the computer as well. Power protection devices offer these benefits:

- Condition the line for both brownouts and spikes
- Provide backup power during a blackout
- Protect against very high spikes that could damage the equipment

When you purchase a UPS, cost often drives the decision about how much and what kind of protection you buy. However, do not buy an inline UPS that runs at full capacity. A battery charger operating at full capacity produces heat, which can reduce the life of the battery. The UPS rating should exceed your total VA or wattage output by at least 25 percent. Also be aware of the degree of line conditioning that the UPS provides. Consider the warranty and service policies as well as the guarantee the UPS manufacturer gives for the equipment that the UPS protects.

FIRE EXTINGUISHERS

A+CORE
3.2

No discussion of working on electrical equipment would be complete without mentioning the importance of having a fire extinguisher handy that is rated to handle fires that are ignited by electricity. The National Fire Protection Association (NFPA), an organization that creates standards for fire safety, says a fire has one of three ratings.

- *Class A.* A fire that is fueled by ordinary combustible materials such as wood, trash, or clothes

- *Class B.* A fire that is fueled by flammable liquids such as oil, gasoline, kerosene, propane gas, and some plastics

- *Class C.* A fire that is ignited and heated by electricity

It's the Class C fire that we are concerned about in this discussion. For a fire to be rated as a Class C fire, regardless of what is burning, the fire must have been ignited by electricity and must keep burning because electrical energy is providing heat. If you take away the electrical current, then the fire becomes a Class A or Class B fire.

Underwriters Laboratories (UL) rates fire extinguishers according to the type of fire they handle and the size of fire they can put out. Ratings are usually displayed on the extinguisher as an icon. (See Figure 11-22.) The class letter is inside a triangle for Class A, a square for Class B, and a circle for Class C. The extinguisher can be rated for more than one type of fire and includes a number for Class A and B fires that indicate what size fire it can handle. A Class C rating is not assigned a number because the size of the fire is determined more by the A or B fuel type. Class A ratings are from 1 to 40 and Class B ratings are from 1 to 640. An excellent choice for a fire extinguisher for home use is one that carries all three ratings. A good example is one rated as 2-A: 10-B: C. This means the extinguisher can handle Class A fires of magnitude 2 on a scale of 1 to 40, Class B fires of magnitude 10 on a scale of 1 to 640, and can handle Class C fires. Fire extinguishers come as either disposable or rechargeable. The rechargeable ones cost more but can be recharged and last longer. Disposable ones lose their pressure after about 12 years and must be replaced.

Mount the fire extinguisher near your workbench but not directly over your work area. If equipment were to catch on fire, you wouldn't want to have to reach over it to get to the fire extinguisher. Know how to use the extinguisher. One good method to remember is the **P-A-S-S** method (**P**ull the pin, **A**im low at the base of the fire, **S**queeze the handle of the extinguisher, and **S**weep back and forth across the base of the fire).

Large computer facilities might have a built-in halon gas system to extinguish fires. Halon does not damage equipment as much as do other types of fire extinguisher chemicals; however, halon is considered an environmental hazard. In 1987, an international agreement, known as the Montreal Protocol, mandated the phaseout of halon fire extinguishing systems in developed countries by the year 2000 and in less-developed countries by 2010, because of the danger halon poses to the ozone layer.

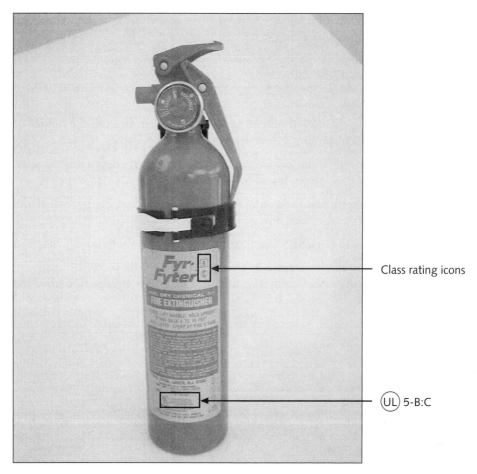

Class rating icons

(UL) 5-B:C

11

Figure 11-22   A fire extinguisher is rated by Underwriters Laboratories. Look for a Class C rating to handle fires ignited by electrical current

CHAPTER SUMMARY

❏ Electricity describes the components necessary for a complete circuit. An electrical circuit is created by a combination of voltage, current, and resistance.

❏ Electrical voltage is a measure of the potential difference in an electrical system.

❏ Electrical current is measured in amps, and electrical resistance is measured in ohms. One volt drives a current of one amp through a resistance of one ohm, which is one watt of power.

❏ Wattage is a measure of electrical power. Wattage is calculated by multiplying volts by amps in a system.

❑ Microcomputers require DC current, which is converted from AC current by the PC's power supply inside the computer case.

❑ A PC power supply is actually a transformer and rectifier rather than a supplier of power.

❑ A multimeter is a device that can measure volts, amps, ohms, and continuity in an electrical system.

❑ Before replacing a damaged system board in a PC, first measure the output of the power supply to make sure that it did not cause the damage.

❑ A faulty power supply can cause memory errors, data errors, system hangs, or reboots, and it can damage a system board or other component.

❑ The U.S. Environmental Protection Agency has established Energy Star standards for electronic devices, to reduce energy consumption.

❑ Devices that are Energy-Star-compliant go into a sleep mode in which they use less than 30 watts of power.

❑ PCs that are Energy-Star-compliant often have CMOS settings that affect the Energy Star options available on the PC.

❑ Devices that control the electricity to a computer include surge suppressors, line conditioners, and UPSs.

❑ A surge suppressor protects a computer against damaging spikes in the electrical voltage.

❑ Line conditioners level out the AC current to reduce brownouts and spikes.

❑ A UPS provides enough power to perform an orderly shutdown during a blackout.

❑ There are two kinds of UPSs: the true UPS, called the inline UPS (or, sometimes, the online UPS) and the standby UPS.

❑ The inline UPS is the more expensive, because it provides continuous power. The standby UPS must switch from one circuit to another when a blackout begins.

❑ An intelligent UPS can be controlled and managed from utility software at a remote computer, or from a computer connected to the UPS through a serial cable.

❑ Data line protectors are small surge suppressors designed to protect modems from spikes on telephone lines.

❑ A Class C fire extinguisher is rated to put out a fire ignited and kept burning by electricity.

KEY TERMS

Alternating current (AC) — Current that cycles back and forth rather than traveling in only one direction. In the U. S., the AC voltage from a standard wall outlet is normally between 110 and 115 V AC. In Europe, the standard AC voltage from a wall outlet is 220 V AC.

Ammeter — A meter that measures electrical current in amps.

Ampere (A) — A unit of measurement for electrical current. One volt across a resistance of one ohm will produce a flow of one amp.

Autorange meter — A multimeter that senses the quantity of input and sets the range accordingly.

Buck-boost regulator — A line-interactive UPS that offers good line conditioning and has an automatic voltage regulator that decreases ("bucks") the voltage during electrical spikes and boosts it during sags.

Capacitor — An electronic device that can maintain an electrical charge for a period of time and is used to smooth out the flow of electrical current. Capacitors are often found in computer power supplies.

Clamping voltage — The maximum voltage allowed through a surge suppressor, such as 175 or 330 volts.

Continuity — A continuous, unbroken path for the flow of electricity. A continuity test can determine whether or not internal wiring is still intact or a fuse is good or bad.

Data line protectors — Surge protectors designed to work with the telephone line to a modem.

Diode — An electronic device that allows electricity to flow in only one direction. Used in a rectifier circuit.

Direct current (DC) — Current that travels in only one direction (the type of electricity provided by batteries). Computer power supplies transform AC current to low DC current.

Display power management signaling (DPMS) — Energy Star standard specifications that allow for the video card and monitor to go into sleep mode simultaneously. *See* Energy Star systems.

11

Double conversion — The process by which the inline UPS converts the AC power to battery power in DC form and then back to AC power.

Doze time — The time before an Energy Star or "Green" system will reduce 80% of its activity.

EMI (electromagnetic interference) — A magnetic field produced as a side effect from the flow of electricity. EMI can cause corrupted data in data lines that are not properly shielded.

Energy Star systems — "Green" systems that satisfy the EPA requirements to decrease the overall consumption of electricity. *See* Green standards.

Ferroresonant regulator — A UPS device that contains a magnetic coil that can retain a power charge that can be used during a brownout to raise the voltage at switching time.

Green Standards — Standards that mean that a computer or device can go into sleep or doze mode when not in use, thus saving energy and helping the environment.

Hard drive standby time — The amount of time before a hard drive will shut down to conserve energy.

Inline UPS — A UPS that continually provides power through a battery-powered circuit, and, because it requires no switching, ensures continuous power to the user.

Intelligent UPS — A UPS connected to a computer by way of a serial cable so that software on the computer can monitor and control the UPS.

Joule — A measure of energy equal to the work done when a current of one ampere is passed through a resistance of one ohm for one second.

Let-through — The maximum voltage allowed through a surge suppressor to the device being protected.

Line conditioners — Devices that regulate, or condition the power, providing continuous voltage during brownouts and spikes.

Line-interactive UPS — A variation of a standby UPS that shortens switching time by always keeping the inverter that converts AC to DC working, so that there is no charge-up time for the inverter.

Multimeter — A device used to measure the various components of an electrical circuit. The most common measurements are voltage, current, and ohms.

Ohms — The standard unit of measurement for electrical resistance. Resistors are rated in ohms.

P-A-S-S — An acronym to help remember how to use a fire extinguisher. (Pull the pin, Aim low at the base of the fire, Squeeze the handle of the extinguisher, and Sweep back and forth across the fire.)

Power conditioners — Line conditioners that regulate, or condition, the power, providing continuous voltage during brownouts.

Rectifier — An electrical device that converts AC to DC. A PC power supply contains a rectifier.

Resistance — The degree to which a device opposes or resists the flow of electricity. As the electrical resistance increases, the current decreases. *See* Ohms and Resistor.

Resistor — An electronic device that resists or opposes the flow of electricity. A resistor can be used to reduce the amount of electricity being supplied to an electronic component.

Sleep mode — A mode used in many "Green" systems that allows them to be configured through CMOS to suspend the monitor or even the drive, if the keyboard and/or CPU have been inactive for a set number of minutes. *See* Green standards.

Standby time — The time before a "Green" system will reduce 92% of its activity. *See* Green standards.

Standby UPS — A UPS that quickly switches from an AC power source to a battery-powered source during a brownout or power outage.

Surge suppressor or **surge protector** — A device or power strip designed to protect electronic equipment from power surges and spikes.

Suspend time — The time before a green system will reduce 99% of its activity. After this time, the system needs a warmup time so that the CPU, monitor, and hard drive can reach full activity.

Transformer — A device that changes the ratio of current to voltage. A computer power supply is basically a transformer and a rectifier.

Transistor — An electronic device that can regulate electricity and act as a logical gate or switch for an electrical signal.

UPS (uninterruptible power supply) — A device designed to provide a backup power supply during a power failure. Basically, a UPS is a battery backup system with an ultra-fast sensing device.

Volt — A measure of potential difference in an electrical circuit. A computer ATX power supply usually provides five separate voltages: +12V, –12V, +5V, –5V, and +3V.

Voltage — Electrical differential that causes current to flow, measured in volts. *See* Volts.

Voltmeter — A device for measuring electrical AC or DC voltage.

Wattage — Electrical power measured in watts.

Watts — The unit used to measure power. A typical computer may use a power supply that provides 200 watts.

REVIEW QUESTIONS

1. Describe three similarities a closed-circuit water system has with a closed-circuit electrical system.
2. Volts are a measure of what characteristic of electricity?
3. What is the normal voltage of house current in the U.S.?
4. Why must an ammeter be installed in line with the circuit in order to measure amps?
5. Which of the three can be measured with the power off, volts, amps, or ohms? Why?
6. Describe the relationship between volts, amps, and ohms in a circuit.
7. What are the five voltages produced by an ATX power supply?
8. What are the four voltages produced by an AT power supply?
9. What is the wattage of a current of 15 amps and a voltage of 120 volts?
10. What is the difference between a transformer and a rectifier? Which are found in a PC power supply?
11. Describe the purpose of the ground line in a house circuit. Show the electrical symbol for ground.
12. What is the basic electronic building block of an integrated circuit?
13. Why is a power supply dangerous even after the power is disconnected?
14. What is the symbol for a diode?
15. What is a simple way to detect EMI?
16. What is a closed connection between two points in a circuit called?
17. What DVM setting do you use to determine if a fuse is good?
18. What DVM voltage range do you use to measure house current voltage, 110V or 120V? Why?
19. With the PC power turned on, if you have set a DVM to measure voltage and place one probe on a ground lead of a hard drive power connection and the other probe on the computer case, what will be the voltage reading?
20. List four computer symptoms that indicate a faulty power supply.
21. If you measure the voltage of a power supply and find it to be within acceptable ranges, why is it still possible that the power supply may be faulty?
22. How much power can a device use in sleep mode if it complies with Green Standards?

11

23. Name one thing that can be set in CMOS that pertains to power management.
24. How can you easily tell if a computer is designed to comply with Green Standards?
25. Name two ways that a surge suppressor is measured.
26. Using a multimeter, what will be the measurement in ohms of a good fuse?
27. What are the two main types of uninterruptible power supplies?
28. How does an intelligent UPS differ from one that is not intelligent?
29. What class fire extinguisher is used for electrical fires?
30. What does the term PASS mean when you are using a fire extinguisher?

PROJECTS

Energy Star Features on a PC

Write down each of the power management and Energy Star features that can be set through CMOS on your home or lab computer.

Price and Value Comparisons

At your local computer vendor(s), compare the prices and ratings of two different surge suppressors.

PC Power Supply Facts

Remove the cover from your home or lab PC and answer the following questions:

1. How many watts are supplied by your power supply? (It is usually printed on the label on the top of the power supply.)
2. How many cables are supplied by your power supply?
3. Where does each cable lead?
4. Is there a switch on the back of the power supply that can be set for 220 volts (Europe) or 110 volts (U.S.)?

Build a Circuit to Turn on a Light

1. From the following components, build a circuit to turn on a light:
   - An AC light bulb or LED (*Note:* A LED has polarity—it must be connected with the negative and positive terminals in the correct positions.)
   - A double-A battery (*Note:* A 9-volt battery can cause some bulbs to blow up.)
   - A switch (A knife switch or even a DIP switch will work.)
   - Three pieces of wire to connect the light, the switch, and the battery
2. Add a second battery to the circuit and record the results.
3. Add a resistor to the circuit and record the results.
4. Place an extra wire in the middle of the circuit running from the battery to the switch (thus making a short) and record the results.

Measure the Output of Your Power Supply

Measure the power output to the system board of your computer and to the floppy drive. Fill in the following chart. Note that red and black leads refer to the color of the probes.

AT System Board

Red Lead	Black Lead	Voltage Measure
3	5	
3	6	
3	7	
3	8	
4	Ground	
9	Ground	
10	Ground	
11	Ground	
12	Ground	

ATX System Board

Red Lead	Black Lead	Voltage Measure
1	4	
1	6	
1	8	
1	14	
1	15	
1	16	
1	18	
2	Ground	
5	Ground	
7	Ground	
9	Ground	
10	Ground	
11	Ground	
12	Ground	
13	Ground	
19	Ground	
20	Ground	

11

Floppy Drive

Red Lead	Black Lead	Voltage Measure
1	3	
4	2	

Research the Market for a UPS for Your Computer System

For a computer system you have access to, determine how much wattage output a UPS should have in the event of a total blackout, and estimate how long the UPS should sustain the power. Research the market and report on the features and prices of a standby UPS and an inline UPS. Include the following information in your report:

❐ Wattage supported

❐ Length of time the power is sustained during total blackout

❐ Line-conditioning features

❐ AC backup present or not present for the inline UPS

❐ Ferroresonant transformer present or not present

❐ Surge suppressor present or not present

❐ Number of power outlets on the box and other features

❐ Written guarantees

❐ Brand name, model, vendor, and price of the device

Using a Multimeter in Troubleshooting

A user comes to you with a problem. He has a cable that connects the serial port of his computer to a serial printer. He needs to order more of the same cables, but he does not know whether this cable is a regular serial cable or a specialized cable made specifically for this printer. One connector on the cable is 9-pin and the other connector is 25-pin. Use a multimeter measuring continuity to answer these questions.

1. Is this a regular serial cable? (*Hint:* Use your pinout results from the project at the end of Chapter 9, and verify with a multimeter that your expectations are correct.)

2. If this is not a regular serial cable, but a specialized cable, give the user the pinouts necessary to order new custom-made cables.

Detecting EMI

Use a small, inexpensive AM radio. Turn the dial to a low frequency, away from a station. Put the radio next to several electronic devices. List the devices in order, from the one producing most static to the one producing least static. Listen to the devices when they are idle and in use.

Total Wattage Used by Your Computer System

Fill in the following chart and then calculate the total wattage requirements of your computer system compared to the rating of your power supply. Include in the chart all devices that draw power from the power supply. Look for a wattage rating printed somewhere on the device.

Component	Wattage	
Hard drive		
Floppy drive		
CD-ROM drive		

Total wattage requirements: _____

Wattage rating of the power supply: _____

This power supply is running at _____ percent of full capacity.

11

12

SUPPORTING WINDOWS 9x

In this chapter, you will learn:

- ◆ About Windows installations and customizing the Windows environment
- ◆ How to install and resolve problems with applications software
- ◆ How to manage Windows resources, including memory and hard drives
- ◆ About ways to optimize Windows performance
- ◆ About the Windows registry and how to repair a corrupted registry
- ◆ How to use some diagnostic software
- ◆ About Plug and Play and how to troubleshoot Plug and Play problems

---

Supporting Windows requires a general knowledge of how hardware works and a detailed knowledge of how Windows and other types of software work. Having a conceptual understanding of how Windows works to manage memory, other hardware devices, and applications software helps in troubleshooting and problem solving.

Before discussing the details of supporting Windows 9x, this chapter explains the fundamental ways in which Windows 9x differs from DOS and Windows 3.x, the variety of software and hardware compatibility problems, and the nature of Windows NT and its successor, Windows 2000. The chapter then turns to ways to support Windows 9x, including installation, memory management, hard disk management, and general troubleshooting.

HOW WINDOWS 9X DIFFERS FROM WINDOWS 3.X AND DOS

Windows 9x is an OS that bridges two worlds. In Figure 12-1, you see that Windows 3.x and DOS constitute a 16-bit world with memory management centered around conventional, upper, and extended memory limitations. Windows 9x, as you have seen throughout several chapters, still has a DOS-based core, uses many 16-bit programs, and must manage base, upper, and extended memory in fundamentally the same way as does DOS. However, Windows 95 introduces 32-bit programming, dynamically loaded device drivers, memory paging, networking, and many other features available in Windows NT and Windows 2000. Windows 9x claims to be completely backward compatible with older software and with hardware designed to work in a DOS and Windows 3.x environment. Windows 9x uses cooperative multitasking when supporting 16-bit applications and preemptive multitasking when supporting 32-bit applications. Windows NT is the break with the past. It does not claim total backward compatibility, because it is a freshly designed OS with new ways of managing software and hardware resources.

A$^+$ OS
1.1

Figure 12-1   Windows 9x is the bridge from DOS to Windows NT

The Windows 9x Core

A$^+$ OS
1.1

Windows 9x has at its core the same three components as Windows 3.x: the user, the kernel, and the GDI. The purposes of each component are listed in Table 12-1.

Figure 12-2 shows the three core portions of the Windows 9x OS. In Figure 12-2, you can see that the basic Windows 9x core component, the kernel, uses mostly 32-bit code. The 16-bit code is only retained as entry points into the kernel from 16-bit application programs. The user portion uses mostly 16-bit code, primarily because it uses less memory than the 32-bit equivalent and does not have a need for significant speed. The GDI core uses a mix of 16-bit and 32-bit code in order to maintain compatibility with 16-bit application programs.

A+ OS
   1.1

Table 12-1   Core components of Windows 9x

Component Name	Main Files Holding the Component	Functions
Kernel	Kernel32.dll, Krnl386.exe	Handles the basic OS functions such as managing memory, file I/O, and loading and executing programs
User	User32.dll, User.exe	Controls the mouse, keyboard, ports, and desktop, including the position of windows, icons, and dialog boxes
GDI	GDI32.dll, GDI.exe	Draws screens, graphics, and lines, and prints them

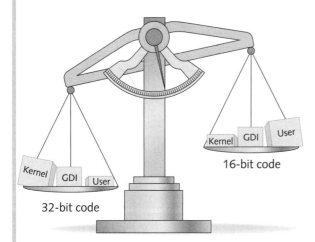

16-bit code

32-bit code

Figure 12-2   Windows 9x uses some 32-bit and some 16-bit code in its three core components

12

The Windows 9x Architecture

The core of Windows 9x consists of the three components described above. This core relates to users, software, and hardware by way of several satellite components, as seen in Figure 12-3. Just as DOS and Windows 3.x each provided a shell for the user to interface with the OS, Windows 9x provides a group of user interface tools and a shell for applications. Configuration data that was once stored in Windows 3.x .ini files is now stored in the Windows 9x registry, a database that also contains the initialization information for applications. There is more about .ini files and the registry later in the chapter.

$A^{+}\,{OS \atop 1.1}$

Figure 12-3   The Windows 9x architecture as it relates to the user, applications software, and hardware

One component manages memory used by other components and applications in a virtual machine environment that is similar to, but more sophisticated than that of Windows 3.x. This component is called the Virtual Memory Manager (VMM).

Another component, called the Installable File System (IFS) Manager, is responsible for all disk access. The Configuration Manager is responsible for the Plug and Play features of Windows 9x and other hardware configuration tasks. In Figure 12-3, the only component that is found in Windows 98, but not Windows 95 is the component responsible for managing device drivers that work under a driver model new to Windows 98, called Win32 Driver Model (WDM) driver manager.

Figure 12-3 serves as a simple, but complete reference point for all the components of Windows 9x, illustrating how they relate to the user, hardware, and software, and to each other. As you can see, Windows 9x architecture uses a modular approach. Keep in mind that Windows 9x is the compromise OS, attempting to bridge two worlds which can, in a simplistic way, be defined as a 16-bit world and a 32-bit world.

16-Bit and 32-Bit Programming

DOS is a 16-bit OS. All portions of the OS are written using 16-bit code, and DOS only supports 16-bit drivers and 16-bit application programs. Windows 3.x also only supports 16-bit applications, but does contain a small amount of 32-bit code. Recall from earlier chapters that Windows for Workgroups 3.11 introduced fast 32-bit programming for disk access, which we now call VFAT, but generally speaking Windows 3.x is a 16-bit program and only supports 16-bit application programs.

Windows 9x contains some 16-bit code and some 32-bit code. Programs written in 32-bit code require more memory and are generally faster than programs written in 16-bit code. Windows 9x supports VFAT, which is written with 32-bit code. Although Windows 9x supports 16-bit device drivers, it's preferable to use the 32-bit drivers supplied with Windows 9x for three main reasons. They are generally much faster, and 32-bit drivers can be stored in extended memory, releasing more of the first MB of memory to application programs. Also, 32-bit drivers can be dynamically loaded, meaning that they are loaded into memory when they are needed and then removed when not needed, thus conserving memory. In contrast, 16-bit drivers must be stored in conventional or upper memory. When Windows 9x is installed over DOS, it searches for these 16-bit drivers and replaces them with 32-bit drivers if it can.

Virtual Machines

A+ OS
1.1,
2.4,
3.1

Another important difference between Windows 9x and DOS with Windows 3.x is that Windows 9x enhances the application of virtual machines. Think of **virtual machines** (VM) as several logical machines within one physical machine, as represented in Figure 12-4, similar in concept to several logical drives within one physical hard drive.

Figure 12-4   Windows 9x uses the virtual machine concept

12

A+ OS
1.1,
2.4,
3.1

In Figure 12-4, the system Virtual Machine can support 32-bit and 16-bit Windows application programs, but DOS programs are put aside into their own virtual machines. Remember that DOS programs don't account for the sharing of resources. A DOS program expects to directly control the hardware of the entire PC, memory included. If a DOS program begins to use memory addresses not assigned to it, errors occur in a multitasking environment. Windows 9x solves this problem by providing the DOS program with its own logical machine. In effect, the application program says, "I want all of memory and all of this and all of that." Windows 9x says, "OK, here they are," and gives the program its own PC, including all the virtual memory addresses it wants from 0 to 4 GB as well as its own virtual hardware! As far as the DOS program is concerned, it can go anywhere and do anything within its own PC. That's a virtual machine! The DOS application program does not try to communicate with any other application program or to access the data of another program, because it thinks there are no other programs—it controls its entire world, and it's the only program in it.

One important result of running DOS programs in their individual virtual machines is that when a program makes an error, the virtual machine it is using hangs, but the rest of the actual PC is isolated from the problem.

Windows 16-bit application programs offer a slightly different challenge to Windows 9x. These programs make some of the same mistakes that DOS programs do and can cause the system to hang. However, they also sometimes expect to access other programs and their data. The 16-bit Windows programs don't expect to control the hardware directly, and are content to route their requests to Windows. Windows 9x places these programs within the system VM because they communicate with hardware through the OS, but Windows 9x puts these programs together in their own memory space so they can share memory addresses.

The result of this arrangement is that, when a 16-bit Windows program causes an error called a Windows Protection Error or a General Protection Fault, it can disturb other 16-bit programs, causing them to fail, but it does not disturb DOS programs in their own VM or 32-bit programs that don't share their virtual memory addresses.

Memory Paging

How does Windows 9x provide virtual memory addresses to DOS and 16-bit Windows application programs? By **memory paging** which is managed by the **Virtual Memory Manager**. Look at Figure 12-5. In the top diagram, you see Windows 3.x with the memory model you have observed in earlier chapters. Application programs in Windows 3.x share the memory addresses that have been assigned to either the physical or virtual memory of a system. For example, in Figure 12-5, 64 MB of memory addresses are available. Although 16-bit programs run in conventional memory (first 640K), they might store their data in extended memory. Of the 64 MB, perhaps half of these addresses are assigned to physical RAM stored on SIMMs or DIMMs, and the other half of the addresses are virtual memory contained in the swap file on the hard drive. In this case, there is only one set of memory addresses, and all application programs must share these addresses.

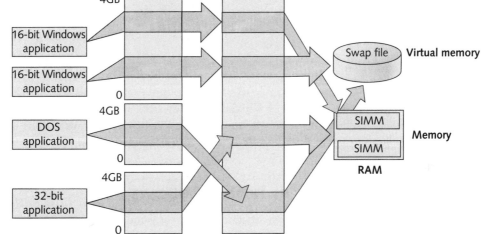

A^+ OS
3.2,
1.1

Figure 12-5 How Windows 9x manages memory differently than does Windows 3.x

As you can see in the lower part of Figure 12-5, Windows 9x not only has virtual memory stored in a swap file, but also provides virtual memory addresses to application programs. In Figure 12-5, you see three sets of virtual memory addresses. Each set can contain 0 to 4 GB of addresses, depending on the amount of virtual memory available. The top set is being used by two 16-bit programs. The second set of virtual addresses is being used by a single DOS program, and a third set of addresses is being used by a 32-bit program. Each VM for DOS has a set of virtual memory addresses. The 16-bit Windows programs share a single set of virtual memory addresses, and each 32-bit program has its own individual set of addresses.

12

A+ *OS*
  3.2,
  1.1

In Figure 12-5, all these virtual addresses map onto the page table, which in turn maps onto either physical memory (RAM) or virtual memory on the hard drive (swap file). Obviously, not all virtual memory addresses in Windows 9x have physical or virtual memory assigned to them. These virtual addresses remain unassigned until an application program uses them.

In Windows 9x, the Virtual Memory Manager controls the page table, moving 4K pages in and out of physical RAM. If a program requests memory that the memory manager knows is stored in the swap file, the manager generates a **page fault**, which causes the manager to go to the drive to return the data from the swap file to RAM. This action is called a **page-in**. If RAM is full, the manager takes a page and moves it to the swap file, which is called a **page-out**.

If RAM is full much of the time, the Virtual Memory Manager might spend excessive time moving pages in and out of RAM, which can cause excessive hard drive use and a decrease in overall system performance and can even cause a system lockup or applications to fail. This situation is sometimes called **disk thrashing** and can cause premature hard drive failure. Symptoms of excessive memory paging are:

- Very high CPU use

- Very slow system response

- Constant hard drive use

The solution is to leave fewer application programs open at the same time or to install more RAM.

Having covered the differences between Windows 95 and Windows 3.x with DOS, the chapter now briefly looks at how Windows 98 differs from Windows 95. The differences are much less significant, as Windows 98 is really just an upgrade from Windows 95.

How Windows 98 Differs from Windows 95

Windows 98 is basically the same operating system as Windows 95, having the same basic core components and providing the same fundamental services to software, hardware, and the user. However, it does offer some added features and improved performance over Windows 95. Some of these features, including FAT32 and support for USB and DVD, became available with Windows 95, Release 2. Windows 98 also includes some new system tools to monitor and improve system performance, new hardware support, and additional Web tools. Table 12-2 summarizes the changes from Windows 95 to Windows 98.

 TIP FAT32 is not compatible with Windows NT or disk compression, including DoubleSpace under Windows 98. To use disk compression or to have a file system compatible with Windows NT, use FAT16. Windows 2000 supports FAT32.

Windows 98 and Window 95 load, run, and install very much the same way. As we continue through this chapter, any significant differences between the two versions will be noted.

Table 12-2   Features new to Windows 98

Feature	Description
Troubleshooting utilities	Windows 95 had a few troubleshooting utilities, but the 15 utilities that come with Windows 98 are more interactive.
Update Wizard	The Update Wizard connects to the Microsoft Web site and automatically downloads any new drivers or fixes.
Maintenance Wizard	The Maintenance Wizard can be used to regularly schedule several maintenance tasks, which include running Disk Defragmenter and ScanDisk, discussed in earlier chapters.
DriveSpace 3	An improved version of DriveSpace for Windows 95, it includes a third level of data compression, called UltraPack which takes up less space per file than does regular compression, called HiPack.
Power management support	Windows 98 supports some power management features, if both hardware and software are present to use them.
Registry Checker	Backs up and restores the registry
Web tools and features	Several Windows 98 features take on an Internet look and feel. Windows 98 also supports viewing TV and interactive programs. You'll need a special TV interface card to do it.
FAT32	Recall that FAT32 is a file system that allows for a smaller cluster size on large drives than the earlier FAT16.
New hardware support	With 1,200 device drivers, Windows 98 supports many more hardware devices than did Windows 95. Also, Windows 98 supports DMA channels for IDE CD-ROM drives, USB, DVD, and multiple video cards supporting multiple monitors.
Win32 Driver Model (WDM)	A new device driver model, also used by Windows NT, makes it possible for the same driver to be used by both operating systems.

12

Windows 98 Upgrades

A+ OS 2.2   Microsoft has produced two upgrades for Windows 98: Windows 98 Second Edition (Windows 98 SE) and Windows Millennium Edition (Windows Me). Each upgrade has significant enhancements over its predecessor.

Windows 98 SE includes several patches, or fixes, for the first edition of Windows 98, updates of existing components, and some new components. Most new features involve networking and Internet access. Improved support for ATM networks includes the addition of Point-to-Point Protocol (PPP) over ATM, which allows a dial-up connection over an ATM network. Security for a dial-up connection over regular phone lines was also upgraded.

A new feature is Internet Connection Sharing (ICS), which makes it possible for a Windows 98 PC to access the Internet through another computer on a local network so that only one computer requires a direct connection to an ISP. This feature means that several PCs on a small home network can share the same access to an ISP without incurring additional charges and without installing third-party software. Support for modems that use a USB port and support for a wake-on-LAN connection are also included. Wake-on-LAN means that a PC can go into a low-power state and then return to standard power when the network card detects activity from another computer on the network.

Windows Me takes us one step closer to the merging of Windows 9x and Windows 2000 as it contains features from each OS, although, at its core, it is still a Windows 9x upgrade. It's designed for the home user and not for business. It focuses on enhancements to multimedia features such as support for video cameras, digital cameras, scanners, and a jukebox recorder. It includes a compression utility for video files and a video editor. True to its goal as a home PC operating system, the OS is very user friendly, including more informative error messages and troubleshooting utilities. Other features unique to Windows Me are discussed at the end of this chapter.

A+ OS
1.1   To know which version of Windows is installed, right-click on the My Computer icon and select **Properties** from the shortcut menu. The System Properties windows opens. Click the **General** tab.

LOADING AND RUNNING WINDOWS 9X

We now turn our attention to what happens when Windows 9x starts up, how a user can alter the startup process, and how the Windows 9x desktop can be customized. With that foundation built, we will then turn our attention to installing Windows 9x, and continue on to a more in-depth look at support issues.

Files Used to Customize the Startup Process

A+ OS
1.1   Before you learn about the startup process, you will learn about the files that Windows 9x uses to control the process. Recall from earlier chapters that DOS requires IO.SYS, MSDOS.SYS, and COMMAND.COM in the root directory of the boot device to load. In addition, AUTOEXEC.BAT and CONFIG.SYS are text files that can contain settings for environmental variables and commands to load drivers and TSRs. If AUTOEXEC.BAT or CONFIG.SYS files are present in the root directory, the command lines in them are executed during the boot. They are used to customize the load. Just as DOS uses text files to contain information about the load, Windows 3.x also uses text files to hold custom settings that help control the loading process. These files are called initialization files, and some of the entries in these files are read and used by Windows 9x. However, most of Windows 9x settings are stored in a database called the Windows registry rather than in text files. You will learn about the Windows registry later in the chapter, but now we turn our attention to how initialization files are organized and how they can be used. The Windows System Configuration Editor (Sysedit) can be used to edit text files. To use Sysedit, type SYSEDIT in the Run dialog box. These files automatically display for editing: Autoexec.bat, Config.sys, Win.ini, and Protocol.ini.

A+ OS
1.1

Initialization Files

An **initialization file**, with an .ini file extension, is a file used by Windows or applications software to store configuration information needed when Windows or an application is first loaded. An application can have its own .ini files and registry and can also store its information in the Windows .ini files and the Windows registry. The contents of files with an .ini extension are organized into sections, which are each given a name. Within a section, values are assigned to variables using this format:

```
[SECTION NAME]

KEYNAME=value
```

Any value to the right of the keyname becomes available to Windows or an applications software program reading the file; in other words, the keyname acts much like the SET command in AUTOEXEC.BAT, which assigns a value to a system variable.

System.ini and Win.ini are used by both Windows 3.x and Windows 9x. A sample Windows 9x System.ini file is shown in Figure 12-6. The two sections that have the most impact on the boot process are [boot] and [386Enh]. Windows 3.x keeps many more entries in these sections than does Windows 9x, which really only uses these files for backward compatibility with older applications.

.ini files are only read when Windows or an application using .ini files starts up. If you change the .ini file for an application, you must restart the software for the change to take effect. If you want the application to ignore a line in the .ini file, you can turn the line into a **comment line**, which is ignored by the software and is used to document the file. To make a line a comment line, put a semicolon at the beginning of the line.

The maximum file size of .ini files is 64K, although files greater than 32K can cause some applications software problems. Most applications have a setup program in their program group that is used to make changes to their .ini files.

TIP   Sometimes it is necessary to manually edit an .ini file that belongs to an application, but you should not edit System.ini or other Windows 9x initialization files because Windows might not run correctly, and because Windows might overwrite these files when changes are made to Windows through the Control Panel.

We now turn our attention to studying the Windows 9x startup process.

The Windows 9x Startup Process

A+ OS
1.1,
2.3

Windows 9x first loads in real mode and then switches to protected mode. With DOS, the two core real-mode system files responsible for starting up the OS, IO.SYS and MSDOS.SYS remain in memory, running even after the OS is running. With Windows 9x, Io.sys is responsible for only the initial startup process performed in real mode, then control is turned over to Vmm32.vxd, which works in protected mode, and Io.sys is terminated. Windows 9x includes a file named **Msdos.sys**, but it is only a text file that contains some parameters and switches that can be set to affect the way the OS boots.

12

A+ OS
1.1,
2.3

Starting up Windows 9x is a five-phase process, as shown in Figure 12-7. We will next look at each phase in turn.

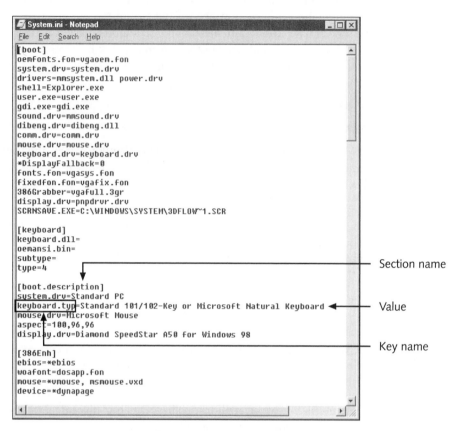

Figure 12-6   A sample Windows 98 System.ini file

A+ OS
1.1,
2.3

Phase 1: BIOS Bootstrap   Startup BIOS begins the process. If the BIOS is **Plug and Play (PnP) BIOS**, then it looks to permanent RAM for information about hardware and configures PnP devices that have their configuration information recorded there. It performs POST and saves information that Windows Configuration Manager later uses to complete the hardware configuration.

Phase 2: DOS Drivers, TSRs and Environmental Settings   In Phase 2, BIOS turns control over to Io.sys, which creates a real-mode operating system environment. It automatically loads several drivers, sets several environmental variables, and executes any commands listed in Config.sys and Autoexec.bat. Config.sys and Autoexec.bat are not used in the same way that they were with DOS, because many of their commands are automatically executed by Io.sys. However, for backward compatibility, any entries in these files are executed.

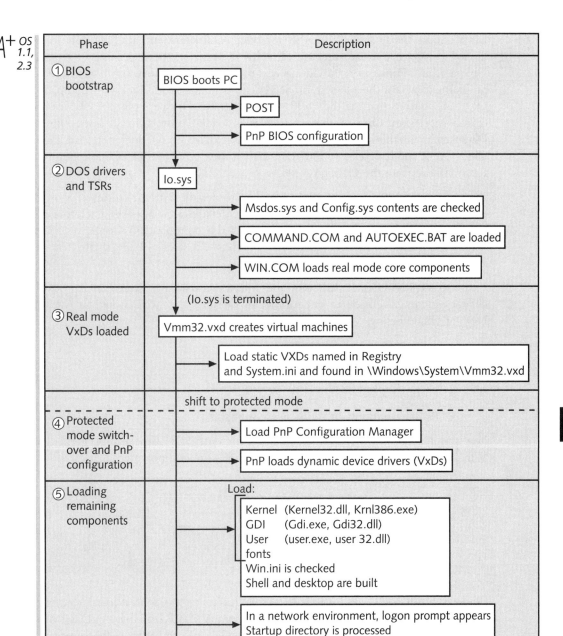

Figure 12-7   Windows 9x core components and the loading process

A+ OS
1.1,
2.3

Io.sys checks the text file Msdos.sys for boot parameters, and automatically loads the fol-lowing drivers if they are present: Himem.sys, Ifshlp.sys, Setver.exe, and Drvspace.bin (or Dblspace.bin). Himem.sys provides access to extended memory. Ifshlp.sys is used by 16-bit programs to access the file system. Setver.exe is included for backward compatibility with DOS applications that use the DOS version number. Drvspace.bin or Dblspace.bin provide disk compression. One of these two files is loaded only if Io.sys finds Dlbspace.ini or Drvspace.ini in the root directory of the boot drive. Io.sys does not load Emm386.exe. Therefore, if you have a 16-bit program that requires emulated, expanded memory, then load Emm386.exe from the Config.sys file.

Io.sys also sets several environmental variables to default settings. Entries in Io.sys cannot be edited, but an entry in Config.sys overrides the default entry in Io.sys. Therefore, if you want to use settings different from the default, put the command in Config.sys. Here are the default Io.sys entries: files=60, lastdrive=z, buffers=30, stacks=9,256, shell=Command.com, and Fcbs=4.

Next, Io.sys loads Command.com, and follows instructions stored in Autoexec.bat. The default assignments made to environmental variables that were stored in Autoexec.bat in DOS are listed below:

- Tmp=c:\windows\temp
- Temp=c:\windows\temp
- Prompt=pg
- Path=c:\windows;c:\windows\command

You can change any of these by making an entry in Autoexec.bat. Next, Io.sys loads Win.com. Then Win.com loads other real-mode core components.

> **TIP** Windows 9x does not need CONFIG.SYS and AUTOEXEC.BAT, but executes them only to provide backward compatibility for older hardware and software. Settings that were once included in CONFIG.SYS and AUTOEXEC.BAT are now built into Io.sys and the registry. However, if you put command lines in either of these two files, they are exe-cuted and override the settings stored in Io.sys and the registry.

Phase 3: Static VxDs   In Phase 3, Io.sys relinquishes control to the Virtual Memory Manager component housed in Vmm32.vxd along with some VxDs. Recall that a VxD is a virtual device driver that works with a virtual machine to provide access to hardware for software running in the VM. Under Windows 3.x, these VxDs were loaded from System.ini and had a 386 file extension. Under Windows 9x, if stored in individual files, they have a .vxd file extension. They are called **static VxDs** because once they are loaded into memory, they remain there. (Conversely, **dynamic VxDs** are loaded into and unloaded from memory as needed.)

Vmm32.vxd was built specifically for this computer when Windows 9x was installed and contains some VxDs critical for a successful boot. (The VxD drivers that are now included in Vmm32.vxd were listed in the [386enh] section of System.ini under Windows 3.x.)

A+ OS
1.1,
2.3

Vmm32.vxd terminates Io.sys and, while still in real mode, loads static VxD device drivers as identified in four different locations. They can be embedded in Vmm32.vxd, named in the registry or System.ini, or stored in the VxD file in the \Windows\System\Vmm32 directory.

If you suspect a problem with a VxD that is part of the Vmm32.vxd file, then store a new version of the file in the \Windows\System\Vmm32 directory. If Windows finds a VxD driver there, it uses that driver instead of the one embedded in Vmm32.vxd. Also, VxD drivers are listed in the registry and also listed in System.ini. Normally, the entries are the same, and entries in System.ini are only listed there for backward compatibility. However, if an entry in System.ini differs from an entry in the registry, the value in System.ini is used.

Phase 4: Protected Mode Switchover and PnP Configuration At the beginning of Phase 4, Vmm32.vxd switches to protected mode and loads Configuration Manager. Configuration Manager is responsible for configuring legacy and PnP devices. It will use any information that PnP BIOS might have left for it, and loads the 32-bit dynamic device drivers (VxDs) for the PnP devices.

Phase 5: Loading Remaining Components In Phase 5, with Vmm32.vxd still in control, the three core components are loaded, fonts and other associated resources are loaded. Win.ini is checked, and commands stored there are executed to allow for backward compatibility. The shell and user desktop are loaded. If the computer is working in a networked environment, a logon dialog box is displayed, and the user can log on to Windows 9x and the network. Finally, any processes stored in the Startup directory are performed.

Microsoft Windows 9x Startup Menu

12

A+ OS
3.1

Normally, when you load Windows, the message, *Starting Windows 98* displays and then the OS loads. However, if you have set up your PC for a dual boot (how to do that was covered in Chapter 7), the following menu is always displayed when you boot. The time that the menu stays on the screen is determined by a setting in Msdos.sys. You can force the menu to display rather than the *Starting Windows 98* message by holding down either the F8 key or the Ctrl key during the boot. The Microsoft Windows 9x Startup Menu options are:

1. Normal

2. Logged (\BOOTLOG.TXT)

3. Safe mode

4. Safe mode with network support

5. Step-by-step confirmation

6. Command prompt only

7. Safe mode command prompt only

8. Previous version of MS-DOS

What to expect when you select each option on the menu is described next.

Option 4 is displayed if the OS is configured for a network, and Option 8 is displayed if a previous version of DOS was retained during the Windows 9x installation.

Normal   In Msdos.sys, if BootGUI=1, then this option starts Windows 9x. If BootGUI=0, then this option will boot to the DOS 7.0 or DOS 7.1 prompt. Either way, the commands in AUTOEXEC.BAT and CONFIG.SYS will be executed.

Logged (\BOOTLOG.TXT)   This option is the same as Normal, except that Windows 9x tracks the load and startup activities and logs them to the bootlog.txt file. This file can be a helpful tool when troubleshooting.

Safe mode   Safe mode starts Windows 9x with a minimum default configuration to give you an opportunity to correct an error in the configuration. Windows 98 includes support for networks, but Windows 95 does not. For example, if you selected a video driver that is incompatible with your system, when Windows 9x starts, it detects the problem and enters Safe mode with a standard VGA driver selected. You can then go to Device Manager, select the correct driver, and restart Windows.

From the Startup menu, you can choose to enter safe mode yourself if you know of a problem you want to correct. For example, if you had previously selected a group of background and foreground colors that makes it impossible to read the screens, you can reboot and choose Safe mode. Safe mode gives you the standard color scheme along with the VGA mode. Go to Display Properties, make the necessary corrections, and reboot.

In safe mode, the commands in AUTOEXEC.BAT and CONFIG.SYS are not executed.

> **TIP**   To load Windows 9x in safe mode, press F5 when the message "Starting Windows 95/98" appears.

Safe mode with Network Support   This option allows access to the network when booting into safe mode. It is useful if Windows 95 is stored on a network server, and you need to download changes to your PC in safe mode. This option is not available in Windows 98.

Step-by-Step Confirmation   The option asks for confirmation before executing each command in Io.sys, CONFIG.SYS, and AUTOEXEC.BAT. You can accomplish the same thing by pressing Shift+F8 when the message "Starting Windows 95/98" appears.

Command Prompt Only   This option executes the contents of AUTOEXEC.BAT and CONFIG.SYS, but doesn't start Windows 9x. You will be given a DOS prompt. Type **WIN** to load Windows 9x. Type WIN to load Windows 9x, which executes the file WIN.COM. When troubleshooting the OS, try these switches with the WIN command: WIN/D:F turns off 32-bit disk access and WIN/D:M starts Windows in Safe Mode.

Safe mode Command Prompt Only   This option does not execute the commands in AUTOEXEC.BAT or CONFIG.SYS. You will be given a DOS prompt.

Previous Version of MS-DOS This option loads a previous version of DOS if one is present. You can get the same results by pressing F4 when the message "Starting Windows 95/98" appears. This option is not available in Windows 98 SE.

Keystroke Shortcuts When Navigating Windows

Table 12-3 lists a few handy keystrokes to use when working with Windows. The function keys used during startup are included to make the table complete. You can also use the mouse to accomplish some of these same tasks, but keystrokes are faster for experienced typists. Also, sometimes in troubleshooting situations, the mouse is not usable. At those times, knowing the keystrokes is very valuable. When using dual monitors, use the mouse to control which screen is active by moving from screen to screen.

Table 12-3 Keystrokes to help make navigating Windows easier

General Action	Keystrokes	Description
While loading Windows	F4	Load previous version of DOS
	F5	Start in Safe Mode
	F8	Display Startup Menu
	Shift + F8	Step-by-Step Confirmation
Working with text anywhere in Windows	Ctrl + C Ctrl + Ins	Shortcut for Copy
	Ctrl + A	Shortcut for selecting all text
	Ctrl + X	Shortcut for Cut
	Ctrl + V Shift + Ins	Shortcut for Paste
	Shift + arrow keys	Hold down the Shift key and use the arrow keys to select text, character by character
Managing programs	Alt + Tab	While holding down the Alt key, press Tab to move from one loaded application to another.
	Ctrl + Escape	Display the Start menu
	Alt + F4	Close a program window, or, if no window is open, shut down Windows
	Double-click	Double-click an icon or program name to execute the program.
	Ctrl + Alt + Del	Display the Task List, which you can use to switch to another application, end a task, or shut down Windows

To control display settings including how the screen displays and what screen saver pattern is used, right click anywhere on the desktop and select Properties from the shortcut menu. To create a screen saver password, click the Screen Saver tab. Select a screen saver and check Password protected. To set the password, click the Change button and then enter and confirm a password. Click OK to save your password and then click OK to exit the Display Properties window.

12

Table 12-3   Keystrokes to help make navigating Windows easier (continued)

General Action	Keystrokes	Description
Selecting items	Shift + click	To select multiple entries in a list (such as filenames in Explorer), click the first item and then hold down the Shift key and click the last item you want to select in the list. All items between the first and last are selected.
	Ctrl + click	To select several items in a list that are not listed sequentially, click the first item to select it. Hold down the Ctrl key as you click other items anywhere in the list. All items you have clicked on are selected.
Using menus	Alt	Press the Alt key to activate the menu bar.
	Alt, letter	After the menu bar is activated, press a letter to select a menu option. The letter must be underlined in the menu.
	Alt, arrow keys	After the menu bar is activated, use the arrow keys to move over the menu tree.
	Alt, arrow keys, enter	After the menu bar is activated and the correct option is highlighted, press Enter to select the option.
	Esc	Press Escape to exit a menu without making a selection.
Managing the desktop	Print Screen	Copy the desktop into the Clipboard
	Ctrl + Esc	Display the Start menu and moves the focus to the menu. (Use the arrow keys to move over the menu.)
	Alt + M	After the focus is on the Start menu, minimizes all windows and moves the focus to the desktop
Using the Windows key	WIN + E	Start Windows Explorer
	WIN + M	Minimize all windows
	WIN + Tab	Move through items on task bar
	WIN + R	Display the Run dialog box
	WIN + Break	Display the System Properties window

Managing the Windows 9x Desktop

From the Windows 9x desktop you can make applications automatically load at startup, create shortcuts to files and applications, and make the environment more user-friendly. You can hide and unhide the taskbar at the bottom of the desktop. To do that, click Start, Settings, Taskbar and Start Menu. Then click the Taskbar Options tab and select Auto hide.

A shortcut on the desktop is an icon that points to a program that can be executed. The user double-clicks the icon to load the software. A shortcut can be created in several ways. One way is to use the Properties option on the taskbar. Right-click the taskbar and select

Properties from the menu that appears (see Figure 12-8). From this window, you can create a shortcut for a program or data file, name it, and select where to place it (either on the desktop or in the Start menu). If you want a program to load whenever Windows 9x starts, create a shortcut and put the shortcut in the StartUp folder of the Start menu. All items in the StartUp folder are automatically executed when Windows 9x starts.

To edit a shortcut, right-click the shortcut and select **Properties** from the menu. To delete a shortcut, select **Delete** from this same menu.

Figure 12-8 To customize the desktop, use the Properties sheet of the Windows 9x taskbar

Troubleshooting Icons on the Desktop An icon on the desktop can be a shortcut to an application or it can represent a file that belongs to an application. The telltale sign of the difference is the small shortcut symbol on the icon, as seen in Figure 12-9. The icon on the right represents the document file MyLetter1.doc stored in the \Windows\Desktop folder, and the icon on the left is a shortcut to the file MyLetter2.doc, which can be stored anywhere on the drive. Also shown in Figure 12-9 are the contents of the \Windows\Desktop folder as seen by Explorer. You can add an icon to the desktop by putting a file in this folder. One way to delete an icon on the desktop is to delete the corresponding file in this folder; however, as you will see, this method can cause problems for the user.

This icon indicates a file is stored in the desktop folder

The small arrow in this icon indicates it is a shortcut

Figure 12-9 One icon is a shortcut, and the other icon represents a file stored in the Desktop folder

In the screen shown in Figure 12-9, it's possible to change the name of either icon so that they read the same on the desktop (to do this, click the icon name, which produces an insertion point), but the meaning of the two icons is still different. If you delete the icon on the right (the document icon), you have deleted the document file, MyLetter1.doc. If you delete the icon on the left (the shortcut), you have only deleted the shortcut, but the document file that it refers to, MyLetter2.doc, still exists somewhere on the drive.

An error can occur if the document file, MyLetter2.doc, is deleted, but the shortcut to the deleted document remains on the desktop. Figure 12-10 shows a sample error message that occurs when this shortcut is used.

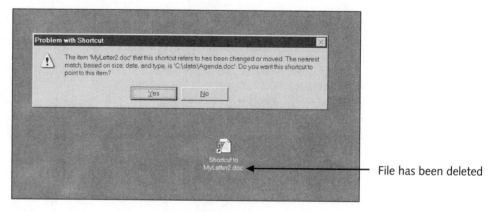

Figure 12-10   The file that the shortcut points to has been deleted, which causes an error when the shortcut is used

Explorer or Program Manager

Windows 3.x uses Program Manager as its primary tool to manage applications and OS components. Program Manager in Windows 3.x is executed by running Progman.exe. Windows 9x uses Explorer as its primary tool for managing applications and OS components. Explorer is executed by running Explorer.exe. Some people who are accustomed to Windows 3.x prefer to use Program Manager instead of Explorer. For these users, you can place a shortcut icon on the desktop to Progman.exe.

INSTALLING AND CONFIGURING WINDOWS 9x

Before installing Windows 9x, verify that the minimum requirements for the hardware are met. In order for Windows 9x to perform satisfactorily, the PC should meet the recommended requirements. Minimum and recommended requirements for Windows 95 and Windows 98 are listed below:

Minimum and recommended requirements for Windows 95:

- 486DX, 25 MHz or higher processor

- 4 MB of RAM (8 MB is recommended)

- 40 to 45 MB of hard disk storage, depending on the installation

Minimum and recommended requirements for Windows 98:

- 486DX, 66 MHz or higher processor

- 24 MB of RAM (32 MB is recommended)

- From 140 to 315 MB of hard disk storage, depending on the installation

Preparing for the Installation

Windows 9x is generally installed as an upgrade to DOS with Windows 3.x, as an upgrade from Windows 95 to Windows 98, or on a clean hard drive. If you have been having problems with the current operating system and applications, consider doing a clean install rather than an upgrade. A clean install requires that you reinstall all applications software after Windows is installed. To do that, first verify that you have all the applications software installation CDs or floppy disks and then back up all data on the drive. Also take the time to verify that the backup of data is good. If you like, you can also format the hard drive. Also, if you suspect a boot sector virus is present, use the FDISK/MBR command discussed in earlier chapters to rewrite the master boot sector program. Then do the clean install.

After Windows 9x is installed, reinstall all the applications software and then, if you formatted the hard drive, restore the data from backups. This method takes longer than an upgrade, but you get the added advantage of a "fresh start" and any problems with corrupted applications or system settings will not follow you into the new installation.

If you are doing an upgrade, before you begin the installation, prepare your hard drive by doing these things:

- Verify that you have enough space on the hard drive. Delete files in the Recycle Bin and temporary directories.

- Run SCANDISK or CHKDSK/F, discussed in Chapter 6, to recover lost clusters, delete the .CHK files created by these programs, and run DEFRAG to defragment your hard drive, which improves overall hard drive performance and possibly allows for a larger swap file.

- Run a current version of antivirus software to check for viruses.

- To ensure that you can backtrack to an earlier version of Windows, save AUTOEXEC.BAT and CONFIG.SYS, found in the root directory, and all files with .ini or .grp file extensions in the \Windows directory to a disk. Files with the .grp file extension are **group files**, which contain information about a program group displayed in Program Manager.

> If you have problems with a Windows 9x installation, you can reinstall the original version of Windows 3.x and copy the .ini files and group files back to the \Windows directory to fully recover from the problem installation.

A^+ OS
2.1

- Check CONFIG.SYS and AUTOEXEC.BAT for potential problems. Before you install Windows, optimize your memory with the methods discussed in Chapter 4, using Memmaker or manually editing these two files.

- If there are TSRs such as QEMM386 (a memory manager by Quarterdeck) loaded from CONFIG.SYS or AUTOEXEC.BAT, and problems arise because they are running during the installation, disable them by converting these lines to comments by typing **REM** at the beginning of the command lines. Later, after the installation, you can activate them again.

- If you are connected to a network, verify that the connection is working. If it is, then Windows setup should be able to reestablish the connection correctly at the end of the installation.

- If you are upgrading from Windows 95 to Windows 98, create a Windows 95 rescue disk for use in the event the installation fails.

- If you are installing Windows on a compressed drive, be aware that the registry can reside on any compressed drive, but the swap file can only reside on a compressed drive that is compressed using protected-mode software such as DriveSpace. DriveSpace marks the area for the swap file as uncompressible. If your drive is compressed with real-mode compression software, such as DoubleSpace, then you should put the swap file on another drive, possibly the host drive. If the host drive is not large enough to hold the file, check the software used to compress the drive, to see if you can increase the size of the host drive.

> **TIP**
> If you used DOS DoubleSpace (available with DOS 6 and 6.2) to compress the drive, type DBLSPACE at the DOS prompt. If you used DriveSpace (available with DOS 6.22), type DRVSPACE. The utilities will give you statistics about the compressed drive and also allow you to change the size of the host drive.

A^+ OS
2.1,
3.2

- Decide if you want to use FAT16 or FAT32 for your file system. If you choose FAT16, you can later convert to FAT32 using the Windows Drive Converter. After Windows 98 is installed, to access the Converter, click **Start**, **Programs**, **Accessories**, **System Tools**, **Drive Converter (FAT32)**. Or you can use the Run dialog box: For the 16-bit version, enter **cvt.exe**, and for the 32-bit version, enter **cvt1.exe** and click **OK**. The Drive Converter wizard steps you through the process.

Performing the Installation

A^+ OS
2.1

If you are performing a clean install on a freshly formatted hard drive, you must boot the PC from a floppy disk. Windows 9x comes on a set of floppy disks or on a CD. If you are installing the OS from floppy disks, boot from the Windows 9x Disk 1 and enter the **A: Setup.exe** command at the DOS prompt (where *A* is the letter of your floppy disk drive). The Windows 9x setup screen appears. Follow the directions on the screen. If you are installing the OS from a CD, after you have booted from a floppy disk, insert the CD in the CD-ROM drive and enter the command **D:\Setup.exe**, substituting the drive letter of your CD-ROM drive in the command line.

$A^+_{2.1}$ OS If this is an upgrade installation, do the following to get to the setup screen:

1. Start the PC, loading the current operating system.

2. Close all open applications including any antivirus software running.

3. Insert the CD in the CD-ROM drive or the floppy disk in the floppy drive. When upgrading from Windows 95 to Windows 98, open the Run dialog box and enter the command **D:\Setup.exe**, substituting the drive letter for the CD-ROM drive or floppy drive in the command line. Click **OK**. When upgrading from Windows 3.x to Windows 9x, enter the same command using File Manager.

4. Follow the instructions on the setup screen.

When installing Windows 9x, you are given the option of creating the Startup disk discussed in earlier chapters. Be sure to do that to help prepare for emergencies. Also during the installation, you will be asked to choose from four setup options:

- *Typical* This option installs all of the components that are usually installed with Windows 9x. Most often, this is the option to choose.

- *Portable* Use this option when installing Windows 9x on a notebook computer.

- *Compact* Use this option if you are short on hard drive space and want the smallest possible installation. No optional components are installed during the installation. After the installation, if you need a component, you can install it by double-clicking the Add/Remove Programs icon in the Control Panel.

- *Custom* Use this option if you know you will need components that are not normally installed under the Typical installation. You are given the opportunity to select any group of components to be included in the installation.

12

Windows 9x Setup begins installation in real mode and then later switches to protected mode. During real mode, it runs ScanDisk, checks for existing Windows software, performs several system checks, loads the extended memory driver, looks for existing TSRs, and starts Windows, if it is not already started. This Windows logo screen is the first thing the user normally sees during the installation. Setup then switches to protected mode.

Setup creates the registry, getting it ready to contain the hardware information, and then searches for hardware. It loads its own drivers for the detected hardware, or, if it cannot detect the hardware, requests the drivers from the user. The drivers are copied to the hard drive.

Up to this point, if Setup fails and you reboot the PC, you boot into DOS. Next Setup alters the boot records on the hard drive to point to the Windows 9x file, Io.sys, rather than to the DOS hidden files. Now, if Setup fails and you reboot, you reboot into Windows 9x.

During a normal installation, the PC reboots and Windows 9x is loaded. Some initial startup programs are run to set the time zone and to change existing application programs to Windows 9x. Depending on the hardware present, the PC may reboot again to load new drivers.

During the installation, Setup is recording information into log files. The primary log file is Setuplog.txt, a text file that is used by Windows to determine how far it got into the installation when it is recovering from a crash. The Detection Log (Detlog.txt) keeps a record of hardware detected. If the system fails to respond during the hardware detection phase, an entry is recorded in Detcrash.log, a binary file used by Windows to help recover from a crash caused by a problem with hardware. Windows does not use the contents of Detlog.txt; it is created only for the benefit of the user.

For example, if Setup suspects that a network card is present, because it sees a network driver installed in CONFIG.SYS, it records in Setuplog.txt and Detlog.txt that it is about to look for the card. If it successfully finds the card, it records the success in Detlog.txt. However, if an error occurs while Setup is searching for the card, an entry is made in the Detcrash.log file.

If the system crashed while trying to detect the network card and then Setup is restarted, it looks at Detcrash.log and Setuplog.txt to determine what it was trying to do at the time of the crash. It skips that step and goes on to the next step, so that it doesn't make the same mistake twice.

Even though Setup might crash several times during the installation process, progress is still being made. By reading the content of the log files, setup is able to skip those steps that caused a problem and move forward. Be careful not to delete the log files during the installation process, especially if you've just experienced a crash. Also, restart by using the power on/power off method so that the ISA bus is fully initialized, which does not always happen during a warm boot.

> **TIP** In certain situations you might want to force Setup to begin installation at the beginning instead of looking to Setuplog.txt for the entry point, for example when you think you might have resolved a problem with hardware and want Setup to attempt to find the hardware again. To do that, delete Setuplog.txt to force a full restart.

Customizing Setup

Windows and other software store information about an installation on the setup CD or floppy disks in information files. These **information files** are text files with an .inf file extension. One .inf file is Msbatch.inf. Information about your installation can be stored in this, which can then be used to do a hands-free installation. All the questions that a user must answer during an installation can be answered by entries in this file so that a user has little to do but begin the installation. For more information about hands-free installations, see the Microsoft Windows 95 or Windows 98 Resource Kit by Microsoft Press.

You can add several switches to the Setup.exe command that starts the setup process. Some of these switches and what they do are listed in Table 12-4.

Configuring the Windows 9x Startup with Msdos.sys

Recall that Msdos.sys plays an entirely different role in the boot process of Windows 9x than it does in the DOS boot process. In Windows 9x, this text file can contain several parameters that mainly affect how the OS boots. The file is a hidden, read-only, system file, so before

Table 12-4   Switches for the Setup command

Switch	Description
Setup /?	Display help for each command-line switch
Setup /D	Don't use the existing version of Windows to begin Setup. Use this option if you suspect corrupted Windows system files when upgrading Windows.
Setup /IC	Perform a clean boot. Use this option if you suspect drivers loaded from Autoexec.bat or Config.sys are causing a problem with the installation.
Setup /IH	Run ScanDisk in the foreground so that you can view results. Use this option if setup failed earlier and you want to check for hard drive corruption.
Setup /IL	Load the driver for a Logitech mouse. Use this option if you are using a Logitech Series C mouse.
Setup /IN	Do not set up the network.
Setup /IS	Do not run ScanDisk.
Setup /PI	Keep hardware settings that are not default settings. Use this option if a previous try of the installation caused a legacy hardware device to fail.

you can edit it, you must first use the ATTRIB command to make the file available for editing. Also, make a backup copy of the file in case you want to revert to the form it was in before the changes were made.

Follow these steps to change the options in Msdos.sys:

- Go to a DOS command prompt.
- Go to the root directory of your hard drive by typing:

    `CD\`

- Make the file available for editing by typing:

    `ATTRIB -R -H -S MSDOS.SYS`

- Make a backup copy of the file by typing:

    `COPY MSDOS.SYS MSDOS.BK`

- Use EDIT.COM to edit the file by typing:

    `EDIT MSDOS.SYS`

- Save the file and return it to a hidden, read-only, system file by typing:

    `ATTRIB +R +H +S MSDOS.SYS`

Table 12-5 lists each entry in the file and its purpose. You can refer back to this table as you read about the different options available when installing and configuring Windows 9x.

TIP In Windows Explorer, by default, Windows 9x hides the file extensions of those files that it knows which application to use to open or execute the file. For example, just after the installation, it hides .exe, .com, .sys, and .txt file extensions, but will not hide .doc, .ppt, or .xls files until the software to open these files has been installed. To display all file extensions, click View, Folder Options and click the View tab. Unselect Hide file extensions for known file types.

12

Table 12-5   Contents of the Msdos.sys file options section

Command Line Variable Name	Purpose of the Values Assigned to the Variable
BootMulti	0 = (Default) Boot only to Windows 9x. 1= Allows for a dual boot
BootWin	1 = (Default) Boot to Windows 9x. 0 = Boot to previous version of DOS.
BootGUI	1 = (Default) Boot to Windows 9x with the graphic user interface. 0 = Boot only to the command prompt for DOS 7.0 or 7.1. (AUTOEXEC.BAT and CONFIG.SYS will be executed, and you will be in real-mode DOS.)
BootMenu	0 = (Default) Don't display the Startup Menu. 1= Display the Startup Menu.
BootMenuDefault	1 through 8 = The value selected from the Startup Menu by Default (Normally this value should be 1.)
BootMenuDelay	n = Number of seconds delay before the default value in the Startup Menu is automatically selected
BootKeys	1= (Default) The function keys work during the boot process (F4, F5, F6, F8, Shift+F5, Ctrl+F5, shift+F8). 0 = Disable the function keys during the boot process. (This option can be used to help secure a workstation.)
BootDelay	n = Number of seconds the boot process waits (when it displays the message "Starting Windows 95" or "Starting Windows 98") for the user to press F8 to get the Startup Menu (default is 2 seconds)
Logo	1= (Default) Display the Windows 9x logo screen. 0 = Leave the screen in text mode. (You can change the logo screen to be another .bmp file. The Windows 9x logo file is stored in Logo.sys in the root directory. Rename it, and name a new .bmp file to Logo.sys to customize this startup screen.)
Drvspace	1= (Default) Load Drvspace.bin, used for disk compression, if it is present. 0 = Don't load Drvspace.bin.
DoubleBuffer	1= (Default) When you have a SCSI drive, enables double buffering for the drive (see the drive documentation) 0 = Don't use double buffering for the SCSI drive.
Network	1= If network components are installed, include the option, "Safe mode with network support" in the Startup Menu. 0 = Don't include the option on the Startup Menu. (This will normally be set to 0 if the PC has no network components installed. The Startup Menu will be renumbered from this point forward in the menu.)
BootFailSafe	1= (Default) Include Safe mode in the Startup Menu. 0 = Don't include Safe mode in the Startup Menu.

Table 12-5   Contents of the Msdos.sys file options section (continued)

Command Line Variable Name	Purpose of the Values Assigned to the Variable
BootWarn	1= (Default) Display the warning message when Windows 9x boots into Safe mode. 0 = Don't display the warning message.
LoadTop	1= (Default) Load COMMAND.COM at the top of conventional memory. 0 = Don't load COMMAND.COM at the top of conventional memory. (Use this option when there is a memory conflict with this area of memory.)

Figure 12-11 shows a sample Msdos.sys file. The lines containing x's at the bottom of the file are used to ensure that the file size is compatible with other programs.

```
[Paths]
WinDir=C:\WIN95
WinBootDir=C:\WIN95
HostWinBootDrv=C

[Options]
BootMulti=1
BootGUI=1
BootMenu=1
Network=0
;
;The following lines are required for compatibility with other programs.
;Do not remove them (MSDOS.SYS needs to be >1024 bytes).
;xxxxxxxxxxxxxxxxxxxxxxxxxxxxxxxxxxxxxxxxxxxxxxxxxxxxxxxxxxxxxa
;xxxxxxxxxxxxxxxxxxxxxxxxxxxxxxxxxxxxxxxxxxxxxxxxxxxxxxxxxxxxxb
;xxxxxxxxxxxxxxxxxxxxxxxxxxxxxxxxxxxxxxxxxxxxxxxxxxxxxxxxxxxxxc
;xxxxxxxxxxxxxxxxxxxxxxxxxxxxxxxxxxxxxxxxxxxxxxxxxxxxxxxxxxxxxd
;xxxxxxxxxxxxxxxxxxxxxxxxxxxxxxxxxxxxxxxxxxxxxxxxxxxxxxxxxxxxxe
;xxxxxxxxxxxxxxxxxxxxxxxxxxxxxxxxxxxxxxxxxxxxxxxxxxxxxxxxxxxxxf
;xxxxxxxxxxxxxxxxxxxxxxxxxxxxxxxxxxxxxxxxxxxxxxxxxxxxxxxxxxxxxg
;xxxxxxxxxxxxxxxxxxxxxxxxxxxxxxxxxxxxxxxxxxxxxxxxxxxxxxxxxxxxxh
;xxxxxxxxxxxxxxxxxxxxxxxxxxxxxxxxxxxxxxxxxxxxxxxxxxxxxxxxxxxxxi
;xxxxxxxxxxxxxxxxxxxxxxxxxxxxxxxxxxxxxxxxxxxxxxxxxxxxxxxxxxxxxj
;xxxxxxxxxxxxxxxxxxxxxxxxxxxxxxxxxxxxxxxxxxxxxxxxxxxxxxxxxxxxxk
;xxxxxxxxxxxxxxxxxxxxxxxxxxxxxxxxxxxxxxxxxxxxxxxxxxxxxxxxxxxxxl
;xxxxxxxxxxxxxxxxxxxxxxxxxxxxxxxxxxxxxxxxxxxxxxxxxxxxxxxxxxxxxm
;xxxxxxxxxxxxxxxxxxxxxxxxxxxxxxxxxxxxxxxxxxxxxxxxxxxxxxxxxxxxxn
;xxxxxxxxxxxxxxxxxxxxxxxxxxxxxxxxxxxxxxxxxxxxxxxxxxxxxxxxxxxxxo
;xxxxxxxxxxxxxxxxxxxxxxxxxxxxxxxxxxxxxxxxxxxxxxxxxxxxxxxxxxxxxp
;xxxxxxxxxxxxxxxxxxxxxxxxxxxxxxxxxxxxxxxxxxxxxxxxxxxxxxxxxxxxxq
;xxxxxxxxxxxxxxxxxxxxxxxxxxxxxxxxxxxxxxxxxxxxxxxxxxxxxxxxxxxxxr
;xxxxxxxxxxxxxxxxxxxxxxxxxxxxxxxxxxxxxxxxxxxxxxxxxxxxxxxxxxxxxs
```

Figure 12-11   A sample Msdos.sys file

12

A+ OS
2.1,
2.2

Installing Windows 9x over DOS and Windows 3.x

If DOS and Windows 3.x reside on the PC prior to installing Windows 9x, you have the choice of installing Windows 9x over DOS and Windows 3.x or installing Windows 9x in a separate directory from Windows 3.x so that you can still run 16-bit programs under Windows 3.x.

The advantages of overwriting Windows 3.x and DOS are:

- Less hard drive space is used.

- Windows 9x Setup copies information about existing application programs from the .ini files of Windows 3.x into the Windows 9x registry, eliminating the need for you to install the existing programs into Windows 9x.

- These programs are added to the Start menu of Windows 9x.

- Existing programs can find their .dlls in the same Windows\System folder as they did with Windows 3.x.

The advantages of installing Windows 9x in a separate directory are:

- You can create a **dual boot** and run the PC with either Windows 3.x or Windows 9x.

- The Windows\System folder of Windows 9x is not cluttered with old, outdated .dlls that current programs no longer use. In effect, you get a "fresh start."

If you install Windows 9x in a separate directory, you must then reinstall each application program that you want to run under Windows 9x, so that it gets information into the Windows 9x registry, its programs are listed under the Start menu, and its .dlls and other supporting files are copied to the Windows\System folder.

Dual Boot Between Windows 9x and DOS with Windows 3.x

You can install DOS with Windows 3.1 and Windows 9x on the same hard drive, so that you can use software made for each operating environment within its native OS. See Chapter 7 for details on how to do this.

PLUG AND PLAY AND HARDWARE INSTALLATIONS

Plug and Play (PnP) is a set of design specifications for both hardware and software that work toward effortless hardware installations. For a system to be truly Plug and Play, it must meet these criteria:

- The system BIOS must be PnP.

- All hardware devices and expansion cards must be PnP-compliant.

- The OS must be Windows 9x or another OS that supports PnP.

- A 32-bit device driver (VxD) must be available (provided by the device manufacturer or Windows).

If all these things are true, hardware installation should be very easy and is only a matter of installing the new hardware device, turning on the PC, and perhaps providing the 32-bit driver, if it is not included with Windows 9x. During the boot process, Windows 9x surveys the devices and their needs for resources and allocates resources to each device. Windows 9x is free to assign these resources to the devices and avoids assigning the same resource to two devices. For PnP to work, each device in the system must be able to use whatever resources the OS assigns to it.

How Plug and Play Works

A+ OS
2.4

A Plug and Play OS like Windows 9x provides two main services: resource management and run-time configuration. **Resource management** occurs at startup as system resources are allocated to devices. **Run-time configuration** is an ongoing process that monitors any changes in system devices, such as the removal of a PC Card on a notebook computer or docking and undocking a notebook computer to and from a docking station. The BIOS must be able to recognize these changes during OS run time (any time the OS is running) and communicate them to the OS.

Windows 9x uses four components in implementing PnP architecture:

- The **configuration manager** controls the configuration process of all devices and communicates these configurations to the devices.

- The **hardware tree** is a database built each time Windows 9x starts up that contains a list of installed components and the resources they use.

- The **bus enumerator** locates all devices on a particular bus and inventories the resource requirements for these devices.

- The **resource arbitrator** decides which resources get assigned to which devices.

When Windows 9x is started, if the system board BIOS is PnP, the configuration manager starts the PnP process by receiving the list of devices from the BIOS. If the BIOS is not PnP, the bus enumerator for each bus on the system provides the information to the configuration manager. The configuration manager oversees the process of assigning resources by loading one device driver after another for each installed device, and instructing the driver to wait until resources have been assigned to it.

The configuration manager performs a process of examining and reexamining required resources until it determines an acceptable configuration of all resources and devices. For example, for ISA devices, according to the PnP standards, each device has a unique 72-bit ID derived from the manufacturer ID, a product ID, and a serial number. Each ISA device competes for resources, and the device with the largest-value ID is assigned resources first. The bus enumerator manages this process and receives the resource assignments from the configuration manager. The configuration manager interacts with the resource arbitrator, allowing the arbitrator to determine what resources are assigned, and then receives that information from the arbitrator, passing it on to the bus enumerator.

12

The bus enumerators collectively build the hardware tree, which is stored in memory. Information to build the hardware tree comes from the configuration at the current moment as well as from information kept in the registry about devices that have been installed, including what device drivers are used to operate the device and user-defined settings for the device. The hardware tree is built each time Windows 9x is started, and is dynamically changed as hardware is plugged and unplugged while the system is running.

Plug and Play BIOS

A+ OS 2.4 | As discussed in previous chapters, BIOS that is PnP-compliant gathers resource configuration information prior to loading Windows 9x, presenting to Windows 9x details it can use to complete the process. System boards manufactured after 1994 most likely contain PnP BIOS. PnP BIOS can also be ESCD (extended system configuration data) BIOS. ESCD BIOS creates a list of configuration changes that you have made manually when installing legacy devices and stores that list on the BIOS chip. Even if the hard drive crashes or you must reload Windows 9x, the configuration changes are still available from the BIOS when it goes through the boot process and presents the information to Windows 9x at startup.

To know if your BIOS is PnP, look for a message about the BIOS type on the startup screen. Information about the BIOS might also be displayed on the CMOS setup screen or written on the BIOS chip (see Figure 12-12). Use MSD and choose Computer from the menu to get information about your BIOS. The documentation for the system board should also say whether or not the BIOS is PnP.

Figure 12-12   Plug and Play BIOS is found on most system boards built after 1994

TIP | If the BIOS is not Plug and Play, you can still use Plug and Play Windows 9x software for hardware devices that are Plug and Play. However, you might need to manually configure the hardware, or, in some cases, disable the Plug and Play features of the interface card.

Installing New Hardware

A+ OS
2.4

Windows 9x provides better support during the installation of new hardware devices than does Windows 3.x. If the computer system is completely PnP-compliant, installations are automated and go very smoothly. However, with older hardware devices and older drivers, problems can occur that must be resolved manually.

This section looks at three sources of problems with hardware installations and what to do about them. Table 12-6 summarizes these problems and their solutions. A device or expansion card that is not PnP is a **legacy** (handed down from the past) device. Legacy devices are not able to have their resources assigned to them by PnP. If the device driver is an older 16-bit driver, there might be a problem with Windows 9x installing and using the driver. Also, Windows 9x might or might not have a built-in driver for the device. Each problem and how to address it is discussed below.

Table 12-6   Hardware device installation problems and solution

Source of the Problem	Nature of the Problem	Solution to the Problem
Unsupported devices	Windows 9x does not have a built-in device driver designed for the device	Provide a device driver from the manufacturer or use a substitute
16-bit drivers	Windows 9x has trouble initially recognizing and installing the driver	First, install the driver using DOS or Windows 3.x
Legacy cards	Can cause a conflict of resources (IRQ, I/O addresses, upper memory addresses) between two devices	Change the DIP switches or jumpers on the card to use different resources

12

Unsupported Devices

New hardware devices are installed from the Control Panel using the Add New Hardware icon. Windows 9x uses the Add New Hardware Wizard to recognize the device, install the correct driver, and allocate the correct resources to the device. The following are general directions to use if Windows 9x does not recognize the device you are installing. After physically plugging in or installing the device, turn on the PC, go to the Control Panel, and choose **Add New Hardware**. When you see the options in Figure 12-13, answer **Yes** to allow Windows to search for the device, and then click **Next**.

If Windows 9x locates a new device and recognizes it to be PnP, as shown in Figure 12-14, simply click **Next** and the work is done.

$A^+_{2.4}^{OS}$

Figure 12-13 Add New Hardware Wizard

Figure 12-14 If Windows 9x recognizes the new device it can complete the installation with no help

If Windows 9x detects the device and recognizes that it is not PnP, it suggests resources that can be assigned to the device, as seen in Figure 12-15. It's left up to you to manually configure the device to use the suggested resources or to select other resources.

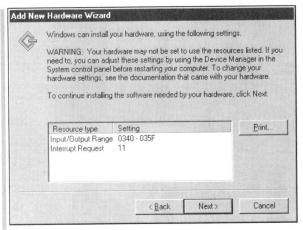

Figure 12-15   If the new device is not PnP, Windows 9x suggests the resources for a legacy device to use

However, if Windows 9x cannot detect a new device, it will ask for your help, as shown in Figure 12-16. When you click **Next**, a list of devices is displayed, as shown in Figure 12-17. Select the device and click **Next**. The list of supported manufacturers and models for that device type is displayed. For example, Figure 12-18 shows a list of CD-ROM drive controllers. You can select a manufacturer and model from the list to use a Windows driver, or you can click **Have Disk** and supply the driver from a device manufacturer's disk or CD-ROM. If you don't have the manufacturer's driver and the device is not listed, try obtaining the driver from the manufacturer's Web site.

12

> **TIP**   When you have a choice between installing a Windows 9x device driver or a driver supplied by the device manufacturer, you will usually get better results using the manufacturer's driver.

Figure 12-16   The new device is not detected or recognized by Windows 9x

A+ OS
2.4

Figure 12-17 When Windows 9x cannot recognize the new hardware, you must select the device

Figure 12-18 List of manufacturers and models of supported CD-ROM drive controllers

Problems with 16-Bit Drivers

A+ OS
3.2

When you supply a device driver to Windows 9x for an unsupported device, Windows 9x copies one or more device driver files to the hard drive and make the appropriate entries in the registry so that it will load the driver each time it starts up. If the driver is a 16-bit

A+ OS
3.2

driver, it also makes the appropriate entries in the AUTOEXEC.BAT and CONFIG.SYS files. If Windows 9x has problems locating and installing a 16-bit driver, then you have three choices. You can contact the manufacturer of the device for an updated driver, you can ask them to recommend a substitute driver, or you can install the driver using DOS or Windows 3.x. If the device driver has an install program, run the install program under either DOS or Windows 3.x, depending on what the install program requires. It makes the correct entries in the AUTOEXEC.BAT and CONFIG.SYS files and copies the driver files to the hard drive. You should then be able to install the device in Windows 9x with no problems.

Problems with Legacy Cards

When you are installing Windows 9x onto a PC that has previously worked well with DOS and Windows 3.x, legacy cards will not normally be a problem because the conflict of resources will usually have already been resolved when the cards were first installed.

A problem arises if the device is a legacy device and requests resources that conflict with another legacy device already installed. You then must intervene and change the jumpers or DIP switches on one of the devices to force it to use a different resource.

Using Device Manager for Troubleshooting

During the installation, Windows 9x might inform you that there is a resource conflict, or the device might simply not work. Use Device Manager as a useful fact-finding tool for the resolution of the problem. Open the **Control Panel**, choose **System**, and select the **Device Manager** tab. The list of devices is displayed, as seen in Figure 12-19. A + beside the device name indicates that you can click the device for a list of manufacturers and models installed. The open diamond symbol indicates a SCSI device. Symbols that indicate a device's status are:

■ A red X through the device name indicates a disabled device.

■ A yellow exclamation point indicates a problem with the device.

■ A blue I on a white field indicates automatic settings were not used, and resources have been manually assigned. It does not indicate a problem with the device.

To see a better explanation of a problem, click the device and select **Properties**. The Device Properties dialog box opens, which can give you helpful information about solving a problem including I/O addresses, DMA channels, and IRQs used by the device as well as the names of devices that are also attempting to use the same resources.

In fact, before you start the hardware installation, you might want to use Device Manager to print a summary of all hardware installed on the PC and resources being used. This printout can be a record of your starting point before the installation as well as a tool to help resolve conflicts during the installation. To print this summary, access Device Manager and click **Print**. From the Print dialog box, select **All Devices and System Summary** for a complete listing.

12

A+ OS
3.2

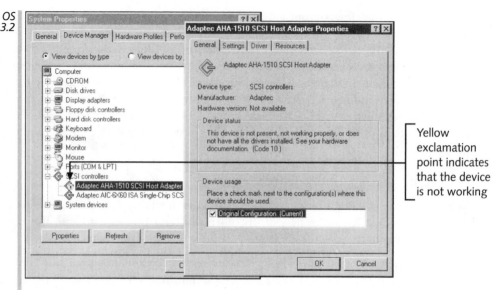

Yellow
exclamation
point indicates
that the device
is not working

Figure 12-19   The Properties box of an installed device that is not working

Troubleshooting with Windows Help

For more information from Windows 9x on how to resolve a problem, click **Start**, click **Help**, and click **Troubleshooting**. The Help information includes suggestions that can lead you to a solution. For example, in Figure 12-20, the Hardware Troubleshooter suggests that you check to see that the device is not listed twice in Device Manager. If this were the case, you would have to remove the second occurrence of the device.

Figure 12-20   Troubleshooter making a suggestion to resolve a hardware conflict

The Windows 9x Registry

The Windows 9x registry is intended to replace the many .ini files that Windows and Windows applications software used under Windows 3.x. Organizing the information contained in these older .ini files is accomplished by using a hierarchical database with a tree-like, top-to-bottom design. All kinds of information is stored in the registry, including system configurations, user settings, Device Manager information, applications software settings, hardware settings, and so on. In this section you will examine how the registry is organized, what kinds of information are in the registry, how and why you might edit the registry, and how to recover from a corrupted registry.

How the Registry Is Organized

A+ OS
1.1

Recall that the Windows 9x System.ini file contains setup parameters. Refer back to Figure 12-6, which shows a portion of the System.ini file. Notice that section names appear in square brackets, key names to the left of the equal signs, and values assigned to these key names to the right of the equal signs. The Windows 9x registry takes on a similar design but enhances it by allowing for keys to cascade to several levels on the tree. Figure 12-21 shows a portion of a Windows 9x registry. Consider names on the left of the window as similar to section names in System.ini; these names are called **keys** by Windows 9x. On the right of the window are value names, such as ScreenSaveTime, and to the right of each name is the **value data** assigned to that name, such as "60." The value names, called values by Windows 9x, are similar to the key names in System.ini, and the value data are similar to the values assigned to key names in System.ini.

Figure 12-21   Structure of the Windows 9x registry

The registry is organized into six major keys or branches of the registry tree, which are listed in Table 12-7. The registry is contained in two files, System.dat and User.dat, located in the Windows directory as hidden, read-only, system files, although the information forms only a single database.

> In a network environment, Windows 9x can use policy files to define user, network, and computer settings. A policy file has a .pol file extension; examples are Policy.pol and Config.pol. Using the System Policy Editor, a network administrator can create a policy file that affects the entire network, a group of users, or a single user on the network. The policy file can reside on the network server and is read when Windows 9x first boots. Entries in the policy file override entries in the Windows 9x registry.

Table 12-7   Six major branches, or keys, of the Windows 9x registry

Key	Description
HKEY_CLASSES_ROOT	Contains information about file associations and OLE data (This branch of the tree is a mirror of HKEY_LOCAL_MACHINE\Software\Classes.)
HKEY_USERS	Includes user preferences, including desktop configuration and network connections
HKEY_CURRENT_USER	If there is only one user of the system, this is a duplicate of HKEY_USERS, but for a multiuser system, this key contains information about the current user preferences.
HKEY_LOCAL_MACHINE	Contains information about hardware and installed software
HKEY_CURRENT_CONFIG	Contains the same information in HKEY_LOCAL_MACHINE\Config and has information about printers and display fonts
HKEY_DYN_DATA	Keeps information about Windows performance and Plug and Play information

Recovering from a Corrupted Registry

Windows 9x maintains a backup copy of the two registry files called System.da0 and User.da0. Each time Windows boots successfully, it makes a backup copy of these two files. If Windows 9x has trouble loading and must start in safe mode, it does not back up the registry files.

If Windows 9x does not find a System.dat when it starts, it automatically replaces it with the backup System.da0. If both System.dat and User.dat are missing, or if the "WinDir=" command is missing in Msdos.sys, Windows 9x tells you that the registry files are missing and starts in safe mode. It then displays the Registry Problem dialog box. Click the **Restore From Backup** and **Restart** buttons. The registry files are restored from System.da0 and User.da0. If these files are also missing, the registry cannot easily be restored. You can either restore the files from your own backups or run Windows 9x Setup. There is another option. Look for the file System.1st in the root directory of the hard drive. This is the System.dat file created when Windows 9x was first installed. In an emergency, you can revert to this file.

A+ OS 3.2 **Windows 98 Registry Checker**   Windows 98 offers a utility that is not available with Windows 95 called the Registry Checker. It automatically backs up the registry each day, and by default, it keeps the last five days of backups. In an emergency, you can recover the registry from one of these backups. You can also tell Registry Checker to make an additional

A+ OS
   3.2

back up on demand, such as when you have just made changes to the registry and want to backup these changes before you make new changes.

To access Registry Checker, select **Start**, point to **Programs**, **Accessories**, **System Tools**, and then click **System Information**. The Microsoft System Information window opens (see Figure 12-22). From the menu bar, select **Tools** and then **Registry Checker**. Registry Checker tells you if the registry is corrupted and will fix it, if allowed. You can also create a new backup at this time.

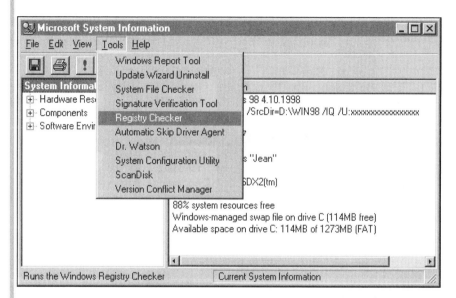

Figure 12-22 The Registry Checker is available under Programs, Accessories, System Tools, System Information Tool; it is used to back up, restore, and repair the Windows 98 registry

Backups are kept in cabinet files in the \Windows\Sysbckup folder as rb001.cab, rb002.cab, and so on. To revert to one of these backups, you must first be in real-mode DOS. Either boot from a bootable disk or boot to a DOS prompt from the Windows 98 startup menu. From the DOS prompt (not a DOS box within a Windows session), use these commands to repair or recover the registry:

- ScanReg/Restore — Restores the registry from a previous backup. A screen is displayed asking you which backup to use.

- ScanReg/Fix — Repairs the corrupted registry. If the problem is inherent to the registry itself, this might work. If the problem is that you want to undo a successful change to the registry, then use the Recover option instead.

- ScanReg/Backup — Creates a new backup of the registry at the DOS prompt. Don't do this if the registry is giving you problems.

A+ OS
  3.2

- ScanReg/Opt   Optimizes the registry. ScanReg will look for and
                             delete information in the registry that is no longer
                             used. This reduces the size of the registry, which
                             might speed up booting.

- ScanReg/?   Help feature of ScanReg

Nuts & Bolts Registry Wizard   Nuts & Bolts Registry Wizard can back up and restore the
registry, clean the registry of unneeded data, search for and repair registry orphans (registry
entries that refer to files that have moved or no longer exist), and tune up and optimize the
registry for better performance. Click **Start**, point to **Programs**, click **Nuts & Bolts**, and
select **Registry Wizard** from the list of Nuts & Bolts utilities. Figure 12-23 shows the opening screen of the Registry Wizard. The best time to use the Registry Wizard is before the
problem occurs by making a backup of the registry before installing new software or hardware, making significant system configuration changes, and before editing the registry.

Figure 12-23   Nuts and Bolts Registry Wizard can back up, restore, clean, repair, and
optimize the Windows 9x Registry

Modifying the Registry

When you make a change in Control Panel or Device Manager or many other places in
Windows 9x, such as happens when you install software, the registry is modified automatically. For most users, this is the only way they will ever change the registry.

However, there are rare occasions when you might need to edit the registry manually. One
example is when you have accidentally deleted the device driver for a hardware device, but
Device Manager says that the device is still installed. Another example is when the wrong
software starts when Windows 9x is loaded and you cannot correct the problem by changing
the Startup folder. Both these problems can be corrected by manually editing the registry.

Editing the Registry

The first step in editing the registry is to back up the two files, System.dat and User.dat. Sometimes the files are small enough to fit on floppy disks and can be copied using Explorer. If the files are too large to copy to floppy disk, copy them to a different folder on the hard drive or use compression software such as PKZIP to copy them to floppy disks. For Windows 98, use Registry Checker to back up the registry. Utility software, including Nuts & Bolts and Norton Utilities, has a registry editor that allows for backing up the registry before entering the editor. The following directions use Windows 9x Regedit to edit the registry.

A^{+} OS 1.1, 3.2

After backing up the registry files, the next step is to use Regedit.exe, located in the Windows folder. You can use Explorer to locate the file, then double-click it, or click **Start**, and then **Run**, and type **Regedit** in the Run dialog box. When you do, the dialog box in Figure 12-24 opens. Open one branch of the tree by clicking on the + sign to the left of the key, and close the branch by clicking on the − sign.

Figure 12-24   The six major keys, or branches, of the registry seen in the Registry Editor

12

To search for an entry in the registry, click **Edit**, and **Find**. The Find dialog box is displayed, as in the screen in Figure 12-25, which is ready to find the text "software" in the registry. Enter the key, the value, or the value data, and click **Find Next**. You can choose to search keys, values, and/or value data by clicking on the check boxes in the dialog box.

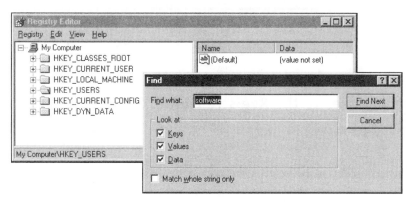

Figure 12-25   Searching for entries in the registry

For example, suppose the wrong programs start when you load Windows 9x. First try to correct the problem without editing the registry. Using Explorer, open the Windows folder and then double-click the **Start Menu** folder. Delete any items that you don't want to start when you load Windows. If this does not correct the problem, the problem might be caused by a wrong entry recorded in the registry. Try editing the registry.

First locate the Shell Folders, which will be in the following branch:
HKEY_CURRENT_USER\Software\Microsoft\Windows\CurrentVersion\Explorer\
Shell Folders

Search for these keys and subkeys one at a time. (Search for HKEY_CURRENT_USER. After you have located it, search for Software, and continue through the list until you come to Shell Folders.)

The value name "Startup=" in the Shell Folders subkey should be "C:\Windows\Start Menu\Programs\Startup." If the data is incorrect, right-click **Startup** and select **Modify** from the shortcut menu. Figure 12-26 shows the Editing dialog box that is displayed. Change the value data and click **OK**.

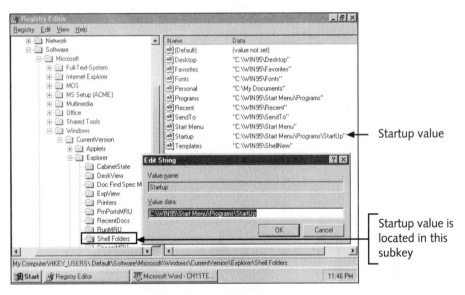

Figure 12-26   Editing an entry in the registry using Regedit.exe

Tracking Changes to the Registry During Software Installation

Two utilities that can track changes not only to the Windows 9x registry but also to .ini files and folders are a shareware program, In Control 4, and Norton Utilities Registry Tracker. To use Norton Utilities Registry Tracker, click **Start**, **Programs**, **Norton Utilities**, **Norton Registry Tracker**, as shown in Figure 12-27. Figure 12-28 shows the Norton Registry Tracker main windows. When the utility first loads, it takes an Activation Snapshot of the system, which it will later use as the baseline to determine if future snapshots have detected any changes.

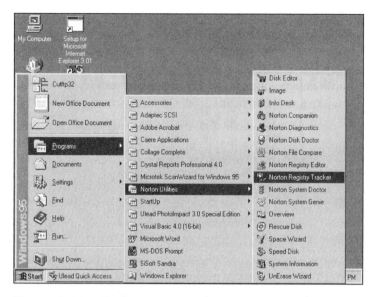

Figure 12-27   Finding Norton Utilities Registry Tracker

Figure 12-28   Norton Utilities Registry Tracker tracks changes to the Windows 9x registry

With the Norton Registry Tracker, you can first choose what it is you want to track and then take a snapshot of the system. Next install the software and then take another snapshot. Compare the two snapshots to see what the installation did to those things you chose to track.

To change the items tracked, click **Options**, and then **Settings** from the Norton Registry Tracker menu. The Tracker Settings screen is displayed, as in Figure 12-29. Select the tab **Registry Keys** to see a list of keys to be tracked. Norton Registry Tracker tracks the two keys and their subkeys, HKEY_LOCAL_MACHINE and HKEY_USERS, because these keys contain the first copy of changes made when software is installed and user settings are changed. In Figure 12-30, the camera and the check mark beside the SOFTWARE subkey indicate that changes to it are to be tracked. If you want to track other keys, select the key and click **Track Key** or **Track Subkey**. On the Folders tab you can choose which folders to track. By default, the Windows folder and the Windows\System folder are tracked. Under text files, AUTOEXEC.BAT, CONFIG.SYS, and the .ini files are tracked. Return to the main window by clicking **OK**.

Figure 12-29   Select what you want Norton Registry Tracker to track during an installation

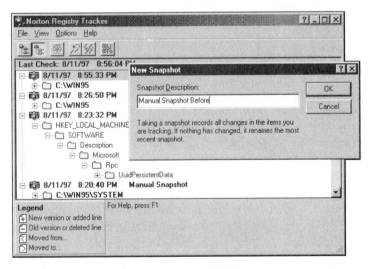

Figure 12-30   Naming the new snapshot

To take a snapshot, select **File**, **New Snapshot**. You see the dialog box in Figure 12-30, asking you to name the snapshot. Enter the name and click **OK**. The snapshot is made and compares the things being tracked to the original activation snapshot made when the utility was first loaded. In the snapshot, changed items are color-coded.

Take a snapshot before the installation, perform the installation, and take another snapshot after the installation. The Norton Registry Tracker can then provide a side-by-side view of the two snapshots to make comparisons easy. Always using Norton Registry Tracker in this way is a good practice whenever installing software.

SUPPORTING APPLICATIONS SOFTWARE WITH WINDOWS 9x

In this section we look at installing applications software, the special needs of DOS applications and problems that can arise when uninstalling software.

Installing Applications Software

A+ OS
2.4

If the software is 32-bit applications software designed to be used with Windows 9x, installation is easily done by using the Add/Remove Programs icon in Control Panel. For older 16-bit software, use the Run dialog box. Before you install any software, do the following:

Check Available Resources Check your computer resources to make sure you have (1) enough space on your hard drive, (2) the minimum requirements for memory, and (3) the proper CPU and video monitor—and that you can fulfill any other requirement of the particular software program. The minimum requirements for the software should be listed in the installation manual. Remember that you should not completely fill the hard drive with software and data.

> **TIP** For best performance with Windows 9x, allow a minimum of 100 MB of unused hard drive space for working temporary files used by applications.

Protect the Original Software For floppy disks, write-protect the original disks before you begin the installation. After the installation is complete, put the original disks or CD-ROM in a safe place.

A+ OS
2.4,
3.2

Back up the Registry and System Configuration Files Many older software packages will want to edit CONFIG.SYS, AUTOEXEC.BAT, Win.sys, and/or System.ini files during the installation. Newer software might add its own entries to the Windows registry. Before you begin the installation, make backup copies of all of these files so that you can backtrack if you want to.

If you are having difficulty with the installation, look at the Readme.htm hypertext file in the \Windows directory, which will point you to the Programs.txt file, also in the \Windows directory. If there is a problem with the software that was known when Windows was

12

shipped, information about the problem and what to do about it might be in these text files. You can also check the web site of the software manufacturer or the Microsoft web site for additional insight.

> **TIP** A hypertext file is a text file that contains hypertext tags to format the file and create hyper links to different points in the file or to other files. Hypertext files are used on the World Wide Web and are read and displayed using a web browser such as Microsoft Internet Explorer or Netscape Navigator. To read a hypertext file using Windows Explorer, double-click the filename and your default browser opens the file.

Install the Software For software designed for Windows 9x, access the Control Panel and double click the Add/Remove Programs icon. Insert the CD in the CD-ROM drive or the floppy disk in the floppy disk drive and click the Install button. Follow directions on the setup screen. Or, for older software, click Start and Run, which displays the Run dialog box. Enter the drive and name of the installation program, for example, A:Install or D:Setup. Either way, the installation program loads and begins executing. If the installation program asks you a question you cannot answer, you can always abandon the installation and try again later.

Most software will ask you for a serial number unique to your copy of the software, which will probably be written on the CD-ROM or on the first floppy disk, or might be stamped on the documentation. Write the serial number on the floppy disk or on the CD case, so that you will still have it if the documentation is later lost. Copyright agreements often allow you to install the software on only one computer at a time. This serial number identifies the copy of the software that you have installed on this machine.

After the installation is complete and the software is working, update your backup copies of AUTOEXEC.BAT, CONFIG.SYS, System.ini, Win.ini, and the registry so that they, too, reflect the changes that the applications software made to these configuration files.

A software installation sometimes leaves files and folders in the Windows temporary directories. To conserve space on the hard drive, delete all files and folders under \Windows\Temp.

> **TIP** If an application locks up when you first open it, try deleting all files and folders under \Windows\Temp.

A troubleshooting tool you can use when you are having problems running an application is Dr. Watson. **Dr. Watson** is a Windows utility that can record detailed information about the system, errors that occur, and the programs that caused them in a log file named \Windows\Drwatson\WatsonXX.wlg, where XX is an incrementing number. Start Dr. Watson and then reproduce the application error. Then look at the events logged in the Dr. Watson window under the Diagnosis tab. Use this information to check the Microsoft web site, support.microsoft.com, for the problem and solution. For errors that you cannot reproduce at will, you can load Dr. Watson each time Windows starts by creating a shortcut to Drwatson.exe in the Startup folder.

> **TIP** Three ways to cause an application to automatically load at startup are to place a shortcut in the Startup folder, put the name of the program file in the Load= or Run= line in Win.ini or manually edit the registry key HKEY_LOCAL_MACHINE\SOFTWARE\Microsoft\Windows\CurrentVersion\Run.

A+ OS
   3.2

Problems with Software Conflicts

Suppose you have Microsoft Word installed correctly on your PC; it has worked well for some time. After you install several new applications, however, Word begins to give you problems. Icons that once were displayed correctly are now displayed as black objects, or, whenever you exit Word, Windows displays a General Protection Fault error message. You attempt to correct the problem by reinstalling Word, but the problem does not go away. What happened to Word, when you installed the other software, that cannot be repaired by reinstalling Word?

The answer is found in the directory \Windows\System. Take a look at this directory, as shown in Figure 12-31. The directory holds files that are used by Windows and other applications software programs. Several programs can use the same files found in this directory. The most common type of file found here has a **.dll** extension, which stands for **dynamic-link library**. These library files contain various programming routines that are used by many application programs to perform such common tasks as opening a database file or displaying a dialog box on the screen. Windows comes with many of these .dll files already installed, but some applications place other .dlls in the \Windows\System directory or replace existing copies of .dll files with more recent versions during installation. Most installations don't save previous copies of .dlls they update; the new application simply overwrites the file with its own version, without informing you of what it's doing.

Figure 12-31   Some DLL files in the \Windows\System directory

Problems arise when an application already installed on the PC uses a .dll that has been updated by the new software, and the new .dll is not compatible with the older software, or the new .dll is corrupted. Reinstalling the older software does not help because it too only updates the .dll if it finds that the .dll file in the \Windows\System directory has an older date than the date of its version.

12

A+ OS
3.2

Finding the .dll that is causing the problem can be like looking for the proverbial needle in a haystack. There are over 700 .dll files in the \Windows\System directory shown in Figure 12-31. It's not uncommon for a small applications software program to install as many as 50 files in this shared directory. Furthermore, when you uninstall an applications software program, the uninstall program probably does not (and should not) erase the .dlls in this shared directory. Over time the directory can get quite large, just as the one in Figure 12-31 has.

Solutions to problems with applications software trying to share .dlls and other files in this directory involve taking more control over the installation process and knowing how to use some utility software to help diagnose software problems. Here are some steps to take to avoid and address software conflicts.

Back up the \Windows\System Directory   If you have the room on your hard drive, you can back up the entire \Windows\System directory before you install new software. After the software is installed, if another program has problems, the older .dlls will be available to you. Perhaps the new software can use an older .dll, and your problem is solved.

However, how do you determine which .dll is causing the problem? First, you must know which .dlls were changed by the new software, and you must know which of these .dlls the old software uses. After that, it's usually a matter of replacing each one in turn until the problem goes away. Things can get even more complicated because .dlls sometimes work as groups. For example, you must keep the four or five files in the OLE group together as a group; exchanging only one file in the group can cause an error.

Monitor the Files Being Updated During the Installation Process   Know what files an application setup program has written to the \Windows\System or any other directory and know the changes made to the Windows .ini files. Some tools you can use for this purpose are Norton Utilities, a shareware program called In Control, and a utility program called DLLaGator.

TIP   Windows 2000 has solved the problems caused by applications sharing .dll files by keeping all the files, including the .dll files, that are installed by each application in a separate folder.

Know What .dlls an Application Uses   Applications load .dlls into memory and unload them throughout installation and during operation. One utility program that lets you view the .dll files currently loaded is DLL Show by Gregory Braun (*www.gregorybraun.com*). See Figure 12-32.

Figure 12-32   Use DLL Show to view .dll files currently in use

Run DLL Show while an application program is loaded. For example, if an applications software program is giving problems, use DLL Show to list the .dlls that might be corrupted. If the software works successfully on one PC, but generates errors on another PC, run DLL Show on the good PC. At the point where the software hangs on the other PC, look for a .dll that is loaded at that time. If you discover one, you probably have identified the file causing the problem.

DLL Show can be a very useful utility to help identify a .dll that has been overwritten by another software installation and is causing problems for the current software. However, DLL Show might not tell the entire story. Sometimes when software loads a .dll, it first reads initialization information from another file in the \Windows\System directory, which might be causing the problem. The file is used by the software but is not listed by DLL Show.

Also, when you see a Windows error message on the screen, if the dialog box offers a Details command button, click the button for more information. Sometimes the name of the .dll causing the problem is listed.

Supporting DOS Applications Under Windows 9x

A+ OS
3.2,
3.1

Windows 3.x used **PIF (program information file)** files to manage the virtual machine environment provided for DOS applications and provided a PIF editor to alter these files. Each application had its own PIF file that was used to specify the DOS environment that Windows 3.x created for it. If an application had no PIF file, Windows 3.x used the settings in the _Default.pif file in the \Windows\System directory.

Windows 9x manages the DOS box environment for DOS applications in a similar, but slightly different fashion. Apps.inf contains a section named [PIF95] that contains a master list of settings to be used for all DOS applications listed in the file.

A+ OS
3.2,
3.1

If you want to customize the settings for a DOS application, use the Properties feature of the DOS program file, which will create an individual PIF for the program file and serves as the PIF editor. Right-click the program filename and select Properties from the menu that is displayed. Windows searches for the program's PIF file and, if none is found, creates one using default values. If Windows 9x was installed over Windows 3.x, then _Default.pif still exists in the \Windows\System directory and default values are read from it. Regardless of where the default values come from, any changes made are stored in the PIF for the application.

For example, if you want a DOS program to run in DOS mode (real mode), follow these directions.

1. Right-click the program filename in Explorer and select **Properties**.

2. Click the **Program** tab and then click **Advanced**. (*Note:* The Program tab will not be present for Windows applications.)

3. Select the **MS-DOS mode** check box, as seen in Figure 12-33.

If you select Use current MS-DOS configuration, Windows executes the contents of Dosstart.bat stored in the Windows folder which is a type of Autoexec.bat file that is executed in two situations: when your select Restart the computer in MS-DOS mode from the shutdown menu or you run a program in MS-DOS mode. This file can be used to load real mode device drivers but SET commands are not executed.

If you select Specify a new MS-DOS configuration, you can make changes to Autoexec.bat and Config.sys files used for this DOS mode only. For example, since the faster 32-bit VCACHE will not be running, you can speed up disk access by loading SmartDrive from this window.

Figure 12-33 Properties sheets for a DOS application affect the way Windows 9x provides an environment for the application

Uninstalling Software

Uninstalling software is clean and easy if the software comes with a well-written uninstall program. Use the Add/Remove Program utility in Control Panel to uninstall it. However, some uninstall programs are not all that great, and sometimes a user will simply delete the folders that contain the software leaving behind .dll files in the \Windows\System directory, entries in the registry, shortcuts on the desktop, and so on for you, the PC technician, to clean up. Even worse, the user or an uninstall program might delete a .dll file needed by another application or make a wrong deletion in the registry.

When software is installed, it can do these things:

- Create new folders that belong to the application only and store files there
- Store files only used by the application in folders also used by other software. An example is an application's .ini file stored in the \Windows folder.
- Create or overwrite files used by other software. An example is \Windows\ system\CTL3D.DLL, a file used by several applications that might be updated by a software installation.
- Make changes to the Windows registry
- Make changes to .ini files that belong to Windows

When software is uninstalled, deleting folders and their contents that belong only to the application is safe. Deleting entire sections in Windows .ini files that are named after the software or a branch in the registry tree that contains the application's name is also safe. But problems might occur when a change is made to a registry entry that other software depends on or when files are deleted that are used by other software.

Figure 12-34 shows the results of such an error. The problem, in this case, can be resolved by reinstalling the OCR software.

12

Cannot find CTL3D.DLL. Windows needs this file to run C:\OPLIMIT\OCRAWARE.EXE.

OK

Figure 12-34 The results of an uninstall program deleting a file needed by another application

MONITORING SYSTEM PERFORMANCE

A+ OS 3.2 Windows 9x offers several tools listed in Table 12-8 to monitor and improve system performance and to help with troubleshooting. Some of these tools have already been discussed and some are covered next. Several of them are only available with Windows 98 and are accessed from the Microsoft System Information window. To access this window, click

A+ OS
3.2

Start, point to **Programs**, **Accessories**, **System Tools**, and click **System Information**. The dialog box illustrated Figure 12-22 opens. The System Information utility is available under Windows 95, but does not include the tools listed in Table 12-8.

Table 12-8 Tools used for troubleshooting and to monitor and improve system performance

Tool	Win95	Win 98	Description
Automatic Skip Driver Agent File name: Asd.exe Location: \windows		X	Automatically skips drivers that prevent Windows from loading and records problems encountered in the log file Asd.log. To run, select **Automatic Skip Driver Agent** from the **Tools** menu of the **System Information** window.
Microsoft System Information File name: MSInfo32.exe Location: \program files\ common files\microsoft shared\msinfo	X	X	Displays system information, including installed hardware and device drivers. To run, click **Start**, **Programs**, **Accessories**, **System Tools**, **System Information**.
Hardware Diagnostic tool (Hwinfo.exe)		X	Displays the same information as System Information, but in text form. Enter **hwinfo/ui** in the Run dialog box.
Registry Checker File name: Scanreg.exe Location: \windows\command		X	Backs up, verifies, and recovers the Registry. To run, select **Registry Checker** from the **Tools** menu of the **System Information** window.
Windows Update File name: Iexplore.exe Location: http://www.microsoft.com/ windows update	X	X	Download service packs (fixes) for Windows from the Microsoft web site.
System options in Control Panel	X	X	Several options in Control Panel can be used in monitoring and tweaking system performance.
System Configuration Utility Filename: MsConfig Location: \windows\system		X	Allows you to temporarily modify the system configuration to help with troubleshooting. To run, select **System Configuration Utility** from the menu **Tools** of the **System Information** window.
System File Checker File name: Sfc.exe Location: \windows\system		X	Verifies system files. This tool scans for changed, deleted, or corrupted system files and restores them from the originals on the Windows CD-ROM. To run, select **System File Checker** from the Tools menu of the **System Information** window.
System Monitor File name: Sysmon.exe Location: \windows		X	System Monitor tracks the performance of some important system components. To run, click **Start**, **Programs**, **Accessories**, **System Tools**, **System Monitor**.
Microsoft Backup (\program files\accessories\ backup\msbackup.exe)	X	X	Backs up files and folders to prevent loss when your hard drive fails. To run, click **Start**, **Programs**, **Accessories**, **System Tools**, **Backup**.
System Recovery File name: pcrestor.bat Location: On the Windows 98 CD in \tools\sysrec		X	Uses a full system backup created by Microsoft Backup to reinstall Windows and restore the system to its state as of the last backup.
Dr. Watson File name: Drwatson.exe Location: \windows		X	Traps errors in log files created by applications and takes a snapshot of the system to use for troubleshooting.
Scheduled Task Wizard File name: Mstask.exe Location: \windows\system	X	X	Schedule tasks such as MS Backup to run at predetermined times.

A+ OS
3.2

Table 12-8 Tools used for troubleshooting and to monitor and improve system performance (continued)

Tool	Win95	Win 98	Description
Version Conflict Manager File name: Vcmui.exe Location: \windows		X	Installs Windows files over a newer file that might be in the \Windows folder and subfolders
System Configuration Editor File name: sysedit.exe Location: \windows\system	X	X	Text editor to edit files that configure how Windows loads. To run it, enter sysedit.exe in the Run dialog box. Sysedit automatically opens protocol.ini, system.ini, win.ini, config.sys and autoexec.bat for editing.
Signature Verification Tool File name: sigverif.exe Location: \windows		X	Checks system drivers for digital signatures given them by Microsoft, which ensures they have been tested by Microsoft. To run it, use the System Information window.
Digital Signature Check		X	Identifies drivers that have been digitally signed by Microsoft to verify their integrity. To use it, enabled this key in the registry: HKEY_LOCAL_MACHINE\Software\Microsoft\Driver Signing

System Options in Control Panel

A+ OS
3.1

In Control Panel, select **System** and click the **Performance** tab. Figure 12-35 shows the results of this action on two computers, one in need of performance tuning and one running at optimal performance. Key messages to look for on this screen (see Figure 12-35a) are "Some drives are using MS-DOS compatibility" under File System, and "MS-DOS compatibility mode" under Virtual Memory. These messages mean that real-mode drivers are being used, which can slow down performance, especially when used with hard drive access. Figure 12-35b indicates that both these components are using 32-bit protected-mode drivers.

12

a. Adjustments are needed in order to use 32-bit protected-mode resource

b. System running at optimal performance

Figure 12-35   The Performance tab under System Properties in Control Panel can tell you if your file system and virtual memory are running at optimal performance

$A^+_{\,OS}$
$_{3.1}$

Whenever you see MS-DOS mode (real mode) being used, make the effort to do whatever you can to see that these drivers are replaced with 32-bit protected-mode drivers. One important tool to use for this process is the file Ios.ini, a text file that contains the Windows 9x Safe Driver List. Windows 9x uses this list to determine if it can safely substitute a protected-mode driver for a real-mode one. Also, if it attempts to make the substitution, but fails, it often records the problem in another file, Ios.log. Check this file for information about the problem.

If a real-mode driver is being used, and you believe that a protected mode driver should be used in its place, first check Ios.log for any error messages. If you don't find an error message, add the real-mode driver name to the safe driver list in the Ios.ini file. Anything following the semicolon on the line is a comment. Sample lines in the file are:

```
[SafeList]
386max.sys      ;      Qualitas
extrados.pro    ;      Qualitas Memory Manager
extrados.max    ;      Qualitas Memory Manager
4dos.com        ;      4DOS shell program
ad-dos.com      ;      Afterdark
ad-wrap.com     ;      Afterdark
adi2.com        ;      Afterdark
aspi3x70.sys    ;      DTC SCSI driver
```

If you are using third-party disk compression software, such as Stacker, make sure to use a 32-bit version of the software. When converting from Windows 3.x to Windows 9x, also upgrade Stacker. If you are still using a 16-bit version of the software, most often an error message about the problem can be found in Ios.log.

System Monitor

$A^+_{\,OS}$
$_{3.2}$

System Monitor allows you to monitor how system resources are being used by applications. It can monitor the file system, memory, the kernel, printer sharing services, and network performance data. System Monitor is not automatically installed in a typical installation. To install it, go to **Control Panel, Add/Remove Programs**. Click **Windows Setup**, and then select **Accessories**. To run System Monitor, click **Start**, point to **Programs**, **Accessories**, **System Tools**, and click **System Monitor**.

Figure 12-36 shows System Monitor tracking the kernel and disk cache hits and misses. Under the File menu you can add and delete items the monitor is tracking. Use System Monitor to help determine if an application is using an inordinate amount of resources or has a memory leak.

Figure 12-36   System Monitor can track the performance of several system resources

System Configuration Utility

A^+ OS 3.2

Similar to loading Windows in safe mode, the System Configuration Utility reduces the startup up process to its essentials. If starting Windows in this condition eliminates the problem, then you can use this utility to add items back one at a time until the problem occurs; the problem source is related to the last item you added. To use the utility, do the following:

1. To access the utility, click **Start**, point to **Programs**, **Accessories**, **System Tools**, and then click **System Information**. The Microsoft System Information window opens (see Figure 12-22). Another way to access the Window is to type MSCONFIG in the RUN dialog box.

2. From the **Tools** menu, select **System Configuration Utility**. The System Configuration Utility dialog box opens, as in Figure 12-37.

3. To diagnose a problem, select **Diagnostic startup – interactively load device drivers and software**, and then click **OK** to restart your computer.

4. If this solves the problem, then the clean start was successful. Next, select **Selective startup** from the screen shown in Figure 12-37 and methodically select first one item and then another to restore, until the problem reappears. Begin by restoring all entries in AUTOEXEC.BAT and CONFIG.SYS, to determine if real-mode drivers and programs loaded from these files are the source of the problem.

5. If the problem still occurs, even with the clean boot, then try these things:

   ■ Scan for a virus, using a current version of antivirus software.

   ■ Use Registry Checker to check for corrupted system files.

   ■ Use System File Checker to check for corrupted system files.

   ■ Check the CMOS setup screen for wrong settings.

12

Figure 12-37   The Windows 98 System Configuration Utility helps troubleshoot Windows configuration problems

WINDOWS ME

Recall that Windows Me is the latest Windows 9x upgrade. Now that you have learned about Windows 95 and Windows 98, you can turn your attention to the features unique to Windows Me that are important if you are supporting the OS. These features include components to protect the system from failure and changes made to the OS that alter the procedures used for troubleshooting.

The Windows Me System Restore component automatically backs up the registry and other system files when the system is idle, at about every 10 hours of operating time. System Restore also prevents a user from deleting important Windows system files. If the system fails but you can still boot into Safe Mode, use the System Restore wizard. You can then choose between earlier versions of the saved system. The damaged system files will be overwritten with these saved ones.

Another feature, System File Protection, which is similar to Windows 2000 System File Protection, prevents system files from being deleted. For example, if you attempt to delete files in the Program Files folder where applications are normally stored, the utility will work in the background to compress and save these files in case you need them later. The utility also prevents an application installation from overwriting newer DLL files with older or non-standard versions.

Windows Me desktop looks more like Windows 2000 than Windows 98 SE, and, just like Windows 2000, the option to boot to the DOS command prompt is not included on the Start menu. That means that you cannot boot Windows Me from the hard drive in true real mode although you do have a MS-DOS Command Prompt window. If you want to get a true real-mode command prompt using Windows Me, create a blank formatted floppy disk, and copy Io.sys and Command.com from the \Windows\Command\EBD folder to the disk, and then boot from this disk.

Windows Me does not allow real-mode device drivers and TSRs to be loaded from Config.sys and Autoexec.bat as does earlier versions of Windows 9x. If you want to run these 16-bit programs, your only option is to load them after Windows Me loads. One way to do this is to include them in a batch file that is listed in the Properties tab of the MS-DOS Command Prompt shortcut.

SUPPORT FROM MICROSOFT

Microsoft offers some excellent support for its products. For those serious about learning to provide professional support for Windows 95 or Windows 98, I highly recommend these books: *Microsoft Windows 95 Resource Kit* and *Microsoft Windows 98 Resource Kit*, both by Microsoft Press.

Another valuable source of information, including software utilities, enhancements, and troubleshooting guidelines for Windows 3.x and Windows 9x is the Microsoft web site. For Microsoft Technical Support Knowledge Base, access this web site:

http://support.microsoft.com/search

Figure 12-38 shows the beginning query screen for this web site. Follow the steps given there to research specific or general topics for the Microsoft products. For example, if you want to learn more about how to optimize Windows 95, choose **Windows 95** in Step 1 of Figure 12-38, and enter **optimize** as the key word to search for. Click **GO**. A list of related articles is displayed. Double-click the article to display it.

12

Figure 12-38   Microsoft Technical Support web site

CHAPTER SUMMARY

❐ Windows 9x, Windows 2000, and Windows NT are the most popular operating systems for new single-user PCs, although DOS and Windows 3.x are still used and supported.

❐ Software stores configuration information in initialization files with an .ini extension that are organized into sections, key names, and values, and can be edited using a text editor.

❐ Lines in .ini files that begin with a semicolon are comments and are ignored by the OS.

❐ Before upgrading Windows, scan and fix the hard drive by removing lost clusters, defragment the drive, and back up Autoexec.bat, Config.sys, System.ini, Win.ini, and the Windows registry files.

❐ Applications software can cause conflicts when, during an installation, the new application overwrites an existing .dll file. The new .dll file might not work correctly with previously installed applications. The .dll files are usually located in the Windows\System directory.

❐ Utility software can track changes to the Windows\System directory and changes to Windows .ini files and the registry during software installation.

❐ PCs can operate in either real mode or protected mode. Real mode limits programs to the first 1 MB of memory, allows direct access to I/O devices, and use a 16-bit data path. Protected mode gives a program access to memory addresses above 1 MB, prevents direct access to I/O devices, and uses a 32-bit data path. Protected mode is generally preferred over real mode because it is faster.

❐ At one time, a General Protection Fault (GPF) error always meant a memory violation by software, but now it can represent many different software errors.

❐ Windows application programs can give insufficient memory errors because a portion of a memory heap is not available, even though not all physical RAM is used yet.

❐ A memory leak is caused when an applications software program does not release a group of memory addresses back to the heap when it unloads.

❐ Windows 3.x is mostly a 16-bit application, whereas Windows 9x is a mixture of 16-bit and 32-bit code.

❐ The core components of Windows 9x are the kernel, the user, and the GDI processes.

❐ Windows 9x, as well as Windows NT and Windows 2000, uses the virtual machine concept to protect against program faults from software currently running.

❐ Memory paging is a Windows 9x method of allocating a different set of memory addresses to different virtual machines.

❐ Windows 9x can be customized by entries in the text file Msdos.sys.

❐ When Windows 9x starts up, static VxDs are loaded in real mode and then the OS switches to protected mode, in which dynamic VxDs are loaded.

❐ Plug and Play requires the use of 32-bit dynamic VxDs.

- Windows 9x and Windows 3.x can coexist on the same PC; this is called a dual boot.

- Press F8 when Windows 9x is loading to view and use the Windows 9x Startup Menu, which can be helpful in troubleshooting Windows problems.

- Plug and Play (PnP) is a group of architectural standards designed to automate the installation of new hardware devices on PCs.

- When using Windows 9x, in order for a PC to be completely Plug and Play-compliant, the system BIOS, all hardware devices, and the OS must be Plug and Play.

- The four components of the OS portion of Plug and Play are the configuration manager, the hardware tree, the bus enumerator, and the resource arbitrator.

- A legacy card is an expansion card that is not PnP-compliant and must be manually configured.

- Windows 9x uses 32-bit drivers stored in extended memory, although it does support older 16-bit drivers stored in the first MB of memory.

- Windows 9x loads older 16-bit drivers from either CONFIG.SYS or AUTOEXEC.BAT.

- The Windows 9x registry keeps information that was previously kept in Windows 3.x .ini files.

- The Windows 9x registry uses six major branches, or keys.

- The Microsoft web site, *support.microsoft.com*, is an excellent source of troubleshooting information for Windows.

- Useful Windows troubleshooting utilities include Automatic Skip Driver Agent, Microsoft System Information, Registry Checker, System options in Control Panel, System Configuration Utility, System File Checker, and System Monitor.

12

KEY TERMS

Bus enumerator — A component of Windows 9x Plug and Play that locates all devices on a particular bus and inventories the resource requirements for these devices.

Comment lines — Documentation lines that are ignored by a program. A REM in front of a line will comment out an AUTOEXEC command. A semicolon will turn an .ini file line into a comment.

Configuration manager — A component of Windows 9x Plug and Play that controls the configuration process of all devices and communicates these configurations to the devices.

Disk thrashing — A condition that results when the hard drive is excessively used for virtual memory because RAM is full. It dramatically slows down processing and can cause premature hard drive failure.

DLL (dynamic-link library) — A file with a .dll file extension that contains a library of programming routines used by programs to perform common tasks.

Dr. Watson — A Windows utility that tracks detailed information into a log file about a failed event and the software that caused it.

Dual boot — The ability to boot using two or more different operating systems, such as Windows NT and Windows 98. However, programs are not easily shared between Windows NT and the other OSs.

Dynamic VxD — A VxD that is loaded and unloaded from memory as needed.

Group files — Windows 3.x files with the .grp file extension that contain information about a program group of Program Manager.

Hardware tree — A database built each time Windows 9x starts up that contains a list of installed components and the resources they use.

Initialization files — Configuration information files for Windows. Win.ini and System.ini are the two most important Windows 3.x initialization files.

Kernel — Core portion of an operating system that loads applications and manages files, memory, and other resources.

Keys — In Windows 9x, section names of the Windows 9x registry.

Legacy — An older device or adapter card that does not support Plug and Play, and might have to be manually configured through jumpers or DIP switches.

Memory leak — A problem caused when an application does not release the memory addresses assigned to it when it unloads, causing the memory heaps to have less and less memory for new applications.

Memory paging — In Windows 9x, swapping blocks of RAM memory to an area of the hard drive to serve as virtual memory when RAM memory is low.

MSDOS.SYS — In DOS, a program file that contains part of the DOS kernel and controls much of the boot process. In Windows 9x, a text file that contains settings used by Io.sys during booting.

Object linking — A method whereby one application can execute a command on an object created by another application.

Page fault — An OS interrupt that occurs when the OS is forced to access the hard drive to satisfy the demand for virtual memory.

Page-in — The process in which the memory manager goes to the hard drive to return the data from a swap file to RAM.

Page-out — The process in which, when RAM is full, the memory manager takes a page and moves it to the swap file.

PIF (program information file) — A file with a .pif file extension that is used by an OS to store the settings of the environment provided to a DOS application.

Plug and Play BIOS — Basic input/output system for Plug and Play devices, which are designed to be automatically recognized by the computer when they are installed.

registry — A database used by Windows to store hardware and software configuration information, user preferences, and setup information. Use Regedit.exe to edit the registry.

Resource arbitrator — A PnP component that decides which resources are assigned to which devices.

Resource management — The process of allocating resources to devices at startup.

Run-time configuration — A PnP ongoing process that monitors changes in system devices, such as the removal of a PC Card on a notebook computer or the docking of a notebook computer to a docking station.

Safe mode — The mode in which Windows 9x is loaded with minimum configuration and drivers in order to allow the correction of system errors. To enter safe mode, press F5 or F8 when "Starting Windows 95/98" is displayed.

Static VxD — A VxD that is loaded into memory at startup and remains there for the entire OS session.

Value data — In Windows 9x, the name and value of a setting in the Registry.

Virtual machines (VM) — Multiple logical machines created within one physical machine by Windows, allowing applications to make serious errors within one logical machine without disturbing other programs and parts of the system.

Virtual memory manager — A Windows 9x program that controls the page table, swapping 4K pages in and out of physical RAM to and from the hard drive.

REVIEW QUESTIONS

1. What Microsoft operating system introduced 32-bit code and protected mode into the OS?

2. Which Microsoft operating systems support 32-bit programs? Which OSs do not allow 32-bit programs?

3. Which Microsoft operating systems do not allow an application program to run in real mode?

4. Which portion of an OS is most likely to interact with the user, the kernel, or the shell? Which is most likely to interact with secondary storage?

5. If Windows runs low on memory while graphics and printing or both are being done, what heap is most likely the problem? What is the solution to the problem?

6. What is the keystroke to move from one program to another program running in a different window?

7. Name two editors that can be used to edit .ini files.

8. What .ini file can contain VxD entries that override the VxD entries in the registry that are loaded when starting Windows 9x?

9. What symbol is used to make a line a comment line in an .ini file?

10. A Windows 9x virtual machine provides an environment for _____ (16 or 32) bit programs.

11. What situation can cause a page fault?

12. What two sections in System.ini have the most impact on the boot process?

13. What is the default path to the Windows temporary directory?

14. How can you change the path to the Windows temporary directory?

15. What are the two files that make up the Windows 9x registry? What type of files in Windows 3.x does the Windows 9x registry replace?

12

16. What is the name of the Windows file that loads VxD drivers each time Windows starts?

17. Windows 9x uses _____ multitasking to provide backward-compatibility with 16-bit applications, but uses _____ multitasking with 32-bit applications.

18. What is the name of the Windows system file that is responsible for the switchover from real mode to protected mode?

19. In what directory are .dll files most often found?

20. What is the name of the file that contains the default settings that Windows 3.x uses to provide an environment for a DOS application?

21. What function key do you press to cause Windows to load in Safe Mode?

22. What is the keystroke shortcut to close a program in Windows?

23. In Windows 9x, what is one reason the user core uses 16-bit code rather than 32-bit code?

24. In Windows 9x, what is one reason the GDI core uses a mix of 16-bit and 32-bit code?

25. In Windows 9x, why do you think the kernel uses mostly 32-bit code?

26. What is a significant benefit to device driver developers when using the Win32 driver model (WDM)?

27. Describe the general difference between a 16-bit DOS application and a 16-bit Windows application.

28. What is disk thrashing? What causes it? What can you do about it?

29. Name three enhancements of Windows 98 over Windows 95.

30. What is the advantage of using FAT32 instead of FAT16 on a hard drive?

31. Static VxDs are loaded in _____ mode, and dynamic VxDs are loaded in _____ mode.

32. How do you force the Startup Menu of Windows 9x to be displayed during booting?

33. Using Device Manager of Windows 9x on your home or lab computer, answer these questions:

    ❏ What are the driver files used by your video system?

    ❏ What I/O addresses does the PCI bus use?

    ❏ What is the name of the driver file that Windows is using to manage the PCI bus?

PROJECTS

Examine Your PC

1. List all of the .ini files stored in your home or lab computer's Windows directory.

2. Print out your home or lab computer's System.ini file and identify each hardware component that is referenced.

3. On a Windows 9x system, click the **Start** button, then click **Run:** and type **Edit C:\Msdos.sys**. Then select **File**, **Print** and print the contents of this file.

4. Follow these steps to list Windows troubleshooting tools:

   a. Click the Windows 9x **Start** button.

   b. Choose the **Settings** option.

   c. Select **Control Panel**.

   d. List at least six Control Panel utilities that can be used to configure hardware and resolve hardware problems.

Windows 9x Start Menu

As soon as your computer displays the message "Starting Windows 95/98" during the boot process, press the F8 function key. Select **Logged(\Bootlog.txt)**. When done, open the file named Bootlog.txt and print out its contents. Shut down Windows, reboot the computer, and press F8 again. Select the **Safe mode** option and note the differences in the screen's appearance. Shut down Windows, reboot the computer, and press F8 again. This time choose the **Step-by-step confirmation** option. Write down each command that executes.

Backing Up Critical Windows 9x Files

Keep a copy of critical Windows 9x files in a separate directory. Each time you install or uninstall hardware or software, redo the backup.

1. Using Windows 9x Explorer, create a new folder called Win-bak.ini.

2. In the C:\Windows folder highlight the System.ini and Win.ini files. Copy them by pressing **Ctrl+C**.

3. Click the **Win-bak.ini** directory, then paste the copied .ini files into the Win-bak.ini file by pressing **Ctrl+V**.

4. Using Explorer, set View, Options to **Show all files**.

5. Copy C:\Windows\System.dat to C:\ Win-bak.ini (do not drag!).

6. Copy C:\Windows\User.dat to C:\ Win-bak.ini (do not drag!).

Monitor a Software Installation

Using utility software such as Norton Utilities, monitor the installation of an applications software package. Install the software following the installation instructions documented with the software. Does the software allow you to customize the environment? What files are used to store the custom configuration? By looking at the date and time stamp on files, how can you guess which files contain custom setup information for this installation of the application?

12

Customizing a Dual Boot

You have your PC set for a dual boot between DOS with Windows 3.1 and Windows 9x. You boot to your previous version of DOS and decide to make a change to the Windows 9x Msdos.sys file. What is the current name of the file? List the steps to edit the file. Verify that your answers are correct by changing the BootMenu option in Msdos.sys. Be certain to first back up the file.

Use Control Panel to Test Your Modem

1. Click the Windows 9x **Start** button.
2. Choose the **Settings** option.
3. Select **Control Panel**.
4. Double-click the **Modems** icon. (This icon only appears when a modem is installed.)
5. Choose the **Diagnostics** tab.
6. Select the appropriate COM port and click the **More Info** button to verify that an OK message is displayed.
7. Click the **Help** button and list at least four problems that the Modem Troubleshooter will help solve.

Mouse Troubleshooting

Assume that your friend is having a difficult time finding and following the mouse pointer on his new laptop computer. Enter Control Panel and list the steps that you would use to make the mouse pointer easier to see. Test your steps on your home or lab computer.

Customizing Windows 9x

Change the Windows 9x logo screen to another .bmp file at startup. (*Hint*: See "Logo" in Table 12-5)

Using Nuts & Bolts to View the Windows 9x Registry

Nuts & Bolts offers a powerful editor for the Windows 9x registry. Use it here to save the registry to a text file (called exporting a registry file) for easy and safe viewing. This text file can later be edited and then imported back into the registry. registry text files are also convenient for transporting portions of a registry from one PC to another. In this example, you export the mouse options set in Control Panel to a registry file and view the text file.

1. Using Windows 9x, click **Start**, **Programs**, **Nuts & Bolts**, and select **Registry Pro** from the Nuts & Bolts utilities.
2. Click **Search**, **Find** and search for the text "mousekeys." The occurrences of mousekeys will be displayed in the key list at the bottom of the editor. Double-click the **HKEY_CURRENT_USER** occurrence of mousekeys. This key should now appear in the editor view window.

3. On the left side of the editor window, you can view the value names and their values for the mouse. Click **File**, **Export Registry File** to save this key to a text file. In the Save As dialog box that is displayed, enter the path and filename for the file and then click **Save**. For example, to save the file to a folder named Data, using MouseSave as the filename, enter **\Data\MouseSave**, and then click **Save**. The editor will assign a .reg file extension to the file.

4. Leaving the Registry Pro editor still on screen, use any text editor or word processor to open the file MouseSave.reg. Print the contents of this text file and compare them to the MouseKeys key values showing in Registry Pro.

5. Exit Registry Pro.

Using Nuts & Bolts Registry Wizard

Use the Registry Wizard of Nuts & Bolts to first make a backup of the registry and then perform the clean, repair, and tune-up procedures shown in Figure 12-39.

1. Back up the registry.

2. Clean the registry of the Recent Docs List. Verify the clean was successful by clicking on **Start**, **Documents**.

3. Repair the registry. Allow the Registry Wizard to search for and fix any orphan entries (entries without associated files) in the registry that it can. How many orphans did it fix?

4. Tune-up the registry. From the Registry Wizard opening screen, select **Tune-up**. Print the Registry Wizard screen showing the values or write down the size of the System.dat and User.dat files before and after the tune-up.

12

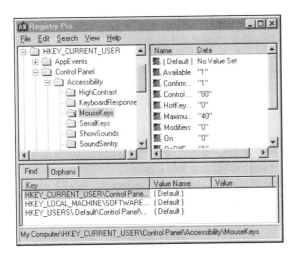

Figure 12-39 Nuts and Bolts offers a powerful registry editor, Registry Pro

Using Program Manager in Windows 9x

Program Manager is sometimes preferred by users who like the look and feel of Windows 3.x. Create a shortcut on the Windows 9x desktop to Program Manager. List the steps you took to do that.

Examine the Windows 95 Registry

Examine the Windows 95 registry to determine if your version of Windows 95 includes support for USB devices. The USB support update module is an add-on module for Windows 95 OSR 2.0. For a PC with Windows 95 to have this support, OSR 2 would have been installed and then the USB update added. To determine the installed version of the OS, look in the registry for these two values:

HKEY_LOCAL_MACHINE\SOFTWARE\Microsoft\Windows\CurrentVersion\Version

HKEY_LOCAL_MACHINE\SOFTWARE\Microsoft\Windows\CurrentVersion\VersionNumber

OSR2.0 with the USB update has the version and version number:

Version "Windows 95" and Version Number "4.03.1212" or "4.03.1214."

Print your screen showing the values for your PC. Do you have USB support installed?

Edit the Windows 9x Registry

Edit the Windows 9x registry to personalize the name of the recycle bin. Rename the recycle bin "Jean's Trash Can", using your own name. (*Hint*: Search the registry for the value "Recycle Bin".) Print the desktop screen showing the newly named recycle bin.

CHAPTER

13

UNDERSTANDING AND SUPPORTING WINDOWS NT WORKSTATION

In this chapter, you will learn:

♦ About the Windows NT environment and its architecture

♦ About the strengths and weaknesses of Windows NT

♦ How to evaluate when Windows NT is the best choice for a PC OS

♦ How to install and customize Windows NT

♦ How to set up a Windows NT environment for a DOS or Windows 3.x application

♦ How to use some Windows NT troubleshooting techniques and tools

---

This chapter provides an introduction to Windows NT Workstation (the NT stands for new technology), including basic architecture, installation, maintenance, and troubleshooting. There are two versions of Windows NT: Windows NT Workstation and Windows NT Server. You can use Windows NT Workstation on a standalone PC or as the operating system on a workstation connected to a network. Windows NT Server, which is not covered in this book, can do the same, as well as provide a domain environment on a network. (A **domain** is a group of computers joined together over a network that share a common database used to control security to each PC on the network.) There have been several upgrades of Windows NT; the last is Version 4, which is the subject of this chapter. The next upgrade of Windows NT is Windows 2000, which is the subject of the next chapter although many of the concepts, processes, and tools introduced in this chapter also apply to Windows 2000.

Windows NT Workstation and Windows NT Server are architecturally built more like the UNIX OS than like other Windows operating systems, such as DOS with Windows 3.x and Windows 9x. Windows NT is designed with a strong emphasis on room for expandability, primarily accomplished by its modular approach to dealing with applications and hardware. Windows NT is also intended to port to several non-Intel-based platforms, provide a high level of security, performance, and reliability, and offer strong networking features.

Assuming that you are familiar with Windows 9x, this chapter often compares Windows NT Workstation to Windows 9x so that you can contrast them and make informed decisions about which best suits your needs. However, comparisons of some features are difficult to make because the two operating systems are fundamentally different. It would be much easier to compare Windows NT to UNIX, particularly when talking about performance, reliability, and networking features. Traditionally, UNIX has not been a viable option for a personal computer operating system, although this is changing somewhat with the growing popularity of Linux. This chapter only compares Windows NT to Windows 9x. Furthermore, to fully appreciate the strengths of Windows NT, you need to go beyond the scope of this chapter to studying networking in detail.

WINDOWS NT VS. WINDOWS 9X

Table 13-1 summarizes how some important Windows NT and Windows 9x features (which will be discussed in this chapter) compare. Remember the following two important points: First, if Windows NT is installed on a PC that is not as powerful as the type of computer it was designed to run on, Windows NT does not perform as well as Windows 9x would on that PC. However, on a powerful workstation PC with a configuration recommended for Windows NT, Windows NT usually performs faster and better than Windows 9x. The second important point is that Windows NT is not another evolution of DOS, Windows 3.x, and Windows 9x. In fact, the opposite is true. Windows NT was developed before Windows 95. Windows 9x and its upgrade, Windows 98, were built as a bridge between the old (DOS with Windows 3.x) and the new (Windows NT). The rest of this section highlights and expands on several of the differences between Windows NT and Windows 9x. While Windows 9x and Windows NT Workstation differ dramatically in underlying architecture and structure, they share many features, including a similar user interface, some of the same utilities (such as Internet Explorer and Microsoft Messaging), and other features (such as system policies, user profiles, and hardware profiles). Windows NT Workstation offers higher performance, reliability, and security than does Windows 9x. On the other hand, Windows 9x has less demanding hardware requirements, offers broad application and device compatibility, and works well on notebook PCs because of better power management features and Plug and Play capability.

The key to appreciating the advantage of Windows NT over Windows 9x is in the platforms and settings that Windows NT targets. Windows NT is designed to satisfy the needs of powerful workstations networked in a corporate environment. Windows 9x, however, is used on low-end PCs dominating the home market, where multimedia applications software and ease of installation are more of an issue than network security and high-end performance.

One major difference between Windows 9x and Windows NT is that Windows NT is a full 32-bit operating system, operating in protected mode as soon as it receives control from BIOS. Recall that Windows 9x begins the boot process in real mode and loads some real-mode components before shifting to protected mode. Windows 9x supports real-mode device drivers; Windows NT does not allow them. Windows 9x uses virtual device drivers (VxDs) that often interact directly with hardware. Windows NT does not allow them, but uses a more layered approach. It does use virtual device drivers, which it calls VDDs, but they are allowed to work only within their virtual machine and must depend on Windows NT device drivers to communicate with the device itself. Table 13-1 lists major differences between Windows NT and Windows 9x.

Table 13-1   Comparing Windows NT to Windows 9x

Feature	Windows 9x	Windows NT
Hardware requirements	Low, requiring a 486 PC with 8–16 MB of RAM	High, requiring a Pentium with 16–32 MB RAM
Hardware compatibility	Supports most legacy devices	Supports most current devices, but does not claim backward compatibility with legacy devices
Software compatibility	Fully backward-compatible with older DOS and Windows 3.x applications	No support for any application that attempts to access hardware directly
Installation	Offers Plug and Play capability	Does not offer Plug and Play and offers less device driver support
Power management	Built-in power management for laptops	None
Performance	Offers multitasking for 32-bit and 16-bit applications	Also offers preemptive multi-tasking for 32-bit applications and cooperative multitasking for 16-bit applications. Has significantly better performance on systems with at least 32 MB of RAM
Reliability and stability	Much better than Windows 3.x	Very high reliability and stability; all applications run in protected memory space
Security	Allows violation of the logon process controlled from a server	Very high security down to the file level

13

Features of Windows NT

A+ OS 1.1 | Windows NT Workstation includes the following features:

- **Desktop performance.** Supports a powerful multitasking environment and multiple microprocessors for true multitasking

- **Hardware profiles.** Can maintain separate hardware profiles for different hardware configurations on the same PC

- **Internet Explorer.** Provides a built-in web browser (Internet Explorer)

- **Peer Web services.** Provides a personal web server

- **Security.** Provides security for individual files, folders, and other resources. User access to a PC's resources can be controlled by user IDs and passwords on the standalone PC or managed from a network controller.

A+ OS
   1.1

- **OS Stability.** Uses protective processing, which prevents applications from causing errors in other applications or in Windows NT itself

Many of these same features, including Internet Explorer, hardware profiles, and user access, are available from Windows 9x as well. Windows 9x allows you to use more hardware devices than does Windows NT, has a simpler installation process, and supports power management features better than does Windows NT. Windows 9x supports Plug and Play technology, but Windows NT does not. Windows NT has higher performance, including faster speed on high-end PCs, higher reliability, and better security than does Windows 9x. The minimum hardware requirements for Windows NT on an IBM-compatible PC are listed below. However, even though Windows NT does run on this minimum hardware configuration, remember that you need a powerful high-end PC to experience the full benefits of Windows NT.

- Pentium-compatible processor or higher
- 16 MB of RAM (32 MB is recommended)
- 110 MB of hard disk space

While the minimum requirements listed above reference IBM-compatible machines, Windows NT can run on other computers as well, providing the same interface and functionality. The main difference between Windows NT running on an IBM-compatible CPU and Windows NT on other computers is in the layer (which is a part of Windows NT) between the OS and the hardware, called the **hardware abstraction layer** or **HAL**. The hardware platforms supported by Windows NT are listed below. This chapter focuses only on the Intel-based CPUs of IBM-compatible machines.

- Intel x86-based (486 or higher) processor
- MIPS R4x00-based processor
- Alpha AXP-based processor
- PReP-compliant PowerPC-based processor

The Windows NT CD-ROM contains three installation directories to choose from, one for each of these types of processors. Each directory contains a different version of HAL (sometimes referred to as the core of the OS). HAL is discussed at greater length later in this chapter.

Hardware Supported by Windows NT. Many hardware device models are not supported by Windows NT. For this reason, before you decide to upgrade a PC to Windows NT, first determine if all components on your PC will work under Windows NT. For instance, you might have to replace a network card, modem, video card, etc., before Windows NT works. To determine if a hardware component is supported by Windows NT, see the **hardware compatibility list** (**HCL**) for Windows NT that comes with the software. The most recent copy is available on the Microsoft Web site at *www.microsoft.com/hcl*. On the list, which you can search by hardware category and/or company name, are all hardware devices supported by Windows 98, Windows NT, and Windows 2000. For instance, Figure 13-1 shows the partial results of a search for modems compatible with Windows NT 4.0. If a device is not on the list, ask the manufacturer if there is a driver specifically for Windows NT (not just Windows 9x). If no driver exists, this device will not work under Windows NT.

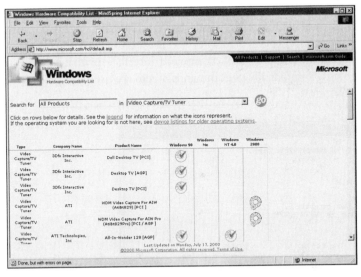

Figure 13-1   Some video capture cards compatible with Windows NT from the HCL

The Windows NT Desktop. Beginning with Windows NT 4.0, the Windows NT desktop took on a similar look and feel to Windows 9x. Figure 13-2 shows the Windows NT desktop with the Start menu and Control Panel showing, both of which work just as they do in Windows 9x, although some Control Panel icons are different. Shortcuts are created the same way as in Windows 9x, and the taskbar works in the same way, too.

13

Figure 13-2   The Windows NT desktop is similar to that of Windows 9x

A+ OS 1.1

The Windows NT Command Prompt. Another similarity between Windows NT and Windows 9x is the command prompt that allows the user to enter DOS-like commands. To access the command prompt, click **Start**, **Programs**, and **Command Prompt** (as in Figure 13-2). The Command Prompt window opens, as in Figure 13-3. From the command prompt, you can enter DOS commands. In Windows 9x, the DOS prompt is actually accessing a version of DOS (Windows 9x uses COMMAND.COM at startup). Windows NT, however, provides a DOS command interface primarily as a convenience for those wanting to use familiar DOS commands. There are no DOS programs underlying and running under Windows NT.

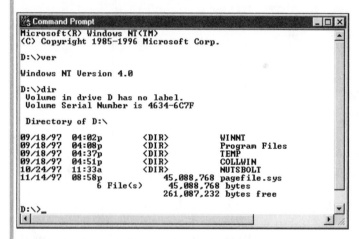

```
Command Prompt                                        _ □ ✕
Microsoft(R) Windows NT(TM)
(C) Copyright 1985-1996 Microsoft Corp.

D:\>ver

Windows NT Version 4.0

D:\>dir
 Volume in drive D has no label.
 Volume Serial Number is 4634-6C7F

 Directory of D:\

09/18/97  04:02p        <DIR>        WINNT
09/18/97  04:08p        <DIR>        Program Files
09/18/97  04:37p        <DIR>        TEMP
09/18/97  04:51p        <DIR>        COLLWIN
10/24/97  11:33a        <DIR>        NUTSBOLT
11/14/97  08:58p             45,088,768 pagefile.sys
              6 File(s)     45,088,768 bytes
                          261,087,232 bytes free

D:\>_
```

Figure 13-3   The Windows NT command prompt uses DOS-like commands

 As a side note, notice in Figure 13-2 that the Control Panel for Windows NT contains an icon, MSDOS, which is labeled Console. Double-click the Console icon to change the properties of the DOS command window. The Console Windows Properties dialog box appears, which allows you to customize the Command Prompt window (see Figure 13-4). If you prefer to use the familiar command prompt often, you can create a shortcut to it by dragging this icon to the desktop.

Choosing Between Windows 9x and Windows NT

When choosing between using Windows 98 or Windows NT as your PC OS, consider the following:

- Does Windows NT support all the hardware devices on your PC? (Check the hardware compatibility list.)

- Is the PC powerful and big enough to support Windows NT? (See the hardware requirements listed earlier in the chapter, and then allow extra resources for your applications.)

Figure 13-4   Customizing the properties of the Command Prompt window

- Will the software you intend to use on the PC work better under Windows 98 or Windows NT? Running older DOS and Windows 16-bit applications might be a problem in a Windows NT environment. Verify that your current, older software works under Windows NT, or plan to replace the current software with 32-bit versions. Be aware, however, that some 32-bit programs written for Windows 9x might not work under Windows NT because of differences in the API calls to the operating system. (An **API** is an application program interface, which is a method by which one program calls another program to perform a task.)

- Is price a factor? Windows NT costs more than Windows 98.

Upgrading from Windows 9x to Windows NT

A+ OS
2.2

Because Windows NT differs so fundamentally from Windows 9x, there is no automatic upgrade path from Windows 9x to Windows NT. When you change a PC from Windows 9x to Windows NT, you can install Windows NT in a different folder. No system settings in Windows 9x will be transferred to Windows NT. After Windows NT is installed, you must reinstall each application on the PC under Windows NT. Windows NT can be present as the only OS on a PC, or it can be installed on the same PC as Windows 9x. (How to set up this "dual boot" is discussed later in this chapter.)

Registries

The main reason Windows 9x cannot be easily upgraded to Windows NT is that their Registries are not compatible, which makes it difficult to transfer information from one to the other. (Remember that a Registry is a database containing all configuration information for the OS.) You do not have this problem when upgrading from Windows 3.x to Windows NT because Windows NT can read the .ini files in Windows 3.x and transfer that information to the Windows NT Registry. Again, realize that Windows NT is not the next stepping stone beyond Windows 98, but a new road altogether.

A Choice of File Systems

Windows NT can work with two types of file systems: the FAT16 file system, which is used by Windows 9x and its predecessors, and the Windows NT file system (NTFS), which works only with Windows NT. Windows NT does not support FAT32. (Recall that FAT32 was introduced by Windows 95 OSR2 and uses 32 bits for each FAT entry.) Windows NT also does not support the High Performance File System (HPFS) used by OS/2. If a hard drive is using HPFS, use the Windows NT convert.exe utility to convert an HPFS partition to an NTFS partition.

> **TIP** Even though Windows NT 4.0 does not support FAT32, you can use third-party utility software packages to manage the interface, making it possible for Windows NT to read from and write to FAT32.

A **file system** is the method used by an OS to manage the data on a drive. The FAT16 file system is backward-compatible with DOS and Windows 9x and uses less overhead than NTFS. The NTFS file system, on the other hand, is more fail-safe, provides more security, and is more efficient with large hard drives. Below, you see how these two file systems are built and then explore what to consider when choosing between the two.

The FAT16 file system uses four components to manage data on a logical drive: the boot record, the FAT, directories, and data files. In contrast, the NTFS file system uses a database called the master file table (MFT) as its core component. The MFT tracks the contents of a logical drive using one or more rows in the table for each file or directory on the drive. As shown in Figure 13-5, the MFT contains in one record, or row, information about each file, including header information (abbreviated H in Microsoft documentation), standard information (SI) about the file (including date and time), filename (FN), security information about the file called the security descriptor (SD), and data about the location of the file. Entries in the MFT are ordered alphabetically by filename to speed up a search for a file listed in the table. When a drive is formatted for NTFS, each cluster on the hard drive can range from 512 bytes on smaller disks to 4K on larger disks. Clusters are numbered sequentially by logical cluster numbers (LCN) from the beginning to the end of the disk.

Referring again to Figure 13-5, notice that the data area in the MFT record is 2K for small hard drives, but can be larger for larger hard drives. For small files, if the data can fit into the 2K area, the file, including its data, is fully contained within the MFT. For small files, all the cluster information for a file can fit into this one data area, including all the cluster numbers for the file. Each cluster number is stored in a 64-bit entry, compared to either 16 bits for FAT16 or 32 bits for FAT32.

If the file is moderately large and the data does not fit into the MFT, the data area in the MFT becomes an extended attribute (EA) of the file, which points to the location of the data. The data itself is moved outside the table to clusters called runs. The record in the MFT for this moderately large file contains pointers to these runs. Each data run, or cluster, assigned to the

A+ OS
1.3

file is assigned a 64-bit virtual cluster number (VCN). The MFT maps the VCNs for the file onto the LCNs for the drive. This mapping is stored in the area of the MFT record that would have contained the data if the file had been small enough.

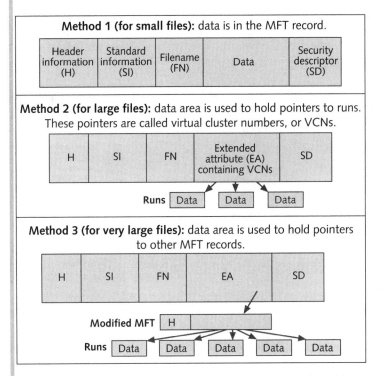

Figure 13-5   The Windows NT file system Master File Table uses three methods to store files, depending on the file size

13

If the file is so large that the pointers to all the VCNs cannot be contained in one MFT record, then additional MFT records are used. The first MFT record is called the base file record and holds the location of the other MFT records for this file.

Advantages of NTFS and FAT16   When choosing between the NTFS file system and the FAT16 file system, consider the advantages that NTFS offers over the FAT:

- NTFS is a recoverable file system. NTFS retains copies of its critical file system data and automatically recovers a failed file system, using this information the first time the disk is accessed after a file system failure.

- NTFS offers increased security over the FAT file system. Security is provided for each file, and auditing information about access to files is more complete.

- NTFS supports mirroring drives, meaning that two copies of data can be kept on two different drives to protect against permanent data loss in case of a hard drive crash. This feature makes the NTFS an important alternative for file servers.

- NTFS uses smaller cluster sizes than does FAT16, making more efficient use of hard drive space when small files are used.
- NTFS supports large-volume drives. NTFS uses 64-bit cluster numbers, whereas FAT16 uses 16-bit cluster numbers. Because the number of bits assigned to hold each cluster number is so large, the cluster number itself can be a large number, and the table can accommodate very large drives with many clusters. NTFS is overall a more effective file system for drives over 1 GB and offers more robust drive compression, allowing compression of individual folders and files.

> **TIP** If the file system for the active partition of a PC is FAT, you can boot from a DOS boot disk and bypass the Windows NT security logon. When you use NTFS, you cannot boot from a DOS boot disk. Use NTFS if you want a high level of security. You can still boot the PC from Windows NT boot disks, but the Windows NT logon is required. In fact, if the one administrator forgets his password to the OS, the only recourse is to reload the OS.

The advantages of the FAT file system over NTFS include:

- The FAT16 file system has less overhead than the NTFS file system and, therefore, works best for hard drives that are less than 500 MB.
- The FAT file system is compatible with other operating systems. If you plan to use either DOS or Windows 9x on the same hard drive as Windows NT, use the FAT file system so that DOS and Windows 9x can access files used by Windows NT.
- In the event of a serious problem with Windows NT, if you are using FAT16 on the active partition of the drive, you can boot the PC from a disk, using DOS, and gain access to the drive.

You can choose to have Windows NT use NTFS by directing it to convert the hard drive from FAT16 to NTFS or by having Windows NT partition a drive so that one partition of the drive uses the FAT format and the other uses the NTFS format. Windows NT allows you to format logical drives with either FAT16 or NTFS on the same extended partition.

Hard Drive Partitions

Windows NT assigns two different functions to its hard drive partitions (see Figure 13-6). The **system partition**, normally drive C, is the active partition of the hard drive. This is the partition that contains the boot record (often called the DOS boot record). Remember that startup BIOS and then the master boot program in the boot sector look to this boot record for the boot program as the first step in turning the PC over to an OS. The other partition, called the **boot partition**, is the partition where the Windows NT operating system is stored. The system partition and the boot partition can be the same partition, or they can be separate partitions. Both can be formatted with either the FAT16 or NTFS. However, only Windows NT can read files formatted with NTFS. If you want another OS to access this hard drive, you must use the FAT16 file system for the partition that another OS accesses.

Recall that Windows 9x, using Fdisk, can create two partitions, a primary and extended partition. The primary partition contains drive C and the extended partition can contain several volumes or logical drives. Also recall that each FAT16 volume can be no larger than 2 GB. Using Windows NT, you can have up to four partitions. The first partition is the primary and can have only a single drive C. One of the other three partitions can be an extended partition, which means it can have several volumes or logical drives. Because of the way Windows NT uses the FAT, each FAT16 volume can be up to 4 GB. The third and fourth partitions in Windows NT can each have a single volume.

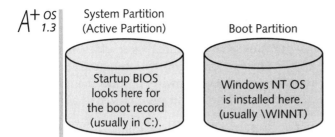

Figure 13-6   Two types of hard drive partitions

> **TIP** Don't be confused by the terminology here. It is really true that, according to Windows NT terminology, the Windows NT OS is on the boot partition, and the boot record is on the system partition, even though that might sound backward. The PC boots from the system partition and loads the Windows NT operating system from the boot partition.

The Dual Boot

Remember that Windows NT can coexist on the same PC with either Windows 9x or DOS. The ability to boot from either Windows NT or another OS, such as Windows 9x or DOS, is called a **dual boot**. In a dual boot arrangement, the system partition must be FAT rather than NTFS, so that the non-NT OS (Windows 9x or DOS) can read it.

> **TIP** Windows NT cannot access a FAT32 drive without third-party software. If you are using Windows 98 with FAT32 and want to create a dual boot with Windows NT, you must first convert to FAT16 or use third-party software to manage the Windows NT and FAT32 interface. To convert from FAT32 to FAT16, use a utility such as Partition Magic.

13

Windows NT resides on the boot partition, which can also be formatted for the FAT16 file system and can share the same partition with the other OS or reside on a second partition, such as drive D. You can format this second partition with either FAT or NTFS. If drive D is NTFS, Windows 9x cannot read any data stored on that drive. If drive D is a FAT16 partition, either OS can read data from either drive.

After both operating systems are installed, a startup menu appears, asking which OS to boot (similar to the menu provided when Windows 9x and DOS are on the same PC). The disadvantage of a dual boot is that applications software cannot be easily shared between the two OSs.

THE WINDOWS NT ENVIRONMENT AND ARCHITECTURE

Understanding the Windows NT environment and architecture begins with understanding the goals and objectives of Windows NT. This section begins by examining some of the objectives of Windows NT, which helps explain why Windows NT works the way it does. Following that discussion is an examination of how Windows NT accomplishes these objectives.

The Goals of Windows NT

Windows NT was conceived when IBM and Microsoft collaborated in building OS/2. While IBM took over OS/2, Microsoft redesigned and added to the original, calling the new OS Windows NT. The next evolution of the OS was called Windows 2000. Windows NT and Windows 2000 have many of the same objectives as UNIX and are considered the primary competitors to UNIX in the client/server industry. Because Windows NT and Windows 2000 also function on a LAN, they are considered competitors of NetWare software by Novell, which is popular for managing LANs. Finally, Windows NT and Windows 2000 compete for some of the standalone PC market, contending with Windows 9x. In this discussion about the goals of Windows NT, the information given also applies to Windows 2000. For an OS to contend for so many markets, its objectives must, by nature, be many, including the following:

- **Room to grow.** Windows NT is designed for expandability, so it can more easily accommodate new hardware and software. The main way that NT does this is by using a modular approach to performing tasks. For example, remember that one way DOS is limited in allowing an application more memory addresses is that real-mode DOS drivers can access memory addresses directly without going through DOS, and thereby can "box in" an application in the first 640K of memory addresses. (Remember from Chapter 4 that memory beginning just above 640K cannot be allocated to applications.) With Windows NT, this "boxing in" can't happen. Applications are required to pass their requests to NT, which processes them. Because of this layer of protection between software and hardware, when hardware requirements change, Windows NT manages the change; the application is insulated from the change. (However, a disadvantage to this approach is that Windows NT must have an interface to all new device drivers before any application operating under Windows NT can use a new device.)

- **Portability to different platforms.** Because of the Windows NT modular approach, it easily ports to different platforms or hardware configurations, including different CPU technologies. Remember that the Windows NT installation CD-ROM comes with three directories ready to accommodate three different CPU technologies. Windows NT can do this by isolating parts of the OS from other parts in a modular fashion. The part of the OS that interacts with the hardware is the HAL, which is available in different versions, each designed to address the specifics of a particular CPU technology. The HAL is the only part of the OS that has to change when platforms change. The other components of the OS need not be changed when the platform changes.

- **Compatibility with other OSs and legacy software.** Because Windows NT had its beginnings in OS/2, Microsoft is committed to Windows NT being compatible with software written for OS/2. As long as DOS applications don't attempt to access resources directly, they too can run under Windows NT. Windows 3.x 16-bit applications can run under Windows NT in a virtual machine environment similar to a Windows 9x virtual machine (discussed at greater length below). Windows NT also supports **POSIX (Portable OS Interface)** based on UNIX, a set of standards adopted by the federal government to better ensure that operating systems and software can port more easily from one platform to another.

- **Security.** Windows NT provides security similar to that on UNIX systems, which is greater than that found in Windows 9x. Windows NT security allows for: (1) the requirement that a user have a logon ID and password to gain access to the PC, (2) security between users on the same PC, so that one user can block another user from data or software, (3) auditing trails to identify security breaches, and (4) memory protection between different applications loaded at the same time.

- **Performance and Reliability.** Although no OS is faultproof, Windows NT provides a much more stable environment than do many OSs, including Windows 9x. Windows NT is less likely to hang, or "lock up," than are other PC OSs. If an application stalls, other applications also loaded are less likely to be affected. When using powerful workstations, Windows NT outperforms Windows 3.x and Windows 9x when running applications written for Windows NT, Windows 3.x, Windows 9x, and DOS.

The Modular Concept of Windows NT

13

Here's an analogy to help you understand the modular concept of Windows NT. The idea is to isolate one process from another so that a change in one process has the least possible effect on the other processes. Consider the self-serve restaurant in Figure 13-7. In the process illustrated in Figure 13-7a, customers arrive for breakfast, walk to the back of the restaurant, tell the cook what they want, wait for him to cook it, take it back to a table, and eat. Customers are responsible for getting their own drinks, silverware, etc. What is the flaw in this design? There are many, but concentrate on only one at this time. Suppose someone in the kitchen moves the silverware or installs a new and different drink-dispensing machine. How many people must learn a new process so the system can continue to work? Every customer. This process is nonmodular and clearly does not minimize the effect that a change in one part of the process has on other parts of the process.

Figure 13-7a   In a nonmodular restaurant model, every customer is responsible for many of the steps in the process

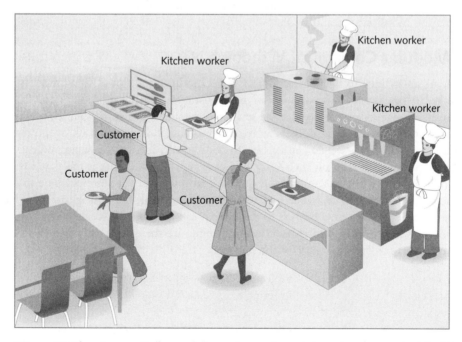

Figure 13-7b   In a partially modular restaurant model, customers are isolated from some processes

Figure 13-7c   In a highly modular restaurant model, employees are grouped by function, and customers interact only with one group of employees. Employee groups are analogous to different parts of the Windows NT operating system

Now consider Figure 13-7b. A counter has been added, and customers are not allowed behind this counter. They come to the counter and tell others in the kitchen what they want to eat, and someone in the kitchen brings the food, drink, and silverware to them at the counter. Things work a little better now. When processes change in the kitchen, only employees who work in the kitchen must be retrained. However, there is still a flaw in the efficiency of this design. Every kitchen worker must know how to cook and make drinks and where the silverware is located. This model introduces some benefits of a modular design, but still has flaws.

Figure 13-7c further refines the process, and our restaurant is now a full-service, highly modular affair. Employees are divided into four groups, each with a different function. The first and second groups of employees—the hosts and hostesses, waiters and waitresses—interact with the customers, greeting them at the door, showing them their seats, taking orders, and serving food. The second group (the waiters and waitresses) also serves as an interface between customers and counter workers. The third group (the counter workers) stands between the kitchen counter and the customer counter, where the drink machines and the silverware are located. The waiters and waitresses pass food requests to the counter workers, who pass the requests to the fourth group, the kitchen workers, who now only prepare the food. When the food is passed back to the counter workers, these workers gather up drinks, silverware, and food and pass them on to the waiters and waitresses, who serve the customers. This model uses a more modular arrangement that provides the benefits of separating processes from each other, even though the overhead (the additional resources needed to implement the new model) is higher than in the other models.

What are the advantages of the last model? If the drink machine is upgraded, only the counter workers must be retrained. If the oven or stove in the kitchen is replaced with an altogether new electronic unit, only the kitchen workers change their methods. The counter workers are unaffected. The waiters and waitresses don't need to know how to communicate with the cook, but can focus on customer service. The customer is isolated from the entire process. In comparing Figures 13-7a and 13-7c, on first appearance it looks as though the process has been complicated. There are more workers, and customers now have to wait to be seated. In fact, a new layer of complexity has been added, and two counters are required. However, it turns out that the advantages of the new system outweigh its disadvantages and overhead. Not only can equipment be easily upgraded without having to retrain so many people or reorient customers to the new procedures, but the integrity of the operation is enhanced: because the processes have been separated from each other, they can now be more easily controlled. Standards and procedures can be more easily applied to each segment of the process because fewer people are involved at each step in the operation, which reduces confusion and improves the overall efficiency of the operation. In summary, the three main reasons to use the highly modular model rather than the nonmodular model are:

- To make upgrades of equipment easier (some employees and all customers are unaffected)

- To increase the overall efficiency of the operation (each part of the process involves fewer people than in the other models)

- To better ensure the integrity of processes (standards are more easily enforced)

The process of running the restaurant can be viewed as analogous to the way operating systems run a computer: the modular approach is analogous to the Windows NT OS, and the nonmodular approaches are analogous to earlier OSs. Customers can be viewed as a combination of users and applications software; employees can be viewed as the OS; the stove, drink machine, silverware stand, etc., can be viewed as the hardware; and the cook can be viewed as those parts of the OS that relate directly to hardware, system BIOS, and device drivers. The process illustrated in Figure 13-7a is most analogous to DOS, in which applications were allowed "behind the counter" to interact directly with BIOS and device drivers, and even to perform some of their own operations with hardware, rather than necessarily turning to the OS to perform hardware operations. For example, in DOS, an application program written to address specific hardware configurations might depend on video BIOS always being found at certain memory addresses, and the program could access that BIOS directly.

The process illustrated in Figure 13-7b is most analogous to a model of the Windows 9x OS, because the customers (the applications) are isolated from some of the interaction with the equipment (hardware), but not all. Notice, for instance, that the silverware stand is still available for customer use; similarly, in Windows 9x, a 16-bit program can interact directly with video memory and other resources.

A+ OS
  1.1

The process illustrated in Figure 13-7c is most analogous to the Windows NT OS, which includes an additional layer between the applications (customers) and hardware (the restaurant equipment); applications (customers) are almost completely isolated from interaction with hardware (restaurant equipment). In fact, the Windows NT architecture is divided into two core components called user mode and kernel mode. **User mode** is a nonprivileged processor mode in which programs have only limited access to system information and can only access hardware through other OS services. **Kernel mode** is a privileged processor mode in which programs have extensive access to system information and hardware.

In the Windows NT analogy, the customers represent users and applications. The user mode includes the hosts and waiters, who represent the different subsystems within user mode (see Figure 13-8). The kernel mode is a combination of the counter workers and the kitchen workers. It is made up of two main parts: the HAL (the kitchen workers) and a part called **executive services** (the counter workers). Applications in user mode have no access to hardware resources. In kernel mode, executive services have limited access to hardware resources, but the HAL primarily interacts with hardware.

Figure 13-8   User mode and kernel mode in Windows NT and how they relate to users, applications software, and hardware

Windows NT was designed to easily port to different hardware platforms. Because only the kernel mode is actually interacting with hardware, it is the only part that needs to be changed when Windows NT moves from one hardware platform to another. For instance, if a major piece of hardware changes (in the restaurant analogy, a new stove in the kitchen), only the HAL must change. Minor hardware changes might cause changes in executive services. When hardware changes are made, the user mode requires little or no change. When

A+ OS
1.1

hardware improves, even though applications have these new resources available to them, they are not responsible for knowing how to interface with them.

Limiting access to the hardware mainly to the HAL increases system integrity because more control is possible. With this isolation, an application cannot cause a system to hang by making illegal demands on hardware. Overall performance is increased because the HAL and executive services can operate independently of the slower, less efficient applications using them.

On the other hand, it is easy to see why Windows NT requires a much more robust system than does Windows 9x or DOS. The increased overhead of this OS only benefits you when hardware and applications software are hefty enough to take advantage of the more powerful OS.

User Mode

In the restaurant analogy in Figure 13-7c, the purpose of the hosts and waiters is to interact with the customers. The purpose of the user mode is to interface with the user and with applications; what you view when running Windows NT is primarily running in user mode. User mode is divided into different modules called **subsystems**. There are two kinds of user mode subsystems, which are defined by their functions. **Environment subsystems** provide an environment for an application to run in; consider an environment subsystem a virtual machine, because it provides a total and complete environment for an application, and, in effect, places the application in "its own little world." One example of a program that is part of the environment subsystem is Explorer. The second group of subsystems is the **integral subsystems**, which are used to provide services to the rest of the system. An example is the security subsystem serving other subsystems by handling the security for files and folders. The Windows NT logon screen belongs to this security subsystem.

In Figure 13-8, note the Win32 subsystem, an environment subsystem, which is probably the most important user mode subsystem because it manages all 32-bit programs and provides the user interface (for example, Explorer). (Remember from Chapter 12 that 32-bit programs are programs written for protected mode using 32-bit code.) The Win32 security subsystem is an integral subsystem and provides logon to the system and other security functions, including privileges for file access. Other subsystems might or might not be running.

All environment subsystems must relate to the executive services by way of the Win32 subsystem, which is itself an environment subsystem. Figure 13-9 shows how various programs that run under Windows NT interact with subsystems. For instance, each DOS application resides in its own **NT virtual DOS machine (NTVDM)**, an environment where a DOS application can only interface with this one subsystem, and cannot relate to anything outside the system. All the 16-bit Windows 3.x applications reside in one NTVDM called a **Win 16 on Win 32 (WOW)** environment. Within the WOW, these 16-bit applications can communicate with one another, and they can communicate with the WOW, but that's as far as their world goes. Because Windows 3.x is itself a DOS application, it must reside in an NTVDM. Figure 13-9 shows three 16-bit Windows 3.x applications residing in a WOW that resides in one NTVDM. Because DOS applications expect to run as the only application on a PC, each has its own NTVDM.

$A^{+}_{1.1}$ OS

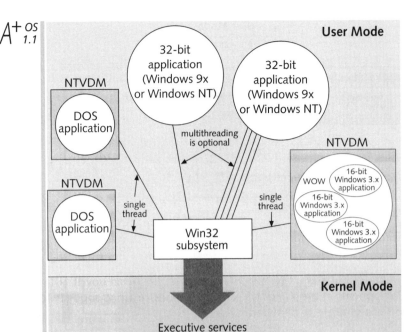

Figure 13-9   Environment subsystems in Windows NT user mode include NTVDMs for DOS and Windows 3.x applications and optional multithreading for 32-bit applications

You can see in Figure 13-9 that 32-bit applications do not require an NTVDM and can relate to the Win32 subsystem directly, because they are written to run in protected mode. The figure shows that 32-bit applications can also use a single line of communication (called single threading) with the Win32 subsystem or can use multiple lines for interfacing (called **multithreading**) with the Win32 subsystem, depending upon what the application requests. An example of multithreading is an application request that the subsystem read a large file from the hard drive while performing a print job at the same time. Single threading happens when the application does not expect both processes to be performed at the same time, but simply passes one request followed by another.

Kernel Mode

Remember that the kernel mode of Windows NT includes executive services and the HAL, which interface more directly with the hardware than does the user mode. Figure 13-10 expands the information from Figure 13-8 to show several of the components of the executive services portion of the kernel mode. Most interaction with the hardware is done by executive services passing the request to the HAL. However, from the diagram, you see that executive services includes device drivers, which have direct access to the hardware.

A+ OS
1.1

Figure 13-10 Components in the Windows NT kernel mode relate to subsystems in user mode and relate to hardware

Only kernel mode components can access hardware. However, in DOS, applications can access hardware resources directly, or they can use an API call to ask DOS to perform the task. In Windows NT, if a DOS application tried to directly access the printer port LPT1, Windows NT would shut down the DOS application. But if the DOS application tried to access the printer by passing a DOS API call to the Windows NT NTVDM, it would be allowed to proceed.

Windows NT Memory Model

An excellent example of how the user mode subsystems, executive services, and the HAL all cooperate and work together is memory management (see Figure 13-11). Windows NT provides memory addresses to an application by way of the WIN32 user mode subsystem. When an application requests the subsystem to write data to some of these assigned addresses, the subsystem turns to the executive services for this service. The component within executive services that manages memory (the virtual memory manager) is responsible for coordinating the interface between the user subsystem and the HAL. This executive service presents the request to the HAL, which is responsible for the actual writing of the data to memory and responds to the executive service when finished. The executive service then reports back to the user subsystem, which, in turn, reports back to the application.

Chapter 4 introduced the Windows NT memory model, which is shown in Figure 13-11. In Figure 13-10, you can see that the virtual memory manager is part of the executive services of the kernel mode. This memory manager interfaces with physical memory in RAM and virtual memory on the hard drive (contained in the Pagefile.sys file) by way of the HAL. Each 32-bit application and NTVDM is assigned its own memory address space, which the virtual memory manager maps onto physical and/or virtual memory. By this method, an application cannot hang the system by storing information in memory that another application or the OS is trying to read, since the application cannot directly access memory.

Figure 13-11   Windows NT memory management

The NT virtual memory manager assigns only one set of memory addresses to each virtual machine, even if more than one application is resident. It is then the job of the resident applications to share the memory. For instance, in Figure 13-9, three 16-bit applications share the same virtual DOS machine inside a WOW. Therefore, the virtual memory manager would have all three 16-bit applications in the WOW share what is considered one virtual address space. These 16-bit applications are responsible for managing their memory addresses so that they do not write to each others' memory addresses and cause another application to hang. The 16-bit applications are sharing memory address space so that they can pass information back and forth through these addresses, as when a spreadsheet passes a graph to a word processor. However, if you want a Windows 16-bit application to have full access to all resources in the NTVDM, you can set the application into its own unique NTVDM apart from other 16-bit Windows applications. Doing so isolates the application from other 16-bit applications and means they cannot share information.

Processes and Threads

Windows NT is a multithreaded OS, which allows for powerful programming so that applications can request more than one event from the CPU to be processed at the same time, and, if the system contains more than one CPU, Windows NT can support this true multitasking environment. Understanding processes and threads is important to grasping the full power of Windows NT. Remember from earlier in the book that a program is a file sitting on secondary storage or ROM BIOS that contains a set of instructions to perform one or more functions. A **process** is a program or group of programs that is running, together with the system resources assigned to it, such as memory addresses, environmental variables, and other resources. Also, more than one process can run for the same program at the same time. For example, in Figure 13-9, each NTVDM and each 32-bit application is a process. Three NTVDM processes are running, even though all three originated from a single NTVDM program stored on the hard drive. The NTVDM process that contains the WOW has at least three (actually more) programs sharing one process. A **thread** is a single task that the process requests from the kernel, such as the task of printing a file. An NTVDM process can only manage one thread at a time. It passes one task to the kernel and must wait for its completion before passing another task. A 32-bit application written for either Windows 9x or Windows NT can pass more than one thread to the kernel at the same time (multithreading). For example, the application might have one thread performing a print job while it continues with another thread to read a file. An application must be specifically written to manage multithreading. If a computer system contains more than one CPU, the kernel mode manages the threads in such a way that one thread is passed to one CPU and another thread is passed to the other CPU, which makes for a true multitasking environment.

Here is an excellent comparison between the potential performance of Windows NT and that of Windows 9x. Compare Figure 13-9 to Figure 12-14 of Chapter 12, where the Windows 9x virtual machine concept is presented. In Windows 9x, all 32-bit and 16-bit applications run in a single virtual machine. With Windows NT, a 32-bit application is not only released from having to share resources with other applications in the Windows 9x virtual machine, but also can use multithreading so that it can make simultaneous requests to the CPU. However, although you can see the potential for more robust performance under Windows NT, the advantage is lost unless the hardware can handle these requests for resources. If the hardware is very limited, the overhead of Windows NT actually slows down performance.

Virtual DOS Machine

Remember that a virtual DOS machine isolates an application from the rest of the system by providing the entire DOS-like environment to the application. Because a common challenge that arises when a system is running Windows NT is having to run 16-bit applications in a Windows NT environment, NTVDMs are explained in more detail below. A Windows NT virtual DOS machine is made up of four main components:

- Ntvdm.exe, which emulates a DOS environment

- Ntio.sys, which performs the same function as IO.SYS in DOS

- Ntdos.sys, which performs the same function as MSDOS.SYS in DOS

- An instruction execution unit, which is only required for RISC-based computers, because DOS applications expect to work on an Intel-based CPU

As you can see from the four components listed above, all the basics of DOS are present in an NTVDM.

In order for a WOW to run within an NTVDM, the following components are also running within this one NTVDM process:

- Wowexec.exe, which emulates the Windows 3.x environment

- Wow32.dll, which emulates the DLL layers of Windows 3.x, which enhance 16-bit applications

- Krnl386.exe, User.exe, and Gdi.exe, which emulate the corresponding three core programs in Windows 3.x

When Windows NT is loaded, a single NTVDM starts, which is then ready to run any 16-bit Windows applications that are loaded. One limitation of a WOW is that there is no communication between a 16-bit application running in the WOW and a 32-bit application or process running outside the WOW. It can be a difficult, if not impossible, chore for these two applications to communicate. (For example, if you are using a 32-bit word processor and have a graph on a spreadsheet that is a 16-bit application, the spreadsheet probably cannot pass the graph to the word processor.) Setting up an NTVDM is covered later in this chapter.

Windows NT Networking

A+ OS
4.1

One of the main reasons Windows NT is chosen as an OS is its strong networking features. Remember that there are two versions of Windows NT: Windows NT Workstation and Windows NT Server. In a general PC environment, a workstation is a desktop PC that both accesses a network and works as a standalone PC. In the most general sense, a server is a computer that contains data, software, and security validation files that are shared simultaneously by workstations on the network. A server on the network is generally not also a workstation. Even though it may have a keyboard and monitor connected to it, these are generally only used by a network administrator to administer and monitor the network; the server is solely dedicated to serving the network.

All the functionality offered by Windows NT Workstation is available with Windows NT Server. The primary difference between the two is that Windows NT Server offers the additional functionality of administering and monitoring the network from this centralized location. However, either OS can be configured to work as one node in a workgroup or as one node on a domain. A **workgroup** is a logical group of computers and users that share resources (Figure 13-12), where the control of administration, resources, and security is distributed throughout the network. A Windows NT **domain** is a group of networked computers that share a centralized directory database of user account information and security for the entire set of computers (Figure 13-13).

When a group of computers is connected to share resources, you can configure these computers as a network using the workgroup model (the network is administered from individual PCs in a workgroup), or use the domain model (the network is administered from a centralized location in the domain). Resources including data, software, and printers can be shared using either model.

13

A^+ $^{OS}_{4.1}$

Figure 13-12 A Windows NT workgroup

Figure 13-13 A Windows NT domain

Also, as you learn about workgroups and domains, remember that in either case, the group of computers is a logical group, not a geographical group. A workgroup of computers can be in a single building, or it can include PCs in other cities. Distance makes no difference, as

A+ OS
4.1

long as there is networked connectivity either over phone lines or by other means. PCs are grouped together to share resources—for example, a sales staff might need to share a marketing database, and the accounting staff of a company might need to share a journals database. People in both groups are spread over several cities. Members of the sales staff make up the sales workgroup, and members of the accounting staff make up the accounting workgroup, so each user can share resources within the appropriate group.

When you implement Windows NT Workstation, it is often necessary to set users up in a workgroup with other PCs using Windows NT or Windows 9x and to configure the PCs to be members of a domain controlled by a Windows NT server. Understanding the concepts of workgroups and domains and how they are managed is the first step in learning how to support them.

Using Workgroups and Domains

In a workgroup, every computer has its own directory database of user accounts and security policies. Each computer in a workgroup manages the accounts on that computer for other users and computers that want to access information on it. If you are a member of a workgroup and want to allow another user on another PC to access files on your PC, you must establish an account for that user. The information about that account is kept only on your PC.

A workgroup can be made up of computers that use either Windows NT Workstation or Windows NT Server. However, PCs that have Windows NT Server installed must be configured as standalone units. A workgroup does not require a Windows NT server to be present. Workgroups have no centralized account management or security. Workgroups are generally used for a small group of workstations, and the PC support person usually manages each user account on each PC in the workgroup. A domain is used for a large number of workstations, and security for the domain shifts to a business-wide or enterprise function of a network administrator controlling security from a single console.

In a Windows NT domain, a network administrator manages access to the network through a centralized database. In Figure 13-13, you see the possible different components of a Windows NT domain. Every domain has a **primary domain controller** (**PDC**), which stores and controls a database of (1) user accounts, (2) group accounts, and (3) computer accounts. This database is called the directory database or the **security accounts manager** (**SAM**) database.

The directory database can be updated by an administrator logged on to any workstation or server on the domain by accessing the PDC, but the domain can have only one PDC. One or more read-only backup copies of the directory database can be kept on other computers. Each computer with a backup of the directory database is called a **backup domain controller** (**BDC**). A system can be set up so that whenever the database on the PDC is updated, copies are written to each BDC, which is called replication or automated duplication. In Figure 13-13, there are two BDCs, each keeping a copy of the directory database. BDCs use their copy of the SAM database to authenticate users as they log on, thereby relieving the PDC of the burden of authentication functions. This sharing of functions improves performance in domains with many (more than 1000) workstations. Workstations on the domain

13

are in the lower part of Figure 13-13. A Windows NT network can contain these OSs functioning in these ways: Windows NT Server functioning as a PDC, a BDC, or as a standalone server (a server on the network that has no domain controller functions); Windows NT Workstation functioning as a workstation or as a standalone server, and Windows 9x.

A^+ OS
    4.1

User Accounts

User accounts are used on PCs to control who has access to what programs, files, and other resources on a PC or network. When using DOS and Windows 9x, the only all-encompassing security is a power-on password, which is a function of the ROM BIOS rather than the OS. Windows NT, however, provides an all-encompassing security feature to the PC. To gain access to a computer, a user must have a **user account** on that computer, which, in a workgroup, must be set up on each computer, or, in a domain, can be set up from the centralized domain server. During the Windows NT installation, an **administrator account** is always created. An administrator has rights and permissions to all computer software and hardware resources.

When Windows NT first boots, someone must log on before the OS can be used. You see the logon screen when you press the **Ctrl+Alt+Del** keys together. (Remember that these keystrokes in the DOS and Windows 9x environment are used to soft boot.) To log on, enter a username and password and click **OK**. Windows NT tracks which user is logged on to the system and grants rights and permissions according to the user's group or to specific permissions granted this user by the administrator.

Administering a Network   Besides access to the network, permissions granted to a user and the OS environment that the user has are also controlled by the administrator. An administrator can create user groups and assign restrictions and rights to the entire group that apply to all users. An administrator can also assign individual restrictions and rights to a single user. A **user profile** is a record of information about an authorized user that is used for security and other reasons. It can include the desktop configuration, sound, color, and resources that should be made available to a particular user. The information is kept in a file with a .usr file extension. The administrator can modify a user profile or group profile to control the types of changes a user can make to his or her environment, including the ability to install or configure software or hardware.

In a typical office environment, a single administrator is responsible for maintaining and supporting the hardware and software of many PCs. An administrator usually controls what users can do through user profiles, most commonly giving users just enough rights and permissions to perform their jobs, but not enough to alter hardware or software settings. Thus, users can be denied the ability to set an environmental variable, install a printer, install software, or do any other chores that change the PC software or hardware environment. In many office environments, gone are the days when employees could bring that favorite screensaver or game to work and install it on their PC.

Using Windows NT Server, an administrator can set profiles for an entire network of workstations from his or her PC. The profiles are stored on the server, which can allow users to move from PC to PC with their profiles following them. These users are known to Windows NT as **roaming users**.

Creating a User Account. User accounts are created and managed by the User Manager portion of Windows NT. Follow these directions to set up a new user account.

1. Click **Start**, point to **Programs**, **Administrative Tools**, and then click **User Manager** (see Figure 13-14). The User Manager screen is displayed. The default user accounts, those that NT sets up as part of installation, are an administrator account and one guest account.

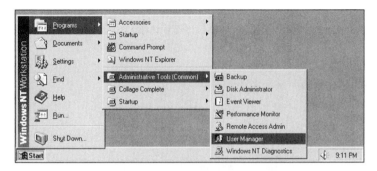

Figure 13-14   The User Manager under Administrative Tools of Windows NT can be used to add a new user

2. To create a new user account, click **User** on the menu bar and then click **New User**. The New User dialog box opens (see Figure 13-15).

Figure 13-15   Use the New User dialog box to provide information about a user

3. Enter the information requested about the user. When logging on, the user will enter the username and password. Notice in Figure 13-15 that the option has been selected that requires the user to change his/her password at the next logon.

4. Click the **Groups** button at the bottom of the dialog box to open the Group Memberships dialog box (see Figure 13-16), showing that in this example the new user JEAN is a member of the Users group, the default choice unless the administrator changes it. The available groups that a user is *not* a member of are listed on the right. The group with the most rights is the Administrators group. The administrator can assign rights to an entire group that apply to all users in that group. Click **OK** to return to the New User dialog box.

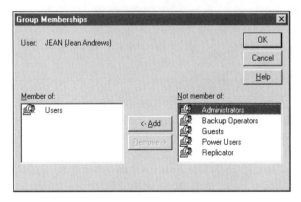

Figure 13-16   Assigning a group membership to a user

5. In the New User dialog box, click the **Dialin** button to open the Dialin Information dialog box (see Figure 13-17).

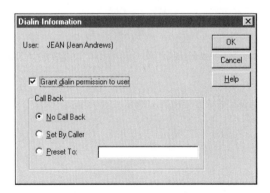

Figure 13-17   Use the Dialin Information dialog box to give a new user permission to dial in to this workstation

6. Check the **Grant dialin permission to user** box to allow the user to access this workstation from a remote PC using a modem.

7. Click **OK** to return to the New User dialog box.

8. In the New User dialog box, click the **Profile** button and enter the path and name of a profile file to apply to this individual user. Then click **OK**.

9. In the New User dialog box, click **OK** to complete the task of adding a new user to the workstation.

To verify that the new account works correctly, log off the system as the administrator and log back on as the new user. To log off, press **Ctrl+Alt+Del**. The Windows NT Security dialog box opens (see Figure 13-18). Click the **Logoff** button. The Windows NT logo screen appears, and no more activity is allowed at this PC until a user logs on. Press **Ctrl+Alt+Del** again to display the logon screen. Enter the new username and password to access the PC under this new user account.

Figure 13-18   Log off the computer using the Windows NT Security dialog box

To demonstrate one way in which Windows NT grants permissions to or withholds permissions from different users, try to establish a new user account different from the JEAN account you just created. From the JEAN account, open the User Manager window again. Click **Start**, point to **Programs**, **Administrative Tools**, and then click **User Manager** to open the window. Click **User** on the menu bar, and then click **New User** (Figure 13-19). Notice that both the New User and Copy options are grayed out on the User menu, because the JEAN account is not allowed to execute these functions. In contrast, the administrator account user menu showed all options in dark type, giving the Administrator access to any of them.

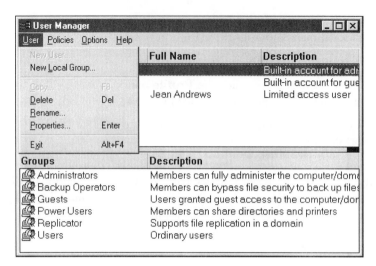

Figure 13-19   Windows NT controls access to options by "graying out" options to users who have not been assigned rights to them

INSTALLING AND CUSTOMIZING WINDOWS NT

This section gives the step-by-step process to install Windows NT. In the following example, we will first examine the system to see if it qualifies for Windows NT and then install the OS.

Preparing for the Installation

Before beginning the installation of Windows NT or upgrading from DOS or Windows 9x to Windows NT, you need to prepare for the installation.

Preparing for Windows NT

To determine if your hardware can support Windows NT, begin by searching the HCL. If a device on your system is not on the HCL, contact the manufacturer for a Windows NT driver. (Remember that if no driver exists, you cannot use the device with Windows NT.) Be sure you have enough hard drive space. Windows NT requires about 120 MB of drive space to install itself, and more if the cluster size is large. A floppy drive and CD-ROM drive are required. For computers without a CD-ROM drive, Windows NT can be installed from a server over a network.

If you are using an Intel-based computer, you can use the **NT Hardware Qualifier (NTHQ)** program found on the Windows NT installation CD-ROM to determine if your system can handle Windows NT. To use Qualifier, boot from a disk onto which you have copied the program, and the utility will examine your system to determine if all hardware present qualifies for NT. Use the following directions to create and use the NT Hardware Qualifier:

Create the NTHQ bootable disk using any computer that has DOS or Windows 9x installed:

1. Insert a bootable disk in drive A.

2. To have Windows NT create the Hardware Qualifier disk, from a DOS prompt or from the Run dialog box of Windows 9x, enter this command substituting the drive letter of your CD-ROM drive:

   `D:\Support\Hqtool\MakeDisk.bat`

3. Using the computer that you want to install Windows NT, boot from the newly created disk. The following message will be displayed on your screen:

   `Preparing NTHQ`

   You can watch as NT tells you it is creating a RAM drive and copying files to it. Next a screen appears informing you that the report the utility generates will take several minutes and will be written to the disk and saved as Nthq.txt.

4. Print the report.

Figure 13-20 contains a portion of a sample report from the NTHQ. Note that the two devices listed at the top were not found in the NTHQ. To determine if these devices will work with Windows NT, check the latest HCL on the Microsoft Web site or contact the manufacturer of each device.

```
Adapter Description: CIRRUS LOGIN PnP V34 MODEM
Adapter Device ID: CIR1000
Listed in Hardware Compatibility List: Not found-check the latest HCL

Adapter Description: OPL3-SAX Sound Board
Adapter Device ID: YMH0024
Listed in Hardware Compatibility List: Not found-check the latest HCL

Adapter Description: S3 Inc. 801/928/964
Listed in Hardware Compatibility List: Yes

Adapter Description: Adaptec AHA-1522
Listed in Hardware Compatibility List: Yes

Adapter Description: Sound Blaster Adapter or compatibles
Listed in Hardware Compatibility List: Yes

Adapter Description: Joystick/game port
Listed in Hardware Compatibility List: Yes
```

13

Figure 13-20   Sample report from the NT Hardware Qualifier

Choosing the Right File System

Remember that when you install Windows NT, you must consider a number of criteria before choosing which of the two available file systems you want, FAT16 or NTFS. If you plan to have a dual boot on your PC with either DOS or Windows 9x, use the FAT16 file system. If you need a high level of security, remember that NTFS offers a higher level of security, including security features unavailable with FAT. If Windows NT is the only OS on the hard drive and security is an issue, then use NTFS. RISC-based computers must use FAT for the active partition.

Step-by-Step Installation

Below is a discussion of how to install Windows NT as the only OS on a system, and as the second OS on a system that already has Windows 9x, creating a dual boot.

Installing Windows NT as the Only OS

Windows NT comes with three disks that contain a simplified version of Windows NT, enough to boot a PC. If the hard drive does not contain an OS, the installation begins by booting from these three disks. After Windows NT has loaded these three disks, it can access the CD-ROM drive, and installation continues from the CD. The program on the CD executed at that point is Winnt.exe. A faster version of Winnt.exe on the CD-ROM named Winnt32.exe also can be used instead of Winnt.exe. Winnt32.exe can be run only after Windows NT has already been installed the first time; it is used to upgrade from an older version of NT to a new version or to reinstall a corrupted version.

The three setup disks can later be used to boot the PC if files on the hard drive become corrupted. You can also create a new set of bootable disks. How to do this is discussed later in the chapter.

Follow these steps to install Windows NT:

1. Insert the Windows NT CD in the CD-ROM drive, insert setup disk 1 into the floppy drive, and boot the PC. You will be asked to insert disk 2.

2. You see a "Welcome to Setup" message. You will be asked to insert disk 3. Press **Enter** to continue. Setup lists the mass storage devices it detected. Press **Enter** to continue.

3. The licensing agreement appears. Scroll to the bottom of the document and press **F8** to indicate your agreement and continue.

4. Setup lists hardware and software components it detected. Press **Enter** to continue.

5. Setup lists existing partitions and space available for creating new partitions. For example, if part of the drive has previously been formatted as drive C with 2047 MB of storage and the other part is still unpartitioned, the following information appears:

```
2442 MB Disk 0 at Id 0 on bus 0 on atapi
C: FAT  2047 MB
Unpartitioned space 394 MB
```

Setup is listing the spaces on the hard drive where it can install the OS, and asking you to make the choice. For this example, highlight **Unpartitioned Space** and press **C** to create a new partition.

6. Setup asks you for the size of the partition, creates it, and informs you it will next format the partition, and prompts you to select a file system for the partition. It then lists the following file systems:

```
Format the partition using the FAT file system
Format the partition using the NTFS file system
```

Select a file system and press **Enter**.

7. After the formatting is completed, Setup asks for this information:

```
Setup installs Windows NT files onto your hard disk.
Choose the location where you want those files to be
installed: \WINNT
```

The default choice is to install Windows NT in the \Winnt directory. Accept the default by pressing **Enter**.

8. Setup now asks for permission to examine the hard drive for corruption. You can either allow it by pressing **Enter** or skip this examination by pressing **Esc**.

9. Setup tells you that it is copying files to the hard drive. After the copying is complete, the following message appears:

```
Press ENTER to restart your computer.
When your computer restarts, Setup will continue.
```

10. Up to this point in the installation, all screens appeared to be DOS-like with little graphic user interface and no use of the mouse. When the PC reboots, you are using a true Windows GUI. The opening screen lists the three steps that Windows NT performs to complete the installation:

```
1) Gathering information about your computer
2) Installing Windows NT networking
3) Finishing Setup
```

The first item in the list is highlighted. Using the mouse, click **Next** to continue the installation.

11. Setup offers four options:

```
* Typical
* Portable
* Compact
* Custom
```

Select **Typical** and click **Next** to continue.

12. Setup requests a name and the name of your organization. Provide them.

13. You are then asked to enter the CD key that identifies the copy of Windows NT being installed. Provide that.

13

14. Setup then requests a computer name. You are told that the name must be 15 characters or less and must be unique for your network. This computer name will later be used to identify this computer on a network. Enter the name and click **Next**.

15. Remember that every Windows NT workstation has an administrator account by default. Setup asks for the password for this account:

    ```
    Administrator Account
    Password:
    Confirm Password:
    ```

    Administrators have full privileges on the workstation. Users have fewer privileges, depending on what the administrator assigns them. If other users who will not have administrator privileges will be using this workstation, or if you are concerned about security at this PC, enter a password. If you are the sole user of this PC and security is not an issue, you do not need to enter a password. Just press **Enter**.

16. Setup gives you the option to create an emergency repair disk (ERD, discussed later in the chapter). Select **Yes** to create the emergency repair disk, and then click **Next** to continue.

17. Setup gives you the option to choose what components to install. Since you can later easily install components not installed during the installation, choose **Install the most common components**.

18. Setup returns to the opening Windows NT setup screen (see Step 11) and continues with Installing Windows NT networking.

19. The choices presented are:

    ```
    Do not connect this computer to a network at this time
    This computer will participate on a network, either:
    Wired to the network (ISDN adapter or network adapter)
    Connected remotely to the network using a modem
    ```

    For this example, choose **Do not connect the computer to a network at this time**, and click **Next** to continue.

20. Setup returns to the opening screen (see Step 11). Click **Finish** to finish Setup. You are asked to select the date and time from the Date/Time Properties sheet. Click **Close**.

21. Setup automatically detects the correct display adapter. You can change any options on the Display Properties sheet and then click **OK**.

22. Setup requests that you insert a blank disk labeled emergency repair disk. Insert a blank disk and click **OK**. Setup creates the repair disk.

23. You are instructed to remove the CD and disk from the drives and restart the PC. The installation is done.

Installing Windows NT as the Second OS on the Hard Drive

Installing Windows NT on a hard drive to create a dual boot begins differently, but is otherwise the same as installing Windows NT as the only OS. The Windows NT installation files are stored in the \I386 directory on the CD-ROM drive. If hard drive space is plentiful, you can copy the contents of the \I386 directory and its subdirectories to the hard drive and perform the installation from there, which is faster because access to the hard drive is faster than access to the CD-ROM drive. If the computer is connected to a network, the contents of the \I386 directory can be copied to the network server, and the Winnt.exe program can be executed from the server to install Windows NT on the PC, if certain conditions exist. (Installations from servers are not covered in this chapter.)

Follow these directions to install Windows NT from the CD-ROM drive as a second OS:

1. Insert the Windows NT installation CD in the drive. If the PC auto-detects the CD, you see the Windows NT opening screen. Click **Windows NT Setup**. If the PC does not auto-detect the CD, click **Start**, **Run** and enter this command in the Run dialog box substituting the drive letter of your CD-ROM drive: **D:\I386\Winnt.exe**.

2. A dialog box appears (Figure 13-21) asking for the location of the installation files. For Intel-based computers, choose the **\I386** directory. Confirm the location of the installation files and press **Enter**. If setup can recognize a formatted hard drive, it copies files from the installation source media (in this example, the CD-ROM drive) to the hard drive.

13

Figure 13-21   The first dialog box of the Windows NT Setup program asking for the location of the installation files

3. Reboot the PC. Then the installation continues as described above beginning with Step 2.

After the installation is complete, when the PC reboots, it detects two OSs, and shows a startup menu (called the **boot loader menu**), giving you the choice between Windows NT Workstation Version 4.0 and Microsoft Windows (Windows 95 or 98). Select **Windows NT Workstation version 4.0**, which then loads.

$A^{+} \frac{OS}{4.1}$ ## Installing a Local or Network Printer

After the Windows NT installation is complete, you can install a printer. Follow these step-by-step directions:

1. Click **Start**, point to **Settings**, and then click **Printers**. The Printers screen opens.

2. Double-click **Add Printer**. The Add Printer Wizard opens, as in Figure 13-22. If this is a local printer operating from the PC's printer port, select **My Computer** and click **Next**.

3. A list of ports is displayed. Select **LPT1**: and click **Next**.

4. A list of manufacturers and printer models is displayed (see Figure 13-23). Select first the manufacturer and then the model from the list. If your printer is not listed, and you have the printer driver for Windows NT on disk or CD-ROM, click **Have Disk**. Drivers designed for Windows 9x might or might not work. If you select a manufacturer and model from the Windows NT list, Windows NT asks for the location of the \I386 directory where driver files are located. Insert the Windows NT CD-ROM and, if necessary, change the path to the files in the dialog box that is displayed.

Figure 13-22   The Add Printer Wizard

 To eliminate the need to have the CD-ROM readily available for installing a device, you can copy the entire contents of the \I386 directory and its subdirectories from the CD to your hard drive or to a server on your network.

A^{+} os
4.1

Add Printer Wizard

Click the manufacturer and model of your printer. If your printer came with an installation disk, click Have Disk. If your printer is not listed, consult your printer documentation for a compatible printer.

Manufacturers:
- Canon
- Citizen
- C-Itoh
- ColorAge
- Compaq
- Dataproducts
- Diconix

Printers:
- Canon Bubble-Jet BJ-10e
- Canon Bubble-Jet BJ-10ex
- Canon Bubble-Jet BJ-10sx
- Canon Bubble-Jet BJ-20
- Canon Bubble-Jet BJ-30
- Canon Bubble-Jet BJ-100
- Canon Bubble-Jet BJ-130

Have Disk...

< Back   Next >   Cancel

Figure 13-23   Select the manufacturer and model of your printer

5. You are asked for the printer name, which will later appear in the list of available printers. Windows NT provides a default name, but you can select your own. Click **Next** to continue.

6. The Add Printer Wizard asks if this printer will be shared with others on a network. If you click Shared, you must enter a printer name unique to the network and the printer is then made available for others on the network. If the printer is to be shared, you have to tell the system what operating systems are on the network that will use the printer. More than one OS can be selected. If the printer is only to be used by your PC, click **Not Shared** and click **Next** to continue.

7. Print a test page. Select **Yes** to print the test page, and then click **Finish** to complete the installation. Close the Printer window.

13

SUPPORTING WINDOWS NT AND APPLICATIONS

Comprehensive coverage of Windows NT administration is beyond the scope of this book, but this chapter does cover a few common procedures that apply to supporting a standalone NT PC using both 16-bit and 32-bit applications. How the boot process works and how to troubleshoot problems during booting is also covered.

The Windows NT Boot Process

Understanding the boot process and making changes to it are critical when supporting Windows NT. (Also, Windows 2000 uses this same boot process.) When an NT PC is first turned on, the boot load menu asks you to select an OS. You can control this menu from the System Properties dialog box of the Control Panel. Click **Start**, point to **Settings**, and then click **Control Panel**. The Control Panel shown in Figure 13-24 allows you to configure Windows NT, add hardware devices and software, and configure the environment for applications.

Figure 13-24   The Windows NT Control Panel

Double-click the **System** icon. The System Properties box opens. Click the **Startup/Shutdown** tab (see Figure 13-25). From the Startup drop-down list, select the OS that you want to start by default. Select the number of seconds you want the system to wait before it chooses the default option. Also from this tab, you can choose what you want the system to do when an error occurs that prevents Windows NT from loading (called a **fatal system error**). You are given the option to "Write an event to the system log" which can later be viewed under the event viewer. When you make changes and click OK, you are told that the system must reboot before the changes take effect.

 If you are having problems booting Windows NT, choose to "Write an event to the system log file" in the System Properties dialog box. Later a Microsoft support person can use this memory dump file to help in diagnosing the boot problem.

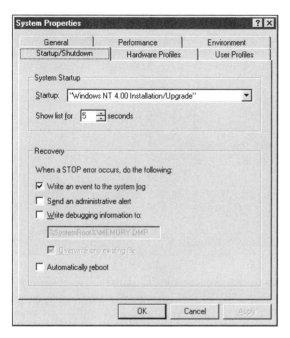

Figure 13-25   System Properties dialog box showing Startup/Shutdown tab

What Happens During the Boot Sequence

The following is a look behind the scenes with a description of each step in the boot process. As you read, refer to Table 13-2 for an outline of the boot sequence for Intel-based computers.

13

Table 13-2   Steps in the Intel-based CPU boot process

Description	Step
POST (power-on self test) is executed.	1. Performed by startup BIOS
MBR (Master Boot Record) is loaded, and the master boot program within the MBR is run. (The master program is at the very beginning of the hard drive, as part of the partition table information. The program searches for and loads the OS boot record of the active partition.)	2. Performed by startup BIOS
Boot sector from active partition is loaded, and program in this boot sector is run.	3. Performed by MBR program
Ntldr (NT Loader) file is loaded and run. (The Ntldr file is the initially executed Windows NT OS file and is similar to Io.sys in DOS and Windows 9x.)	4. Performed by boot sector program
Processor is changed from real mode to flat memory mode, in which 32-bit code can be executed.	5. Performed by Windows NT loader

A+ OS
1.1

Table 13-2 Steps in the Intel-based CPU boot process (continued)

Description	Step
Minifile system drivers (described below) are started so files can be read.	6. Performed by Windows NT loader
Read Boot.ini file and build the boot loader menu described in the file. (This menu is discussed later in the chapter.)	7. Performed by Windows NT loader
If user chooses Windows NT, then run Ntdetect.com to detect hardware present; otherwise, run Bootsect.dos.	8. Performed by Windows NT loader
Ntldr reads information from the Registry about device drivers and loads them. Also loads the Hal.dll and Ntoskrml.exe.	9. Performed by Windows NT loader
Ntldr passes control to Ntoskrml.exe; load is complete.	10. Last step performed by the loader

BIOS executes POST. First, Startup BIOS performs POST, which happens just as it would regardless of the OS present. After POST, BIOS turns to the hard drive to load an OS. Remember from earlier chapters that BIOS looks for the partition information at the beginning of the hard drive.

BIOS executes the MBR program. The first thing in the partition information that BIOS needs is the MBR (Master Boot Record) containing the master boot program. Remember from earlier chapters that the master boot program is the very first thing written in the first sector of a hard drive. The master boot program is followed by the partition table itself, and both are stored in the master boot sector. BIOS executes this master boot program, which examines the partition table, looking for the location of the active partition on the drive, and then turns to the first sector of the active partition to find and load the program in the boot sector of that active partition. So far in the boot process, nothing is different between Windows NT and other OSs.

The MBR program executes the OS boot program. Remember that when DOS or Windows 9x boots, the DOS boot sector contains the name of the initial OS load program, Io.sys. When Windows NT is installed, it edits this boot sector of the active partition, instructing it to load the Windows NT program Ntldr at startup, instead of Io.sys. (It does this even when the PC is configured for a dual boot.)

The boot program executes Ntldr. With the execution of Ntldr, Windows NT then starts its boot sequence. This program is responsible for loading Windows NT and performing several chores to complete the load. It then passes off control to the OS.

Ntldr changes the processor mode and loads a file system. Up to this point, the CPU has been processing in real mode; every program had complete access to system resources. Windows NT does not process in real mode. Ntldr is a 32-bit program and begins by changing the CPU mode from real mode to a 32-bit mode called **32-bit flat memory mode**, in order to run its 32-bit code. Next a temporary, simplified file system called the **minifile system** is started so that Ntldr can read files from either a FAT or an NTFS file system.

A+ OS
1.1

Ntldr reads and loads the boot loader menu. Ntldr then is able to read the Boot.ini file, a hidden text file that contains information needed to build the boot loader menu discussed earlier. The menu is displayed, and the user can make a selection or, after the preset time expires, the default selection is used.

Ntldr uses Ntdetect.com. If Ntldr is to load Windows NT as the OS, Ntldr runs the program Ntdetect.com, which checks the hardware devices present and passes the information back to Ntldr. This information will later be used to update the Windows NT registry concerning the last-known good hardware profile used (the registry is discussed later in the chapter).

Ntldr loads the OS and device drivers. Ntldr then loads Ntoskrnl.exe, Hal.dll, and the System hive. The System hive is a portion of the Windows NT registry that includes hardware information that is now used to load the proper device drivers for the hardware present.

Ntldr passes control to Ntoskrnl.exe. Ntldr then passes control to Ntoskrnl.exe, and the boot sequence is complete.

An operating system other than Windows NT is chosen. If a selection was made from the boot loader menu to load an OS other than Windows NT, such as DOS or Windows 9x, Ntldr does not load Ntdetect.com or complete the remaining chores to load Windows NT, but loads and passes control to the program Bootsect.dos, which is responsible for loading the other OS.

> **TIP** When repairing a corrupted hard drive, a support person often copies files from one PC to another. However, the Bootsect.dos file contains information from the partition table for this particular hard drive and cannot be copied from another PC.

13

The files needed to successfully boot Windows NT are listed in Table 13-3. (In the table, references to *winnt_root* follow Microsoft documentation conventions and mean the name of the directory where Windows NT is stored, which is \Winnt by default.)

Table 13-3   Files needed to successfully boot Windows NT

File	Location
Ntldr	Root directory of the system partition (usually C:\)
Boot.ini	Root directory of the system partition (usually C:\)
Bootsect.dos	Root directory of the system partition (usually C:\)
Ntdetect.com	Root directory of the system partition (usually C:\)
Ntbootdd.sys*	Root directory of the system partition (usually C:\)
Ntoskrnl.exe	*winnt_root*\system32 directory of the boot partition
Hal.dll	*winnt_root*\system32 directory of the boot partition
System	*winnt_root*\system32\config of the boot partition
Device drivers	*winnt_root*\system32\drivers of the boot partition

*Ntbootdd.sys is only used with a SCSI boot device.

Troubleshooting the Boot Process

Windows NT offers several tools and methods to aid in troubleshooting and fixing problems that happen during the boot process. For instance, each time the OS boots and the first logon is made with no errors, the OS saves a copy of the hardware configuration from the registry, which is called the Last Known Good configuration. The next time the PC boots, if an error occurs, it can use the Last Known Good configuration. Windows NT also offers a set of boot disks and an emergency rescue disk. If the emergency rescue disk has been kept up to date, it can be invaluable in solving boot problems. This section discusses how to use all three of these tools in troubleshooting the boot process.

Last Known Good Configuration   The key in the registry that contains the Last Known Good configuration is:

```
HKEY_LOCAL_MACHINE\HARDWARE
```

You can select the Last Known Good configuration from the Windows NT menu that displays when a problem is encountered during the boot process. For example, if you install a new device driver, restart Windows NT, and find that the system hangs, you can use the Last Known Good configuration to revert back to the previous configuration.

Because the configuration information is not saved to the Last Known Good area until after the logon, if you are having trouble with the boot, don't attempt to log on. Doing so will cause the Last Known Good to be replaced by the current configuration, which might have errors.

For example, if you have installed a new video driver and you restart Windows, but the screen is very difficult to read, don't log on. Instead, press the reset button to reboot the PC. When given the choice, select Last Known Good from the startup menu.

To prevent hard drive corruption, if you are having problems booting Windows NT, wait for all disk activity to stop before pressing the reset button or turning off the PC, especially if you are using the FAT file system.

If you accidentally disable a critical device, Windows NT decides to revert to the Last Known Good for you. You are not provided with a menu choice.

Reverting to the Last Known Good causes the loss of any changes made to the hardware configuration since the Last Known Good was saved. Therefore, it is wise to make one change at a time to the hardware configuration and reboot after each change. That way, if problems during booting are encountered, only the most recent change is lost.

 If you are having problems booting in Windows NT, don't log on, because if you do, you will overwrite your previous Last Known Good.

Windows NT Boot Disks   With Windows 9x and DOS, any single disk could be formatted as a boot disk or system disk. Windows NT is different. It requires three disks to hold enough of Windows NT to boot. However, formatting a disk to just hold data or software can be done using Explorer.

A+ OS
3.1

When a disk is formatted by Windows NT, the boot sector is written to boot the Ntldr program instead of Io.sys, as DOS and Windows 9x do. To format a disk, use Windows NT Explorer. Right-click the **3½ Floppy (A:)** line in Explorer and choose **Format** from the shortcut menu. Figure 13-26 is displayed.

Figure 13-26   Windows NT dialog box used to format a disk

The only file system available for a disk is FAT. Note in the figure that there is no option to make the disk a system disk or boot disk. If you try to boot from a disk that has been formatted by Windows NT, this error message displays:

```
BOOT: Couldn't find NTLDR
Please insert another disk
```

Creating boot disks is done by a different method. Remember that Windows NT comes with a set of three disks that are initially used to boot the machine before the installation continues from the CD-ROM. After the OS is installed, you can use these disks in an emergency to boot the OS. These three disks come with Windows NT, but you can make extra sets. The set of boot disks is the same no matter what PC you are using. The disks contain no special information about your system.

If the original three disks to boot Windows NT become corrupted or are lost, you can make extra copies using Winnt32.exe if you are running Windows NT, or using Winnt.exe if you are running another OS, such as DOS or Windows 9x (explained below). You do not have to be working on the PC where you intend to use the disks in order to make them, since the disks don't contain unique information for a PC. Proceed as follows to create boot disks using Windows NT:

   1. Click **Start**, **Run** and enter the path and name of the program with the /OX
      parameters. These parameters say to only create the set of three disks without

13

A+ OS
3.1

performing a complete installation. Note the E:\I386\winnt32.exe/ox entry in the Run dialog box of Figure 13-27. This is the command line from within Windows NT used to create the disks when drive E contains the Windows NT installation CD.

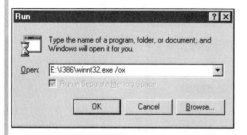

Figure 13-27 Using Winnt32.exe to create a set of boot disks

2. The program asks for the location of the installation files. In this example, enter **E:\I386**. You are then prompted to insert three disks. The program creates the disks beginning with disk 3.

Windows NT does not have a Safe Mode as does Windows 98, so, if the PC later cannot boot Windows NT from the hard drive, these three disks can be used to load Windows NT, which loads using a generic VGA mode. After Windows NT is loaded, use the Emergency Repair Disk to restore critical system files to their state at the time the last update was made to the emergency repair disk.

The Windows NT Emergency Repair Disk A fourth important disk is the Emergency Repair Disk (ERD), which does contain information unique to your OS and hard drive. You are given the opportunity to create the disk during installation. Always create this disk, because it is your record of critical information about your system that can be used to fix a problem with the OS.

The ERD is, in effect, a backup of the Windows NT registry on your hard drive, which contains all the configuration information of Windows NT. In addition, information that is used to build a NTVDM to run DOS applications is also included on the disk. The files on the ERD are listed in Table 13-4. More about each file is covered later in the chapter when the registry is discussed. Files stored on the ERD are also written to the hard drive during the installation process. Using Explorer, you can see the files listed in the \winnt_root\repair folder.

After the installation, you can create a new ERD or update the current one by using the Rdisk.exe utility in the \winnt_root\system32 folder. You should update the disk any time you make any major changes to the system configuration. To use the Rdisk.exe utility, click **Start**, **Run**, and then either click **Browse** or enter the path to the utility. Add the /S option so that the utility also updates the SAM, Default, and Security files of the Registry.

If Windows NT is stored on drive D, the command line is:

```
D:\WINNT\System32\rdisk.exe /s
```

A+ OS
  3.1

Files are first updated to the *winnt_root*\repair directory, and then you are given the opportunity to create a new ERD.

Using the boot disks and ERD to recover from failed boot. If you cannot recover Windows NT from the Last Known Good hardware profile, the next step is to boot from the set of three boot disks that come with the Windows NT CD-ROM or that you made using either Winnt.exe or Winnt32.exe. The Windows NT programs on these disks may also request that you provide the ERD. Insert the first boot disk and reboot. You will be prompted to insert disk 2, followed by disk 3. The Setup menu in Figure 13-28 is then displayed.

Table 13-4   Files on the Emergency Repair Disk

File	Description
Setup.log	A read-only, hidden system file that is used to verify the files installed on a system
System._	A compressed file containing the HKEY_LOCAL_MACHINE\SYSTEM Registry key
Sam._	A compressed file containing the security accounts manager HKEY_LOCAL_MACHINE\SAM Registry key
Security._	A compressed file containing security information from the HKEY_LOCAL_MACHINE\SECURITY Registry key
Software._	A compressed file containing software information from the HKEY_LOCAL_MACHINE\SOFTWARE Registry key
Default._	A compressed copy of the Default hive of the Registry
Config.nt	The Windows NT version of CONFIG.SYS (\winnt_root\Systems32\Config.nt), used for creating a virtual DOS machine (NTVDM)
Autoexec.nt	The Windows NT version of AUTOEXEC.BAT (\winnt_root\Systems32\ Autoexec.nt) used for creating a virtual DOS machine
Ntuser.da_	A compressed copy of \winnt_root\profiles\defaultuser\ntuser.dat

13

```
Windows NT Workstation Setup

Welcome to Setup.
The Setup program for the Microsoft(R) Windows NT(TM) OS version 4.0
prepares Windows NT to run on your computer.

        *To learn more about Windows NT Setup before continuing, press F1
        *To set up Windows NT now, press ENTER
        *To repair a damaged Windows NT version 4.0 installation, press R
        *To quit Setup without installing Windows NT, press F3
```

Figure 13-28   Windows NT Workstation Setup menu

Select the option to repair a damaged installation by pressing **R**. When you press R, the following list of optional tasks is displayed:

```
(X) Inspect registry files
(X) Inspect startup environment
```

A+ OS
3.1

```
(X) Verify Windows NT system files
(X) Inspect boot sector
Continue (perform selected tasks)
```

Table 13-5 summarizes the purpose of each task on the Repair menu.

Table 13-5 The purpose of each task on the repair menu

Repair Menu Option	Description
Inspect registry files	This task prompts you before you replace each registry file stored on the ERD. Any changes to security and SAM are lost, and they revert to the state they were in at system installation. Changes to software and system are restored to the last update made to the ERD.
Inspect startup environment	Inspects the Boot.ini file and edits it so that Windows NT is added as an option if it is not already present
Verify Windows NT system files	Identifies and offers to replace files that have been altered from the original files on the Windows NT CD-ROM. Includes verifying files needed to boot.
Inspect boot sector	Verifies that the boot sector on the active partition has the reference to Ntldr and puts it there if needed. This action can correct the problem caused by someone using the DOS SYS command that changes the boot sector to reference a DOS file instead of Ntldr.

By default, all optional tasks listed above are selected. You can choose not to perform a task by highlighting it and pressing **Enter**, which removes the selection mark, X. After you have selected your options, highlight **Continue** and press **Enter**.

Files are copied from the boot disks, as needed, to repair the startup environment. Some of the options listed above use the ERD. You are asked if you have the disk; if you answer positively, you will be asked to insert the disk. For example, boot sector information used to perform the task "Inspect boot sector" is included in the files on the ERD. Setup asks for the disk and restores the boot sector from the information on the disk.

Table 13-6 lists some error messages that might display during the boot process when critical files are missing or corrupted. In all cases listed in the table, the solution is to boot from the boot disks and provide the CD-ROM or ERD when requested by the setup program.

Table 13-6 Some Windows NT errors at startup

Error Message	Missing or Corrupted File
BOOT: Couldn't find NTLDR. Please insert another disk.	Ntldr
NTDETECT V1.0 Checking Hardware ... NTDETECT failed	Ntdetect.com
Windows NT could not start because the following file is missing or corrupt: \winnt_root\system32\ntoskrnl.exe. Please re-install a copy of the above file	Ntoskrnl.exe
I/O Error accessing boot sector file multi(0) disk (0) rdisk (0) partition (1):\bootsect.dos	Bootsect.dos

Managing Legacy Software in the Windows NT Environment

Even though it would be convenient if all software running under Windows NT were written in the newer 32-bit code used by Windows 9x and Windows NT, this doesn't always happen. As explained in the discussion above, Windows NT makes provisions for running DOS applications by creating a separate NTVDM for each application, so that each program can run in its native environment. Windows 16-bit applications can run in individual NTVDMs, or several 16-bit Windows applications can run in the same NTVDM so they can share resources. How to do this is discussed next.

Customizing an NTVDM for a DOS Application

To prepare to run a DOS application with Windows NT, first create a shortcut to the DOS application. For example, a quick and easy way to place a shortcut on the desktop is to use Explorer. From Explorer, click the name of the executable file and drag it to the desktop. A shortcut is immediately created. You can edit the name of the shortcut on the desktop by clicking inside the name area, which creates an insertion point in the text.

Next edit the properties of the shortcut. Right-click the shortcut icon. You see a shortcut menu, as in Figure 13-29. Select **Properties** from the menu. In the Properties dialog box, click the **Program** tab. Click **Windows NT** to open the Windows NT PIF Settings dialog box (see Figure 13-30). Notice the .nt file extension on the Autoexec and Config files in the *winnt_root*\system32 folder. From this dialog box, you can edit the names and locations of these files. Click **OK** to return to the DOS Properties sheet.

Figure 13-29   Right-click a shortcut icon to see the icon's shortcut menu

Each DOS application can have individual initialization files, but by default, they all use these two, AUTOEXEC.NT and CONFIG.NT. You can edit the contents of these two files and put any DOS command compatible with DOS 5.0 in them. These commands will be executed when the NTVDM is first loaded.

To configure memory for a DOS application to run under Windows NT, click the **Memory** tab (see Figure 13-31). In most cases, you should leave the conventional memory at Auto to allow Windows NT to make the selection.

13

Figure 13-30   Setting the location of initialization files for a DOS application

Figure 13-31   The Memory tab of the DOS Properties dialog box

Customizing an NTVDM for 16-bit Windows Applications

As with customizing Windows NT for DOS applications, the first step in customizing Windows NT for 16-bit Windows applications is to create a shortcut for the application. Then you can right-click the **shortcut** and choose **Properties** from the menu. You see the

Windows Properties dialog box. Select the **Shortcut** tab (see Figure 13-32). To run the application in its own individual NTVDM, check **Run in Separate Memory Space**. If you are running a 16-bit application from the Start menu, as in Figure 13-33, when Windows NT recognizes the application to be a 16-bit Windows application, it makes the check box available so that you can choose to run the application in its own memory address space. The box is grayed out if the application is a 32-bit or DOS application.

Figure 13-32   Properties dialog box for a 16-bit Windows application

Figure 13-33   Windows NT allows a 16-bit application to run in a separate memory space

Why Applications Might Not Work with Windows NT

The following is a list of reasons that applications might not work with Windows NT:

- DOS applications that try to access hardware directly are shut down by Windows NT.

- A 16-bit Windows application that uses virtual device drivers (VxD) will fail because the virtual device drivers attempt to access hardware directly.

- A 32-bit application that was developed on a different hardware platform than the current PC might not run under Windows NT.

- Some OS/2 applications are not compatible with Windows NT.

THE WINDOWS NT REGISTRY

The **Windows NT Registry** is a hierarchical database containing all the hardware, software, device drivers, network protocols, and user configuration information needed by the OS and applications. Many components depend on the registry for information about hardware, software, users, security, and much more. The Windows NT Registry provides a secure and stable location for configuration information about these entities. Table 13-7 lists ways in which some components use the registry.

The registry is a hierarchical database that follows an upside-down tree structure similar to that used by folders and subfolders. In the next section, you will look at how the registry is organized, how to view the contents of the registry, how to back up and recover the registry, and how Windows NT makes changes to the registry.

How the Registry is Organized

When studying how the registry is organized, keep in mind that there are two ways to look at this organization, the physical organization and the logical organization.

Table 13-7   Components that use the Windows NT Registry

Component	Description
Setup programs for devices and applications	Setup programs can record configuration information in the Registry and query the Registry for information needed to install drivers and applications.
User profiles that are maintained and used by the OS	Windows NT maintains a profile for each user that determines the user's environment. User profiles are kept in files, but, when a user logs on, the profile information is written to the Registry, where changes are recorded, and then later written back to the user profile file. The OS uses this profile to control user settings and other configuration information specific to this user.
When Ntldr is loading the OS	During the boot process, Ntdetect.com surveys present hardware devices and records that information in the Registry. Ntldr loads and initializes device drivers using information from the Registry, including the order in which to load them.
Device drivers	Device drivers both read and write configuration information from and to the Registry each time they load. The drivers read hardware configuration information from and to the Registry to determine the proper way to load.

Table 13-7   Components that use the Windows NT Registry (continued)

Component	Description
Hardware profiles	Windows NT can maintain more than one set of hardware configuration information (called a **hardware profile**) for one PC. The data is kept in the Registry. An example of a PC that has more than one hardware profile is a PC that is also a docking station. Two hardware profiles describe the PC, one docked and the other undocked. This information is kept in the Registry.
Application programs	Many application programs read the Registry for information about the location of files the program uses and various other parameters that are stored in .ini files under Windows 3.x and Windows 9x.

Logical Organization of the Registry

Logically, the organization of the Registry looks like a tree with five branches, called keys or subtrees (see Figure 13-34), which are categories of information stored in the registry. Each key is made up of several subkeys that may also have subkeys under them. Subkeys lead to values. Each value has a name and data assigned to it. Data in the registry is always stored in values, the lowest level of the tree.

Figure 13-34   The Windows NT Registry is logically organized in an upside-down tree structure of keys, subkeys, and values

Figure 13-35 shows the Windows NT Registry Editor, the window you see when you first open the editor: the subtree level has five cascading windows, one for each subtree. The first window in the figure shows the HKEY_CURRENT_USER subtree and a list of the subkeys in this subtree. Notice in the figure that some subkeys have plus (+) signs in the icon. A + sign indicates that this subkey has subkeys under it. Later in the chapter you will see how to move down these subkeys to the lowest level of the tree, where the values are stored.

Figure 13-35   The five subtrees of the Windows NT Registry

A+ OS
1.1,
3.2

Physical Organization of the Registry

The physical organization of the registry is quite different from the logical organization. Physically, the registry is stored in five files called **hives**. There is not a one-to-one relationship between the subtrees and these five files, even though there are five of each. Figure 13-36 shows the way the subtrees are stored in hives, summarized as follows:

- HKEY_LOCAL_MACHINE consists of four hives, the SAM hive, the Security hive, the Software hive, and the System hive.

- HKEY_CURRENT_CONFIG data is kept in portions of two hives, the Software hive and the System hive.

- HKEY_CLASSES_ROOT data is kept in a portion of the Software hive.

- HKEY_USERS data is kept in the Default hive.

- HKEY_CURRENT_USER data is kept in a portion of the Default hive.

From Figure 13-36, you can also see that physically, some subtrees use data that is contained in other subtrees. For instance, the HKEY_CURRENT_USER data is a subset of the data in the HKEY_USERS subtree. HKEY_CURRENT_CONFIG and HKEY_CLASSES_ROOT subtrees use data that is contained in the HKEY_LOCAL_MACHINE subtree. However, don't let this physical relationship cloud your view of the logical relationship among these subtrees. Even though data is shared among the different subtrees, logically speaking, none of the five subtrees is considered subordinate to any other.

Figure 13-36   The relationship between Registry subtrees (keys) and hives

The Registry hives are stored in the *winnt_root*\system32\config folder as a group of files (see Figure 13-37). In a physical sense, each hive is a file. Each hive is backed up with a log file and a backup file, which are stored in the *winnt_root*\system32\config folder.

In addition, registry information about each user who has ever logged on to this workstation is permanently stored in a file named Ntuser.dat located in the *winnt_root*\profiles folder. The ..\profiles subfolder has the same name as the username. For example, for the username JEAN, the path and name to the file is:

```
C:\WINNT\Profiles\JEAN\Ntuser.dat
```

The information in this file is the same as that temporarily kept in the HKEY_CURRENT_USER subtree while the user is logged on.

A Closer Look at Subkeys and Values

Now let's go back to the logical organization of the registry. The five subtrees of the registry, displayed in Figure 13-35, are listed in Table 13-8 together with their primary functions. As you can notice from the table, the HKEY_LOCAL_MACHINE subtree is the supporting mainstay key of the registry.

13

Figure 13-37   The registry is stored in the *winnt_root*\\system32\\config folder

Table 13-8   The five subtrees of the Windows NT Registry

Subtree (Main Keys)	Primary Function
HKEY_CURRENT_USER	Contains information about the currently logged-on user. Similar information about each user who has ever logged on to this workstation is also kept in a file called Ntuser.dat in a folder with the same name as the username.
HKEY_CLASSES_ROOT	Contains information about software and the way software is configured. This key points to data stored in HKEY_LOCAL_MACHINE.
HKEY_CURRENT_CONFIG	Contains information about the active hardware configuration, which is extracted from the data stored in the HKEY_LOCAL_MACHINE subkeys called SOFTWARE and SYSTEM.
HKEY_USERS	Contains only two subkeys: information used to build the logon screen and the ID of the currently logged-on user.
HKEY_LOCAL_MACHINE	This key contains all configuration data about the computer, including information about device drivers and devices used at startup. The information in this key does not change when different users are logged on.

A+ OS
1.1,
3.2

Windows NT offers two Registry Editors, each with a slightly different look and feel, although they both accomplish the same thing. They are:

- Regedt32.exe located in the *winnt_root*\\system32 folder, which shows each key in a separate window (recommended by Microsoft)

A+ OS
1.1,
3.2

- Regedit.exe located in the \winnt_root folder, which shows all keys in the same window and has a look and feel similar to Explorer

In the example below, we use Regedt32.exe to view the Registry to get a close look at registry values. Even though the Registry Editors allow you to make changes to the registry, this should only be done as a last resort, and usually only when you are instructed to do so by a network administrator or Microsoft technical support. *Never* make changes to the Registry without first creating a current ERD.

Figure 13-38 shows a view of the registry using Regedt32.exe all the way down to the value level. Double-click the filename in Explorer or use this command from the Start, Run dialog box to access the Registry Editor.

```
\winnt_root\System32\regedt32.exe
```

Figure 13-38   Registry Editor showing subkeys and values

When you don't plan to make changes to the registry, set the editor to read-only mode to avoid making changes unintentionally. For example, follow these directions to view the HKEY_LOCAL_MACHINE portion of the registry as read-only.

1. Select the **Options** menu and check **Read Only Mode** to avoid making changes unintentionally.

2. Reduce to icons all subtree windows except HKEY_LOCAL_MACHINE.

3. Maximize the HKEY_LOCAL_MACHINE window. The HKEY_LOCAL_MACHINE key has five subkeys. The hardware subkey is the only one that does not relate to a hive. This key is built each time Windows NT is loaded, from information gathered during the boot. (As you work with the Registry Editor, double-click a yellow folder on the left side of the screen to expand the folder, and double-click it again to reduce it.)

4. Double-click **Hardware**, then **Description**, then **System**. Figure 13-38 shows the results of this action; you can now see values within the system subkey on the right side of the Registry Editor screen. Each entry of a value includes a name, a data type, and the value itself, which is sometimes called the **configuration parameter**. The value name is listed first, followed by the data type of the value, followed by the value itself.

5. If you need to edit a value, you can do so by double-clicking the value to open the edit box. You can make changes and click **OK** to record the changes. Because you are in read-only mode, if you double-click a value now, a warning will be displayed saying that your changes will not be saved.

6. Exit the editor by clicking on the **Registry** menu and choosing **Exit**.

Backing Up the Registry

Before editing the registry directly using Regedt32.exe or changing it by installing hardware or software, make a backup of the registry. To back up the registry, use Rdisk.exe (discussed earlier in the chapter) to create an ERD, which also makes a copy of the Registry files to the *winnt_root*\repair folder. After you have confirmed that your changes to the registry are functioning correctly, once again make a new ERD so that your registry backup is up to date.

INSTALLING SOFTWARE AND HARDWARE

Hardware and software are installed using the Windows NT Control Panel, which looks like, and works in a similar way to, that of Windows 9x (see Figure 13-24). As both are done, changes are made to the Registry. We next look at examples of each.

Installing Software

Software is installed from the Control Panel using the Add/Remove Programs icon. Installation works very much the same way as under Windows 9x. Access the Control Panel by clicking **Start**, pointing to **Settings**, and clicking **Control Panel**. From the Control Panel, double-click the **Add/Remove Programs** icon. The Add/Remove Programs Properties dialog box opens. Any software that installs with a Setup.exe or Install.exe program can be installed using this dialog box. Click **Install**, and the dialog box requests the location of the setup program.

To add new components to Windows NT that were not installed when Windows NT was originally installed, click the **Windows NT Setup** tab of the Add/Remove Programs Properties dialog box. You see a list of all of the Windows NT components. From this list, you can select to install new components or to uninstall components that are already installed.

Installing Hardware Devices

Windows NT builds its list of available hardware devices each time it is booted. This list is not permanently kept in the registry. However, when a new hardware device is installed, device driver information is kept in the registry. New hardware devices are installed from the Control Panel. The steps below describe the installation of a sound card, because this installation is typical of many hardware devices.

1. To install a sound card, access the **Control Panel** and double-click the **Multimedia** icon. The Multimedia Properties dialog box is displayed.

2. Click the **Devices** tab to see a list of multimedia devices.

3. Select **Audio Devices** and click the **Add** button. The Add dialog box opens. You can either select a device driver from the list or click **Unlisted or Updated Driver** to install your own device driver from disk or CD-ROM.

4. If you choose to install your own driver, click **Unlisted or Updated Driver** and click **OK**. The Install Driver dialog box is displayed, asking for the location of the driver. As the example shown in Figure 13-39 shows, the vendor-provided driver is selected. Several versions of the driver (for each of the OSs supported) are located in directories on the CD-ROM that comes with the sound card.

Figure 13-39   When installing a device driver, you can use a driver provided by Windows NT or one from the device vendor

5. In the example CD, the location for the driver is E:\nt\. Enter the path and click **OK** to continue the installation. If Windows NT already has the driver you are installing, the OS gives you the choice to use the driver provided by the vendor or the Windows NT driver.

6. The driver is copied to the hard drive, and then the hardware setup dialog box is displayed, as seen in Figure 13-40. The suggested I/O address, IRQ, and DMA channel are selected, but you can change these values if you are aware of a conflict. Otherwise, leave the values as suggested and click **OK** to complete the installation.

7. The Windows NT Registry is then updated, and you are asked to restart the PC so the changes to the registry can take effect.

8. Install the CD Player component of Windows NT to use the new sound card. As with many devices, software is necessary to use the sound card. The next step is to double-click the Add/Remove Programs icon of the Control Panel and install

the CD Player component of Windows NT in order to use the sound card to play audio CDs. This installation window works just as with Windows 9x.

Figure 13-40   Windows NT suggests a hardware setup for the new device

This example is typical of many hardware installations. The Control Panel was used to install the device driver, and you saw how Windows NT suggests the hardware setup resources to use. Next time the PC boots, the registry communicates to the Ntldr program to load the sound card device driver. As the driver loads, it looks to the registry for the list of resources that it will use.

The software to use the CD player is also installed from the Control Panel. This information is now kept in the registry to be used each time the OS loads. The OS uses this registry information to provide the CD Player option under Start, Accessories, Multimedia.

WINDOWS NT DIAGNOSTIC TOOLS

Windows NT provides several diagnostic tools to help support users, the OS, and applications, and to help with troubleshooting. Three tools are discussed below: the Task Manager, the Event Viewer, and Windows NT Diagnostics.

The Task Manager

The Task Manager is a tool that was first introduced with Windows NT 4.0 and is included with Windows 98 and Windows 2000. It allows you to monitor processes and applications running on the PC, and to start and stop them. It also displays performance measurements, including processor time, main memory and virtual memory size, and number of threads, to help in diagnosing problems with poor performance. There are three ways to access Task Manager:

right-click the taskbar and select Task Manager from the shortcut menu, press CTRL, ALT and DEL and select Task Manager from the Security window, or press CTRL, SHIFT and ESCAPE. Either way, the utility Taskman.exe is executed. Click the **Applications** tab to display a list of applications currently running. For instance, in Figure 13-41, three applications are running. This window is actively monitoring all tasks as they are started and stopped by other means than the Task Manager. However, you can end a task, switch from one task to another, and start a new task from this tab as well.

Figure 13-41   The Task Manager lists applications currently running

Click the **Processes** tab to see a list of current processes (see Figure 13-42). In the figure, two programs are subordinate to the Ntvdm.exe process, which provides a NTVDM. Capture.exe is a 16-bit, Windows 3.x application that requires a WOW to run in an NTVDM. Wowexec.exe provides the WOW.

From this tab, you can monitor CPU time and memory used by processes, end processes by clicking on End Process, and see, in a visual format, how some programs are related to others within a process.

Click the **Performance** tab to see a graphical representation of how system resources are being used. CPU usage and memory usage are graphed, and other statistics are displayed at the bottom of the sheet. In Figure 13-43, the sudden jump in CPU usage shown in the graph was caused when a print job with graphics (this screen capture) was sent to the printer. Use the Task Manager to end applications that have locked up, to monitor processes and applications that are draining computer resources, and to search for potential problems with memory and the CPU.

Figure 13-42 The Task Manager tracks current processes and how they are using system resources

Figure 13-43 The Task Manager monitors system performance

> **TIP** Another diagnostic tool in the Administrative Tools group that measures component and application performance is Performance Monitor. It can track percent processor time indicating how busy the CPU is, interrupts/second indicating performance of hardware devices, and processor queue length indicating CPU performance.

The Event Viewer

A+ OS
3.1

One of the most important uses of the Event Viewer is to view a log that Windows NT created because of a failed event. Most information can be found here to help resolve the failed event. Access the Event Viewer by clicking **Start**, pointing to **Programs**, **Administrative Tools**, and clicking **Event Viewer** in the menu list. The Event Viewer tracks events as they are performed by the applications, the OS, services, or processes, and by user actions. When an attempted action causes a problem, this event, as well as significant successful events, is recorded in the Event Viewer. In Figure 13-44, a failed event is indicated by a stop sign in front of the event line; the eighth event in the log failed. Near the bottom of the list, a possible future problem with an event is indicated by an exclamation point. Events are marked with the letter "i" to indicate that the event completed successfully. To see the details of an event, double-click the event line in the log. For example, to see a description of the problem for the event that failed, double-click that line. The details for the failed event of Figure 13-44 are shown in Figure 13-45. Using the log Menu in the Event viewer window, you can save the log to a log file, open a previously-saved log file, and clear all events from the current log. (Windows 2000 uses the action menu for these same functions.).

13

Figure 13-44   The Event Viewer tracks failed events and many successful ones

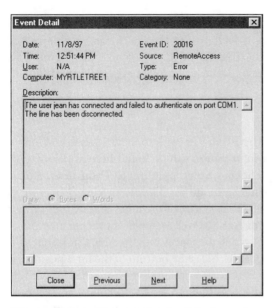

Figure 13-45   The details of a failed event

Windows NT Diagnostic

The Windows NT Diagnostic utility is a graphical view of the Windows NT Registry show-ing hardware and OS data, which can be used to resolve conflicts, diagnose failed hardware, view information about drivers and services that are loaded, and much more. The utility is located in the Administrative Tools group. Click on **Start**, point to **Programs**, **Administrative Tools**, and click **Windows NT Diagnostics**. Information cannot be updated using this utility, but it is a convenient way to view the information. For example, click the **Resources** tab to see a list of different resources. By using the buttons at the bot-tom of this sheet, you can see a list of IRQs (see Figure 13-46), I/O ports, DMA channels, memory, and devices in use. Browsing through the Windows NT Diagnostic tabs allows you to see a thorough overview of the hardware and OS configurations.

Figure 13-46   The Windows NT Diagnostics utility shows information from the registry

CHAPTER SUMMARY

❑ Windows NT comes in two versions, Windows NT Workstation and Windows NT Server.

❑ Both versions can operate on standalone PCs or on a network, but Windows NT Server can also operate as a controller in a network domain.

❑ The next evolution of Windows NT after Version 4 is Windows 2000.

❑ Windows NT does not claim to be fully backward-compatible with legacy hardware and software, as does Windows 9x.

❑ Windows NT requires at least a 486DX Intel-based CPU, 12 MB of RAM, and 120 MB of hard drive space.

❑ Windows NT is written for different CPU technologies. The installation information for three different CPU types is contained on the CD-ROM.

❑ The hardware compatibility list (HCL) is maintained by Microsoft and is a list of devices that, according to Microsoft, are compatible with Windows NT.

❑ Windows NT and Windows 9x have a similar desktop; many functions look and act the same way.

❑ Windows NT can operate using two different file systems: FAT16 and NTFS. NTFS offers more security and power than does FAT16, but FAT16 is backward-compatible with older OSs.

13

❑ A PC can be configured to dual boot between Windows NT and either DOS or Windows 9x.

❑ Windows NT works on different platforms and with different software because of its modular approach to interfacing with both.

❑ The two architectural modes of Windows NT are user mode and kernel mode. Kernel mode is further divided into two components: executive services and the hardware abstraction layer (HAL).

❑ A process is a unique instance of a program running together with the program resources and other programs it may use.

❑ An NTVDM provides a DOS-like environment for DOS and Windows 3.x applications.

❑ Windows 3.x 16-bit applications run in a WOW.

❑ A workgroup is a group of computers and users sharing resources. Each computer maintains a list of users and their rights on that particular PC.

❑ A domain is a group of computers and users that is managed by a centralized controlling database on a computer called the primary domain controller (PDC).

❑ Of all Windows NT accounts, the administrator account has the most privileges and rights and can create new user accounts and assign them rights.

❑ The NT Hardware Qualifier is on the Windows NT CD-ROM and can be used to survey the hardware devices on a PC to determine if they qualify to run under the Windows NT OS.

❑ Four disks are important to recover from a failed Windows NT boot. Three disks are required to boot Windows NT, and an emergency repair disk (ERD) can be prepared to recover critical system files on the hard drive.

❑ The Windows NT Registry is a database containing all the hardware, software, and user configuration information on the PC. The Registry is stored in five files called hives.

❑ Windows NT makes most changes to the Registry when you change the system configuration from the Control Panel.

❑ Three diagnostic utilities included with Windows NT are the Event Viewer, Windows NT Diagnostics, and the Task Manager.

KEY TERMS

32-bit flat memory mode — A protected processing mode used by Windows NT to process programs written in 32-bit code early in the boot process. NT is a full 32-bit OS.

Administrator account — An account that grants to the administrator(s) rights and permissions to all hardware and software resources, such as the right to add, delete, and change accounts and to change hardware configurations.

API (application program interface) — A method used by an application program to call another program to perform a utility task.

Backup domain controller (BDC) — A computer on a network that holds a read-only copy of the SAM (security accounts manager) database.

Boot loader menu — A startup menu that gives the user the choice between Windows NT Workstation Version 4.0 and another OS, such as Windows 98.

Boot partition — The hard drive partition where the Windows NT OS is stored. The system partition and the boot partition may be different partitions.

Configuration parameter — Another name for the value names and values of the Registry; information in the Windows NT Registry.

Domain — A logical group of networked computers, such as those on a college campus, that share a centralized directory database of user account information and security for the entire domain.

Dual boot — The ability to boot using either of two different OSs, such as Windows NT and Windows 98. Note that programs cannot be easily shared between Windows NT and the other OS.

Environment subsystems — A user-mode process in which a subsystem runs an application in its own private memory address space as a virtual machine. (Compare to integral subsystems.)

Event Viewer — A utility that tracks and logs events as they are performed by the applications, processes, or user actions. Accessed by clicking Start, Programs, Administrative Tools, and then selecting Event Viewer.

Executive services — In Windows NT, a subsystem running in kernel mode that interfaces between the user mode and HAL.

Fatal system error — An error that prevents Windows NT from loading. An example is a damaged Registry.

File system — The overall structure that an OS uses to name, store, and organize files on a disk. Examples of files systems are FAT16, FAT32, and NTFS.

Hardware abstraction layer (HAL) — The low-level part of Windows NT, written specifically for each CPU technology, so that only the HAL must change when platform components change.

Hardware compatibility list (HCL) — The list of all computers and peripheral devices that have been tested and are officially supported by Windows NT (see *www.microsoft.com/hcl*).

Hardware profiles — Configuration information about memory, CPU, and OS, for a PC. A PC may have more than one profile. For example, a docking station PC may have two profiles, one with and one without the notebook PC docked.

Hive — A physical segment of the Windows NT Registry that is stored in a file.

Integral subsystems — Processes used to provide services to the rest of the system and the applications the system supports. (Compare to environment subsystems.)

Kernel mode — A Windows NT "privileged" processing mode that has access to hardware components.

Minifile system — A simplified file system that is started so that Ntldr (NT Loader) can read files from either a FAT16 or an NTFS file system.

13

Multithreading — The ability to pass more than one function (thread) to the OS kernel at the same time, such as when one thread is performing a print job while another reads a file.

NT Hardware Qualifier (NTHQ) — A utility found on the NT installation CD-ROM that examines your system to determine if all hardware present qualifies for NT.

Ntldr (NT Loader) — Ntldr is the OS loader used on Intel systems.

NT virtual DOS machine (NTVDM) — An emulated environment in which a 16-bit DOS application or a Windows 3.x application resides within Windows NT with its own memory space or WOW (Win 16 application on a Win 32 platform). (*See* WOW.)

Portable Operating System Interface (POSIX) — A set of standards adopted to allow operating systems (such as UNIX and NT) and their applications to port from one platform to another.

Primary domain controller (PDC) — The computer that controls the directory database of user accounts, group accounts, and computer accounts on a domain.

Process — An executing instance of a program together with the program resources. There can be more than one process running for a program at the same time. One process for a program happens each time the program is loaded into memory or executed.

Roaming users — Users who can move from PC to PC within a network, with their profiles following them.

SAM (security accounts manager) — A portion of the Windows NT Registry that manages the account database that contains accounts, policies, and other pertinent information about the domain.

Subtree — One of five main keys that make up the Windows NT Registry. Examples are HKEY_CURRENT_USER and HKEY_LOCAL_MACHINE.

System partition — The active partition of the hard drive containing the boot record and the specific files required to load Windows NT.

Thread — A single task that is part of a larger task or program.

User account — The information, stored in the SAM database, that defines an NT user, including username, password, memberships, and rights.

User mode — Provides an interface between an application and an OS, and only has access to hardware resources through the code running in kernel mode.

User profile — A personal profile about the user, kept in the NT Registry, which enables the user's desktop settings and other operating parameters to be retained from one session to another.

Windows NT file system (NTFS) — A file system first introduced with Windows NT that provides improved security, disk storage, file compression, and long filenames.

Windows NT Registry — A database containing all configuration information, including the user profile and hardware settings. The NT Registry is not compatible with the Windows 9x Registry.

Workgroup — A logical group of computers and users in which administration, resources, and security are distributed throughout the network, without centralized management or security.

WOW (Win 16 on Win 32) — A group of programs provided by Windows NT to create a virtual DOS environment that emulates a 16-bit Windows environment, protecting the rest of the NT OS from 16-bit applications.

REVIEW QUESTIONS

1. What are the two versions of Windows NT 4.0?
2. Which OS is more backward-compatible, Windows 98 or Windows NT?
3. Why can't a 16-bit device driver work under Windows NT?
4. What layer of Windows NT is responsible for interacting with hardware?
5. What is one reason that interaction with hardware is limited to only one layer of the OS?
6. Before you install Windows NT, how can you determine if all the hardware on your PC is supported by the OS?
7. What is one reason not to upgrade from Windows 98 to Windows NT?
8. What is one reason to upgrade from Windows 98 to Windows NT?
9. What two file systems are supported by Windows NT?
10. If you have Windows 98 installed on a PC using FAT32 and you are creating a dual boot with Windows NT, what must you do first?
11. If you are upgrading a PC from Windows 98 with FAT32 to Windows NT, how will having FAT32 on the hard drive change the results of the upgrade, as opposed to an installation that begins with FAT16?
12. Which is more likely to hang, or lock up, Windows NT or Windows 98?
13. How many bits are used to store a cluster number in the Windows NT NTFS file system?
14. What is the file system that is common to DOS, Windows 9x, and Windows NT?
15. What file system cannot be read by DOS or Windows 9x, but can be used by Windows NT?
16. Which file system can be read by some versions of Windows 9x, but not DOS or Windows NT?
17. Windows NT is installed using a system partition and a boot partition. Which of these partitions must be the active partition of the hard drive?
18. Which part of the Windows NT architecture makes it possible for Windows NT to port to more than one platform?
19. What are the two core components, or modes, of the Windows NT architecture?
20. Which of these two modes contains the NTVDM?
21. Why do 32-bit applications not need to reside in an NTVDM?
22. What is one function of a backup domain controller in a Windows NT domain?
23. In a Windows NT workgroup, where is access to an individual workstation on the network controlled?
24. In a Windows NT domain, where is access to an individual workstation on the network controlled?

13

25. If you are working from home and want to log on to a Windows NT network at your workplace, how do you get access to the network?

26. What is the first Windows NT program that is loaded and run when Windows NT is booted?

27. How many floppy disks are needed in order to boot Windows NT from disk?

28. What is the command to back up the Windows NT Registry to disk?

29. Of the five subtrees of the Windows NT Registry, which one is most important in retaining information about hardware?

30. Which subtrees contain information in the software hive?

31. In what folder is information stored by each user who logs on to the Windows NT workstation?

32. What Windows NT utility do you use to look for information about a failed event?

33. What Windows NT utility do you use to help solve problems with system resource conflicts?

34. A software developer comes to you with a problem. She has been asked to convert software that she has written for Windows 9x to Windows NT. The software consists of two 16-bit programs that work equally well under Windows 3.x and Windows 9x. She was able to convert one of the programs to a 32-bit version, but had to leave the other program in 16-bit code. Both programs run at the same time and share data in memory. However, when she runs the two programs under Windows NT, the 32-bit program cannot read data written to memory by the 16-bit program. Why not? What should she do so that the two programs can work under Windows NT?

PROJECTS

Using the Control Panel

1. Shut down and restart Windows NT and observe the number of seconds that the boot loader program waits until Windows NT is loaded. Key in the number of seconds to wait so that the number of seconds is doubled. Verify that the change is made, by rebooting. When you have verified the change, return the number of seconds to the original value.

2. Check under the Accessories and Games sections of Windows NT and install a new game or accessory. Verify that the program is installed.

3. Change the colors in the Display Properties box and verify the changes.

Troubleshooting the Boot Process

Prepare a copy of the three Windows NT setup disks and an emergency repair disk, and then reproduce one of the errors listed in Table 13-6. Use the disks to recover from the error.

Editing the Windows NT Registry

Be sure you have an updated copy of the three boot disks and the Emergency Repair Disk before editing the registry. Insert a CD-ROM that has autorun and verify that autorun is working. Then make a change to the registry to disable autorun from a CD-ROM by editing this subkey:

HKEY_LOCAL_MACHINE\System\CurrentControlSet\Services\CdRom\Autorun = 0

Use the Internet for Problem Solving

Access the *www.microsoft.com* web site for Windows NT Workstation support. Print one example of a frequently asked question and its answer.

Using the Windows NT Diagnostic Utility

1. Using Windows NT Diagnostics, print out information about memory for your PC.

2. List the IRQs currently not used by your system.

3. List the DMA channels that are currently being used, and explain how each is used.

Windows NT and 16-bit Applications

Try running a DOS utility such as MSD or SANDRA (from Chapter 1) under Windows NT. What error message do you get? Why?

Using the Internet for Research

You want to install Windows NT on a PC using a dual boot with Windows 98. The Windows 98 logical drive is using FAT32, and you want Windows NT to be able to access the data files on this logical drive. Using the Internet, look for third-party software that will allow Windows NT to read from and write to FAT32 volumes. Answer these questions:

1. What software allows Windows NT to read FAT32 volumes? How much does it cost? What URL did you use to answer the question?

2. What software allows Windows NT to read from and write to FAT32 volumes? How much does it cost? What URL did you use to answer the question?

13

14

SUPPORTING WINDOWS 2000 PROFESSIONAL

In this chapter, you will learn:

♦ About the different operating systems within the Windows 2000 suite
♦ About the differences and similarities among Windows 98, Windows NT, and Windows 2000 Professional
♦ How to install Windows 2000 Professional
♦ About the Windows 2000 boot process, management tools, and problem-solving tools
♦ How to troubleshoot problems with Windows 2000

Windows 2000 is the culmination of the evolution of Microsoft operating systems from the 16-bit DOS operating system to a true 32-bit, module-oriented operating system complete with desktop functionality, user-friendly Plug and Play installations, and other easy-to-use features. As a personal computer operating system, Windows 2000 is the next generation of Windows NT Workstation. While taking advantage of the user-friendly features of Windows 98, Windows 2000 is founded on the new technology of Windows NT, and is committed to leaving behind the compromises Windows 9x made with legacy hardware and applications software. In addition, Windows 2000 introduces many new features, including a new approach to managing hard drive storage, called dynamic storage. This chapter looks at the similarities and differences among Windows 98 discussed in Chapter 12, Windows NT Workstation discussed in Chapter 13, and Windows 2000. You will learn about Windows 2000, how it manages hardware and software, and how you can support it. Windows 2000 is really a suite of operating systems, each designed for a different size computer and level of computing needs. We first turn our attention to an overview of each operating system before we begin a detailed study of Windows 2000 Professional, the operating system designed for personal computers.

SUITE OF OPERATING SYSTEMS

Windows 2000 is a series of operating systems, each designed for a particular size computer and type of computing needs. Windows 2000 includes four operating systems:

- *Windows 2000 Professional* This OS is designed to ultimately replace both Windows 98 and Windows NT Workstation as a personal computer desktop OS in a business environment. It is an improved version of Windows NT Workstation, using the same kernel approach to hardware and software, and includes all the popular features of Windows 98. Some of the new features include Plug and Play, a Control Panel with an Add/Remove Hardware icon, an improved backup utility, a FAT32 file system, virtual private network support, and improved security features. Windows 2000 Professional works well as an OS for notebook computers, with excellent power management features. The minimum system requirements are 133 MHz Pentium-compatible CPU, 64 MB RAM, and 650 MB hard drive storage. Recommended requirements are 300 MHz Pentium-compatible CPU, 128 MB of RAM, and 2 GB hard drive storage.

- *Windows 2000 Server* This OS is the improved version of Windows NT Server and is designed as a network operating system for low-end servers. Just as with Windows NT Server, Windows 2000 Server can be a domain controller for a network and is a powerful file server and printer-sharing server. It is intended to be used in a small business environment as the network operating system for a small LAN. The minimum system requirements are 133 MHz Pentium-compatible CPU, 256 MB RAM, and 1 GB hard drive storage. Recommended requirements are 400 MHz Pentium-compatible CPU, 256 MB of RAM, and 2 GB hard drive storage.

- *Windows 2000 Advanced Server* This network operating system has the same features as Windows 2000 Server, but is designed to run on more powerful servers. Windows 2000 Advanced Server supports up to eight processors in a single system and up to 8 GB of memory. It is designed to support high volumes of users and complex applications in e-commerce and medium-size business environments. The minimum system requirements are 133 MHz Pentium-compatible CPU, 256 MB RAM, and 1 GB hard drive storage. Recommended requirements depend on how the system is used.

- *Windows 2000 Datacenter Server* This network operating system is another step up from Windows 2000 Advanced Server and is designed to support up to 32 processors and 64 GB of memory. It is intended to be used in large enterprise operations centers such as those needed to support data warehousing, Internet service providers (ISPs), and application service providers (ASPs). The minimum and recommended requirements depend on how the system is used.

Table 14-1 shows the maximum number of CPUs supported in a single system and the maximum amount of memory supported by the four operating systems. Hardware and software must qualify for all the Windows 2000 products just as they must qualify for Windows NT. For hardware, check the Hardware Compatibility List at *www.microsoft.com/hcl*. For software applications, search the list of compatible software applications list at *www.microsoft.com/windows2000/upgrade/compat*.

Table 14-1 Comparing Windows 2000 products

Description	Windows 2000 Professional	Windows 2000 Server	Windows 2000 Advanced Server	Windows 2000 Datacenter Server
Maximum RAM supported	4 GB	4 GB	8 GB	64 GB
Maximum CPUs in one system	2	4	8	32

Microsoft has announced intentions to market a home personal computer version of Windows 2000, which is expected to replace Windows 98 in the personal computer market for low to mid-range systems. The suite of Windows 2000 operating systems will ultimately replace all Windows NT and Windows 9x operating systems.

COMPARING WINDOWS 2000 TO WINDOWS NT AND WINDOWS 98

A+ OS 1.1 This section looks at the differences between Windows 2000 and its predecessor, Windows NT, and also compares Windows 2000 to Windows 98.

Windows 2000 and Windows 98

A+ OS 1.1 Windows 2000 was built on Windows NT and is basically the next evolution of Windows NT with the added user-friendly features of Windows 98. Windows 2000 Professional is probably the best choice of operating systems for the business or corporate desktop computer, and Windows 98 the best choice for home users. Because of the power management improvements Windows 2000 has over Windows 98, Windows 2000 is the best choice for notebook computers. For the business environment, Windows 2000 offers better support for very large hard drives, more security, and better reliability. For home users, Windows 98 works best with games, music, and video, and offers the best support for the most hardware and software products.

Windows 2000 is more reliable than Windows 98. Recall that Windows 98 is a combination 16-bit and 32-bit operating system, but Windows 2000 is a true 32-bit OS. Windows 2000 supports true multithreading and isolates 32-bit applications in different processes so that one bad application cannot hang the entire system. When Windows 2000 installs an application, it keeps separate versions of the application DLLs so that two applications that use a DLL with the same name can coexist on a system. By comparison, Windows 98 allows one application to overwrite the DLL files of another. Drivers and Windows system files under Windows 2000 are protected from being altered by applications and users, which prevents corruption and improves system reliability. By contrast, Windows 98 does not always ask for your permission before allowing an application to alter or overwrite a critical system file. Also, Windows 2000 has some new tools to help application developers build installation disks for their products and troubleshoot application problems. One of these products is Dependency Walker, which is discussed later in the chapter.

14

A+ OS
1.1

Windows 2000 offers better security than previous operating systems. The NTFS file system inherited from Windows NT gives better security. Windows 2000 has its own data encryption system and uses Kerberos (a security standard) to encrypt a user ID and password as the user logs on to the network from a Windows 2000 workstation. None of these features are available under Windows 98.

Although both Windows 2000 and Windows 98 use Plug and Play, the Windows 2000 version is significantly advanced over that of Windows 98. You will learn more about Windows 2000 Plug and Play later in the chapter. Windows 2000 includes a personalized Start menu that only shows the applications used most often so that the menus are not cluttered with applications seldom used. See Figure 14-1. The down arrows indicate that more applications are in the list but are hidden from view. To see these applications, hold your cursor over the menu for a brief moment.

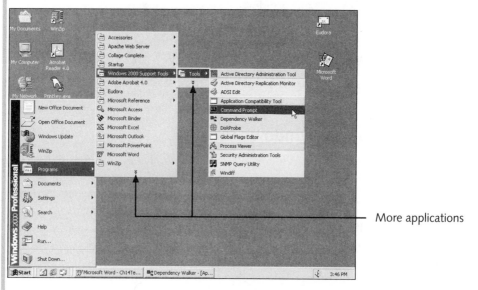

More applications

Figure 14-1   The Windows 2000 personalized Start menu does not initially show applications that are not often used

As with Windows NT, Windows 2000 has an advantage over Windows 98 when deploying the operating system over multiple desktop computers in a corporate or educational setting. Windows 2000 has built-in disk duplication support so that you can copy the OS from one hard drive to another with a minimum of interaction. Also, you can perform unattended installations, meaning you can install the OS to a computer from across a network without interacting with the software. Windows 2000 also has new support tools for troubleshooting problems with the OS.

Windows 2000 and Windows 98 use Advanced Configuration and Power Interface (ACPI), which enables a computer to power down unused devices to conserve power, and gives the user much more control over power to the system. The Windows 2000 features for ACPI are improved over those of Windows 98. Both require the cooperation of ACPI-compliant system BIOS. For example, on a PC with ACPI BIOS, to set the Power Options of Windows 2000,

A+ OS
  1.1

open the **Control Panel** shown in Figure 14-2. Double-click the **Power Options** icon. The Power Options Properties dialog box opens. Click the **Advanced** tab (see Figure 14-3). From the list of power options, select what will happen when you press the power button on your computer case. For example, you can set the computer to change to Standby mode when you press the power button. On the Hibernate tab, you can also control when and how the system goes into hibernation. On the UPS tab, you can control and monitor an intelligent UPS device, if one is attached.

ACPI specifications were developed by Compaq, Intel, Microsoft, Phoenix, and Toshiba to allow for reliable power management through hardware and software cooperation. For more information about ACPI, see *www.teleport.com/~acpi*.

Figure 14-2   Windows 2000 Control Panel

14

Also notice in Figure 14-2 that the Network and Dial-Up Connections and Scheduled Tasks icons are in the Windows 2000 Control Panel rather than in the My Computer window of Windows 98. This is a much more logical place to put them because they control system resources.

TIP   A user might forget their Windows 2000 password. If you have Administrator privileges, you can reset a password using the Users and Passwords icon in Control Panel. Double click on the icon, select a user from the list of users and click Set Password.

A+ OS
1.1

Figure 14-3   Windows 2000 offers several features to control power available from the Power Options icon of Control Panel

Another major change in how windows are accessed to control resources is the window to identify a computer on a network. In Windows 98, to name the computer on a network, you open the Network Properties dialog box and click the **Identification** tab. (Recall that to access the Network Properties window in Windows 98, you right-click the Network Neighborhood icon and select Properties from the shortcut menu.) With Windows 2000, to assign a name to your computer on a network, you use the System Properties dialog box. To access the window, you can right-click the **My Computer** icon on the desktop or you can double-click the **System** icon in Control Panel. The System Properties dialog box opens, as shown in Figure 14-4. Click the **Network Identification** tab to view and change the computer name and to join a workgroup or domain.

Computer names are also different in Windows 2000. Windows 9x and Windows NT assume that a computer is using NetBIOS for applications to access resources on a network and, therefore, assume that this computer name is a NetBIOS name. A NetBIOS name can have up to 15 characters, for example, joesmith. NetBIOS is being replaced by another application programming interface (API) called Windows Sockets (WinSock for short) that uses domain names, the name convention used on the Internet. Windows 2000 assumes that a computer name is a domain name, which uses a hierarchical format such as joesmith.mycompany.com.

Accessing Device Manager is also different under Windows 2000. From the Control Panel, double-click the **System** icon. The System Properties dialog box opens (see Figure 14-5). Click the **Hardware** tab, and then click the **Device Manager** button. The Device Manager window opens (see Figure 14-6). Right-click a device to view its Properties dialog box. Figure 14-6 shows the Properties dialog box for a modem. Each hardware Properties dialog box provides access to the Windows 2000 Troubleshooter for that device.

A+ OS
1.1

Figure 14-4   The Network Identification tab is a part of the System Properties dialog box of Windows 2000

Figure 14-5   Use the Hardware tab of the System Properties dialog box to access Device Manager

14

Figure 14-6   Device Manager and a hardware Properties dialog box

A+ OS
  1.1

The Troubleshooter is more comprehensive than Windows 98 or Windows NT (see Figure 14-7). Use it for suggestions of things to do and try to resolve problems with hardware.

Figure 14-7   Windows 2000 has a comprehensive Troubleshooter

Because Windows 2000 uses NT technology, it does not support 16-bit legacy device drivers, nor does it support all legacy devices or software. If you have a legacy application or device, you might have to use Windows 98. To determine if your hardware and software qualify for Windows 2000, see the Microsoft web site. You will learn more about the process later in the chapter.

Windows 2000, as well as Windows 98 and Windows NT offer user profiles that allow the system to restore user preferences each time a user logs onto the system. A user profile can include software and hardware settings such as how the desktop displays, what shortcuts are on the desktop and what printers or other hardware devices are available for a user. When several users use the same computer, user profiles can be a handy way for each user to keep individual settings. Also, on a network, a roaming profile follows the user from computer to computer on the network. Users profiles can be collected into a group profile so that changes to the group profile affect all users assigned to that group.

Windows 2000 for Notebook Computers

The following features are available for notebook computers using Windows 2000, but are not a part of Windows 98:

- A feature called Offline Files and Folders allows you to download files and folders from a network to the PC so you can work on them offline. When the PC is later connected to the network, the files and folders can be uploaded to the network so that any changes are kept current on the network.

- The technology is included in Windows 2000 to allow a notebook to connect to a virtual private network (VPN) so that a user can work from home and connect to the corporate network over the Internet in a secure connection. To do this, Windows 2000 encrypts data before it is transmitted over the Internet using Point-to-Point Tunneling Protocol (PPTP), Layer Two Tunneling Protocol (L2TP), and Internet Protocol security (IPSec).

- The power management features of Windows 2000 are enhanced and improved over those of Windows 98.

In summary, Windows 2000 Professional is designed as a desktop computer operating system for a large network in a corporate or educational environment. Windows 98 is best used on a PC in a home or on a small network. Finally, for a notebook computer, Windows 2000 is the best choice.

Windows 2000 and Windows NT

A+ OS
1.1,
3.1,
3.2

Windows 2000 is the next upgrade of Windows NT. It contains the same core technology and provides a number of new capabilities. Windows 2000 supports the FAT16, FAT32, and the NTFS file systems. The Windows 2000 registry is organized and edited the same way as the Windows NT registry. Utilities, such as Event Viewer and Dr. Watson, also work the same way with major changes. It provides an encrypted file system for added security and support for virtual private networks. Windows 2000 Help and Troubleshooter utilities are much more comprehensive than the Windows NT or Windows 98 utilities. Windows 2000 supports multiple monitors, IEEE 1394 (FireWire), USB, and ACPI. Network Neighborhood is replaced by My Network Places, which intelligently shows recently visited network resources and lets you assign user-friendly names to these resources. See Figure 14-8.

Recall that Windows NT does not support Plug and Play. Windows 2000 uses an advanced version of Plug and Play that does all the work for configuring a system and does not use the Plug and Play programs in system BIOS.

Another feature new to Windows 2000 is **Active Directory**, a service that allows for a single point of administration for all shared resources on a network. Active Directory can track the location of files; peripheral devices, including printers; scanners, and other hardware; databases; web sites; users; services; and so forth. It uses a locating method similar to that used by the Internet. Windows 2000 Server provides Active Directory, and Windows 2000 Professional acts as an Active Directory client, or user of the directory.

14

Figure 14-8   My Network Places window intelligently shows resources recently visited

Recall from Chapter 13 that a Windows NT client/server network has one primary domain controller and may have one or more backup domain controllers. A Windows NT network can have no more than one primary domain controller, which maintains the only copy of the directory database that can be edited. When the directory database is changed, such as when a new user is added to the network, only the directory database on the primary domain controller is updated. The directory databases on the backup domain controllers are updated by the primary domain controller. With Windows 2000, a network can have any number of domain controllers, each keeping a copy of the directory that can be edited (see Figure 14-9). An administrator can update the directory on any one of these domain controllers, which will then communicate the change to the other domain controllers on the network.

When both Windows NT and Windows 2000 domain controllers are on the same network, conflicts can result because of the differences in the way the domain controllers work. For this reason, Windows 2000 runs in two modes, mixed mode and native mode. **Native mode** is used when no Windows NT domain controllers are present and **mixed mode** is used when there is at least one Windows NT domain controller on the network. Mixed mode is necessary in a situation where a large network is being upgraded from Windows NT to Windows 2000, and some servers have received the upgrade but others have not.

Windows 2000 includes several new diagnostic and recovery tools, including Recovery Console, Safe Mode (similar to Windows 98 Safe Mode), and File Protection (which prevents system files from being corrupted or erased). For backups, Windows NT provides a backup utility to tape only, but Windows 2000 allows backups to tape, Zip drives, recordable CD-ROMs, and external hard drives. Windows 2000 uses the **Internet Printing Protocol** (**IPP**), so users can print directly to a printer's URL anywhere on the Internet. In addition, several other features new to Windows 2000 are designed to support and improve Internet services to users.

Figure 14-9   Windows 2000 allows for multiple domain controllers, each keeping a read/write copy of the domain database

Windows 2000 offers two ways to configure a hard drive: basic disk and dynamic disk. Basic disk is the same as the configuration used with DOS, Windows 9x, and Windows NT. By default, Window 2000 uses basic disk configuration. Dynamic disks don't use partitions or logical drives. Data to configure the disk is stored in a disk management database that resides in the last 1 MB of storage space at the end of a hard drive. Dynamic disks cannot be read by DOS, Windows 9x, or Windows NT.

A dynamic volume is contained within a dynamic disk and is a logical volume similar to a logical drive in a basic disk. It can be used as one of several volumes that makes up a striped volume set. A striped volume is a way of writing data across several hard drives as though they were a single drive. The purpose of striped volumes is to increase the overall size of the storage space, making several hard drives appear as one logical drive to a system. Striped volumes have been around for a long time, but dynamic disks are a new way that Windows 2000 implements these striped volumes and allows for other methods of providing redundancy and very large amounts of hard drive storage.

A+ OS
1.2

Another feature new to Windows 2000 is Encrypting File System (EFS). EFS can only be used with the NTFS file system, and uses a public key encryption method to encrypt files and folders. Public key encryption requires a public key installed on the computer doing the encryption and a private key on the computer decrypting the files. If the files are encrypted and then decrypted on the same computer, it must have both the public and private key. A public or private key is binary data stored in the Windows Registry that belongs to a single user; it's the user's responsibility to protect a key.

To encrypt a folder or file, using Windows Explorer, right-click on the file or folder name and select **Properties** from the shortcut menu. Select the **General** tab and click the **Advanced** button. Select **Encrypt contents to secure data**.

14

INSTALLING WINDOWS 2000 PROFESSIONAL

A+ OS
  2.2

This section looks at installing Windows 2000 on a system with a newly installed hard drive, called a **clean installation**, and also installing Windows 2000 as an upgrade from Windows 9x or Windows NT, called an **upgrade installation**. Also, just as with Windows NT, Windows 2000 can be installed to be dual-booted with another OS. As you read the following instructions, notice the similarities to the installation process for Windows NT Workstation discussed in Chapter 13.

Plan the Installation

Windows 2000 has its roots in Windows NT. Just as with Windows NT, it does not use system BIOS to interface with hardware devices. For that reason, a hardware device must be designed to specifically interact with Windows 2000. Use the Hardware Compatibility List (HCL) to determine if all the hardware devices in your system qualify for Windows 2000. A version of the HCL is on the Windows 2000 CD in the \Support folder. See Figure 14-10. However, the list is constantly being updated. To see the latest version of the list, check the Microsoft web site at *www.microsoft.com/hcl*. Don't assume that because a device is compatible with Windows NT, it will work with Windows 2000. There are some instances in which this is not the case, so check the HCL for Windows 2000 to be sure.

Figure 14-10 Before installing Windows 2000, verify that hardware devices qualify by checking the Hardware Compatibility List (HCL)

Software applications must also qualify for Windows 2000. To verify that all the applications you intend to use on the Windows 2000 PC are certified to work with Windows 2000, search the list of compatible software applications list at *www.microsoft.com/windows2000/upgrade/compat*. If an application is not on the list, it might still work with Windows 2000. You can verify that by checking with the application manufacturer's web site or technical support, or you can just install the application under Windows 2000 and test it yourself.

A+ OS
2.4

To take full advantage of Windows 2000 power management abilities, your system BIOS must be ACPI-compliant. Some BIOS manufacturers offer a BIOS upgrade to make older systems compliant. Most system BIOS made after January, 1999 are compliant. To learn if your BIOS is compliant, if you are upgrading from Windows 98 to Windows 2000, you can check for the ACPI feature under the Windows 98 Device Manager. Look for ACPI, Advanced Configuration and Power Management Interface in the Device Manager list of devices. Because Windows 95 and Windows NT do not support ACPI, it is not listed under these OS installations. You can also check the web site of the BIOS manufacturer or the Microsoft web site.

Microsoft calls a BIOS that is ACPI-compliant a good BIOS and puts it on the Good BIOS list. The Microsoft site allows you to search for ACPI-compatible computers. When you search by model and manufacturer, the Microsoft web site tells you if the system is compatible with Windows 2000 and sometimes provides a link to the BIOS web site where you can download an upgrade to the BIOS. If you are upgrading BIOS, do that before you begin the Windows 2000 installation. If the system is not ACPI-compliant, you can still install Windows 2000 but you cannot use some of the power management features.

For Microsoft links to hardware, software, and BIOS compatibility checks, see this URL:

> *www.microsoft/windows2000/upgrade/compat/default.asp*

Also plan which partition on the hard drive will hold Windows 2000 and what file system you will use on that partition. Windows 2000 supports the FAT16, FAT32, and NTFS file systems. For compatibility with Windows 98, use the FAT32 file system. For compatibility with DOS or Windows 95, use FAT16, and for the most security, use NTFS. If the hard drive is not yet partitioned or formatted, Windows 2000 does that for you during the installation, or you can use FDISK to create partitions before you begin the installation.

Installing Windows 2000 on Networked Computers

If you are installing Windows 2000 on a network PC, consider where the Windows 2000 installation files are stored. You can install the OS from a CD in the computer's CD-ROM drive or you can store the files on a file server on the network and perform the installation from the file server. If you will be doing multiple installations on the network, consider using a file server. Copy all the files from the \i386 folder on the Windows 2000 CD to a folder on the file server and then share that folder on the network. Later, during the installation, when you are ready for the CD, point the setup program to the file server folder instead.

Windows 2000 offers a number of options for installation that can be automated without requiring someone to sit at the computer responding to the questions that setup asks during the installation process. One method is called an **unattended installation** and is performed by storing the answers to installation questions in a text file or script that Windows 2000 calls an **answer file**. A sample answer file is stored on the Windows 2000 CD. If you must perform many installations on computers that have the same Windows 2000 setup, it might be worth your time to develop an answer file to perform unattended installations. How to set up unattended installations is beyond the scope of this chapter.

14

When installing Windows 2000 on a network, just as with other operating systems, you need to know how to configure the computer to access the network. You should know these things before you begin the installation:

- The computer name and workgroup name for a peer-to-peer network
- The user name, user password, and host name for a domain network
- For TCP/IP networks, how the IP address is assigned, either dynamically (gets its IP address from a server when it first connects to the network) or statically (IP address is permanently assigned to the workstation). If the IP addresses are statically assigned, then have the IP address to assign the workstation.

Upgrade or Clean Install

If you are installing Windows 2000 on a new hard drive, then you are doing a clean install, but if Windows 9x or Windows NT is already installed on the hard drive, then you have three choices. You can perform a clean install, overwriting the existing operating system and applications; you can install Windows 2000 in a second partition on the hard drive and create a dual-boot situation; or you can perform an upgrade installation. There are advantages and disadvantages to each. If you perform an upgrade, you must begin the installation while you are in the current OS. Therefore, if you are working from a remote location on the network, you cannot do an upgrade.

Clean Install, Erasing Existing Installations If the hard drive does not have a lot of important data on it or if the data can be backed up, a clean install overwriting the existing installation has some advantages. One advantage is that you get a fresh start. With an upgrade, problems with applications or the OS might follow you into the Windows 2000 load. If you erase everything (format the hard drive), then you are assured that the registry as well as all applications are as clean as possible. The disadvantage is that, after Windows 2000 is installed, you must reinstall applications software on the hard drive and restore the data from backups. If you do a clean install, you can choose to format the hard drive first or simply do a clean install on top of the existing installation. If you don't format the drive, the data will still be on the drive, but the previous operating system settings and applications installations will be lost.

If you decide to do a clean install, verify that you have all the applications software CDs or floppy disks and software documentation. Back up all the data and verify that the backups are good. Then, and only then, format the hard drive or begin the clean install without formatting the drive.

Upgrade the Existing Operating System The advantages of upgrading are that all applications and data are carried forward into the new Windows 2000 environment, most OS settings carry forward, and the installation is faster.

Create a Dual Boot Don't create a dual boot unless you need two operating systems. Windows 2000 does not support a second operating system on the same partition, so you must use at least two partitions on the hard drive. All applications must be installed on each partition to be used by each OS.

A+ OS
1.3

You must decide what file system to use for the Windows 2000 partition: FAT16, FAT32, or NTFS. If you choose to use a dual boot with DOS, use FAT16 for the Windows 2000

A+ OS
    1.3

partition so that DOS can read the partition. For Windows 9x, use either the FAT16 or FAT32 file system, not NTFS, so that Windows 9x can read the Windows 2000 partition.

Windows 2000 uses the latest version of NTFS that was first introduced by Windows NT Server 4.0, NTFS Version 5.0 (NTFS5). NTFS4 is used by Windows NT Workstation 4.0. The NTFS5 version includes numerous enhancements over previous versions, but cannot be read by Windows NT Workstation 4.0 unless Windows NT 4.0 Service Pack 4 is applied. For this reason, if you create a dual boot between Windows 2000 and Windows NT using NTFS for both operating systems, the file system data structures might not be the same, disk utilities such as Chkdsk under Windows NT might not work on the drive, and encrypted files and folders cannot be read by Windows NT. For this reason, using a dual boot between Windows 2000 and Windows NT is not recommended.

We first look at how to do a clean install, and then at how to do an upgrade.

Step-by-Step Instructions for a Clean Installation

The Windows 2000 package comes with documentation and a CD. For United States distributions, the package includes a floppy disk to provide 128-bit data encryption. (This disk is not included in distributions to foreign countries because of laws that prohibit 128-bit data encryption software from leaving the United States.)

If your PC is capable of booting from a CD, then insert the CD and turn on the PC. The Welcome to the Windows 2000 Setup Wizard screen appears. See Figure 14-11. Select **Install a new copy of Windows 2000**, and then click **Next** and proceed to Step 6 below. However, if your PC does not boot from a CD and you have a clean, empty hard drive, then first create a set of Windows 2000 setup disks to boot the PC and to begin the installation process. The remaining installation will be done from the CD.

14

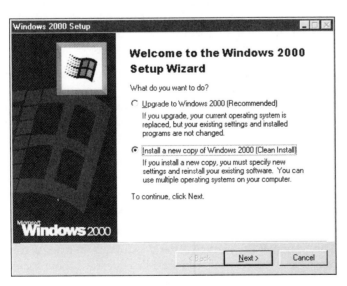

Figure 14-11   Using the Setup Wizard, you can do an upgrade, do a clean install, or create a dual boot

A+ OS
2.2,
2.3

To make the four setup disks, follow these directions:

1. Format four floppy disks.

2. Using a working PC, place the Windows 2000 CD in the CD-ROM drive and a formatted floppy disk in the floppy disk drive. For Windows 9x, click **Start**, **Run** and enter this command in the Run dialog box:

   `D:\bootdisk\makeboot.exe A:`

   (Substitute the drive letter of the CD-ROM drive for D: and the letter of the floppy drive for A: in the command line.)

3. Insert new disks in the drive as requested. Label the disks Windows 2000 Setup Disks 1, 2, 3, and 4.

A+ OS
2.1,
2.2,
2.3

4. Now begin the Windows 2000 installation. Boot the PC from the first setup disk created above. You will be asked to insert each of the four disks in turn and then asked for the Windows 2000 CD.

5. The Windows 2000 license agreement appears. Accept the agreement and then the Welcome screen appears, shown in Figure 14-11. The setup process is now identical to that of booting directly from the CD. Save the four setup floppy disks in case you have future problems with Windows 2000.

6. Windows 2000 searches the hard drive for partitions and asks which partition to use. If the partitions are not created, it creates them for you. You are asked to decide which file system to use. If the hard drive has already been formatted with the FAT16 or FAT32 file system, you are asked if you want to upgrade to the NTFS file system. Be aware that if you convert the file system to NTFS, you cannot revert to FAT16 or FAT32. You can also convert from FAT16 or FAT32 to NTFS after the installation is complete. If the hard drive is already partitioned and contains a partition larger than 2 GB and if you select the FAT file system, then Windows 2000 automatically formats the drive using the FAT32 file system. It puts the entire partition into one logical FAT32 drive.

7. During the installation, you are given the opportunity to change your keyboard settings for different languages, enter your name and company name, and enter the product key found on the CD case. You are also given the opportunity to enter date and time settings and an Administrator password. Be sure to remember the password. If you forget it, the only recourse may be to reinstall Windows 2000.

8. If setup recognizes that you are connected to a network, it provides the Networking Settings window to configure the computer to access the network. If you select Typical settings, then setup automatically configures the OS for your network. After the installation, if the configuration is not correct, you can make changes.

9. At this point in the installation, you are asked to remove the Windows 2000 CD and click **Finish**. The computer then restarts. After Windows 2000 loads, it completes the process of connecting to the network. You are asked questions about the type of network (for example, does the network use a domain or workgroup?). When the configuration is complete, verify that you have access to the network if there is one.

$A+$ *OS*
2.1,
2.2,
2.3

Clean Install When the Hard Drive Has an Operating System Installed

Using Windows 9x, if your PC automatically detects a CD in the CD-ROM drive, follow these directions to do a clean install when another OS is already installed:

1. Insert the Windows 2000 CD in the CD-ROM drive. If your PC detects the CD, a window opens with the message "This CD-ROM contains a newer version of Windows that the one you are presently using. Would you like to upgrade to Windows 2000?" Answer **No**. The Install Windows 2000 window appears (see Figure 14-12).

2. Click **Install Windows 2000**. The Windows Setup Wizard opens, as in Figure 14-11. Select **Install a new copy of Windows 2000 (Clean Install)**. You will be asked to accept the license agreement, which is displayed, enter the product key from the back of the CD case, and given the opportunity to select special options. After a reboot, the installation process continues as described above.

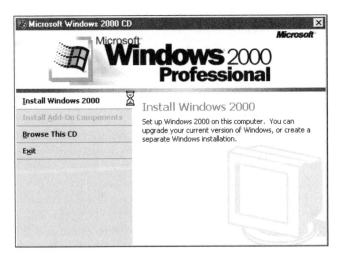

Figure 14-12 Windows 2000 setup window

$A+$ *OS*
2.2,
2.1

If your PC does not automatically recognize a CD, then insert the CD in the CD-ROM drive and do the following:

1. Click **Start**, **Run**. In the Run dialog box, enter the command: **D:\i386\winnt32.exe**. Substitute the drive letter of the CD-ROM drive for D:.

2. The Windows 2000 Setup Wizard appears, as in Figure 14-11. Select **Install a new copy of Windows 2000 (Clean Install)**. The installation process continues as described above.

14

Step-by-Step Instructions for an Upgrade Installation

Recall that devices, device drivers, and applications must all be Windows 2000-compatible for a successful installation. When you are checking applications and devices for compatibility, you might be provided with a fix from the hardware or software manufacturer in order to achieve compatibility. During the upgrade, if Windows 2000 Setup detects a problem, it gives you the opportunity to provide the files for the fix.

To upgrade your operating system from Windows 9x or Windows NT using the Windows 2000 CD, first prepare for the installation by doing the following:

1. Verify that all devices and applications are Windows 2000-compatible.

2. Verify that you have at least 650 MB of free space on your hard drive. (Recall that you also must have at least 64 MB of RAM and a 133 MHz Pentium-compatible CPU.)

3. Using antivirus software, scan memory and your hard drive for viruses.

4. Back up all critical system files and data files. Back up the registry in case you need to backtrack to the current installation. If you have important data on your hard drive, back up the data.

5. Close all applications and disable any virus-scanning software. If the hard drive is compressed, decompress the drive.

A+ OS
2.2

You are now ready to perform the upgrade. Do the following:

1. Insert the Windows 2000 CD in the CD-ROM drive. If your system is set to automatically detect the CD, it runs the setup program and shows a message asking if you want to upgrade your computer to Windows 2000. Answer **Yes**, and the installation process begins. If Windows does not detect the CD, then click **Start**, **Run**, enter **D:\i386\winnt32.exe** in the Run dialog box, and click **OK**. Substitute the drive letter of the CD-ROM drive for D:. On the Welcome to Windows 2000 Setup Wizard Screen, select **Upgrade to Windows 2000 (Recommended)**. Follow the directions on the screen.

2. Windows 2000 Setup performs the upgrade in two major stages: the Report phase and the Setup phase. During the Report phase, Windows 2000 Setup scans the hardware, device drivers, current operating system, and applications for compatibility. Also, in the Report phase, you are given the opportunity to provide third-party DLL files that make a device driver or application Windows 2000-compatible, if Setup recognizes that the device driver or application will not work without the fix. Next, Setup generates a report of its findings. If findings indicate that an unsuccessful installation is likely to happen, you can abandon the installation and perhaps check with hardware and software manufacturers for fixes. In the Report phase, Setup also creates an answer file that it will use during the Setup phase, installs the Windows 2000 boot loader, and copies Windows 2000 installation files to the hard drive.

3. The PC reboots and the Setup phase begins, which has two parts: the Text mode and the GUI mode. In the Text mode, Setup installs a Windows 2000 base in the same folder that the old OS is in, usually C:\Windows for Windows 9x and

$A^+_{2.2}$ ^{OS}

C:\WINNT for Windows NT. This target folder cannot be changed at this point. Setup then moves the Windows registry and profile information to %windir%\setup\temp, which most likely is C:\Windows\setup\temp.

4. The PC reboots again, and the GUI mode of Setup begins. Setup reads information that it saved about the old Windows system and makes appropriate changes to the Windows 2000 registry. It then migrates application DLLs to Windows 2000 and reboots for the last time. The upgrade is now done.

TROUBLESHOOTING PROBLEMS WITH WINDOWS 2000

As with other operating systems, problems can be grouped as those that prevent the operating system from loading properly and those that occur after loading. This section looks at both categories, beginning with problems loading Windows 2000. But first, as you know, the best way to solve a problem is to be prepared before the problem occurs. No problem-solving tool is better than a good backup of critical system files, so we first look at Windows 2000 provisions for backing up critical system files.

Backing Up the System State

Windows 2000 calls the files critical to a successful operating system load the **System State data**. This includes all files necessary to boot the OS, the Windows 2000 registry, and all system files in the %SystemRoot% folder (the folder in which Windows 2000 is installed, most likely C:\WINNT). When you perform a backup of the System State data, you cannot select which of these files you want to back up because Windows 2000 will always back up all of them. Here is the process:

1. Click **Start**, point to **Programs**, **Accessories**, and **System Tools** and then click **Backup**. The Backup dialog box opens. Click the **Backup** tab. See Figure 14-13.

14

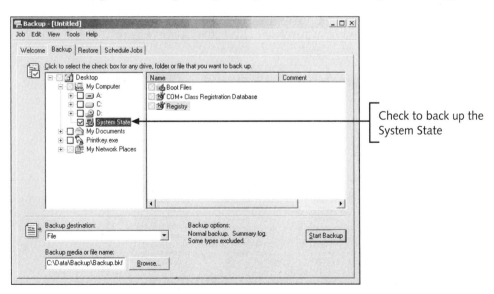

Figure 14-13   Back up the Windows 2000 Registry and all critical system files

2. Check the **System State** box in the list of items you can back up. Notice in Figure 14-13 that the System State includes the boot files and the registry. It also includes the COM+ (Component Object Model) Registration Database, which contains information about applications and includes files in the Windows folders.

3. Select the destination for the backup. You can back up to any media, including a folder on the hard drive, Zip drives, tape drives, or a network drive. Click **Start Backup** to begin the process.

Later, if you have problems with a corrupted Windows 2000 installation, you can click the Restore tab in the Backup window illustrated in Figure 14-13 to restore the system to its state at the last backup.

When you back up the System State, the registry is also backed up to the folder %SystemRoot%\repair\RegBack. If you later have a corrupted registry, you can copy files from this folder to the registry folder, which is %SystemRoot%\System32\Config. You will learn more about this later in the chapter.

We now turn our attention to understanding the boot process and the tools offered by Windows 2000 to solve problems when booting the OS.

Understanding the Boot Process

A+ OS
1.1

The Windows 2000 boot process proceeds just as does the Windows NT process. You can review these steps in Chapter 13. In this section, we look at some of the troubleshooting tools provided by Windows 2000 to solve boot problems.

Just as with Windows NT, Windows 2000 can be installed in two partitions, the system partition and the boot partition. The system partition is the active partition and contains the files necessary to boot Windows 2000 in the root directory. The boot partition contains the main Windows 2000 directory and usually contains the page file, which is used as virtual memory. For personal computers, most likely all files are contained in a single partition, which is both the system and boot partition. This is the case in Figure 14-14, which shows the files in the root directory.

Figure 14-14   Files in the root directory of a Windows 2000 system

A+ OS
  1.1

The steps to booting are:

1. System BIOS performs POST and then turns to the MBR on the hard drive for an OS.

2. The MBR looks to the bootstrap loader program in the boot sector of the active partition. The bootstrap loader program executes ntldr, the Windows 2000 boot loader program.

3. Ntldr reads Boot.ini and provides a boot loader menu for a dual booting system, if so indicated by the entries in Boot.ini.

4. Ntldr executes NTDetect.com to detect and configure the hardware present, reads information from the registry about device drivers, and loads them.

5. Ntldr loads the Windows 2000 kernel, including the Hal.dll and Ntoskrnl.exe files, and passes control to Ntoskrnl.exe, the kernel-controlling module.

Troubleshooting the Boot Process

A+ OS
  3.2

When problems arise with booting, as with all PC problems, try the simple things first. Turn off the power and restart. Check for loose cables, switches not on, stuck keys on the keyboard, a wall outlet switch turned off, and similar easy-to-solve problems. The next step is to determine at what point in the boot process the system fails. Ask what has happened since the last successful boot. Has new hardware or software been installed? Has there been a power surge or electrical storm? Has an inexperienced user tinkered with the system? If you cannot pinpoint the source of the problem, then you have several tools to help you troubleshoot the boot process. Windows 2000 offers an Advanced Options Menu, which includes starting the computer in Safe Mode. Use this option to prevent many device drivers and system services that normally load during the boot process from loading. You can then correct or disable these devices or services once the OS loads. The second utility, called the Recovery Console, is new to Windows 2000. It provides a command-line interface for you to perform maintenance and repairs to the hard drive. Another tool is the Emergency Startup Disk, which is used to recover from problems with corrupted or missing operating system files or a corrupted hard drive boot sector. These three tools are discussed next.

Advanced Options Menu

As a PC boots, when the message, Starting Windows, appears at the bottom of the screen, press the F8 key to display the Windows 2000 **Advanced Options Menu** shown in Figure 14-15. As with the Windows 9x Startup Menu, this menu can be used to diagnose and fix problems when booting Windows 2000. Here is the purpose of each option on the menu:

14

A+ OS
  3.2

```
Windows 2000 Advanced Options Menu
Please select an option:

        Safe Mode
        Safe Mode with Networking
        Safe Mode with Command Prompt

        Enable Boot Logging
        Enable VGA Mode
        Last Known Good Configuration
        Directory Services Restore Mode (Windows 2000 domain controllers only)
        Debugging Mode

        Boot Normally

Use ↑ and ↓ to move the highlight to your choice.
Press Enter to choose.
```

Figure 14-15   Press the F8 key at startup to display the Windows 2000 Advanced Options Menu

A+ OS
  2.3,
  3.1

Safe Mode   Safe Mode boots the OS with a minimum configuration and can be used to solve problems when a new hardware installation is causing problems. Safe Mode boots with the mouse, monitor with basic video, keyboard, and mass storage drivers loaded. It uses the default system services (it does not load any extra services) and does not provide access to a network. When you boot in Safe Mode, you see "Safe Mode" in all four corners of your screen. You have a GUI interface in Safe Mode. Once the OS loads in Safe Mode, you can disable the problem device, scan for viruses, run diagnostic software, or take other appropriate action to diagnose and solve problems. When you load Windows 2000 in Safe Mode, all files used for the load are recorded in the Ntbtlog.txt file.

Safe Mode with Networking   Use this option when you are solving a problem with booting and need access to the network to solve the problem. For example, if you have just attempted to install a printer which is causing the OS to hang when it boots and the printer drivers are downloaded from the network, boot into Safe Mode with Networking. Uninstall the printer and then install it again from the network. Also use this mode when the Windows 2000 installation files are not loaded from CD, but from the network, and you need to access these files.

Safe Mode with Command Prompt   This Safe Mode option does not automatically load a GUI desktop. Use it to get a command prompt. If Safe Mode does not load the OS, then try this option.

Enable Boot Logging   When you boot with this option, Windows 2000 loads normally and you access the regular desktop as usual. However, all the files used during the load process are recorded in a file, Ntbtlog.txt. Use this option to see what did and did not load during the boot process. If you are having a problem getting a device to work, check the file for its driver files. Boot logging is much more effective if you have a copy of the file that was made when everything was working as it should, and then you can compare the good load to the bad load, looking for the differences.

Enable VGA Mode   Use this option when the video setting is such that you can't see well enough to fix a bad setting. This can happen because of a corrupted video driver or when a user has created a desktop with black fonts on a black background, or something similar. Booting in this mode gives you a very plain VGA video. Go to the Display settings, correct the problem, and reboot normally.

Last Known Good Configuration   Just as with Windows NT, Windows 2000 keeps the Last Known Good Configuration in the registry. Use this option if you suspect the system was configured incorrectly. Windows 2000 will be restored to the settings of the last successful boot and all system setting changes made after this last successful boot are lost.

Directory Services Restore Mode (Windows 2000 Domain Controllers Only)   This option only applies to domain controllers and is used as one step in the process of recovering from a corrupted Active Directory domain database. The details of how all this works are beyond the scope of this chapter.

Debugging Mode   This mode gives you the opportunity to move system boot logs from the failing computer to another computer for evaluation. Connect a computer to this computer by way of the serial port. In this mode, Windows 2000 sends all the boot information to the serial port. The details of how to do this can be found in the Windows 2000 Professional Resource Kit by Microsoft.

A^{+} *OS*
3.2

Recovery Console

The Advanced Options menu can help if the problem is with a faulty device driver or system service. However, if the problem goes deeper than that, the next tool to use is the **Recovery Console**. Use it when the operating system does not start properly or hangs during the load. The Recovery Console does not use a GUI, and with it you can access the FAT16, FAT32, and NTFS file systems.

The purpose of the Recovery Console is to allow you to use tools to repair a damaged registry, system files, and file system on the hard drive. You must enter the Administrator password in order to use the Console. If the registry is so corrupted that the Recovery Console cannot read the password in order to validate it, you are not asked for the password but you are limited in what you can do at the Console. You are not allowed into all folders, and you cannot copy files from the hard drive to a floppy disk without setting certain parameters.

The Recovery Console software is on the Windows 2000 CD and also on the four Windows 2000 setup disks. If you have not already created the setup disks, you can go to a working Windows 2000 PC and create the disks by following the directions given earlier in the chapter. Follow these steps to load Windows 2000 from the disks and access the Recovery Console:

1. Insert the first of the four setup disks and restart the PC. You are directed to insert each of the four disks in turn, and then the Setup screen appears as shown in Figure 14-16.

14

Windows 2000 Professional Setup
_____

Welcome to Setup

This portion of the Setup program prepares Microsoft®
Windows 2000 (TM) to run on your computer.

- To set up Windows 2000 now, press ENTER.
- To repair a Windows 2000 installation, press R.
- To quit Setup without installing Windows 2000, press F3.

_____
ENTER=Continue   R=Repair   F3=Quit

Figure 14-16   Use this Windows Setup screen to access the Recovery Console

  2. Type **R** to select the To repair a Windows 2000 installation option. The
     Windows 2000 Repair Options window opens. See Figure 14-17. Type **C** to
     select the Recovery Console.

Windows 2000 Professional Setup
_____

Windows 2000 Repair Options:

- To repair a Windows 2000 installation by using
  the recovery console, press C.

- To repair a Windows 2000 installation by using
  the emergency repair process, press R.

If the repair options do not successfully repair your system,
run Windows 2000 Setup again.

_____
C=Console   R=Repair   F3=Quit

Figure 14-17   Windows 2000 offers two repair options

  3. The Windows 2000 Recovery Console window opens. See Figure 14-18. The
     Recovery Console looked at the hard drive and determined that there was only a
     single Windows 2000 installation on the drive installed in the C:\WINNT folder.
     (The WINNT folder might be on a different drive on your machine.) Press **1**
     and press **Enter** to select that installation.

Microsoft Windows 2000 (TM) Recovery Console.

The Recovery Console provides system repair and recovery functionality.

Type EXIT to quit the Recovery Console and restart the computer.

1: C:\WINNT

Which Windows 2000 installation would you like to log onto
(To cancel, press ENTER)? 1
Type the Administrator password:
C:\WINNT>

Figure 14-18   The Windows 2000 Recovery Console command prompt

4. Enter the Administrator password and press **Enter**. If you don't know the password, you cannot use the console.

You now have a command prompt. You can use a limited group of DOS–like commands at this point to recover a failed system. These commands are listed and described in Table 14-2.

 At the command prompt, to retrieve the last command entered, press the F1 key to retrieve one character at a time.

Table 14-2   Commands available from the Recovery Console

Command	Description
Attrib	Changes the attributes of a file or folder (works the same as the DOS version, as in the following example): `Attrib -r -h -s filename` This command removes the read, hidden, and system attributes from the file.
Batch	Carries out commands stored in a batch file: `Batch file1 file2` The commands stored in file1 are executed and the results written to file2. If no file2 is specified, results are written to screen.
Cd	Displays or changes the current directory
Chkdsk	Checks a disk and repairs or recovers the data
Cls	Clears the screen
Copy	Copies a single file: `Copy File1 File2` You can include paths to either file. No wildcard characters are allowed.
Del	Deletes a file: `Del File1`
Dir	Lists files and folders
Disable	Disables a Windows 2000 system service or driver: `Disable servicename`
Diskpart	Creates and deletes partitions on the hard drive. Enter the command with no arguments to display a user interface.
Enable	Enables a Windows 2000 system service or driver: `Enable servicename`

14

Table 14-2   Commands available from the Recovery Console (continued)

Command	Description
Exit	Quits the Recovery Console and restarts the computer
Expand	Expands a compressed file. For example: `Expand file1`
Fixboot	Rewrites the OS boot sector on the hard drive. If a drive letter is not specified, the system drive is assumed. `Fixboot C:`
Fixmbr	Rewrites the master boot record boot program. This command is the same as FDISK/MBR.
Format	Formats a logical drive. If no file system is specified, NTFS is assumed: `Format C:/fs:FAT32` Uses FAT32 file system `Format C:/fs:FAT` Uses FAT16 file system
Help	Help utility appears for the given command: `Help Fixboot`
Listsvc	Lists all available services
Logon	Allows you to log on to an installation with the Administrator password
Map	Lists all drive letters and file system types
Md or Mkdir	Creates a directory: `MD C:\TEMP`
More or Type	Displays a text file on screen: `TYPE filename.ext`
Rd or Rmdir	Deletes a directory: `RD C:\TEMP`
Rename or Ren	Renames a file: `Rename File1.txt File2.txt`
Set	Displays or sets Recovery Console environmental variables
Systemroot	Sets the current directory to the directory where Windows 2000 is installed

If you suspect that the registry is damaged, you can use these commands to restore the registry from the last backup that you have created in the %SystemRoot%\Repair\RegBack folder. To do so, first rename the registry files so that you can backtrack if necessary. From the Recovery Console command prompt, perform the steps outlined in Table 14-3. These actions will restore the registry to its state at the time of the last backup.

Table 14-3   Steps to restore the registry

Command	Description
1. Systemroot	Makes the Windows folder the current folder
2. CD System32\Config	Makes the Windows registry folder the current folder

3. Ren Default Default.save
   Ren Sam Sam.save
   Ren Security Security.save
   Ren Software Software.save
   Ren System System.save
	Renames the five registry files

4. Systemroot	Returns to the Windows folder

Table 14-3   Steps to restore the registry (continued)

Command	Description
5. CD repair\RegBack	Makes the registry backup folder the current folder
6. Copy default C:\WINNT\system32\config Copy Sam C:\WINNT\system32\config Copy Security C:\WINNT\system32\config Copy Software C:\WINNT\system32\config Copy System C:\WINNT\system32\config	Copies the five registry files from the backup folder to the registry folder

To leave the Recovery Console and start Windows 2000, type **Exit** at the command prompt.

$A^{+OS}_{2.3}$ ## Emergency Repair Process

If options on the Advanced Options menu fail to recover the system and the Recovery Console fails, your next option is the **Emergency Repair Process**. You only want to use this option as a last resort because it restores the system to the state it was in immediately after the Windows 2000 installation. All changes since the installation will be lost. The process uses an Emergency Repair Disk (ERD), but the disk does not contain the same information as does the Windows NT ERD (Windows NT Emergency Repair Disk).

Recall that the Windows NT ERD contains a copy of the registry and that you should update the disk any time you make significant changes to the registry. You can then use the disk to repair a corrupted registry, restoring it to its state when you last updated the ERD.

The Windows 2000 ERD contains information about your current installation, but does not contain a copy of the registry because it is too large to fit on a single floppy disk. Rather the ERD only points to a folder on the hard drive where the registry was backed up when Windows 2000 was installed. This folder is %SystemRoot%\repair, and its contents are shown in Figure 14-19.

14

Figure 14-19   Windows 2000 backs up the registry and system data to %SystemRoot%\repair during the installation process

A+ OS
2.3

Using the ERD to recover from a corrupted registry returns you to the installation version of the registry, and you lose all changes to the registry since that time. Because of the way the ERD works, you do not need to remake the disk once you've created it. Before a problem occurs, follow these directions to create the disk:

1. Click **Start**, point to **Programs**, **Accessories**, and **System Tools**, and then click **Backup**. The Backup window appears with the Welcome tab selected. See Figure 14-20. Select **Emergency Repair Disk**.

2. The Backup tab and the Emergency Repair Diskette dialog box open. See Figure 14-21. If you check the box shown in Figure 14-21, the system backs up your registry to a folder under the Repair folder, %SystemRoot%\repair\RegBack (refer back to Figure 14-19).

3. Click **OK** to create the disk. Label the disk Windows 2000 Emergency Repair Disk, and keep it in a safe place.

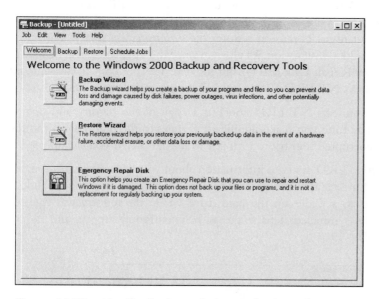

Figure 14-20   Use the Backup window to back up the registry and create an Emergency Repair Disk

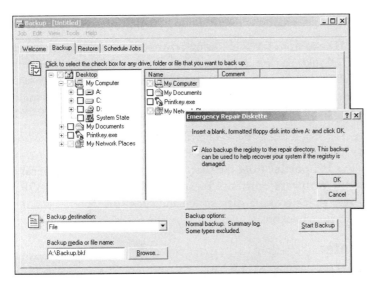

Figure 14-21   Create an ERD and back up the registry to the hard drive

If your hard drive fails, you can use the disk to restore the system, including system files, boot files, and the registry, to its state at the end of the Windows 2000 installation. To do that follow these steps:

1. Boot the PC from the four Windows 2000 setup disks. The Setup menu appears (refer back to Figure 14-16). Select option **R**.

2. When the Windows 2000 Repair Options window opens (refer back to Figure 14-17), select option **R**.

3. You are instructed to insert the Emergency Repair Disk. Follow the instructions on the screen to repair the installation.

If this process does not work, then your next option is to reinstall Windows 2000. Be sure to use ScanDisk to scan the drive surface for errors before you do the installation. If you suspect that a virus has damaged the hard drive file system, also use the FDISK/MBR command discussed in earlier chapters to replace the master boot program in case it has been corrupted by the virus. Windows 2000 also offers a utility called InoculateIT Antivirus AVBoot, which is a command-line tool that can scan memory, the MBR sector, and OS boot sectors for viruses. You will learn to use the utility in a project at the end of the chapter.

Problems After the Operating System Loads

Windows 2000 offers several maintenance tools that can help prevent and solve problems after the system loads. Some are similar to Windows 9x, Windows NT, and DOS tools, and some are new to Windows 2000. Several are discussed next.

A+ OS 1.3 **Chkdsk**   Chkdsk is located in the %SystemRoot%\System32 folder. It scans a floppy disk or hard drive for lost clusters and cross-linked files and repairs them if you have included the /F option in the command line. Enter this command in the Run dialog box: **C:\WINNT\ system32\chkdsk.exe/ F**

Substitute the drive and folder name where Windows 2000 is installed, in the command line.

$A^+_{1.1}^{OS}$ **CMD** Executing **CMD.exe** from the Run dialog box opens a command interpreter window where you can use DOS-like commands at a command prompt. A command window is also available under Start, Programs, Accessories, Command Prompt. Type **Exit** to close the window. You can also execute single commands from the Run dialog box without having to open the command window. Use the CMD command with the /C option like this: CMD /C CHKDSK

$A^+_{1.2}^{OS}$ **Compress** To save disk space, using the NTFS file system, you can compress an entire volume, individual files or folders. Using Windows Explorer, right-click on the volume, folder or file name and select **Properties** from the shortcut menu. Select the **General** tab and, for a file or folder, check **Compress contents to save disk space** and click **OK**. For a volume, check **Compress drive to save disk space** and click **OK**. Later, if you decide to not use compression, clear the checkbox.

$A^+_{1.3,}^{OS}$
$_{3.2}$ ## Disk Defragmenter

To run Disk Defragmenter, click **Start**, point to **Programs**, **Accessories**, and **System Tools**, and then click **Disk Defragmenter**. Just as with Windows 98, this tool reorganizes files on the hard drive to eliminate fragmented files and gives you a nice graphical view of the process as it works.

Another way to access Disk Defragmenter is from Explorer. Right-click a logical drive letter in Explorer and select **Properties** from the shortcut menu. The drive Properties window opens (see Figure 14-22). Select the **Tools** tab. From this window you can access the Windows 2000 Backup utility to back up folders on the drive, defragment the drive using Disk Defragmenter, and scan the drive for errors using ScanDisk.

Figure 14-22 The Tools tab of a local disk Properties dialog box has tools to back up and manage the hard drive

Windows Update

You can quickly download service packs (fixes to known Windows 2000 bugs) from the *windowsupdate.microsoft.com* web site by clicking **Start**, **Windows Update** (see Figure 14-23). Internet Explorer opens and displays the web site. Download the latest service pack, which downloads the file to a directory on your hard drive. If you think you might later want to uninstall the fix, when given the opportunity, select the **Save uninstall information** option.

Later, to uninstall the fix, again execute the downloaded file. When given the option, select **Uninstall a previously installed service pack**.

$A^{+OS}_{3.2}$ ## System File Checker

System File Checker is part of the new Windows 2000 utility that protects system files, called **Windows File Protection** (**WFP**). WFP runs in the background and alerts a user when a system file has been altered. The message you see is:

A file replacement was attempted on the protected system file <filename>. To maintain system stability, the file has been restored to the correct Microsoft version. If problems occur with your application, please contact the application vendor for support.

If you see this message, carefully note what application was working at the time and what had just happened before the message. Suspect a virus or bad application software.

Figure 14-23   Windows Update accesses the web site *windowsupdate.microsoft.com*

$A^{+OS}_{3.2}$ If you suspect that system files have become corrupted or deleted, use System File Checker. Click **Start**, **Run**, and enter this command in the Run dialog box: **C:\WINNT\ system32\sfc.exe /scannow**. If the utility cannot retrieve a copy of a corrupted system file from its cache, it requests that you insert the Windows 2000 CD in the CD-ROM drive.

14

A+ OS
1.1

Computer Management

Computer Management is a window that consolidates several tools that you can use to manage the local PC or other computers on the network. It combines several Windows 2000 administrative tools. To access Computer Management, click **Start**, point to **Programs**, **Administrative Tools**, and then click **Computer Management**. The Computer Management window appears. See Figure 14-24. Some of the tasks you can perform from this window include monitoring problems with hardware, software, and security. You can share folders, view device configurations, add new device drivers, start and stop services, and manage server applications.

Figure 14-24   Computer Management combines several administrative tools into a single easy-to-access window

Microsoft Management Console

When Windows combines several administrative tools into a single window, the window is called a **console**. Individual tools within the console are called **snap-ins**. For example, Computer Management is a console, and Event Viewer and System Information are two snap-ins in that console. Another example of a console is Recovery Console, which contains a set of commands, or tools, you can use to recover from a failed Windows 2000 boot.

You can use Microsoft Management Console to create your own customized consoles. You can also save the console to a file, which is assigned a .msc file extension. Store the file in the *system-drive*\Documents and Settings*user*\Start Menu\Programs\Administrative Tools folder to make it open as a program when you click Start, and point to Programs, Administrative Tools. In the path, substitute the drive letter of the system drive and the name of the user. For example, if the system drive is C and the user is Administrator, the path to the .msc file is C:\Documents and Settings\Administrator\Start Menu\Programs\Administrative Tools. Once you create a console, you can copy the .msc file to any computer or place a shortcut to it on the desktop. To create a shortcut, right click on the file name and select Create Shortcut and then drag the shortcut to the desktop. You can also use your right mouse button to drag the file to the desktop and then select Create Shortcut Here from the menu that appears when you drop the file on the desktop.

Follow these directions to create a console that contains some popular utility tools:

1. Click **Start**, **Run**, enter **MMC** in the Run dialog box and click **OK**. An empty console window appears as seen in Figure 14-25.

2. Click **Console** on the menu bar, and then click **Add/Remove Snap-in**. The Add/Remove Snap-in window opens. The window illustrated in Figure 14-26 is empty because no snap-ins have been added to the console.

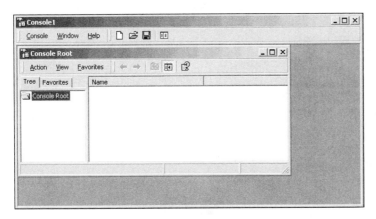

Figure 14-25   An empty console

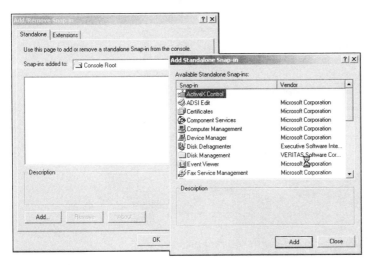

Figure 14-26   List of snap-ins available to be added to a console

3. Click **Add**. You see a list of snap-ins that can be added to a console, as shown in Figure 14-26. Select a snap-in and click **Add**.

4. A dialog box opens that allows you to set the parameters for the snap-in. The dialog box offers different selections depending on the snap-in being added. A sample dialog box is shown in Figure 14-27. When you have made your selections, click **Finish**. The new snap-in appears in the Add/Remove Snap-in window.

5. Repeat Steps 3 and 4 until you have added all the snap-ins that you want to the console. When you are finished, from the Add Standalone Snap-in window illustrated in Figure 14-26, click **Close** then click **OK**.

6. Figure 14-28 shows a console with four snap-ins added. To save the console, click **Console** on the menu bar, and then click **Save As**. The Save As dialog box opens.

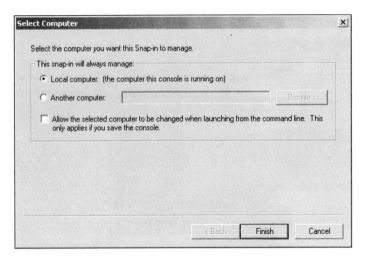

Figure 14-27   Set the parameters for the snap-in

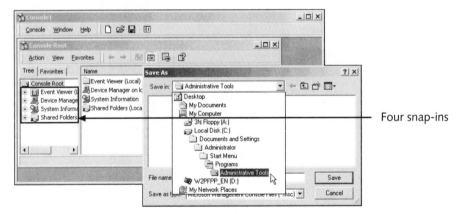

Figure 14-28   Saving a console with four snap-ins

7. The default location for the console file is shown in Figure 14-28—the location that ensures the console appears as an option under Administrative Tools on the Start menu. Select this location for the file, name the file, and click **Save**.

8. Close the console window by clicking **Console**, **Exit**.

In this example, the console file was named My Console. Figure 14-29 shows the console listed under **Start**, **Programs**, **Administrative Tools**.

Figure 14-29   New console is listed under Administrative Tools

Windows 2000 Support Tools

A+ OS 2.4 Windows 2000 offers several support tools that you can install. They are located in the \Support\Tools folder of the Windows 2000 CD. To install them, run the Setup program in that folder. Enter this command in the Run dialog box: **D:\Support\Tools\Setup.exe**. Substitute the drive letter of the CD-ROM drive in the command line. The list of tools installed is shown in Figure 14-30.

Figure 14-30   Windows 2000 support tools

14

A+ OS
2.4

One of these utilities is Dependency Walker, which lists all the files used by an application. It can be useful when troubleshooting a failed application installation if you have a report of files used by the application on a computer where the installation is good. Recall from Chapter 12 that software applications often use DLL files for added functionality and to relate to the operating system. To use the utility, click **Start**, point to **Programs**, **Windows 2000 Support Tools**, and **Tools**, and then click **Dependency Walker**. Figure 14-31 shows the resulting Dependency Walker window. Click **File**, **Open**, and select the main executable file for an application. In the figure, Apache.exe is selected. Apache is a popular Web server application. The window lists all supporting files that Apache.exe uses and how they are dependent on one another.

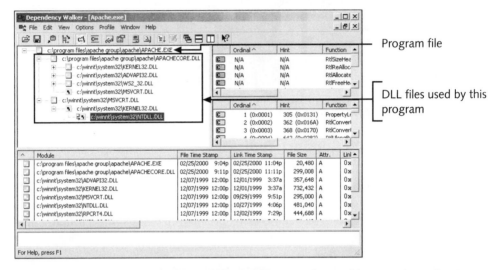

Figure 14-31   You can use dependency Walker to solve problems with applications

Other Sources of Support

Two important sources of information about Windows 2000 are the Microsoft web site at *support.microsoft.com* and the *Windows 2000 Professional Resource Kit* by Microsoft Press. The *Resource Kit* includes a CD that contains additional Windows 2000 utilities. These resources can further help you understand Windows 2000 and solve problems with the OS.

CHAPTER SUMMARY

❑ Windows 2000 is the next evolution of Windows NT with the added user-friendly features of Windows 98.

❑ Windows 2000 is a suite of four operating systems, each designed for a different size computer system. The suite includes Windows 2000 Professional, Windows 2000 Server, Windows 2000 Advanced Server, and Windows 2000 Datacenter Server.

❑ Windows 2000 Professional is designed for the corporate desktop computer and provides more security and reliability than Windows 98 and has added support for large hard drives.

❑ The minimum requirements for Windows 2000 Professional are 133 MHz Pentium-compatible CPU, 64 MB RAM, and 1 GB of hard drive storage. Recommended requirements are 300 MHz Pentium-compatible CPU, 128 MB of RAM, and 2 GB of hard drive storage.

❑ Windows 98 is recommended for home computers over Windows 2000 because it supports legacy devices and software and manages games and similar multimedia applications better than Windows 2000.

❑ Because of the improvements in power management over Windows 98, Windows 2000 is the recommended operating system for notebook computers.

❑ Windows 2000 offers several ways to deploy the OS in a corporate setting, including unattended installations and disk duplication support.

❑ Windows 2000 makes use of ACPI-compliant system BIOS in order to fully enable power management features.

❑ If a system does not have ACPI BIOS, upgrade the BIOS before you do the installation, if the BIOS manufacturer offers the upgrade.

❑ Network Identification, Device Manager, Dial-Up Networking, and Scheduled Tasks are some utilities that are not located on the desktop in the same places in Windows 2000 as they are in Windows 98.

❑ Windows 2000 supports virtual private networks so that a worker can access a corporate network from across the Internet using a secure connection.

❑ Windows 2000 Active Directory is a new feature of Windows 2000 that provides a centralized point of administration for all shared resources on a network.

❑ Windows 2000 can have more than one domain controller, whereas Windows NT can have only a single primary domain controller.

❑ Windows 2000 allows for printing to a URL so that you can send a print job to anywhere on the Internet.

❑ Windows 2000 offers a clean install and an upgrade installation. A clean install overwrites all information from previous operating system installations on the hard drive.

❑ Both hardware and software must be compatible with Windows 2000. Check the HCL and the Compatible Software Applications list on the Microsoft web site before beginning an installation.

❑ Windows 2000 supports the FAT16, FAT32, and NTFS file systems.

❑ Windows 2000 supports a dual boot, but each operating system must be installed in its own partition, and an application must be installed twice—once for each OS.

❑ A Windows 2000 upgrade installation is done in two phases, the Report phase and the Setup phase.

14

❏ Back up the Windows 2000 System State on a regular basis using the Backup utility. This backup includes system files, files to load the OS, and the registry.

❏ The Windows 2000 boot process works like the Windows NT process. The boot loader program is Ntldr, which gives control to Ntoskrnl.exe when the boot completes.

❏ Tools to use to troubleshoot problems loading Windows 2000 are the Advanced Options menu, the Recovery Console, and the Emergency Repair Process.

❏ Press F8 when starting Windows 2000 to access the Advanced Options menu.

❏ The Advanced Options menu includes Safe Mode, Safe Mode with Networking, Safe Mode with Command Prompt, Enable Boot Logging, Enable VGA Mode, Last Known Good Configuration, Directory Services Restore Mode, and Debugging Mode.

❏ The Recovery Console is a command interface with a limited number of commands available to troubleshoot a failing Windows 2000 load. The console requires that you enter the Administrator password.

❏ Access the Recovery Console by first booting from the Windows 2000 CD or from the four setup disks.

❏ Using the Recovery Console, you can restore the registry to the state it was in at the time of the last backup of the registry.

❏ The Emergency Repair Process lets you restore the system to its state at the end of the Windows 2000 installation. Don't use it unless all other methods fail because you will loose all changes made to the system since the installation. It requires the Emergency Startup Disk.

❏ Utilities that can help solve problems after a system loads include Chkdsk, Disk Defragmenter, Windows Update, and System File Checker.

❏ Windows File Protection (WFP) protects the system files against an application, virus, or user changing or deleting them.

❏ Windows 2000 Support Tools can be installed from the Windows 2000 CD and include several utilities to support hardware and applications.

❏ Sources of support for Windows 2000 include the support web site at *support.microsoft.com* and the *Windows 2000 Professional Resource Kit* by Microsoft.

KEY TERMS

Active Directory — A Windows 2000 service that allows for a single point of administration for all shared resources on a network, including files, peripheral devices, databases, Web sites, users, and services.

Advanced Options Menu — A Windows 2000 menu that appears when you press F8 when Windows starts. The menu can be used to troubleshoot problems when loading Windows 2000.

answer file — A text file that contains information that Windows 2000 requires in order to do an unattended installation.

clean installation — A Windows 2000 installation that overwrites all previous installations on the hard drive partition.

console — An administrative tool contains two or more individual administrative tools. For example, Recovery Console contains a set of commands designed to manage a failed Windows 2000 boot, and Computer Management is a console that contains several tools to monitor and manage hardware and software.

Emergency Repair Process — A Windows 2000 process that restores the OS to its state at the completion of a successful installation.

Internet Printing Protocol (IPP) — A protocol used to send print jobs across the Internet. A printer is addressed by its URL (uniform resource locator)—for example, *www.ourdomain.com/printer4.*

mixed mode — A Windows 2000 mode for domain controllers used when there is at least one Windows NT domain controller on the network.

native mode — A Windows 2000 mode used by domain controllers when there are no Windows NT domain controllers present on the network.

Recovery Console — A Windows 2000 command-interface utility that can be used to solve problems when the OS cannot load from the hard drive.

Snap-in — An administrative tool that is contained within a console. For example, Event Viewer is a snap-in in the Computer Management console.

System File Checker — System File Checker is part of the new Windows 2000 utility to protect system files, called Windows File Protection (WFP).

System State data — All files that Windows 2000 requires to load and perform successfully. The System State data is backed up using the Backup utility.

unattended installation — A Windows 2000 installation that is done by storing the answers to installation questions in a text file or script that Windows 2000 calls an answer file so that the answers do not have to be typed in during the installation.

upgrade installation — A Windows 2000 installation that carries forward all previous operating system settings and applications installed under the previous operating system.

Windows File Protection (WFP) — A Windows 2000 feature that protects system files from being corrupted or erased by applications or users.

14

REVIEW QUESTIONS

1. List the four operating systems that make up the Windows 2000 suite.

2. What are the minimum system requirements for Windows 2000 Professional?

3. What is the maximum amount of RAM that Windows 2000 Professional can support?

4. Which OS is better for home computing, Windows 98 or Windows 2000? Why?

5. What is the purpose of Kerberos?

6. What is required before Windows 2000 can provide full power management functionality?

7. What five manufacturers were responsible for the initial development of ACPI?

8. Under what circumstances must you use Windows 98 rather than Windows 2000 Professional for a personal computer OS?

9. What is a virtual private network and how does Windows 2000 support one?

10. What three file systems does Windows 2000 support?

11. Explain the difference between Windows 2000 native mode and mixed mode.

12. When you print to a printer URL on the Internet, what protocol are you using?

13. If you are installing Windows 2000 on a new hard drive and your system cannot boot from a CD, how do you begin the installation?

14. If you want to access a hard drive using either DOS or Windows 2000, what file system must you use?

15. If you install Windows 2000 on an 8 GB hard drive, use a single partition for the drive, and choose not to use the NTFS file system, what file system will Windows 2000 automatically use?

16. If your BIOS is not ACPI-compliant, what should you do before you install Windows 2000?

17. What does %SystemRoot% mean?

18. List the steps to back up the Windows 2000 System State data.

19. In what folder does Windows 2000 store a backup of the registry?

20. Which loads first, Ntldr or Ntoskrnl.exe?

21. What is the purpose of NTDetect.com in the load process?

22. What is the purpose of Safe Mode with Networking under the Advanced Options menu?

23. What is the name of the log file that Windows 2000 uses when booting in Safe Mode?

24. At what point in the Windows 2000 load process is the Last Known Good Configuration saved?

25. List the steps to load the Recovery Console.

26. Why is the Administrator password required in order to use the Recovery Console?

27. In Question 26 above, under what circumstances is the password not required?

28. What is the purpose of the Systemroot command under the Recovery Console?

29. Under the Recovery Console, what is the command that gives the same results as FDISK/MBR?

30. List the five files that make up the Windows 2000 registry.

31. Before you can perform the Windows 2000 Emergency Repair Process, what disk must you have? What is contained on the disk?

32. When would you use System File Checker? What is the command to execute it?

33. What is the command to install the Windows 2000 Support Tools?

PROJECTS

Preparing for Windows 2000

Use the Microsoft web site to research whether your home or lab PC qualifies for Windows 2000. Fill in the following table and print the web pages showing whether each hardware device and application installed on your PC qualifies for Windows 2000.

Hardware Device or Application	Specific Device Name or Application Name and Version	Does It Qualify for Windows 2000?
System board BIOS		
Video card		
Modem card (if present)		
Sound card (if present)		
Printer (if present)		
Network card (if present)		
CD-ROM drive (if present)		
DVD drive (if present)		
SCSI hard drive (if present)		
Other device		
Application 1		
Application 2		
Application 3		

14

Installing Windows 2000 Professional

Do the following to install Windows 2000 Professional and then test different startup options:

1. Install Windows 2000 Professional as the second OS in a dual boot with your current operating system.

2. Boot to the Windows 2000 Advanced Options Menu. Boot using each option on the menu and write a short description of what you see during and after the boot.

3. Create an Emergency Repair Disk and print the contents of the files on that disk. If the contents of a file are longer than one page, only print the first page.

4. Using the Recovery Console, copy the registry files to a backup folder on the hard drive.

Using the Microsoft Knowledge Base

Using the Microsoft support web site (*support.microsoft.com*), print information about the following:

1. Troubleshooting IEEE 1394 devices running under Windows 2000 Professional

2. How to set up Windows 2000 to support multiple CPUs.

3. Information on how to set up and troubleshoot multiple monitors with Windows 2000 Professional.

Using DiskProbe to Back Up the MBR

DiskProbe is a powerful disk editor similar to DEBUG, which is described in Appendix F. DiskProbe edits individual sectors on a hard drive and can edit the MBR, boot sectors, the FATs and NTFS file system tables as well as data files. Research DiskProbe and find the directions that show you how to back up the MBR, which contains the partition table. Follow these directions and answer these questions:

1. Find the document Dskprtrb.doc in the C:\ProgramFiles\Support Tools folder, which describes how to use DiskProbe. Print the page from the document that describes how to save the MBR record to a floppy disk.

2. If the Windows 2000 Support Tools are not installed, install them now.

3. Execute DiskProbe (click **Start**, point to **Programs**, **Windows 2000 Support Tools**, and **Tools**, and then click **DiskProbe**).

4. Follow these directions to save the MBR, including the partition table, to a floppy disk.

5. How many bytes of data are included in the MBR? What is the size of the file?

6. What is the disadvantage of using DiskProbe to restore the MBR in the event it becomes corrupted?

Creating a Windows 2000 Antivirus Boot Disk

Windows 2000 offers an antivirus program that can scan memory, the MBR sector, and OS boot sectors for viruses. Follow these directions to create the boot disk and scan your system for viruses. Use the disk when you suspect that a virus has attacked your Windows 2000 hard drive.

1. Insert the Windows 2000 CD in the CD-ROM drive and insert an empty floppy disk in the floppy disk drive.

2. Click **Start**, **Run**. From the Run dialog box, enter this command:

   D:\VALUEADD\3RDPARTY\CA_ANTIV\Makedisk.bat

   Substitute the drive letter for your CD-ROM drive for D:.

3. Label the disk Windows 2000 AVBoot.

4. Boot from the floppy disk. When the scan is completed, Windows 2000 will automatically load.

Note: If your PC is not set to boot from a floppy disk before booting from the hard drive, change the boot sequence in CMOS setup.

Using Dependency Walker

Follow these steps to use Dependency Walker to list the files used by Internet Explorer:

1. If the Windows 2000 Support Tools are not installed, install them now.
2. Execute Dependency Walker (click **Start**, point to **Programs**, **Windows 2000 Support Tools**, and **Tools**, and click **Dependency Walker**).
3. Set Dependency Walker to show all the supporting files used by Internet Explorer.
4. List the files or print the screen showing them.

Examining the Ntbtlog.txt File

Using the Windows 2000 Advanced Options menu, boot with Enable Boot Logging. Print the Ntbtlog.txt file created. Then boot with Safe Mode. Again print the Ntbtlog.txt file. Compare the two files and mark the differences. Keep these two reports in case you ever have problems booting this system since they can provide a picture of what a normal boot should be.

14

15

PURCHASING A PC OR BUILDING YOUR OWN

In this chapter, you will learn:

♦ Some guidelines to use when purchasing a PC

♦ Reasons why you might choose to assemble a PC yourself

♦ How to assemble a PC from separately purchased parts

This chapter presents guidelines to follow when purchasing a new PC and also presents detailed, step-by-step procedures for building a PC from parts. If you need a computer for your own personal use, consider assembling it yourself, not necessarily to save money, but to benefit in other ways. If you don't want to build a PC, you must choose between purchasing a brand-name PC or a clone.

After-sales service and support are probably the most important criteria to consider when purchasing a PC. In general, a brand-name PC (such as IBM or Compaq) might cost more, but will provide better service and support than a PC built with parts manufactured by companies whose names you don't recognize. Important reasons for choosing to build your own PC rather than buying a comparable preassembled one are the knowledge gained and the fact that you will have complete control over every part purchased to make your own customized integrated system.

SELECTING A PERSONAL COMPUTER TO MEET YOUR NEEDS

So far, this book has been chock-full of information to help you make decisions concerning which computers, peripheral devices, operating systems, and software to buy and how to manage and maintain them once they are yours. However, hardware and software are changing daily, and it's important to stay informed if you make buying decisions or give purchasing advice on an ongoing basis. You can choose one of three alternatives when selecting a PC: buy a brand-name PC, buy a clone, or buy parts and assemble a PC yourself—which, in effect, results in your own personally designed clone.

A **brand-name PC**, sometimes called an IBM-compatible PC, is a PC manufactured by a company with a recognizable name such as Compaq, Packard Bell, Dell, Gateway, or IBM. A **clone** is generally understood to mean a PC that has been assembled by a local company with parts manufactured by several companies. (The terms *brand-name PC* and *clone* once had entirely different meanings. Originally, the one and only brand-name PC was the IBM, and all other personal computers were called clones.) There are advantages and disadvantages to purchasing both brand-name and clone PCs, in the areas of warranties, service contracts, and ease of obtaining replacement and additional parts. For instance, while it may seem advantageous that brand-name PCs and most clones come with some software already installed, the software is not necessarily standard, brand-name software. The preinstalled software can be any variety of shareware, unknown software, etc., and the documentation and original installation disks for the software may not be included in the total package.

When selecting a computer system that will include both hardware and software, begin by taking a high-level view of the decisions you must make. Start by answering these questions:

- How will the computer be used now and in the future?
- What functionality do you want the computer to have (within its intended use)?
- What hardware and software do you need to meet this functionality?
- What is your budget?
- If you determine that a clone meets your needs, do you want to assemble it yourself?

In order to make the best possible decision, consider the first question to be the most important, the second question the next most important, and so on. For example, if you intend to use the computer for playing games and accessing the Internet, the functionality required is considerably different than for a computer used for software development. Listed below are some examples of possible answers to the first question:

- To access the Internet
- To play games
- To use software stored on a file server while connected to a LAN
- For Windows software development
- For business applications on a standalone PC or on a LAN
- For computing-intensive engineering or mathematical applications such as CAD/CAM

- To provide help-desk support with online remote control of other computers
- For multimedia presentations before large and small groups
- For use in a retail store (including cash register support)
- For network administration

After you have identified the intended purpose of the computer, list the functionality required to meet the needs of the intended purpose. For example, if the computer is to be used for playing games, some required functionality might be:

- Ability of the hardware to support game software
- Excellent video and sound
- Sophisticated input methods

If the computer is to be used for Windows software development, required functionality might include:

- The ability to support the standard hardware and software environment that most customers using the developed software might have
- The ability to run software development tools and hardware to support the software
- A comfortable keyboard and mouse for long work hours
- A removable, high-capacity storage device for easy transfer and storage of developed software
- Reliable warranty and service to guarantee minimal "downtime"

Once the required functionality is defined, the next step—defining what hardware and software are needed—is much easier. For example, if a comfortable keyboard designed for long work hours is a required functionality, begin by researching the different types of keyboards available, and try out a few in the stores if necessary. It would be a mistake to purchase the cheapest keyboard in the store for this intended purpose. However, for game playing, an expensive, comfortable keyboard is probably not needed because most games use other input devices. Spending your resources on a sophisticated joystick probably makes more sense.

As noted above, the least possible amount of downtime is a required functionality for software development. This is also true for many business-use computers, and it is the most important reason a business chooses a brand-name computer over a clone.

Purchasing a Brand-Name PC vs. a Clone PC

As you have most likely noticed, brand-name PCs generally cost more than clone PCs with similar features. One reason for this is that you are paying extra money for after-sales service. For example, an IBM PC comes with a three-year warranty, a 24-hour-service help line with a toll-free number, and delivery of parts to your place of business. A clone manufacturer might also give good service, but this may be due to the personalities of a few employees, rather than to company policies. Most likely, clone company policies are not as liberal and all-encompassing as those of a brand-name manufacturer. Typically, most brand-name manufacturers provide

15

additional support not provided by clone manufacturers, such as functional Web sites, updated drivers and utilities, and online troubleshooting or user manuals.

On the other hand, many brand-name manufacturers use nonstandard parts with their hardware and nonstandard approaches to setting up their systems, making their computers more proprietary than clones. **Proprietary** systems are ones that are unique to a particular vendor (or proprietor), often forcing customers to use only parts and service from that vendor. One of the most common ways for a brand-name manufacturer to make its computer more proprietary is to put components directly on the system board rather than use more generic expansion cards. Remember from earlier chapters that an easy way to tell if ports are coming directly off a system board is to look at the back of the PC. If ports are aligned horizontally on the bottom of a desktop PC or vertically down the side of the tower-case PC, these ports most likely come directly off the system board, and the board is more likely to be proprietary.

For example, a brand-name system can include video, sound, or network logic on the system board rather than on an expansion card. Or, rather than being updated by a setup program in BIOS, the CMOS setup program might be stored on the hard drive. The shape and size of the computer case might be such that a standard system board does not fit; only the brand-name board will do. These practices can make upgrading and repairing brand-name PCs more difficult, because you are forced to use the brand-name parts and brand-name service. Also, in some areas of the country, it might be difficult to find authorized dealers and service centers for brand-name PCs.

Selecting Software

When selecting software, review the required functionality you identified, which drives your decisions about software selection. Choose the operating system first, according to guidelines presented in Chapter 2. When choosing applications software consider these questions:

- What do you want the software to do? (This will be defined by your answer to the functionality question above.)
- Is compatibility with other software or data required?
- Is training available, if you do not already have the skills needed to use the software?
- How good is the program's documentation?
- What are the company's upgrade policies?
- How well known or popular is the software? (The more popular, the more likely you'll find good training materials, trained people, technical support, and other compatible software and hardware.)

Caution is in order if you are buying a brand-name or clone computer that has preinstalled software that you are not familiar with. The software may not provide the functionality that you need, and may not have good documentation or reliable upgrades or support. Unless you feel that you have the skill to manage this software, you're probably better off staying with mainstream-market software. One way to identify which brand of software is the most prevalent in the industry is to browse the computer books section of a local bookstore, looking for the software that has the most "how to" books written about it. Also see trade magazines, the Internet, and your local retailer.

Selecting Hardware

The two most important criteria to consider when selecting hardware are compatibility and functionality. Begin by considering the system board. (See Chapter 3 for more information about how to select one.) Here are other topics you should consider:

- If you plan to use Windows 9x on a PC, choosing a PC that is made up of 100% Plug and Play components is of value, but not necessary. Be certain, however, that the BIOS is Plug and Play.

- If you intend to use the PC for multimedia applications, including games, you will want MMX technology or better for the CPU, and plenty of memory and drive space.

- If you plan to use the PC for heavy network use, buy a PC with plenty of processing power.

- If Internet access is important, don't skimp on the modem, and, if it's an external modem, be sure to include a high-speed serial port.

- When selecting a computer case, keep in mind that tower cases generally offer more room than desktop units, and are easier to work with when adding new devices. Make sure the case has a reset button and, if security is an issue, a key lock in order to limit access to the inside of the case. Some cases even have a lock on the floppy drive to prevent unauthorized booting from a floppy disk.

Selecting a Total Package

When selecting a complete computer package, including hardware and software, consider these points:

- Are the hardware and software compatible with those found on the general market? (For example, if you wanted to upgrade your video card or word processor, how difficult would that be?)

- What is the warranty and return or exchange policy?

- What on-site or local service is available? Do you know of anyone who has used this service, and was it satisfactory?

- Is the system Energy Star compliant? (For information about Energy Star, see Chapter 11.)

- What software comes preinstalled?

- What documentation or manuals come with the system?

- Does the manufacturer maintain a Web site with useful support features, utilities, and updates?

- Does the system board allow for expansion of both DRAM and SRAM?

- What expansion slots are not being used? (Always allow for some room to grow.)

15

- Can features such as video on the system board be disabled if necessary? (Refer back to Chapter 3 for other guidelines on selecting system boards.)

- How much does the system cost?

When considering price, keep in mind that high-priced to middle-range-priced PCs are most likely to be network-compatible and easily expandable; they offer a broader range of support, and have had extensive testing of vendor products for reliability and compatibility. Low-priced PCs may not have been tested for network compatibility; they offer a limited range of support, and the quality of components may not be as high.

When considering preinstalled software, remember that sometimes unneeded software is more of a hindrance than a help, needlessly taking up space. For example, it is not uncommon for a brand-name computer to come with three or four applications for Internet access (for example, America Online, CompuServe, Prodigy, and Microsoft Network) because of licensing agreements distributors have with online providers. Typically, only one is needed. Sometimes having more than one on your computer can cause problems.

PREPARING TO BUILD YOUR OWN PC

Assembling your own PC takes time, skill, and research, but it can be a great learning experience. You might even want to consider it your "rite of passage" toward being a PC technician. All the skills needed to be a PC technician are tested: research, knowledge of user needs and the computer market, planning, organization, patience, confidence, problem solving, and extensive knowledge of both hardware and software. If you intend to become a corporate-level technician, you most certainly should put together at least one whole PC before starting your first job.

However, don't build your PC in order to save money, because you probably won't. The total price of all parts usually about equals the price of a comparable clone PC that is prebuilt. Here are a few good reasons to assemble your own PC:

- The whole process can be quite fun.

- Knowledge is power. The knowledge and experience gained in researching the parts to buy, studying the documentation, and finally assembling the PC can't be overemphasized.

- When you buy all the parts and software for a PC individually, you are also getting the documentation for each hardware component. This is most likely not the case when you buy a PC already assembled. If you plan to upgrade your PC later, having this documentation can be very valuable.

- Many prebuilt PCs come with software already preloaded. You may not receive the original CDs or disks or the documentation for these programs, which can be a problem when you try to maintain your system. However, when you buy each software package individually, you have the installation disks, CDs, and documentation.

- When you purchase each computer part individually, you are more likely to understand exactly what you are buying, and you can be more particular about the selection of each component. You have control over the brand and features of each component in the PC.

Here are a few reasons why you might *not* want to build your own PC:

- If you are in a rush to get a PC up and running, assembling your own is probably not a good idea, especially if you are a first-time builder. The process takes time and requires patience, and the first time you do it, you most likely will make a few mistakes that will need to be resolved.

- Individual parts may be warrantied, but if you build your own PC, there is no overall warranty on the PC. If a warranty or a service agreement is important, then look for a ready-built PC with these services included.

- Clone PCs have been tested to assure that individual components are compatible. When building your own PC, it is possible you might select components that are incompatible. For this reason, buy quality mainstream components to best ensure compatibility.

- Don't plan to assemble a PC for the first time unless you have access to an experienced technician or a technical service center you can consult if you encounter a problem you cannot resolve. For example, you may buy all the parts from a store that has a service center. The store may offer to assemble the PC for you for a charge ($50 to $75 is about right). If you find you cannot resolve a problem, you can always go back to the store for this service.

- Remember, don't assemble the PC to save money, because you probably won't.

Getting Ready for Assembly: Selecting Parts

If you have decided to buy parts and assemble a PC, expect the process to take some time. The system board and expansion cards are full of jumper switches, connections, and ports, and the documentation must be carefully read to determine just how to configure the system board and all components to work together. Technicians in service centers can assemble a PC in less than an hour—but they have already assembled the same group of parts many times!

Planning the assembly of a PC is like packing for a camping trip to a remote location. You must plan for everything you will need before you begin. As you select and purchase each part, two things are important: part functionality and compatibility with other parts.

Almost every computer needs these essentials: system board, CPU, RAM, hard drive, CD-ROM drive (or you can substitute a DVD drive or CD-RW drive for added functionality), floppy drive, case, power supply, video card, monitor, keyboard, and mouse. And, most likely, you will also want a sound card and modem. Make careful and informed decisions about every part you buy. Selecting each component requires reviewing your functionality, compatibility, and budget needs and determining what parts meet your criteria. Select the system board first, and then select the rest of the parts around this one most important component. Remember from Chapter 3 that the Intel chip set is preferable to other brands of chip sets.

When selecting parts, including the system board, carefully examine the documentation. Look for good documentation that you can understand without struggling. When buying parts for your first assembly, you should probably not use mail order. Buy from a reputable local dealer who will allow you to examine a part and look at the documentation, and who is willing and able to answer any technical questions you may have. Know the return policy of the store and the manufacturer's warranty for the part.

If you can buy the system board, CPU, and memory from the same dealer, who can help you determine that all three are compatible, do so to avoid later problems with compatibility. The documentation for the system board is quite valuable. Make sure it's readable and complete. Does the CPU need a voltage regulator, heat sink, or fan? Ask the dealer for recommendations, and read the documentation for the CPU. Often a dealer will sell a system board with the CPU and fan already installed and jumpers on the system board set correctly.

After you have selected the system board, RAM, and CPU, select the case and accompanying power supply. Remember the two rules: the case must meet your predetermined functionality, and it must be compatible with other parts (especially the system board). Next, select the hard drive and other drives. Does your BIOS on the system board support the IDE or SCSI hard drive selected? Is there an IDE adapter on the system board? Are connections available for the CD-ROM drive, floppy drive, removable drive, and the like? If the video logic is not included on the system board (for clone system boards it probably will not be), select the video card next, and make sure that you have an AGP or a PCI slot to accommodate it. Next, select the hard drive, CD-ROM drive, and floppy drive and then the peripherals, including a mouse, keyboard, and monitor.

Getting Ready for Assembly: Final Preparations

When all parts are purchased, prepare for the assembly well. Prepare a work area that is well lit and uncluttered. Read all the documentation and plan the assembly through, from beginning to end, before you start. If you have questions or are unsure how to proceed, find the answers to your concerns before you begin. For example, if you're not sure how to set the jumpers on the system board, even after you have read the documentation, take the documentation to your technical support (dealer, service center, a knowledgeable friend) and ask for help in interpreting the settings in the documentation before you start the work. Often you can find a detailed diagram of the system board on the manufacturer's Web site complete with proper settings for specific CPUs.

While working, don't get careless about protecting against static electricity (review the safety precautions at the beginning of this book). Always use the ground strap on your wrist.

BUILDING A PERSONAL COMPUTER, STEP BY STEP

This section is a step-by-step, detailed description of building a Pentium II PC designed for multimedia applications, from parts—including a hard drive, floppy drive, DVD drive, Zip drive, modem, sound card, video camera, and SCSI card to support a scanner. Depending on what you have decided you want your computer for, and what functionality and budget you are operating with, you may choose to build a slightly different PC, with a different CPU and different parts. We selected this particular Pentium II system board so that you can see a typical configuration using jumpers. At the end of the chapter, you will see a Pentium II system board that has a much easier jumper-free configuration. While we do not have the space to provide instructions on the assembly of many different PCs, the examples below will provide you with background and guidance, and demonstrate how to approach the task at hand.

The text describes some of the problems actually encountered during an assembly. I wish I could invite you to work beside me, reading the documentation for that jumper setting, deciding just which card should go in which slot for the best overall fit, and enjoying the pleasure of turning on the PC and seeing it boot up for the first time. However, the best I can do is invite you into the experience through this book. My hope is that you will one day have the opportunity to experience it for yourself.

Overview of the Assembly Process

Once the research is done and the parts purchased, organize everything you'll need to assemble the PC. Have the parts with the accompanying documentation and software available, together with your PC tools. You'll need a safe place to work, with a ground mat and ground strap. Be careful to follow all the safety rules and precautions discussed at the beginning of this book. Work methodically and keep things organized. If you find yourself getting frustrated, take a break. Remember, you want the entire experience to be fun!

The parts purchased for the PC before the beginning of the assembly are listed below. Since the system includes a DVD drive that can read a CD, a CD-ROM drive is not needed. The parts to be installed inside the case are shown in Figure 15-1.

- 17-inch monitor
- ATX case with power supply
- System board
- Pentium II CPU that runs at 350 MHz
- One 64–MB DIMM
- AGP video card
- Hard drive
- Floppy drive
- DVD drive kit
- Zip drive
- Sound card
- Modem card
- SCSI host adapter (to interface with a scanner)
- Video camera with USB connection
- Mouse and keyboard

15

Figure 15-1   The parts of a PC before assembly

The general steps to assemble the PC are as follows:

1. Set the jumpers on the system board.
2. Install the CPU and CPU fan.
3. Install RAM on the system board.
4. Verify that the system board is working by performing a memory test.
5. Install the system board in the computer case.
6. Connect the power cord and front panel connectors to the system board.
7. Install the floppy drive, hard drive, and Zip drive.
8. Install the video card, modem card, sound card, and SCSI adapter.
9. Install the DVD subsystem, including DVD drive, controller card, and cords.
10. Connect essential peripherals.
11. Install the operating system.
12. Connect remaining peripherals and install device drivers.

Step 1: Setting the Jumpers on the System Board

A+CORE
1.2

This section describes how to set jumpers on the system board to configure hardware; the jumpers and their functions are listed in Table 15-1. Figure 15-2 shows a diagram of the system board with the main parts identified. When doing an installation, read the system-board documentation carefully, looking for the type of information in the table, and set the jumpers according to the hardware you will be installing, which may differ from what appears here.

1. CPU Slot 1
2. DIMM Sockets 1,2,3
3. PCI Slots 1,2,3,4
4. ISA Slots 1,2,3
5. AGP slot
6. Floppy drive connector (34 pin)
7. Primary/secondary IDE connectors (40 pin)
8. ATX power connector (20 pin)
9. External ports
10. Panel connectors
11. Flash EEPROM BIOS
12. Jumpers, bus speed
13. Jumpers, CPU multiplier
14. Jumper, clear RTC
15. Jumper, keyboard power-up

Figure 15-2   System-board layout including jumper definitions

15

A+CORE
   1.2

For example, although this system board does not require that a jumper be set to indicate what type of CPU is installed, many system boards do have a jumper for this purpose. Also, a system board might require you to use jumper settings to regulate the voltage to the CPU. When making this kind of selection, read the documentation that comes with the CPU to learn the voltage requirements. If the system board has L2 cache, then there will most likely be jumper settings to indicate how much cache memory is installed.

Table 15-1   Jumper settings on the system board

Jumper Groups on the System Board	Description
CPU memory bus frequency (Item 12 in Figure 15-2)	This group of nine pins controls the speed (frequency) of the bus between the CPU and memory.
CPU core bus frequency multiple (Item 13 in Figure 15-2)	This group of 12 pins controls the ratio of CPU core speed to memory bus speed (i.e., the multiplier).
Clear CMOS RAM (Item 14 in Figure 15-2)	This is one jumper, which, when closed, will clear CMOS settings including the real time clock.
Keyboard power-up (Item 15 in Figure 15-2)	This jumper group consists of three pins with two possible settings to enable and disable the feature to allow the Spacebar on the keyboard to power up the PC. Requires a power supply that supports the feature.

One of the most time-consuming steps of assembling a PC can be setting the jumpers on the system board, or rather studying the system-board documentation to learn how to set the jumpers. (Once you know how to set them, doing so is quick and easy.) The documentation for the system board used here is really very good. Every jumper is clearly marked, and the settings for the jumper are clearly explained. That is not always the case.

First, locate the four jumper groups on the system board (see Figure 15-2), as listed in Table 15-1. Each jumper group will be discussed in turn to determine what it does and what settings it should have. As each jumper set in the documentation is examined, one setting for each jumper group will be marked as a default setting. This is usually the factory setting (the setting on the system board when it is shipped). However, if you want to use the default setting, check to see that the jumper is set as indicated, because sometimes the factory sets the jumpers differently from what is listed in the documentation as the default.

Also, occasionally the wrong documentation will be shipped with a system board, or the documentation will have an error. After power-up, if you have problems because the system is incorrectly sensing your system-board configuration, double-check your settings. If you don't find an error, suspect the problem may be with the documentation. If your system-board manufacturer has a Web site, check it for the latest information about jumper settings.

Jumpers are set to the closed position by placing a small cap across a pair of pins. An open jumper has no cap across the pair. If you want to set the jumper to open, you can place the unused cap on one of the two pins, so you won't lose it. This is called "parking" the jumper. Set the following jumpers:

A+CORE
1.2
Jumper to Clear CMOS RAM

Closing the "Clear real-time clock" jumper (labeled CLRTC in the documentation) clears CMOS RAM, which may be necessary in order to remove a forgotten password or erase improper, but forgotten, CMOS changes. To clear CMOS RAM, turn off the PC and unplug the AC outlet. Short the CLRTC jumper by placing a cap over it. Remove the cap and power up. When you boot, enter CMOS setup to reenter setup preferences. Leave the jumper open (uncapped) for now. Park the jumper cap on one pin.

Jumper Setting for Keyboard Power-Up

The keyboard power-up feature allows you to power up the PC by pressing the Spacebar on the keyboard. In order to use this feature, your power supply must support it. If the documentation for the computer case and power supply does not tell you if the feature is supported, disable it. If it is enabled and the feature is not supported by your power supply, the system will not come on.

Figure 15-3 shows the two different configurations for these jumpers, where dark shading over two pins indicates that they are closed. The darkened pins will always be in pairs, because a jumper cap closes two pins by connecting the pair. Also, sometimes in documentation, pin 1 is marked as a square and other pins as circles. On the system board, a very small 1 is sometimes imprinted next to pin 1 in a group of pins, or the name of the group is imprinted next to the entire group of three or four pins. Set the jumper to disable the keyboard power-up feature:

- Locate the jumper group on the system board.

- Place the jumper cap to disable the feature, as indicated in the documentation (in this case across pins 1 and 2).

Figure 15-3   Keyboard power-up feature is enabled or disabled with this jumper group

15

Jumper Settings for CPU Bus Frequency and CPU Multiplier

Before we continue with setting jumpers, a quick review of terms and relationships is in order. System-board documentation does not always use the most common terminology, which can lead to confusion. Also, terms used on one page or diagram might not be the same as the terms used on another page or diagram. Now, let's turn to our review: Recall that the CPU speed is the internal speed of the processor and is really a "frequency" rather than a "speed," because it is rated as MHz (million cycles per second). Also recall that the CPU communicates with

A+CORE
1.2

RAM over the memory bus, which is sometimes called the CPU bus, the clock bus, the system-board bus, the host bus, the system bus, and so on. The two most popular ratings for this memory bus are 66 MHz and 100 MHz. Also recall that the memory bus runs in sync with the CPU, and the CPU speed is determined by multiplying a factor times the memory bus speed, called the multiplier. This system-board documentation expresses that multiplier as a ratio, which, of course it really is. The documentation expresses this ratio using the colon, like this: "CPU core:bus frequency." In our example, 350:100 yields the multiple of 3.5 for a 350-MHz CPU and 100-MHz memory bus speed. And finally, recall that the PCI bus also runs in sync with the CPU, but at half or a third the rating of the memory bus.

As seen in Figure 15-4, this system board can run at recommended speeds of either 100 MHz or 66 MHz and can support multipliers of 3.5, 4.0, 4.5, and 5.0. As you can see from the jumper settings in the lower part of Figure 15-4, the jumpers can also be set so that the bus runs as high as 133 MHz, although the system-board documentation says that this speed is not supported by the Intel chip set on the board and is not guaranteed to be stable. The board accommodates Pentium II or Pentium II Celeron CPUs rated from 266 MHz to 450 MHz. In order to use the faster bus speed of 100 MHz, the CPU must be rated for at least 350 MHz.

The jumpers on this board must be set to determine the memory bus speed and the multiplier. Begin with the rating of the CPU, which in our case is 350 MHz. Look in Figure 15-4 and select the correct row in the diagram for the 350 MHz CPU. From that row, read that the ratio (or multiplier) must be 3.5 and the bus frequency (memory bus speed) must be set to 100 MHz. The settings for each jumper are written at the end of this row, but it's easier to locate them in the diagram in the lower part of the figure. To set the jumpers for the CPU multiplier (see the jumper part of the diagram), we selected the fourth group of the first row of possible selections because it is labeled with 3.5, which is the multiplier we need. For the bus frequency, select the fourth group in the one row of possible selections, because it is labeled with the appropriate speed. You have selected the multiplier to be 3.5, bus speed to be 100 MHz, and PCI bus speed to be 33.3 MHz. (For the PCI selection, look carefully at the very last row of the figure labeled PCI.) The PCI bus will be running at one-third the speed of the memory bus.

To complete this step of setting CPU bus frequency and CPU multiplier (your system board may have an entirely different grouping of jumpers to specify memory bus speed and multiplier):

- Locate the jumpers on the system board.
- Set them just as they are in our selections.

A+CORE
   1.2

❶ Begin with the speed of your CPU
❷ The CPU speed determines the ratio (multiplier)
❸ The CPU speed also determines the bus frequency

Set the jumpers by the iInternal speed of your processor as follows:

Intel CPU Model	Freq.	Ratio	BUS F.	(BUS Freq.) FS0	FS1	FS2	(Freq. Ratio) BF0	BF1	BF2	BF3
Pentium II	450MHz	4.5x	100MHz	[1-2]	[1-2]	[1-2]	[1-2]	[2-3]	[1-2]	[2-3]
Pentium II	400MHz	4.0x	100MHz	[1-2]	[1-2]	[1-2]	[2-3]	[2-3]	[1-2]	[2-3]
Pentium II	350MHz	3.5x	100MHz	[1-2]	[1-2]	[1-2]	[1-2]	[1-2]	[2-3]	[2-3]
Pentium II/Celeron	333MHz	5.0x	66MHz	[1-2]	[1-2]	[2-3]	[2-3]	[1-2]	[1-2]	[2-3]
Pentium II/Celeron	300MHz	4.5x	66MHz	[1-2]	[1-2]	[2-3]	[1-2]	[2-3]	[1-2]	[2-3]
Pentium II/Celeron	266MHz	4.0x	66MHz	[1-2]	[1-2]	[2-3]	[2-3]	[2-3]	[1-2]	[2-3]

Jumper settings

2.0X (2/1)   2.5X (5/2)   3.0X (3/1)   3.5X (7/2)   4.0X (4/1)   4.5X (9/2)   5.0X (5/1)

5.5X (11/2)   6.0X (6/1)   6.5X (13/2)   7.0X (7/1)   7.5X (15/2)   8.0X (8/1)
CPU Core:BUS Frequency Multiple

P2B CPU

66.8MHz	75MHz	83.3MHz	100.2MHz	103MHz	112MHz	133MHz ← CPU
33.4MHz	37.5MHz	41.65MHz	33.3MHz	33.4MHz	37.3MHz	33.3MHz/ ← PCI
						44.3MHz

CPU External Clock (BUS) Frequency Selection

Figure 15-4   Based on the advertised speed of your CPU, select the multiplier and the bus frequency from the table, which then determines the jumper settings to use

15

Figure 15-5 shows the final settings for one of the jumper groups, the CPU core to memory bus speed ratio.

A+CORE
1.2,
1.8

Figure 15-5   Jumper group that controls CPU core:bus frequency. Compare this photo to the diagram in Figure 15-4. The jumpers are set for the multiplier = 3.5.

Step 2: Install the CPU and CPU Fan

This system board has a Slot 1 for the Pentium II, which comes packaged either in a single edge contact cartridge (SECC) or a single edge processor package (SEPP) for the Celeron processor. For either processor, the system board uses a universal retention mechanism (URM), which is preinstalled on the board. Follow these steps to install the fan on the side of the processor first, and then install the processor on the system board.

- Unfold the URM arms. Flip both arms up until they lock into position (Figure 15-6).

- Examine the fan and processor to see how the fan brace lines up with holes in the side of the SECC (see Figure 15-7). Place the fan directly on the side of the SECC. The two should fit tightly together, with absolutely no space between them.

Figure 15-6   Preparing URM arms to receive the CPU. The arms are in the upright position.

Figure 15-7 The braces on the fan align with holes in the side of the SECC

15

A+CORE
1.2,
1.8

- After the fan and SECC are fitted together, place the SECC on a table and push the clamp on the fan down and into place, to secure the fan to the SECC (see Figure 15-8).

Push clamp down

Figure 15-8 Push the clamp on the fan down until it locks in place, locking the fan to the SECC

- Insert the fan and SECC into the supporting arms (Figure 15-9). The SECC should fit snugly into Slot 1, similarly to the way an expansion card settles down into an expansion slot. The arms should snap into position when the SECC is fully seated. Be certain you have a good fit here.

Fan and SECC

Supporting arms

Slot 1

Figure 15-9   Insert the fan and SECC into the supporting arms and Slot 1

■ Lock the SECC into position by pulling the SECC locks outward until they lock into the supporting arm lock holes. See Figure 15-10. (Incidentally, this figure shows a good view of the ports coming off the system board, which are labeled in the photo.)

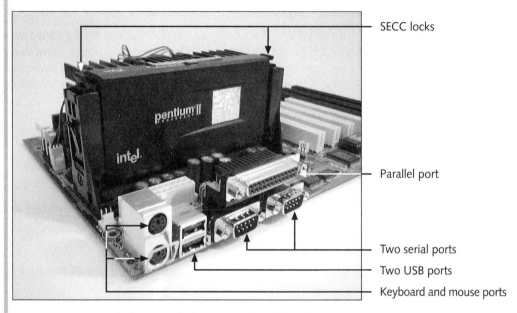

SECC locks

Parallel port

Two serial ports

Two USB ports

Keyboard and mouse ports

Figure 15-10   Push the SECC locks outward until they lock into the supporting arm lock holes

■ Connect the power cord coming from the fan to the power connection on the system board (Figure 15-11). Look for the power connection near Slot 1. If you have trouble locating it, see the system-board documentation.

15

Power for CPU fan

Figure 15-11   Connect the fan power cord to system board

Step 3: Installing RAM on the System Board

A+CORE
1.2

From discussions in Chapter 4, you know how to select the right kind of RAM and the right amount for your system board, and you know that you should be careful to match size, manufacturer, production batch, and mode.

Our system board has three DIMM sockets, and each socket can hold DIMMs that contain either 8, 16, 32, 64, 128, or 256 MB of memory. Therefore, the amount of memory installed on this board can range from a minimum of one DIMM with 8 MB to a maximum of three DIMMs each having 256 MB, for a total of 768 MB. In our example, we are installing a single 64-MB SDRAM DIMM that is PC100-compliant, meaning that it is rated to work at the memory bus speed of 100 MHz.

As shown in Figure 15-12, insert the DIMM into DIMM Slot 1 (the DIMM slots are labeled 1, 2, and 3), following these directions:

- Pull the supporting arms on the sides of the slot outward.

- Look on the DIMM edge connector for the notches, which will help orient the DIMM correctly over the slot.

- Insert the DIMM straight down into the slot.

- When the DIMM is fully inserted, the supporting arms should pop back into place.

Figure 15-12   Insert the DIMM into the slot by pressing straight down until the supporting arms lock into position

Figure 15-13 shows the DIMM installed.

Figure 15-13 One DIMM installed in DIMM Slot 1. Can you look at the DIMM and tell if it is ECC-compliant?

Step 4: Verify That the System Board Is Working by Performing a Memory Test

Before we get too far along in the details of installation, do a quick verification that the critical components are working. To do this test, connect the video card and connect power to the system board, plug in the monitor, and turn on the PC and the monitor. You should get a good memory test (before the first error occurs, saying that BIOS cannot find a boot device). By getting a good memory test, you know that the BIOS, RAM, CPU, most of the system board, and video are all working. If any one of these components fails, there is no point in continuing the installation until the problem is located or the part replaced.

Caution is in order here because some power supplies cannot handle this test. Less expensive power supplies will not work or might even be damaged if they are turned on without a full power load applied. For these power supplies, a full load must include a hard drive or a similar device that will draw +12V. If you are using a very inexpensive power supply, skip this memory test and proceed to Step 5.

The system board is very vulnerable during this test, so you want to be careful, especially when the power is on. Set the system board on an antistatic mat as you work. Because the port side of the video card will protrude down below the system board when it is fully inserted in the expansion slot, the system board must be sitting higher than the table surface. (For our memory test, we set the system board on top of its shipping box with an antistatic mat under it.) When the power is on, don't touch the system board, the video card, or any system-board components.

15

Installing the Video Card

The next step for your test is to temporarily install the video card on the system board. Proceed as follows:

As in Figure 15-14, place the video card into position. When seating a card, push the card directly down into the expansion slot, as the photo illustrates.

Skirt at end of card

AGP edge connector

AGP slot

Figure 15-14   Insert the video card in the AGP slot

An expansion card inserted into a system board that is not already installed in a case is vulnerable to damage. Be careful that you don't move the system board much once the card is installed, so that the card is not bent as the system board is moved about.

Powering Up and Watching for the POST Memory Test

In this next step, we connect the system board to the power supply and to the monitor, and perform POST in order to verify that critical parts are working.

- Set the system board near enough to the computer case so that the power cords can reach the power connections on the system board.

- Connect the power cord, which will only go into the P1 power connector in one direction (Figure 15-15).

Figure 15-15   Connect the power cord to the system board

- This ATX power supply requires that the ATX power switch be connected to the system board. The switch wire comes from the front of the case and connects to the system board at the panel connections (Item 10 in Figure 15-2). Connect the switch wire to the panel connection, as seen in Figure 15-16. (An AT power supply does not have this switch wire.)

Figure 15-16   Connect the ATX power switch to the system board in preparation for the memory test

- Plug the video cable into the video port of the video card. Figure 15-17 shows all connections to the system board ready for the test.

- Connect the power cords from the case and monitor to a wall outlet or surge suppressor.

- Before turning on the power, check again that all connections are secure, unused power cords are tucked safely out of harm's way, and the system-board components are not touching anything metallic or conductive that would ground them or cause a short.

- Turn on the monitor and the PC and watch startup BIOS perform POST (see Figure 15-18).

15

Figure 15-17   All connections to the system board are ready for the memory test

Figure 15-18   Memory test is successful

- Look for POST to count up a full 64 MB of RAM on the monitor screen. Also look for POST to display the speed of the CPU and confirm that the speed is correct in order to verify your jumper settings on the system board. Next, POST looks for hard drives and finds none, and then gives an error message when it also cannot detect a floppy drive or keyboard. This is all to be expected; however, the memory test does prove that the critical components of the system already installed are working, and that you can continue with the installation.

- Turn the computer and monitor off, remove the video card, and disconnect the power cords (including the power cord from the power supply to the system board) before continuing the installation.

Step 5: Installing the System Board in the Computer Case

A^{+}CORE
1.2

Installing the system board in the computer case may take more patience than installing other components. The case comes with the necessary spacers and screws, and most system boards align well with most cases. However, sometimes the holes are difficult to align, and screws and spacers difficult to install. Some system boards use a small faceplate that is installed between the system-board ports and the case, which creates a well-fitted enclosure around the ports. First, install the faceplate at the rear of the case and then install the standoffs. A **standoff** (or spacer) is a small plastic or metal peg that separates the system board from the case and holds the system board in place. Standoffs are necessary so that components on the bottom of the system board don't touch the case, which can cause a short on the system board.

Select the correct faceplate for the rear of the case and install it:

- This system board comes with three faceplates to cover the ports that come directly off the system board. Select the one faceplate that fits the ports for this system board (see Figure 15-19). The other faceplates can then be discarded.

Hole inside of case to receive a faceplate

Ports on system board will later show through holes in faceplate

15

Faceplates

Figure 15-19   The computer case comes with several faceplates. Select the faceplate that fits over the ports that come off the system board. The other plates can be discarded.

A+CORE
    1.2

- Insert the faceplate in the hole at the back of the case (see Figure 15-20).

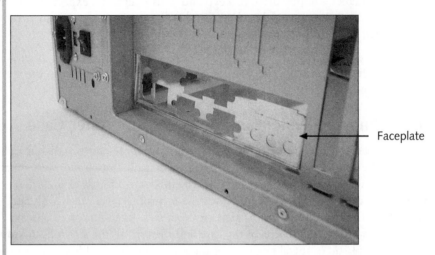

Faceplate

Figure 15-20   Install the faceplate in the hole at the rear of the computer case

The next step is to select the holes for the standoffs, install the standoffs, place the system board in the case, and use screws to hold it in place.

- To determine in which holes to use the standoffs, align the system board with the case and consider the position of the board in the case. To help orient the board to the case, align the ports coming off the system board to the faceplate just installed. Because a case is designed to fit more than one type of system board, there will be unused screw holes on the case. If you cannot locate a screw hole on the case, try tipping the case on its end so that you can see the bottom, where the holes are.

- Screw the standoffs into the slots on the bottom of the case. Figure 15-21 shows how the standoff is positioned correctly so that when the system board is moved into position the standoff will line up directly underneath the hole in the system board where a screw will be inserted into the standoff.

- Use as many standoffs as there are aligned holes in the system board and in the case. With this case and board, six standoffs can be used, but don't settle for fewer than four.

- If you need to remove a standoff to move it to a new slot, needle-nose pliers work well to unscrew the standoff so that you can move it to a new hole.

- After the standoffs have been installed in the case, place the system board inside the case and use screws to attach the system board to the case, using the standoffs to receive the screws. Figure 15-22 shows the system board sitting in the computer case. Three standoffs and four screw holes are visible where the board must be moved slightly left and down in order to align the holes over the standoffs.

$A^{+CORE}_{1.2}$

Figure 15-21 Select the positions of each standoff so that holes in the system board will align directly over the standoff. The system board will later be held in place with screws in the standoffs.

Figure 15-22 Three standoffs and four screw holes are visible

15

Step 6: Attaching the Power Cord and Front Panel Connectors to the System Board

A+CORE 1.2 Connect the power cord to the P1 power connection on the system board. The cord can only connect in one direction. (Recall that for an AT system board there are two power connections, P8 and P9, which are connected using the black-to-black rule.)

On the front panel of the computer case are several lights and one switch, and the speaker is nearby. The switches are inputs to the system board, while the lights and speaker are outputs from the system board, which are all connected to the system board by wires. The case comes with these wires permanently attached, but the leads on the ends of each wire must be connected to pins on the system board. The next step to complete the installation of the system board is to connect the wire leads from the front panel of the case to the system board. You can see the front panel connectors as Item 10 in the diagram in Figure 15-2. A close-up of these pins with the one power switch wire attached is shown in Figure 15-16, and the purpose of each connection is labeled in Figure 15-23. The wires coming from the front panel of the case are also labeled in Figure 15-24.

Figure 15-23   Panel connections on the system board

There are five wires coming from the front panel. The five connectors are:

- **Reset switch.** Used to reboot the computer

- **HDD LED.** Controls a light on the front panel that lights up when any IDE device is in use. (LED stands for light-emitting diode; an LED is a light on the front panel.)

- **Speaker.** Controls the speaker

Figure 15-24 Five wires from the front panel connect to the system board

- **Power LED.** Light indicating that power is on

- **Remote switch.** Controls power to the system board; must be connected for the PC to power up

Because the computer case and the system board were not made by the same manufacturer, the labels on the connectors are not the same as the labels on the system board or in the documentation for the system board. A little experience will quickly help you make the translation, but it's okay to guess when connecting a wire to a connection. If it doesn't work, no harm is done.

The connectors are really pins. A lead wire from the front panel may have pin holes for two, three, or four pins. The speaker uses a 4-pin connector, and the power LED uses a 3-pin connector. The reset switch, HDD LED, and remote switch all use 2-pin connectors. A 3-pin connector similar to the power LED is shown in Figure 15-25.

Figure 15-25 Look for the small triangle embedded on the wire lead connectors to correctly orient the connector to the system-board connector pins

To help orient the connector on the system-board pins, look for a small triangle embedded on the connector that marks one of the outside wires as pin 1. Sometimes the documentation will mark pin 1 as a square pin in the diagram, rather than round like the other pins.

A+CORE
1.2

Also, the wires coming from the connector are color-coded, although the coding scheme for the wires is often not included in the computer case documentation. Some connectors have the name of the lead printed or embedded on the connector; the case we use does have that. But if the purpose of the wire is not written on the connector to show which wire lead goes to which connector on the system board, you must trace the wire back to its source on the front panel. You might need to do a little guessing until you get the right lead wires connected to the right location on the system board. Sometimes you will not know if your guess is right until you power up and check out the reset button and LED lights on the front of the case. In general, proceed as follows:

- If the purpose of the wire lead is not written on the wire connector, then trace it back to its source on the front of the computer case to determine which lead belongs where.

- Orient the lead to the pins by looking for the triangle on the lead connection and orienting it according to the documentation. Or try orienting the connector to the pins by using the color of the wire.

- If neither method of orientation works, then guess. Later, if one of the wires does not work, reverse the connector. For example, later, when the PC is up and working but the hard drive light does not come on, reverse the HDD LED connector on the pins.

For this installation, using the documentation in Figure 15-23, we see that the five wires in Figure 15-24 fit the pins in the right corner of the system board this way:

- Reset switch wire in Figure 15-24 matches "Reset SW" in Figure 15-23

- HDD LED wire in Figure 15-24 matches "IDE LED" in Figure 15-23

- Speaker wire in Figure 15-24 matches "Speaker connector" in Figure 15-23

- Power LED wire in Figure 15-24 matches "Power LED" in Figure 15-23

- Remote switch wire in Figure 15-24 matches "ATX Power Switch" in Figure 15-23

 TIP   If the ATX Power Switch is not connected correctly, later when the PC is turned on, it will appear "dead." There will be no video, no beeps, no lights.

Step 7: Installing the Floppy Drive, Hard Drive, and Zip Drive

Installing the floppy drive is generally easy to do, but the other three drives (hard drive, Zip drive, and DVD drive) require a little planning because they are all IDE devices. However, we cover the floppy drive, hard drive, and Zip drive as a group here because they all fit together into a removable bay. The DVD drive will be covered later as part of the complete DVD subsystem.

A+CORE
1.2

Set IDE Jumpers on Each IDE Drive in the System

Before we get into the details of installing the drives, let's quickly review IDE installations previously covered in Chapter 7. Recall that there can be up to two IDE controllers on a system board, the primary and secondary IDE controller. Each controller can support up to two drives, a master and a slave, for a total of up to four IDE drives in a system. When possible, leave the hard drive as the single drive on one controller so that it does not compete with another drive for access to the controller and possibly slow down performance. Recall that each IDE drive must be configured as single, master, or slave. Configuration is normally done by setting jumpers on the drive housing, and the explanation of the jumper settings is most often printed somewhere on the housing.

In our installation, we will set the hard drive as the single drive on the primary controller, and the Zip drive will be set to master and the DVD drive to slave on the secondary controller. Figure 15-26 shows the back of the Zip drive. There is a group of three jumpers, and printed on the top of the drive is an explanation of each setting. The rightmost pins in the group are closed in the photo, which is the setting for master. This drive is typical of most IDE drives in that there are a 40-pin IDE data connection, jumpers, and a power connection on the backside of the drive.

Jumper setting explained

Power connection
Jumper group
IDE 40-pin data connection

Figure 15-26   Jumpers on the Zip drive housing are used to configure an IDE drive as single, master, or slave

In a similar fashion, the hard drive jumpers are set to a single IDE drive, and the DVD drive jumpers are set to slave. Later, when we connect data cables to the drives, the hard drive will have its own data cable, and the Zip drive and DVD drive will share a cable.

Installing Drives in the Removable Bay

There are two bays in this computer case (Figure 15-27). The top bay is designed for large drives, such as a DVD or CD-ROM drive, and is not removable. The lower bay is narrow, designed for small drives, such as floppy drives and hard drives, and is removable. This bay has

15

$A^{+CORE}_{\ \ 1.2}$ room for three drives; the top two positions are accessible from the front of the case and will be used for the floppy drive and Zip drive, while the lower position, which is not accessible from the front of the case, will be used for the hard drive. When installing drives, be sure to use short screws that will not protrude too deeply into the drive and damage it. Follow these steps to install the three small drives in the lower bay:

- Place the floppy drive in the bay and align the drive flush with the front of the computer case (Figure 15-27), noting where the screw holes in the drive align with the side of the bay.

Stationary bay for large drives

Floppy drive

Removable bay for small drives

Figure 15-27   Line up the floppy drive in the removable bay, flush with the front of the case

- Remove the bay and secure the floppy drive to the bay with four screws, two on each side of the bay (Figure 15-28).

- Install the Zip drive underneath the floppy drive; align it flush with the floppy drive, and secure it with four screws.

- Install the hard drive in the last position (Figure 15-29). Position the hard drive flush with the end of the bay so that it will butt up against the computer case once the bay is in position.

A+CORE
1.2

Screws

Floppy drive

Bay

Figure 15-28 Secure the floppy drive to the removable bay with four screws, two on each side of the bay

Floppy drive

Zip drive

Hard drive

15

Figure 15-29 Position the hard drive flush with the end of the bay

- Next, install the data cables to each drive (Figure 15-30). The floppy drive has its own cable. Install the end of the cable with the twist so this drive will be drive A in the final configuration. Look on the drive for a small 1 that indicates pin 1 and align that with the colored edge of the data cable. (In most cases, pin 1 is next to the power connection on a floppy drive and oriented in the opposite direction from that of IDE drives.)

A$^{+CORE}_{1.2}$

Connected to Zip drive

Twist in cable for drive A

Hard drive cable

For DVD drive

Figure 15-30   Connect the cables to all three drives

- Connect the first IDE cable to the hard drive and the second IDE cable to the Zip drive. Make sure the pin 1 label on the drive housings is aligned with the colored edge of the data cables.

- Plan for the second IDE data cable connected to the Zip drive to also connect to the DVD drive, which will later be installed just above it.

- Place the bay back into position and secure the bay with the bay screw (Figure 15-31).

Figure 15-31 Secure the bay with the bay screw

- Install a power connection to each drive (Figure 15-32). The floppy drive will use the small power connection, and the other drives use the larger ones. It doesn't matter which of the power cords you use, because they all produce the same voltage.

- Connect the floppy drive data cable to the floppy drive connection on the system board, the hard drive data cable to the primary IDE connection, and the Zip drive data cable to the secondary IDE connection on the system board (see Figure 15-33). For each cable, look for pin 1 labeled on the system board and align it with the colored edge of the data cable.

A+CORE 1.2

15

A+CORE
1.2

Figure 15-32   Connect a power cord to each drive

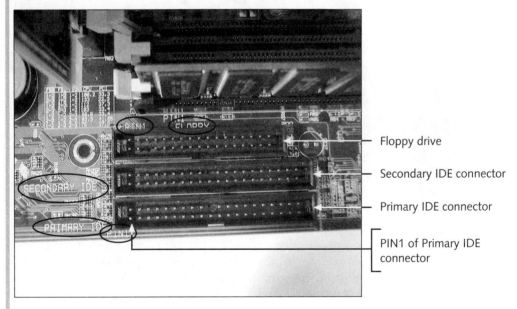

Figure 15-33   Floppy drive and two IDE connectors on the system board

Step 8: Installing the Video Card, Sound Card, Modem Card, and SCSI Adapter

The next step is to install the expansion cards, including the video, sound, modem, and SCSI cards. In general, when installing an expansion card, first read the documentation for the card and set any jumper switches or DIP switches on the card. (Most cards today are Plug and Play and have no jumpers.) Next, select the expansion slot you plan to use on the system board, remove the faceplate for the selected slot from the computer case, and insert the card in the slot. When inserting a card in an expansion slot, press the card straight down into the slot. As you insert the card, don't allow the card to wobble in the slot, because that could widen the slot and prevent a tight fit. Make sure the card is inserted solidly in the slot and then, using the same screw that held the faceplate in position, screw the card to the computer case.

Follow these directions to install the four expansion cards:

Installing the Video Card

The video card has no jumpers to set and goes into the single AGP slot on the system board, so installation is straightforward. Remove the faceplate from the opening on the back of the computer case for this slot. Insert the card in the slot and secure it with a screw (Figure 15-34). That's it.

15

Figure 15-34   Secure the video card in the slot with a screw

Installing the Sound Card

The Sound Blaster sound card shown in Figure 15-35 has three internal connections (connections to something inside the case) and one jumper group that enables or disables a speaker amplifier.

Figure 15-35   The Sound Blaster sound card has three internal connections and one jumper group that controls amplifier support

In a system using a CD-ROM drive, an audio cord would run from the CD-ROM drive to the CD audio connector (center connector in the group of three) to receive audio input directly from the CD-ROM. However, in our installation, we're using a DVD drive, which reads CDs as well as DVDs. The DVD drive requires a DVD decoder card to decode the audio and video data, so the setup will be slightly different from one that has a CD-ROM drive, which does not require a decoder card. There will be an audio cord that will transmit audio directly from the DVD drive to the DVD decoder. The decoder card will decode the audio data, and then another audio cord will send the decoded data from the DVD decoder card to the sound card (more about this DVD installation later in the chapter). Since we will be using a speaker system with an amplifier, we want to disable the amplifier on the card. Therefore, proceed as follows:

- Set the jumper on the sound card to disable amplifier support (jumper cap in lower position).

- Connect the audio wire to the center connector labeled CD audio (Figure 15-36).

Figure 15-36   Connect the audio card to the sound card

- Remove the faceplate from an ISA slot and insert the card in the slot.

- Secure the card to the computer case with a screw.

Installing the Modem Card

The modem we're installing is the 3Com U.S. Robotics 56K Winmodem. It comes with a phone cord and two floppy disks. One disk contains the User Guide, and the other contains driver files. The modem is Plug-and-Play-compliant and uses an ISA slot. There are no jumpers or switches to set on the card, so the physical installation is simple. (If you are installing a modem card that is not Plug and Play, read the documentation to see how to set jumpers for the IRQ and I/O address that you will use for the card.) Select an ISA slot and remove its faceplate. Insert the modem card in the slot and secure the card with a screw.

Installing the SCSI Host Adapter

Next is the installation of an SCSI host adapter. The SCSI host adapter we use is shown in Figure 15-37 and supports only one single-ended SCSI device, as evidenced by the 25-pin port on the back of the card. (Remember that differential SCSI devices use a 50-pin connection.) The card is set to use SCSI ID 7 and (since it will always be on one end of the SCSI chain) to provide termination on the SCSI bus. Figure 15-38 shows a diagram of the card with the jumpers marked. The card is not Plug-and-Play-compliant, so there are several jumpers on the card, which collectively make up the card configuration, including the IRQ, I/O address, SCSI parity, and SCSI disconnection.

15

Figure 15-37   SCSI host adapter card

Figure 15-38   Diagram of the SCSI host adapter showing jumper positions on the card

Figure 15-39 shows a table of jumper settings similar to that in the card documentation. After reviewing our options, we choose the default settings, which are IRQ 10, I/O address 140h, SCSI parity enabled, and SCSI disconnection disabled. When you're installing any card, don't forget to mark the selections you have made on the documentation. Later, if you want to know what settings have been chosen, you can look at the documentation rather than having to remove the case cover to see the card. Proceed as follows:

- Even though the jumpers should already be set to these settings according to the table in Figure 15-39, verify that they are set correctly on the card.

SCSI Disconnection	J2	I/O Port Address	J5	SCSI Parity	J7
Enabled	Off	140h*	On	Enabled*	On
Disabled*	On	340h	Off	Disabled	Off

	IRQ Channel	J3	J4	J12	J11	J10	J9
On = Jumper	9	On	On	Off	Off	Off	On
Off = No Jumper	10*	Off	On	Off	Off	On	Off
	11	On	Off	Off	On	Off	Off
	12	Off	Off	On	Off	Off	Off

Figure 15-39   Table of jumper settings for the host adapter

- Install the card in a 16-bit ISA expansion slot.

Step 9: Installing the DVD Subsystem

This multimedia PC includes a DVD drive. We're installing the Creative PC-DVD Encore by Creative Labs, Inc. Besides the documentation and a sample DVD game disc, the parts that are included in the DVD drive kit are shown in Figure 15-40. The data coming from the DVD drive is split into video data and sound data. Recall from Chapter 10 that video data must be decoded before output to the monitor, and sound data must be decoded before output to a regular sound card (one that does not process Dolby sound). Both are accomplished by the DVD decoder card. Figure 15-41 shows the flow of data in the completed system.

15

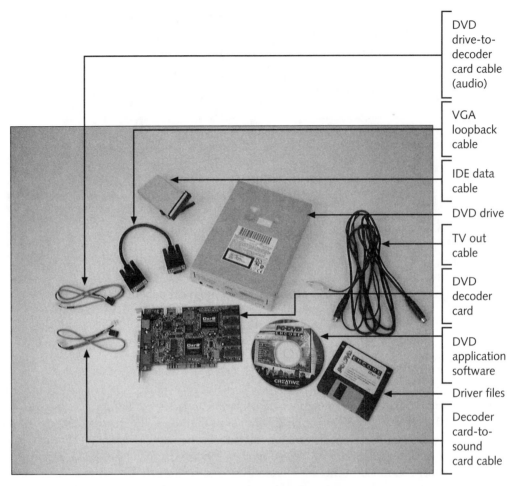

DVD drive-to-decoder card cable (audio)

VGA loopback cable

IDE data cable

DVD drive

TV out cable

DVD decoder card

DVD application software

Driver files

Decoder card-to-sound card cable

Figure 15-40   Parts that are included in the DVD drive kit

Figure 15-41   Data flow in the DVD subsystem

To help make the final installation of parts easier to visualize, we set up the installation outside the case and took the photo shown in Figure 15-42. This photo was taken simply to help you understand the final installation. No power was turned on while the components were in this position!

Video data "loops back" to DVD decoder

Decoded audio data to sound card

Video card

Sound card

DVD decoder card

IDE data cable carries video data

DVD drive

Audio data to decoder

VGA output to monitor

Audio output to speakers

Figure 15-42   The complete DVD subsystem, including the drive (right) and various components installed on the system board (left)

The DVD decoder card (Figure 15–43) has connections for audio in, audio out, video in, and video out. In addition, there are two other external ports, one for TV out and one for Dolby digital sound out. Use the TV out port to play DVD movies from your PC, and the Dolby port if you have a Dolby speaker system. Recall from Chapter 10 that a Dolby sound system, which is the standard sound for DVD audio data, can use up to six speakers on six separate audio tracks to provide a rich theater-like sound.

Output to a Dolby digital sound device

Audio out (to sound card)

Audio in (from DVD drive)

PCI connection

VGA in (from video card using loopback cable)

VGA out (to monitor)

TV out (using TV cable provided)

Figure 15-43   DVD decoder card

The rear of the DVD drive is shown in Figure 15-44, and a diagram of the rear panel is shown in Figure 15-45. Looking closely at Figure 15-44, note that the jumper is set so that the drive will be a slave on the IDE connection.

IDE connection

15

Power

Jumper in "slave" position

Audio out

Figure 15-44   Rear of DVD drive (see Figure 15-45 for an explanation of each connection)

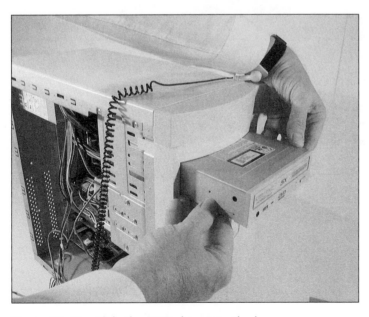

Figure 15-45 Rear panel of the DVD drive

Looking at the location of the bay for the DVD drive, we decide to connect the audio cable first, slide the drive into the bay, and then connect the remaining cable and cord. Survey your own situation for the best approach. Follow these steps to install the DVD components:

- Confirm that the jumper on the DVD drive is set to slave (the default setting).

- Connect the DVD drive audio cord to the analog audio connection on the rear of the drive.

- Remove the faceplate on the front of the computer case covering the bay opening.

- Slide the drive into the bay from the front of the bay (Figure 15-46).

Figure 15-46 Slide the DVD drive into the bay

- Secure the drive in the bay with two screws on each side of the drive.

- Attach the IDE data cable to the drive, being careful to align the edge color of the cable with pin 1 on the drive (Figure 15-47).

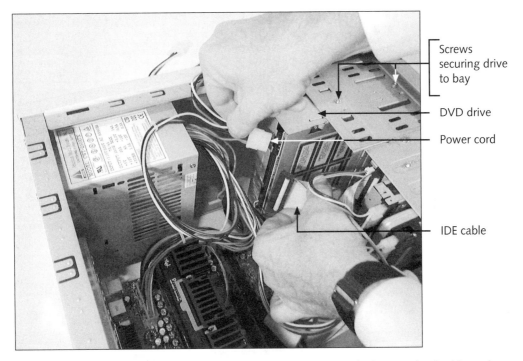

Screws securing drive to bay

DVD drive

Power cord

IDE cable

Figure 15-47 After the DVD drive is secured in its bay, attach the IDE data cable and power cord

- Connect a power cord to the power connection on the drive.

- Connect the audio cord coming from the DVD drive to the audio in connection on the DVD decoder card.

- Connect the second audio cord first to the audio out connection on the DVD decoder card and then to the audio in connection on the sound card (refer back to Figure 15-42). The cord has two plugs at the sound-card end. Select the plug that fits the sound-card connection.

- Insert the DVD decoder card in a PCI expansion slot and secure it with a screw.

That completes the DVD subsystem installation inside the computer case. Later, when you are ready to use the DVD system, install the video loopback cable (see Figure 15-48), which presents video data to the DVD decoder for decoding before the decoder sends the video data on to the monitor.

15

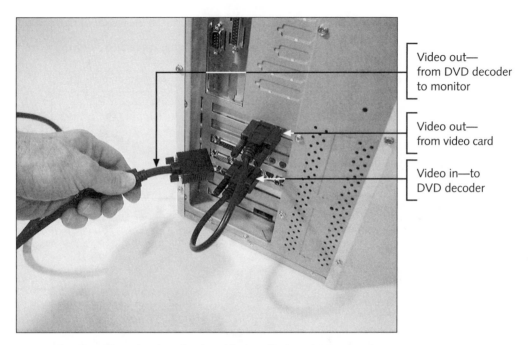

Video out—
from DVD decoder
to monitor

Video out—
from video card

Video in—to
DVD decoder

Figure 15-48   The video loopback cable installed in the DVD subsystem

Step 10: Connecting Other Essential Peripherals

The installation inside the case is now complete (Figure 15-49). Install the case cover next. In our installation, the case cover is two panels that fit on each side of the case. Slide the panels into position (Figure 15-50) and secure them with screws on the back of the case. Next, connect the mouse, keyboard, speakers, and monitor, and then install the operating system and drivers for each hardware device that needs one, and then the applications software. You might want to power up the PC and make sure it is operating before you install the case cover, in order to ensure that everything inside the case is working.

SCSI host in
ISA slot

DVD decoder
card in PCI slot

Video card in
AGP slot

DVD drive

Pentium II

Floppy drive

Zip drive

Hard drive

Sound card
in PCI slot

Modem card
in ISA slot

Figure 15-49   All components installed inside the case

Slide to front

15

Figure 15-50   Install the panels on the sides of the computer case

With older system boards, when you first turn on the PC, you must go to CMOS setup and configure the system. With newer system boards using autodetection, this should not be necessary.

Step 11: Installing the Operating System

A+ OS
2.1

When you first turn on a brand-new PC, nothing is written to the hard drive, so you must boot from a floppy disk. We are installing Windows 98 from a CD and are using the DVD drive to read the CD. The floppy disk must have the necessary drivers on it to support the DVD drive while Windows 98 is being installed. (The same files that support a CD-ROM drive can support a DVD drive so the drive can read a CD.) Later, after the OS is installed, we can then install the DVD drivers under Windows.

We need a boot disk that contains enough DOS to partition and format the hard drive, and drivers to support the DVD drive in order to read a CD from which Windows 98 can be installed. Table 15-2 lists the files on the disk that are required. In addition, it is wise for the disk to have other files that Windows normally puts on an emergency startup disk.

The command in AUTOEXEC.BAT to load the DOS CD-ROM extender is:

```
MSCDEX.EXE /D:MYTAG /L:E /M:10
```

The command in CONFIG.SYS to load the CD-ROM driver is:

```
DEVICE=MTMCDAI.SYS /D:MYTAG
```

Including the /L parameter in the first command will assign E as the drive letter for the DVD drive. For more information about CD-ROM drivers, see Chapter 10.

Table 15-2   Files needed on the bootable disk to start the load process

Files	Description
COMMAND.COM, IO.SYS, MSDOS.SYS	DOS 7.1 files necessary to boot
AUTOEXEC.BAT and CONFIG.SYS	Needed to load device driver to support the DVD drive and to load Himem.sys so there is enough memory available to DOS to support the DVD drive and format the hard drive
MSCDEX.EXE and MTMCDAI.SYS	DOS extender and a device driver that together allow the DVD drive to "act like" a CD-ROM drive (just about any CD-ROM driver would work in place of the MTMCDAI.SYS file used here)
HIMEM.SYS	Allows access to extended memory that is needed by DOS and drivers
FDISK.EXE and FORMAT.COM	Needed to partition and format the hard drive

Follow these steps to format the hard drive and load the operating system:

- Prepare a bootable disk with the files listed in Table 15-2.

$A^+ \begin{smallmatrix} OS \\ 2.1 \end{smallmatrix}$

- Turn on the PC. You should see the BIOS count up memory to 64 MB, recognize the three IDE devices, and list the PCI devices installed, together with the resources assigned to them. It should then boot from the floppy disk and come to an A prompt.

- Run FDISK and partition the hard drive.

- Run FORMAT C:/S to format the hard drive and enable it to boot DOS 7.

- Run Windows 98 Setup from the CD in the DVD drive.

Step 12: Connecting Remaining Peripherals and Installing Device Drivers

After Windows 98 is installed, install the drivers for the sound card, video card, DVD drive, Zip drive, and modem. Next, connect the remaining peripherals, including the speakers and scanner. When connecting the scanner to the SCSI connection, include a terminating resistor at the scanner end. Figure 15-51 shows the terminating resistor being attached to the end of the SCSI cable that will then attach to the scanner.

15

Figure 15-51   Include a terminating resistor at the scanner end of the SCSI chain

Connect the video camera to the USB port and install the video camera software. Figure 15-52 shows the completed system.

Figure 15-52   The completed system

JUMPERFREE SYSTEM BOARD INSTALLATION

A+CORE
1.2,
1.8

Some system boards do not use jumpers to configure the system board and CPU frequencies. For example, look at the system board shown in Figure 3-3 in Chapter 3, which has a Pentium III processor installed. The processor runs at 667 MHz, and the system board is configured to run at 133 MHz. You can configure the system board by using a bank of DIP switches on the board, as shown in Figure 15-53, or you can use CMOS setup to configure the board, which is called JumperFree mode. The board has a single group of jumpers, shown in Figure 15-54. Use this group of jumpers to enable and disable JumperFree mode. When the cap is over pins 1 and 2, JumperFree mode is enabled; when the cap is over pins 2 and 3, JumperFree Mode is disabled.

A+CORE
  1.2,
  1.8

Figure 15-53   A system board can use a bank of DIP switches for configuration settings

Cap over pins 1 and 2

Pin 3

15

Figure 15-54   Because pins 1 and 2 are covered, the JumperFree mode is enabled

If you do not want to use JumperFree mode, set the jumpers to disable the feature and use the DIP switches to control the configuration. Figure 15-55 shows the documentation for this system board with the possible configurations for the system. Because this system has a 667 MHz Pentium III processor, the second row is selected in the table, and the ten DIP switches are then set to off, off, off, off, on, off, off, on, on, and off, according to the table.

A+CORE
1.2,
1.8

Intel CPU Model	Freq.	Mult.	BUS F.	(CPU BUS Freq.)				(Freq. Multiple)				AGP	
				7	8	9	10	1	2	3	4	5	6
Pentium III	733MHz	5.5x	133MHz	[OFF]	[OFF]	[OFF]	[OFF]	[OFF]	[OFF]	[OFF]	[ON]	[ON]	[OFF]
Pentium III	667MHz	5.0x	133MHz	[OFF]	[OFF]	[OFF]	[OFF]	[ON]	[OFF]	[OFF]	[ON]	[ON]	[OFF]
Pentium III	700MHz	7.0x	100MHz	[OFF]	[OFF]	[OFF]	[ON]	[ON]	[OFF]	[ON]	[OFF]	[ON]	[OFF]
Pentium III	650MHz	6.5x	100MHz	[OFF]	[OFF]	[OFF]	[ON]	[OFF]	[ON]	[ON]	[OFF]	[ON]	[OFF]
Pentium III	600MHz	6.0x	100MHz	[OFF]	[OFF]	[OFF]	[ON]	[ON]	[ON]	[ON]	[OFF]	[ON]	[OFF]
Pentium III	550MHz	5.5x	100MHz	[OFF]	[OFF]	[OFF]	[ON]	[OFF]	[OFF]	[OFF]	[ON]	[ON]	[OFF]
Pentium III	500MHz	5.0x	100MHz	[OFF]	[OFF]	[OFF]	[ON]	[ON]	[OFF]	[OFF]	[ON]	[ON]	[OFF]
Pentium II/III	450MHz	4.5x	100MHz	[OFF]	[OFF]	[OFF]	[ON]	[OFF]	[ON]	[OFF]	[ON]	[ON]	[OFF]
Pentium II	400MHz	4.0x	100MHz	[OFF]	[OFF]	[OFF]	[ON]	[ON]	[ON]	[OFF]	[ON]	[ON]	[OFF]
Pentium II	350MHz	3.5x	100MHz	[OFF]	[OFF]	[OFF]	[ON]	[OFF]	[OFF]	[ON]	[ON]	[ON]	[OFF]
Celeron	466MHz	7.0x	66MHz	[OFF]	[OFF]	[ON]	[ON]	[ON]	[OFF]	[ON]	[OFF]	[ON]	[OFF]
Celeron	433MHz	6.5x	66MHz	[OFF]	[OFF]	[ON]	[ON]	[OFF]	[ON]	[ON]	[OFF]	[ON]	[OFF]
Celeron	400MHz	6.0x	66MHz	[OFF]	[OFF]	[ON]	[ON]	[ON]	[ON]	[ON]	[OFF]	[ON]	[OFF]
Pentium II/Celeron	333MHz	5.0x	66MHz	[OFF]	[OFF]	[ON]	[ON]	[ON]	[OFF]	[OFF]	[ON]	[ON]	[OFF]
Pentium II/Celeron	300MHz	4.5x	66MHz	[OFF]	[OFF]	[ON]	[ON]	[OFF]	[ON]	[OFF]	[ON]	[ON]	[OFF]
Pentium II/Celeron	266MHz	4.0x	66MHz	[OFF]	[OFF]	[ON]	[ON]	[ON]	[ON]	[OFF]	[ON]	[ON]	[OFF]
Pentium II	233MHz	3.5x	66MHz	[OFF]	[OFF]	[ON]	[ON]	[OFF]	[OFF]	[ON]	[ON]	[ON]	[OFF]

Use this selection for a Pentium III CPU rated at 677Mhz

For updated processor settings, visit the ASUS Web site

Figure 15-55   When not using JumperFree mode, set DIP switches according to the internal speed of your processor

To use JumperFree mode, set the jumpers to JumperFree mode and set all DIP switches to off. When you boot the PC, access CMOS setup and configure the system board by using the Advanced Setup screen, shown in Figure 15-56. For example, for this system board, set the CPU Speed to 667 MHz, the CPU System Frequency Multiple to 5.0x, and System/PCI Frequency to 133.9/33.25 MHz. To select these settings, follow the directions at the bottom of the setup screen.

Incidentally, this system board has a unique way to reset CMOS when you need to erase a forgotten password and return the CMOS settings to the default values. Rather than using two jumper pins as does the system board shown earlier in the chapter, this system board uses two solder pads positioned very close to the round lithium battery. Turn the system off, place a small screwdriver across the pads, remove the screwdriver, and reboot the system.

A^{+CORE}
1.2,
1.8

```
                        AwardBIOS Setup Utility
  Main     Advanced     Power      Boot      Exit

  CPU Speed                      [Manual]        Item Specific Help
  CPU:System Frequency Multiple  [4.0x]
  System/PCI Frequency (MHz)     [133.9/33.25]   To make changes to the
  System/SDRAM Frequency Ratio   [4/3]           first 4 fields, the
  CPU Vcore                      [2.00V]         motherboard must be set
  CPU Level 1 Cache              [Enabled]       to jumperfree mode.
  CPU Level 2 Cache              [Enabled]
  CPU Level 2 Cache ECC Check    [Disabled]      To set the following 2
  Processor Serial Number        [Disabled]      fields, the CPU speed  1
  Bios Update                    [Enabled]       must be set to [Manual]o
  PS/2 Mouse Function Control    [Auto]          If the frquency is
  USB Legacy Support             [Auto]          adjusted too high, the
  OS/2 Onboard Memory > 64M      [Disabled]      system may hang. Please
► Chip Configuration                             turn off the system and
► I/O Device Configuration                       then restart to set the
► PCI Configuration                              frequency.
► Shadow Configuration


  F1   Help   ↑↓  Select Item  -/+    Change Values    F5   Setup Defaults
  ESC  Exit   ←→  Select Menu  Enter  Select ► Sub-Menu F10  Save and Exit
```

Figure 15-56   When the system board is set to JumperFree mode, use CMOS setup to select CPU speed and frequency ratios

CHAPTER SUMMARY

❑ The most common reason to buy a brand-name PC rather than a clone is after-sales service.

❑ Many brand-name PCs use proprietary designs that force you to use only that particular brand name's parts and service when upgrading or maintaining the PC.

❑ Middle-range PCs offer more network capability, more expandability, more support, and more prior testing than do low-end PCs.

❑ Some reasons to build your own PC are the knowledge you will gain, the control you will have over the choice of individual parts, the availability of documentation and original software disks, and the satisfaction of having built the PC yourself.

❑ When choosing to build your own PC, be aware that the process will take time, that you will likely encounter problems along the way, that there will be no warranty on the assembled product, and that you probably will not save money.

❑ Plan the project of assembling a PC well. Get answers to any questions you may have on the details before you begin. Keep things organized as you work. Expect the project to be fun.

❑ When assembling a PC, follow this general plan:

  - Study the system-board documentation and set all jumpers.

  - Verify that the system board, CPU, and memory are all working before installing the system board in the case.

15

- Install the system board, panel connections, and power cord.

- Install the drives (floppy drive, hard drive, CD-ROM drive, etc.).

- Install the sound card, modem, and any other cards, including the video card.

- Connect the peripherals.

- Install the operating system and device drivers.

KEY TERMS

Clone — Originally, a computer that was compatible with IBM computer hardware and MS-DOS software. Today, the word *clone* often refers to no-name Intel and Microsoft compatibles.

IBM-compatible — A computer that uses an Intel (or compatible) processor and can run DOS and Windows.

Proprietary — A term for products that a company has exclusive rights to manufacture and/or market. Proprietary computer components are typically more difficult to find and more expensive to buy.

Standoffs — Small plastic or metal spacers placed on the bottom of the main system board, to raise it off the chassis, so that its components will not short out on the metal case.

REVIEW QUESTIONS

1. What are the advantages of buying a well-known, brand-name computer?

2. What are the advantages of buying a less-expensive PC clone?

3. List three reasons why it may be wise to build your own PC. List three reasons, other than fear, why you may not want to build your own PC.

4. When building a new computer, you may have to change jumper settings on the system board. List two reasons for this.

5. What rule must be followed when connecting the power supply cables to the system board?

6. What is the maximum number of IDE devices that can be installed on a system?

7. What should you do before switching on the power of a freshly assembled system?

8. List several LED connectors that are typically attached to a system board.

9. What rule must be followed when attaching drive cables?

10. List five port connectors that are commonly built into most system boards today.

11. Is floppy drive A attached to the middle cable connector or the end cable connector of the floppy drive cable?

12. In a system that uses a CD-ROM drive instead of a DVD drive, the audio wire connects the _____ to the _____.

13. What will be the SCSI ID of a host adapter on the SCSI chain?

14. Where and when are SCSI terminating resistors attached?

15. Assume that you are shopping for a new personal computer. Answer the following questions to help in making the best buying decision.

   a. What is the intended purpose or purposes of the computer?

   b. What functions must the computer have to satisfy each intended purpose?

   c. What hardware and software components are needed to perform each function?

   d. For each hardware and software component, what is one question that you want answered about the component before you make your decision?

16. What is the maximum number of PCI cards that can be installed in the PC system assembled in this chapter?

17. What is the purpose of performing the memory test before installing the system board in the computer case?

18. If the memory test failed, list three possible causes of the failure.

19. What would be the jumper settings for the SCSI card if configured to use IRQ 11?

20. If the floppy drive cable were installed with the edge color opposite pin 1 instead of next to it, what would be the result?

PROJECTS

Practicing Computer Assembly Skills

Work with a partner. With your partner not watching, carefully write down where every wire and cable inside your computer is connected. Disconnect all cable connections: power, drives, and LED indicators. Have your partner replace each connection without your help. Work together with your partner to carefully inspect the connections, using your diagram as an aid. Reboot and test the computer.

15

Planning an Upgrade

Using a system-board manual, write down what jumper changes must be made to upgrade a CPU or to upgrade memory cache.

Troubleshooting an Assembly Problem

After assembling the PC shown in this chapter, we found that the floppy drive did not work, and the light on the front of the drive stayed on. Troubleshoot the problem by comparing Figure 15-30 to the rear of a floppy drive.

Planning to Buy Parts for a PC

Price the following parts needed to build a PC:

❏ System board for a Pentium CPU

❏ Pentium III CPU

❏ 128 MB of RAM

❏ Hard drive with at least 8 GB of storage

❏ Floppy disk drive

❏ CD-ROM drive

❏ Computer case and power supply

❏ Video controller card

❏ Sound card

List the features of the system board, CPU, and RAM you chose.

What speed is the CD-ROM drive you selected?

Identify and price at least one other device to install inside the computer case that you would want on your own PC.

As you price each part, if you select a high-end (more expensive) part rather than a low-end (less expensive) one, list the feature on the part that caused you to plan to spend the extra money.

Upgrading Memory

Looking back at the documentation in the chapter for the system board, what memory modules would you buy, and how much would it cost to upgrade RAM from 64 MB to 128 MB?

16

COMMUNICATING OVER PHONE LINES

In this chapter, you will learn:

♦ The basics of how computers communicate with each other

♦ About the problems faced by systems communicating over phone lines

♦ How modems work and what features and protocols modems use

♦ How to configure a modem, using Windows 9x, Windows NT, or Windows 2000

♦ The features of different communications software programs and how to use one of the more popular (pcANYWHERE) programs

♦ How to troubleshoot modem operations

♦ About high-speed digital communication lines, including ISDN, DSL, and cable modem

---

Most personal computers today have modems. In fact, modems are almost considered standard equipment on new PCs that target the home market because of the popularity of e-mail, the Internet, and the World Wide Web, and also because telecommuting employees offer advantages to their companies. However, there is a speed ceiling on regular phone lines, which is resulting in an emphasis on the development of digital alternatives, such as ISDN and DSL—digital replacements for regular phone lines and cable modems. This chapter discusses some of the alternatives to phone lines, how they work, and what is needed on a PC to support them.

The ultimate goal of many PC users is to use their modems and phone lines to access a network, either the Internet or a private business network. However, this chapter focuses on installing and configuring modems on phone lines, and leaves the subject of networking, including accessing the Internet, for the next chapter.

COMMUNICATIONS LAYERS

The morning paper arrives filled with all the latest news; readers quickly turn to the editorial section to see what the editors are thinking today. Seldom do they stop to think about the systems, methods, people, and equipment required for that morning paper, with its interesting editorials, to arrive at the door. They probably understand that layers of systems are in place to make it possible for this single event (the arrival of the paper at your door), and many more like it, to occur. As you look at Figure 16-1, consider the systems that transport the paper to your door. News editors create the material sent to the press. Workers at the press distribution center load the papers onto trucks that carry them to distribution points in the city. Delivery people pick up the papers and use their own system to disperse them.

As you read an editorial, the news editor is communicating with you, even though you recognize that this communication is not direct (face to face) but logical, or virtual (by indirect methods). Another way of saying this is that virtual communication takes place between the editor and the reader by way of direct, or physical, communication, through systems that the two people might or might not recognize. The editor is aware of the printing process and communicates with that system, and the reader is aware of the delivery person on the bicycle and communicates with him or her. However, neither the reader nor the editor needs to be aware of, or communicate with, the other systems in the diagram.

Now think of communication in the above example in terms of layers. To transport papers, a delivery system often depends on a supporting system to make it work. For example, the distribution department depends on the truck drivers and their trucks. The truck system is dependent on the road system. If a bridge goes out, a truck can't pass over it, the truck driver cannot perform his or her duty, the person at the distribution center cannot fill an order at a distribution point, and the morning paper does not arrive. As you study communication over phone lines, remember this analogy of layers of transport systems being dependent on other layers of supporting systems. This concept is often referred to as communications layers. Four communications layers in the newspaper analogy are: the editor and reader, the distribution system, the trucking system, and the road system.

Figure 16-2 illustrates direct communication over phone lines between systems. One computer sends data to its modem, which transmits that data over phone lines to a modem on the other end, which transmits the data to a receiving computer. The figure also indicates that the mode of communication differs at different stages in the process: PC-to-modem communication is digital, but modem-to-modem communication is analog.

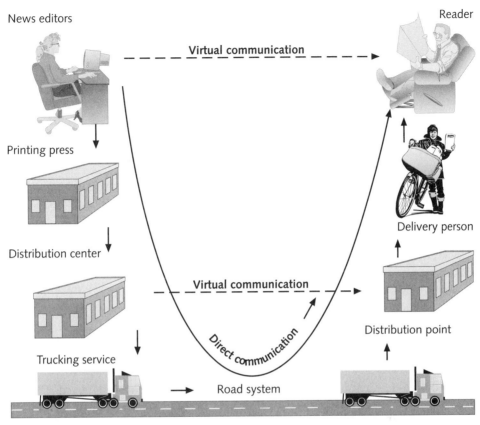

Figure 16-1   Virtual (logical) communication between editor and reader is possible because of direct communication between adjacent systems

Figure 16-2   Communicating over phone lines can be viewed as direct or virtual

Even though communications over phone lines are customarily thought of as direct, this communication can also be considered virtual. Look at Figure 16-3, where two users are communicating by way of their PCs and modems. The communication between the two users is virtual and is possible because of the underlying supporting layers of adjacent systems, which are communicating directly.

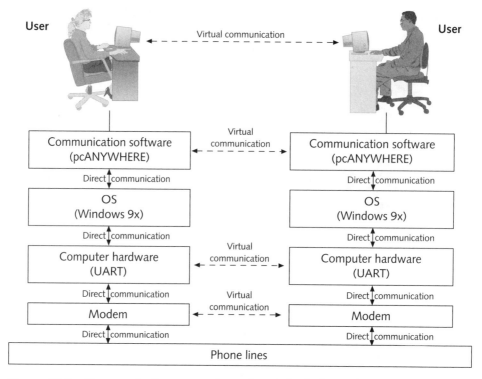

Figure 16-3 Communications over phone lines is both direct (between adjacent systems) and virtual (between similar systems)

One user enters data into his or her communications applications software, such as pcANYWHERE or ProComm Plus. The communications applications software communicates with the OS, which communicates with the computer hardware. The computer hardware communicates with a modem, which uses phone lines to send the information to a remote modem, with communication passing from computer hardware to the OS to communications software, and finally to a remote user.

In the newspaper analogy in Figure 16-1, virtual communication is taking place between reader and editor, but other underlying systems are also communicating with their counterpart systems at remote locations. For example, the distribution center receives an order for newspapers from a remote distribution point in the city, and the center fills the order, sending newspapers to the remote point. This, too, can be seen in the drawing as virtual communication.

Virtual communication at different levels of data communication also occurs. In Figure 16-3, the communications software on one end says to the communications software at the other end, "I want the such-and-such file." The remote software responds and sends the file. As you read this chapter, you see virtual communication taking place computer-hardware-to-computer-hardware, as well as modem-to-modem. This communication between correlating systems on corresponding layers of each side of the drawing is virtual, but communication from one layer to the next adjacent layer in the drawing is direct.

The remainder of this chapter examines each layer, or level of communication, shown in Figure 16-3, beginning with the modem layer and working up the diagram to computer hardware, OS, and finally communications software.

ALL ABOUT MODEMS

The **modem** is a device used by a PC to communicate over a phone line. A modem can be an external device (see Figure 16-4) or a modem card (see Figure 16-5). A modem card uses either an ISA or PCI slot.

Figure 16-4   SupraSonic external modem

Flash ROM microchip

Figure 16-5   3Com U.S. Robotics 56K Winmodem modem card

16

To reduce the total cost of a computer system, some system boards have a small expansion slot, less than half the length of a PCI slot, called an **audio/modem riser (AMR)** (See Figure 16-6) slot or a **communication and networking riser (CNR)** slot. The small slot accommodates a small, inexpensive type of modem card called a **modem riser card**. In addition, the AMR slot can support an audio riser card, and the CNR slot can support an audio riser card or a networking riser card. A riser card has part of the audio, modem, or networking logic on the card and part on a controller on the system board.

Figure 16-6   An audio/modem riser slot can accommodate an inexpensive modem riser card

A+CORE 1.1 | Regardless of the type of modem card or external device, a modem is both hardware and firmware. On the device is firmware on ROM chips that contains the protocol and instructions needed to format and convert data so that it can be transported over phone lines to a receiving modem on the other end. In general, modems are considered to be hardware, but it is fundamental to an understanding of communications to also consider them to be firmware.

Computers are digital; regular phone lines are analog. Earlier chapters discussed the difference between digital data and analog data, and Figure 16-2 shows how this concept applies to phone lines. Recall that data is stored inside a PC and communicated to a modem as binary or digital data—0s and 1s. A modem converts this binary, or digital, data into an analog signal (the process is called **modulation**) that can travel over a phone line, and then the modem at the receiving end converts it back to digital (this process is called **demodulation**) before passing it on to the receiving PC. The two processes of MOdulation/DEModulation lead to the name of the device: modem.

Recall that an analog signal is made up of an infinite number of possible values in its range of values, but a **digital signal** has only a finite number of values in its range of values. Remember also that phone lines were designed to transmit sound (that is, the human voice, which is analog). Sound traveling over regular phone lines is transmitted as analog signals, meaning that there are an infinite number of sound values, just as there are an infinite number of sound values in the human voice. When data is transmitted over phone lines, even though the data from a PC is inherently digital, it, too, must be converted to an analog signal in order to use telephone technology. Think of PC data as being converted from two simple states or measurements (0 and 1, or off and on) to waves (like sound waves), which have a potentially infinite number of states or measurements. Modems use different characteristics of waves to correspond with the 0s and 1s of digital communication.

A+CORE 1.4
Two PCs communicate over phone lines by using either internal or external modems. Either way, the modem provides a connection for a regular phone line called an **RJ-11** connection, which is the same type of connection that you see for a regular phone wall outlet (Figure 16-7). In addition to a line-in connection from the wall outlet, a modem also has an extra RJ-11 connection for a telephone.

A+CORE 6.1
A modem must be able to both receive and transmit data. Communication in which there can be transmission in only one direction at a time is called **half-duplex**; an example of this type of communication is a CB radio. A modem that can only communicate in one direction at a time is called a half-duplex modem. Communication that allows transmission in both directions at the same time is called **full-duplex**; regular voice phone conversations are an example of full-duplex communication. If a modem can communicate in both directions at the same time, it is called a full-duplex modem.

Figure 16-7 An RJ-11 connection on a modem is the same as that used for a regular phone connection

16

How Modems Are Rated

A PC initiates a phone call by instructing its modem to make the call. The modem makes the call, and a modem on the remote end answers the call and passes notification of this event on to its PC. The two PCs communicate with one another by using the modems as their interpreters, or translators. Because information traveling over phone lines is analog in nature and data processed by a PC must be digital, the two PCs can communicate only if the modems between them are translating data from digital to analog before sending it onto the phone lines, and then translating received data back to digital before the PC sees it.

A modem can translate digital data into an analog signal in many ways so that a receiving modem can understand it, quality of transmission can be assured, and the best possible transmission speeds can be attained. Using Windows 9x, you can view the properties of an installed modem on a PC. Many people install their modems by simply choosing settings supplied by others, or by allowing the installation program to use default selections. (They may not even understand what these modem properties mean or why certain selections, such as transmission speed and method of controlling data flow, are made.) This section explains what each modem property means and how it affects the modem's performance and compatibility with other modems in order to make communication possible.

Getting Started

When you first use a modem to make a dial-up call to another PC, you hear the modem making noises as the dial-up is completed. The two modems are establishing the rules of communication between them. What you hear are the sounds being sent over the phone lines as the two modems negotiate these rules. The process is called **training** or **handshaking**. Modems use one of many protocols (agreed-on methods of communication) to communicate, and, in this handshaking phase, the calling modem and the receiving modem are communicating the protocols and speeds they can support, and arriving at the best possible common solution. The decisions made about protocols include how to handle data compression and error checking, and what methods of data transfer will be used.

Modem Speeds

A+CORE
1.1

The speed at which a modem passes data over phone lines is partly determined by the transmission standard the modem is using. Modem speed is measured either in **baud rate** (named after the inventor, J. M. E. Baudot), which is the number of times a signal changes in one second, or in **bits per second (bps)**; bps is the more common unit of measurement. For slower baud rates, one signal represents one bit (in which case baud rate is equal to bps rate); slower modems are often measured in baud rates. For faster baud rates, one signal can represent more than one bit, so faster modems are measured in bps (and baud rates may differ from bps rates). When measuring modem speed using baud rate, the number of bps will always be equal to or a multiple of the baud rate. The most commonly rated speeds of modems in use today are 14.4 Kbps, 28.8 Kbps, 33.6 Kbps, and 56.6 Kbps.

The maximum speed of a modem is often written into the manufacturer's name for the modem. To see what your modem rating is when using Windows 9x, click **Start**, point to **Settings**, click **Control Panel**, and double-click **Modems**. You see the Modems Properties dialog box in Figure 16-8. The installed modem is labeled as a 3334 33.6 FDSP Fax Modem. The 33.6 portion of the name indicates the maximum speed of the modem: 33.6 Kbps.

Figure 16-8   The maximum modem speed is often included in the modem name
(in this case 33.6 Kbps)

The Ceiling on Modem Speeds

Many factors contribute to limitations on modem speeds. One of these limitations is caused not by the limits of modem technology, but rather by the nature of regular phone lines and what they are designed to do. Analog phone lines were designed to provide only sufficient audio signal quality to support the transmission of the human voice. This limited quality of audio signals affects our ability to attain high transmission speeds for data. In addition to the limitations on analog lines, newer digital phone lines have limitations as well. Older phone lines (before 1940) were analog from beginning to end, with no digital components. This is not true today; regular (analog) telephone lines are always analog as they leave a house or office building. However, the analog signals are almost always converted to a digital signal at some point in the transmission. These digital signals are then transmitted, using sophisticated computing equipment and methods, and converted back to analog signals at some point before traveling the last step between a local central telephone company office and the phone of the person receiving the call.

One limitation on modem speeds using regular phone lines results from the method used when an analog signal is converted to a digital signal somewhere along the phone line route. This is how it's done: the phone company takes a sampling of the analog signal (8,000 samples every second) and converts each sample to an 8-bit byte. So, modem transmission is limited to this 8,000 bytes/second (64,000 bits/second) transmission of the digital signal.

16

TIP Because of the sampling rate used by phone companies when converting an analog signal to digital, taking into account the overhead of data transmission (bits and bytes sent with the data that are used to control and define transmissions), the maximum transmission rate that a modem can attain over a regular phone line is about 56,000 bps or 56 Kbps.

Other factors further limit modem speed. For a modem to achieve this high a transmission rate, the conversion by the phone company from analog to digital can only take place once during the transmission. Also, if the lines in your neighborhood are multiplexed (several logical phone lines sharing a common physical line), the 56K speed cannot be attained. The line also often has some disturbance, called **noise**, which can be caused by lines bumping against one another in the wind, fluorescent lighting, nearby radios or TVs, bad wiring, lightning, and so forth. This reduction in line quality is called a dirty or noisy line. A line that consistently produces high-quality results is called a clean line.

Modem Standards

The telecommunications industry sets several modem standards to determine modem speed and protocols. The industry-approved standards for international communication were written by **Comité Consultatif Internationale de Télégraphique et Téléphonique (CCITT)**. In 1992, the CCITT organization was incorporated into the **International Telecommunications Union (ITU)**, an intergovernmental organization approved by the United Nations to be responsible for adopting standards governing telecommunications. You might see the standards used by modems referred to as the CCITT standards (more common) or as the ITU standards. The CCITT standards are listed in Table 16-1.

 Avoid purchasing a modem using a proprietary standard because it may only be able to communicate with another modem by the same manufacturer.

Table 16-1   Transmission standards used by modems

Standard	Applies Mainly to	Description
Bell 212A	Speed (up to 1,200 bps)	An older standard that supports 1,200 bps
CCITT V.32	Speed (up to 9,600 bps)	This standard runs at 9,600 bps, includes error checking, and can negotiate standards with other modems. V.32 uses 2,400 baud, transmits 4 bits per each baud, or 9,600 bps. This standard was used for quite some time.
HST	Speed (up to 14.4 Kbps)	An older proprietary standard that supports 9,600 or 14,400 bps, created by U.S. Robotics. (U.S. Robotics also supports the CCITT standards.)
CCITT V.32bis	Speed (up to 14.4 Kbps)	This standard is an improvement over V.32 (bis means "second" in Latin), and has a speed of 14,400 bps. It transmits at a 2,400 baud rate and transmits 6 bits per baud, or 14,400 bps.
CCITT V.34	Speed (up to 33.6 Kbps)	This standard transmits at 28,800 bps, or 28.8 Kbps. Optional higher speeds are 31.2 Kbps and 33.6 Kbps. This standard prevails today.

Table 16-1   Transmission standards used by modems (continued)

Standard	Applies Mainly to	Description
MNP Class 4	Error correction	Developed by Microcom, Inc. and called the Microcom Networking Protocol (MNP), this standard provides error detection and correction, and also automatically adjusts the speed of transmission based on the quality of the phone line. Earlier classes of MNP standards for error correction are Class 2 and Class 3.
CCITT V.42	Error correction	This is an error-correcting standard that adopted the methods used by MNP Class 4. Data that is corrupted during transmission is automatically retransmitted using this standard. A modem can use this standard for error correction and one of the standards listed above for speed.
MNP Class 5	Data compression	MNP Class 5 standard provides data compression, which can double normal transmission speeds between modems. It is common to see both MNP Class 4 and MNP Class 5 supported by a modem. They are sometimes called MNP-4 and MNP-5.
CCITT V.42bis	Data compression	An improved version of V.42 that also uses data compression. Many modems use the V.42bis standard for data compression and error checking and, at the same time, use the V.34 standard for data transmission protocols.
K56flex	Speed (up to 56 Kbps)	One of two earlier standards used to attain a speed of 56 Kbps. This standard was backed by Lucent Technologies and Rockwell International Corp.
x2	Speed (up to 56 Kbps)	One of two earlier standards that support a speed of 56 Kbps. This standard was supported by U.S. Robotics.
V.90	Speed (up to 56 Kbps)	The current standard used to attain speeds of 56 Kbps. It replaces both K56flex and x2.

$A^{+CORE}_{1.1}$

16

When one modem dials another modem, during the handshake they attempt to establish a communications protocol or standard at the fastest speed that both can support. The receiving modem takes the lead in negotiating these protocols by offering its best solution. If the calling modem does not respond to this protocol, the receiving modem continues to offer a slower protocol until they agree on the fastest possible solution common to both. Data-compression and error-checking protocols are also negotiated and agreed upon during the handshake, if both modems can support the same standards for these features. More details about handshaking are covered later in the chapter.

Here's one example of the many standards that might be supported by a single modem. Listed in Figure 16-9 are the standards supported by the 3Com U.S. Robotics 56K

Winmodem shown in Figure 16-5. Note in Figure 16-9 the many different modulation schemes (which indicate speed) that the modem can support. The fastest standard, ITU-T V.90, is the standard that the modem first uses when trying to establish communication with another modem, unless specified otherwise in the modem setup. Note on the right side of Figure 16-9 the different speeds that can be supported under each standard and in the lower-left corner of the figure the different error-control and data-compression standards supported. The more standards a modem supports, the more likely it will be able to establish good communication with any other modem.

Modulation Schemes	Fax Modulation Schemes	V.34+ Link Rates
ITU-T V.90 3Com 56K technology ITU-T V.34+ ITU-T V.34 ITU-T V.32bis ITU-T V.32 ITU-T V.23 ITU-T V.22bis ITU-T V.22 Bell 212A ITU-T V.21 Bell 103	ITU-T V.17 ITU-T V.29 ITU-T V.27ter ITU-T V.21 **Fax Standards** EIA 578 Class 1 FAX EIA 592 Class 2.0 FAX **Front Channel Link Rates**	4800, 7200, 9600, 12000, 14400, 16800, 19200, 21600, 24000, 26400, 28800, 31200, 33600 **V.32bis Link Rates** 4800, 7200, 9600, 12000, 14400 **Additional Link Rates**
Error Control and Data Compression Schemes ITU-T V.42 ITU-T V.42bis MNP 2-5	28000, 29333, 30666, 32000, 33333, 34666, 36000, 37333, 38666, 40000, 41333, 42666, 44000, 45333, 46666, 48000, 49333, 50666, 52000, 53333, 54666, 56000, 57333 **Back Channel Link Rates** 4800, 7200, 9600, 12000, 14400, 16800, 19200, 21600, 24000, 26400, 28800, 31200	300, 1200/75 (V.23), 1200, 2400 **Fax Link Rates** 2400, 4800, 7200, 9600, 12000, 14400

Figure 16-9   Specifications for a 56K modem

You can force a modem to use a particular standard that it supports. For example, if you want to force this modem to communicate with another modem using the Bell proprietary standard, in Windows 9x, follow these steps:

1. Click **Start**, point to **Settings**, click **Control Panel**, and then double-click **Modems**. The Modems Properties dialog box opens.

2. Select the modem from the list of installed modems, and then click **Properties**. You see the Properties dialog box for the selected modem, as shown in Figure 16-10. Note in this figure that the maximum speed of the modem is set to 115,200 bps; this speed is not attainable over phone lines. You can, however, use this dialog box to offset problems with a dirty phone line by forcing the modem to transmit at a slower

speed than it normally would. Slowing down the speed of your modem might solve the problem.

3. Click the **Connection** tab of the modem Properties dialog box. Figure 16-11 shows the connection preferences supported by this modem. These preferences are discussed later in the chapter.

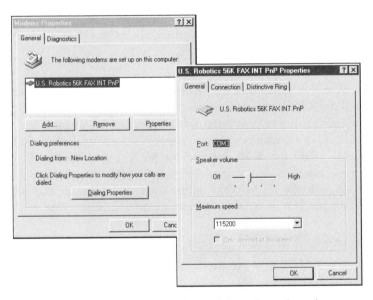

Figure 16-10   The Properties box of the selected modem

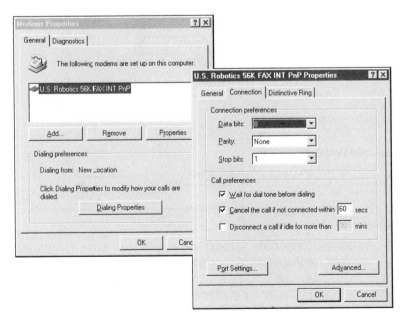

Figure 16-11   Connection preferences supported by the installed modem

4. Click the **Advanced** button. Figure 16-12 shows the advanced connection settings, which let you select a modulation standard for this modem. The figure shows the drop-down list of standards. You can select Non-standard or Standard. The standard selection for this modem causes the modem to function according to one of the CCITT modulation standards listed in Figure 16-8. If you select the Non-standard setting, this modem attempts to communicate using the Bell212/103 standard listed in Figure 16-9 under "Modulation schemes."

5. Leave the Modulation type set to Standard and click **Cancel** to exit the dialog box.

Modems with 56 Kbps Speeds

A+CORE
1.1

Before 1998, there were two standards for 56-Kbps transmission, the x2 standard supported by U.S. Robotics and the K56flex standard supported by Lucent Technologies and Rockwell International Corp. These two standards were not compatible with one another. Because of this incompatibility, all three companies agreed to support a third standard for 56 Kbps transmission. This standard, called the **V.90** standard for 56 Kbps, was published by ITU in February 1998. If you have a modem that uses either the x2 or the K56flex standard, it is likely that you can upgrade the Flash ROM on the modem card to use the new standard. See the Web site of the modem manufacturer for more information.

Figure 16-12 Advanced Connection Settings allows you to select a transmission standard for the installed modem

Another concern about buying a 56-Kbps modem is that, if your phone line is too noisy, the modem cannot attain the high speed. 3Com, a modem manufacturer, offers a way for you to test your phone line to determine if it qualifies, before you buy a 56-Kbps modem. With a modem using the V.34 standard, access the 3Com Web site (*www.3com.com/56k/need4_56k/linetest.html*) and read and follow the directions to have the 3Com program analyze your line.

Although modems are rated and advertised to transmit at 56 Kbps, this speed is seldom accomplished. When one PC is communicating with another, even if both PCs are equipped with 56K modems and using clean phones lines, most likely the actual attained speed will not exceed 34 Kbps. When a PC is connected to an Internet service provider (ISP), to come close to the 56-Kbps transmission, the ISP's incoming lines must be digital rather than analog. Even so, the transmission from the provider to the PC (called downstream transmission) is only about 53 Kbps, and the transmission from the PC to the provider (called upstream transmission) does not exceed 34 Kbps.

 TIP Before upgrading to a 56-Kbps modem, check with your ISP and find out if they support this speed.

Data Compression

Recall the concept of communications layers presented earlier in the chapter. The next discussion focuses on the direct communication between the two adjacent layers represented by the modem and the phone lines. The modem includes the firmware (permanent programming) housed on the modem, which can perform error correction and data compression. These and other functions of data communication can be performed by either hardware (firmware on the modem) or software (programs on the PC).

When data compression is performed by a modem, it applies to all data that is transmitted by the modem. If data compression is performed by the software on the PC, it applies to single-file transfer operations. Software protocols used to compress data will be addressed later in the chapter.

Data compression done by the modem follows either the MNP-5, CCITT V.42, or V.42bis protocol. All three of these protocols also perform error correction. A modem using one of these methods of data compression is communicating to its computer at higher speeds than it is communicating to the phone line. This is because the data is being compressed at the modem and, therefore, there are more bits coming from the local computer into the modem than are being transmitted over the phone line (assuming, of course, that few errors occur). This fact may cause the overall speed of the data transmission at the PC to appear much faster than the actual phone line transmission rate.

The compression ratio of MNP-5 is 2:1, and V.42bis can have up to a 4:1 compression ratio. MNP-5 also has more overhead in its compression methods, and sometimes, if a file is already compressed (such as a ZIP file), because of this overhead, the actual transmission time increases because MNP-5. V.42 can determine if a file is already compressed, and therefore does not compress it a second time.

16

If you are sending files that are already compressed over a modem, and the only compression standard your modem supports is MNP-5 compression, disable MNP-5 compression to speed up data transmission.

Error Correction

As seen in Table 16-1, the standards that include error correction are MNP-4, CCITT V.42, and CCITT V.42bis. One modem often supports all three standards. If it doesn't, during the handshaking process, the answering modem tries to establish an error-correction protocol with the other modem by first suggesting the fastest, best standard. If the calling modem responds by accepting that standard, then it is used by both. If the calling modem does not support the suggested protocol, then the two modems negotiate to find the best protocol they both can use, or simply decide not to use error correction.

Look back at Figure 16-12: the Advanced Connection Settings for the installed modem. From this dialog box, you can click **Use error control** to determine if the modem can use error control, if it can negotiate a protocol with the other modem. You can also specify from this dialog box that error control is required to connect. (Click **Required to connect** under **User error control** in the dialog box in Figure 16-12.) If the other modem cannot use error control, then this modem does not complete the connection. Also note that data compression cannot be selected unless error control is evoked.

Error correction works by breaking data up into small packets called **frames**. The sending modem performs some calculations on a frame of data and sums these calculations into a checksum. A **checksum** is a summary calculation of data and will later be used to check or verify the accuracy of the data when received. Checksum works somewhat like a parity bit, except that it is a little more complicated and applies to more data. The checksum is attached to the data frame, and they are transmitted together. The receiving modem performs the same calculations and compares its answer to the checksum value received. If they do not agree, then the receiving modem requests a new transmission of the packet. This process does slow down the transmission of data, especially on dirty or noisy phone lines, but accuracy is almost 100% guaranteed.

More About Handshaking

Now that you understand several of the different protocols that must be established between two modems before they can communicate data, you can more carefully examine the handshaking process in which these protocols are agreed upon. Follow the step-by-step process of two modems performing a handshake:

1. The calling modem dials a phone number, and the phone rings at the other end.

2. The answering modem picks up. The answering modem sends a modem tone, sometimes called a **guard tone**, which the calling modem recognizes as another modem and not a human voice, and so it does not break the connection.

3. The answering modem sends a signal called the **carrier**. This is an unmodulated (unchanging) or continuous tone at a set frequency (also called pitch), which

depends on the speed of communication the answering modem is attempting to establish with the calling modem. This process, called establishing carrier, sounds like static, which you hear during handshaking.

4. The answering modem keeps sending one unmodulated carrier (or signal) after another until the calling modem responds.

5. If the calling modem responds with the same carrier, both modems use it. If the calling modem does not respond, the answering modem simply drops this particular carrier and tries another.

6. After carrier is established, the two modems enter the equalization stage, which sounds like hissing or buzzing on the line. The modems are both testing the line quality and compensate for poor quality by changing the way they transmit.

7. Having established carrier and adjusted for line quality, the two modems have now agreed on a speed of data transmission between them, called the **modem speed** or the **line speed**.

8. The speakers on the modems are now turned off. Next the modems begin to talk about how they will transmit data. The answering modem asks if the other modem can support MNP-4, MNP-5, V.42, V.42bis, and so on. After some interchange, the methods of data transmission are agreed upon, and the handshaking is complete. The two modems can now communicate.

External modems give you the status of what is happening by turning on and off lights on the front of the modem and displaying messages on an LCD panel (called a display readout). Internal modems, of course, don't have these lights available for you to see, so communications software sometimes displays a pseudo-modem-panel on your computer screen. The modem lights were listed in Table 9-3 of Chapter 9 and are discussed in more detail later in this chapter.

When a modem is first activated (turned on), it initializes itself and then raises (turns on) its Clear to Send (CTS) signal and, for an external modem, the CTS light also goes on. When the PC receives the CTS signal from its modem, it will raise its Request to Send (RTS) signal in order to begin a call. For external modems, the RTS or RS light goes on.

16

TIP   Communications technicians use the terms "raising" and "dropping" signals to mean that the signal is either started or stopped, respectively.

After the handshaking explained in Step 7 above, when carrier between the two modems is established, if the modems are external modems with status lights, each modem turns on its Carrier Detect (CD) light, which stays on as long as the modems are connected. When a communications technician sees this light, he or she will say that carrier is up. Not only does the light come on, but the CD signal transmitted to the PC over the serial port cable is also raised, letting the computer know that communication has been established, and that data can now be sent. Data transmission can be detected by looking at the external modem lights, TXD and RXD (or they may be TD and RD) for transmitting and receiving data.

If error correction or data compression is used, the communication established will most likely be synchronous over the phone line, which means that data is sent from one modem to the other as blocks of data based on timed intervals. Clocks on each modem are used to synchronize the transmissions. Asynchronous communication relies on bits being sent before and after the data to communicate when each modem should transmit. These bits are called **stop bits** and **start bits**. Asynchronous communication can also use parity checking.

Modem Features

In addition to the speed, protocols, data compression, and error correction that are used to rate a modem, there are other features. Some additional abilities you might want to look for in a modem are:

- **Caller ID** (provided that you subscribe to that service from the phone company) is supported.

- **Display readout** on external modems provides information about the status of the modem. (See Chapter 9, Table 9-3, for a list of modem lights and their meanings. The modem can also have an LCD panel for messages such as Training or Idle.)

- **Flash ROM** allows you to upgrade your modem to support future standards.

- **Plug and Play for Windows 9x** makes modem installation more automatic.

- **Voice/data capability** allows the modem to also serve as a telephone, complete with built-in speaker and microphone.

- **Auto-answer** makes it possible for the modem to receive incoming calls while you are away from the PC.

Computer-Hardware-to-Modem Communication

Looking back to the newspaper analogy (see Figure 16-2), the newspaper distribution system must coordinate its efforts with the trucking system. In data communication with computers, this coordination can be equated to the computer hardware coordinating its communication with its modem. Between the PC hardware layer and the modem layer, communication is digital. How the PC hardware and the modem communicate is the subject of this section.

A+CORE
1.1

Figure 16-13 shows an overview of the way that PCs and modems communicate. The computers are classified as **data terminal equipment (DTE)**, and the modems are called **data communications equipment (DCE)**.

PCs don't communicate with modems in the same way that modems communicate with other modems. Transmission speeds, error checking, and data format from the PC to the modem (DTE to DCE) are different than they are between a modem and another modem (DCE to DCE). Remember that a modem may be an internal or an external modem. As you study communication between DTEs and DCEs, the concepts are easier to visualize if you think of a PC and an external modem sitting beside it connected by a serial cable. However, the same concepts apply to an internal modem as to an external modem, even though the modem card and the PC are not connected by a cable.

Figure 16-13   A computer communicates with a modem differently from the way a modem communicates with another modem

Transmission Speed

Data transmission involves three speeds (see Figure 16-13): the speed between the calling PC and its modem (called the **port speed**), the speed between the two modems (called the modem speed or the line speed), and the port speed between the answering PC and its modem. The overall speed of data transmission is affected by each of these speeds.

Look back at the modem properties for a 56K modem in Figure 16-10. Notice that the maximum speed that is available for this modem is 115200. This speed is given in bps, and you naturally may wonder why it is so much higher than the rated speed of the modem. The answer is that this speed is referring to the transmission speed from the PC to the modem (the port speed), which may very well be this high.

Now turn back to Figures 16-10 and 16-13. The speed labeled "Maximum speed" in Figure 16-10 refers to communication between a DTE (computer) and a DCE (modem) and is called the DTE speed, or the port speed, because the PC is using a serial port to communicate with the modem. The port speed must be significantly higher than the modem speed in order for the PC to take advantage of data compression performed by the modem.

As a general rule, port speed should be at least four times as fast as modem speed.

16

For example, for a 28.8 Kbps modem, set the port speed to 115.2 Kbps. The speed seen in Figure 16-10 is the port speed that is supported by this particular modem. Modem speed (line speed) is determined by several factors, including the rated speed of the modem, the line quality, and the speed of the remote modem.

The UART

Recall from Chapter 9 that the chip responsible for any communication over a serial port is the UART (universal asynchronous receiver-transmitter), sometimes called an ACIA (asynchronous communications interface adapter). The UART controls the port speed as well as other features of serial port communications. Table 16-2 summarizes the speeds and different models of the UARTs.

Table 16-2   Maximum port speeds of UARTs

UART	Maximum Speed	FIFO Buffering	Comments
8250, an 8-bit chip	38.4 Kbps	None	Improvements to this chip are the 8250A and 8250B.
16450, a 16-bit chip	38.4 Kbps	None	This chip fixed bugs in the 8250 chip and improved performance.
16550, a 16-bit chip	115.2 Kbps	Has a 16-byte buffer	The 16550A version of this chip fixed a bug in the 16550. 16550AF chip improves on the 16550A chip.
16650, a 16-bit chip	230 Kbps and higher	Has a 32-byte buffer	Performance is improving as new technologies arise.
16750	Up to 1 Mbaud	Has a 64-byte buffer	Produced by Texas Instruments

Remember from Chapter 9 that the FIFO (first-in-first-out) buffer is needed by the UART chip to temporarily hold data as it is being received or transmitted. If your UART chip has a buffer, you can control its size as well as the port speed from the Modems Properties box of Windows 9x. Follow these directions:

1. Click **Start**, point to **Settings**, click **Control Panel**, and then double-click the **System** icon. Select the **Device Manager** tab.

2. Click the **+** sign beside **Ports (COM & LPT)** to display a list of ports.

3. Select the COM port used by your modem and then click **Properties**. Figure 16-14 shows the COM1 Properties dialog box. From here, you can select the port speed in bits per second.

4. Click the **Advanced** button to open the Advanced Port Settings dialog box, as in Figure 16-15. From here, you can control the size of the FIFO buffer of the 16550 UART and establish whether to use the buffer.

5. Click **OK** to close the dialog box.

Other settings on the Communications Port Properties box are discussed later in the chapter.

As you can see in Table 16-2, if you have a very fast external modem with data compression, but your UART cannot support the same speed, the modem cannot attain its maximum speed. The solution may be to upgrade your UART or to install an I/O controller card with a fast UART chip. Remember from Chapter 9 that you can use MSD (Microsoft Diagnostics) utility to determine which UART you have on your PC. When reading documentation about the speed of communication over phone lines, you may see the UART or port speed referred to as the DTE speed, and the modem or line speed called the DCE speed.

Figure 16-14   The COM1 Properties box lets you control port settings, including the port speed in bits per second

16

Figure 16-15   Selecting the FIFO buffer size of a 16550 UART chip

The UART Chip on External and Internal Modems

Let's now consider the different ways internal and external modems use the UART. Figure 16-16 shows the differences between an external and internal configuration of the UART. Almost all system boards sold today contain either a UART or the UART logic somewhere within the chip set on the system board. External modems connect to a PC by way of a serial port, and therefore use the UART on the system board that controls this serial port. In this case, data from the system board travels over the serial cable to the modem in digital form, so the external modem must have a UART in it to receive the digital data. Sometimes the external modem may combine the UART logic into other chips in the modem.

A+CORE
1.3

Internal modems are expansion cards that connect to the system board by way of an ISA or a PCI expansion slot. Internal modems have their own UART on the modem card and provide their own serial port logic to the computer system. This is why an internal modem must be configured to have its own COM port assigned to it for its UART to control. A typical configuration for a PC is to have COM1 assigned to the serial mouse and COM2 assigned to the internal modem. (An external modem does not need a COM port assigned to it, because it uses the existing COM port already configured on the system.) The UART on the system board holding the internal modem is not used by the modem, because the modem is not using the COM ports on the system board.

Figure 16-16 For an external modem, digital data is controlled by the UART chip on the system board; for an internal modem, the controlling UART chip is on the modem card

TIP Sometimes a COM port on a system board can compete for resources with the COM port on an internal modem, causing a conflict. In this case, use CMOS setup to disable the conflicting COM port on the system board.

The UART on an internal modem and the UART chip on a system board supporting an external modem basically perform the same function—controlling digital data sent from the CPU to the modem. Either of these UARTs may perform error checking and control the flow of data. In the discussions that follow about the functions of the UART chip in modem communication, the same principles apply to either an external or an internal modem. The difference is the location of the UART performing the function.

In speaking of the need to upgrade a slow UART, a slow UART chip on an internal modem has the same effect as a slow UART chip on a system board supporting an external modem. A UART chip on an internal modem is also controlling the speed at which data is transferred from the system bus to the modem. If this UART is not fast enough, then your only recourse is to replace the modem card.

Flow Control

Recall that three speeds affect the overall speed of data transmission, line speed and the port speeds of the sending and receiving computers. Because each speed can differ, a way is needed to stop the data from flowing when either the DTE or DCE needs to catch up. For example, if the receiving modem is receiving data faster than it can uncompress it and pass it off to its PC, it must stop the flow coming from the remote modem long enough to catch up. **Flow**

16

control is a method of controlling the flow of data by sending a message to stop data flow. Either the receiving PC or the receiving modem can initiate a flow control message.

There are two methods of flow control: flow control over software channels, called Xon/Xoff protocol, and flow control over hardware channels, called RTS/CTS protocol. Looking back at Figure 16-12, you can see the two choices for flow control under Advanced Connection Settings. Figure 16-17 illustrates the difference between the two methods: Software flow control uses the same methods to send stop and start messages as it does to send data. Hardware flow control uses the same methods used by the modem (hardware) to initially establish communication.

In software flow control, the receiving device transmits a message to the sending device to pause transmission by sending a special control character within the same channel (frequency) in which data is sent. This method is called **in-band signaling**. The control character to stop the data from flowing, Xoff, is Control-S, sent as an ASCII character whose ASCII value is 19. (See Appendix C for information about ASCII characters.) The Xon control character is Control-Q, or ASCII value 17, which tells the sending device to begin sending data again. This method of flow control works well as long as only ASCII data is being transmitted, but if data is being transmitted in some other coding format, the control characters themselves may be valid data and may be mistakenly included in the data stream as regular data, which will cause problems with communication. Another problem with software flow control is that data needs to be continually monitored to detect the signals, and, at the high speeds at which data is transmitted today, the control character may not be detected in time to stop the data.

Instead of embedding signals within data, hardware flow control uses electrical signals from a PC to its modem that are not part of the data flow channel; this is called **out-of-band signaling**. Hardware flow control is a way for a PC to tell its modem to stop the other modem from sending data. When the first (receiving) modem receives the signal from its PC, it just deactivates the line between the two modems (how it does that is addressed below), forcing the other modem to wait. In order to understand how hardware flow control works, turn your attention back to a subject from an earlier chapter: serial port communication.

Software Flow Control

Sending PC   Flow control signal   Cable   Receiving PC

Modem   Modem

The sending modem or PC receives   Data   The receiving PC sends a signal
the stop data signal (control S) or   to the sending PC or modem to
start data signal (control Q) from   stop (control S) or start (control Q)
the receiving PC   data flow

Hardware Flow Control

Sending PC   Flow control signal
                 Cable   Receiving PC
Modem   Modem

                           Data
                                    The receiving PC sends an
                                    electrical signal to the receiving
                                    modem to activate (start data)
                                    or deactivate (stop data) the line

Figure 16-17   Software flow control sends in-band software messages from the receiving
PC to the sending device; hardware flow control sends out-of-band electrical
signals only from the receiving PC to the receiving modem

RS-232c Serial Port Communication

Remember from Chapter 9 that serial port communication on PCs follows the RS-232c standard, which specifies how information and commands travel over nine wires in the serial cable. All RS-232c serial communication is controlled by the UART chip. Hardware flow control is accomplished by the UART chip, using two of these wires: one to stop and one to start the data.

As you can see from Figure 16-17, with hardware flow control the signal to stop or start data flow need only travel from the receiving PC to the receiving modem. Remember that the cable uses nine wires and can have either a DB25 (25-pin) or a DB9 (9-pin) connection at either end. Table 16-3 lists the purpose of each of these nine wires and the pin connection for both the DB9 and DB25 connectors at the computer or DTE end. On a PC, serial port communication is asynchronous, meaning that data flow does not stay in sync with a clock. The RS-232c standard includes pin outs used to synchronize data transmission with the receive and transmit clocks, but, since PCs don't use this feature, only nine pins are used, making possible the more convenient 9-pin connection for PCs rather than always requiring a 25-pin port.

16

Table 16-3   RS-232c standard for serial port cable pins

Pin Number for 9-Pin Connector	Pin Number for 25-Pin Connector	Pin Use	Description	Modem Lights
1	8	Carrier detect	Connection with remote is made	CD or DCD
2	3	Receive data	Receiving data	RD-RXD
3	2	Transmit data	Sending data	SD or TXD
4	20	Data terminal ready	Computer is ready to control modem	TR or DTR
5	7	Signal ground	Not used with PCs	
6	6	Data set ready	Modem is able to talk	MR or DSR
7	4	Request to send	Computer wants to talk	RTS
8	5	Clear to send	Modem is ready to talk	CTS
9	22	Ring indicator	Someone is calling	AA or RI

Looking back at flow control settings in Figure 16-12, you can see which of the two pins in Table 16-3 is used for hardware flow control: RTS and CTS. RTS is used by the computer, and CTS is used by the modem. In most cases, RTS and CTS stay on the entire time a communication session is active. Also, remember that between the two modems, carrier (indicating that the line is still open) from each modem must also stay up for communication to take place. When the receiving computer wants to stop receiving data, it drops the RTS signal. Its modem responds by dropping the CTS signal and refusing to acknowledge the receipt of data from the sending modem, thus stopping communication. When the receiving computer is ready for more data, it raises RTS, and the receiving modem responds by raising CTS and, once again, acknowledges received data. Communication resumes.

Additional UART Protocols

When a UART chip from a sending device sends digital data to a sending modem, it first prepares the data to be received by the UART chip on the other end. When the UART chip on the receiving end of the transmission receives digital data from its modem, it performs some error checking based on information sent to it from the sending UART chip. Think of this process as another communication layer: UART-to-UART, as seen in Figure 16-3.

Just as the two modems agree to use the same protocols, both the sending and receiving UART chips must have determined to use the same protocol to send and receive data, for communication to take place. The five protocols for digital communication between two PCs, as controlled by their UART chips, are listed in Table 16-4. Figure 16-14 shows the Windows 9x screen where these protocols are set for the UART chip and its COM port. The resulting selections are known as the **port settings**.

Don't confuse the modem settings with the port settings. Modem settings control modem-to-modem communication, and port settings control UART-to-UART communication.

Table 16-4   Communication protocol between two UART chips

Port Setting	Description	Common Values
Bits per second (port speed)	What will be the speed of transmission in bps?	2400; 4800; 9600; 19,200; 38,400; 57,600; 115,200; 230,400; 460,800; 921,600 bps
Data bits	How many bits are to be used to send a single character of data?	7 or 8 bits
Parity	Will there be error checking, and if so, what will be its format?	Odd, even, or none
Stop bits	What will be the code to indicate that a character (its string of bits) is starting or ending?	1, 1.5, or 2 bits
Flow control	How will the flow of data be controlled?	Xon/Xoff or hardware

The first and last items in this table (speed and flow control) have already been discussed. This section covers the other three settings.

Data Bits   Back when most data sent across modems was in ASCII format, the question arose: How many bits are necessary to send one ASCII character? The answer to this question was critical because the maximum number of bits needed to represent one ASCII character is 7 bits, not 8. (To understand this point, see Appendix C, and convert the largest hex value to binary.) Therefore, to transmit in ASCII really requires that only 7 bits be used per character. The choice, therefore, for character transmission is either 7 or 8 data bits. Most often today, you should choose 8 data bits unless you know that you are only transmitting in ASCII.

Parity   Parity checking in telecommunications is performed in much the same way that memory on a system board checks parity. When you are using 7 data bits, add an extra bit, which can be 0 or 1 to make either odd or even parity. The receiving UART chip compares the parity to its count of odd or even bits to check the data bits for errors. In most cases today, you don't want the UART chip to use parity checking. Error checking as well as error correction can be better performed by the modem.

Stop Bits   Whenever the sending UART chip is ready to send a group of data bits (a character) to the receiving UART chip, it puts one start bit in front of the data bits to indicate to the receiving UART chip that a character is starting. In most cases, the UART chip also sends one stop bit to indicate that the character is complete, although two stop bits can be selected.

Installing and Configuring a Modem

A+CORE 1.7   Follow these steps to install an internal modem:

1. Read the modem documentation.

2. Determine which serial port is available on your system.

16

A+CORE
1.7

3. Set any jumpers or DIP switches on the modem card. (See your documentation for details about your card. An example is shown in Figure 16-18. Common jumper and DIP switch settings are for COM ports, IRQ, and I/O addresses, and to indicate whether or not the card will use Plug and Play.)

Jumper bank for IRQ setting

Jumper bank for COM port selection

Figure 16-18 A modem will have jumpers to set IRQ and COM values. The default jumper settings should be set to use Plug and Play rather than dictate these values

4. Turn off your computer and remove the case. Find an empty slot, remove the faceplate, and save the screw. Mount the card firmly into the slot, and replace the screw to anchor the card.

5. Replace the cover. (You can test the modem before replacing the cover.)

6. Plug the telephone line from the house into the line jack on the modem. The second RJ-11 jack on the modem is for an optional telephone. It connects a phone so that you can more easily use this same phone jack for voice communication.

For an external modem, follow these steps:

1. You need an RS-232c serial cable to connect the modem to the serial port. If the modem does not come with a cable, don't skimp on price here; buy a good quality cable. Connect the cable to the modem and to the serial port.

2. Plug the electrical cord from the modem into a 110V AC outlet.

3. Plug the telephone line from the house into the line jack on the modem. The second jack on the modem is for an optional telephone.

Turn on your computer and follow these steps to configure the modem under the OS. Begin with Step 1 for Windows NT, with Step 12 for Windows 9x, and with Step 14 for Windows 2000.

1. For Windows NT, click **Start**, point to **Settings**, click **Control Panel**, and then double-click **Modem**. You see the Install New Modem dialog box, as in Figure 16-19. If you want Windows NT to detect and install the modem for you, click **Next** and go to Step 3. If you want to provide the installation disk for the modem, click **Don't detect my modem: I will select it from the list**, and proceed to Step 2.

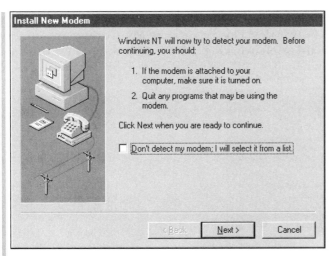

Figure 16-19   Installing a new modem

2. Either select the modem from the list of modems provided by Windows NT or, if you have an installation disk provided with the modem, click **Have Disk** and provide the location of the files. Go to Step 4.

 Sometimes an installation disk has several directories, one for each operating system it supports. For example, for Windows NT 4.0, look for a directory named \NT40.

3. After the modem is detected, Windows NT requests the location of the Windows NT \I386 directory on the Windows NT installation CD-ROM from which it copies the necessary drivers. Place the CD in the drive and enter the location of the directory, using the drive letter of your CD-ROM (for example, D:).

4. After the modem drivers are installed, configure the modem. Click **Start**, point to **Settings**, click **Control Panel**, and then double-click **Modem**. The modem Properties box opens, which looks and works about the same as it does in Windows 9x. Click the installed modem and then click **Properties**.

5. Use the properties listed below unless you have a specific reason to do otherwise (such as to compensate for a noisy phone line).

   ■ Set the modem speed at the highest value in the drop-down list, which is the highest value supported by this modem.

   ■ Set the port protocol at "8, No, and 1," which is computer jargon for 8 bits, no parity, and 1 stop bit.

   ■ Use hardware flow control.

6. If you want to use Windows NT to make calls without using other software, install Dial-Up Networking. Double-click the **My Computer** icon, and then double-click **Dial-Up Networking**. You see the dialog box illustrated in Figure 16-20, and Windows NT tells you that you can now install the service.

Figure 16-20   Windows NT instructs the user to install Dial-Up Networking before the modem can be used

7. Click **Install**.

8. Windows NT requests the location of the \I386 directory. Insert the CD-ROM and enter the location of the directory.

9. When Windows NT asks you to select the RAS (Remote Access Service, pronounced "razz") device, select the newly installed modem and click **OK** to continue.

10. When you are asked to select the type of communication protocols that you want to use when connected, select two, NetBEUI and TCP/IP (Dial-Up Networking is covered in detail in Chapter 17).

11. Reboot the PC. The configuration is now complete for Windows NT.

12. For Windows 9x, turn on the PC. Windows 9x Plug and Play detects a new hardware device. Allow the OS to identify the modem and install the drivers, or provide your own disk. You might have to boot twice: once to allow Plug and Play to detect the UART and again to detect the modem.

13. After the modem drivers are installed, configure the modem. Use the same method as for Windows NT, beginning in Step 4. The Windows 9x installation is now complete.

14. For Windows 2000, installation is performed as it is for Windows 9x because both OSs use Plug and Play. However, some options in the modem Properties dialog box are slightly different. To configure the modem, click **Start**, point to **Settings**, click **Control Panel**, and double-click the **Phone and Modem Options** icon. When the Phone and Modem Options dialog box opens, click the **Modems** tab. Select the modem and click **Properties**. The modem Properties dialog box opens. Configure the modem using this dialog box.

What can go wrong during modem installation and how to detect and resolve conflicts are covered under the Troubleshooting section later in the chapter. The last step after the modem installation is complete is to test the modem using communications software.

An excellent software utility you can use to test a modem is HyperTerminal, a quick and easy way to make a phone call from a Windows 9x PC. Follow these steps to test your modem using Windows 9x:

1. For Windows 98, click **Start**, point to **Programs**, **Accessories**, **Communications**, and click **HyperTerminal**. For Windows 95, click **Start**, point to **Programs**, **Accessories**, and click **HyperTerminal**.

2. Double-click the **Hypertrm.exe** icon in the HyperTerminal window.

3. When you see the Connection Description dialog box, enter a descriptive name for your connection and select an icon for the shortcut. Click **OK**.

4. Enter the phone number to dial and select the modem from the list of dial-up devices (most likely it's the only entry). Click **OK**.

5. Click **Dial** to make the call. Even if you dial an out-of-service number, you can still hear your modem make the call. This confirms that your modem is installed and configured to make an outgoing call.

COMMUNICATIONS SOFTWARE

You have seen how one modem communicates with another modem and how computer hardware (a UART controlling a COM port) communicates with a modem. You have also seen how one computer's hardware communicates with another computer's hardware (UART-to-UART). Now take this process a step further up the communications layers to where hardware communicates with an OS, which communicates with communications software, as shown in Figure 16-3. The UART chip is sending and receiving data only because the software on the PC is communicating with it. Windows 9x, Windows NT, and Windows 2000 support communication using modems without any other communications software. These operating systems communicate with modems by using the **Telephony Application Programming Interface (TAPI)**, a standard jointly developed by Intel and Microsoft, used by Windows to connect a PC to telephone services. **Telephony** is a term describing the technology of converting sound to signals that can travel over telephone lines (the technology of telephones), and TAPI is a type of API (application programming interface) that Windows can call when it needs to make a telephone connection.

Even though you can make phone calls from your PC using only the operating system, using an application specifically designed to manage communications enhances communication in several ways, as you will see later in the chapter. Two examples of communications software programs are ProComm Plus and pcANYWHERE. These two applications software programs can be used to send files back and forth between computers, control remote computers, and perform a variety of other communications tasks.

16

This section looks at how communications software communicates with a modem (by way of a UART chip) and at how communications software on one PC communicates with the same or similar software on another PC.

Software-to-Modem Communication

In previous sections you have seen how one modem communicates with another modem, and how a PC and a modem communicate with each other, using the RS-232c standard for out-of-band signaling. Sometimes the commands that a PC needs to send to a modem cannot fit into the pinouts provided by the RS-232c standard, such as the command to make a call or what phone number to dial. This type of information needs to be sent to a modem as characters, but the modem must distinguish between the characters it is receiving from the computer that are commands and the characters that are simply being sent along as data and don't need to be interpreted.

One of the pioneers in modem communications, Hayes Microcomputer Products, developed a language for PCs to use to control modems. Hayes did not patent or copyright the language, so most modems today are built to understand this language. Any modem that contains the logic to understand this language is said to be Hayes-compatible, and the language has become a *de facto* standard. (A **de facto standard** is a standard that does not have official backing, but is considered a standard because of widespread use and acceptance by the industry.)

The Hayes language for modem control is called the **AT command set** because, when the modem is receiving commands, each command line is prefaced with AT for ATtention. A modem that uses this language stays in command mode at any time that it is not connected to another modem. When a modem is in command mode and bits and bytes are sent to it from a PC, the modem interprets the bytes as commands to be followed, rather than as data to be sent over a phone line. It leaves command mode when it either receives an incoming call or dials out, and returns to command mode when a call is completed or a special escape sequence is sent to it by its computer.

Other manufacturers of modems have added to the Hayes AT command set, but Table 16-5 lists a few of the core AT commands that most modems understand. The commands that begin with the ampersand character (&) are part of the extended command set; the others are part of the basic command set. When a modem is in command mode, it responds to each command with OK or gives the results after performing the command. You can type a command from a communications software window to be executed immediately or enter a command from a dialog box for the modem configuration to be executed later, when the modem makes a call.

Table 16-5   AT commands for Hayes-compatible modems

Command	Description	Some Values and Their Meanings
+++	**Escape sequence:** tells the modem to return to command mode. You should pause at least 1 second before you begin the sequence. After you end it, wait another second before you send another command. Don't begin this command with AT.	
On	**Go online:** tells the modem to return to online data mode. This is the reverse command for the escape sequence above.	O0 Return online O1 Return online and retrain (perform training or handshaking again with the remote modem)
A/	**Repeat last command:** repeat the last command performed by the modem. Don't begin the command with AT, but do follow it with Enter. Useful when redialing a busy number.	
In	**Identification:** instructs the modem to return product identification information	I0 Return the product code I3 Return the modem ROM version
Zn	**Reset:** instructs the modem to reset and restore the configuration to that defined at power on	Z0 Reset and return to user profile 0 Z1 Reset and return to user profile 1
&F	**Factory default:** instructs the modem to reload the factory default profile. In most cases, use this command to reset the modem rather than using the Z command.	
A	**Answer the phone:** instructs the modem to answer the phone, transmit the answer tone, and wait for a carrier from the remote modem	
Dn	**Dial:** tells the modem to dial a number. There are several parameters that can be added to this command. A few are listed on the right.	D5551212 Dial the given number D, Causes the dialing to pause DP Use pulse dialing DT Use tone dialing DW Wait for dial tone D& Wait for the credit card dialing tone before continuing with the remaining dial string
Hn	**Hang up:** tells the modem to hang up	H0 Hang up H1 Hang up and enter command mode
Mn	**Speaker control:** instructs the modem as to how it is to use its speaker	M0 Speaker always off M1 Speaker on until carrier detect M2 Speaker always on

16

Table 16-5   AT commands for Hayes-compatible modems (continued)

Command	Description	Some Values and Their Meanings
Ln	**Loudness:** sets the loudness of the modem's speaker	L1 Low L2 Medium L3 High
Xn	**Response:** tells the modem how it is to respond to a dial tone and busy signal	X0 Blind dialing; the modem does not need to hear the dial tone first and will not hear a busy signal X4 Modem must first hear the dial tone and responds to a busy signal (this is the default value)

For example, to use HyperTerminal to control a modem using the AT command set, follow these steps.

1. For Windows 98, click **Start**, point to **Programs**, **Accessories**, **Communications**, and click **HyperTerminal**. For Windows 95, click **Start**, point to **Programs**, **Accessories**, and click **HyperTerminal**.

2. Double-click the **Hypertrm.exe** icon in the HyperTerminal window.

3. When the Connection Description dialog box opens, click **Cancel**. You see an empty HyperTerminal window. Type **AT** and press **Enter**. The modem responds with OK to acknowledge the command session. See Figure 16-21.

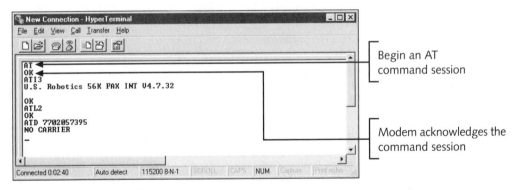

Figure 16-21   HyperTerminal can be used to control a modem using the AT command set

4. Enter any AT command. For example, in Figure 16-21, the ATI3 command causes the modem to report its ROM version, the ATL2 command sets the loudness to medium, and the ATD command followed by a phone number causes the modem to dial a number. Notice in the figure that the modem responds that no modem was connected on the other end (NO CARRIER).

Table 16-6 shows an example of an interchange between a modem and a user. Other examples of AT commands and their meanings are listed in Table 16-7.

Table 16-6 An example of a dialog between a user and a modem

Source	Command or Response	Description
From user	ATD 5551221 [enter]	Dial the given number.
From modem	CONNECT 19200	Modem responds with the agreed-on bps. At this point, you can transfer data using a utility provided by the communications software. Then wait at least 1 second before the next command.
From user	+++	Escape sequence telling the modem to return to command mode (then pause 1 second).
From modem	OK	Modem responds by giving you the OK response.
From user	ATH0 [Enter]	Disconnect the line.
From modem	OK	Modem responds by giving you the OK response.

Table 16-7 Some examples of AT commands

Command	Description
ATDT 5552115	Dial the given number using tone dialing.
ATDP 5552115	Dial the given number using pulse dialing.
ATD 9,5552115	Dial 9 and pause, then dial the remaining numbers (use this method to get an outside line from a business phone).
AT &F1DT9,5552115	Restore the default factory settings. Dial using tone dialing. Pause after dialing the 9. Dial the remaining numbers.
ATM2L2	Always have the speaker on. Set loudness of speaker at medium.
ATI3	Report the modem ROM version.

Even though you can communicate with a modem using AT commands, most often when working with modems, you are using communications software that is providing a more user-friendly interface than just a window for AT commands. For example, when using pcANYWHERE, you can tell the software to dial up a remote computer by clicking on a button and typing a phone number to dial. The software performs the dial-up in the background for you by sending the appropriate AT commands to the modem.

16

Using pcANYWHERE for Windows 3.x, follow the steps below to establish a connection to a remote PC. (The Windows 9x version of pcANYWHERE works similarly, except that the modem dialog box showing AT commands does not appear.)

1. Double-click the **pcANYWHERE** icon in Program Manager. The pcANYWHERE opening screen appears, as in Figure 16-22.

Figure 16-22   Opening screen of pcANYWHERE for Windows 3.1

2. Click **Call a Host PC** and select **pcANYWHERE Host via modem** from the Host PC Directory. Click **Call**.

3. Enter the phone number to dial and click **OK**. pcANYWHERE does the rest. The Connecting dialog box opens, as in Figure 16-23, showing the dialog between the software and its modem. Notice in the Modem dialog box of Figure 16-23 that some of the AT command strings contain "Sn = number," where n is a number. These commands set the modem's internal registers, which are memory locations in the modem where it temporarily keeps configuration information. For example, the AT command S7 = 30 in Figure 16-23 says to store the value 30 in modem register 7. Modem register 7 is used to keep the number of seconds that the modem is to wait for a carrier from the other modem before assuming that the modem is not there. The value is set to 30 seconds. For a complete listing of the modem registers and the values they support, see your modem manual.

Figure 16-23   Sample dialog between the communications software and its modem shows modem registers being set

4. After the connection is made, pcANYWHERE creates a window on your screen that is an exact replica of the remote PC's screen.

Software-to-Software Communication

Even though you know that software cannot communicate directly with software on another computer without going through modems, logically this fact can be masked so that there can be virtual communication between the software programs. Return to the newspaper analogy in Figure 16-1: The distribution center at the newspaper press headquarters receives a request for papers from a remote distribution point in the city. The center fills the order and responds that the newspapers are on the way. The truck and road systems are involved in this transaction, yet the two distribution points communicate and do business at a high level where trucks and the road system supporting them are not even considered; however, they are part of the transaction, but are transparent to the two distributors.

This concept is also true of two communications applications communicating. One application sends its data to another application, which receives the data and responds. This higher communication layer is the beginning of the software realm of data communication. There are basically two ways that software communicates with other software:

- **Remote control.** In this mode, the remote PC controls the host PC. The remote PC sends commands to the host PC. The host PC uses these commands to execute software on the host PC and passes the results of the commands back to the remote PC. This method passes commands from the remote PC to the host. The host PC cannot pass commands to the remote PC.

16

- **Data transfer.** In this mode, the remote PC requests data from the host computer, and the host computer sends the requested data to the remote PC. File transfer is one example of this type of communication. This method passes requests for data from the remote PC to the host. The host computer cannot request data from the remote PC. (Downloading a file from an Internet Web site is an example of data transfer.)

The first method is usually slower than the second method, but offers more power to the remote PC. This section looks at an example of each type of software-to-software communication, using pcANYWHERE.

File Transfer with pcANYWHERE

Sharing data between two PCs is one of the most common tasks of communications software. Most communications applications provide file-transfer utilities that have their own look and feel, but the basics of file transfer are the same from one utility to another. The file-transfer function of pcANYWHERE for Windows 9x is the example used below. pcANYWHERE on one computer can make a connection to another PC in one of three ways:

- A remote PC can call a host PC.

- A host PC can call a remote PC.

- A PC can call an online service.

In the explanation below, the terminology used by pcANYWHERE is followed. The two PCs are called the host PC and the remote PC. The host follows the commands of or processes requests for data from the remote PC. The first instance listed above is used for the example below: a remote PC calling a host PC. If you are sitting at a PC making a call to another PC, your PC is called the remote PC, even though it is not "remote" to you, but rather is your local PC; the other PC is called the "host" PC. The connection is made as follows:

1. Call the host PC. The connection is made at the modem-to-modem level. A window opens that is a replica of the host PC's screen. An example is shown in Figure 16-24.

2. Select the **File Transfer** option. The window illustrated in Figure 16-25 opens.

3. In this pcANYWHERE File Manager window, you see your directories and files on the left side of the window (called the Remote side) and the files on the other PC on the right (called the Host side). Commands are listed at the bottom of the window. To copy a file from the Remote side to the Host side, select the file on the left and drag it to the right side, or can use the Send button on the bottom of the window.

4. Exit the utility by selecting **File, Exit** from the menu at the top of the window.

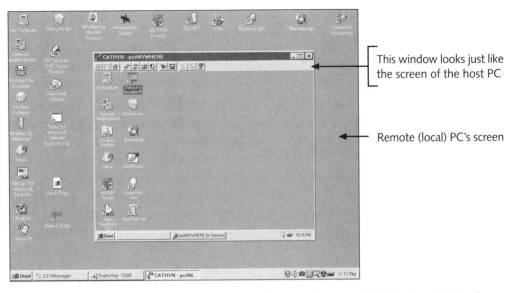

This window looks just like the screen of the host PC

Remote (local) PC's screen

Figure 16-24   pcANYWHERE provides a window on the remote PC that replicates the screen on the host PC. From this window, the remote user can control the host PC.

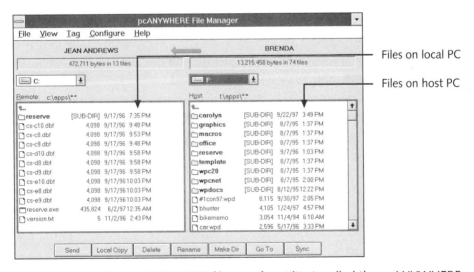

Files on local PC

Files on host PC

Figure 16-25   The pcANYWHERE file transfer utility is called the pcANYWHERE File Manager

Remote Control with pcANYWHERE

One very useful tool for software communication, especially for a PC support person, is remote control. With remote control, a person sitting at one PC (called the remote) can dial another PC (called the host) and remotely control the other PC. The user can execute software on the host PC just as though he or she were sitting at the host PC, and even reboot the host PC. Help-desk personnel find this kind of control very useful when supporting a user and PC at a remote location. A person working from home or off-site can dial into his or her computer at work and perform tasks on that PC that can also be performed while sitting in front of it, although the speed of response does limit how productive that work can be.

In Figure 16-24, a connection is established between the remote (local) and the host (the other end). If the Host window shown in the figure is the active window, any mouse move-ment or keyboard strokes that are performed at the remote PC are passed to the host com-puter to be executed. If the Host window is not active, then the user is controlling his or her own computer locally.

Remote control requires that both computers have pcANYWHERE installed. When you pur-chase pcANYWHERE, you are purchasing two licenses, one for the remote PC and one for the host. ProComm Plus also offers a remote control utility with a similar licensing policy. With both applications, a PC can be set up to be either the remote or the host, but can't be both at the same time. The host serves the remote, passing data to it or performing commands it receives from the remote. The remote PC has more control over what is being done than does the host.

To make your computer a host computer, you must set pcANYWHERE to be a host and leave the application open and waiting for a call. To do so, follow these steps:

1. Using Windows 9x, start pcANYWHERE.

2. Click **Be a Host PC**. The dialog box shown in Figure 16-26 opens.

3. To require a password for the caller or limit the caller to only certain directories or drives on your PC, click **Settings**.

4. After you specify settings, click **Wait for Call**. pcANYWHERE initializes the modem, reduces itself to an icon and waits, as in Figure 16-27.

5. You can use the PC in any other way while the PC is listening for a call. When a call from a remote PC is in progress, you can watch what is happening at the host end.

Figure 16-26   Setting up a PC to be a host using pcANYWHERE

Figure 16-27   "pcANYWHERE waiting" in the taskbar indicates that this host PC is waiting for an incoming call

TROUBLESHOOTING GUIDELINES

A+CORE
2.1

This section provides a guide to solving problems with modems and communicating over phone lines. Some keys to troubleshooting are: determine what works and what doesn't work, find out what has worked in the past that doesn't work now, and establish what has changed since things last worked. Much of this can be determined by asking the user and yourself questions and by trying the simple things first. Below is a list of problems you may encounter with your modem and suggestions on how you can proceed.

16

The modem does not respond.

1. Make sure the modem is plugged into the phone jack.

2. If you are using an external modem, make sure it is plugged into the computer and that the connection is solid.

3. There are two RJ-11 ports on a modem. Check that the phone line from the wall outlet is connected to the line-in port.

A+CORE
2.1

4. Plug a phone directly into the wall jack you are using and make sure that there is a dial tone.

5. If necessary, make sure to instruct the modem to dial an extra character to get an outside line, such as 9 or 8.

6. If this is a new installation that has never been used before, check these things:

   - Make sure the modem is set to the same COM port and IRQ that the software is set to.

   - Make sure that no other device is configured to the same COM port or IRQ as the modem.

   - For an internal modem, check that the DIP switches and jumpers agree with the modem properties in the OS.

   - For an internal modem, using CMOS setup, disable the COM port the modem is set to use so there will be no conflicts. For an external modem, verify that the COM port the modem is using is enabled.

   - If you are using an internal modem, try installing it in a different expansion slot. If you are using an external modem using a serial port card, move the serial port card to a different slot and try to install the modem. If you are using an external modem, substitute a known-good serial cable.

   - Check that the software correctly initialized the modem. If you did not give the correct modem type to the software, it may be trying to send the wrong initialization command. Try AT&F. (Under Windows 9x, click **Start**, point to **Settings** and click **Control Panel**. Double-click **Modems**. Select the modem and click **Modem Properties**, **Connection**, **Advanced**. The dialog box in Figure 16-28 opens. Enter the AT&F command under Extra settings.) Retry the modem.

   - Make sure you have enough RAM and hard drive space. Then close all other applications currently running, reboot the PC, and try the modem again.

The modem says there is no dial tone, even though you can hear it.

1. Make sure the phone cord from the wall outlet is plugged into the line jack on the modem.

2. The modem might not be able to detect the dial tone even if you can hear it. Try unplugging any other equipment plugged into this same phone line, such as a fax machine.

3. Try giving the ATX0 command before you dial. Enter the command under Advanced Settings, as in Figure 16-28. If that doesn't help, then remove the ATX0 command.

4. Straighten your phone lines! Don't let them get all twisted and crossed up with other heavy electrical lines.

A+CORE
2.1

5. If there has been a recent lightning storm, the modem may be damaged. Replace the modem with one you know works.

Figure 16-28 The Extra settings box allows you to send extra AT commands to the modem on any call

The modem dials and then says that the other end is busy, even when you know that it is not.

1. This can happen with international calls if the modem does not recognize the signal as a ring. Try giving the ATX0 command first.

2. Straighten the phone lines and remove extra equipment, as described above.

The sending modem and the receiving modem take a very long time to negotiate the connection.

1. This is probably because of a noisy phone line. Try calling again or using a different number.

2. Remove other equipment from your line. A likely suspect is a credit card machine.

3. Try turning off data compression and try again.

4. Turn off error correction and try again.

5. Try forcing your modem to use a slower speed.

During a connection, it sounds as if the handshaking starts all over again. Modems normally do this if the phone line is noisy and would cause a lot of data to become corrupted; it's called retraining, and it sometimes can solve the problem as the modems renegotiate, compensating for the noisy line. Do the things listed above to clear your line of equipment and twisted phone lines.

16

A+CORE
2.1

File transfers are too slow.   Make sure your modem is configured to use data compression, if possible.

The modem loses connection at odd times or is slow.

1. Check the communications software for the speed assigned to it. Many times people set the communications software speed for the modem speed instead of for what the software is asking for, the port speed, which should be about four times the modem speed.

2. You may have a noisy phone line. Try the connection using the same brand and model of modem on both lines. If performance is better, the problem is most likely the phone line.

3. Is the phone line from the modem to the jack too long? About 4 feet is the limit; otherwise, electromagnetic interference may be the problem.

4. Straighten the phone lines and clear the line of any extra equipment.

5. Reinstall the modem. Allow Windows 9x to detect the modem for you and install its own drivers.

The modem drops the connection and gives the NO CARRIER message.

1. Most likely the connection was first dropped by the remote modem. Is someone trying to use a phone extension on this line?

2. Disable call waiting. To do this, put *70 before the dialing number. Some communications software has a setting to disable call waiting. If not, you can put these three characters in the Extra settings box of Advanced Connections Settings (see Figure 16-28).

3. Remove extra equipment from the line and straighten the phone lines.

4. Check the modem settings and make sure "Error control required to connect" is not checked.

5. Try using a different modulation type under Advanced Connection Settings of your modem properties.

6. The remote modem may not support the high speeds used. Try reducing the port speed to 9600 or lower.

Whenever the weather is bad, the connection disconnects often.   This is caused by a dirty phone line. Remove any extra equipment and straighten the lines.

Whenever large files are downloaded, some of the data is lost.   Make sure that hardware flow control is on, and that software flow control is off, for the software, the COM port, and the modem. (Use software settings options, the COM port Properties box, and the modem Properties box.)

A+CORE
2.1

The connection fails whenever large files are uploaded or downloaded. There may be a buffer overflow. Try these things to gain better control of data flow:

1. Make sure that hardware flow control is on, and that software flow control is off, for the software, the COM port, and the modem.

2. Is the serial port speed set too high for the UART chip you have? Lower the port speed.

3. For an external modem, try a different serial port cable.

You get nothing but garbage across the connection.

1. Check the port settings. Try 8 data bits, no parity, and one stop bit (8, No, and 1).

2. Slow down the port speed.

3. Slow down the modem speed.

4. Try a different modulation type.

FASTER THAN PHONE LINES

A+CORE
6.1

The speed of communicating data is constantly improving. Looking back at Figure 16-3, you can see that no matter how fast communication is between the computer and its modem, the speed between one modem and another can be no faster than the limited speed of the regular analog phone lines to which they are connected. You also learned in this chapter that phone lines most often become digital once they reach a central office of the phone company or some other centralized location. The phone company transports voice and data digitally over long distances and then converts it back to an analog signal just before it reaches the customer location, which is usually done at the customer's central office.

The problem with slow analog lines can be greatly improved by making the phone lines digital all the way from one customer to the next. This was first done for large commercial customers. One example of a digital line is called a T1 line, which carries the equivalent of 24 phone circuits and can transmit data at 1.5 million bps. Prices for T1 lines vary and are somewhere around $1000 per month. These lines are sometimes installed as private circuits connecting two locations of the same company.

A T1 line is too expensive for personal or small business users, so several technologies have emerged to compete for the home and small business market for high-speed data transmission. The data transmission capacities for several of these technologies are listed in Table 16-8. When referring to digital data communication, data transfer capacity is called **bandwidth**.

16

 TIP

When referring to analog data communication, bandwidth has a different meaning than it does when applied to digital communication. With analog communication, bandwidth is the range of frequencies that can travel over the analog line. For example, regular telephone lines can accommodate frequencies between 300 Hz and 3,300 Hz, so the bandwidth of a regular phone line is 3,000 Hz.

Table 16-8   Bandwidth technologies for personal and small business users

Technology	Access Method	Attainable Speeds	Comments
Regular phone line	Dial-up	Up to 53 Kbps	POTS — "plain old telephone service"
ISDN	Dial-up	64 Kbps to 128 Kbps	Requires a leased line from phone company. It can be used by a medium-sized business to access an ISP.
DSL	Direct connect	Varies greatly; 1 Mbps upstream and up to 32 Mbps downstream	Requires a leased line from phone company. There are several versions of DSL on the market.
Cable modem	Direct connect	512 Kbps to 5 Mbps	Uses TV cable system to provide home or small business access to ISP
Satellite	Direct connect	400 Kbps	Only works downstream; upstream transmission requires a dial-up

Integrated Services Digital Network (ISDN)

A+CORE 6.1

A technology developed in the 1980s that uses regular phone lines and is accessed by a dial-up connection was developed using an accepted international standard called **Integrated Services Digital Network** or **ISDN**. An ISDN line is fully digital and consists of two channels, or phone circuits, on a single pair of wires. Each line can support speeds up to 64,000 bps. The two lines can be combined so that, effectively, data travels at 128,000 bps, which is about five times the speed of regular phone lines.

Because ISDN lines are designed for small business and home use, the two lines can support voice communication, fax machines, and computers. Logically, the two circuits are two phone lines, which can each have different phone numbers, although most often only one number is assigned to both lines. Because an ISDN line must have little noise on it, only a single jack for the line—which initially connects to one device—is allowed at a customer location.

In order to use an ISDN line at your business or home, you must have these things:

- An ISDN line leased from the phone company

- An ISDN device on your computer (comparable to a modem for a regular phone line)

- ISDN software on your PC to manage the connection

If you plan to use an ISDN line to access the Internet, then, in order for you to see a performance gain, your service provider must also have an ISDN line. If you plan to use the ISDN line for telecommuting, then your place of business must also have ISDN in order for performance to improve.

The single ISDN device that connects to the ISDN line at your home can be an expansion card inside your PC or can be an external device. Communications software, the OS, and computer hardware relate to an ISDN device for digital phone lines just as they relate to a modem for analog phone lines (see Figure 16-3). The communications software and the OS must support the ISDN device. If the device is external and using the COM port on the computer system, then the UART chip controlling that COM port does not make a distinction between communicating with an ISDN device and with a modem, since all its communication is digital in either case. There are three choices as to how you can connect to ISDN:

- **Internal card.** An internal card is less expensive than the other two choices, but limits the use of the ISDN to when your computer is on.

- **External device.** An external device requires a connection to your PC. If you connect the device by way of your serial port, you have a bottleneck at the serial port; the device can communicate to your PC only as fast as the serial port speed.

- **External device and network card.** You can use an external device connected to your PC by way of a network card. The price is higher, but this solution offers the most advantages: the PC does not have to be on to use the ISDN line, and the network card is faster than a serial port.

Figure 16-29 shows one setup for an ISDN external device. The external ISDN device can also function as a bridge between a LAN in your building and the ISDN line. (In networking, a bridge is a device that connects two networks so that communication can take place between them.) Every PC would then connect to the ISDN line by way of its network card, which is also its access to the LAN. Some of these external ISDN devices also supply ordinary phone jacks so that ordinary telephones can also be connected to the ISDN line without having to go through a PC in your building.

The ISDN device, be it internal or external, in North America is technically an NT1 (network termination 1) device, but the term heard most often in referring to this device is a terminal adapter (TA). The two major manufacturers of TAs in the U.S. are Eicon Technologies and 3Com. (See their Web sites at *www.eicon.com* and *www.3com.com* for more information.)

You may hear an external TA called an ISDN modem or an ISDN box. An internal TA may be called an ISDN card or an ISDN modem. Call it a box or a card or a device, but calling it an ISDN modem is not correct! A modem converts digital to analog and analog to digital. An ISDN circuit is digital all the way. No modems are needed.

16

Figure 16-29   An external ISDN device serves as a connection point for
PCs and telephones

Cable Modem

A+CORE
6.1

Regular phone lines and ISDN both require a dial-up connection. In moving to the next generation of data transmission for the home and small business, the choice is a direct connection and speeds measured in Mbps (million bits per second) rather than Kbps (thousand bits per second). A direct connection means that the line is always up rather than having to be established as a connection with a dial-up. **Cable modem**, a popular technology that is direct connect, uses cable lines that already exist in millions of households in the U.S. Just as with cable TV, cable modems are always connected. Simply turn on the PC and you're up. Cable modems use a technology called **Data Over Cable Service Interface Specifications (DOCSIS)**.

With cable modem, you install an Ethernet network interface card in your PC. When the cable company installs the service in your home, they provide an external modem that converts the analog signal coming over the cable to digital before it is sent to the Ethernet NIC in your PC. The modem designed for the DOCSIS interface is likely to be leased to you as part of the cable modem service.

A very few cable companies don't provide upstream service (data flowing *from* your PC *to* your ISP) by cable. The connection downstream (data flowing *from* the ISP *to* your PC) is a direct connect by cable, but the service upstream is by regular dial-up phone lines. This means that you can receive data over the cable, but to transmit, you must use a regular dial-up. Be sure you understand what you're getting before you lease.

A+CORE
6.1

When you lease cable modem service, you are most likely also agreeing to use the service provider as your ISP. Two popular cable modem providers are @Home and MediaOne Express. See their Web sites at *www.home.net* and *www.mediaoneexpress.com* for more information. The cost for cable modem service, including ISP cost, is in the range of $35–$90 per month. How to connect to the Internet using cable modem is covered in the next chapter.

Digital Subscriber Line (DSL)

In the race to produce a fast data transmission technology that is affordable for home use and offers a direct connection rather than a dial-up, the telephone industry has developed several technologies, which are collectively called **Digital Subscriber Line** or **DSL**. (ISDN is an early example of DSL.)

One prominent version of DSL is **Asymmetric Digital Subscriber Line (ADSL)**, which is 50 times faster than ISDN and is direct connect. (Asymmetric refers to the fact that upstream transmission is not necessarily run at the same speed as downstream transmission.) When using the Internet, most transmission is downstream (downloading Web pages), so the asymmetric technology is a viable option for home use if the emphasis is on using the Internet. ADSL uses a new standard for transmission called **G.Lite** sponsored by ITU. To have a DSL connection, you must lease the line from the phone company, which provides a converter box on-site. From the box, the line connects to an Ethernet NIC in your PC just like cable modem. The cost of an ADSL line varies greatly, anywhere from $75 to $850 per month, depending on your location. How to connect to the Internet using DSL is covered in the next chapter.

Satellite

One last way to attain high-speed data transmission is by using satellites. You lease the service from a provider and mount a satellite dish on your premises. One service provider is DirecPC Satellite Service by Hughes (see the Web site *www.direcpc.com*). Using a satellite connection for downstream transmission of data is not a good option unless you need high-speed transmission and live in a remote location that doesn't offer other alternatives. The installation can be complicated and requires a dial-up connection for data to travel upstream.

16

CHAPTER SUMMARY

❑ Communicating over phone lines involves both virtual communication and direct communication. Virtual communication takes place between counterpart layers at each end of a transmission, and direct communication occurs between adjacent layers.

❑ A modem is a device used to convert digital data from a PC to analog signals suitable for transmission over phone lines, and to convert analog data from phone lines back to digital signals for a PC.

❐ When two modems first connect, they must decide how data will be transmitted. This process is called training or handshaking. The handshaking between two modems can be heard as hissing sounds when the two modems first connect.

❐ Computers communicating through modems are called data terminal equipment (DTE). The modems are called data communications equipment (DCE).

❐ Modems can perform data compression to speed up transmission, and error correction to ensure the integrity of the data.

❐ The speed that data can travel over phone lines is called modem speed or line speed and is measured in baud rates or bits per second (bps).

❐ The limitation of modem speeds is partly determined by the analog quality of phone lines and the way data is converted to digital signals during transmission over the phone lines.

❐ Modem standards have been set by CCITT (Comité Consultatif Internationale de Télégraphique et Téléphonique), and are now called either CCITT standards or ITU standards.

❐ Modem standards include standards for speed, data compression, and error correction.

❐ The protocols used by modems are factory-set into the modem's firmware, but can be partially controlled by settings in the operating system or communications software.

❐ Error correction performed by modems is done by dividing data into packets or frames and calculating a checksum on each packet. The checksum is calculated again at the receiving end. If the two checksums differ, another transmission is requested by the receiving modem.

❐ Overall transmission speed is determined by the port speed, which is the speed of the UART chip controlling the communications port used by the modem, and the line speed, which is the speed from modem to modem over phone lines.

❐ Both internal and external modems use a UART chip to control the transmission of digital data from the computer.

❐ The method that a receiving modem or PC uses to stop and start the flow of data to it is called flow control.

❐ Flow control can be performed by a computer or by a modem. Two methods of flow control are software flow control and hardware flow control. Hardware flow control is the preferred choice.

❐ Serial ports use the RS-232c standard for communication. Hardware flow control uses two of the connections in the RS-232c standard.

❐ The UART chip controls data transmission speed, parity checking, start and stop bits, and flow control.

❐ Communications software can either provide remote control to a host PC or pass data from one PC to another. Remote control is usually the slower of the two methods.

❏ Most communications software communicates to modems using a modem language developed by Hayes called the AT command set. Modems that use this language are said to be Hayes-compatible.

❏ Some technologies that offer higher data transmission speeds than regular phone lines are cable modem, ISDN, ADSL, and satellite.

❏ ISDN is a dial-up connection. Cable modem, ADSL, and satellite are direct connections.

❏ ISDN is a faster alternative to regular analog phone lines because it is digital and provides two lines rather than only the single line provided by regular phone lines.

❏ In order to benefit from using ISDN technology, both the sending and receiving computers must have an ISDN connection. Each computer must use an ISDN device and ISDN software.

❏ A cable modem is leased from a cable television company and usually comes bundled with service from an Internet service provider.

❏ A cable modem requires an external modem to receive the incoming signal that connects to an Ethernet NIC in your PC.

❏ ADSL is about 50 times faster than ISDN. It connects to your PC by way of an Ethernet NIC.

❏ Satellite data transmission is only for downstream transmission. Upstream transmission must be by some other method such as dial-up on a regular phone line.

KEY TERMS

ADSL (asymmetric digital subscriber line) — A method of data transmission over phone lines that is digital, allows for a direct connection, and is about 50 times faster than ISDN.

AT command set — A set of commands used by a PC to control a modem. AT is the ATtention command, which alerts a modem to prepare to receive additional commands. For example, ATDT means attention and listen for a dial tone.

Audio/modem riser (AMR) — A specification for a small slot on a system board to accommodate an audio or modem riser card. A controller on the system board contains some of the logic for the audio or modem functionality.

Bandwidth — For digital data transmission, the data transfer capacity (for example, a T1 line has a bandwidth of 1.544 Mbps). For analog data transmission, the difference between the highest and lowest frequency that the technology accommodates (for example, a regular telephone line has a bandwidth of 3,000 Hz).

Baud rate — A measure of line speed between two devices such as a computer and a printer or a modem. This speed is measured in the number of times a signal changes in one second. *See* bps.

bps (bits per second) — A measure of data transmission speed. (Example: a common modem speed is 56,000 bps or 56 Kbps.)

16

Cable modem — A method of data transmission over cable TV lines that requires a modem and an Ethernet network interface card to receive the transmission.

Carrier — A signal used to activate a phone line to confirm a continuous frequency; used to indicate that two computers are ready to receive or transmit data via modems.

Checksum — A method of error checking transmitted data, whereby the digits are added up and their sum compared to an expected sum.

CCITT (Comité Consultatif Internationale de Télégraphique et Téléphonique) — An international organization that was responsible for developing standards for international communications. This organization has been incorporated into ITU. *See* ITU.

Communication and networking riser (CNR) — A specification for a small expansion slot on a system board that accommodates a small audio, modem, or network riser card. Part of the logic for the card is contained in a controller on the system board.

Data communications equipment (DCE) — The hardware, usually a dial-up modem, that provides the connection between a data terminal and a communications line.

Data terminal equipment (DTE) — This term refers to both the computer and a remote terminal or other computer to which it is attached.

De facto standard — A standard that does not have an official backing, but is considered a standard because of widespread use and acceptance by the industry.

Demodulation — When digital data that has been converted to analog data is converted back to digital data. *See* Modulation.

Digital signal — A signal that has only a finite number of values in the range of possible values. An example is the transmission of data over a serial cable as bits, where there are only two values: 0 and 1.

Digital subscriber line (DSL) — A type of technology that is used by digital telephone lines that direct connect rather than dial-up.

DOCSIS (Data Over Cable Service Interface Specifications) — The communications standard used by cable modems.

Error correction — The ability of some modems to identify transmission errors and then automatically request another transmission.

Flow control — When using modems, a method of controlling the flow of data from a sending PC by having the receiving PC send a message to the sending device to stop or start data flow. Xon/Xoff is an example of a flow control protocol.

Frame — A small, standardized packet of data that also includes header and trailer information as well as error-checking codes.

Full-duplex — Communication that happens in two directions at the same time.

G.Lite — A communications standard sponsored by ITU that is used by ADSL.

Guard tone — A tone that an answering modem sends when it first answers the phone, to tell the calling modem that a modem is on the other end of the line.

Half-duplex — Communication between two devices whereby transmission takes place in only one direction at a time.

Handshaking — When two modems begin to communicate, the initial agreement made as to how to send and receive data. It often occurs when you hear the modem making noises as the dial-up is completed.

In-band signaling — In modem communication, the name of the signaling used by software flow control, which pauses transmission by sending a special control character in the same channel (or band) that data is sent in.

ISDN (Integrated Services Digital Network) — A communications standard that can carry digital data simultaneously over two channels on a single pair of wires, at about five times the speed of regular phone lines.

ITU (International Telecommunications Union) — The international organization responsible for developing international standards of communication. Formerly CCITT.

Line speed — *See* Modem speed.

Modem — From MOdulate/DEModulate. A device that modulates digital data from a computer to an analog format that can be sent over telephone lines, then demodulates it back into digital form.

Modem speed — The speed a modem can transmit data along a phone line measured in bits per second (bps). Two communicating modems must talk at the same speed for data transmission to be successful. Also called line speed.

Modem riser card — A small modem card that uses an AMR or CNR slot. Part of the modem logic is contained in a controller on the system board.

Modulation — Converting binary or digital data into an analog signal that can be sent over standard telephone lines.

Noise — An extraneous, unwanted signal, often over an analog phone line, that can cause communication interference or transmission errors. Possible sources are fluorescent lighting, radios, TVs, lightning, or bad wiring.

Out-of-band signaling — The type of signaling used by hardware flow control, which sends a message to pause transmission by using channels (or bands) not used for data.

Port settings — The configuration parameters of communications devices such as COM1, COM2, or COM3, including IRQ settings.

Port speed — The communication speed between a DTE (computer) and a DCE (modem). As a general rule, the port speed should be at least four times as fast as the modem speed.

RJ-11 — A phone line connection found on a modem, telephone, and house phone outlet.

Start bit — A bit that is used to signal the approach of data.

Stop bit — A bit that is used to signal the end of a block of data.

Telephony — A term describing the technology of converting sound to signals that can travel over telephone lines.

Telephony Application Programming Interface (TAPI) — A standard developed by Intel and Microsoft that can be used by 32-bit Windows 9x communications programs for communicating over phone lines.

Training — *See* Handshaking.

V.34 standard — A communications standard that transmits at 28,800 bps and/or 33,600 bps.

V.90 — A standard for data transmission over phone lines that can attain a speed of 56 Kbps. It replaces K56flex and x2 standards.

16

REVIEW QUESTIONS

1. How is communication over phone lines both direct and virtual? Give an example of each.

2. Converting a digital signal to analog is called _____. Converting analog back to digital is called _____.

3. Communication in only one direction at a time is _____ communication. Communication in both directions at the same time is _____ communication.

4. Why is the maximum transmission rate of today's modems limited to 56.6 Kbps?

5. How does the V.34 standard differ from the V.90 standard?

6. What two standards does the V.90 standard replace?

7. What organization is responsible for setting telecommunications standards?

8. Name two standards that pertain to data compression.

9. Why is a modem required to support more than one standard for transmission speed?

10. Name two reasons why a 56K modem might not transmit data at its maximum rated speed.

11. What happens when the receiving modem finds that the checksum is incorrect during data transmission with error checking?

12. On external modems, what is the purpose of the TD and RD lights?

13. Describe the difference between port speed and modem speed.

14. What chip controls a serial port?

15. When an external modem connects to a PC, what port is normally used? Describe the shape and name of the port connection.

16. During data transmission, what two devices can initiate a flow control message?

17. Why is hardware flow control better than software flow control?

18. Which two pins on a 9-pin serial cable are used for hardware flow control? What are these two pins called?

19. Why is it best to not have the UART chip perform parity checking?

20. What company invented the AT command set for a PC to communicate with a modem?

21. What is a dial-up, digital data transmission technology that is faster than regular phone lines?

22. Name two data-transmission technologies that offer a direct, "always up" connection.

23. List three hardware reasons why a modem might not respond.

24. List three software reasons why a modem might not respond.

25. Which is faster, an ISDN line or an ADSL line?

PROJECTS

Quick Modem Test

Use Windows HyperTerminal to make a call from your computer to any phone number. Describe what happens. What does this test confirm and not confirm about your modem and its setup?

Does Your Phone Line Qualify for a 56-Kbps Line?

You must have a V.34 standard modem for this project. Determine if your phone line is clean enough to support a 56-Kbps modem. Access the 3Com Web site at *www.3com.com*, search the site for "linetest", and follow the directions on the screen. Get a printed screen of your results.

Find Out About Your Modem

1. Open the Control Panel: Click **Start**, point to **Settings**, and click **Control Panel**.
2. Double-click **Modems**.
3. Click the **Diagnostics** tab.
4. Under Port, click the port that shows the installed modem.
5. Click the **More Info** button
   a. What DOS port does the modem use?
   b. What interrupt does the modem use?
   c. What port address does the modem use?
   d. What UART chip is used?
   e. What is the highest possible speed supported by the UART chip?
   f. What model of modem is installed?
   g. List several types of information stored under the Command and Response headings.
6. Click **OK**. Select the **General** tab, then click the **Dialing Properties** button. If you are using a business phone, how do you tell the computer what to do to access an outside line?

16

Change Your Modem's Connection Settings

Following the directions in the troubleshooting guidelines, change your modem's connection settings so that the modem speaker remains on the entire time that the modem is connected, by using the ATM2 command under the Extra settings box of Advanced Connection Settings.

Make a call with this setting. After you have finished the call, remove the extra setting.

Modem Troubleshooting

In the Advanced Connections Settings dialog box, check the box **Record a log file** for Windows 95 or **Append to Log** for Windows 98. This action causes Windows 9x to create a log file named Modemlog.txt in the folder where Windows is installed. Make a phone call using the modem and then disconnect. Print the log file that is created.

Simulating Modem Problems

Work with a partner on this project. Using a computer with an internal modem and a phone line, simulate a problem with the modem, as your partner does the same with another PC. Don't tell your partner what you did to your modem, and then exchange PCs. Troubleshoot the problem created by your partner. Here are some examples of problems to create:

◻ Change a jumper or DIP switch on the modem. (Don't do this without first carefully writing down the original setting.)

◻ Disable the COM port the modem is using.

◻ Uninstall the modem in the operating system.

◻ Loosen the modem card from its expansion slot.

◻ Disconnect the phone line.

◻ Insert the phone line in the wrong jack on the modem.

As you work to troubleshoot the problem caused by your partner, keep notes of what you discover and what you try. Begin by answering these questions:

1. Describe exactly what happens when you attempt to make a call.
2. List what you know works with the modem and the software.
3. List what you suspect the problem might be.
4. List the steps you take to correct the problem.
5. What was the source of the problem (not your partner!)?

Using Nuts & Bolts to Get Serial Port Information

Using Nuts & Bolts, access Discover Pro. From the Discover Pro main screen, click the **Diagnostics** tab, and then click **Advanced**. Select **Serial Diag** from the icons on the left side of the advanced diagnostics screen. Figure 16-30 is displayed. Perform the serial port test, and then print the test results. What does the term "external loopback" mean?

Figure 16-30   Nuts & Bolts advanced diagnostics can test a serial port

Cable Modem Research

Research what is involved for a cable modem connection to your home. Answer these questions:

1. Is the service available to your home?

2. How much does it cost?

3. What is provided with the service?

4. What equipment is needed that is not included with the service, and how much does it cost?

5. What software is required to use the service?

6. Does the company also serve as an Internet service provider?

7. Is transmission both upstream and downstream?

Research on the Internet

A customer asks you to install an ISDN TA device on his PC. Research how much the device costs, what features the device offers, and what software is included. Give the customer two options, one from 3Com and one from Eicon. Use their Web sites for your research. See *www.3com.com* and *www.eicon.com*.

16

17

NETWORKING FUNDAMENTALS AND THE INTERNET

In this chapter, you will learn:

♦ About the typical hardware components of a network

♦ How several popular network technologies manage data traffic

♦ How data is transmitted over several interconnected networks

♦ How communications layers and their protocols are used on a network

♦ About many of the popular applications used on a network

♦ How to connect to a network using a modem and a phone line

♦ About the Internet and how to support PCs connected to the Internet

More and more PC users are connecting to the Internet from a home PC or connecting to a network at their places of business. So, you have to understand networking if you plan to manage and maintain a personal computer. This chapter first looks at the fundamentals of the hardware and software that make up networks, and then turns to the largest network of all, the Internet, and explains how to support a PC that interfaces with the Internet.

AN OVERVIEW OF NETWORKING

Networking is a means of connecting computers together so that they can share data, such as files and programs, and resources, such as printers and modems. As with all other computer-related subjects, networking can be separated into two categories: network hardware and network software. This chapter addresses both the hardware and software used by networks, with the focus on how networking relates to personal computers.

Network architecture is the overall design of the network, including the physical components, network technologies, interfacing software and their protocols needed to establish reliable communication among each computer or workstation, which is called a network station, a **node**, or a **host**. Data is sent over a network as bits and bytes that have been translated into electronic signals. Before being transmitted, data is first divided into segments, each of which has a header and trailer attached. The headers and trailers are called a **frame** and the entire unit is called a **packet**. Each data packet is sent as an independent unit over the network. At the receiving end, the header and trailer information is removed, and the data within the several packets is reassembled into contiguous data.

You can think of this process of sending data over a network as similar to that of shipping a computer to a destination. The computer is first disassembled and packed into several boxes. When the boxes all arrive, the components are unpacked and reassembled into a complete computer. Think of the computer as data, its various components as data segments, and the shipping boxes with address labels as the headers and trailers. The units (the combination of shipping boxes, labels, and computer components) are the data packets. While in transit, the computer (or data) cannot function as a computer because it has been temporarily disassembled. But once it arrives at its destination, the packing is removed, and the computer is reassembled and made ready for use.

Just as an address is information written on a shipping box, a **header** is information sent in front of data to identify for receiving protocols the data destination and the protocols that the packet is using. A **trailer** follows the data and contains information used by some protocols for error checking. For example, in PCs, the firmware on the network card breaks the data into segments and encloses each segment between headers and trailers, thus creating individual packets. In addition, on the receiving end, the firmware on the network card reassembles the segments back into contiguous data. In the computer shipping analogy, think of the network card in the sending PC as the packing and shipping department, and the network card in the receiving PC as the person who receives the boxes, unpacks them, and assembles the computer system.

Remember that there are two approaches to managing a network: a peer-to-peer network where each individual workstation manages its own security and resources, and a client-server network that is managed by a server. As you learned in Chapter 13, Windows NT calls these two types of networks workgroups and domains, respectively.

The OSI Layer Network Model

In the 1970s, when manufacturers were beginning to build networking software, firmware, and hardware to connect computers, each manufacturer developed its own standards of communication within its proprietary network design. In the early 1980s, manufacturers began to make attempts to standardize networking so that networks from different manufacturers could communicate. Two bodies that were leaders in this standardization are the International Organization for Standardization (ISO) and the Institute of Electrical and Electronics Engineers (IEEE). For example, one major effort of the IEEE was to standardize **Token Ring** and **Ethernet** protocols, which are both considered industry standards for network cards and other network hardware devices that together make up the physical devices that form a network. Ethernet and Token Ring networks are discussed later in the chapter.

Proposed new standards are presented to the industry in the form of a **Request for Comment** (**RFC**), which is assigned a number to identify it. The RFC is publicized and discussed at large, and either adopted or rejected by the industry. You can search for and view the many RFCs that pertain to networking and the Internet at this web site: *www.rfc-editor.org*.

In an overall effort to identify and standardize all the levels of communication needed in networking, ISO developed a networking model called the **Open Systems Interconnect** (**OSI**) reference model, which is illustrated in Figure 17-1. This model breaks down the communication needed for one user or application to communicate with another over a network into seven logical levels. This model can be understood in much the same way as the model for communications over phone lines shown in Chapter 16, Figure 16-3, except that the OSI model covers strictly software and firmware, not hardware. Communication between adjacent layers is considered direct, but communication between matching layers is considered logical or virtual.

When studying the OSI model, remember that not all networks have a separate software or firmware layer that matches each of the seven layers. Realistically, no network in use today perfectly follows the model. However, the model does serve the networking industry as a reference point for discussing different levels or layers in a network. For example, firmware on a network card operates in the physical layer and the data-link layer in the model. From Figure 17-1, we see that the data-link layer is responsible for disassembling data into segments to be assigned to separate packets and later reassembling packets into contiguous data. The physical layer is responsible for passing packets to and receiving packets from the network media or cabling.

For our discussions, it would be unproductive to try to distinguish which portion of firmware on a Token Ring or Ethernet network interface card (NIC) is the data-link layer, and which portion is the physical layer. However, it is useful to talk about Token Ring and Ethernet covering these two layers and then to look for other software or firmware on the network that is managing the layers higher up in the model. For example, once you know that an Ethernet network handles the bottom two layers of data transmission, you can ask the question, "What software on the network determines the best possible route to send a packet so it can arrive at its destination?" This question is addressed by the network layer. The answer will not be found on the firmware of the Ethernet card, because Ethernet does not

17

encompass the network layer of the OSI model. By referring to the OSI model, manufacturers have a structure from which to work as they develop and enhance new networking software, protocols, and designs.

Without getting too deeply into the details of the OSI model, the following provides an overview of the role each layer plays in a network, starting at the top.

Figure 17-1 The OSI reference model identifies seven layers of network communication within software and firmware

Application Layer

The **application layer** of the OSI model is responsible for interfacing with the applications software using the network. For example, suppose you are using a word processor such as Microsoft Word. Word can open a document file that is stored on your hard drive (drive C), and it can just as easily open a document file stored on a file server connected to the LAN. The file server is known to the word processor as just another drive, such as drive F. You can open C:\Data\Myfile.doc or F:\Data\Myotherfile.doc. When the word processor attempts to open the file on drive F (which is the file server), it communicates the request to the application layer of the network software. The communication over the network is transparent to the application from that point forward. The file is retrieved over the network and presented to the word processor by the OSI application layer. An example of software that handles the application layer is NFS for Chameleon by NetManage (NFS stands for Network File Service).

Presentation Layer

The **presentation layer** receives requests for files from the application layer and presents the requests to the session layer (described below). Any reformatting, compressing, or encryption of data is performed by the presentation layer in order for the application layer and the session layer to communicate, for the data to be sent faster, or to secure the data.

Session Layer

The **session layer** is responsible for establishing and maintaining a session between two networked stations or nodes. A session over a network works somewhat like a telephone call over phone lines. The caller makes a call; someone answers on the other end. After both parties know that communication is established, conversation goes in both directions until either the caller or receiver ends the phone call. The session layer performs similar duties. An attempt is made to establish a session between two nodes on a network. Both nodes acknowledge the session, and the session is usually assigned an identifying number. Either node can disconnect a session when communication in both directions is completed. Sometimes a session between two nodes on a network is called a **socket**. When a session is established, a socket is opened. A disconnected session is called a closed socket.

Transport Layer

The **transport layer** is responsible for error checking and requests retransmission of data if errors are detected. The transport layer guarantees successful delivery of data.

Network Layer

The **network layer** is responsible for finding the best possible route by which to send frames over an internetwork (a network of networks). The two most common protocols that make up both the transport layer and the network layer are **TCP/IP (Transmission Control Protocol/Internet Protocol)** and **IPX/SPX (Internetwork Packet Exchange/Sequenced Packet Exchange)**, which are both supported by Windows NT,

17

Windows 2000, and Windows 9x. For TCP/IP, which is used by the Internet, the TCP portion of the protocol is responsible for error checking, and therefore operates in the transport layer. The IP portion of the protocol makes up the network layer and is responsible for routing. IPX/SPX is used by NetWare by Novell, one of the most popular network operating systems for LANs. The IPX portion of the protocol is the network layer responsible for routing, and the SPX portion of the protocol manages error checking, making it the transport layer. These network protocols are further discussed later in the chapter.

Data-Link Layer

The **data-link layer** is responsible for receiving data packets from the network layer and splitting them up into segments of bits to be presented to the physical layer for transport. When data is received from the physical layer, the bits are reconstructed into packets to be presented to the network layer. Token Ring and Ethernet firmware on network cards are examples of code that handles both the data-link and physical layers of the OSI model.

Physical Layer

The OSI **physical layer** on a PC is controlled by the firmware on the network card. It includes the IEEE specifications for cabling types connected to the card and other media definitions. This layer controls how data is transmitted over the physical media. At this level, data is nothing but indistinguishable bits. Remember that data is packaged within frames before it is transmitted. This packaging of data has already occurred before this layer; the physical layer does not distinguish the frame header or trailer from the payload, or data, within the frame. The physical layer sees all of it as just bits that need to be passed on.

Data Frames

Remember that data is segmented and enclosed in frames before it is transmitted over a network as data packets. Each layer in the seven-layer model can add information to the beginning and ending of a data packet to be read by the counterpart layer on the receiving workstation. In practice, however, only the data link layer adds both a header and a trailer. The physical layer adds neither, and the other layers might or might not add a header. At its most complex stage, a packet may look like that in Figure 17-2, in which each layer that adds a header or trailer has added its identifying information to the packet.

Later, when the packet is presented to the counterpart layer on the receiving station, that layer interprets any information in the header and trailer intended for that layer. Then it strips off that header and trailer and passes the packet to the next higher layer in the model. For packets to transmit successfully, each layer of the OSI model must communicate using the same protocol as its counterpart layer on the remote computer.

A single data packet

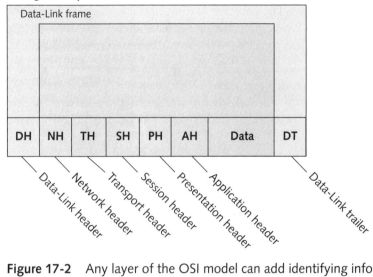

Figure 17-2 Any layer of the OSI model can add identifying information to a single data packet, either as a header or trailer, although, in practice, only the data-link layer uses both a header and a trailer and the physical layer uses neither

The rest of this chapter is generally organized around the OSI networking model, starting at the bottom. You will first learn about the bottom two layers—the physical and data-link layers—of the OSI model and also study the different hardware components (network cards, cables, and so forth) that these layers connect to. Then the chapter turns to the next two layers in Figure 17-1, the network and transport layers, and discusses the most popular protocol at these layers, TCP/IP, which is used by the Internet. Lastly, the chapter focuses on the session, presentation, and application layers, the layers we, as users, are most familiar with, including OS functionality, web browsers, e-mail software, and the like.

NETWORK TECHNOLOGIES

The two bottom levels of the OSI model, the data-link layer and the physical layer are more directly connected to the physical hardware devices that form a network than other layers in the OSI model. Which device drivers and network card firmware operate at the data-link layer and physical layer is determined by the physical technologies used to create the network. These physical technologies and related network hardware devices are the subjects of this section.

The three most popular physical network technologies are Ethernet, Token Ring, and Fiber Distributed Data Interface (FDDI). A relatively new type of network is Asynchronous Transfer Mode (ATM), which is a very fast network that works well over both short and long distances. An older type of network is Attached Resource Computer network (ARCnet), which is seldom seen today. Each type of technology is designed to solve certain network

17

problems, and each has its own advantages and disadvantages. Network technologies differ from each other in many ways. The coverage of some detailed differences is beyond the scope of this book. However, two basic differentiating characteristics—how computers are logically connected and how traffic is controlled on the network—are discussed here.

A network can be a LAN (local area network, typically a network in a single building or adjacent buildings, with nodes connected by cables) or a WAN (wide area network, covering a large geographical area, with nodes connected by methods other than cables, such as microwave signals). Several networks of either type can be tied together, which is called an **internetwork**.

Ethernet

Ethernet is the most popular network technology used today. Ethernet networks can be configured as either a bus topology or a star topology. **Topology** is the arrangement or shape used to physically connect devices on a network to one another. Figure 17-3 shows an example of a bus and a star topology. A **bus topology** connects each node in a line and does not include a centralized point of connection. Cables just go from one computer, to the next one, and the next. A **star topology** connects all nodes to a centralized **hub**. PCs on the LAN are like the points of a star around a central hub.

Bus design

Terminator   Terminator

a) Ethernet can be constructed with a bus design.

Star design

Hub

b) Ethernet can be constructed with a star design using a hub.

Figure 17-3   Ethernet is a simple and popular networking topology

The star arrangement is more popular because it is easier to wire and to maintain than is the bus arrangement. In a bus arrangement, the failure of one node affects all the other nodes. In a star arrangement, some hubs are called **intelligent hubs** because they can be remotely controlled from a console, using network software. Intelligent hubs can monitor a network and report errors or problems. With intelligent hubs, stations that are having problems can be remotely disabled from network access without affecting the rest of the network.

An Ethernet network is a passive network, meaning that the networked computers, rather than a dedicated network device, originate the signals that manage the network. (A dedicated network device is a device, such as a hub, used solely to support a network; other devices on the network, such as PCs, have functions other than networking.) Ethernet works much like an old telephone party line, where each computer is like a party line caller. When someone on a party line wanted to use a phone, he or she would pick up and listen. If there was a dial tone (carrier), then the person could make a call. If someone else was talking, the person would hang up and try again later. If two people attempted to make a call at the same time, both calls would fail. They would each need to hang up and begin again. The first one back on the line would be able to make a call.

A+CORE
6.1

Similarly, a computer that wants to send packets over Ethernet will first listen on the network for silence. If it hears nothing, it begins to transmit. As it transmits, it is also listening. If it hears something other than its own data being transmitted, it stops transmitting and sends out a signal that there has been a **collision**, which occurs when two computers attempt to send data at the same time. A collision can corrupt packets the computers recently sent. Each computer waits for a random amount of time and then tries to transmit again, first listening for silence. This type of network technology is called a **contention-based** system because each computer must contend for an opportunity to transmit on the network. Computers using Ethernet are said to gain access to the network using the **Carrier Sense Multiple Access with Collision Detection (CSMA/CD)** method. The name of the method suggests three characteristics of the way computers communicate on Ethernet: (1) a computer must sense that the network is free to handle its transmission before initiating a signal (carrier sense), (2) many computers use the same network (multiple access), and (3) each computer must detect and manage collisions (collision detection).

A+CORE
1.4

Ethernet can use any one of six cabling systems, which are described in Table 17-1. Figure 17-4 shows an example of each of these cables. The two most popular Ethernet cabling systems are 10BaseT and 10Base2 (Thinnet).

17

A+CORE
1.4,
6.1

Table 17-1   Cabling systems used by Ethernet

Cable System	Cable and Connectors	Description
10Base5 (Thicknet) Speed = 10 Mbps	Thick coaxial cable uses an AUI 15-pin D-shaped connector.	Coaxial cable is made of two conductors: a center wire and a metallic braid that surrounds the center wire. Foam insulation separates the two. The maximum segment length of Thicknet is 500 meters.
10Base2 (Thinnet) Speed = 10 Mbps	Thin coaxial cable uses a **BNC connector** (T-connector).	A less expensive, smaller coaxial cable than Thicknet, with a maximum segment length of 185 meters. Thinnet and Thicknet are sometimes used on the same network.
10BaseT (Twisted pair) Speed = 10 Mbps	Unshielded twisted-pair (UTP) cable uses an **RJ-45 connector**.	Two pairs of wire, each insulated from the other and twisted together inside a plastic casing to lessen crosstalk and outside interference. (**Crosstalk** is the interference that each wire produces in the other.) There are several grades of UTP. (A lower grade of UTP not suitable for 10BaseT is often used for telephone wire.)
100BaseT (Fast Ethernet) Speed = 100 Mbps	Unshielded twisted pair (UTP) or Shielded twisted pair (STP) cable with RJ-45 connector. Category 5 (Cat-5) UTP cable is most common.	STP costs more than UTP and thin coaxial cable, but less than thick coaxial cable and fiber-optic cable. STP is rigid and thick and has a shielding around the twisted wires to protect them from outside interference. (Sometimes a very high grade of UTP can also be used for Fast Ethernet for local connections.)
10BaseFL and 100BaseFX (Fiber-optic) Speeds = 10 Mbps or 100 Mbps	Optical fiber (fiber-optic cable) uses an ST or SC fiber-optic connector.	These cables use light rather than electricity to transmit signals. A glass or plastic fiber in the center of the cable, about the same diameter as a human hair, transmits the light.

A+CORE
1.4,
6.1

a) Coaxial cable

b) Unshielded twisted pair (UTP)

c) Fiber-optic cables with tight and loose sheaths

d) Shielded twisted pair (STP)

Figure 17-4   Networking cables

The "10" in 10BaseT comes from the speed of transmission (10 Mbps). The "Base" comes from **baseband**. Ethernet is a baseband network, which carries data over wire a single message at a time in digital form. Contrast baseband to a **broadband** network such as ATM or cable modem that carries multiple messages over wire, each message traveling on its own frequency in analog form. The "T" in 10BaseT stands for twisted-pair cabling.

A 10BaseT network uses a star topology (see Figure 17-5) with each PC on the network connected to a hub, although it is possible to connect two PCs together for a simple 10BaseT network without a hub. 10BaseT networks use RJ-45 connectors, which look like large phone jack connectors.

Figure 17-5 The popular Ethernet 10BaseT network uses unshielded twisted-pair (UTP) wire, RJ-45 connectors, and a star topology commonly using a hub

Thinnet (10Base2) networks use coaxial cables and BNC connectors, which are sometimes shaped like Ts (see Figure 17-6). Thinnet networks use a bus topology with terminators at each end of the bus that twist into the T-connectors at the back of the two end PCs. The BNC port on the network card looks like a cable TV connection.

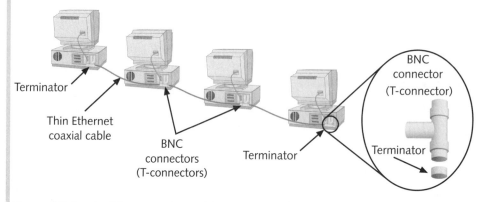

Figure 17-6 An Ethernet 10Base2 (Thinnet) network uses coaxial cables and BNC connectors, with terminators at each end of the network bus

Because signals transmitted over long distances on a network can weaken, devices are added to strengthen the signals. For example, for a 10BaseT Ethernet cable, if the cable exceeds 100 meters (328 feet), signal strengthening is required. A **repeater** is a device that strengthens signals on a network. There are two kinds of repeaters. An **amplifying repeater** simply amplifies the incoming signal, noise and all. A **signal-regenerating repeater** "reads" the signal and then creates an exact duplicate of the original signal before sending it on. Baseband networks such as Ethernet use a signal-regenerating repeater and broadband networks such as ATM use amplifier repeaters.

A+CORE
1.4,
6.1

Each of the cable systems listed in the table can support only a limited number of nodes. As the number of nodes increases, performance speed and reliability can drop for the overall network. One method used to prevent this kind of congestion is **segmentation**. Segmentation splits a large Ethernet into smaller Ethernet segments. Each segment contains two or more computers and is connected to the other segments by a **router**, **switch, gateway**, or **bridge**. The differences among these devices are discussed later in the chapter. Stations on a single segment only need to contend with other stations on the same segment to send their packets. For example, in Figure 17-7, a router connects two Ethernet segments. The router transfers packets to another segment only when it knows that the packet is addressed to a station outside its segment. All other network traffic is contained within the segment. Don't let the two T shapes in Figure 17-7a confuse you. The Ts logically exist, but do not physically exist. If you were to wire these four PCs and one router together, the physical diagram could look like Figure 17-7b. You will learn more about routers later in the chapter.

a) Logically, a bridge connects two Ethernet segments.

b) Physically, the PCs and bridge can be cabled together in this manner.

Figure 17-7   A bridge connects two Ethernet segments

Token Ring

Token Ring networking, which was developed by IBM, is more complex and expensive, but more robust and reliable, than Ethernet. Because of its complexity, it is more difficult to maintain than Ethernet.

Connecting Components on a Token Ring

Logically, Token Ring networks are rings. However, physically, stations are connected to the network in a star formation. Each station connects to a centralized device called a **controlled-access unit** (**CAU**), a **multistation access unit** (**MSAU** or sometimes just **MAU**), or a smart multistation access unit (SMAU). Figure 17-8 shows one Token Ring configuration using two IBM 8228 MSAUs. Each MSAU shown in the figure can connect eight workstations to the network, and, with this type of MSAU, there can be as many as 33 MSAUs on one Token Ring network. One MSAU can connect to another by a cable called a patch cable. One end of each MSAU has a Ring In (data flows into the MSAU) or Ring Out (data flows out from the MSAU) connection. The main ring is composed of the MSAUs and the cables connecting them, which are together referred to as the main ring cable. (The cable connecting the last MSAU Ring Out to the first MSAU Ring In is not considered a patch cable.) The main ring cable can be fiber-optic.

Figure 17-8   A Token Ring network uses one or more centralized hubs called multistation access units

The entire token ring is made up of not only the main ring, but also the cabling to each PC on the token ring. Each workstation contains a Token Ring LAN card with a 9-pin connector for the Token Ring cable, which connects each workstation to an MSAU. Each Token Ring network card has a unique address, which is assigned to it during manufacturing and encoded on the card's firmware. Token Ring cables can be either UTP or STP cables that have two twisted pairs, or four total wires in the cable.

Looking at Figure 17-8, you can see why a Token Ring network is said to be a physical star but a logical ring. All workstations connect to a centralized MSAU (in this case, two MSAUs), but you can also follow the ring path around the entire network. The ring path in the figure goes from the first MSAU to each PC and back again, across the patch cable to the next MSAU, from this MSAU to each PC connected to it and back again, and finally, around the main ring cable back to the first MSAU.

Communication on a Token Ring

Communication and traffic on a Token Ring network are controlled by a **token**, which is a small frame with a special format that travels around the ring in only one direction. One station receives the token from the preceding station, called its **nearest active upstream neighbor (NAUN)**, and passes it on to the next station on the ring, called its **nearest active downstream neighbor (NADN)**. As one station passes the token to the next station, it can attach data in a frame to the token. The next station receives the token together with the data frame and reads this data frame. If the frame is intended for it, it changes 2 bits in the frame to indicate that the data has been read by the intended station. It then passes the token and the data frame on. When the token and frame are received by the station that sent the frame, it sees that the frame was successfully received and does not send the frame again. In this case, it releases the token by passing it on to the next PC, without a data frame attached. However, if the amount of data requires more than one frame, instead of releasing the token, the PC sends the next frame with the token. In either case, the token is passed on to the next PC, and data is never on the ring without the token preceding it.

Any PC receiving a token with no data frame attached is free to attach a data frame before passing on the token. The token is busy and not released to another PC until the sending PC has received word that the data was successfully received at its destination. In other words, the only PC that should remove a data frame from behind the token is the PC that attached it in the first place.

FDDI

Fiber Distributed Data Interface (FDDI, pronounced "fiddy") is a ring-based network, like Token Ring, but does not require a centralized hub, making it both a logical and physical ring. FDDI provides data transfer at 100 Mbps, which is much faster than Token Ring or regular Ethernet, and a little faster than Fast Ethernet, which also runs at about 100 Mbps. At one time, FDDI used only fiber-optic cabling, but now it can also run on UTP. FDDI is often used as a backbone network. A **backbone** is a network used to link several networks together. For example, several Token Ring and Ethernet networks can be connected using a single FDDI backbone.

17

FDDI uses a token-passing method to control traffic, but FDDI is more powerful and sophisticated than Token Ring. FDDI stations can pass more than one frame of data along the ring without waiting for the first frame to return. Once the frames are transmitted, the sending station can pass the FDDI token to the next station, so more than one station can have frames on the ring at the same time. With Token Ring, a data frame is only found traveling behind the token. With FDDI, data frames travel on the ring without the token. A PC keeps the token until it has sent out its data and then passes the token on. Possessing the token gives a PC the right to send data. A token is released (sent on) when the PC has finished transmitting.

Look at Figure 17-9, which shows a FDDI network with five stations. There are three frames of data currently on the ring, all sent from Station 1 to Station 5. Because Station 1 is finished sending its data, it has passed the FDDI token to Station 2. If Station 2 is ready to send data, it can do so now, although data from Station 1 is still on the ring. Another optional feature of FDDI is multiframe dialogs. **Multiframe dialogs** allow one station to send a **limited token** to another station. With this limited token, the second station can communicate only with the first station, not with other stations on the network. This "private conversation" allows for continuous communication between two stations without interference from other stations. At the same time, the main token can be active on the ring, allowing other frames to be passed among other stations.

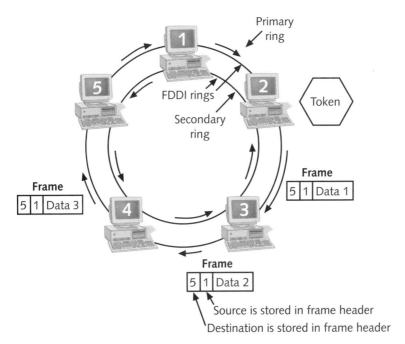

Figure 17-9   A FDDI network can have more than one frame of data on the rings. Shown here are three frames of data moving clockwise around the ring

One important strength of FDDI is its dual counter-rotating rings, as seen in Figure 17-9. Instead of a single ring like the one the Token Ring uses, FDDI has two rings linking each device on the network, a primary ring and secondary ring. Data normally travels on the primary ring. However, if a break occurs on the FDDI ring, any device can switch the data to the secondary ring, which causes the data to travel in the opposite direction back around the ring, as shown in Figure 17-10. When the data reaches the break coming from the other direction, a station switches the data back to the primary ring, and it continues in the opposite direction again. In this way, communication continues even with a break in one FDDI ring.

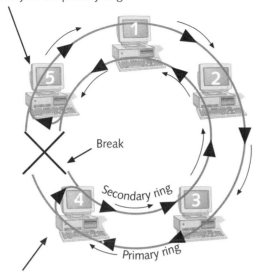

Station 5 diverts the data from
the secondary to the primary ring

Break

Secondary ring

Primary ring

Station 4 diverts the data from the primary
to the secondary ring

Figure 17-10   A break in the FDDI ring causes stations to divert data from one ring
to another

Summary of Network Technologies

Table 17-2 shows a comparison and summary of the three network technologies discussed above.

Table 17-2   Comparing three popular network architectures

Item	Ethernet	Token Ring	FDDI
Logical topology or shape	Bus	Single ring	Dual ring
Physical topology or shape	Star or bus	Ring or star	Ring
Media	Twisted-pair, coaxial, or fiber-optic cable	Twisted-pair or fiber-optic cable	Primarily fiber-optic cable
Standard bandwidth	10 Mbps or 100 Mbps	4 or 16 Mbps	100 Mbps to 200 Mbps
How token is released	Not applicable	After receive	After transmit

17

Table 17-2   Comparing three popular network architectures (continued)

Item	Ethernet	Token Ring	FDDI
Maximum number of nodes	500	260	1024
Advantages	Of the three networks, Ethernet is the least expensive, simplest, and most popular solution.	Token Ring operates more reliably under heavy traffic than does Ethernet, but can be difficult to troubleshoot.	FDDI is much faster than Token Ring and regular Ethernet and faster than 100BaseT (Fast Ethernet).

NETWORKING HARDWARE

Almost all LANs and WANs today are designed using a Token Ring, Ethernet, FDDI, or possibly ATM technology. Besides network cards in the PCs and cabling connecting them, there are other devices needed to physically construct a network. It is beyond the scope of this book to cover all the many hardware components needed to make a LAN or WAN work, but this chapter introduces a few common components. Recall that, for a PC, the direct connection to a network is by way of a network interface card (NIC). Sometimes the logic normally contained on the NIC is on the system board, with a network port coming directly off the system board. This is a common practice for Compaq and Macintosh computers. Hubs are used to provide the centralized location for nodes to connect on a star network. Bridges, switches, routers, and gateways connect one network to another, each performing a slightly different function when connecting like and unlike networks.

Network Interface Card (NIC)

A+CORE
6.1,
4.1

A **network interface card** (**NIC**) plugs into a system board and provides a port or ports on the back of the card for connection to a network. A NIC manages the communication and network protocol for the PC. A NIC is designed to support Ethernet, Token Ring, or FDDI network topologies, but not all three. However, it might be designed to handle more than one cabling system. See Figure 17-11 for some examples of network cards. The network card and the device drivers controlling the network card are the only components in the PC that are aware of the type of network being used. In other words, the type of network in use is transparent to the applications software using it.

a. FDDI

b. Token Ring

c. Ethernet

Figure 17-11   Three different types of network cards: (a) FDDI, (b) Token Ring, and (c) Ethernet

A network card sends and receives data to and from the system bus in parallel, and sends and receives data to and from the network in series (Figure 17-12). In addition, the network card is responsible for converting the data it is transmitting into a signal that is in a form appropriate to the network. For example, a fiber-optic FDDI card contains a laser diode that converts data to light pulses before transmission, and a twisted-pair Ethernet card that converts data from the 5-volt signal used on the computer to the voltage used by twisted-pair cables. The component on the card that is responsible for this signal conversion is called the **transceiver**. It is common for an Ethernet card to contain more than one transceiver, each with a different port on the back of the card, in order to accommodate different cabling media. This type of Ethernet card is called a **combo card** (see Figure 17-13).

17

Figure 17-12   Network cards communicate with the network in serial, and with the computer in parallel

Figure 17-13   This Ethernet combo card can use either a BNC or RJ-45 connection, depending on the cabling system used

Different networks have different ways of identifying each node on the network. Ethernet and Token Ring cards have unique addresses hard-coded on the card by the manufacturer. Called **media access control** (**MAC**) addresses, **adapter addresses**, or, in the case of Ethernet, Ethernet addresses, these addresses are 6-byte hex addresses unique to each card. Part of the MAC address contains the manufacturer, and part of the address is unique to each card; therefore, no two adapters should have the same MAC address.

Network cards require an IRQ, an I/O address, and, for DOS and Windows 9x real mode, upper memory addresses. If the network card is on the PCI bus, then the PCI bus controller manages the IRQ and I/O address requirements. (See Chapter 9 for more information about

A+CORE
6.1,
4.1

configuring PCI devices.) Network cards may be Plug and Play, or they can use jumpers or DIP switches on the card to determine which resources to request. When selecting a network card, three things are important:

- The type of network you are attaching to (for example, Ethernet, Token Ring, FDDI, or a proprietary network standard)

- The type of media you are using (for example, shielded twisted-pair, coaxial, or fiber-optic cable)

- The type of I/O bus you are attaching the card to (for example, PCI or ISA. When selecting the bus to use, recall that PCI is faster than ISA and is the preferred choice. FDDI is much too fast a network for an ISA bus; always use a PCI bus with FDDI cards.)

Bridges, Switches, Routers, and Gateways

Remember that when more than one network is connected, the networks form an internetwork. For instance, a large Ethernet network can be broken into smaller, more easily managed segments, and a device is needed to bridge them. When two networks use different methods of transmission, such as Ethernet and Token Ring, then a device is needed to translate between the two networks. When many networks are interconnected, a device is needed that can choose the best route over these networks.

To satisfy these requirements, bridges, switches, routers, and gateways are used to connect networks and network segments to each other. Two reasons to internetwork are: (1) to extend the geographical area beyond what a single LAN can support, such as to different floors in a building or to other buildings, and (2) to decrease the amount of traffic on a single LAN by dividing the LAN into more than one network.

Bridges and switches connect network segments and work at the lower two layers of the OSI model. When a bridge or switch receives signals from one network segment, it makes an intelligent decision as to whether to pass the signals on to the next segment, based on the destination MAC address. In this way, the bridge or switch limits network traffic across it to only traffic going from one network segment to another, thus making the network more efficient. Using a bridge or switch on a network can improve network performance if the device is strategically placed in the network so that most traffic remains contained on its own side of the device. An example of breaking up a network to improve performance is when you isolate a group of computers that shares the same printers or files. The heavy traffic of this group communicating within itself does not affect the rest of the network.

Routers also connect networks, but work at the Network and Transport layers of the OSI model. Routers can also make intelligent decisions about how to route packets to other networks. For example, large networks are often logically divided into many smaller separate networks, and each small network is identified by a logical network address. These smaller networks are sometimes called **subnetworks**, or **subnets**. Now each packet or frame, in addition to having a physical device address, also has a logical network or subnet address. A router can make decisions as to which neighboring network to send a packet to, based on its ultimate destination subnet address.

17

Routers can be computers with operating systems and special network software, or they can be other dedicated devices built by network manufacturers. Routers hold tables of network addresses, along with the best possible predetermined routes to these networks. These **router tables** can also contain the cost of sending data to a network. The cost can be expressed in one of two ways (hop count is the more common method):

- **Hop count:** The number of routers a packet must pass through in order to reach its destination

- **Tick count:** The time required for a packet to reach its destination. One tick equals 1/18 second.

The routing tables are modified every few minutes to reflect changes in the networks. When a router rebuilds its router table based on new information, the process is called **route discovery**.

A **gateway** connects networks that use different protocols and translates these protocols. For example, a gateway can convert e-mail messages written in a proprietary e-mail format on a corporate WAN to a format that can be sent over the Internet before leaving the WAN. The gateway translates the outgoing network traffic to the protocol needed by the destination network. Gateways can even function so that a computer on one network that uses one protocol can use data from an application stored on a computer on another network that uses a different protocol. The term gateway also is sometimes loosely used to describe any device that acts as the entry or exit point for a network.

Networking Software Overview

Each of the seven layers in the OSI model uses different methods of communicating to its counterpart layer. These methods are called **protocols**. From the preceding discussion, you can see why there are many different protocols simultaneously in use when a network is working. You have seen that the two lowest layers (the physical and data-link layers) are controlled by the firmware on the network cards. However, most of the layers of the OSI model are controlled by the OS managing the network. The best-known network operating systems in the PC world are the UNIX operating system, NetWare by Novell, Microsoft Windows NT and Windows 2000. In addition to the OS that is managing the network, applications software such as Web browsers and e-mail clients are working at the top layers of the model. This section first looks at an overview of all the network software components, and then looks in detail at several of the more popular products used at the topmost layers of the OSI model, the ones users are most accustomed to seeing and using.

A map showing how the components of a network relate to one another and to the OSI model is shown in Figure 17-14. The figure is not intended to be comprehensive. There are user and applications services other than the ones listed, and networks other than Ethernet, Token Ring, FDDI, and phone lines. However, this figure shows how real-life networks map to the OSI model, moving from the lowest level at the bottom of the figure to the highest level at the top.

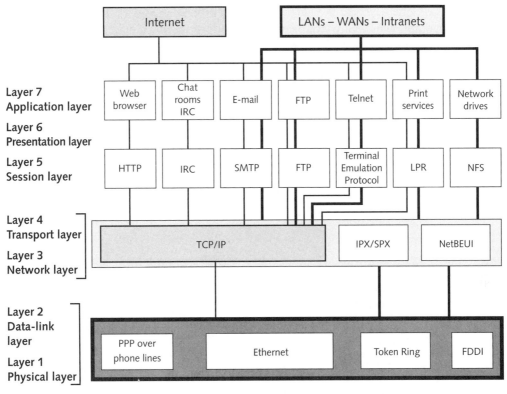

Figure 17-14   An overview of networking software showing the relationships among components

Network Protocol

A+CORE
6.1,
OS
4.1

The three network technologies shown in the bottom layer (physical and data-link layers) of Figure 17-14 have already been discussed: Ethernet, Token Ring, and FDDI. Also shown at the bottom layer is **PPP** (**Point-to-Point Protocol**) over phone lines, which is a protocol PCs with modems use to connect to a network. The Point-to-Point Protocol is the most popular protocol for managing network transmission from one modem to another. The next level up in the figure shows the network and transport layers, showing TCP/IP as the protocol used by the Internet. It is also used on LANs, WANs, and intranets. (An **intranet** is a private TCP/IP network used by a large company.) The IPX/SPX protocol is used primarily on Novell LANs. Since TCP/IP is becoming the most popular protocol at this level, Novell also supports TCP/IP as an alternate protocol. Less significant, but shown in the figure, is the **NetBEUI** protocol (**NetBIOS Extended User Interface**, pronounced "net-boo-ee"), a proprietary Microsoft protocol used only by Windows-based OSs (such as Windows for Workgroups) and limited to LANs, since it does not support routing. Other proprietary protocols that can be used at this level are XNS, DECnet, Vines, and AppleTalk for Apple and Macintosh computers.

17

A+CORE
6.1,
OS
4.1
The higher layers in the network model shown in Figure 17-14 also use protocols to communicate with their counterpart services on the receiving node of the network. For example, when you send e-mail across a network, the e-mail is sent using **SMTP (Simple Mail Transfer Protocol)**, which operates on the session layer. Network drives use NFS protocol, and the World Wide Web on the Internet uses **HTTP (Hypertext Transfer Protocol)**, both of which operate on the session layer as well. Transferring files across the Internet is most often done using **FTP (File Transfer Protocol)**. E-mail, the World Wide Web, and FTP are all discussed later in the chapter.

Network Services

At the highest level of the OSI model are the application and presentation layers. Users access some of these components directly, and others are designed to be interfaces between the network and applications software. Some of the more popular network applications offered at this level are listed below:

- **Web browsers**: Provide primary access to the Internet

- **Chat rooms**: Provide online, interactive communication among several people on the Internet

- **E-mail**: Provides electronic mail (which consists of text files) across the Internet or other networks

- **FTP**: Provides a method of transferring files from one computer to another

- **Telnet**: Provides a console session from a computer to a remote computer. (For example, a user can sit at a PC and use Telnet to connect to a remote UNIX computer and display a window on the PC screen that looks and acts just like the UNIX OS console. Using this window, the user can issue UNIX commands to control the UNIX computer from the PC.)

- **Print services**: Refers to sharing printers across a network

- **Network drive**: Hard drive space on one computer on the network made available to another computer as a virtual or logical drive for the remote computer

Two Network Configurations

A+CORE
6.1
Using Figure 17-14 as an anchor point, recall from Chapter 13 that a network can be logically configured either as a peer-to-peer network or as a network using a dedicated server. Figure 17-15 shows an example of a peer-to-peer network. Users at each workstation can use shared printers and files on each others' computers. The services on a peer-to-peer network are often limited to FTP, print services, and network drives. Nodes on a peer-to-peer network can communicate with any other node on the network and access files and other resources on that node, subject to security limitations. Each node is responsible for the security of its own resources.

A_+^{CORE} 6.1

Figure 17-15   A peer-to-peer network allows all computers to share and use resources

A dedicated-server network, seen in Figure 17-16, has at least one computer, or server, on the network that serves the other computers on the network. If the server contains applications software together with data that is shared by other computers on the network (called clients, or workstations), then the network is called a client/server network. The application on the client that makes use of data stored on the server is called the **front end**. The application on the server that processes requests for data is called the **back end**.

Figure 17-16   A dedicated-server network allows a server to make resources available to all workstations on the network

Dedicated-server networks can be used in one of two ways. If data is processed by the front end, and the server only holds the data, processing can be very slow because the client and server need to interact repeatedly. In a true client/server environment, the front end passes all information that is needed to process the data to the back end, and the back end does the processing. When the back end is finished, it can pass a positive response or a calculated answer back to the client. This last method requires less network traffic and is considered a better use of the network.

Looking back at Figure 17-14, all the programs listed at the application layer can operate on either a dedicated-server or peer-to-peer network. However, the World Wide Web, chat rooms, and e-mail always involve at least one dedicated server. A service that is not listed in the figure, but is used in a client/server environment, is the software necessary for an application on a

17

A+CORE
   6.1
client to pass requests to a server, and for a server to respond with data. This type of software is called **middleware**. One popular example of middleware is Microsoft's Open Database Connectivity (ODBC) software. For instance, with ODBC, a front-end application on a client passes a request to update or query a database on the server. The ODBC back-end version of the software processes the request on the dedicated server and returns an answer to the client.

NETWORKING WITH WINDOWS 9x, WINDOWS NT WORKSTATION, AND WINDOWS 2000

This section discusses how Windows 9x, Windows NT, and Windows 2000 workstations can connect to a network, how to install a network card, and what you need to know when supporting PCs on a network. To connect to a network with Windows 9x or Windows NT Workstation, the networking portion of the OS must be enabled. Sometimes this process is more automatic than at other times. The proper hardware must be installed, along with the device drivers to use that hardware. The device drivers and firmware on modems and network cards generally operate at the physical and data-link layers of the network. The Transport and Network protocols must be installed and then bound to the modem or NIC.

At the transport and network layers, Windows 9x and Windows NT support three different transport and network protocols: TCP/IP, IPX/SPX, and NetBEUI. In addition, Windows 2000 supports AppleTalk. Each protocol can use three different methods for connecting to a network: (1) a network card (either Ethernet, Token Ring, or some other network technology), (2) direct cable connect (for example, using a serial or parallel port), and (3) dial-up networking (using a modem and phone lines). This section addresses these three methods of connecting to a network at this lowest level of networking.

Dial-Up Networking

A+CORE
   6.1
When a Windows PC connects to a network using a modem and regular phone line, the process is called **dial-up networking** (**DUN**). In effect, the modem on the PC acts like a network card, providing the physical connection to the network and the firmware at the lowest level of communication. After the dial-up connection is made, the PC's applications software relates to the network as though it were directly connected to the network using a network card, but a network card is not needed. The modems and phone lines in between are transparent to the user, although transmission speeds with direct network connections are much faster than with dial-up connections. This section covers how to use Windows 9x, Windows NT, and Windows 2000 Dial-Up Networking utilities.

How Dial-Up Networking Works

Dial-up networking works by using PPP (Point-to-Point Protocol) to send packets of data over phone lines. The network protocol packages the data, making it ready for network traffic, and then PPP frames these packets. Figure 17-17a shows how this works. The data is presented to the network protocols, either TCP/IP, NetBEUI, or IPX/SPX, which add their frame

A+CORE
6.1 information. Then the packet is presented to the line protocol, PPP, which serves as the data-link layer in the OSI model. The packet is encapsulated in the PPP header and trailer and then presented to the modem for delivery over phone lines to a modem on the receiving end.

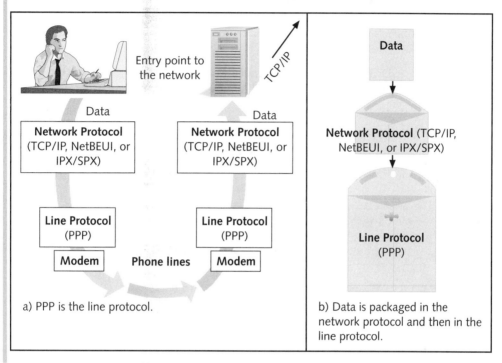

a) PPP is the line protocol.

b) Data is packaged in the network protocol and then in the line protocol.

Figure 17-17   PPP allows a PC to connect to a network using a modem

The modem on the receiving end is connected to a PC or server. The receiving computer strips off the PPP header and trailer information and sends the packet on to the network still packaged in the TCP/IP protocols, or whatever other protocols the network is using. In Figure 17-17b, you can see how these two protocols act like envelopes. Data is put into a TCP/IP envelope for travel over the network. This envelope is put into a PPP envelope for travel over phone lines. When the phone line segment of the trip is completed, the PPP envelope is discarded.

PPP is sometimes called a bridging protocol or, more commonly, a **line protocol**. An earlier version of a line protocol is **Serial Line Internet Protocol** (**SLIP**), which is seldom used today.

A+ OS
4.1 ## Creating a Dial-Up Connection

To use Windows 9x or Windows NT Workstation to communicate to a network over phone lines; Dial-Up Networking must be installed as an OS component on your PC. (Windows 2000 Network and Dial-Up Connections is installed by default.) After installation, you then create an icon in the Dial-Up Networking group, and then use the icon to

17

$A+\ OS$
4.1

make a connection. After the connection is made, any network service available on your network can be used if you have the software on your PC to support it. For example, a network drive is a useful method of passing files back and forth to and from a host computer or other computers on the network. However, experience says that FTP is a more reliable way to transmit files; the choice is yours. If you are using Windows 9x, follow these directions to create a connection using Dial-Up Networking. Windows 98 is used in this example, but Windows 95 works the same way:

1. If Dial-Up Networking is not installed, click **Start**, point to **Settings**, and click **Control Panel**. Double-click **Add/Remove Programs**.

2. In the Add/Remove Programs dialog box, select the **Windows Setup** tab.

3. Select **Communications** and click **Details**. The dialog box on the right in Figure 17-18 shows the components of the Communications group of Windows 98.

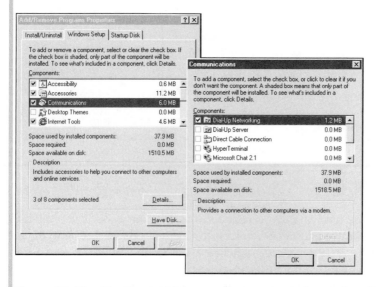

Figure 17-18   Use the Add/Remove Programs window to install Dial-Up Networking

4. If the Dial-Up Networking box is not checked, check it now, and click **OK** to install the component. You might be asked for the Windows 98 CD-ROM or disks.

5. After Dial-Up Networking is installed, click **Start**, point to **Programs**, **Accessories**, **Communications**, and then click **Dial-Up Networking**. The Dial-Up Networking dialog box appears, as in Figure 17-19.

6. Double-click **Make New Connection**. The Make New Connection dialog box appears, also shown in Figure 17-19.

A+ OS
4.1

Figure 17-19   Creating a Dial-Up Networking Connection icon

7. Enter a description of the computer you will be dialing. If your modem is already installed, it appears in the modem list. If not, see Chapter 15 about installing modems.

8. If a logon is required, either before or after you dial into the network, you can request a logon window. Click **Configure** to see the Modem Properties dialog box shown in Figure 17-20.

Figure 17-20   When setting up the logon interface, you can request that a terminal window be displayed before or after dialing

9. Click the **Options** tab, as in Figure 17-20. Select the option to display a terminal window before or after dialing, according to what the network needs. Click **OK** to return to the previous screen. Click **Next** to continue.

17

$A^+ \!\!\!\begin{array}{c} OS \\ 4.1 \end{array}$

10. In the next dialog box, type the phone number to dial, and click **Next** to continue.

11. Click **Finish** to build the icon. The icon is displayed in the Dial-Up Networking window.

12. Dial-Up Networking uses default values for the properties of this icon. To view these values, right-click the icon and select **Properties** from the drop-down menu.

13. Click **Server Type**. Figure 17-21 shows the resulting dialog box. Notice that all three network protocols are selected, meaning that the connection supports whichever of the three the network is using. PPP for Windows 98, Windows NT Server, or the Internet is the selected Dial-Up Server. Click **Cancel** twice to return to the Dial-Up Networking window.

Figure 17-21   Properties of a Dial-Up Networking icon showing server types

14. To make a connection, double-click the icon you just created, and then click **Connect**. You should now hear the modem making the connection.

Dial-Up Adapter

When Windows 9x installs Dial-Up Networking, it also "installs" a Dial-Up Adapter. In terms of function, think of a Dial-Up Adapter as a virtual network card. It is a modem playing the role of a network card for Dial-Up Networking. After DUN is installed, open the Device Manager to see your "new" Dial-Up Adapter listed under Network adapters, as in Figure 17-22. You can also see it listed as an installed network component in the Network window of the Control Panel.

A+ OS
   4.1

Figure 17-22   After Dial-Up Networking is installed, a new virtual network device, Dial-Up Adapter, is listed as an installed hardware device

After the Connection is Made

After you make a dial-up connection, you can do three things, depending on the type of computer or network you dialed. Each of the options listed below is discussed in more detail later in the chapter.

- If you are connected to an Internet service provider, you can use Internet programs installed on your PC such as e-mail or a web browser.

- If you are connected to another PC also running Windows 98, you can use files and printers on the other PC if the other PC has designated them for sharing. How to share resources between two computers is discussed under "Direct Cable Connect," coming up next.

- If you are connected to a LAN such as when you dial into a network at your workplace, from home or another remote location, you can gain access to resources on the LAN by using Network Neighborhood.

17

You can set up your PC to allow another computer to dial in. When using Windows 95, run the Microsoft Plus! utility. For Windows NT, install RAS, and for Windows 98, install Windows 98 Dial-Up Server. For Windows 2000, remote access is installed by default.

Direct Cable Connection

A+ CORE 6.1, OS 4.1

Windows 9x, Windows NT, and Windows 2000 offer a direct cable connection service that allows you to connect two PCs, using either a null modem cable (a cable that connects two PCs using their serial ports) or a parallel cable. When using Windows 9x, follow these directions to use this handy utility (for example, when all you need to do is have two PCs share files or printers, and a cable can reach between them). You can also use this method to allow a guest computer to access shared network resources that a host computer can access.

1. For Windows 98, if it is not already installed, install Direct Cable Connection. Click **Start**, point to **Settings**, click **Control Panel**, and then double-click **Add/Remove Programs**.

2. Click the **Windows Setup** tab.

3. Select **Communications** and click **Details** (see Figure 17-18). Select **Direct Cable Connection** and check it if it is not already checked.

4. Once a connection is made, install Windows 9x File-and-printer-sharing component so you can share files and printers. To install this network component, click **Start**, point to **Settings**, and click **Control Panel**.

5. Double-click the **Network** icon. Select the **Configuration** tab. If File and printer sharing for Microsoft Networks is not already installed, click **Add**.

6. Select **Service** from the list of components. Click **Add**.

7. From the list of network services, select **File and printer sharing for Microsoft Networks**, and click **OK**. You might be asked to provide the Windows 9x CD-ROM or disks and to restart your computer to complete the installation.

8. After you have installed File and printer sharing, open Windows Explorer. Right-click the drive or folder you want to share, and select **Sharing** from the drop-down menu. Select **Shared as** and click **OK**. A folder that is shared has a hand at the bottom of the folder's icon in Explorer.

9. To use the Direct Cable Connection, click **Start**, point to **Programs**, **Accessories**, **Communications**, and then click **Direct Cable Connection**. The Direct Cable Connection dialog box appears, as in Figure 17-23.

10. You must run Direct Cable Connection on both computers. Select one computer as the host and the other computer as the guest. The host computer will listen for the guest computer. Configure the computer that is to share its resources as the host computer, and the one that is to use these shared resources as the guest computer. Click **Next** to continue.

A+CORE
6.1,
OS
4.1

Figure 17-23   Direct Cable Connection is a quick and easy way to connect two computers

11. Select the port you want to use, either a serial port or a parallel port. To use the parallel ports, both computers must have bidirectional parallel ports. Parallel port connections require a parallel cable, and serial port connections require a null modem cable. A printer cable will not work as this parallel cable, because the connection at the printer end of the cable will not fit a PC's parallel port. Buy a parallel cable with two DB-25 male/male connections, or buy an adapter for a printer cable. Connect the cable to both computers and click **Next** to continue.

12. Click **Finish**. For the host computer, the Direct Cable Connection tells you that it is now listening for the guest computer. When you click **Finish** on the guest computer, it attempts to make the connection.

13. After the connection is made, use Windows Explorer on the guest computer to view the shared folders on the host computer. The guest computer can now use resources on the host computer that have been designated for sharing.

Installing Network Adapters Using Windows 9x, Windows NT, or Windows 2000

17

The most powerful and direct access to a network is achieved using a network adapter, or network card. A network adapter may be FDDI, Ethernet, Token Ring, or some other type of network technology. Earlier, the chapter discussed how to select a NIC and configure it. This section moves forward to the next step, installing the NIC using Windows 9x, Windows NT, or Windows 2000.

A+CORE
6.1,
OS
4.1

Installing a NIC under Windows NT

Before purchasing a network adapter to be used with Windows NT, check the Windows NT Hardware Compatibility List to make sure that the card is supported by Windows NT. (See Chapter 13 for details of how to do this.) Follow these directions to install a network adapter under Windows NT:

1. Based on information in the card documentation, set DIP switches or jumpers on the card to configure the IRQ and I/O addresses used by the card. Physically install the card in an expansion slot.

2. Turn on the PC and open the Network window: click **Start**, point to **Settings**, click **Control Panel**, and then double-click **Network**.

3. Click the **Adapters** tab. From this tab you can add, remove, and change the settings of adapter cards.

4. Click **Add**. A list of NICs supported by Windows NT appears, as shown in Figure 17-24. Either select the network adapter from the list or click **Have Disk** if your adapter is not in the list and you have on disk the drivers that are designed to work under Windows NT. If you select an adapter from the list, you are asked to supply the location of the Windows NT CD-ROM and the location of files on the CD. For example, if your CD-ROM drive is drive E, type E:\i386. (The folder i386 is used for Intel-based processors.)

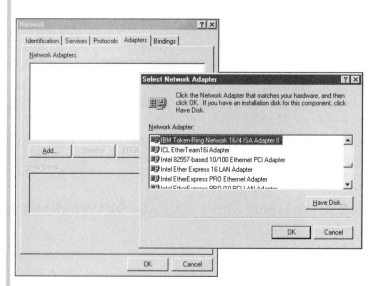

Figure 17-24   Selecting a network adapter supported by Windows NT

5. Windows NT then displays a dialog box (see Figure 17-25) showing the suggested resources to be assigned to the card. You need to know the type of cabling connected to the card and the IRQ and I/O address that the card is configured to use. Click **OK** when you're finished.

A+CORE
6.1,
OS
4.1

Figure 17-25 Assigning resources to a network card under Windows NT

6. If Windows NT recognizes that the PC has more than one bus, it asks you to select the bus that you are using for the card (as determined by the expansion slot you used). Do so and click **OK**. The card will now be listed under the Adapters tab as an installed card. Reboot the PC.

Installing a NIC Under Windows 9x

Windows 95 supports Ethernet, Token Ring, and ARCnet networking cards. Windows 98 supports ATM, Ethernet, Token Ring, FDDI, IrDA (Infrared Data Association standards for infrared communications), and ARCnet networking cards. In most situations, Windows 9x detects a network card when the PC is first turned on, and automatically configures the card for you. However, for legacy cards you can configure the adapter settings yourself using the Control Panel, as follows:

1. Set DIP switches or jumpers and physically install the network card in the PC. If the card is Plug and Play, it most likely will not have jumpers or DIP switches to set.

2. Turn on the PC. Windows 9x detects the new device and configures it for you. You can check the settings by using the Control Panel: click **Start**, point to **Settings**, click **Control Panel**, and then double-click **Network**.

3. Select the **Configuration** tab. The network card should be in the list of installed network components.

4. Select the card from the list and click **Properties**. Figure 17-26 is displayed.

5. The IRQ and the I/O address of the card are showing. If this is not a Plug and Play card, and you know what the card DIP switches and jumpers are set to, you can compare those values to the values shown here. If Windows 9x did not make a correct match, you can change the settings now. From Configuration type, select **Basic Configuration**, so that you can change the IRQ and I/O address settings. Click **OK** when done.

6. Click **OK** again to save your changes. Reboot the PC to give the NIC its best opportunity to synchronize with the network.

17

A+CORE
6.1,
OS
4.1

Figure 17-26 A network adapter's resources show in the properties option of the network window

 If a network card cannot make a successful connection to the network, the problem **TIP** might be an IRQ conflict. Try disabling PCI bus IRQ steering (use Device Manager). For more information on resource conflicts under Windows 9x, see Chapter 12.

Installing a NIC Under Windows 2000

After the card is physically installed and the PC is turned on, Windows 2000 automatically detects the card and guides you through the process of installing drivers. After the installation, verify the card is installed. One way to do so is by using Device Manager. To access Device Manager from the Windows 2000 desktop, right-click the **My Computer** icon and select **Properties** from the drop-down menu. The System Properties dialog box opens. Click the **Hardware** tab and then click the **Device Manager** button. The network card should be listed under Network adapters. Right-click the card and select **Properties** to view the card's properties. Another way to access the NIC Properties dialog box is from the Control Panel. Open the **Control Panel** and double-click the **Network and Dial-up Connections** icon. When the dialog box opens, right-click the Local Area Connection icon and select **Properties** to view the card's properties. If you make changes to the properties, reboot the PC.

Using Resources on a Network

You have learned how to access a network either by way of a network card or by way of Dial-Up Networking. After gaining access to the network, software is needed to manage the interface between the network and the OS. This software layer, called network client software, is responsible for determining how your computer will make use of the network protocols to initiate and maintain communication. Windows 2000, Windows NT, and Windows 9x provide client software for several networks, or you can use third-party software. When you

A+CORE
6.1,
OS
4.1

install this client software as an add-on component to the OS, the OS provides the Network Neighborhood icon on the desktop. (Windows 2000 calls this icon My Network Places.) Using Network Neighborhood or My Network Places, you can access printers, servers, other PCs, and other resources on the network.

The directions below describe how to install client software that is bundled with Windows 98. This Windows 98 computer is connected to a Microsoft Windows NT network. Follow these directions:

1. Click **Start**, point to **Settings**, and click **Control Panel**. Double-click **Network**. The Network window in Figure 17-27 appears. If client software is already installed, it is listed under installed components. (Note that none is listed in Figure 17-27, so we will add it.)

Figure 17-27   Use the Network window of Control Panel to install client software so that the PC can use resources on a LAN

2. Click **Add**. The Select Network Component Type dialog box appears, as shown in Figure 17-27. Select **Client** and click **Add**.

3. The list of network manufacturers that Windows 98 supports is displayed (see Figure 17-28). Notice that Windows 98 supports three network manufacturers: Banyan, Microsoft, and Novell. For a Microsoft Windows NT network, select **Microsoft** as the manufacturer on the left, and **Client for Microsoft Networks** on the right as the network. Click **OK** to continue. Click **OK** a second time to close the Network window. You will be prompted to restart your computer before changes will take effect.

17

$A+$CORE
6.1,
OS
4.1

Figure 17-28   Windows 98 supports networks from three manufacturers; network client software must be installed to use these networks

4. After the installation is completed, Client for Microsoft Networks appears as an installed network component, as seen in Figure 17-29. Also notice in the figure that a new icon has appeared on the desktop: Network Neighborhood. Use this icon to access resources on the LAN. When you double-click the icon, the Network Neighborhood window opens, showing available network resources.

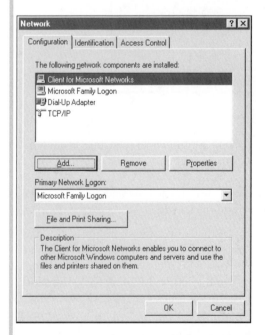

Figure 17-29   After Network client software is installed, it is listed in the Network window and the Network Neighborhood icon appears on the desktop

Servicing PCs on a Network

As a PC technician, you will be expected to troubleshoot and repair PCs connected to networks. You will need to know how to recognize that a PC is connected to a network and how to verify that the connection is working. If the local hard drive loses data or is replaced, you will need to know how to recover the network configuration that was originally on the drive. When the repair is made, you must restore the PC to the network and verify that the connection is again working. Below are general step-by-step directions for a typical situation in which you must remove a PC from a network, make repairs, and then restore the PC to the network.

A network administrator is responsible for the network configuration on the PC and is your resource for specific questions about the network. If, while repairing the PC, you lose the network software and configuration data, work with the network administrator to restore them. Also, when the repairs are made and you are ready to test the network connection, the PC must be logged back on to the network with a valid user ID and password. The PC's end user will have that information. If he or she is not available, see the network administrator.

The steps to disconnect a PC from a network, repair the PC, and reconnect it to the network with the least possible disturbance of the network configuration are summarized in this section:

1. If possible, verify that the PC is network-ready.
2. Log off the network.
3. Save the network files and parameters to disk if you think you might destroy them on the hard drive as you work.
4. Disconnect the network cable and repair the PC.
5. Restore the network configurations.
6. Reconnect the PC to the network.
7. Verify that network resources are available to the PC.

Step 1: Verify That the PC Is Network-Ready

A PC is network-ready if a NIC and client software are installed and the software is configured for a network connection. When you first arrive on-site, check if the PC is connected to a network (look for an installed NIC with an attached cable). Even if a network cable is not attached, the PC might still have network client software installed and configured. If the PC is not working, but the hard drive information is still intact, you can look on it to determine if the PC has client software installed. If the hard drive needs replacing or reformatting, you still might be able to save network configuration information to disk, to make restoring the PC to the network easier.

To verify that a PC is network-ready for DOS and possibly for Windows 9x, look for entries in the CONFIG.SYS and AUTOEXEC.BAT files that execute network software. Also, look in File Manager or Explorer for a network drive. (Remember that a network drive is space

17

on a network server that appears to be a logical drive on the PC.) Common drive letters for network drives are F or J. If you double-click the drive in File Manager or Explorer and see a list of folders available on the server for this PC, the PC is connected to a network.

For Windows 9x, look for a Network Neighborhood icon on the desktop. Double-click the icon to open the Network Neighborhood window. Double-click the Entire Network icon to see resources on the network that are available to this PC.

Step 2: Log Off the Network

Before you turn off a PC connected to a network, it is important to actually issue the logoff command so that the current session is properly terminated at the network server. If you simply turn off the PC without first logging off the network, the network session may not immediately be terminated. Then, if the user attempts to log on to the network again after the reboot, the user's new session may not be allowed, since the network server thinks there is still an active session.

To log off using NetWare by Novell, Inc. (the most popular LAN software for DOS and Windows 9x systems), access a DOS command prompt and type LOGOFF and press enter. For Windows NT systems, press CTRL-ALT-DEL and choose logoff from the dialog box that appears.

Step 3: Save the Network Files and Parameters to Disk

Because the most popular network software for DOS and Windows 95 PCs is Novell, the files, commands, and data used by Novell are described below. Novell and Windows NT networking software is also described for Windows 98 and Windows NT workstations.

Using DOS or Windows 95   NetWare by Novell uses entries in CONFIG.SYS and AUTOEXEC.BAT for DOS and Windows 95, to load network software and drivers and to provide a logon screen for the user to log on to the network. You will want to preserve these entries without changes to restore the network connection after the repair. The NetWare software, by default, is located in the directory \NWCLIENT, although another directory name can be used. Expect to see four to six command lines in the AUTOEXEC.BAT file placed there by NetWare or by the network administrator, and one command line in CONFIG.SYS. The one entry in CONFIG.SYS is LASTDRIVE=Z: (or some other letter), which allows for network drive letters.

An example of a group of startup commands for NetWare that typically might be found in AUTOEXEC.BAT is shown below:

```
SET NWLANGUAGE=English
C:\NWCLIENT\LSL.COM
C:\NWCLIENT\3C5X9.COM
C:\NWCLIENT\IPXODI.COM
C:\NWCLIENT\VLM.EXE
F:\LOGIN JANDREWS
```

The commands might be grouped together in AUTOEXEC.BAT, and preceded by remarks indicating that they are used to load the client software. IPXODI.COM and VLM.EXE (lines 4 and 5 above) are the two main programs of the NetWare client software. The third line above loads a driver for the network card. Sometimes the command lines will include LH at the beginning of the command line, to cause the program to load into upper memory.

The last command line in the list provides a logon screen for the user. The username is included in the command line (JANDREWS in this example) so that the user only needs to enter his or her password. The username can be omitted in the command line and entered from the prompt. The F:\ at the beginning of the command line tells NetWare to access the NetWare server to run the logon program to log on to the network. Figure 17-30 shows the results after entering the command LOGIN without the username included. (Different versions of NetWare may have different login boxes than the one shown in the figure.) The user enters the username and password just as they are recorded on the NetWare server.

```
                        Novell NetWare
  Enter your login name:JANDREWS
```

Figure 17-30   Netware provides a logon screen to log on to a Novell LAN

Sometimes you will see the command lines listed above stored in a batch file, and the batch file referenced in AUTOEXEC.BAT. For example, a batch file named START.BAT might be in the \NWCLIENT directory, and the command C:\NWCLIENT\START in the AUTOEXEC.BAT file.

You may need to replace or reformat the hard drive. If so, be sure to preserve the network settings. The easiest way to do this is to back up the CONFIG.SYS and AUTOEXEC.BAT files, including the network commands. In addition to these two files, one important file in the \NWCLIENT directory is NET.CFG, which contains the specific network configuration information for this PC. If you are having problems with the hard drive, but you have the opportunity to save just a few files, consider this one file important, because it contains information specific to this PC's network configuration.

Using Windows 98, Windows NT, Windows 2000   You can connect a Windows 98, Windows NT, or Windows 2000 workstation to a network in two ways: using the client software included with Windows, or using client software from Novell or some other third-party network client. For a Windows NT workstation on a Novell NetWare network, if Microsoft's Windows NT client software is used instead of Novell's, then you will see the CSNW

17

(Client Service for NetWare) icon in the Control Panel. For a Windows 2000 workstation using CSNW on a NetWare network, look for CSNW installed under the Network and Dial-Up Connections icon in Control Panel. If Microsoft's Windows 98 client software for Novell is used, look for Novell NetWare as an installed network component in the Network window under Control Panel. In any case, if the hard drive of a PC using one of these OSs looses the client software installation, ask the network administrator for assistance to reinstall either the Windows or Novell client software. It will not be possible to simply copy files back to the hard drive, as with DOS or Windows 95, because Windows 98, Windows NT and Windows 2000 store network settings in the Registry.

Step 4: Disconnect the Network Cable and Repair the PC

After you have logged off the network and saved configuration information to disk, disconnect the network cable (called a patch cable) and repair the PC. If you must exchange the NIC, use an identical card with identical jumper and DIP switch settings, because the drivers on the PC are set up specifically for this card. If you are exchanging one type of NIC for another, ask the network administrator to help you reconfigure the PC for the new type of card.

Step 5: Restore the Network Configurations

Reboot the PC without reconnecting the network cable, and restore the network files and parameters, including the commands in CONFIG.SYS and AUTOEXEC.BAT for a DOS or Windows 95 PC, to load the network software and provide a logon screen. The network administrator may provide you with network software to reinstall, or may simply ask you, for a Novell network, to restore the \NWCLIENT directory together with the OS startup files, CONFIG.SYS, and AUTOEXEC.BAT. For Windows 2000, Windows NT, or Windows 98, ask the network administrator to help reinstall the network software.

Step 6: Reconnect the PC to the Network

Turn the PC off, reconnect the network cable, and then turn the PC back on. When the PC boots, the network software should load, and a logon screen should be displayed to reestablish a network session. If you are rebooting the PC with NetWare, the login screen in Figure 17-30 appears. Have the user log on to the network with his or her user ID and password, or use one provided to you by the network administrator for testing. NetWare displays a message saying that you are logged on, and then Windows is loaded.

For DOS and Windows 95, if the network software loads, but the logon screen does not appear, you can issue the LOGIN command from the command prompt. Just enter the command as it appears in the AUTOEXEC.BAT file. For Windows 2000, Windows NT, and Windows 98, if the workstation is connected to a Microsoft network, the logon to the workstation will also log the workstation on to the network. For NetWare networks, the logon may be two different logons, one to the workstation and the other to the NetWare network, or the logon may be synchronized so that both logons occur simultaneously.

Step 7: Verify That Network Resources Are Available to the PC

To verify that all is well with the network, look in Explorer and verify that the network drive is present. Look for drive F or drive J, or some other drive letter representing a network drive. You can find the network drive letter by looking either in AUTOEXEC.BAT at the LOGIN command, or at the contents of NET.CFG in the \NWCLIENT directory for a NetWare network. Network drives are covered in more detail later in the chapter. For Windows NT and Windows 98, check Network Neighborhood for networking resources to determine if the network is functioning correctly. For Windows 2000, check My Network Places. If you don't find resources there, try rebooting the PC.

PCs AND THE INTERNET

A+ OS 4.2

The **Internet** is the largest network in the world. To be more accurate, it is the largest grouping of many networks internetworked together. The software and protocols used by the Internet include all the OSI layers from the application layer through the network layer (see Figure 17-14). At the foundation of the Internet is TCP/IP, which operates at the OSI transport and network layers. TCP/IP was developed in 1969 by the U.S. Department of Defense (DOD) to provide a decentralized and fast network to connect networks. The network was originally called ARPANET (Advanced Research Project Agency network), from which the civilian Internet evolved. DOD wanted decentralized data transfers so that communication would not be dependent on any one server or network, backbone network, or centralized geographic location in order to function. This decentralized concept means that, even if many networks fail, data will still arrive at its destination. Originally, this design was intended to protect data communications in case of a major military attack on the United States, in which many networks might be put out of service. Another goal of decentralization was to allow any one communication to travel from source to destination through any number of different paths, or to be broken into parts that travel different paths, and come together at their single destination.

The Internet is a web of interconnecting, yet independent, networks. Many people confuse the Internet with the World Wide Web (WWW). Again, note in Figure 17-14 that the Web operates at the OSI application and presentation layers and is only one service of many services that use TCP/IP. The Web presents data to Internet users as pages—called web pages—displayed on computer monitors. These pages of information can contain graphics and texts with links to sound files, video files, animation, all types of graphics, other web pages, and other programs. The Web is only one way to communicate over the Internet at the user, or application, level. Other ways, also shown in Figure 17-14, are chat rooms, e-mail, and FTP.

The Internet is a network of networks, and TCP/IP is designed to work in a mixture of several types of networks. Underneath TCP/IP is some other protocol such as PPP, Ethernet, Token Ring, or FDDI, providing the bottom two layers of the OSI model (again, see Figure 17-14). TCP/IP enables packets of data to traverse many networks to arrive at their destination. To understand how these packets can be routed all the way around the world is to understand TCP/IP. One way of looking at this relationship between TCP/IP and network protocols at the

17

A+ OS
4.2

data-link and physical layers is to consider that the Internet, using TCP/IP, uses these underlying networks like a shipping department uses different transportation systems. For example, a package is shipped first by truck, then by train, then by plane, and again by truck before arriving at its destination. In this analogy, TCP/IP is like the shipping box that encloses the contents and the mailing label that identifies the package, its sender, and its destination to all the subsystems sending it on its way. The subsystems are the protocols in the data-link and physical layers of the OSI model.

How the Internet Works

Figure 17-31 shows a simplified, bird's-eye view of how networks work together to send data over the Internet. A user in California accesses a server in New York by traversing many networks. Each network operates independently of all other networks but can also receive a packet from another network and send it on to a third network, while it also manages its own routine, internal traffic. Networks are connected by routers, which belong to more than one network. In Figure 17-31, Network B contains four routers: Routers 1, 2, 3, and 4. But Routers 3 and 4 also belong to Network C. Network C contains Router 8, which also belongs to the same network as the server in New York that the user wants to access.

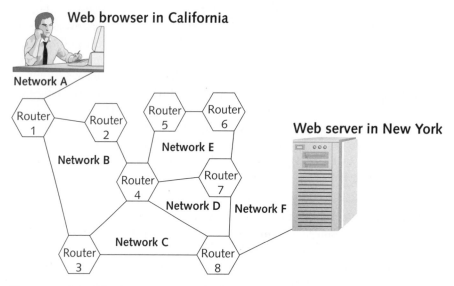

Figure 17-31 The Internet is a web of interconnecting, yet independent, networks

How many paths are there on the Internet by which the user in California can access the server in New York? One path is through Router 1, then 3, then 8, and finally to the server. Data going from the server to the user may travel a different path than data traveling from the user to the server. In fact, if there is a lot of data divided into several packets, each packet may take a different route, and the packets may not arrive at the user's PC in the same order in which they were sent. It's up to the lower layers in the OSI model to sort it all out and reassemble the data before it's presented to the application layer to be presented to the user.

Connecting to the Internet

A+ OS
4.2

There is a variety of ways for a PC to access the Internet. Most people access the Internet through an **Internet service provider** (**ISP**). For a monthly fee, the service provider gives you a username and password, and an access phone number, and may include necessary software for your PC. In addition to providing access to the Internet, the larger ISPs also provide online services, an infrastructure that enables subscribers to communicate with one another, to get stock quotes and news, and to use community bulletin boards. The largest ISPs that also provide online services are America Online, Microsoft Network, and CompuServe. For a listing of over 3000 ISPs, see the web site *www.thelist.internet.com*.

In Figure 17-31, a router that belongs to a network has a network address on that network. However, a router can have more than one network address. Router 4, in the diagram, belongs to four networks (B, C, D, and E), and would, therefore, have four network addresses. On the Internet, each device that can be addressed by TCP/IP is assigned a combination address containing both the network address (which identifies the network) and the host address (which identifies the individual device or computer). (More about network and host addresses below.) This combination address is called an **Internet Protocol address** (**IP address**). A host on the Internet is defined as any computer or device that can have an IP address. Therefore, in Figure 17-31, Router 4 is a host that has four IP addresses. The network portion of each IP address corresponds to each of the four networks it belongs to, and the host portion of each IP address is unique for the given network.

This section looks at the basics of the Internet, how IP addresses on the Internet are determined, how TCP/IP uses these IP addresses to route data, and the details of connecting a PC to the Internet.

IP Addresses

The Internet and the UNIX operating system use Transmission Control Protocol/Internet Protocol (TCP/IP) as their network protocol. TCP/IP requires that each node on a network be assigned a unique numeric address, called an IP address. The organization that keeps track of all IP address assignments is Network Solutions, Inc. (NSI), working under an agreement with the National Science Foundation. The work is done at the **Internet Network Information Center** (**InterNIC**) in Menlo Park, California. When a company, college, or some other organization applies for IP addresses, InterNIC assigns a range of addresses appropriate to the number of hosts on the organization's networks. For more information about InterNIC, see its web site, *www.internic.com*.

An IP address is 32 bits long, made up of four 8-bit numbers separated by periods. The largest possible 8-bit number is 11111111, which is equal to 255 in decimal, so the largest possible IP address in decimal is 255.255.255.255. Each of the four numbers separated by periods is called an **octet** (for 8 bits) and can be any number from 0 to 255, making for a total of 4.3 billion potential IP addresses (256 x 256 x 256 x 256). (However, because of the allocation scheme used to assign these addresses, not all of them are readily available for use.)

17

Classes of IP Addresses

IP addresses are divided into three classes—Class A, Class B, and Class C—based on the number of possible IP addresses in each network within each class. IP addresses are assigned to these classes according to the scheme outlined in Table 17-3. A Class A license assigns a single number to be used in the first (leftmost) octet of the address, which is the network address. (The first bit of the first octet for a Class A IP address is always zero.) The remaining three octets of the IP address can be used for host addresses that uniquely identify each host on this network. The first octet of a Class A license is a number between 0 and 126. For example, if a company is assigned 87 as its Class A network address, then 87 is used as the first octet for every host on this one network. Examples of IP addresses for hosts on this network are 87.0.0.1, 87.0.0.2, and 87.0.0.3 (the last octet does not use 0 or 255 as a value, so 87.0.0.0 would not be valid). Therefore, one Class A license can have approximately 256 2 256 2 254 node addresses, or about 16 million IP addresses.

Table 17-3   Classes of IP addresses

Class	Network Octets (blanks in the IP address are used for octets identifying hosts)	Total Number of Possible Networks or Licenses	Host Octets (blanks in the IP address are used for octets identifying networks)	Total Number of Possible IP Addresses in Each Network
A	0.___.___.___ to 126.___.___.___	127	___.0.0.1 to ___.255.255.254	16 million
B	128.0.___.___ to 191.255.___.___	16,000	___.___.0.1 to ___.___.255.254	65,000
C	192.0.0.___ to 254.255.255.___	2,000,000	___.___.___.1 to ___.___.___.254	254

A Class B license assigns a number for each of the first two leftmost octets, leaving the third and fourth octets for host addresses. (The first two bits of the first octet for a Class B IP address are always 10.) The number of possible values for two octets is about 256 2 256 (some IP addresses are reserved, so these numbers are approximations), or about 65,000 host addresses in a single Class B license. However, the first octet of a Class B license is a number between 128 and 191, which gives about 63 different values for a Class B first octet. The second number can be between 0 and 255, so there are approximately 63 2 256, or about 16,000, Class B networks. For example, suppose a company is assigned 135.18 as the network address for its Class B license. The first two octets for all hosts on this network are 135.18, and the company uses the last two octets for host addresses. Examples of IP addresses on this company's Class B network are 135.18.0.1, 135.18.0.2, 135.18.0.3, and so forth.

A Class C license assigns three octets as the network address. (The first three bits of the first octet for a Class C IP address are always 110.) With only one octet used for the host addresses, there can be only 254 host addresses on a Class C network. The first number of a Class C license is between 192 and 254. For example, if a company is assigned a Class C license for its network with a network address of 200.80.15, some IP addresses on this Class C network would be 200.80.15.1, 200.80.15.2, and 200.80.15.3.

When a small company is assigned a Class C license, it obtains 254 IP addresses for its use. If it only has a few nodes (say, less than 25 on a network), many IP addresses go unused, which is one of the reasons that there is a shortage of IP addresses. If the company grows and now has 300 workstations on the network, it runs out of IP addresses. Most companies solve this problem by assigning their own private IP addresses. The following IP addresses are not used on the Internet and can be assigned to any private network:

- 10.0.0.0 through 10.255.255.255

- 172.16.0.0 through 172.31.255.255

- 192.168.0.0 through 192.168.255.255

How does a PCs with private IP addresses access the Internet? By making its request to a server that communicates with the Internet on its behalf, using its own public IP address for the request. This server is called a **proxy server** and uses a method called **Network Address Translation (NAT)**. Hosts on the Internet only communicate with this one proxy server instead of every PC on the private network, which brings a degree of security to the private network. In addition, the entire network requires only a single publicly assigned IP address, which, in many cases, will be assigned by the ISP. Windows 98 SE and Windows 2000 include proxy server software called **Internet Connection Sharing**. One PC must be configured as the proxy server and others on the network are configured to access the Internet through the proxy server.

When assigning private IP addresses to a network, keep in mind that a few IP addresses are reserved for special use by TCP/IP and should not be used. They are listed in Table 17-4.

Table 17-4   Reserved IP addresses

IP Address	How It Is Used
255.255.255.255	Broadcast messages
0.0.0.0	A currently unassigned IP address
127.0.0.1	Indicates your own workstation; yourself

Dynamically Assigned IP Addresses

An IP address permanently assigned to a workstation is called a **static IP address**, but, for a large network, it can become very difficult to manually keep track of each IP address assigned to each PC. Another solution is to have a server automatically assign an IP address to a workstation every time it comes online to the network, using an IP address from a range of IP addresses allotted the service. These IP addresses are called **dynamic IP addresses**.

17

The server that manages these dynamically assigned IP addresses is called a **Dynamic Host Configuration Protocol** (**DHCP**) server. In this arrangement, workstations are called DHCP clients. DHCP software resides on both the client and the server to manage the dynamic assignments of IP addresses. DHCP client software is built into Windows 9x, Windows NT, and Windows 2000. Many Internet service providers (ISPs) use dynamic IP addressing for their dial-up users.

Plans for New IP Addresses

Because of an impending shortage of IP addresses, a new scheme of IP addresses is currently being developed. Called the IP version 6 (IPv6) standard, it will use 128 bits (four 32-bit segments) instead of 32 bits (four 8-bit segments). Ipv6 will have the added advantage over current IP addressing that it can automatically assign an IP address to a network device.

Domain Names

A+ OS
4.2

Because IP addresses are numbers and sometimes difficult to remember, and because companies might want to change their IP addresses without also changing the name that Internet users recognize, hosts are sometimes given alphabetic, or word-based, names called **domain names**. Domain names are an alternate way of addressing a host on the Internet, but all domain names must eventually be mapped onto a host's IP address before contact with the host can take place. Think of a domain name as a pseudonym or an alias; the real name of the host computer is its IP address.

The last segment of a domain name tells you something about the host. Domain names in the United States end in .edu (for educational institution), .gov (for government institution), .com (for commercial institution), .org (for nonprofit institution), and .net (for Internet provider). There are other endings as well, including codes for countries, such as .uk for the United Kingdom. Examples of domain names are course.com, microsoft.com, and leeuniversity.edu. The enormous demand for commercial domain names, combined with a shortage of acceptable domain names, has led to upcoming new domain name suffixes and longer lengths for domain names.

Domain Name Resolution

There is not necessarily a fixed relationship between a domain name and an IP address. A host computer can have a certain domain name and can be connected to one network and assigned a certain IP address, and then be moved to another network and assigned a different IP address. The domain name can stay with the host while it connects to either network. It is up to a name resolution service to track the relationship between a domain name and the current IP address of the host computer.

Two name resolution services track relationships between computer names and IP addresses. **Domain Name System**, also called **Domain Name Service (DNS)** tracks domain names, and Microsoft's **Windows Internet Naming Service (WINS)**, used only on Microsoft networks, tracks NetBIOS names.

At the heart of DNS is a distributed database, which must initially be updated manually. When a new domain name is assigned, that name and its corresponding IP address are

A+ OS
4.2

entered into a database on a top-level domain name server. When a remote computer tries to access your host by using your domain name, if that remote computer does not know the IP address currently assigned to that domain name, it queries its DNS server. If the DNS server does not have the information in its DNS database, it contacts another DNS server for that information and updates its database. This second DNS server is designated as its top-level DNS server and can contain the initial manual entry into the Internet system that relates a domain name to an IP address. The local DNS server is also informed, and then tells the remote computer the IP address of the domain name.

Recall that when a computer is configured for a network, it is assigned a computer name so that other computers and devices on the network can access this computer without knowing its IP address. Windows 9x and Windows NT assume this name is a NetBIOS name and use WINS as its default name resolution process. If that fails, it turns to DNS to resolve the name. Windows 2000 assumes its computer name is a domain name and uses DNS as its default name resolution process. If that fails, it turns to NetBIOS WINS resolution to resolve the name.

The Internet, Networks, and Subnets

All the networks that make up the Internet use the TCP/IP protocol suite. When you understand how TCP/IP addresses networks and host computers and routes data around the Internet, the task of configuring Windows to connect to the Internet becomes much clearer. This section begins by introducing the many different protocols that make up the TCP/IP protocol suite, and then discusses how TCP/IP uses the IP address system.

Routing Using TCP/IP

TCP/IP uses routers to transfer packets of data from network to network in such a way that the overall transmission makes all these networks appear to be one large network. Each protocol of the TCP/IP suite is designed to perform a single task—such as error checking or sending error messages back to the sending host—as part of the overall stupendous task of routing packets around the world. TCP and IP are the two principal protocols of the suite, but there are others.

The Suite of TCP/IP Protocols   TCP/IP can use more than one protocol at each OSI layer that it supports. However, when data is being transmitted, only one protocol is used at each layer. The choice of which protocol to use depends on what type of data is being transmitted and on what applications software is interfacing with the network.

Figure 17-32 shows the protocols of the TCP/IP suite supported by Windows. The Windows Sockets protocol (sometimes called WinSock) is designed to interface with applications that rely on sockets, or sessions, to connect to a remote computer. Browser software for the World Wide Web is one example of software that uses sockets. **NetBIOS over TCP/IP** (**NetBT**) is another applications protocol designed to interface with applications that rely on NetBIOS for communication. There is more information about applications protocols later in the chapter.

17

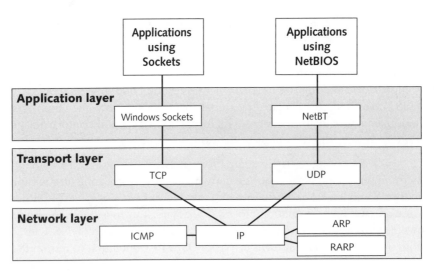

Figure 17-32   Protocols of the TCP/IP suite supported by Windows 9x and Windows NT

There are two protocols at the transport layer, TCP and UDP. **User Datagram Protocol (UDP)** is a **connectionless protocol**, meaning that it does not require a connection to send a packet and does not guarantee that the packet will arrive at its destination. UDP is used to send broadcast messages over the network when responses from each node are not required. One service at the application layer that uses UDP is a network drive map, which uses UDP because it does its own verifying that the packets have arrived safely. (A network drive map makes space on a remote computer's hard drive, to look like a hard drive on the local computer.) TCP is a **connection protocol**, meaning that data is guaranteed to arrive at its destination. Most network applications use TCP rather than UDP. To understand the difference in sending data over a network with or without a connection, think of the difference between a radio broadcast and a telephone call. The radio broadcast does not require a connection at the remote end to confirm receipt of the signal. It is therefore, a type of connectionless communication. On the other hand, a telephone call requires a connection at both ends for data to be communicated, and is an example of communication with a connection.

At the network layer, **Address Resolution Protocol (ARP)** converts IP addresses into physical network addresses such as Ethernet IDs or Token Ring MAC addresses. A counterpart protocol, **Reverse Address Resolution Protocol (RARP)** does the reverse and converts physical network addresses into IP addresses. Also at the network layer is **Internet Control Message Protocol (ICMP)**, which transmits error messages and other control messages to hosts and routers. For example, if a router is unable to deliver a packet, it informs the sender of the failure using ICMP.

IP Addresses and Physical Addresses   Fundamental to the design of TCP/IP is the concept of routing packets across networks by using IP addresses that relate to physical network adapter addresses. The routers of each network are responsible for routing packets from outside the networks to the hosts within their own network. These routers may or may not know the adapter address of the host but will "learn" the address the first time a packet is sent to it. Other routers outside the network also might know the adapter addresses of hosts within this one network.

Think of IP addresses and adapter addresses as phone numbers and street addresses of houses, respectively, as seen in Figure 17-33. A house on a certain street of a city may have one phone number today, but another one tomorrow if new owners move in, or if the present owner has his or her phone number changed. However, the street and city address of this house will most likely never change.

IP address

These numbers may change

130.45.120.40

Phone number

404-555-1800

Adapter address

Physical address is unlikely to change

Ethernet network card address
04-EF-88-4B-8C-A8

Street address

325 N. Maple St.
My City, USA

Figure 17-33   IP addresses and physical network addresses can be compared to phone numbers and street addresses

An IP address is assigned to a host just as a phone number is assigned to a house (no inherent relationship), and both the IP address and phone number can easily change. An adapter address is like the physical address of the host and only changes if the network adapter card is exchanged, just as the street address of a house seldom, if ever, changes. Think of adapter addresses as the permanent physical network addresses of hosts.

We can take the analogy one step further. An IP address is made up of a network and host address, just as phone numbers consist of area codes followed by seven-digit numbers. The area code generally identifies the approximate location of the house, just as the network portion of an IP address generally identifies the location of the network where the host resides.

When configuring a workstation to use TCP/IP, one step in the configuration is to associate an adapter address to an IP address. This process is called binding the adapter address to the IP address. When an IP address is bound to the adapter address, TCP/IP data that is addressed to this IP address now has a physical computer or adapter address to send the data to. (In general, the term **binding** refers to associating any OSI layer in the network to a layer just above it or just below it. For example, an application protocol can be bound to a transport protocol,

17

and a transport protocol can be bound to a network protocol. When the two layers are bound, communication continues between them until they are unbound or released.)

How TCP/IP Routing Works   Figure 17-34 shows an example of two TCP/IP networks connected by a router. The router (Computer C) belongs to both networks and has an IP address for each network. Think of it as the intersection point of the two networks.

Figure 17-34   Two networks using TCP/IP connected by a router

Suppose both these networks are Ethernet, and Host A wants to send data to Host B, which is on the same network. Host A knows the IP address of Host B. It would also need to know the Ethernet address (adapter address) of Host B in order to send the packet. This is what happens:

1. Host A knows the Host B IP address and turns the job of discovering the adapter address over to ARP (Address Resolution Protocol), which looks up the IP address of Host B in its routing tables on the Host A PC.

2. If ARP does not find the IP address of Host B in its tables, it sends out a broadcast message to the entire network (Hosts B and C in this case), containing a request for the adapter address of Host B.

3. Host B recognizes its IP address and responds with its Ethernet adapter address.

4. Host A receives the packet and updates its routing tables.

5. Host A sends its packet to Host B.

Now suppose that Host A is now ready to send a packet to Host E, which is on the other network. Here's what happens:

1. Host A looks at the IP address of Host E and recognizes that Host E does not belong to its network. (How it recognizes that is coming up.)

2. Because Host A is trying to communicate with a different network, it sends the packet to the router of its network, in this case, Host C. Host A knows the Ethernet address of its router, so it knows where to send the packet. (Host A did not attempt to broadcast for a response from Host E because it recognized that Host E would not hear the broadcast message, since it is on a different network.)

3. Host C receives the packet and looks at the destination IP address. Host C recognizes that the destination IP address is on its second network, so it sends the packet to Host E, just as Host A sent the packet to Host C. In other words, it will first look in its router table. If it doesn't find the IP address of Host E, it will send out a broadcast message to Host E's network.

Also note that in this example, Host C is an IP router but is also called a gateway, because it serves as the connection point of two networks.

Default Gateways   Sometimes a large network will have more than one router, as seen in Figure 17-35. The network in the upper left of the figure is 250.1.2 and has two routers (D and E), each belonging to other networks. Host E is designated as the **default gateway**, meaning that hosts on the 250.1.2 network will send packets addressed to other networks to this gateway first. The other router, Host D, is called the **alternate gateway** and will be used if communication to the default gateway fails.

Suppose Host A on network 250.1.2 wants to send a packet to Host K on Network 210.1.3 in the figure. Host A first sends its packet to the default gateway. If that fails, Host A will try the alternate gateway. Sometimes the default gateway knows that a packet should be routed through an alternate gateway. If so, it will send an ICMP redirect packet back to Host A, telling Host A to use the alternate gateway when addressing Host K. The next time Host A attempts to send a packet to Host K, it reads from its routing table to use the alternate gateway.

Network Mask   Comparing the network addresses in Figure 17-35 to those of Table 17-3, you can see that networks 250.1.2 and 210.1.3 are Class C networks, and network 130.5 is a Class B network. Also remember that Host A had to determine that Host K was not on its network, but was on a foreign network. How did it know that? By comparing Host K's IP address to the network mask. A **network mask** is that part of the IP address that identifies the network rather than the host. Host A's network address is 250.1.2. Host A compared these values to the first three octets of Host K's IP address. Since they were not the same, Host A knew that Host K was on another network.

Also notice in Figure 17-35 that the three network addresses are 250.1.2, 210.1.3, and 130.5. The first two networks are Class C networks because three octets are used in the network address, and the third network is a Class B network because the network address only has two octets. You can also identify the class of a network address by the first number; 250 and 210 fall within the range for Class C addresses, and 130 falls within the range of a Class B address.

17

Figure 17-35   A network can have more than one router; one router of the network will be the default gateway

Subnets

In configuring TCP/IP on a workstation, besides entering the IP address, you must also enter one or more subnet masks. A **subnet mask** looks like an IP address because it has four numbers separated by periods, but it is not an IP address. It's a number that defines which portion of an IP address identifies the network (including the subnet) and which portion identifies the host. (It does not contain a network address; that's in an IP address.)

Remember, from our earlier discussions in the chapter, that an IP address contains two parts, a network address and a host address. When a large company applies for a single class license, it is assigned a single network address from which it can create many IP addresses unique to each host in its network. The company may have many networks, and many workstations within these networks need these IP addresses. In order to take full advantage of the routing abilities of TCP/IP, each of these networks is assigned a group of IP addresses within the one class license. Each group is called a **subnet**. A single Class A, B, or C license can be divided into several subnets. Each subnet is a network segment or single network of the company. Traffic can be better controlled using subnets because local traffic can be contained within its own subnet and routers can be effectively used to route traffic from subnet to subnet.

TCP/IP can manage this by using not only network addresses, but subnet addresses as well. A few bits at the beginning of the host portion of the IP address are borrowed from the host and used to identify the subnet, and the subnet mask tells how many of these bits are used for that purpose. An example of a subnet mask is 255.255.240.0. When converted to bits, it looks like this: 11111111.11111111.11110000.00000000.

All subnet masks, when converted to bits, will have all ones on the left and all zeroes on the right. The ones define the network portion (including the subnet) of the mask, and the zeroes define the host portion. A host uses its subnet mask to decide if a destination host is in its subnet. It determines how many bits in a destination IP address belong to the network address by the number of ones in its subnet mask. Once it knows what portion of the destination IP address is the network address, it compares that portion of the address to its own address to decide if the destination address is inside its own subnet. If it is, it will attempt to communicate with it directly. If the IP address is outside its subnet, it will communicate through the router.

Let's look at one example, using these values:

- Sending IP address: 130.5.206.189
- Destination IP address: 130.5.194.5
- Subnet mask: 255.255.240.0

Here's what the sending host does:

1. The sending host IP address, the destination host IP address, and the subnet masks are all converted to bits:

    Sending IP address: 130.5.206.189 = 10000010.00000101.11001110.10111101

    Destination IP address: 130.5.194.5 = 10000010.00000101.11000010.00000101

    Subnet mask: 255.255.240.0 = 11111111.11111111.11110000.00000000

2. From the subnet mask, the host knows that the first 20 bits of the IP addresses are the network address so it only uses those bits to make the comparison between its IP address and the destination IP address:

    Sending IP address, network portion: 10000010.00000101.1100

    Destination IP address, network portion: 10000010.00000101.1100

3. The network portions of the two IP addresses are the same, so the sending host attempts to communicate directly with the destination host.

When configuring a computer for TCP/IP using static IP addressing, remember that the PC must know the subnet mask to determine if an IP address it wants to communicate with is inside or outside its subnet.

WAN Connections

A company that supports a WAN often uses subnets to help manage a group of networks, each with its own network technology. It is also common for every PC on a WAN to need

17

access to the Internet although not all individual networks in the WAN have this direct connection. A company might not own an entire Class A, Class B, or Class C license, but might lease IP addresses from an ISP. This section looks at how a small WAN might be configured to manage these possibilities.

When a service provider owns several Class C network addresses and subleases or subnets them to small companies, these addresses are called **classless addresses** because they are used on networks with subnet masks that don't fall on full octets. The service provider might also lease out an IP address that serves as a gateway to the Internet. This static IP address on a server at the ISP will belong to a subnet at the company site. For example, in Figure 17-36, a small organization has two networks, a Token Ring and an Ethernet. It leases IP addresses from an ISP with an ISDN direct line to an Internet gateway to the ISP. The company uses a subnet mask of 255.255.255.192 (11111111.11111111.11111111.11000000) so that it can have each network on a different subnet. (In this case, the subnet portion of the host address is the first 2 bits of the fourth, or rightmost, octet.) Another computer serves as a router connecting the two networks. It has an Ethernet card to connect to the Ethernet LAN and a Token Ring card to connect to the Token Ring. The Ethernet card is associated with or bound to the IP address 240.10.12.65. The fourth octet in this IP address is 0100 0001, which is decimal 65. The first 2 bits are the subnet address, and the remaining bits are the host address. All hosts on the Ethernet use these same subnet bits.

Figure 17-36   A small organization may use classless addresses with a gateway to the Internet

The router's Token Ring card is associated with an IP address of 240.10.12.2. The Token Ring network also uses a subnet mask of 255.255.255.192 for all hosts on this network. The router has one more communication card, an ISDN card to communicate with the ISP gateway to the Internet. This ISDN card uses a third IP address, 250.2.3.252, to associate with the subnet that the gateway to the Internet is on. The router, therefore, belongs to three subnets.

A+ OS 4.2 Configuring TCP/IP with Windows 9x, Windows NT, and Windows 2000

This section contains instructions to configure TCP/IP using Windows 9x, Windows NT, and Windows 2000.

TCP/IP and Windows 9x To use TCP/IP with the networking software that comes with Windows 9x, install and configure TCP/IP under the Network window of the Control Panel. Follow these directions:

1. Click **Start**, point to **Settings**, click **Control Panel**, and then double-click **Network**. Click the **Configuration** tab.

2. If TCP/IP is not already installed, click **Add** and select **Protocol** from the list of network components. Click **Add**.

3. The Select Network Protocol dialog box appears, as in Figure 17-37. Select **Microsoft** from the list of manufacturers. Select **TCP/IP** from the list of network protocols. (Notice that NetBEUI and IPX/SPX are also choices now.) Click **OK**. You will be asked to provide the Windows 9x CD-ROM or disks.

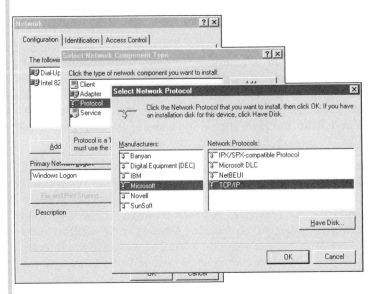

Figure 17-37   Installing TCP/IP from the Network window of the Control Panel

4. When you return to the Network window, notice that TCP/IP is automatically bound to the two adapters already installed: a network card (Intel 82595-Based Ethernet) and Windows Dial-Up Adapter (see Figure 17-38). Windows treats the

A^{+} OS
4.2

Dial-Up Adapter just as though it were a network card. Think of it as the software that turns your modem into a NIC.

Figure 17-38   TCP/IP is automatically bound to the two network adapters already installed

5. The next step is to configure TCP/IP for each of the bindings listed that you will use. (Recall that when an IP address is associated with a network card, ISDN card, or modem, the process is called binding.) If you plan to use TCP/IP with the network card (so that the PC can communicate over networks other than its LAN), then click that selection in the list. In this case, select **TCP/IP -> Intel 82595-Based Ethernet** from the list in Figure 17-38 and then click **Properties**. The TCP/IP Properties dialog box appears, as in Figure 17-39.

6. The information in this Properties dialog box must be provided by your network administrator. For the IP Address tab, you must know if your network uses static or dynamic IP addressing. If static IP addressing is used, then click **Specify IP address** and enter the IP Address and Subnet Mask as supplied by your administrator. If dynamic IP addressing is used, click **Obtain an IP address automatically**. This will most likely be your selection when connecting to the Internet. Other tabs under this TCP/IP Properties window are discussed later in the chapter.

7. When finished, click **OK** to exit the Properties dialog box.

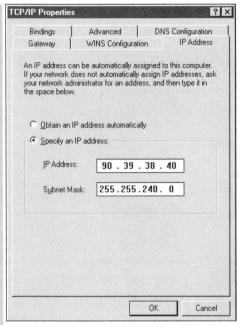

A+ OS
4.2

Figure 17-39   Configuring TCP/IP for static IP addressing

Using TCP/IP with Windows NT   To use TCP/IP with Windows NT, first install and configure the TCP/IP protocol, and then bind it to the appropriate adapters. Follow these directions:

1. Click **Start**, point to **Settings**, click **Control Panel**, and then double-click the
   Network icon. The Network window opens. Click the **Protocols** tab.

2. If TCP/IP is not already listed as an installed protocol, click **Add**. A list of network protocols supported by Windows NT appears, as in Figure 17-40.

3. Select **TCP/IP Protocol** and click **OK**.

4. During the installation, Windows NT asks if you plan to use a DHCP (Dynamic
   Host Configuration Protocol) server. If you plan to use static IP addressing,
   answer **No**, but if you plan to use dynamic IP addressing, as you may when connecting to the Internet, answer **Yes**.

5. You will be asked to provide the Windows NT CD-ROM and to indicate the
   drive and directory of the installation files. For example, for a CD-ROM drive E,
   enter E:\i386.

6. Click the **Close** button to close the Network window and complete the installation.

7. You can then use the TCP/IP Properties dialog box (see Figure 17-41) to configure TCP/IP for any network adapters that Windows NT detects are already
   installed. Again, you must choose between static and dynamic IP addressing. If
   you choose static, by selecting Specify an IP address, enter the IP Address, Subnet
   Mask, and Default Gateway for this PC. Obtain this information from your network administrator.

17

A+ OS
  4.2

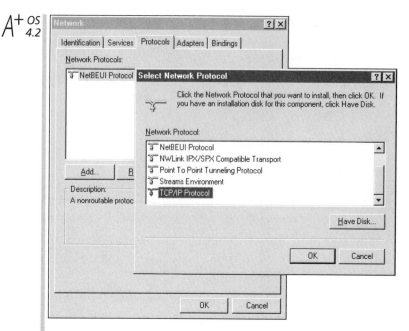

Figure 17-40   For Windows NT, install TCP/IP from the Network window of the
Control Panel

Figure 17-41   Configuring TCP/IP for Windows NT for static IP addressing

A+ OS
4.2

Using TCP/IP with Windows 2000 TCP/IP is installed by default with most Windows 2000 installations. However, if you find it missing, follow these directions to install it, and then bind the TCP/IP properties to the NIC.

1. Using Control Panel, double-click the **Network and Dial-up Connection** icon. Right-click the connection you want to change and select **Properties** from the drop-down menu.

2. If the TCP/IP component is not listed, click **Install**. At this point, the TCP/IP installation works as it does for Windows 9x.

To set the TCP/IP properties for the connection follow the steps below.

1. Select (**Internet Protocol**) **TCP/IP** from the list of installed components and click the **Properties** button. The TCP/IP Properties dialog box opens. See Figure 17-42.

2. For dynamic IP addressing, select **Obtain an IP address automatically**. For static IP addressing, select **Use the following IP address** and enter the IP address, Subnet mask, and Default gateway.

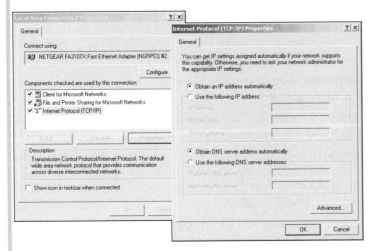

Figure 17-42   Configure a TCP/IP connection using Windows 2000

17

Connecting to the Internet

When you are supporting personal computers in a business environment where PCs are connected to a company LAN or corporate WAN, the network administrator is the final authority and is responsible for the overall support of the network. However a PC support person often is called on to help a home or small office user connect to the Internet through a dial-up connection. In this case, you are often on your own, without the help of a network administrator. You may or may not be able to call on technical support from the Internet service provider. This section looks at the process of connecting a PC running Windows 9x to the Internet, using Dial-Up Networking to make the connection.

A+ OS
   4.2
Establishing Dial-up Connection to the Internet Using Windows 9x

Creating a dial-up connection to the Internet for web access and e-mail when using Windows 9x is a four-step process:

1. Install and configure your modem.
2. Configure Dial-Up Adapter.
3. Configure Dial-Up Networking.
4. Install applications software to use the Internet.

The text below describes how to do each step. Step 1 (installing and configuring a modem) is covered in Chapter 16. Once the modem is installed, follow these directions to connect to the Internet using Windows 9x:

Step 2: Configure the Dial-Up Adapter   Remember that a Dial-up Adapter is Windows 9x terminology for making a modem act like a network card. The Dial-Up Adapter is automatically installed when Dial-Up Networking or Direct Cable Connection is installed. However, someone might have accidentally removed it after the installation of DUN or DCC. If necessary, you can reinstall Dial-Up Adapter from the Control Panel. Also, in Windows 95, when DUN and DCC are installed, network protocols IPX/SPX and NetBEUI are automatically installed, but not TCP/IP. Windows 98, on the other hand, automatically installs TCP/IP when DUN and DCC are installed. For Windows 98, to install TCP/IP and then bind it to the Dial-Up Adapter, follow these procedures:

1. From the **Control Panel**, open the **Network** window . If Dial-Up Adapter is not listed as an installed network component, click **Add**.
2. Select **Adapter** from the list of components to install, and then click **Add**. Manufacturers and network cards that are supported by Windows 98 are listed.
3. Select **Microsoft** as the manufacturer on the left and **Dial-Up Adapter** from the list on the right. Click **OK**. You will be asked to provide the Windows 98 CD-ROM or disks. You will then be returned to the Network window, and Dial-Up Adapter should be listed along with IPX/SPX and NetBEUI protocols.
4. To use the Internet, you need TCP/IP. Click **Add**, select **Protocol** from the list to install, and click **Add**.
5. Click **Microsoft**. From the list of supported protocols, select **TCP/IP** and click **Add**. You will be asked for the Windows 98 CD-ROM or disks.
6. After TCP/IP is installed, you are returned to the Network window. Select **TCP/IP** and then click **Properties** to configure the protocol. The Properties dialog box appears.
7. On the IP Address tab, select **Obtain an IP Address automatically**.
8. On the WINS Configuration tab, select **Disable WINS Resolution**.
9. On the Gateway tab, no installed gateways should be listed.
10. On the DNS Configuration tab, select **Disable DNS**.
11. Click **OK** to close the Properties dialog box.
12. Click **OK** to close the Network window. You might be asked to reboot the PC.

A^{+} OS
  4.2

Step 3: Configure Dial-Up Networking If Dial-Up Networking is not installed, follow the directions earlier in the chapter to install it, then follow the directions below to create a dial-up icon for your ISP:

1. Click **Start**, point to **Programs**, **Accessories**, **Communications**, and click **Dial–Up Networking**. Double-click **Make New Connection**.

2. Verify that the modem listed under **Select a device** is the correct modem installed on your PC and enter in a name for the connection. Click **Next**.

3. Enter the phone number of your ISP and click **Finish**. The new dial-up icon appears in the Dial-Up Networking window.

4. Right-click the icon and select **Properties** from the drop-down menu. Click the **Server Types** tab (see Figure 17-43), and verify that these choices are made:

   ■ Type of Dial-Up Server: PPP Internet, Windows NT Server, Windows 98

   ■ Advanced Options: Select Enable software compression (software compression is most likely to be enabled, but this option really depends on what the ISP is doing) and Log on to network.

   ■ Allowed Network Protocols: TCP/IP

Figure 17-43   Configuring the server type for a connection to the Internet

17

A+ OS
4.2

5. Click **TCP/IP Settings** to open TCP/IP Settings dialog box, as in Figure 17-44. Verify that these settings are chosen:

- Server assigned IP address
- Specify name server addresses
- Use IP header compression
- Use default gateway on remote network

Figure 17-44   TCP/IP settings for a connection to the Internet

6. Enter the IP addresses of the Primary and Secondary DNS servers. (This information is provided by your ISP.)

7. Click **OK** two times to complete building the Dial-Up Networking connection.

8. You should now be able to dial up your ISP and see the connection complete. Once connected, however, you will not be able to use the Internet until you have installed some application-level software to access it.

Step 4: Install applications software to use the Internet

- For web browsing, install Windows 9x Internet Explorer, Netscape Navigator, or some other software provided by your ISP.

- For access to e-mail, install Windows 9x Windows Messaging (Inbox) or some other e-mail software, such as Eudora Light.

Most ISPs provide you with a web browser and e-mail software, and probably will include other software as well, such as chat room software. Install this software following the directions given to you by the ISP.

A+ OS
  4.2

If you are using Internet Explorer, after you have installed the software, you can upgrade your version with the latest version of Internet Explorer from Microsoft. See directions on the company's web site, *www.microsoft.com*, to download the latest version. Internet Explorer is free to all who have a license to use a Windows OS.

There are many e-mail software programs available. A popular freeware is Eudora Light, which is likely to be included with the software from your ISP. You can download the latest version from the web site *www.eudora.com*. After you download the compressed file, execute it by double-clicking on it from Explorer. The file will decompress and a setup program executes.

Cable Modem and DSL Connections to the Internet

When connecting to the Internet using a cable modem, the service provider provides the cable modem, which is an external device that sits near your PC. The cable modem has a connection to the TV cable system of your home that connects to the ISP, and an Ethernet port to connect to your PC. An Ethernet cable connects the cable modem to a network card installed in your PC. Bind TCP/IP to this network card according to the parameters the ISP gives you.

DSL works the same way in that a device sits next to your PC, which connects to the DSL line on one side and to a network card installed in your PC on the other side. Bind TCP/IP to the network card according to the parameters the ISP gives you.

SOME EXAMPLES OF NETWORK SERVICES

At the highest level of the OSI model is the application layer, which interfaces with users and with applications software that uses networks. Figure 17-14 shows some of the more common application services: For the Internet, there are web browsers, chat rooms, e-mail, and FTP. For LANs, WANs, and corporate intranets, there are e-mail, FTP, Telnet, print services, and network drives. You have also learned from this chapter that other application-level software exists, such as middleware used to pass requests for data between a client PC and a network server. This section looks at several of the more common network services, most of which function at the top three layers of the OSI model: the application, presentation, and session layers. (Print services, an important service provided on a LAN, are covered in Chapter 18.)

Upper-Level Protocols

A+ OS
  4.2

Also shown in Figure 17-14 are several upper-level protocols that function at the session and presentation layers of the OSI model, including **Hypertext Transfer Protocol** (**HTTP**) used by the World Wide Web, File Transfer Protocol (FTP) used to transfer files, and Simple Mail Transfer Protocol (SMTP) used to transfer e-mail. Sometimes these protocol names are placed in front of a computer's domain address when one computer is addressing another. The protocol, domain name, and a path or filename are collectively called a **Uniform Resource Locator** (**URL**). The domain name is the only portion of a URL that is always required. An example of a URL with the three parts labeled is shown in Figure 17-45. This URL is pointing to a Web site that uses HTTP, as seen by the protocol portion of the address.

17

A+ OS
4.2

The path or filename portion of the URL includes a filename and file extension, document.html.

Figure 17-45   A Uniform Resource Locator (URL) can include protocol, domain name, and specific path and filename information

At the application, presentation, and session layers of the OSI model, protocols use one of two methods to establish communication with lower-level protocols: sockets or NetBIOS. Network Basic Input/Output System (NetBIOS) is mostly used on LANs for PC-based networking. It is a network extension of the older DOS BIOS used by applications software to interact with hardware. NetBEUI (NetBIOS Extended User Interface) protocol at the transport and network layers was written to interface with NetBIOS working at the session, presentation, and application layers.

Recall that a **socket** is a virtual connection (the computers are logically connected, but not necessarily physically connected) from one computer to another, such as from a PC to a server. The session-layer protocol HTTP uses the socket method to establish communication. For instance, let's look at what happens when a user requests information from a web server over the Internet. HTTP sends a request to the server to open a socket, and the socket is assigned a number for the current session. HTTP can then refer to this number when sending a GET command to the web server. The socket software then in turn uses TCP to segment and send the data. (See Figure 17-31, where the application using a socket is a web browser.) Internet protocols making connections to remote computers mostly use the socket method rather than NetBIOS. However, as you can see in Figure 17-32, the TCP/IP protocol suite includes support for NetBIOS; the protocol of TCP/IP that supports NetBIOS is NetBT.

One more concept is needed before looking at examples of network services. For all these network services, there must be a program running on both nodes of the network, for the service to work. For example, for FTP to work, FTP Client must be running at one end and FTP Server at the other. When using the World Wide Web, web browser software must be running at one end and web service software must be running on the other end. (The web service will most likely be running on a more powerful computer than a desktop PC.) Likewise, for a network drive map to work, the network drive service must be running on the host PC, and the network drive client software must be running on the client PC. Looking back at Figure 17-1, you can see this concept depicted in the diagram as the application layer on one computer logically communicating with the application layer on the other computer.

World Wide Web Browsers

Web browser software is designed to provide an interface between web sites and PCs. A web site resides on a server, has a domain name and a static IP address, and provides web pages to those computers requesting them. Using the Internet, a web browser can access a server by either its IP address or its domain name. The browser can also further identify files and folders to access by putting an extension, containing paths and filenames, on the domain name. The domain name is followed by a forward slash and the path or filename to be selected.

Communication over the Web by web browsers consists of passing document files from the web server host site to the PC. The protocol used to request and pass these documents on the Web is HTTP. Often these documents are hypertext files. **Hypertext** is text that contains links or pointers to other text, files, or graphics. Hypertext is intended to be read interactively as the reader moves about over the document in a nonsequential way by selecting links either to items outside of the document or to some other point within the document. **HTML (Hypertext Markup Language)** is used to create hypertext and provides a way to tag links in the document. HTML documents have an .html file extension or, for DOS applications, have an .HTM file extension.

> **TIP** If a browser is slow, try emptying the browser cache. For Internet Explorer, click Tools, Internet Options, Delete Files, OK. You can also reduce the size of the cache to save disk space. To do that, click Tools, Internet Options, Settings, and change the size. Also, if images do not display, verify the browser setting to show pictures. To do that, click Tools, Options icon, Advanced. Under the Multimedia group check Show Pictures. The Internet Options window can also be accessed from the Control Panel.

File Transfer

A common task of communications software is file transfer, the passing of files from one computer to another. For file transfer to work, the software on both ends must be using the same protocol. The most popular way to transfer files over the Internet is with File Transfer Protocol (FTP), which is used to transfer files between two computers using the same or different operating systems. A popular use of the Internet is for companies to provide files for customers to download to their PCs, such as when new upgrades for software become available. This service is commonly provided by Windows 2000, Windows NT or UNIX servers that provide access to files using FTP and are called **FTP servers** or **FTP sites**. These commercial FTP sites only provide the ability to download a file to your PC. However, FTP offers more power than just that. A user who has first logged on to a remote computer can use FTP utility software to copy, delete, and rename files, make directories, remove directories, and view details about files and directories.

Most communications applications provide a file transfer utility that has its own look and feel, but the basics of file transfer are the same from one utility to another. The text below discusses a couple of examples of file transfer utilities, highlighting their similarities and differences.

File Transfer from a Command Prompt

FTP can be initiated at a DOS, Windows 9x, Windows NT, or Windows 2000 command prompt, if a connection is established to a network or the Internet. Operating FTP from a command prompt is a quick-and-dirty way to transfer files when the computer does not have more user-friendly FTP software installed. For example, Windows NT Workstation has FTP available at the command prompt, but a GUI version of FTP is not packaged with the OS and must be installed. The FTP DOS commands work like the dialog in Table 17-5.

17

A+ OS
4.2

Table 17-5   A sample FTP session from a DOS command prompt

Command Entered at the DOS Command Prompt	Description
FTP	Execute the DOS FTP utility
OPEN 110.87.170.34	Open a session with a remote computer having the given IP address
LOGIN: XXXXXX	The host computer provides a prompt to enter a user ID for the computer being accessed.
PASSWORD: XXXXXX	The host computer requests the password for that ID. Logon is then completed by the host computer.
CD /DATA	Change directory to the /DATA directory
GET YOURFILE.DAT	Copy the file YOURFILE.DAT (or whatever file you want) from the remote computer to my computer
PUT MYFILE.DAT	Copy the file MYFILE.DAT (or whatever file you want) from your computer to the remote computer
BYE	Disconnect the FTP session

File Transfer Using FTP Software

FTP client software can be downloaded from the Internet or directly from your ISP. This example looks at how to execute FTP using such software:

1. Start the FTP utility software. The FTP utility screen appears similar to the one in Figure 17-46.

2. Click **Connect** to log on to an FTP site. A Session Profile dialog box appears, such as the one in Figure 17-46.

3. Enter the Host Name, for example ftp.course.com. Enter the User ID and Password for this host computer, and then click **OK**.

4. The connection is made, and your ID and password are passed to the host. After you have been authenticated by the host computer, a screen similar to that in Figure 17-47 is displayed.

5. The files on the left belong to you, and the files on the right belong to the remote host computer. You can drag and drop files either to or from the other computer, or you can use the commands at the bottom of the window. Notice in Figure 17-47 the choices toward the bottom of the window: ASCII, Binary, or Auto. These choices refer to the format that is to be used to transfer the files. Use ASCII only for text files, and use Binary for all others. If you are not sure which to use, choose **Auto**.

6. When transferring files is complete, click **Exit** to leave the utility.

Figure 17-46   A typical FTP utility provided by an Internet service provider

Figure 17-47   An FTP utility screen showing local and remote files

Many web pages provide the ability to download a file. It is likely that this file is not being downloaded from the web server, but the author of the web page has programmed a link from the web page to an FTP server. When you click the filename on the web page, the program controlling the page executes FTP commands to the FTP server to download the file to you. If you receive an error, you can sometimes solve the problem by going directly to the company's FTP server and using an FTP utility (such as the one described here) to download the file or even see a list of other files that you might also like to download.

Network Drive Map

A+ OS
4.1

A network drive map is one of the most powerful and versatile methods of communicating over a network. By using network file service (NFS) software, the network drive map makes one PC appear to have a new hard drive, such as drive E, that is really hard drive space on another host computer. Even if the host computer is using a different OS, such as UNIX, the drive map still functions. Using a network drive map, files and folders on a host computer are available even to network-unaware DOS applications. The path to a file simply uses the remote drive letter instead of a local drive such as drive A or drive C.

The following example connects two computers, using Dial-Up Networking. The host computer is using Windows NT, and the local computer is using Windows 95 (although Windows 98 works just the same way). The Windows 95 PC will map a network drive to the Windows NT PC.

Preparing a Windows NT Host Computer for a Network Drive Map

For Windows NT to allow a remote PC to dial in, Remote Access Service (RAS) must be installed and running. The remote user must have been set up with a user ID and password, and drives and/or folders must be shared, meaning that other computers are allowed to have access to them.

Follow these directions for setting up a Windows NT PC to allow a remote PC to map a network drive using Windows 95:

1. To install RAS, click **Start**, point to **Settings**, click **Control Panel**, and then double-click the **Network** icon.

2. Select the **Services** tab. If Remote Access Service is not already listed as being installed, click **Add**. From the list of Network services, select **Remote Access Service** and click **OK** to install the service. You will be asked to supply the Windows NT CD-ROM and the path to the \i386 directory on the CD.

3. From the Network window, select **Remote Access Service** and click **Properties**. The Remote Access Setup dialog box appears, as in Figure 17-48.

4. Click **Configure**. The Configure Port Usage dialog box appears, as in Figure 17-49. Select **Dial out and Receive calls**. Click **OK**.

A^+ OS
4.1

Figure 17-48   Remote Access Service allows another PC to dial in to a Windows NT PC

Figure 17-49   Configuring RAS under Windows NT to allow both incoming and dial-out calls

17

5. From the Remote Access Setup dialog box, click **Network**. The dialog box shown in Figure 17-50 appears, including the three network protocols for dial-out or dial-in calls. For one PC to connect to another, NetBEUI is the most efficient

A+ OS
4.1

choice. You can select only NetBEUI or leave others selected as well. For a Novell LAN, use IPX, and use TCP/IP to connect to the Internet. Click **OK** and then **Continue** to return to the Control Panel.

Figure 17-50 Windows NT RAS supports three network protocols

6. Once RAS is installed, it can be set to start automatically each time you boot, or you can start it manually. To start the RAS service, click **Start**, point to **Settings**, click **Control Panel**, and double-click **Services**. Select **Remote Access Server** and then click **Start**.

7. Follow instructions from Chapter 13 to set up a user ID and password from the User Manager. (Click **Start**, point to **Programs**, **Administrative Tools**, and click **User Manager**.) Be sure to grant the user the permission to dial in from a remote PC.

8. To establish which drives and/or folders you want the remote user to access, open Explorer, and then right-click the drive or folder you want to share. Select **Sharing** from the drop-down menu. Select **Shared As** and give the resource a name, such as MarketFolder or C. The workstation is now set to allow a dial-in. The next time you want to allow the remote use of the PC, all that you must do is start RAS.

A+ OS
4.1

Mapping the Network Drive from a Remote to a Host Computer

To set up a host computer and to allow a network drive to map to your hard drive, or to access the network drive from a remote computer, each computer must be running network drive software. Windows NT and Windows 9x include support to map network drives to other Windows PCs. To map network drives to computers using other OSs, you must use third-party software.

The remote computer can use either a regular network connection or Dial-Up Networking to connect to the host computer. After you are connected, to map a network drive on your computer, use Windows Explorer. Follow these directions:

1. While connected to a network, access Windows Explorer. Click the **Tools** menu shown in Figure 17-51. Select **Map Network Drive**.

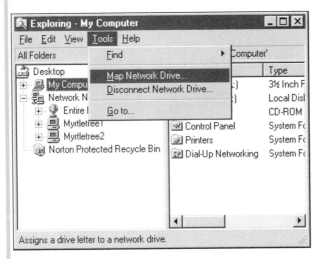

Figure 17-51   Mapping a network drive to a remote computer, using Windows Explorer

2. The Map Network Drive dialog box appears, as in Figure 17-52. Select a drive letter from the drop-down list.

3. Enter a path to the host computer. Use two backslashes, followed by the name of the host computer, followed by a backslash and the drive or folder to access on the host computer. For example, to access drive C on the computer named MyrtleTree1, enter **\\MYRTLETREE1\C** and then click **OK**.

4. Figure 17-53 shows the results of the drive map. There is a new drive E displayed in Windows Explorer. Folders listed on the right side of the figure are on the host PC.

17

A+ OS
4.1

Figure 17-52 To map a network drive, enter a drive letter to use on your PC and the path to the remote computer

Figure 17-53 Folders listed on the right side of Windows Explorer belong to the remote computer. This computer sees them belonging to its drive E.

Linux Operating System

Network services often are provided by a computer running the Linux operating system. Linux is well-suited to support web servers, FTP servers, and file servers. Because Linux is very reliable and does not require a lot of computing power, it is sometimes used as a desktop OS, although it is not as popular for this purpose because it is not easy to use. As a PC support technician, you should know a little about Linux, including a few basic commands.

Recall from earlier chapters that an operating system is composed of a kernel, which interacts with the hardware and other software, and a shell, which interacts with the user and the kernel. Linux is a UNIX-like operating system, and, just as with other versions of UNIX, can use more than one shell. The default shell for Linux is the Bash shell. The name stands for "Bourne Again Shell" and takes the best features from two previous shells, the Bourne and the Korn shells.

The system administrator is responsible for a Linux or UNIX server. This person installs updates to the OS (called patches), manages backup processes, supports the installation of software and hardware, sets up user accounts, resets passwords, and generally supports users. The system administrator has root privileges, which means that he or she can access all the functions of the OS and the principal user account called the root account. The administrator protects the password to the root account because this password gives full access to the system. When the administrator is logged on, he or she is logged on as the user root. For example, you can use the who command to show a list of all users currently logged on to the system. Type **who** to see that three users are currently logged on: the root, james, and susan.

```
who
root      tty1      Oct 12 07:56
james     tty1      Oct 12 08:35
susan     tty1      Oct 12 10:05
```

The command prompt for the root is different from the command prompt for ordinary users. The root command prompt is # and other users have the $ command prompt.

The main directory in UNIX is the root directory and is written with a forward slash. For example, use the ls command, which is similar to the DOS DIR command, to list the contents of the root directory. The command (ls -l /) and its results are shown in Figure 17-54. Notice that the -l parameter is added to the command, which displays the results using the long format. Also notice in the figure the format used to display the directory contents. The d at the beginning of each entry indicates that the entry is a directory, not a file. The other letters in this first column have to do with the read and write privileges assigned to the directory and the right to execute programs in the directory. The name of the directory is in the last column. The rights assigned the directory can apply to the owner of the directory, other users, or to an entire group of users.

17

UNIX Commands

This section describes some basic UNIX commands together with simple examples of their use. As you read along, know that all commands entered in Linux or UNIX are case sensitive.

Figure 17-54   Use the ls command to display directory contents

Table 17-6   Some common UNIX commands

Command	Description
echo	Displays information on the screen. For example, to display which shell is currently being used, enter this command: `echo $SHELL`
clear	Clears the screen
man	Displays the online help manual called the man pages. For example, to get information about the echo command: `man echo` The manual program displays information about the command. To exit the manual program, `type q`.
whatis	Use the whatis command to display a brief overview of a command. For example, to get quick information about the echo command: `whatis who`

cat	The cat command lets you view the contents of a file. For example, to display a file:
	`cat /etc/shells`
	This command displays the contents of the file named shells which is located in the /etc directory. Use the forward slash when giving the path to a file rather than the back slash used by Windows.
	Many UNIX commands can use the redirection symbol > to redirect the output of the command. For example, use the redirection symbol with the cat command to copy a file:
	`cat /etc/shells > newfile`
	The contents of the shells file is written to newfile.

Table 17-6   Some common UNIX commands (continued)

Command	Description
cd	Change directory. For example, cd /etc changes the directory to /etc.
ls	The ls command is similar to the DOS DIR command. For example, to list all files in the /etc directory, using the long parameter for a complete listing: ls -l /etc
chmod	This command changes the attributes assigned to a file and is similar to the DOS ATTRIB command. For example, to grant read permission to the file myfile: Chmod +r myfile

Managing Processes

If the Linux system is a web or e-mail server, then the web or e-mail server application runs as a process in the background. When a process runs in the background, no information is displayed on the screen about that process. When you initiate a process to run in the background, enter the name of the process at the command prompt followed by the &. For example, to run the program myserver in the background, enter this command:

> **$ myserver &**
> **862**

Linux starts the process and responds with a number, which is the process identifying number (PID). This number can be different each time the process is started. You can use this PID to later stop the process.

To get a listing of all currently running processes together with their PIDs, use the ps command like this:

```
$ ps
PID        TTY        TIME        CMD
648        pts/0      00:00:00    bash
709        pts/0      00:00:00    ps
862        pts/0      00:00:00    myserver
```

To stop a process, use the kill command. To kill a process, you can refer to the process name or the PID. If the process name is used in the kill command, precede the name with the %. For example, to kill the process myserver, use either command:

> **kill 862**
> **kill %myserver**

Windows Managers

Because many users prefer a Windows desktop, several applications have been written to provide a GUI shell for UNIX and Linux. These shells are called X Windows. A typical X Window screen is shown in Figure 17-55. One popular desktop environment software that runs on top of a windows manager is GNU Network Object Model Environment (GNOME). GNOME (pronounced "guh-nome") provides a desktop that looks and feels

17

like Windows 98, and is free software designed to use a Linux kernel. The major components of a GNOME window are showing in Figure 17-56. For more information about GNOME, see the organization's web site at *www.gnu.org*.

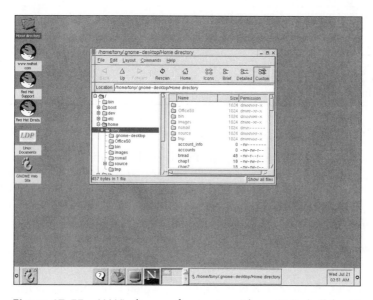

Figure 17-55   X Windows software provides a GUI shell for Linux and UNIX users

Figure 17-56   GNOME is popular desktop environment software used on Linux systems

NETWORK TROUBLESHOOTING GUIDELINES

This section covers some guidelines to use when troubleshooting network problems.

Windows 9x Dial-Up Problems

A+ OS
3.2,
4.2

Below are Windows 9x dial-up problems you will face and suggestions for solving them.

Modem problems

Problems that arise when dialing into a host computer using Windows 95 Dial-Up Networking may be caused by the modem. See Chapter 16 for troubleshooting guidelines for modems.

Cannot make a connection Sometimes a computer cannot connect to the network. Because Dial-Up Networking involves so many different components, first find out what works and what doesn't work. Find out the answers to these questions:

- Does the modem work? Compare the printout of a Modemlog.txt file that was made during a successful connection at another PC to the Modemlog.txt file of this PC, to identify the point in the connection at which an error occurs. (For Windows 9x, to log modem events to the Modemlog.txt file, double-click **Modems** in Control Panel, then select the modem, click **Properties**, **Connection**, **Advanced**, and turn on **Recording to a log file**.)

- Are all components installed? Check for the Dial-Up Adapter and TCP/IP, and check the configuration of each.

- Check the Dial-Up Networking connection icon for errors. Is the phone number correct? Does the number need to include a 9 to get an outside line? Has a 1 been added in front of the number by mistake?

- Reboot your PC and try again.

- Try removing and reinstalling each network component. Begin with TCP/IP.

- Try dialing the number manually from a phone. Do you hear beeps on the other end?

- Try another phone number.

- Sometimes older copies of the Windows socket DLL may be interfering with the current Windows 9x socket DLL. (Windows 9x may be finding and executing the older DLL before it finds the newer one.) Search for and rename any files named Winsock.dll except the one in the Windows\System directory.

17

$A{+\atop}$ OS
3.2,
4.2

You can connect, but you get the message "Unable to resolve hostname..."   This error message means that TCP/IP is not able to determine how to route a request to a host. Right-click the **Dial-Up Networking** connection icon, select **Properties**, and check for these things:

- Under Server Type, try making TCP/IP the only network protocol allowed.
- Under TCP/IP settings, check the IP addresses of the DNS servers.
- Make sure **Using the default gateway** is selected.
- Try *not* selecting IP header compression.

After connecting, you get the error message "Unable to establish a compatible set of network protocols"   This error is most likely to be caused by a problem with the installation and configuration of Dial-Up Networking and/or TCP/IP. Try these things:

- Verify that Dial-Up Adapter and TCP/IP are installed and configured correctly.
- Remove and reinstall TCP/IP. Be sure to reboot after the installation.
- Try putting the Windows 9x PCs in different workgroups.
- Windows 9x can write the events of PPP processing a call to a log file. Create the Ppplog.txt file on a PC that makes a successful connection, and compare it to the log file of your bad connection to see exactly when the problem began. To turn on the logging of events to the file, double-click the **Network** icon in Control Panel. Click **Dial-Up Adapter**, click **Properties**, select the **Advanced** tab and select **Record a log file**. On the Value list, click **Yes**, then click **OK**. Reboot the PC. The file Ppplog.txt is created in the Windows folder as the connection is made and used.

When you double-click the network browser, the modem does not dial automatically. When this occurs, right-click the network browser icon and select **Properties** from the drop-down menu. Under the Connection tab, check **Connect to the Internet as needed**.

Problems with TCP/IP

Windows 9x and Windows NT offer several utilities that can help in troubleshooting TCP/IP. Some are introduced here.

Problems with TCP/IP Configuration or Suspected Network Problems

A useful diagnostic tool for either Windows 9x or Windows NT is **Packet Internet Groper** (**PING**), which tests connectivity. PING sends a signal to a remote computer. If the remote computer is online and hears the signal, it will respond. Ipconfig under Windows NT and Windows 2000 and Winipcfg under Windows 9x test TCP/IP configuration. Try these things:

- For Windows NT, at the command prompt, enter **Ipconfig**, or, for Windows 9x, click **Start**, **Run** and enter **WinIPcfg** in the Run dialog box and click **OK**. If the TCP/IP configuration is correct, for static IP addressing, the IP address, subnet

A+ OS
3.2,
4.2

mask, and default gateway appear along with the adapter address. If DHCP is used for dynamic IP addressing and no IP address has yet been assigned, the IP address should read 0.0.0.0.

- Try to release the IP address and request a new one, which might reestablish a connection. On the WinIPcfg window, select the network adapter and click Release and Renew.

- Next try the loopback address test. Enter the command PING 127.0.0.1. This IP address refers to you. It should respond with a reply message from you. If this works, TCP/IP is likely to be configured correctly.

- If you have been assigned an IP address, PING it. If you get any errors up to this point, then assume that the problem is on your PC. Check the installation and configuration of each component. Remove and reinstall each component and watch for error messages. Compare the configuration to that of a PC that is working on the same network.

- Next PING the IP address of your default gateway. If it does not respond, then the problem may be with the gateway or with the network to the gateway.

- Now try to PING the host computer you are trying to reach. If it does not respond, then the problem may be with the host computer or with the network to the computer.

- If you substitute a URL for the IP address in the PING command, and the PING works, then you can conclude that DNS works. If an IP address works, but the URL does not work, the problem lies with DNS. Try this: PING *microsoft.com*.

- Use Tracert to trace the route to the remote computer: Try tracert microsoft.com or substitute an IP address in the command line.

- Under Windows 2000, to resolve a problem with DNS, use Nslookup to display information about a domain name kept on a DNS server. Try Nslookup microsoft.com

CHAPTER SUMMARY

- A network can be either a LAN or a WAN. Connecting LANs and WANs together is called internetworking.

- The three most popular network technologies today are Ethernet, Token Ring, and FDDI. Each is designed to satisfy a different networking need. ATM is a relatively new network technology that is faster than the other three.

- Ethernet can follow either a bus or star physical design and is the least expensive and most popular network type. Token Ring is more reliable, but more expensive and difficult to maintain. FDDI is used to fill massive networking needs over a wide area, for example, serving as the backbone network between smaller networks in a large building complex such as a large hospital.

- There are several kinds and grades of networking cables, including coaxial cable, unshielded twisted-pair (UTP) cable, shielded twisted-pair (STP) cable, and fiber-optic cable.

- Segmentation is a method of breaking a large network into smaller segments in order to control traffic over the network.

17

◻ Bridges, routers, switches, and gateways are used to interconnect networks.

◻ Repeaters are used to amplify signals that are traveling a long distance on a network.

◻ A network interface card (NIC) prepares data for transmission by disassembling the data into data segments and encapsulating the packet with header and trailer information. It then transmits the data packet over cabling media, and reassembles the data back into a contiguous stream at the receiving end.

◻ Each NIC has embedded on it at the factory a unique identifying 6-byte hex number called the media access control (MAC), or adapter, address. This number uniquely identifies the NIC on the network and physically identifies the node on the network.

◻ The seven-layer OSI network model is used as a guideline for discussing the different protocols, software, and firmware of a network. Mapping the many different components onto the model helps in understanding how they interrelate and what function each serves for the network.

◻ Examples of networking software components that satisfy the bottom two layers of the OSI model (physical and data-link layers) are Ethernet, Token Ring, FDDI, and PPP over phone lines. Examples of protocols that work at the network, transport, and session layers are TCP/IP, IPX/SPX, and NetBEUI. Software examples of the top OSI layers (presentation and application) are web browsers, e-mail and chat room software, and Telnet.

◻ Windows 9x, Windows NT, and Windows 2000 support phone line access to networks. This OS service is called Dial-Up Networking, and it makes a modem appear to be a NIC on the network.

◻ Windows 9x, Windows NT, and Windows 2000 also support direct cable connection, a method of networking two PCs with a serial or parallel cable.

◻ The Internet is a huge interconnection of many networks. It provides a decentralized way to successfully route data over many networks that use varying protocols, software, and hardware. The principal protocol of the Internet is TCP/IP, which identifies each node on the network with an IP address that ultimately must match up with the computer's MAC address.

◻ An IP address has two parts: a network address identifying the network, and a host address identifying the individual PC on the network. Sometimes the network address also includes a subnet address to allow a network to be broken up into logical segments in order to control traffic within the network.

◻ IP addresses can be permanently assigned to PCs (called static IP addressing) or dynamically assigned. When IP addresses are dynamically assigned, a different IP address is assigned to a host each time the host goes online to the network. Servers that manage dynamic assignments of IP addresses are called DHCP (Dynamic Host Configuration Protocol) servers.

◻ A domain name is a convenient and user-friendly method of naming a host on a network. A domain name must ultimately be mapped to the IP address of the host before data can be routed to the host. Two services that track domain names and their corresponding IP addresses are DNS (Domain Name Service) and WINS (Windows Internet Naming Service).

❑ TCP/IP is really a suite of protocols that satisfy differing needs of a network and include the network, transport, and session layers of the OSI model.

❑ Once connection to the Internet is made using TCP/IP and PPP (with a modem), software at the higher layers of the OSI model is used to send and receive data over the network. Different types of Internet software access different Internet services, including web browsing, e-mail, and FTP.

❑ Important networking services typically used on smaller networks are network drive maps and print services.

KEY TERMS

Adapter address — A 6-byte hex hardware address unique to each NIC and assigned by manufacturers. The address is often printed on the adapter. An example is 00 00 0C 08 2F 35. Also called MAC address.

Address Resolution Protocol (ARP) — A method used by TCP/IP that dynamically or automatically translates IP addresses into physical network addresses such as Ethernet IDs or Token Ring MAC addresses.

Alternate gateway — An alternate router that is used if the default gateway is down. *See* Gateway.

Amplifying repeater — A repeater used on a broadband network that amplifies whatever it receives regardless of its source.

Application layer — The layer of the OSI model responsible for interfacing with the user or application using the network.

Back end — In a client/server environment, the application on the server that processes requests for data from the client.

Backbone — A network used to link several networks together. For example, several Token Ring and Ethernet LANs may be connected using a single FDDI backbone.

Baseband — Relating to a communications system which carries only a single message at a time over wire. Ethernet uses baseband technology. Compare to broadband.

Binding — Associating an OSI layer to a layer above it or below it. For example, associating a protocol type such as TCP/IP to a NIC driver.

BNC connector — A connector used on an Ethernet 10Base2 (Thinnet) network. A BNC connector looks like a TV cable connector.

Bridge — A hardware device or box, coupled with software at the data-link layer, used to connect similar networks and network segments. A bridge uses a MAC address to determine which network gets a packet.

Broadband — Relating to a communications system such as cable modem or ATM networks that carry multiple messages over wire, each message traveling on its own frequency. Compare to baseband.

17

Bus network topology — A network design in which nodes are connected in line with one another, with no centralized point of contact.

Carrier Sense Multiple Access with Collision Detection (CSMA/CD) — A feature used in Ethernet networks whereby packets are sent after the sending node listens for silence, and are resent if a collision is detected.

Classless addresses — Class C network addresses that are used in subnets where the subnet masks don't fall on full octets

Collision — In an Ethernet network, a collision occurs when transmitted packets of data are sent at the same time and collide. Ethernet will first listen for silence before it transmits, and it will stop and resend if a collision occurs.

Combo card — An Ethernet card that has more than one port to accommodate different cabling media.

Connection protocol — In networking, confirming that a good connection is made before transmitting data to the other end. To accomplish this, most network applications use TCP rather than UDP.

Connectionless protocol — When UDP is used and a connection is not required before sending a packet. Consequently, there is no guarantee that the packet will arrive at its destination. An example of a UDP transmission is a broadcast to all nodes on a network.

Contention-based system — A system in which each computer contends for the opportunity to transmit on the network. If there is a collision, a computer waits a random amount of time and resends.

Controlled-access unit (CAU) — A centralized hub on a Token Ring network. *See* Multistation access unit.

Crosstalk — The interference that one wire, in a twisted pair, may produce in the other.

Data-link layer — The OSI layer that disassembles packets and reassembles data into packets.

Default gateway — The main gateway or unit that will send or receive packets addressed to other networks.

Dial-Up Networking (DUN) — A Windows application that allows a PC to remotely connect to a network through a phone line. A Dial-Up Network icon can be found under My Computer.

Domain name — A unique, text-based name that identifies an IP (Internet address). Typically, domain names in the United States end in .edu, .gov, .com, .org, or .net. Domain names also include a country code, such as .uk for the United Kingdom.

Domain Name System or **Domain Name Service (DNS)** — A database on a top-level domain name server that keeps track of assigned domain names and their corresponding IP addresses.

Dynamic Host Configuration Protocol (DHCP) — The protocol of a server that manages dynamically assigned IP addresses. DHCP is supported by Windows 9x, Windows NT, and Windows 2000.

Dynamic IP address — An assigned IP address that is used for the current session only. When the session is terminated, the IP address is returned to the list of available addresses.

Ethernet — The most popular network topology used today. It uses Carrier Sense Multiple Access with Collision Detection (CSMA/CD) and can be physically configured as a bus or star network.

FDDI (Fiber Distributed Data Interface) — Pronounced "fiddy." A ring-based network, similar to Token Ring, that does not require a centralized hub. FDDI often uses fiber-optic cabling.

Frame — The header or trailer information added to data to encapsulate it before it is sent over a network.

Front end — In a client/server environment, the application on the client that makes use of data stored on the server.

FTP (File Transfer Protocol) — An Internet standard that provides for the transfer of files from one computer to another. FTP can be used at a command prompt, or with a GUI interface, which is available with FTP software or with a web browser. When using a web browser, enter the command "ftp" in the browser URL line instead of the usual "http://" used to locate a web site.

FTP server or **FTP site** — A computer that stores files that can be downloaded by FTP.

Gateway — A device or process that translates protocol types between networks.

Header — Information sent ahead of data being transferred over a network to identify it to receiving protocols. An IP header consists of items such as header and data packet length, flags, checksum, addresses, and so on.

Hop count — The number of routers a packet must pass through in a network in order to reach its destination.

HTML (Hypertext Markup Language) — The language used to create hypertext documents commonly used on web sites. HTML documents have an .html file extension.

HTTP (Hypertext Transfer Protocol) — The common transfer protocol used by Internet browsers on the World Wide Web.

Hub — A network device or box that provides a central location to connect cables.

Hypertext — Text that contains links to remote points in the document or to other files, documents, or graphics. Hypertext is created using HTML and is commonly distributed from web sites.

Intelligent hubs — Network hubs that can be remotely controlled at a console, using network software. These hubs can monitor a network and report errors or problems.

Internet — The worldwide collection of over a million hosts that can communicate with each other using TCP/IP. The lowercase *internet* simply means multiple networks connected together.

Internet Control Message Protocol (ICMP) — Part of the IP layer that is used to transmit error messages and other control messages to hosts and routers.

Internet service provider (ISP) — A commercial group that provides a user with Internet access for a monthly fee. AOL, Prodigy, GTE, and CompuServe are four large ISPs.

Internetwork — Two or more networks connected together, such as a LAN and a WAN joined together.

Intranet — A private internet used by a large company.

17

IP (Internet Protocol) address — A 32-bit "dotted-decimal" address consisting of four numbers separated by periods, used to uniquely identify a device on a network that uses TCP/IP protocols. The first numbers identify the network; the last numbers identify a host. An example of an IP address is 206.96.103.114.

IPX/SPX — A protocol developed and used by Novell NetWare for LANs. The IPX portion of the protocol works at the network layer, which is responsible for routing, and the SPX portion of the protocol manages error checking at the transport layer.

Limited token — Applies to a FDDI network. A token sent that allows a receiving station to communicate only with the sending station, thus providing continuous communication between the two stations.

Line protocol — A protocol used over phone lines to allow a connection to a network. Also called a bridging protocol. The most popular line protocol is PPP (Point-to-Point Protocol).

MAC (media access control) — An element of data-link layer protocol that provides compatibility with the NIC used by the physical layer. A network card address is often called a MAC address. *See* Adapter address.

Middleware — Software necessary for an application on a client to pass requests to a server, and for a server to respond with data. Microsoft's Open Database Connectivity (ODBC) is an example of middleware.

Multiframe dialog — When a limited token is sent that allows a receiving station to communicate only with the sending station, thus providing continuous communication between the two stations.

Multistation access unit (MSAU or **MAU)** — A centralized device used to connect IBM Token Ring network stations.

Nearest active downstream neighbor (NADN) — The next station to receive a token in a token ring.

Nearest active upstream neighbor (NAUN) — The station that has just sent a token to the nearest active downstream neighbor in a token ring.

NetBEUI (NetBIOS Extended User Interface) — A proprietary Microsoft networking protocol used only by Windows-based systems, and limited to LANs because it does not support routing.

NetBT (NetBIOS over TCP/IP) — An alternate Microsoft NetBEUI component designed to interface with TCP/IP networks.

Network interface card (NIC) — A network adapter board that plugs into a computer's system board and provides a port on the back of the card to connect a PC to a network.

Network layer — The OSI layer responsible for routing packets.

Network mask — The portion of an IP address that identifies the network.

Node — Each computer, workstation, or device on a network.

Octet — A traditional term for each of the four 8-bit numbers that make up an IP address. For example, the IP address 206.96.103.114 has four octets.

Open Systems Interconnect (OSI) — A seven-layer (application, presentation, session, transport, network, data-link, physical) model of communications supported by a network. Refers to software and firmware only.

Packets — Network segments of data that also include header, destination addresses, and trailer information.

Physical layer — The OSI layer responsible for interfacing with the network media (cabling).

PPP (Point-to-Point Protocol) — A common way PCs with modems can connect to an internet. The Windows Dial-Up Networking utility, found under My Computer, uses PPP.

Presentation layer — The OSI layer that compresses and decompresses data and interfaces with the Application layer and the session layer.

Protocol — A set of preestablished rules for communication. Examples of protocols are modem parity settings and the way in which header and trailer information in a data packet is formatted.

Repeater — A device that amplifies weakened signals on a network.

Request for Comment (RFC) — A document presented to the technical community to propose and describe in detail a new standard to be adopted by the community at large. Search for and view RFCs at *www.rfc-editor.org*.

Reverse Address Resolution Protocol (RARP) — Translates the unique hardware NIC addresses into IP addresses (the reverse of ARP).

RJ-45 connector — A connector used on an Ethernet 10BaseT (twisted-pair cable) network. An RJ-45 port looks similar to a large phone jack.

Route discovery — When a router rebuilds its router tables on the basis of new information.

Router — A device or box that connects networks. A router transfers a packet to other networks only when the packet is addressed to a station outside its network. The router can make intelligent decisions as to which network is the best route to use to send data to a distant network and works at the Transport and Network layers of the OSI model.

Router table — Tables of network addresses that also include the best possible routes (regarding tick count and hop count) to these networks. *See* Tick count and Hop count.

Segmentation — To split a large network into smaller segments that are connected to each other by routers. This is done to prevent congestion as the number of nodes increases.

Session layer — The OSI layer that makes and manages a connection between two nodes of the network.

Signal-regenerating repeater — A repeater that "reads" the signal on a baseband network and then creates an exact duplicate of the signal, thus amplifying the signal without also amplifying unwanted noise that is mixed with the signal.

17

SLIP (Serial Line Internet Protocol) — An early version of line protocol designed for home users connecting to the Internet. SLIP lacks reliable error checking and has mostly been replaced by PPP.

SMTP (Simple Mail Transfer Protocol) — A common protocol used to send e-mail across a network.

Socket — A virtual connection from one computer to another such as that between a client and a server. Higher-level protocols such as HTTP use a socket to pass data between two computers. A socket is assigned a number for the current session, which is used by the high-level protocol.

Star topology — A network design in which nodes are connected at a centralized location.

Static IP addresses — IP addresses permanently assigned to a workstation. In Windows 9x, this can be done under Dial-Up Networking, Server Type, TCP/IP settings. Specify an IP address.

Subnet mask — Defines which portion of the host address within an IP address is being borrowed to define separate subnets within a network. A 1 in the mask indicates that the bit is part of the network address, and a 0 indicates that the bit is part of the host address. For example, the subnet mask 255.255.192.0, in binary, is 11111111.11111111.11000000.00000000. Therefore, the network address is the first two octets and the subnet address is the first two bits of the third octet. The rest of the IP address refers to the host.

Subnetworks or **subnets** — Divisions of a large network, consisting of smaller separate networks (to prevent congestion). Each subnetwork is assigned a logical network IP name.

Switch — A device that is used to break a large network into two smaller networks in order to reduce traffic congestion. A switch uses MAC addresses to determine which network to send a packet.

TCP/IP (Transmission Control Protocol/Internet Protocol) — The suite of protocols developed to support the Internet. TCP is responsible for error checking, and IP is responsible for routing.

Tick count — The time required for a packet to reach its destination. One tick equals 1/18 of a second.

Token — A small frame on a Token Ring network that constantly travels around the ring in only one direction. When a station seizes the token, it controls the channel until its message is sent.

Token ring — A network that is logically a ring, but stations are connected to a centralized multistation access unit (MAU) in a star formation. Network communication is controlled by a token.

Trailer — The part of a packet that follows the data and contains information used by some protocols for error checking.

Transceiver — The bidirectional (transmitter and receiver) component on a NIC that is responsible for signal conversion and monitors for data collision.

Transport layer — The OSI layer that verifies data and requests a resend when the data is corrupted.

URL (Uniform Resource Locator) — A unique address that identifies the domain name, path, or filename of a World Wide Web site. Microsoft's URL is: *http://www.microsoft.com/*

User Datagram Protocol (UDP) — A connectionless protocol that does not require a connection to send a packet and does not guarantee that the packet arrives at its destination. (A data packet was once called a datagram.)

Windows Internet Naming Service (WINS) — A Microsoft resolution service with a distributed database that tracks relationships between domain names and IP addresses. Compare to DNS.

REVIEW QUESTIONS

1. What happens if an Ethernet network detects a transmission collision?
2. List and describe three types of cables that can be used on an Ethernet network.
3. What is the function of a router in a network environment? How is a router different from a bridge?
4. What type of connector is used on Ethernet Thinnet? On Ethernet 10BaseT?
5. What Windows 9x utility enables you to easily connect two PCs with a parallel or serial cable?
6. When computer A initates a connection to computer B, then computer A is called the _____ computer and computer B is called the _____ computer.
7. A device that belongs to more than one network and serves as the connection point between the two is called a _____.
8. In a star topology, the device that all computers connect to is called the _____.
9. The OSI layer responsible for error checking and guaranteeing successful delivery of data is the _____ layer.
10. A network card manages the _____ and _____ layers of the OSI model.
11. What is the reserved IP address that is used to refer to yourself?
12. List and briefly describe the seven network layers.
13. Describe a client/server network.
14. Use Windows Help, and describe how to use FTP to obtain a missing driver from the Microsoft web site.
15. List three of the largest ISPs.
16. Give an example of a Class C Internet address.
17. What organization is responsible for regulating the assignments of Internet addresses?
18. What are the advantages of dynamically assigned IP addresses?
19. List five main domain name extensions used in the United States.
20. What is the domain name extension for Harvard University? For Microsoft Corporation? For the White House?
21. What class does the IP address 130.200.50.3 belong in?
22. What is the subnet mask for Class C IP addresses on a network where 1 bit of the host address is used for the subnet address? How many subnets are possible using this arrangement?
23. Why would an organization use a WAN? What type of organization would use a WAN?
24. What utility is commonly used to "transfer" files on the Internet?
25. What is the purpose of Telnet?

17

Projects

Practice Dial-Up Networking Skills with Windows 9x

1. Open My Computer and open the Dial-Up Networking folder.
2. Double-click the **Make New Connection** option.
3. Enter the name **TEST** for the name of the computer that you are dialing. Click **Next**.
4. Enter your home phone number. Click **Next**.
5. Click the **Finish** button to create the Test dial-up.
6. Double-click the newly created Test dial-up icon, and confirm that it dials out correctly. Describe what happens.

Use the PPPLog.txt File for Troubleshooting

Set Windows 9x so that the PPPLog.txt file is used to record events. Reboot the PC and make a good connection to the Internet, using a modem. Print the log file. This printout of a good connection can later be used to compare to a log file of a bad connection to help identify problems.

Now cause an error to occur in the dial-up connection to the Internet by setting a wrong configuration for TCP/IP (make a note of the correct configuration before you change it!). Attempt the connection. Print the log file for the bad connection and compare the two files. At what point during the connection did it fail? Restore the TCP/IP configuration to the correct value and verify that all is well.

Practice TCP/IP Networking Skills

While using TCP/IP on a network with or without Dial-Up Networking (such as while connected to the Internet), answer these questions:

1. What is your current IP address?
2. Disconnect and reconnect. Now what is your IP address?
3. Are you using dynamic or static IP addressing? How do you know?
4. What is your adapter address?
5. What is your default gateway IP address?
6. What response do you get when you PING the default gateway?

Using Windows 9x Help

Click the **Start** button and select **Help**. Search for "Internet," and write down a step-by-step set of directions that can be used to connect to the Internet using Dial-Up Networking.

Direct Cable Connection

Using either a null modem cable or a parallel cable, connect two computers using direct cable connection under Windows 9x. After the connection is made, use Explorer on the guest computer to copy a file from the host computer. Next, reverse roles, making the host the guest computer, and the guest the host computer. Copy a file from the host to the guest computer.

Dial-Up Networking

Work with a partner on this project. You each need a PC with Windows 9x or Windows NT, a modem, and a phone line. For two computers with Windows 95, one of the PCs must have Microsoft Plus! in order to be set up to receive incoming calls. Follow the directions in the chapter to connect the two computers using Dial-Up Networking over phone lines. After the connection is made, use Explorer to share files between the two computers.

Using a Null Modem Cable with Windows NT

A null modem cable can be used by Windows NT to communicate to another PC over a serial port. Install a null modem cable as though it were a modem. In the list of supported modems, select **Standard Modem Types** as the manufacturer, and select **Dial-Up Networking Serial Cable between 2 PCs** as the modem model.

Using two Windows NT PCs and a null modem cable, install and run Dial-Up Networking to establish communication between the PCs. Map a network drive from one PC to the other.

Building a Peer-to-Peer Network

Follow these directions to build a peer-to-peer network using network cards and a Microsoft network:

1. Obtain the following materials:

    ❑ Two computers with Windows 9x

    ❑ Network cards for each computer

    ❑ Cabling and connectors for the network cards

2. Install the NICs. Check the configuration in Windows 9x against the card documentation.

3. Select the client software to be **Client for Microsoft Networks**.

4. Add the service **File and Printer Sharing**. Verify that File and Printer Sharing is running from the Network window.

5. Share a folder or folders on the hard drive. If you have a printer connected, share the printer.

6. Reboot both PCs and verify that you are connected, by browsing the Network Neighborhood of each PC.

17

Back Up Network Files

Look on a PC that is connected to a Novell NetWare LAN. Which entries in the AUTOEXEC.BAT file can you identify as commands used to load network software? Which directory contains the NetWare software? Print the contents of NET.CFG in this directory. What is the drive letter of the network drive used to log on to the LAN?

18

PRINTERS AND NOTEBOOK COMPUTERS

In this chapter, you will learn:

♦ How printers, including laser printers and ink-jet photo-quality printers, work

♦ How to support and troubleshoot printers

♦ About the special needs of supporting printers on a network

♦ How to upgrade memory on a notebook

♦ How Windows 98 supports notebooks and about notebook support new to Windows 2000

♦ About power management features of notebooks

♦ How to support PC Cards for notebooks

A PC technician's job requires familiarity with a wide range of technologies: not just computers, but networks, telecommunications, data formatting, and so on. Technicians are often called on to support printers and notebook computers. This chapter first covers supporting printers and then addresses the special needs of notebook computers.

PRINTERS

A+CORE
5.1

Chapter 8 covered the fundamentals of supporting printers. This chapter provides more detail, covering how printers work and how to support them, including those on a network. Printers connect to a PC by way of a parallel port, serial port, USB port or a wireless connection using an infrared port. A PC can then share its printer with others on a network.

How Printers Work

A+CORE
5.1

This section focuses on laser, ink jet, and dot-matrix printers. You will examine how these printers work and how to maintain them.

Laser Printers

Laser printers are a type of electrophotographic printers and range from small, personal desktop models to large network printers capable of printing handling large volumes continuously. Figure 18-1 shows an example of a typical laser printer for a desktop computer system, the Hewlett-Packard LaserJet 4050.

Figure 18-1   The HP LaserJet 4050 desktop laser printer

Laser printers require the interaction of mechanical, electrical, and optical technologies to work. Understanding how they work will help you support and service them. It also explains why the safety precautions stated in laser printer user manuals are necessary.

How a Laser Printer Works   Laser printers work by placing toner on an electrically charged rotating drum and then depositing the toner on paper as the paper moves through the system at the same speed the drum is turning. Figure 18-2 shows the six steps of laser printing. The first four use the printer components that undergo the most wear. They are

A+CORE
5.1

contained within the removable cartridge to increase the life of the printer. The last two steps are performed outside the cartridge. Follow the steps of laser printing below while you refer to Figure 18-2:

1. **Cleaning**. The drum is cleaned of any residual toner and electrical charge.

2. **Conditioning**. The drum is conditioned to contain a high electrical charge.

3. **Writing**. A laser beam discharges the high charge down to a lower charge, only in those places where toner is to go.

4. **Developing**. Toner is placed onto the drum where the charge has been reduced.

5. **Transferring**. A strong electrical charge draws the toner off the drum onto the paper. This is the first step that takes place outside the cartridge.

6. **Fusing**. Heat and pressure fuse the toner to the paper.

Figure 18-2   The six progressive steps of laser printing

Note that Figure 18-2 shows only a cross-section of the drum, mechanisms, and paper. As you visualize the process, remember that the drum is as wide as a sheet of paper. The mirror, blades, and rollers in the drawing are also as wide as paper. First note the location of the removable cartridge in the drawing, the photosensitive drum inside the cartridge turning in a clockwise direction, and the path of the paper, which moves from right to left.

Step 1: Cleaning. Figure 18-3 shows a clear view of the cleaning step. First a sweeper strip cleans the drum of any residual toner, which is swept away from the drum by a sweeping blade. A cleaning blade completes the physical cleaning of the drum. Next the drum is cleaned of any electrical charge by erase lamps (located in the hinged top cover of the printer), which light the surface of the drum to neutralize any electrical charge left on the drum.

18

Sweeping blade

Cleaning blade

Drum

Sweeper strip

Figure 18-3 The cleaning step cleans the drum of toner and electrical charge

Step 2: Conditioning. The conditioning step puts a uniform electrical charge of −600 V on the drum. The charge is put there by a primary charging roller or primary corona, which is charged by a high-voltage power supply assembly. The primary charging roller in Figure 18-2 is inside the toner cartridge, and regulates the charge on the drum, ensuring that it is a uniform −600 V.

Step 3: Writing. In the writing step, the uniform charge that was applied in Step 2 is discharged only where you want the printer to print. This is done by controlling mirrors to reflect laser beams onto the drum in a pattern that recreates the image desired. This is the first step in which data from the computer must be transmitted to the printer. Figure 18-4 shows the process: Data from the PC is received by the formatter (1) and passed on to the DC controller (2) that controls the laser unit (3). The laser beam is initiated and directed toward the octagonal mirror called the **scanning mirror**. The scanning mirror (4) is turned by the scanning motor in a clockwise direction. There are eight mirrors on the eight sides of the scanning mirror. As the mirror turns, the laser beam is directed in a sweeping motion that can cover the entire length of the drum. The laser beam is reflected off the scanning mirror, focused by the focusing lens (5), and sent on to the mirror (6), which is also shown in Figure 18-2. The mirror deflects the laser beam to a slit in the removable cartridge and on to the drum (7).

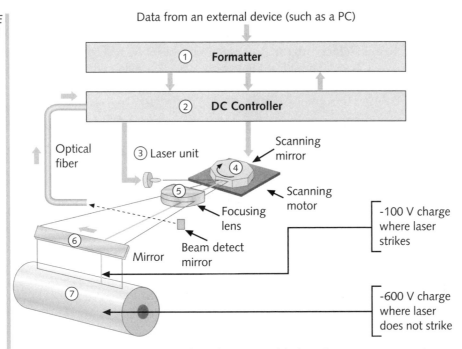

Figure 18-4   The writing step, done by an invisible laser beam, mirrors, and motors, causes a discharge on the drum where the image will be recaptured

The speed of the motor turning the drum and the speed of the scanning motor turning the scanning mirror are synchronized so that the laser beam completes one pass, or scanline, across the drum and returns to the beginning of the drum (right side of the drum in Figure 18-4) to begin a new pass until it completes the correct number of passes for each inch of the drum circumference. For example, for a 300 dots per inch (dpi) printer, the beam makes 300 passes for every one inch of the drum circumference. The laser beam is turned on and off continually as it makes a single pass down the length of the drum, so that dots are written along the drum on every pass. For a 300 dpi printer, 300 dots are written along the drum for every inch of linear pass. The 300 dots per inch down this single pass, along with 300 passes per inch of drum circumference, together accomplish the resolution of 300 X 300 dots per square inch of many desktop laser printers.

TIP   A laser printer can produce better quality printouts than dot matrix printers, even when printing at the same dpi, because it can vary the size of the dots it prints, creating a sharp, clear image. HP calls this technology of varying the size of dots **RET (resolution enhancement technology)**.

In a laser printer, where the laser beam strikes the surface of the drum, the drum discharges from its conditioned charge of −600 V down to −100 V where toner will be placed on the drum. Toner does not stick to the highly charged areas of the drum.

18

A+CORE 5.1

Just as the scanning laser beam is synchronized to the rotating drum, the data output is synchronized to the scanning beam. Before the beam begins moving across the scanline of the drum, the **beam detect mirror** detects the laser beam by reflecting it to an optical fiber. The light travels along the optical fiber to the DC controller, where it is converted to an electrical signal that synchronizes the data output. The signal is also used to diagnose problems with the laser or scanning motor.

The laser beam has written an image to the drum surface as a −100 V charge. The −100 V charge on this image area will be used in the developing stage to transmit toner to the drum surface.

Step 4: Developing. Figure 18-5 shows the developing step, in which toner is applied by the developing cylinder to the discharged (−100 V) areas of the drum. Toner transfers from the cylinder to the drum as the two rotate very close together. The cylinder is coated with a layer of toner, made of black resin bonded to iron, which is similar to the toner used in photocopy machines. The toner is held on the cylinder surface by its attraction to a magnet inside the cylinder. (A **toner cavity** keeps the cylinder supplied with toner.) A **control blade** prevents too much toner from sticking to the cylinder surface. The toner on the cylinder surface takes on a negative charge (between −200 V and −500 V) because the surface is connected to a DC power supply called the DC bias.

Figure 18-5 In the developing step, charged toner is deposited onto the drum surface

The negatively charged toner is more negative than the −100 V on the drum surface but less negative than the −600 V surface. This means the toner is attracted to the −100 V area of the drum surface (the −100 V area is positive *relative to* the toner). The toner is repelled from the

A+CORE 5.1

−600 V part of the drum surface, which is negative *relative to* the toner. The result is that toner sticks to the drum where the laser beam has hit and is repelled from the area where the laser beam has not hit.

You can adjust printer density manually at the printer or through software controlling the printer. With laser printers, when you adjust print density, you are adjusting the DC bias charge on the developing cylinder, which controls the amount of toner attracted to the cylinder, which, in turn, results in a change in print density.

Step 5: Transferring. In the transferring step, the transfer charging roller or transfer corona (shown in Figure 18-2) produces a positive charge on the paper that pulls the toner from the drum onto the paper when it is passed between the transfer charging roller and the drum. The static charge eliminator (refer again to Figure 18-2) weakens the positive charge on the paper and the negative charge on the drum so that the paper does not adhere to the drum—which it would otherwise do because of the difference in charge between the two. The stiffness of the paper and the small radius of the drum also help the paper move away from the drum and toward the fusing assembly. Very thin paper can wrap around the drum, which is why printer manuals usually instruct you to use only paper designated for laser printers.

Step 6: Fusing. The fusing step causes the toner to bond with the paper. Up to this point, the toner is merely sitting on the paper. The fusing rollers apply both pressure and heat to the paper. The toner melts, and the rollers press the toner into the paper. The temperature of the rollers is monitored by the printer. If the temperature exceeds an allowed maximum value (410° F for some printers), the printer shuts down.

The previous steps describe how a black and white printer works. Color laser printers work in a similar way except that the writing process repeats four times, one for each toner color of cyan, magenta, yellow, and black. Then the paper passes to the fusing stage where the fuser bonds all toner to the paper and aids in blending the four tones to form specific colors.

A+CORE 5.2

Supporting Laser Printers   All of the major mechanical printer components that normally create problems are conveniently contained within the replaceable toner cartridge. In most cases, the solution to poor quality printing is to replace this cartridge. Follow these general guidelines:

- If the print is faded, smeared, wavy, speckled, or streaked, the toner may be low. Remove the toner cartridge and gently rock it from side to side to redistribute the toner. Replace the cartridge. If this solves the problem, plan to replace the toner cartridge soon.

- If this doesn't solve the problem, try replacing the toner cartridge.

- EconoMode (a mode that uses less toner) may be on; turn it off.

- On some laser printers, you can clean the mirror. Check the user guide for directions.

- A single sheet of paper may be defective. Try new paper.

- The paper may not be of high enough quality. Only use paper recommended for use in a laser printer.

18

A+CORE 5.2

- Try a different brand of paper.

- Clean the inside of the printer with a dry, lint-free cloth. Don't touch the transfer roller.

- If the transfer roller is dirty, the problem will probably correct itself after printing several sheets. If not, then take the printer to an authorized service center.

A+CORE 5.1

Ink-Jet Printers

Ink-jet printers don't normally provide the quality resolution of laser printers, but are popular because they are small and can print color inexpensively. Ink-jet printers tend to smudge on inexpensive paper, and they are slower than laser printers. The quality of the paper used with ink-jet printers significantly affects the quality of printed output. Only use paper designed for an ink-jet printer, and to get the best results, use a high-grade paper. Figure 18-6 shows one example of an ink-jet printer.

Figure 18-6 An example of an ink-jet printer

How an Ink-Jet Printer Works An ink-jet printer resembles a dot-matrix printer in several ways. Both printers use a print head that moves across the paper, creating one line of text with each pass. Also, both types of printer put ink on the paper using a matrix of small dots, although ink-jet printers use much smaller dots than do dot-matrix printers.

Different types of ink jet printers form their droplets of ink in different ways. Printer manufacturers use several technologies, but the most popular is the bubble jet. Bubble jet printers use tubes of ink that have tiny resistors near the end of each tube. These resistors heat up and cause the ink to boil. Then, a tiny air bubble of ionized ink (which means that it has an electrical charge) is ejected onto the paper. A typical bubble jet print head has 64 or 128 tiny nozzles, and all can fire a droplet simultaneously. Plates carrying a magnetic charge direct the path of ink onto the paper to form shapes.

A+CORE
5.1

Ink jet printers include one or more cartridges of ink. When purchasing an ink jet printer, look for the kind that uses two separate cartridges, one for black ink and one for three-color printing. If an ink-jet printer does not have a black ink cartridge, then it produces black by combining all colors of ink to produce a dull black. Having a separate cartridge for black ink means that it prints a true black and, more importantly, does not use the more expensive colored ink. You can replace the black cartridge without also replacing the colored ink cartridge.

Figure 18-7 shows the two ink cartridges for the Hewlett-Packard DeskJet 712C. The cartridge on the left contains red, blue, and yellow ink (official names are magenta, cyan, and yellow), and the cartridge on the right contains black ink. The print head assemblage in the figure is located in the center position because the top cover has been lifted. Normally when the printer is not in use, the head assemblage sits to the far right of the printing area. This is called the home position and helps protect the ink in the cartridges from drying out.

Print head assemblage

Black ink cartridge

Color ink cartridge

Top cover

Figure 18-7   The ink-jet cartridges of an ink-jet printer

Photo-Quality Ink-Jet Printers   A new generation of ink-jet printers has emerged that can give photo-quality results, especially when used with photo-quality paper. Until this new technology, increasing the quality of an ink-jet printer meant increasing the dpi (dots per inch). Earlier ink-jet printers used 300 dpi, but ink-jet printers today can use as many as 1400 dpi. Increasing the dpi has its drawbacks. Doing so increases the amount of data sent to the printer for a single page, and all those dots of ink on the page can produce a wet page. An improved technology that gives photo-quality results mixes different colors of ink to produce a new color that then makes a single dot. Hewlett-Packard calls this PhotoREt II color technology. HP mixes as many as 16 drops of ink to produce a single dot of color on the page, producing up to 30 times as many shades of color as conventional ink-jet printing does.

18

A+*CORE*
5.1,
5.2

The results are dramatic, and the cost of an ink-jet printer using photo-quality technology is not significantly different from that of a standard printer.

Supporting an Ink-Jet Printer   Sometimes dust or dirt gets down into the print head assemblage, which can cause streaks or lines on the printed page. See the printer guide to see how to clean the print cartridges and their cradles.

Correcting Missing Lines or Dots on the Printed Page   The ink nozzles on an ink-jet cartridge occasionally dry out, especially when the printer sits unused for a long time. Symptoms of this are missing lines or dots on the printed page. With older ink-jet printers, you had to clean the ink-jet nozzles manually, but now newer printers often let you clean the nozzles automatically, using software or buttons on the front panel of the printer. This section describes how to use supporting software to clean the nozzles on one ink-jet printer. For more information about how to clean the nozzles on your printer, see the printer documentation.

Using Software to Clean Ink-Jet Nozzles   For the HP 710C series of printers, you can use the software that accompanies the printer to clean the ink-jet nozzles automatically. When the printer software was installed, it placed a printer toolbox icon on the desktop and added several tabs to the printer Properties dialog box. Use a tab on the printer Properties dialog box to clean the ink-jet nozzles. Here is what you do:

1. Click **Start**, point to **Settings**, and click **Printers**. The Printers window opens. Right-click the ink-jet printer icon and select **Properties** from the shortcut menu.

2. Click the **Services** tab. Figure 18-8 shows the list of services available for this printer.

3. Click **Clean the print cartridges** to clean the ink-jet nozzles automatically.

4. A test page prints. If the page prints sharply with no missing dots or lines, then you are finished. If the page does not print correctly, perform the auto-clean again.

5. You might need to perform the auto-clean procedure six or seven times to completely clean the nozzles. If the problem persists, don't attempt to manually clean the nozzles—contact the manufacturer or vendor for service.

Correcting Ink Streaks   Follow the manufacturer's directions to clean the print cartridge assemblage. Use clean distilled water and cotton swabs to clean the cartridge cradle and the face and edges of the print cartridge, being careful not to touch the nozzle plate. To prevent the ink-jet nozzles from drying out, don't leave the print cartridges out of their cradle for longer than 30 minutes.

A+CORE
5.2

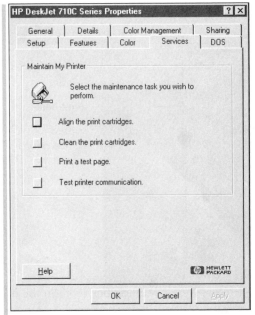

Figure 18-8   Use the Services tab under the printer Properties box to auto-clean the ink-jet nozzles

A+CORE
5.1

Dot-Matrix Printers

Dot-matrix printers are less expensive than other types of printers, but they don't give nearly the print quality. The one reason you still see so many around is that they are impact printers and can print multicopy documents. A dot-matrix printer has a print head that moves across the width of the paper using pins to print a matrix of dots on the page. The pins shoot against a cloth ribbon, which hits the paper, depositing the ink. The ribbon provides both the ink for printing and the lubrication for the pin heads.

Occasionally, you should replace the ribbon of a dot matrix printer. Although the print head can wear out, replacing it is probably not cost-effective because it costs almost as much as the printer itself. If the print head fails, buy a new printer. Overheating can damage a print head (see Figure 18-9). Keep the print head as cool as possible so that it will last longer. Keep the printer in a cool, well-ventilated area and don't use it to print more than 50 to 75 pages without allowing the head to cool down.

18

$A^{+CORE}_{5.2}$

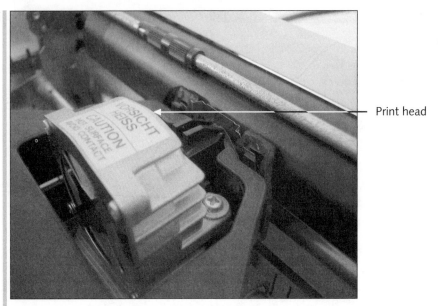

Print head

Figure 18-9   Keep the print head of a dot-matrix printer as cool as possible so that it will
last longer

Supporting Printers

$A^{+}_{}$ OS
2.4   This section briefly introduces how Windows 9x prints, and then discusses how to improve
printer performance and troubleshoot printer problems.

Printing Using Windows 9x

Windows 9x manages print jobs in one of three ways:

- For Windows applications using a non-PostScript printer, the print job data is
  converted to **enhanced metafile format** (**EMF**). This format embeds print
  commands in the data to help speed up printing.

- For Windows applications using a PostScript printer, the print job data is converted to the PostScript language. (Recall that a PostScript printer is a printer that
  uses a special language for data communication called PostScript.)

- For DOS applications, data is not converted, but sent to the printer as is (this is
  called raw data).

When Windows 9x receives a print job from an application, it places the job in a queue and
prints from the queue, so that the application is released from the printing process as soon as
possible. Several print jobs can accumulate in the queue, which you can view in the Printer
window. This process of queue printing jobs is called **spooling**. (The word "spool" is an
acronym for simultaneous peripheral operations on line.) Most printing from Windows 9x
uses EMF spooling.

A+ OS
   2.4
If the parallel port, printer cable, and printer all support bidirectional communication, the printer can communicate with Windows. For example, Windows 9x can ask the printer how much printer memory is available and what fonts are installed. The printer can send messages to the OS such as an out-of-paper or paper jam message. Bidirectional communication for parallel ports and parallel data cables was discussed in Chapter 9.

A+ OS
   3.2
Improving Printer Performance

The speed of a small, desktop printer depends on the speed of the computer and the printer itself. Laser printers are rated by two speed properties: the time it takes to print the first page measured in seconds and the print speed measured in pages per minute. If the printer is very slow, upgrading the computer's memory or the CPU can help. Printer speed can also be improved by lowering the printer resolution and the print quality.

To speed up a laser printer, besides lowering the printer resolution and the print quality (which lowers the RET settings), you can try adding more memory to the printer.

If the bottom portion of a page on a laser printer does not print, the problem is that either the PC or the printer needs more memory. Upgrading memory on either the PC or the printer might solve the problem.

The quality of paper determines the final print quality, especially with ink-jet printers. In general, the better the quality of the paper used with an ink-jet printer, the better the print quality. Do not use less than 20-lb paper in any type of printer, unless the printer documentation specifically says that a lower weight is satisfactory.

Troubleshooting Guidelines for Printers

When resolving printer problems, begin by finding the problem. It may be with the printer, the PC hardware or OS, the application using the printer, the printer cable, or, in the case of a printer installed on a network, the network. This section first addresses how to isolate the problem and then discusses troubleshooting each of the possible sources of the problem. Problems with printers on a network are covered later in the chapter. Follow the steps in Figure 18-10 to isolate the problem to one of the following areas:

- The application attempting to use the printer
- The OS and printer drivers
- Connectivity between the PC and the printer
- The printer

18

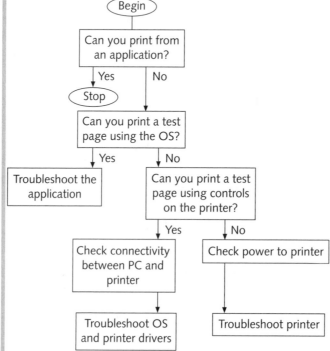

Figure 18-10   How to isolate a printer problem

Operating System Test Page   If you can print a test page from the operating system, you have eliminated every possible source of the problem except the applications software that is trying to print.

1. To print a test page using the OS, click **Start**, point to **Settings**, and click **Printers**. The Printers window opens.

2. Right-click the icon for the printer you are testing. The printer Properties dialog box opens, as in Figure 18-11. Click **Print Test Page**.

3. This test page is different from the one that prints from the printer self-test. This test page contains a list of driver files that the OS is using to communicate with the printer, and the port and the name of the driver the OS is using.

If you cannot print successfully, Windows 9x will automatically launch its troubleshooting tool to help you troubleshoot the problem. It will make suggestions and ask questions to help discover the solution to the problem.

If the operating system test page printed correctly, turn to the applications software and begin troubleshooting there.

A^{+} OS
3.2

Click here to print
a test page

Figure 18-11   If a **Print Test Page** command is successful, then the OS, device drivers,
communications, and the printer are all working properly

Problems with the Printer   To eliminate the printer as the problem, print a test page at
the printer. If this test page prints correctly, it confirms that the printer is working correctly.

TIP   When troubleshooting problems with printer drivers, check the web site of the printer
manufacturer to download the latest driver. Also, look for troubleshooting suggestions
in the site's FAQs. You might also be able to get help by e-mailing technical support.

Printer Self-Test Page   Follow these steps to print a self-test page.

1. For directions to print a self-test page, see the user guide for the printer. One
   example, the HP LaserJet 5L, prints a test page if you hold down the button on
   the front panel until the front panel lights begin to blink.

2. A printer test page generally prints some text and some graphics and prints information about the printer such as the printer resolution and how much memory
   is installed.

3. Verify that the information on the test page is correct. For example, if you know
   that the printer should have 2 MB of on-board printer memory, but it only
   reports 1 MB, then there is a problem with memory.

18

A+ OS
  3.2

If the test page does not print, or prints incorrectly (for example, it has missing dots or smudged streaks through the page), troubleshoot the printer until you can successfully print a good test page:

- Turn the printer off and disconnect it from the PC. Turn the printer back on and try to print another self-test page.

- Does the printer have paper? Is the paper installed correctly? Is there a paper jam?

- Reset the printer.

- For a laser printer, check that a toner cartridge is installed. For an ink jet printer, check that ink cartridges are installed.

- Check that power is getting to the printer.

- Try another power cable.

For some laser printers, if the printer does not have enough memory to hold the entire page, an error occurs. For others, only a part of the page prints.

Some HP LaserJet printers that don't have a control panel on the front of the printer signal errors by a flashing amber light. For some HP LaserJet printers that have a control panel, the error message for low memory is "20 Mem Overflow." The solution is to install more memory or only print simple pages with few graphics.

Print a self-test page to verify how much memory is installed. Check the printer guide to determine how much memory the printer can support and what kind of memory to buy.

A+CORE
  5.2

Problem with the Printer Cable   If the printer self-test worked, but the OS printer test did not work, the problem might be with the printer cable.

- Check that the cable is firmly connected at both ends.

- Many businesses use a switch box (sometimes called a T-switch) to share one printer between two computers. A printer cable connects to the printer port of each computer. The two cables connect to the switch box. A third cable connects from the switch box to the printer. A switch on the front of the box controls which computer has access to the printer. Switch boxes were built with older dot-matrix printers in mind. Some switch boxes are not recommended for ink-jet or laser printers that use a bidirectional parallel cable, and can even damage a printer. For these printers, remove the switch box.

- Try a different cable.

- Try printing using the same printer and printer cable, but a different PC.

- Enter CMOS setup of the PC and check how the parallel port is configured. Is it disabled? Set to ECP or bidirectional? Recall from Chapter 9 that an ECP parallel port requires the use of a DMA channel. Try setting the port to bidirectional.

A^+ OS
3.2

Problem with the OS or Device Drivers If the printer self-test worked, but the OS printer test did not work, the problem might be with the operating system or device drivers.

- Try rebooting and then print another OS test page.

- Try printing from DOS. Access a DOS prompt (real-mode DOS, not a DOS box) and print a directory list. Use the command **DIR > LPT1**. If nothing prints, press the Form Feed button. Sometimes a partial page needs to be ejected by this method before it prints when using DOS.

- If you can print from DOS, but not from Windows, try removing and reinstalling the printer driver. To uninstall the printer driver, right-click the printer icon in the Printers window, select **Delete** to remove the printer, and then reinstall the printer.

- Check the configuration of the parallel port in CMOS setup.

- Try another printer driver. It may not print graphics correctly, but if another driver does work at all, then you can conclude that you have a faulty driver. For example, if you have an HP LaserJet 5L, try using the HP LaserJet III driver.

- Verify printer properties. Try lowering the resolution or printing a different document.

- Try printing from NotePad. If you can print from NotePad, the problem is with the application. Reboot the PC and try to print from the application again.

- In the printer Properties dialog box, try disabling "Check Port State Before Printing."

- Reboot the PC. Immediately print a text document in NotePad or WordPad.

- If you can print from DOS, but not from Windows, try disabling printer spooling. Go to the printer Properties dialog box and select **Print Directly to the Printer**. Spooling holds print jobs in a queue for printing, so if spooling is disabled, printing from an application can be slower.

- The print spool might be stalled. Try deleting all print jobs in the printer's queue. Double-click the printer icon in the Printers window. Select **Printer**, **Purge Print Documents**.

- Also in the printer Properties dialog box, click **Disable bidirectional support for this printer**. The PC and printer might have a problem with bidirectional communication.

- Check the resources assigned to the printer port. Open **Device Manager**, select **LPT1**, and click **Properties**. Verify that the resources are assigned correctly for LPT1 (I/O addresses are 0378 to 037B) and that Device Manager reports "No conflicts."

18

A+ OS
3.2

Problem with the Applications Software

- If you can print from NotePad or WordPad, but cannot print from another application, try closing and reopening the application.

- Verify that the correct printer is selected in the Print Setup dialog box. To set the printer as the default printer for Windows, using the Printer Window, right-click on the printer icon and select **Set as Default** from the shortcut menu.

- Try printing a different application file.

- Try creating new data in a new file and printing it. Keep the data simple.

- Try printing from another application.

- If you can print from other applications, but not this one application, consider reinstalling the application.

Sharing Printers over a Network

A+ OS
2.4,
4.1

Printers can be shared on a network using one of three basic methods.

- A regular printer can be attached to a PC using the PC's parallel port, and then that PC can share the printer with the network.

- A network printer with embedded logic to manage network communication can be connected directly to a network.

- A computer called a print server can control several printers connected to a network. For example, HP has software called HP JetDirect, designed to support HP printers in this manner.

This section explains how to make a printer connected directly to a PC available to the network and how to gain access to a shared printer on the network.

Print Services

Network print services allow a computer to share a printer connected to it, and to use printers that are connected to other computers on the network or connected directly to the network. In Windows 9x and Windows NT, you can share a printer as you share a file or folder: allow sharing and give the printer a name so that another user can identify the printer to the network. (Recall that if the remote user connects using a modem, you must also grant the right for the user to dial in.)

To Share a Printer   To allow a remote PC to use a printer connected to a Windows 9x computer, do the following:

1. On the Windows 9x computer, make sure that File and Printer Sharing is installed. Click **Start**, point to **Settings**, click **Control Panel** and then double-click the **Network** icon.

2. If **File and Printer Sharing for Microsoft Networks** is not listed, click **Add** to install the component.

A+ OS
2.4,
4.1

3. Select **Service** and click **Add**. From the list of network services, select **File and Printer Sharing for Microsoft Networks** and click **OK**. You might be asked to insert the Windows 9x CD and to reboot the PC for the changes to take effect.

Once File and Printer Sharing is installed, share the printer by doing the following:

4. Click **Start**, point to **Settings**, and click **Printers**. The Printers window opens.

5. Right-click the printer you want to share. From the shortcut menu, select **Sharing**. (This Sharing option is grayed out if File and Printer Sharing is not installed.)

6. The Properties dialog box opens with the Sharing tab selected (see Figure 18-12).

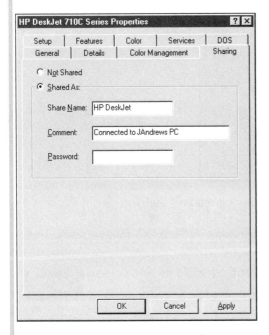

Figure 18-12   When using Windows 98, use the printer Properties window to share a connected printer with other computers on the network

7. Select **Shared As** and give the printer a **Share Name**. Click **OK** to exit.

8. The printer is listed in the Network Neighborhood group of other computers on the network.

To allow a remote PC to use a printer connected to a Windows NT workstation, do the following:

1. On the Windows NT PC, allow print sharing: click **Start**, point to Settings, and click **Printers**. The Printers window opens. Right-click the printer you want to share, and select **Sharing** from the shortcut menu. The printer Properties dialog box opens, as seen in Figure 18-13. Select **Shared** and enter a name for the printer. Click **OK** when done.

18

A^{+} *OS*
  2.4,
  4.1

2. The Windows NT PC must be connected to a network either directly or through RAS.

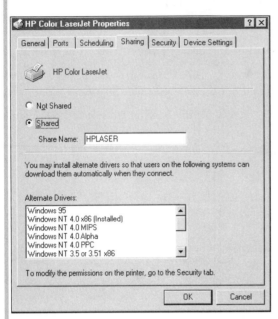

Figure 18-13   Windows NT printer sharing requires that you give the printer a name

To Use a Shared Printer   On the Windows 9x local PC, follow these directions to use a shared printer on another PC:

1. Connect to the host computer by modem or by connecting directly to a LAN.

2. Add a new printer: click **Start**, point to **Settings**, and click **Printers**. Double-click **Add Printer**. The Add Printer Wizard window opens. Click **Next**.

3. In response to the question, "How is this printer attached to your computer?", select **Network printer**. Click **Next**. The wizard window in Figure 18-14 opens.

4. Enter the host computer name and printer name. Begin with two backslashes and separate the computer name from the printer name with a backslash. Or you can click **Browse** and search the list of shared printers on the network, selecting the printer to install. If you plan to print from DOS applications, select yes to the question, "Do you print from MS-DOS based programs?" Click **Next**.

   (If your network is using static IP addressing and you know the IP address of the host PC, you can enter the IP address instead of the host name in this step.)

5. Select the printer manufacturer and then the printer model from the list of supported printers. Click **Next** when finished.

6. Enter a name for the printer. You might include the location of the printer, such as 3rd Floor Laser or John's Laser. Click **Next** to continue.

7. Print a test page, and then click **Finish**. The network printer is now available for use.

Figure 18-14   To use a network printer under Windows 9x, enter the host computer name followed by the printer name

$A+$ OS 3.2 | **Problems with Network Printers**   If you are having problems with network printers, first rule out a physical problem with the printer. See guidelines on how to do that, earlier in this chapter. Problems with network printing can be caused by the printer, the network to the printer, or the computer trying to use the printer. You can isolate the problem by finding the answers to the following questions:

- Is the printer online?

- Is the network printer on the remote PC configured correctly?

- Is the correct network printer selected on the remote PC?

- Is there enough hard disk space available on the remote PC?

- Can you print successfully from another application on the remote PC?

- Can you print successfully from the host PC using the identical application?

- Can you print to a file and then send the file to the host PC to successfully print? If this works, then the problem is with data transmission. If this does not work, then the problem is with the application or print driver on the remote PC.

- For DOS applications, you may need to exit the application before printing occurs. Try capturing the printer port. To do that, go to the printer Properties window, click the Details tab, click Capture Printer Port and select the port. Type the network path and click OK. Under "Print to the following port," select the port you mapped.

18

NOTEBOOK COMPUTERS

Supporting notebook computers is another essential task of a PC technician. This section discusses the special needs of supporting notebooks including adding memory to a notebook, changing power management options, understanding and supporting PC Cards, and using special Windows 98 components available for supporting notebooks.

Notebooks use the same technology as do PCs, but with modifications so as to use less voltage, take up less space, and work when on the move.

 A **notebook** or **laptop computer** is a computer designed for travel (see Figure 18-15). Notebooks use thin LCD panels instead of CRT monitors for display, compact hard drives that can withstand movement even during operation, and small memory modules and CPUs that require less voltage than regular components. Recall from Chapter 9 that notebook LCD panels use several different technologies, and that active matrix (sometimes called thin film transistor or TFT) technology generally gives better quality than does passive matrix (sometimes called dual-scan twisted nematic or DSTN) technology.

Notebooks cost more than PCs with similar features, because components are designed to be more compact and to endure movement and even jars when in use. The types and features of notebooks vary widely as they do for PCs. However, notebooks are generally purchased as a whole unit, including both hardware and software, and you are not likely to upgrade a notebook's hardware and OS, as you would with a PC. In fact, some notebook manufacturers no longer support a notebook that has had the OS upgraded or new hardware components added. In contrast, recall that PCs are highly modular, letting you easily interchange, upgrade, and enhance components. In fact, PCs are often assembled from components purchased from various vendors and manufacturers. Notebook computers, on the other hand, are designed with a different goal in mind and can be very proprietary in design, which means the skills needed to support them are brand-specific. In this chapter, we'll look at universal support issues, but remember that procedures can vary from one notebook brand to another.

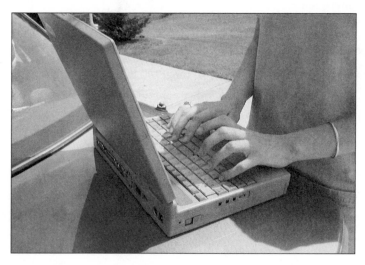

Figure 18-15   A notebook is a computer designed for travel

A+CORE 1.1

TIP   The LCD panels on notebooks are fragile and can be damaged. Take precautions against damaging the notebook's LCD panel with rough use.

Windows 98 and Windows 2000 Professional offer features designed specifically for notebooks, and these are covered as well as managing power, upgrading memory, adding peripheral devices, and supporting PC Cards.

When supporting any notebook, pay careful attention to the stipulations on the warranty that accompanies it. Some warranties are voided if you open the notebook case or install memory, batteries, or a hard drive that was not made by, or at least authorized by, the notebook manufacturer. Almost all operating system installations on notebooks are customized by the manufacturer, and a floppy disk comes with the notebook that contains data and utilities specific to the configuration. Read the supporting documentation for the notebook before you consider upgrading or reinstalling the OS.

Windows 98 Notebook Features

The Windows 98 features designed to support notebooks include:

- Multilink Channel Aggregation, a feature that allows you to use two modem connections at the same time to speed up data throughput when connected over phone lines. It works on both regular analog phone lines and ISDN. To use the feature, you must have two phone lines and two modem cards that are physically designed to connect two phone lines at the same time. You will learn more about PC Card modems later in the chapter.

- **ACPI (Advanced Configuration and Power Interface)** developed by Intel, Microsoft, and Toshiba to control power on a notebook and other devices. ACPI allows a device to turn on a notebook or allows a notebook to turn on a device. For example, if you connect an external CD-ROM drive to the notebook, it can turn on the notebook, or the notebook can cycle up and turn on an external CD-ROM drive. The BIOS of the notebook and the device must support ACPI for it to work.

- Several improvements over Windows 95 for managing power consumption for notebooks. Windows 98 automatically powers down a PC Card modem when not in use, supports multiple battery packs, and lets you create individual power profiles. Power profiles are described in the next section.

- Improved support for PC Cards, adding several new drivers.

- Microsoft Exchange lets a user select what e-mail to download when traveling with a notebook. Downloading large e-mail messages with attachments takes a long time over a modem. You might prefer to leave this e-mail to download when you are later connected directly to the network.

When returning from a trip with a notebook, you might want to update your desktop PC with all e-mail documents and other files created or updated during the trip. To do this, use Windows 9x **Briefcase**, a system folder used to synchronize files between two computers. Briefcase automatically updates files on the original computer to the most recent version. You can use a null modem cable, disk, or network for the file transfer.

18

Power Management

A+CORE
1.2

A notebook can be powered by a battery pack or an AC adapter connected to a power source. The length of time that a battery pack can power the notebook before being recharged varies according to the quality of the battery, the power consumption as determined by the devices being used, and how power is being managed.

Windows 98 has features to help manage power consumption. The goal is to minimize power consumption to increase the time before a battery pack needs recharging. Using Windows 98, to access the power management window, click **Start**, point to **Settings**, click **Control Panel** and double-click the **Power Management** icon. Figure 18-16 shows the Power Management Properties dialog box for one notebook. (Other brands of notebooks may have different tabs in their Properties dialog box.) Use this dialog box to create, delete, and modify multiple power management schemes to customize how Windows 98 manages power consumption.

Figure 18-16   The Power Management Properties box of Windows 98 allows you to create and manage multiple power schemes

For example, one power-saving feature of Windows 98 puts a notebook into **hibernation**. When a computer hibernates, it stores whatever is currently in memory and then shuts down. When it returns from hibernating, it restores everything to the way it was before the shutdown. When hibernating, the notebook is not using power. When you step away from the notebook for a few minutes and direct the notebook to hibernate, you save power.

To configure Windows 98 to cause the notebook to hibernate when you close the lid of the notebook, do the following:

1. In the Power Management Properties dialog box, click the **Hibernate** tab (see Figure 18-17) and verify that hibernate support is enabled.

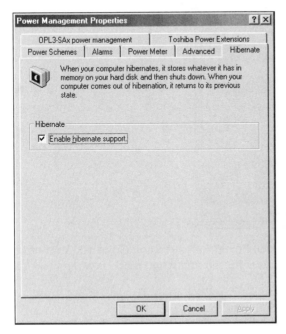

Figure 18-17   Verify that hibernate support is enabled

2. Click the **Advanced** tab. Figure 18-18 shows the Advanced page which you use to control what happens when you press the shut down button or close the lid of the notebook.

3. Click the list arrow for "When I close the lid of my portable computer" and select **Hibernate**. See Figure 18-19.

4. Click **Apply** and **OK** to close the Properties dialog box, saving your changes.

18

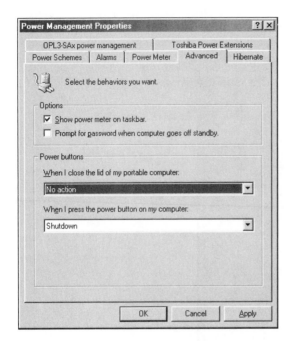

Figure 18-18   The Advanced tab of Power Management allows you to control the behavior of the power button and what happens when you close the lid of your notebook

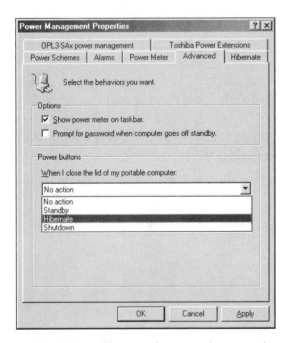

Figure 18-19   Choices of action when you close the lid of your notebook

A+CORE
1.2,
1.8

If you need to use the notebook for extended periods away from an electrical outlet, you can use extra battery packs. When the notebook signals that power is low, remove the old battery and replace it with a charged one. See the notebook user guide for directions. Here is an example of directions for exchanging the battery pack for one notebook:

1. Save your work and turn off the notebook.

2. Remove all cables connected to the notebook.

3. Set the notebook on its back, as in Figure 18-20.

Figure 18-20   Slide the battery release panel to the left to expose the battery pack

4. Slide the battery release panel to the left to expose the battery.

5. Lift the battery out of the computer.

6. Before placing a new battery in the slot, clean the edge connectors of the battery with a clean cloth.

Windows 2000 Notebook Features

18

Windows 2000 Professional has several new features designed to support notebooks. When choosing between Windows 98 and Windows 2000 Professional for a notebook OS, use Windows 98 for low-end notebooks and Windows 2000 for high-end notebooks that are used in a business environment in which security is important. Windows 2000 has stronger power management and security features. The features new to Windows 2000 include:

■ Offline Files, which replaces Briefcase, stores shared network files and folders in a cache on the notebook hard drive so you can use them offline. When you reconnect to the network, Offline Files synchronizes the files in the cache with those on the network.

■ Hibernate mode, support for ACPI and APM (Advanced Power Management) have been improved.

■ Improved battery support includes the ability to use two batteries and to monitor battery performance with greater control.

■ Hot swapping of IDE devices and floppy disk external drives is a new feature.

■ Folder redirection lets you point to an alternate location on a network for a folder. This feature can make the location of a folder transparent to the user.

Upgrading Memory

A+CORE 1.8 Notebooks use proprietary (built by the manufacturer of the notebook) memory modules that are smaller than regular SIMMs or DIMMs called **SO-DIMMs** (small outline DIMMs), which have 72 pins and support 32-bit data transfers (see Figure 18-21). Before upgrading memory, make sure you are not voiding your warranty. Search for the best buy, but make sure you use memory modules made by the notebook manufacturer and designed for the exact model of your notebook. Installing generic memory might save you money, but might also void the warranty of the notebook.

Figure 18-21   An SO-DIMM memory module for a notebook computer

To install memory, see the notebook user guide for directions. The following is an example of how to install memory on one notebook. Directions vary from one computer to another.

1. Turn off the notebook and remove all cables.

2. Lift the keyboard brace, as shown in Figure 18-22.

Figure 18-22 Lift the keyboard brace

3. Turn the keyboard over and toward the front of the notebook. See Figure 18-23. The keyboard is still connected to the notebook by the ribbon cable.

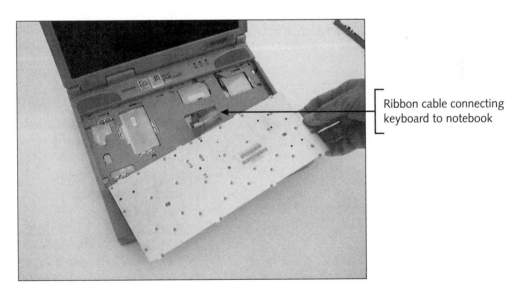

Ribbon cable connecting keyboard to notebook

18

Figure 18-23 Turn the keyboard over toward the front of the notebook to expose memory module sockets

4. Lift up the plastic sheet covering the memory module socket.

5. Insert the SO-DIMM module into the socket. See Figure 18-24. The socket braces should snap into place on each side of the module when the module is in position.

Figure 18-24   Install the SO-DIMM into the memory socket

6. Replace the keyboard and keyboard brace.

7. When you power up the notebook, it detects the new memory.

Connecting Peripheral Devices to Notebooks

A+CORE
1.3,
1.7

A notebook provides ports on its back or sides (see Figure 18-25). With the exception of the infrared port, all these ports have been discussed in earlier chapters. An infrared port connects devices to notebooks or other computers without cabling. A printer, keyboard, microphone, mouse, or other device can communicate with the laptop by using an infrared signal over a short distance. With special software, the notebook can communicate with another computer using the infrared port. Windows 98 and Windows 2000 support infrared devices. To activate an infrared device, double-click the Infrared icon in Control Panel. The most popular way to add peripheral devices to a notebook is by using PC Card slots.

A+CORE
1.2,
4.3

PC Cards (PCMCIA Cards)

Unlike PCs, notebooks don't have the traditional expansion slots that connect to an I/O bus to add peripheral devices to a system. Rather, notebook computers contain special bus expansion slots called **PC Card slots** (see Figure 18-26), formally called **PCMCIA slots**, that connect to the 16-bit PCMCIA I/O bus on the notebook system board.

A+*CORE*
1.2,
1.7

VGA port (video out)

Parallel port

USB port (presently covered)

Keyboard and/or mouse port

AC adapter connection

Infrared port

Serial port

Figure 18-25   Ports on the back of a notebook

Figure 18-26   Most peripheral devices are added to a notebook using a PC Card slot; here, a modem PC Card is inserted in a PC Card slot

18

A+*CORE*
1.7,
1.8
The PCMCIA organization (Personal Computer Memory Card International Association) has developed four standards for these slots. Once intended only for memory cards (cards that add additional memory to a notebook), these PC Card slots can now be used by many devices, including modems, network cards, CD-ROMs, sound cards, and hard disks. Some docking station PCs also have a PC Card slot, so that the device you use with your notebook can also be attached to the docking station. (A **docking station** or port replicator such as the one shown in Figure 18-27 is a special device that allows a notebook to easily connect to a full-sized monitor, keyboard, and other peripheral devices.) The latest PCMCIA specification is called

A+CORE
1.7,
1.8

CardBus and improves I/O speed, increases the bus width to 32 bits, and supports lower-voltage PC Cards while maintaining backward compatibility with earlier standards.

IBM ThinkPad notebook computer

Port replicator

Figure 18-27   A docking station or port replicator makes it convenient to connect a notebook computer to resources and peripherals at your office

A+CORE
1.8

Three standards for the PCMCIA slots pertain to size and are named Type I, Type II, and Type III. Generally, the thicker the PC Card, the higher the standard. A thick hard drive card might need a Type III slot, but a thin modem card might only need a Type II slot. The PC Card is about the size of a credit card, but thicker, and inserts into the PC Card slot. Type I cards can be up to 3.3-mm thick and are primarily used for adding RAM to a notebook PC. Type II cards can be up to 5.5-mm thick and are often used as modem cards. Type III cards can be up to 10.5-mm thick, which is large enough to accommodate a portable disk drive. When buying a notebook PC, look for both Type II and Type III PC Card slots. Often one of each is included. For improved performance, look for the slots to be 32-bit CardBus slots.

The operating system must provide two services for the PC Card, a socket service and a card service. The socket service manages the socket, closing (establishing) the socket when the card is inserted and opening (disconnecting) the socket when the card is removed. The card service provides the device driver to interface with the card once the socket is closed.

The PC Card might contain a data cable to an external device, or it might be self-contained. For example, in Figure 18-28, the PC Card on the left is the interface between the notebook PC and the CD-ROM external drive. Insert the PC Card in the PC Card slot. The data cable from the PC Card connects to the external CD-ROM drive, which requires its own power supply that must be connected into a wall outlet. On the other hand, the PC Card on the right in Figure 18-28, is the actual modem. Insert the card in the PC Card slot (Figure 18-27) and connect the telephone line to the modem PC Card (Figure 18-29).

Connection into
the PC Card slot

Connection into
the PC Card slot

PC Card for
CD-ROM
interface

PC Card is a
modem

Connector for
telephone line

CD-ROM
drive

Transformer

Figure 18-28 Two examples of PC Cards, one self-contained (the modem), the other
connected to an external device (the CD-ROM)

A+CORE
1.8

One worthwhile feature in PC Card slots is **hot swapping** (which means you can install a
device while a computer is running, and the computer will recognize the device without having to reboot). Hot swapping allows you to remove one card and insert another without powering down the PC. For example, if you are currently using a modem in the PC Card slot
and want to switch to the CD-ROM, first turn off the modem card (open the socket) by
using the PC Card icon in the Windows 9x Control Panel (see Figure 18-30). Then remove
the modem card and insert the CD-ROM card with the attached external CD-ROM drive.

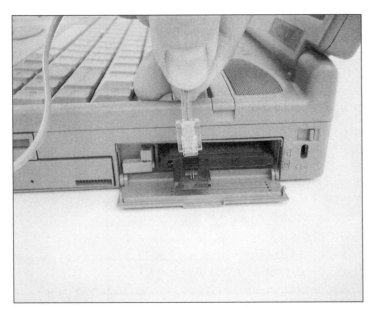

18

Figure 18-29 Connect the phone line to the modem PC Card

Figure 18-30   Before removing a PC Card from the notebook, stop the Card (open the socket) from the PC Card Properties box

A+CORE
1.7   Another popular use of a PC Card is to interface with a network. Figure 18-31 shows a PC Card that serves as the NIC to an Ethernet 10BaseT network. The RJ-45 connection is at the end of a small cord connected to the PC Card. This small cord is called a dongle or pigtail, and is used so that the thick RJ-45 connection does not have to fit flat against the PC Card.

Figure 18-31   This PC Card serves as a NIC for an Ethernet 100BaseT network

Supporting Notebooks

A+CORE
1.2,
1.8

Except for the differences discussed in this section, notebooks work identically to desktop PCs, and the troubleshooting guidelines in previous chapters also apply to notebooks. When troubleshooting notebooks, be especially conscious of warranty issues; know what you can do within the guidelines of the warranty. The documentation that comes with a notebook is much more comprehensive than what comes with a PC and most often contains troubleshooting guidelines for the notebook. Remember that the loaded OS and the hardware configuration are specific to the notebook, so you can rely on the notebook manufacturer for support more than you can for a desktop PC. Sometimes a notebook is designed so that the hard drive can be replaced or upgraded without violating warranties. See the notebook documentation for details. For questions about supporting a notebook that are not answered in the documentation, see the web site of the notebook manufacturer. Popular manufacturers of notebooks and their web sites are listed in Table 18-1.

Table 18-1   Notebook manufacturers

Manufacturer	Web Site
Acer America	www.acer.com
ARM Computer	www.armcomputer.com
Compaq Computer	www.compaq.com
Dell Computer	www.dell.com
FutureTech Systems	www.futuretec.com
Gateway	www.gateway.com
Hewlett-Packard	www.hp.com
IBM	www.ibm.com
Micron Electronics	www.micronpc.com
PC Notebook	www.pcnotebook.com
Sony	www.vaiodirect.sel.sony.com
Toshiba America	www.csd.toshiba.com
WinBook	www.winbook.com

Personal Digital Assistant (PDA)

A **personal digital assistant** (**PDA**) such as a Palm Pilot or a Pocket PC is a small handheld computer that has its own operating system and applications. You can use a PDA to store addresses and phone numbers, manage a calendar, run word processing, send e-mail, access web sites, play music, and exchange information with a desktop computer. A PDA most likely uses either the Palm operating system for Palm Pilot devices or Microsoft Windows CE. Some PDAs come with all application software preinstalled and others require the user to download applications at additional cost. Some PDAs allow you to download e-mail or web site content from a desktop computer or a notebook, and others can access the Internet directly by way of a modem or wireless connection. Not all web sites are designed to be

18

accessed by a PDA and the web content readable by a PDA is more limited than that readable by a desktop computer or notebook.

Typically, a PDA comes with a cable to connect to a desktop computer or notebook by way of a serial or USB port, or a PDA might use an infrared connection. Special software such as ActiveSync by Microsoft might be needed to perform the synchronization. Similar to a notebook, a PDA is battery powered, uses either a grayscale or color active matrix or dual scan passive matrix display, and can sometimes benefit from additional memory.

CHAPTER SUMMARY

Printers

- ❏ The three most popular printers are dot-matrix, ink-jet, and laser. Laser printers produce the highest quality, followed by ink-jet printers. Dot-matrix printers have the advantage of printing multicopy documents.

- ❏ The six stages that a laser printer uses to print are cleaning, conditioning, writing, developing, transferring, and fusing. The first four stages are performed inside the removable toner cartridge.

- ❏ Ink-jet printers print by shooting ionized ink at a sheet of paper.

- ❏ The nozzles of an ink-jet printer tend to clog, especially when the printer remains unused. The nozzles can be cleaned automatically through printer software or by buttons on the front panel of the printer.

- ❏ Dot-matrix printers print by projecting pins from the print head against an inked ribbon that deposits ink on the paper.

- ❏ When troubleshooting printers, first isolate the problem. Narrow the source to the printer, cable, PC hardware, operating system including the device driver, applications software, or network.

- ❏ When computers are connected with a modem or a network, printers can be shared among computers.

- ❏ A printer can be shared on a network in three ways: as a regular printer connected to a PC's parallel port, serial port, USB port, or 1394 port (access to this printer is by way of the PC it's connected to), as a network printer connected directly to the network, or as a printer controlled by a print server.

- ❏ When a printer is connected to a PC port, install File and Printer sharing to share that printer using Windows 9x. The person using the PC connected to the printer must name the shared printer. This name, together with the computer name, identifies the printer on the network.

Notebook Computers

❏ A notebook is a computer designed for travel. Notebooks cost more than comparable PCs because they are more compact and can withstand movement and jars even when in use. Notebooks don't contain expansion slots for I/O devices, but rather use PC Card slots.

❏ Windows 98 offers several features to support notebooks, including using multiple modems for faster data transmission, ACPI and other power management features, improved support for PC Cards, and improved e-mail services.

❏ Use hibernation to manage power consumption on notebooks. With hibernation, the notebook takes a "snapshot" of the open applications before it shuts down and then returns you to that same state after a power-up.

❏ Notebooks use a memory module called a SO-DIMM, which is smaller than a regular SIMM or DIMM.

❏ Upgrading memory on a notebook varies from one notebook to another, so see the user guide for a notebook for specific instructions.

❏ When upgrading components on a notebook, including memory, use the same brand of components as the notebook, or only use components recommended by the notebook manufacturer.

❏ PC Cards are a popular way to add peripheral devices to notebooks. There are three types of PC Cards, which vary in thickness: Types I, II, and III.

KEY TERMS

ACPI (Advanced Configuration and Power Interface) — Specification developed by Intel, Microsoft, and Toshiba to control power on notebooks and other devices. Windows 98 supports ACPI.

Beam detect mirror — Detects the initial presence of a laser printer's laser beam by reflecting the beam to an optical fiber.

Briefcase — A Windows 9x system folder used to synchronize files between two computers. When files are transferred from one computer to another, Briefcase automatically updates files on the original computer to the most recent version.

Control blade — A laser printer component that prevents too much toner from sticking to the cylinder surface.

Docking station — A device designed to connect to a portable, or notebook, computer to make it easy to connect the notebook to peripheral devices.

Enhanced metafile format (EMF) — A format used to print a document that contains embedded print commands. When printing in Windows, EMF information is generated by the GDI portion of the Windows kernel.

Hibernation — A power-saving notebook feature. When a computer hibernates, it stores whatever is currently in memory and then shuts down. When it returns from hibernating, it restores everything back to the way it was before the shutdown.

18

Hot swapping — The ability of a computer to use a device, such as a PC Card on a notebook, that is inserted while the computer is running without the computer needing to be rebooted.

Laptop computer — *See* Notebook.

Notebook — A personal computer designed for travel, using less voltage and taking up less space than a regular PC. Also called a laptop computer.

PC Card — A credit-card-sized adapter card that can be slid into a slot in the side of many notebook computers and is used for connecting to modems, networks, and CD-ROM drives. Also called PCMCIA Card.

PC Card slot — An expansion slot on a notebook computer, into which a PC Card is inserted. Also called a PCMCIA Card slot.

PCMCIA (Personal Computer Memory Card International Association) card — *See* PC Card.

PCMCIA Card slot — *See* PC Card slot.

RET (resolution enhancement technology) — The term used by Hewlett-Packard to describe the way a laser printer varies the size of the dots used to create an image. This technology partly accounts for the sharp, clear image created by a laser printer.

Scanning mirror — A component of a laser printer. An octagonal mirror that can be directed in a sweeping motion to cover the entire length of a laser printer drum.

SO-DIMM (small outline DIMM) — A small memory module designed for notebooks that have 72 pins and support 32-bit data transfers.

Spooling — Placing print jobs in a print queue so that an application can be released from the printing process before printing is completed. Spooling is an acronym for simultaneous peripheral operations online.

Toner cavity — A container filled with toner in a laser printer. The black resin toner is used to form the printed image on paper.

REVIEW QUESTIONS

1. List the six steps used by a laser printer to print a page.

2. Which document exhibits better quality, one printed with 300 dpi or one printed with 600 dpi? Why?

3. During the laser printing process, what determines when the toner sticks to the drum and when it does not stick to the drum?

4. Why is it less expensive to maintain an ink-jet printer that has a black ink cartridge than one that does not?

5. What technology makes an ink-jet printer a photo-quality ink-jet printer?

6. What should you do if an ink-jet printer prints with missing dots or lines on the page?

7. What should you do if an ink-jet printer prints with ink streaks on the page?

8. What can you do to help a dot-matrix printer last longer?

9. When you are isolating a printer problem, what are the four major possible sources of the problem?

10. How can you eliminate the printer as the source of a printing problem?

11. If you can print a test page from the operating system successfully, then what is the likely source of a printer problem?

12. How can you be sure that a printer cable is not the source of a printer problem?

13. What are two possible settings in CMOS for parallel port mode?

14. List two possible ways to improve printing speed.

15. When a laser printer is short on memory, what is a possible symptom of this problem?

16. Why are notebooks usually more expensive than PCs with comparable power and features?

17. What type of memory module is used in a notebook?

18. How are battery packs used in a notebook?

19. What type of monitor does a notebook use?

20. When a battery pack discharges and you need to continue working on a notebook, what are your two choices?

21. What is the thickness of a Type I PC Card? Of a Type III PC Card?

22. What term refers to a PC Card you can remove and replace without powering off?

23. What two services must an OS provide for a PC Card to work?

24. What is the small cord sometimes found on the end of a PC Card called?

PROJECTS

Installing a Printer

Practice installing a printer by uninstalling a printer and then reinstalling it. If the printer is not supported by your OS, you will need the CD or disk that contains the driver software.

Research Printer 1394 Connections

Your company wants to improve the printing speed on its network and has asked you to do some research on the Internet. You are considering using IEEE 1394 for your printer connection to a PC that currently does not have a 1394 port. Research the Unibrain web site (*www.unibrain.com*) and provide the following:

1. Print the web page of a card that can be installed in a PC to provide a 1394 port for a printer.

2. Print the web page of a card that can be installed in a printer to provide the 1394 connection.

3. Research a printer manufacturer web site (for example, HP at *www.hp.com*), and print the web page for a printer that can support this 1394 connection.

18

Troubleshooting Skills

Practice troubleshooting skills by doing the following. Begin with a printer connected to a PC that is printing properly.

1. Turn off spooling to the printer. Print several files from an application. What difference do you see between spooling and not spooling the documents?

2. In CMOS setup, disable the parallel port being used by the printer. What happens when you attempt to print?

3. In CMOS setup, change the mode of the parallel port. Try printing a document with each mode selected. What happens when you attempt to print using each mode?

Printer Maintenance

For an ink-jet printer, follow the procedures in the printer's user guide to clean the printer nozzles and ink cartridges. For a laser printer, follow the procedures in its user guide to clean the inside of the printer where the toner cartridge is installed.

Power Management Features of a Notebook

Using a notebook, change the power management options to support hibernation. If the notebook supports it, set hibernation to start when the notebook lid is closed. Open one or more applications that include current data on the screen. Close the lid or, if that is not supported, wait the specified time until hibernation begins. Start up the notebook again (you can use the power on switch) and verify that applications and data are restored to their status when hibernation began.

Notebook Batteries

Practice replacing a dead battery on a notebook by removing and replacing the battery. Using the model number on the battery, find out the current price of a new battery unit. See the Web site of the notebook manufacturer for this information.

Research PC Card Modems

Some employees in your company spend much time on the road and, while traveling, need easy access to the Internet. Research how they could use a cellular phone to connect a notebook computer to the Internet. Using the Motorola web site (*www.motorola.com*) or a similar site, provide the following:

1. Print the web page of a modem card for a notebook computer that can accommodate a cellular phone connection.

2. Print the web page of a cellular phone that can accommodate a modem card connection to a notebook.

3. Print the page that shows or describes the cord that connects the modem card to the cellular phone.

19

VIRUSES, DISASTER RECOVERY, AND A MAINTENANCE PLAN THAT WORKS

In this chapter, you will learn:

- ♦ About preventive maintenance and procedures designed to protect systems
- ♦ How to develop a preventive maintenance plan
- ♦ How systems become infected with viruses and other infestations
- ♦ How viruses work, how to protect systems against them, and how to deal with them when they infect your system
- ♦ About the strengths and weaknesses of different backup procedures and systems, and how to use backup software
- ♦ How to develop a disaster recovery plan

When you are responsible for a computer, regular maintenance can help prevent disaster, lower repair costs, and make problems less disruptive. Two important tasks in preventive maintenance are making regular backups of hard drives and dealing with viruses. These two tasks, as well as routine hardware maintenance and designing a disaster recovery plan, are addressed in detail in this chapter.

PREVENTIVE MAINTENANCE

If you are responsible for the PCs of an organization, make and implement a preventive maintenance plan to help prevent failures and reduce repair costs and downtime. In addition, you need a disaster recovery plan to manage failures when they occur. PC failures are caused by many different environmental and human factors, including heat, dust, magnetism, power supply problems, static electricity, human error (such as spilled liquids or an accidental change of setup and software configurations), and viruses. The goals of preventive maintenance are to reduce the likelihood that the events that cause PC failures will occur and to lessen the damage if they do occur. When designing a preventive maintenance plan, consider what you can do to help prevent each cause, and write into the plan the preventive actions you can take. Think through the situation caused by each problem. What would happen to the PC, the software, the data, the user's productivity, and so on, if a failure occurred? What would you do and what materials would you like to have in that situation? What can you do ahead of time to help make the situation less disastrous? Your answers to those questions will lead you to create effective preventive maintenance and disaster recovery plans. This section focuses on the preventive maintenance plan.

For example, consider the problem caused by a user accidentally changing CMOS setup. What can you do to prevent that from occurring? If it does occur, how can you solve the problem? What can you do now to prepare for that event? By answering these three questions, you might arrive at these preventive maintenance and recovery procedures: (1) make a backup copy of setup to floppy disk, (2) label the disk and keep it in a safe place, (3) educate the user about the importance of not changing setup, and (4) keep a maintenance record of this PC, including the last time setup was backed up.

A Preventive Maintenance Plan

If your company has established written guidelines for PC preventive maintenance, read them and follow the necessary procedures to make them work. If your company does not have an established plan, make your own. A preventive maintenance plan tends to evolve from a history or pattern of malfunctions within the organization. For example, dusty environments can mean more maintenance, whereas a clean environment can mean less maintenance. Table 19-1 lists some guidelines for developing a preventive maintenance plan that may work for you.

$A^{+\,CORE}_{\;\;3.1}$ Dust is not good for a PC because it acts like a blanket, insulating PC parts, which can cause them to overheat; therefore, ridding the PC of dust is an important part of preventive maintenance. Some PC technicians don't like to use a vacuum inside a PC because they're concerned about ESD that the vacuum might produce. Use compressed air to blow the dust out of the chassis, power supply and fan, or use a special anti-static vacuum designed to be used around sensitive electronic equipment.

A+*CORE*
3.1,
5.2

Table 19-1   Guidelines for developing a PC preventive maintenance plan

Component	Maintenance	How Often
Inside the case	▪ Make sure air vents are clear. ▪ Use compressed air to blow the dust out of the case, or use a vacuum to clean vents, power supply, and fan. ▪ Ensure that chips and expansion cards are firmly seated. ▪ Clean the contacts on expansion cards.	Yearly
CMOS setup	Keep a backup record of setup (for example, use Nuts & Bolts rescue disk).	Whenever changes are made
Floppy drive	Only clean the floppy drive head when the drive does not work.	When the drive fails
Hard drive	▪ Perform regular backups. ▪ Automatically execute a virus scan program at startup. ▪ Defragment the drive and recover lost clusters regularly. ▪ Don't allow smoking around the PC. ▪ Place the PC where it will not be jarred, kicked, or bumped.	At least weekly At least daily Monthly Always Always
Keyboard	▪ Keep the keyboard clean. ▪ Keep the keyboard away from liquids.	Monthly Always
Mouse	▪ Clean the mouse rollers and ball (see Chapter 8).	Monthly
Monitor	▪ Clean the screen with a soft cloth.	At least monthly
Printers	▪ Clean out the dust and bits of paper, using compressed air or a vacuum. Small pieces of paper can be removed with tweezers. ▪ Clean the paper and ribbon paths with a soft lint-free cloth. ▪ Don't re-ink ribbons or use recharged toner cartridges. ▪ If the printer uses an ozone filter, replace it as recommended by the manufacturer.	At least monthly or as recommended by the manufacturer
Software	▪ If directed by your employer, check that only authorized software is present. ▪ Regularly delete files from the recycle bin and \Temp directories. ▪ Delete any temporary files in the \DOS directory.	At least monthly
Written record	▪ Keep a record of all software, including version numbers and the OS installed on the PC. ▪ Keep a record of all hardware components installed, including hardware settings. ▪ Record when and what preventive maintenance is performed. ▪ Record any repairs done to the PC.	Whenever changes are made

19

A+CORE
3.1

The general idea of preventive maintenance is to do what you can to make a PC last longer and give as little trouble as possible. You may also be responsible for ensuring that data is secure and backed up, that software copyrights are not violated, and that users are supported. As with any plan, when designing your preventive maintenance plan, first define your overall goals, and then design the plan accordingly. The guidelines listed in Table 19-1 address primarily the problems that prevent a PC from lasting and from performing well.

Recordkeeping and protecting software and hardware documentation are often overlooked during preventive maintenance. A record of what is done to a PC is valuable when solving problems or considering an upgrade. Secure all manufacturer hardware documentation, such as for a sound card or modem, to prevent accidental loss or destruction. You can file these documents in an envelope with a log of everything you have done to the PC for regular maintenance, installations, and repairs. Be sure to include a boot disk that contains a copy of CMOS setup for this PC. Consider taping the envelope to the inside of the computer case, especially when you are responsible for PCs at off-site locations where you might not have assigned filing cabinet space. You can also keep this information in a notebook along with other similar notebooks at your workstation. Label each notebook to identify the PC that it tracks. You can also keep records on a separate PC.

Tidy the hard drive after installing an OS or an application. For example, after installing Windows 9x, delete temporary files from the \DOS directory and from the \Windows\Temp directory. Also, when you initially set up a PC, if you are using an older version of DOS, check the SET TEMP command in the AUTOEXEC.BAT file. If it reads SET TEMP=C:\DOS, change it to SET TEMP=C:\TEMP and create a \TEMP directory. Storing temporary files in the \DOS directory can create problems. In addition to the list in Table 19-1, encourage users to follow routine steps as part of your preventive maintenance plan. For instance, ask a user to conserve hard drive space by regularly deleting the files in the \TEMP or \Windows\Temp directory. For Windows 9x, Windows NT, and Windows 2000, regularly empty the Recycle Bin by deleting its files. Routinely back up the hard drive (for a more efficient backup process, you can back up only directories that contain data). You will learn more about hard drive backups later in the chapter. Ask the user not to block the air vents on the back of the monitor or computer case and not to place the case on the floor where it can be kicked.

When Moving Equipment

When shipping a PC, rough handling can cause damage, as can exposure to water, heat, and cold. The PC can also be misplaced, lost, or stolen. When you are preparing a PC for shipping, take extra precautions to protect it and its data. Follow these general guidelines when preparing to ship a PC:

- Back up the hard drive onto a tape cartridge. If you don't have access to a tape cartridge, back up important system and configuration files to a floppy disk. Whatever you do, don't ship a PC that has the only copy of important data on the hard drive or data that should be secured from unauthorized access.

- Remove any floppy disks, tape cartridges, or CDs from the drives. Make sure that the tapes or disks holding the backup data are secured and protected during transit. Consider shipping them separately.

- Turn off power to the PC and all other devices.

- Disconnect power cords from the electrical outlet and the devices. Disconnect all external devices from the computer.

- If you think someone might have trouble later identifying which cord or cable belongs to which device or connection, label the cable connections with white tape or white labels.

- Coil all cords and secure them with plastic ties or rubber bands.

- Pack the computer, monitor, and all devices in their original shipping cartons or similar boxes with enough packing material to protect them.

Disposing of Used Equipment

A+CORE
3.2

As a PC technician, it will often be your responsibility to dispose of used equipment and consumables, including batteries, printer toner cartridges, and monitors. Table 19-2 lists items and how to dispose of them. Manufacturer documentation and local environmental regulators can also provide disposal instructions or guidance. Monitors and power supplies can contain a charge even after the devices are unplugged. To discharge the capacitors in either device, place a screwdriver across a hot prong and the ground prong of the electrical connections as shown in Figure 19-1. To discharge the actual CRT in a monitor, the monitor must be opened. Ask a technician trained to fix monitors to do this for you.

19

Figure 19-1   Discharge the capacitors in a monitor before disposal

A+CORE
3.2

A **material safety data sheet (MSDS)** explains how to properly handle substances such as chemical solvents. An MSDS includes information such as physical data, toxicity, health effects, first aid, storage, disposal, and spill procedures. It comes packaged with the chemical, or you can order one from the manufacturer, or find one on the Internet (see *www.ilpi.com/msds*).

Table 19-2   Computer parts and how to dispose of them

Part	How to Dispose
• Alkaline batteries including AAA, AA, A, C, D, and 9 volt	Normal trash
• Button batteries used in digital cameras, Flash Path, and other small equipment • Battery packs used in notebooks	These batteries can contain silver oxide, mercury, lithium, or cadmium and are considered hazardous waste. Dispose of these either by returning them to the original dealer or taking them to a recycling center. To recycle them, pack them separately from other items. If you don't have a recycling center nearby, contact your county for local regulations for disposal.
• Laser printer toner cartridges	Return to the manufacturer or dealer to be recycled
• Ink-jet printer ink cartridges • Computers • Monitors • Chemical solvents and cans	Check with local county or environmental officials for laws and regulations in your area for proper disposal of these items. The county might provide a recycling center that will receive them. Before disposing of a monitor, first discharge the monitor.

VIRUSES AND OTHER COMPUTER INFESTATIONS

A+ OS
3.2

A computer support person needs to know how to protect computers against computer infestations (including viruses), how to recognize them, and how to get rid of them. Understanding what infestations are, how they work, and where they hide helps technicians deal with them successfully. A computer **infestation** is any unwanted program that is transmitted to a computer without the knowledge of the user or owner, and is designed to do varying degrees of damage to data and software. Computer infestations do not damage PC hardware, although, when boot sector information is destroyed on a hard drive, it can appear as though the hard drive is physically damaged. What most people refer to as viruses really fall into four categories of computer infestations: viruses, Trojan horses, worms, and logic bombs. The four types of infestations differ in the way they spread, what damage they do, and how they hide.

Because viruses are by far the most common of the four kinds of computer infestations, one of the most important defenses against computer infestations is **antivirus (AV)** software that is designed to discover and remove a virus. This section looks at several AV programs and how to use them effectively.

Understanding Computer Infestations

A+ OS 3.2

A **virus** is a program that can replicate by attaching itself to other programs. The infected program must be executed for a virus to run. The virus might then simply replicate, or also do damage by immediately performing some harmful action. A virus might be programmed to perform a negative action in the future, such as on a particular date (for instance, Friday the 13th), or when some logic within the host program is activated. A virus is different from a **worm**, a program that spreads copies of itself throughout a network without a host program. A **Trojan horse** is a third type of computer infestation that, like a worm, does not need a host program to work—rather it substitutes itself for a legitimate program. Trojan horses cannot replicate themselves. (This last statement has some exceptions. One Trojan horse program was disguised as an automatic backup utility downloadable from the Internet. When used, it created backups and replicated itself to the backups. It was programmed to damage several systems on Friday the 13th. In this case, the Trojan horse program is also considered a virus because of its ability to replicate.) A worm is seldom seen except on a network, where it creates problems by overloading the network as it replicates. Worms do damage by their presence rather than by performing a specific damaging act, as a virus does. A worm overloads memory or hard drive space by replicating repeatedly. Because Trojan horse infestations cannot replicate and require human intervention to move from one location to another, they are not as common as viruses.

Sometimes problems on a PC caused by an error or software bug can look and act like viruses, even when no virus is involved. Sometimes software is altered with malicious intent. A **logic bomb** is dormant code added to software and is triggered by a predetermined time or event. For example, an employee might put code into a program to destroy important files if his or her name is ever removed from the payroll file. Also, viruses, Trojan horses, logic bombs, and worms can occur in combination such as when a virus gains access to a network by way of a Trojan horse. The virus plants a logic bomb within applications software on the network that sets off a worm when it executes.

Where Viruses Hide

A program is called a virus because (1) it has an incubation period (does not do damage immediately), (2) it is contagious (can replicate itself), and (3) it is destructive. Viruses are often programmed to hide to avoid detection by antivirus software. A virus can hide in four ways. Sometimes a virus can use more than one method at the same time.

Boot Sector Virus   A **boot sector virus** hides in a boot sector program. It can hide on a hard drive either in the program code of the Master Boot Record or in the boot record program that loads the OS on the active partition of the hard drive. On a floppy disk, a boot sector virus hides in the boot program of the boot sector. One of the most common ways a virus spreads is from a floppy disk used to boot a PC. When the boot program is loaded into memory, so is the virus, which can then spread to other programs.

However, a floppy disk does not have to be bootable to spread a virus. All floppy disks have a boot sector that contains a boot program. If a PC is configured to first boot from drive A then drive C, and a floppy disk is in the drive when the PC is booted, BIOS executes the boot program on the disk. If the disk is not bootable, this program displays an error message,

19

A+ OS
3.2

such as "Nonsystem disk or disk error." If the user removes the disk and presses any key, the PC boots from the hard drive. However, if the boot program of the floppy disk contains a boot sector virus, the virus might already have been loaded into memory. When the system boots from the hard drive, the virus is then spread to the boot sector of the hard drive.

To prevent this kind of infection, after unsuccessfully trying to boot from the floppy disk, don't press a key that instructs the PC to turn to the hard drive to boot. Also, pressing CTRL+ALT+DEL might not be enough to prevent the problem, because the loaded virus can still hide in memory and some viruses intercept a CTRL+ALT+DEL to take control of the PC. The best way to proceed is to use a cold boot—turn the PC off, remove the floppy disk, and turn the PC back on. The danger of virus infection from a floppy is a good reason to configure your computer to always boot from the hard drive first, and then, if the hard drive is not bootable, to boot from the floppy drive. This boot order normally prevents BIOS from reading a boot sector of a floppy disk that is inserted during boot. The order of booting from the A and C drives is determined in CMOS setup.

Incidentally, many CMOS setups have an option that prevents writing to the boot sector of the hard drive, which can protect against some boot sector viruses. This feature must be turned off before installing Windows 9x, Windows NT, or Windows 2000, which must write to the boot sector during installation. Windows 9x does not tell you that you must turn the feature off and start the installation over until about halfway through the installation.

File Viruses A **file virus** hides in an executable (.exe or .com) program or in a word-processing document that contains a macro. A **macro** is a small program contained in a document and can be automatically executed when the document is first loaded, or later by pressing a key combination. For example, a word-processing macro might automatically read the system date and copy it into a document when you open the document. Viruses that hide in macros of document files are called **macro viruses**. Macro viruses are the most common viruses spread by e-mail, hiding in macros of attached document files.

One well-known example of a macro virus is Melissa, first introduced on Friday, March 26, 1999, in a Word 97 macro. The virus immediately spread around the world within one working day. The e-mail that initially spread Melissa looked like this:

```
From: (name of infected user)
Subject: Important Message From (name of infected user)
To: (50 names from alias list)
Here is that document you asked for ... don't show anyone
else ;-)
Attachment: LIST.DOC
```

When the recipient opened the document, a macro executed and immediately e-mailed the LIST.DOC to 50 e-mail addresses listed in the user's address book. The virus infected other Word documents, which, when e-mailed, also spread the virus.

Melissa drops its payload, or activates, when a document is opened when the minutes of the hour match the day of the month (for example, at 09:18 on the 18th day of a month). It then inserts a phrase from the *Simpsons* TV show into the current document.

One type of file virus searches a hard drive for files with .exe file extensions and then creates another file with the same filename with a .com file extension, and stores itself there. When the user launches a program, the OS first looks for the program name with the .com file extension. It then finds and executes the virus. The virus is loaded into memory and loads the program with the .exe extension. The user appears to have launched the desired program. The virus is then free to do damage or spread itself to other programs.

A virus cannot work if it is contained in a data file with no embedded macros. Sometimes a virus copies itself to a data file by mistake, where it cannot do much damage, since the data is not a program and cannot be executed from memory. However, the virus can corrupt data by overwriting what was already in the file.

Multipartite Viruses   A **multipartite virus** is a combination of a boot sector virus and a file virus. It can hide in either type of program.

Cloaking Techniques

A virus is programmed to attempt to hide from antivirus (AV) software. AV software can only detect viruses that are identical or similar to ones it has been programmed to search out and recognize. AV software detects a known virus by looking for distinguishing characteristics called the **virus signature**, which is why it is important to update your AV software.

> **TIP**   Antivirus software cannot detect a virus it does not know to look for. Therefore, continue to upgrade your AV software as new viruses are discovered.

A virus attempts to hide from AV software in two ways: by changing its distinguishing characteristics (its signature) and by attempting to mask its presence. Three types of viruses that are categorized according to their cloaking techniques are polymorphic, encrypting, and stealth viruses, which are discussed next.

Polymorphic Viruses   A **polymorphic virus** changes its distinguishing characteristics as it replicates. Mutating in this way makes it more difficult for AV software to recognize the presence of the virus.

Encrypting Viruses   One key symptom AV software looks for a program that can replicate itself. An **encrypting virus** can transform itself into a nonreplicating program to avoid detection. However, it must revert to a replicating program to spread or replicate, when it can be detected by AV software.

Stealth Viruses   A **stealth virus** actively conceals itself, using one or more of the following techniques:

- Because AV software can detect a virus by noting the difference between a program's file size before the virus has infected it and after the virus is present, the virus alters OS information to mask the size of the file it is hiding in.

19

- The virus monitors when files are opened or closed. When it sees that the file it is hiding in is about to be opened, it temporarily removes itself or substitutes a copy of the file that does not include the virus. The virus keeps a copy of this uninfected file on the hard drive just for this purpose.

The Damage an Infestation Can Cause

Viruses, worms, and Trojan horses have not been known to physically damage a hard drive or other hardware device. The damage they do ranges from minor, such as displaying bugs crawling around on a screen, to major, such as erasing everything written on a hard drive. Infestation damage is called the payload and can be accomplished in a variety of ways. A virus can be programmed to drop its payload only in response to a triggering event such as a date, opening a certain file, or pressing a certain key. Figures 19-2 and 19-3 show the results of two harmless viruses that simply display garbage on the screen.

Figure 19-2   The harmless, or benign, Walker virus displays a man walking across the screen

How Infestations Spread

A+ OS 3.2   Understanding how infestations spread is essential to understanding how to protect your computer against them. Some computers are more vulnerable than others, depending on user habits. Below is a list of user activities that make a computer susceptible to infestations.

- Trading floppy disks containing program files

- Connecting the computer to an unprotected network

- Buying software from unreliable sources

- Downloading programs from the Internet

Figure 19-3   The crash virus appears to be destructive, making the screen show only garbage, but does no damage to the hard drive data

A+ OS
  3.2

- Using floppy disks from unknown sources

- Using shared network programs

- Using used, preformatted floppy disks

- Reading e-mail that automatically executes a word processor to read attached files

- Not write-protecting original program disks

How a Virus Replicates   Once a program containing a virus is copied to your PC, the virus can spread only when the infected program is executed. The process is shown in Figure 19-4. Recall from earlier chapters that the first step in executing a program, whether it is stored in a program file or in a boot sector, is to load the program into memory. Viruses hidden in a program can then be executed from memory. A virus can either be a **memory-resident virus** and stay in memory, still working, even after the host program is terminated, or a **non-memory-resident virus**, which means that it is terminated when the host program is closed.

After a virus is loaded into memory, it looks for other programs that are loaded into memory. When it finds one, it copies itself there and into that same program file on disk. From Figure 19-4, you can see that a virus becomes more dangerous the longer it stays loaded into memory and the more programs that are opened while it is there. For this reason, if you want to use a computer that has been used by other people, such as in a computer lab, always reboot before you begin work to clear memory of programs. Use a hard boot, not just a soft boot, to erase that all memory-resident programs (including a memory-resident virus) from memory.

19

A^+ *OS*
      3.2

> **TIP**   When using a computer in a computer lab, always hard boot the PC before you begin work to protect against viruses.

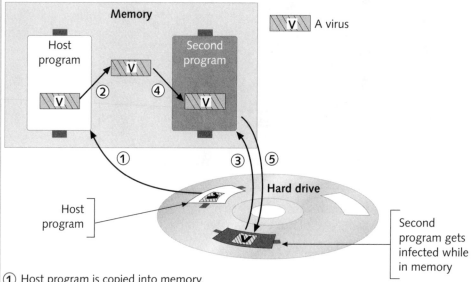

① Host program is copied into memory.
② The virus may or may not move itself to a new location in memory.
③ A second program is opened and copied into memory.
④ The virus copies itself to the second program in memory.
⑤ The newly infected second program is written back to the hard drive.

Figure 19-4   How a virus replicates

How a Trojan Horse Gets into Your Computer   A Trojan horse is an infestation that masquerades as a legitimate program. One interesting example of a Trojan horse is the AOL4FREE program. Originally this was an illegal program that could provide unauthorized access to America Online. After the program's usefulness was blocked by AOL, a new program emerged, also called AOL4FREE, which was not an online access program, but a destructive Trojan horse. People passed the program around, thinking that it would provide illegal access to AOL; however, if executed, it actually erased files on their hard drives.

Virus Hoaxes   A virus hoax is a letter or e-mail warning about a nonexistent virus. The warning is itself a pest because it overloads network traffic. Here's an example of a virus hoax e-mail message I received:

There is a new virus going around in the last couple of days!! DO NOT open or even look at any mail that you get that says: "Returned or Unable to Deliver." The virus will erase your whole hard drive and attach itself to your computer components and render them useless. Immediately delete any mail items that say this. AOL has indicated this is a very dangerous

A+ OS
3.2
virus, and there is NO remedy for it at this time. Please be careful and forward to all your online friends ASAP. This is a new email virus and not a lot of people know about it; just let everyone know, so they won't be a victim. Please forward this email to your friends!!!

First, don't believe the part about a virus rendering computer components useless. No virus has been known to actually do physical damage to hardware, although viruses can cause a PC to be useless by destroying programs or data. Second, don't believe the part that says the virus will be activated just because you open an e-mail message. An e-mail message is text, not a program, and a virus can't hide there. (It can, however, hide in word-processing documents containing macros that are attached to an e-mail message.) And third, don't be gullible and take the bait by forwarding the message to someone else. The potential damage a hoax like this can do is to overload an e-mail system with useless traffic, which is the real intent of the hoax. When I received this e-mail, there were over a hundred names on the distribution list.

Protecting Against Computer Infestations

You can do a lot to protect your computer against viruses and other infestations. Your first line of defense is to regularly make backups and use virus scan software. After that, use wisdom when managing programs. Here are some general guidelines:

- Buy antivirus software and set your computer to automatically run the AV program at startup.

- Keep your AV software current by periodically downloading upgrades from the Internet.

- Set a virus scan program to automatically scan word-processor documents as they are opened.

- Establish and faithfully execute a plan to make scheduled backups of your hard drive to protect against potential infestation damage.

- Only buy software from reputable vendors.

- Don't trade program files on floppy disks.

- Don't use floppy disks from unknown sources, and always scan floppy disks for viruses no matter where they came from.

- Download software from the Internet sparingly, and then *always* scan program files for viruses before executing them.

- Never use pirated software.

- Format floppy disks before first use.

- Write-protect original program disks.

- In a business environment, adopt strict company policies against using unauthorized software.

19

- Before using a running computer that others have already used, hard boot the computer.

- Set your computer CMOS settings to boot from drive C, then drive A.

- Turn on antivirus protection for your MBR in the CMOS settings, if available.

Virus Symptoms

A+ OS
  3.2

Know what to expect when a virus is replicating or dropping its payload. Here are some warnings that suggest a virus is at work:

- A program takes longer than normal to load.

- The number and length of disk accesses seem excessive for simple tasks.

- Unusual error messages occur regularly.

- Less memory than usual is available.

- Files mysteriously disappear or appear.

- Strange graphics appear on your computer monitor, or the computer makes strange noises.

- There is a noticeable reduction in disk space.

- The system cannot recognize the hard drive when you have booted from a floppy disk.

- The system cannot recognize the CD-ROM drive, although it has worked earlier.

- Executable files have changed size.

- Executable files that once worked no longer work and give unexpected error messages.

- The access lights on the hard drive and floppy drive turn on when there should not be any activity on that device. (However, sometimes an OS will perform routine maintenance on the drive when the system has been inactive for a while.)

- Files constantly become corrupted.

- Strange or bizarre error messages appear.

- DOS or Windows error messages about the FAT or partition table are displayed.

- The hard drive boots but hangs up before getting a DOS prompt or Windows desktop.

- File extensions or file attributes change without reason.

- A message is displayed from the virus scanner software.

- The number of bad sectors on the hard drive continues to increase.

- The DOS MEM command reveals unfamiliar TSRs loaded into memory.

What to Do When You Suspect a Virus Infestation

If you suspect a virus, run a virus scan program to detect and delete the virus. If the antivirus software is not already installed, you can still use it. Consult the documentation for instructions on how to proceed. In many cases, the installation process detects the virus and eliminates it before continuing the installation. However, if the AV software does not recognize the virus, or if the virus successfully hides, the AV program cannot detect the virus. If the AV software found nothing, but you still suspect a virus, get the latest upgrade of your AV software and try it or another AV program.

Protecting Against Viruses

Antivirus software cannot prevent a Trojan horse program from being copied to your computer, tell you that an e-mail message is a hoax, or force you to use wisdom in handling software. However, aside from taking precautions to prevent a virus from entering your system, using antivirus software is your best line of defense against a virus. Table 19-3 lists some popular antivirus software and Web sites that provide information about viruses.

Table 19-3   Antivirus software and information

Antivirus Software and Information	Web Site
Command AntiVirus by Command Software Systems	www.commandcom.com
Datafellows (virus information)	www.datafellows.com
Dr. Solomon's Software	www.drsolomon.com
eSafe by Aladdin Knowledge Systems, Ltd.	www.esafe.com
F-PROT by FRISK Software International	www.complex.is
McAfee VirusScan by McAfee Associates, Inc. (a version is included on the CD-ROM with this book)	www.mcafee.com
NeaTSuite PC-cillin by Trend Micro	www.antivirus.com
Norton AntiVirus by Symantec Corporation	www.symantec.com
Patricia Hoffman's Virus Summary (virus information)	www.vsum.com

When selecting antivirus software, look for the ability to do the following:

- Download new software upgrades from the Internet so that your software knows about new viruses

- Automatically execute at startup

- Detect macros in a word-processing document as it is loaded by the word processor

- Automatically monitor files being downloaded from the Internet

19

Using Antivirus Software

A+ OS
3.2

Antivirus software can work at different times to scan your hard drive or a floppy disk for viruses. Most AV software can be configured to scan memory and the boot sector of your hard drive for viruses each time your PC is booted. Often it's not practical to have it scan

A+ OS
3.2

the entire hard drive each time you boot, because that takes too much time. Consider sched-uling the AV software to run at the same time every day, such as during the lunch hour.

Some AV software can run continuously in the background and scan all programs that are executed. However, the software can cause problems with other software, especially during installations. If you are having a problem installing a new application, try terminating your AV software first.

Make sure your AV software can scan files as they are downloaded from the Internet or a network, and can scan documents for macro viruses each time a document is opened by a word processor. Make sure the AV software can scan both files and boot sectors of hard dri-ves and disks. A version of McAfee VirusScan software is included with Nuts & Bolts on the CD-ROM accompanying this book. Using this software, follow these directions to scan a hard drive for viruses:

1. For Windows 9x, click **Start**, point to **Programs**, **Nuts & Bolts**, **McAfee VirusScan**, and then click **McAfee VirusScan**.

2. When the software first executes, it lets you log on to the McAfee web site and download any updates to the software (see Figure 19-5). You must be connected to the Internet before you click **Update** to download the files.

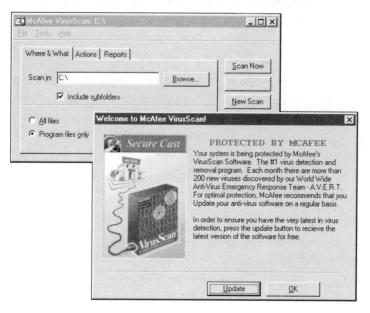

Figure 19-5   McAfee VirusScan allows you to update the software from the McAfee Web site to ensure protection against newly discovered viruses

3. The McAfee VirusScan window opens, as shown in Figure 19-6. Select the drive to scan, what to do when a virus is detected, what reports to create and where, and what type of files to scan.

4. Click **Scan Now** to begin scanning.

5. Any viruses that are detected are listed in the box at the bottom of the screen.

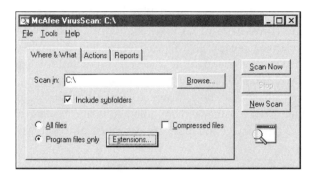

Figure 19-6   McAfee VirusScan software ready to perform a scan for viruses

ALL ABOUT BACKUPS AND FAULT TOLERANCE

There's nothing like a rousing discussion of computer viruses to make a PC support person appreciate hard drive backups and other methods of protecting data. With data and software, a good rule of thumb is: if you can't get along without it, back it up. This section covers the hardware and software needed to make backups of data and software from a hard drive. Windows 9x, Windows NT, and Windows 2000 offer backup tools, which are also covered in this section. Another feature of preventive maintenance is to make hard drives more fault tolerant. **Fault tolerance** is the ability of a computer to respond to a fault or catastrophic event, such as a hardware failure or power outage, in such a way that data is not lost. Several approaches to making hard drives more fault tolerant are collectively called **RAID**. The term first stood for **redundant array of inexpensive disks**, but has recently been updated to mean **redundant array of independent disks**. The different methods of RAID are also discussed in this section.

Backup Hardware

Popular hardware devices used for making hard drive backups on standalone personal computers or small servers include tape, Zip, and Jaz drives, and read-write CDs. However, in a business environment, if a PC is connected to a file server, the most practical backup approach is to back up data from the PC's hard drive to the file server. Data on both the PC and the file server can become corrupted. However, the file server most likely uses its own automated backup utility to back up to either tape or a larger mainframe computer.

19

Regardless of the backup medium, it is practical to back up only the data and not the software on a regular basis. You might choose to back up software one time immediately after installation. Later, if the software becomes corrupted, it can be reinstalled.

This section first discusses using tape drives and then using removable drives for backups.

Tape Drives

Tape drives (Figure 19-7) are an inexpensive way of backing up an entire hard drive or portions of it. Tape drives are more convenient for backups than floppy disks or other types of removable disks, and they are relatively inexpensive. Tapes have capacities anywhere from several hundred kilobytes to several gigabytes and come in several types and formats. Although tape drives don't require that you use special backup software to manage them, most likely you will want to invest in specialized backup software to make backups as efficient and effortless as possible. Many tape drives come with bundled software. Several of the more common standards and types of tape drives and tapes are described in this section.

Figure 19-7   An external tape drive

The biggest disadvantage of using tape drives is that data is stored on tape by **sequential access**, meaning that, in order to read data from anywhere on the tape, you must start at the beginning of the tape and read until you come to the sought-after data. Sequential access makes recovering files slow and inconvenient, which is why tapes are not used for general-purpose data storage.

How a Tape Drive Interfaces with a Computer   A tape drive can be external or internal. An external tape drive costs more but can be used by more than one computer. A tape drive can interface with a computer in these ways:

- An external tape drive can use the parallel port (see Figure 19-8) with an optional pass-through to the printer (so that the drive and the printer can use the same parallel port).

- An external or internal drive can use a SCSI bus. This method works well if the tape drive and the hard drive are on the same SCSI bus, which contains a data pass-through just to the SCSI system.

- An external or internal drive can use its own proprietary controller card or the floppy drive interface.

- An internal drive can use the IDE ATAPI interface.

External tape drive

Parallel port

Figure 19-8   An external tape drive can use the parallel port for input/output, with an optional pass-through to the printer

Currently, the most popular tape drive interfaces are SCSI and IDE ATAPI. Figure 19-9 shows the rear of an ATAPI tape drive. You can see the connections for a power supply and 40-pin IDE cable and jumpers to set the drive to master, slave, or cable select. This setup is similar to any IDE device. When installing an ATAPI tape drive, avoid putting the drive on the same IDE data cable as the hard drive to prevent hindering the hard drive's performance. A typical configuration is to put the hard drive as the sole device on the primary IDE channel and put a CD-ROM drive and tape drive sharing the second channel. Set the CD-ROM drive to master and the tape drive to slave on that channel.

19

Jumper bank to set master, slave, or cable select

40-pin connection for IDE cable

Power supply connection

Figure 19-9   The rear of an ATAPI IDE tape drive

The Tapes Used by a Tape Drive   Tape drives accommodate one of two kinds of tapes: full-sized **data cartridges** are 4 × 6 × ⅝ inches, and the smaller **minicartridges**, like the one in Figure 19-10, are 3¼ × 2½ × ⅝ inches. Minicartridges are more popular because their drives can fit into a standard 5½-inch drive bay of a PC case.

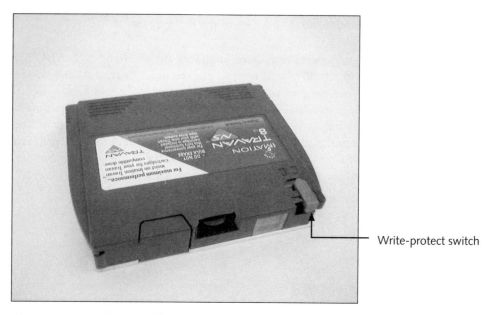

Write-protect switch

Figure 19-10   Minicartridge for a tape drive has a write-protect switch

The technology used by tape drives to write to tapes is similar to that used by floppy drives (see Chapter 5). A FAT at the beginning of the tape tracks the location of data and bad sectors on the tape. The tape must be formatted before data can be written to it. Buy factory formatted tapes to save time.

Standards for writing data to tapes have not developed as well as consumers would like, making it necessary to carefully match tapes to tape drives when purchasing and using them. Several standards exist, which have been promoted by different organizations as well as by individual manufacturers. Figure 19-11 shows two tables, each from a different tape drive manufacturer, showing the tape formats and tape types that are supported by their tape drives. Figure 19-11a shows that the Seagate Travan 8 or 20 GB drives that can support QIC-3080 and TR-5 tapes. Figure 19-11b shows that the Eagle TR-3 tape minicartridge tape drive can use either the QIC-3010 or QIC-3020 format and five tape types. Note that these drives are also likely to be able to read other formats that are compatible with these formats.

a) Tape formats for the Seagate Travan 8 GB and 20 GB tape drives

Tape Drive	Tape Format	Capacity	Tape Function
Travan NS 8 GB drive	Travan 8 (TR-4)	8 GB	Read and write
	QIC-3080	3.2 GB	Read and write
	QIC-Wide (3080)	4 GB	Read and write
Travan 20 GB drive	Travan 20 (TR-5)	20 GB	Read and write
	Travan 8 (TR-4)	8 GB	Read only

b) Minicartridge capacities obtained by the Eagle TR-3 tape drive using five different tape types

Tape Format	Travan TR-3	QIC Wide	MC 3000XL	TR-3 Extra	MC 3020 Extra
QIC-3020*	3.2 GB	1.7 GB	1.4 GB	4.4 GB	3.2 GB
QIC-3020	1.6 GB	850 MB	680 MB	2.2 GB	1.6 GB
QIC-3010*	1.6 GB	840 MB	680 MB	2.2 GB	1.6 GB
QIC-3010	800 MB	420 MB	340 MB	1.1 GB	800 MB

*Using software compression with an assumed 2:1 compression ratio

Figure 19-11   Tables from two tape drive manufacturers indicate the multitude of formats used when reading and writing to tapes

Tape Formats and Tape Types   One of the first efforts to standardize the way data is written to tape was established around 1983 by a group of manufacturers who formed Quarter-Inch Cartridge Drive Standards, Inc. These standards are sometimes called the **Quarter-Inch Committee (QIC)**, or quarter-inch cartridge (standards). Many QIC standards have been developed, but only a few are used today. 3M developed a standard, called Travan, based on the QIC format. Travan has been backed by many leaders in the tape drive industry. There are different levels of Travan standards, called TR-1 through TR-5, each based on a different QIC standard.

19

Looking at the second column of Figure 19-11a, showing tape types, and at the column headings of Figure 19-11b, you can see that there are several types of tape available. Although most manufacturers suggest that you use a tape cartridge they manufacture for their drive, tape drives often support a variety of tape types. Even though a tape drive can use a minicartridge rather than a data cartridge, not all minicartridge tapes can be used in any one drive. Consult the tape drive's user guide to find out which tape types you can use with the drive. Minicartridge tape drives use more than one type of tape drive mechanism, and more than one density is used to write data to a tape, just as there is more than one density for floppy disks. Also, some tape drives don't format tapes, meaning that you must buy preformatted tapes to use the drive.

Troubleshooting Guide for Tape Drives

A+CORE
2.2

The following is a list of possible tape drive problems you might encounter and suggestions for dealing with them.

A minicartridge does not work

- If you are trying to write data, verify that the minicartridge is write-enabled.

- Are you inserting the minicartridge correctly? Check the user guide.

- Check that you are using the correct type of minicartridge. See the user guide.

- Is the minicartridge formatted? The software performs the format and can take an hour or more.

- Retension the tape. Use the backup software to do this. Some tape drives require this, and others do not. **Retensioning** fast-forwards and rewinds the tape to eliminate loose spots.

- Take the minicartridge out and reboot. Try the minicartridge again.

- Try using a new minicartridge. The old one may have worn out.

- As with floppy disks, if the tape was removed from the drive while the drive light was on, the data being written at that time may not be readable.

Data transfer is slow

- Does the tape software have an option for optimizing speed or data compression? Try turning one, and then the other, off and on.

- Some tape drives can use an optional accelerator card to speed up data transfer. See the tape drive user guide.

- Try a new minicartridge.

- If the tape drive can do so, completely erase the tape and reformat it. Be sure that the tape drive can perform this procedure before you tell the software to do it.

- If you have installed an accelerator card, verify that the card is connected to the tape drive.

- Check that there is enough memory for the software to run.

$A^{+CORE}_{2.2}$ **The drive does not work after the installation**

- Check that pin 1 is oriented correctly to the data cable at both ends.
- Check for a resource conflict. The tape drive normally requires an IRQ, DMA channel, and I/O address.
- For DOS, check the entries in CONFIG.SYS and AUTOEXEC.BAT.

The drive fails intermittently or gives errors

- The tape might be worn out. Try a new tape.
- Clean the read/write head of the tape drive. See the tape drive user guide for directions.
- For an external tape drive, move the drive as far as you can from the monitor and computer case.
- Reformat the tape.
- Retension the tape.
- Verify that you are using the correct tape type and tape format.

Removable Drives

$A^{+}_{1.3}^{OS}$ New media such as read-writable CDs or Jaz drives are becoming popular for PC backups because they can be used for other purposes as well, and because their prices have recently been reduced. As discussed in Chapter 6, Zip drives come in 100-MB or 250-MB sizes. SuperDisk holds 120 MB of data, and Jaz drives hold 1 GB or 2 GB of data. These removable drives are ideal for backups as long as the data fits on one disk. When data can fit on a single removable disk, a quick and easy method of backing up data to one of these disks is to create a shortcut on your desktop that executes a small batch file (text file with .BAT file extension). The example below demonstrates how to create a shortcut to back up the \Data directory, its files, and subdirectories:

1. Using Notepad or WordPad, type this command line, where the removable drive is E and the /S parameter tells the OS to include subdirectories when copying (Hidden files will not be copied, but data is not usually hidden.):

   ```
   XCOPY C:\DATA\*.* E: /S
   ```

2. Save the file as **\Data\BATCH.BAT** and exit the editor.

3. Create a shortcut to the BATCH.BAT file.

4. Since .BAT files are DOS files, the icon on the desktop will be the MSDOS icon. To change the icon, right-click the icon, select **Properties** from the shortcut menu, click the **Program** tab, and click **Change Icon** (see Figure 19-12). Select an icon, then click **OK** twice to return to the desktop.

19

Figure 19-12   Change the icon for the BACKUP.BAT shortcut

5. Whenever you want to back up your data, place a disk in the drive and double-click the shortcut icon.

TIP
The batch file just created is very simple and only uses DOS commands. Window a much more sophisticated tool, Windows Scripting Host (WSH), to execute scrip programmers have written using a scripting language such as VBScript or JScri script is stored in a file that can be placed as an icon on the desktop. To run script, type **wscript.exe filename** in the Run dialog box, substituting filename w name of the script file or double-click on the desktop icon.

Backup Methods

You can use more sophisticated methods to create backups in which the backup process is selective, only backing up what's changed, what has not been recently backed up, and so forth. Traditionally, these methods all involve backing up to tapes, because a tape is more likely to be large enough to contain an entire backup. In discussing these methods, we use tapes as our medium. These backup methods are designed to reuse tapes and to make the backup process more efficient. The child, parent, grandparent method is a plan for reusing tapes. Full, incremental, and differential backup methods speed up the backup process, and scheduled backups minimize the inconvenience to users. Selective backups only back up data that changes often on the hard drive. By selecting only certain critical folders on the drive to back up, the backup routine goes much faster, and recovery of lost data is much easier.

The Child, Parent, Grandparent Method

Before you perform routine hard drive backups, devise a backup plan or procedure. One common plan, called the **child, parent, grandparent method**, makes it easy to reuse tapes. This method is explained in Table 19-4. Put the plan in writing and keep a log of backups performed.

Table 19-4   The child, parent, grandparent backup method

Name of Backup	How Often Performed	Storage Location	Description
Child backup	Daily	On-site	Keep four daily backup tapes and rotate them each week. Label the four tapes Monday, Tuesday, Wednesday, and Thursday. A Friday daily (child) backup is not made, because on Friday you'll make the parent backup.
Parent backup	Weekly	Off-site	Perform the weekly backup on Friday. Keep five weekly backup tapes, one for each Friday of the month, and rotate them each month. Label the tapes Friday 1, Friday 2, Friday 3, Friday 4, and Friday 5.
Grandparent backup	Monthly	Off-site, in a fireproof vault	Perform the monthly backup on the last Friday of the month. Keep 12 tapes, one for each month. Rotate them each year. Label the tapes January, February, and so on.

Full, Incremental, and Differential Backups

A+ OS
1.3

Some backup methods are more efficient because they do not always create a complete backup of all data. A **full backup** backs up all data from the hard drive. An **incremental backup** backs up only files that have changed or that have been created since the last backup, *whether that backup is itself an incremental or full backup.* **Differential backups** back up files that have changed or been created since the last *full* backup.

Begin by performing a full backup. The next time you back up, choose the incremental method to back up only files that have changed or been created since the full backup. The second time you perform an incremental backup, you back up only the files that have changed or been created since the last incremental backup.

For example, using the child, parent, grandparent method, you can perform a full backup each Friday. Monday through Thursday, you perform incremental backups. The advantage of this method is that incremental backups are faster and require less tape space than full backups. The disadvantage is that, to recover data, you must begin with the last full backup and work your way forward through each incremental backup until the time that the data was lost. This process can be time consuming. Plan to make a full backup after at least every sixth or seventh incremental backup. The Windows 9x, Windows NT, and Windows 2000 backup utilities support incremental backups.

If you create differential backups with the child, parent, grandparent method, create a full backup on Fridays. On Monday, do a differential backup to back up all files that have changed since Friday. On Tuesday, a differential backup also backs up all files that have changed since Friday (the full backup). Differential backups don't consider whether other differential backups have been performed, but compare data only to the last full backup, which is how differential backups and incremental backups differ. Another difference is that incremental backups mark

19

files as backed up by clearing the archive bit in the attribute byte, but the differential backup does not mark a file as having been backed up. The advantage of differential backups over incremental ones is that if you need to recover data, you only need to recover from the last full backup and the last differential backup. Differential backups are not supported by Windows 95, but are supported by Windows 98, Windows NT, and Windows 2000.

Scheduling Backups

A+ OS
1.3

Backups can be performed manually by a user sitting at the computer or can be scheduled to run automatically without user interaction. A scheduled backup is automatically performed by software when the computer is commonly not in use, such as during the middle of the night. Windows 98, Windows NT, and Windows 2000 support scheduling any program (including backup tasks) to execute at designated dates and times without user intervention. Using Windows 98, do the following to schedule the BATCH.BAT program created earlier in the chapter to run at 11:59 p.m. every Monday night:

1. Double-click **My Computer** on the desktop, and then double-click **Scheduled Tasks** to open the Scheduled Tasks window (see Figure 19-13).

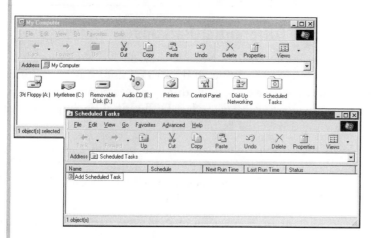

Figure 19-13   Add a scheduled task under Windows 98

2. Double-click **Add Scheduled Task**. The Scheduled Task Wizard appears (see Figure 19-14). Select the program to schedule: Click **Browse**, find and click the **BATCH.BAT** file in the \Data folder, and click **Open**.

3. Enter a name for the scheduled task, select how often to perform the task, and then click **Next**.

4. Enter the start time and select the day of the week for the task to execute. For example, enter **11:59 PM every Monday**. Click **Next**.

5. The wizard reports the scheduled task parameters. Click **Finish**.

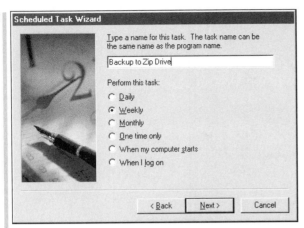

Figure 19-14   Name the scheduled task and select how often it runs

6. To change the settings for a scheduled task, double-click **My Computer**, double-click **Scheduled Tasks**, and right-click the task in the Scheduled Task window. Select **Properties** from the shortcut menu (see Figure 19-15). The task Properties dialog box opens (see Figure 19-16).

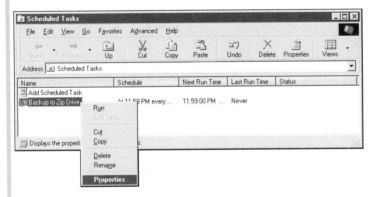

Figure 19-15   To change the task settings, use the Properties box of the task listed in the Scheduled Tasks window

7. Click the **Settings** tab to change the task settings. Notice at the bottom of the Settings sheet that you can direct the scheduler to wake the computer to perform the task. This feature requires a system board that supports the option for software to power up the PC. To know if your system board supports the feature, see CMOS setup or the system-board documentation. If not, then the PC must be turned on for the scheduler to work.

19

A+ OS
1.3

Figure 19-16 With some computers, the task scheduler can power up the computer to run the task

Backup Software

A+ OS
1.3

Most tape drives come with some backup software. You can also purchase third-party backup software or use Windows 9x, Windows NT, or Windows 2000 for backing up your hard drive. Because the software only backs up files that are not currently in use, close all files before performing a backup.

Windows 9x Backup Utility

Windows 9x offers a backup utility that can back up to floppy disks and tape drives. Windows 98 supports many popular backup devices that Windows 95 did not, including those using parallel ports, IDE/ATAPI, and SCSI devices. To use drives and tapes not supported by Windows 9x, you also must use third-party backup software.

If the Windows 9x Backup component is not installed under Windows 9x, you can install it as follows:

1. Click **Start**, point to **Settings**, click **Control Panel**, and double-click **Add/Remove Programs**.

2. Click the **Windows Setup** tab.

3. Under **Disk Tools** for Windows 95 or **System Tools** for Windows 98, select **Backup**. Click **OK** and then click **Apply** to install the component. Supply the original Windows 9x floppy disks or CD so that the OS can complete the installation.

A+ OS
1.3

To use the Windows 98 Microsoft Backup utility, do the following:

1. Click **Start**, point to **Programs**, **Accessories**, **System Tools**, and click **Backup**. The Backup Wizard first searches for backup devices such as Zip or tape drives. If it finds none, it asks if you want to install one. Otherwise, it displays a window asking if you want to create a new backup job or open an existing job. The Backup utility keeps information about backup jobs under a name that you give it, so you can use the same job many times. Select **Create a new backup job** and click **Next** to continue.

2. The Backup Wizard asks you questions about what type of backup you want (for example, back up all files or only those files that have changed since the last backup). Make your selections and then click **Next**.

3. The Microsoft Backup utility opens the Backup window, as shown in Figure 19-17.

Figure 19-17 Windows 98 Microsoft Backup allows you to select files and folders to back up

4. To back up only certain folders, files, or logical drives, check the boxes to the left of their names. To display a list of all subfolders under a folder, click the box with the + sign in it. Backup indicates that only parts of a folder or drive are selected for backup by placing a gray check in the box.

19

A+ OS
1.3

5. From the **Where to back up** list box of the Backup window shown in Figure 19-17, select the medium and directory to use. In the figure the medium is drive D, a Zip drive. The backup file will go into a folder named \Backup.

6. Click **Start** to begin the backup.

To recover files, folders, or the entire hard drive from backup using the Windows 98 Backup utility, follow these directions:

1. On the Backup utility window, shown in Figure 19-17, click the **Restore** tab. Select the backup job to use for the restore process. The Backup utility displays the folders and files that were backed up with this job. You can select the ones that you want to restore.

2. Click **Start** to restore the files.

Disk Cloning Software

You can back up a hard drive to replicate the drive to a new computer, such as when you deploy a new operating system with applications software on multiple computers in a corporate or educational lab. This process is called **disk cloning** or **disk imaging** and is best done with software designed for that purpose. Examples of disk imaging software are Drive Image by PowerQuest (see *www.powerquest.com*), ImageCast by Innovative Software (see *www.imagecast.com*), and Norton Ghost by Symantec Corp (see *www.symantec.com*).

RAID

Besides maintaining good backups, you can also protect data by continuously writing two copies of the data, each to a different hard drive. This method is most often used on high-end, high-cost file servers, but it is occasionally appropriate for a single-user workstation.

Collectively, these several methods, used to improve performance and/or automatically recover from a failure, are called RAID (redundant array of independent disks). There are several levels of RAID, but this section discusses only the three most commonly used (Table 19-5). Only the first level is financially practical for a standalone workstation.

RAID Level 0 increases the logical drive capacity by treating two drives as a single logical drive, but it includes only one copy of data. Therefore, it does not let you recover from a failure (an important feature of fault tolerance). RAID 0 is one method of **disk striping**, in which more than one hard drive is treated as a single volume. For an array of two hard drives, some data is written to one hard drive and some to the other; both drives make up one logical drive, or volume, and data is only written once. RAID 0 is supported by Windows NT and Windows 2000, but not by Windows 9x.

RAID Level 1 is designed to protect data from a hard drive failure by writing the data twice, once to each of two drives. One type of RAID Level 1 is called **disk mirroring**, in which the two hard drives both use the same adapter card.

Table 19-5 The three most common RAID levels

RAID Level and Common Name	Intended Purpose	Description
RAID 0: Disk striping without parity (striping refers to writing data across more than one physical drive)	Increases system performance and volume capacity	Data is written to two or more hard drives. The set of drives is treated as a single volume (a single virtual drive). Because more than one drive is doing the work, performance improves.
RAID 1: Disk mirroring or disk duplexing	Provides fault tolerance	Data is written twice, once to each of two drives. Disk mirroring uses only a single HD adapter. Disk duplexing uses two adapters, one for each drive.
RAID 5: Disk striping with parity	Increases performance and volume capacity and provides fault tolerance	Data is written to three or more drives, and parity information is distributed across these drives so that, if one drive fails, the other drives can re-create the data stored on the failed drive.

The advantages of RAID 1 disk mirroring are:

- If either drive fails, the data is still safe on the other drive.

- Disk reads are speeded up because the adapter has two places to read from.

The disadvantages of RAID 1 are:

- Having two hard drives in the same computer is more expensive.

- Because the data is written twice, hard drive capacity is, in effect, cut in half.

- Disk writes are slowed down because the data must be written twice.

One weakness in drive mirroring is that both hard drives are using the same adapter. If the adapter fails, neither hard drive is accessible. An improvement of disk mirroring, also considered RAID 1, is **duplexing**, in which each hard drive has its own adapter card. The initial cost is higher, but if one adapter fails, you are protected from losing the data on both drives. If a workstation cannot backup to a server on a network, disk mirroring or duplexing might be appropriate (if the data is considered valuable enough to merit the added expense).

Windows NT Workstation does not support RAID 1, so to use it on a workstation, the two hard drives must be managed by firmware on the controllers rather than by the OS. The more sophisticated hard drive controller increases the hardware expense. Windows NT Server supports RAID 1 and RAID 5.

RAID 5, or disk striping with parity, is an interesting variation of RAID 0 combined with RAID 1 and RAID 4, and improves fault tolerance and drive capacity. RAID 5 requires at

19

least three hard drives. To understand RAID 5, we must first examine how RAID 4 works. In Figure 19-18, RAID 4 uses four hard drives grouped as one virtual hard drive. When any data is written to this one drive, the data is divided into three segments. Each segment is written to one of the first three drives, and parity information about the three segments is written to the fourth drive.

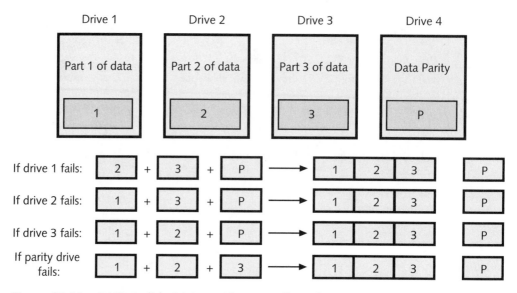

Figure 19-18   RAID 4, disk striping with parity, allows for increased drive capacity as well as fault tolerance: any one drive can fail and data can still be re-created

If any of the four drives fails, the data can be recovered from the other three drives using the method illustrated in the lower half of Figure 19-18. Using any two segments and the parity information, the three segments can be recreated, or, if the parity drive fails, the three segments are still safely stored on the first three drives. With RAID 5, rather than storing all parity information on a single, dedicated parity drive, parity information is distributed over all the drives, thus removing the performance bottleneck created by having a single parity drive.

To understand how data is recovered using parity information, consider this simple example. Suppose three numbers are stored on three different drives. If you store the sum of the three numbers on the fourth, or parity, drive, you can use the information you have to calculate a missing number. For example, let's say the three numbers are 1, 2, and 6, you store their sum (9) on the parity drive. If the first number is lost, you can calculate it from the sum and the other two numbers.

When a drive fails, the data can be regenerated on the replacement drive using information from the other drives. First replace the failed drive with a new drive. To generate the data on the new drive when using Windows NT Server, go to the Disk Administrator of the Administrator Tools and execute a Regenerate command. Windows NT does the rest. The action is automatic, and you can still use the computer for other operations while regenerating is taking place.

For file servers using RAID 5 that must work continuously, it might be practical to use hardware that allows for hard drive hot swapping, which means that you can remove one hard drive and insert another without powering down the computer. However, hard drives that can be hot swapped cost significantly more than regular hard drives.

Windows 2000 Dynamic Drives

Windows 2000 offers a new feature called dynamic drives that protects the information stored in partition tables of traditional drives. (Using Windows 2000 terminology, hard drives that use partition tables are called **basic drives**.) Recall from earlier chapters that the partition table shares the same first sector at the beginning of the drive with the master boot program. Because the master boot program is often the target of boot sector viruses, the partition table is vulnerable to attack. Windows 2000 solves this by storing information about partitions in a 1-MB database written at the end of the hard drive, rather than at the beginning. The hard drive is then called a **dynamic drive** and the partitions are called **volumes**. When you upgrade a hard drive from basic to dynamic, the information in the partition table is moved to the database at the end of the drive. DOS and Windows 9x can have only two partitions; Windows NT can have up to four, but Windows 2000 can have up to 26 volumes, limited only by the number of letters in the alphabet.

Windows 2000 Professional can also link several volumes spread across multiple hard drives, called **spanned volumes**, which creates one logical drive. Windows 2000 Professional supports RAID 0 and calls it a striped volume. In addition to spanned volumes and striped volumes, Windows 2000 Server supports RAID 1, which it calls a mirrored volume, and RAID 5, which it calls RAID-5 volume.

To create any type of RAID volume under Windows 2000, you must use dynamic drives, although, if you are upgrading from Windows NT to Windows 2000 and already have a RAID system set up, Windows 2000 supports the setup using basic drives. The primary advantage of using dynamic drives over basic drives is that the 1-MB database not only contains information about the volumes on its hard drive, but also automatically contains information about all volumes on all hard drives in the system. This database is automatically replicated on all drives. If one database fails, it is quickly and automatically restored using a copy of the database on another drive. Dynamic drives have little advantage for a system with only a single hard drive, especially considering that only Windows 2000 can read dynamic drives.

Planning for Disaster Recovery

The time to prepare for a disaster is before it occurs. If you have not prepared, the damage from a disaster will probably be greater than if you had made and followed disaster plans. Suppose the hard drive on your PC stopped working and you lost all its data. What would be the impact? Are you prepared for this event? Backups are important, but you should also know how to use them to recover lost data. Also know when the backup was made and what to do to recover information entered since the last backup. Here's where careful record-keeping can pay off.

When you perform a backup for the first time or set up a scheduled backup, verify that you can use the backup tape or disks to successfully recover the data. This is a very important step

19

in preparing to recover lost data. After you have created a backup tape, erase a file on the hard drive, and use the recovery procedures to verify that you can recreate the file from the backup. This verifies that the tape or floppy disk works, the recovery software is effective, and that you know how to use it. After you are convinced that the recovery works, document how to perform the recovery.

TIP   Verify that your recovery plan will work by practicing it before a disaster occurs.

Always record your regular backups in a table with the following information: the folders or drives backed up, the date of the backup, the type of backup, and the name of the tape used. Refer to this table to recover data that was lost days or weeks before you discovered that should be recovered. Keep the records in a notebook. You can also store the records in a log file (a file where events are logged or recorded) each time you back up; always keep hard copies of log files in a paper file. The log-file method might be too time-consuming to do daily. Even though the software automatically records events to the log file, the backup will take longer because of the extra writing, and printing the file later will also consume time.

Periodically fully restore a hard drive that you back up. Use the tape made from a full backup and a different hard drive. Restore the first hard drive to the new hard drive and compare the results so you are confident that your backups can recover from a disaster.

CHAPTER SUMMARY

- ❏ PC failures are caused by many environmental and human factors, including heat, dust, magnetism, power supply problems, static electricity, spilled liquids, viruses, and human error.

- ❏ The goals of preventive maintenance are to make PCs last longer and work better, protect data and software, and reduce the cost of repairs.

- ❏ A PC preventive maintenance plan includes blowing dust from the inside of the computer case, cleaning the contacts on expansion cards, keeping a record of setup, backing up the hard drive, and cleaning the mouse, monitor, and keyboard.

- ❏ Protecting software and hardware documentation is an important preventive maintenance chore.

- ❏ Never ship a PC when the only copy of important data is on its hard drive.

- ❏ Computer infestations include viruses, Trojan horses, and worms, which are categorized by how they are transmitted.

- ❏ Antivirus software is your best defense against the damage caused by viruses.

- ❏ Viruses can hide in program files, boot sectors, and documents that contain macros. They attempt to cloak themselves from antivirus software by changing their distinguishing characteristics and masking their presence.

❏ Some viruses are relatively harmless, only displaying garbage on the computer screen. Others can be so destructive they erase everything on a hard drive, including partition table information.

❏ Steps you can take to prevent viruses from infesting your computer include not trading floppy disks, buying software from reliable sources, downloading programs from reliable sites on the Internet, and using networks with caution.

❏ A virus hoax is intended to overload network traffic. It works by tricking people into forwarding e-mail messages about viruses.

❏ To protect against damage by viruses, use antivirus software and back up your hard drive regularly.

❏ Tape drives are the most common hardware devices used to back up a hard drive, and come in many types and formats.

❏ Use RAID (redundant array of independent disks) to mirror data stored on a hard disk and to increase hard drive capacity by making more than one hard drive work as a single virtual drive.

❏ Use the child, parent, grandparent method of backing up data to reuse tapes according to a straightforward and easy-to-follow plan.

❏ Using a full backup, followed by incremental or differential backups, speeds up the time it takes to make a backup.

❏ Scheduled backups are performed when no one is using the computer.

❏ Windows 9x, Windows NT and Windows 2000 include a Backup utility that can be used with tape drives. In addition, Windows 9x Backup can use floppy disks, and Windows 2000 Backup can use several types of storage media including those on a network.

❏ When planning for disaster recovery, keep careful records of backups and periodically test your backup method to ensure that you can successfully recover lost data. Have a written disaster recovery plan.

KEY TERMS

Antivirus (AV) software — Utility programs that prevent infection, or scan a system to detect and remove viruses. McAfee Associates VirusScan and Norton AntiVirus are two popular AV packages.

Basic drive — In Windows 2000, a drive that uses a partition table at the beginning of the drive to hold information about the drive's primary and extended partitions. Compare to dynamic drive.

Boot sector virus — An infectious program that can replace the boot program with a modified, infected version of the boot command utilities, often causing boot and data retrieval problems.

Child, parent, grandparent backup method — A plan for backing up and reusing tapes or removable disks by rotating them each week (child), month (parent), and year (grandparent).

19

Data cartridge — A type of tape medium typically used for backups. Full-sized data cartridges are 4 × 6 × ⅜ inches in size. A minicartridge is only 3¼ × 2½ × ⅗ inches.

Differential backup — Backs up only files that have changed or have been created since the last *full* backup. When recovering data, only two backups are needed: the full backup and the last differential backup.

Disk cloning — Making an exact image of a hard drive including partition information, boot sectors, operating system installation and applications software to replicate the hard drive on another system or recover from a hard drive crash. Also called disk imaging.

Disk duplexing — An improvement of disk mirroring, whereby redundant data is written to two or more drives, and each hard drive has its own adapter card. This provides greater protection than disk mirroring.

Disk imaging — *See* disk cloning

Disk mirroring — A strategy whereby the same data is written to two hard drives in a computer, to safeguard against hard drive failure. Disk mirroring uses only a single adapter for two drives.

Disk striping — Treating multiple hard drives as a single volume. Data is written across the multiple drives in small segments, in order to increase performance and logical disk volume, and, when parity is also used, to provide fault tolerance. RAID 5 is disk striping with an additional drive for parity.

Dynamic drive — In Windows 2000, a hard drive that uses a 1-MB database written at the end of the drive to hold information about volumes on the drive and RAID setup information.

Encrypting virus — A type of virus that transforms itself into a nonreplicating program in order to avoid detection. It transforms itself back into a replicating program in order to spread.

Fault tolerance — The degree to which a system can tolerate failures. Adding redundant components, such as disk mirroring or disk duplexing, is a way to build in fault tolerance.

File virus — A virus that inserts virus code into an executable program and can spread whenever that program is accessed.

Full backup — A complete backup, whereby all of the files on the hard drive are backed up each time the backup procedure is performed. It is the safest backup method, but it takes the most time.

Incremental backup — A time-saving backup method that only backs up files changed or newly created since the last full *or* incremental backup. Multiple incremental backups might be required when recovering lost data.

Infestation — Any unwanted program that is transmitted to a computer without the user's knowledge and that is designed to do varying degrees of damage to data and software. There are a number of different types of infestations, including viruses, Trojan horses, worms, and time bombs, among others.

Macro — A small sequence of commands, contained within a document, that can be automatically executed when the document is loaded, or executed later by using a predetermined keystroke.

Macro virus — A virus that can hide in the macros of a document file. Typically, viruses do not reside in data or document files.

Material safety data sheet (MSDS) — A document that provides information about how to properly handle substances such as chemical solvents including physical data, toxicity, health effects, first aid, storage, disposal, and spill procedures.

Memory-resident virus — A virus that can stay lurking in memory, even after its host program is terminated.

Minicartridge — A tape drive cartridge that is only 3¼ × 2½ × ⅗ inches. It is small enough to allow two drives to fit into a standard 5½-inch drive bay of a PC case.

Multipartite virus — A combination of a boot sector virus and a file virus. It can hide in either type of program.

Non-memory-resident virus — A virus that is terminated when the host program is closed. Compare to memory-resident virus.

Polymorphic virus — A type of virus that changes its distinguishing characteristics as it replicates itself. Mutating in this way makes it more difficult for AV software to recognize the presence of the virus.

Quarter-Inch Committee or **quarter-inch cartridge (QIC)** — A name of a standardized method used to write data to tape. Backups made with the Windows 9x System Tools Backup utility have a .qic extension.

RAID (redundant array of inexpensive disks or **redundant array of independent disks)** — Several methods of configuring multiple hard drives to store data to increase logical volume size and improve performance, and to ensure that if one hard drive fails, the data is still available from another hard drive.

Retension — A tape maintenance procedure that fast-forwards and then rewinds the tape to eliminate loose spots on the tape.

Sequential access — A method of data access used by tape drives whereby data is written or read sequentially from the beginning to the end of the tape or until the desired data is found.

Spanned volumes — Windows 2000 method of linking several volumes across multiple hard drives into a single logical drive

Stealth virus — A virus that actively conceals itself by temporarily removing itself from an infected file that is about to be examined, and then hiding a copy of itself elsewhere on the drive.

Trojan horse — A type of infestation that hides or disguises itself as a useful program, yet is designed to cause damage at a later time.

Virus — A program that often has an incubation period, is infectious, and is intended to cause damage. A virus program might destroy data and programs or damage a disk drive's boot sector.

Virus signature — The distinguishing characteristics or patterns of a particular virus. Typically, AV signature updates for new viruses can be downloaded monthly from the Internet.

Volumes — In Windows 2000, a partition on a hard drive that is formatted as a dynamic drive.

Worm — An infestation designed to copy itself repeatedly to memory, on drive space, or on a network until little memory or disk space remains.

19

REVIEW QUESTIONS

1. List one or two preventive maintenance measures that help protect each of the following: computer case, CMOS setup, floppy drive, hard drive, keyboard, mouse, printer, and software.

2. List three things that should be done before moving or shipping a computer.

3. How do you properly dispose of a battery pack from a notebook computer? A broken monitor? A toner cartridge from a laser printer?

4. List and describe three types of viruses.

5. List three ways to "catch" a virus.

6. List three ways to prevent a virus.

7. List three symptoms or problems that indicate that a virus might be present.

8. How is disk mirroring different from disk duplexing?

9. When one hard drive can be removed and another hard drive inserted without powering down a computer, this is called _____.

10. Clearly explain how the child, parent, grandparent method works as a plan for reusing tapes.

11. How are differential backups different from full backups, and what are the advantages of each?

12. How are differential backups different from incremental backups, and what are the advantages of each?

13. Why would you want to "retension" a backup tape?

14. Give two reasons why you would want to schedule a hard drive backup to occur during the night.

15. Why is it important to verify that your disaster recovery plan works and to put it in writing?

PROJECTS

Hands-on
Project

Creating a Preventive Maintenance and Disaster Recovery Plan

Assume that you are a PC technician responsible for all of the 30 to 35 PCs of a small organization. The PCs are networked to a file server that is backed up each evening. No PC has power protection or line conditioning. Although some users make backups of data on their PC to tape drives or Zip drives, the company does not have a procedure to back up data or software. Your supervisor has asked you to submit a preventive maintenance and disaster recovery plan for these PCs and to estimate the amount of time you will spend each month for the next 12 months on preventive maintenance. She has also asked you to submit a suggested PC data backup plan for all users to follow, which will become a company policy. Do the following to create these plans and estimate your time.

1. List the possible causes of PC failures.

2. Using the list above, list what you can do to prevent these problems. Divide the list into two categories: what you plan to do one time for each PC or user, and what you plan to do on a routine or as-needed basis.

3. For each PC, estimate the amount of time you need to implement the one-time-only plan and the amount of time you need each year for ongoing maintenance.

4. Based on your answers to Question 3, how much time do you plan to spend, on average, each month for the next 12 months on preventive maintenance?

5. In response to the request for a recommended company policy to back up PC data, write a policy for users to follow to back up data on their PCs. Since all PCs are networked to the file server, suggest that company policy be that data on a PC should be backed up to the file server, where it will be backed up nightly in case of a file server failure. Write the backup policy and instructions on how to use it.

Using the Internet to Learn About Viruses

The classic source of information about viruses on the Web is Data Fellows. Go to the web site *www.datafellows.com/vir-info/*, shown in Figure 19-19, for information about viruses; the viruses are listed in alphabetical order with complete descriptions, including any known source of the virus. Print a description of three viruses from this web site:

1. One virus that destroys data on a hard drive

2. One harmless virus that only displays garbage on the screen

3. One virus that hides in a boot sector

Figure 19-19   For complete virus information, see the Data Fellows web site

19

Download the Latest Update of AV Software

If you own antivirus software, download the latest antivirus definition list from the Internet. For example, for Norton AntiVirus, follow these directions:

1. Log on to the AV site:

   www.symantec.com/avcenter

2. Click **Download Updates**. Answer the required questions, such as:

   Product: NAV for Windows 95

   Language: English, US

   Operating Environment: Windows 95

3. Follow the directions to download the latest update and signature list for the particular version of your AV software.

4. While online, see if the site offers information on virus hoaxes and create a list of hoaxes if it does.

Using Nuts & Bolts, McAfee VirusScan Software

Using the McAfee VirusScan software, scan a floppy disk for viruses.

Research the Market for a Tape Drive

To evaluate two tape drives for possible purchase, fill in the following table. Which drive seems more appropriate for a standalone PC that is used heavily for data entry and needs data backed up daily? Why?

	Tape Drive 1	Tape Drive 2
Product name		
Manufacturer		
Price		
Accelerator (yes/no/optional)		
Software included		
Type (internal/external)		
Warranty (1year/2 years/lifetime)		
Tape formats supported		
Maximum capacity (also indicate the tape format required to meet this maximum capacity, for example: 4.4 GB using QIC-3020)		
Types of cartridges supported		

Using Windows 98 to Back Up Files and Folders

This exercise lets you practice using Windows 98 Microsoft Backup and see how the Backup utility manages several situations.

Part I

1. Using Windows Explorer, create a folder called Backtest on a hard drive.

2. Use Explorer to find a .BAT file, and copy it to the new folder. Copy two other files to the Backtest folder. Make a subfolder called Subfolder in Backtest and copy a fourth file to C:\backtest\subfolder.

3. Right-click the .BAT file and rename it Overwrite.txt. Right-click the second file and rename it Delete.txt. Rename the third file NoChange.txt. The fourth file can be left alone for now. Use Explorer and write down the file sizes before the backup.

4. Click **Start**, **Programs**, **Accessories**, **System Tools**, and **Backup**.

5. Use the directions provided in this book to back up the folder Backtest to a floppy disk. Use Explorer and compare the backup file size to the original file sizes. How are they different?

6. Delete the file **Delete.txt**. Edit and change the contents of the file Overwrite.txt. Make no changes to the file NoChange.txt. Delete **Subfolder**.

7. Using Windows 98 Backup, restore the files from the backup to their original folder.

   a. What did Backup do with the Delete.txt file?

   b. What did Backup do with the Overwrite.txt file?

   c. What did Backup do with the NoChange.txt file?

   d. What did Backup do with the missing Subfolder and missing file?

   e. What is the name of the backup file on the floppy disk?

   f. What are the name and path to the error log created by Backup?

   g. Print the error log.

Part II

8. Use Windows Explorer to copy the Backtest folder to a second floppy disk.

9. Delete all the files in the Backtest folder on the hard drive.

10. Use Windows Explorer to copy the three files back to the Backtest folder.

11. Delete the files in the Backtest folder on the hard drive.

12. Open the Recycle Bin and restore the three files to the Backtest folder by highlighting the selected files and using the File, Restore option. Did they return to the correct folder?

13. Once again, delete the files in the Backtest folder on the hard drive.

14. Highlight the three files in the Recycle Bin, and choose **File**, **Delete**. Can you still restore the files?

19

Disposal Rules in Your Community

Research the laws and regulations in your community concerning the disposal of batteries and old computer parts. Answer these questions regarding your community:

1. How do you properly dispose of a monitor?

2. How do you properly dispose of a battery pack used by a notebook computer?

3. How do you properly dispose of a large box of assorted computer parts including hard drives, floppy drives, computer cases, and circuit boards?

20

THE PROFESSIONAL PC TECHNICIAN

In this chapter, you will learn:

- ♦ How to make and keep excellent customer relationships
- ♦ How to maintain a successful help desk
- ♦ How professional organizations and certifications can help you be a better PC technician
- ♦ About software copyrights and software piracy
- ♦ About how to stay abreast of new technology

As a professional PC technician, manage your professional career by staying abreast of new technology and striving for top professional certifications. In addition, you should maintain excellent customer relationships and professionalism, and seek opportunities for joining professional organizations. In Chapter 8, "Troubleshooting Fundamentals," you learned how to work with customers while trying to solve a problem for them. The chapter discussed what types of questions to ask, how to pose them, and how to maintain good customer relations. This chapter builds on that information, also addressing other topics that will help establish you as a high-quality PC professional.

As you know, PC technicians provide service to customers over the phone, in person on-site, and sometimes in a shop where they have little customer contact. While each setting poses specific challenges, almost all of the recommendations made in this chapter apply across the board. After all, even if your company is contracted to provide on-site service, you most likely will try to help solve problems first by phone. And even if you work in a shop, you might get calls from customers with questions or complaints. Focus on polishing all the skills needed in all the service settings in which you may find yourself.

WHAT CUSTOMERS WANT: BEYOND TECHNICAL KNOW-HOW

Probably the most significant indication that a PC technician is doing a good job is that his or her customers are consistently satisfied. The principle to follow to satisfy your customers is simple: provide excellent service and treat customers as you would want to be served and treated in a similar situation. Think about when you have been dependent on service technicians for help. Some probably helped you quickly, some needed a bit more time, and in some situations, the technician had to turn to someone else to help you. Many factors most likely affected your level of satisfaction, but one characteristic probably determined whether you were satisfied with the service you received: if you believed that the person did his or her best for you in your situation, you were much more likely to be satisfied with his or her performance. The right attitude from a service technician can be the deciding factor between satisfied and dissatisfied customers.

People who are personally committed to doing their very best in every situation tend to be the successful ones. If you have not already done so, make the personal commitment right now to always give your best in your profession, whether you plan on being a PC technician or not; this one decision can catapult you to success.

Part of giving your best is to be prepared, both technically and nontechnically. Being prepared includes knowing what customers want, what they don't like, and what they expect from a PC technician.

Your customers can be "internal" (you both work for the same company) or "external" (your customers come to you or your company for service). Customers can be highly technical or technically naive, represent a large company or simply own a home PC, be prompt or slow at paying their bills, want only the best (and be willing to pay for it) or be searching for bargain service, be friendly and easy to work with or demanding and condescending. In each situation, the key to success is always the same: don't allow circumstances or personalities to affect your personal commitment to excellence.

We've all heard, "If a job's worth doing, it's worth doing well." A disgruntled coworker once told me, "I'll do the job, but don't expect me to give my best. It just won't happen." Think of the worst situation you could be in with a customer—one that would cause you to take the same attitude as my disheartened coworker. Now that you've pictured that situation, see yourself doing your very best in it, not because of the situation or people involved, but because of *you* and *your* personal commitment to excellence. See the difference? A person's professional (or unprofessional) response should have nothing to do with specific circumstances and everything to do with the person. Incorporate this principle into your work, and you'll be an asset to your organization, personally successful, and favored in your profession. Up to this point, this book has emphasized your becoming a competent PC technician; the value of this cannot be overemphasized. However, all customers, whether technical or nontechnical, want more from you than technical proficiency. Listed below are qualities that distinguish one competent technician from another in the eyes of the customer. Specific ways to reinforce these qualities in your service are discussed later under "Learning to Be a Better Communicator."

- **Positive and Helpful Attitude.** A positive and helpful attitude helps to establish good customer relationships. Customers appreciate a friendly disposition and positive outlook. Smile. Don't belittle your customer's choice of hardware or software. Don't complain. Give compliments and state things positively when you can. Be empathic; put yourself in the customer's situation and respect his or her needs. Express your concern, especially when you are the bearer of bad news. A brief but sincere apology for the customer's complaint might take care of the customer, and can allow you to move forward and solve the problem quickly.

- **Dependability.** Customers appreciate those who do as they say. If you promise to be back at 10:00 the next morning, be back at 10:00 the next morning. If you cannot keep your appointment, never ignore your promise. Call, apologize, let the customer know what happened, and reschedule your appointment.

- **Being Customer-Focused.** When you're working with or talking to a customer, focus on him or her. Don't be distracted. Listen; take notes if appropriate. Make it your job to satisfy this person—not just your organization, your boss, your bank account, or the customer's boss. It might not always be possible to give customers exactly what they ask for, especially when a customer is not paying the bill directly, but try your best.

- **Credibility.** Convey confidence to your customers. Being credible means being technically competent and knowing how to do your job well, but a credible technician also knows when the job is beyond his or her level of expertise and when to ask for help. In most organizations, if you cannot address a customer's problem, you follow policies and procedures to pass the problem to more experienced or resourceful personnel. This process of passing the problem up organizational levels is often called **escalating**. Don't be afraid to escalate when you have exhausted your efforts or knowledge. Customers appreciate a technician who cares enough about their problem to take it to his or her boss.

- **Integrity and honesty.** Don't try to hide your mistakes—not with your customer or with your boss. Everyone makes mistakes, but don't compound them with a lack of integrity or failing to assume responsibility. Accept responsibility and do what you can to correct the error. When you take this approach to your mistakes, your credibility with your customer (and your boss) rises.

- **Know the law with respect to your work.** For instance, observe the laws concerning the use of software. Don't use or install pirated software (copies of software made in violation of the licensing agreement with the original purchaser). See the "Protecting Software Copyrights" section for details. You are expected to know what is legal and illegal in a software installation. Set an example by personally committing yourself to using only legally obtained software on your own PC and on your company's or customers' PCs. When asked if certain actions are legal, have the answer or know how to get it. You will be viewed by others as someone who can be trusted.

20

- **Professionalism.** Customers want a technician to look and behave profession-ally. Dress appropriately for the environment. For example, don't arrive at a cus-tomer site in a T-shirt and shorts or use the phone without permission. Consider yourself a guest at the customer site. See Chapter 8 concerning how to handle yourself on a site visit: what to do and not to do.

- **Perform your work in a professional manner.** If a customer is angry, allow the customer to vent, keeping your own professional distance. Remain calm and undefensive. (You do, however, have the right to expect a customer not to talk to you in an abusive way.)

SUPPORT CALLS: PROVIDING GOOD SERVICE

Customers want good service. Even though each customer is different and might expect dif-ferent results, the following characteristics consistently constitute good service in the eyes of most customers.

- The technician responds and completes the work within a reasonable time.

- For on-site visits, the technician is prepared for the service call.

- The work is done right the first time.

- The price for the work is reasonable and competitive.

- The technician exhibits good interpersonal skills.

- If the work extends beyond a brief on-site visit or phone call, the technician keeps the customer informed about the progress of the work.

Planning for Good Service

Whether you support PCs on the phone, on-site, or in a shop, you need a plan to follow when you approach a service call. Chapter 8 gave many guidelines and specific suggestions about PC troubleshooting from a technical point of view. This section surveys the entire service situation—from the first contact with the customer to closing the call. Follow these general guidelines when supporting computers and their users.

Taking the Initial Call

Almost every support project starts with a phone call, and your company likely has a policy with specific instructions on the information you should take when answering that initial call. Follow the guidelines of your company.

Don't assume that an on-site visit is necessary until you have asked questions to identify the problem and asked the caller to check and try some simple things while on the phone with you. For example, the customer can check cable connections, power, and monitor settings, and can look for POST error messages. Only after you have determined that the problem cannot be easily resolved on the phone should you make an appointment to go to the customer's location or ask the customer to bring the PC to you. If an on-site visit is needed, make an appointment and fill out the proper documentation (discussed below) while the caller is on the phone.

Customer Service Policies

Be familiar with your company's customer service policies. You might need to refer questions about warranties, licenses, documentation, or procedures to other support personnel or customer relations personnel. Your organization might not want you to answer some questions, such as questions about upcoming releases of software or new products, or what your personal or company experience has been supporting particular hardware or software.

Be clear on how your organization wants you to handle these situations, and stay current with new information. You might find it helpful to get to know other employees at your company and their specialties. Then you will know who to call when confronted with a difficult or critical situation that is beyond your expertise.

Troubleshooting

A+ OS
3.2

CORE
2.2

After reviewing your company's service policies, follow these general guidelines for effective troubleshooting:

- Let the customer explain the problem in his or her own way. Take notes, and then interview the customer about the problem so you understand it thoroughly. Have the customer reproduce the problem and carefully note each step taken and its results. This process gives you clues about the problem and about the technical proficiency of the customer, which helps you know how to communicate with the customer. (See Chapter 8 for specific questions you can ask.)

- Search for answers. If the answers to specific questions or problems are not evident, become a researcher. Learn to use online documentation, expert systems, and other resources that your company provides. See the "Recordkeeping and Information Tools" section for more details.

- Develop your troubleshooting skills. Isolate the problem. Check for user error. What works and what doesn't work? What has changed since the system last worked? Reduce the system to essentials. Check the simple things first. Use the troubleshooting guidelines in Appendix E to help you think of approaches to test and try.

- If you have given the problem your best, but still haven't solved it, ask for help, as discussed below.

Asking for Help

You learn when to ask for help from experience. Once you have made a reasonable effort to help, and it seems clear that you are unlikely to be successful, don't waste a customer's time. Ask a coworker for help or escalate the problem according to your company's policy. Many times, describing the problem to a coworker helps you think through it more thoroughly, and reminds you of the solution you already know.

20

Documentation and Other Aids

After a call, create a written record to build your own knowledge base. Record the initial symptoms of the problem, the source of the problem you actually discovered, how you made that discovery, and how the problem was finally solved. Don't waste time researching a problem more than once. Write down what you know so you retain the knowledge you have gained.

Organize your documentation for quick reference. For example, you can file documentation according to symptoms or according to solutions. In your documentation, carefully record the problem's symptoms and what you did to solve them. Later, you can save time by following your own instructions created from past calls.

Making a Service Call

When a technician makes an on-site service call, customers expect him or her to have both technical and interpersonal skills. Prepare for a service call by reviewing information given you by whoever took the call. For example:

- Know the problem you are going to address.
- Know what computer, software, and hardware need servicing.
- Know the urgency of the situation.
- Arrive with a complete set of equipment appropriate to the visit, which might include a tool kit, flashlight, multimeter, grounding strap and mat, and bootable disks that have been scanned for viruses.
- As discussed earlier, dress in an appropriate manner.

A+CORE 2.2   Set a realistic time for the appointment (one that you can expect to keep) and arrive on time. If you are unavoidably delayed, call the customer and let him or her know what to expect. When you arrive at the customer's site, greet the customer in a friendly manner. Use Mr. or Ms. and last names rather than first names when addressing the customer, unless you are certain that the customer expects you to use first names. The first thing you should do is listen— save the paperwork for later.

- Listen carefully to the customer explain the problem.
- Allow the customer to say everything he or she wants to say before you make suggestions or offer solutions.
- When talking with the customer, judge the technical knowledge that the customer has, and speak with the customer at that level.
- Never respond to the customer in a condescending or patronizing way.

As you work, be as unobtrusive as possible. Don't make a big mess. Keep your tools and papers out of the customer's way. Don't use the phone or sit in the customer's desk chair without permission. If the customer needs to attend to his or her own work while you are present, do whatever is necessary to accommodate that. Remember that you are a guest at the customer's site, and act accordingly.

Express genuine concern for the customer's problem and predicament. Although you want a customer to have confidence in your skills to resolve the problem, do not project the attitude that the problem is not serious.

Keep the customer informed:

- Once you have collected enough information, explain to the customer what the problem is and what you must do to fix it, giving as many details as the customer wants.

- When a customer must make a choice, state the customer's options so that you are not unfairly favoring the solution that makes the most money for you as the technician or for your company.

Allow the customer time to be fully satisfied that all is working before you close the call. Does the printer work? Print a test page. Does the network connection work? Can the customer log on to the network and access data on it? If you changed anything on the PC after you booted it, reboot one more time to make sure that you have not caused a problem with the boot. It's tempting to stop when you have fixed the problem. However, double-check that you have not inadvertently caused a new problem. Take the time to convince yourself and the customer that he or she can simply go back to work after you leave.

After the problem is solved and the fix tested, one of your final steps should be to review the service call with the customer. Summarize the instructions and explanations you have given during the call. This is an appropriate time to fill out your paperwork and explain to the customer what you have written. However, if the customer is not interested or does not have the time to listen, then don't pressure him or her to do so.

Before you leave, if you see things that the customer can do to prevent this same problem or some other problem from occurring, share that knowledge with the customer. Explain preventive maintenance to the customer (such as deleting temporary files from the hard drive or cleaning the mouse). Most customers don't have preventive maintenance contracts for their PCs and appreciate your time to show them how they can take better care of their computers.

Phone Support

Providing phone support requires more interaction with customers than any other type of PC support. To give clear instructions, you must be able to visualize what the customer is seeing at his or her PC. Customers might have technical knowledge, or might be only slightly computer literate. Patience is required if the customer must be told each key to press or command button to click. Help-desk support requires excellent communication skills, good phone manners, and lots of patience and empathy.

During the call, follow the guidelines outlined in the "Be a Better Communicator" section. Make few, if any, assumptions. Have the caller check simple things, such as making sure that

20

the PC or monitor is plugged into a power source and that cables are securely and correctly connected. As your help-desk skills improve, you will learn to think through the process as though you were sitting in front of the PC yourself. Drawing diagrams and taking notes as you talk can be very helpful.

As with on-site service calls, let the user make sure that all is working before you close the phone call. If you end the call too soon and the problem is not completely resolved, the customer can be frustrated, especially if it is difficult to contact you again.

If you spend many hours on the phone at a help desk, use a headset instead of a regular phone to reduce strain on your ears and neck. Learn how to use your telephone system well so that you don't accidentally disconnect someone. If you are accidentally disconnected, call back immediately. Don't eat or drink while on the phone. If you must put callers on hold, tell them how long it will be before you get back to them. When the call is over, wait for the caller to hang up first. Don't complain about your job, your company, or other companies or products to your customers. A little small talk is okay and is sometimes beneficial in easing a tense situation, but keep it upbeat and positive.

Be a Better Communicator

Most people assume they are good communicators—that others understand what they are saying and that they in turn understand others. However, almost anyone can improve his or her communication skills by following some specific guidelines; this section presents those guidelines as they apply to PC support technicians. For the PC technician, on-the-job training often involves only technical knowledge and skills, not communication skills. Yet, without good communication skills, even a good technician can't effectively deliver his or her support. Customers often form their opinion of your organization on the basis of the way you communicate with them.

Communicating on the Phone

When someone calls asking for support, you must control the call, especially at the beginning. Follow these steps at the beginning of a service call.

- Identify yourself and your organization. (Follow the guidelines of your employer as to what to say.)

- Ask for and write down the name and phone number of the caller. Ask for spelling if necessary. If your help-desk supports businesses, get the name of the business that the caller represents.

- Your company might require that you obtain a licensing or warranty number to determine if the customer is entitled to receive your support free of charge, or that you obtain a credit card number, if the customer is paying by the call. Get whatever information you need at this point to determine that you should be the one to provide service before you start to address the problem. It might be necessary to refer the call to someone else in the organization, such as a customer service representative.

- Open up the conversation for the caller to describe his or her problem.

Be certain to write down a caller's name correctly, and use that name as you speak. Ask for a phone number in case you are disconnected during the call or need to call back later. As a caller describes his or her problem, listen carefully, focus on the call, and don't allow yourself to be distracted.

Show Concern for the Customer's Situation

Empathy promotes communication. You can communicate with empathy by saying things like, "I understand," "You've really had it rough!" "That's terrible," "I know you must be frustrated," and "I'm sorry you're having such a hard time." On the other hand, if you really don't care, don't try to fake it with one of these phrases because you'll most likely sound patronizing and insincere, which can alienate your customer.

Express Confidence

You can communicate confidence to your customer in the following ways:

- Speak calmly.

- Ask questions in a systematic way. A good way to do this is to have a written list of questions.

- Take your time, and pause when necessary. Don't allow the urgency of a situation to fluster you.

- Plan ahead how you will handle a situation in which you don't know what to do. For example, you can say, "Excuse me while I check with my coworkers," or you can say, "I've got to research this; I'll get back to you shortly." Be sure to say exactly when you will call back or return to the customer's desk.

- Don't be defensive about the software or hardware you are supporting, or about your own degree of knowledge or experience.

- Adjust your communication to your customer's level of technical ability.

Handling Difficult Situations

Be prepared to handle difficult situations when communicating with a customer on the phone or face to face. Here are a few guidelines.

When the Customer Is Not Knowledgeable A help-desk call is the most difficult situation to handle when a customer is not knowledgeable about how to use a computer. When on-site, you can put a PC in good repair without depending on a customer to help you, but when you are trying to solve a problem over the phone, with a customer as your only eyes, ears, and hands, a computer-illiterate user can present a very challenging situation. Here are some tips for handling this situation.

20

- Don't use computer jargon while talking. Describe things in a way that the customer can understand. For example, instead of saying, "Open File Manager," say,

"Do you see the yellow filing cabinet that has File Manager written underneath? Using your left mouse button, double-click on it."

- Don't ask the customer to do something that might destroy settings or files, without first having him or her back them up carefully. If you think the customer can't handle what you need done, then ask for some on-site help.

- Frequently ask the customer what he or she sees on the screen to help you track the keystrokes and action.

- Follow along at your own PC. It's easier to direct the customer, keystroke by keystroke, if you are doing the same things.

- Give the customer plenty of opportunity to ask questions.

- Compliment the customer whenever you can, to help the customer gain confidence.

- If you determine that the customer cannot help you solve the problem without a lot of coaching, you may need to request that the caller have someone with more experience call you. Do this in a tactful manner, using expressions such as, "I think I need to discuss your problem with your on-site technical support. Could you have him or her call me?" This might become necessary if your time or the customer's time is valuable, and you simply cannot take extra time to guide him or her through each step.

 When solving computer problems in an organization other than your own, check with technical support instead of only working with the PC user. Policies may have been set on the PC that prevent changes to the OS, hardware, or applications software of which the user is not aware.

When the Customer Is Overly Confident Sometimes a customer is proud of what he or she knows about computers and wants to give advice, take charge of a call, withhold information that he or she judges you don't need to know, or execute commands at the computer without letting you know, so that you don't have enough information to follow along. A situation like this must be handled with tact and respect for the customer. Here are a few tips.

- When you can, compliment the customer concerning his or her knowledge, experience, or insight. Let the customer know that you respect what he or she knows. If the customer does not feel that he or she must prove or establish his or her knowledge, then it is much easier for the customer to relax and be more helpful.

- Ask the customer's advice. Say something like, "What do you think the problem is?" Do this to let customers know that you respect their knowledge, and because they might have the answer. (However, don't ask this question of customers who are not confident because they most likely don't have the answer and might lose confidence in you.)

- Slow the conversation down. You can say, "Please slow down. You're moving too fast for me to follow. Help me understand."

- Don't back off from using problem-solving skills. You must still have the customer check the simple things, but direct the conversation with tact. For example, you can say, "I know you've probably already gone over these simple things, but could we just do them again together?"

- Be careful not to accuse the customer of making a mistake.

- Use technical language in a way that conveys that you expect the customer to understand you.

When the Customer Complains When you are on-site or on the phone, a customer might complain to you about your organization, products, service, or the service and product of another company. Studies have shown that a dissatisfied customer who complains is more likely to continue to use your product or service than a dissatisfied customer who does not let you know. Consider the complaint to be helpful feedback that can lead to a better product or service and better customer relationships. A PC support person is expected to handle these complaints in a professional manner. Here are a few suggestions on to how to do that.

- Listen to the complaint. Consider it valuable feedback.

- Remember that a genuine, empathic apology for whatever the customer has experienced can be very helpful. See if that allows you to move on to solving the problem. If it does, don't spend a lot of time finding out exactly whom the customer dealt with and what exactly happened to upset him or her.

- Don't be defensive. Everyone and every company makes mistakes. It's better to leave the customer with the impression that you and your company are listening and willing to admit mistakes and learn from them than to defend yourself, your product, or your company.

- Empathize with the customer. Show that you are concerned about the problem.

- If the customer is complaining about a product or service that is not from your company, don't start off by saying, "That's not our problem." Instead, listen to the customer complain. Don't appear as though you don't care.

- If the complaint is against you or your product, identify the underlying problem if you can. Ask questions and take notes. Then pass these notes on to whoever in your organization needs to know. The complaint might be used to improve the product or service.

When the Customer Is Angry I once worked as the fourth and final level of support at a help desk. When calls arrived at my desk, three tiers of support had already given up. The customer was at the highest level of frustration and impatience. In a situation like this, if the customer is also angry, you must give special consideration. Allow the customer to be angry. You might be angry, too, in a similar situation. Listen carefully to what the customer is saying. Ask

20

questions. Be an active listener, and let the customer know that he or she is not being ignored. Look for the underlying problem and take notes if the customer is also complaining. Stay calm. Don't take the anger personally. Give the customer a little time to vent, and apologize when you can. Then start the conversation from the beginning, asking questions, taking notes, and solving problems. When the customer realizes that you are helping, doing your best, respecting his or her needs, and solving the problem, the anger will subside. Sometimes simply making progress or reducing the problem to a manageable state for the customer reduces his or her anxiety.

When the Customer Does Not Want to End a Phone Call   Some customers like to talk and don't want to end a phone call. In this situation, when you have finished the work and are ready to hang up, you can ease the caller into the end of the call by doing these things:

- Ask if there is anything that needs more explanation.

- Briefly summarize the main points of the call, and then say something like, "That about does it. Call if you need more help."

- Be silent about new issues. Answer only with "yes" or "no." Don't take the bait by engaging in a new topic.

- Don't get frustrated. As a last resort, you can say, "I'm sorry, but I must go now."

When a Customer Is Beginning to Get Upset   When you sense that a customer is beginning to get angry or upset, try these approaches to control the situation and get things back on track.

- If you have made a mistake, admit it and apologize.

- Apologize for the situation even if you don't think you're at fault.

- Summarize what you have both agreed on or observed so far in the conversation. This establishes and reinforces points of agreement.

- Point out ways that you think communication could be improved. For example, you might say, "I'm sorry, but I'm having trouble understanding what you want. Could you please slow down, and let's take this one step at a time."

- Reassure the customer that you will work on the problem until it is solved.

When You Can't Solve the Problem

You are not going to solve every computer problem you encounter. Knowing how to escalate a problem to those higher in the support chain is one of the first things you should learn on a new job. Each organization will have procedures in place as to how to do this, and it is essential that you familiarize yourself with your company's specific escalation policies and procedures. When escalation involves the customer, generally follow these guidelines:

- Before you escalate, first ask knowledgeable coworkers for suggestions toward solving the problem, which might save you and your customer the time and effort it takes to escalate.

- Know your company's policy as to how to escalate. What documents do you fill out? Who gets them? Do you remain the responsible "support" party, or does the person now addressing the problem become the new contact? Are you expected to still keep in touch with the customer and the problem, or are you totally out of the picture?

- Document the escalation. In the documentation, describe the problem as clearly as you can while keeping the description brief and concise. It's very important to include the detailed steps necessary to reproduce the problem, which can save the next support person lots of time. Engineers and other support personnel are normally very busy people and don't have the time to read long pages of information, but they also don't have the time to investigate for information that you already knew but failed to pass on.

- Pass the problem on according to the proper channels of your organization. This might mean a phone call, an online entry in a database, or an e-mail message.

- Tell the customer that you are passing the problem on to someone who is more experienced and has access to more extensive resources. Let the customer know when he or she should expect this new support person to call. In most cases, the person who receives the escalation will immediately contact the customer and assume responsibility for the problem. However, you should follow through, at least to the point where you know that the new person and the customer have made contact.

- If you check back with the customer only to find out that the other support person has not called or followed through to the customer's satisfaction, don't lay blame or point fingers. Just do whatever you can within your company guidelines to help. Your call to the customer will go a long way toward helping in the situation.

RECORDKEEPING AND INFORMATION TOOLS

If you work for a service organization, it will probably have most of the tools you will need to do your job, including forms, online recordkeeping, procedures, and manuals. In some cases, help-desk support personnel may have software to help them do their jobs, such as programs that support the remote control of customers' PCs (one example is pcANYWHERE), an online help utility, or a problem-solving tool developed specifically for their help desk.

There are several types of resources, records, and information tools that can help you with your work supporting PCs. These include:

20

- Copies of software or hardware you are expected to support. Specific software or hardware that you support must be available to you to test, observe, and study, and to use to re-create a customer's problem whenever possible.

- **User documentation.** You should have a copy of the same documentation that the user sees and be familiar with it.

- Technical documentation. Products, including both hardware and software, will likely have more **technical documentation** than just a user manual. This technical documentation should be made available to you by a company when you support its product.

- Online help. Online help targeted specifically to field technicians and help-desk technicians is often available. This online help will probably include a search engine that works by topics, words, error messages, and the like. An additional feature of some online help software is the ability of support personnel to write annotations directly into the online text, so that they and other technicians can benefit from new information. Some organizations have one or more persons whose sole responsibility is to keep this online help current.

- Expert systems. **Expert systems** software is designed and written to help solve problems. It uses databases of known facts and rules to simulate human experts' reasoning and decision-making processes. Expert systems for PC technicians work by posing questions about a problem, to be answered either by the technician or by the customer. The response to each question will trigger another question from the software, until the expert system arrives at a possible solution or solutions. Many expert systems are "intelligent," meaning that the system will record your input and use it in subsequent sessions to select more questions to ask and approaches to try. Expert systems are fun to use and develop, and they can be wonderful assets in a support organization.

- Call tracking. **Call tracking** can be done online or on paper. Most organizations will have a call-tracking system that tracks (1) the date, time, and length of help-desk or on-site calls, (2) causes of and solutions to problems already addressed, (3) who did what, and when, and (4) how each call was officially resolved. Call-tracking software or documents can also be vehicles used to escalate calls when necessary and to track the escalation. In addition, if an organization knows who its customers are (for example, who the registered users of its software are), this information will probably be made available to the call-tracking system. For small organizations, you might have to develop your own call-tracking system.

PROFESSIONAL ORGANIZATIONS AND CERTIFICATIONS

The work done by PC technicians has been viewed as a profession only within the past few years. As with other budding professions, professional organizations and certifications have taken a while to develop and to become recognized by the industry. The one most significant certifying organization for PC technicians is the **Computing Technology Industry Association** (**CompTIA**, pronounced "comp-TEE-a"). CompTIA sponsors the **A+ Certification** Program, including managing the A+ Service Technician Certification Examination, which measures the knowledge of job tasks and behaviors expected of entry-level technicians. This book prepares you for this exam. To become certified, you must pass two test modules: the core test and the DOS/Windows test. This book is designed to fully prepare you for both exams. A+ Certification is gaining increasing industry recognition, so it should be your first choice for certification as a PC technician. As evidence of this industry recognition, these companies now include A+ Certification in their requirements for employment:

- Compaq Computer Corporation requires that all work done under its warranty agreements be done by A+ Certified personnel.

- Digital Equipment Corporation requires A+ Certification for all international and domestic warranty work.

- ENTEX Information Services requires that all service employees have A+ Certification.

- GE Capital Services requires that all service employees have A+ Certification one year after hire.

- Inacom requires A+ Certification as a core competency for all service providers.

- Okidata requires that all field service technicians have A+ Certification.

- Packard Bell requires all employees to be certified within 90 days of hire.

Some other companies where A+ Certification is mandatory are:

- Aetna U.S. Healthcare

- BancTec, Inc.

- Computer Data, Inc.

- Computer Sciences Corp.

- Delta Airlines

- Dow Jones & Company

- FBI, U.S. Department of Justice

- Gateway 2000

- New Horizons

- Tandy Corporation

- TSS IBM

- US Airways

- Vanstar

- Wang

20

CompTIA has over 6,000 members, which include every major company that manufactures, distributes, or publishes computer-related products and services. For more information about CompTIA and A+ Certification, see the CompTIA Web site at *www.comptia.org*.

Other certifications are more vendor specific. For example, Microsoft, Novell, and Cisco offer certifications to use and support their products. These are excellent choices for additional certifications when your career plan is to focus on these products.

Why Certification?

Many people work as PC technicians without any formal classroom training or certification. However, by having certification or an advanced technical degree, you prove to yourself, your customers, and your employers that you are prepared to do the work and are committed to being educated in your chosen profession. Here are some reasons for seeking certification and advanced degrees:

- They are recognized proof of competence and achievement.
- They improve your job opportunities.
- They create a higher level of customer confidence.
- They often qualify you for other training and/or degrees.

STAYING ABREAST OF NEW TECHNOLOGY

In addition to becoming certified and seeking advanced degrees, the professional PC technician should also stay abreast of new technology. With the ever-changing technology of today, this can be quite a challenge. Helpful resources include: on-the-job training, books, magazines, the Internet, trade shows, interaction with colleagues, seminars, and workshops. Some magazines that routinely include excellent articles explaining new technology in detail are *PC Magazine*, *PC Today*, *Computer Shopper*, *PC Computing*, and *PC World*. Probably the best-known trade show is COMDEX and Windows World, where you can view the latest technology, hear industry leaders speak, and network with vast numbers of organizations and people. For more information about COMDEX and Windows World, see the Web site *www.comdex.com*.

Throughout this book you'll find references to Web sites for more information about a particular technology. In addition, try the Web sites listed in Table 20-1 for excellent up-to-date technical information about PCs.

Staying up to date concerning new technology begins with an attitude and commitment to self-improvement. Your education is primarily your own responsibility, and only secondarily the responsibility of your employer. Take advantage of opportunities presented by your employer for training, but remember that a personal commitment to continue to learn is more important than any training program offered by your employer.

Table 20-1   Technical support Web sites

Organization	Web Site
Advanced Services Network	www.aserve.net
BYTE Magazine	www.byte.com
CNET, Inc.	www.cnet.com
COOK Network Consultants (Internet glossary)	www.cookreport.com
CyberCollege	www.cybercollege.com
DataFellows, Inc.	www.datafellows.com
internet.com Corporation	www.pcwebopedia.com
Kingston Technology (information about memory)	www.kingston.com
Microsoft technical resources	msdn.microsoft.com
MK Data	www.karbosguide.com
O'Reilly and Associates (PC hardware glossary)	www.oreilly.com/reference/dictionary
PC Guide	www.pcguide.com
PC Today Online	www.pc-today.com
PC World	www.pcworld.com
Sangoma Technologies, Inc.	www.sangoma.com
Steve Jenkins and Jenesys, LLC	www.winfiles.com
Tom's Hardware Guide	www.tomshardware.com
ZDNet (Publishes several technical magazines)	www.zdnet.com
Zoom Telephonics, Inc.	www.modems.com

PROTECTING SOFTWARE COPYRIGHTS

As a computer support technician, you will be faced with the legal issues and practices surrounding the distribution of software. When someone purchases software from a software vendor, that person has only purchased a **license** for the software, which is the right to *use* the software, and does not legally *own* the software; he or she therefore does not have the right to distribute the software. The right to copy the work, called a **copyright**, belongs to the creator of the work or others he or she has transferred this right to. A professional PC technician should understand and follow the laws that apply to the sale and distribution of software.

As a PC technician you will be called upon to install, upgrade, and customize software. You need to know where your responsibility lies in upholding the law, especially as it applies to software copyright. Copyright is intended to legally protect the intellectual property rights of organizations or individuals to creative works, whether they be books, images, or, in the case of this discussion, software. While the originator of a creative work is the original owner of a copyright, copyright can be transferred from one entity to another.

The Federal Copyright Act of 1976 was designed in part to protect **software copyrights** by requiring that only legally obtained copies of software be used; the law also allows for one

20

backup copy of software to be made. Making unauthorized copies of original software violates the Federal Copyright Act of 1976, and is called **software piracy**, or, more officially, software copyright infringement. Making a copy of software and then selling it or giving it away is a violation of the law. Because it is so easy to do this, and because so many people do it, many people don't realize that they're breaking the law. Normally only the person who violated the copyright law is liable for infringement; however, in some cases, an employer or supervisor is also held responsible, even when the copies were made without the employer's knowledge. The Business Software Alliance (a membership organization of software manufacturers and vendors) has estimated that 26% of the business software in the United States is obtained illegally and that, in 1995, the worldwide illegal use of software cost the software industry more than $13 billion.

Vendors may sometimes sell counterfeit software by installing unauthorized software on computers for sale. This practice is called **hard-disk loading**. Vendors have even been known to counterfeit disk labels and Certificates of Authenticity. Warning signs that software purchased from vendors is pirated include:

- No end-user license is included.

- There is no mail-in product registration card.

- Software is installed on a new PC, but documentation and original disks are not included in the package.

- Documentation is photocopied, or disks have handwritten labels.

Several technological methods have been attempted to prevent people from making copies of software. These methods include making distribution disks copy-resistant and putting **holographic images** on software packages. Nontechnical methods include stiffer fines and sentences for infringement and more aggressive lawsuits.

In the past few years, site licensing, whereby a company can purchase the rights to use multiple copies of software, has grown in popularity. There are many ways that software is licensed today in order to accommodate the growing demands of companies that distribute software to PCs from network servers or execute software directly off the server. Read the licensing agreement of any software to determine the terms of distribution.

One of two associations committed to the prevention of software piracy is the Software Information Industry Association, a nonprofit organization that educates the public and enforces copyright laws. Their Web address is *www.siia.net*, and their antipiracy hotline is 1-800-388-7478. Another organization is the Business Software Alliance, which manages the BSA Anti-Piracy Hotline at 1888NOPIRACY. The BSA can also be reached at their e-mail address: software@bsa.org. Their Web site is *www.bsa.org*. These associations are made up of hundreds of software manufacturers and publishers in North and Latin America, Europe, and Asia. They promote software raids on large and small companies, and, in the U.S., they receive the cooperation of the United States government to prosecute offenders.

What Does the Law Say?

The Federal Copyright Act of 1976 protects the exclusive rights of copyright holders. It gives legal users of software the right to make one backup copy. Other rights are based on what the copyright holder allows. In 1990, the United States Congress passed the Software Rental Amendment Act, which prevents the renting, leasing, lending, or sharing of software without the expressed written permission of the copyright holder. In 1992, Congress instituted criminal penalties for software copyright infringement, which include imprisonment for up to five years and/or fines of up to $250,000, for the unlawful reproduction or distribution of 10 or more copies of software. In short, it is illegal for a person to give an unauthorized copy of software to another individual, even if they both work for the same organization.

What Are Your Responsibilities to the Law?

Your first responsibility as an individual user is to use only software that has been purchased or licensed for your use. As an employee of a company that has a site license to use multiple copies of the software, your responsibility is to comply with the license agreement, whatever that is. It is also your responsibility to purchase only legitimate software. Purchasers of counterfeit or copied software face the risk of corrupted files, virus-infected disks, inadequate documentation, and lack of technical support and upgrades, as well as the legal penalties for using pirated software.

CHAPTER SUMMARY

- Customers want and expect more than just technical proficiency from a PC technician.
- Customers expect a technician to keep a positive and helpful attitude, to remain professional at all times, and to put the needs of the customer above all else.
- A PC technician is expected to respond to a call for service within a reasonable time, to be prepared for the service call, and to do the work right the first time.
- Good communication skills are an important attribute of a PC technician.
- A PC technician is a guest at the customer site and should act like a guest.
- Keeping records of service calls, help-desk calls, and bench work is important to identify trends and the need for training or information, and to help with future problem solving.
- When tracking a service call, a phone call, or bench work, always record the symptoms, the originating problem, and the solution. This information will help in future problem solving.
- CompTIA (Computing Technology Industry Association) sponsors A+ Certification, the industry-accepted certification for the PC technician.
- Staying abreast of new technology can be done by attending trade shows, reading trade magazines, researching on the Internet, and attending seminars and workshops.

20

◘ Software piracy—the use of software obtained in violation of the copyright owner's specific terms—is against the law. A professional PC technician is committed to not using or installing pirated software.

◘ The Business Software Alliance and the Software Publishers Association are two associations committed to controlling software piracy.

KEY TERMS

A+ Certification — A certification awarded by CompTIA (The Computing Technology Industry Association) that measures a PC technician's knowledge of the skills and behaviors expected of entry-level PC technicians. Many companies require that their service technicians have A+ Certification.

Call tracking — A system that tracks the dates, times, and transactions of help-desk or on-site PC support calls, including the problem presented, the issues addressed, who did what, and when and how each call was resolved.

Computing Technology Industry Association (CompTIA) — A membership trade association that sponsors A+ Certification, a valuable certification for PC technicians.

Copyright — An individual's right to copy his/her own work. No one else, other than the copyright owner, is legally allowed to do so without permission.

Escalating — The process by which a technician passes a customer's problem to higher organizational levels, if he or she cannot address the problem.

Expert systems — Computerized software that uses a database of known facts and rules to simulate a human expert's reasoning and decision-making processes.

Hard-disk loading — The illegal practice of installing unauthorized software on computers for sale. Hard-disk loading can typically be identified by the absence of original disks in the original system's shipment.

Holographic image — A three-dimensional image (created by holography) that is made up of a light-interference pattern preserved in a medium such as photographic film and that changes when the angle of view changes. Because making unofficial copies of holographic images is extremely difficult, they are often used to tag products, such as software packages, as original, making it difficult to distribute illegal copies.

License — Permission for an individual to use a product or service. A manufacturer's method of maintaining ownership, while granting permission for use to others.

Software copyrights — Copyright is a legal concept (covered by the Federal Copyright Act of 1976) that encompasses the protection of the rights of an originator of a creative work, which can include software. With the exception of archival backups, copyrighted programs are illegal to copy without specific authorization from the copyright holder.

Software piracy — Making unauthorized copies of original copyrighted software.

Technical documentation — The technical reference manuals, included with software packages and peripherals, that provide directions for installation, usage, and troubleshooting.

User documentation — Manuals, online documentation, instructions, and tutorials designed specifically for the user.

REVIEW QUESTIONS

1. Assume that you are a customer who wants to have a personal computer repaired. List five main characteristics that you would want to see in your PC repairperson.

2. List and briefly discuss five practices that should be followed to make a technician a better customer-oriented service person.

3. What is one thing you should do when you receive a phone call requesting on-site support, before you make an appointment?

4. What can you do if you have made every effort to solve a problem, but it is still not solved?

5. You make an appointment to do an on-site repair, but you are detained and find out that you will be late. What is the best thing to do?

6. When you arrive for an on-site service call, how important is your greeting? What would be a good greeting to start off a good business relationship?

7. When making an on-site service call, what should you do before making any changes to software, or before taking the case off a computer?

8. What should you do after finishing your PC repair?

9. What is a good strategy to follow if a conflict arises between you and your customer?

10. When someone calls your help desk, what is the first thing you should do?

11. List the items of information that you would want to record at the beginning of a help-desk call.

12. What is one thing you can do to help a caller who needs phone support and is not a competent computer user?

13. Describe what you should do when a customer complains to you about a product or service that your company provides.

14. What are some things you can do to make your work at a help desk easier?

15. What is one printed source that you can use to stay abreast of new technology?

16. Why is it important to be a certified technician?

17. Examine the software license of some software currently installed on your PC. Is it legal to have this software installed on your PC at work and also installed on your PC at home?

18. List three things to check when you are considering the purchase of software to verify that the software is not pirated.

19. What two associations educate about and protect against software piracy?

20. What organization offers PC technician certification?

20

PROJECTS

A+ Certification

Go to CompTIA's Web site, *www.comptia.org*, and print out sample test questions for the A+ Certification exam. Include questions from the core and the operating system sample tests. Answer the questions for these sample tests. On the basis of the sample tests, how prepared do you think you are to take the A+ exam?

Practicing Help-Desk Skills

Work with a partner. One of you play the role of the customer, and the other the role of the help-desk technician. The customer calls, saying, "My computer won't work." The technician should lead the conversation by asking questions. Ask the appropriate questions to determine exactly what the problem is, and then check all cable connections for PC, monitor, mouse, keyboard, and power. Write down the questions you ask. (Don't forget to ask the customer's name, phone number, and so on.)

Customer Relationships

Work in a small discussion group of three to four people. Come prepared by writing a paragraph describing the worst situation in which you might realistically find yourself when servicing a PC. Read the paragraph to the group. Have the group discuss what would be the appropriate thing to do in this situation. Under the paragraph, write two column headings, Do and Don't. Write down the suggestions of the group for each column. For example, here is one sample paragraph for your discussion:

You respond to a customer call by traveling across town in heavy traffic to the customer's place of business. He insisted that you arrive promptly that same day, even though the call didn't come until 4:00 P.M. The customer told you on the phone that the PC would not boot. You had him check all connections and switches, but all seemed well. When you get to the site, the customer is angry because you took so long arriving and threatens to report you. When you check the PC, you discover that the monitor cable is not plugged into the computer case. What do you say and do?

A Self-Study of New Technology

Select a new hardware or software feature or product and do a self-directed study of the subject. Use magazines, books, and the Internet. Collect the information in a file folder and let it be the first folder of many that you keep on new technology. Some suggestions for your study are:

- Digital cameras
- FireWire
- Linux
- Windows 2000

Illegal Software

1. Search in Windows 9x Help for ways to identify illegal Microsoft software. Print out the warning signs that might indicate that software installed on your newly purchased PC, or available on a retail store shelf, might be illegal.

2. If you believe you have unknowingly purchased illegal software, see the Software Publishers Association Web site at *www.siia.net* to find out what you can do about your situation.

Internet Search

1. Log on to the Internet and do a Web search. Enter the key words PC+troubleshooting, and list and describe five of the sites found. Also enter the key words PC+certification, and list three sites found.

2. In this chapter, under the heading, "Staying Abreast of New Technology," select three of the Web sites listed and access the sites. Write one paragraph for each site, describing what type of technical information is available on the site to help a PC technician.

A

ERROR MESSAGES AND
THEIR MEANINGS

A+ OS
3.1,
3.2,
CORE
2.1

The following table of error messages and their meanings can help when you are diagnosing computer problems.

Error Message	Meaning of the Error Message and What to Do
Bad sector writing or reading to drive	Sector markings on the disk may be fading. Try ScanDisk or reformat the disk.
Bad command or file not found	The DOS command just executed cannot be interpreted, or DOS cannot find the program file specified in the command line. Check the spelling of the filename and check that the path to the program file has been given to DOS.
Beeps during POST	Before the video is checked, during POST, the ROM BIOS communicates error messages with a series of beeps. Each BIOS manufacturer has its own beep codes, but the following are examples of some BIOS codes. For specific beep codes for your system board, see the Web site of the system-board manufacturer.
One single beep followed by three, four, or five beeps	System-board problems, possibly with DMA, CMOS setup chip, timer, or system bus
Two beeps	The POST numeric code is displayed on the monitor.
Two beeps followed by three, four, or five beeps	First 64K of RAM has errors.
Three beeps followed by three, four, or five beeps	Keyboard controller failed or video controller failed.
Four beeps followed by two, three, or four beeps	Problem with serial or parallel ports, system timer, or time of day
Continuous beeps	Problem with power supply
Configuration/CMOS error	Setup information does not agree with the actual hardware the computer found during boot. May be caused by a bad or weak battery or by changing hardware without changing setup. Check setup for errors.
Insufficient memory	This error happens under Windows when too many applications are open. Close some applications. A reboot may help.
Hard drive not found	The OS cannot locate the hard drive, or the controller card is not responding.

A1

A+ OS
3.1,
3.2,
CORE
2.1

Error Message	Meaning of the Error Message and What to Do
Fixed disk error	The PC cannot find the hard drive that setup told it to expect. Check cables, connections, power supply, and setup information.
Incorrect DOS version	When you execute a DOS external command, DOS looks for a program file with the same name as the command. It finds that this file belongs to a different version of DOS than the one that is now running. Use the DOS software from the same version that you are running.
Invalid drive specification	The PC is unable to find a hard drive or a floppy drive that setup tells it to expect. Look for errors in setup, or the hard drive may have a corrupted partition table.
Invalid or missing COMMAND.COM	This may be caused by a nonbooting disk in drive A. Remove the disk and boot from drive C. COMMAND.COM on drive C may have been erased or the path could not be found.
No boot device available	The hard drive is not formatted, or the format is corrupted, and there is no disk in drive A. Boot from a floppy and examine your hard drive for corruption.
Non-system disk or disk error	COMMAND.COM or one of two DOS hidden files is missing from the disk in drive A or the hard drive. Remove the disk in drive A and boot from the hard drive. Use the SYS command to restore system files
Not ready reading drive A: Abort, Retry, Fail?	The disk in drive A is missing, is not formatted, or is corrupted. Try another disk.
Numeric codes during POST	Sometimes numeric codes are used to communicate errors at POST. Some examples for IBM XT/AT error codes include:
Code in the 100 range	System-board errors
Code in the 200 range	RAM errors
Code in the 300 range	Keyboard errors
Code in the 500 range	Video controller errors
Code in the 600 range	Floppy drive errors
Code in the 700 range	Coprocessor errors
Code in the 900 range	Parallel port errors
Code in the 1100–1200 range	Async (communications adapter) errors
Code in the 1300 range	Game controller or joystick errors
Code in the 1700 range	Hard drive errors
Code in the 6000 range	SCSI device or network card errors
Code in the 7300 range	Floppy drive errors
Track 0 bad, disk not usable	This usually occurs when you attempt to format a floppy disk using the wrong format type. Check the disk type and compare to the type specified in the format command.

A+ OS
3.1,
3.2,
CORE
2.1

A

Error Message	Meaning of the Error Message and What to Do
Write-protect error writing drive A:	Let the computer write to the disk by setting the switch on a 3½-inch disk or removing the tape from a 5¼-inch disk.
Missing operating system, error loading operating system	The MBR is unable to locate or read the OS boot sector on the active partition or there is a translation problem on large drives. Boot from a floppy and examine the hard drive file system for corruption
Unknown error at Post	See the Web site of the system BIOS manufacturer: • AMI BIOS: *www.ami.com* • Award BIOS and Phoenix BIOS: *www.phoenix.com* • Compaq: *www.compaq.com* • Dell: *www.dell.com* • IBM: *www.ibm.com*
Error in CONFIG.SYS line xx	There is a problem loading a device driver or with the syntax of a command line. Check the command line for errors. Verify the driver files are in the right directory. Reinstall the driver files.
HIMEM.SYS not loaded, missing or corrupt HIMEM.SYS	HIMEM.SYS is corrupted, not in the right directory, or not the right version for the currently loading OS. Verify HIMEM.SYS.

B

HARD DRIVE TYPES

As you recall, if your system BIOS does not use autodetection, you must tell it what hard drive type you are using when you set up your system. System BIOS provides you with a list of drive types to select from, as well as the option of specifying a user-defined drive type. This appendix lists various hard drive types and their parameters, including the number of tracks, heads, sectors per track, and so on. Nowadays, these drive types are rarely used; today's hard drives are much larger than any on the BIOS drive list, so the user-defined drive type is usually used, which is usually type 47 or 48. Nonetheless, the BIOS of almost every PC continues to offer the same list of "old" drive types, and it is still helpful to understand where the list comes from and what it means.

The first hard drive types were established by IBM, and a list of them was first included in its BIOS for IBM XT 286 computers in 1985. When a hard drive is installed on a PC, setup is told the drive type (or autodetection automatically detects the type) and this information is then written to CMOS. The system BIOS then knows the logical layout and size of the hard drive. As the variety of hard drives increased, the list of drive types grew. IBM later added more types to its list, and Compaq and other manufacturers introduced their own lists. Other companies writing BIOSs also introduced their own lists.

Following are two tables, the first listing drive types from the IBM BIOS list, and the second listing drive types from the Phoenix BIOS list. Other BIOSs may have different hard drive tables. For a listing of the hard drive types supported by your BIOS, see CMOS setup.

Table B-1   IBM hard drive types

Drive Type	Tracks	Heads	Sectors Per Track	Write Precomp	Capacity (MB)
1	306	4	17	128	10
2	615	4	17	300	20
3	615	6	17	300	32
4	940	8	17	512	64
5	940	6	17	512	48
6	615	4	17	None	20
7	462	8	17	256	30
8	733	5	17	None	30
9	900	15	17	110	112
10	820	3	17	None	20
11	855	5	17	None	35
12	855	7	17	None	50
13	306	8	17	128	20
14	733	7	17	None	40
15	Not used				
16	612	4	17	0	20
17	977	5	17	300	40
18	977	7	17	None	56
19	1024	5	17	512	60
20	733	5	17	300	30
21	733	7	17	300	42
22	733	5	17	300	30
23	306	4	17	0	10
24	612	4	17	305	21

Table B-2   Phoenix BIOS drive types

Drive Type	Tracks	Heads	Sectors Per Track	Write Precomp	Capacity (MB)
25	615	4	17	0	20
26	1024	4	17	None	35
27	1024	5	17	None	44
28	1024	8	17	None	70
29	512	8	17	256	35
30	615	2	17	615	10
31	989	5	17	0	42
32	1020	15	17	None	130
33	615	4	26	None	32
34	820	6	26	None	65
35	1024	9	17	1024	80
36	1024	5	17	512	44
37	1024	5	26	512	68
38	823	10	17	256	70
39	615	4	17	128	21
40	615	8	17	128	42
41	917	15	17	None	120
42	1023	15	17	None	132
43	823	10	17	512	71
44	820	6	17	None	42
45	1024	5	17	None	44
46	925	9	17	None	71
47	699	7	17	256	42
48	User-defined				

B

C

ASCII CHARACTER SET AND ANSI.SYS

ASCII (American Standard Code for Information Interchange) is a coding system that is used by personal computers to store character data, such as letters of the alphabet, numerals, some symbols, and certain control characters. There are 128 characters defined by the standard ASCII character set. Each ASCII character is assigned an 8-bit code that converts to a decimal number from 0 to 127. The first 31 values, which are non-printable codes, are used for control characters and can be used to send commands to printers or other peripheral devices. Files that store data as ASCII characters are sometimes called ASCII files, ASCII text files, or simply text files. ASCII can be read by most editors and word processors and is considered the universal file format for personal computers. AUTOEXEC.BAT is one example of an ASCII file.

In addition to the standard ASCII character set, some manufacturers use an extended ASCII character set that is specific to their equipment and is not necessarily compatible with other computers. The extended ASCII character sets use the codes 128 through 255.

The American National Standards Institute (ANSI), an organization responsible for many computer standards, developed an extended character set using codes 128 through 255 that includes special characters such as letters in an international alphabet and accents, currency symbols, and fractions. ANSI also defined a series of control codes that can be used to control the monitor. For example, a sequence of control codes can clear the monitor, cause characters to display upside down, or put color on a DOS screen. ANSI.SYS is a device driver that, when loaded in a DOS environment, provides these monitor and keyboard functions. ANSI.SYS is loaded from the CONFIG.SYS file with this command:

```
DEVICE=C:\DOS\ANSI.SYS
```

Some DOS programs need ANSI.SYS loaded in order to interpret the extended character set entered from the keyboard, display these characters on the screen, and control the monitor in other ways.

The table below lists the standard ASCII character set. Note that items 2 through 32 are not included; these represent non-printable ASCII control characters that are used to communicate with peripheral devices.

Table C-1   Standard ASCII character set

Item Number	Symbol	Meaning	ASCII in Decimal Representation	ASCII in Binary Representation	ASCII in Hex Representation
1	.	Null	0	0000 0000	0
33	b/	Space	32	0010 0000	20
34	!	Exclamation point	33	0010 0001	21
35	"	Quotation mark	34	0010 0010	22
36	#	Number sign	35	0010 0011	23
37	$	Dollar sign	36	0010 0100	24
38	%	Percent sign	37	0010 0101	25
39	&	Ampersand	38	0010 0110	26
40	'	Apostrophe, prime sign	39	0010 0111	27
41	(	Opening parenthesis	40	0010 1000	28
42	)	Closing parenthesis	41	0010 1001	29
43	*	Asterisk	42	0010 1010	2A
44	+	Plus sign	43	0010 1011	2B
45	,	Comma	44	0010 1100	2C
46	-	Hyphen, minus sign	45	0010 1101	2D
47	.	Period, decimal point	46	0010 1110	2E
48	/	Slant	47	0010 1111	2F
49	0		48	0011 0000	30
50	1		49	0011 0001	31
51	2		50	0011 0010	32
52	3		51	0011 0011	33
53	4		52	0011 0100	34
54	5		53	0011 0101	35
55	6		54	0011 0110	36
56	7		55	0011 0111	37
57	8		56	0011 1000	38
58	9		57	0011 1001	39
59	:	Colon	58	0011 1010	3A
60	;	Semicolon	59	0011 1011	3B

Table C-1   Standard ASCII character set (continued)

Item Number	Symbol	Meaning	ASCII in Decimal Representation	ASCII in Binary Representation	ASCII in Hex Representation
61	<	Less than sign	60	0011 1100	3C
62	=	Equal sign	61	0011 1101	3D
63	>	Greater than sign	62	0011 1110	3E
64	?	Question mark	63	0011 1111	3F
65	@	Commercial at sign	64	0100 0000	40
66	A		65	0100 0001	41
67	B		66	0100 0010	42
68	C		67	0100 0011	43
69	D		68	0100 0100	44
70	E		69	0100 0101	45
71	F		70	0100 0110	46
72	G		71	0100 0111	47
73	H		72	0100 1000	48
74	I		73	0100 1001	49
75	J		74	0100 1010	4A
76	K		75	0100 1011	4B
77	L		76	0100 1100	4C
78	M		77	0100 1101	4D
79	N		78	0100 1110	4E
80	O		79	0100 1111	4F
81	P		80	0101 0000	50
82	Q		81	0101 0001	51
83	R		82	0101 0010	52
84	S		83	0101 0011	53
85	T		84	0101 0100	54
86	U		85	0101 0101	55
87	V		86	0101 0110	56
88	W		87	0101 0111	57
89	X		88	0101 1000	58
90	Y		89	0101 1001	59
91	Z		90	0101 1010	5A
92	[	Opening bracket	91	0101 1011	5B
93	\	Reverse slant	92	0101 1100	5C
94	]	Closing bracket	93	0101 1101	5D

C

Table C-1   Standard ASCII character set (continued)

Item Number	Symbol	Meaning	ASCII in Decimal Representation	ASCII in Binary Representation	ASCII in Hex Representation
95	^	Caret	94	0101 1110	5E
96	_	Underscore	95	0101 1111	5F
97	`	Acute accent	96	0110 0000	60
98	a		97	0110 0001	61
99	b		98	0110 0010	62
100	c		99	0110 0011	63
100	d		100	0110 0100	64
102	e		101	0110 0101	65
103	f		102	0110 0110	66
104	g		103	0110 0111	67
105	h		104	0110 1000	68
106	i		105	0110 1001	69
107	j		106	0110 1010	6A
108	k		107	0110 1011	6B
109	l		108	0110 1100	6C
110	m		109	0110 1101	6D
111	n		110	0110 1110	6E
112	o		111	0110 1111	6F
113	p		112	0111 0000	70
114	q		113	0111 0001	71
115	r		114	0111 0010	72
116	s		115	0111 0011	73
117	t		116	0111 0100	74
118	u		117	0111 0101	75
119	v		118	0111 0110	76
120	w		119	0111 0111	77
121	x		120	0111 1000	78
122	y		121	0111 1001	79
123	z		122	0111 1010	7A
124	{	Opening brace	123	0111 1011	7B
125			Split vertical bar	124	0111 1100	7C
126	}	Closing brace	125	0111 1101	7D
127	~	Tilde	126	0111 1110	7E
128	Δ	Small triangle	127	0111 1111	7F

D

THE HEXADECIMAL NUMBER SYSTEM AND MEMORY ADDRESSING

Fundamental to understanding how computers work is understanding the number system and the coding system that computers use to store data and communicate with each other. Early attempts to invent an electronic computing device met with disappointing results as long as inventors tried to use our own decimal number system, with the digits 0–9. No electronic device could be invented that would dependably hold 10 different numeric values. Attempts during the 1940s involved using vacuum tubes that held varying quantities of electrical charge. A very small charge would be a 1, a little more would be a 2, and so on up to 9, the strongest charge. Measuring the charge to determine what number it represented just wasn't reliable, however, because the electrical charges fluctuated too much. Then John Atanasoff came up with the brilliant idea of not measuring the charge at all. He proposed using a coding system that expressed everything in terms of different sequences of only two numerals: one represented by the presence of a charge and one represented by the absence of a charge. The existing technology could handle that. The numbering system that can be supported by the expression of only two numerals is the base 2, sometimes called binary, numbering system, invented by Ada Lovelace many years before, using the two numerals 0 and 1. Under Atanasoff's design, all numbers and other characters would be converted to this binary number system, and all storage, comparisons, and arithmetic would be done using it. Even today, this is one of the basic principles of computers. Every character or number entered into a computer is first converted into a series of 0s and 1s. Many coding schemes and techniques have been invented to manipulate these 0s and 1s, called **bits** for **bi**nary dig**its**.

The most widespread binary coding scheme for microcomputers, which is recognized as the microcomputer standard, is called the ASCII (American Standard Code for Information Interchange) coding system. (Appendix C lists the binary code for the basic 127-character set.) In ASCII, each character is assigned an 8-bit code called a **byte**. Table D-1 lists the terms used in the discussion of how numbers are stored in computers. The byte has become the universal single unit of storage for data in computers everywhere.

Table D-1   Computer terminology

Term	Definition
Bit	A numeral in the binary number system: a 0 or a 1
Byte	8 bits
Kilobyte	1,024 bytes, which is 2^{10}, often rounded to 1,000 bytes
Megabyte	Either 1,024 kilobytes or 1,000 kilobytes, depending on what has come to be standard practice in different situations. For example, when calculating floppy disk capacities, 1 megabyte = 1,000 kilobytes; when calculating hard drive capacity, traditionally, 1 megabyte = 1,024 bytes.
Gigabyte	1,000 megabytes or 1,024 megabytes, depending on what has come to be standard practice in different situations
ASCII	American Standard Code for Information Interchange coding scheme used for microcomputers, which assigns a 7- 8-bit code to all characters and symbols. See Appendix C for more information.
Hex	Short for hexadecimal. A number system based on 16 values (called base 16), which is explained in detail below. Uses the sixteen numerals 0, 1, 2, 3, 4, 5, 6, 7, 8, 9, A, B, C, D, E, and F. Hex numbers are often followed by a lowercase h to indicate they are in hex (example: 78h).

Human beings are accustomed to the decimal number system, and working with the binary number system is quite tedious, mostly because of the sheer volume of bits that have to be managed. But computers use the binary number system, and the calculations to convert binary to decimal are relatively complex. Therefore, a compromise arose. Computers convert binary data into the hexadecimal number system (shortened to hex system) because it is much less complex for computers to convert binary numbers into hex numbers than into decimal numbers, and it is much easier for human beings to read hex numbers than to read binary numbers. This way, even though the actual processing and inner workings of computers use the binary system, they often display information using the hex system.

Learning to "Think Hex"

One skill a knowledgeable computer support person must have is the ability to read hex numbers and convert hex to decimal and decimal to hex. Once you understand one numbering system (decimal), you can understand any numbering system (including binary and hexadecimal), because they all operate on the same basic principle: place value. So we begin there.

Place Value

A key to understanding place value is to think of a number system as a method of grouping multiple small units together until there are enough of them to be packed into a single larger group, then grouping multiple larger groups together until there are enough of them to form an even larger group, and so on. In our (decimal) number system, once there are 10 units of any group, that group becomes a single unit of the next larger group. So, groups of 10 units are packed into groups of tens; groups of ten tens are packed into groups of hundreds; groups of 10 hundreds are packed into groups of thousands, and so forth.

An easy way to understand number systems is to think of the numbers as being packaged for shipping, into boxes, cartons, crates, truckloads, and so on. For the decimal numbering system, consider packing widgets (units) into boxes (tens) which are packed into cartons (100s) which are packed into crates (1000s), and so forth. The same analogy works for binary, decimal, and all other number systems.

Our friend Joe, in Figure D-1, is a widget packer in the shipping department of the ACE Widget Co. Joe can ship single widgets, or he can pack them in boxes, cartons, crates, and truckloads. He can fit three, and only three, widgets to a box; three, and only three, boxes into one carton ($3 \times 3 = 9$ widgets); three, and only three, cartons into one crate ($3 \times 9 = 27$ widgets); and three, and only three, crates into one truck ($3 \times 27 = 81$ widgets). He is not allowed to pack more widgets into boxes, cartons, crates, or truckloads than those specified. Neither is he allowed to send out a box, carton, crate, or truckload that is not completely filled.

1 truckload
holds 3 crates
(81 widgets)

1 crate
holds 3 cartons
(27 widgets)

1 carton
holds 3 boxes
(9 widgets)

1 box
holds 3
widgets

single
widgets

Figure D-1 Joe in the shipping department groups widgets in singles, boxes, cartons, crates, and truckloads—all in groups of three

Joe receives an order to ship out 197 widgets. How does he ship them? The answer is shown in Figure D-2. Joe sends out 197 widgets grouped into 2 truckloads ($2 \times 81 = 162$ widgets), 1 crate (27 widgets), no cartons, 2 boxes ($2 \times 3 = 6$ widgets), and 2 single widgets. We can write this grouping of widgets as 21022, where the "place values" from left to right are truckloads, crates, cartons, boxes, and units, which in this case are (in decimal) 81 widgets, 27 widgets, 9 widgets, 3 widgets, and single widgets. Notice that each "place value" in our widget-packing system is a multiple of 3, because the widgets are grouped into three before they are packed into boxes; the boxes are grouped into three before they are packed into cartons, and so on. By grouping the widgets into groups of 3s in this manner, we converted the decimal number (base 10) 197 into the ternary number (base 3) 21022. Joe's widget-packing method is a base three, or ternary, system. The numerals in the ternary number system are 0, 1, and 2. When you get to the next value after 2, instead of counting on up to 3, you move one place value to the left and begin again with 1 in that position, which represents 3. So, counting in base 3 goes like this: 0, 1, 2, 10, 11, 12, 20, 21, 22, 100, 101 and so on. This is the same as Joe's never shipping out 3 of any one group unless they are packed together into one larger group. For example, Joe wouldn't ship 3 individual boxes, he would ship one carton.

| 2 trucks | 1 crate | 0 cartons | 2 boxes | 2 singles |

Figure D-2   Joe's shipment of 197 widgets: 2 trucks, 1 crate, 0 cartons, 2 boxes, and a group of 2 singles

You can easily apply the widget-packing analogy to another base. If Joe packed 7 (and only 7) units to a box, 7 (and only 7) boxes to a carton, 7 (and only 7) cartons to a crate, and 7 (and only 7) crates to a truck, then his packing system would be operating using base seven rules. If he used 10 instead of seven, he would be using base ten (decimal) rules. So, numbering systems differ by the different numbers of units they group together. In the hex number system, we group by 16. So, if Joe were shipping in groups of 16, as in Figure D-3, single widgets could be shipped out up to 15, but 16 widgets would make one box. Sixteen boxes would make one carton, which would contain 16×16, or 256, widgets. Sixteen cartons would make one crate, which would contain 16×256, or 4,096, widgets.

Suppose Joe receives an order for 197 widgets to be packed in groups of 16. He will not be able to fill a carton (256 widgets), so he ships out 12 boxes (16 widgets each) and 5 single widgets:

$12 \times 16 = 192$, and $192 + 5 = 197$

Figure D-3   Widgets displayed in truck loads, crates, cartons, boxes, and singles grouped in 16s

You approach an obstacle if you attempt to write the number in hex. How are you going to express 12 boxes and 5 singles? In hex, you need single numerals in hex to represent the numbers 10, 11, 12, 13, 14, and 15 in decimal. Hex uses letters for these numerals. A, B, C, D, E, and F are used for the numbers 10 through 15. Table D-2 shows values expressed in the decimal, hex, and binary numbering systems. In the second column in Table D-2, you are counting in the hex number system. For example, 12 is represented with a C. So you say that Joe packs C boxes and 5 singles. The hex number for decimal 197 is C5 (see Figure D-4).

Table D-2   Decimal, hex, and binary values

Decimal	Hex	Binary	Decimal	Hex	Binary	Decimal	Hex	Binary
0	0	0	14	E	1110	28	1C	11100
1	1	1	15	F	1111	29	1D	11101
2	2	10	16	10	10000	30	1E	11110
3	3	11	17	11	10001	31	1F	11111
4	4	100	18	12	10010	32	20	100000
5	5	101	19	13	10011	33	21	100001
6	6	110	20	14	10100	34	22	100010
7	7	111	21	15	10101	35	23	100011
8	8	1000	22	16	10110	36	24	100100
9	9	1001	23	17	10111	37	25	100101
10	A	1010	24	18	11000	38	26	100110
11	B	1011	25	19	11001	39	27	100111
12	C	1100	26	1A	11010	40	28	101000
13	D	1101	27	1B	11011			

For a little practice, calculate the hex values of the decimal values 14, 259, 75, and 1,024 and the decimal values of FFh and A11h.

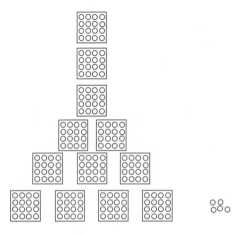

Figure D-4   Hex C5 represented as C boxes and 5 singles = 197 decimal

How Exponents Are Used to Express Place Value

If you are comfortable with using exponents, you know that writing numbers raised to a power is the same thing as multiplying that number times itself the power number of times. For example, $3^4 = 3 \times 3 \times 3 \times 3 = 81$. Using exponents in expressing numbers can also help us easily see place value, because the place value for each place is really the base number multiplied by itself a number of times, based on the place value position . For instance, look back at Figure D-1. A truckload is really $3 \times 3 \times 3 \times 3$, or 81, units, which can be written as 3^4. A crate is really $3 \times 3 \times 3$, or 27, units. The numbers in Figure D-1 can therefore be written like this:

Truckload = 3^4 Crate = 3^3 Carton = 3^2 Box = 3^1 Single = 3^0

(Any number raised to the 0 power equals 1.) Therefore, we can express the numbers in Figure D-2 as multiples of truckloads, crates, cartons, boxes, and singles like this:

	Truckloads	Crates	Cartons	Boxes	Singles
21022 (base 3)	2×3^4	1×3^3	0×3^2	2×3^1	2×3^0
Decimal equivalent	162	27	0	6	2

When we sum up the numbers in the last row above, we get 197. We just converted a base 3 number (21022) to a base 10 number (197).

Binary Number System

It was stated earlier that it is easier for computers to convert from binary to hex or from hex to binary than to convert between binary and decimal. Let's see just how easy. Recall that the binary number system only has two numerals, or bits: 0 and 1. If our friend Joe in shipping operated a "binary" shipping system, he would pack like this: 2 widgets in a box,

2 boxes in one carton (4 widgets), two cartons in one crate (8 widgets), and two crates in one truckload (16 widgets). In Figure D-5, Joe is asked to pack 13 widgets. He packs 1 crate (8 widgets), 1 carton (4 widgets), no boxes, and 1 single. The number 13 in binary is 1101:

$$(1 \times 2^3)+(1 \times 2^2)+(0 \times 2^1)+(1 \times 2^0)= 8 + 4 + 0 + 1 = 13$$

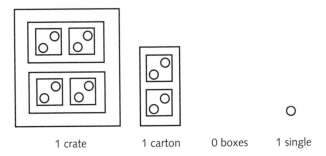

    1 crate   1 carton   0 boxes   1 single

Figure D-5   Binary 1101 = 13 displayed as crates, cartons, boxes, and singles

Now let's see how to convert binary to hex and back again. The largest 4-bit number in binary is 1111. This number in decimal and hex is:

```
binary 1111 = 1 group of 8 = 8
              1 group of 4 = 4
              1 group of 2 = 2
                  1 single = 1
              _____
              TOTAL = 15 (decimal)
Therefore, 1111 (binary) = 15 (decimal) = F (hex)
```

This last calculation is very important when working with computers: F is the largest numeral in the hex number system and it only takes 4 bits to write this largest hex numeral: F (hex) = 1111 (binary). So, every hex numeral (0, 1, 2, 3, 4, 5, 6, 7, 8, 9, A, B, C, D, E, and F) can be converted into a 4-bit binary number. Look back at the first 16 entries in Table D-2 for these binary values. Add leading zeroes to the binary numbers as necessary.

When converting from hex to binary, take each hex numeral and convert it to a 4-bit binary number and string all the 4-bit groups together. Fortunately, when working with computers, you will almost never be working with more than 2 hex numerals at a time. Here are some examples:

1. To convert hex F8 to binary, do the following: F = 1111, and 8 = 1000. Therefore, F8 = 11111000 (usually written 1111 1000).

2. To convert hex 9A to binary, do the following: 9 = 1001, and A = 1010. Therefore, 9A = 1001 1010.

Now try converting from binary to hex:

1. To convert binary 101110 to hex, first group the bits in groups of 4, starting at the right and moving left, adding leading zeros as necessary: 0010 1110.

2. Then convert each group of 4 bits in binary to a single hex numeral: 0010 = 2, and 1110 = E. The hex number is 2E.

Writing Conventions

Sometimes when you are dealing with hex, binary, and decimal numbers, it is not always clear which number system is being used. If you see a letter in the number, you know the number is a hex number. Binary numbers are usually written in groups of four bits. This book follows the convention of placing a lowercase h after a hex number, like this: 2Eh.

Memory Addressing

Computers often display memory addresses in the hex number system. You must either "think in hex" or convert to decimal. It's really easier, with a little practice, to think in hex. Here's the way it works:

Memory addresses are displayed as two hex numbers. An example is C800:5

The part to the left of the colon (C800) is called the **segment address**, and the part to the right of the colon (5) is called the **offset**. The offset value can have as many as four hex digits. The actual memory address is calculated by adding a zero to the right of the segment address and adding the offset value, like this: C800:5 = C8000 + 5 = C8005

The first 640K of memory is called conventional memory. Look at how that memory is addressed, first in decimal and then in hex (assuming 1 kilobyte = 1,024 bytes):

640K = 640 × 1,024 = 655,360

There are 655,360 memory addresses in conventional memory, where each memory address can hold 1 byte, or 8 bits, of either data or program instructions. The decimal value 655,360 converted to hex is A0000 (10×16^4). So, conventional memory addresses begin with 00000h and end with A0000h minus 1h or 9FFFFh. Written in segment-and-offset form, conventional memory addresses range from 0000:0 to 9FFF:F.

Recall that upper memory is defined as the memory addresses from 640K to 1,024K. The next address after 9FFF:F is the first address of upper memory, which is A0000, and the last address is FFFFF. Written in segment-and-offset terms, upper memory addresses range from A000:0 to FFFF:F.

Here is one way to organize the conversion of a large hex value such as FFFFF to decimal (remember F in hex equals 15 in decimal).

FFFFF converted to decimal:

$$
\begin{array}{llr}
15 \times 16^0 = 15 \times 1 = & & 15 \\
15 \times 16^1 = 15 \times 16 = & & 240 \\
15 \times 16^2 = 15 \times 256 = & & 3,840 \\
15 \times 16^3 = 15 \times 4096 = & & 61,440 \\
15 \times 16^4 = 15 \times 65,536 = & & 983,040 \\
\end{array}
$$

$$\text{TOTAL} = 1,048,575$$

Remember that FFFFF is the last memory address in upper memory. The very next memory address is the first address of extended memory, which is defined as memory above 1 MB. If you add 1 to the number above, you get 1,048,576, which is equal to 1024 × 1024, which is the definition of 1 megabyte.

Displaying Memory with DOS DEBUG

In Figure D-6 you see the results of the beginning of upper memory displayed. The DOS DEBUG command displays the contents of memory. Memory addresses are displayed in hex segment-and-offset values. To enter DEBUG, type the following command at the C prompt and press **Enter**:

C:\> DEBUG

Type the following dump command to display the beginning of upper memory (the hyphen in the command is the DEBUG command prompt) and press **Enter**:

-d A000:0

Memory is displayed showing 16 bytes on each line. The A area of memory (the beginning of upper memory) is not used unless the computer is using a monochrome monitor or this area is being used as an upper memory block. In Figure D-6, the area contains nothing but continuous 1s in binary or Fs in hex. The ASCII interpretation is on the right side. To view the next group of memory addresses, you can type **d** at the hyphen and press **Enter**. DEBUG displays the next 128 addresses.

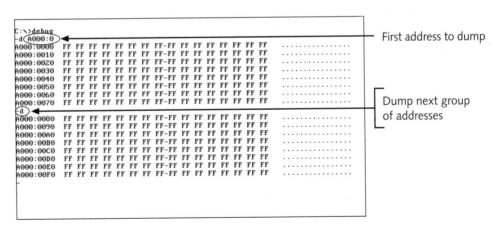

Figure D-6   Memory dump: −d A000:0

The A and B ranges of upper memory addresses (upper memory addresses that begin with A or B when written in hex) are used for monochrome monitors. The C range contains the video BIOS for a color monitor. Figure D-7 shows the dump of the beginning of the C range.

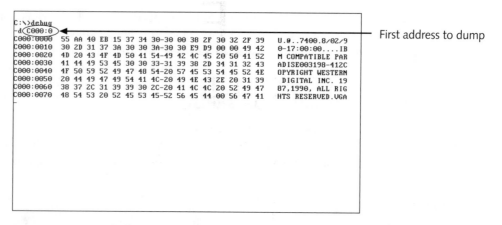

First address to dump

Figure D-7   Memory dump: -d C000:0

There is more than one way—in fact there are many ways—to identify the same segment-and-offset value. Try these commands to display the same upper memory addresses:

-d C000:0

-d BFF1:00F0

-d BFFF:0010

-d BEEE:1120

In summary, reading and understanding binary and hex numbers are essential skills for managing computers. All data is stored in binary in a computer and is often displayed in hex. Memory addresses are often displayed in hex segment-and-offset terms. An address in memory can be written in a variety of segment-and-offset values. The actual memory address is calculated by placing one zero to the right side of the segment address and adding the resulting value to the offset value. To exit DEBUG, type **q** for quit at the hyphen prompt. For more information about DEBUG, see Appendix F.

E

TROUBLESHOOTING GUIDELINES

This appendix brings together all the troubleshooting guidelines covered in the text and is designed to serve as a central point of reference when you are solving computer problems. The appendix is divided into sections by topic to help you locate information, but when you are not certain of the source of the problem, try browsing through the entire appendix, which may help you identify the source of the problem you are addressing. The suggestions made here are only meant to be summary guidelines. See the related chapters for complete explanations and procedures.

The following table is a detailed index to this appendix, listing the problems you may find yourself solving. It indicates both where in the appendix you can find troubleshooting guidance, and which chapter in the book contains more details about how to solve the problem.

If you find items in these guidelines that need to be updated, visit the Course Technology Web site at *www.course.com/pcrepair* to submit an item to be included in future versions of the guidelines.

CAUTION

Don't open your computer's case until you read this warning. Removing, replacing, and modifying pieces of hardware inside your computer without following the necessary precautions can cause you and your computer serious damage. The most common risk to a computer is posed by the discharge of static electricity, which can destroy circuit boards and chips. However, accessing the insides of the power supply or monitor can pose serious safety risks to you as well. These dangers can be avoided. To ensure safety in your work setting, follow every precaution listed in the Read This Before You Begin section at the beginning of this book.

Description of Problem	Appendix E Page	Chapter Reference
The computer does not boot	E2	2 (boot process); 12 (software problems under Windows 9x); 13 (software problems under Windows NT); 14 (software problems under Windows 2000)
Problems after the computer boots	E5	12 (software problems under Windows 9x); 13 (software problems under Windows NT); 14 (software problems under Windows 2000)
Memory problems with DOS	E6	4
Power supply problems	E7	11
Floppy drive problems	E8	5
Problems with the mouse	E10	9
Hard drive problems	E11	6, 7
Keyboard problems	E12	8, 9
Monitor problems	E14	8, 9
Printer problems	E17	8, 18
Modem problems	E21	16
CD-ROM drive problems	E23	10
Backup tape drive problems	E26	19
Problems that interrupt setup during a Windows 9x installation	E27	12
Software installation problems	E27	12, 13, 14
Hardware device installation problems under Windows 9x	E28	9, 12
Windows NT boot problems	E29	13
Windows 2000 boot problems	E29	14
Network problems	E30	17

The Computer Does Not Boot

Recall that the startup BIOS first performs POST before it turns to secondary storage for an OS. During POST, errors are communicated as a series of beeps, called beep codes, until video is checked. After video is running, errors are displayed on the screen. When POST completes with no errors, it sounds a single beep indicating all is well. Below is a list of the various ways things can go wrong between power on and a successful boot.

Blank screen, the PC appears "dead"

- Are there any burnt parts or odors?
- Are there any loose cable connections?
- Is the computer plugged in?

- Are all the power switches turned on? Remember to check the computer, the monitor, the surge protector, and the uninterruptible power supply.

- In some cases, a PC may appear to be dead because of a bad monitor. If you hear a single beep, can see lights on the front panel, and can hear a spinning hard drive, check for a bad monitor or a faulty monitor connection.

- Is there a separate circuit breaker that should be checked?

- Is the wall outlet (or surge protector) good?

- If the fan is not running, turn off the computer, open the case, and check the connections to the power supply. Are they secure? Are all cards securely seated? Are there any loose parts inside the case or on the system board?

- In some cases, a PC may appear to be dead because of a bad monitor. If you hear a single beep, see lights on the front panel, and can hear a spinning hard drive, check for a bad monitor or a faulty monitor connection.

- For an ATX system board, there is a wire that runs from the power switch on the front of the case to the system board. This wire must be connected properly, and the power switch on the front of the case must be turned on before the power comes up. This wire and its system-board connection might be labeled "REMOTE SW," "PWR SW," or something like that.

- Remove memory modules and reseat them. For a DIMM, try a different memory slot.

- Check the voltage output from the power supply. (How to do this is covered in Chapter 11.)

- Blow out the dust from the power supply's fan vent. Excessive dust causes overheating.

A+CORE 2.1
- Remove all nonessential expansion cards (modem, sound card, mouse) one at a time. Verify that they are not drawing too much power and pulling the system down. It is possible that the expansion cards are all good, but that the power supply is not capable of supplying enough current for all the add-on boards.

- It may be that there are too many cards and the computer is overheating. The temperature inside the case should not exceed 113° F.

- Trade the power supply for one you know is good. For AT system boards, be certain to follow the black-to-black rule when attaching the power cords to the system board.

- Is there strong magnetic or electrical interference? Sometimes an old monitor will emit too much static and EMF (electromagnetic force) and bring a whole system down.

- If the fan is running, reseat or trade the CPU, BIOS, or RAM. A POST code diagnostic card is a great help at this point.

- Sometimes a dead computer can be fixed by simply disassembling it and reseating cables, adapter cards, socketed chips, and memory modules. Bad connections and corrosion are common problems.

- Check jumpers, DIP switches, and CMOS settings.

- Is the system in a Doze or Sleep mode? Many "green" systems can be programmed through CMOS to suspend the monitor or even the hard drive if the keyboard and/or CPU has been inactive for a few minutes. Pressing any key will usually resume exactly where the user left off.

A+CORE 2.1

- A dying or dead battery may cause problems. Sometimes, if the computer hasn't been used for a few days, a weak battery will cause the CMOS to forget its configuration.

- Use a POST code diagnostic card to check system-board components.

- Exchange the system board, but before you do that, measure the output voltage of the power supply in case it is producing too much power and has damaged the board.

The computer does not recognize all installed RAM or SIMMs

- Are CMOS settings correct?

- Run diagnostic software such as PC-Technician to test memory.

- Are DIMM or SIMM modules properly seated?

- Look for bent pins, or chips installed the wrong way, on cache memory. Look for loose memory modules.

- Place your fingers on the individual chips. Sometimes a bad chip will be noticeably hotter than the other chips.

- Make sure the DIMMs or SIMMs have the correct or consistent part number. For example, if there are four installed SIMMs, they usually must be the same size (in megabytes) and same speed (in nanoseconds).

- Replace memory modules one at a time. For example, if the system only recognizes 6 out of 8 megabytes of RAM, swap the last two SIMM modules. Did the amount of recognized RAM change?

- Use SIMM modules with the same part number. (See Chapter 4 for details.)

- A trace on the system board may be bad. If this is the case, you may have to replace the entire system board.

Error messages appear during booting

- When a PC boots, one beep after POST indicates that all is well. If you hear more than one beep, look up the beep code in Appendix A.

- If error messages appear on the screen, then video is working. Look up the error message in Appendix A if you don't understand it.

- If a problem arises during a soft boot, try a hard boot. A soft boot may not work because TSRs are not always "kicked out" of RAM with a soft boot, or an ISA bus may not be initialized correctly.

- If new hardware has just been installed, disconnect it. If this solves the problem, troubleshoot the new device.
- For Windows 9x, try to boot into Safe Mode.
- Boot from a floppy disk. You should boot to an A prompt. If you are successful, the problem is in the hard drive subsystem and/or the software on the drive.

After booting from the floppy drive, consider the following:

- Can you access the hard drive from the A prompt?
- If you can get a C prompt, then the problem is in the software that is used on the hard drive to boot, such as the partition table, Master Boot Record, operating system hidden files, or command interface files. See the suggestions for hard drive problems.
- Run diagnostic software (Nuts & Bolts or PC-Technician) to test for hard drive hardware problems.
- Open the case, check all connections, and reseat all boards.
- Reduce the system to essentials. Remove any unnecessary hardware, such as expansion cards, and then try to boot again.

Windows 9x does not load correctly

A+CORE
2.1

- Boot into Safe Mode and then try booting normally. While in Safe Mode, if any changes were made in Control Panel just before the problem occurred, undo the changes.
- Boot from a rescue disk and run a current version of antivirus software.
- For Windows 98, use the System Configuration Utility to troubleshoot the load process. For more information, see Chapter 12.
- Try booting from the Nuts & Bolts rescue disk.

Problems after the Computer Boots

- If you suspect that software may be the source of the problem, try diagnostic software such as Nuts & Bolts Disk Tune or ScanDisk before reloading the software package.
- If you are having a problem with a hardware device, suspect the applications software using the device. Try another application or reinstall the software.
- If you suspect that hardware is the source of the problem, first isolate the problem by removing devices and substituting good components for suspected bad ones, one at a time. Be aware that the problem may be a resource conflict.
- Check the voltage output from the power supply with a multimeter.
- Check jumpers, DIP switches, and CMOS settings for the devices.
- Suspect a corrupted device driver. Reinstall the driver.

E

Memory Problems with DOS

A TSR will not load high

$A^{+CORE}_{2.1}$

- Are all command lines present in CONFIG.SYS and AUTOEXEC.BAT?
- Make sure that the DEVICEHIGH= commands in CONFIG.SYS are ordered so that the larger TSRs are placed first in the larger UMBs. There may not be enough upper memory addresses available to load the last ones.
- Try using MEMMAKER, which does a very good job of choosing the best order of loading TSRs.
- Some TSRs do not work from upper memory, so test them before assuming that all is well.

A device does not work or the system hangs

When a device doesn't work, suspect a resource conflict that may cause a device to stop working or the system to hang. Some common ones include:

- Two expansion boards are using the same I/O address, upper memory addresses, IRQ, or DMA channel.
- DOS has created and is using a UMB in the same memory addresses used by an expansion board, causing a memory conflict.

Two expansion boards are using the same resource

- Use MSD or Device Manager to determine what resources are being used.
- Some devices display the resources they are using during the boot process. Carefully watch for this information during booting.
- Read the documentation for each board to determine what resources are used and to look for the possibility of using alternate resources.
- Some expansion boards have DIP switches or jumpers that allow you to substitute one set of resources for another. Change the settings to avoid the conflict.
- For a memory address conflict, you may change the memory addresses by adding a parameter to the command line that loads the device driver for the expansion board.

When UMBs and expansion board memory addresses conflict

- Read the documentation for each board, use MSD or Device Manager, or watch for the displayed information while booting to determine the upper memory addresses in use.
- Use the Exclude option to the EMM386.EXE command line. For example, to exclude CC000–CFFFF from the addresses used by UMBs, use this command line:

```
DEVICE=C:\DOS\EMM386.EXE. NOEMS X=CC00 - CFFF
```

- Reboot your computer to activate the change. For more information on memory address conflicts, see Chapter 4.

Power Supply Problems

A+CORE 2.1 | Symptoms of problems with the power supply or the house current to the PC are:

- The computer stops or hangs for no reason. Sometimes it may even reboot itself.
- During booting, the system might hang, but after several tries, it boots successfully.
- During booting, beep codes occur, but the errors come and go.
- Memory errors appear occasionally.
- Data is written incorrectly to the hard drive.
- The keyboard stops working at odd times.
- The system board fails or is damaged.
- The power supply overheats and becomes hot to the touch.

Try these things:

- What other devices are using the same house circuit? Remove a copy machine, laser printer, or other heavy equipment from the circuit.
- Measure the voltage output of the power supply, or exchange it for one you know is good.
- Install an electrical conditioner to monitor and condition the voltage to the PC.

The fan on the power supply stops working

Usually just before a fan stops working, it hums or whines. If this has just happened, replace the fan or the entire power supply. If you replace the power supply or fan and the fan still does not work, the problem may not be the fan or power supply. It may be caused by a short somewhere else in the system drawing too much power. This section is about troubleshooting a short somewhere else in the system.

- Don't operate the PC with the fan not working. Computers without cooling fans can quickly overheat and damage chips.
- Turn the power off and remove all power cord connections to all components, including power to the system board, and all power cords to drives. Turn the power back on. If the fan comes on, the problem is probably with one of the systems you disconnected, not with the power supply.
- Turn the power off and reconnect the power cords to the drives. If the fan comes on, you can eliminate the drives as the problem. If the fan does not come on, try one drive after another until you identify the drive with the short.
- If the drives are not the problem, suspect the system-board subsystem. With the power off, reconnect all power cords to the drives.

- Turn the power off and remove the power to the system board by disconnecting P8 and P9 or P1. Turn the power back on.
- If the fan comes back on, the problem is probably not the power supply but a short in one of the components powered by the power cords to the system board. The power to the system board also powers interface cards.
- Remove all interface cards and reconnect plugs to the system board.
- If the fan still works, the problem is with one of the interface cards. If the fan does not work, the problem is with the system board or something still connected to it.
- Check for missing standoffs that may be allowing a system-board component to improperly ground to the computer case.
- Look for damage on the bottom side of the system board that may be causing shorted circuits on the board.
- Frayed wires on cable connections can also cause shorts. Disconnect hard drive cables connected directly to the system board. Power up with power to the system board connected, but all cables disconnected from the system board. If the fan comes on, the problem is with one of the systems you disconnected.
- Never replace a damaged system board with a good one without first testing the power supply. You don't want to subject another good board to possible damage.

Floppy Drive Problems

A+CORE 2.1 | Below is a list of errors you may encounter, created by floppy drive problems.

General failure reading drive A: Abort, Retry, Fail?

The problem may come from several sources, including:

- An error in the application you are currently running
- The operating system you are currently running
- The system BIOS or CMOS setup (they may not be correctly configured)
- The floppy disk in the drive
- The floppy drive
- The floppy drive controller card
- The cable from the controller card to the drive
- The power supply
- The power supply cable to the drive (it may be loose or disconnected)
- The command just issued (it may contain a mistake or may be the wrong command)
- The drive latch (it may not be closed, or the disk may be incorrectly inserted)
- The drive read/write head (it may be dirty)

A^{+}_{CORE} 2.1   Try the following:

- Remove the floppy disk. Does the shuttle window move freely?
- Do you see any dirt, hair, or trash on the disk's Mylar surface?
- Does the disk spin freely inside the housing cover?
- Some new disks simply need a little loosening up. Put the disk back in the drive and try again.
- Does the light on the correct drive go on when you try to access it? Maybe you are trying to access the B drive, but the disk is in the A drive.
- Will another disk work in the drive? If so, the problem is probably caused by the disk, not the drive. There is an exception to this statement. The drive may be out of alignment. If it is, the drive will be unable to read a floppy disk formatted in another drive that has a different (correct) alignment, although it may read a disk that is formatted with its own alignment. To test this possibility, try several disks, and note if the drive only reads those disks that it has recently formatted. If so, then you've probably located the problem. You probably will want to replace the drive.
- Does the drive light come on at all? If not, then the problem may be with the software or the hardware. Try to access the disk with a different software program.
- What does work? Can DOS access the drive with a simple DIR A:? Can File Manager or Explorer access the disk? How about CHKDSK A:?
- Reboot the machine and try again. Many problems with computers disappear with a simple reboot. If a soft boot doesn't do it, try a hard boot.
- If the light doesn't come on even then, suspect that the source of your problem is the power to the drive or the hardware connections inside the case.
- Does a second floppy drive work? If both lights refuse to come on, suspect the power supply or the floppy drive controller card.
- Has this drive been used recently? Perhaps the system setup has lost CMOS data. The system may think it has a 720K drive when it really has a 1.44-MB drive. Access Setup and check the drive specifications.
- Try cleaning the drive's read/write heads. Use a head-cleaning kit that includes a paper disk and a cleaning solution.

If none of the above solves the problem, it is time to go inside the case. Turn off the computer and open the computer case.

- Check every connection from the system board to the drive.
- Check the power cable connection.
- If the drive uses a controller card, remove the card. Using a clean white eraser, erase and clean the edge connector and reseat the board.
- Take the power cable from a second, working floppy drive and put it on the non-working one to eliminate the power cable as the problem.

- Replace the data cable and try the drive again. Exchange the controller card. If that does not work, exchange the drive itself and try again.
- If the drive still does not work, suspect the system board or the ROM BIOS on the system board.

A^+ OS
    3.1

Non-system disk or disk error. Replace and strike any key when ready

This error message appears when you are booting from a disk that does not have the operating system on it. Use a different disk and try to boot again.

Invalid or missing COMMAND.COM

This error message appears when DOS is loading and the two hidden files are present, but COMMAND.COM is not present, is corrupt, or is the wrong version. Boot from a bootable disk that has COMMAND.COM, and then copy the file to the disk that you want to be bootable or use the SYS command to restore the file.

Invalid Drive Specification

This error message appears when you are trying to access a drive that the operating system does not know is available.

Not ready reading drive A: Abort, Retry, Fail?

This error occurs when the disk in drive A is not readable. Maybe the disk is missing or is inserted incorrectly. The disk may have a bad boot record, errors in the FAT, or bad sectors. Try using Nuts & Bolts to examine the disk for corruption.

Track 0 bad, disk not usable

This message typically appears when you are trying to format a disk using the wrong disk type.

Write-protect error writing drive A:

This error occurs when the disk is write-protected, and the application is trying to write to it.

Problems with the Mouse

A^+ CORE
    2.1

The most common problem created by the mouse: the cursor on the screen is difficult to move with the mouse

The rollers inside the mouse housing collect dirt and dust and occasionally need cleaning. Remove the cover to the mouse ball from the bottom of the mouse. These usually come off with a simple press and shift motion. Clean the rollers with a cotton swab dipped in a very small amount of liquid soap.

Hard Drive Problems

A+CORE
2.1

When troubleshooting hard drive problems, always begin by interviewing the user, asking questions such as the following:

- Was the computer recently moved?
- Was any new hardware recently installed?
- Was any new software recently installed?
- Was any software recently reconfigured or upgraded?
- Does the computer have a history of similar problems?

Below is a list of hard drive problems you may encounter while supporting PCs.

Hard drive does not boot

This error may occur for any number of reasons. Try the following:

- Confirm that both the monitor and computer switches are turned on.
- Prepare for the presence of a virus by write-protecting your bootable rescue disk. Then try booting from this boot disk and logging on to drive C. If you have a Windows 9x rescue disk, you can use ScanDisk, Chkdsk, or Fdisk to examine the system.
- If the PC will not boot from the bootable floppy disk, verify that the boot disk is good. Try using it in a different computer.
- After booting from the rescue disk, run a current version of an antivirus program.
- Check to be sure that the power cable and disk controller cable connections are good and are correctly oriented.
- If the drive still does not boot, try performing the following procedures in order:
  - Reconnect or swap the drive data cable.
  - If the drive uses an adapter card, reseat or exchange it.
  - Exchange the hard drive with one you know is in working condition, and try to boot from that.
- A bad power supply or a bad system board also may cause a disk boot failure. If the problem is solved by exchanging one of the above modules, try reinstalling the old module to verify that the problem was not caused by a bad connection.
- For DOS, boot from a floppy disk, run SCANDISK, and restore hidden system files on drive C with the command: A:\>SYS C:.
- Boot from the Nuts & Bolts rescue disk.
- Check CMOS setup to confirm that BIOS recognizes the drive.

E

$A^{+CORE}_{2.1}$ ## Drive retrieves and saves data slowly

This may be caused by fragmented files that have been updated, modified, and spread over different portions of the disk. Run DEFRAG to rewrite fragmented files to contiguous sectors.

- Verify that the hard disk drivers are properly installed.
- If the PC uses disk caching software, verify that it loads and is operational.
- Use a current version of anti-virus software to check for viruses.

Computer will not recognize a newly installed hard disk

If the disk is brand new or has no information you want to keep on it, consider the following:

- Does the hard disk manual state that you must first do a "low-level" format or run Disk Manager before using the disk? IDE drives are already low-level formatted. Older drives require the user to perform this task.
- Has the FDISK utility been successfully run? Choose Display Partition Information from the FDISK menu to verify the status.
- FORMAT C:/S is the last required "format" step. Has this been done?
- Has the CMOS setup been correctly configured?
- Verify in CMOS setup that power management features are disabled.
- Verify that the drive spins up when power is turned on.
- Are there any drivers to install?
- Are there any DIP switches or jumpers that must be set?
- Has the data cable been properly connected? Verify that the colored edge of the cable is connected to pin 1 on the edge connectors of both the card and cable.
- Call the drive manufacturer if the above steps don't fix the problem.

Keyboard Problems

Because keyboards are relatively inexpensive, the most common solution to a keyboard problem is to replace it. However, there are a few simple things you can do to repair a keyboard that is not working.

A few keys don't work

- Remove the cap on the bad key with a chip extractor. Spray contact cleaner into the key well. Repeatedly depress the contact in order to clear it out. Don't use rubbing alcohol to clean the key well, because it can add a residue to the contact.
- If this method of cleaning solves the problem, then clean the adjacent keys as well.

The keyboard does not work at all

- Is the cable plugged in securely?

- If the cable connection is good and the keyboard still does not work, connect a working keyboard of the same type to the computer. If the second keyboard works, you have verified that the problem is in the keyboard and not in the computer.

- If the second keyboard does not work, connect the first keyboard to a computer that works properly. If this works, then the problem must be with the original computer.

- If the problem is in the keyboard, if possible, swap the existing cable with a cable known to be good, perhaps from an old, discarded keyboard. Sometimes a wire in a PC keyboard cable becomes pinched or broken. Most cables can be easily separated and detached from the keyboard by removing the few screws that hold the keyboard case together, then simply unplugging the cable. Be careful as you work; don't allow the key caps to fall out!

- If the problem is not the cable, replace the keyboard.

- If the problem is with the computer, consider the following: On the system board, the two chips that affect the keyboard functions are the keyboard chip and the ROM BIOS chip. You might choose to swap each of these chips on the system board. Otherwise the entire system board may have to be replaced.

Key continues to repeat after being released

- The problem may be a dirty contact. Some debris has conductive properties and can therefore short the gap between the contacts, causing the key to repeat. Try cleaning the key switch with contact cleaner.

- Very high humidity and excess moisture may short key switch contacts and cause keys to repeat. The problem will usually resolve itself once the humidity level returns to normal. You can hasten the drying process by using a fan (not a hot hair dryer) to blow air at the keyboard.

Keys produce the wrong characters

This problem is usually caused by a bad chip on the keyboard. Try swapping the keyboard for one you know is good. If the problem goes away, replace the original keyboard with a new one.

Major spills on the keyboard

For major spills on the keyboard, unplug the keyboard and thoroughly rinse it in running water. Give the board about two days to dry. You can speed up the process if you set it out in the sun or in front of a fan.

Monitor Problems

CAUTION
Don't open the monitor case unless you are trained to work inside the case.

Poor cable connections or bad contrast/brightness adjustments cause many monitor problems. Below is a list of some common monitor problems and how to address them.

Power light (LED) does not go on, no picture

- Is the monitor plugged in?
- Verify that the wall outlet works by plugging in a lamp, radio, or other device.
- If the monitor power cord is plugged into a power strip or surge protector, verify that the power strip is turned on, and the monitor is also turned on.
- If the monitor power cord is plugged into the back of the computer, verify that the connection is tight, and that the computer is turned on.
- Check for a fuse in the monitor. If one is present, it should be visible from the back of the monitor. Look for a black knob that you can remove (no need to go inside the monitor cover). Check the fuse for a broken wire indicating a bad fuse.
- Check for a switch on the back of the monitor for choosing between 110 volts and 220 volts. Check that the switch is in the correct position.
- If none of these things works, take the monitor to a service center.

Power LED light is on, no picture on power up

- Check the contrast adjustment. If there's no change, then leave it at a middle setting.
- Check the brightness adjustment. If there's no change, then leave it at a middle setting.
- Is the cable connected securely to the computer?
- If the monitor-to-computer cable detaches from the monitor, exchange it for a cable you know is good, or check the cable for continuity (Chapter 11).
- If this solves the problem, reattach the old cable to verify that the problem was not simply a bad connection.
- Confirm that the proper system configuration has been set up. Some older system boards have a jumper or DIP switch that can be used to select the monitor type.
- Test the monitor that isn't working on a computer that works with another monitor.
- Test a monitor you know is good on the computer you suspect to be bad. If you think the monitor is bad, make sure that it also fails to work on a good computer.

- Check the software configuration on the computer. For Windows 9x, boot into Safe Mode, which forces the OS to use a generic video driver and low resolution. If this works, then change the driver and resolution.

- Test the video card you think is bad on a computer that works. Test a video card you know is good on the computer that you suspect may be bad. Whenever possible, try to do both. If the card you think is bad works on a computer you know is good, then the card is good. If the card doesn't work on either machine, you have probably found the source of your problem.

- If the video card has some socketed chips that appear dirty or corroded, consider removing them and trying to clean the pins. You can use a clean pencil eraser to do this. But normally, if the problem is a bad video card, the most cost-effective measure is to replace the card.

- Go into Setup and disable the shadowing of video ROM.

- Use Nuts & Bolts Discover Pro to test the RAM on the system board.

- Trade the system board for one you know is good. Sometimes, though rarely, a peripheral chip on the system board of the computer causes the problem.

E

Power on, but monitor displays the wrong characters

- Wrong characters are usually not the result of a bad monitor, but a problem with the video card. Trade the video card for one you know is good.

- If the new video card doesn't work, exchange the system board. Sometimes a bad chip, ROM, or RAM on the system board will display the wrong characters on the monitor.

Monitor flickers and/or has wavy lines

- Check the cable. Monitor flicker can be caused by poor cable connections.

- Does the monitor have a degauss button to eliminate accumulated or stray magnetic fields? If so, press it.

- Check if something in the office is providing a lot of electrical noise. For example, you may be able to stop a flicker by moving the office fan to a different outlet. Bad fluorescent lights or large speakers have also been known to cause interference. Two monitors placed very closely together may also cause problems.

- If the vertical scan frequency (the refresh rate at which the screen is drawn) is below 60 Hz, a screen flicker may appear in the normal course of operation.

- Try using a different refresh rate if your monitor supports it. In Windows 9x, right-click on the desktop and select Properties from the menu.

- Try a different monitor set in the same location. Does the same thing happen to the new monitor? If so, suspect interference.

A+CORE
    2.1

- Check Control Panel, Display, Settings to see if a high resolution (greater than 800 × 600 with more than 256 colors) is selected. Consider these issues:
    - The video card may not support this resolution/color setting.
    - There may not be enough video RAM; 2 MB or more may be required.
    - The monitor may not support this resolution or refresh rate.
    - The added (socketed) video RAM may be of a different speed than the soldered memory.

No graphics display, or the screen goes blank when loading certain programs

- A special graphics or video accelerator card is defective or not present.
- The software is not configured to do graphics, or the software does not recognize the installed graphics card.
- The video card may not support this resolution and/or color setting.
- There may not be enough video RAM; 2MB or more may be required.
- The added (socketed) video RAM may be of a different speed than the soldered memory.
- The wrong adapter/display type may be selected. Start Windows 9x from Safe Mode to reset display. ("How to" is covered in Chapter 12.)

Screen goes blank 30 seconds or one minute after you last touched the keyboard

- A "green" system board (which follows energy-saving standards) used with an Energy Star monitor can be configured to go into a Standby or Doze mode after a period of inactivity.
- Try to change the doze features in CMOS, using a menu option such as Power Management, or in Windows 9x, using Control Panel, Display, Screen Saver.
- Some monitors have a Power Save switch on the back of the monitor. This may not be switched to your desired setting.

Poor quality color display

- Read the documentation for the monitor for explanations of the color-adjusting buttons on the outside of the monitor, which are used to fine-tune the color.
- Exchange video cards.
- Add more video RAM; 2, 4, or 8 MB may be required for higher resolutions.
- Check if there is a fan or large speaker (which has large magnets) or another monitor nearby that may be causing interference.
- Less expensive monitors and video cards don't use quality components, which can cause perceived degradation. Try a quality monitor to determine if the image is affected.

Picture out of focus, or out of adjustment

- Check the adjustment knobs on the control panel on the outside of the monitor.

- Change the refresh rate. Sometimes this can make the picture appear more in focus.

- There are adjustments that can be made inside the monitor that may solve the problem. If you have not been trained to work inside the monitor, take the monitor to a service center for adjustments.

Crackling sound

An accumulation of dirt or dust inside the unit may cause a crackling sound. Someone trained to work on the inside of the monitor can vacuum the inside.

Printer Problems

When troubleshooting printer problems, first determine that the problem is truly with the printer. The problem may be the computer hardware communicating with the printer, the applications software using the printer, the printer driver, the printer cable, or the printer. Ask these questions and try these approaches:

- Is the printer turned on, and is the printer online?

- Is the correct printer selected as the default printer?

- Will the printer work with an application program other than the one currently running? If so, then suspect the currently-running application to be the problem.

- Is the printer using the correct driver? Does the driver need updating? Is the driver correctly installed?

- Is there enough available hard drive space for the software to create temporary print files?

- Can you move the printer to another computer and print from it? Will another printer work on this computer? Answering these two questions can isolate the problem to either the printer or the computer.

After you are convinced that the problem is not with the computer hardware or software, but is indeed a problem with the printer itself, you are ready for the following troubleshooting guide. Also see the printer documentation for troubleshooting steps to solve printer problems.

Laser printer problems

The printer documentation can be very helpful and most often contains a phone number for technical support from the printer manufacturer. A good test for a printer is to print a test page from the PC, not just directly from the printer. From Windows 9x, access **Control Panel** and double-click on **Printers**. Right-click on the printer you want to test. Select the **Properties** options. Click on **Print Test Page** to send a test page to the printer.

A+CORE
5.1

Printer never leaves warm-up mode

The warming up message should disappear as soon as the printer establishes communication with the PC. If it doesn't, try the following:

- Turn the printer off and disconnect the cable to the computer.

- Turn on the printer. If it now displays a Ready message, the problem is communication between the printer and the computer.

- Verify that the cable is connected to the correct printer port, not to a serial port.

- Verify that data to the installed printer is being sent to the parallel port. For example, access the Properties box of the installed printer as described above. Verify that the print job is being sent to LPT1.

- Replace the cable.

A Paper Out message displays

- Remove the paper tray. Be sure there is paper in the tray. Carefully replace the tray, being certain that the tray is fully inserted in the slot.

- Check the lever mechanism that falls into a slot on the tray when no paper is present. Is it jammed or bent?

- Turn the printer off and back on.

A Toner Low message displays, or print is irregular or light

- Remove the toner cartridge from the printer, shake the cartridge from left to right to redistribute the toner supply evenly over the bottom of the bin, and replace it in the printer. To avoid flying toner, don't shake the cartridge too hard. This is really just a temporary fix for a cartridge low on toner. Plan to replace the toner cartridge in the printer soon.

- Extreme humidity may cause the toner to clump in the cartridge and give the same error message.

A Paper Jam message displays

- If paper is jammed inside the printer, follow the directions in the printer documentation to remove the paper. Don't jerk the paper from the printer mechanism, but pull it out carefully and evenly. Check for paper jams coming from the input tray and going to the output bin.

- If there is no jammed paper, then remove the tray and check the metal plate at the bottom of the tray. Can it move up and down freely? If not, replace the tray with a new tray.

- When you insert the tray in the printer, does the printer lift the plate as the tray is inserted? If not, the lift mechanism may need repairing.

A+CORE
5.1

One or more white streaks appear in the print

- Remove the toner cartridge, tap it to redistribute the toner supply, and replace the cartridge.
- Check the printer manual for specific directions as to what part may need replacing when this problem occurs.

Print appears speckled

- Try replacing the cartridge. If the problem continues, the power supply assembly may be damaged.

Printed images are distorted

- Check for debris that might be interfering with the printer operation.
- Replace the toner cartridge.

Dot matrix printer problems

A number of problems can arise with dot matrix printers.

Print quality is poor

- Begin with the ribbon. Does it advance normally while the carriage moves back and forth? Is it placed correctly in the ribbon guide? Replace the ribbon.
- If the new ribbon still does not advance properly, check the printer's advance mechanism.
- Adjust the print head spacing. There is usually a lever adjustment that can alter the distance between the print head and the plate.
- Check the print head for dirt. Make sure it's not hot before you touch it. If there is a build-up, wipe off each wire with a cotton swab dipped in alcohol or contact cleaner.

Printer self-test works, but printing from a computer application program does not work

- To perform a printer self-test, see the printer documentation. If this test indicates that the printer itself is functioning correctly, communication from the PC may be the problem.
- Check cable connections. Is the printer online?

Print head moves back and forth, but nothing prints

- Check the ribbon. Is it installed correctly between the plate and the print head?
- Does the ribbon advance properly?
- Try a new ribbon.

E

A+CORE
5.1

Ink-jet printer problems

A number of problems can arise with ink-jet printers.

Print quality is poor

- The paper being used should be specifically designed for ink-jet printers.
- Is the ink supply low, or is there a partially clogged nozzle? (This may happen if the printer has been idle for several days.) If so, follow the printer's documentation to clean each nozzle.
- Remove and reinstall each cartridge.
- Change the print quality selection for the printer. (Use the Printer Properties window.)
- Is the print head too close to, or too far from, the paper?
- If you are printing on transparencies, try changing the fill pattern in your application.

Printing is intermittent or absent

- Make sure the correct printer driver is installed.
- Is the ink supply low?
- Are nozzles clogged?
- Replace the ink cartridges or replenish the ink supply. Follow the directions in the printer documentation.

Network Printer Problems

First determine that the problem is not a physical problem with the printer. Problems with network printing may be caused by the printer, the network, or the computer trying to use the printer. You can isolate the problem by finding the answers to the following questions:

- Is the printer online?
- Is the network printer on the remote PC configured correctly? Try uninstalling and reinstalling the printer.
- Is the correct network printer selected on the remote PC?
- Is there enough hard disk space available on the remote PC?
- Can you print successfully from another application on the remote PC?
- Can you print successfully from the host PC using the identical application?
- If you print to a file and then send the file to the host PC, does it print successfully? If this works, then the problem is with data transmission to the network printer. If this does not work, then the problem is with the application or print driver on the remote PC.

- For DOS applications, you may need to exit the application before printing will work. Is the network printer configured to handle DOS printing?

Modem Problems

A+ OS 3.2 The text below describes how to address modem problems you may encounter.

The modem does not respond

To address this problem, answer the following questions and try the following approaches:

- Make sure the modem is plugged into the phone jack.
- If you are using an external modem, make sure it is plugged into the computer and that the connection is solid.
- There are two jacks on a modem. Are the lines reversed?
- Is the phone line working? Plug in a phone. Is there a dial tone?
- Do you need to dial an extra character (such as 9 or 8) to get an outside line?
- Has the modem ever worked, or is this a new installation? If it is a new installation, check the following:
  - Is the computer short on RAM or hard drive space? Try closing all other applications currently running.
  - Is the modem set to the same COM port and IRQ that the software is set to?
  - Is another device also configured to the same COM port or IRQ that the modem is using?
  - For an internal modem, check the DIP switches and jumpers. Do they agree with the modem properties in the OS?
  - Try moving an internal modem to a different expansion slot. For an external modem using a serial port card, move the serial port card to a different slot.
  - For an external modem, use a different serial cable.
  - Did the software correctly initialize the modem? If you did not give the correct modem type to the software, it may be trying to send the wrong initialization command. Try AT&F. (Under Windows 9x, click **Start**, **Settings**, **Control Panel**. Double-click **Modem**. Select the modem and click **Modem Properties**, **Connections**, **Advanced Connection Settings**. Enter the **AT** command under Extra Settings.) Retry the modem.

The modem says that there is no dial tone, even though you can hear it

- The modem may not be able to detect the dial tone, even if you can hear it. Try unplugging any other equipment plugged into this same phone line, such as a Fax machine.
- Try giving the ATX0 command before you dial. Enter the command under Advanced Settings, as described above.

E

- Straighten your phone lines! Don't let them get all crossed and twisted up with other heavy electrical lines.

The modem dials and then says that the other end is busy, even when you know that it is not

- This can happen with international calls; the modem does not recognize the signal as a ring. Using communications software that allows you to enter AT commands (such as ProCom Plus), try entering the ATX0 command before entering the command to dial.
- Straighten the phone lines and remove extra equipment, as described above.

The modem and the receiving modem take a very long time to negotiate the connection

- This is probably due to a noisy phone line. Try calling again or using a different number.
- Remove other equipment from your line. A likely suspect is a credit card machine.
- Turn off data compression and try again.
- Turn off error correction and try again.
- Try forcing your modem to use a slower speed.

During a connection, it sounds as if the handshaking starts all over again

- Modems normally do this if the phone line is noisy and causes a lot of data to get corrupted; it's called **retraining**, and sometimes it can solve the problem as the modems renegotiate, compensating for the noisy line. Do the things listed above to clear your line of equipment and twisted phone lines.

File transfers are too slow

- Does your modem support data compression? Check that the modem is configured for it.

The modem loses connection at odd times or is slow

- Check the communications software for the speed assigned to the modem. Many times people set the communications software speed for the modem speed instead of for the port speed, which is what the software is asking for. (It should be about four times the modem speed.)
- You may have a noisy phone line. Try the connection using modems of the same brand and model on both ends. If performance is better, the problem is most likely the phone line, because two modems of the same brand and model are best able to compensate for a noisy phone line.
- Is the phone line from the modem to the jack too long? About 4 feet is the upper limit; otherwise, electromagnetic interference may be the problem.

- Straighten the phone lines and clear the line of any extra equipment.
- Reinstall the modem. Allow Windows 9x to detect the modem for you and install its own drivers.
- Search the Web site of the modem manufacturer for a new driver and install that.

The modem drops the connection and gives the NO CARRIER message

- Most likely the connection was first dropped by the remote modem. Is someone trying to use a phone extension on this line?
- Disable call waiting. Some communications software has a setting to disable call waiting. If not, you can put *70 in the Extra Settings box of Advanced Connections Settings.
- Remove extra equipment from the line and straighten the phone lines.

When the weather is bad, the connection often disconnects

- This is caused by a dirty phone line. Does your line make extra noises at these times? Remove any extra equipment and straighten the lines.

Whenever large files are downloaded, some of the data is lost

- Make sure that hardware flow control is on and that software flow control is off, for the software, the COM port, and the modem.

The connection fails whenever large files are uploaded or downloaded

- There may be a buffer overflow. Try these approaches to gain better control of data flow:
  - Make sure that hardware flow control is on and that software flow control is off, for the software, the COM port, and the modem.
  - Is the serial port speed set too high for the UART chip you have? Lower the port speed.
  - For an external modem, try a different serial port cable.

You get nothing but garbage across the connection

- Check the port settings. Try 8 databits, no parity, and one stop bit (8, No, and 1).
- Slow down the port speed.
- Slow down the modem speed.

CD-ROM Drive Problems

Problems with the CD-ROM can arise in a number of different settings.

Problems when installing the CD-ROM drive

Real-mode CD-ROM drivers can be loaded from the AUTOEXEC.BAT and CONFIG.SYS files. See the CD-ROM installation guide for specific commands for your drive. Here are two examples:

In the CONFIG.SYS file: `DEVICE=C:\CDSYS\SLCD.SYS /D:MSCD001`

In AUTOEXEC.BAT: `C:\DOS\MSCDEX.EXE /D:MSCD001 /L:D /M:8`

Try creating a bootable disk with these commands and the referenced files. (Modify the paths to point to drive A.)

The error message (Invalid Drive Specification) appears while the system is trying to access the drive

- Does the eject button work on the drive? If not, then check the power connection to the drive.

- Check that there are no errors in the command lines in the CONFIG.SYS or AUTOEXEC.BAT file, according to the documentation that came with the CD-ROM. Did you get an error message during booting, such as Bad Command or File Not Found?

- If an adapter card is used, reseat it and check cable connections.

- The MSCDEX.EXE program may not be loaded. The entry in AUTOEXEC.BAT needs to come before the command to load Windows.

- Try a different version of MSCDEX. Look for this file in the \DOS directory and change the path in front of the filename in AUTOEXEC.BAT to point to that version.

- Reinstall the drivers. Check the Web site of the drive manufacturer for updated driver files.

The install process is terminated with the message "MSCDEX.EXE not found"

- For DOS and Windows 3.x, MSCDEX.EXE must be copied onto the hard drive. Put it in the \DOS directory, then restart the install process. Sometimes MSCDEX is placed in the Windows directory, and sometimes a copy is put in the newly created CD-ROM directory.

The error message "Not Enough Drive Letters" appears during booting

- Increase the number of allowed drive letters with the LASTDRIVE line in CONFIG.SYS:
  LASTDRIVE=Z

Conflict errors exist

- These will appear during booting as error messages, or they will cause some other device to fail to operate. The IRQ and the I/O address of your CD-ROM should be in the documentation. If not, call the manufacturer's technical support for this information or check the manufacturer's Web site.

■ For Windows 9x, see Device Manager for resources used. Search Device Manager for resource conflicts.

Computer does not recognize CD-ROM (no D: prompt in DOS or no drive D listed in Windows 9x Explorer)

A+ OS
2.1

E

■ Check the following configurations:

- When using DOS, does the CONFIG.SYS file contain a CD device command line? Does the AUTOEXEC.BAT file call MSCDEX.EXE? Is MSCDEX.EXE placed in the correct directory? (A correct Windows 9x installation will not need MSCDEX.EXE or entries in AUTOEXEC.BAT or CONFIG.SYS.)

- For Windows 9x, has the CD-ROM driver been installed? Look in Device Manager.

- Check to see if another device is using the same port settings or IRQ number. Look in Device Manager.

■ Check the following connections:

- Is the power cable attached to the CD-ROM?

- Is the data cable attached to the CD-ROM and to the controller?

- Is the stripe on the data cable correctly aligned to pin 1? (Look for an arrow or small 1 printed on the drive. For a best guess, pin 1 is usually next to the power connector.)

- For IDE drives, is the correct master/slave jumper set? For example, if both the hard drive and the CD-ROM drive are hooked up to the same ribbon cable, one must be designated master and the other slave.

- For IDE drives, verify the IDE connection is enabled in CMOS setup.

- For SCSI drives, is the proper ID set and the device terminated if it's on the end of the SCSI chain?

■ Suspect a boot virus. Run a current version of an antivirus program.

No sound

■ Is the sound cable attached between the CD-ROM and the analog audio connector on the sound card?

■ Are the speakers turned on?

■ Make sure the speaker volume is turned up. (Check both the speaker itself and the OS volume control.)

■ Make sure the speakers are plugged into the line "Out" or "Spkr" port of the sound card.

- Is the transformer for the speaker plugged into an electrical outlet on one end and into the speakers on the other end?
- Is the volume control for Windows turned down? (To check, click **Start**, **Programs**, **Accessories**, **Entertainment**, **Volume Control**.)
- Does the sound card have a "diagnose" file on the installation floppy disk?
- Reinstall the sound card drivers.
- Is another device using the same I/O address or IRQ number? Look in Device Manager.
- To check for a bad connection, remove and reinstall the sound card.
- Replace the sound card with one you know is good.

Backup Tape Drive Problems

There are a number of different tape drives that may cause different types of problems.

A minicartridge does not work

- Verify that the minicartridge is write-enabled if you are trying to write data.
- Are you inserting the minicartridge correctly? Check the user guide.
- Check that you are using the correct type of minicartridge. See the user guide.
- Is the minicartridge formatted? The format is done by the software and can take an hour or more.
- Retension the tape. Use the backup software to do this. Some tape drives require this, and others do not. Retension fast-forwards and rewinds the tape to eliminate loose spots.
- Take the minicartridge out and reboot. Try the minicartridge again.
- Try using a new minicartridge. The old one may have worn out.
- Just as with floppy disks, if the tape was removed from the drive while the drive light was still on, the data being written at that time may not be readable.

Data transfer is slow

- Does the tape software have an option for optimizing speed or data compression? Try turning one and then the other off and on.
- Some tape drives can use an optional accelerator card to speed up data transfer. See the tape drive user guide.
- Try a new minicartridge.
- If the tape drive can do so, completely erase the tape and reformat it. Be sure that the tape drive has the ability to perform this procedure before you tell the software to do so.

E

- If you have installed an accelerator card, verify that the card is connected to the tape drive.
- Check that there is enough memory for the software to run.

The drive does not work after the installation

- Check that pin 1 is oriented correctly to the data cable at both ends.
- Check for a resource conflict. The tape drive normally requires an IRQ, DMA channel, and I/O address.
- For DOS, check the entries in CONFIG.SYS and AUTOEXEC.BAT.

The drive fails intermittently or generates errors

- The tape might be worn out. Try a new tape.
- Clean the read/write head of the tape drive. See the tape drive user guide for directions.
- For an external tape drive, move the drive as far as you can from the monitor and computer case.
- Reformat the tape.
- Retension the tape.
- Verify that you are using the correct tape type and tape format.

Problems That Interrupt a Windows 9x Installation

A+ OS
2.1

- Setup is probably having trouble detecting the hardware present. Begin the installation again. Setup might recover from the error and continue normally.
- Another possibility is a virus. Run a virus scan program on the hard drive from the DOS prompt.
- The existing version of Windows might have corrupted system files. To eliminate using the existing version of Windows early in the installation, use this command to run Setup: Setup /D.
- To watch for errors during the installation that can be caused when ScanDisk runs, use this command to run ScanDisk in the foreground: Setup /IH.

Software Installation Problems

A+ OS
3.2

A number of different problems can arise during software installation.

Setup continues to ask for the same installation disk

Remove the disk from the floppy drive and verify that you have the correct disk. Open and close the shuttle window several times, and try the disk again. The disk may be defective.

$A^{+}_{}$ $\begin{smallmatrix} os \\ 3.2 \end{smallmatrix}$ ## You don't have enough hard drive space for the installation

- Erase lost clusters and defragment the drive before the installation.
- Look for temporary files or applications software that you no longer use, and delete them.
- Run a Custom Setup that allows you to install only some of the application.

The problem is unknown; the software just does not work after the installation

- Wrong configuration information may have been given to the installation program. If you suspect that this is the problem, begin again, giving the correct information.
- Try reinstalling the software, and carefully watch for error messages. Before you begin again, use the uninstall program that comes with the software to completely uninstall the software. If you suspect the uninstall utility is not working properly, restore the Windows registry to its state before the installation.
- If there is no uninstall program, use a third-party uninstaller, or erase all files in directories on the hard drive created by the installation program, remove the directories it created, and restore the Windows registry to its state before the installation.
- For legacy software, look in AUTOEXEC.BAT and CONFIG.SYS files for errors. Restore the original AUTOEXEC.BAT, CONFIG.SYS, Win.ini, Progman.ini, and System.ini files, and begin again, at the beginning of the installation process.
- Try to execute some portion of the software, such as the Help utility. Look for information about installation requirements. Consult your documentation and technical support for the software.
- After the installation is complete and the software is working, update your backup copies of AUTOEXEC.BAT, CONFIG.SYS, System.ini, Win.ini, and the Windows registry so that they, too, reflect the changes the applications software made to these configuration files.

Hardware Device Installation Problems Under Windows 9x

Hardware installation problems under Windows 9x arise in a number of different settings.

The device is not in the list of supported devices

When Windows 9x cannot identify a new hardware device, you can select the device from the list of devices supported by the OS. If your device is not in the list, provide a device driver from the manufacturer (click Have Disk), or use a Windows 9x substitute (see the device documentation for a recommendation). When possible, use the manufacturer's driver rather than a Windows 9x driver.

$A^+_{2.1}$ *OS* ## Windows 9x cannot use a 16-bit driver

- Contact the manufacturer of the device for an updated driver, or ask the manufacturer to recommend a substitute driver.

- If the 16-bit device driver has an install program, run the install program under either DOS or Windows 3.x, depending on what the install program requires. It makes the correct entries in the AUTOEXEC.BAT and CONFIG.SYS files and copies the driver files to the hard drive. You should then be able to install the device in Windows 9x with no problems.

Problems installing a legacy card (not Plug and Play)

- Problems installing a legacy card under Windows 9x are generally caused by resource conflicts with other legacy cards.

- See Device Manager for the resources being used by other legacy cards already installed.

- Change the jumpers or DIP switches on one of the devices to force it to use a different resource.

- Disable PCI bus IRQ steering (see Chapter 9 for more information).

Windows NT Boot Problems

$A^+_{2.2}$ *OS* A number of problems can arise when booting Windows NT.

Errors display during the boot process

$A^+_{2.2}$ *OS*
- Don't attempt to log on. Reboot and select the Last Known Good configuration at bootup.

- Use antivirus software to scan for viruses.

- If the active partition is FAT, boot from a floppy disk and run Scandisk to check for surface errors.

Windows NT will not boot

Boot using the three Windows NT boot disks. Have the Windows NT emergency repair disk available. When the Start menu displays, select all options for repair and execute the menu. Follow the directions on the screen. You may be asked to provide the original Windows NT CD-ROM or a previously prepared Windows NT emergency repair disk.

Windows 2000 Boot Problems

What to do when solving problems booting Windows 2000 Professional depend on at what point in the boot process the problem occurs. Try these things in this order to recover from a failed boot:

- Boot into Safe Mode and run antivirus software.

A+ OS
2.1

- Boot to the Advanced Options Menu (press F8 during booting) and select the Last Known Good Configuration to restore the registry to its state during the last successful boot.

- If you have other backups of the registry, try restoring the registry from these backups.

- Boot from the Windows 2000 CD or from the four Windows 2000 Setup disks. From the Windows Setup menu select "To repair a Windows 2000 installation." The Windows 2000 Repair Options window opens. Type C to select the Recovery Console. Use the Recovery Console to restore the Registry to its state at the end of the installation process.

- Use the Emergency Rescue Disk to fully recover the system to its state at the completion of the installation.

- Reinstall Windows 2000

Network Problems

Network problems can arise in a variety of settings.

Windows 9x dial-up problems

Problems encountered when dialing into a host computer using Windows 9x Dial-Up Networking may be caused by the modem. See the troubleshooting guidelines for modems, above, to eliminate the modem as the source of the problem.

Cannot make a connection

Because Dial-Up Networking involves so many different components, first find out what works and what doesn't work. Find out the answers to these questions:

- Does the modem work? Compare the printout of a Modemlog.txt file that was made during a successful connection from another PC to the Modemlog.txt file generated when trying to connect from this PC, to identify at what point in the connection an error occurs. (For Windows 9x to log modem events to the Modemlog.txt file, double-click on **Modems** in Control Panel, and then select the modem, click **Properties**, **Connection**, **Advanced**, and turn on **Recording to a log file**.)

- Are all components installed? Check for the Dial-Up Adapter and TCP/IP, and check the configuration of each.

- Check the Dial-Up Networking connection icon for errors. Is the phone number correct? Does the number need to include a 9 for you to get an outside line? Has a 1 been added in front of the number by mistake?

- Reboot your PC and try again.

- Try removing and reinstalling each network component. Begin with TCP/IP.

- Try dialing the number manually from a phone. Do you hear beeps on the other end?

- Try another phone number.
- Sometimes older copies of the Windows socket DLL may be interfering with the current Windows 9x version. (Windows 9x may be finding and executing the older DLL before it finds the newer one.) Search for and rename any files named Winsock.dll except the one in the Windows\System directory.

You can connect, but you get the message, "Unable to resolve hostname..."

This means that TCP/IP is not able to determine how to route a request to a host. Right-click on the **Dial-Up Networking** connection icon, select **Properties**, and check for these things:

- Under Server Type, is TCP/IP the only network protocol allowed?
- Under TCP/IP settings, check the IP addresses of the DNS servers.
- Is **Using the default gateway** selected?
- Try *not* selecting IP header compression.

After connection, you get the error: "Unable to establish a compatible set of network protocols"

- The error is most likely to be caused by a problem with the installation and configuration of Dial-Up Networking and/or TCP/IP. Try these approaches:
- Verify that Dial-Up Adapter and TCP/IP are installed and configured correctly.
- Remove and reinstall TCP/IP. Be sure to reboot after the installation.
- Try putting the PCs in different workgroups. Sometimes problems arise when two PCs using Windows 9x are in the same workgroup.
- Windows 9x can write the events of PPP processing a call to a log file. Create the PPPLog.txt file on a PC that makes a successful connection, and compare it to the log file of your bad connection. You might be able to see exactly when the problem began. To turn on **Logging events to the file**, double-click the **Network** icon in **Control Panel**. Click **Dial-Up Adapter**, click **Properties**, select the **Advanced** tab, and select **Record a log file**. On the Value list, click **Yes**, and then click **OK**. Reboot the PC. The file PPPLog.txt is created in the Windows folder as the connection is made and used.

When you double-click on the network browser, the modem does not dial automatically

Right-click on the network browser icon and select **Properties** from the drop-down menu. Under the Connection tab, check **Connect to the Internet as needed**.

Problems with TCP/IP Under Windows 9x, Windows NT, or Windows 2000

- For Windows 2000 or Windows NT, at the command prompt, enter **IPCONFIG**, or, for Windows 9x, from a Run dialog box enter **WinIPcfg** and click **OK**. If the TCP/IP configuration is correct, then for static IP addressing, the IP address, subnet mask, and default gateway will be displayed, along with the adapter address. If DHCP is used for dynamic IP addressing and the PC is unable to connect with the DHCP server, then the IP address might read 0.0.0.0, or for automatic IP configuration, the IP address will have the form 169.254.x.x.

- Next try the loopback address test. Enter the command PING 127.0.0.1. If this works, most likely TCP/IP is configured correctly.

- If you have been assigned an IP address, PING it. If you get any errors up to this point, then assume that the problem is on your PC. Check the installation and configuration of each component. Remove and reinstall each component and watch for error messages. Compare the configuration to that of a PC that is working, on the same network.

- Next PING the IP address of your default gateway. If it does not respond, then the problem may be with the gateway or with the network to the gateway.

- Now try to PING the host computer you are trying to reach. If it does not respond, then the problem may be with the host computer or with the network to the computer.

- If you substitute a URL for the IP address in the PING command, and the PING works, then you can conclude that DNS works. If an IP address works, but the URL does not work, the problem lies with DNS. Try this: PING Microsoft.com.

F

BEHIND THE SCENES WITH DEBUG

This appendix uses DEBUG, a DOS and Windows 9x editor, to view and manipulate the components of the file system on floppy disks and hard drives, including the FAT, the directories, the boot record, and files. Many good data recovery software products are available today that can recover data automatically, and you don't have to understand exactly what is going on behind the scenes to use them. If you do want a more hands-on sense of the process, however, this appendix describes how to interpret what's written on the disk, how a disk becomes damaged, and a manual method of data recovery that gives you the most control over what is happening. This approach is not always the best or fastest way to recover lost data, but it is certainly the most reliable.

The reasons for using the not-too-user-friendly DOS and Windows 9x DEBUG utility are (1) everyone who has DOS or Windows 9x on his or her computer has DEBUG, and (2) with DEBUG, you can see and learn at the "grass roots" level what is written on a disk. Learning about data recovery using DEBUG provides the strong technical insight that you need to use more user-friendly utility software, such as Nuts & Bolts, Norton, and Lost & Found, and to be confident that you understand how it works. The better you understand how data is constructed on the disk and exactly what problems can arise, the better your chances of recovering lost or damaged data.

Introducing the DEBUG Utility

The DOS and Windows 9x DEBUG utility is a tool that displays for you the hex values of the contents of memory or anything written to a floppy disk or hard drive including the FAT, directories, boot record, data, and so on. This information appears exactly as it is written to the drive.

Using DEBUG is not difficult if you grasp one concept: DEBUG is an editor. It is just like any other editor except that it displays and works with hex values rather than filenames or numbers or other familiar terminology. For instance, when you use Notepad to open a file and edit it, these events occur: The file is "opened" by copying it from the hard drive or disk into memory. Notepad, an ASCII editor, displays the contents of memory to you in ASCII form and allows you to edit what is in memory. When you "save" the file, Notepad copies the contents of memory back to the floppy disk or hard drive. DEBUG performs similar functions only in hexadecimal, but the commands are written differently. DEBUG works beyond the concept of a file, looking directly at the bits stored in sectors on the hard drive, converting them to hex before displaying them. DEBUG "opens" a sector by copying the sector from the disk or hard drive into memory and then displaying the contents of memory. You must tell DEBUG which sector to read from the drive and which memory addresses to copy the sector into. You can display and edit the contents of these memory addresses and then command DEBUG to copy the contents of memory back to the drive, which is similar to the "save" concept in Notepad.

The advantages of using DEBUG are that (1) you circumvent the limitation placed on you by the OS and software applications, which only let you view files; with DEBUG, you can look at any sector on the hard drive or disk regardless of its function, and (2) by viewing critical sectors that are used to organize the data on a hard drive, you gain knowledge invaluable to you when using Nuts & Bolts or Norton Utilities to recover the data on a damaged hard drive or floppy disk.

Table F-1 compares the functions of Notepad and DEBUG to further help you become comfortable with this interesting tool.

Using DEBUG

To use DEBUG you need to understand the hexadecimal number system and how memory is addressed in microcomputers by using the segment address followed by a colon and the offset. Appendix D covers these topics. If you have not already done so, read that appendix before proceeding. Follow these steps:

To begin, shut down, power off your computer, then power on your computer with only the essential software loaded, so that memory is relatively free and easily identified as unused. This makes it easier to find some unused part of memory to use as a "scratch pad" as you work. The easiest way to boot with only essential software loaded is to boot from a floppy disk.

When you boot from a floppy disk, you will be at an A prompt. Go to the C prompt by typing **C:**

Table F-1   Notepad and DEBUG are both editors

Notepad Function	DEBUG Function	Description of Functions
Open a file. (Use the **File, Open** command.)	Copy a sector from disk to specified memory addresses. (Use the **L** or **Load** command.)	Gives you a "snapshot" of data written on a disk
Display contents of file now stored in memory. (Notepad does this automatically.)	Display the contents of the memory addresses above. (Use the **D** or **Dump** command.)	Displays contents of memory
Edit a file.	Change the contents of memory. (Use the **E** or **Enter** command.)	Changes the data displayed that is stored in memory, but does not change the data on the disk
Save or close a file. (Use the **File, Save** or **File, Close** command.)	Write the contents of memory back to the disk. (Use the **W** or **Write** command.)	Writes data from memory to disk
Exit the Notepad editor. (Use the **File, Exit**, command.)	Exit the DEBUG editor. (Use the **Q** or **Quit** command.)	Exits the editor

Execute DEBUG. The DEBUG program should be stored in the \DOS directory of your hard drive for DOS, and in the \WINDOWS\COMMAND directory for Windows 9x. (Later, to exit DEBUG, type **Q** to quit.) The paths should be:

```
\DOS\DEBUG
```

or

```
WINDOWS\COMMAND\DEBUG
```

Next, look for an area of memory where you can store whatever it is you will be examining. Suppose you plan to examine the boot record of the floppy disk that you booted from. You know that the boot record is one sector long, which is 512 bytes. Therefore, you need 512 bytes of unused memory to store the boot record. Use the DUMP command to search for an unused area of memory. Near the top of conventional memory is a good place to look for some empty area to use as a "scratch pad." Try the memory location 5000:0. If you find data there, keep looking until you find an empty area of memory. Enter this dump command:

```
-d5000:0
```

You should now see 128 bytes of memory beginning with the location 5000:0. When you press **d** followed by no parameters, DEBUG gives you the contents of the next 128 bytes of memory. In Figure F-1, you see that memory is clean (i.e., filled with zeroes and containing no data) from 5000:0000 through 5000:00FF. That equals 256 bytes. Because a sector on a 3½-inch high-density disk is 512 bytes, issue the DUMP command twice more to make sure that a total of 512 bytes of memory is unused:

```
-d
-d
```

You now know that copying the boot record into this area of memory will not overwrite something important. If your dump displays data in memory at this location, try some other area until you find 512 free bytes.

Figure F-1   Empty area of memory from 5000:0 through 5000:00FF (two dump commands)

Next we examine the boot record of a floppy disk. You could examine the boot record of a logical drive on a hard drive using the same basic approach.

THE BOOT RECORD

This section uses DEBUG to examine a good boot record of a floppy disk and then repair a corrupted one. Recall from Chapter 5 that a 3½-inch floppy disk has 512 bytes in each allocation unit or cluster, which means there is one sector in each cluster. Also, there are 2,847 clusters or sectors on the disk.

To examine the boot record, first execute DEBUG and then load the boot record into an unused area of memory. Use this command:

```
-L5000:0  0  0  1
```

The command line is interpreted as follows:

L5000:0	Load into the area of memory beginning at location 5000:0.
0	Load from the disk in drive A (drive B is 1, and drive C is 2).
0	Begin with sector 0.
1	Load 1 sector.

Look at the contents of memory using the DUMP command:

```
-d5000:0
```

Follow this with three more **d** commands to see the entire 512-byte sector. Figure F-2 shows the first 128 bytes of the boot record of a 3½-inch disk formatted with DOS. Figure F-3 shows the beginning of the boot record for the same size disk formatted with Windows 95, for comparison. On the diskette, when more than one byte is used to express a number, the least significant byte is written first, which is the reverse of the way we normally write a value. Values shown on the right side of these two figures are written with the most significant byte first, followed by the least significant byte. For example, the first value at the top of Figure F-2, bytes per sector, is written on the diskette as 00 02. To write the hex value, reverse the bytes, which gives 0200h as the number of bytes per sector. Note that most of the data on the right side of the screen cannot be interpreted by the editor. This section is converting the contents of memory in hex numbers to their ASCII representation, as described in Appendix C; most of this data is not ASCII code and, therefore, makes no sense when converted to ASCII.

Figure F-2   The first 128 bytes of the boot record of a 3½-inch floppy disk formatted with DOS

Figure F-3   The first 128 bytes of the boot record of a 3½-inch floppy disk formatted with Windows 95

The figure labels highlight some interesting entries at the beginning of the record. Table 6-4 of Chapter 6 shows the complete record layout for the boot record. The medium descriptor byte tells DOS what type of disk this is. The values of this descriptor byte are shown in Table 6-5 of Chapter 6.

The program code that loads DOS starts at location 5000:0200. In the last 128 bytes of the record shown in Figure F-4, you can see that the message that prints if this program does not find the hidden files that it needs to load DOS is as follows:

```
Non-System disk or disk error..Replace and press any key
when ready...
```

At the bottom of the record are the names of the files that it is searching for, in this case IO.SYS and MSDOS.SYS. Continue to use the DUMP command until you can see all of these entries. Figure F-5 shows a similar presentation of this message for a Windows 95 disk.

Figure F-4   "Non-system disk" message for a DOS disk

Figure F-5   "Invalid system disk" message for a Windows 95 disk

To repair a damaged boot record using DEBUG, follow this procedure:

- Find or make a disk of the same size and density as the damaged disk.

- Using the procedure above, load this good boot record into memory.

- Copy the good boot record from memory to the damaged disk, using this command:

    ```
    -W5000:0 0 0 1
    ```

The command line is interpreted as:

W5000:0 Write beginning with the data located at memory address 5000:0.
0   Write to drive A (B = 1 and C = 2).
0   Write to sector 0.
1   Fill one sector.

F

THE FILE ALLOCATION TABLE (FAT)

After the boot record, the next file system component on a disk or drive is the FAT. This section explains how a 16-bit FAT on a hard drive actually appears by viewing the FAT with DEBUG. First look at Figure F-6, where a FAT is shown that contains two files. Figure F-7 shows the same information as a screenshot of the beginning of a 16-bit FAT for a hard drive created using DEBUG. Compare the two figures as you read this section and notice precisely what the FAT looks like to the OS. The memory dump displayed in Figure F-7 was created using the DEBUG utility with these commands:

Figure F-6   FAT showing two files

Command	Description
C:\>DEBUG	Execute DOS DEBUG.
–L9000:0 2 1 1	From drive 2 (drive C), beginning with sector 1 and reading 1 sector, load contents into memory addresses beginning with 9000:0 (Or substitute another area of memory if this area is used).
–D9000:0	Dump to screen the contents of memory beginning at 9000:0.

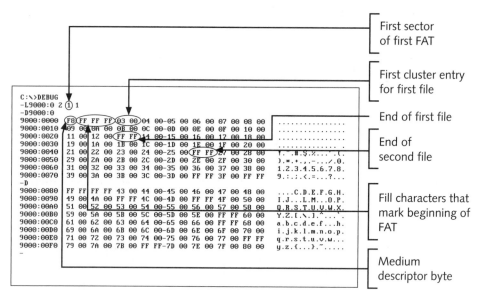

Figure F-7   Beginning of a 16-bit FAT on a hard drive

Here is what the data in the dump means. The first byte in Figure F-7 is F8, the byte that identifies what medium is used—in this case, a hard drive. The next three bytes are FF FF FF, which indicate the beginning of the FAT. Each of the following entries in the FAT uses two bytes. The next few bytes describe the location of the first file on the disk, which begins at cluster 2. The entry for cluster 2 is 03 00. Because the contents of memory are written from right to left, you must reverse the order of the two bytes to read the cluster number. Thus, you read the 03 00 entry as 00 03, which means that the next cluster used by this file is cluster 3. The file occupies 17 clusters, ending at cluster 12h with FF FF, which indicates the end of the file. The clusters used, then, are numbered 2 through 12 (hex) or 2 through 18 (decimal). This file occupies 2,048 bytes/cluster × 17 clusters, or 34,816 bytes of disk space. In a later section, we will look at the file's entries in the root directory.

In Figure F-7 the next file begins at cluster 13h and continues through cluster 25h. A quick count shows that this second file occupies 19 clusters, which equal 2,048 bytes/cluster × 19 clusters, or 38,912 bytes of disk space.

The FAT begins at sector 1. This particular hard drive's logical geometry is 1,024 cylinders, 17 sectors per track, and 12 heads. (To find out how many cylinders, sectors per track, and heads your hard drive has, so that you can make similar calculations, see your CMOS setup.)

How many individual sectors and how many clusters are there, and how long is the FAT in the example discussed here? You calculate as follows:

1,024 tracks × 17 sectors/track × 12 heads = 208,896 sectors
208,896 sectors / 4 sectors per cluster = 52,224 clusters

This hard drive can accommodate only 52,224 files and subdirectories, which equals the total number of clusters. Each cluster has a 2-byte entry in the FAT, making the size of the FAT as follows:

52,224 FAT entries × 2 bytes/FAT entry = 104,448 bytes
104,448 bytes / 512 bytes per sector = 204 sectors

A hard drive keeps two copies of the FAT, just as disks do, so you can expect the second copy of the FAT to begin at sector 205. Use DEBUG to verify your calculation for your machine. To use the Load command in DEBUG, you must convert 205 to hex, which is CDh. You can use these commands to display the second copy of the FAT, shown in Figure F-8.

```
C:\>DEBUG-L9000:0 2 CD 1
```

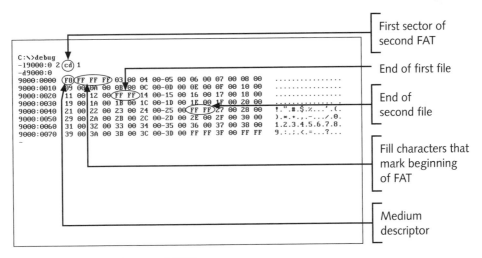

Figure F-8   Second copy of FAT

Execute DEBUG. Load into memory beginning with memory address 9000:0 the contents of disk 2 (drive C) beginning with sector CDh and continuing for 1 sector.

```
-D9000:0
```

Dump the contents of memory beginning with 9000:0.

How a Floppy Disk FAT is Written and Used

This section is designed to help you understand how the FAT is written to a floppy disk and how it is used. This will allow you to better use Norton Disk Editor or similar editors to recover data from a disk and ultimately from a hard drive. The discussion below uses DEBUG as a tool to demonstrate what these editors are really doing. The discussion first takes a look at some healthy FATs.

Figure F-9 shows a FAT of a Windows 98 freshly formatted disk that does not contain system files; this is the emptiest FAT possible. The same results can be obtained using DOS to format the disk.

Figure F-9   Empty 12-bit FAT on a floppy disk

The FAT in Figure F-9 can be produced using this procedure:

1. Format a 3½-inch high–density floppy disk using Windows 9x Explorer.

2. Load the first copy of the FAT into an empty area of memory, using the following command substituting a different area of memory as necessary:

```
C:\>\WINDOWS\COMMAND\DEBUG
-L5000:0 0 1 1
```

An explanation of the command line is as follows:

L5000:0   Load data into memory addresses beginning at 5000:0.
0   Load from the disk in Drive A (A = 0, B = 1, C = 2).
1   Begin the load with sector 1.
1   Load one sector.

Remember that the boot record is located at sector 0, and the FAT begins at sector 1. Looking at Figure F-9, you see that the first byte is the medium descriptor byte, which tells DOS what kind of disk is being used. The next two bytes are called fill characters and are always FF FF for a 12-bit FAT, and FF FF FF for a 16-bit FAT. The rest of the FAT is empty.

Next WordPad is used to create a file on this disk and save the file as a DOS text file using the choices given in the WordPad Save As command. Name the file MYFILE.TXT and put in it the five characters "HAPPY". Figure F-10 shows the result of the DOS DIR command and the newly dumped FAT. Note first in Figure F-10 the difference between the number of free bytes on the disk and the number of free bytes before you created the five-character file:

```
1,457,664 bytes — 1,457,152 bytes = 512 bytes
```

Figure F-10   Directory of disk showing MYFILE.TXT followed by a DEBUG dump
displaying FAT with five-character file

The five-character or five-byte file took up 512 bytes of disk space! Disk space is wasted because one file allocation unit or one cluster on this disk equals 512 bytes. Compare the FAT in Figure F-10 with the one in Figure F-9. Note that two bytes are now altered, and read

```
FF 0F
```

Before you begin interpreting these two bytes, four facts need to be pointed out:

- All floppy disks have 12-bit FATs, and each entry in the table is 12 bits long. These 12 bits equal 1.5 bytes.

- Entries in a FAT are written in reverse order. In other words, if you label two bytes 1 and 2 in the FAT, you read the bytes as 2 and 1 when reading the FAT entry. In Figure F-10, you read the second byte first, so the bytes are read 0F FF.

- The end of a file in the FAT is written as all 12 bits filled with 1s. This record (1111 1111 1111) is converted to FFF in hex, which is what you see in the FAT entry.

- Clusters are numbered in the FAT beginning with cluster 2. Cluster 2 in a FAT entry is really not physically the second cluster on the disk, because the boot record, the two copies of the FAT, and the directory table all come before the data files. Windows 9x and DOS both number the clusters allocated for data beginning with 2.

Now back to Figure F-10. You know that your file only takes up one cluster, or one sector, and you would expect that to mean only one entry in the FAT. You interpret the first 2 bytes in reverse order as 0F FF. One entry is 12 bits, or 1.5 bytes, long, and the end of a file is identified with FFF. You see then that this file has the one entry, FFF.

Next, you copy to the disk a second file named Long Word File.doc that uses a long file name and contains 4,608 characters, or bytes. Examining the result of the CHKDSK command in Figure F-11, you see the short DOS version of the filename and see that the number of clusters, or sectors, required by this second file is:

```
4608 bytes/512 bytes per cluster = 9 clusters
```

Figure F-11   Disk with two files

Since you can't allocate partial clusters, if the number of clusters had been a fractional number you would have rounded up to the nearest whole cluster; this file, however, requires exactly nine clusters. Adding one cluster for your original file, you get a total of 10 clusters used on the disk. Figure F-12 shows a dump of the FAT with the two files stored on the disk. Since the FAT entries are 1.5 bytes long, you will first divide these bytes into groups of 3 bytes apiece. Each group of 3 bytes contains two FAT entries and can be interpreted as follows:

        AB CD EF = DAB EFC

Figure F-12   Dump of the FAT showing two files

AB CD EF represents two FAT entries of 1½ bytes each. The first entry is AB and half of the next entry, CD. However, since the entries are written reversed, the part of the CD entry that belongs to the first FAT entry is the D, not the C. Also, the first entry is written going from byte 2 (CD) to byte 1 (AB) so that the entry is DAB. Similarly, the second entry begins with the EF and ends with C.

For example, say the first 3 bytes are FF 4F 00. We reverse these bytes and read them as FFF 004. The first entry marks the end of the first file, which is one cluster long. The second entry points to cluster 4. Remember that DOS begins with 2 when counting clusters. These two entries contain the pointers for cluster 2 and cluster 3. Cluster 3, the first cluster of Long Word File.doc, tells DOS to continue on to cluster 4 to find more of Long Word File.doc. Reading from Figure F-12, you see that cluster 4 points to 5, 5 points to 6, 6 points to 7, 7 points to 8, 8 points to 9, 9 points to A, A points to B, and B marks the end of the file with FFF.

Restoring a Damaged FAT Using DEBUG

With a great deal of patience, you could (1) read a disk sector by sector marking the beginning and ending of a file, (2) calculate the FAT entries, and (3) reconstruct a damaged FAT by editing it using DEBUG. To do this (besides needing tons of patience), you only need one more DEBUG command, the E or ENTER command, which allows you to change the contents of memory. You can load a damaged FAT into memory, make the necessary changes with the ENTER command, and write the corrected FAT back to the disk.

For example, suppose you decide to limit the file Long Word File.doc to three clusters. You want to put the FFF at the FAT table entry 5 so that only clusters 3, 4, and 5 are allocated to the file. The command is:

```
-E5000:0007
```

DEBUG responds with 5000:0007 60.

Whatever you now type replaces the 60 currently at this location. You respond with 5000:0007 60.F0 (typing only the F0).

Pressing the Spacebar, you can continue to enter new data that replaces whatever is stored in memory from this location forward. Therefore, instead of only typing F0, you can correct both bytes like this:

```
5000:0007 60.F0
5000:0008 00.FF
```

In the first line, everything up to the first period was displayed. You typed F0 and one space. DEBUG responded with the contents of the next byte, which was 00 followed by a period. You then typed FF and pressed **Enter**, which changed the second byte and terminated the command.

In the last step, you write the altered FAT to disk with this command:

```
-W5000:0 1 1 1
```

The command causes the one sector to be written to sector 1 of the A drive disk.

There is only one problem. Windows 9x or DOS is expecting a file that is 4,608 bytes long, but you have given it only three clusters, which is not enough. There is one last thing to do: you must alter the root directory to change the size of the file, so that the OS will expect to find three clusters when reading the file. Editing a directory table is coming up.

Second Copy of the FAT

Recall that Windows 9x and DOS keep a second copy of the FAT immediately following the first copy. Without utility software, this second copy is not available to you if the first copy is damaged. You can look at the second copy of the FAT on a 3½-inch high-density disk with this DEBUG command:

```
-L5000:0 0 A 1
```

The second FAT begins with sector A in hex or 10 in decimal. The first FAT began at sector 1. A quick calculation tells you that the first FAT requires 9 sectors or 512 bytes/sector × 9 sectors = 4,608 bytes. You see this must be so because this disk has 80 tracks/head × 18 sectors/track × 2 heads/disk, or 2,880 sectors (see Table 5-1 of Chapter 5). Because one sector equals one cluster, the FAT has 2,880 entries. Since each entry is 1.5 bytes long, the FAT contains 4,320 bytes, which is equal to 8.44 sectors. Hence, 9 sectors for one FAT are all accounted for. If you're reconstructing a FAT using DEBUG, don't forget to alter the second FAT as well as the first.

Even more important, maybe the second FAT isn't damaged. Load it into memory and see. If it isn't damaged, write it to the disk into the first FAT's location, and your disk is restored.

EXAMINING AND REPAIRING DIRECTORIES

Recall that the root directory is created when a floppy disk or logical drive is first formatted. Later, subdirectories are created under the root which have a similar structure. This section describes how to examine and repair the root directory and subdirectories using DEBUG.

The Root Directory

The root directory is written on a hard drive immediately after the second copy of the FAT. For the hard drive FAT shown in Figure F-8, the second copy of the FAT ends at sector 408, and the root directory begins at sector 409, which is 199h. The dump of the beginning of a root directory is shown in Figure F-13. You saw in Figure F-7 that the first file on this hard drive occupies 34,816 bytes of disk space and begins at cluster 2. The second file on the hard drive begins at cluster 13h and occupies 38,912 bytes of disk space. You would expect this information to be confirmed by entries in the root directory. Looking at Figure F-13, you can see that the entries for the first two files are as shown in Table F-2.

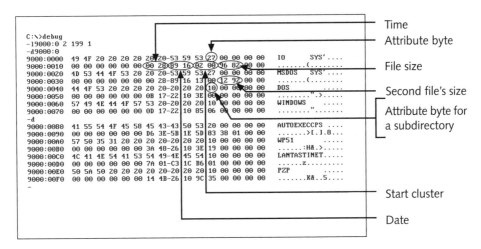

Figure F-13   A root directory

Table F-2   Example of directory entries for first two files in root directory

	File 1	File 2
Filename	IO	MSDOS
File extension	SYS	SYS
Attribute byte	27 = 0010 0111	27 = 0010 0111
Time	00 28	00 28
Date	89 16	89 16
Starting cluster number	00 02	00 13
Size of file	96 82	12 92

The hard drive is loaded with DOS and Windows 3.1. Not surprisingly, then, the first two files stored on this disk are the two DOS hidden files used to boot DOS. The attribute byte is interpreted in Table 5-5 of Chapter 5. From this Table 5-5 you can, therefore, deduce that the two files are system files that are not to be archived, and that they are hidden, read-only files.

According to what you saw in the FAT, the first file begins at cluster 2, and its size is written as 96 82. First reverse the bytes and then convert the hex number to decimal. The calculations for the hex number 8,296 are as follows:

$8 \times 4,096$	=	32,768
2×256	=	512
9×16	=	144
6×1	=	6
TOTAL:		33,430

You saw from the FAT that this file occupies 17 clusters × 2,048 bytes/cluster, or 34,816 bytes of disk space. The unused part of the last cluster is the wasted space. The second file shows a size of 9,212h bytes, which is 37,394 in decimal. The file requires 19 clusters, or 38,912 bytes of space.

Some entries in the root directory are subdirectories rather than files. The third entry in Figure F-13 is the \DOS subdirectory. Note that the attribute byte for this entry is 10h, or 0001 0000 in binary. Table 5-5 of Chapter 5 shows that having the fourth bit on and all other bits off indicates a subdirectory entry. The starting cluster number for this entry is 00 3E, which is the beginning of the directory table for the \DOS subdirectory. It would be interesting to dump this sector of the hard drive and read this directory. Also note that the size of the file is zero for a subdirectory entry because DOS does not use this information.

You have seen that the root directory begins at logical sector 409. Where does it end, and where do data files begin? To calculate this, you need to know that there is room for 512 entries, or blocks, and that each entry is 32 bytes long. The root directory, then, occupies 512 entries × 32 bytes/entry = 16,384 bytes. To convert bytes to sectors, you divide 16,384 by 512 and see that the root directory is exactly 32 sectors long. Adding that to the starting sector 409, you find that the root directory ends at the 440th sector, and the data files begin at sector 441. In the FAT, sector 441 is named cluster 2. Therefore, to read a cluster number in the FAT table and to convert this number to a logical sector number on the hard drive you must use the following conversion expression, where 4 is the number of sectors in one cluster:

(cluster number − 2) × 4 + 441 = sector number

Examining the information at the beginning of a hard drive can be tedious, but knowledge is power. When you have to recover data from a damaged hard drive, skills learned here will make your work much easier.

Subdirectories

In Figure F-14 you see the DEBUG dump of the \GAME directory table. Note that the . and .. entries look just like file and subdirectory entries. Both show 10 or 0001 0000 as their attribute byte, indicating they are subdirectory entries rather than files. The starting cluster number of the . entry is 00 41, which is equal to 65 decimal. This byte marks the beginning of this directory table. The same 00 41 cluster number is found in the root directory as the starting cluster number of the \GAME directory. To use the DEBUG command to create the screen in Figure F-14, you need to locate this directory table. Convert the cluster number in decimal to the logical sector number according to the formula explained earlier:

(65 − 2) × 4 + 441 = 693 (decimal) = 2B5 (hex)

The DEBUG commands used to view the subdirectory table in Figure F-14 then look like this:

```
—L9000:0  2  2B5  1
—D9000:0
```

Figure F-14   Dump of subdirectory table C:\GAME

Directory Repair

This section gives you an in-depth look at the entries in a directory, to help you understand what happens when a utility like Norton Utilities repairs a directory. You can also use this information to help in the recovery of a corrupted file using Norton Disk Editor.

On the 3½-inch high-density disk used in the example below, the directory begins at sector 13h. Remember that the second copy of the FAT began at sector A and was nine sectors long. Thus, it ends at sector A + 8 or 12 in hex (10 + 8 = 18 in decimal), and the root directory begins with sector 13h. Figure F-15 is a memory dump of the root directory of the disk with the two files, MYFILE.TXT and Long Word File.doc. The root directory was first loaded into memory using this DEBUG command:

```
-L5000:0 0 13 1
```

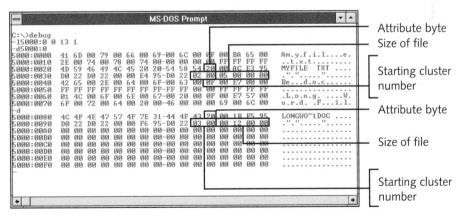

Figure F-15   Memory dump of a root directory containing two files

The layout of each entry in a directory for a file is listed in Tables 5-4 and 5-5 in Chapter 5. The first 32 bytes of the root directory contain the volume label of the disk. Each entry after that is also 32 bytes long for DOS and longer for Windows 9x when using long filenames. The extra information for the long filename is listed in the root directory before the 32 bytes used by both DOS and Windows 9x for each file entry.

Look at the entries for MYFILE.TXT and Long Word File.doc in Figure F-15. The attribute byte, starting cluster number, and size of the file are labeled for each of the two files listed in this root directory. The second file has a long filename together with its short DOS filename. The size of the file Long Word File.doc is stored in 4 bytes at the end of the 32-bit entry of the file that follows the long filename information (see addresses 5000:0080 of the dump). These four bytes read:

    00 12 00 00

To interpret them, you must read in reverse order like this:

    00 00 12 00

You can then convert the hex 1200 to decimal, which is 4,608, the size of the file.

In Figure F-15, the attribute byte for this file is at memory location 5000:008B. The byte reads 20 in hex. Converting 20h to binary so that you can read each bit, you take each hex number and convert it to binary like this:

2 in hex = 0010 in binary, and 0 in hex = 0000 in binary, therefore the byte is 0010 0000

Looking back at Table 5-5 in Chapter 5, you can interpret each of these 8 bits, reading from left to right, in the following way:

- 0   Not used
- 0   Not used
- 1   To be archived
- 0   A file, not a directory
- 0   A normal directory entry, not a volume label
- 0   A normal file, not a system file (like IO.SYS)
- 0   Not hidden
- 0   Read/write file, not read-only

By understanding how to interpret each item in the directory entry, you can reconstruct a damaged directory table if you need to. Again, you may never use DEBUG to repair a directory because utility software is so much easier to use, but the purpose of using it here is to learn exactly how entries are written to the directory, so you can understand what these utilities are doing for you. Norton Utilities Disk Editor makes reading and writing to directories very easy to do. This editor converts the entries to decimal for display, accepts your decimal entry, and converts it to hex and binary before writing it to the disk.

G

INTERRUPT VECTORS

A+CORE
1.3

Most microcomputer activity is interrupt-driven. This means that the CPU performs a task in response to an interrupt. Hardware, software, or the CPU itself can initiate an interrupt. An interrupt initiated by the CPU is called an "exception," and most often is the result of a problem or error, such as when the CPU is instructed to divide by zero.

Hardware interrupts begin when the BIOS controlling the hardware device raises its IRQ line. The interrupt controller receives the IRQ and signals the CPU that a hardware interrupt has occurred. The CPU responds by signaling to the interrupt controller that it will process the interrupt. The interrupt controller or the hardware BIOS then sends an interrupt value to the CPU. This interrupt value is used by the CPU to point to a row in the interrupt vector table. This row contains the memory location of the request handler that will service the hardware device. Software can also initiate an interrupt, but does not need or use the IRQ lines to do so, because the software is already running when the interrupt is issued, and so already has the attention of the CPU.

The memory locations listed in the interrupt vector table and the BIOS and device drivers assigned to these memory locations are determined during booting, but can be changed later. Software can make changes to the interrupt vector table to create its own user software interrupts, which it can later use to gain access to hardware devices. This ability of software to alter the interrupt vector table is sometimes used by a virus to replicate itself. Whether the CPU, hardware, or software initiates the interrupt, the same interrupt values are used, which are listed in the table below. These functions for the interrupt values are not universal; there are some variations.

Interrupt Value	Function
0	Divide by zero (exception interrupt)
1	Single step
2	Nonmaskable interrupt
3	Break point instruction
4	Overflow
5	Print screen

A+CORE
1.3

Interrupt Value	Function
6	Invalid opcode
7	Math coprocessor not present
8	System timer interrupt (IRQ 0)
9	Keyboard data ready (IRQ 1)
A	Reserved (IRQ 2) cascade from slave interrupt controller
B,C	Hardware interrupt for serial communication
D	Parallel port hardware interrupt (IRQ 5, LPT 2)
E	Diskette controller hardware interrupt (IRQ 6)
F	Printer hardware interrupt (IRQ 7, LPT 1)
10	Software interrupt to use video
11	Equipment check call
12	Memory check call
13	Software interrupt to use hard drive
14	Software interrupt to use serial port
15	Not used
16	Keyboard software interrupt
17	Software interrupt to use printer
18	ROM basic entry call
19	Bootstrap loader
1A	Time of day call
1B	Get control on keyboard break
1C	Get control on timer interrupt
1D	Pointer to video initialization table
1E	Pointer to diskette parameter table
1F	Pointer to graphics character generator
20–3F	Used by DOS
40	Reserved
41	Fixed disk parameter table
46	Fixed disk parameter table
47–5F	Reserved
60–67	Reserved for user software interrupts
68–6F	Not used
70	Real time clock hardware interrupt
72	Reserved (IRQ 10)
73	Reserved (IRQ 11)
74	Reserved (IRQ 12)
76	Fixed disk controller (IRQ 14)
77	Reserved (IRQ 15)
80–F0	Used by BASIC programs and interpreter
F1–FF	Not used

GLOSSARY

3D RAM — Special video RAM designed to improve 3D graphics simulation.

32-bit flat memory mode — A protected processing mode used by Windows NT to process programs written in 32-bit code early in the boot process.

A+ Certification — A certification awarded by CompTIA (The Computing Technology Industry Association) that measures a PC technician's knowledge of the skills and behaviors expected of entry-level PC technicians. Many companies require that their service technicians have A+ Certification.

Accelerated graphics port (AGP) — A slot on a system board for a video card that provides transfer of video data from the CPU that is synchronized with the memory bus.

ACPI (Advanced Configuration and Power Interface) — Specification developed by Intel, Microsoft, and Toshiba to control power on notebooks and other devices. Windows 98 supports ACPI.

Active Directory — A Windows 2000 service that allows for a single point of administration for all shared resources on a network, including files, peripheral devices, databases, Web sites, users, and services.

Adapter address — A 6-byte hex hardware address unique to each NIC and assigned by manufacturers. The address is often printed on the adapter. An example is 00 00 0C 08 2F 35. Also called MAC address.

Adapter card — Also called an interface card. A small circuit board inserted in an expansion slot and used to communicate between the system bus and a peripheral device.

Address Resolution Protocol (ARP) — A method used by TCP/IP that dynamically or automatically translates IP addresses into physical network addresses such as Ethernet IDs or Token Ring MAC addresses.

Administrator account — In Windows NT, an account that grants to the administrator(s) rights and permissions to all hardware and software resources, such as the right to add, delete, and change accounts and to change hardware configurations.

ADSL (asymmetric digital subscriber line) — A method of data transmission over phone lines that is digital, allows for a direct connection, and is about 50 times faster than ISDN.

Advanced Options Menu — A Windows 2000 menu that appears when you press F8 when Windows starts. The menu can be used to troubleshoot problems when loading Windows 2000.

Advanced SCSI programming interface (ASPI) — A popular device driver that enables operating systems to communicate with a SCSI host adapter. (The "A" originally stood for Adaptec.)

Advanced Transfer Cache (ATC) — A type of L2 cache contained within the Pentium processor housing that is embedded on the same core processor die as the CPU itself.

Alternate gateway — An alternate router that is used if the default gateway is down. See Gateway.

Alternating current (AC) — Current that cycles back and forth rather than traveling in only one direction. Normally between 110 and 115 AC volts are supplied from a standard wall outlet.

Ammeter — A meter that measures electrical current in amps.

Ampere (A) — A unit of measurement for electrical current. One volt across a resistance of one ohm will produce a flow of one amp.

Amplifier repeater — A repeater that amplifies whatever it receives regardless of its source.

Amplifying repeater — A repeater used on a broadband network that amplifies whatever it receives regardless of its source.

Analog-to-digital converter (A/D or ADC) — A component on a sound card that samples and converts analog sound into digital values that can be stored in a file.

ANSI (American National Standards Institute) — A nonprofit organization dedicated to creating trade and communications standards.

answer file — A text file that contains information that Windows 2000 requires in order to do an unattended installation.

Antivirus (AV) software — Utility programs that prevent infection, or scan a system to detect and remove viruses. McAfee Associates VirusScan and Norton AntiVirus are two popular AV packages.

API (application program interface) — A method used by an application program to call another program to perform a utility task.

Application layer — The layer of the OSI model responsible for interfacing with the user or application using the network.

Asynchronous SRAM — Static RAM that does not work in step with the CPU clock and is, therefore, slower than synchronous SRAM.

AT command set — A set of commands used by a PC to control a modem. AT is the ATtention command, which alerts a modem to prepare to receive additional commands. For example, ATDT means attention and listen for a dial tone.

ATAPI (Advanced Technology Attachment Packet Interface) — An interface standard that is part of the IDE/ATA standards, which allows tape drives and CD-ROM drives to be treated like an IDE hard drive by the OS.

ATTRIB command — A DOS command that can display file attributes and even lock files so that they are "read-only" and cannot be modified (for example, ATTRIB +R FILENAME).

Audio/modem riser (AMR) — A specification for a small slot on a system board to accommodate an audio or modem riser card. A controller on the system board contains some of the logic for the audio or modem functionality.

Auto detection — A feature on newer system BIOS and hard drives that automatically identifies and configures a new hard drive in the CMOS setup.

AUTOEXEC.BAT — One startup file on an MS-DOS computer. It tells the computer what commands or programs to execute automatically after bootup.

Autorange meter — A multimeter that senses the quantity of input and sets the range accordingly.

Back end — In a client/server environment, the application on the server that processes requests for data from the client.

Back up, Backup — When used as a verb, to make a duplicate copy of important files or data. When used as a noun, refers to the file created when backing up. Backups can be made by saving a file with a different name or by copying files to a different storage media.

Backbone — A network used to link several networks together. For example, several Token Rings and Ethernet LANS may be connected using a single FDDI backbone.

Backside bus — The bus between the CPU and the L2 cache inside the CPU housing.

Backup domain controller (BDC) — In Windows NT, a computer on a network that holds a read-only copy of the SAM (security accounts manager) database.

Backward compatible — Refers to new hardware and software that is able to support older, existing technologies. This is a common choice of hardware and software manufacturers.

Bandwidth — The range of frequencies that a communication cable or channel can carry. In general use, the term refers to the volume of data that can travel on a bus or over a cable.

Bank — An area on the system board that contains slots for memory modules (typically labeled bank 0, 1, 2, and 3).

Base memory — *See* Conventional memory.

Baseband — Relating to a communications system which carries only a single message at a time over wire. Ethernet uses baseband technology. Compare to broadband.

Basic drive — In Windows 2000, a drive that uses a partition table at the beginning of the drive to hold information about the drive's primary and extended partitions. Compare to dynamic drive.

Batch file — A text file containing a series of DOS instructions to the computer, telling it to perform a specific task (for example, AUTOEXEC.BAT, which contains a series of startup commands).

Baud rate — A measure of line speed between two devices such as a computer and a printer or a modem. This speed is measured in the number of times a signal changes in one second. *See* bps.

Beam detect mirror — Detects the initial presence of a laser printer's laser beam by reflecting the beam to an optical fiber.

Binary number system — The number system used by computers where there are only two numbers, 0 and 1, called binary digits, or bits.

Binding — Associating an OSI layer to a layer above it or below it. For example, associating a protocol type such as TCP/IP to a NIC driver.

BIOS (basic input/output system) — Firmware that controls much of a computer's input/output functions, such as communication with the floppy drive, RAM chips, and the monitor. Also called ROM BIOS.

Bit-map file — A type of graphics file in which the image is written as a series of 0s and 1s. These files have the extension .bmp and can be loaded into paint programs to be edited and printed.

Block mode — A method of data transfer between hard drive and memory that allows multiple data transfers on a single software interrupt.

BNC connector — A connector used on an Ethernet 10Base2 (Thinnet) network. A BNC connector looks like a TV cable connector.

Boot loader menu — A startup menu that gives the user the choice between Windows NT Workstation Version 4.0 and another OS, such as Windows 98.

Boot partition — The hard drive partition where the Windows NT OS is stored. The system partition and the boot partition may be different partitions.

Boot record (of hard drives) — The first sector of each logical drive in a partition that contains information about the logical drive. If the boot record is in the active partition, then it is used to boot the OS. Also called OS boot record or volume boot record.

Boot sector virus — An infectious program that can replace the boot program with a modified, infected version of the boot command utilities, often causing boot and data retrieval problems.

Bootable disk — For DOS, a floppy disk that can upload the OS files necessary for computer startup. It must have the two hidden system files IO.SYS and MSDOS.SYS, and also COMMAND.COM.

Booting — The process that a computer goes through when it is first turned on to get the computer ready to receive commands.

Bps (bits per second) — A measure of data transmission speed. (Example: a common modem speed is 56,000 bps or 56 Kbps.)

Break code — A code produced when a key on a computer keyboard is released. *See* Make code.

Bridge — A hardware device or box, coupled with software at the data-link layer, used to connect similar networks and network segments. *See* Router.

Briefcase — A Windows 9x system folder used to synchronize files between two computers. When files are transferred from one computer to another, Briefcase automatically updates files on the original computer to the most recent version.

Broadband — Relating to a communications system such as cable modem or ATM networks that carry multiple messages over wire, each message traveling on its own frequency. Compare to baseband.

Buck-boost regulator — A line-interactive UPS that offers good line conditioning and has an automatic voltage regulator that decreases ("bucks") the voltage during electrical spikes and boosts it during sags.

Buffer — A temporary memory area where data is kept before being written to a hard drive or sent to a printer, thus reducing the number of writes to the devices.

Burst EDO (BEDO) — A refined version of EDO memory that significantly improved access time over EDO. BEDO is not widely used today because Intel chose not to support it. BEDO memory is stored on 168-pin DIMM modules.

Burst SRAM — Memory that is more expensive and slightly faster than pipelined burst SRAM. Data is sent as a two-step process; the data address is sent, and then the data itself is sent without interruption.

Burst transfer — A means of sending data across the bus, with one packet immediately following the next, without waiting for clock beats and/or addressing of the information being sent.

Bus — Strips of parallel wires or printed circuits used to transmit electronic signals on the system board to other devices. Most Pentium systems use a 32-bit bus.

Bus enumerator — A component of Windows 9x Plug and Play that locates all devices on a particular bus and inventories the resource requirements for these devices.

Bus mouse — A mouse that plugs into a bus adapter card and has a round, 9-pin mini-DIN connector.

Bus network architecture — A network design in which nodes are connected in line with one another, with no centralized point of contact.

Bus network topology — A network design in which nodes are connected in line with one another, with no centralized point of contact.

Bus speed — The speed or frequency at which the data on the system board is moving.

Cabinet file — A file that contains one or more compressed files, and is often used to distribute software on disk. The Extract command is used to extract one or more files from the cabinet file.

Cable modem — A method of data transmission over cable TV lines that requires a modem and an Ethernet network interface card to receive the transmission.

Cache memory — A kind of fast RAM that is used to speed up memory access because it does not need to be continuously refreshed.

Call tracking — A system that tracks the dates, times, and transactions of help-desk or on-site PC support calls, including the problem presented, the issues addressed, who did what, and when and how each call was resolved.

Capacitor — An electronic device that can maintain an electrical charge for a period of time and is used to smooth out the flow of electrical current.

Cards — Adapter boards or interface cards placed into expansion slots to expand the functions of a computer, allowing it to communicate with external devices such as monitors or speakers.

Carrier Sense Multiple Access with Collision Detection (CSMA/CD) — A feature used in Ethernet networks whereby packets are sent after the sending node listens for silence, and are resent if a collision is detected.

Carrier — A signal used to activate a phone line to confirm a continuous frequency; used to indicate that two computers are ready to receive or transmit data via modems.

CCITT (Comité Consultatif Internationale de Télégraphique et Téléphonique) — An international organization that was responsible for developing standards for international communications. This organization has been incorporated into ITU. *See* ITU.

CD or CHDIR command — A DOS command to change directories (for example, CD\WINDOWS changes the directory to the Windows directory, and CD\ returns to the Root directory).

CD-R (recordable CD) — A CD drive that can record or write data to a CD. The drive may or may not be multisession, but the data cannot be erased once it is written.

CD-RW (rewritable CD) — A CD drive that can record or write data to a CD. The data can be erased and overwritten. The drive may or may not be multisession.

Chain — A group of clusters used to hold a single file.

Checksum — A method of error checking transmitted data, whereby the digits are added up and their sum compared to an expected sum.

Child directory — *See* Subdirectory.

Child, parent, grandparent backup method — A plan for backing up and reusing tapes or removable disks by rotating them each week (child), month (parent), and year (grandparent).

Chip set — A group of chips on the system board that relieves the CPU of some of the system's processing tasks, providing careful timing of activities and increasing the overall speed and performance of the system.

CHS (cylinders, heads, sectors) mode — The traditional method by which BIOS reads from and writes to hard drives by addressing the correct cylinder, head, and sector. Also called normal mode.

Circuit boards — Computer components, such as the main system board or an adapter board, that have electronic circuits and chips.

Clamping voltage — The maximum voltage allowed through a surge suppressor, such as 175 or 330 volts.

Classless addresses — Class C network addresses that a service provider owns and then subleases to small companies.

clean installation — A Windows 2000 installation that overwrites all previous installations on the hard drive partition.

Client — In a network, a computer that is connected to another computer and uses programs and/or data stored on the other computer.

Clock speed — The speed or frequency that determines the speed at which devices on the system bus operate, usually expressed in MHz. Different components on a system board operate at different speeds, which are determined by multiplying or dividing a factor by the clock speed. The clock speed is itself determined by a crystal or oscillator located somewhere on the system board.

Clone — Originally, a computer that was compatible with IBM computer hardware and MS-DOS software. Today, the word clone often refers to no-name Intel and Microsoft compatibles.

Cluster — One or more sectors that constitute the smallest unit of space on a disk for storing data (also referred to as a file allocation unit). Files are written to a disk as groups of whole clusters.

Cluster chain — A series of clusters used to hold a single file.

CMOS (complementary metal-oxide semiconductor) — One of two types of technologies used to manufacture microchips (the other type is TTL or transistor-transistor logic chips). CMOS chips require less electricity, hold data longer after the electricity is turned off, are slower, and produce less heat than do TTL chips. The configuration or setup chip is a CMOS chip.

COAST (cache on a stick) — Memory modules that hold memory used as a memory cache. *See* Cache memory.

CODEC (compressor/decompressor) — Compressing and later decompressing sound, animation, and video files. MPEG is a common example. Also stands for coder/decoder when referring to digital-to-analog conversion.

Cold Boot — *See* Hard boot.

Collision — In an Ethernet network, a collision occurs when transmitted packets of data are sent at the same time and collide. Ethernet will first listen for silence before it transmits, and it will stop and resend if a collision occurs.

Color depth — The number of possible colors used by a monitor. Determines the number of bits used to compose one pixel. One of two characteristics (the other is resolution) that determines the amount of data sent to the video card to build one screen.

Color space conversion — Converting images to RGB values before they are displayed. Processing is faster if the video card does the conversion instead of the CPU.

Combo card — An Ethernet card that has more than one port to accommodate different cabling media.

Comment lines — Documentation lines that are ignored by a program. A REM in front of a line will comment out an AUTOEXEC command. A semicolon will turn an .ini file line into a comment.

Common access method (CAM) — A standard adapter driver used by SCSI.

Communication and networking riser (CNR) — A specification for a small expansion slot on a system board that accommodates a small audio, modem, or network riser card. Part of the logic for the card is contained in a controller on the system board.

Compressed drive — A drive whose format has been reorganized in order to store more data. A compressed drive is really not a drive at all; it's actually a type of file, typically with a host drive called H.

Computing Technology Industry Association (CompTIA) — A membership trade association that sponsors A+ Certification, a valuable certification for PC technicians.

Configuration data — Also called setup information. Information about the computer's hardware, such as what type of hard drive or floppy drive is present, along with other detailed settings.

Configuration manager — A component of Windows 9x Plug and Play that controls the configuration process of all devices and communicates these configurations to the devices.

Configuration parameter — In Windows NT, another name for the value names and values of the Registry; information in the Windows NT Registry.

Connection protocol — In networking, confirming that a good connection is made before transmitting data to the other end. To accomplish this, most network applications use TCP rather than UDP.

Connectionless protocol — When UDP is used and a connection is not required before sending a packet. Consequently, there is no guarantee that the packet will arrive at its destination. An example of a UDP transmission is a broadcast to all nodes on a network.

console — An administrative tool contains two or more individual administrative tools. For example, Recovery Console contains a set of commands designed to manage a failed Windows 2000 boot, and Computer Management is a console that contains several tools to monitor and manage hardware and software.

Constant angular velocity (CAV) — A technology used by hard drives and newer CD-ROM drives whereby the disc rotates at a constant speed.

Constant linear velocity (CLV) — A CD-ROM format in which the spacing of data is consistent on the CD, but the speed of the disc varies depending on whether the data is reading near the center or the edge of the disc.

Contention-based system — A system in which each computer contends for the opportunity to transmit on the network. If there is a collision, a computer waits a random amount of time and resends.

Continuity — A continuous, unbroken path for the flow of electricity. A "continuity test" can determine whether or not internal wiring is still intact.

Control blade — A laser printer component that prevents too much toner from sticking to the cylinder surface.

Controlled-access unit (CAU) — A centralized hub on a Token Ring network. *See* Multistation access unit.

Conventional memory — Memory addresses between 0 and 640K. Also called base memory.

Cooperative multitasking — A type of pseudomultitasking whereby the CPU switches back and forth between programs loaded at the same time. One program sits in the background waiting for the other to relinquish control. Also called task switching.

Coprocessor — A chip or portion of the CPU that helps the microprocessor perform calculations and speeds up computations and data manipulations dramatically.

COPY command — A command that copies files from one location to another (for example, COPY FILE.EXT A: is used to copy the file named FILE.EXT to the floppy disk in drive A).

Copyright — An individual's right to copy his/her own work. No one else, other than the copyright owner, is legally allowed to do so without permission.

Corrupted files — Data and program files that are damaged for any of a variety of reasons, ranging from power spikes to user error.

CPU (central processing unit) — Also called a microprocessor. The heart and brain of the computer, which receives data input, processes information, and executes instructions.

Cross-linked clusters — Errors caused when files appear to share the same disk space, according to the file allocation table.

Crosstalk — The interference that one wire, in a twisted pair, may produce in the other.

CVF (compressed volume file) — The file on the host drive of a compressed drive that holds all compressed data.

DAC (digital-to-analog converter) — A component that converts digital data back into analog signals just before output from the computer. For example, DAC technology is used to convert digital sound to analog sound just before playback to the speakers.

Data cartridge — A type of tape medium typically used for backups. Full-sized data cartridges are $4 \times 6 \times \frac{3}{8}$ inches in size. A minicartridge is only $3\frac{1}{4} \times 2\frac{1}{2} \times \frac{3}{8}$ inches.

Data communications equipment (DCE) — The hardware, usually a dial-up modem, that provides the connection between a data terminal and a communications line.

Data compression — Reducing the size of files by various techniques such as using a shortcut code to represent repeated data.

Data line protectors — Surge protectors designed to work with the telephone line to a modem.

Data path — The number of bits of data transmitted simultaneously on a bus. The size of a bus, such as a 32-bit-wide data path in a PCI bus.

Data terminal equipment (DTE) — This term refers to both the computer and a remote terminal or other computer to which it is attached.

Data-link layer — The OSI layer that assembles data into packets, addresses data, and manages the flow of transmission between devices.

Datagrams — Packets of data that travel between networks from a sender to a receiver. A datagram typically includes an IP header, address information, a checksum, and data.

DEBUG utility — A DOS utility that shows exactly what is written to a file or memory, using the hexadecimal numbering system to display memory addresses and data.

De facto standard — A standard that does not have an official backing, but is considered a standard because of widespread use and acceptance by the industry.

Default directory — The directory that DOS automatically uses to save and retrieve files.

Default drive — The drive that DOS automatically uses to save and retrieve files.

Default gateway — The main gateway or unit that will send or receive packets addressed to other networks.

Default printer — The printer that Windows software will use unless the user specifies another printer.

Defragment — To "optimize" or rewrite a file to a disk in one contiguous chain of clusters, thus speeding up data retrieval.

DEL command — A command that deletes files (for example, DEL A:FILE.EXT deletes the file named FILE.EXT from drive A).

DELTREE command — A command used to delete a directory, all its subdirectories, and all files within it (for example, DELTREE DIRNAME deletes the directory named DIRNAME and everything in it).

Demodulation — When digital data that has been converted to analog data is converted back to digital data. *See* Modulation.

Desktop — The initial screen that is displayed when an OS that has a GUI interface is loaded.

Device driver — A small program stored on the hard drive that tells the computer how to communicate with an input/output device such as a printer or modem.

Diagnostic cards — Adapter cards designed to discover and report computer errors and conflicts at POST time (before the computer boots up), often by displaying a number on the card.

Diagnostic software — Utility programs that help troubleshoot computer systems. Some DOS diagnostic utilities are CHKDSK and SCANDISK. PC-Technician is an example of a third-party diagnostic program.

Dial-Up Networking (DUN) — A Windows application that allows a PC to remotely connect to a network through a phone line. A Dial-Up Network icon can be found under My Computer.

Differential backup — Backs up only files that have changed or have been created since the last full backup. When recovering data, only two backups are needed: the full backup and the last differential backup.

Digital diagnostic disk — A floppy disk that has data written on it that is precisely aligned, which is used to test the alignment of a floppy disk drive.

Digital signal — A signal that has only a finite number of values in the range of possible values. An example is the transmission of data over a serial cable as bits, where there are only two values: 0 and 1.

Digital subscriber line (DSL) — A type of technology that is used by digital telephone lines that direct connect rather than dial-up.

Digital video disc (DVD) — A faster, larger CD-ROM format that can read older CDs, store over 8 gigabytes of data, and hold full-length motion picture videos.

DIMM (dual inline memory module) — A miniature circuit board used in newer computers to hold memory. DIMMs can hold 16, 32, 64, or 128 MB of RAM on a single module.

Diode — An electronic device that allows electricity to flow in only one direction. Used in a rectifier circuit.

DIP (dual in-line package) switch — A switch on a circuit board or other device that can be set on or off to hold configuration or setup information.

Direct Rambus DRAM — A memory technology by Rambus and Intel that uses a narrow, very fast network-type memory bus. Memory is stored on a RIMM module. Also called RDRAM or Direct RDRAM.

Direct current (DC) — Current that travels in only one direction (the type of electricity provided by batteries). Computer power supplies transform AC current to low DC current.

Directory — An OS table that contains file information such as name, size, time and date of last modification, and the cluster number of the file's beginning location.

Discrete L2 cache — A type of L2 cache contained within the Pentium processor housing, but on a different die, with a cache bus between the processor and the cache.

Disk Editor by Norton — A powerful tool for editing any part of a disk, including the partition table, directory entries, DOS boot record, and FAT.

Disk cache — A method whereby recently retrieved data and adjacent data are read into memory in advance, anticipating the next CPU request.

Disk cloning — Making an exact image of a hard drive including partition information, boot sectors, operating system installation and applications software to replicate the hard drive on another system or recover from a hard drive crash. Also called disk imaging.

Disk compression — Compressing data on a hard drive to allow more data to be written to the drive.

Disk duplexing — An improvement of disk mirroring, whereby redundant data is written to two or more drives, and each hard drive has its own adapter card. This provides greater protection than disk mirroring.

Disk imaging — *See* disk cloning

Disk mirroring — A strategy whereby the same data is written to two hard drives in a computer, to safeguard against hard drive failure. Disk mirroring uses only a single adapter for two drives.

Disk striping — Treating multiple hard drives as a single volume. Data is written across the multiple drives in small segments, in order to increase performance and logical disk volume, and, when parity is also used, to provide fault tolerance. RAID 5 is disk striping with an additional drive for parity.

Disk thrashing — A condition that results when the hard drive is excessively used for virtual memory because RAM is full. It dramatically slows down processing and can cause premature hard drive failure.

DISKCOPY command — A command that copies the entire contents of one disk to another disk of the same type, while formatting the destination disk so that the two will be identical (for example, DISKCOPY A: A: uses drive A to duplicate a disk).

Display adapter — *See* Video controller card.

Display power management signaling (DPMS) — Energy Star standard specifications that allow for the video card and monitor to go into sleep mode simultaneously. *See* Energy Star systems.

DLL (dynamic-link library) — A file with a .dll file extension that contains a library of programming routines used by programs to perform common tasks.

DMA (direct memory access) controller chip — A chip that resides on the system board and provides channels that a device may use to send data directly to memory, bypassing the CPU.

Docking station — A device designed to connect to a portable, or notebook, computer in order to make it easy to connect the notebook to peripheral devices.

DOCSIS (Data Over Cable Service Interface Specifications) — The communications standard used by cable modems.

Documentation — Manuals, tutorials, and Help files that provide information that a user needs in order to use a computer system or software application.

Domain — In Windows NT, a logical group of networked computers, such as those on a college campus, that share a centralized directory database of user account information and security for the entire domain.

Domain name — A unique, text-based name that identifies an IP (Internet address). Typically, domain names in the United States end in .edu, .gov, .com, .org, or .net. Domain names also include a country code, such as .uk for the United Kingdom.

Domain Name System or Domain Name Service (DNS) — A database on a top-level domain name server that keeps track of assigned domain names and their corresponding IP addresses.

Dot pitch — The distance between the dots that the electronic beam hits on a monitor screen.

Double conversion — The process by which the inline UPS converts the AC power to battery power in DC form and then back to AC power.

Double-data rate SDRAM (DDR SDRAM or SDRAM II) — A type of memory technology used on DIMMs that runs at twice the speed of the system clock.

Doze time — The time before an Energy Star or "Green" system will reduce 80% of its activity.

DriveSpace — A utility that compresses files so that they take up less space on a disk drive, creating a single large file on the disk to hold all the compressed files.

Drop height — The height from which a manufacturer states that its drive can be dropped without making the drive unusable.

Dual boot — The ability to boot using either of two different OSs, such as Windows NT and Windows 98. Note that programs cannot be easily shared between Windows NT and the other OS.

Dual ported — When the video chip set (input) and the RAM DAC (output) can access video memory at the same time. A special kind of video RAM is required.

Dual voltage CPU — A CPU that requires two different voltages, one for internal processing and the other for I/O processing.

Dynamic drive — In Windows 2000, a hard drive that uses a 1-MB database written at the end of the drive to hold information about volumes on the drive and RAID setup information.

Dynamic Host Configuration Protocol (DHCP) — The protocol of a server that manages dynamically assigned IP addresses. DHCP is supported by both Windows 9x and Windows NT, and Windows 2000.

Dynamic IP address — An assigned IP address that is used for the current session only. When the session is terminated, the IP address is returned to the list of available addresses.

Dynamic RAM (DRAM) — The most commonly used type of system memory, with access speeds ranging from 70 to 50 nanoseconds. It requires refreshing every few milliseconds.

Dynamic routing — Routing tables that are automatically updated as new information about routes becomes known and is shared by one router with another. Compare to Static routing.

Dynamic VxD — A VxD that is loaded and unloaded from memory as needed.

ECC (error checking and correction) — A chip set feature on a system board that checks the integrity of data stored on DIMMs and can correct single-bit errors in a byte. More advanced ECC schemas can detect, but not correct, double-bit errors in a byte.

ECHS (extended CHS) mode — A mode of addressing information on a hard drive by translating cylinder, head, and sector information in order to break the 528 MB hard drive barrier. Another name for large mode.

ECP (extended capabilities port) — A bidirectional parallel port mode that uses a DMA channel to speed up data flow.

EDO (extended data output) memory — A type of RAM that may be 10–20% faster than conventional RAM because it eliminates the delay before it issues the next memory address.

EEPROM (electrically erasable programmable ROM) chip — A type of chip in which higher voltage may be applied to one of the pins to erase its previous memory before a new instruction set is electronically written.

EISA (extended industry standard architecture) bus — A 32-bit bus that can transfer 4 bytes at a time at a speed of about 20 MHz.

Electrostatic discharge (ESD) — Another name for static electricity, which can damage chips and destroy system boards, even though it might not be felt or seen with the naked eye.

Embedded SCSI devices — A SCSI device designed to be a stand-alone SCSI device with some of the host adapter logic built in.

Emergency Repair Process — A Windows 2000 process that restores the OS to its state at the completion of a successful installation.

Emergency startup disk (ESD) — A Windows 9x system disk that also contains some Windows 9x diagnostic and utility files. The ESD serves Windows 9x as a rescue disk. *Also see* Rescue disk.

EMI (electromagnetic interference) — A magnetic field produced as a side effect from the flow of electricity. EMI can cause corrupted data in data lines that are not properly shielded.

EMM386.EXE — A DOS utility that provides both emulated expanded memory (EMS) and upper memory blocks (UMBs).

Encrypting virus — A type of virus that transforms itself into a nonreplicating program in order to avoid detection. It transforms itself back into a replicating program in order to spread.

Energy Star systems — "Green" systems that satisfy the EPA requirements to decrease the overall consumption of electricity. *See* Green standards.

Enhanced BIOS — A newer BIOS that has been written to accommodate larger-capacity gigabyte drives.

Enhanced IDE technology — A newer drive standard that allows systems to recognize drives larger than 504 MB/528 MB and to handle up to four devices on the same controller.

Enhanced metafile format (EMF) — A format used to print a document that contains embedded print commands. When printing in Windows, EMF information is generated by the GDI portion of the Windows kernel.

Environment — As related to OSs, the overall support that an OS provides to applications software.

Environment subsystems — In Windows NT, a user-mode process in which a subsystem runs an application in its own private memory address space as a virtual machine. (Compare to integral subsystems.)

EPP (enhanced parallel port) — A parallel port that allows data to flow in both directions (bidirectional port) and is faster than original parallel ports on PCs that only allowed communication in one direction.

EPROM (erasable programmable ROM) chip — A type of chip with a special window that allows the current memory contents to be erased with special ultraviolet light so that the chip can be reprogrammed. Many BIOS chips are EPROMs.

ERASE command — Another name for the DEL command.

Error correction — The ability of some modems to identify transmission errors and then automatically request another transmission.

Escalating — The process by which a technician passes a customer's problem to higher organizational levels, if he or she cannot address the problem.

ESCD (extended system configuration data) — A list written to the BIOS chip of what you have done manually to the system configuration that Plug and Play does not do on its own.

ESD (electrostatic discharge) — *See* Electrostatic discharge.

Ethernet — The most popular network topology used today. It uses Carrier Sense Multiple Access with Collision Detection (CSMA/CD) and can be physically configured as a bus or star network.

Event Viewer — In Windows NT, a utility that tracks and logs events as they are performed by the applications, processes, or user actions. Accessed by clicking Start, Programs, Administrative Tools, and then selecting Event Viewer.

Executive services — In Windows NT, a subsystem running in kernel mode that interfaces between the user mode and HAL.

Expanded memory (EMS) — Memory outside of the conventional 640K and the extended 1024K range that is accessed in 16K segments, or pages, by way of a window to upper memory.

Expansion bus — A bus that does not run synchronized with the system clock.

Expansion card — A circuit board inserted into a slot on the system board to enhance the capability of the computer.

Expansion slot — A narrow slot on the system board where an expansion card can be inserted. Expansion slots connect to a bus on the system board.

Expert systems — Computerized software that uses a database of known facts and rules to simulate a human expert's reasoning and decision-making processes.

Extended memory — Memory above the initial 1024 KB, or 1 MB, area.

External cache — Static cache memory, stored on the system board or inside CPU housing, that is not part of the CPU (also called level 2 or L2 cache).

Fatal system error — An error that prevents Windows NT from loading. An example is a damaged Registry.

Fault tolerance — The degree to which a system can tolerate failures. Adding redundant components, such as disk mirroring or disk duplexing, is a way to build in fault tolerance.

FDDI (Fiber Distributed Data Interface) — Pronounced "fiddy." A ring-based network, similar to Token Ring, that does not require a centralized hub. FDDI often uses fiber-optic cabling.

Ferroresonant regulator — A UPS device that contains a magnetic coil that can retain a power charge that can be used during a brownout to raise the voltage at switching time.

Field replaceable unit — A component in a computer or device that can be replaced with a new component without sending the computer or device back to the manufacturer. Example: a DIMM memory module on a system board.

File allocation table (FAT) — A table on a disk that tracks the clusters used to contain a file.

File allocation units — See Cluster.

File extension — A three-character portion of the name of a file that is used to identify the file type. The file extension follows the filename under DOS naming conventions.

File system — The overall structure that an OS uses to name, store, and organize files on a disk. Examples of files systems are FAT16, FAT32, and NTFS.

File virus — A virus that inserts virus code into an executable program and can spread whenever that program is accessed.

File — A collection of related records or lines that can be written to disk and assigned a name (for example, a simple letter or a payroll file containing data about employees).

Filename — The first part of the name assigned to a file. In DOS, the filename can be no more than 8 characters long and is followed by the file extension.

Fire Wire — An expansion bus that can also be configured to work as a local bus. It is expected to replace the SCSI bus, providing an easy method to install and configure fast I/O devices. Also called IEEE 1394.

Firmware — Software that is permanently stored in a chip.

Flash ROM — ROM that can be reprogrammed or changed without replacing chips.

Flash memory — A type of RAM that can electronically hold memory even when the power is off.

Flat panel monitor — A desktop monitor that uses an LCD panel.

Flow control — When using modems, a method of controlling the flow of data from a sending PC by having the receiving PC send a message to the sending device to stop or start data flow. Xon/Xoff is an example of a flow control protocol.

FM (frequency modulation) method — A method of synthesizing sound by making a math-ematical approximation of the musical sound wave. MIDI may use FM synthesis or wavetable synthesis.

Folder — A Windows directory for a collection of related files (for instance, a person may find it convenient to create a Mydata directory, or folder, in which to store personal files). For example, ATDT means attention and listen for a dial tone.

Formatting (a floppy disk) — To prepare a new floppy disk for use by placing tracks or cylinders on its surface to store information (for example, FORMAT A:). Old disks can be reformatted, but all data on them will be lost.

FPM (fast page mode) memory — An earlier memory mode used before the introduction of EDO memory.

Fragmentation — The distribution of data files, such that they are stored in noncontiguous clusters.

Fragmented file — A file that has been written to different portions of the disk so that it is not in contiguous clusters.

Frame — A small, standardized packet of data that also includes header and trailer information as well as error-checking codes. See also Packets.

Frame — The header or trailer information added to data to encapsulate it before it is sent over a network.

Front end — In a client/server environment, the application on the client that makes use of data stored on the server.

Frontside bus — The bus between the CPU and the memory outside the CPU housing.

FTP (File Transfer Protocol) — An Internet standard that provides for the transfer of files from one computer to another. FTP can be used at a command prompt, or with a GUI interface, which is available with FTP software or with a Web browser. When using a Web browser, enter the command "ftp" in the browser URL line instead of the usual "http://" used to locate a Web site.

FTP server or **FTP site** — A computer that stores files that can be downloaded by FTP.

Full backup — A complete backup, whereby all of the files on the hard drive are backed up each time the backup procedure is performed. It is the safest backup method, but it takes the most time.

Full-duplex — Communication that happens in two directions at the same time.

G.Lite — A communications standard sponsored by ITU that is used by ADSL.

Gateway — A device or process that connects networks with different protocols. See Bridge and Router.

General Protection Fault (GPF) error — A Windows error that occurs when a program attempts to access a memory address that is not available or is no longer assigned to it.

Genlock — A standard for video-capturing cards that refers to the ability of the card to capture a single unique frame of video, rather than "sampling" pieces of adjoining frames.

Graphics accelerator — A type of video card that has an on-board processor that can substantially increase speed and boost graphical and video performance.

Green Standards — Standards that mean that a computer or device can go into sleep or doze mode when not in use, thus saving energy and helping the environment.

Ground bracelet — An antistatic wrist strap used to dissipate static electricity. Typically grounded by attaching an alligator clip to the computer chassis or to a nearby ground mat.

Ground mat — An antistatic mat designed for electronic workbenches to dissipate static electricity. It often uses a wire attached to the ground connection in an electrical outlet.

Group files — Windows 3.x files with the .grp file extension that contain information about a program group of Program Manager.

Guard tone — A tone that an answering modem sends when it first answers the phone, to tell the calling modem that a modem is on the other end of the line.

GUI (graphical user interface) — A user interface, such as the Windows interface, that uses graphics or icons on the screen for running programs and entering information.

Half-duplex — Communication between two devices whereby transmission takes place in only one direction at a time.

Half-life — The time it takes for a medium storing data to weaken to half of its strength. Magnetic media, including traditional hard drives and floppy disks, have a half-life of five to seven years.

Handshaking — When two modems begin to communicate, the initial agreement made as to how to send and receive data. It often occurs when you hear the modem making noises as the dial-up is completed.

Hard boot — Restart the computer by turning off the power or by pressing the Reset button. Also called cold boot.

Hard copy — Output from a printer to paper.

Hard drive — The main secondary storage device of a PC, a sealed case that contains magnetic coated platters that rotate at high speed.

Hard drive controller — A set of microchips with programs that control a hard drive. Most hard drive controllers today are located inside the hard drive housing.

Hard drive standby time — The amount of time before a hard drive will shut down to conserve energy.

Hard-disk loading — The illegal practice of installing unauthorized software on computers for sale. Hard-disk loading can typically be identified by the absence of original disks in the original system's shipment.

Hardware — The physical components that constitute the computer system, such as the monitor, the keyboard, the system board, and the printer.

Hardware abstraction layer (HAL) — The low-level part of Windows NT, written specifically for each CPU technology, so that only the HAL must change when platform components change.

Hardware cache — A disk cache that is contained in RAM chips built right on the disk controller.

Hardware compatibility list (HCL) — The list of all computers and peripheral devices that have been tested and are officially supported by Windows NT (See *www. microsoft.com/hwtest*).

Hardware interrupt — An event caused by a hardware device signaling the CPU that it requires service.

Hardware profiles — In Windows NT, configuration information about memory, CPU, and OS, for a PC. A PC may have more than one profile. For example, a docking station may have two profiles, one with and one without the notebook PC docked.

Hardware tree — A database built each time Windows 9x starts up that contains a list of installed components and the resources they use.

Head — The top or bottom surface of one platter on a hard drive. Each platter has two heads.

Header — Information sent ahead of data being transferred over a network to identify it to receiving protocols. An IP header consists of items such as header and datagram length, flags, checksum, addresses, and so on.

Heap — A memory block set aside for a program's data. If the heap fills up, an "Out of memory" error might occur, even if there is plenty of regular RAM left, especially in 16-bit applications.

Heat sink — A piece of metal, with cooling fins, that can be attached to or mounted on an integrated chip (such as the CPU) to dissipate heat.

Hertz (Hz) — Unit of measurement for frequency, calculated in terms of vibrations, or cycles, per second. For example, a Pentium CPU may have a speed of 233 MHz (megahertz). For 16-bit stereo sound, 44,100 Hz is used.

Hibernation — A power-saving notebook feature. When a computer hibernates, it stores whatever is currently in memory and then shuts down. When it returns from hibernating, it restores everything back to the way it was before the shutdown.

Hidden file — A file that is not displayed in a directory list. To hide or display a file is one of the file's attributes kept by the OS.

High memory area (HMA) — The first 64K of extended memory. The method of storing part of DOS in the high memory area is called loading DOS high.

High-level format — Format performed by the OS that writes a file system to a logical drive. For DOS and Windows 9x, the command used is FORMAT, which writes a FAT and a directory to the drive. Also called OS format.

HIMEM.SYS — A device driver that manages memory above 640K. It is often executed by the line DEVICE = C:\DOS\HIMEM.SYS in a CONFIG.SYS file.

Hive — A physical segment of the Windows NT Registry that is stored in a file.

Holographic image — A three-dimensional image (created by holography) that is made up of a light interference pattern preserved in a medium such as photographic film and that changes when the angle of view changes. Because making unofficial copies of holographic images is extremely difficult, they are often used to tag products, such as software packages, as original, making it difficult to distribute illegal copies.

Hop count — The number of routers a packet must pass through in a network in order to reach its destination.

Host adapter — The circuit board that controls a SCSI bus that supports as many as eight or 16 separate devices, one of which is a host adapter that controls communication with the PC.

Host drive — Typically drive H on a compressed drive. *See* Compressed drive.

Hot swapping — The ability of a computer to use a device, such as a PC Card on a notebook, that is inserted while the computer is running without the computer needing to be rebooted.

Hot-pluggable — A characteristic of 1394 devices that let you plug in the device without rebooting your PC and remove the device without receiving an error message.

HTML (Hypertext Markup Language) — The language used to create hypertext documents commonly used on web sites. HTML documents have an .html file extension.

HTTP (Hypertext Transfer Protocol) — The common transfer protocol used by Internet browsers on the World Wide Web.

Hub — A network device or box that provides a central location to connect cables.

Hypertext — Text that contains links to remote points in the document or to other files, documents, or graphics. Hypertext is created using HTML and is commonly distributed from Web sites.

I/O addresses — Numbers that are used by devices and the CPU to manage communication between them.

I/O card — A card that often contains serial, parallel, and game ports on the same adapter board, providing input/output interface with the CPU.

IBM-compatible — A computer that uses an Intel (or compatible) processor and can run DOS and Windows.

IEEE 1284 — A standard for parallel ports developed by the Institute for Electrical and Electronics Engineers and supported by many hardware manufacturers.

IEEE 1394 — *See* Fire Wire.

In-band signaling — In modem communication, the name of the signaling used by software flow control, which pauses transmission by sending a special control character in the same channel (or band) that data is sent in.

Incremental backup — A time-saving backup method that only backs up files changed or newly created since the last full or incremental backup. Multiple incremental backups might be required when recovering lost data.

Infestation — Any unwanted program that is transmitted to a computer without the user's knowledge and that is designed to do varying degrees of damage to data and software. There are a number of different types of infestations, including viruses, Trojan horses, worms, and time bombs, among others.

Initialization files — Configuration information files for Windows. Win.ini and System.ini are the two most important Windows 3.x initialization files.

Inline UPS — A UPS that continually provides power through a battery-powered circuit, and, because it requires no switching, ensures continuous power to the user.

Instruction set — The set of instructions, on the CPU chip, that the computer can perform directly (such as ADD and MOVE).

Integral subsystems — In Windows NT, processes used to provide services to the rest of the system and the applications the system supports. (Compare to environment subsystems.)

Integrated Device Electronics (IDE) — A hard drive whose disk controller is integrated into the drive, eliminating the need for a controller cable and thus increasing speed, as well as reducing price.

Intelligent hubs — Network hubs that can be remotely controlled at a console, using network software. These hubs can monitor a network and report errors or problems.

Intelligent UPS — A UPS connected to a com-puter by way of a serial cable so that software on the computer can monitor and control the UPS.

Interlace — A display in which the electronic beam of a monitor draws every other line with each pass, which lessens the overall effect of a lower refresh rate.

Interleave — To write data in nonconsecutive sectors around a track, so that time is not wasted waiting for the disk to make a full revolution before the next sector is read.

Internal cache — Memory cache that is faster than external cache, and is contained inside 80486 and Pentium chips (also referred to as primary, Level 1, or L1 cache).

Internal DOS commands — DOS commands whose coding is contained within COMMAND.COM and are, therefore, automatically loaded into memory when COMMAND.COM is loaded.

Internet — The worldwide collection of over a million hosts that can communicate with each other using TCP/IP. The lowercase internet simply means multiple networks connected together.

Internet Control Message Protocol (ICMP) — Part of the IP layer that is used to transmit error messages and other control messages to hosts and routers.

Internet Network Information Center (InterNIC) — The central group that assigns and keeps track of all Internet IP addresses on the organizational level.

Internet Printing Protocol (IPP) — A protocol used to send print jobs across the Internet. A printer is addressed by its URL (uniform resource locator)—for example, *www.ourdomain.com/printer4*.

Internet service provider (ISP) — A commercial group that provides a user with Internet access for a monthly fee. AOL, Prodigy, GTE, and CompuServe are four large ISPs.

Internetwork — Two or more networks connected together, such as a LAN and a WAN joined together.

Interpolative scaling — A method used to fill in the gaps in an image to produce a more realistic-looking display when a small video window is enlarged to full-screen size.

Interrupt handler — A program (either BIOS or a device driver), that is used by the CPU to process a hardware interrupt.

Interrupt vector table — A table that stores the memory addresses assigned to interrupt handlers. Also called a vector table.

Intranet — A private internet used by a large company.

IP (Internet Protocol) address — A 32-bit "dotted-decimal" address consisting of four numbers separated by periods, used to uniquely identify a device on a network that uses TCP/IP protocols. The first numbers identify the network; the last numbers identify a host. An example of an IP address is 206.96.103.114.

IPX/SPX — A protocol developed and used by Novell NetWare for LANs. The IPX portion of the protocol works at the network layer, which is responsible for routing, and the SPX portion of the protocol manages error checking at the transport layer.

IRQ (interrupt request number) — A line on a bus that is assigned to a device and is used to signal the CPU for servicing. These lines are assigned a reference number (for example, the normal IRQ for a printer is IRQ 7).

ISA bus — An 8-bit industry standard architecture bus used on the original 8088 PC. Sixteen-bit ISA buses were designed for the 286 AT, and are still used in Pentiums for devices such as modems.

ISDN (Integrated Services Digital Network) — A communications standard that can carry digital data simultaneously over two channels on a single pair of wires, at about five times the speed of regular phone lines.

Isochronous data transfer — A method used by IEEE 1394 to transfer data continuously without breaks.

ITU (International Telecommunications Union) — The international organization responsible for developing international standards of communication. Formally CCITT.

Joule — A measure of energy equal to the work done when a current of one ampere is passed through a resistance of one ohm for one second.

JPEG (Joint Photographic Experts Group) — A "lossy" graphical compression scheme that allows the user to control the amount of data that is averaged and sacrificed as file size is reduced. It is a common Internet file format. *See* Lossy compression.

Jumper — Two wires that stick up side by side on the system board that are used to hold configuration information. The jumper is considered closed if a cover is over the wires, and open if the cover is missing.

Kernel — Core portion of an operating system that loads applications and manages files, memory, and other resources.

Kernel mode — A Windows NT "privileged" processing mode that has access to hardware components.

Keyboard — A common input device through which data and instructions may be typed into computer memory.

Keys — In Windows 9x, section names of the Windows 9x Registry.

Land — Microscopic flat areas on the surface of a CD or DVD that separate pits. Lands and pits are used to represent data on the disc.

Laptop computer — *See* Notebook.

Large mode — A format that supports hard drives that range from 504 MB to 1 GB, mapping the data to conform to the 504-MB barrier before the address information is passed to the operating system.

Legacy — An older device or adapter card that does not support Plug and Play, and might have to be manually configured through jumpers or DIP switches.

Let-through — The maximum voltage allowed through a surge suppressor to the device being protected.

Level 1 cache — *See* Internal cache.

Level 2 cache — *See* External cache.

License — Permission for an individual to use a product or service. A manufacturer's method of maintaining ownership, while granting permission for use to others.

Limited token — Applies to a FDDI network. A token sent that allows a receiving station to communicate only with the sending station, thus providing continuous communication between the two stations.

Line conditioners — Devices that regulate, or condition the power, providing continuous voltage during brownouts and spikes.

Line protocol — A protocol used over phone lines to allow a connection to a network. Also called a bridging protocol. The most popular line protocol is PPP (Point-to-Point Protocol).

Line speed — *See* Modem speed.

Line-interactive UPS — A variation of a standby UPS that shortens switching time by always keeping the inverter that converts AC to DC working, so that there is no charge-up time for the inverter.

Load size — The largest amount of memory that a driver needs to initialize itself and to hold its data. It is almost always a little larger than the size of the program file.

Loading high — The process of loading a driver or TSR into upper memory.

Local bus — A bus that operates at a speed synchronized with the CPU speed.

Local I/O bus — A local bus that provides I/O devices with fast access to the CPU.

Logical block addressing (LBA) — A method in which the operating system views the drive as one long linear list of LBAs, permitting larger drive sizes (LBA 0 is cylinder 0, head 0, and sector 1).

Logical drive — A portion or all of a hard drive partition that is treated by the operating system as though it were a physical drive containing a boot record, FAT, and root directory.

Logical geometry — The number of heads, tracks, and sectors that the BIOS on the hard drive controller presents to the system BIOS and the OS. The logical geometry does not consist of the same values as the physical geometry, although calculations of drive capacity yield the same results.

Logical unit number (LUN) — A number from 0 to 15 (also called the SCSI ID) assigned to each SCSI device attached to a daisy chain.

Lossless compression — A method that substitutes special characters for repeating patterns without image degradation. A substitution table is used to restore the compressed image to its original form.

Lossy compression — A method that drops unnecessary data, but with some image and sound loss. JPEG allows the user to control the amount of loss, which is inversely related to the image size.

Lost allocation units — *See* Lost clusters.

Lost clusters — Lost file fragments that, according to the file allocation table, contain data that does not belong to any file. In DOS, the command CHKDSK/F can free these fragments.

Low insertion force (LIF) — A socket feature that requires the installer to manually apply an even force over the microchip when inserting the chip into the socket.

Low-level format — A process (usually performed at the factory) that electronically creates the hard drive cylinders and tests for bad spots on the disk surface.

MAC (media access control) — An element of data-link layer protocol that provides compatibility with the NIC used by the physical layer. A network card address is often called a MAC address. *See* Adapter address.

Macro — A small sequence of commands, contained within a document, that can be automatically executed when the document is loaded, or executed later by using a predetermined keystroke.

Macro virus — A virus that can hide in the macros of a document file. Typically, viruses do not reside in data or document files.

Main board — *See* System board.

Make code — A code produced by pressing a key on a computer keyboard. *See* Break code.

Master boot record (MBR) (of a floppy disk) — The record written near the beginning of a floppy disk, containing information about the disk as well as the startup operating system programs.

Master boot record (MBR) (on a hard drive) — The first sector on a hard drive, which contains the partition table and other information needed by BIOS to access the drive.

Material safety data sheet (MSDS) — A document that provides information about how to properly handle substances such as chemical solvents including physical data, toxicity, health effects, first aid, storage, disposal, and spill procedures.

MCA (micro channel architecture) bus — A proprietary IBM PS/2 bus, seldom seen today, with a width of 16 or 32 bits and multiple master control, which allowed for multitasking.

MD or MKDIR command — A command used to create a directory on a drive (for example, MD C:\MYDATA).

MEM command — A DOS utility used to display how programs and drivers are using conventional, upper, and extended memory (Example: MEM/C/P).

MemMaker — A DOS utility that can increase the amount of conventional memory available to DOS-based software applications, by loading drivers and TRSs into upper memory.

Memory — Physical microchips that can hold data and programming located on the system board or expansion cards.

Memory address — A number that the CPU assigns to physical memory to keep track of the memory that it has access to.

Memory bus — The bus between the CPU and memory on the system board. Also called the system bus or the host bus.

Memory cache — A small amount of faster RAM that stores recently retrieved data, in anticipation of what the CPU will request next, thus speeding up access.

Memory caching — Using a small amount of faster RAM to store recently retrieved data, in anticipation of what the CPU will next request, thus speeding up access.

Memory leak — A problem caused when an application does not release the memory addresses assigned to it when it unloads, causing the memory heaps to have less and less memory for new applications.

Memory management — The process of increasing available conventional memory, required by DOS-based programs, accomplished by loading device drivers and TSRs into upper memory.

Memory mapping — Assigning addresses to both RAM and ROM during the boot process.

Memory paging — In Windows 9x, swapping blocks of RAM memory to an area of the hard drive to serve as virtual memory when RAM memory is low.

Memory-resident virus — A virus that can stay lurking in memory, even after its host program is terminated.

Middleware — Software necessary for an application on a client to pass requests to a server, and for a server to respond with data. Microsoft's Open Database Connectivity (ODBC) is an example of middleware.

MIDI (Musical Instrument Digital Interface) — Pronounced "middy," a standard for transmitting sound from musical devices, such as electronic keyboards, to computers where it can be digitally stored.

Minicartridge — A tape drive cartridge that is only $3\frac{1}{4} \times 2\frac{1}{2} \times \frac{3}{5}$ inches. It is small enough to allow two drives to fit into a standard $5\frac{1}{2}$-inch drive bay of a PC case.

Minifile system — In Windows NT, a simplified file system that is started so that Ntldr (NT Loader) can read files from either a FAT16 or an NTFS file system.

MIRROR command — An old DOS command that saves information about deleted files as they are deleted. This information can be used later by the UNDELETE command to recover a deleted file. The command can be used to save the partition table to a floppy disk.

mixed mode — A Windows 2000 mode for domain controllers used when there is at least one Windows NT domain controller on the network.

MMX (Multimedia Extensions) technology — A variation of the Pentium processor designed to manage and speed up high-volume input/output needed for graphics, motion video, animation, and sound.

Modem — From MOdulate/DEModulate. A device that modulates digital data from a computer to an analog format that can be sent over telephone lines, then demodulates it back into digital form.

Modem eliminator — A technique that allows two data terminal equipment (DTE) devices to communicate by means of a null modem cable in which the transmit and receive wires are cross-connected, and no modems are necessary.

Modem riser card — A small modem card that uses an AMR or CNR slot. Part of the modem logic is contained in a controller on the system board.

Modem speed — The speed a modem can transmit data along a phone line measured in bits per second (bps). Two communicating modems must talk at the same speed for data transmission to be successful. Also called line speed.

Modulation — Converting binary or digital data into an analog signal that can be sent over standard telephone lines.

Monitor — The most commonly used output device for displaying text and graphics on a computer.

Motherboard — *See* System board.

Mouse — A pointing and input device that allows the user to move a cursor around a screen and select programs with the click of a button.

MP3 — A method to compress audio files that uses MPEG level 3. It can reduce sound files as low as a 1:24 ratio without losing sound quality.

MPC (Multimedia Personal Computer) guidelines — The minimum standards created by Microsoft and a consortium of hardware manufacturers for multimedia PCs.

MPEG (Moving Pictures Experts Group) — A processing-intensive standard for data compression for motion pictures that tracks movement from one frame to the next, and only stores the new data that has changed.

MSDOS.SYS — In DOS, a program file that contains part of the DOS kernel and controls much of the boot process. In Windows 9x, a text file that contains settings used by Io.sys during booting.

Multibank DRAM (MDRAM) — A special kind of RAM used on video cards that is able to use a full 128-bit bus path without requiring the full 4MB of RAM.

Multiframe dialog — When a limited token is sent that allows a receiving station to communicate only with the sending station, thus providing continuous communication between the two stations.

Multimedia — A type of computer presentation that combines text, graphics, animation, photos, sound, and/or full-motion video.

Multimeter — Either a voltmeter or an ammeter that can also measure resistance in ohms or as continuity, depending on a switch setting.

Multipartite virus — A combination of a boot sector virus and a file virus. It can hide in either type of program.

Multiplier — On a system board, the factor by which the bus speed or frequency is multiplied to get the CPU clock speed.

Multiscan monitor — A monitor that can work within a range of frequencies, and thus can work with different standards and video cards. If offers a variety of refresh rates.

Multisession — A feature that allows data to be read (or written) on a CD during more than one session. This is important if the disc was only partially filled during the first write.

Multistation access unit (MSAU or MAU) — A centralized device used to connect IBM Token Ring network stations.

Multitasking — When a CPU or an OS supporting multiple CPUs can do more than one thing at a time. The Pentium is a multitasking CPU.

Multithreading — The ability to pass more than one function (thread) to the OS kernel at the same time, such as when one thread is performing a print job while another reads a file.

native mode — A Windows 2000 mode used by domain controllers when there are no Windows NT domain controllers present on the network.

Nearest active downstream neighbor (NADN) — The next station to receive a token in a token ring.

Nearest active upstream neighbor (NAUN) — The station that has just sent a token to the nearest active downstream neighbor in a token ring.

NetBEUI (NetBIOS Extended User Interface) — A proprietary Microsoft networking protocol used only by Windows-based systems, and limited to LANs because it does not support routing.

NetBT (NetBIOS over TCP/IP) — An alternate Microsoft NetBEUI component designed to interface with TCP/IP networks.

Network interface card (NIC) — A network adapter board that plugs into a computer's system board and provides a port on the back of the card to connect a PC to a network.

Network layer — The OSI layer responsible for routing packets.

Network mask — The portion of an IP address that identifies the network.

Node — Each computer, workstation, or device on a network.

Noise — An extraneous, unwanted signal, often over an analog phone line, that can cause communication interference or transmission errors. Possible sources are fluorescent lighting, radios, TVs, lightning, or bad wiring.

Non-interlace — A type of display in which the electronic beam of a monitor draws every line on the screen with each pass. See Interlace.

Non-memory-resident virus — A virus that is terminated when the host program is closed. Compare to memory-resident virus.

Nonparity memory — Slightly less expensive, 8-bit memory without error checking. A SIMM part number with a 32 in it (4 2 8 bits) is nonparity.

Nonvolatile — Refers to a kind of RAM that is stable and can hold data as long as electricity is powering the memory.

Normal mode — See CHS.

North bridge — That portion of the chip set hub that connects faster I/O buses (e.g., AGP bus) to the system bus. Compare to South bridge.

Notebook — A personal computer designed for travel, using less voltage and taking up less space than a regular PC. Also called a laptop computer.

NT Hardware Qualifier (NTHQ) — A utility found on the Windows NT installation CD-ROM that examines your system to determine if all hardware present qualifies for NT.

NT virtual DOS machine (NTVDM) — An emulated environment in which a 16-bit DOS application or a Windows 3.x application resides within Windows NT with its own memory space or WOW (Win 16 application on a Win 32 platform). (See WOW.)

Ntldr (NT Loader) — In Windows NT, the OS loader used on Intel systems.

Null modem cable — See Modem eliminator.

Object linking — A method where one application can execute a command on an object created by another application.

Octet — A traditional term for each of the four 8-bit numbers that make up an IP address. For example, the IP address 206.96.103.114 has four octets.

Ohms — The standard unit of measurement for electrical resistance. Resistors are rated in ohms.

On-board BIOS — See System BIOS.

On-board ports — Ports that are directly on the system board, such as a built-in keyboard port or on-board serial port.

Open Systems Interconnect (OSI) — A seven-layer (application, presentation, session, transport, network, data-link, physical) model of communications supported by a network. Refers to software and firmware only.

Operating system format — See High-level format.

OS format — See High-level format.

Out-of-band signaling — The type of signaling used by hardware flow control, which sends a message to pause transmission by using channels (or bands) not used for data.

Overclocking — Running a system board at a speed that is not recommended or guaranteed by CPU or chipset manufacturers.

P-A-S-S — An acronym to help remember how to use a fire extinguisher. (Pull the pin, Aim low at the base of the fire, Squeeze the handle of the extinguisher, and Sweep back and forth across the fire.)

P1 connector — Power connection on an ATX system board.

Packets — Network segments of data that also include header, destination addresses, and trailer information. Also called Frames.

Page — Memory allocated in 4K or 16K segments within a page frame.

Page-in — The process in which the memory manager goes to the hard drive to return the data from a swap file to RAM.

Page-out — The process in which, when RAM is full, the memory manager takes a page and moves it to the swap file.

Page fault — An OS interrupt that occurs when the OS is forced to access the hard drive to satisfy the demands for virtual memory.

Page frame — A 64K upper memory area divided into four equal-sized pages through which the memory manager swaps data.

Parallel port — A female port on the computer that can transmit data in parallel, 8 bits at a time, and is usually used with a printer. The names for parallel ports are LPT1 and LPT2.

Parity — An error-checking scheme in which a ninth, or "parity," bit is added. The value of the parity bit is set to either 0 or 1 to provide an even number of ones for even parity and an odd number of ones for odd parity.

Parity error — An error that occurs when the number of 1s in the byte is not in agreement with the expected number.

Parity memory — Nine-bit memory in which the 9th bit is used for error checking. A SIMM part number with a 36 in it (4 2 9 bits) is parity. Older DOS PCs almost always use parity chips.

Partition — A division of a hard drive that can be used to hold logical drives.

Partition table — A table at the beginning of the hard drive that contains information about each partition on the drive. The partition table is contained in the master boot record.

Passive network — A network, such as Ethernet, in which the computers, not dedicated network devices, drive the signals over the network.

Path — The drive and list of directories pointing to a file.

PC Card — A credit-card-sized adapter card that can be slid into a slot in the side of many notebook computers and is used for connecting to modems, networks, and CD-ROM drives. Also called PCMCIA Card.

PC Card slot — An expansion slot on a notebook computer, into which a PC Card is inserted. Also called a PCMCIA Card slot.

PCI (peripheral component interconnect) bus — A bus common on Pentium computers that runs at speeds of up to 33 MHz, with a 32-bit-wide data path. It serves as the middle layer between the memory bus and expansion buses.

PCI bus IRQ steering — A feature that makes it possible for PCI devices to share an IRQ. System BIOS and the OS must both support this feature.

PCMCIA (Personal Computer Memory Card International Association) card — *See* PC Card.

PCMCIA Card slot — *See* PC Card slot.

Peripheral devices — Devices that communicate with the CPU, but are not located directly on the system board, such as the monitor, floppy drive, printer, and mouse.

Physical geometry — The actual layout of heads, tracks, and sectors on a hard drive. *See* Logical geometry.

Physical layer — The OSI layer responsible for interfacing with the network media (cabling).

PIF (program information file) — A file with a .pif file extension that is used by an OS to store the settings of the environment provided to a DOS application.

Pin grid array (PGA) — A feature of a CPU socket where the pins are aligned in uniform rows around the socket.

Pipelined burst SRAM — A less expensive SRAM that uses more clock cycles per transfer than nonpipelined burst, but does not significantly slow down the process.

Pit — Recessed areas on the surface of a CD or DVD, separating lands, or flat areas. Lands and pits are used to represent data on the disc.

Pixel — Small spots on a fine horizontal scan line that are illuminated to create an image on the monitor.

Plug and Play — A technology in which the operating system and BIOS are designed to automatically configure new hardware devices to eliminate system resource conflicts (such as IRQ and port conflicts).

Plug and Play BIOS — Basic input/output system for Plug and Play devices, which are designed to be automatically recognized by the computer when they are installed.

Polling — A process by which the CPU checks the status of connected devices to determine if they are ready to send or receive data.

Polymorphic virus — A type of virus that changes its distinguishing characteristics as it replicates itself. Mutating in this way makes it more difficult for AV software to recognize the presence of the virus.

Port — A physical connector, usually at the back of a computer, that allows a cable from a peripheral device, such as a printer, mouse, or modem, to be attached.

Port settings — The configuration parameters of communications devices such as COM1, COM2, or COM3, including IRQ settings.

Port speed — The communication speed between a DTE (computer) and a DCE (modem). As a general rule, the port speed should be at least four times as fast as the modem speed.

Portable Operating System Interface (POSIX) — A set of standards adopted to allow operating systems (such as UNIX and NT) and their applications to port from one platform to another.

POST (power-on self test) — A self-diagnostic program used to perform a simple test of the CPU, RAM, and various I/O devices. The POST is performed when the computer is first turned on and is stored in ROM-BIOS.

Power conditioners — Line conditioners that regulate, or condition, the power, providing continuous voltage during brownouts.

Power supply — A box inside the computer case that supplies power to the system board and other installed devices. Power supplies provide 3.3, 5, and 12 volts DC.

Power-on password — *See* Startup password.

PPP (Point-to-Point Protocol) — A common way PCs with modems can connect to an internet. The Windows Dial-Up Networking utility, found under My Computer, uses PPP.

Preemptive multitasking — A type of pseudomultitasking whereby the CPU allows an application a specified period of time and then preempts the processing to give time to another application.

Presentation layer — The OSI layer that compresses and decompresses data and interfaces with the Application layer and the Session layer.

Primary cache — *See* Internal cache.

Primary domain controller (PDC) — In a Windows NT network, the computer that controls the directory database of user accounts, group accounts, and computer accounts on a domain.

Primary storage — Temporary storage on the system board used by the CPU to process data and instructions.

Printer — A peripheral output device that produces printed output to paper. Different types include dot matrix, ink-jet, and laser printers.

Process — An executing instance of a program together with the program resources. There can be more than one process running for a program at the same time. One process for a program happens each time the program is loaded into memory or executed.

Processor speed — The speed or frequency at which the CPU operates. Usually expressed in MHz.

Program — A set of step-by-step instructions to a computer. Some are burned directly into chips, while others are stored as program files. Programs are written in languages such as BASIC and C++.

Program file — A file that contains instructions designed to be executed by the CPU.

Program jump — An instruction that causes control to be sent to a memory address other than the next sequential address.

Program Information File (PIF) — A file used by Windows to describe the environment for a DOS program to use.

Proprietary — A term for products that a company has exclusive rights to manufacture and/or market. Proprietary computer components are typically more difficult to find and more expensive to buy.

Protected mode — An operating mode that supports multi-tasking whereby the OS manages memory, programs have more than 1024K of memory addresses, and programs can use a 32-bit data path.

Protocol — A set of preestablished rules for communication. Examples of protocols are modem parity settings and the way in which header and trailer information in a data packet is formatted.

PS/2 compatible mouse — A mouse that uses a round mouse port (called a mini-DIN or PS/2 connector) coming directly off the system board.

Pulse code modulation (PCM) — A method of sampling sound in a reduced, digitized format, by recording differences between successive digital samples instead of their full values.

Quarter-Inch Committee or quarter-inch cartridge (QIC) — A name of a standardized method used to write data to tape. Backups made with the Windows 9x System Tools Backup utility have a .qic extension.

RAID (redundant array of inexpensive disks or redundant array of independent disks) — Several methods of configuring multiple hard drives to store data to increase logical volume size and improve performance, and to ensure that if one hard drive fails, the data is still available from another hard drive.

RAM (random access memory) — Temporary memory stored on chips, such as SIMMs, inside the computer. Information in RAM disappears when the computer's power is turned off.

RAM drive — A RAM area configured as a virtual hard drive, such as drive D, so that frequently used programs can be accessed faster. It is the opposite of virtual memory.

RD or RMDIR command — A DOS command to remove an unwanted directory (for example, RD C:\OLDDIR). You must delete all files in the directory to be removed, prior to using this command.

Re-marked chips — Chips that have been used and returned to the factory, marked again, and resold. The surface of the chips may be dull or scratched.

Read/write head — A sealed, magnetic coil device that moves across the surface of a disk either reading or writing data to the disk.

Real mode — A single-tasking operating mode whereby a program only has 1024K of memory addresses, has direct access to RAM, and uses a 16-bit data path.

RECOVER command — A command that recovers files that were lost because of a corrupted file allocation table.

Recovery Console — A Windows 2000 command-interface utility that can be used to solve problems when the OS cannot load from the hard drive.

Rectifier — An electrical device that converts AC to DC. A PC power supply contains a rectifier.

Reduced write current — A method whereby less current is used to write data to tracks near the center of the disk, where the bits are closer together.

Refresh — The process of periodically rewriting the data for instance, on dynamic RAM.

Registry — A database used by Windows to store hardware and software configuration information, user preferences, and setup information. Use Regedit.exe to edit the Registry.

Removable drives — High-capacity drives, such as Zip or Jaz drives, that have disks that can be removed like floppy disks.

Repeater — A device that amplifies weakened signals on a network.

Request for Comment (RFC) — A document presented to the technical community to propose and describe in detail a new standard to be adopted by the community at large. Search for and view RFCs at *www.rfc-editor.org.*

Rescue disk — A floppy disk that can be used to start up a computer when the hard drive fails to boot. *Also see* Emergency startup disk.

Resistance — The degree to which a device opposes or resists the flow of electricity. As the electrical resistance increases, the current decreases. *See* Ohms and Resistor.

Resistor — An electronic device that resists or opposes the flow of electricity. A resistor can be used to reduce the amount of electricity being supplied to an electronic component.

Resolution — The number of spots called pixels on a monitor screen that are addressable by software (example: 1024×768 pixels).

Resource arbitrator — A PnP component that decides which resources are assigned to which devices.

Resource management — The process of allocating resources to devices at startup.

RET (resolution enhancement technology) — The term used by Hewlett-Packard to describe the way a laser printer varies the size of the dots used to create an image. This technology partly accounts for the sharp, clear image created by a laser printer

Retension — A tape maintenance procedure that fast-forwards and then rewinds the tape to eliminate loose spots on the tape.

Reverse Address Resolution Protocol (RARP) — Translates the unique hardware NIC addresses into IP addresses (the reverse of ARP).

RISC (reduced instruction set computer) chips — Chips that incorporate only the most frequently used instructions, so that the computer operates faster (for example, the PowerPC uses RISC chips).

RJ-11 — A phone line connection found on a modem, telephone, and house phone outlet.

RJ-45 connector — A connector used on an Ethernet 10BaseT (twisted-pair cable) network. An RJ-45 port looks similar to a large phone jack.

Roaming users — Users who can move from PC to PC within a network, with their profiles following them.

ROM (read-only memory) — Chips that contain programming code and cannot be erased.

ROM BIOS — *See* BIOS.

Root directory — The main directory created when a hard drive or disk is first formatted.

Route discovery — When a router rebuilds its router tables on the basis of new information.

Router — A device or box that connects networks. A router transfers a packet to other networks when the packet is addressed to a station outside its network. The router can make intelligent decisions as to which network is the best route to use to send data to a distant network. *See* Bridge.

Router table — Tables of network addresses that also include the best possible routes (regarding tick count and hop count) to these networks. *See* Tick count and Hop count.

Run-time configuration — A PnP ongoing process that monitors changes in system devices, such as the removal of a PC Card on a notebook computer or the docking of a notebook computer to a docking station.

Safe mode — The mode in which Windows 9x is loaded with minimum configuration and drivers in order to allow the correction of system errors. To enter safe mode, press F5 or F8 when "Starting Windows 95/98" is displayed.

SAM (security accounts manager) — A portion of the Windows NT Registry that manages the account database that contains accounts, policies, and other pertinent information about the domain.

Sample size — Refers to samples taken when converting a signal from analog to digital. Sample size is a measure of the amount of storage allocated to a single measurement of a single sample. The larger the sample size, the more accurate the value and the larger the file sizes needed to store the data.

Sampling — Part of the process of converting sound or video from analog to digital format, whereby a sound wave or image is measured at uniform time intervals and saved as a series of smaller representative blocks. *See* Sampling rate.

Sampling rate — The rate of samples taken of an analog signal over a period of time, usually expressed as samples per second, or Hertz. For example, 44,100 Hz is the sampling rate used for 16-bit stereo.

SCAM (SCSI configuration automatically) — A method that follows the Plug and Play standard, to make installations of SCSI devices much easier, assuming that the device is SCAM-compatible.

Scanning mirror — A component of a laser printer. An octagonal mirror that can be directed in a sweeping motion to cover the entire length of a laser printer drum.

SCSI (small computer system interface) — A faster system-level interface with a host adapter and a bus that can daisy-chain as many as seven or 15 other devices.

SCSI ID — *See* Logical unit number.

SCSI bus — A bus standard used for peripheral devices tied together in a daisy chain.

SCSI bus adapter chip — The chip mounted on the logic board of a hard drive that allows the drive to be a part of a SCSI bus system.

SC330 (Slot Connector 330) — A 330-pin system board connector used to contain the Pentium III Xeon. Also called Slot 2.

SECC (Single Edge Contact Cartridge) — A type of cartridge that houses the Pentium III processor.

Secondary storage — Storage that is remote to the CPU and permanently holds data, even when the PC is turned off.

Sector — On a disk surface, one segment of a track, which almost always contains 512 bytes of data. Sometimes a single wedge of the disk surface is also called a sector.

Segmentation — To split a large Ethernet into smaller segments that are connected to each other by bridges or routers. This is done to prevent congestion as the number of nodes increases.

Sequential access — A method of data access used by tape drives whereby data is written or read sequentially from the beginning to the end of the tape or until the desired data is found.

Serial mouse — A mouse that uses a serial port and has a female 9-pin DB-9 connector.

Serial ports — Male ports on the computer used for transmitting data serially, one bit at a time. They are called COM1, COM2, COM3 and COM4.

Server — A microcomputer or minicomputer that stores programs and data to be used remotely by other computers.

Session layer — The OSI layer that makes and manages a connection between two nodes of the network.

SGRAM (synchronous graphics RAM) — Memory designed especially for video card processing that can synchronize itself with the CPU bus clock. They are commonly used for modems and mice, and in DOS are called COM1 or COM2.

Shadow RAM or shadowing ROM — The process of copying ROM programming code into RAM to speed up the system operation, because of the faster access speed of RAM.

Signal-regenerating repeater — A repeater that "reads" the signal on the network and then creates an exact duplicate of the signal, thus amplifying the signal without also amplifying unwanted noise that is mixed with the signal.

SIMM (single inline memory module) — A miniature circuit board used in a computer to hold RAM. SIMMs hold 8, 16, 32, or 64 MB on a single module.

Single voltage CPU — A CPU that requires one voltage for both internal and I/O operations.

Single-instruction, multiple-data (SIMD) — An MMX process that allows the CPU to execute a single instruction simultaneously on multiple pieces of data rather than by repetitive looping.

Slack — Wasted space on a hard drive caused by not using all available space at the end of clusters.

Sleep mode — A mode used in many "Green" systems that allows them to be configured through CMOS to suspend the monitor or even the drive, if the keyboard and/or CPU have been inactive for a set number of minutes. *See* Green standards.

SLIP (Serial Line Internet Protocol) — An early version of line protocol designed for home users connecting to the Internet. SLIP lacks reliable error checking and has mostly been replaced by PPP.

SMARTDrive — A hard drive cache program that comes with Windows 3.x and DOS that can be executed as a TSR from the AUTOEXEC.BAT file (for example, DEVICE=SMARTDRV.SYS 2048).

SMTP (Simple Mail Transfer Protocol) — A common protocol used to send e-mail across a network.

Snap-in — An administrative tool that is contained within a console. For example, Event Viewer is a snap-in in the Computer Management console.

Socket — A virtual connection from one computer to another such as that between a client and a server. Higher-level protocols such as HTTP use a socket to pass data between two computers. A socket is assigned a number for the current session, which is used by the high-level protocol.

SO-DIMM (small outline DIMM) — A small memory module designed for notebooks that has 72 pins and supports 32-bit data transfers.

Soft boot — To restart a PC by pressing three keys at the same time (Ctrl, Alt, and Del). Also called warm boot.

Software — Computer programs, or instructions to perform a specific task. Software may be BIOS, OSs, or applications software such as a word-processing or spreadsheet program.

Software cache — Cache controlled by software whereby the cache is stored in RAM.

Software copyrights — Copyright is a legal concept (covered by the Federal Copyright Act of 1976) that encompasses the protection of the rights of an originator of a creative work, which can include software. With the exception of archival backups, copyrighted programs are illegal to copy without specific authorization from the copyright holder.

Software interrupt — An event caused by a program currently being executed by the CPU signaling the CPU that it requires the use of a hardware device.

Software piracy — Making unauthorized copies of original copyrighted software.

South bridge — That portion of the chip set hub that connects slower I/O buses (e.g., ISA bus) to the system bus. Compare to North bridge.

Spanned volumes — Windows 2000 method of linking several volumes across multiple hard drives into a single logical drive

Spooling — Placing print jobs in a print queue so that an application can be released from the printing process before printing is completed. Spooling is an acronym for simultaneous peripheral operations online.

SSE (streaming SIMD extension) — A technology used by the Intel Pentium III designed to improve performance of multimedia software.

Staggered pin grid array (SPGA) — A feature of a CPU socket where the pins are staggered over the socket in order to squeeze more pins into a small space.

Standby time — The time before a "Green" system will reduce 92% of its activity. *See* Green standards.

Standby UPS — A UPS that quickly switches from an AC power source to a battery-powered source during a brownout or power outage.

Standoffs — Small plastic or metal spacers placed on the bottom of the main system board, to raise it off the chassis, so that its components will not short out on the metal case.

Star network architecture — A network design in which nodes are connected at a centralized location.

Star topology — A network design in which nodes are connected at a centralized location.

Start bit — A bit that is used to signal the approach of data. *See* Stop bit.

Startup BIOS — Part of system BIOS that is responsible for controlling the PC when it is first turned on. Startup BIOS gives control over to the OS once it is loaded.

Startup password — A password that a computer requires during the boot process used to gain access to the PC. Also called power-on password.

Static electricity — *See* Electrostatic discharge.

Static IP addresses — IP addresses permanently assigned to a workstation. In Windows 9x, this can be done under Dial-Up Networking, Server Type, TCP/IP settings. Specify an IP address.

Static RAM (SRAM) — RAM chips that retain information without the need for refreshing, as long as the computer's power is on. They are more expensive than traditional DRAM.

Static routing — When routing tables do not automatically change and must be manually edited. Windows NT and Windows 95 support only static routing. Compare to Dynamic routing.

Static VxD — A VxD that is loaded into memory at startup and remains there for the entire OS session.

Stealth virus — A virus that actively conceals itself by temporarily removing itself from an infected file that is about to be examined, and then hiding a copy of itself elsewhere on the drive.

Stop bit — A bit that is used to signal the end of a block of data.

Streaming audio — Downloading audio data from the Internet in a continuous stream of data without first downloading an entire audio file.

Subdirectory — In DOS, a directory that is contained within another directory. Also called a child directory.

Subnet mask — Defines which portion of the host address within an IP address is being borrowed to define separate subnets within a network. A 1 in the mask indicates that the bit is part of the network address, and a 0 indicates that the bit is part of the host address. For example, the subnet mask 255.255.192.0, in binary, is 11111111.11111111.11000000.00000000. Therefore, the network address is the first two octets and the subnet address is the first two bits of the third octet. The rest of the IP address refers to the host.

Subnetworks or **subnets** — Divisions of a large network, consisting of smaller separate networks (to prevent congestion). Each subnetwork is assigned a logical network IP name.

Subtree — One of five main keys that make up the Windows NT Registry. Examples are HKEY_CURRENT_USER and HKEY_LOCAL_MACHINE.

Suite — As applies to software, a collection of applications software sold as a bundle, whose components are designed to be compatible with one another. An example is Microsoft Office.

Surge suppressor or surge protector — A device or power strip designed to protect electronic equipment from power surges and spikes.

Suspend time — The time before a green system will reduce 99% of its activity. After this time, the system needs a warmup time so that the CPU, monitor, and hard drive can reach full activity.

Swap file — A file on the hard drive that is used by the OS for virtual memory.

Swapping — A method of freeing some memory by moving a "page" of data temporarily to a swap file on the hard drive; it can later be copied from disk back into memory.

Switch — A device that is used to break a large network into two smaller networks in order to reduce traffic congestion. A switch uses MAC addresses to determine which network to send a packet.

Synchronous DRAM (SDRAM) — A type of memory stored on DIMMs that run in sync with the system clock, running at the same speed as the system board. Currently, the fastest memory used on PCs.

Synchronous SRAM — SRAM that is faster and more expensive than asynchronous SRAM. It requires a clock signal to validate its control signals, enabling the cache to run in step with the CPU.

System BIOS — Basic input/output system chip(s) residing on the system board that control(s) normal I/O to such areas as system memory and floppy drives. Also called on-board BIOS.

System File Checker — System File Checker is part of the new Windows 2000 utility to protect system files, called Windows File Protection (WFP).

System State data — All files that Windows 2000 requires to load and perform successfully. The System State data is backed up using the Backup utility.

System board — The main board in the computer, also called the motherboard. The CPU, ROM chips, SIMMs, DIMMs, and interface cards are plugged into the system board.

System bus — Today the system bus usually means the memory bus. However, sometimes it is used to refer to other buses on the system board. *See* memory bus.

System clock — A line on a bus that is dedicated to timing the activities of components connected to it. The system clock provides a continuous pulse that other devices use to time themselves.

System disk — A floppy disk containing enough of an operating system to boot.

System partition — The active partition of the hard drive containing the boot record and the specific files required to load Windows NT.

System variable — A variable that has been given a name and a value; it is available to the operating system and applications software programs.

System-board mouse — A mouse that plugs into a round mouse port on the system board. Sometimes called a PS/2 mouse.

Task switching — *See* Cooperative multitasking.

TCP/IP (Transmission Control Protocol/Internet Protocol) — The suite of protocols developed to support the Internet. TCP is responsible for error checking, and IP is responsible for routing.

Technical documentation — The technical reference manuals, included with software packages and peripherals, that provide directions for installation, usage, and troubleshooting.

Telephony Application Programming Interface (TAPI) — A standard developed by Intel and Microsoft that can be used by 32-bit Windows 9x communications programs for communicating over phone lines.

Telephony — A term describing the technology of converting sound to signals that can travel over telephone lines.

Temp directory — A location to which inactive applications and data can be moved as a swap file, while Windows continues to process current active applications. (Avoid deleting Temp swap while Windows is running.)

Temporary file — A file that is created by Windows applications, to save temporary data, and may or may not be deleted when the application is unloaded.

Terminating resistor — The resistor added at the end of a SCSI chain to dampen the voltage at the end of the chain. *See* Termination.

Termination — A process necessary to prevent an echo effect of power at the end of a SCSI chain resulting in interference with the data transmission. *See* Terminating resistor.

Thread — A single task that is part of a larger task or program.

Tick count — The time required for a packet to reach its destination. One tick equals 1/18 of a second.

Token — A small frame on a Token Ring network that constantly travels around the ring in only one direction. When a station seizes the token, it controls the channel until its message is sent.

Token ring — A network that is logically a ring, but stations are connected to a centralized multistation access unit (MAU) in a star formation. Network communication is controlled by a token.

Toner cavity — A container filled with toner in a laser printer. The black resin toner is used to form the printed image on paper.

Trace — A wire on a circuit board that connects two components or devices together.

Track — The disk surface is divided into many concentric circles, each called a track.

Trailer — The part of a packet that follows the data and contains information used by some protocols for error checking.

Training — *See* Handshaking.

Transceiver — The bidirectional (transmitter and receiver) component on a NIC that is responsible for signal conversion and monitors for data collision.

Transformer — A device that changes the ratio of current to voltage. A computer power supply is basically a transformer and a rectifier.

Transistor — An electronic device that can regulate electricity and act as a logical gate or switch for an electrical signal.

Translation — A technique used by system BIOS and hard drive controller BIOS to break the 504 MB hard drive barrier, whereby a different set of drive parameters are communicated to the OS and other software than that used by the hard drive controller BIOS.

Transport layer — The OSI layer that verifies data and requests a resend when the data is corrupted.

TREE command — A DOS command that shows the disk directories in a graphical layout similar to a family tree (for example, TREE/F shows every filename in all branches of the tree).

Trojan horse — A type of infestation that hides or disguises itself as a useful program, yet is designed to cause damage at a later time.

TSR (terminate-and-stay-resident) — A program that is loaded into memory but is not immediately executed, such as a screen saver or a memory-resident antivirus program.

Turbo mode — A means of doubling the clock speed by pressing a button on the case of some older computers.

UART (universal asynchronous receiver/transmitter) chip — A chip that controls serial ports. It sets protocol and converts parallel data bits received from the system bus into serial bits.

UPS (uninterruptible power supply) — A device designed to provide a backup power supply during a power failure. Basically, a UPS is a battery backup system with an ultrafast sensing device.

URL (Uniform Resource Locator) — A unique address that identifies the domain name, path, or filename of a World Wide Web site. Microsoft's URL is: *http://www.microsoft.com/*

Unattended installation — A Windows 2000 installation that is done by storing the answers to installation questions in a text file or script that Windows 2000 calls an answer file so that the answers do not have to be typed in during the installation.

UNDELETE command — A command that resets a deleted file's directory entry to normal, provided the clusters occupied by the file have not been overwritten and the file entry is still in the directory list.

UNFORMAT command — A DOS command that performs recovery from an accidental FORMAT, and may also repair a damaged partition table if the partition table was previously saved with MIRROR/PARTN.

Universal serial bus (USB) — A bus that is expected to eventually replace serial and parallel ports, designed to make installation and configuration of I/O devices easy, providing room for as many as 127 devices daisy-chained together. The USB uses only a single set of resources for all devices on the bus.

Upper memory block (UMB) — A group of consecutive memory addresses in RAM from 640K to 1 MB that can be used by device drivers and TSRs.

Upper memory — The memory addresses from 640K up to 1024K, originally reserved for BIOS, device drivers, and TSRs.

upgrade installation — A Windows 2000 installation that carries forward all previous operating system settings and applications installed under the previous operating system.

URL (Uniform Resource Locator) — A unique address that identifies the domain name, path, or filename of a World Wide Web site. Microsoft's URL address is: *http://www.microsoft.com/*

User Datagram Protocol (UDP) — A connectionless protocol that does not require a connection to send a packet and does not guarantee that the packet arrives at its destination. (A data packet was once called a datagram.)

User account — The information, stored in the SAM database, that defines a Windows NT user, including user name, password, memberships, and rights.

User documentation — Manuals, online documentation, instructions, and tutorials designed specifically for the user.

User mode — Provides an interface between an application and an OS, and only has access to hardware resources through the code running in kernel mode.

User profile — A personal profile about the user, kept in the Windows NT Registry, which enables the user's desktop settings and other operating parameters to be retained from one session to another.

Utility software — Software packages, such as Nuts & Bolts or Norton Utilities, that provide the means for data recovery and repair, virus detection, and the creation of backups.

V.34 standard — A communications standard that transmits at 28,800 bps and/or 33,600 bps.

V.90 — A standard for data transmission over phone lines that can attain a speed of 56 Kbps. It replaces K56flex and x2 standards.

Value data — In Windows 9x, the name and value of a setting in the registry.

VCACHE — A built-in Windows 9x 32-bit software cache that doesn't take up conventional memory space or upper memory space, as SmartDrive does.

Vector table — *See* Interrupt vector table.

VESA (Video Electronics Standards Association) VL bus — A local bus used on 80486 computers for connecting 32-bit adapters directly to the local processor bus.

Video card — An interface card installed in the computer to control visual output on a monitor.

Video controller card — An interface card that controls the monitor. Also called video card or display adapter.

Video driver — A program that tells the computer how to effectively communicate with the video adapter card and monitor. It is often found on a floppy disk or CD that is shipped with the card.

Video RAM or VRAM — RAM on video cards that holds the data that is being passed from the computer to the monitor and can be accessed by two devices simultaneously. Higher resolutions often require more video memory.

Virtual device driver (VDD) or VxD driver — A 32-bit device driver running in protected mode.

Virtual file allocation table (VFAT) — A variation of the original DOS 16-bit FAT that allows for long filenames and 32-bit disk access.

Virtual machines (VM) — Multiple logical machines created within one physical machine by Windows, allowing applications to make serious errors within one logical machine without disturbing other programs and parts of the system.

Virtual memory manager — A Windows 9x program that controls the page table, swapping 4K pages in and out of physical RAM to and from the hard drive.

Virtual memory — A method whereby the OS uses the hard drive as though it were RAM.

Virtual real mode — An operating mode in which an OS provides an environment to a 16-bit program that acts like real mode.

Virus — A program that often has an incubation period, is infectious, and is intended to cause damage. A virus program might destroy data and programs or damage a disk drive's boot sector.

Virus signature — The distinguishing characteristics or patterns of a particular virus. Typically, AV signature updates for new viruses can be downloaded monthly from the Internet.

Voice — A group of samples for a musical instrument stored in a wavetable.

Volatile — Refers to a kind of RAM that is temporary, cannot hold data very long, and must be frequently refreshed.

Volt — A measure of electrical pressure differential. A computer ATX power supply usually provides five separate voltages: +12V, −12V, +5V, −5V, and +3V.

Voltage — Electrical differential that causes current to flow, measured in volts. *See* Volts.

Voltmeter — A device for measuring electrical voltage.

Volumes — In Windows 2000, a partition on a hard drive that is formatted as a dynamic drive.

Wait state — A clock tick in which nothing happens, used to ensure that the microprocessor isn't getting ahead of slower components. A 0-wait state is preferable to a 1-wait state. Too many wait states can slow a system down.

Warm boot — *See* Soft boot.

Wattage — Electrical power measured in watts.

Watts — The unit used to measure power. A typical computer may use a power supply that provides 200 watts.

Wavetable — A table of stored sample sounds used to synthesize sound by reconstructing the sound from digital data using actual samples of sounds from real instruments.

Window RAM (WRAM) — Dual-ported video RAM that is faster and less expensive than VRAM. It has its own internal bus on the chip, with a data path that is 256 bits wide.

Windows Custom Setup — A setup feature that allows user customization of such things as directory locations, wallpaper settings, font selections, and many other features.

Windows Express Setup — A setup feature that automatically installs Windows in the most commonly used fashion.

Windows File Protection (WFP) — A Windows 2000 feature that protects system files from being corrupted or erased by applications or users.

Windows Internet Naming Service (WINS) — A Microsoft resolution service with a distributed database that tracks relationships between domain names and IP addresses. Compare to DNS.

Windows NT Registry — A database containing all configuration information, including the user profile and hardware settings. The NT Registry is not compatible with the Windows 9x Registry.

Windows NT file system (NTFS) — A file system first introduced with Windows NT that provides improved security, disk storage, file compression, and long filenames.

Workgroup — In Windows NT, a logical group of computers and users in which administration, resources, and security are distributed throughout the network, without centralized management or security.

Worm — An infestation designed to copy itself repeatedly to memory, on drive space, or on a network until little memory or disk space remains.

WOW (Win 16 on Win 32) — A group of programs provided by Windows NT to create a virtual DOS environment that emulates a 16-bit Windows environment, protecting the rest of the NT OS from 16-bit applications.

Write precompensation — A method whereby data is written faster to the tracks that are near the center of a disk.

XCOPY command — A faster external DOS COPY program that can copy subdirectories (/S) (for example, XCOPY *.* A:/S).

Zero insertion force (ZIF) — A socket feature that uses a small lever to apply even force when installing the microchip into the socket.

Zone bit recording — A method of storing data on a hard drive whereby the drive can have more sectors per track near the outside of the platter.

INDEX